Fodor's

THE COMPLETE GUIDE TO THE NATIONAL PARKS OF THE WEST

Welcome to the National Parks of the West

Awe-inspiring landscapes and unlimited recreational opportunities make a trip to any Western national park a grand adventure. You can raft the raging Colorado River as it pushes through the Grand Canyon, view wildlife in Yosemite while you hike, or watch Yellowstone's Old Faithful geyser in action. Places such as Mesa Verde also preserve the long history of life in the West. Wherever you explore in the parks, these sprawling treasures invite you to discover nature's stunning variety and reconnect with the great outdoors. As you plan your travels, please confirm that places are still open and let us know when we need to make updates by writing to us at editors@fodors.com.

TOP REASONS TO GO

★ **Wildlife:** From bison to bald eagles to bears, the parks shelter amazing species.

★ **Hiking:** Countless scenic trails for all levels inspire and challenge walkers.

★ **Geology:** Unique formations like Oregon's Crater Lake and Utah's Arches astound.

★ **Great Views:** Mountain peaks and scenic overlooks reward climbers and drivers alike.

★ **History:** Monuments and outposts trace the settling of the former Wild West.

★ **Luxury Lodges:** Famous hotels pair old-school grandeur with splendid surroundings.

Contents

Fodor's Features

MAPS

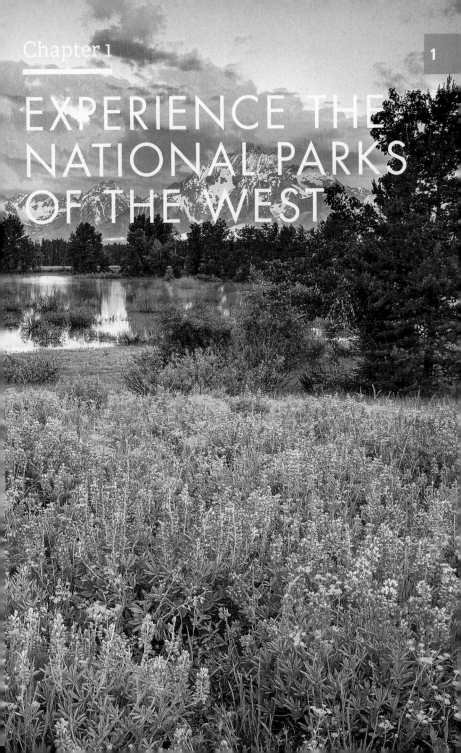

Chapter 1

EXPERIENCE THE NATIONAL PARKS OF THE WEST

36 ULTIMATE EXPERIENCES

The National Parks of the West offers terrific experiences that should be on every traveler's list. Here are Fodor's top picks for a memorable trip.

1 | Day climb in the Tetons

Grand Teton National Park, Wyoming. Known for having some of the country's best rock climbing, the gold standard at this park is a trip 13,776 feet up the Grand Teton, which, if you go with one of the park's two approved outfitters, is open to beginners but may be better suited for those with some climbing experience. *(Ch. 17)*

2 Witness the beauty of the Big Room

Carlsbad Caverns National Park, New Mexico. The massive cavern's most beautiful section is a softly lit ballroom of sparkling speleothems called the Big Room, ringed with a paved path. *(Ch. 11)*

3 Visit four distinct districts

Canyonlands National Park, Utah. The Green and Colorado Rivers divide the park into districts of canyons, mesas, arches, and hoodoos. Most accessible is Island in the Sky, a sandstone mesa. *(Ch. 9)*

4 See unusual boxwork cave formations

Wind Cave National Park, South Dakota. This is the seventh-longest cave system in the world, with roughly 150 surveyed miles of underground passageways. It's the densest "maze cave" on Earth. *(Ch. 35)*

5 See Delicate Arch and the Windows Section

Arches National Park, Utah. The sandstone arches here, famous symbols of the American Southwest, have been carved by thousands of years of wind, water, and ice. *(Ch. 4)*

6 Discover extinct creatures

Badlands National Park, South Dakota. This landscape of eroded rock formations preserves the remains of mammals 33 million years old. See replicas of some of the fossils discovered here. *(Ch. 5)*

7 Ogle General Sherman

Sequoia National Park, California. The General Sherman tree is the largest living tree in the world, at 275 feet tall and 36 feet in diameter at its roots. *(Ch. 32)*

8 Hike Half Dome

Yosemite National Park, California. The 16-mile round-trip trail to the top of Half Dome climbs nearly 5,000 feet. The challenge rewards hikers with unparalleled views of the Yosemite Valley. *(Ch. 37)*

9 Investigate coastal tide pools

Olympic National Park, Washington. Along the park's rocky coastal outcroppings are tidepools full of giant green anemone, sea stars, and other intertidal species. *(Ch. 26)*

10 Hike into the Canyon

Grand Canyon National Park, Arizona. Views along the well-maintained, 12-mile (round-trip) Bright Angel Trail are unforgettable, whether you go the distance or just do a segment. *(Ch. 16)*

11 Drive the Going-to-the-Sun Road

Glacier National Park, Montana. Construction began in 1921 on the 50-mile long road, which spans the width of the park. See the park's most famous features and wildlife. *(Ch. 15)*

12 Hike to the Santa Elena Canyon

Big Bend National Park, Texas. The sheer cliffs of the dramatic Santa Elena Canyon flank the Rio Grande, forming the boundary between Mexico and Texas in the park. *(Ch. 6)*

13 See volcanic erosion

Pinnacles National Park, California. This moonscape of eroded volcanic detritus is frequented by roughly 200 condors. See them at High Peaks or from the Peaks View scenic overlook. *(Ch. 28)*

14 Explore Wizard Island

Crater Lake National Park, Oregon. At the west end of Crater Lake, an extinct volcano and the deepest lake in the United States, is Wizard Island, which is capped with a 100-foot deep crater. *(Ch. 13)*

15 Look into the past

Petrified Forest National Park, Arizona. Thousands of years of human history is scattered across the desert landscape; over 600 archaeological and petroglyph sites have been found. *(Ch. 27)*

16 See one of the world's oldest organisms

Great Basin National Park, Nevada. Pine trees make up Nevada's ancient forest. The Bristlecone pine is the world's longest-living tree and likely its oldest living organism. *(Ch. 18)*

17 Watch hoodoos change color

Bryce Canyon National Park, Utah. Bryce Canyon has the largest concentration of hoodoos in the world. At sunset they are ablaze with pinks, oranges, yellows, and reds. *(Ch. 8)*

18 See the country's largest cactus

Saguaro National Park, Arizona. The Saguaro cactus, the largest succulent in the United States, grows in abundance in this slice of the Sonoran Desert. The plants can grow up to 40 feet. *(Ch. 31)*

19 See the South Rim Drive's 12 unique views

Black Canyon of the Gunnison National Park, Colorado. The 7-mile South Rim Drive has 12 separate overlooks, each offering a different view of the park's famous gorge. *(Ch. 7)*

20 Explore a geologic wrinkle in the Earth

Capitol Reef National Park, Utah. Utah's Waterpocket Fold is a geological wrinkle in the Earth's crust where shifting tectonic plates sent sedimentary rocks upwards into a spiny plateau. *(Ch. 10)*

21 Trek to the summit of the Lassen Peak

Lassen Volcanic National Park, California. Lassen Peak is the world's largest "plug dome" volcano. Though dormant, it's the southernmost active volcano in the Cascade Range. *(Ch. 22)*

22 Hike one of the most dangerous volcanoes

Mount Rainier National Park, Washington. Mt. Rainier is considered one of the most dangerous volcanoes in the world due to its large film of glacial ice. *(Ch. 24)*

23 Explore desertscapes and ghost towns

Death Valley National Park, California. Mining towns sprang up in Death Valley when there was gold in the Panamint Mountains, but were abandoned once the riches ran out in the late 1800s. *(Ch. 14)*

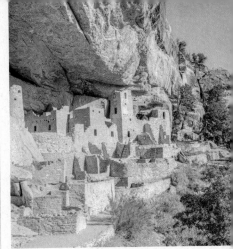

24 Kayak around Santa Cruz Island

Channel Islands National Park, California. Due to thousands of years of isolation, these islands are inhabited by plants and animals found nowhere else on Earth. Rent a kayak and explore. *(Ch. 12)*

25 Explore Cliff Palace

Mesa Verde National Park, Colorado. Cliff Palace was inhabited by 100 people for over a century before it was abandoned during 13th-century droughts. *(Ch. 23)*

26 Watch the goings on at Prairie Dog Town

Theodore Roosevelt National Park, North Dakota. The official "Prairie Dog Town" is less than a mile down the Buckhorn Trail from the Caprock Coulee Trailhead. *(Ch. 33)*

27 Hike the Pacific Crest Trail

Kings Canyon National Park, California. Through the High Sierra, a landscape of steep peaks and deep valleys, the trail hits its formidable highest point at Forester Pass, 13,153 feet above sea level. *(Ch. 32)*

28 Hike to the "Top of Texas"

Guadalupe Mountains National Park, Texas. Guadalupe Peak is the highest point in the state of Texas, a whopping 8,751 feet above sea level. If you're game enough to make it to the top, you'll climb 3,000 feet. *(Ch. 20)*

29 Hike The Narrows

Zion National Park, Utah. The only way to pass through The Narrows, a gorge so slim that it's less than 30 feet wide at some points, is by walking in the Virgin River. *(Ch. 38)*

30 Backpack beneath mountain glaciers

North Cascades National Park, Washington. Envisioned as an undeveloped backcountry, 94% of the park remains untouched, dotted with alpine lakes, forests, and 300 glaciers. *(Ch. 25)*

31 See the desert in bloom

Joshua Tree National Park, California. This rocky park is known for its unusual Joshua tree, a tall, stately yucca plant. In the springtime, cacti, succulents, and the Joshua trees are in full bloom. *(Ch. 21)*

32 Explore Fern Canyon

Redwood National and State Parks, California. In this 325-million-year-old stream canyon, cliff walls with ancient ferns frame the gorge. *(Ch. 29)*

33 Sand sled down dunes

Great Sand Dunes National Park, Colorado. The sand dunes, the steepest in North America, are made up of 5 billion cubic meters of sand once found at the bottom of mountain lakes. *(Ch. 19)*

34 Drive through the Dunes

White Sands National Park, New Mexico. As you curve around one set of towering white dunes after another, it feels as though you're driving through a snowy winter wonderland. *(Ch. 34)*

35 See Grand Prismatic

Yellowstone National Park, Wyoming. Grand Prismatic Spring is the largest hot spring in the United States, and third largest in the world. *(Ch. 36)*

36 Ride across the park on horseback

Rocky Mountain National Park, Colorado. Ride on horseback through 415 square miles of incredible alpine beauty. Two stables offer guided tours in the summer. *(Ch. 30)*

WHAT'S WHERE

Parks in this section are organized by state.

WASHINGTON

24 Mount Rainier. The fifth-highest mountain in the Lower 48, Mt. Rainier has temperate rain forest, old-growth forests of hemlock and fir, high meadows, and tundra—not to mention hot springs, glaciers, lakes, and waterfalls. **Best Paired With:** North Cascades and Olympic

25 North Cascades. Hiking on a real glacier is a memorable experience—especially if you add in marmots, golden eagles, and coyotes, and North Cascades is home to several hundred of them. **Best Paired With:** Mount Rainier and Olympic

26 Olympic. Centered on Mt. Olympus and framed on three sides by water, this park is known for its temperate rain forests, rugged coastal expanses, Sol Duc hot springs, and hiking (or skiing) at Hurricane Ridge. **Best Paired With:** North Cascades and Mount Rainier

OREGON

13 Crater Lake. Crater Lake is a geological marvel—the 21-square-mile sapphire-blue lake inside a caldera is the nation's deepest. The park itself includes about 90 miles of trails. **Best Paired With:** Mount Rainier and Olympic or Redwood and Lassen Volcanic

MONTANA

15 Glacier–Waterton Lakes. The rugged mountains that weave their way through the Continental Divide in northwest Montana are the backbone of Glacier and its sister park in Canada, Waterton Lakes. The park's Going-to-the-Sun Road is a spectacular drive that crosses the crest of the Continental Divide. **Best Paired With:** Yellowstone

NORTH DAKOTA

33 Theodore Roosevelt. Theodore Roosevelt is known for chunks of badlands on the Little Missouri River and the 26th president's beloved Elkhorn Ranch. This is one of the more isolated parks in the Lower 48, but South Dakota's Badlands is only 5½ hours to the southeast. **Best Paired With:** Badlands

WYOMING

17 Grand Teton. With no foothills, the unimpeded view of the Teton Range rising out of Jackson Hole is stunning. Wildlife from short-tailed weasels to grizzly bears abounds. **Best Paired With:** Yellowstone

36 Yellowstone. Best known for Old Faithful, the world's most famous geyser, flowing hot springs, and mud pots, Yellowstone is the oldest national park in the world. Spotting the abundant wildlife, like bison, elk, moose, and bears, is the other main draw. **Best Paired With:** Grand Teton

SOUTH DAKOTA

5 Badlands. The park's eroded buttes and spires cast amazing shades of red and yellow across the South Dakota prairie. In addition to scenery, it has some of the world's richest mammal fossil beds. **Best Paired With:** Wind Cave

35 Wind Cave. One of the largest caves in the world, with beautiful cave formations including boxwork (3-D calcite honeycomb patterns on cave walls and ceilings), Wind Cave is the place to go spelunking. **Best Paired With:** Badlands

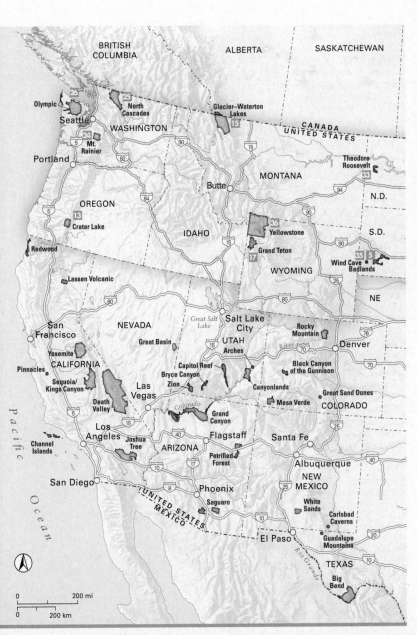

WHAT'S WHERE

NEVADA

18 Great Basin. It may be one of the nation's least visited national parks, but the stalactites, stalagmites, and popcorn in Lehman Caves and the solitude of backcountry treks are big draws. **Best Paired With:** Bryce Canyon

UTAH

4 Arches. Four hours (235 miles) from Salt Lake City, this park has the world's largest concentration of natural sandstone arches, including that most famous symbol of Utah, Delicate Arch. Nearby is Moab, an adventure hot spot, with world-class white-water rafting on the Colorado River, rock climbing, four-wheeling, and mountain biking. **Best Paired With:** Canyonlands

8 Bryce Canyon. Exploring the hoodoos (spectacular columns of rock) at this park is like wandering through a giant maze. Bryce is within a few hours of Utah's other national parks and near Kodachrome Basin State Park and Grand Staircase–Escalante National Monument. **Best Paired With:** Capitol Reef and Zion

9 Canyonlands. Biking on White Rim Road, white-water rafting in Cataract Canyon—plus spires, pinnacles, cliffs, and mesas as far as the eye can see—are the top reasons to go. **Best Paired With:** Arches

10 Capitol Reef. Seven times larger than nearby Bryce Canyon and much less crowded, Capitol Reef is known for its 100-mile-long Waterpocket Fold, a monocline (or "wrinkle" in the Earth's crust). It has many options for day hikes as well as backcountry trips into slot canyons, arches, cliffs, domes, and slickrock. **Best Paired With:** Bryce Canyon and Zion

38 Zion. Sheer 2,000-foot cliffs and river-carved canyons are what Zion is all about, and hiking the Narrows and the Subway are on many an adventurer's bucket list. Zion is right next to hospitable Springdale, which is full of amenities and charm. **Best Paired With:** Bryce Canyon and Grand Canyon

COLORADO

7 Black Canyon of the Gunnison. This steep and narrow river gorge has sheer cliffs and a drop twice as high as the Empire State Building. **Best Paired With:** Arches

19 Great Sand Dunes. The roughly 30 square miles of landlocked dune fields are an impressive sight. Aside from the dunes, there are eight different life zones to explore, ranging from salty wetlands to alpine peaks.

23 Mesa Verde. Located in the Four Corners region—the junction of Utah, Colorado, New Mexico, and Arizona—this park houses an amazing collection of Ancestral Puebloan dwellings, some carved directly into cliff faces, and ancient artifacts. **Best Paired With:** Arches or Canyonlands

30 Rocky Mountain. Alpine lakes, mountain peaks, and wildlife such as elk and bighorn sheep draw visitors to the park. There are more than 350 miles of trails leading to meadows filled with wildflowers and crystal lakes and 14,259-foot Long's Peak to summit.

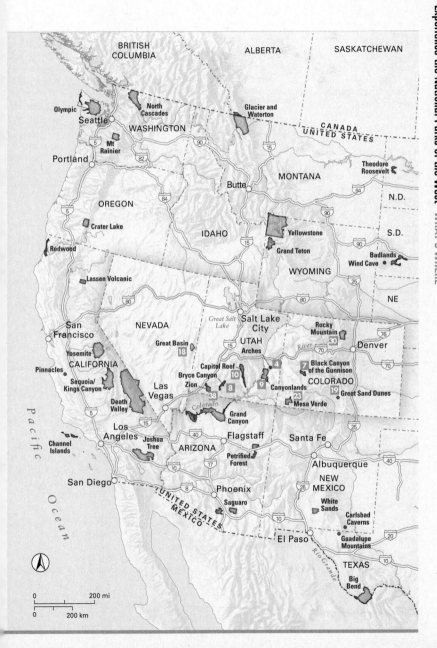

WHAT'S WHERE

CALIFORNIA

12 Channel Islands. You must take a boat or plane to reach the five islands, which are home to many species of terrestrial plants and animals found nowhere else on Earth. You're bound to see wildlife such as dolphins, sea lions, island foxes, and pelicans, and can kayak, dive, and go whale-watching. **Best Paired With:** Yosemite and Sequoia and Kings Canyon

14 Death Valley. This is a vast, lonely, beautiful place with breathtaking vistas, blasting 120-degree heat, and mysterious moving rocks. The desert landscape is surrounded by majestic mountains, dry lakebeds, spring wildflowers, and Wild West ghost towns. **Best Paired With:** Joshua Tree and Zion

21 Joshua Tree. Large stands of Joshua trees gave the park its name, but it's also a great spot for bouldering and rock climbing. Brilliant wildflower displays and starry nights add to the draw. **Best Paired With:** Death Valley

22 Lassen Volcanic. Lassen Peak, a dormant plug dome volcano that last erupted in 1915, and every other type of known volcano (shield, cinder cone, and composite) is here, as well as roiling mud pots and hissing steam vents. **Best Paired With:** Redwood and Crater Lake or Yosemite

28 Pinnacles. Hiking among rugged volcanic spires is the most popular activity at Pinnacles, and the best chance you'll have at encountering one of the extremely rare California condors that make their home here. **Best Paired With:** Yosemite

29 Redwood. Redwood is home to the world's tallest trees: giant coast redwoods, which grow to more than 300 feet tall. **Best Paired With:** Lassen Volcanic and Crater Lake

32 Sequoia and Kings Canyon. Sequoias are the big trees here, which have monstrously thick trunks and branches. The Generals Highway, which connects the two parks, features many of these natural marvels. The Kings Canyon Scenic Byway offers views into a canyon deeper than the Grand Canyon. **Best Paired With:** Yosemite National Park

37 Yosemite. Dozens of famed features, from the soaring granite monoliths of Half Dome and El Capitan, to shimmering waterfalls like Yosemite Falls and Bridalveil Fall, lie within reach in the Yosemite Valley. **Best Paired With:** Sequoia and Kings Canyon

ARIZONA

16 Grand Canyon. The Grand Canyon both exalts and humbles the human spirit. You can view the spectacle from the South Rim, the less-traveled North Rim, or hike or take a mule ride into the canyon for a richer experience. For adventure junkies, rafting the Colorado River through the canyon can't be beat. **Best Paired With:** Petrified Forest or Zion

27 Petrified Forest. This park is known for fallen and fossilized trees, which look like they are made of colorful stone. **Best Paired With:** Grand Canyon

31 Saguaro. The park takes its name from the saguaro cactus, the largest of its kind in the United States, found here. The park is split into two districts bookending Tucson (about 30 miles apart); the better collection of cacti is found in the west district.

NEW MEXICO

11 Carlsbad Caverns. The park's 119 caves, bizarre underground rock formations, and roughly 400,000 diving, dipping, sonar-blipping bats are the main draws. **Best Paired With:** Guadalupe Mountains and/or White Sands

34 White Sands. You can wander amid, or climb up and sled down the massive dunes contained within this 150,000-acre windswept expanse of powdery gypsum. **Best Paired With:** Carlsbad Caverns and/or Guadalupe Mountains

TEXAS

6 Big Bend. In a remote location, with the Rio Grande along its southern border, its limitless skies and ample space are two of its strongest selling points. **Best Paired With:** Guadalupe Mountains

20 Guadalupe Mountains. This remote park draws thousands of visitors every fall, when the hardwoods of McKittrick Canyon burst into flaming color. The park is home to the Guadalupe Peak, the highest point in the state. **Best Paired With:** Carlsbad Caverns and/or White Sands

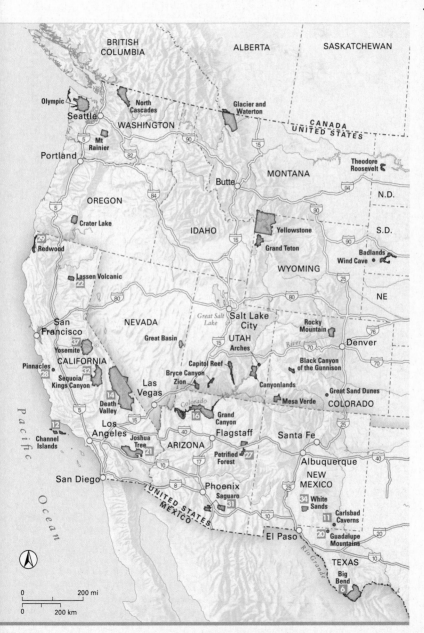

The Best National Parks of the West Lodges

JENNY LAKE LODGE
Grand Teton National Park, Wyoming
East Coast "dudes" began this homestead in 1922, back when there were just two cabins. Hiking trails accessible from the grounds offer views of Grand Teton and Mt. Moran, and guests can ride horses and cruiser-style bikes around the grounds.

THE INN AT DEATH VALLEY
Death Valley National Park, California
This 1927 Spanish Mission–style inn underwent renovations and reopened in 2018 with luxurious new casitas around the historic Oasis Gardens. Explore the winding trails of Mosaic Canyon.

PARADISE INN
Mount Rainier National Park, Washington
Visitors began staying at the timber-frame inn here in 1917, and it hasn't changed much since then. A restaurant complete with park views and a cozy fireplace serves appropriately hearty fare like mac and cheese or bison Bolognese.

ZION LODGE
Zion National Park, Utah
The only place to stay in the park, this 1920s-era lodge is framed by lofty sandstone cliffs. Rustic cabins offer porches with incredible views and stone fireplaces. Bonus: at night, you can watch deer grazing on the lawn in the moonlight.

THE AHWAHNEE HOTEL
Yosemite National Park, California
Built in 1927, the hotel blends art deco and Native American design elements—some of which inspired the fictional Overlook Hotel in *The Shining.* Stay in a main lodge room for classic decor, or a cozy cottage with a fireplace.

EL TOVAR HOTEL
Grand Canyon National Park, Arizona
Situated a short stroll from the Grand Canyon's famed South Rim, it's all about location at El Tovar. The canyon empties of tourists after sunset, so you'll have the place all to yourself.

OLD FAITHFUL INN
Yellowstone National Park, Wyoming
The lobby, built in 1904 and flanked by gigantic stone fireplaces, is one of the biggest log structures in the world. In the 1950s, a printing press in the basement supplied nightly dinner menus. Comfortably furnished rooms here face the famous geyser.

THE AHWAHNEE HOTEL in Yosemite National Park.

MANY GLACIER HOTEL
Glacier National Park, Montana
Glacial peaks provide a grand backdrop for this rustic lodge beside Swiftcurrent Lake in Glacier National Park's northeastern section. The series of Swiss chalet–style buildings house modestly decorated guest rooms.

KALALOCH LODGE
Olympic National Park, Washington
Come to this serene ocean-front setting to explore rain forests, glaciers, and protected coastline. Spend a day at Ruby Beach or Lake Crescent, before enjoying sustainable seafood and Washington State wines at Creekside Restaurant back at the lodge.

CRATER LAKE LODGE
Crater Lake National Park, Oregon
Gaze on the deepest lake in the U.S. from this rustic lodge perched on the southwest rim of the caldera. The vivid blue water is due to the lake's depth—nearly 2,000 feet—and the surrounding volcanic peaks only add to the dramatic beauty.

DRAKESBAD GUEST RANCH
Lassen Volcanic National Park, California
Electricity here is scarce, so many guests use kerosene lamps, and some showers are in a shared bathhouse. A hot spring pool turns into a giant hot tub at night, and meals are inlcuded.

ROSS LAKE RESORT
North Cascades National Park, Washington
Hike or take a ferry to this secluded resort. Cabins sit along the lake shore overlooking the Pacific Northwest landscape of blue water and rolling evergreen Cascades. Guests must bring their own food, and all cabins have full kitchens.

The Best Campgrounds in the National Parks of the West

JENNY LAKE CAMPGROUND
Grand Teton National Park, Wyoming
A short walk from glacial Jenny Lake, this campground is a favorite among kayakers and canoers, anglers in search of lake trout, hikers, climbers, and bikers.

WHITE RIVER CAMPGROUND
Mount Rainier National Park, Washington
Three thousand feet into a glacial canyon, 112 campsites for tents and smaller RVs (no hookups) make up Mount Rainier National Park's White River Campground. White River is nestled in a forest with soaring pine-laden slopes.

JUMBO ROCKS CAMPGROUND
Joshua Tree National Park, California
This campground is woven among the stacked and strewn oversized volcanic boulders unique to Joshua Tree National Park, which change color in the shifting evening light. Several hiking trails begin here.

CHISOS BASIN CAMPGROUND
Big Bend National Park, Texas
Surrounded by rugged cliffs high in the Chisos Mountains, this campground is a picturesque slice of montane shrubland, all Arizona cypress, and desert-hardy mesquite trees. It's perfectly positioned close to the park's most popular trails.

SLOUGH CREEK CAMPGROUND
Yellowstone National Park, Wyoming
The 16 sites at Slough Creek can accommodate tents and small RVs. The campground is in the heart of the Lamary Valley, one of the best places for wildlife viewing in the park.

FRUITA CAMPGROUND
Capitol Reef National Park, Utah
Fed by the Fremont River, which meanders along the campground's edge, Fruita is literally an oasis in the desert, surrounded by the cool, green shade of historic orchards.

NORTH RIM CAMPGROUND
Grand Canyon National Park, Arizona
The fairly quiet North Rim Campground sits at 8,200 feet in elevation bordering the Transept Canyon, an offshoot of the main canyon. Many campsites have fantastic views.

Fruita Campground

MORAINE PARK CAMPGROUND

Rocky Mountain National Park, Colorado

This beautiful campground is spread out through a Douglas fir and pine forest, surrounded by a meadow of tall grasses and wildflowers and sheltered by craggy peaks rising up to 14,000 feet.

KINTLA LAKE CAMPGROUND

Glacier National Park, Montana

Just south of the Canadian border, Kintla Lake is the park's most remote developed campground. Perched on the edge of the pristine lake, this 13-site, RV-free campground offers campers serene solitude.

AZALEA CAMPGROUND

Kings Canyon National Park, California

Sheltered by towering pines and sequoias, Azalea is hilly and dotted with massive boulders, creating a sense of privacy among its 110 first-come, first-served sites.

KALALOCH CAMPGROUND

Olympic National Park, Washington

For truly epic sunset views, the Kalaloch Campground can't be beat. Overlooking the Pacific Ocean, this 170-site campground is right on the edge of North America.

TEXAS SPRINGS CAMPGROUND

Death Valley National Park, California

The massive size of this place, the quickly shifting shades of the desert, will take your breath away.

WATCHMAN CAMPGROUND

Zion National Park, Utah

This massive, 213-site campground, a quarter of a mile from the south entrance and visitor center, sits in the shadow of the famous Zion rock formation. Reserve well in advance.

Field Guide: Geology and Terrain

GEOTHERMAL FEATURES

Hissing geysers, gurgling mud pots, and steaming hot springs have fascinated travelers ever since mountain man John Coulter described them to an unbelieving public in 1810. Today, these "freaks of a fiery nature," as Rudyard Kipling characterized them, are created when superheated water rises to the Earth's surface from a magma chamber below. In the case of geysers, the water is trapped under the surface until the pressure is so great that it bursts through. Mud pots, also known as paint pots, are a combination of hot water, hydrogen sulfide gas, and dissolved volcanic rock.

CRATERS AND CALDERAS

A crater is a bowl-shape depression that's left behind when a volcano erupts. A caldera (Spanish for "cooking pot" or "cauldron") is essentially a big, sunken crater in which the volcano's inner magma chamber has also collapsed.

MONUMENT

This general term applies to two distinct geologic formations: those that are much taller than they are wide and those that resemble man-made structures.

MESAS AND CUESTAS

A mesa is an isolated hill with a smooth, flat top and steeply sloping sides. Its topmost layer is composed of rock that protects the lower layers from erosion. A cuesta is essentially a mesa that dips slightly to one side. A single mesa or cuesta may cover hundreds of square miles.

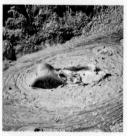

VOLCANOES AND VOLCANISM

Volcanoes are openings in Earth's crust where magma reaches the surface. Volcanic activity, or volcanism, can create many geologic formations like batholiths (large, rounded domes) or dikes and sills (banded, sheetlike formations).

GLACIERS AND GLACIAL FEATURES

Heavy snow compacted by centuries of pressure forms the slow-moving river of ice known as a glacier. Although most of the glaciers of North America have retreated, you can still see them in some of the Western parks.

Geothermal Features

BUTTES AND SPIRES

Buttes are isolated hills with very steep sides and flat tops (they're defined as a hill that's higher than it is wide). They are formed in sedimentary (layered) rock by erosion, when wind or water wear away softer layers to leave a section of harder rock behind. As a butte erodes, it may become one or more spires, which look like giant stone columns (with a uniform thickness and smooth profile that tapers slightly at the top).

DESERT VARNISH

This reddish-brown or black coating, sometimes called rock varnish, drips down arid canyon walls. Windblown dust or rain containing iron and manganese, along with microorganisms living on the rock's surface, create the color. Ancestral Pueblo and other ancient Native Americans scratched petroglyphs into it.

PLAYAS

Shallow lake beds known as playas ("beaches" in Spanish) commonly lie in the low points of arid Southwestern valleys. These sedimentary basins often fill with rainwater, then dry again as the water evaporates.

ARCHES AND BRIDGES

An arch is a window in a rock wall that typically forms through erosion, when wind and/or water wear away the surface to create a hole all the way through. A natural bridge is a type of arch created by rushing water. Together, they are called windows.

Wildlife in the Parks

EAGLES
With a wingspan of up to 7½ feet, the adult golden eagle has dark plumage, except for a golden head. Golden eagles are seen in Mount Rainier, Redwood, Sequoia and Kings Canyon, Theodore Roosevelt, and Yellowstone; you might see a bald eagle, distinguished by their white heads, in North Cascades, Olympic, Redwood, Sequoia and Kings Canyon, Yellowstone, and Zion.

BISON
Yellowstone is the only place in the country where bison have lived continuously since prehistoric times; currently, the park's two herds have about 4,800 animals. Bison can also be seen at Badlands, Grand Teton, Great Sand Dunes, Theodore Roosevelt, and Wind Cave.

GRAY WOLF
These impressive canines, listed as threatened or endangered in parts of the United States, communicate with each other through body language, barks, and howls. Wolves are wary of humans, but you might spot one at Grand Teton, Mount Rainier, North Cascades, and Yellowstone.

MOOSE
Feeding on fir, willows, and aspens, the moose is the largest member of the deer family: the largest bulls stand 7 feet tall at the shoulders and weigh up to 1,600 pounds. Look for moose in Glacier, Grand Teton, Rocky Mountain, and Yellowstone.

BIGHORN SHEEP
Clambering along rocky ledges, bighorn sheep fascinate with their ability to travel so easily where the rest of us can't. In winter, the docile herd animals descend to lower elevations. Many of the national parks of the West are home to a few varieties of bighorn sheep. They rut in autumn, when antlered males fight each other dramatically over mates.

GRIZZLY BEAR
A male grizzly can weigh 700 pounds and reach a height of 8 feet when standing on its hind legs. After hibernation (November to March), they emerge hungry, sometimes prompting trail closures.

MOUNTAIN GOAT
Not really goats at all (they're actually related to antelope), these woolly mountaineers live in high elevations throughout the northwestern United States. Look for them in Glacier, Mount Rainier, North Cascades, and Yellowstone.

ELK
Elk congregate where forest meets meadows. In September and October, bulls attract mating partners by bugling, a loud whistling. Elk are residents of many national parks.

MOUNTAIN LION
Although mountain lions live throughout the American West, from northern Canada through the South American Andes, chances are you won't see them at most of the parks due to their elusive nature. Also called cougars, these enormous carnivores can be 8 feet long and weigh up to 200 pounds. They're capable of taking down a mule deer or elk.

COYOTE
As big as a mid-size dog, coyotes thrive in the western U.S. and at many national parks. They travel most often alone or in pairs, but occasionally form small packs for hunting. Although they pose little threat to humans, never approach one.

What to Read and Watch

OUR NATIONAL PARKS
BY JOHN MUIR

As a naturalist and early advocate for the protection of America's Western forests, John Muir has become synonymous with America's national parks. This collection of essays celebrates the beauty of the nation's untamed. In terms of the environment, Muir was very much ahead of his time, helping to form the Sierra Club and inspiring other conservation initiatives. But Muir was also very much a man *of* his time, espousing hurtful views of Native and African Americans. In 2020, the Sierra Club itself not only apologized for these views but also pledged to make amends by adopting new, more-inclusive policies and employment practices.

YOSEMITE AND THE RANGE
OF LIGHT BY ANSEL ADAMS

This collection of more than 150 black-and-white photos conveys the jaw-dropping majesty of the High Sierras as only a master photographer can. Ansel Adams's camera captured both the grandeur of Yosemite's mountains and valleys and the intimate nature of the relationship between people and the natural world.

DESERT SOLITAIRE BY
EDWARD ABBEY

Arches National Park serves as the stunning backdrop of Edward Abbey's account as a park ranger. The essays describe both the hostility and the beauty of the American Southwest with funny, poetic, and often elegiac prose. Although first published in 1968, Abbey's advocacy on behalf the country's natural wonders is as prescient today as it was more than 50 years ago.

GLORYLAND BY
SHELTON JOHNSON

When Yellowstone was first established, the park was patrolled by a regiment of Buffalo Soldiers. This historical novel by Shelton Johnson (a Yosemite park ranger himself) tells the story of one soldier who finds a home among the mountains and rivers of Yosemite when his regiment is assigned to guard the park.

BUTCH CASSIDY AND
THE SUNDANCE KID

George Roy Hill's 1969 Western tells the (mostly) real-life story of outlaws Robert Leroy Parker (a.k.a. Butch Cassidy) and Harry Alonzo Longabaugh (a.k.a. the Sundance Kid). Over the course of the film, Paul Newman and Robert Redford are chased by lawmen, rob trains, and banter against the backdrop of Zion National Park and in the ghost town of Grafton, a few miles south of Zion.

THE RIVER WILD

Meryl Streep and Kevin Bacon star in this 1994 thriller about a family's whitewater rafting vacation going awry when they cross paths with a pair of on-the-lam criminals. It was shot on the Middle Fork of the Flathead River, which forms part of the southern boundary of Glacier National Park.

THELMA AND LOUISE

The quintessential road trip movie, *Thelma and Louise* follows the titular friends as they make their way from Arkansas to the Grand Canyon. Parts of the film were shot in Arches and Canyonlands National Park. But that iconic final scene was actually filmed at Dead Horse Point State Park in Utah.

STAR WARS: A NEW HOPE

You could be forgiven for thinking that the arid Death Valley National Park looks like something from a galaxy far, far away. It did, after all, serve as the location for the desert planet of Tatooine in *Star Wars: A New Hope* and *Return of the Jedi*.

Chapter 2

PLANNING YOUR VISIT

Know Before You Go

What are the must-see sights? What the are best hikes? Are there any scenic drives? Where can you eat in the park? Where can you stay in the park? What park-based activities are available? We've got answers and a few tips to help you make the most of your visit.

SEASONS AND WEATHER WORK DIFFERENTLY HERE

National parks are places of extremes—extreme beauty and extreme weather. In May, for example, you'll see snow at Yellowstone and North Cascades; while down at Guadalupe Mountains on the Texas/New Mexico border, the unrelenting sun has already dried out the landscape; and in Death Valley, average temperatures are already in the 90s. No matter which park you visit, prepare for both excessive heat and brutal cold.

PLAN AHEAD FOR THE MOST ADVENTUROUS PARK EXPERIENCES

National park rangers protect the parks' ecologies from the millions of tourists who visit annually. This means that for some of the most popular adventures in the park—kayaking up-bay at Glacier Bay or exploring Slaughter Canyon Cave at Carlsbad Caverns—there are only a handful of spots open and they fill up well in advance, so be sure to reserve early on the park's website. In some places, like at Yosemite's Half Dome, the required permit is accessible only via a lottery system, with just 300 winners a day.

LEAVE NO TRACE

Anything you bring into the park must be carried back out or put in the appropriate garbage or recycling receptacle. Don't pick up any rocks or artifacts or fossils; don't collect flowers or firewood; and never touch or interact with a wild animal.

SOME CAMPSITES ARE RESERVED FOR WALK-UPS

Most parks reserve campsites for first-come, first-served walk-ups. As long as you get there as early in the morning as possible, you're likely to get a spot, even on weekends. They aren't always the most desirable campgrounds in the park, though—at Yosemite, for example, most of the walk-up sites are located in high country and not in the Yosemite Valley— but it's much better than staying home.

RECOGNIZE AND RESPECT THE PARK'S INDIGENOUS HISTORY

For many centuries, the only visitors to this nation's wilderness were the indigenous peoples of North America. Evidence of settlement and exploration by Native Americans in the national parks dates back more than 10,000 years. Thanks to a mandate that enforces management of cultural and ecological resources in the parks, artifacts left behind have been well preserved. For some of the best insight into Native American history, plan a visit to Mesa Verde, the Grand Canyon, Badlands, or the Utah triad—Arches, Zion, and Canyonlands. If you find an artifact while hiking or backpacking in a national park, never pick it up; artifacts are useless to archaeologists unless they are discovered in situ.

FIRES ARE A HUGE CONCERN

Although wildfires have always been an issue, particularly during June and July, in recent years, hot, dry conditions, overgrown forests, and unhealthy trees have turned the West into a tinderbox, and wildfires have ravaged the landscape year-round. In 2017, more than 12,000 acres of Glacier National Park were destroyed by the Howe Ridge Fire; in 2018, Yosemite closed for the first time since 1990 due to the nearby Ferguson Fire; and in 2020, it seemed as if all of California was ablaze. It's critical that you be mindful of fire alerts and that you follow fire-prevention protocols. Most parks still allow campfires in designated fire pits, while others have charcoal grills. Outside of these designated areas, fires are both illegal and incredibly dangerous. If you plan to camp in the backcountry and need fire for cooking, bring a small camp stove or propane burner.

DON'T SKIP THE VISITOR CENTER

At most national parks, the visitor center is more than just a place to get information on the best hiking trails. Here you'll often find museum-quality displays on the park's ecology, geology, and biology; some even have archaeological artifacts on view.

TAKE WARNING SIGNS AND RANGER ADVICE SERIOUSLY

National parks are among the few remaining places in the United States that have not been entirely engineered for your safety; in some cases the only thing that stands between you and certain death is a sign. Visitors die every year in climbing and hiking accidents and animal encounters in America's national parks. Always take precautionary signs and ranger advice seriously.

FIND BEAUTY AND SOLITUDE AWAY FROM THE FAMOUS SITES

It's kind of a catch-22: you go to a national park to experience the beauty and solitude of the natural world only to discover that everyone else had the same plan. Rather than visiting the most popular sites, hit the trails (or water), particularly routes that are longer than 3 miles and can't be traversed by baby carriages and large tour groups. They may not be listed as the park's must-see locations, but they're almost guaranteed to be just as spectacular, yet apart from the crowds.

GET A GOOD LOOK AT WHAT WE COULD LOSE AS CLIMATE CHANGE PROGRESSES

National parks are ground zero for the environmental havoc wrought by climate change. These extreme environments are seeing rapid change as glaciers melt (Glacier Bay) and wildfires rage (Yosemite and Glacier). While this is devastating to watch, visiting the national parks reminds us what we have to lose.

PETS IN THE PARK

Generally, pets are allowed only in developed areas of the national parks, including drive-in campgrounds and picnic areas. They must be kept on a leash at all times. With the exception of guide dogs, pets are not allowed inside buildings, on most trails, on beaches, or in the backcountry. They also may be prohibited in areas controlled by concessionaires, such as restaurants. Some national parks have kennels; call ahead to learn the details and to see if there's availability. Some of the national forests (⊕ www.fs.fed.us) surrounding the parks have camping and are more lenient with pets, although you should not plan to leave your pet unattended at the campsite.

TRAVELING WITH KIDS

If you plan to travel with kids, check out these websites before heading out for ways to entertain and educate. ⊕ smokeybear. com/en/smokey-for-kids; ⊕ www.nationalparks. org/our-work/programs/ npf-kids; ⊕ www.nps.gov/ kids/junior-ranger-online. htm; ⊕ www.doi.gov/public/ teachandlearn

USE MAPS

If you plan to do a lot of hiking or mountaineering, especially in the backcountry, invest in detailed maps and a compass. Topographical maps are sold in well-equipped outdoor stores (REI and Cabela's, for example). Maps in different scales are available from the U.S. Geological Survey. To order, go to ⊕ www.usgs. gov/pubprod/maps.html or call ☎ 888/275–8747.

THE PARKS AND COVID-19

The United States was gravely impacted by the COVID-19 virus in 2020, and the national parks were not spared. If you're currently planning a visit, remember to call ahead to verify open hours, which parts of the park are open, and how reservation protocols have been affected.

Park Passes

NATIONWIDE PASSES

Although not all national parks charge admission—and children under age 16 always enter free—many do. If you're visiting several American national parks in one vacation or over the course of a year, you can save money with one of the America the Beautiful (all called Interagency) passes, which generally cover the cardholder and all others in a single vehicle (or the cardholder and up to three other passengers age 16 and older at places that charge per person).

What's more, the passes are valid for entry to more than 2,000 federal recreation sites managed by six participating agencies. These include the NPS as well as the Bureau of Land Management, Bureau of Reclamation, Fish and Wildlife Service, U.S. Army Corps of Engineers, and USDA Forest Service.

Although the NPS (⊕ *www.nps.gov/ planyourvisit/passes.htm*) has pass details, and you can buy passes on location at some participating sites, the United States Geological Survey (USGS) is the primary source for information and purchase (☎ *888/275–8747, Option 2* ⊕ *store.usgs.gov/pass*). Another good source is Recreation.gov (☎ *877/444– 6777* reservations, ☎ *606/515–6777* international ⊕ *www.recreation.gov*).

Although USGS phone and online orders incur a $5 or $10 handling charge, they do include a free brochure and vehicle hang tags (if you're driving a motorcycle or an open-top vehicle, inquire about free decals). All passes are nontransferable and nonrefundable (lost or stolen passes must be repurchased), and you must show photo ID with your pass at entrances.

Access Pass. United States citizens or permanent residents with disabilities medically determined to be permanent (documentation required) can acquire this free lifetime pass. At some locations, it might also allow for discounts on camping, tour, and other amenities.

Annual Pass. Available to anyone age 16 or older, this pass costs $80 and is valid for a year from the date of purchase. It can be shared by two "owners," who need not be related or married (both must sign the back of the pass).

Every Kid Outdoors Pass. This free pass (⊕ *everykidoutdoors.gov*) is available to U.S. students in their fourth-grade school year (i.e., it's valid Sept.–Aug.) and covers three accompanying family members or friends.

Senior Pass. If you're 62 or older and are a U.S. citizen or permanent resident, you can buy an annual $20 pass or a lifetime $80 pass. At some sites, this pass might also allow for discounts on some amenities and services such as camping and guided tours; discounts vary from park to park. In addition, senior citizens can acquire passes via a mail-in application (⊕ *store.usgs.gov/s3fs-public/ senior_pass_application.pdf*); additional fees apply.

Volunteer Pass. Look into this free, annual pass if you've logged 250 volunteer hours at recreation sites or lands overseen by one of the six federal pass-program agencies.

Military Pass. This pass is free to current members (and members' dependents) of the Army, Navy, Air Force, Marines, and Coast Guard, as well as the Reserves and National Guard.

TIP→ The Golden Eagle, Golden Age, and Golden Access passes have been discontinued. These passes can be used for park entrance if they are still valid according to the pass's original provisions.

INDIVIDUAL PARK PASSES

Most national parks offer individual annual passes. Prices vary but hover around $35 to $70 (⊕ *www.nps.gov/aboutus/ entrance-fee-prices.htm*). In a few cases these passes include admission to two sites (say, a national park and a national monument, recreation area, or forest) that are near each other. If you might visit a particular park more than once in a year, look into its annual pass. Sometimes, there's only a small difference between a single day's and a year's admission. For example, Bryce Canyon, charges $35 per vehicle for a seven-day permit but only $5 more for the annual pass, meaning a $30 savings if you return to the park within the year.

In other cases, the entrance fee to one park includes admission to other federally managed sites nearby: a $55 Southeast Utah Parks Pass gets you into Arches and Canyonlands, plus Natural Bridges National Monument, for a year; any paid entrance to Sequoia and Kings Canyon includes access to the Hume Lake District of Sequoia National Forest/Giant Sequoia National Monument; and for an extra $5, you can add unlimited access to Arapahoe National Recreation Area to your $70 Rocky Mountain NP annual pass.

CANADIAN NATIONAL PARKS

If you're planning to travel to Canadian national parks, Parks Canada (☎ *877/737-3783* in North America, ☎ *519/826-5391* elsewhere ⊕ *www.pc.gc.ca*), the Canadian equivalent of the NPS, issues an annual Discovery Pass (⊕ *www.commandesparcs-parksorders.ca*) that allows free entry to 80 parks and other sites. Prices range from about US$45 to US$106.

FREE ADMISSION

Each year, the national parks designate a handful of "Free Entrance Days" (check the NPS website, ⊕ *www.nps.gov/findapark/feefreeparks.htm*, for the most updated list). In addition, many parks—312 of the 421 NPS properties—never charge an admission fee. They include:

- Channel Islands*
- Great Basin*
- Redwood
- Wind Cave*

There is a fee for transportation to Channel Islands; cave tours at Great Basin and Wind Cave have a fee.

Family Fun

TOP 5 TIPS

1. Plan ahead. At many parks, rooms and campsites fill up fast, so make your reservations as early as you can. Many parks will have every room and camp-site booked several months in advance (weekends are especially popular). We recommend booking at least six months ahead, and more if you plan to visit one of the more popular parks, such as Grand Canyon, Grand Teton, Rocky Mountain, Yellowstone, or Yosemite. If you plan on staying outside the park, check with the hotels you're considering as far ahead as you can, as these places can fill up fast as well. You can also go online. All the national parks have websites—links to all of them are at the National Park Service page (⊕ *www.nps.gov*).

2. Get the kids involved. It might seem easier to do the planning yourself, but you'll probably have a better time—and your kids definitely will—if you involve them. No matter how old they are, children ought to have a good idea of where you're going and what you're about to experience. It will help get them excited beforehand and will likely make them feel like they have a say and a stake in the trip. Discuss the park's attractions and give your kids a choice of two or three options (that are all amenable to you, of course). Many of the parks' sites have links with advice on family travel or info on children's activities.

3. Know your children. Consider your child's interests. This will help you plan a vacation that's both safe and memorable (for all the right reasons). For starters, if you have kids under four, be honest with yourself about whether the national park itself is an appropriate destination. Parents are notorious for projecting their awe for majestic scenery and overall enthusiasm for sightseeing on their younger kids, who might be more interested in cataloging the snacks in the hotel room's minibar. Likewise, be realistic about your child's stamina and ability. If your children have never been hiking, don't expect them to be able to do a long hike at a higher altitude than they are used to. Remember: Children's first experience hiking can make them a lover or a hater of the activity, so start off slowly and try some practice hikes near home.

4. Pack wisely. Be sure you're bringing kid-size versions of the necessities you'll pack for yourself. Depending on the park you're visiting (and the activities you're planning), that will probably include sturdy sandals or hiking shoes, sunglasses, sunscreen, and insect repellent. You'll almost certainly need a few layers of clothing and plenty of water and snacks. In terms of hydration, the American Academy of Pediatrics recommends giving children ages 9 to 12 about 3 to 8 ounces of water or another beverage every 20 minutes during strenuous exercise; adolescents should drink 34 to 50 ounces every hour.

5. Develop a Plan B. National parks are natural places, meaning they change dramatically with the seasons and the weather, so you should plan on alternate activities if Mother Nature isn't cooperative. And if you've already talked with your kids about your options, you can pick a new plan that appeals to everyone.

BUDGETING YOUR TRIP

Like most vacations, a trip to a national park can be as frugal, or as fancy, as you like. Here are a few things to consider:

Getting in. Individual admission costs vary by park and range from free to $35 per vehicle (or $10–$15 per person and $15–$30 per motorcycle). You also can buy an America the Beautiful Pass for $80, which will get you and three other adults (kids 15 and under are free) into any national park (as well as other designated federal lands) for one year.

Sleeping. Fewer than half of the parks charge for camping; the cost is typically less than $25 per night. In many parks, you also can stay at a lodge, where prices run from $120 to $500 a night. Most parks have several accommodation options outside the park, as well.

Eating. In each of the parks, all the in-park concessions are run by companies under contract with the National Park Service, meaning their prices are set by the government. Generally speaking, prices are a bit higher than what you'd pay outside the park, but not significantly so. You also can bring in your own food and eat at one of the park's picnic areas.

Entertainment. Just looking at the wonders of the park is entertainment enough for many youngsters, but the many sports and outdoor activities—from hiking and bicycling to horseback riding and cave touring, depending on the park— help children stay active while exploring. Many park visitor centers also have films; some parks, such as Grand Canyon and Zion, even have IMAX movies. Cost for these offerings varies, ranging from free to a couple hundred dollars for more involved programs, such as a white-water rafting trip.

Sample Budget for a Family of Four

Here is an idea of what a family of four might spend on a three-day trip to Grand Canyon National Park, during which they stay and eat all their meals within the park. Depending on your accommodations and dining-out options, the total you spend can vary dramatically.

Admission: $35 per car; admission covers seven days in the park.

Lodging: A standard double room in one of the in-park lodges on the popular South Rim ranges from approximately $118 to $360 a night. Total for three nights: $354 to $1,080; double that ($708 to $2,160) if you have older children in a separate room.

Meals: Dining options in the park range from no-frills snack bars to upscale restaurants. Per-meal costs average $20 to $50 or more, per person (you might be able to spend less if you're cooking meals over your campfire or packing bag lunches). Total (three meals per person, per day for three days): $720 to $1,800.

Souvenirs: Budget $10 to $15 per person per day for souvenirs so that everybody can get something small each day, or one or two larger items per trip. Total: $120 to $180.

TOTAL COST: $1,194 to $3,060 (more if older children have a separate room)

Souvenirs. All the parks have gift shops, and many stock items that are actually useful. For example, you'll find things like kid-size binoculars, fanny packs, and magnifying glasses, all of which can make your child's visit even more enjoyable. Budget $10 or $15 to cover one item (maybe something you might have bought for your child anyway, like a new sun hat).

KIDS' PROGRAMS
Roughly two-thirds of the 421 U.S. National Park Service units (national parks as well as historic sites, national monuments, preserves, and other significant places) are part of the Junior Ranger Program, which offers kids the opportunity to learn about individual parks by filling out a short workbook or participating in an activity such as taking a hike with a park ranger. After completing the program, kids get a badge (or a pin or patch, depending on the park). For availability, check with the ranger station or visitor center when you arrive; you can also check online ahead of time (⊕ *www.nps.gov/kids/parks-with-junior-ranger-programs.htm*). Kids can also complete Junior Ranger activities online (⊕ *www.nps.gov/kids/junior-ranger-online.htm*).

In addition to the Junior Ranger Program, kids can find a variety of activities in the parks designed just for them. Some parks, such as Olympic, loan "Discovery Backpacks" filled with kid-friendly tools like magnifying glasses (check ahead for availability). Other parks, like Grand Teton, have smartphone apps with information on park sites, current events, and history, as well as photo-editing features that allow for creative social-media sharing.

Many ongoing general-interest or park-specific programs—stargazing in Bryce Canyon, say, or rock climbing in Yosemite—will also be of interest to kids.

■ TIP→ **If your child is in the fourth grade, don't forget to get the free Every Kid Outdoors Pass. For more details visit everykidoutdoors.gov.**

What to Pack

TOP 10 ESSENTIALS

Packing lists for any trip vary according to the individual and his or her needs, of course, but here are 10 essential things to include in your luggage for a national parks vacation.

1. Binoculars. Many of the parks are a bird- (and animal-) watcher's dream. A pair of binos will help you spot feathered friends as well as larger creatures. Binoculars are sold according to power, or how much the objects you're viewing are magnified (i.e., 7x, 10x, 12x), and the diameter of objective lens, which is the one on the fat end of the binoculars; 10x is a good choice for magnification, field of view, and steadiness.

2. Clothes that layer. In much of the West (especially at higher elevations), days are often warm while nights turn chilly. The weather also can change quickly, with things going from dry and sunny to windy and wet in a matter of minutes. This means you need to pack with both warm and cold (as well as wet and dry) weather in mind. The easiest solution is to dress in layers. Experts suggest synthetics such as polyester (used in Coolmax and other "wicking" fabrics that draw moisture away from your skin, and fleece, which is an insulator) and lightweight merino wool. Look for socks in wicking wool or polyester. Don't forget a waterproof poncho or jacket.

3. Long pants and long-sleeve shirts. It's wise to minimize exposed skin when hiking, especially in areas with poison ivy and/or ticks and at higher elevations, where the sun's radiation is much stronger. Convertible pants (the bottom portion zips off, leaving you in a pair of shorts) are another good option—they're often made of quick-drying and rugged material and allow you the flexibility of pants or shorts at a moment's notice.

4. Sturdy shoes or sandals. If you plan to do any hiking, be sure your footwear has rugged soles, a necessity on unpaved trails. Be sure to break in your shoes before the trip.

5. Insect repellent. If you're hiking or camping in an area with lots of mosquitoes, a good bug spray can help keep your trip from being a swatting marathon. A repellent also helps deter ticks. Most experts recommend repellents with DEET (N,N-diethyl-m-toluamide); the higher the level of DEET, the longer the product will be effective. Just be sure to use a separate sunscreen, not a single product with both ingredients (this is because you're supposed to reapply sunscreen every few hours, but doing so with DEET could deliver a dangerous dose of the chemical).

6. Skin moisturizer, sunscreen, and lip balm. In the parks, you're likely to be outside for longer—and in higher altitudes and drier climates—than you're used to. All of this can leave your skin and lips parched and burned. Sunscreen should provide both UVA and UVB protection, with an SPF of at least 15; look for a lotion marked "sweatproof" or "sport" and be sure to reapply throughout the day.

7. Sunglasses and hat. Higher elevation means more ultraviolet radiation; research shows there's an 8% to 10% increase in UV intensity for every 1,000 feet in elevation gain. Look for sunglasses that provide 100% UV protection.

8. Journal and camera. When your jaw drops at the glorious vistas and your head clears from all the fresh air, you may want to try your hand at sketching what you see or jotting down your thoughts. And of course, you'll want to get photographs.

9. Snacks and water. National parks by their nature are remote, and some are lacking in services. Bring plenty of water and healthy snacks (or meals, depending on how long you plan to be out and what you're likely to find in the park). When hiking in hot weather, experts recommend ½ to 1 quart of water (or another fluid) per person, per hour, to prevent potentially dangerous dehydration. The risk of dehydration is greater at elevations above 8,000 feet. Even if you're not hiking, have water and food in the car for long drives where facilities might be scarce.

10. First-aid kit. A solid kit should contain a first-aid manual, aspirin (or ibuprofen), razor blades, tweezers, a needle, scissors, adhesive bandages, butterfly bandages, sterile gauze pads, 1-inch-wide adhesive tape, an elastic bandage, antibacterial ointment, antiseptic cream or spray, antihistamines, calamine lotion, and moleskin (for blisters).

HIKING ITEMS

For vacations where you'll be hiking for longer than an hour or two at a time, consider investing in the following:

■ a **compass and map**

■ a **daypack** with enough room for everybody's essentials

■ **energy bars** (they may not be five-star dining, but they do give you energy and keep your kids—and you—from getting cranky)

■ a **hiking stick or poles**, especially if you've got bad knees

■ a **water filter** to treat water

■ **bear bells** if you're in bear country

■ **reusable water bottles**

CAMPING GEAR

Planning on roughing it on your national parks vacation? In addition to a working tent (check the zipper before you go!), sleeping bags and pillows, and, of course, the ingredients for s'mores (graham crackers, chocolate bars, and marshmallows), here are some things veteran campers recommend be among your gear:

■ **camping chairs** (folding or collapsible)

■ **camp stove and fuel**

■ **cooking utensils, plates, and cups**

■ **duct tape** (great for covering tears)

■ **flashlight, headlamp, and lantern**

■ **matches**

■ **paper towels, napkins, wet wipes**

■ a **multipurpose knife and cutting board**

■ a **rope** (for laundry or to help tie things down; pack **clothespins**, too)

■ a **sleeping pad or air mattress**

■ a **tarp** (will help keep the bottom of your tent—and you—dry)

■ a **cooler**

■ **toilet paper**

■ a **shovel** (to bury waste) or **plastic bags** (to haul it out)

Photography Tips

Today's digital cameras make it difficult to take a truly lousy picture, but there are still some things even the best models can't do on their own. The tips here (some of them classic photography techniques) won't turn you into the next Ansel Adams, but they might prevent you from being upstaged by your eight-year-old with her smartphone.

The Golden Hours. The best photos are taken when most of us are either snoozing or eating dinner: about an hour before and after sunrise and sunset. When the light is gentle and golden, your photos are less likely to be overexposed or filled with harsh shadows and squinting people.

Divide to Conquer. You can't go wrong with the Rule of Thirds: When you're setting up a shot, mentally divide your picture area into thirds, horizontally and vertically, which will give you nine squares. Any one of the four places where the lines intersect (the four corners of the center square) represents a good spot to place your primary subject. (If all this talk of imaginary lines makes your head spin, just remember not to automatically plop your primary focal point in the center of your photos.)

Lock Your Focus. To get a properly focused photo using a camera with auto-focus, press the shutter button down halfway and wait a few seconds before pressing down completely. (On most cameras, a light or a beep will indicate that you're good to go.)

Circumvent Auto-Focus. If your camera isn't homing in on your desired focal point, center the primary subject smack in the middle of the frame and depress the shutter button halfway, allowing the camera to focus. Then, without lifting your finger, compose your photo properly (moving your camera so the focal point isn't in the center of the shot), and press the shutter all the way down.

Jettison the Jitters. Shaky hands are among the most common causes of out-of-focus photos. If you're not good at immobility, invest in a tripod or rest the camera on something steady—such as a wall, a bench, or a rock—when you shoot. If all else fails, lean against something sturdy to brace yourself.

Consider the Imagery. Take a moment or two to consider *why* you're shooting what you're shooting. Once you've determined this, start setting up your photo. Look for interesting lines that curve into your image—such as a path, the shoreline, or a fence—and use them to create the impression of depth. You can do the same thing by photographing people with their bodies or faces positioned at an angle to the camera.

Ignore All the Rules. Sure, thoughtful contemplation and careful execution are likely to produce brilliant images, but there are times when you just need to capture the moment. If you see something wonderful, grab your camera and just get the picture. If the photo turns out to be blurry, off-center, or over- or underexposed, you can always Photoshop it later.

Smartphone Tips: When possible, don't use the zoom tool. This reduces the picture's resolution and can lead to fuzzy photos. Instead, it's best to crop your photos manually. Also, it's helpful to turn on the grid feature, which helps you compose your shots.

Special Considerations. If you're going to any Native American reservations (many are near national parks), check the rules before you take photographs. In many cases you must purchase a permit.

Staying Healthy, Playing It Safe

ALTITUDE SICKNESS
Altitude sickness can result when you've moved to high elevations without having time to adjust. When you're at a mile (5,280 feet) or more above sea level, and especially when you're higher than 8,500 feet, you may experience shortness of breath, light-headedness, nausea, fatigue, headache, and insomnia. To help your body adjust, drink lots of water, avoid alcohol, and wait a day or two before attempting vigorous activity. If your symptoms are severe, last several days, or worsen, seek medical attention.

ANIMAL BITES
Although animals abound in the national parks, the odds of your meeting one face to face, let alone sustaining a bite, are slim (especially if you follow the rules about not feeding them). But if you are bitten or scratched by any wild animal—even a small one—seek medical attention. You may need stitches and antibiotics, or a rabies or tetanus shot. If that animal is a snake, stay calm (if the snake is venomous, a lot of movement can spread the poison). Have someone else get medical help for you right away.

DEHYDRATION
If your body doesn't have the fluids it needs, you're dehydrated. Symptoms can range from minor (a dull headache) to life-threatening (seizures, coma). Dehydration is often caused by excessive sweating coupled with inadequate fluid intake, and is a real concern in the national parks, where visitors are generally active (hiking, climbing) but not good at carrying and drinking water. Dehydration is a particular problem for children and seniors and for anyone exercising in dry climates; it's also more likely at high altitudes. To counter a mild case, drink water or another beverage. Take small sips over a period of time instead of trying to force down a large amount. A serious case requires immediate medical attention. To prevent dehydration, be sure to bring and consume enough water: ½ to 1 quart per person for each hour of exercise.

DON'T FEED THE ANIMALS
It's dangerous—and illegal (you'll be fined). Animals in many national parks are used to humans being around and may not flee at your presence. But feeding wild animals habituates them to humans and teaches them to look to us for food. When that happens, they lose the ability to hunt or forage on their own, meaning they might starve to death or be hit by cars when looking for handouts. Feeding animals also causes them to be more aggressive, and thus more dangerous, to future visitors. Aggressive animals are removed from areas where they'll have contact with people; in some cases, they're relocated, but in others, they're put down.

HEAT-RELATED ILLNESS
Typically caused by excessive exertion in high temperatures such as a strenuous hike in the desert, heat exhaustion or more serious heatstroke can cause nausea, headaches, and dizziness—and even seizures, unconsciousness, and death. If you suspect heat-related illness, rest in a cool, shady place and drink water. Dehydration is often a factor in heat exhaustion and heatstroke. Apply cool compresses to the head, forehead, and trunk. If the victim is unconscious or confused, seek medical help immediately.

HYPOTHERMIA
When your body gets too cold for too long, hypothermia can develop. Symptoms are chills, fatigue, shivering, and lack of mental clarity. If symptoms develop, seek shelter, remove any wet clothes, and wrap yourself in warm blankets.

GREAT ITINERARIES

Vast wilderness and endless recreation opportunities make it easy to spend an entire trip exploring just one national park. But adventurous travelers looking to discover more of the West can take on a bigger itinerary involving several parks, plus a couple of other destinations (national monuments, state parks, scenic byways, and the like) that show off some of the most impressive scenery America has to offer. We've put together a collection of these itineraries, aimed at the most popular (and feasible) routes taken by curious explorers.

Most of the national parks are so large you need a vehicle to properly explore, so planning a driving trip to visit them is a no-brainer. Whether you fly into the nearest airport and rent a car or drive all the way in your own vehicle, these itineraries can help you plan your route—and your time in the parks—to give you the best experience possible. Each itinerary is meant to be used for inspiration in planning your own trip, tailored to your interests and your travel style. We suggest you pick the parks that most appeal to you and linger a little longer there. That being said, those who want to see more in less time will prefer the tours just as they are.

We've developed these itineraries based on the idea that you'll be traveling during the summer, when you'll find most roads and facilities open in the parks. If you'll be traveling at another time of year, be sure to check with the park(s) you'll be visiting about road conditions and closures. Many parks are in remote and/or mountainous areas, accessible by roads that are subject to seasonal closures.

You should also note that "summer" can mean something different in different parts of the West; warm weather typically arrives much later in the year in the northern United States than it does in Arizona and New Mexico. Additionally, we're assuming you'll be traveling in a passenger car. If you're driving an RV (or pulling a trailer), check ahead on the proper routing for your particular rig, and check with the park(s) to see if they have any size or other vehicle restrictions.

Washington State National Parks Road Trip Itinerary, 8 Days

A trip to Washington's three national parks—plus a visit to Mount St. Helen's National Volcanic Monument—takes you through rugged Pacific coastline and high alpine terrain as well as lush temperate rain forest, glaciers, waterfalls, and some of the largest remnants of ancient forests in the U.S.

For those coming from out of state, the nearest airport is **Seattle-Tacoma International,** where you can start your journey by picking up a rental car. Depending on when your flight gets in, you can rest up at a nearby hotel for the night or make

the 85-mile, 1½-hour drive to **Sedro-Woolley,** Washington, where you can spend the night.

46 miles or about an hour drive from Sedro-Woolley.

From Sedro-Woolley, drive east for 46 miles along Route 20, also known as the North Cascades Highway, to the entrance of **North Cascades National Park.** Take your first stroll through an old-growth forest on the Skagit River Loop (1.8 miles), which starts at the visitor center near the town of Newhalem, about 9 miles from the entrance, then devote the rest of the day to driving through the park on Route 20, stopping at various overlooks. Exit the park and continue through the scenic Methow Valley and on to **Chelan** (about 190 miles from the park's western boundary) to stay the night.

205 miles or a 3-hour, 45-minute drive from Chelan; 136 miles or a 2-hour, 45-minute drive from Arlington.

From Chelan, get an early start to drive to Ohanapecosh, the southeastern entrance to **Mount Rainier National Park.** When you arrive, take a drive on the spectacular Sunrise Road (about 30 miles round-trip), which reveals the "back" (northeast) side of Rainier. Book a room in nearby **Ashford** (about 19 miles east of the park's Nisqually entrance) and make that your base for the next two nights.

The next day, energetic hikers will want to tackle one of the four- to six-hour trails that scale the park's many peaks. Less ambitious visitors can take one of the shorter hikes in the Paradise Inn area or join a ranger-led walk through wildflower meadows. Another option is to hike to Panorama Point (a strenuous 4-mile round-trip), near the foot of the Muir Snowfield, for breathtaking views of the glaciers and high ridges of Rainier. Finish your day with dinner at the Paradise Inn, where you can watch the sunset on the peak.

120 miles or a 2½-hour drive from Mount Rainier; 245 miles or a 4½-hour drive north from Mount St. Helens to Port Angeles.

Today, drive south to spend the day visiting the **Mount St. Helens National Volcanic Monument,** where you can enter from the west side via Route 504 and see the destruction caused by the 1980 eruption. After leaving the monument, follow Route 504 back to Interstate 5 and head north to Olympia, winding through scenic Puget Sound countryside, skirting the Olympic foothills, and periodically dipping down to the waterfront en route to **Port Angeles,** where you'll spend the night.

19½ miles (40 minutes) south from Port Angeles to Hurricane Ridge; 69 miles (1½ hours) southwest from Port Angeles to La Push; 72 miles (1 hour, 40 minutes) south from Hoh Rain Forest to Lake Quinault.

The next morning, launch into a full day at **Olympic National Park.** From the Port Angeles entrance, drive south to Hurricane Ridge, where you'll find several trails taking you through meadows and subalpine forest. The Hurricane Hill Trail (3.2 miles round-trip) delivers panoramic views of the mountains and ocean. Afterward, head back to Port Angeles for the night.

On Day 7, follow U.S. 101 west to **La Push,** a skinny satellite of coastal land that's part of the national park. From La Push, hike 1.4 miles to Third Beach for a taste of the wild Pacific coastline. Back on U.S. 101, head south to the town of Forks and then east to the **Hoh Rain Forest,** also part of Olympic National Park. Explore the moss-covered alders and big-leaf maples, then follow a circular route on U.S. 101 to **Lake Quinault,** winding west toward the coast, then back to the lake and the national park. Check into the Lake Quinault Lodge, then drive up the river to access one of several trails—the Graves Creek Trail is a popular choice—through the lush Quinault Valley.

Catch your flight back home from Seattle–Tacoma International, about 130 miles (a 2½-hour drive) from Olympic via I-5.

Yellowstone and Grand Teton National Parks Road Trip Itinerary, 7 Days

A visit to these two parks takes you through one of the last remaining natural ecosystems in this region of the world. Here, you'll see wildlife ranging from beavers, bison, and bears to weasels and wolves, plus pristine mountain lakes, bubbling mud pots, and the world's biggest collection of geysers.

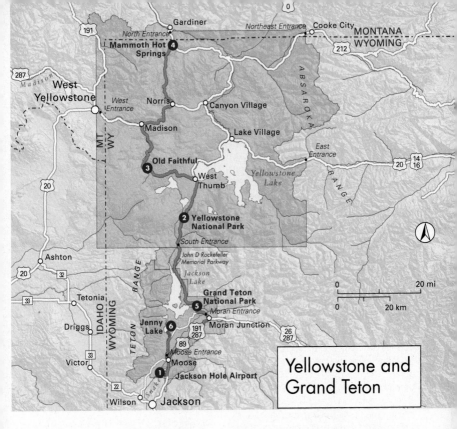

Yellowstone and Grand Teton

If you'll be flying, the **Jackson Hole Airport** in Jackson, Wyoming, is probably the best place to start, as it's only an hour from the southern entrance of Yellowstone. You'll find plenty of lodging options in Jackson for your first night, or you can book a room at one of the park's nine lodges—perhaps, the centrally located Lake Hotel or the iconic Old Faithful Inn.

Dedicate the next three days to **Yellowstone National Park,** which, because of its sheer size and incredibly diverse wildlife and scenery, could take a lifetime to explore. Spend your first day on the park's 142-mile Grand Loop Road. This road forms a big figure-eight as it passes nearly every major Yellowstone attraction, and offers interpretive displays, overlooks, and short trails along the way.

On your second day in the park, visit **Old Faithful** and take a short hike (about 2½

miles round-trip) around Mystic Falls, then head up to the Canyon Village section of the park for a look at the Grand Canyon of Yellowstone, with its two separate waterfalls. For a more strenuous option, hike from Dunraven Pass to the summit of Mt. Washburn for wildflowers, wildlife, and panoramic views (6.2 miles round-trip).

For your third day, explore the northern part of the park, starting with the **Mammoth Hot Springs** area, with its terraced limestone formations. From there, head past Tower-Roosevelt to the Lamar Valley in the far northeast corner of the park for gorgeous mountain views, enormous herds of bison, and your best chance to spot wolves. Then check out the Mud Volcano and Sulphur Caldron in the Hayden Valley area, just south of Canyon Village.

7 miles from Yellowstone's southern entrance to the northern boundary of Grand Teton.

Leaving Yellowstone, drive south into **Grand Teton National Park.** The sheer ruggedness of the Tetons makes them seem imposing and unapproachable, but a drive on Teton Park Road, with frequent stops at scenic turnouts, will get you up close and personal with the peaks. The Jenny Lake Scenic Drive delivers fantastic views as well; just north of **Jenny Lake,** pull over to the Leigh Lake Trailhead for a hike. You can take the 3.8-mile loop around String Lake, or head north, then take the right-hand branch of the trail and follow the eastern shore of the lake (turn around at the campground on Trapper Lake) for a 9-mile hike. Spend your two nights at any of the excellent lodges or cabins in the park.

Your second day in the park, head back to Jenny Lake and catch a shuttle boat across to the western side, where you can take either a short hike along the Cascade Canyon Trail (2 miles round-trip) or hike the Forks of Cascade Canyon, a 9.6-mile trip that's well worth the effort. If you'd rather explore Jenny Lake from the water, rent a canoe or kayak or take a guided tour.

When your visit to Grand Teton is complete, getting back to the Jackson Hole Airport couldn't be simpler: it's actually inside the park boundary, about 4 miles from the southern entrance.

Black Hills and Badlands National Parks Road Trip Itinerary, 6 Days

The national parks of southwestern South Dakota—along with the state park and two national memorials nearby— deliver a surprising variety of sights: the swaying grasses and abundant wildlife of one of the country's few remaining intact prairies, the complex labyrinth of passages and unique geologic formations in one of the world's longest caves, and some of the richest fossil beds on Earth.

The closest commercial airport is **Rapid City Regional Airport,** about 70 miles northeast from Wind Cave. Arrive in the morning to pick up your rental car and make the 1½-hour drive to **Wind Cave National Park,** with more than 33,000 acres of wildlife habitat above ground (home to bison, elk, pronghorn, and coyotes) and one of the world's longest caves below. Take an afternoon cave tour and a short drive through the park. Spend the night in **Hot Springs,** about 10 miles from the park's southern boundary.

36 miles or a 45-minute drive northeast from Hot Springs.

Spend today at **Custer State Park,** which is adjacent to Wind Cave. The 71,000-acre park has exceptional drives, lots of wildlife (including a herd of 1,400 bison), and fingerlike granite spires rising from the forest floor (they're the reason this is called the Needles region of South Dakota). While you're in the park, be sure to visit Limber Pine Natural Area, a National Natural Landmark containing spectacular ridges of granite. If you have time, check out the Cathedral Spires trail, 3 miles round-trip. Overnight in one of five mountain lodges at the Custer State Park Resort.

About 28 miles (40 minutes) west from Custer State Park to Jewel Cave; 20 miles northeast from Jewel Cave to Crazy Horse Memorial.

Today, venture down U.S. 16 to **Jewel Cave National Monument,** 13 miles west of the town of Custer, an underground wilderness where you can see beautiful nailhead and dogtooth spar crystals lining its more than 195 miles of passageways.

After visiting Jewel Cave, head back to Custer and take U.S. 16/385 to **Crazy**

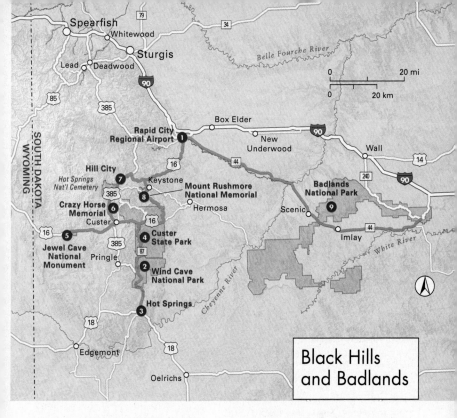

**Black Hills
and Badlands**

Horse Memorial (about 7 miles north of Custer), home to a colossal mountain carving of the legendary Lakota leader and the Indian Museum of North America. Afterward, head 12 miles north to the former gold and tin mining town of **Hill City,** where you'll spend the night.

12 miles or about a 30-minute drive northwest from Hill City.

This morning, travel to **Mount Rushmore National Memorial,** where you can view the huge carved renderings of presidents Washington, Jefferson, Theodore Roosevelt, and Lincoln. Afterward, head northwest for 23 miles back to **Rapid City,** the eastern gateway to the Black Hills. Spend the night here.

62 miles or a 1-hour drive southeast from Rapid City to the northeast entrance of Badlands.

Begin your day early and drive east (via Interstate 90) to **Badlands National Park,** a 244,000-acre geologic wonderland. The Badlands Highway Loop Road (Highway 240) wiggles through the moonlike landscape of the park's north unit for 32 miles. Stop in at Ben Reifel Visitor Center, at the far eastern edge of the park, to pick up a trail map and head out on a hike. The Notch Trail, 1½ miles round-trip, offers spectacular views of the White River Valley, but is definitely not for anyone with a fear of heights. The Cliff Shelf trail, ½ mile round-trip, is a more mellow option that showcases rock formations and juniper forest, as well as occasional wildlife sightings.

After you leave the park, head back to Rapid City to spend the night.

The airport in Rapid City is about 10 minutes southeast of town.

California National Parks Road Trip Itinerary, 9 Days

This trip takes you to California's most popular national parks. Yosemite is a nearly 1,200-square-mile expanse in the western Sierras filled with meadows, waterfalls, and spectacular granite domes and canyons. Nearby Sequoia and Kings Canyon national parks deliver spectacular alpine scenery along with the world's largest trees. And Death Valley is a land of extremes, with its impossibly dry (and hot) below-sea-level basin alongside high mountain peaks and diverse wildlife.

If you're planning to start this trip with a flight, your best bet would be to arrive at **Fresno Yosemite International Airport,** which is about 70 miles from the southern entrance to Yosemite (your first stop) and 80 miles from the northern entrance to Sequoia and Kings Canyon (your last).

From the airport, head north toward **Yosemite National Park** and its **Mariposa/Wawona Entrance,** following Highway 41. Depending on how much time you've got, either do some exploring (head for the Yosemite Valley Visitor Center, about 32 miles from the Wawona entrance) or look for lodging. You can stay in the park (there are several options, from primitive camping to luxury rooms at the Ahwahnee Hotel) or in **Mariposa,** about 43 miles (1 hour) west of the Wawona Entrance on Route 140.

126 miles, a 2-hour drive, southeast from Yosemite's Tioga Pass Entrance to Lone Pine.

Early in the morning of Day 2, head into Yosemite Valley, near the center of the park, and take a hike on Lower Yosemite Fall Trail, an easy 1.1-mile loop. If you've got more time and ambition, continue on for the first mile of the Upper Fall Trail to Columbia Rock, where you'll be rewarded with spectacular views of both the upper and lower sections of the highest waterfall in North America. Afterward, stop in at the historic Ahwahnee Hotel, then attend one of the ranger programs or a presentation at Yosemite Theater.

On your second day in the park, head back to the Yosemite Valley area, and take an easy hike around Mirror Lake (5 miles round-trip) or a more strenuous trek to Vernal Fall (2.5 miles round-trip), then drop in at the Yosemite Museum (next to the visitor center) and the nearby reconstructed Indian Village. Drive up to Glacier Point for a valley-wide view, timing your arrival for sunset.

On your last day in the park, head east to Tuolumne Meadows, where you can stretch your legs with a hike (an easy option is the 1½-mile round-trip trail to Soda Springs and historic Parsons Lodge). Then take a drive on Tioga Road (check ahead to make sure it is not closed), a 59-mile stretch through the high country that takes you over Tioga Pass (9,941 feet) and along the highest stretch of road in California. Leave the park through the **Tioga Pass Entrance,** then drive to the town of **Lone Pine,** where you'll spend the night.

53 miles or a 60-minute drive southwest from Lone Pine to the park's western Panamint entrance; 280 miles (about 4½ hours) northwest from Panamint entrance to Sanger.

On Day 5, drive to **Death Valley National Park,** known as the lowest, driest, and hottest place in North America. Covering more than 5,300 square miles, it's also the biggest national park in the lower 48, with vast expanses of desert and mountain ranges extending as far as the eye can see. ■TIP→ **The best time to hike Death Valley is November–March, as hiking in the summer heat can be hazardous.**

Begin in the Furnace Creek area, roughly in the middle of the park. If you're getting

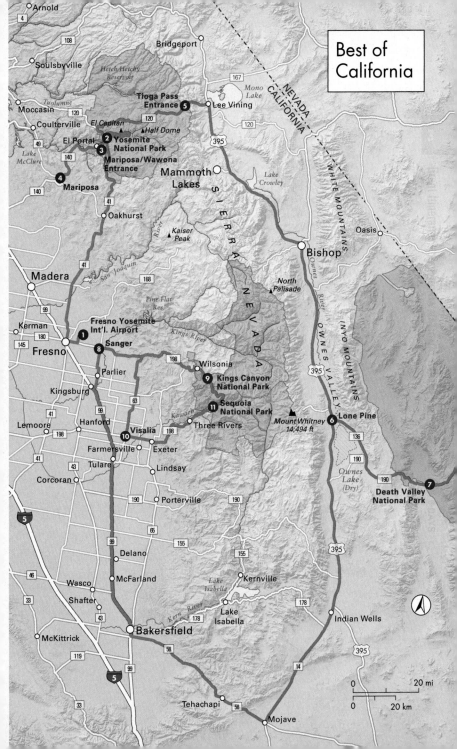

Best of California

an early start, hike into Golden Canyon by taking the 1-mile-long interpretive trail, which starts 2 miles south of Highway 190 on Badwater Road. From there, head to Devil's Golf Course (11 miles south of Furnace Creek) to see millions of tiny salt pinnacles and, if you get up close, a mass of perfectly round holes. Badwater Basin, 8 miles farther south, has expansive saltwater flats and the lowest point in the park, which is 282 feet below sea level. Then go to the highest spot—Dante's View, 5,000 feet above the valley floor—for the best views and blessedly cooler temperatures (the lookout is about 20 miles southeast of Furnace Creek). If you want to hike, there's a trail leading from the parking area onto Dante's Ridge that offers even more spectacular vistas (it's ½ mile to the first summit, then another 4 miles to Mt. Perry).

On your second day in Death Valley, explore the northern section of the park, by driving about 53 miles north of Furnace Creek on Ubehebe Crater Road to its namesake crater. From there, if your car has high clearance and good tires, you can drive 27 miles southwest on a rough dirt road to the Racetrack, a phenomenal dry lake bed famous for its mysterious moving rocks (to see the rocks, drive 2 miles past the Grandstand parking area).

Leave the park via the western (Panamint) entrance and head southwest toward Sequoia and Kings Canyon. Stop in **Sanger** to spend the night.

41 miles or a 50-minute drive east from Sanger to Kings Canyon; 35 miles or a 40-minute drive southwest from Sequoia to Visalia.

From Sanger, drive east to the Big Stump Entrance of **Kings Canyon National Park.** Inside the park, head to Grant Grove Village and stop at the visitor center there, then take the Kings Canyon Scenic Byway (Route 180) along the Kings River and its giant granite canyon that is well

over a mile deep at some points. Stop along the way at pull-outs for long vistas of some of the highest mountains in the United States. Hike the Zumwalt Meadow Trail (1½ miles), which starts just before the end of the road, 4½ miles from Cedar Grove Village, for gorgeous views of the park's largest meadow, plus high granite walls, talus, and the river below. At the end of the day, follow Route 180 back to Grant Grove Village and take Generals Highway south into Sequoia National Park. Leave through the Ash Mountain Entrance and head to the nearby town of **Visalia** for the night.

Spend the next day exploring **Sequoia National Park,** where some of the world's oldest and largest trees stand. Driving the winding, 40-mile-long Generals Highway takes about two hours. Be sure to stop at the Redwood Mountain Overlook, just outside Cedar Grove Village, for terrific views of the world's largest sequoia grove. Take a hike on the Congress Trail (2 miles), which starts at the General Sherman Tree, the world's largest tree, just off the Generals Highway near Wolverton Road. At the end of the day, head back to Sanger for the night.

From Sanger, it's a short 13-mile drive (about 20 minutes) to the Fresno airport.

Utah and Arizona National Parks Road Trip Itinerary, 9 Days

This itinerary takes you through Zion's massive sandstone cliffs and narrow slot canyons, the hoodoos (odd-shape pillars of rock left by erosion) of Bryce Canyon, and the overwhelming majesty of the Grand Canyon, close to 300 river miles long, 18 miles wide, and a mile deep.

45 miles or about a 50-minute drive northeast from St. George airport to the south entrance of Zion National Park.

Best of Utah and Arizona

Plan to fly into and out of **St. George Regional Airport** in St. George, Utah. It's close to all three parks, with Zion a little more than an hour away.

From the airport, head east toward **Zion National Park,** about 46 miles. Depending on how much daylight you've got, you can start exploring the park—enter at the south entrance and head to the Zion Canyon Visitor Center—or find a room for the next three nights in **Springdale,** the bustling town just outside the park (1.1 miles from the south entrance).

74 miles or about a 1-hour, 25-minute drive northeast from the east entrance of Zion to Bryce Canyon.

Start your day at the visitor center, just inside the south entrance, south of the junction of the Zion–Mount Carmel Highway and the Zion Canyon Scenic Drive.

Then explore the scenic drive, either in your own vehicle (January through early February only) or via the park's shuttle, which costs $1 per person per day (though there might be same-day "walk-up" availability, tickets should be purchased in advance through Recreation.gov as they are not sold in the park). Shuttles typically run every five minutes from 7 am to 5 pm mid-February through Thanksgiving and over the year-end holiday season, and a round-trip ride takes about 80 minutes. Intrepid hikers will want to tackle the Narrows, Zion's infamous 16-mile-long gorge cut by the Virgin River, which requires hikers to spend more than half of their time walking, wading, or swimming in the fast-flowing river. For everyone else, Zion offers plenty of other hiking options. The Emerald Pool trails (about 1 mile each) take you on a fairly easy hike from Zion Lodge, about

3 miles from Canyon Junction, to Lower and Upper Emerald Pool and waterfalls.

Spend the next day exploring the Kolob Canyons, in the northwestern corner of the park about 40 miles from Canyon Junction. Take the Kolob Canyons Road 5 miles to its end at the Kolob Canyons Viewpoint, where you'll get fabulous views of the surrounding red rock canyons. For a spectacular 5-mile hike, drive about 2 miles back on the Kolob Canyons Road to the Taylor Creek Trail, which takes you past historic homesteaders' cabins and through a narrow box canyon to the Double Arch Alcove, a large arched grotto.

At the end of the day, leave the park via the beautiful Zion–Mount Carmel Highway and its historic mile-long tunnel. You'll pass through slickrock country, with huge, petrified sandstone dunes etched by ancient waters, and head to Bryce Canyon, where you'll spend the night (you've got a few lodging options, both inside and just outside the park in the town of Bryce Canyon).

75 miles or about a 1-hour, 30-minute drive southwest from Bryce Canyon to Kanab.

Start your tour of **Bryce Canyon National Park** at the visitor center, about 1 mile past the park entrance. Central to your tour of Bryce Canyon is the 18-mile-long main park road, where numerous scenic turnouts reveal vistas of bright red-or-ange rock. ■TIP→ **If you're visiting from mid-April to late October, the free Bryce Canyon Shuttle will take you to many of the park's most popular attractions.** Trails worth exploring include the 1-mile Bristlecone Loop Trail and the 1.3-mile Navajo Loop Trail, both of which will get you into the heart of the park.

At the end of the day, leave the park and head toward **Kanab** to spend the night en route to the Grand Canyon.

294 miles or a 5-hour drive south from Kanab to the South Rim of the Grand Canyon.

Today, you'll drive from Kanab to **Grand Canyon National Park.** Check into a hotel in Grand Canyon Village on the **South Rim** or in **Tusayan,** a few miles to the south, for the next two nights. If you've got time, hike (or take the shuttle) to Yavapai Point, just west of the visitor center in the South Rim Village, to catch the sunset.

284 miles or about a 4-hour, 40-minute drive north from the South Rim to Fredonia.

If you didn't make it yesterday, begin today's tour with a stop at the Grand Canyon Visitor Center, near Mather Point in the South Rim Village, for the latest maps and information. While you're there, check out the Historic District, with its early-19th-century train depot and other buildings, many built by the Santa Fe Railroad. Get your bearings with a drive (or, if you're visiting early spring–late fall, a free shuttle ride on the red line) on the 7-mile-long Hermit Road. Hike the Rim Trail, a nearly flat path (much of which is paved) that hugs the edge of the canyon from the Village to Hermit's Rest, 2.8 miles to the west.

On your second day in the park, tackle the upper section of one of the "Corridor Trails"—South Kaibab or Bright Angel—which start at the South Rim and meet in the Bright Angel Campground at the bottom of the canyon (the third Corridor Trail, North Kaibab, connects the bottom of the canyon to the North Rim). Bright Angel, the easier of the two, is one of the most scenic paths into the canyon; the trailhead is near Kolb Studio, at the western end of the Village.

For your last day in the park, sign up for an interpretive ranger-led program; they cover a wide variety of subjects, including geology, history, and wildlife, so pick up a list at the Grand Canyon Visitor Center. Afterward, you can spend the

Best of Utah and Colorado

night in (or near) the park again, or start your drive back toward the airport in St. George. The town of **Fredonia, Arizona,** would be a good stopping point for the night.

The St. George Regional Airport is 77 miles (1 hour, 20 minutes) northwest of Fredonia.

Utah and Colorado National Parks Road Trip Itinerary, 6 Days

With this itinerary, you'll get to experience two of Utah's best parks. There's Arches, famous for its spectacular colors and unique landforms—natural stone arches, soaring pinnacles, plus giant fins

and balanced rocks—and Canyonlands, with a wilderness of canyons and buttes carved by the Colorado River and its tributaries. A few hours away, Colorado's Mesa Verde offers a peek into the lives of the Ancestral Pueblo people, who made it their home from AD 600 to 1300.

18 miles or a 20-minute drive southeast from Canyonlands Field airport to Moab.

The closest airport to your first two destinations is **Canyonlands Field,** also known as Moab Airport, where you can get flights to and from Denver. After you land and get your rental car, head into **Moab,** where you'll find plenty of options for food and lodging. Book yourself a room for the next three nights.

5 miles from Moab.

Your trip begins at **Arches National Park,** which holds the world's largest concentration of natural rock windows or "arches." Start with a guided hike in the Fiery Furnace, a maze of sandstone canyons and fins that is considered one of the most spectacular hikes in the park. On your second day, explore the Devil's Garden and Windows sections of the park. Head back to Moab for the night.

30 miles or about a 40-minute drive southwest from Moab; 106 miles or roughly a 2-hour drive southeast from Canyonlands to Cortez, CO.

From Moab, head to **Canyonlands National Park.** Start at the park's Island in the Sky District, at the northern end of the park (about 30 miles from Moab). Explore the area from the road, which has many overlooks, or hike the first section of the Upheaval Dome Trail, an 8.3-mile loop that starts at Whale Rock, about 11 miles from the visitor center and spotlights an enormous syncline, or downward fold in the Earth's crust (there are overlooks ½ mile and 1 mile from the trailhead). At the end of the day, on your way back to Moab, take a detour into **Dead Horse Point State Park,** about 11 miles from the Canyonlands entrance, and head up to the top of the mesa for magnificent views of the Colorado River as it goosenecks through the canyons below.

On Day 5, head to the Needles District, at the southwest corner of the park, and hike the Slickrock Trail (2.4 miles round-trip), keeping an eye out for bighorn sheep. At the end of the day, drive to **Cortez, Colorado** where you can find a hotel for the night.

11 miles east from Cortez to Mesa Verde; 142 miles or a 2½-hour drive northwest from Mesa Verde to Canyonlands Field airport.

From Cortez, drive to **Mesa Verde National Park,** with 5,000 archaeological sites (including 600 cliff dwellings) left behind by the Ancestral Pueblo people, who lived here more than 1,000 years ago. Begin your visit at the visitor center, just before the entrance station, to get the latest park information and purchase tour tickets for some of the more popular tours (to get the most out of your visit, plan to take at least one ranger-led tour). Inside the park, stop at the Chapin Mesa Museum.

After exploring Mesa Verde, you can spend the night at the Far View Lodge inside the park or head back to Cortez. Or, if you've got an early flight in the morning, you can drive back to Moab.

Chapter 4

ARCHES NATIONAL PARK

Updated by
Stina Sieg

4

UTAH

⛺ Camping	🛏 Hotels	🏃 Activities	👁 Scenery	🎭 Crowds
★★☆☆☆	★★★★☆	★★★☆☆	★★★★★	★★★★★

WELCOME TO ARCHES NATIONAL PARK

TOP REASONS TO GO

★ **Arch appeal:** Nowhere in the world has as large an array or quantity of natural arches.

★ **Legendary landscape:** A photographer's dream— no wonder it's been the chosen backdrop for many Hollywood films.

★ **Treasures hanging in the balance:** Landscape Arch and Balanced Rock look like they might topple any day. And they could—the features in this park erode and evolve constantly.

★ **Fins and needles:** Fins are thin, parallel walls of eroding rock that slowly disintegrate into towerlike "needles." The spaces around and between them will carve their way into your memories like the wind and water that formed them.

1 Devils Garden. Eighteen miles from the visitor center, this is the end of the paved road in Arches. It has the park's only campground, a picnic area, and access to drinking water. Trails in Devils Garden lead to Landscape Arch and several other noteworthy formations.

2 Fiery Furnace. About 14 miles from the visitor center this area is so labeled because its orange spires of rock look much like tongues of flame. Reservations are required, and can be made up to six months in advance, to join the twice-daily ranger-guided treks. Or you can obtain a permit to visit Fiery Furnace on your own, but only experienced, well-prepared hikers should attempt this option.

3 Delicate Arch/Wolfe Ranch. A spur road about 11.7 miles from the visitor center leads to the moderately strenuous 3-mile round-trip trail and viewpoints for the park's most famous feature— Delicate Arch. To see it from below, follow the road to the viewpoint, then walk to either easily accessible viewing area.

4 The Windows. Reached on a spur 9.2 miles from the visitor center, here you can see many of the park's natural arches from your car or on an easy rolling trail.

5 Balanced Rock. This giant rock teeters atop a pedestal, creating a 128-foot formation of red rock grandeur right along the roadside, about 9 miles from the visitor center.

6 Petrified Dunes. Just a tiny pull-out about 5 miles from the visitor center, stop here for pictures of acres and acres of petrified sand dunes.

7 Courthouse Towers. The Three Gossips, Sheep Rock, and Tower of Babel are all here. Enter this section of the park 3 miles past the visitor center. The Park Avenue Trail winds through the area.

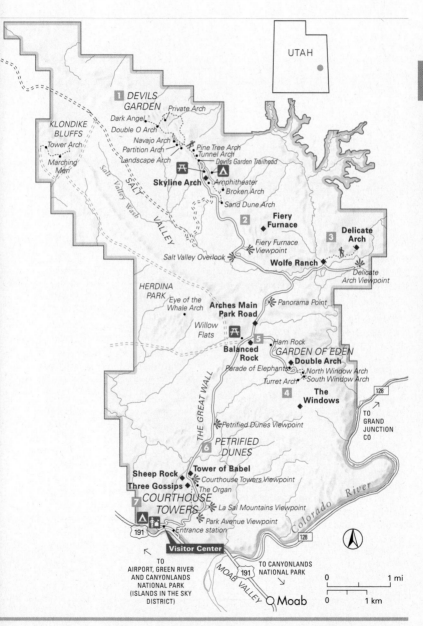

UTAH

1 DEVILS GARDEN

Private Arch
Dark Angel
Double O Arch
Navajo Arch
Partition Arch
Landscape Arch
Pine Tree Arch
Tunnel Arch
Devils Garden Trailhead

KLONDIKE BLUFFS

Tower Arch

Marching Men

SALT VALLEY WASH

SALT VALLEY

Skyline Arch

Amphitheater

Broken Arch

Sand Dune Arch

2

Fiery Furnace

Fiery Furnace Viewpoint

Salt Valley Overlook

Wolfe Ranch

3 Delicate Arch

Delicate Arch Viewpoint

HERDINA PARK

Eye of the Whale Arch

Arches Main Park Road

Panorama Point

Willow Flats

5

Ham Rock

GARDEN OF EDEN

Balanced Rock

Double Arch

North Window Arch

South Window Arch

Parade of Elephants

Turret Arch

4

The Windows

128

TO GRAND JUNCTION CO

Petrified Dunes Viewpoint

THE GREAT WALL

6 PETRIFIED DUNES

Tower of Babel

Sheep Rock

Courthouse Towers Viewpoint

Three Gossips

The Organ

7 COURTHOUSE TOWERS

La Sal Mountains Viewpoint

Park Avenue Viewpoint

191

Entrance station

Visitor Center

TO AIRPORT, GREEN RIVER AND CANYONLANDS NATIONAL PARK (ISLANDS IN THE SKY DISTRICT)

Colorado River

128

TO CANYONLANDS NATIONAL PARK

MOAB VALLEY

191

Moab

0   1 mi

0   1 km

More than 1.5 million visitors come to Arches annually, drawn by the red rock landscape and its wind- and water-carved rock formations. The park is named for the 2,000-plus sandstone arches that frame horizons, cast precious shade, and are in a perpetual state of gradual transformation, the result of constant erosion.

Fancifully named attractions like Three Penguins, Queen Nefertiti, and Tower of Babel stir curiosity, beckoning visitors to stop and marvel. Immerse yourself in this spectacular landscape, but don't lose yourself entirely—summer temperatures frequently exceed 100°F, and water is hard to come by inside the park boundaries.

It's easy to spot some of the arches from your car, but take the time to step outside and walk beneath the spans and giant walls of orange rock. This gives you a much better idea of their proportion. You may feel as writer Edward Abbey did when he awoke on his first day as a park ranger in Arches: that you're walking in the most beautiful place on Earth.

It's especially worthwhile to visit as the sun goes down. At sunset, the rock formations glow, and you'll often find photographers behind their tripods waiting for magnificent rays to descend on Delicate Arch or other popular sites. The Fiery Furnace earns its name as its narrow fins glow red just before the sun dips below the horizon. Full-moon nights are particularly dramatic in Arches as the creamy white Navajo sandstone reflects light, and eerie silhouettes are created by towering fins and formations.

Planning

When to Go

The busiest times of year are spring and fall. In the spring blooming wildflowers herald the end of winter, and temperatures in the 70s and 80s bring the year's largest crowds. The crowds remain steady in summer as the thermostat often exceeds 100°F and above in July and August. Sudden dramatic cloudbursts create rainfalls over red rock walls in late-summer "monsoon" season.

Fall means clear, warm days and crisp, cool nights. The park is much quieter in winter, and from December through February you can hike many of the trails in relative solitude. Snow occasionally falls in the valley beneath La Sal Mountains, and when it does, Arches is a photographer's paradise, with a serene white dusting over slickrock mounds and natural rock windows.

AVERAGE HIGH/LOW TEMPERATURES					
JAN.	**FEB.**	**MAR.**	**APR.**	**MAY**	**JUNE**
44/22	52/28	64/35	71/42	82/51	93/60
JULY	**AUG.**	**SEPT.**	**OCT.**	**NOV.**	**DEC.**
100/67	97/66	88/55	74/42	56/30	45/23

Getting Here and Around

AIR

Moab is served by tiny Canyonlands Field Airport, which has daily service to Denver on United Airlines and a couple of car rental agencies. The nearest midsize airport is Grand Junction Regional Airport in Grand Junction, Colorado, which is approximately 110 miles from Moab and is served by several major airlines.

CAR

The park entrance is just off U.S. 191 on the north side of downtown Moab, 28 miles south of Interstate 70 and 130 miles north of the Arizona border. Arches is also about 30 miles from the Island in the Sky section and 80 miles from the Needles District of Canyonlands National Park. If you're driving to Arches from points east on Interstate 70, consider taking Exit 214 in Utah (about 50 miles west of Grand Junction), and continuing south on picturesque Highway 128, the Colorado River Scenic Byway, about 50 miles to Moab. Bear in mind that services can be sparse on even major roads in these parts.

Branching off the main 18-mile park road—officially known as Arches Scenic Road—are two spurs, one 2½ miles to the Windows section and one 1.6 miles to Delicate Arch trailhead and viewpoint. There are several four-wheel-drive roads in the park; always check at the visitor center for conditions before attempting to traverse them. The entrance road into the park can back up mid-morning to early afternoon during busy periods. You'll encounter less traffic early in the morning or at sunset.

TRAIN

The *California Zephyr,* operated by Amtrak (☎ *800/872–7245*), stops daily in Green River, about 50 miles northwest of Moab.

Inspiration

127 Hours: Between a Rock and a Hard Place by Aron Ralston. This true story—made into a movie of the same name starring James Franco—took place southeast of Arches and is a modern-day survivor story of solitary man in nature.

Canyon Country Wildflowers, by Damian Fagan, can help you name the colorful blossoms you see during wildflower season (spring and early summer).

Desert Solitaire. Eminent naturalist Edward Abbey's first ranger assignment was Arches; this classic is a must-read.

Road Guide to Arches National Park, by Peter Anderson, has basic information about the geology and natural history in the park.

Park Essentials

ACCESSIBILITY

Not all park facilities meet federally mandated accessibility standards, but as visitation to Arches increases, the park continues efforts to increase accessibility. Visitors with mobility impairments can access the visitor center, all park restrooms, and two campsites at the Devils Garden Campground (4H is first-come, first served, while site 7 can be reserved up to six months in advance Mar.–Oct.). The Park Avenue

Arches in One Day

There's no food service in the park, so pack snacks, lunch, and plenty of water and electrolytes before you head into Arches. Also plan ahead to get tickets to the daily ranger-led Fiery Furnace walks, held spring through fall. It's a highlight for those who are adventurous and in good shape (see *Ranger Programs* for details). The one-day itinerary below is based on what to do on a day that you can't visit Fiery Furnace. If you do take a Fiery Furnace walk, you should also have time to drive the park road and perhaps walk on the Park Avenue Trail. If you have a third day, take a rafting trip on the nearby Colorado River.

Start as early as sunrise for cool temperatures and some of the best natural light, and head out on the 3-mile round-trip hike on the **Delicate Arch Trail.** The route is strenuous but extremely rewarding. Next head to **Devils Garden**, another great spot for morning photography, where you'll also find the easy, primarily flat trail to **Landscape Arch**, the second of the park's two must-see arches. If you're a fairly experienced hiker, continue on to **Double O**, but note that this portion of the trail is moderately difficult. Along the way, picnic in the shade of a juniper or in a rock alcove. By the time you return you'll be ready to see the rest of the park by car, with some short strolls on easy paths.

In the mid- to late afternoon, drive to **Balanced Rock** for photos, then on to **Windows.** Depending on what time the sun is due to set, go into Moab for dinner before or after you drive out to Delicate Arch or along the park road to watch the sun set the rocks aglow.

Viewpoint is a paved path with a slight decline near the end, and both Delicate Arch and Balanced Rock viewpoints are partially hard-surfaced. For those with visual disabilities, visitor center exhibits include audio recordings and some tactile elements. You can also request an audio version of the park brochure (or listen to it on the park website ⊕ *www.nps.gov/arch*). Large-print and braille versions of park information are also available at the visitor center.

PARK FEES AND PERMITS

Admission to the park is $30 per vehicle, $25 per motorcycle, and $15 per person entering on foot or bicycle, valid for seven days. To encourage visitation to the park during less busy times, a $50 local park pass grants you admission to both Arches and Canyonlands parks as well as Natural Bridges and Hovenweep national monuments for one year.

PARK HOURS

Arches National Park is open year-round, seven days a week, around the clock. It's in the Mountain time zone.

CELL PHONE RECEPTION

Cell phone reception is spotty in the park and in general is strongest whenever the La Sal mountains are visible. There are pay phones outside the visitor center.

Hotels

Though there are no hotels or cabins in the park itself, in the surrounding area every type of lodging is available, from economy chain motels to B&Bs and high-end, high-adventure resorts. It's important to know when popular events are held, however, as accommodations can, and do, fill up weeks ahead of time.

Restaurants

In the park itself, there are no dining facilities and no snack bars. Supermarkets, bakeries, and delis in downtown Moab will be happy to make you food to go. If you bring a packed lunch, there are several picnic areas from which to choose.

Visitor Information

The park's visitor center is in the southern part of the park, near Balanced Rock and the park's southern entrance.

PARK CONTACT INFORMATION Arches National Park. ⊠ *N. U.S. 191* ☎ *435/719–2299* ⊕ *www.nps.gov/arch.*

Devils Garden

18 miles north of the visitor center.

At the end of the paved road in Arches, Devils Garden is the most developed area of the park, with the park's only campground and drinking water. It's also the site of the busiest trailheads.

◉ Sights

GEOLOGICAL FORMATIONS
Skyline Arch
NATURE SITE | FAMILY | A quick walk from the parking lot at Skyline Arch, 16½ miles from the park entrance, gives you closer views and better photos. The short trail is less than a ½ mile round-trip and takes only a few minutes to travel. ⊠ *Devils Garden Rd.*

SCENIC DRIVES
★ Arches Main Park Road
SCENIC DRIVE | The main park road and its two short spurs are extremely scenic and allow you to enjoy many park sights from your car. The main road leads through Courthouse Towers, where you can see Sheep Rock and the Three Gossips, then alongside the Great Wall, the Petrified

Dunes, and Balanced Rock. A drive to the Windows section takes you to attractions like Double Arch, and you can see Skyline Arch along the roadside as you approach the Devils Garden campground. The road to Delicate Arch allows hiking access to one of the park's main features. Allow about two hours to drive the 45-mile round-trip, more if you explore the spurs and their features and stop at viewpoints along the way. ⊠ *Arches National Park.*

PICNIC AREAS
★ Devils Garden
LOCAL INTEREST | FAMILY | There are grills, water, picnic tables, and restrooms here and, depending on the time of day, some shade from junipers and rock walls. It's a good place for lunch before or after a hike. ⊠ *End of main road, 18 miles from park entrance.*

TRAILS
Broken Arch Trail
TRAIL | An easy walk across open grassland, this loop trail passes Broken Arch, which is also visible from the road. The arch gets its name because it appears to be cracked in the middle, but it's not really broken. The trail is 1¼ miles round-trip, but you can extend your adventure to about 2 miles round-trip by continuing north past Tapestry Arch and through Devils Garden Campground. *Easy.* ⊠ *Arches National Park* ⊹ *Trailhead: off Devils Garden Rd., 16½ miles from park entrance.*

★ Devils Garden Trail
TRAIL | Landscape Arch is a highlight of this trail but is just one of several arches within reach, depending on your ambitions. It's an easy ¾-mile one-way (mostly gravel, relatively flat) trip to Landscape Arch, one of the longest stone spans in the world. Beyond Landscape Arch the scenery changes dramatically and the hike becomes more strenuous, as you must climb and straddle slickrock fins and negotiate some short, steep inclines. Finally, around a sharp bend, the stacked spans that compose Double O Arch

come suddenly into view. Allow up to three hours for this round-trip hike of just over 4 miles. For a still longer (about a 7-mile round-trip) and more rigorous trek, venture on to see a formation called Dark Angel and then return to the trailhead on the primitive loop, making the short side hike to Private Arch. The hike to Dark Angel is a difficult route through fins. Other possible (and worthwhile) detours lead to Navajo Arch, Partition Arch, Tunnel Arch, and Pine Tree Arch. Allow about five hours for this adventure, take plenty of water, and watch your route carefully. Pick up the park's useful guide to Devils Garden, or download it from the website before you go. *Moderate–Difficult.* ⊠ *Arches National Park* ⟡ *Trailhead: on Devils Garden Rd., end of main road, 18 miles from park entrance.*

Landscape Arch

TRAIL | This natural rock opening, which measures 306 feet from base to base and looks like a delicate ribbon of rock bending over the horizon, is the longest geologic span in North America. In 1991, a slab of rock about 60 feet long, 11 feet wide, and 4 feet thick fell from the underside, leaving it even thinner. You reach it via a rolling, gravel, 1.6-mile-long trail. *Easy–Moderate.* ⊠ *Arches National Park* ⟡ *Trailhead: at Devils Garden Rd., at end of main road, 18 miles north of park entrance.*

Tower Arch Trail

TRAIL | Check with park rangers before attempting the dirt road through Salt Valley to Klondike Bluffs parking area. If rains haven't washed out the road, a trip to this seldom-visited area provides a solitude-filled hike culminating in a giant rock opening. Allow from two to three hours for this 3½-mile round-trip hike, not including the drive. *Moderate.* ⊠ *Arches National Park* ⟡ *Trailhead: at Klondike Bluffs parking area, 24½ miles from park entrance, 7¾ miles off main road.*

Fiery Furnace

14 miles north of hte park entrance.

Fewer than 10% of the park's visitors ever descend into the chasms and washes of Fiery Furnace (a permit or a ranger-led hike is the only way to go), but you can gain an appreciation for this twisted, unyielding landscape from the Overlook. At sunset, the rocks glow a vibrant flamelike red, which gives the formation its daunting moniker.

Sights

TRAILS
Fiery Furnace

TRAIL | This area of the park has taken on a near-mythical lure for park visitors, who are drawn to challenging yet breathtaking terrain. Rangers strongly discourage inexperienced hikers from entering here—in fact, you can't enter without watching a video about how to help protect this very special section of the park and obtaining a permit ($6). Reservations can be made up to six months in advance to get a spot on the 2-mile round-trip ranger-led hikes ($16), offered mid-April–September, through this unique formation. A hike through these rugged rocks and sandy washes is challenging but fascinating. Hikers will need to use their hands at times to scramble up and through narrow cracks and along vertigo-inducing ledges above drop-offs, and there are no trail markings. If you're not familiar with the Furnace you can easily get lost or cause damage, so watch your step and use great caution. For information about reservations, see Ranger Programs Overview above. The less intrepid can view Fiery Furnace from the Overlook off the main road. *Difficult.* ⊠ *Arches National Park* ⟡ *Trailhead: off main road, about 14 miles from park entrance.*

Sand Dune Arch Trail

TRAIL | FAMILY | You may return to the car with shoes full of bright red sand from this giant sandbox in the desert—it's fun exploring in and around the rock. Set aside five minutes for this shady, 530-yard walk and plenty of time if you have kids, who will love playing amid this dramatic landscape. Never climb on this or any other arch in the park, no matter how tempting—it's illegal, and it could result in damage to the fragile geology or personal injury. The trail intersects with the Broken Arch Trail—you can visit both arches with an easy 1½-mile round-trip walk. *Easy.* ☒ *Arches National Park* ⊹ *Trailhead: off Arches Scenic Dr., about 16½ miles from park entrance.*

Delicate Arch/ Wolfe Ranch

13 miles north of the park entrance.

The iconic symbol of the park and the state (it appears on many of Utah's license plates), Delicate Arch is tall and prominent compared with many of the spans in the park—it's big enough that it could shelter a four-story building. The arch is a remnant of an Entrada Sandstone fin; the rest of the rock has eroded and it now frames La Sal Mountains in the background. Drive 2.2 miles off the main road to the viewpoint to see the arch from a distance, or hike right up to it from the trailhead that starts near Wolfe Ranch. The trail, 1.2 miles off the main road, is a moderately strenuous 3-mile round-trip hike with no shade or access to water. It's especially picturesque shortly after sunrise or before sunset.

Sights

HISTORIC SIGHTS

Wolfe Ranch

HISTORIC SITE | Civil War veteran John Wesley Wolfe and his son started a small ranch here in 1888. He added a cabin in 1906 when his daughter Esther and her family came west to live. Built out of Fremont cottonwoods, the rustic one-room cabin still stands on the site. Look for remains of a root cellar and a corral as well. Even older than these structures is the nearby Ute rock-art panel by the Delicate Arch trailhead. About 150 feet past the footbridge and before the trail starts to climb, you can see images of bighorn sheep and figures on horseback, as well as some smaller images believed to be dogs. ☒ *Off Delicate Arch Rd.*

TRAILS

★ Delicate Arch Trail

TRAIL | To see the park's most famous freestanding arch up close takes effort and won't offer you much solitude—but it's worth every step. The 3-mile round-trip trail ascends via steep slickrock, sandy paths, and along one narrow ledge (at the very end) that might give pause to anyone afraid of heights. Plus, there's almost no shade. First-timers should start early to avoid the midday heat in summer. Still, at sunrise, sunset, and every hour in between, it's the park's busiest trail. Bring plenty of water, especially in the warmer months, as heatstroke and dehydration are very real possibilities. Allow two to three hours, depending on your fitness level and how long you care to linger at the arch. If you go at sunset or sunrise, bring a headlamp or flashlight. Don't miss Wolfe Ranch and some ancient rock art near the trailhead. *Moderate–Difficult.* ☒ *Arches National Park* ⊹ *Trailhead: on Delicate Arch Rd., 13 miles from park entrance.*

The Windows

11¾ miles north of the park entrance.

As you head north from the park entrance, turn right at Balanced Rock to find this concentration of natural windows, caves, and needles. Stretch your legs on the easy paths that wind between the arches and soak in a variety of geological formations.

Sights

GEOLOGICAL FORMATIONS

Double Arch

NATURE SITE | In the Windows section of the park, 11¾ miles from the park entrance, Double Arch has appeared in several Hollywood movies, including *Indiana Jones and the Last Crusade*. From the parking lot you can also take the short and easy Window Trail to view North Window, South Window, and Turret Arch. ⊠ *The Windows Rd.*

TRAILS

Double Arch Trail

TRAIL | FAMILY | If it's not too hot, it's a simple walk to here from Windows Trail. This relatively flat trek leads to two massive arches that make for great photo opportunities. The ½-mile round-trip gives you a good taste of desert flora and fauna. *Easy.* ⊠ *Arches National Park ✥ Trailhead: 2½ miles from main road, on Windows Section spur road.*

The Windows

TRAIL | FAMILY | An early stop for many visitors to the park, a trek through the Windows gives you an opportunity to get out and enjoy the desert air. Here you'll see three giant openings in the rock and walk on a trail that leads right through the holes. Allow about an hour on this gently inclined, 1-mile round-trip hike. As most visitors don't follow the "primitive" trail around the backside of the two windows, take advantage if you want some desert

solitude. The primitive trail adds an extra half hour to the hike. *Easy.* ⊠ *Arches National Park ✥ Trailhead: on the Windows Rd., 12 miles from park entrance.*

Balanced Rock

9¼ miles north of the park entrance.

One of the park's favorite sights, this rock is visible for several minutes as you approach—and just gets more impressive and mysterious as you get closer. The formation's total height is 128 feet, with the huge balanced rock rising 55 feet above the pedestal. Be sure to hop out of the car and walk the short (⅓-mile) loop around the base.

Sights

PICNIC AREAS

Balanced Rock Picnic Area

VIEWPOINT | The view is the best part of this picnic spot opposite Balanced Rock parking area. There's no water, but there are tables. If you sit just right you might find some shade under a small juniper; otherwise, this is an exposed site. Pit toilets are nearby. ⊠ *9¼ miles from park entrance on main road.*

TRAILS

Balanced Rock Trail

TRAIL | FAMILY | You'll want to stop at Balanced Rock for photo ops, so you may as well walk the easy, partially paved trail around the famous landmark. This is one of the most accessible trails in the park and is suitable even for small children. The 15-minute stroll is only about ⅓ mile round-trip. *Easy.* ⊠ *Arches National Park ✥ Trailhead: approximately 9¼ miles from park entrance.*

Park Avenue Trail

TRAIL | The first named trail that park visitors encounter, this is a relatively easy, 2-mile round-trip walk (with only one small hill but a somewhat steep

Plants and Wildlife in Arches

As in any desert environment, the best time to see wildlife in Arches is early morning or evening. Summer temperatures keep most animals tucked away in cool places, though ravens and lizards are exceptions. If you happen to be in the right place at the right time, you may spot one of the beautiful turquoise-necklace-collared lizards. It's more likely you'll see the western whiptail. Mule deer, jackrabbits, and small rodents are usually active in cool morning hours or near dusk. You may spot a lone coyote foraging day or night. The park protects a small herd of desert bighorns, and some of their tribe are sometimes seen early in the morning grazing beside U.S. 191 south of the Arches entrance. Never approach bighorns, which have been known to charge people who attempt to get too close, or any other animals in the park. Ravens, mule deer, and small mammals such as chipmunks are very used to seeing people and will get close to you, but don't feed them.

descent into the canyon) amid walls and towers that vaguely resemble a New York City skyline. You'll walk under the gaze of Queen Nefertiti, a giant rock formation that some observers think has Egyptian-looking features. If you are traveling with companions, make it a one-way, 1-mile downhill trek by having them pick you up at the Courthouse Towers Viewpoint. Allow about 45 minutes for the one-way journey. *Easy–Moderate.* ⊠ *Arches National Park* ✛ *Trailhead: 2 miles from park entrance on main park road.*

VISITOR CENTERS

Arches Visitor Center

With well-designed hands-on exhibits about the park's geology, wildlife, and history; helpful rangers; a water station; and a bookstore; the center is a great way to start your park visit. It also has picnic tables and something that's rare in the park: cell service for many carriers. ⊠ *N. U.S. 191* ☎ *435/719–2299* ⊕ *nps.gov/arch.*

Petrified Dunes

5 miles north of the visitor center.

Sights

Petrified Dunes

NATURE SITE | FAMILY | Just a tiny pull-out, this memorable stop features acres upon acres of reddish-gold, petrified sand dunes. There's no trail here, so roam as you like while keeping track of where you are. If you do lose your way, heading west will take you back to the main road. ⊠ *Arches National Park* ✛ *6 miles from park entrance.*

Courthouse Towers

3 miles north of the visitor center.

This collection of towering rock formations looks unreal from a distance and even more breathtaking up close. The Three Gossips does indeed resemble a gaggle of wildly tall people sharing some kind of secret. Sheep Rock is right below, with the massive Tower of Babel just a bit north. Enter this section of the park 3 miles past the visitor center. The extremely popular Park Avenue Trail winds through the area.

 ## Sights

SCENIC STOPS
Courthouse Wash
NATURE SITE | Although this rock-art panel fell victim to an unusual case of vandalism in 1980, when someone scoured the petroglyphs and pictographs that had been left by four cultures, you can still see ancient images if you take a short walk from the parking area on the left-hand side of the road, heading south. ✉ *U.S. 191, about 2 miles south of Arches entrance.*

Activities

Arches lies in the middle of one of the adventure capitals of the United States. Deep canyons and towering walls are everywhere you look. Thousand-foot sandstone walls draw rock climbers from across the globe. Hikers can choose from shady canyons or red rock ridges that put you in the company of the West's big sky. The Colorado River forms the southeast boundary of the park and can give you every grade of white-water adventure. Moab-based outfitters can set you up for just about any sport you may have a desire to try: mountain biking, ATVs, dirt bikes, four-wheel-drive vehicles, kayaking, climbing, stand-up paddleboarding, and even skydiving. Within the park, it's best to stick with basics such as hiking, sightseeing, and photography. Climbers and other adventure seekers should always inquire at the visitor center about restrictions, which can also be seen on the park's website.

BIRD WATCHING
Within the park you'll definitely see plenty of the big, black, beautiful ravens. Look for them perched on top of a picturesque juniper branch or balancing on the bald knob of a rock. Noisy black-billed magpies populate the park, as do the more melodic canyon and rock wrens. Lucky visitors may spot a red-tailed hawk and hear its distinctive call. Serious birders will have more fun visiting the Nature Conservancy's Scott M. Matheson Wetlands Preserve, 5 miles south of the park. The wetlands is home to more than 200 species of birds including the wood duck, western screech owl, indigo bunting, and plumbeous vireo.

CAMPING
Campgrounds in and around Arches range from sprawling RV parks with myriad amenities to quaint, shady retreats near a babbling brook. The Devils Garden Campground in the park is a wonderful spot to call home for a few days, though it is often full and lacks an RV dump station. More than 350 campsites are operated in the vicinity by the Bureau of Land Management—their sites on the Colorado River and near the Slickrock Trail are some of the nicest (and most affordable, at just $20/night) in the area. The most centrally located campgrounds in Moab generally accommodate RVs.

Devils Garden Campground. This campground is one of the most unusual—and gorgeous—in the West, and in the national park system, for that matter. ✉ *End of main road, 18 miles from park entrance* ☎ *435/719–2299, 877/444–6777 for reservations* ⊕ *www.recreation.gov.*

EDUCATIONAL PROGRAMS
As you explore Arches, look for sandwich boards announcing "Ranger Sightings" and stop for a 3- to 10-minute program led by park staff. Topics range from geology and desert plants to mountain lions and the Colorado River. Most nights, spring through fall, more in-depth campfire programs are available at Devils

Garden Campground amphitheater. You may also find guided walks (in addition to the beloved Fiery Furnace walk) during your visit. For information on current schedules and locations of park programs, contact the visitor center or check the bulletin boards throughout the park.

Junior Ranger Program

NATIONAL/STATE PARK | FAMILY | Kids of all ages can pick up a Junior Ranger booklet at the visitor center. It's full of activities, word games, drawings, and thought-provoking material about the park and the wildlife. To earn your Junior Ranger badge, you must complete several activities in the booklet, attend a ranger program, or watch the park film and pick up some trash in the park. ⊠ *Arches National Park.*

Red Rock Explorer Pack

NATIONAL/STATE PARK | FAMILY | Families can check out a youth backpack filled with tools for learning about both Arches and Canyonlands national parks. A guide for naturalists, a three-ring binder of activities, hand lens magnifier, and binoculars are just some of the loaner items. Backpacks can be returned to either Arches or Island in the Sky visitor center. Use of the backpack is free. ⊠ *Arches National Park.*

FOUR-WHEELING

With thousands of acres of nearby Bureau of Land Management lands to enjoy, it's hardly necessary to use the park's limited trails for four-wheel adventures. You can, however, go backcountry riding in Arches on the Willow Flats Road. Parallel to the Salt Valley Road is also a dirt track simply called the 4 Wheel Drive Road, which is very sandy and requires experienced drivers. Don't set out for an expedition without first stopping at the visitor center to learn of current conditions.

HIKING

Getting out on any one of the park trails will surely cause you to fall in love with this Mars-like landscape. But remember, you are hiking in a desert environment and approximately 1 mile above sea level. Many people succumb to heat and dehydration because they do not drink enough water. Park rangers recommend a gallon of water per day per person, plus electrolytes.

★ Fiery Furnace Walk

TOUR—SIGHT | Join a park ranger on a 2½-hour scramble through a labyrinth of rock fins and narrow sandstone canyons. You'll see arches and other eye-popping formations that can't be viewed from the road. You should be very fit and not afraid of heights or confined spaces for this moderately strenuous experience. Wear sturdy hiking shoes, sunscreen, and a hat, and bring at least a liter of water. Guided walks into the Fiery Furnace are offered mid-April through September, usually a few times a day (hours vary), and leave from Fiery Furnace Viewpoint, about 15 miles from the park visitor center. Tickets for the morning walks must be reserved (at ⊕ *www.recreation. gov*) and are available beginning six months in advance and up to four days before the day of the tour. Tickets for afternoon Fiery Furnace walks must be purchased in person at the park visitor center, ideally as soon as you arrive in Moab and as far ahead as seven days before your hike. Children ages 5–12 are charged half price; kids under 5 are not allowed. Book early as the program usually fills months prior to each walk. ⊠ *Arches National Park ✛ Trailhead: on Arches Scenic Dr. ⊠ $16 ⊘ Guided hikes not offered Oct.–mid-April.*

ROCK CLIMBING AND CANYONEERING

Rock climbers travel from across the country to scale the sheer red rock walls of Arches National Park and surrounding areas. Most climbing routes in the park require advanced techniques. Permits are not required, but climbers are encouraged to register for a free permit, either online or at a kiosk outside the visitor center. Climbers are responsible for knowing park regulations, temporary route closures, and restricted routes. Two popular routes ascend Owl Rock in the Garden of Eden (about 10 miles from the visitor center); the well-worn route has a difficulty of 5.8, while a more challenging option is 5.11 on a scale that goes up to 5.13-plus. Many climbing routes are available in the Park Avenue area, about 2.2 miles from the visitor center. These routes are also extremely difficult climbs. No commercial outfitters are allowed to lead rock-climbing excursions in the park, but guided canyoneering (which involves ropes, rappelling, and some basic climbing) is allowed, and permits are required for canyoneering. Before climbing, it's imperative that you stop at the visitor center and check with a ranger about climbing regulations.

Desert Highlights

CLIMBING/MOUNTAINEERING | This guide company takes adventurous types on descents and ascents through canyons (with the help of ropes), including those found in the Fiery Furnace at Arches National Park. Full-day and multiday canyoneering treks are available to destinations both in and near the national parks. ⌧ 16 S. 100 E, Moab ☎ 435/259–4433 ⊕ www.deserthighlights.com ✉ From $105.

Nearby Towns

Moab is the primary gateway to both Arches and Canyonlands national parks. Don't let its outsize image and status as Grand County seat fool you: only about 5,200 people live here year-round—compared with the 1.5 million who visit annually. Near the Colorado River in a beautiful valley between red rock cliffs, Moab is an interesting, eclectic place to visit, and it's home to a mix of both super-casual and hip restaurants, plus Southwestern-inspired souvenirs, art galleries, tour operators, recreation outfitters, and a selection of lodging options.

The next-closest town to Arches, about 50 miles to the northwest, is **Green River,** a fairly sleepy little town with some less expensive—but also less noteworthy— dining and lodging options and the excellent John Wesley Powell River History Museum. Each September the fragrance of fresh cantaloupe, watermelon, and honeydew fills the air, especially during Melon Days, a family-fun harvest celebration on the third weekend of September. As Moab hotels have become more expensive and crowded spring through fall, many park visitors have taken to staying farther south in the small southeastern Utah towns of **Monticello, Blanding,** and **Bluff,** and even 110 miles away up in **Grand Junction, Colorado,** a lively and attractive small city of about 62,000 with a bustling historic downtown and some great, reasonably priced dining and lodging options and close proximity to gorgeous Colorado National Monument.

BADLANDS NATIONAL PARK

Updated by
Carson Walker

SOUTH
DAKOTA

🏕 Camping	🛏 Hotels	🤸 Activities	👁 Scenery	👥 Crowds
★★★☆☆	★★★☆☆	★★★☆☆	★★★★★	★★★★☆

WELCOME TO BADLANDS NATIONAL PARK

TOP REASONS TO GO

★ **Fossils:** From the mid-1800s, the fossil-rich Badlands area has welcomed paleontologists, research institutions, and fossil hunters who have discovered the fossil remnants of numerous species from ancient days.

★ **A world of wildlife:** Badlands National Park is home to a wide array of wildlife: bison, pronghorn, deer, black-footed ferrets, prairie dogs, rabbits, coyotes, foxes, and badgers.

★ **Missiles:** The Minuteman Missile National Historic Site, north of the entrance to the park, represents the only remaining intact components of a nuclear missile.

★ **Stars aplenty:** Due to its remote location and vastly open country, Badlands National Park contains some of the clearest and cleanest air in the country, which makes it perfect for viewing the night sky.

★ **Moonscape:** With hundreds of square miles of ragged ridgelines and sawtooth spires, Badlands National Park touts a landscape that is otherworldly.

1 North Unit. This is the most accessible unit and includes the Badlands Wilderness Area.

2 Palmer Creek Unit. This is the most isolated section of the park—no recognized roads pass through its borders. You must obtain permission from private landowners to pass through their property (contact the White River Visitor Center). Allot one day to hike in and one day to hike out.

3 Stronghold Unit. This was used as a gunnery range for the United States Air Force and the South Dakota National Guard from 1942 until the late 1960s. Discarded remnants and unexploded ordnance make this area potentially dangerous. Do not handle fragments; report the location to a ranger instead.

Sceni

Sheep Mountain Table

Pine Ridge Indian Reservation Boundary

3
Stronghold Unit ◆

Stronghold Table

2

TO WOUNDED KN

SOUTH
DAKOTA

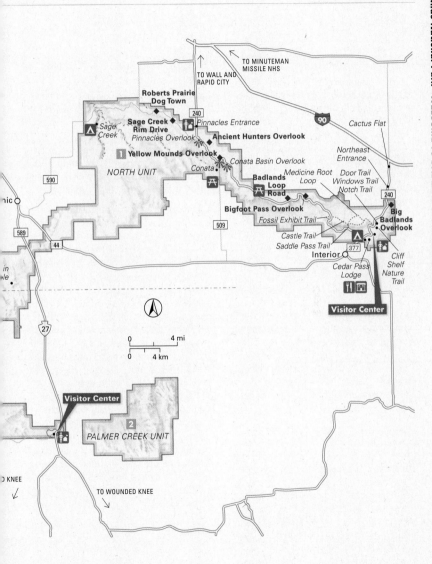

TO MINUTEMAN
MISSILE NHS

TO WALL AND
RAPID CITY

Roberts Prairie
Dog Town

240

Pinnacles Entrance

Cactus Flat

Sage Creek
Rim Drive

Sage
Creek

Pinnacles Overlook

Ancient Hunters Overlook

Northeast
Entrance

1 Yellow Mounds Overlook

Conata Basin Overlook

NORTH UNIT

Conata

Medicine Root
Loop

Door Trail
Windows Trail
Notch Trail

590

Badlands
Loop
Road

240

Bigfoot Pass Overlook

509

Big
Badlands
Overlook

Fossil Exhibit Trail

589

Castle Trail

44

Saddle Pass Trail

377

Interior

Cliff
Shelf
Nature
Trail

Cedar Pass
Lodge

Visitor Center

27

0   4 mi

0   4 km

Visitor Center

2

PALMER CREEK UNIT

KNEE

TO WOUNDED KNEE

Ravaged over time by wind and rain, the 380 square miles of chiseled spires, ragged ridge lines, and deep ravines of South Dakota's Badlands continue to erode and evolve.

Prairie creatures thrive on the untamed territory, and animal fossils abound. The rugged, desolate terrain looks more like moonscape than prairie. The South Dakota Legislature summarized its value well in a 1909 petition to Congress: "This formation is so unique, picturesque, and valuable for the purpose of study that a portion of it should be retained in its native state." After several tries, the area was ultimately designated a national monument in 1939 and national park in 1978.

Badlands National Park features the largest mixed-grass prairie in the National Park System. It's home to prairie dog towns as well as bison, bighorn sheep, pronghorn antelope, mule deer, coyotes, jackrabbits, the endangered black-footed ferret, and numerous bird species. There's also fossil evidence of prehistoric creatures, including the three-toed horse, camel, sabre-toothed cat, and an ancestor of the rhinoceros.

Despite its vastness, most of the park is relatively accessible. Several shorter trails are wheelchair-friendly, and visitors are allowed to walk through formations made of sand, silt, and clay that have been cemented into solid form. Though there are only about 20 miles of formal trails, hikers and backpackers are free to explore and camp off the paths because of an open-hike policy. The North Unit, one of three that comprise the park, attracts the most visitors. It's home to the park headquarters and offers the easiest access by vehicle over the Badlands Loop Road. Buffalo Gap National Grassland surrounds most of the North Unit. The other two units to the south, Stronghold and Palmer Creek, lie within the Pine Ridge Indian Reservation, and the Oglala Sioux Tribe can limit access, so check the park website for updates.

The area around Badlands National Park is rich in Native American and Cold War history. In the 1890s, Sioux warriors performed the Ghost Dance rituals on what is now the Stronghold Unit. When they refused to end the practice, the U.S. Army was called in. On Dec. 29, 1890, soldiers shot and killed 150 to 300 Lakota men, women and children at nearby Wounded Knee, the last confrontation between Native Americans and the United States Army. If you do venture to the park's southern districts, you can visit the Wounded Knee Massacre Memorial, which marks the mass grave and is a somber reminder of that part of our nation's history. North of the park, the Minuteman Missile National Historic Site is a decommissioned nuclear missile site with a visitor center. An hour's drive west are Rapid City and the Black Hills, home to Mount Rushmore and the Crazy Horse Memorial.

AVERAGE HIGH/LOW TEMPERATURES					
JAN.	FEB.	MAR.	APR.	MAY	JUNE
34/11	40/16	48/24	62/33	72/44	82/56
JULY	AUG.	SEPT.	OCT.	NOV.	DEC.
91/60	92/55	81/46	65/34	48/21	39/17

Planning

When to Go

Most visitors see the park between Memorial Day and Labor Day. The park's vast size and isolation prevent it from ever being too packed—though it is usually crowded the first week of August, when hundreds of thousands of motorcycle enthusiasts flock to the Black Hills for the annual Sturgis Motorcycle Rally (⇨ see Wind Cave chapter for more info). In summer, temperatures typically hover around 90°F—though it can get as hot as 116°F—and sudden mid-afternoon thunderstorms are not unusual. Storms put on a spectacular show of thunder and lightning, but it rarely rains for more than 10 or 15 minutes (the average annual rainfall is 16 inches). Autumn weather is generally sunny and warm. Snow usually appears by late October. Winter temperatures can be as low as −40°F. Early spring is often wet, cold, and unpredictable. By May the weather usually stabilizes, bringing pleasant 70°F days.

FESTIVALS AND EVENTS

Badlands Quilters Weekend Getaway. A display of the region's finest hand- and machine-made quilts, plus quilting classes by expert quilters, demonstrations, and sales are held in Wall's community center the second weekend in March. ⊕ www.badlandsquilters.com.

Black Hills Stock Show and Rodeo. Watch world-champion wild-horse races, bucking horses, timed sheepdog trials, draft-horse contests, and steer wrestling during this two-week-long professional rodeo at the Rushmore Plaza Civic Center in Rapid City and Central States Fairgrounds (the festival's headquarters). ⊕ www.blackhillsstockshow.com.

Central States Fair & Rodeo. Held every August, the fair features a midway with rides and games; concerts and the Range Days Rodeo; craft, art, and culinary exhibits; cattle shows; horse events; and kids' entertainment. ⊕ www.centralstatesfair.com.

Red Cloud Indian Art Show. Native American paintings and sculptures by both emerging and professional artists are the focus of this 11-week-long exhibition, beginning on the first Sunday in June, at the Red Cloud Indian School in Pine Ridge. ⊕ www.redcloudart.show.

Getting Here and Around

CAR

The North Unit of Badlands National Park is 75 miles east of Rapid City (with a regional airport) and about 140 miles northeast of Wind Cave National Park in western South Dakota. It's accessed via Exit 110 or 131 off I–90, or Route 44 east to Route 377. Few roads, paved or otherwise, pass within the park. Badlands Loop Road (Route 240) is the most traveled and the only one that intersects I–90. It's well maintained and rarely crowded. Parts of Route 44 and Route 27 run at the fringes of the badlands, connecting the visitor centers and Rapid City. Unpaved roads should be traveled with care when wet. Sheep Mountain Table Road, the only public road into the Stronghold Unit, is impassable when wet, with deep ruts—sometimes only high-clearance vehicles

Badlands in One Day

With a packed lunch and plenty of water, arrive at the park via the northeast entrance (off I–90 at Exit 131) and follow Badlands Loop Road (Route/Highway 240) southwest toward the **Ben Reifel Visitor Center.** You can pick up park maps and information here, and also pay the park entrance fee (if the booth at the entrance is closed).

Next, stop at the **Big Badlands Overlook,** just south of the northeast entrance, to get a good feel for the landscape. As you head toward the visitor center, hike any one of several trails you'll pass, or if you prefer guided walks, arrive at the visitor center in time to look at the exhibits and talk with rangers before heading over to the **Fossil Exhibit Trail.** The badlands are one of the richest fossil fields in the world, and along the trail are wayside exhibits describing creatures that once lived here. After your walk, drive a couple of miles to the **Big Foot Pass Overlook,** up on the right. Picnic tables here let you enjoy a packed lunch amid grassy prairies, with the rocky badland formations all around you.

After lunch, continue driving along Badlands Loop Road, stopping at the various overlooks for views and a hike or two. Near the Conata Picnic Area, you'll find the **Big Pig Dig,** a fossil site that was excavated by paleontologists through the summer of 2008. When you reach the junction with **Sage Creek Rim Road,** turn left and follow it along the northern border of the 100-square-mile **Badlands Wilderness Area,** which is home to hundreds of bison.

Provided the road is dry, take a side trip 5 miles down Sage Creek Rim Road to **Roberts Prairie Dog Town,** inhabited by a huge colony of the chattering critters. Children will love to watch these small rodents, which bark warning calls and dive underground if you get too close to their colony. The animals built burrow networks that once covered the Great Plains, but since European settlers established ranches in the region during the late 19th century, prairie dogs have become a far rarer sight. The park is less developed the farther you travel on Sage Creek Rim Road, allowing you to admire the sheer isolation and untouched beauty of badlands country. Hold out for a glorious sunset over the shadows of the nearby Black Hills, and keep your eyes open for animals stirring about.

can get through. Off-road driving is prohibited. There's free parking at visitor centers, overlooks, and trailheads.

Inspiration

Badlands National Park, by Jan Cerney and part of the Images of America Series, uses historical photography to help shed light on a ruggedly surreal landscape that has, over the centuries, been traversed by Native Americans, fur traders, cattlemen, homesteaders, and fossil hunters.

Mount Rushmore, Badlands, Wind Cave: Going Underground, by Mike Graf, with illustrations by Marjorie Leggitt, takes kids on national park learning adventures with the Parker family.

Several movies have featured scenes from South Dakota's badlands, including *Nomadland, Dances With Wolves, Starship Troopers, Armageddon, How the West Was Won, Thunderheart,* and *Badlands.*

Park Essentials

ACCESSIBILITY

Cedar Pass Lodge, the visitor centers, and most overlooks are wheelchair accessible. The Fossil Exhibit Trail and the Window Trail have reserved parking and are accessible by ramp, although they are quite steep in places. The Door and Cliff Shelf trails are accessible by boardwalk. Cedar Pass Campground has two fully accessible sites, plus many other sites that are sculpted and easily negotiated by wheelchair users; its office and amphitheater also are accessible. The Bigfoot Picnic Area has reserved parking, ramps, and an accessible pit toilet. Other areas can be difficult or impossible to navigate by those with limited mobility.

PARK FEES AND PERMITS

The entrance fee is $12 per person or $25 per vehicle, and is good for seven days. An annual park pass is $50. A backcountry permit isn't required for hiking or camping in Badlands National Park, but check in at park headquarters before setting out on a backcountry journey. Backpackers may set up camps anywhere except within a half mile of roads or trails. Open fires are prohibited.

PARK HOURS

The park is open 24/7 year-round and is in the Mountain time zone. Ranger programs are offered late May to early September. For offerings and times, check at the Ben Reifel Visitor Center and the Cedar Pass Lodge; a schedule might also be posted at the Cedar Pass Campground kiosk.

CELL PHONE RECEPTION

Cell phone service has improved measurably over the last decade in western South Dakota, but you may not get a signal in much of the park. The closest pay phone you'll find will likely be in Wall.

Hotels

If you're determined to bed down within park boundaries, you have only one choice: Cedar Pass Lodge. Though rustic, it's comfortable, inexpensive, and has eco-friendly cabins.

The rustic-but-comfy formula is repeated by the area's few motels, hotels, and inns. Most are chain hotels grouped around the interstate. Whether you stay inside or outside the park, you shouldn't have to worry about making reservations very far in advance, except during the first full week of August, when the entire region is inundated with motorcyclists for the annual Sturgis Motorcycle Rally. Rooms for miles around book up more than a year in advance. *Hotel reviews have been shortened. For full information, visit Fodors.com.*

What It Costs			
$	$$	$$$	$$$$
RESTAURANTS			
under $13	$13–$20	$21–$30	over $30
HOTELS			
under $101	$101–$150	$151–$200	over $200

Restaurants

Dining on the prairies of South Dakota has always been a casual and family-oriented experience, and in that sense little has changed in the past century. Even the fare, which consists largely of steak and potatoes, has stayed consistent (in fact, in some towns, "vegetarian" can be a dirty word). But for its lack of comparative sophistication, the grub in the restaurants surrounding Badlands National Park is typically very good. You'll probably never have a better steak—beef or buffalo—outside this area. You should also try cuisine influenced by Native

American cooking. In the park itself there's only one restaurant. The food is quite good, but don't hesitate to explore other options farther afield. *Restaurant reviews have been shortened. For full information, visit Fodors.com.*

Tours

Affordable Adventures Badlands and Wall Drug Tour

TOUR—SIGHT | Take a seven-hour narrated tour through the park and surrounding badlands, with a stop at the famous Wall Drug Store for lunch (not included in the fee), the Minuteman II Missile Museum, and the Prairie Homestead Sod House Historical Site. Tours can easily be customized and are available year-round; there's hotel pickup in Rapid City. ⊠ *5542 Meteor St., Rapid City* ☎ *605/342–7691, 888/888–8249* ⊕ *www.affordableadventuresbh.com* ⌨ *$145.*

Visitor Information

A free park newspaper, *Badlands Visitor Guide,* is available at the park's visitor centers and by request. Several park brochures on such topics as geology, photography, and horseback riding in the park are free at the visitor centers and from ⊕ *www.nps.gov/badl.*

PARK CONTACT INFORMATION Badlands National Park. ☎ *605/433–5361* ⊕ *www. nps.gov/badl.* **Black Hills, Badlands & Lakes Association.** ⊠ *1851 Discovery Circle, Rapid City* ☎ *605/355–3700, 888/945–7676* ⊕ *www.blackhillsbadlands.com.*

North Unit

34 miles from Wall (northeast entrance).

The North Unit hosts most of the major attractions and is most accessible from Interstate 90. The Badlands Loop Road has numerous overlooks that offer varying views as well as the park's formal hiking trails. Ben Reifel Visitor Center is a must-stop with museum exhibits, a fossil preparation lab, a film about the park, and bookstore.

While not technically part of the Badlands National Park, Minuteman Missile National Historic Site and Visitor Center is a prominent fixture close to the northeast park entrance road and definitely worth a stop to learn about the area's prominent role in the Cold War.

Sights

HISTORIC SITES

Ancient Hunters Overlook

VIEWPOINT | Perched above a dense fossil bed, this overhang, adjacent to the Pinnacles overlook, is where prehistoric bison hunters drove herds of buffalo over the edge. ⊠ *Badlands National Park* ✛ *22 miles northwest of the Ben Reifel Visitor Center* ⊕ *www.nps.gov/badl.*

Big Pig Dig

ARCHAEOLOGICAL SITE | Until 2008, paleontologists dug for fossils at this site near the Conata Picnic Area. It was named for a large fossil originally thought to be of a prehistoric pig (it turned out to be a small, hornless rhinoceros). Wayside signs and exhibits, including a mural, provide context on the area and its fossils. ⊠ *Badlands National Park* ✛ *17 miles northwest of Ben Reifel Visitor Center.*

Minuteman Missile National Historic Site

HISTORIC SITE | This remote piece of United States history just north of Badlands National Park gives visitors the opportunity to tour a decommissioned Minuteman II intercontinental ballistic missile (ICBM) site, the first national park in the world dedicated to the Cold War. Start at the visitor center at I-90 Exit 131 to watch a film and view informative exhibits. The second site is the Delta 01-Lanch Control Facility at Exit 127. It's open only to visitors with tickets to the ranger-led tour that are available at the visitor center on a first-come, first-served basis. The next stop west, at Exit 116, is the Delta-09 missile silo, which has exhibits and a self-guided cell phone tour that describe the site and give visitors a view down into the silo. ⊠ *Interstate 90 Exit 126* ☎ *605/433–5552* ⊕ *nps.gov/mimi.*

PICNIC AREAS

Bigfoot Pass Overlook

LOCAL INTEREST | There is only a handful of tables here and no water or restrooms, but the incredible view makes it a lovely spot to have lunch. ⊠ *Badlands Loop Rd.* ⊹ *7 miles northwest of Ben Reifel Visitor Center.*

Conata Picnic Area

LOCAL INTEREST | A half-dozen or so covered picnic tables are scattered over this area, which rests against a badlands wall ½ mile south of Badlands Loop Road. There's no potable water, but there are bathroom facilities and you can enjoy your lunch in peaceful isolation at the threshold of the Badlands Wilderness Area. The Conata Basin area is to the east, and Sage Creek area is to the west. ⊠ *Conata Rd.* ⊹ *15 miles northwest of Ben Reifel Visitor Center* ⊕ *www.nps.gov/badl.*

SCENIC DRIVES

For the average visitor, a casual drive is the essential means by which to see Badlands National Park. To do the scenery justice, drive slowly, and don't hesitate to get out and explore on foot when the occasion calls for it.

★ Badlands Loop Road

SCENIC DRIVE | The simplest drive is on two-lane Badlands Loop Road (Route/Highway 240). The drive circles from Exit 110 off I–90 through the park and back to the interstate at Exit 131. Start from either end and make your way around to the various overlooks along the way. Pinnacles and Yellow Mounds overlooks are outstanding places to examine the sandy pink- and brown-toned ridges and spires

distinctive to the badlands. The landscape flattens out slightly to the north, revealing spectacular views of mixed-grass prairies. The Cedar Pass area of the drive has some of the park's best trails. ⊠ *I–90, Exit 110* ⊕ *www.nps.gov/badl.*

Sage Creek Rim Drive

SCENIC DRIVE | This gravel route near the Pinnacles entrance follows the road less traveled and covers rougher terrain than Badlands Loop Road. Sage Creek Rim Road is completely negotiable by most vehicles, but should be avoided during a thunderstorm when the sudden rush of water may cause flooding. It might also close temporarily after snowstorms. A vast mixed-grass prairie covers the rest. Keep an eye out for free-roaming bison. ⊠ *Badlands National Park* ⊕ *www.nps. gov/badl.*

SCENIC STOPS

★ Badlands Wilderness Area

NATURE PRESERVE | Covering about a quarter of the park, this 100-square-mile area is part of the country's largest prairie wilderness. About two-thirds of the Sage Creek region is mixed-grass prairie, making it the ideal grazing grounds for bison, pronghorn, and other native animals. The Hay Butte Overlook (2 miles northwest on Sage Creek Rim Road) and the Pinnacles Overlook (1 mile south of the Pinnacles entrance) are the best places to get an overview of the wilderness area. Feel free to park at an overlook and hike your own route into the untamed, unmarked prairie. ⊠ *Badlands National Park* ⊹ *25 miles northwest of Ben Reifel Visitor Center* ⊕ *www.nps.gov/badl.*

Big Badlands Overlook

VIEWPOINT | From this spot just south of the park's northeast entrance, the vast majority of the park's 1 million annual visitors get their first views of the White River Badlands. ⊠ *Badlands National Park* ⊹ *5 miles northeast of the Ben Reifel Visitor Center.*

The two-lane Badlands Loop Road has more than a dozen scenic overlooks that provide amazing views of the spires and ridges that make the Badlands so distinct.

Big Foot Pass Overlook

VIEWPOINT | See where Sioux Chief Big Foot and his band traveled en route to the battle at Wounded Knee, December 29, 1890. ⊠ *Badlands National Park ✛ 7 miles northwest of the Ben Reifel Visitor Center.*

Roberts Prairie Dog Town

NATURE PRESERVE | FAMILY | Once a homestead, the site today contains one of the country's largest (if not the largest) colonies of black-tailed prairie dogs. ⊠ *Sage Creek Rim Rd. ✛ 5 miles west of Badlands Loop Rd.*

Yellow Mounds Overlook

VIEWPOINT | Contrasting sharply with the whites, grays, and browns of the Badlands' pinnacles, the mounds viewed from here greet you with soft yet vivid yellows, reds, and purples. ⊠ *Badlands National Park ✛ 16 miles northwest of Ben Reifel Visitor Center.*

TRAILS

Castle Trail

TRAIL | The park's longest hike runs 5 miles one-way between the Fossil Exhibit trailhead on Badlands Loop Road and the parking area for the Door and Windows trails. Although the Castle Trail is fairly level, allow at least three hours to cover the entire 10 miles out and back. If you choose to follow the Medicine Root Loop, which detours off the Castle Trail, you'll add ½ mile to the trek. Experienced hikers will do this one more quickly. *Moderate.* ⊠ *Badlands National Park ✛ Trailhead: 5 miles north of Ben Reifel Visitor Center, off Hwy. 240.*

Cliff Shelf Nature Trail

TRAIL | This ½-mile loop winds through a wooded prairie oasis in the middle of dry, rocky ridges and climbs 200 feet to a peak above White River Valley for an incomparable view. Look for chipmunks, squirrels, and red-winged blackbirds in the wet wood, and eagles, hawks, and vultures at hilltop. Even casual hikers can complete this trail in far less than an

Plants and Wildlife in Badlands

The park's sharply defined cliffs, canyons, and mesas are near-deserts with little plant growth. Most of the park, however, is made up of mixed-grass prairies, where more than 460 species of hardy grasses and wildflowers flourish in the warmer months. Prairie coneflower, yellow plains prickly pear, pale-green yucca, buffalo grass, and sideoats grama are just a few of the plants on the badlands plateau. Trees and shrubs are rare and usually confined to dry creek beds. The most common trees are Rocky Mountain junipers and plains cottonwoods.

It's common to see pronghorn antelope and mule deer dart across the flat plateaus, bison grazing on the buttes, prairie dogs and sharp-tailed grouse, and, soaring above, golden eagles, turkey vultures, and hawks. Also present are coyotes, swift foxes, jackrabbits, bats, gophers, porcupines, skunks, bobcats, horned lizards, bighorn sheep, and prairie rattlers. The latter are the only venomous reptiles in the park—watch for them near rocky outcroppings and in prairie-dog towns. Backcountry hikers might consider heavy boots and long pants reinforced with leather or canvas. Although rarely seen, weasels, mountain lions, and the endangered black-footed ferret roam the park.

hour, but if you want to observe the true diversity of wildlife present here, stay longer. *Moderate.* ⊠ *Badlands National Park* ✛ *Trailhead: 1 mile east of Ben Reifel Visitor Center, off Hwy. 240.*

Door Trail

TRAIL | The ¾-mile round-trip trail leads through a natural opening, or door, in a badlands rock wall. The eerie sandstone formations and passageways beckon, but it's recommended that you stay on the trail. The first 100 yards of the trail are on a boardwalk. Even a patient and observant hiker will take only about 30 minutes. *Easy.* ⊠ *Badlands National Park* ✛ *Trailhead: 2 miles east of Ben Reifel Visitor Center, off Hwy. 240.*

★ Fossil Exhibit Trail

TRAIL | FAMILY | The trail, in place since 1964, has fossil replicas of early mammals displayed at wayside exhibits along its ¼-mile length, which is completely wheelchair accessible. Give yourself at least an hour to fully enjoy this popular hike. *Easy.* ⊠ *Badlands National Park*

✛ *Trailhead: 5 miles northwest of Ben Reifel Visitor Center, off Hwy. 240.*

Notch Trail

TRAIL | One of the park's more interesting hikes, this 1½-mile round-trip trail takes you over moderately difficult terrain and up a ladder. Winds at the notch can be fierce, but it's worth lingering for the view of the White River Valley and the Pine Ridge Indian Reservation. With breaks to enjoy the views, you'll probably spend more than an hour on this hike. *Moderate–Difficult.* ⊠ *Badlands National Park* ✛ *Trailhead: 2 miles north of Ben Reifel Visitor Center, off Hwy. 240.*

Saddle Pass Trail

TRAIL | This route, which connects with Castle Trail and Medicine Root Loop, is a steep, ¼-mile round-trip route up and down the side of "The Wall," an impressive rock formation. Plan on spending about an hour on this climb. *Difficult.* ⊠ *Badlands National Park* ✛ *Trailhead: 2 miles west of Ben Reifel Visitor Center, off Hwy. 240 ⊕ www.nps.gov/badl.*

Window Trail

TRAIL | This ¼-mile round-trip trail ends at a natural hole, or window, in a rock wall. You'll see more of the distinctive badlands pinnacles and spires. *Easy.* ✉ *Badlands National Park* ✣ *Trailhead: 2 miles north of Ben Reifel Visitor Center, off Hwy. 240.*

VISITOR CENTERS

Ben Reifel Visitor Center

INFO CENTER | Open year-round, the park's main information hub has brochures, maps, and information on ranger programs. Check out exhibits on geology and wildlife, and watch paleontologists at work in the Fossil Prep Lab (June–September). View the film, *Land of Stone and Light,*in the 95-seat theater, and shop in the Badlands Natural History Association Bookstore. The facility is named for a Sioux activist and the first Lakota to serve in Congress. Born on the nearby Rosebud Indian Reservation, Ben Reifel also served in the Army during World War II. ✉ *Badlands National Park* ✣ *Badlands Loop Rd., near Hwy. 377 junction, 8 miles from northeast entrance* ☎ *605/433–5361*.

Minuteman Missile Visitors Center

HISTORIC SITE | This modern visitor center is full of Cold War history. If you were alive during the Cold War era (or are a fan of *War Games*), it's a must-see trip back in time, with immersive displays that capture the history of the United States' nuclear standoff with the former Soviet Union. For children and grandchildren, the site does a great job explaining this not-too-distant piece of history that gives context to the country's relationship with the USSR. While the visitor center (and two accompanying sites) aren't in Badlands National Park, it's less than 10 minutes from the northeast entrance, making it a perfect stop before or after your park visit. ✣ *Interstate 90 Exit 131* ☎ *605/433–5552* 🌐 *www.nps.gov/mimi.*

🍴 Restaurants

Cedar Pass Lodge Restaurant

$ | **AMERICAN** | **FAMILY** | Cool off within dark, knotty-pine walls under an exposed-beam ceiling, and enjoy a hearty meal of steak or tacos and fry bread. **Known for:** locally sourced fish, meat, and produce; fresh fry bread; decent selection of vegetarian and gluten-free dishes. [$] *Average main: $9* ✉ *20681 Hwy. 240, Interior* ☎ *605/433–5460* 🌐 *www.cedarpasslodge.com* 🕒 *Closed Nov.–mid-Apr.*

🛏 Hotels

Cedar Pass Lodge

$$$ | **HOTEL** | Besides impressive views of the badlands, these cabins include modern touches like flat-screen TVs and Wi-Fi connections. **Pros:** new cabins; the best stargazing in South Dakota. **Cons:** remote location; long drive to other restaurants. [$] *Rooms from: $176* ✉ *20681 Hwy. 240, Interior* ☎ *605/433–5460, 877/386–4383* 🌐 *www.cedarpasslodge.com* 🕒 *Closed Nov.–mid-Apr.* 🛏 *26 cabins* 🍴 *No meals.*

Palmer Creek Unit

26 miles from Kyle.

This is a very remote part of the park and accessible only with permission to cross private land. Backcountry camping is allowed, but you have to hike in and follow all rules and regulations.

Stronghold Unit

4 miles from Scenic and 34 miles from Ben Reifel Visitor Center in the North Unit.

With few paved roads and no campgrounds, the park's southwest section is difficult to access without a four-wheel-drive vehicle. If you're willing to trek, its isolation provides a rare opportunity to explore the Badlands rock formations and prairies completely undisturbed. From 1942 to 1968, the U.S. Air Force and South Dakota National Guard used much of the area as a gunnery range. Hundreds of fossils were destroyed by bomber pilots, who frequently targeted the large fossil remains of an elephant-size titanothere (an extinct relative of the rhinoceros). Beware of unexploded bombs, shells, rockets, and other hazardous materials. Steer clear of it and find another route.

⊙ Sights

PICNIC AREAS

White River Visitor Center Picnic Tables

LOCAL INTEREST | Directly behind this visitor center are four covered tables, where you can picnic simply and stay protected from the wind. There are also restroom facilities. ⊠ *Rte. 27 ⊹ 25 miles south of Rte. 44.*

SCENIC STOPS

Stronghold Table

HISTORIC SITE | Within the Stronghold Unit, the Stronghold Table, a 3-mile-long plateau, can be reached only by crossing a narrow land bridge just wide enough to let a wagon pass. It was here, just before the Massacre at Wounded Knee in 1890, that some 600 Sioux gathered to perform one of the last known Ghost Dances, a ritual in which the Sioux wore white shirts that they believed would protect them from bullets. ⊠ *Badlands National Park ⊹ North and west of White River Visitor Center; entrance off Hwy. 27* ⊕ *www.nps.gov/badl.*

TRAILS

Sheep Mountain Table Road

TRAIL | This 7-mile dirt road in the Stronghold Unit is ideal for mountain biking, but should be attempted only when dry, and riders must stay on the road. The terrain is level for the first 3 miles, then it climbs and levels out again. At the top you can take in great views of the area. ⊠ *Badlands National Park ⊹ About 14 miles north of White River Visitor Center.*

VISITOR CENTER

White River Visitor Center

INFO CENTER | Open in summer, this small center serves almost exclusively serious hikers and campers venturing into the Stronghold or Palmer unit. If that's you, stop here for maps and details about road and trail conditions. The center is on the Pine Ridge Indian Reservation. While you're here you can see fossils and Lakota artifacts, and learn about Sioux culture. ⊠ *Badlands National Park ⊹ 25 miles south of Hwy. 44 via Hwy. 27* ☎ *605/455–2878* ⊕ *www.nps.gov/badl.*

Activities

BIKING

Bicycles are permitted only on designated roads, which may be paved or unpaved. They are prohibited from closed roads, trails, and the backcountry. Flat-resistant tires are recommended.

Two Wheeler Dealer Cycle and Fitness

BICYCLING | Family-owned and-operated Two Wheeler Dealer Cycle and Fitness, based in Spearfish, stocks hundreds of bikes for sale and plenty of them to rent. The service is exceptional. ⊠ *305 Main St. Suite 1, Spearfish* ☎ *605/642–7545* ⊕ *www.twowheelerdealer.com.*

BIRD-WATCHING

Especially around sunset, get set to watch the badlands come to life. More than 215 bird species have been recorded in the area, including herons, pelicans, cormorants, egrets, swans, geese, hawks, golden and bald eagles, falcons, vultures, cranes, doves, and cuckoos. Established roads and trails are the best places from which to watch for nesting species. The Cliff Shelf Nature Trail and the Castle Trail, which both traverse areas with surprisingly thick vegetation, are especially good locations. You may even catch sight of a rare burrowing owl at the Roberts Prairie Dog Town.

CAMPING

Pitching a tent and sleeping under the stars is one of the greatest ways to fully experience the sheer isolation and unadulterated empty spaces of Badlands National Park. You'll find two relatively easy-access campgrounds within park boundaries, but only one has any sort of amenities. The second is little more than a flat patch of ground with some signs. Unless you desperately need a flush toilet to have an enjoyable camping experience, you're just as well off hiking into the wilderness and choosing your own campsite. You can set up camp anywhere that's at least a half mile from a road or trail and is not visible from any road or trail.

Cedar Pass Campground. With tent sites and 20 RV sites as well as coin-operated showers, this is the most developed campground in the park, and it's near Ben Reifel Visitor Center, Cedar Pass Lodge, and a half-dozen hiking trails. ⊠ *Rte. 377, ¼ mile south of Badlands Loop Rd.* ☎ *605/433–5361* ⊕ *www.cedarpasslodge.com.*

Sage Creek Primitive Campground. If you want to get away from it all, this lovely, isolated spot surrounded by nothing but fields and crickets is the right camp for you. ⊠ *Sage Creek Rim Rd., 25 miles west of Badlands Loop Rd.* ☎ *No phone.*

EDUCATIONAL PROGRAMS

Evening Program and Night Sky Viewing
TOUR—SIGHT | Watch a 45-minute presentation on the wildlife, natural history, paleontology, or another aspect of the Badlands. Shows typically begin around 9 pm. Stick around afterward for the Night Sky Viewing, a star-gazing interpretive program complete with telescopes. ⊠ *Cedar Pass Campground amphitheater, 20681 Hwy. 240* ⊕ *www.nps.gov/badl.*

Fossil Talk
TOUR—SIGHT | What were the Badlands like many years ago? This 20-minute talk about protected fossil exhibits will inspire and answer all your questions. It's usually held at 10:30 am and 1:30 pm daily at the Fossil Exhibit Trail. ⊠ *Badlands National Park* ⊹ *Fossil Exhibit Trail, Badlands Loop Rd., 5 miles northwest of Ben Reifel Visitor Center* ⊕ *www.nps.gov/badl.*

Geology Walk
TOUR—SIGHT | Learn the geologic story of the White River Badlands in a 45-minute walk, generally departing from the Door Trailhead daily at 8:30 am. The terrain can be rough in places, so be sure to wear hiking boots or sneakers. A hat is a good idea, too. ⊠ *Badlands National Park* ⊹ *Door and Window trails parking area, Badlands Loop Rd., 2 miles south of the northeast entrance* ⊕ *www.nps.gov/badl.*

Junior Ranger Program
TOUR—SIGHT | FAMILY | Children ages 7–12 can join in this daily, 30-minute adventure, typically a short hike, game, or other hands-on activity focused on badlands wildlife, geology, or fossils. Parents are welcome. Meet at the visitor center at 11 am, and wear closed-toe shoes. ⊠ *Ben Reifel Visitor Center, 25216 Hwy. 240* ☎ *605/433–5361* ⊕ *www.nps.gov/badl.*

HIKING

The otherworldliness of the badlands is best appreciated with a walk through them. Take time to examine the dusty rock beneath your feet, and be on the lookout for fossils and animals. Fossil Exhibit Trail and Cliff Shelf Nature Trail are must-dos, but even these popular trails tend to be primitive. You'll find bathrooms at Fossil Exhibit Trail. Both trails feature boardwalks, so you won't be shuffling through dirt and gravel. Door Trail and Window Trail are also short, easy, and easily accessible treks on the east end of the North Unit. Notch Trail is nearby but is more of a strenuous hike that offers an awesome view of the White River Valley. Castle Trail, the park's longest, takes you deep into the badlands. Extend your hike by connecting with Medicine Root Trail or Saddle Pass Trail. Thanks to Badlands National Park's open-hike policy, you can also venture off the trails. One area to consider is the Sage Creek Wilderness Area where the park's bison live.

Because the weather here can be so variable, be prepared for anything. Wear sunglasses, a hat, and long pants, and have rain gear available. It's illegal to interfere with park resources, which include everything from rocks and fossils to plants and artifacts. Stay at least 100 yards away from wildlife. Due to the dry climate, open fires are never allowed. Tell friends, relatives, and the park rangers if you're going to embark on a multiday expedition. Assume that your cell phone, if you've brought one, won't get a signal in the park. But most important of all, be sure to bring your own water. Sources of water in the park are few and far between, and none of them are drinkable. All water in the park is contaminated by minerals and sediment, and park authorities warn that it's untreatable. If you're backpacking into the wilderness, bring at least a gallon of water per person per day. For day hikes, rangers suggest you drink at least a quart per person per hour.

OUTFITTERS
Scheels All Sport

HIKING/WALKING | In the Rushmore Crossing Mall, off I–90 at the East-North Street or Lacrosse Street exit, this enormous shop carries a wide selection of all-weather hiking gear, footwear, and clothes as well as binoculars suitable for bird-watchers. ⊠ *1225 Eglin St., Rapid City* ☎ *605/342–9033* ⊕ *www.scheels.com.*

HORSEBACK RIDING

The park has one of the largest and most beautiful territories in the state in which to ride a horse. Riding is allowed in most of the park except for some marked trails, roads, and developed areas. The mixed-grass prairie of the Badlands Wilderness Area is especially popular, though the weather can be unpredictable. Only experienced riders or people accompanied by experienced riders should venture far from more developed areas.

There are several restrictions and regulations that you must be aware of if you plan to ride your own horse. Potable water for visitors and animals is a rarity. Riders must bring enough water for themselves and their stock. Only certified weed-free hay is approved in the park. Horses are not allowed to run free within the borders of the park.

Gunsel Horse Adventures

HORSEBACK RIDING | The company customizes backcountry trips throughout the Black Hills and Badlands. Bring your sleeping bag. ☎ *605/343–7608* ⊕ *www. gunselhorseadventures.com* ✉ *Call for pricing.*

Nearby Towns

Located off I–90, 50 miles east of the edge of the Black Hills (and **Rapid City,** the largest community on this side of the state), Badlands National Park allows travelers a unique stop in a highly dense area of national parks, monuments, and memorials including Mount Rushmore National Memorial, Wind Cave National Park, Jewel Cave National Monument, Devils Tower National Monument, and Custer State Park. The Black Hills provide a wonderful backdrop for the dry canyon and dusty buttes of the badlands. Park entrances along I-90 are near the towns of **Wall** on the west (home to the famous Wall Drug) and Kadoka on the east, which have lodging, restaurants, gas and auto repair, and other support services.

Rapid City

80 miles to the Badlands National Park's Interior entrance; 56 miles to Wall on I–90.

Called the "City of Presidents" because of the life-size bronze statues of U.S. presidents that adorn virtually every downtown street corner, Rapid City is the largest urban center in a 350-mile radius. The city is an excellent base from which to explore the treasures of the state's southwestern corner, including Mount Rushmore (25 miles south) and Wind Cave National Park (50 miles south).

GETTING HERE AND AROUND

Most Black Hills travelers come by RV, passenger vehicle, or motorcycle. If you're driving, Rapid City is a five hour drive west of Sioux Falls on I-90 and a six-hour drive northwest of Sioux City, Iowa via I-90 W. If you're coming from the east, Billings, Montana is five hours southeast of Rapid City via US-212 E and I-90 E; from the south, Denver is six hours via I-25 N and US-85 N.

CONTACTS Rapid City Regional Airport. *(RAP)* ✉ *4550 Terminal Rd., Rapid City* ☎ *605/393–9924* ⊕ *www.rapairport.com.*

TOURS
City View Trolley
GUIDED TOURS | Walking is the best way to see Rapid City's downtown, but taking the City View Trolley is the easiest way to see other attractions in town. The narrated tour includes 15 stops at points of interest and historical sites. The tour begins and ends downtown at the transportation center (though you can board it at any of the stops) and includes the Dahl Arts Museum, Journey Museum, Storybook Island, and Dinosaur Park. Tours run Monday through Saturday, June through August. ✉ *Rapid City* ☎ *605/394–6631* ⊕ *www.rapidride.org/city-view-trolley* ⊠ *$2.*

VISITOR INFORMATION
Rapid City Convention and Visitors Bureau. ✉ *512 Main St., Suite 240, Rapid City* ☎ *605/718–8484, 800/487–3223* ⊕ *www.visitrapidcity.com.*

Sights

Art Alley
ARTS VENUE | This outdoor gallery started organically and evolved as artists and community members worked with city leaders to turn the back of the buildings into a canvas that includes social commentary, Native American culture, and even Yoda. ✉ *Rapid City* ✛ *Between 6th and 7th, and Main and Saint Joseph streets* ⊕ *www.artalleyrc.com.*

★ Bear Country U.S.A.
ZOO | FAMILY | Encounter black bear, elk, sheep, and wolves at this drive-through wildlife park, which has been entertaining guests for more than 40 years. There's also a walk-through wildlife center with red foxes, porcupines, badgers, bobcats, and lynx. The Babyland area features bear cubs and young otters. ✉ *13820 S. U.S. 16, Rapid City* ☎ *605/343–2290* ⊕ *www.bearcountryusa.com* ⊠ *$18, with a maximum per vehicle of $65* ⊗ *Closed late Nov.–late Apr.*

Black Hills Caverns
CAVE | FAMILY | Amethysts, logomites, calcite crystals, and other specimens fill this cave, first discovered by gold-seekers in 1882. Half-hour and hour tours, as well as gemstone and fossil mining, are available. ✉ *2600 Cavern Rd., Rapid City* ☎ *605/343–0542, 800/837–9358* ⊕ *www.blackhillscaverns.com* ⊠ *From $17* ⊗ *Closed Nov.–mid-May.*

Black Hills National Forest
NATIONAL/STATE PARK | Hundreds of miles of hiking, mountain-biking, and horseback-riding trails crisscross this million-acre forest on the state's western edge. Entry points include Custer,

Deadwood, Hill City, Hot Springs, Lead, Rapid City, Spearfish, and Sturgis. The visitor center (open seasonally) is west of Rapid City at Pactola Reservoir. ⊠ *U.S. 385 W, Rapid City* ☎ *605/673–9200 supervisor's office in Custer* ⊕ *www. fs.usda.gov/blackhills* ⊠ *Free.*

Black Hills Petrified Forest

NATURE SITE | A 15-minute video and a self-guided nature walk teach you about the geologic evolution of western South Dakota. Allow about an hour for your visit to this forest, which opened to the public in 1929, and is about halfway between Rapid City and Sturgis. ⊠ *Elk Creek Resort, 8220 Elk Creek Rd., Piedmont* ☎ *605/787–4560* ⊕ *elkcreekresort.net/ petrified-forest/* ⊠ *$7* ⊙ *Closed Oct.–Apr.*

Chapel in the Hills

RELIGIOUS SITE | Hidden away in a residential neighborhood lies this most unexpected gem—an exact replica of the Borgan Stavkirke in Norway. Built in 1960 as place for the areas numerous Norwegian Lutherans to worship, if you're looking for a bit of calm, are a fan of unique architecture, love finding unexpected places, or want to take in a service, you won't be sorry. There's a prayer walk around the property, as well as a museum and a charming Nordic- (and religious-) theme gift shop. ⊠ *3788 Chapel Ln., Rapid City* ☎ *605/342–8281* ⊕ *www.chapel-in-the-hills.org* ⊙ *Closed Oct.–May.*

City of Presidents

HISTORIC SITE | Started in 2000 to honor "the legacy of the American presidency," a visit to this series of life-size bronze statues ties in nicely with a visit to Mount Rushmore. Located throughout downtown Rapid City, the statues of the country's past presidents can be found on the downtown's street corners. Each privately funded sculpture has a creative nod to each president: JFK is with his son, Ronald Regan has a cowboy hat, and Gerald Ford is with his dog. Check out the web site for information about each statue, as well as an interactive

map that shows each statue's location. ⊠ *Rapid City* ⊹ *Downtown Rapid City's street corners* ⊕ *presentsrc.com.*

Ft. Hays Dances with Wolves Movie Set

FILM STUDIO | Starting with movie sets from the epic *Dances with Wolves,* this attraction is evolving into the South Dakota Film Museum, chronicling some 50 films produced in the state since 1914. See props, posters, and historical photos. A seasonal chuck-wagon dinner show is also held here. ⊠ *2255 Fort Hayes Dr., Rapid City* ☎ *605/343–3113* ⊕ *www.mountrushmoretours.com* ⊠ *Free; chuck-wagon dinner and show, $29* ⊙ *Closed mid-Oct.–mid-May.*

Journey Museum

MUSEUM | FAMILY | The interactive exhibits at this museum explore the history of the Black Hills from the age of the dinosaurs to the days of the pioneers. Its five permanent collections cover Native American and pioneer history, geology, paleontology, and archaeology. Special programming and exhibitions occur throughout the year. ⊠ *222 New York St., Rapid City* ☎ *605/394–6923* ⊕ *www. journeymuseum.org* ⊠ *$10.*

Museum of Geology

MUSEUM | This museum, affiliated with the South Dakota School of Technology & Mines, has a fine collection of fossilized bones from giant dinosaurs. It also contains extensive collections of agates, fossilized cycads, rocks, gems, and minerals. Younger travelers love the hands-on Kids' Zone exhibits. Shop for a sparkly treasure in the gift shop. ⊠ *O'Harra Memorial Building, 501 E. St. Joseph St., Rapid City* ☎ *605/394–2467* ⊕ *www.sds-mt.edu/Academics/Museum-of-Geology/ Home/* ⊠ *Free.*

South Dakota Air and Space Museum

MUSEUM | See General Dwight D. Eisenhower's B-25 Mitchell bomber, a B-1 Bomber, and more than 32 planes, helicopters, and missiles. From mid-May to mid-September, tours of a Minuteman

II missile silo on Ellsworth Air Force Base are also available for a nominal fee. ✉ *Ellsworth Air Force Base, 2890 Rushmore Dr., Box Elder* ☎ *605/385–5189* 🌐 *www.sdairandspacemuseum.com* 🎟 *$10.*

🍴 Restaurants

Delmonico Grill

$$$ | STEAKHOUSE | Recharge from your busy day in style with an elegant steak dinner; there are plenty of sensibly sized rib-eye options available, along with a smattering of additional entrées, upscale burgers, and even vegetarian options. If you're somehow not starving, consider the honey bourbon steak tips with peppers and cornbread or the "609" burger for a (somewhat) lighter taste of the house's specialty. **Known for:** steak for two is the signature splurge; meat, meat, and more meat; the Delmonico ribeye, a minimum 32-ounce tomahawk-cut steak. [$] *Average main: $35* ✉ *609 Main St., Rapid City* ☎ *605/791–1664* 🌐 *www.delmonicogrill.com.*

Firehouse Brewing Company

$ | AMERICAN | Brass fixtures and firefighting equipment ornament the state's first brewpub, located in a 1915 firehouse. The five house-brewed beers are the highlight here, and the menu includes such hearty pub dishes as pastas, salads, and gumbo. [$] *Average main: $0* ✉ *610 Main St., Rapid City* ☎ *605/348–1915* 🌐 *www.firehouse-brewing.com* 🕓 *No lunch Sun.*

Golden Phoenix

$ | CHINESE | Great food, low prices, and relaxed, friendly, and quick service make this one of South Dakota's best Chinese restaurants. The chef-owner, who socializes with the locals who frequent his establishment, seasons traditional dishes from all over China with spices from his native Taiwan. **Known for:** efficient service; loved by locals; wallet-friendly prices. [$] *Average main: $10* ✉ *2421 W. Main St., Rapid City* ☎ *605/348–4195* 🌐 *goldenphoenixrc.com.*

Millstone Family Restaurant

$ | AMERICAN | Depending on your early morning energy level, walk or drive to the Millstone for a satisfying country breakfast before starting your day. Breakfast is so beloved here that it's served all day and includes an extensive array of omelets, waffles, pancakes, and more, but the skillets menu is most worth your attention. **Known for:** all day breakfast; the breakfast skillets;. [$] *Average main: $10* ✉ *1520 N. Lacrosse St., Rapid City* ☎ *605/348–9022* 🌐 *bhmillstone.com.*

Murphy's Pub and Grill

$ | AMERICAN | Chow down on Rapid City flavors featuring local ingredients that produce hearty regional favorites like buffalo stew and buffalo meatloaf. Be sure to start with the restaurant's famous Dakota Pulled Pork Chips, hand-cut and topped with slow-roasted, red-wine pork and cheese. **Known for:** great appetizers like Mom's Deviled Eggs and the Redneck Sausage Sampler ; storied history in Rapid City; great beers on tap. [$] *Average main: $10* ✉ *510 9th St., Rapid City* ☎ *605/791–2244* 🌐 *www.murphyspubandgrill.com.*

☕ Coffee and Quick Bites

Black Hills Bagels

$ | AMERICAN | Start your day early at this local favorite breakfast spot, where more than 20 varieties of bagels range from cinnamon raisin to white chocolate chip and can be enhanced with an array of toppings on the build-your-own sandwich menu (or just choose from the five signature sandwiches if endless options aren't your thing). If you're heading off to explore the Badlands or Mount Rushmore, take your breakfast sandwich to-go, and consider grabbing something extra for the long morning ahead. **Known for:** more than 20 bagel varieties; great to-go options for breakfast and lunch; serves Dark Canyon coffee. [$] *Average main: $9* ✉ *913 Mt Rushmore Rd., Rapid City* ☎ *605/399–1277* 🌐 *www.blackhillsbagels.com.*

Hotels

Holiday Inn Rushmore Plaza
$$$ | **HOTEL** | This eight-story hotel has a central lobby with an atrium, glass elevators, and a 60-foot waterfall. **Pros:** excellent atrium and waterfall; good food in restaurant; nice bartenders in lounge. **Cons:** sterile feel; fairly long walk to restaurants; limited parking. [$] *Rooms from: $180-229* ✉ *505 N. 5th St., Rapid City* ☎ *605/348–4000, 800/315–2621* 🌐 *www.rushmoreplaza.com* 🛏 *205 rooms, 1 suite* 🍴 *No meals.*

Hotel Alex Johnson Rapid City
$$$ | **HOTEL** | Part of the Curio Collection by Hilton, the hotel was built in 1928 by Alex Johnson, vice president of the Chicago and Northwestern Railroad, as a tribute to the Native Americans and South Dakota's Black Hills which can be seen in the hotel's common areas. **Pros:** updated rooms in a historic property; pets are allowed; central location. **Cons:** it's said to be haunted by several spirits, which might not be everyone's cup of tea; rooms are on the small side. [$] *Rooms from: $173* ✉ *523 6th St., Rapid City* ☎ *605/342–1210* 🌐 *www.alexjohnson.com* 🛏 *143 rooms* 🍴 *No meals.*

Shopping

★ **Prairie Edge Trading Company and Galleries**
CRAFTS | One of the world's top collections of Plains Native American artwork and crafts makes Prairie Edge Trading Company and Galleries seem more like a museum than a store. The collection ranges from books to stunning artwork representing the Lakota, Crow, Cheyenne, Shoshone, Arapaho, and Assiniboine tribes of the Great Plains. ✉ *6th and Main Sts., Rapid City* ☎ *605/342–3086* 🌐 *www.prairieedge.com.*

Wall

8 miles from the Pinnacles entrance to the Badlands National Park's North Unit via Highway 240.

Built against a steep ridge of badland rock, Wall was founded in 1907 as a railroad station. Today, it's home to about 850 residents and the world-famous Wall Drug Store, best known for its fabled jackalopes and free ice water.

GETTING HERE AND AROUND
If you're coming from Rapid City in the west, Wall is 50 miles east on I-90. From the east on I-90, Wall is 95 miles from Murdo and 290 miles from Sioux Falls on the far eastern end of South Dakota. Just look for the giant dinosaur and the numerous signs for Wall Drug.

VISITOR INFORMATION Wall–Badlands Area Chamber of Commerce. ✉ *501 Main St., Wall* ☎ *605/279–2665, 888/852–9255* 🌐 *www.wall-badlands.com.*

Sights

★ **Wall Drug Store**
STORE/MALL | **FAMILY** | This South Dakota original got its start in 1931 by offering free ice water to road-weary travelers. Today its four dining rooms seat 530 visitors at a time. A life-size mechanical Cowboy Orchestra and Chuckwagon Quartet greet you inside, and, in the back, you'll find an animated T. rex, a replica of Mount Rushmore, and a panning and mining experience. The attached Western Mall has 14 shops selling all kinds of keepsakes from cowboy hats, boots, and Black Hills gold jewelry to T-shirts and fudge. Just don't skip the donuts. ✉ *510 Main St., Wall* ☎ *605/279–2175* 🌐 *www.walldrug.com* 🎟 *Free.*

Wounded Knee: The Museum
MUSEUM | This modern facility interprets the history of the December 29, 1890, Wounded Knee Massacre through interactive exhibits with historical photos and

documents. Many visitors choose to stop at this convenient location off I–90 in lieu of a stop at the isolated battleground 80 miles to the south. ✉ *207 10th Ave., Wall* ☎ *605/279–2573* ⊕ *www.wounded-kneemuseum.org* 💲 *$6* ⊙ *Closed Mon. and early Oct.–late May.*

🍴 Restaurants

Western Art Gallery Restaurant

$ | AMERICAN | More than 200 original oil paintings, all with a Western theme, line the dining room of this eatery in the Wall Drug building. For a tasty meal, try a hot beef sandwich or a buffalo burger. **Known for:** road-trip classic; Western memorabilia; friendly service. 💲 *Average main: $12* ✉ *510 Main St., Wall* ☎ *605/279–2175* ⊕ *www.walldrug.com.*

Pine Ridge

About 35 miles south of Badlands National Park's Stronghold Unit.

If you're traveling from (or to) Denver en route to the badlands, you'll probably pass through the tiny town of Pine Ridge, which is on the cusp of Pine Ridge Indian Reservation. The town was established in 1877 as an Indian agency for Chief Red Cloud and his band of followers. With 2,800 square miles, the reservation—home, and headquarters of the Oglala Sioux—is second in size only to Arizona's Navajo Reservation. There aren't any lodging options in Pine Ridge, and only a few franchise food restaurants, so it's really only a good place to refuel before the park.

GETTING HERE AND AROUND

The only transportation to Pine Ridge is by car. If you're coming from Hot Springs, in the southern Black Hills, take Highway 18 east for 64 miles. From Ben Reifel Visitor Center, it's 86 miles south.

TOURS
White Thunder Ranch

DRIVING TOURS | This tour operator offers several vehicle tours of the Pine Ridge Reservation and offer sights and history related to the Oglala Lakota Nation. ☎ *605/455–2343* ⊕ *www.vwhitethunder. com/tours.*

VISITOR INFORMATION
Pine Ridge Area Chamber of Commerce ✉ *7900 Lakota Prairie Dr., Kyle* ☎ *605/455–2685* ⊕ *www.pineridgechamber.com.*

◉ Sights

Oglala Sioux Tribe (Pine Ridge)

NATIVE SITE | The Pine Ridge Reservation is home to more than 40,000 Oglala Lakota, members of a major Sioux division known as the Western or Teton Sioux, who live in nine tribal districts on 1.4 million acres of land. They are led by a Tribal Council President who is advised by an executive committee and a tribal council. ✉ *Pine Ridge* ☎ *605/867–5821* ⊕ *www.oglalalakotanation.info.*

Red Cloud Indian School Heritage Art Museum

MUSEUM | Changing exhibits highlight Native American culture and art; the permanent collection has 10,000 contemporary and historical pieces. The gift shop sells locally made Lakota crafts and fine or decorative works of art. ✉ *100 Mission Dr., Pine Ridge* ☎ *605/867–8257* ⊕ *www. redcloudschool.org/museum* 💲 *Free.*

Wounded Knee Historical Site

NATIVE SITE | A stone obelisk commemorates the site of the 1890 massacre at Wounded Knee, the last major conflict between the U.S. military and Native Americans. Only a handful of visitors make pilgrimages to the remote site today, which is simple and largely unchanged from its 1890 appearance. ✉ *U.S. 18, Pine Ridge* ⊹ *12 miles northwest of Pine Ridge* 💲 *Free.*

Chapter 6

BIG BEND
NATIONAL PARK

6

Updated by
Andrew Collins

TEXAS

🏕 Camping   🏨 Hotels   🤸 Activities   👁 Scenery   👥 Crowds
★★★★☆   ★★★★☆   ★★★★★   ★★★★★   ★★★★☆

WELCOME TO
BIG BEND NATIONAL PARK

TOP REASONS TO GO

★ **Varied terrain:** Visit a desert of prickly cacti, a fabled international-border river, bird-abundant woods, and mountain spirals all in the same day.

★ **Wonderful wildlife:** Catch sight of the park's extremely diverse animals, including fuzzy tarantulas, bands of swarthy javelinas, reclusive mountain lions, and lumbering black bears.

★ **Bird-watching:** Spy a pied-billed grebe or another member of the park's more than 450 bird species, including the Lucifer hummingbird and the unique-to-this-area *pato mexicano* (Mexican duck).

★ **Hot spots:** Dip into the natural hot springs (105°F) near Rio Grande Village.

★ **Mile-high mountains:** Lace up your hiking boots and climb the Chisos Mountains, reaching almost 8,000 feet skyward in some places and remaining relatively cool except May–October, when temperatures reach into the upper 90s even at high elevations.

1 Chisos Basin. This bowl-shape canyon amid the Chisos Mountains—along with nearby Panther Junction—is at the heart of Big Bend. It's a base for numerous hikes and a prime place to watch a sunset through a "fracture" in the bowl known as the Window.

2 Castolon. Just east of Santa Elena Canyon, this cluster of adobe dwellings, once used by ranchers and the U.S. military, anchors the park's west side.

3 Rio Grande Village. Tall, shady cottonwoods highlight the park's eastern fringe along the Mexican border and Rio Grande. It's popular with bird-watching and camping enthusiasts.

4 Persimmon Gap. The park's engaging Fossil Discovery Exhibit is a highlight of this arid northern portion of the park that includes the Persimmon Gap entrance and several remote back roads where nomadic warriors once traveled to Mexico via the Comanche Trail.

TEXAS

Study Butte
Terlingua
118
170
0   5 mi
0   5 km
Lajitas
Luna's Jacal
Santa Elena Canyon Overlook
Santa Elena Canyon
Castolo
San
Eler

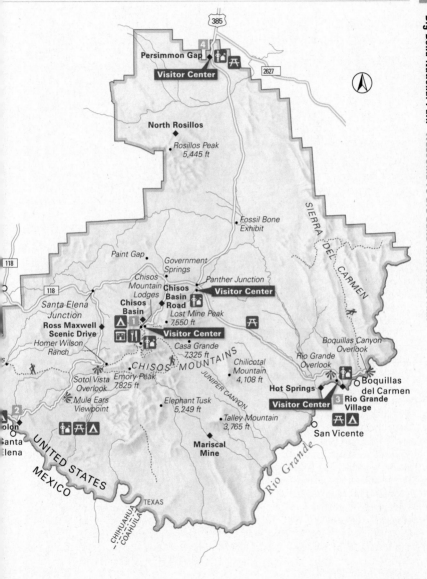

Persimmon Gap
Visitor Center
385
2627

North Rosillos
Rosillos Peak
5,445 ft

SIERRA DEL CARMEN

Fossil Bone
Exhibit

Paint Gap
118
118
*Government
Springs*
Chisos
Mountain
Lodges
Panther Junction
Chisos
Basin
Road
Visitor Center
*Santa Elena
Junction*
**Chisos
Basin**
**Ross Maxwell
Scenic Drive**
Lost Mine Peak
7,550 ft
*Homer Wilson
Ranch*
Visitor Center
Casa Grande
7,325 ft
CHISOS
Chilicotal
Mountain
4,108 ft
Boquillas Canyon
Overlook
Rio Grande
Overlook
*Sotol Vista
Overlook*
MOUNTAINS
JUNIPER CANYON
Hot Springs
Visitor Center
Boquillas
del Carmen
Emory Peak
7,825 ft
*Mule Ears
Viewpoint*
Elephant Tusk
5,249 ft
**Rio Grande
Village**
San Vicente
Talley Mountain
3,765 ft
olon
anta
lena
**Mariscal
Mine**
UNITED STATES
MEXICO
Rio Grande
TEXAS
CHIHUAHUA
COAHUILA

Cradled in the southwestern elbow of Texas, this 801,163-acre park hugs a wild and undeveloped 118-mile span of the Rio Grande, which separates it from northern Mexico's isolated deserts. Containing both the craggy, forested Chisos Mountains and the flat, starkly beautiful plains of the Chihuahuan Desert, Big Bend is one of the nation's largest and most geographically diverse parks.

Big Bend is the kind of park that rewards visitors almost exponentially the more time they spend here. There's simply too much to see and explore to fully appreciate the park in a day or two. Start by exploring the canyons along the Rio Grande at the park's western and eastern reaches, and you'll come away with an entirely different sense of Big Bend than if you spend a day trekking through the alpine forests of the Chisos Mountains, which rise some 6,200 feet above the river. This part of Texas is incredibly vast and untouched, even as you travel for hundreds of miles outside the park—just 15 miles west of the national park, for example, you'll find Big Bend Ranch State Park, which preserves another 311,000 acres of unspoiled wilderness. With its grand scale in mind, and keeping in mind that there's much to see and do in the nearby town of Marathon, Alpine, and Marfa, do try to budget at least three days and as much as a week for a truly satisfying Big Bend experience.

The region has always felt vast and untamed. Although archaeological evidence documents the presence of local human activity as far back as 6500 BC, the harsh terrain and climate helped deter significant development. The Spaniards who arrived in 1535 encountered several bands of nomadic hunters whom they dubbed the Chisos, and both Mescalero Apache and Comanche tribes regularly passed through the region en route to Mexico's interior until well into the 19th century, but large-scale permanent settlements were never established in this land the Spaniards referred to as El Despoblado, or The Uninhabitable. The first nonnatives to take any real interest in Big Bend began arriving in the mid-19th century, and they engaged in two principle activities: mining and ranching. You can find remnants of both endeavors in many parts of the park, including Mariscal Mine, Sam Nail Ranch, and the Castolon Historic District.

AVERAGE HIGH/LOW TEMPERATURES					
JAN.	FEB.	MAR.	APR.	MAY	JUNE
62/38	68/42	75/48	84/56	89/63	95/70
JULY	AUG.	SEPT.	OCT.	NOV.	DEC.
93/71	92/71	86/65	81/57	71/47	63/39

Efforts to preserve Big Bend as a park—in recognition of its breathtakingly diverse wildlife, flora, and geography—began in the 1930s. Hundreds of mostly Hispanic young men employed by the Civilian Conservation Corps (CCC) carved out trails, built visitor facilities, and constructed what remains one of Big Bend's signature features, the curving 7-mile road that climbs from the high desert near Panther Junction up into the crisp-aired peaks of the Chisos Basin. The Texas state government purchased more than 600,000 acres of private land in the early 1940s, and on June 12, 1944, Big Bend National Park welcomed its first visitors. Although the park enjoys a devoted following, its remoteness also helps to keep it from feeling overrun. Fewer than a half-million visitors pass through this massive preserve each year, a tiny fraction of the number of who visit much smaller parks in the West. This fact may not offer you much comfort when Chisos Mountains Lodge is fully booked, or you can't snag a parking space at the Lost Mine Trailhead. But take heart—if you're willing to venture out into Big Bend's more remote backcountry, the promise of solitude and spectacular natural beauty await, even during the busiest times.

Planning

When to Go

There is never a bad time to make a Big Bend foray—but during Thanksgiving, Christmas, and spring break, be aware that competition for rooms at Chisos Mountains Lodge, campsites, and nearby hotels is fierce—with reservations needed up to a year in advance.

Depending on the season—and sometimes even the day—Big Bend can be hot, dry, cold, or rainy. Many shun the park in late spring and summer, because temperatures skyrocket (up to 120°F down along the river) from May through August, and the Rio Grande lowers. In winter, temperatures rarely dip below 30°F. During those few times the mercury takes a dive, visitors might be rewarded with a rare snowfall at upper elevations. The mountains routinely are 5 to 20 degrees cooler than the rest of the park, while the sweltering stretches of the Rio Grande are 5 to 10 degrees warmer.

FESTIVALS AND EVENTS
Terlingua International Chili Championship. On the first Saturday of November, top chefs spice up cooling weather with chili cooking, bragging, and partying at this spicy chili cook-off held behind the Terlingua Store in Terlingua ghost town. Some of the prize-winning cooks dole out samples. And this is Texas, pardner: no beans allowed. ⊕ www.abowlofred.com.

Big Bend National Park PLANNING

6

Big Bend in One Day

Big Bend is the seventh largest park in the Continental United States. The west-side and east-side routes to its storied attraction branch apart at the foot of **Chisos Basin Road** in the heart of the park. Attempting both in one day, covering an aggregate 110 miles, could be hectic and ultimately frustrating, and you'll miss the striking details that bring the park and its history to life. Whichever side you decide to focus on, do spend half your day amid the mountain peaks and rugged trails of **Chisos Basin.** To the west, the goal is **Santa Elena Canyon**, carved by the Rio Grande. From Chisos Mountains Lodge, drive 7 miles north on **Chisos Basin Road,** turn west on Route 118 and connect with **Ross Maxwell Scenic Drive,** which curls past silent deserted homesteads, stunning overlooks, and the Castolon Historic District's ancient old adobe buildings near the Rio Grande. Explore as many overlooks and historical sites as time allows on this 30-mile stretch, then hike the spectacular **Santa Elena Canyon Trail** (1.6 miles round-trip). During rainy periods, you might need to wade Terlingua Creek before ascending a short but moderately steep trail cut into the canyon, which eventually steps down to a sandy riverside clearing. The majestic canyon is framed by gargantuan 1,500-foot-tall cliffs flanking the Rio Grande. Back at the trailhead, return to Chisos Basin Ross Maxwell Scenic Drive or the slower but picturesque unpaved Old Maverick Road (14 miles, and best managed by driving a high-clearance vehicle).

An alternative one-day option is to explore the east side of the park: head east from **Chisos Basin** toward **Rio Grande Village,** along the way exploring Panther Junction Visitor Center, Dugout Wells, Mariscal Mine, Hot Springs, and Boquillas Canyon. At Rio Grande Village, stroll through cottonwoods by the river, home to many birds. There's also a well-stocked convenience store and gas station for a midday snack. If you have time and a passport, cross the river at nearby Boquillas Crossing and while away a few hours in the rustic village of Boquillas del Carmen, Mexico. Return to Chisos Basin by the same route, hopefully in time to hike the short Window View Trail, where prime-time hues are captured at sunset.

Viva Big Bend. This West Texas showcase of Lone Star music features rock, blues, country, Latin, and beyond, on stages in Alpine, Fort Davis, Marathon, Lajitas, and Marfa, both in large paid-admission venues and free concerts on hotel patios. ⊕ *www.vivabigbend.com.*

Getting Here and Around

AIR

The nearest major airport is in Midland, four hours north of the park, but many visitors fly into El Paso, five hours northwest, which is served by more flights and airlines.

CAR

It can take 90 minutes to cross this huge park, but you'll be treated to gorgeous scenery. Big Bend's northern entrance is 39 miles south of Marathon via U.S. 385, but it's another 45 minutes drive to reach central Chisos Basin. To the western entrance, it's 80 miles from Alpine via Highway 118 and 70 miles from Presidio on Highway FM 170. Paved park roads have twists and turns, some very extreme in higher elevations; if you have an RV longer than 24 feet or a trailer longer than 20 feet, you should avoid Chisos Basin Road into higher terrain in the park's center. Four-wheel-drive vehicles are needed for many backcountry roads.

Inspiration

Naturalist's Big Bend, by Roland H. Wauer and Carl M. Fleming, paints a picture of the park's diverse plants and animals.

Big Bend: The Story Behind the Scenery, by Carol E. Sperling, is rife with colorful photos illustrating the park's history and geology.

For gleeful and awestruck thoughts on the Big Bend wilderness, check out *God's Country or Devil's Playground,* which collects the writing of nearly 60 authors.

The Natural History Association's *Backcountry Road Guide* gives in-depth information on the web of paved and improved dirt roads running through the park—and the views you can see from them. Find it on sale at park visitor centers.

Although not many movies have filmed directly in the park, several have been shot in and around Marfa, to the north. The most famous is *Giant,* the epic 1956 James Dean and Elizabeth Taylor epic, but the town and surrounding region has appeared prominently in *No Country for Old Men* and *There Will Be Blood,* both produced in 2007, and *Fandango* in 1985.

Park Essentials

ACCESSIBILITY

Visitor centers and some campsites at Rio Grande Village and Chisos Basin are wheelchair accessible. The Founder's Walk and Panther Path at Panther Junction, Window View Trail at Chisos Basin, and Rio Grande Village Nature Trail boardwalk are wheelchair-accessible trails. The Rio Grande and Chisos Basin amphitheaters also are accessible.

PARK FEES AND PERMITS

It costs $30 to enter at the gate by car, and your pass is good for seven days. Entry on foot, bicycle, or commercial vehicle is $15; entry by motorcycle is $25. Camping fees in developed campgrounds are $16 per night, while backcountry camping is $10 for up to 14 days. Mandatory backcountry camping, boating, and fishing permits are available at visitor centers.

PARK HOURS

Big Bend National Park never closes. Visitor centers at Rio Grande Village, Persimmon Gap, and the Castolon Historic District close in summer. The park is in the Central time zone.

CELL PHONE RECEPTION

Cell phone reception is spotty in much of the park, though service is generally more reliable near the visitor centers and on some of the higher-elevation trails in the Chisos Mountains.

Hotels

At the Chisos Mountains Lodge, the only hotel in the park, you can select from a freestanding stone cottage or a motel-style room, both within a pace or two of popular trailheads and spectacular views—Chisos sunsets and sunrises are not to be missed. The region flanking Big Bend retains its grand historic hotels, such as the glamorous Hotel Paisano in Marfa (which now competes with some very hip design hotels), the Gage Hotel in Marathon, and the Holland Hotel in Alpine. But you'll also find the well-outfitted Lajitas Golf Resort and some distinctive—some spendy, some not—options near the park in Terlingua. *Hotel reviews have been shortened. For full information, visit Fodors.com.*

What It Costs			
$	$$	$$$	$$$$
RESTAURANTS			
under $16	$16–$22	$23–$30	over $30
HOTELS			
under $120	$120–$180	$181–$240	over $240

Restaurants

Although the park itself has just one no-frills restaurant, albeit with stunning Chisos Basin views, little Terlingua—just outside the park entrance, has a few more interesting options. And the towns along the U.S. 90 corridor north of the park, including Marathon, Alpine, and Marfa, have a mix of noteworthy eateries, ranging from historic steak-focused hotel dining rooms to hip Austin-style contemporary bistros and mod coffeehouses. *Restaurant reviews have been shortened. For full information, visit Fodors.com.*

Visitor Information

There are five visitor centers in Big Bend: Panther Junction, considered park headquarters, at the intersection of Western Entrance Road (which Hwy. 118 becomes) and Persimmon Road (which U.S. 385 becomes); Persimmon Gap at the park's northern entrance at U.S. 385; Rio Grande Village, on the eastern border near Boquillas Canyon and Mexico; the Castolon Historic District on Ross

Maxwell Scenic Drive, near Santa Elena Canyon in the southwestern corner of the park; and up high in Chisos Basin, by Chisos Mountains Lodge. Rio Grande Village, Castolon, and Persimmon Gap are closed May–October.

CONTACTS Big Bend National Park.
☎ 432/477–2251 ⊕ www.nps.gov/bibe.

Chisos Basin

30 miles east of Terlingua, 68 miles south of Marathon, 103 miles southeast of Alpine.

The geographical heart of this enormous park, and the best place to begin your explorations, also encompasses its highest points—the mountains surrounding the Chisos Basin. It's here that you'll find the park's only lodging and restaurant and some of its most rewarding hikes and scenery. There's a small visitor center in Chisos Basin as well, and 10 miles north at the junction of the park's main roads you can visit Big Bend's main visitor center at Panther Junction and stock up on fuel and basic snacks at an adjacent gas station.

◉ Sights

PICNIC AREAS
Dugout Wells Area
LOCAL INTEREST | There is a picnic table under the shady cottonwoods off the Dugout Wells Trail loop, plus a vault toilet. ⊠ *Rio Grande Village Rd.* ✛ *6 miles southeast of Panther Junction.*

SCENIC DRIVES

★ **Chisos Basin Road**
MOUNTAIN—SIGHT | This 7-mile road climbs majestically from Chisos Basin Junction to Chisos Mountains Lodge, with a spur leading to a campground. In these higher elevations you're slightly more likely to spot mountain lions and bears as well as white-tailed deer amid juniper and pinyon pines. You'll also see smooth, red-barked

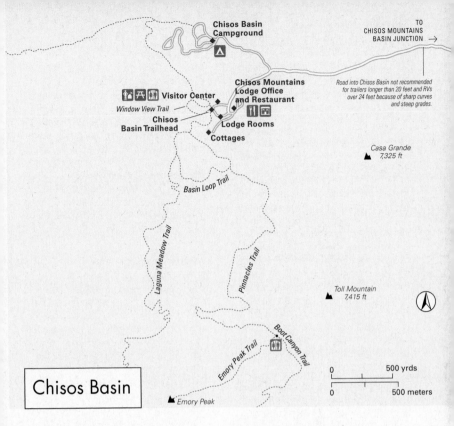

Texas madrone along with some Chisos oaks and Douglas fir trees. Roadside exhibits explain the various ecosystems. Because of sharp curves and switchbacks, this drive is not suitable for RVs longer than 24 feet. ☒ *Big Bend National Park* ✛ *3 miles west of Panther Junction.*

SCENIC STOPS

★ Chisos Basin

NATURE SITE | Panoramic vistas, a restaurant with an up-close view of jagged mountain peaks, and glimpses of the Colima warbler (which summers in Big Bend) await in the forested Chisos Basin. The spiritual heart of Big Bend, at an elevation of 5,400 feet, it's ringed by taller peaks and has a lodge, a campground, a grocery store, an amphitheater, a visitor center, and access to some of the park's best hiking trails. Winter sometimes brings snow, but in summer this is where you can find relief from the desert heat below. ☒ *Big Bend National Park* ✛ *End of Chisos Mountain Rd.*

TRAILS

Chihuahuan Desert Nature Trail

TRAIL | FAMILY | A windmill and spring form a desert oasis, a refreshing backdrop to a ½-mile round-trip, hot and flat nature trail; wild doves are abundant, the hike is pleasant, and kids will do just fine. Keep an eye out for the elf owl, one of the sought-after birds in the park. *Easy.* ☒ *Big Bend National Park* ✛ *Trailhead: Dugout Wells, 6 miles southeast of Panther Junction.*

Chisos Basin Loop Trail

TRAIL | FAMILY | This forested 2-mile round-trip romp that begins at 5,400-foot elevation affords sweeping views of the lower desert and distant volcanic mountains. The loop intersects with a few longer trails but offers a good sense of the basin if you have only an hour or so. *Easy–moderate, elevation gain 500 feet.* ⊠ *Big Bend National Park* ✛ *Trailhead: west end of Chisos Basin parking lot.*

★ Emory Peak Trail

TRAIL | Give yourself about seven hours to complete this rugged 10½-mile round-trip alpine trek to the park's highest peak, at 7,832 feet. The initial 3½-mile stretch follows the Pinnacles Trail, which eventually leads to the South Rim—a rewarding 12- to 14½-mile round-trip adventure that can be done in a very long full day but is more easily managed with a night of camping. For Emory Peak, you pick up a 1-mile spur that affords some dazzling vistas as it zigzags up to the summit. Note there's a bit of scrambling over rocks the final 25 feet, but the panoramic views are worth the effort. *Difficult, 2,400-foot elevation gain.* ⊠ *Big Bend National Park* ✛ *Trailhead: west end of Chisos Basin parking lot.*

★ Grapevine Hills Trail to Balanced Rock

TRAIL | FAMILY | This memorable ramble to one of the park's most distinctive rock formations begins with a 6½-mile drive along a maintained but slightly rough dirt road across a yucca and sagebrush desert north of Chisos Mountains Basin Junction. From the parking area, a relatively flat and easy 2.2-mile round-trip trail leads to a wonderland of igneous *laccolith* rock spires and boulders. Near the end of the trail, you'll scramble a bit up a rocky slope to balanced rock, a giant stone wedged rather improbably across vertical rock piles, creating a "window" through which you can see across the park's southeastern reaches. Although the drive can be managed in a standard car, it's easier with a high-clearance vehicle, especially during wet conditions. ⊠ *Big Bend National Park* ✛ *Trailhead: Mile 6.4 of Grapevine Hills Rd.*

★ Lost Mine Trail

TRAIL | Set aside about three hours to explore the nature of the Chisos Mountains along this 4.8-mile round-trip trail. It starts at 5,700 feet and climbs 1,100 feet to an even loftier vantage point that takes in spectacular, soaring peaks and colorful rock formations. There's a breathtaking view at marker 10, about a mile up—a nice photo op if you haven't time for the full hike. Try to get here early, as the parking lot is small and often fills up quickly. *Moderate–difficult.* ⊠ *Big Bend National Park* ✛ *Trailhead: mile marker 5, Chisos Basin Rd.*

Window View Nature Trail

TRAIL | FAMILY | This 0.3-mile round-trip paved nature trail is wheelchair accessible and also great for little ones. Take in the beautiful, craggy-sided Chisos and look through the V-shape rock-sided "Window" framing the desert below (you can hike to this very point via the quite rewarding, moderately difficult 5.6-mile round-trip Window Trail, which is accessed from the same trailhead). This self-guided trail, which is especially captivating at sunset, is easily accomplished in 20 minutes. Be on the lookout for wild javelina, which occasionally root through here. They're not normally aggressive, but give them a respectful distance. *Easy.* ⊠ *Big Bend National Park* ✛ *Trailhead: west end of Chisos Basin parking lot.*

VISITOR CENTERS

Chisos Basin Visitor Center

INFO CENTER | The small but informative center, by the park's only lodge, is one of the better equipped, with an interactive computer exhibit and a bookstore. An adjacent general store has camping supplies and basic groceries. There are nods to the wild, with natural resource and geology exhibits, a map of bear and mountain lion sightings, and a larger-than-life representation of a mountain lion. The center sponsors educational activities

Bluebonnets: The Pride of Texas

Ever since men first explored the prairies of Texas, the bluebonnet has been revered. Native Americans wove folktales around this bright bluish-violet flower; early-day Spanish priests planted it thickly around their newly established missions; and the cotton boll and cactus competed fiercely with it for the state flower—the bluebonnet won the title in 1901.

Nearly half a dozen varieties of the bluebonnet, distinctive for flowers resembling pioneers' sunbonnets, exist throughout the state. From mid-January until late March, at least one of the famous flowers carpets the park: the Big Bend (also called Chisos) bluebonnet has been described as the most majestic species, as its deep-blue flower spikes can shoot up to three feet in height. The Big Bend bluebonnets can be found beginning in late winter on the flats of the park as well as along El Camino del Rio (FM 170), which follows the legendary Rio Grande between Lajitas and Presidio, Texas.

here and at the nearby Chisos Basin Amphitheater. ✉ *End of Chisos Basin Rd.* ☎ *432/477–2251* 🌐 *www.nps.gov/bibe.*

★ **Panther Junction Visitor Center**
INFO CENTER | FAMILY | The park's main visitor center, near the base of the Chisos Mountains, contains a bookstore and impressive exhibits on the park's mountain, river, and desert environments. An elegantly produced 22-minute film detailing the wonders of the park shows every half-hour in the theater, and there's a sprawling replica of the park's topographical folds. Nearby, a gas station offers limited groceries. ✉ *1 Panther Junction Dr.* ☎ *432/477–2251* 🌐 *www.nps.gov/bibe.*

🍴 Restaurants

Chisos Mountains Lodge Restaurant
$$ | AMERICAN | FAMILY | The star attraction here, whether you dine inside or on the gracious patio, is the signature view through three walls of windows that bring the craggy Chisos Mountains to your table. They serve decent, tried-and-true American food, with a few Mexican specialties; the staff is friendly and efficient. **Known for:** astounding views from dining room and patio; nice selection of Texas craft beers; tasty soups of the day. [$] *Average main: $16* ✉ *End of Chisos Mountain Rd.* ☎ *432/477–2291* 🌐 *www.chisosmountainslodge.com.*

🛏 Hotels

★ **Chisos Mountains Lodge**
$$ | HOTEL | FAMILY | With ranger talks just next door at the visitor center, miles of hiking trails to suit all levels of fitness, and plenty of wildlife nearby, these comfortable no-frills rooms—some of which have been nicely remodeled—are a great place for families. **Pros:** sweeping mountain views from many rooms; steps from numerous hikes; reasonable rates for the dramatic setting. **Cons:** no phones or TVs; Wi-Fi is weak or nonexistent in many rooms; small, basic bathrooms. [$] *Rooms from: $155* ✉ *End of Chisos Basin Rd.* ☎ *432/477–2291 desk, 877/386–4383 Forever Resorts* 🌐 *www.chisosmountainslodge.com* 🛏 *72 rooms* 🍴 *No meals.*

Castolon

35 miles southwest of Panther Junction and Chisos Basin, 40 miles south of Terlingua.

Big Bend's southwestern section, which includes the spectacular viewpoints and hiking trails along Ross Maxwell Scenic Drive as well as the breathtaking views of Santa Elena Canyon, is anchored by the Castolon Historic District, with its visitor center and general store. The area from Castolon west to Santa Elena Canyon, along a pretty stretch of the Rio Grande, is quite a bit warmer than the rest of the park and more enjoyable to visit fall through spring (the visitor center is closed in summer, too).

 Sights

HISTORIC SITES
Castolon Historic District
HISTORIC SITE | Adobe buildings and wooden shacks serve as reminders of the farming and military community of Castolon, near the banks of the Rio Grande. Although a 2019 wildfire caused significant damage to the district, including the destruction of the building that housed the Castolon Visitor Center and La Harmonia general store, firefighters saved many artifacts and buildings, including the Magdalena House, which contains historical exhibits. The old Officer's Quarters building now temporarily houses the visitor center, and a temporary building contains the general store. Eventual plans call for relocating these operations permanently inside the historic Garlick House. ⊠ *Big Bend National Park* ✛ *Ross Maxwell Scenic Dr.*

PICNIC AREAS
Santa Elena Canyon Trailhead
LOCAL INTEREST | **FAMILY** | Two tables sit in the shade—with views toward the canyon—next to the parking lot at the trailhead. There is a vault toilet. ⊠ *Big Bend National Park* ✛ *End of Ross Maxwell Scenic Dr.*

SCENIC DRIVES
⭐ **Ross Maxwell Scenic Drive**
FARM/RANCH | **FAMILY** | Although it extends only 30 miles, you can easily spend a full day on this winding ribbon of blacktop soaking up soaring alpine views, exploring historic sites, taking short hikes, and earning a true Big Bend education. There are scenic overlooks, a magnificent western perspective of the Chisos Mountains, informative exhibit signs, and the ruins of old homesteads. Top waysides along this route that don't take more than a half-hour or so to explore include Sam Nail Ranch, the remains of an adobe homestead in a shady grove with a creek that draws myriad birdlife; Sotol Vista Overlook, a grand promontory with sweeping views of the southwestern side of the park (including Santa Elena Canyon); and Tuff Canyon, a striking steep-walled volcanic-rock canyon. Slightly longer but highly worthwhile excursions include the 1-mile round-trip hike into a green valley to Blue Creek Ranch (aka Homer Wilson Ranch), and the 1-mile round-trip ramble to Lower Burro Mesa Pouroff, a sheer box canyon reached via a 1½-mile side road. Mile Ears Viewpoint, which entails a 4-mile round-trip hike to a gurgling desert spring, is another intriguing side adventure. If you have plenty of time and don't mind driving on a bumpy, washboard gravel road, you can make this drive a loop by reconnecting with West Entrance Road (near Highway 118) from Santa Elena Canyon via unpaved Old Maverick Road for 14 miles—allow an hour for this road, and avoid it if you're driving an RV or there's been a lot of rain. ⊠ *Big Bend National Park* ✛ *Off West Entrance Rd., 12 miles west of Panther Junction.*

TRAILS
⭐ **Santa Elena Canyon Trail**
TRAIL | **FAMILY** | A 1.7-mile round-trip crosses marshy Terlingua Creek, scales a rocky staircase, and deposits you on the banks of the Rio Grande for a cathedral-like view of stunning 1,500-foot cliff walls boxing in the river. Try to visit near

West Texas fauna include prairie dogs, jackrabbits, and roadrunners, while its flora include yuccas.

sunset, when the sun stains the cliffs a rich red-brown chestnut. In clear weather, an overlook on the Ross Maxwell Scenic Drive affords a panoramic view into the canyon. Summer can feel like a sauna, but you might have this secluded place to yourself, and the trail sometimes closes due to mud and flooding following heavy rains. *Easy–moderate.* ⊠ *Big Bend National Park* ✚ *Trailhead: end of Ross Maxwell Scenic Dr.*

VISITOR CENTERS
Castolon Visitor Center
HISTORIC SITE | FAMILY | Temporarily housed in the old Officer's Quarters building following its destruction during a 2019 wildfire, this visitor center in the Castolon Historic District contains hands-on exhibits of fossils, plants, and implements used by the farmers and miners who settled here in the 1800s and early 1900s. There's also an old adobe gallery displaying poster boards explaining the U.S.–Mexico "transparent border." ⊠ *Ross Maxwell Scenic Dr.* ☎ *432/477–2251* ⊕ *www.nps.gov/bibe* ⊗ *Closed May–Oct.*

Rio Grande Village

21 miles southeast of Panther Junction, 89 miles southeast of Marathon.

As with the Castolon area, Rio Grande Village is the base for exploring a long stretch of the river for which it's named—and from here you can access a number of interesting sites in the park's southeastern quadrant, including Boquillas Canyon, a natural hot springs, and the eerily abandoned Mariscal Mine. Despite the name, Rio Grande Village isn't a village per se so much as a cluster of services that include RV and tent campgrounds, an amphitheater, a boat launch, a summer-only visitor center, and a gas station and small grocery store. A grove of giant cottonwood trees alongside the river makes for cooling shadows in this area of the park that can be unbearably hot in summer, and the grassy picnic area is highly recommended for bird-watching. Just east of the village, you can cross

Border Crossing at Big Bend

Once upon a time, Big Bend visitors could splash across the Rio Grande and into the confines of Boquillas and Santa Elena, small Mexican towns that buttered their bread by selling Americans handicrafts. Now, if you want to visit one of the border towns, you must do so by entering official checkpoints in Texas; closed after 9/11, the Boquillas Crossing, at the park's southeastern edge, reopened in 2013 and is open during the day, Friday–Monday in summer and Wednesday–Sunday in winter.

You'll take a row boat the short distance across the Rio Grande to reach Boquillas ($5 round-trip), then walk, take a burro ($5), the back of a pickup ($5), or ride a horse ($8) the remaining ¾-mile to town, where you'll find a few bars, restaurants, and shops. To reenter the United States, you'll need a passport.

Once you get to Mexico, don't fret about language difficulties or money incompatibility. Boquillas is very tourist-friendly, and most there speak English. U.S. currency is accepted.

into Boquillas del Carmen, Mexico, by row boat through the only official U.S. Customs port of entry in the park.

Sights

HISTORIC SITES

Boquillas del Carmen, Mexico Crossing
NATIONAL/STATE PARK | If you have a valid passport, you can use this crossing, about 2 miles east of Rio Grande Village, to visit the village of Boquillas del Carmen. Check the park website for current hours, but generally the crossing is open May–October from 9 am to 6 pm, Friday through Monday, and the rest of the year from 8 am to 5 pm, Wednesday through Sunday. Once a mining boomtown that fed off rich minerals and silver, Boquillas has shrunk to a small village, but there is a restaurant and bar along with a few shops. U.S. citizens can bring back up to $200 in merchandise duty-free. To get across, you can access a $5 round-trip row boat across the river and a $3 entrance fee to enter the Mexican Protected Area that the village is located in. The remaining ¾-mile to the village can be made on foot, by donkey ($5 round-trip), pickup truck ($5), or horseback ($8).

⚠ If you do not return to the border in time, you may be stuck in Mexico for two or three days. ✛ Off Boquillas Canyon Rd.

★ **Hot Springs**
HOT SPRINGS | FAMILY | Follow this 1-mile loop trail to soak in 105°F waters along-side the Rio Grande (bring a swimsuit), where petroglyphs coat the canyon walls nearby. The remains of a post office, motel, and bathhouse point to the old commercial establishment operating here in the early 1900s. Along the hike, you can hear the Rio Grande at every turn, and low trees occasionally shelter the walkway. The 1.6-mile dirt road leading to the Hot Springs trailhead from Rio Grande Village Road cannot accommodate RVs and is best avoided after rainstorms. Also, don't leave valuables in your car, especially during the slow season. Temperatures can soar to 120°F, so hike in the morning or during cooler months. You can also hike to the springs via the more challenging 6-mile Hot Springs Canyon Trail, the trailhead of which is at Daniel's Ranch, on the west side of Rio Grande Village ⊠ End of Hot Springs Rd.

Mariscal Mine

MINE | Hard-working men and women once coaxed cinnabar, or mercury ore, from the Mariscal Mine, located at the north end of Mariscal Mountain, in the southern reaches of the park. The mines and surrounding stone buildings were abandoned in the 1940s. If you visit, take care not to touch the timeworn stones, as they may contain poisonous mercury residue. You need a high-clearance vehicle to navigate the 20-mile road, which begins 5 miles west of Rio Grande Village; check with park rangers for current road conditions, and allow a half-day for this fascinating but remote adventure. ⊠ *End of River Rd. E.*

PICNIC AREAS

Rio Grande Village Area

LOCAL INTEREST | **FAMILY** | Half a dozen picnic tables are scattered under cottonwoods south of the convenience store. Half a mile away at Daniels Ranch there are two tables and a grill. Wood fires aren't allowed (charcoal and propane are). ⊠ *Rio Grande Village Rd.*

TRAILS

★ Boquillas Canyon Trail

TRAIL | After climbing over a rocky bluff with sweeping views of the Rio Grande and the desert in Mexico beyond it, this picturesque 1.4-mile round-trip trek drops into a lush sandy canyon and parallels the river. Soaring cliffs rise on either side, and the trail ends at a scenic point where the canyon narrows dramatically. *Easy–Moderate.* ⊠ *Big Bend National Park* ✛ *Trailhead: parking lot at end of Boquillas Canyon Spur Rd.*

Rio Grande Village Nature Trail

TRAIL | **FAMILY** | Down by the Rio Grande, this short, ¾-mile loop trail packs a powerful wildlife punch. The village is one of the best spots in the park to see rare birds, and other wildlife isn't in short supply either. Keep a lookout for coyotes, javelinas (they look like wild pigs), and other mammals. This is a good trail for kids, so expect higher traffic. Restrooms are nearby, and the trail can be done in less than an hour. The first ¼ mile is wheelchair accessible. *Easy.* ⊠ *Big Bend National Park* ✛ *Trailhead: Site #18 of Rio Grande Village Campground.*

VISITOR CENTERS

Rio Grande Village Visitor Center

INFO CENTER | At this seasonal center you take in the videos of Big Bend's geological and natural features at the minitheater and view exhibits on the Rio Grande. ⊠ *End of Rio Grande Village Rd.* ☎ *432/477–2251* ⊕ *www.nps.gov/bibe* ⊙ *Closed May–Oct.*

Persimmon Gap

27 miles north of Panther Junction, 41 miles south of Marathon.

With few services and not too many trails or formal sites, Big Bend's northern section—which contains the Persimmon Gap entrance as well as a small summer-only visitor center—offers a quieter and more introspective sense of the park. Flanked by the North Rosillos, Santiago, and Sierra Del Carmen mountains, the area is bisected by the main park road from Marathon along with a few rough but picturesque unpaved roads that are best tackled with a high-clearance vehicle. The area's must-see is the Fossil Discovery Exhibit, just off the main park road.

⦿ Sights

HISTORIC SITES

★ Fossil Discovery Exhibit

ARCHAEOLOGICAL SITE | **FAMILY** | This covered, open-air building with a beautiful contemporary design contains renderings, infographic displays, and touch-friendly models of the dinosaur fossils that have been discovered here just off the road between Persimmon Gap and Panther Junction. The imaginatively presented exhibits clearly explain

6

Big Bend National Park PERSIMMON GAP

Plants and Wildlife in Big Bend

Because Big Bend contains habitats as diverse as spent volcanoes, slick-sided canyons, and the Rio Grande, it follows that species here are extremely diverse, too. Among the park's most notable residents are endangered species like the Mexican long-nosed bat (which feasts on the nectar of agave and cacti), shadow-dappled peregrine falcon, swarthy javelina, and fat-bellied horned lizard (Texans call them "horny toads"). More than 450 species of birds wing throughout the park, including the black-capped vireo and the turkey vulture, which boasts a 6-foot wingspan.

In the lower desert, be aware of scorpions and rattlesnakes, especially in the summer at dusk and dawn. The vipers aren't normally aggressive, so try to refrain from sudden movement and give them a wide berth.

In the highlands mountain lions lurk, while black bears loll in the crags and valleys. Your chances of spotting the reclusive creatures are slim, though greater at dusk and dawn. If you do encounter either, don't run away. Instead, stand tall, shout, throw rocks if necessary, and look as scary as possible.

Also very watch-worthy are the plants populating the region. Supremely adapted to the arroyos, valleys, and slopes, local flora range from the endangered Chisos Mountains hedgehog cactus (found only in the park) to the towering rasp of the giant dagger yucca. Also here are 60 types of cacti—so be careful where you tread.

Big Bend's ancient geological history, dating back some 130 million years to when a vast, shallow inland sea covered the area. Scientists have recovered fossils of sharks, sea urchins, and oysters as well as of the dinosaurs and giant alligators who roamed the landscape after the sea receded. Kids can climb on fossil-inspired structures beside the exhibit space, where you'll also find a shaded picnic area and a short nature trail that leads to a sweeping overlook of Big Bend's key geological features. The exhibit area is open dawn to dusk. ⊠ *Off Park Rd.* ✛ *18 miles south of Persimmon Gap.*

PICNIC AREAS

Fossil Discovery Exhibit Picnic Area

LOCAL INTEREST | This peaceful covered picnic area between the Persimmon Gap and Panther Junction visitor centers is beside the parking lot for the Fossil Discovery Exhibits. There's a pit toilet. ⊠ *Main Park Rd.* ✛ *18 miles south of Persimmon Gap Visitor Center.*

VISITOR CENTERS

Persimmon Gap Visitor Center

INFO CENTER | Complete with exhibits and a bookstore, this seasonal visitor center is the northern gateway into miles of flatlands that surround the more scenic heart of Big Bend. ⊠ *Big Bend National Park* ✛ *On Main Park Rd. (U.S. 385)* ☎ *432/477–2251* ⊕ *www.nps.gov/bibe* ⊘ *Closed May–Oct.*

Activities

Spectacular and varied scenery plus more than 300 miles of roads spell adventure for hikers, bikers, horseback riders, or those simply seeking a ramble on foot or by Jeep. A web of dusty, unpaved roads lures adventuresome drivers and experienced hikers deep into the backcountry, while paved roads lead to most of the park's better-known and more established trails and scenic overlooks. Because the park has nearly half of the bird species in North America, birding ranks high. Boating is popular along the Rio Grande, where you can view some of the park's most striking features.

BIKING

Mountain biking the backcountry roads can be so solitary that you're unlikely to encounter another human being; note that bikes are not permitted off-road or on trails. The solitude also means you should prepare for the unexpected with ample supplies, especially water and sun protection (summer heat is brutal, and shade is scarce). Biking is recommended only during the cooler months (October–April).

On paved roads, a regular road bike should suffice, but you'll have to bring your own—outfitters in the area tend to rent only mountain bikes. For an easy ride on mostly level ground, try the 14-mile (one-way) unpaved **Old Maverick Road** on the west side of the park, connecting Santa Elena Canyon Road and West Entrance roads. For a challenge, take the unpaved **Old Ore Road** for 27 miles from the park's northern reaches to near Rio Grande Village on the east side.

BIRD-WATCHING

Situated on north–south migratory pathways, Big Bend attracts approximately 450 species of birds—more than any other national park. In fact, the birds that flit, waddle, soar, and swim in the park represent more than half the bird species in North America, including the Colima warbler, found nowhere else in the United States. To glimpse darting Lucifer hummingbirds, turkey vultures, golden eagles, and the famous Colima, look to the Chisos Mountains. To spy woodpeckers and scaled quail (distinctive for dangling crests), look to the desert scrub. And for cuckoos, cardinals, and screech owls, you must prowl along the river,

especially around Rio Grande Village, where you might spy summer tanagers and vermilion flycatchers. Rangers often lead birding talks.

BOATING AND RAFTING

The watery pathway that is the Rio Grande is one of Big Bend's most spectacular "trails" of a sort. The river's 118 miles that border the park form its backbone, defining the vegetation, landforms, and animals found at the park's southern rim. By turns shallow and deep, the river flows through stunning canyons and picks up speed over small and large rapids.

Alternately soothing and exciting (Class II and III rapids develop here, particularly after the summer rains), the river can be traversed in several ways, from guided rafting tours to more strenuous kayak and canoe expeditions. In general, rafting trips spell smoother sailing for families, though thrills are inherent when soaring over the river's meringue-like tips and troughs.

You can bring your own raft to the boat launch at the Rio Grande, but you must obtain a river-use permit (free for dayuse, $10 if you plan to camp overnight along the river) from a visitor center, where you should also check with staff to make sure river levels are appropriate for an outing (neither too low nor too high). No motorized craft are allowed on the Rio Grande. For less fuss, go with a tour guide or outfitter—most of these are just outside the park around Terlingua and Lajitas. Guided trips can last from a few hours to several days (these longer adventures can cost thousands of dollars). Most outfitters also rent rafts, canoes, kayaks, and inflatable kayaks (nicknamed "duckies") for when the river is low. Personalized river tours are available all year, and they might include gourmet rafting tours that end with filet mignon and live country music.

Buffalo Soldiers

During the American Indian Wars of 1866 through 1892, the U.S. government enlisted vast numbers of black soldiers to serve in its cavalry. Those who entered the Army were confined to all-black regiments led by white officers, and were treated as third-rate citizens. Despite many hardships—including poor rations, little respect, and cavalry mounts sometimes described as "old and half-dead"—soldiers in two Texas all-black regiments persevered and became known as the Buffalo Soldiers (the same Buffalo Soldiers immortalized in the Bob Marley song).

Explanations diverge for how these brave men (and one barely documented woman) of the 9th and 10th cavalry units received their unique name. Some say that the Native Americans they fought—and also protected—gave them this name out of respect for their courage and fortitude, traits their culture associated with buffalo.

These units were given the toughest, most inhospitable terrain to guard—including the severe, cactus-covered desert plains that comprise modern-day Big Bend National Park. They protected this land, wrestled rustlers, and even strung telegraph lines. In West Texas, the government put them to work rounding up the intractable Apache and Comanche peoples that inhabited the region.

Despite adversity from adversaries, the weather, the terrain, and racist attitudes, the Buffalo Soldiers' units are said to have had the lowest desertion rates in the Army. They were eventually rewarded for their contribution in the late 1880s, when several became the first African-Americans to receive the Congressional Medal of Honor—only 20-plus years after the Civil War, and nearly a century before the civil rights movement. The Buffalo Soldiers of the 19th and early 20th centuries segued into all-black units that finally were dissolved in the 1950s. The last living Buffalo Soldier, Mark Matthews, died in 2005 at the age of 111 and was interred in Arlington National Cemetery.

While there are no longer any living soldiers to recall the wild, harsh time of the Comanche Wars, Texas strives to keep their memory alive through events, plaques, signs, and demonstrations at the forts where they served. Visitors to West Texas can explore this history through events at Fort Concho in San Angelo, Fort Lancaster near Sheffield, Fort Stockton in the city of Fort Stockton, and in displays at the Museum of the Big Bend in Alpine and the Frontier Texas! museum in Abilene. Big Bend National Park's visitor centers also have informative exhibits.

—Jennifer Edwards

CAMPING

The park's copious campsites are separated, roughly, into two categories—frontcountry and backcountry. Each of its four frontcountry sites, except Rio Grande Village RV Campground, has toilet facilities at a minimum. Inside the park, rates are $16 for tent sites and $36 for the RV sites at Rio Grande Village. Far more numerous are the primitive backcountry sites, which require $10 permits from the visitor center. Primitive campsites with spectacular views are accessed via River Road, Glenn Springs, Old Ore Road, Paint Gap, Old Maverick Road, Grapevine Hills, Pine Canyon, and Croton Springs.

Chisos Basin Campground. Scenic views and cool shade are the highlights here, as well as access to some of the best alpine hiking in the park. About half of these sites can be reserved. ⊠ *End of Chisos Basin Rd.* ☎ *877/444–6777* ⊕ *www.recreation.gov.*

Cottonwood Campground. This 24-site, first-come, first-served spot near Castolon Visitor Center is popular for bird-watching near the Rio Grande. ⊠ *Off Ross Maxwell Scenic Dr.* ☎ *877/444–6777* ⊕ *www.recreation.gov*

Maverick Ranch RV Park. Just outside the park at Lajitas Golf Resort, this layout has 100 RV sites and 18 primitive camping sites. There's a clubhouse, deli, hot showers, laundry facilities, picnic area, and hiking trails. It's also pet-friendly. ⊠ *10 Main St., Lajitas* ☎ *432/424–5182* ⊕ *www.lajitasgolfresort.com*

Rio Grande Village Campground. This shady oasis is a popular birding spot. It's also a great site for kids and seniors, due to the ease of accessing facilities. There are 100 campsites with coin-operated showers, restrooms, and laundry. ⊠ *End of Rio Grande Village Rd.* ☎ *877/444–6777* ⊕ *www.recreation.gov.*

Rio Grande Village RV Park. Often full during holidays, this is one of the best sites for families because of the minitheater and proximity to the hot spring, which is fun to soak in at night. There are 25 RV sites with full hookups. ⊠ *End of Rio Grande Village Rd.* ☎ *432/477–2293.*

EDUCATIONAL PROGRAMS

★ Interpretive Activities

INFO CENTER | FAMILY | Ranger-guided activities are held throughout the park, indoors and outdoors, and include slideshows, talks, and walks on cultural and natural history, including wildlife and birds. Check visitor centers and campground bulletin boards for event postings, which are usually updated every two weeks. ⊠ *Big Bend National Park.*

Junior Ranger Program

INFO CENTER | FAMILY | This self-guided program for kids of all ages is taught through a free booklet of nature-based activities (available at visitor centers). Upon completion of the course, kids are given a Junior Ranger badge or patch. ⊠ *Big Bend National Park.*

HIKING

Each of the park's zones has a wealth of intriguing trails. The east side offers rigorous mountain hikes, border canyons, limestone aplenty, and sandy washes with neat geographic formations. West-side trails access the striking scenery of Santa Elena Canyon and venture out through volcanic rock formations and past abandoned ranches along Ross Maxwell Scenic Drive. The heart of the park has abandoned mines, pine-topped vistas, scrub vegetation around the Chisos, and vast deserts with massive boulders and colorful cacti lying just north of the Chisos Mountains, out in the Grapevine Hills. ■TIP→ **Carry enough drinking water—a gallon per person daily (more when extremely hot).**

While Big Bend certainly has "expedition level" trails to test the most veteran backpacker, many are very demanding and potentially dangerous—attempt these only if you're quite experienced. The trails we've included in this chapter are best suited to moderately active hikers, but a few easy ones are appropriate even for novices and young kids.

HORSEBACK RIDING

At Big Bend, you can bring your own horses or book a guided excursion, which can last from two hours to several days, through an outfitter. The going might be slow in some parts, as horses aren't allowed on paved roads. If you're bringing your own horses for the day, you must obtain a free backcountry permit from a visitor. You may camp with your horse at any of the park's primitive campsites, but not in the developed areas. There's a primitive campsite with corrals for eight horses about 5 miles north of Panther Junction at Hannold Draw; it can be reserved up to 180 days in advance at ☎ 432/477–1158 ⊕ www.recreation.gov; the cost is $10 per night.

HORSEBACK OUTFITTERS
Big Bend & Lajitas Stables
HORSEBACK RIDING | FAMILY | This outfitter with locations at Lajitas Resort and in Study Butte offers trail rides on the western edge of the national park and the eastern edge of Big Bend Ranch State Park. Rides range from one to five hours with lunch. ⊠ Hwy. 118 at FM 170, Study Butte ☎ 432/371–3064, 800/887–4331 ⊕ www.lajitasstables.com ⊑ From $47.

JEEP TOURS

Wheeled traffic is welcome in the park, up to a point. RVs, trucks, cars, and Jeeps are allowed on designated paved and dirt roads, though personal ATV use is prohibited. Jeep rental isn't available inside the park, but Jeep, SUV, and ATV tours just outside the park are possible through outfitters. Jeep tours can cost as little as about $85 for a three-hour tour, while ATV tours start at about $180.

MULTISPORT OUTFITTERS
Angell Expeditions
TOUR—SPORTS | A smaller outfitter based between Lajitas and Presidio in tiny Redford, Angell customizes river- (kayaking and rafting) and land-based (jeep and hiking) tours at both Big Bend National Park and Big Bend Ranch State Park—or at regional destinations beyond park boundaries. ⊠ Redford ☎ 432/384–2307 ⊕ www.angellexpeditions.com ⊑ From $140.

★ **Big Bend River Tours**
TOUR—SPORTS | FAMILY | Exploring the Rio Grande is this outfitter's specialty. Custom tours can be half a day up to 10 days and include rafting, canoeing, and hiking and horseback trips combined with a river float. ⊠ 23331 FM 170, Terlingua ☎ 800/545–4240, 432/371–3033 ⊕ www. bigbendrivertours.com ⊑ From $82.

Desert Sports
TOUR—SPORTS | From rentals—mountain bikes, boats, and inflatable kayaks—to experienced guides for multiday mountain-bike touring, boating, and hiking, this outfitter has it covered. The company prides itself on its small size and personal touch. ⊠ 22937 FM 170, Terlingua ☎ 432/371–2727 ⊕ www.desertsportstx. com ⊑ From $150.

Far Flung Outdoor Center
TOUR—SPORTS | FAMILY | Call these pros for personalized nature, historical, and geological trips via rafts, ATVs, and 4X4s. Trips include gourmet rafting tours with cheese and wine served on checkered tablecloths alongside the river, and sometimes spectacular star viewing at night. The property also offers overnight casitas with kitchenettes and a full range of amenities. ⊠ 23310 FM 170, Terlingua ☎ 432/371–2633 ⊕ www.bigbendfar-flung.com ⊑ From $84.

Nearby Towns

The handful of towns nearest (and just west of) the park are quite tiny and include a now defunct quicksilver mining town **Terlingua** and its neighbor **Study Butte,** which contain a smattering of places to stay and eat as well as several local tour operators. The combined Terlingua–Study Butte population is about 190, many of them iconoclasts and big-city refugees. Follow FM 170 west from Terlingua for 13 miles to the flat-rock formations of tiny **Lajitas,** an erstwhile U.S. Cavalry outpost that's been converted into a sprawling golf and equestrian resort. Lajitas and the border town of **Presidio,** 65 miles to the west, are gateways to enormous Big Bend Ranch State Park.

Although they're 45 minutes to a couple of hours from the park, the historic West Texas towns along U.S. 90 are extremely popular with visitors to Big Bend, in part because each of these communities has its own rich history and distinctive personality—and this area abounds with intriguing dining and lodging options. **Marathon,** just a 45-minute drive from the northern entrance, is the closest of these to the park's northern (Permisson Gap) entrance and has a fun Old West railroad vibe and the iconic Gage Hotel. A half-hour west, **Alpine** sits amid the Davis Mountains, some 80 miles north of the park's western entrance. It's known for Sul Ross State University, with its excellent Museum of the Big Bend, and you'll find a few notable eateries, galleries, and hotels. Another half-hour west is **Marfa,** a middle-of-nowhere West Texas hamlet with a world-renowned contemporary arts scene and an increasingly hip and stylish clutch of restaurants, art galleries, hotels, and boutiques. Its spooky, unexplained "Marfa lights" are attributed to everything from atmospheric disturbances to imagination. From Marfa and Alpine, it's about a half-hour north to **Fort Davis,** a scenic and historic town in the Davis Mountains that's also home to several worthwhile attractions and historic lodgings.

Marathon

68 miles north of Panther Junction, 330 miles west of San Antonio.

The closest town to Big Bend's northern entrance, this historic ranching community with magnificently dark, starry night skies and one of the state's most alluring historic accommodations—the Gage Hotel—is a peaceful and picturesque hub for exploring the park. With just under 400 residents, it's a quiet place, but there are some great restaurants, most of them affiliated with the Gage.

GETTING HERE AND AROUND

At the confluence of U.S. 90 and U.S. 385 (which leads south to Big Bend's Persimmon Gap entrance), Marathon is the first of the region's towns that most visitors reach if driving from San Antonio, Austin, and points east.

🍴 Restaurants

Brick Vault Brewery and Barbecue

$ | **BARBECUE** | Run by the owners of the iconic Gage Hotel just down the street, this lively microbrewery serves reliably good Texas-style barbecue, including brisket, turkey, ribs, and sausages with a nice selection of sides (skillet green beans, green chile mac and cheese). Set in an 1880s building that once housed a mercantile establishment and later a service station, the space has a fun retro-funky vibe and turns out interesting craft beer. **Known for:** tender brisket; Capt. Shepard's Pecan Porter; attractive outdoor patio. [$] *Average main: $14* ✉ *103 1st St., Marathon* ☎ *432/386–4205* 🌐 *www.brickvaultbreweryandbbq.com* 🕒 *Closed Mon.–Wed. No dinner Sun.*

★ **12 Gage Restaurant**

$$$$ | **MODERN AMERICAN** | When the sun sets, this intimate, fireplace-warmed indoor-outdoor restaurant is the best place to eat and socialize in Marathon. The innovative menu, featuring fresh produce from the Gage Hotel Garden across the railroad tracks, changes with the season but maintains a Southwestern flair. **Known for:** beef tenderloin fillet; extensive wine list; Mexican chocolate brownie with ice cream and homemade cajeta (Mexican caramel) sauce. [$] *Average main: $33* ✉ *101 N.W. 1st St., Marathon* ☎ *432/386–4205* 🌐 *www.gagehotel.com.*

Hotels

Eve's Garden B&B

$$ | **B&B/INN** | This whimsical, color-saturated property built with recycled building materials and lots of imagination creates an entirely singular lodging experience. **Pros:** warmly decorated rooms; breakfast features delicious local, organic ingredients; short walk to several restaurants. **Cons:** a bit quirky for some; not a good fit for families; two-night minimum for some rooms. [$] *Rooms from: $171* ✉ *200 N.W. 3rd St., Marathon* ☎ *432/386–4165* 🌐 *www.evesgarden.org* 🛏 *7 rooms* 🍴 *Free Breakfast.*

★ **Gage Hotel**

$$$ | **HOTEL** | Cowboy, Native American, and Hispanic cultures are reflected in the furnishings and artwork of this gorgeously restored historic hotel, built in the 1920s by renowned architect Henry Trost, across from the downtown railroad tracks. **Pros:** amazing architecture; outstanding restaurant, bar, and coffeehouse; well-equipped pool, fitness room, and spa. **Cons:** often reserved well in advance; expensive for the area; sometimes booked full for weddings and events. [$] *Rooms from: $195* ✉ *102 N.W. 1st St., Marathon* ☎ *432/386–4205, 800/884–4243* 🌐 *www.gagehotel.com* 🛏 *46 rooms* 🍴 *No meals.*

Alpine

30 miles west of Marathon, 103 miles northwest of Panther Junction.

Nestled amid the plum and tan beauty of the Davis Mountains, historic Alpine has just shy of 6,000 residents, many of them faculty or students at Sul Ross State University. The school and the relative proximity to Big Bend have helped imbue Alpine with an increasingly hip vibe, as has its relative proximity to Marfa. Several arts and cultural festivals take place here throughout the year, and colorful murals cover the walls of many downtown buildings, some of which house cool cafés, bars, and boutiques.

GETTING HERE AND AROUND

U.S. 90 cuts east–west through town, and Highway 118 runs north to Fort Davis and south to Big Bend's western entrance, near Terlingua. Alpine is also a stop on Amtrak's Sunset Limited and Texas Eagle routes, and there is a car-rental agency in town.

VISITOR INFORMATION Alpine Chamber of Commerce. ☎ *432/837–4144, 800/561–3712* 🌐 *www.alpinetexas.com.*

Sights

★ **Museum of the Big Bend**

MUSEUM | **FAMILY** | This expansive history-lover's haven has exhibits representing the life and cultures of the region and sponsors an annual show on ranching handiwork (such as saddles, reins, and spurs) held in conjunction with the Cowboy Poetry Gathering each February. The map collection is renowned. ✉ *Sul Ross State University, 400 N. Harrison St., Alpine* ☎ *432/837–8143* 🌐 *www.museumofthebigbend.com* 🎟 *Free* 🕒 *Closed Mon.*

Restaurants

★ Reata

$$ | SOUTHWESTERN | A favorite of many West Texans spending the day in Alpine, Reata ("rope" in Spanish) feels both welcoming and upscale, with big, wooden tables and a pleasant rancher/cowboy vibe. It's a "howdy"-type place with prompt, down-home service and a menu that emphasizes creative Southwestern and Tex-Mex fare, such as tortilla soup, calf fries with cream gravy, and beef tamales with pecan mash, plus generously portioned steaks from a legendary ranch in the nearby Davis Mountains. **Known for:** West Texas buttermilk pecan pie; jalapeño-and-bacon mac and cheese; well-chosen wine list. $ *Average main: $21 ⊠ 203 N. 5th St., Alpine ☎ 432/837–9232 ⊕ www.reata.net ⊗ Closed Sun.*

☕ Coffee and Quick Bites

★ Cedar Coffee Supply

$ | CAFÉ | Coffee connoisseurs and java junkies flock from nearby towns to this minimalist third wave café that turns out some of the finest single-origin sips in West Texas, from straightforward macchiatos to lattes with organic honey-lavender syrup. Cedar Coffee also serves up a limited selection of exceptionally tasty breakfast and lunch items, including savory and sweet crepes and Belgian waffles with berries. **Known for:** potent cold brew (it's available bottled, too); house-made horchata; adjoins a great bookstore. $ *Average main: $6 ⊠ 103 N. 4th St., Alpine ⊕ www.cedarcoffeesupply.com ⊗ Closed Sun.*

🛏 Hotels

★ Holland Hotel

$$ | HOTEL | Once a stop on the transcontinental railroad, the rancher-themed Holland Hotel is now a historic landmark still hung with its original sign on the bustling main drag in downtown Alpine—just doors down from shops, cafés, and galleries. **Pros:** inviting lobby and courtyard; excellent spa and restaurant; swimming pool available at the co-owned Maverick Inn. **Cons:** noise from nearby trains (earplugs provided in rooms); older property with a few quirks; breakfast is on the meager side. $ *Rooms from: $140 ⊠ 209 W. Holland Ave., Alpine ☎ 432/837–2800, 800/535–8040 ⊕ www.thehollandhoteltexas.com ⇌ 27 rooms ⦿ Free Breakfast.*

Maverick Inn

$ | HOTEL | A self-described "roadhouse for wanderers," the Maverick is an updated motor lodge that defines Alpine's artful personality. **Pros:** retro-stylish ambience; some rooms have kitchenettes; close to good restaurants. **Cons:** on a busy road; small and somewhat dated bathrooms; very basic breakfast. $ *Rooms from: $105 ⊠ 1200 E. Holland Ave., Alpine ☎ 432/837–0628 ⊕ www.themaverickinn.com ⇌ 21 rooms ⦿ Free Breakfast.*

Marfa

26 miles west of Alpine, 195 miles southeast of El Paso.

Three hours from the nearest commercial airport (in El Paso), this cultural oasis enjoys a devoted following among artists, hipsters, LGBTQ folks, and free spirits. Its relative proximity to Big Bend as well as the Davis and Guadalupe mountain ranges has also made this offbeat design mecca with about 1,750 residents a favorite destination with hikers and other outdoors enthusiasts, too. With its clutch of avant-garde galleries, ranch-chic restaurants and indie hotels, and endless opportunities for people-watching—from poetry readings to gallery openings to bar-hopping—Marfa is the kind of place you may want to spend a few days in.

GETTING HERE AND AROUND

Located at the junction of U.S. 90 and U.S. 67, Marfa is the closest town in the area to El Paso (about a three-hour drive). The fastest route to Big Bend is through Alpine, but you can also get there by following U.S. 67 south to Presidio, and then turning east on FM 170 through Big Bend Ranch State Park.

VISITOR INFORMATION Visit Marfa. ⊠ 302 S. Highland Ave., Marfa ☎ 432/729–4772 ⊕ www.visitmarfa.com.

Sights

★ Chinati Foundation

MUSEUM | With one of the largest permanent installations of contemporary art in the world, the Chinati Foundation displays works by American minimalist Donald Judd and others in buildings spread over 340 acres of the former Ft. D. A. Russell. The Judd collection includes 15 concrete works outdoors, plus 100 aluminum pieces housed in two converted artillery sheds. You'll also see 25 sculptures by John Chamberlain and an installation by Dan Flavin that occupies six former army barracks. The museum's comprehensive guided tours require a significant commitment of time—six hours, including a two-hour break for lunch—and energy to walk up to 1½ miles over uneven terrain. While self-guided tours are always an option, space on the guided tours is limited. ⊠ 1 Cavalry Row, Marfa ☎ 432/729–4362 ⊕ www.chinati.org ☜ $15 self-guided tours ⊗ Closed Mon.–Tues.

 Restaurants

★ Convenience West

$$ | BARBECUE | Named for the prosaic old convenience store–gas station that it occupies on the west side of Marfa, this cozy counter-service restaurant with a few indoor and outdoor tables fires up some of the best barbecue in the region. Dig into a platter of slow-smoked ribs, whole chicken, brisket-cheddar crunchy tacos, or jalapeño-cheddar-beef sausage, and don't overlook the unusual sides, like roasted beets with sriracha mayo and green-chile mac and cheese. **Known for:** short but well-chosen beer and wine list; inspired side dishes; lemon curd hand pies and other fine desserts. $ Average main: $17 ⊠ 1411 W. San Antonio St., Marfa ⊕ www.conveniencewest.com ⊗ Closed Mon.–Thurs. No lunch.

LaVenture

$$$ | MODERN AMERICAN | The urbane restaurant just off the lobby at Marfa's design-driven Hotel Saint George wouldn't feel out of place in Austin or Brooklyn, its softly illuminated brick walls hung with bold contemporary local art. The seasonal, market-inspired cuisine, from lighter wood-fired pizzas and cheese-charcuterie boards to more substantial plates of grass-fed bone-in rib eye and pappardelle pasta with garlic-fennel sausage, is accompanied by a well-curated wine list and first-rate cocktails. **Known for:** locally sourced seasonal ingredients; house-made desserts; Texas wagyu beef tartare. $ Average main: $26 ⊠ Hotel Saint George, 105 S. Highland Ave., Marfa ☎ 432/729–3700 ⊕ marfasaintgeorge.com.

Pizza Foundation

$ | PIZZA | FAMILY | Set in a sleekly industrial warehouse-style building on the east edge of downtown Marfa, Pizza Foundation appeals to families with its casual atmosphere and the quality thin-crust pizza the native Rhode Island owners turn out. They close for the evening when they run out of pizza, so you call ahead before you go. **Known for:** Jarritos Mexican soft drinks; Big Bend Brewery beers on tap; white pizza with ricotta, spinach, and olive oil. $ Average main: $11 ⊠ 305 S. Spring St., Marfa ☎ 432/729–3377 ⊗ Closed Mon.–Thurs.

Coffee and Quick Bites

★ Aster Marfa

$ | **CAFÉ** | The hearty fare, potent coffee, and fresh-squeezed juices served in this small patio café across from the Presidio County Courthouse will help you fuel up for a day of hiking or art-touring. Good bets include the Bernese rösti potato pancakes with ham, Gruyère, and eggs, while the vegan Swiss Müsli with coconut yogurt is a bit on the lighter side. **Known for:** made-from-scratch baked goods; rösti potato pancakes; cheerful patio. [$] *Average main: $11* ✉ *215 N. Highland Ave., Marfa* ☎ *432/729–4500* 🌐 *www.astermarfa.com* 🕒 *Closed Mon.–Tues. No dinner.*

Hotels

El Cosmico

$$ | **HOTEL** | An unusual setup that suits Marfa's quirky personality, hipster-approved El Cosmico is a nomadic draw for glamping adventurers, with safari tents, tepees, campsites, a yurt, and 1950s-style trailers that provide surprising comfort. **Pros:** rugged-chic, laid-back environment; "well-behaved" dogs are welcome; set on 21 scenic acres with great high-desert views. **Cons:** not well-suited to families; when the temperature dips below freezing, which is often in winter, the pipes in the outdoor bath houses can freeze; Wi-Fi can be spotty or slow in some units. [$] *Rooms from: $125* ✉ *802 S. Highland Ave., Marfa* ☎ *432/729–1950, 877/822–1950* 🌐 *www.elcosmico.com* 🔑 *26 rooms* 🍴 *No meals.*

Hotel Paisano

$$ | **HOTEL** | Once the playground of Liz Taylor, Rock Hudson, and James Dean, who stayed here while filming *Giant,* the Paisano has maintained its glamour with glistening Mediterranean architecture, a fountain in the courtyard dining area, and dress and jewelry shops in downstairs hallways. **Pros:** filled with Hollywood memorabilia; in the center of town; bar and restaurant are great for people-watching. **Cons:** no elevator; some rooms and bathrooms are quite small; not much of a view from most rooms. [$] *Rooms from: $144* ✉ *207 N. Highland Ave., Marfa* ☎ *432/729–3669, 844/476–2732* 🌐 *www.hotelpaisano.com* 🔑 *40 rooms* 🍴 *No meals.*

★ Hotel Saint George

$$$$ | **HOTEL** | The region's swankiest lodging, in the heart of downtown Marfa, has an airy lobby and common spaces hung with museum-quality local contemporary artwork, and houses Bar Saint George, LaVenture restaurant, and renowned Marfa Book Company. **Pros:** hip design and muted color palette; beautiful pool and bar; ultracomfy beds and fancy amenities. **Cons:** on the pricey side; contemporary style feels out of place to some; the adult vibe isn't conducive to families. [$] *Rooms from: $255* ✉ *105 S. Highland Ave., Marfa* ☎ *432/729–3700* 🌐 *www.marfasaintgeorge.com* 🔑 *55 rooms* 🍴 *No meals.*

Fort Davis

24 miles northwest of Alpine, 21 miles north of Marfa

Situated at about 5,000 feet elevation and surrounded by the dramatic David Mountains, this mountain town established as a military outpost in the mid-19th century is about as far north as you'd want to stay if visiting Big Bend National Park. Its charmingly historic downtown and scenic attractions—including McDonald Observatory and Fort Davis National Historic Site—make it worth the added driving distance.

GETTING HERE AND AROUND

Set at the junction of Highways 118 and 17, Fort Davis is about three hours southeast of El Paso, and a little under two hours north of Big Bend's western entrance (reached by heading south on Highway 118).

VISITOR INFORMATION Fort Davis Chamber of Commerce. ☎ *432/426–3015, 800/524–3015* 🌐 *www.fortdavis.com.*

Sights

★ **Fort Davis National Historic Site**
HISTORIC SITE | FAMILY | Fort Davis (also the city's namesake) provides a history lesson on this late 1800s region, with exhibits and many original buildings preserved. You can spend hours touring the sprawling grounds, which include barracks, the post hospital, the visitor center, and servants' quarters. ✉ *101 Lt. Henry Flipper Dr., Fort Davis* ☎ *432/426–3224* 🌐 *www.nps.gov/foda* 🎟 *$10 per person, $20 per vehicle.*

★ **McDonald Observatory Visitors Center**
INFO CENTER | FAMILY | Check out exhibits, examine sunspots and flares safely via film, or peer into the workings of giant research telescopes. Guided tours of the domed observatories are given several days a week following programs at 11 and 2. After nightfall, the observatory offers star parties (usually Tuesday, Friday, and Saturday). Online reservations are required for all public programs. It's a beautiful 15-mile drive from Fort Davis to the visitor center, at 6,235 elevation. ✉ *3640 Dark Sky Dr., Fort Davis* ☎ *432/426–3640, 877/984–7827* 🌐 *www.mcdonaldobservatory.org* 🎟 *$3; tours $10, star parties $25.*

Hotels

Indian Lodge
$$ | HOTEL | FAMILY | Built of adobe in the 1930s by the Civilian Conservation Corps, this handsome old lodge nestled within 2,700-acre Davis Mountain State Park makes for a distinctive, out-of-the-way Southwestern experience. **Pros:** swimming pool; numerous hiking trails nearby; central air and heat. **Cons:** no pets allowed; about 100 miles from nearest Big Bend National Park entrance; decidedly rustic. [$] *Rooms from: $105* ✉ *Davis Mountains State Park, 16453 Park Rd. 3, Fort Davis* ☎ *432/426–3254, 800/792–1112* 🌐 *www.tpwd.texas.gov/state-parks/indian-lodge* 🛏 *39 rooms* 🍴 *No meals.*

Presidio

60 miles south of Marfa, 91 miles west of Panther Junction.

A quiet border town with relatively few services, Presidio is nonetheless worth checking out if you plan to explore Big Bend Ranch State Park just to the east.

GETTING HERE AND AROUND
Presidio lies at the southern end of U.S. 67, at the U.S. border crossing into Ojinaga, Mexico. To reach Big Bend's western entrance, drive east 70 miles along FM 170 through Lajitas and Terlingua.

VISITOR INFORMATION Presidio Tourism. ✉ *507 W. O'Reilly St., Presidio* ☎ *432/229–3517* 🌐 *www.presidiotx.us.*

Sights

★ **Big Bend Ranch State Park**
NATIONAL/STATE PARK | FAMILY | The largest state park in Texas serves as an enormous western buffer to Big Bend National Park. This rugged desert wilderness extends along the Rio Grande across more than 300,000 acres from east of Lajitas to Presidio. It's far less developed than the national park (if that seems possible) and nearly one-third as large, and it's filled with amazing opportunities to hike, mountain bike, backpack, raft, and ride horseback. A collection of hiking trailheads spoke off from FM 170 across from the Barton Warnock Visitor Center at Lajitas, which serves as the park's eastern information post and contains excellent exhibits on the region as well as a covered picnic area. The western visitor center is at 23-acre Fort Leaton State Historical Site near Presidio and contains a thick-walled adobe fort and trading post that dates back to pioneer

days, plus exhibits, a ½-mile nature trail, and picnic sites. ✉ *FM 170, Presidio* ☎ *432/358–4444* 🌐 *www.tpwd.texas.gov* 🎟 *$5 peak.*

🍴 Restaurants

The Bean Cafe

$ | SOUTHWESTERN | This homey, modest roadside café is a good bet for sustenance before visiting Big Bend Ranch State Park. Open daily for breakfast and lunch, the Bean serves up hearty stick-to-your-ribs fare, such as *machaca* (spicy dried beef) omelets, Reuben sandwiches, and salads topped with crispy-fried chicken. **Known for:** Mexican-American breakfast fare; chicken-fried steak; friendly, down-home service. [$] *Average main:* ✉ *201 W. O'Reilly St., Presidio* ☎ *432/229–3131* 🕓 *No dinner.*

Terlingua

62 miles east of Presidio, 30 miles west of Panther Junction

Popular for its funky ghost town vibe as well as its close proximity to the western entrance to Big Bend National Park, Terlingua began life around the turn of the 20th century as a source of mining for cinnabar. A little under 200 residents live here, many of them involved in tourism related to the park, running everything from tour agencies to guest houses. The adjacent Study Butte area has a few basic services, including a gas station and shares Terlingua's rich mining history. About 13 miles west, tiny Lajitas is home to a popular golf and spa resort and acts as the eastern gateway to Big Bend Ranch State Park.

GETTING HERE AND AROUND

Terlingua is on FM 170, just west of Highway 118, which leads to the western entrance of Big Bend.

VISITOR INFORMATION Big Bend Chamber of Commerce. 🌐 *www.bigbendchamberofcommerce.org.*

🍴 Restaurants

Starlight Theatre

$$ | SOUTHWESTERN | This convivial restaurant-saloon with live-music is ground zero for all the ghosts and other characters of Terlingua. The menu includes plenty of local flavor, such as Terlingua chili and chicken-fried wild boar with Terlingua gold beer gravy. **Known for:** the mixed grill of wild boar–venison sausage, grilled quail, and steak; mesquite-smoked brisket; ice cold local beers. [$] *Average main: $19* ✉ *631 Ivey Rd., Terlingua* ☎ *432/371–3400* 🌐 *www.thestarlighttheatre.com* 🕓 *No lunch.*

☕ Coffee and Quick Bites

Espresso y Poco Mas

$ | CAFÉ | For some of the tastiest breakfast fare close to the park, try this funky down-home spot in Terlingua ghost town, which makes everything from scratch, including the flour tortillas used for hearty breakfast burritos. The coffee is the best in town, and the desserts are homemade. **Known for:** several types of breakfast burritos; overstuffed sandwiches; organic coffee from Big Bend Roasters. [$] *Average main: $7* ✉ *45 Milagro Way, Terlingua* ☎ *432/371–3044* 🌐 *www.laposadamilagro.com* 🕓 *No dinner.*

🛏 Hotels

Big Bend Casitas at Far Flung

$$$ | B&B/INN | FAMILY | Next door to Far Flung Outdoor Center and just 3 miles from the western boundary of Big Bend National Park, the outfitter operates 12 freestanding casitas with hardwood floors, flat-screen TVs, kitchenettes, two pillow-top queen beds, and back porches with rocking chairs. **Pros:** homey atmosphere; activity package deals available with outfitter; grills and a kitchenette for self-catering. **Cons:** no restaurant on-site, but there are a few nearby; no pets; two-night minimum stay. [$] *Rooms* *from: $205 ✉ 23310 FM 170, Terlingua ☎ 800/839–7238, 432/371–2633 🌐 www.bigbendfarflung.com 🛏 12 rooms 🍴 No meals.*

Lajitas Golf Resort & Spa

$$$ | **RESORT** | The former cavalry post turned ghost town is now a privately owned collection of Western-theme tourist attractions with a golf resort, spa, riding stables, convenience store, RV park, and hiking trails, adding up to the nicest place to eat, shop, and overnight within 25 miles of the park. **Pros:** resort is a town unto itself, with many activities; outstanding golf course; near both national park and Big Bend Ranch State Park. **Cons:** pricey rooms for the area; no elevator; not much to do in this tiny town. [$] *Rooms from: $219 ✉ 21701 FM 170, Lajitas ☎ 432/424–5000, 877/525–4827 🌐 www.lajitasgolfresort.com 🛏 102 rooms 🍴 No meals.*

La Posada Milagro

$$$ | **B&B/INN** | As charmingly rustic, yet comfortable, as Terlingua gets, this cozy compound has all the amenities and views that you could hope for in such a faraway outpost. **Pros:** short drive from Big Bend National Park; some rooms have fireplaces; terrific café. **Cons:** far from many services; shared bathrooms for some rooms are located in separate building; breakfast costs extra. [$] *Rooms from: $185 ✉ 100 Milagro Rd., Terlingua ☎ 432/371–3044 🌐 www.laposadamilagro.net 🛏 6 casitas 🍴 No meals.*

★ Willow House

$$$$ | **B&B/INN** | It's a bit of a surprise finding this minimalist compound of neomodern concrete casitas in funky Terlingua, just a few miles from Big Bend's Maverick Entrance Station no less—indeed, this exquisitely designed and decorated complex on a 287-acre spread with panoramic views of the Chisos Mountains is quite posh by any standard. **Pros:** the communal spaces and kitchen make it ideal for groups; stunning design; very close to Big Bend. **Cons:** not suitable for younger kids; often booked weeks in advance; steep rates. [$] *Rooms from: $315 ✉ 23112 FM170, Terlingua ☎ 432/213–2270 🌐 www.willowhouse.co 🛏 12 rooms 🍴 No meals.*

Chapter 7

BLACK CANYON OF THE GUNNISON NATIONAL PARK

7

Updated by
Kellee Katagi

COLORADO

🏕 Camping   🏨 Hotels   🏃 Activities   👁 Scenery   🎡 Crowds
★★★★☆   ★★☆☆☆   ★★★☆☆   ★★★★★   ★★☆☆☆

WELCOME TO BLACK CANYON OF THE GUNNISON NATIONAL PARK

TOP REASONS TO GO

★ **Sheer of heights:** Play it safe, but edge as close to the canyon rim as you dare and peer over into an abyss that's more than 2,700 feet deep in some places.

★ **Rapids transit:** Experienced paddlers can tackle Class V rapids and 50°F water with the occasional portage past untamable sections of the Gunnison River.

★ **Fine fishing:** Fish the rare Gold Medal Waters of the Gunnison. Of the 27,000 miles of trout streams in Colorado, only 329 miles have this "gold medal" distinction.

★ **Triple-park action:** Check out Curecanti National Recreation Area and Gunnison Gorge National Conservation Area, which bookend Black Canyon.

★ **Cliff-hangers:** Watch experts climb the Painted Wall—Colorado's tallest vertical wall at 2,250 feet—and other challenging rock faces.

1 East Portal. The only way you can get down to the river via automobile in Black Canyon is on the steep East Portal Road. There's a campground and picnic area here, as well as fishing and trail access. Check the park website before you go, however; a repaving project will be closing the road for an extended time.

2 North Rim. If you want to access this side of the canyon from the South Rim, you will have to leave the park and wend around it to either the west (through Montrose and Delta) or to the east (via Highway 92); expect a drive of at least two hours. The area's remoteness and difficult location mean the North Rim is rarely crowded; the road is partially unpaved and closes in the winter. There's also a small ranger station here.

3 South Rim. This is the main area of the park. The park's only visitor center is here, along with a campground, a few picnic areas, and many hiking trails. The South Rim Road closes at Gunnison Point in the winter, when skiers and snowshoers take over.

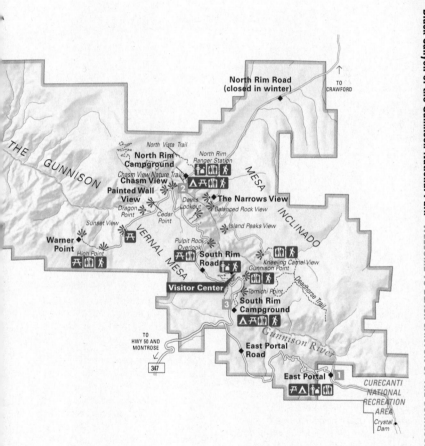

North Rim Road
(closed in winter)

TO
CRAWFORD

THE GUNNISON

North Vista Trail

North Rim
Campground

North Rim
Ranger Station

Chasm View Nature Trail
Chasm View

MESA INCLINADO

Painted Wall
View

Dragon
Point

Cedar
Point

Devils
Lookout

Balanced Rock View

The Narrows View

Sunset View

Island Peaks View

VERNAL MESA

Warner
Point

High Point

Pulpit Rock
Overlook

South Rim
Road

Kneeling Camel View

Gunnison Point

Deadhorse Trail

Visitor Center

Tomichi Point

South Rim
Campground

TO
HWY 50 AND
MONTROSE

347

East Portal
Road

Gunnison River

East Portal

CURECANTI
NATIONAL
RECREATION
AREA

Crystal
Dam

The Black Canyon of the Gunnison River is one of Colorado's most awe-inspiring places—a vivid testament to the powers of erosion, the canyon is roughly 2,000 feet deep. The steep angles of the cliffs allow little sunlight, and ever-present shadows blanket the canyon walls, leaving some of it in almost perpetual darkness and inspiring the canyon's name. And while this dramatic landscape makes the gorge a remarkable place to visit, it also has prevented any permanent occupation—there's no evidence that humans have ever taken up residence within the canyon's walls.

Spanish explorers encountered the formidable chasm in 1765 and 1776, and several other expeditions surveyed it from the mid-1800s to the early 1900s. The early groups hoped to find a route suitable for trains to transport the West's rich resources and the people extracting them. One such train—the Denver and Rio Grande narrow-gauge railroad, completed in 1882—did succeed in constructing a line through the far eastern reaches of the canyon, from Gunnison to Cimmaron, but ultimately concluded that the steepest and deepest part of the canyon, which is now the national park, was "impenetrable." Even so, the rail line's views were majestic enough and the passages narrow enough to earn it the moniker "Scenic Line of the World."

In the late 1800s Black Canyon explorers had another goal in mind: building a tunnel through the side of the canyon to divert water from the Gunnison River into the nearby Uncompahgre Valley, to nurture crops and sustain settlements, such as Montrose. To this day, water still flows through the tunnel, located at the Black Canyon's East Portal, to irrigate the valley's rich farmland.

Once the tunnel was complete, the focus shifted from esteeming the canyon for its resources to appreciating its aesthetic and recreational value. In 1933, Black Canyon of the Gunnison was

AVERAGE HIGH/LOW TEMPERATURES					
JAN.	**FEB.**	**MAR.**	**APR.**	**MAY**	**JUNE**
37/14	42/16	50/18	47/23	67/37	75/44
JULY	**AUG.**	**SEPT.**	**OCT.**	**NOV.**	**DEC.**
84/51	81/50	72/42	62/31	48/23	37/12

designated a national monument, and from 1933 to 1935, Civilian Conservation Corps crews built the North Rim Road, under the direction of the National Park Service. More than 60 years later, in 1999, the canyon was redesignated as a national park. Today, the canyon is far enough removed from civilization that its unspoiled depths continue, as an 1883 explorer wrote, to "arouse the wondering and reverent amazement of one's being."

Planning

When to Go

Summer is the busiest season, with July experiencing the greatest crowds. However, a spring or fall visit gives you two advantages: fewer people and cooler temperatures. In summer, especially in years with little rainfall, daytime temperatures can reach into the 90s. Winter brings even more solitude, as all but one section of campsites are shut down and only about 2 miles of South Rim Road, the park's main road, are plowed.

November through March is when the snow hits, with an average of about 3 to 8 inches of it monthly. March through April and July and August are the rainiest, with about an inch of precipitation each month. June is generally the driest month. Temperatures at the bottom of the canyon are about 8 degrees warmer than at the rim.

FESTIVALS AND EVENTS

Cattleman's Days. Held in July at the Gunnison fairgrounds, this 120-year-old rodeo is the nation's oldest continuous rodeo and the fourth-oldest professional rodeo. Other events include a horse show and a parade. ⊕ www.cattlemensdays.com

Paonia Cherry Days. One of Colorado's longest-running annual events, this small-town festival on the 4th of July includes a parade, food, crafts, sidewalk sales, and a variety of entertainment celebrating local cherry crops (and the other fruits that have made Paonia famous). ⊕ www.paoniacherrydays.com.

Getting Here and Around

AIR

The Black Canyon of the Gunnison lies between the cities of Gunnison and Montrose, both with small regional airports.

CAR

The park has three roads. South Rim Road, reached by Route 347, is the primary thoroughfare and winds along the canyon's South Rim. From about late November to early April, the road is not plowed past the visitor center at Gunnison Point. North Rim Road, reached by Route 92, is usually open from April through Thanksgiving; in winter, the road is unplowed. On the park's south side, the serpentine East Portal Road descends abruptly to the Gunnison River below. The road is usually open from April through the end of November. Because of the grade, vehicles or vehicle-trailer combinations longer than 22 feet are not permitted. The park has no public transportation.

Black Canyon of the Gunnison in One Day

Pack a lunch and head to the canyon's South Rim, beginning with a stop at the South Rim Visitor Center. Before getting back into the car, take in your first view of Black Canyon from Gunnison Point, adjacent to the visitor center. Then set out on a driving tour of the 7-mile South Rim Road, allowing the rest of the morning to stop at the various viewpoints that overlook the canyon. Don't miss Chasm View and Painted Wall View, and be sure to stretch your legs along the short (0.4 mile round-trip) Cedar Point Nature Trail. If your timing is good, you'll reach High Point, the end of the road, around lunchtime. After lunch, head out on Warner Point Nature Trail for an hour-long hike (1½ miles round-trip). Then retrace your drive along South Rim Road back to the visitor center.

Inspiration

The Gunnison Country, by Duane Vandenbusche, contains nearly 500 pages of historical photographs and essays on the park.

The Essential Guide to Black Canyon of the Gunnison National Park, by John Jenkins, is one of the definitive guides to the park.

The *South Rim Driving Tour Guide* is enlivened by David Halpern's evocative black-and-white images.

A Kid's Guide to Exploring Black Canyon of the Gunnison National Park, by Renee Skelton, is perfect for the 6–12 set.

Park Essentials

ACCESSIBILITY
South Rim Visitor Center is accessible to people with mobility impairments, as are most of the sites at South Rim Campground. Drive-to overlooks on the South Rim include Tomichi Point, the alternate gravel viewpoint at Pulpit Rock (the main one is not accessible), Chasm View (gravel), Sunset View, and High Point.

Balanced Rock (gravel) is the only drive-to viewpoint on the North Rim. None of the park's hiking trails are accessible by car.

PARK FEES AND PERMITS
Entrance fees are $25 per week per vehicle. Visitors entering on bicycle, motorcycle, or on foot pay $15 for a weekly pass. To access the inner canyon, you must pick up a wilderness permit (no fee).

PARK HOURS
The park is open 24/7 year-round. It's in the Mountain time zone.

CELL PHONE RECEPTION
Cell phone reception in the park is unreliable and sporadic, but the most common spot for visitors to find a cell signal is at High Point, near the end of the South Rim Road, 6 miles from the visitor center.

Hotels

Black Canyon is devoid of hotels. Smaller hotels and rustic lodges are nearby, as are a few of the larger chains. *Hotel reviews have been shortened. For full information, visit Fodors.com.*

What It Costs

	$	$$	$$$	$$$$
RESTAURANTS				
	under $13	$13–$18	$19–$25	over $25
HOTELS				
	under $121	$121–$170	$171–$230	over $230

Restaurants

The park itself has no eateries, but nearby towns have choices ranging from traditional American to an eclectic café and bakery.

There are, however, a variety of picnic areas in the park, all with pit toilets; all are closed when it snows. *Restaurant reviews have been shortened. For full information, visit Fodors.com.*

Visitor Information

PARK CONTACT INFORMATION Black Canyon of the Gunnison National Park. ✛ *7 miles north of U.S. 50 on CO Hwy. 347* ☎ *970/641–2337* ⊕ *www.nps.gov/blca.*

East Portal

15 miles from Montrose; 7 miles from the South Rim Visitor Center.

This area of the park offers the only opportunity for visitors to experience the bottom of the canyon, without attempting a highly technical rock scramble or tackling Class V rapids. A steep, five-mile road—to the right immediately past the park's south entrance—leads down to the Gunnison River, where you'll find picnic areas, a campground, a short riverside trail, and world-class fishing.

◉ Sights

PICNIC AREAS

East Portal

RESTAURANT—SIGHT | This picnic area, located at the bottom of the canyon at a bend in the river, accommodates large groups. There are tables, a large shaded shelter, and outhouses. ⊠ *East Portal Rd. at the Gunnison River* ⊙ *Closed Nov.–mid-Apr.*

SCENIC DRIVES

East Portal Road

SCENIC DRIVE | The only way to access the Gunnison River from the park by car is via this paved route, which drops approximately 2,000 feet down to the water in only 5 miles, giving it an extremely steep grade. Vehicles longer than 22 feet are not allowed on the road. If you're towing a trailer, you can unhitch it near the entrance to South Rim campground. The bottom of the road is actually in the adjacent Curecanti National Recreation Area. There you'll find a picnic area, a campground, a primitive riverside trail, and beautiful scenery. A tour of East Portal Road, with a brief stop at the bottom, takes about 45 minutes. Immediately after arrival through the park's South entrance, take a right on East Portal Road. ⊙ *Closed mid-Nov.–mid.-Apr.*

SCENIC STOPS

Curecanti National Recreation Area

BODY OF WATER | This recreation area, part of the National Park Service, encompasses three reservoirs along 40 miles of the Gunnison River and can be accessed at the bottom of the East Portal Road. Blue Mesa, nearly 20 miles long, is the largest body of water in Colorado; Morrow Point and Crystal are fjordlike reservoirs set in the upper Black Canyon of the Gunnison. All three reservoirs provide water-based recreational opportunities, including fishing, boating, and paddling, but only Blue Mesa offers boat ramps. Excellent fly fishing can be found upstream (east) of Blue Mesa Reservoir along the Gunnison

River. A variety of camping and hiking opportunities are also available. The Elk Creek Visitor Center on U.S. 50 is available year-round for trip-planning assistance. ✉ *102 Elk Creek, Gunnison* ☎ *970/641–2337* ⊕ *www.nps.gov/cure* 🖾 *Free.*

North Rim

27 miles south of Paonia; 77 miles from South Rim Visitor Center.

Black Canyon's North Rim is much less frequented, but no less spectacular—the walls here are nearly vertical—than the South Rim. To reach the 15½-mile-long North Rim Road, take the signed turnoff from Route 92 about 3 miles south of Crawford. The road is paved for about the first 4 miles; the rest is gravel. After 11 miles, turn left at the intersection (the North Rim Campground is to the right). There are six overlooks along the road as it snakes along the rim's edge. Kneeling Camel, at the road's east end, provides the broadest view of the canyon. Set aside about two hours for a tour of the North Rim.

⊙ Sights

PICNIC AREAS
North Rim campground
LOCAL INTEREST | This small campground is nestled among pine trees near the North Rim Road. Feel free to use unoccupied camping sites for picnicking. There are tables, fire grates, and bathrooms. ✉ *Crawford* ✛ *West end of North Rim Rd.* ☺ *Closed Nov.–mid-April.*

SCENIC STOPS
Narrows View
VIEWPOINT | Look upriver from this North Rim viewing spot and you'll be able to see into the canyon's narrowest section, just a slot really, with only 40 feet between the walls at the bottom. The canyon is also taller (1,725 feet) here than it is wide at the rim (1,150 feet).

Wildlife in Black Canyon

You may spot peregrine falcons nesting in May and June. Other raptors (red-tailed hawks, Cooper's hawks, golden eagles) circle above year round. In summer, turkey vultures join the flying corps, and in winter, bald eagles. Mule deer, elk, and the very shy bobcat also call the park home. In spring and fall, look for porcupines among pinyon pines on the rims. Listen for the chirp of the yellow-bellied marmot on sunny, rocky outcrops. Though rarely seen, mountain lions and black bears also live in the park.

✉ *North Rim Rd., First overlook along the left fork of the North Rim Rd.*

TRAILS
Chasm View Nature Trail
TRAIL | The park's shortest trail (0.3 mile round-trip) starts at North Rim Campground and offers an impressive 50-yard walk right along the canyon rim as well as an eye-popping view of Painted Wall and Serpent Point. This is also an excellent place to spot raptors, swifts, and other birds. *Moderate.* ✉ *Black Canyon of the Gunnison National Park* ✛ *Trailhead: at North Rim Campground, 11¼ miles from Rte. 92.*

Deadhorse Trail
TRAIL | Despite its name, the 6-mile Deadhorse Trail is actually a pleasant hike, starting on an old service road from the Kneeling Camel view on the North Rim Road. The trail's farthest point provides the park's easternmost viewpoint. From this overlook, the canyon is much more open, with pinnacles and spires rising along its sides. *Easy.* ✉ *Black Canyon of the Gunnison National Park* ✛ *Trailhead: at the southernmost end of North Rim Rd.*

North Vista Trail

TRAIL | The round-trip hike to Exclamation Point is 3 miles; a more difficult foray to the top of 8,563-foot Green Mountain (a mesa, really) is 7 miles. The trail leads you along the North Rim; keep an eye out for especially gnarled pinyon pines—the North Rim is the site of some of the oldest groves of pinyons in North America, between 700 and 900 years old. *Moderate.* ⊠ *Black Canyon of the Gunnison National Park* ⚓ *Trailhead: at North Rim ranger station, off North Rim Rd., 11 miles from Rte. 92 turnoff.*

VISITOR CENTERS
North Rim Ranger Station

INFO CENTER | This small facility on the park's North Rim is open sporadically and only in summer. Rangers can provide information and assistance and can issue permits for wilderness use and rock climbing. If rangers are out in the field, which they often are, guests can find directions for obtaining permits posted in the station. ⊠ *North Rim Rd., 11 miles from Rte. 92 turnoff* ☏ *970/641–2337.*

South Rim

15 miles from Montrose.

The South Rim is the hub of the park, a seven-mile stretch that houses the Visitor Center; 12 canyon overlooks; a campground; multiple hiking trails; and opportunities for ranger-led talks, hikes, and kids programs.

Sights

PICNIC AREAS
High Point

RESTAURANT—SIGHT | When the sun is unforgiving, this overlook offers more shade than most of the other picnic areas. There are tables and bathrooms but no fire grates. This spot also has the park's most reliable cell phone reception. ⊠ *West end of South Rim Rd.*

South Rim campground

LOCAL INTEREST | Feel free to use unoccupied camping sites for picnicking. There are tables, fire grates, and bathrooms. ⊠ *Black Canyon of the Gunnison National Park* ⚓ *About 1 mile east of South Rim Visitor Center on South Rim Rd.*

Pulpit Rock

RESTAURANT—SIGHT | There are tables and bathrooms at this overlook. ⊠ *Black Canyon of the Gunnison National Park* ⚓ *2 miles west of the South Rim Visitor Center.*

Sunset View

RESTAURANT—SIGHT | There are tables and bathrooms at this overlook. ⊠ *Black Canyon of the Gunnison National Park* ⚓ *About 1 mile east of High Point on South Rim Rd.*

SCENIC DRIVES
South Rim Road

SCENIC DRIVE | This paved 7-mile stretch from Tomichi Point to High Point is the park's main road. The drive follows the canyon's level South Rim; 12 overlooks are accessible from the road, most via short gravel trails. Several short hikes along the rim also begin roadside. Allow between two and three hours round-trip.

SCENIC STOPS
Chasm and Painted Wall Views

VIEWPOINT | At the heart-in-your-throat Chasm viewpoint, the canyon walls plummet 1,820 feet to the river, but are only 1,100 feet apart at the top. As you peer down into the depths, keep in mind that this section is where the Gunnison River descends at its steepest rate, dropping 240 feet within the span of a mile. A few hundred yards farther is the best place from which to see Painted Wall, Colorado's tallest cliff. Pinkish swaths of pegmatite (a crystalline, granitelike rock) give the wall its colorful, marbled appearance. ⊠ *Black Canyon of the Gunnison National Park* ⚓ *Approximately 3½ miles from the Visitor Center on South Rim Rd.*

Warner Point

NATURE SITE | This viewpoint, at the end of the Warner Point Nature Trail, delivers awesome views of the canyon's deepest point (2,722 feet), plus the nearby San Juan and West Elk mountain ranges. ⊠ *End of Warner Point Nature Trail, westernmost end of South Rim Rd.*

TRAILS

Cedar Point Overlook Trail

TRAIL | **FAMILY** | This 0.4-mile round-trip interpretive trail leads out from South Rim Road to two overlooks. It's an easy stroll, and signs along the way detail the surrounding plants. *Easy.* ⊠ *Black Canyon of the Gunnison National Park* ⊹ *Trailhead: off South Rim Rd., 4¼ miles from South Rim Visitor Center.*

Oak Flat Loop Trail

TRAIL | This 2-mile loop is the most demanding of the South Rim hikes, as it brings you about 400 feet below the canyon rim. In places, the trail is narrow and crosses some steep slopes, but you won't have to navigate any steep drop-offs. Oak Flat is the shadiest of all the South Rim trails; small groves of aspen and thick stands of Douglas fir along the loop offer some respite from the sun. *Difficult.* ⊠ *Black Canyon of the Gunnison National Park* ⊹ *Trailhead: just west of the South Rim Visitor Center.*

Rim Rock Nature Trail

TRAIL | The terrain on this 1-mile round-trip trail is primarily flat and exposed to the sun, with a bird's-eye view into the canyon. The trail connects the visitor center and the campground. There's an interpretive pamphlet, which corresponds to markers along the route, available at both destinations. *Moderate.* ⊠ *Black Canyon of the Gunnison National Park* ⊹ *Trailheads: at Tomichi Point overlook or Loop C in South Rim Campground.*

Bridge Over the ◉ River Gunnison?

A bridge that would span the canyon's two rims was proposed in the 1930s. The bad news is that it was never built, so it'll take you two to three hours to drive from one rim around to the other. The good news for the long trek is all the unforgettable scenery along the way.

★ Warner Point Nature Trail

TRAIL | The 1½-mile round-trip hike starts from High Point. It provides fabulous vistas of the San Juan and West Elk mountains and Uncompahgre Valley. Warner Point, at trail's end, has the steepest drop-off from rim to river: a dizzying 2,722 feet. *Moderate.* ⊠ *Black Canyon of the Gunnison National Park* ⊹ *Trailhead: at the end of South Rim Rd.*

VISITOR CENTERS

South Rim Visitor Center

INFO CENTER | The park's only visitor center offers interactive exhibits and an introductory film detailing the park's geology and wildlife. Inquire at the center about free informational ranger programs. ⊠ *Black Canyon of the Gunnison National Park* ⊹ *1½ mile from the entrance station on South Rim Rd.* ☎ *970/249–1914.*

Activities

BIKING

Bikes are not permitted on any of the trails, but cycling along the South Rim or North Rim Road is a great way to view the park. ■**TIP**→ **Be careful: the roads are fairly narrow.**

BIRD-WATCHING

The sheer cliffs of Black Canyon, though not suited for human habitation, provide a great habitat for birds. Peregrine falcons, white-throated swifts, and other cliff-dwelling birds revel in the dizzying heights, while at river level you'll find American dippers foraging for food in the rushing waters. Canyon wrens, which nest in the cliffs, are more often heard than seen, but their hauntingly beautiful songs are unforgettable. Dusky grouse are common in the sagebrush areas above the canyon, and red-tailed and Cooper's hawks and turkey vultures frequent the canyon rims. The best times for birding are spring and early summer.

BOATING AND KAYAKING

With Class V rapids, the Gunnison River is one of the premier kayak challenges in North America. The spectacular 14-mile stretch of the river that passes through the park is so narrow in some sections that the rim seems to be closing up above your head. Once you're downstream from the rapids (and out of the park), the canyon opens up into what is called the Gunnison Gorge National Conservation Area. The rapids ease considerably, and the trip becomes more of a quiet float on Class I to Class IV water. Access to the Gunnison Gorge is only by foot or horseback. However, several outfitters offer guided raft and kayak trips in the Gunnison Gorge and other sections of the Gunnison River.

Kayaking the river through the park requires a wilderness use permit (and lots of expertise); rafting is not allowed. You can, however, take a guided pontoon-boat trip into the eastern end of the canyon via Morrow Point Boat Tours, which launch from the Curecanti National Recreation Area, east of the park.

Lake Fork Marina

BOATING | Located on the western end of Blue Mesa Reservoir off U.S. 92, the Lake Fork Marina rents all types of boats. If you have your own, there's a ramp at the marina and slips for rent. Guided fishing excursions can also be booked here. ☒ *Off U.S. 92, near Lake Fork Campground, Gunnison* ☎ *970/641–3048* ⊕ *www.thebluemesa.com.*

Morrow Point Boat Tours

BOATING | Starting in neighboring Curecanti National Recreation Area, these guided tours run twice daily (except Tuesday) in the summer, at 10 am and 1 pm. Morrow Point Boat Tours take passengers on a 90-minute trip into the Black Canyon via pontoon boat. Passengers must walk 1 mile in each direction to and from the boat dock (includes quite a few stairs), and reservations are required. ☒ *Pine Creek Trail and Boat Dock, U.S. 50, milepost 130, 25 miles west of Gunnison, Gunnison* ☎ *970/641–2337* ⊕ *www.nps.gov/cure* ☒ *$25* ⊘ *Closed mid-Sept.–May.*

Dvorak Expeditions

WHITE-WATER RAFTING | The outfitter offers rafting trips through the Gunnison Gorge, just northwest of the Black Canyon. Excursions last from one to three days and can be combined with fishing- or photography-focused excursions. ☒ *17921 U.S. 285, Nathrop* ☎ *719/539–6851, 800/824–3795* ⊕ *www.dvorakexpeditions.com* ☒ *From $229.*

Wilderness Aware Rafting

KAYAKING | Wilderness Aware Rafting takes visitors on single- or multiday trips through the Gunnison Gorge (there is no commercial rafting in the Black Canyon). ☒ *12600 U.S. Hwy. 285, Buena Vista* ☎ *800/462–7238, 719/395–2112* ⊕ *www.inaraft.com* ☒ *From $274.*

CAMPING

There are three campgrounds in Black Canyon national park. The small North Rim Campground is first come, first served, and is closed in the winter. Vehicles longer than 35 feet are discouraged from this campground. South Rim Campground is considerably larger and has a loop that's open year-round. Reservations are accepted in South Rim Loops A and B. Power hookups exist only in Loop B. The East Portal campground is at the bottom of the steep East Portal Road and is open whenever the road is open. It offers 15 first-come, first-served tent sites in a pretty, riverside setting. Water has to be trucked up to the campgrounds, so use it in moderation; it's shut off in mid-to-late September. Generators are not allowed at the South Rim and are highly discouraged on the North Rim.

East Portal Campground. Its location next to the Gunnison River makes it perfect for fishing. ⊠ *East Portal Rd., 5 miles from the main entrance.*

North Rim Campground. This small campground, nestled amid pine trees, offers the basics along the quiet North Rim. ⊠ *North Rim Rd., 11¼ miles from Rte. 92.*

South Rim Campground. Stay on the canyon rim at this main campground right inside the park entrance. Loops A and C have tent sites only. The RV hookups are in Loop B, and those sites are priced higher than those in other parts of the campground. It's possible to camp here year-round (Loop A stays open all winter), but the loops are not plowed, so you'll have to hike in with your tent. ⊠ *South Rim Rd., 1 mile from the visitor center.*

EDUCATIONAL OFFERINGS

Junior Ranger Program. Kids of all ages can participate in this program with an activities booklet to fill in while exploring the park. Inquire at the South Rim Visitor Center.

FISHING

The three dams built upriver from the park in Curecanti National Recreation Area have created prime trout fishing in the waters below. Certain restrictions apply: Only artificial flies and lures are permitted, and a Colorado fishing license is required for people ages 16 and older. Rainbow trout are catch-and-release only, and there are size and possession limits on brown trout (check at the visitor center). Most anglers access the river from the bottom of East Portal Road; an undeveloped trail goes along the riverbank for about ¾ of a mile.

HIKING

All trails can be hot in summer and most don't receive much shade, so bring water, a hat, and plenty of sunscreen. Dogs are permitted, on leash, on Rim Rock, Cedar Point Nature, and Chasm View Nature trails, and at any overlook. Venturing into the inner canyon, while doable, is not for the faint of heart—or slight of step. Six named routes lead down to the river, but they are not maintained or marked, and they require a wilderness permit. In fact, the park staff won't even call them trails; they refer to them as "Class III scrambles" These supersteep, rocky routes vary in one-way distance from 1 to 2¾ miles, and the descent can be anywhere from 1,800 to 2,722 feet. Your reward, of course, is a rare look at the bottom of the canyon and the fast-flowing Gunnison. ■TIP➔ **Don't attempt an inner-canyon excursion without plenty of water (the park's recommendation is one gallon per person, per day).** For descriptions of the routes and the necessary permit to hike them, stop at the visitor center at the South Rim or the North Rim ranger station. Dogs are not permitted in the inner canyon.

HORSEBACK RIDING

Although its name might indicate otherwise, Deadhorse Trail is actually the only trail in the park where horses are allowed. Although no permit is required, the park has no riding facilities.

TOURS
Elk Ridge Trail Rides

HORSEBACK RIDING | You can take 90-minute trail rides at this ranch just outside the Black Canyon National Park. ⊠ *10203 Bostwick Park Rd., Montrose* ☎ *970/240–6007* ⊕ *www.elkridgeranchinc.com* ⊒ *$75. Reservations required.*

Did You Know?

Though you won't likely see them, coyotes live in the canyon. The size of medium dogs, coyotes are largely nocturnal; listen for their distinctive howls and high-pitched yelps, which you can usually hear in the early evening. Coyotes also bark when protecting their dens or food.

ROCK CLIMBING

Rock climbing in the park is for experts only, but you can do some bouldering at the Marmot Rocks area, about 100 feet south of South Rim Road between Painted Wall and Cedar Point overlooks (park at Painted Wall). Four boulder groupings offer a variety of routes rated from easy to very difficult; a pamphlet with a diagrammed map of the area is available at the South Rim Visitor Center.

Irwin Guides

CLIMBING/MOUNTAINEERING | Intermediate and expert climbers can take full-day rock-climbing guided tours in the Black Canyon on routes rated from 5.8 to 5.13. ⌧ *330 Belleview Ave., Crested Butte* ☎ *970/349–5430* ⊕ *www.irwinguides. com* ⊠ *$550 for one person; $500 for two or more.*

WINTER ACTIVITIES

From late November to early April, South Rim Road is not plowed past the visitor center, offering park guests a unique opportunity to cross-country ski or snowshoe on the road. The Park Service also grooms a cross-country ski trail and marks a snowshoe trail through the woods, both starting at the visitor center. It's possible to ski or snowshoe on the unplowed North Rim Road, too, but it's about 4 miles from where the road closes, through sagebrush flats, to the canyon rim.

Nearby Towns

The primary gateway to Black Canyon is **Montrose,** 15 miles west of the park. The legendary Ute chief, Ouray, and his wife, Chipeta, lived near here in the late 1800s. Today, Montrose straddles the important agricultural and mining regions along the Uncompahgre River, and is the area's main shopping hub. Northeast on Route 92 (20 miles) is **Paonia,** a unique

and charming blend of the old and new West. About 60 miles to the east, along Highway 50, lies the town of **Gunnison,** home to Western Colorado University and a low-key hub for outdoor enthusiasts. Black Canyon visitors coming from Denver often stop off for a day or two in Gunnison and the skiing and mountain biking paradise that is **Crested Butte.**

Crested Butte

28 miles north of Gunnison via Hwy. 135; 92 miles northeast of Montrose via U.S. 50 and Hwy. 135.

Like Aspen, the town of Crested Butte was once a small mining village (albeit for coal, not silver). The Victorian gingerbread-trim houses remain, many of them now painted in whimsical shades of hot pink, magenta, and chartreuse. Unlike Aspen, however, Crested Butte has retained much of its small-town charm despite its development as a ski area.

The setting is serenely beautiful. The town sits at the top of a long, broad valley that stretches 17 miles south toward Gunnison. Mount Crested Butte, which looms over the town, is the most visible landmark. It's surrounded by the Gunnison National Forest and the Elk Mountain Range.

It's as an extreme-skiing playground that Crested Butte earned its reputation with some of the best skiers in the land. Over the years, Crested Butte has steadily increased its adventure-skiing terrain to nearly 550 ungroomed acres. Although this area, known as the Extreme Limits, should only be attempted by experts, there are plenty of cruise-worthy trails for skiers of all levels. The groomed trails are rarely crowded, which allows for plenty of long, fast, sweeping turns.

GETTING HERE AND AROUND

Crested Butte is just over the mountain from Aspen, but there are no paved roads—just unpaved routes over the challenging Pearl, Taylor, and Schofield passes and hiking trails through White River National Forest. If you're coming from the north or west, the most direct route is over Kebler Pass. The drive is one of Colorado's prettiest, passing through one of the state's largest stands of aspens. If you're coming from the east, the beautiful Cottonwood Pass will deposit you on Highway 135, just south of town. Both graded gravel roads are closed in winter, making it necessary to take a circuitous route on U.S. 24 and U.S. 50 through Poncha Springs and Gunnison, and then up Highway 135 to Crested Butte.

Alpine Express will transport you between the Gunnison–Crested Butte Regional Airport and the resort for around $80 round-trip. Mountain Express is a reliable free shuttle bus that travels the 3 miles between the town and the resort throughout the year.

WHEN TO GO

Ski season—mid-December to mid-April—is definitely the busiest time in Crested Butte. The weeks between Memorial Day and Labor Day are hopping, as well. Things slow down dramatically in the in-between times, with some businesses closing completely.

ESSENTIALS

TRANSPORTATION CONTACTS Alpine Express. ☎ *970/641–5074, 800/822–4844* 🌐 *www.alpineexpressshuttle.com.* **Mountain Express.** ✉ *2 N. 8th St., Bldg. D* ☎ *970/349–5616* 🌐 *www.mtnexp.org.*

VISITOR INFORMATION Crested Butte Visitor Center. ✉ *601 Elk Ave.* ☎ *970/349–6438, 855/681–0941* 🌐 *www.cbchamber.com.* **Crested Butte Snow Report.** ☎ 🌐 *www.skicb.com/snow.* **Crested Butte Vacations.** ✉ *12 Snowmass Rd.* ☎ *855/969–3022* 🌐 *www.skicb.com.*

Sights

Crested Butte Mountain Heritage Museum

MUSEUM | Housed in an 1893 hardware store, this museum showcases the essentials for life in an 1880s mining town, such as clothing, furniture, and household items. There's an intricate diorama of the town in the 1920s, complete with a moving train, plus exhibits on skiing, sledding, biking, and Flauschink, a quirky local ceremony that welcomes the return of spring. ✉ *331 Elk Ave.* ☎ *970/349–1880* 🌐 *www.crestedbuttemuseum.com* 🎟 *$5* 🕒 *Closed mid-Nov.*

Crested Butte Mountain Resort Adventure Park

AMUSEMENT PARK/WATER PARK | FAMILY | Make a day of it at Crested Butte Mountain Resort Adventure Park, where, for one ticket price, you can access unlimited lift-served hiking and biking, mini-golf, bungee trampolines, a climbing wall, an inflated-bag jump, and a hands-on kids' mining exhibit. A la carte pricing and guided hiking are also available. The lift-served hiking and biking are summer-only, but the rest of the Adventure Park is open both winter and summer. ✉ *12 Snowmass Rd., Mt. Crested Butte* ☎ *855/969–3022* 🌐 *www.skicb.com* 🎟 *From $47, kids from $40* 🕒 *Closed early Apr.–late May; late Oct.–late Nov.*

Restaurants

Django's Kitchen

$$$$ | **MODERN AMERICAN** | Delectable small plates and a wide-ranging wine list star at this sophisticated, modern eatery on the town's main street. The offerings change with the seasons but always include meat and seafood, as well as creative salads and veggie dishes. **Known for:** classy atmosphere; creekside patio; tip included in prices. [$] *Average main: $30* ✉ *209 Elk Ave.* ☎ *970/765–8864* 🌐 *www.djangos.us* 🕒 *Closed Mon.–Tues., and mid-Apr.–early June and Nov. No lunch.*

Montanya Distillers Tasting Room

$ | **TAPAS** | Stop here for artisan cocktails and tasty tapas before dinner and it just might end up being your dinner spot. The rum is divine (ask for a free tasting)—there's a light and a dark, both skillfully distilled on-site in copper stills from Portugal using fresh local-spring water (come by between noon and five Wednesday through Saturday for a distillery tour). **Known for:** Maharaja cocktail; Asian-style rice and noodle bowls; live music. [$] *Average main: $12* ✉ *212 Elk Ave.* ☎ *970/799–3206* 🌐 *www.montanyarum.com.*

Secret Stash

$ | **PIZZA** | Sit inside beneath sweeping tapestries in a Japanese-style booth (seating on the floor) or opt for a table on the deck to enjoy amazing pizza in a mind-bending array of formulations—from the "Notorious F.I.G." (prosciutto, dried figs, and truffle oil) to the "Mac Daddy" (with Thousand Island, shaved rib eye, pickles, and a sesame seed crust). **Known for:** gluten-free crusts available; extensive bar menu; breakfast and brunch available. [$] *Average main: $12* ✉ *303 Elk Ave.* ☎ *970/349–6245* 🌐 *www.secretstash.com.*

The Slogar

$$$ | **AMERICAN** | In a lovingly renovated Victorian tavern awash in handmade lace and stained glass, this restaurant is just plain cozy. A menu with a comfort-food bent spotlights family-style options, such as skillet-fried chicken, rib-eye steak, and ribs, paired with sides like fresh biscuits, creamy mashed potatoes, gumbo, and mac 'n' cheese. **Known for:** family-style comfort food; Creole Sunday brunch; historic building. [$] *Average main: $26* ✉ *517 2nd St., at Whiterock Ave.* ☎ *970/349–5765* 🌐 *www.slogarcb.com* 🕒 *Closed mid-Oct.–Nov. and mid-Apr.–mid-May. No lunch.*

★ Soupçon

$$$$ | **FRENCH** | "Soup's on" (get it?) occupies two intimate rooms in a historic cabin tucked away in an alley and dishes up five courses of Nouveau American cuisine with a strong French accent. Organic herbs grown on the premises accent local produce, and everything, including soups, stocks, and sauces, is made from scratch. **Known for:** award-winning wine cellar; Colorado lamb; artistic presentation. [$] *Average main: $50* ✉ *127A Elk Ave.* ☎ *970/349–5448* 🌐 *www.soupconcb.com* 🕒 *Closed Mon.–Tues.; Nov. and mid-Apr.–mid-May.*

Sunflower

$$$$ | **MODERN AMERICAN** | This small, simple-looking restaurant on Crested Butte's main street serves up perhaps the valley's best gourmet farm-to-table fare. New menus are printed regularly—creatively crafted to accommodate the fresh, organic meats and produce available that day from local farm suppliers—but they always feature a few delicious entrées, along with a generous selection of smaller plates. **Known for:** extremely fresh ingredients; a well-curated wine list; delicious homemade desserts. [$] *Average main: $34* ✉ *214 Elk Ave.* ☎ *970/417–7767* 🌐 *www.sunflowercb.com* 🕒 *Closed Mon. No lunch.*

Teocalli Tamale

$ | **MEXICAN** | Known as "Teo's," this Mexican restaurant is housed in a small, historic building and is a local favorite for tasty takeout (or a claustrophobic eat-in experience). You can get a generous portion of tamales, burritos, or tacos for about $10. **Known for:** flavorful homemade salsas; mahimahi tacos; margaritas. [$] *Average main: $11* ✉ *311 Elk Ave.* ☎ *970/349–2005* 🌐 *www.teocallitamale.com.*

Hotels

Cristiana Guesthaus

$$ | **B&B/INN** | With a huge stone fireplace in a wood-beamed lobby, this alpine-style ski lodge provides a cozy, unpretentious haven. **Pros:** close to downtown and hiking, biking, and ski trails; knowledgeable hosts; hot tub on deck has mountain views. **Cons:** TV only in common area; no air-conditioning; no hot items at breakfast. [$] *Rooms from: $145* ✉ *621 Maroon Ave.* ☎ *970/349–5326* 🌐 *www.cristiana-guesthaus.com* ⏲ *Closed early Apr.* 🛏 *21 rooms* 🍴 *Free Breakfast.*

Elevation Hotel & Spa

$$$ | **HOTEL** | Top-notch service, mountain-modern luxury, and ample amenities make this upscale ski-in ski-out hotel worth the splurge. **Pros:** Indoor and outdoor hot tubs; complimentary ski valet and storage; restaurant and beauty salon on-site. **Cons:** parking is $20 per day; pool is small; no meals included. [$] *Rooms from: $186* ✉ *500 Gothic Rd., Mt. Crested Butte* ☎ *970/251–3000* 🌐 *www.elevationresort.com* 🛏 *311 rooms* 🍴 *No meals.*

Elk Mountain Lodge

$$$ | **B&B/INN** | Built in 1919 as a boardinghouse for miners, this historic hotel has been painstakingly renovated; step into the lobby and you will encounter a slower pace of life and extraordinary attention to detail. **Pros:** good, full breakfast; intimate feel; provides locked ski storage on-site and on-mountain. **Cons:** 3 miles from ski area; no elevator; stairs are a bit steep. [$] *Rooms from: $200* ✉ *129 Gothic Ave.* ☎ *970/349–7533, 800/374–6521* 🌐 *www.elkmountainlodge.com* 🛏 *19 rooms* 🍴 *Free Breakfast.*

Grand Lodge Crested Butte

$$$ | **HOTEL** | A warm stone-and-log lobby with a huge fireplace welcomes guests to this comfortable lodge in the mountain's base village. **Pros:** close to ski lift; rooms have many amenities; terrific restaurant. **Cons:** some of the basic rooms are small; can feel impersonal; fitness center is small. [$] *Rooms from: $199* ✉ *6 Emmons Loop, Mt. Crested Butte* ☎ *866/823–4446, 970/349–8000* 🌐 *www.skicb.com* 🛏 *228 rooms* 🍴 *No meals.*

Old Town Inn

$ | **B&B/INN** | An excellent in-town location makes this a great base for adventures in town or the mountains, but the real draws are unique touches like the free-for-loan "townie" bikes, sleds, and snowshoes for guests' use; concierge services; and delicious homemade cookies each afternoon. **Pros:** good deluxe Continental breakfast; outdoor hot tub; convenient location. **Cons:** no pool; no elevator to second story; ski storage on-mountain only. [$] *Rooms from: $119* ✉ *708 6th St.* ☎ *970/349–6184, 888/349–6184* 🌐 *www.oldtowninn.net* 🛏 *33 rooms* 🍴 *Free Breakfast.*

★ **Pioneer Guest Cabins**

$$$ | **B&B/INN** | On a creekside meadow about 8 miles from Crested Butte, this pleasant getaway for outdoors lovers has rustic but comfortable two- and three-bed log cabins, and you can hike, bike, snowshoe, or cross-country ski from trails that start right at your door. **Pros:** secluded setting; close to trails and fishing; each cabin has a fully equipped kitchen and outdoor fire pit. **Cons:** bedrooms are small; no restaurant, TVs, or phones; minimum stay required. [$] *Rooms from: $229* ✉ *2094 Cement Creek Rd.* ☎ *970/349–5517* 🌐 *www.pioneerguest-cabins.com* 🛏 *8 cabins* 🍴 *No meals.*

Nightlife

Kochevar's Saloon and Gaming Hall

BARS/PUBS | An 1899 cabin built from hand-hewn logs, Kochevar's is a classic saloon where locals play pool. ✉ *127 Elk Ave.* ☎ *970/349–7117.*

Public House

BARS/PUBS | A classy, modern spin on a Western saloon, this pub has live music and serves draft beers and higher-end bar food, such as elk chili and cornbread. ✉ *202 Elk Ave.* ☏ *970/349–0173* ⊕ *www. publichousecb.com.*

Wooden Nickel

BARS/PUBS | This popular place is packed for happy hour each day from 4 to 6. Stay for dinner, as the steaks are terrific. ✉ *222 Elk Ave.* ☏ *970/349–6350* ⊕ *www. woodennickelcb.com* ⊗ *Closed mid-Apr.– early May.*

Activities

BACKCOUNTRY SKIING

Crested Butte Nordic Center

SKIING/SNOWBOARDING | FAMILY | Crested Butte abounds with backcountry possibilities. You can rent cross-country skis or snowshoes, and then head out on one of the Forest Service roads that radiate from town—particularly Washington Gulch, Slate River Road, and Gothic Road. The Crested Butte Nordic Center offers half-day ski or snowshoe packages that include transportation, guides, and equipment. ✉ *620 2nd St.* ☏ *970/349–1707* ⊕ *www.cbnordic.org* ✉ *Tours from $90.*

DOWNHILL SKIING AND SNOWBOARDING

Crested Butte Mountain Resort

SKIING/SNOWBOARDING | The skiing here has a split personality, which is plain to see when you check out the skiers who descend on the place year after year. Its mellow half is the network of trails on the front side of the mountain, characterized by long intermediate runs. Families flock to Crested Butte for these trails, as well as the children's ski-school facilities and the laid-back and friendly vibe.

The wilder side of Crested Butte's personality is the **Extreme Limits,** nearly 550 acres of backcountry-like terrain (all double black diamond), with steep bowls,

gnarly chutes, and tight tree skiing. It's some of the toughest in-bounds skiing in North America. Sign up for one of the guided programs for expert instruction (and insider info on the best powder stashes on the mountain).

The best expert skiing on the front side of the mountain is off the Silver Queen high-speed quad, which shoots you up 2,078 vertical feet in one quick ride. For beginners there's a wonderful expanse of easy terrain from the Red Lady Express lift. **Facilities:** 121 trails; 1,547 acres; 2,755-foot vertical drop; 15 lifts. ✉ *12 Snowmass Rd.* ☏ *855/969–3022* ⊕ *www. skicb.com* ✉ *Lift ticket from $117.*

Crested Butte Ski and Ride School

SKIING/SNOWBOARDING | FAMILY | A half-day adult group lesson starts at $140 (lift ticket not included). For kids ages 5 through 17, Camp CB offers single all-day lessons starting at $175, which includes lunch. One-hour private lessons for 3- and 4-year-olds start at $135. ✉ *12 Snowmass Rd.* ☏ *855/969–3022* ⊕ *www.skicb.com.*

Crested Butte Rental and Demo Center

SKIING/SNOWBOARDING | Full rental packages (including skis, boots, helmet, and poles), as well as snowshoes, snowboard equipment, and tuning, are available at this outfitter. Packages start at $37 per day. ■TIP➜ For best prices, reserve ahead at rentskis.com. ✉ *10 Crested Butte Way* ☏ *970/349–2240* ⊕ *www.skicb.com.*

FISHING

Almont

FISHING | Located where the East and Taylor rivers join to form the Gunnison River, this tiny angler-oriented hamlet is one of Colorado's top fly-fishing centers. It's also one of the most crowded. Local fishing outfitters rent equipment, teach fly-fishing, and lead guided wading or float trips to both public and private waters. ✉ *Almont.*

Almont Anglers

FISHING | This outfitter and guide has a solid fly and tackle shop with an enormous selection. There are clinics for beginners as well as guided wading and float-fishing excursions on the East, Taylor, and Gunnison rivers. ✉ *10209 Hwy. 135, Almont* ☎ *970/641–7404* ⊕ *www. almontanglers.com* ✉ *Lessons from $80; trips from $270.*

Dragonfly Anglers

FISHING | Crested Butte's oldest year-round guide service and fly-fishing outfitter, Dragonfly Anglers offers guided walk-wade trips and float trips to choice fly-fishing spots, including the famed Gunnison Gorge. The shop sells a wide variety of rods and has a solid selection of reels, flies, and outdoor gear, including Patagonia items. ✉ *307 Elk Ave.* ☎ *970/349–1228, 800/491–3079* ⊕ *www. dragonflyanglers.com* ✉ *From $295; from $425 for Black Canyon excursions.*

Willowfly Anglers at Three Rivers Resort

FISHING | A branch of Three Rivers Resort and Outfitting, the Orvis-endorsed Willowfly Anglers offers half- and full-day guided trips for all skill levels and has a full-service fly shop. Trip prices include all necessary equipment. ✉ *130 County Rd. 742, Almont* ☎ *970/641–1303, 888/761–3474* ⊕ *www.willowflyanglers. com* ✉ *Trips start at $300.*

FOUR-WHEELING

Colorado Adventure Rentals

FOUR-WHEELING | Choose from a variety of one- to four-person ATVs to explore the rugged terrain around Crested Butte and Gunnison. Insurance, helmets, gas, and basic instruction are included, and snowmobiles are available in the winter. ✉ *23044 County Rd. 742, Almont* ☎ *970/641–3525* ⊕ *www.coloradoad-venturerentals.com* ✉ *From $139 for a two-hour rental.*

GOLF

★ The Club at Crested Butte

GOLF | Golf legend Robert Trent Jones Jr. designed this ravishing 18-hole course surrounded by gorgeous mountain peaks. The first nine holes follow a traditional format, but the back nine offer a Highlands-style surprise with a Scottish-links design. Water hazards are present on 14 of the 18 holes, so be sure to bring extra balls. The semiprivate course belongs to the country club, but it's open to the public daily after 11:30. The dress code bars denim and mandates stand-up collars for all. ✉ *385 Country Club Dr.* ☎ *970/349–8601* ⊕ *www.theclubatcrestedbutte. com* ✉ *$99 for 9 holes, $179 for 18 holes* ⚑ *18 holes, 7208 yards, par 72* ⚐ *Reservations essential* ☞ *Rates include golf cart and practice balls.*

HIKING

Judd Falls

HIKING/WALKING | **FAMILY** | One of the area's easiest—and most kid-friendly—hiking trails is the 2 miles round-trip to Judd Falls, located within the Gunnison National Forest near the former mining town of Gothic. The path slices through groves of aspen and, in summer, a crop of more than 70 local wildflower varieties. At the end, look over Judd Falls from a bench named after Garwood Judd, "the man who stayed" in the old mining town. ✉ *Gunnison National Forest, off Gothic Rd.* ☎ *970/874–6600* ⊕ *www.fs.usda.gov/ gmug.*

HORSEBACK RIDING

Fantasy Ranch

HORSEBACK RIDING | **FAMILY** | Riding a horse is one of the best ways to see the Crested Butte area. Fantasy Ranch gives guided horseback tours into the Elk Mountains, Maroon Bells, and Gunnison National Forest. Trips range from 90-minute trail rides to full-day wilderness adventures. Riders must be at least 10 years old, but younger children can do 20-minute pony rides. ✉ *935 Gothic Rd., Mt. Crested Butte* ☎ *970/349–5425*

⊕ www.fantasyranchoutfitters.com
🗠 From $75 in winter; from $85 spring through fall.

ICE-SKATING

Crested Butte Nordic Center

ICE SKATING | FAMILY | If you're eager to practice a figure eight, the Crested Butte Nordic Center operates a covered, outdoor skating rink. Skating is free and open to the public when the rink isn't reserved for hockey. The center rents skates for $10–$20. ✉ 620 2nd St. ☎ 970/349–1707 ⊕ www.cbnordic.org 🗠 Free ⊗ Closed Mar.–Nov.

KAYAKING AND RAFTING

Three Rivers Resort & Outfitting

KAYAKING | The rivers around Crested Butte are at their best from May through early August. Three Rivers offers rafting trips, kayaking lessons, and stand-up paddleboard rentals on the Taylor and Gunnison rivers. ✉ 130 County Rd. 742, Almont ☎ 970/641–1303, 888/761–3474 ⊕ www.3riversresort.com 🗠 Raft trips start at $55.

MOUNTAIN BIKING

Crested Butte is the mountain-biking center of Colorado. This is a place where there are more bikes than cars, and probably more bikes than residents. Many locals own two: a cruiser (or "townie") for hacking around and a mountain bike for *serious* hacking around. Nearby Pearl Pass is known as the route that got the fat-tire craze started.

Crested Butte Mountain Bike Park

BICYCLING | Crested Butte Mountain Resort maintains 30 miles of downhill and cross-country singletrack, from green to black diamond. There are also two skills zones for riders to work on fundamentals. ✉ 12 Snowmass Rd., Mt. Crested Butte ☎ 855/969–3022 ⊕ www.skicb.com ⊗ Closed Nov.–May.

Upper Loop

BICYCLING | Great for beginners, the Upper Loop is a popular 1½-mile ride that will help orient you to the area. The views up the Slate River valley to the peaks of Paradise Divide are wonderful. **Tony's Trail** consists of a short, moderate climb leading to an intersection with the Upper Upper Loop Trail. Here you can take in the view of the town below and the mountains above, and then enjoy a fun descent or venture farther in either direction on the Upper Upper Loop. ✉ Crested Butte ⊕ www.travelcrestedbutte.com.

Irwin Guides

BICYCLING | Guided rides on the area's legendary singletrack trails are available for riders of all skill levels. Irwin offers instruction, half- and full-day tours, and overnight tours with meals, lodging, and transportation included. ✉ 330 Belleview Ave. ☎ 970/349–5430 ⊕ www.irwinguides.com 🗠 From $175 per person for a half day.

Big Al's Bicycle Heaven

BICYCLING | This full-service downtown bike shop, a favorite with locals, sells and rents all manner of two-wheelers, from knock-around "townies" to state-of-the-art mountain bikes, as well as bike trailers to haul kids. The shop also carries road and cross-country bikes and a full line of clothing, helmets, and other necessities. Best of all, the staff is willing to share the inside scoop on local trails. ✉ 207 Elk Ave. ☎ 970/349–0515 ⊕ www.bigalsbicycleheaven.com.

Crested Butte Sports

BICYCLING | Come here to rent Orbea and Transition mountain bikes, plus helmets and other gear. It also has a full repair shop. ✉ 35 Emmons Loop Rd. ☎ 970/349–7516, ⊕ crestedbuttesports.com ☞ From $50 for four hours.

SPAS
Elevation Spa

SPA/BEAUTY | With an elevation of 9,385 feet, Mount Crested Butte can drain the life out of your skin. The energizing atmosphere and treatments of the Elevation Spa can bring it back. The 11,000-square-foot spa is simply decorated, but provides all the amenities you need to unwind: robes, sandals, steam rooms, and three relaxation rooms—men's, women's, and coed—plus a large, well-equipped fitness center overlooking the slopes. ⊠ *500 Gothic Rd., Mt. Crested Butte* ☎ *970/251–3500* ⊕ *www.elevationspa.com* ☞ *$115 50-min massage, $295 2-hr massage and facial package. Hot tubs (indoor and outdoor), indoor pool, saunas, steam rooms. Gym with: cardiovascular machines, free weights, weight-training equipment. Services: body wraps and scrubs, facials, massage.*

TRACK SKIING
Crested Butte Nordic Center

SKIING/SNOWBOARDING | **FAMILY** | The community-owned Crested Butte Nordic Center maintains 31 miles of cross-country ski and snowshoe trails, many of which start from town. The trails cover flat and moderately rolling terrain across meadows and through aspen groves. A one-day adult trail pass costs $20, although there are six miles of groomed trails that don't require a pass. Group classic lessons and private skate or classic lessons are offered daily, as well as training groups for adults and kids. You can also reserve a spot for a dinner at the Magic Meadows Yurt, which includes a 1-mile trek to a cozy yurt for a five-course dinner prepared by local chefs and accompanied by live music; the $185 per-person cost includes a trail pass, equipment rentals, and gratuity. You can also buy hot drinks, soups, and pastries every Sunday from 10 to 2 at the Magic Meadows Yurt. ⊠ *620 2nd St.* ☎ *970/349–1707* ⊕ *www.cbnordic.org.*

RENTALS
The Alpineer

SKIING/SNOWBOARDING | This iconic Crested Butte shop rents top-notch backcountry and telemark equipment, as well as classic Nordic and skate skis. The staff offers expert advice on routes and snow conditions. ⊠ *419 6th St.* ☎ *970/349–5210* ⊕ *www.alpineer.com* ☞ *Closed Sun.*

ZIPLINING
Crested Butte Mountain Resort Zipline Tour

ADVENTURE TOURS | **FAMILY** | Friendly guides and superior views make this two-hour, five-line tour worth your time. The tour runs in the summer at the base of the mountain, where you can watch the bikers below as you zip from tree to tree. ⊠ *12 Snowmass Rd., Mt. Crested Butte* ⊕ *www.skicb.com* ✉ *A two-hour tour costs $65.*

Gunnison

64 miles east of Montrose via U.S. 50; 28 miles south of Crested Butte via Hwy. 135.

At the confluence of the Gunnison River and Tomichi Creek, Gunnison is an old mining and ranching community and college town. It's been adopted by nature lovers because of the excellent outdoor activities, including hiking, climbing, fishing, and hunting. In fact, long before any settlers arrived, the Ute Indians used the area as summer hunting grounds. Gunnison provides economical lodging and easy access to Crested Butte and Blue Mesa Reservoir. Locals (for good reason) call it "Sunny Gunny," despite its claim to fame of having recorded some of the coldest temperatures ever reported in the continental United States.

GETTING HERE AND AROUND

Getting in and out of Gunnison is a breeze. U.S. 50 travels right through town, heading east to I–25 in Pueblo and northwest to I–70 in Grand Junction. U.S. 50 goes by the name Tomichi Avenue as it travels 18 blocks through town. Western State Colorado University and the Pioneer Museum are on the east side of town, and the rodeo grounds and airport are to the south.

ESSENTIALS
VISITOR INFORMATION Gunnison County Chamber of Commerce. ✉ *500 E. Tomichi Ave.* ☎ *970/641–1501* ⊕ *www.gunnison-crestedbutte.com.*

Sights

Curecanti National Recreation Area
BODY OF WATER | This recreation area, part of the National Park Service, encompasses three reservoirs along 40 miles of the Gunnison River and can be accessed at the bottom of the East Portal Road. Blue Mesa, nearly 20 miles long, is the largest body of water in Colorado; Morrow Point and Crystal are fjordlike reservoirs set in the upper Black Canyon of the Gunnison. All three reservoirs provide water-based recreational opportunities, including fishing, boating, and paddling, but only Blue Mesa offers boat ramps. Excellent fly fishing can be found upstream (east) of Blue Mesa Reservoir along the Gunnison River. A variety of camping and hiking opportunities are also available. The Elk Creek Visitor Center on U.S. 50 is available year-round for trip-planning assistance. ✉ *102 Elk Creek* ☎ *970/641–2337* ⊕ *www.nps.gov/cure* 🎫 *Free.*

Gunnison Pioneer Museum
MUSEUM | FAMILY | Anyone interested in the region's history shouldn't miss the Pioneer Museum. The complex spreads across 6 acres and includes an extensive collection of vehicles, from Model Ts to 1960s sedans. There are also two old schoolhouses; an impressive display of arrowheads; mining exhibits; and a train, complete with coal tender, caboose, and boxcar. ✉ *803 E. Tomichi Ave.* ☎ *970/641–4530* ⊕ *www.gunnisonpioneermuseum.com* 💲*$10* 🕙 *Closed Oct.–mid-May* 🎫 *Cash only.*

Hartman Rocks Recreation Area
PARK—SPORTS-OUTDOORS | This free recreation area is a haven for mountain bikers, hikers, horseback riders, rock climbers, and ATV riders in the summer and Nordic skiers and snowshoers in the winter. With 8,000 acres of public land, encompassing 40 miles of single-track trails and 33 miles of road, there's enough room for everyone. ✉ *Gunnison* ✛ *3 miles south of U.S. 50, via County Road 38* ⊕ *www.blm.gov/visit/hartman_rocks.*

🍴 Restaurants

Blackstock Bistro
$$ | **CONTEMPORARY** | The atmosphere and food at this modern, airy bistro are about as sophisticated as you'll find in Gunnison. It serves an innovative selection of small and large plates, but the real gem is the happy hour (3 to 6 pm every day and from 9 to close Friday and Saturday), which offers hearty portions at very reasonable prices. **Known for:** delectable ramen bowls; innovative small plates; truffle fries. 💲 *Average main: $15* ✉ *122 W. Tomichi Ave.* ☎ *970/641–4394* ⊕ *www.blackstockbistro.com* 🕙 *Closed Sun. No lunch.*

Garlic Mike's
$$$ | **ITALIAN** | The menu at this unpretentious Italian spot is surprisingly rich and complex, featuring traditional favorites, as well as suprises like the scrumptious garlic-roasted prime rib. The atmosphere is especially delightful in summer, when you can dine on the outdoor patio overlooking the Gunnison River and enjoy an after-dinner libation at the River Bar. **Known for:** live music on Friday nights in summer; Float & Dine pre-dinner raft trip; riverside patio. 💲 *Average main: $23* ✉ *2674 Hwy. 135* ☎ *970/641–2493* ⊕ *www.garlicmikes.com* 🕙 *No lunch.*

Hotels

The Inn at Tomichi Village

$$ | **HOTEL** | The rooms at this updated hotel feature modern-rustic decor, comfortable beds (including a variety of pillow styles to suit various tastes), and amenities such as refrigerators and microwaves. **Pros:** ample amenities; large indoor pool; on-site restaurant. **Cons:** motel-style entrances; bathrooms are a bit dated; a little outside of town. *Rooms from: $129 41883 U.S. 50 E 970/641–1131 www.theinntv.com 51 rooms Free Breakfast.*

Rockey River Resort

$ | **RESORT** | **FAMILY** | A tetherball on the turf, a riverside fire pit, and welcoming front porches: these are just a few of the touches that make this old homestead a uniquely pleasant place to stay. **Pros:** close to fishing; a lot of activities available on the property; pet-friendly. **Cons:** 6 miles from Gunnison; TV only in common areas; some cabins are a bit dated. *Rooms from: $95 4359 County Rd. 10 970/641–0174 www.gunnisoncabins.com Closed Nov.–Apr. 14 cabins No meals.*

Activities

FISHING

Gunnison Sports Outfitters

FISHING | Take a guided fishing trip on the Gunnison River or the Blue Mesa Reservoir, which teems with brown trout, rainbow trout, and kokanee salmon. Full-day trips are $345 per person; half-day are $295. Kids 12 and younger are free with a paying adult. *201 W. Tomichi Ave. 970/641–1845 www.gunnisonsportsoutfitters.com.*

HORSEBACK RIDING

Tenderfoot Outfitters

HORSEBACK RIDING | With a variety of guided backcountry trail rides ranging from three hours to a full day, Tenderfoot Outfitters also offers camping trips with comfortable tents and real beds, starting at $190, including meals. Rides start at $75. *Gunnison 800/641–0504 www.tenderfoot-outfitters.com.*

WATER SPORTS

At 20 miles long, with 96 miles of shoreline, Blue Mesa Reservoir ranks as Colorado's largest body of water. Located within Curecanti National Recreation Area, the reservoir was created in the mid-1960s when the Gunnison River was dammed as part of the Colorado River Storage Project. This cold-water reservoir has become a mecca for water-sports enthusiasts. Anglers are drawn by the 3 million stocked kokanee salmon, as well as rainbow, lake, brown, and brook trout.

Five boat ramps and two marinas operate through the summer with varying hours and amenities. Boat permits are required and are available at the Elk Creek Visitor Center. A two-day boat permit is $4, and a two-week permit is $10. Annual boat permits run $30.

Elk Creek Marina

WATER SPORTS | About 16 miles west of Gunnison, this marina on Blue Mesa Reservoir offers a range of services: boat and slip rentals, mechanical and towing services, gas, ice, bait, and supplies. You can also book guided fishing trips here. A small restaurant, Pappy's, is located above the dock, where you can enjoy a light meal while watching anglers try their luck. *24830 U.S. 50 970/641–0707 www.thebluemesa.com Closed Oct.–Apr.*

Montrose

15 miles west of Black Canyon of the Gunnison National Park; 64 miles west of Gunnison; 22 miles south of Delta, all via U.S. 50.

The "Home of the Black Canyon" sits amid glorious surroundings, but it's otherwise a typical Western town with a small historic center, where you'll find a smattering of trendy shops and restaurants, and a collection of truck stops, strip malls, and big-box stores along its outskirts. Montrose also has a small airport that's a major gateway for skiers heading to Telluride and Crested Butte.

GETTING HERE AND AROUND
U.S. 550 enters Montrose from the south; it's known as Townsend Avenue as it passes through town. At Main Street, U.S. 550 merges with U.S. 50, which continues north to Delta and east to Black Canyon of the Gunnison National Park and the town of Gunnison.

VISITOR INFORMATION Montrose Visitor Center. ✉ *107 S. Cascade Ave., Montrose* ☎ *970/497–8558* 🌐 *www.visitmontrose.com.*

👁 Sights

Museum of the Mountain West

MUSEUM | FAMILY | Run by a retired archaeologist, the museum depicts life in Colorado from the late 1800s to the 1940s. It features roughly 500,000 artifacts and 23 buildings, including a schoolhouse, church, carriage works, and jail cell, as well as homesteads and tepee replicas. ✉ *68169 E. Miami Rd., Montrose* ✣ *2 miles east of Montrose, off U.S. 50* ☎ *970/240–3400* 🌐 *www.museumofthemountainwest.org* 🎟 *$10* 🕒 *Closed Sun.*

Ute Indian Museum

MUSEUM | If you're interested in the lives of the region's original residents, stop by the renovated Ute Indian Museum, 3 miles south of town. The museum contains several dioramas and the most comprehensive collection of Ute materials and artifacts in Colorado. It's housed in the 1956 homestead of Ute Chief Ouray and his wife, Chipeta. Today, the complex includes the Chief Ouray Memorial Park, Chipeta's Crypt, a native plants garden, picnic areas, and shaded paths linked to the citywide walking trail. ✉ *17253 Chipeta Rd., Montrose* ☎ *970/249–3098* 🌐 *www.historycolorado.org* 🎟 *$6.*

🍴 Restaurants

Camp Robber

$$ | SOUTHWESTERN | This simply decorated restaurant serves some of Montrose's most creative cuisine, such as its famous green-chile chicken and potato soup or shrimp, avocado, and prosciutto pasta (gluten-free options available too). At lunch, salads with house-made dressings, hearty sandwiches, and blue-corn enchiladas fuel hungry hikers. **Known for:** New Mexican dishes; house-made salsa and desserts; shaded patio. [$] *Average main: $15* ✉ *1515 Ogden Rd., Montrose* ☎ *970/240–1590* 🌐 *www.camprobber.com* 🕒 *No dinner Sun.*

Colorado Boy Pizzeria & Brewery

$ | PIZZAPIZZA | The dough is house-made (with Italian-imported flour) and the beer is home-brewed at this trendy downtown pizzeria with high ceilings, brick walls, and contemporary decor. Sit at the pizza bar in the back and enjoy an English-style ale while you watch the chefs craft your tasty pie. **Known for:** home-brewed ales; growlers and cans to go; house-made sausage. [$] *Average main: $10* ✉ *320 E. Main St., Montrose* ☎ *970/240–2790* 🌐 *www.coloradoboy.com* 🕒 *No lunch Mon.–Fri.*

Hotels

Country Lodge

$ | HOTEL | A log cabin–style building and rooms ringing a pretty garden and pool make this hotel feel remote even though it's on Montrose's main drag. **Pros:** great value; intimate feel; nice pool and hot tub. **Cons:** small bathrooms and TVs; on main highway, so it can sometimes be noisy; breakfast is basic. $ *Rooms from: $90* ⊠ *1624 E. Main St., Montrose* ☎ *970/249–4567* ⊕ *www.country-lodgecolorado.com* ⇆ *23 rooms* ⊚ *Free Breakfast.*

Red Arrow Inn & Suites

$$ | HOTEL | This low-key establishment offers reasonable prices for one of the nicest lodgings in the area, mainly because of the large, pretty rooms filled with handsome wood furnishings. **Pros:** good breakfast; outdoor fire pit; pleasant outdoor pool. **Cons:** motel-style entrances; next to busy street; decor doesn't offer much local flavor. $ *Rooms from: $140* ⊠ *1702 E. Main St., Montrose* ☎ *970/249–9641* ⊕ *www.redarrowinn.com* ⇆ *59 rooms* ⊚ *Free Breakfast.*

Paonia

24 miles north of the north entrance of the Black Canyon of the Gunnison National Park, via Crawford Rd. and Fruitland Mesa Rd.

Vineyards, orchards, and farms surround this small town, which encompasses a little over a square mile in the midst of a verdant valley. A pleasant but unassuming main street, called Grand Avenue, features shops and restaurants, many of which provide opportunities to enjoy the agricultural bounty of the area, including wines from some of the highest-altitude vineyards in the Northern Hemisphere.

VISITOR INFORMATION

North Fork Valley Tourism. ☎ *970/872–3226* ⊕ *www.northforkvalley.net.*

Sights

Big B's Delicious Orchards

FARM/RANCH | This lovely orchard one mile west of Paonia markets its own organic apples, apricots, cherries, peaches, pears, and plums throughout the summer. You can pick them yourself, along with a variety of other produce, or buy them in the shop in the form of homemade organic juices or hard cider; you'll also find local wines, art, honey, and more. The café serves tasty sandwiches, salads, and Colorado-style Mexican entrées that can be enjoyed indoors or out. There's live music outdoors on many summer evenings, and kids will keep themselves entertained on the variety of tree swings. Camping is also available. ⊠ *39126 Hwy. 133, Hotchkiss* ☎ *970/527–1110* ⊕ *www.bigbs.com* ⊙ *Closed Dec.–Mar.*

Orchard Valley Farms & Market and Black Bridge Winery

FARM/RANCH | Family fun takes an organic approach at this friendly farm. Take a stroll through the gardens and orchards and pick your own fruits and vegetables, or choose from a nice selection at the farm market, which also features a broad selection of other local products. Enjoy your bounty immediately at creekside picinc tables. The on-site Black Bridge Winery offers $5 tastings of its Chardonnay, Riesling, Merlot, Pinot Noir, and other wines. ⊠ *15836 Black Bridge Rd., Paonia* ☎ *970/527–6838* ⊕ *www.orchardvalleyfarms.com* ⊙ *Closed Nov.–late May.*

Stone Cottage Cellars

WINERY/DISTILLERY | This winery, three miles north of town (a mile of it up a steep, narrow dirt road), is in an idyllic setting, featuring old world–style stone cottages the owner made himself. Specialties include Chardonnay, Merlot, Syrah, Pinot Noir, Pinot Gris, and Gewürztraminer varietals. Stop by for a free vineyard tour and wine tasting; don't miss the delicious small plates as well. If you plan ahead, you can book a night in the two-bedroom guest cottage. ✉ *41716 Reds Rd., Paonia* ☎ *970/527–3444* 🌐 *www.stonecottagecellars.com* 🕒 *Closed Nov.–Apr.*

🍴 Restaurants

Flying Fork Cafe & Bakery

$$ | **ITALIAN** | This charming café serves tasty Italian fare in a comfortable dining room and, in the summer, a shady outdoor garden. Local ingredients are used whenever possible, and the house-made fettuccine noodles are delicious. **Known for:** gluten-free pasta and pizza options; homemade fettuccine noodles; vegetarian lasagna. [$] *Average main: $18* ✉ *101 3rd St., Paonia* ☎ *970/527–9075* 🌐 *www.flyingforkcafe.com* 🕒 *Closed Mon.–Tues.*

The Living Farm Café

$$ | **ECLECTIC** | Housed in a historic building at the end of the main drag, this farm-to-table eatery infuses local and organic fare throughout its menu—much of it from its own namesake farm nearby. There are salads, burgers, and sandwiches aplenty, along with a smattering of international selections, including Mexican, Indian, and Chinese. **Known for:** fresh-from-the-farm organic ingredients; vegan and gluten-free options aplenty; half portions available. [$] *Average main: $$17* ✉ *120 Grand Ave., Paonia* ☎ *970/527–3779* 🌐 *www.thelivingfarmcafe.com* 🕒 *Closed Tue.–Wed.*

🛏 Hotels

Bross Hotel

$$ | **B&B/INN** | On a quiet, shady street in downtown Paonia, this brick hotel was opened in 1906 by the local deputy sheriff. **Pros:** lovely hotel with genuine period ambience; excellent full breakfast in a large, classy breakfast room; outdoor hot tub and small fitness center. **Cons:** no a/c in the dog days of summer can be a drag; no elevator and narrow staircase; breakfast is at specific seating times versus at your leisure. [$] *Rooms from: $155* ✉ *312 Onarga St., Paonia* ☎ *970/527–6776* 🌐 *www.paonia-inn.com* 🛏 *10 rooms* 🍽 *Free Breakfast.*

Chapter 8

BRYCE CANYON NATIONAL PARK

8

Updated by
Shelley Arenas

UTAH

🔺 **Camping**
★★★☆☆

🏨 **Hotels**
★★★☆☆

🎯 **Activities**
★★★☆☆

👁 **Scenery**
★★★★★

👥 **Crowds**
★★★★☆

WELCOME TO BRYCE CANYON NATIONAL PARK

TOP REASONS TO GO

★ **Hoodoo heaven:** The boldly colored, gravity-defying limestone tentacles reaching skyward—called hoo-doos—are Bryce Canyon's most recognizable attraction.

★ **Famous fresh air:** With some of the clearest skies in the nation, the park offers views that, on a clear day, can extend more than 100 miles and into three states.

★ **Spectacular sunrises and sunsets:** The deep orange and crimson hues of the park's hoodoos are intensified by the light of the sun at either end of the day.

★ **Dramatically different zones:** From the highest point of the rim to the canyon base, the park spans 2,000 feet, so you can explore three unique climatic zones: spruce-fir forest, ponderosa-pine forest, and pinyon pine-juniper forest.

★ **Snowy fun:** Bryce gets an average of 87 inches of snowfall a year, and is a popular destination for skiers and snow-shoe enthusiasts.

1 Bryce Canyon North. Bryce Amphitheater is the heart of the park. From here you can access the historic Bryce Canyon Lodge as well as Sunrise, Sunset, and Inspiration points. Walk to Bryce Point at sunrise to view the mesmerizing collection of massive hoodoos known as Silent City. The 23-mile Under-the-Rim Trail is the best way to reach Bryce Canyon backcountry. It can be a challenging three-day adventure or half day of fun via one of the four access points from the main road. Several primitive campgrounds line the route.

2 Bryce Canyon South. Rainbow and Yovimpa Points are at the end of the scenic road, but not of the scenery. Here you can hike a trail to see some ancient bristlecone pines and look south into Grand Staircase-Escalante National Monument.

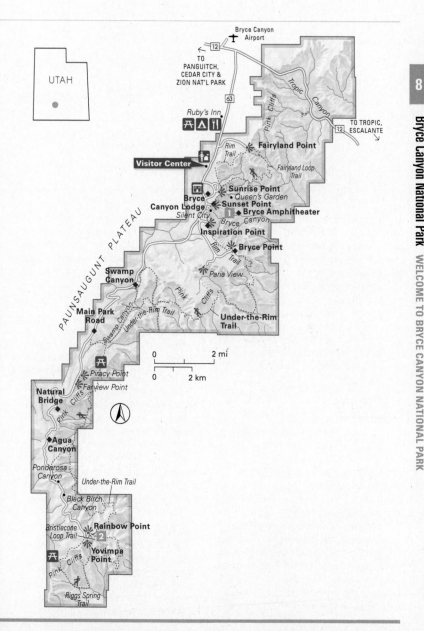

UTAH

Bryce Canyon Airport

12

TO PANGUITCH, CEDAR CITY & ZION NAT'L PARK

63

Ruby's Inn

Tropic Canyon

Pink Cliffs

TO TROPIC, ESCALANTE

12

Rim Trail

Fairyland Point

Visitor Center

Fairyland Loop Trail

Sunrise Point

• Queen's Garden

Bryce Canyon Lodge

Silent City

Sunset Point

Bryce Amphitheater

Bryce Canyon

Inspiration Point

Bryce Point

Rim Trail

Paria View

PAUNSAUGUNT PLATEAU

Swamp Canyon

Pink Cliffs

Swamp Canyon

Under-the-Rim Trail

Main Park Road

Under-the-Rim Trail

0   2 mi

0   2 km

Piracy Point

Fairview Point

Natural Bridge

Pink Cliffs

Agua Canyon

Ponderosa Canyon

Under-the-Rim Trail

Black Birch Canyon

Bristlecone Loop Trail

Rainbow Point

2

Yovimpa Point

Pink Cliffs

Riggs Spring Trail

A land that captures the imagination and the heart, Bryce is a favorite among the Southwest's national parks. Although its splendor had been well known for decades, Bryce Canyon wasn't designated a national park until 1928. Bryce Canyon is famous for its fanciful hoodoos, best viewed at sunrise or sunset, when the light plays off the red rock.

In geological terms, Bryce is actually an amphitheater, not a canyon. The hoodoos in the amphitheater took on their unusual shapes because the top layer of rock—cap rock—is harder than the layers below it. If erosion undercuts the soft rock beneath the cap too much, the hoodoo will tumble. Bryce continues to evolve today, but the hoodoos are a permanent feature; old ones may die, but new ones are constantly forming as the amphitheater rim recedes.

Planning

When to Go

Around Bryce Canyon National Park and the nearby Cedar Breaks National Monument area, elevations approach and surpass 9,000 feet, making for temperamental weather, intermittent and seasonal road closures due to snow, and downright cold nights well into June. The air is cooler on the rim of the canyon than it is at lower altitudes. ■TIP→ **If you choose to see Bryce Canyon April through October, you'll be visiting with the rest of** the world. **During this period, traffic on the main road can be heavy and parking limited, so consider taking one of the park shuttle buses. RV access is also limited to a handful of lots and camping areas, most of them near the park entrance, during these months.**

If it's solitude you're looking for, come to Bryce any time between November and February. The park is open all year long, so if you come during the cooler months you might just have a trail all to yourself.

FESTIVALS AND EVENTS

Bryce Canyon Winter Festival. This event at the Best Western Ruby's Inn features cross-country ski races, snow-sculpting contests, ski archery, ice-skating, and kids' snow boot races. Clinics to hone skills such as snowshoeing and photography also take place, and there's plenty of entertainment, too. ⊕ *www. rubysinn.com.*

Quilt Walk Festival. During the bitter winter of 1864, Panguitch residents set out over the mountains to fetch provisions from the town of Parowan, 40 miles away. Legend says the men, frustrated and ready to turn back, laid a quilt on the snow and knelt to pray. Soon they

AVERAGE HIGH/LOW TEMPERATURES					
JAN.	FEB.	MAR.	APR.	MAY	JUNE
37/15	38/17	45/23	54/29	64/37	75/45
JULY	AUG.	SEPT.	OCT.	NOV.	DEC.
80/53	77/50	70/42	58/32	45/23	36/15

realized the quilt had kept them from sinking into the snow. Spreading quilts before them as they walked, leapfrog style, the men traveled to Parowan and back. This four-day event in June commemorates the event with quilting classes, a tour of pioneer homes, tractor pull, dinner-theater, and other events. ⊕ www.quiltwalk.org.

Getting Here and Around

AIR
The nearest commercial airport to Bryce Canyon, Cedar City Regional Airport is 80 miles west and has daily direct flights from Salt Lake City. The airports in Salt Lake City and Las Vegas are the closest major ones to the park—each is about a four-hour drive.

BUS
A shuttle bus system operates in Bryce Canyon from mid-April through mid-October. Buses start at 8 am and run every 10 to 15 minutes until 8 pm in summer and 6 pm in early spring and October; they're free once you pay park admission. The route begins at the Shuttle Station north of the park, where parking is available (visitors can also park at Ruby's Inn or Ruby's Campground outside the park entrance and catch the shuttle there). It stops at the visitor center, lodge, campgrounds, and all the main overlooks and trailheads.

CAR
The closest major cities to Bryce Canyon are Salt Lake City and Las Vegas, each about 270 miles away. You reach the park via Highway 63, just off of Highway 12, which connects U.S. 89 just south of

Panguitch with Torrey, near Capitol Reef National Park. You can see the park's highlights by driving along the well-maintained road running the length of the main scenic area. Bryce has no restrictions on automobiles on the main road, but from spring through fall you may encounter heavy traffic and full parking lots—it's advisable to take the shuttle bus at this time.

Inspiration

Bryce Canyon Auto and Hiking Guide, available from the Bryce Canyon Natural History Association, has info on the geology and history of the area.

Park Essentials

ACCESSIBILITY
Most park facilities were constructed between 1930 and 1960. Some have been upgraded for wheelchair accessibility, while others can be used with some assistance. The Sunset campground offers two sites with wheelchair access. Few of the trails, however, can be managed in a standard wheelchair due to the sandy, rocky, or uneven terrain. The section of the Rim Trail between Sunrise and Inspiration points is wheelchair accessible. The 1-mile Bristlecone Loop Trail at Rainbow Point has a hard surface and could be used with assistance, but several grades do not meet accessibility standards. Accessible parking is marked at all overlooks and public facilities.

PARK FEES

The entrance fee is $35 per vehicle for a seven-day pass and $20 for pedestrians or bicyclists, and includes unlimited use of the park shuttle. An annual Bryce Canyon park pass, good for one year from the date of purchase, costs $40. If you leave your private vehicle outside the park at the shuttle staging area or Ruby's Inn or Campground, the one-time entrance fee is $35 per party and includes transportation on the shuttle.

A $5 backcountry permit, available from the visitor center, is required for camping in the park's interior, allowed only on Under-the-Rim Trail and Rigg's Spring Loop, both south of Bryce Point. Camp-fires are not permitted.

PARK HOURS

The park is open 24/7, year-round. It's in the Mountain time zone.

CELL PHONE RECEPTION

Cell phone reception is hit-or-miss in the park, with some of the higher points along the main road your best bet. The lodge and visitor center have limited (it can be slow during busy periods) Wi-Fi, and there are pay phones at a few key spots in the park, but these are gradually being removed.

Hotels

Lodgings in and around Bryce Canyon include both rustic and modern options, but all fill up fast in summer. Bryce Canyon Lodge is the only hotel inside the park, but there are a number of options in Bryce Canyon City, just north of the park's entrance. Nearby Panguitch and Tropic, and Escalante a bit farther away, are small towns with a number of additional budget and mid-range hotels, and these places tend to have more last-minute availability. *Hotel reviews have been shortened. For full information, visit Fodors.com.*

What It Costs			
$	$$	$$$	$$$$
RESTAURANTS			
under $16	$16–$22	$23–$30	over $30
HOTELS			
under $125	$125–$175	$176–$225	over $225

Restaurants

Dining options in the park proper are limited to a few options in or near Bryce Canyon Lodge; you'll also find a handful of restaurants serving mostly standard American fare within a few miles of the park entrance, in Bryce Canyon City. Venture farther afield—to Tropic and Escalante to the east, and Panguitch and Hatch to the west—and the diversity of culinary offerings increases a bit. *Restaurant reviews have been shortened. For full information, visit Fodors.com.*

Tours

Bryce Canyon Airlines & Helicopters
TOUR—SPORTS | For a bird's-eye view of Bryce Canyon National Park, take a dramatic helicopter ride or airplane tour over the fantastic sandstone formations. Longer full-canyon tours and added excursions to sites such as the Grand Canyon, Monument Valley, and Zion are also offered. Flights last from 35 minutes to four hours. ☎ *435/834–8060* ⊕ *www.rubysinn.com/scenic-flights* ✈ *From $110.*

Visitor Information

PARK CONTACT INFORMATION Bryce Canyon National Park. ☎ *435/834–5322* ⊕ *www.nps.gov/brca.*

Bryce Canyon in One Day

Begin your day at the **visitor center** to get an overview of the park and to purchase books and maps. Watch the 20-minute film and peruse the excellent exhibits about the natural and cultural history of Bryce Canyon. Then, proceed to the historic **Bryce Canyon Lodge**. From here, stroll along the relaxing **Rim Trail**. If you have the time and stamina to walk into the amphitheater, the portion of the Rim Trail near the lodge gets you to the starting point for either of the park's two essential hikes, the **Navajo Loop Trail** from **Sunset Point** or the **Queen's Garden Trail** that connects Sunset to **Sunrise Point.**

Afterward (or if you skip the hike), drive the 18-mile **main park road**, stopping at the overlooks along the way. Allowing for traffic, and if you stop at all 13 overlooks, this drive will take you between two and three hours.

If you have the time for more walking, a short, rolling hike along the **Bristlecone Loop Trail** at **Rainbow Point** rewards you with spectacular views and a cool walk through a forest of bristlecone pines.

End your day watching the sunset at **Inspiration Point** or dining at Bryce Canyon Lodge.

Bryce Canyon North

Bryce Ampitheater is the central part of the park. Here you'll find the visitor center, lodge, campgrounds, and many of the most popular trails and viewpoints. A convenient free shuttle runs a loop through this area, stopping at eight main spots where you can get out and explore. It also runs through the nearby town of Bryce Canyon City, so you don't need to bring your vehicle if you're staying at one of the hotels just outside the park.

Bryce Canyon's longest trail leads backpackers under the rim of the park's plateau that edges the natural amphitheater. Hiking the full 23-mile Under the Rim Trail will require an overnight stay, though there are some shorter trails to access parts of this area on day hikes. On clear nights, the stargazing can be amazing.

Sights

HISTORICAL SIGHTS
Bryce Canyon Lodge
BUILDING | The lodge's architect, Gilbert Stanley Underwood, was a national park specialist, having designed lodges at Zion and Grand Canyon before turning his T-square to Bryce in 1924. The results are worth a visit as this National Historic Landmark has been faithfully restored, right down to the lobby's huge limestone fireplace, and log and wrought-iron chandelier. Inside the historic building, the only remaining hotel built by the Grand Circle Utah Park Company, are a restaurant and gift shop, as well as information on park activities. The lodge operation includes several historic log cabins and two motels nearby on the wooded grounds, just a short walk from the rim trail. Everything but the Sunset Motel (which is open early March–late December) shuts down from early November through late March. ⊠ *Off Hwy. 63* ☎ *435/834–8700* ⊕ *www.bryce-canyonforever.com.*

8

Bryce Canyon National Park   BRYCE CANYON NORTH

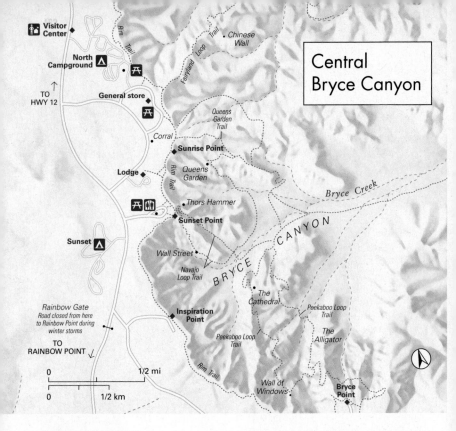

SCENIC DRIVES

⭐ Main Park Road

SCENIC DRIVE | Following miles of canyon rim, this thoroughfare gives access to more than a dozen scenic overlooks between the park entrance and Rainbow Point. Major overlooks are rarely more than a few minutes' walk from the parking areas, and many let you see more than 100 miles on clear days. Remember that all overlooks lie east of the road. To keep things simple, proceed to the southern end of the park and stop at the overlooks on your northbound return; they will all be on the right side of the road. Allow two to three hours to travel the entire 36-mile round trip. The road is open year-round, but may close temporarily after heavy snowfalls. Keep your eyes open for wildlife as you drive. Trailers are not allowed at Bryce Point and Paria View, but you can park them at the parking lot across the road from the visitor center. RVs can drive throughout the park (with limited parking options spring through fall), and vehicles longer than 25 feet are not allowed at Paria View. ✉ *Bryce Canyon National Park.*

SCENIC STOPS

Agua Canyon

VIEWPOINT | This overlook in the southern section of the park, 12 miles south of the park entrance, has a nice view of several standout hoodoos. Look for the top-heavy formation called the Hunter, which actually has a few small hardy trees growing on its cap. As the rock erodes, the park evolves; snap a picture because the Hunter may look different the next time you visit. ✉ *Bryce Canyon National Park* ⊕ *www.nps.gov/brca/planyourvisit/ aguacanyon.htm.*

Bryce Point

VIEWPOINT | After absorbing views of the Black Mountains and Navajo Mountain, you can follow the Under-the-Rim Trail and go exploring beyond Bryce Amphitheater to the cluster of top-heavy hoodoos known collectively as the Hat Shop. Or, take a left off the Under-the-Rim Trail and hike the challenging Peekaboo Loop Trail with its geological highlight, the **Wall of Windows.** Openings carved into a wall of rock illustrate the drama of erosion that formed Bryce Canyon. ⊠ *Inspiration Point Rd., 5½ miles south of park entrance.*

Fairyland Point

VIEWPOINT | Best visited as you exit the park, this scenic overlook adjacent to Boat Mesa, ½ mile north of the visitor center and a mile off the main park road, has splendid views of Fairyland Amphitheater and its delicate, fanciful forms. The Sinking Ship and other formations stand before the grand backdrop of the Aquarius Plateau and distant Navajo Mountain. Nearby is the Fairyland Loop trailhead—it's a stunning five-hour hike in summer and a favorite of snowshoers in winter. ⊠ *Off Hwy. 63.*

★ Inspiration Point

VIEWPOINT | Not far (1½ miles) east along the Rim Trail from Bryce Point is Inspiration Point, site of a wonderful vista on the main amphitheater and one of the best places in the park to see the sunset. (You will have plenty of company and hear a variety of languages as the sun goes down.) ⊠ *Inspiration Point Rd.* ⊕ *www.nps.gov/brca/planyourvisit/inspiration.htm.*

Natural Bridge

VIEWPOINT | Formed over millions of years by wind, water, and chemical erosion, this 85-foot rusty-orange arch formation—one of several rock arches in the park—is an essential photo op. Beyond the parking lot lies a rare stand of aspen trees, their leaves twinkling in the wind. Watch out for distracted drivers at this stunning viewpoint. ⊠ *Main park road, 11 miles south of park entrance* ⊕ *www.nps.gov/brca/planyourvisit/naturalbridge.htm.*

North Campground Viewpoint

VIEWPOINT | **FAMILY** | Across the road and slightly east of the Bryce Canyon Visitor Center, this popular campground has a couple of scenic picnic areas plus a general store and easy trail access. ⊠ *Main park road* ⊕ *½ mile south of visitor center.*

★ Sunrise Point

VIEWPOINT | Named for its stunning views at dawn, this overlook a short walk from Bryce Canyon Lodge is one of the park's most popular stops. It's also the trailhead for the Queen's Garden Trail and the Fairyland Loop Trail. You have to descend the Queen's Garden Trail to get a glimpse of the regal **Queen Victoria,** a hoodoo that appears to sport a crown and glorious full skirt. The trail is popular and marked clearly, but a bit challenging with 350 feet of elevation change. ⊠ *Off Hwy. 63.*

Sunset Point

VIEWPOINT | Watch the late-day sun paint the hoodoos here. You can see **Thor's Hammer,** a delicate formation similar to a balanced rock, from the rim, but when you hike 550 feet down into the amphitheater on the Navajo Loop Trail you can walk through the famous and very popular Wall Street—a deep, shady "slot" canyon. The point is near Bryce Canyon Lodge. ⊠ *Bryce Canyon National Park.*

TRAILS

Fairyland Loop Trail

TRAIL | Hike into whimsical Fairyland Canyon on this trail that gets more strenuous and less crowded as you progress along its 8 miles. It winds around hoodoos, across trickles of water, and finally to a natural window in the rock at Tower Bridge, 1½ miles from Sunrise Point and 4 miles from Fairyland Point. The pink-and-white badlands and hoodoos surround you the whole way. Don't feel like you have to go the whole distance to make it worthwhile. But if you do, allow at least five hours round-trip with 1,700 feet of elevation change. *Difficult.* ⊠ *Bryce Canyon National Park* ✛ *Trailheads: at Fairyland Point and Sunrise Point.*

Hat Shop Trail

TRAIL | The sedimentary haberdashery sits 2 miles from the trailhead. Hard gray caps balance precariously atop narrow pedestals of softer, rust-color rock. Allow three to four hours to travel this somewhat strenuous but rewarding 4-mile round-trip trail, the first part of the longer Under-the-Rim Trail. *Moderate.* ⊠ *Bryce Canyon National Park* ✛ *Trailhead: at Bryce Point, 5½ miles south of park entrance.*

Navajo Loop Trail

TRAIL | FAMILY | One of Bryce's most popular and dramatic attractions is this steep descent via a series of switchbacks leading to Wall Street, a slightly claustrophobic hallway of rock only 20 feet wide in places with walls 100 feet high. After a walk through the Silent City, the northern end of the trail brings Thor's Hammer into view. A well-marked intersection offers a shorter way back via Two Bridges Trail or continuing on the Queen's Garden Trail to Sunrise Point. For the short version allow at least an hour on this 1½-mile trail with 550 feet of elevation change. *Moderate.* ⊠ *Bryce Canyon National Park* ✛ *Trailhead: at Sunset Point, near Bryce Canyon Lodge.*

★ Navajo/Queen's Garden Combination Loop

TRAIL | FAMILY | By walking this extended 3-mile loop, you can see some of the best of Bryce; it takes a little more than two hours. The route passes fantastic formations and an open forest of pine and juniper on the amphitheater floor. Descend into the amphitheater from Sunrise Point on the Queen's Garden Trail and ascend via the Navajo Loop Trail; return to your starting point via the Rim Trail.

Moderate. ⊠ *Bryce Canyon National Park* ✛ *Trailheads: at Sunset and Sunrise points, 2 miles south of park entrance.*

★ Peekaboo Loop

TRAIL | The reward of this steep trail is the Wall of Windows and the Three Wise Men. Horses use this trail in spring, summer, and fall and have the right-of-way. Start at Bryce, Sunrise, or Sunset Point and allow four to five hours to hike the 5-mile trail or 7-mile double-loop. *Difficult.* ⊠ *Bryce Canyon National Park* ✛ *Trailheads: at Bryce Point, 5½ miles south of park entrance; Sunrise and Sunset points, near Bryce Canyon Lodge.*

Queen's Garden Trail

TRAIL | FAMILY | This hike is the easiest way down into the amphitheater, with 350 feet of elevation change leading to a short tunnel, quirky hoodoos, and lots of like-minded hikers. It's the essential Bryce "sampler." Allow two hours total to hike the 1½-mile trail plus the ½-mile rimside path and back. *Easy.* ⊠ *Bryce Canyon National Park* ✛ *Trailhead: at Sunrise Point, 2 miles south of park entrance.*

Under-the-Rim Trail

TRAIL | Starting at Bryce Point, the trail travels 23 miles to Rainbow Point, passing through the Pink Cliffs, traversing Agua Canyon and Ponderosa Canyon, and taking you by several springs. Most of the hike is on the amphitheater floor, characterized by up-and-down terrain among stands of ponderosa pine; the elevation change totals about 1,500 feet. It's the park's longest trail, but four trailheads along the main park road allow you to connect to the Under-the-Rim Trail and cover its length as a series of day hikes. Allow at least two days to hike the route in its entirety, and although it's not a hoodoo-heavy hike there's plenty to see to make it a more leisurely three-day affair. *Difficult.* ⊠ *Bryce Canyon National Park* ✛ *Trailheads: at Bryce Point, Swamp Canyon, Ponderosa Canyon, and Rainbow Point.*

VISITOR CENTERS
★ Bryce Canyon Visitor Center
INFO CENTER | FAMILY | Even if you're anxious to hit the hoodoos, the visitor center—just to your right after the park entrance station—is the best place to start if you want to know what you're looking at and how it got there. Rangers staff a counter where you can ask questions or let them map out an itinerary of "must-sees" based on your time and physical abilities. There are also multimedia exhibits, Wi-Fi, books, maps, backcountry camping permits for sale, and the Bryce Canyon Natural History Association gift shop, whose proceeds help to support park programs and conversation. ⊠ *Hwy. 63* ☎ *435/834–5322* ⊕ *www.nps.gov/brca.*

 Restaurants

★ Bryce Canyon Lodge Restaurant
$$$ | AMERICAN | With a high-beam ceiling, tall windows, and a massive stone fireplace, the dining room at this historic lodge set among towering pines abounds with rustic western charm. The kitchen serves three meals a day (reservations aren't accepted, so be prepared for a wait), and the dishes—highlights of which include buffalo sirloin steak, burgundy-braised bison stew, and almond-and-panko-crusted trout—feature organic or sustainable ingredients whenever possible. **Known for:** good selection of local craft beers; delicious desserts, including fudge brownie sundae and six-layer carrot cake; hearty breakfasts. $ *Average main: $28* ⊠ *Off Hwy. 63* ☎ *435/834–8700* ⊕ *www.brycecanyonforever.com/dining* ☉ *Closed early Nov.–late Mar.*

Valhalla Pizzeria & Coffee Shop
$ | PIZZA | FAMILY | A quick and casual 40-seat eatery across the parking lot from Bryce Canyon Lodge, this pizzeria and coffee shop is a good bet for an inexpensive meal, especially when the lodge dining room is too crowded. Coffee shop choices include an espresso bar, housemade pastries, and fresh fruit, or kick back on the tranquil patio in the evening and enjoy fresh pizza or salad. **Known for:** convenient and casual; decent beer and wine selection; filling pizzas. $ *Average main: $13* ⊠ *Off Hwy. 63* ☎ *435/834–8709* ⊕ *www.brycecanyonforever.com/pizza* ☉ *Closed mid-Sept.–mid-May.*

 Hotels

★ Bryce Canyon Lodge
$$$ | HOTEL | This historic, rugged stone-and-wood lodge close to the amphitheater's rim offers western-style rooms with semi-private balconies or porches in two motel buildings, suites in the historic inn, and cozy, beautifully designed lodgepole pine–and–stone cabins, some with cathedral ceilings and gas fireplaces. **Pros:** close proximity to canyon rim and trails; lodge is steeped in history and has loads of personality; cabins have fireplaces and exude rustic charm. **Cons:** closed in winter; books up fast; no TVs or air-conditioning. $ *Rooms from: $223* ⊠ *Off Hwy. 63* ☎ *435/834–8700, 877/386–4383* ⊕ *www.brycecanyonforever.com* ☉ *Closed Jan.–early Mar.* ↪ *113 rooms* ⊠ *No meals.*

Shopping

Bryce Canyon Lodge Gift Shop
CONVENIENCE/GENERAL STORES | Here you can buy Native American and Southwestern crafts such as pottery and jewelry, T-shirts, jackets, dolls, and books. ⊠ *Bryce Canyon Lodge, Hwy. 63, 2 miles south of park entrance* ☎ *435/834–8700* ☉ *Closed mid-Nov.–late Mar.*

Bryce Canyon Pines General Store
CONVENIENCE/GENERAL STORES | Buy groceries, T-shirts, hats, books, postcards, and camping items that you might have left behind, as well as snacks, drinks, juices, and quick meals at this multipurpose facility at Sunrise Point. Picnic tables under pine trees offer a shady break. ⊠ *Bryce Canyon National*

Plants and Wildlife in Bryce Canyon

With elevations approaching 9,000 feet, many of Bryce Canyon's 400 plant species are unlike those you'll see at less lofty places. Look at exposed slopes and you might catch a glimpse of the pygmy pinyon, or the gnarled, 1,000-year-old bristlecone pine. At lower altitudes are the Douglas fir, ponderosa pine, and the quaking aspen, which sit in groves of twinkling leaves. No fewer than three kinds of sagebrush—big, black, and fringed—grow here, as well as the blue columbine.

Mule deer and chipmunks are common companions on the trails and are used to human presence. You might also catch a glimpse of the endangered Utah prairie dog. Give them a wide berth; they may be cute, but they bite (and it's illegal to approach or feed wildlife in any national park). Other animals include elk, black-tailed jackrabbits, and the desert cottontail. More than 210 species of bird live in the park or pass through as a migratory stop. Bird-watchers are often rewarded handsomely for their vigilance: eagles, peregrine falcons, and even the rare California condor have all been spotted in the park.

Park ⊹ About ½ mile off the main park road, 2 miles south of the park entrance ☎ 435/834–5441.

Visitor Center Bookshop
BOOKS/STATIONERY | The Bryce Canyon Natural History Association runs a bookstore inside the park visitor center where you can find maps, books, videos, stuffed animals, CDs, clothing, and postcards. ⊠ Bryce Canyon Visitor Center, 1 mile south of park entrance ☎ 435/834–4783, 888/362–2642 ⊕ www.nps.gov/brca.

Bryce Canyon South

Heading south from park entrance, this is as far as you can drive on the 18-mile park road. The area includes a short, easy trail through the forest as well as a longer difficult trail. The viewpoints at Rainbow and Yovimpa look to the north and south, so you'll want to visit both. Many visitors like to drive to this part of the park first, then drive back north.

◉ Sights

SCENIC DRIVES AND OVERLOOKS
★ Rainbow and Yovimpa Points
VIEWPOINT | Separated by less than half a mile, Rainbow and Yovimpa points offer two fine panoramas facing opposite directions. Rainbow Point's best view is to the north overlooking the southern rim of the amphitheater and giving a glimpse of Grand Staircase–Escalante National Monument; Yovimpa Point's vista spreads out to the south. On an especially clear day you can see all the way to Arizona's highest point, Humphrey's Peak 150 miles away. Yovimpa Point also has a shady and quiet picnic area with tables and restrooms. You can hike between them on the easy Bristlecone Loop Trail or tackle the more strenuous 9-mile Riggs Spring Loop Trail, which passes the tallest point in the park. This is the outermost auto stop on the main road, so visitors often drive here first and make it their starting point, then work their way back to the park entrance. ⊠ End of main park road, 18 miles south of park entrance.

Yovimpa Point looks to the south of Bryce Canyon, offering a spectacular view.

TRAILS

Bristlecone Loop Trail

TRAIL | This 1-mile trail with a modest 200 feet of elevation gain lets you see the park from its highest points of more than 9,000 feet, alternating between spruce and fir forest and wide-open vistas out over Grand Staircase–Escalante National Monument and beyond. You might see yellow-bellied marmots and dusky grouse, critters not found at lower elevations in the park. Plan on 45 minutes to an hour. *Easy.* ⊠ *Bryce Canyon National Park* ✛ *Trailhead: at Rainbow Point parking lot, 18 miles south of park entrance.*

Riggs Spring Loop Trail

TRAIL | One of the park's two true backpacker's trails, this rigorous 9-mile path has an overnight option at the Yovimpa Pass, Riggs Spring, or Corral Hollow campsites. You'll journey past groves of twinkling aspen trees and the eponymous spring close to the campsite. Start at either Yovimpa or Rainbow point and be prepared for 1,500 feet of elevation change. Campers need to check in at the visitor center ahead of time for backcountry permits. *Difficult.* ⊠ *Bryce Canyon National Park* ✛ *Trailheads: at Yovimpa and Rainbow points, 18 miles south of park entrance.*

Activities

Most visitors explore Bryce Canyon by car, but the hiking trails are far more rewarding. At these elevations, you'll have to stop to catch your breath more often if you're used to being closer to sea level. It gets warm in summer but rarely uncomfortably hot, so hiking farther into the depths of the park is not difficult, so long as you don't pick a hike that is beyond your abilities.

BIRD-WATCHING

More than 210 bird species have been identified in Bryce. Violet-green swallows and white-throated swifts are common, as are Steller's jays, American coots, rufous hummingbirds, and mountain bluebirds. Lucky bird-watchers will see golden eagles floating across the skies above the pink rocks of the amphitheater, and experienced birders might spot an osprey nest high in the canyon wall. The best time in the park for avian variety is from May through July.

CAMPING

The two campgrounds in Bryce Canyon National Park fill up fast, especially in summer, and are family-friendly. All are drive-in, except for the handful of backcountry sites that only backpackers and gung-ho day hikers ever see.

North Campground. A cool, shady retreat in a forest of ponderosa pines, this is a great home base for campers visiting Bryce Canyon. You're near the general store, The Lodge, trailheads, and the visitor center. Reservations are accepted for some RV sites; for the rest it's first-come, first-served, and the campground usually fills by early afternoon in July, August, and September. Just be aware that some sites feel crowded and not private. ⊠ *Main park road, ½ mile south of visitor center* ☎ *435/834–5322.*

Sunset Campground. This serene alpine campground is within walking distance of Bryce Canyon Lodge and many trailheads. Most of the 100 or so sites are filled on a first-come, first-served basis, but 20 tent sites can be reserved up to six months in advance. The campground fills by early afternoon in July though September, so secure your campsite before you sightsee. Reservations are required for the group site. As one of the most accessible hiking areas of the park, it can be crowded. ⊠ *Main park road, 2 miles south of visitor center* ☎ *435/834–5322.*

EDUCATIONAL PROGRAMS
RANGER PROGRAMS
Campfire and Auditorium Programs. Bryce Canyon's natural diversity comes alive in the park's North Campground amphitheater, the Visitor Center Theater, or in the Bryce Canyon Lodge Auditorium.

Ranger talks, multimedia programs, and guided walks introduce you to geology, astronomy, wildlife, history, and many other topics related to Bryce Canyon and the West. ⊕ *www.nps.gov/brca/planyourvisit/ranger-programs.htm.*

Geology Talks. Rangers host free 20-minute discussions twice a day about the long geological history of Bryce Canyon. These interesting talks are held at Sunset Point and no reservations are needed. ⊕ *www.nps.gov/brca/planyourvisit/ranger-programs.htm.*

Junior Ranger Program. Kids can sign up to be Junior Rangers at the Bryce Canyon Visitor Center. They have to complete several activities in their free Junior Ranger booklet and attend a ranger program, visit the park museum, or watch the park movie. Allow three to six hours total to earn the park's Junior Ranger badge. Ask a ranger about each day's schedule of events and topics, or look for postings at the visitor center, Bryce Canyon Lodge, and campground bulletin boards. ⊕ *www.nps.gov/brca/learn/kidsyouth/beajuniorranger.htm.*

Telescopes Program. City folk are lucky to see 2,500 stars in their artificially illuminated skies, but out here among the hoodoos you see three times as many. The 90-minute program at the visitor center includes low-key ranger talks on astronomy, followed by telescope viewing (weather permitting). The program is typically offered on Thursday–Saturday nights at 10 pm from Memorial Day through Labor Day weekends and some Saturdays during the rest of the year. Check the visitor center for details. ⊕ *www.nps.gov/brca/planyourvisit/ranger-programs.htm.*

HIKING

To get up close and personal with the park's hoodoos, set aside a half day to hike into the amphitheater. Remember, after you descend below the rim you'll have to get back up. The air gets warmer the lower you go, and the altitude will have you huffing and puffing unless you're very fit. The uneven terrain calls for lace-up shoes on even the well-trodden, high-traffic trails and sturdy hiking boots for the more challenging ones. No below-rim trails are paved. For trail maps, information, and ranger recommendations, stop at the visitor center. Bathrooms are at most trailheads but not down in the amphitheater. ⇨ *For more information on hiking trails, see the Sights sections, above.*

RANGER-LED HIKES
★ **Full Moon Hike**

Rangers lead guided hikes on the nights around each full moon (two per month). You must wear heavy-traction shoes, and reserve a spot on the day of the hike. In peak season the tickets are distributed through a lottery system. Schedules are posted at the visitor center and on the park's website. No flashlights are allowed and children must be at least 8 years old. ⊠ *Bryce Canyon National Park* ⊕ *www. nps.gov/brca/planyourvisit/fullmoonhikes. htm.*

Rim Walk

Join a park ranger for a ½-mile, 75-minute-long stroll along the gorgeous rim of Bryce Canyon starting at the Sunset Point overlook. Reservations are not required for the walk, which is offered twice daily from Memorial Day through Labor Day weekends, then usually daily the rest of the year. Check with the visitor center or the park website for details. ⊠ *Bryce Canyon National Park* ⊕ *www.nps.gov/ brca/planyourvisit/ranger-programs.htm.*

HORSEBACK RIDING

Many of the park's hiking trails were first formed beneath the hooves of cattle wranglers. Today, hikers and riders share the trails. A number of outfitters can set you up with a gentle mount and lead you to the park's best sights. Not only can you cover more ground than you would walking, but equine traffic has the right-of-way at all times. Call ahead to the stables for reservations to find a trip that's right for you, from 90 minutes to all day. The biggest outfitters have more than 100 horses and mules to choose from. People under the age of seven or who weigh more than 220 pounds are prohibited from riding.

Canyon Trail Rides

HORSEBACK RIDING | Descend to the floor of the Bryce Canyon amphitheater via horse or mule—most visitors have no riding experience so don't hesitate to join in. A two-hour ride ambles along the amphitheater floor through the Queen's Garden before returning to Sunrise Point. The half-day expedition follows Peekaboo Loop Trail, winds past the Fairy Castle, and passes the Wall of Windows before returning to Sunrise Point. Two rides a day of each type leave in the morning and early afternoon. There are no rides in winter. ⊠ *Bryce Canyon Lodge, Off Hwy. 63* ☏ *435/679–8665, 435/834–5500 Bryce Canyon reservations* ⊕ *www. canyonrides.com* ☏ *From $65.*

Ruby's Horseback Adventures

HORSEBACK RIDING | **FAMILY** | Ride to the rim of Bryce Canyon, venture through narrow slot canyons in Grand Staircase–Escalante National Monument, or even retrace the trails taken by outlaw Butch Cassidy more than 100 years ago. Rides last from 90 minutes to all day. Kids must be seven or older to ride, in some cases 10. Wagon rides to the rim of Bryce Canyon are available for all ages, as are sleigh rides in winter. ⊠ *Bryce Canyon National Park* ☏ *866/782–0002* ⊕ *www. horserides.net* ☏ *From $68.*

WINTER ACTIVITIES
Ruby's Winter Activities Center

SKIING/SNOWBOARDING | **FAMILY** | This facility grooms miles of private, no-cost trails that connect to the ungroomed trails inside the park. Rental snowshoes, ice skates, and cross-country ski equipment are available. ⊠ *Hwy. 63, 1 mile north* *of park entrance, Bryce Canyon City* ☏ *435/834–5341, 866/866–6616* ⊕ *www. rubysinn.com/winter-activities.*

Nearby Towns

Just a few miles from the visitor center and right on the shuttle route, **Bryce Canyon City** was incorporated in 2007 by the owners of the Ruby's Inn nearly a century after it first began welcoming guests. Though there are less than 200 year-round residents, thousands of tourists stay here each year to explore the adjacent park and partake in events like the town's winter festival.

The small town of **Panguitch** is 25 miles northwest of Bryce Canyon. It has restaurants, motels, gas stations, and trinket shops. You'll find a few more eateries and other businesses in tiny **Hatch,** 15 miles south of Panguitch. Just 10 miles east of the park, little **Tropic** has a handful of noteworthy lodgings and eateries. Continue about 37 miles northeast to reach **Escalante,** a western gateway to the Grand Staircase–Escalante National Monument with several good places to stay and eat. From Interstate 15, **Cedar City** is where you exit to Bryce (it's a 90-minute drive). With a population of 31,200, it's the region's largest city and the home of Southern Utah University and the Utah Shakespeare Festival, which draws theater buffs from all over.

Bryce Canyon City

Right outside the park, this village has several lodging and dining options, shops, gas, tourist attractions, and other helpful amenities for park visitors. The park shuttle bus makes several stops in the town.

Sights

Bryce Wildlife Adventure
MUSEUM | FAMILY | Imagine a zoo frozen in time: this 14,000-square-foot private museum contains more than 1,600 butterflies and 1,000 taxidermy animals in tableaux mimicking actual terrain and animal behavior. The animals and birds come from all parts of the world. An African room has baboons, bush pigs, Cape buffalo, and a lion. There's also a collection of living deer that kids delight in feeding, and ATV and bike rentals for touring scenic Highway 12 and the Paunsaugunt Plateau. ⊠ *1945 W. Hwy. 12, Bryce Canyon City* ☏ *435/834–5555* ⊕ *www.brycewildlifeadventure.com* ⊡ *$8* ⊙ *Closed mid-Nov.–Mar.*

U.S. 89/Utah's Heritage Highway
LOCAL INTEREST | Winding north from the Arizona border all the way to Spanish Fork Canyon, an hour south of Salt Lake City, U.S. 89 is known as the Heritage Highway for its role in shaping Utah history. At its southern end, Kanab (see the Zion National Park chapter) is known as "Little Hollywood," having provided the backdrop for many famous Western movies and TV commercials. The town has since grown considerably into a major recreation hub and a base for visiting Zion, Bryce, and the North Rim of the Grand Canyon. Other towns north along this famous road may not have the same notoriety in these parts, but they do offer eye-popping scenery as well as some lodging and dining options relatively close to Bryce Canyon.

 Restaurants

Bryce Canyon Pines Restaurant
$$ | AMERICAN | Inside the Bryce Canyon Pines Motel, about 6 miles northwest of Bryce Canyon National Park, this down-home, family-friendly roadhouse decorated with Old West photos and

memorabilia serves reliably good stick-to-your-ribs breakfasts, hefty elk burgers, rib-eye steaks, and Utah rainbow trout. But the top draw here is homemade pie, which comes in a vast assortment of flavors, from banana-blueberry cream to boysenberry. **Known for:** delectable pies; friendly staff; plenty of kids' options. $ *Average main: $16* ✉ *Hwy. 12, mile marker 10, Bryce Canyon City* ☎ *435/834–5441* ⊕ *www.brycecanyon-restaurant.com.*

Hotels

Best Western Bryce Canyon Grand Hotel
$$$ | HOTEL | If you appreciate creature comforts but can do without much in the way of local personality, this four-story hotel just outside the park fits the bill—rooms are relatively posh, with comfortable mattresses, pillows, and bedding, spacious bathrooms, and modern appliances, and there's an outdoor pool and pleasant patio. **Pros:** clean, spacious rooms; lots of amenities and activities; short drive or free shuttle ride from Bryce Canyon. **Cons:** no pets allowed; pricey during busy times; standard chain ambience. $ *Rooms from: $220* ✉ *30 N. 100 E, Bryce Canyon City* ☎ *866/866–6634, 435/834–5700* ⊕ *www.brycecanyongrand.com* ⤴ *164 rooms* ⦿| *Free breakfast.*

Best Western Plus Ruby's Inn
$$$ | HOTEL | FAMILY | This bustling Southwestern-themed hotel has expanded over the years to include various wings with rooms that vary widely in terms of size and character. **Pros:** lots of services and amenities; short drive or free shuttle ride into the park; nice indoor pool. **Cons:** can get very busy, especially when the big tour buses roll in; too big for charm or a quiet getaway; uneven quality of restaurants. $ *Rooms from: $190* ✉ *26 S. Main St., Bryce Canyon City* ☎ *435/834–5341, 866/866–6616* ⊕ *www.rubysinn.com* ⤴ *368 rooms* ⦿| *Free breakfast.*

Bryce Canyon Pines
$$ | HOTEL | Most rooms in this motel complex tucked into the woods 6 miles southwest of the park entrance have excellent mountain views. **Pros:** guided horseback rides; outdoor pool and hot tub; lively restaurant famed for homemade pies. **Cons:** thin walls; room quality varies widely; furnishings are a bit dated. $ *Rooms from: $150* ✉ *Hwy. 12, mile marker 10, Bryce Canyon City* ☎ *800/892–7923* ⊕ *www.brycecanyon-motel.com* ⤴ *46 rooms* ⦿| *No meals.*

Shopping

Ruby's General Store
CONVENIENCE/GENERAL STORES | It may not be one of the area's geological wonders, but this giant mercantile center almost has to be seen to be believed. On a busy evening it is bustling with tourists plucking through souvenirs that range from sweatshirts to wind chimes. There is also Western wear, children's toys, a holiday-gift gallery, and groceries. Even the camping equipment is in ample supply. Need a folding stove, sleeping bag, or fishing gear? You will find it at Ruby's. You can also cross Main Street to where this ever-expanding complex has added a line of shops trimmed like an Old West town, complete with candy store and rock shop. ✉ *26 S. Main St., Bryce Canyon National Park* ☎ *435/834–5484.*

Cedar City

 Restaurants

Milt's Stage Stop
$$$ | STEAKHOUSE | Cabin decor, friendly service, and canyon views are the hallmarks of this dinner spot 10-minutes southeast of downtown Cedar City by car. Expect traditional, hearty steak house cuisine: rib-eye steaks, prime rib, and seafood dishes, accompanied by loaded baked potatoes, deep-fried

zucchini, and similar sides. **Known for:** scenic alpine setting; hefty steaks and seafood; chocolate lava cake. $ *Average main: $27* ⊠ *3560 E. Hwy. 14, Cedar City* ☎ *435/586–9344* ⊕ *www.miltsstagestop. com* ⊗ *No lunch.*

Escalante

 Hotels

Circle D Motel

$ | **HOTEL** | Although there's nothing fancy about this low-slung adobe motel on the edge of downtown Escalante, the simple rooms have all the basics you need for a comfortable night or two, including microwaves, fridges, coffeemakers, HDTVs, and individual climate control, and one larger suite can sleep six and has a kitchenette. **Pros:** short walk from downtown businesses; casual restaurant with a pleasant patio; among the lowest rates in the area. **Cons:** standard rooms are small; no pool or gym; no breakfast. $ *Rooms from: $85* ⊠ *475 W. Main St., Escalante* ☎ *435/826–4297* ⊕ *www. escalantecircledmotel.com* ⇋ *22 rooms* ⦾ *No meals.*

CANYONLANDS NATIONAL PARK

Updated by
Stina Sieg

UTAH

⛰ Camping	🛏 Hotels	🏃 Activities	👁 Scenery	👥 Crowds
★★☆☆☆	★★★☆☆	★★★★☆	★★★★☆	★★★★☆

WELCOME TO CANYONLANDS NATIONAL PARK

TOP REASONS TO GO

★ **Endless vistas:** The view from Island in the Sky stretches for miles as you look out over millennia of sculpting by wind and rain.

★ **Seeking solitude:** Needles, an astoundingly beautiful part of the park to explore on foot, sees very few visitors—it can sometimes feel like you have it all to yourself.

★ **Radical rides:** The Cataract Canyon rapids and the White Rim Trail are world-class adventures by boat or bike.

★ **Native American artifacts:** View rock art and Ancestral Pueblo dwellings in the park.

★ **Wonderful wilderness:** Some of the country's most untouched landscapes are within the park's boundaries, and they're worth the extra effort needed to get there.

★ **The night skies:** Far away from city lights, Canyonlands is ideal for stargazing.

1 Island in the Sky. From any of the overlooks here you can see for miles and look down thousands of feet to canyon floors. Chocolate-brown canyons are capped by white rock, and deep-red monuments rise nearby.

2 Needles. Pink, orange, and red rock is layered with white rock and stands in spires and pinnacles around grassy meadows. Extravagantly red mesas and buttes interrupt the horizon as in a picture postcard of the Old West.

3 The Maze. Only the most intrepid adventurers explore this incredibly remote mosaic of rock formations. There's a reason Butch Cassidy hid out here.

4 Horseshoe Canyon. Plan on several hours of dirt-road driving to get here, but the famous rock-art panel "Great Gallery" is a grand reward at the end of a long hike.

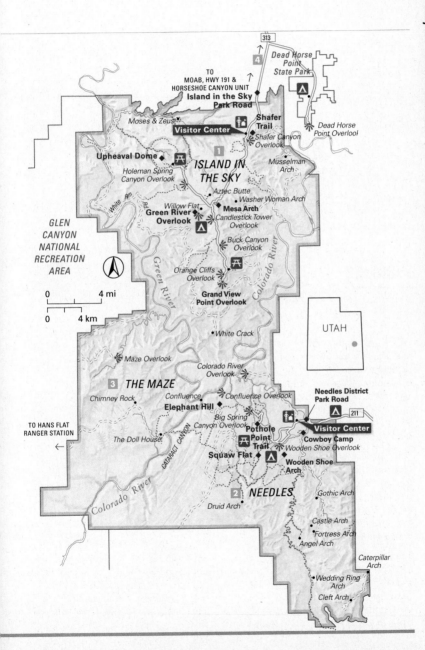

313

Dead Horse
Point State Park

4

TO
MOAB, HWY 191 &
HORSESHOE CANYON UNIT
**Island in the Sky
Park Road**

Moses & Zeus

**Shafer
Trail**

Visitor Center

Shafer Canyon
Overlook

Dead Horse
Point Overlook

Upheaval Dome

*ISLAND IN
THE SKY*

Holeman Spring
Canyon Overlook

Musselman
Arch

White Rim Rd

Aztec Butte

Washer Woman Arch

Willow Flat

**Green River
Overlook**

Mesa Arch

Candlestick Tower
Overlook

Buck Canyon
Overlook

*GLEN
CANYON
NATIONAL
RECREATION
AREA*

Green River

Colorado River

Orange Cliffs
Overlook

**Grand View
Point Overlook**

0 ____ 4 mi

0 ____ 4 km

UTAH

White Crack

Maze Overlook

Colorado River
Overlook

3 *THE MAZE*

Chimney Rock

Confluence

Elephant Hill

Confluence Overlook

**Needles District
Park Road**

211

Visitor Center

TO HANS FLAT
RANGER STATION

Big Spring
Canyon Overlook

**Pothole
Point
Trail**

Cowboy Camp

Wooden Shoe Overlook

The Doll House

CATARACT CANYON

Squaw Flat

**Wooden Shoe
Arch**

2 *NEEDLES*

Gothic Arch

Colorado River

Druid Arch

Castle Arch

Fortress Arch

Angel Arch

Caterpillar
Arch

Wedding Ring
Arch

Cleft Arch

Canyonlands is truly four parks in one, but the majority of visitors drive through the panoramic vistas of Island in the Sky and barely venture anywhere else. Plan a day to explore the Needles district and see the park from the bottom up. Float down the Green and Colorado rivers on a family-friendly rafting trip, or take on the white water in the legendary Cataract Canyon.

Planning

When to Go

Gorgeous weather means that spring and fall are most popular. Canyonlands is seldom crowded, but in spring backpackers and four-wheelers populate the trails and roads. During Easter week, some of the four-wheel-drive trails in the park are used for Jeep Safari, an annual event drawing thousands of visitors to Moab.

The crowds thin out by July as the thermostat reaches 100°F and higher for about four weeks. It's a great time to get out on the Colorado or Green River winding through the park. October can be a little rainy, but the region receives only 8 inches of rain annually.

The well-kept secret is that winter, except during occasional snow storms, can be a great time to tour the park. Crowds are gone, snowcapped mountains stand in the background, and key roads in Island in the Sky and Needles

are well-maintained (although it's wise to check the park website for conditions). Winter here is one of nature's most memorable shows, with red rock dusted white and low-floating clouds partially obscuring canyons and towers.

Getting Here and Around

AIR
Moab is served by tiny Canyonlands Field Airport, which has daily service to Denver on SkyWest/United Airlines and a couple of car rental agencies. The nearest mid-sized airport is Grand Junction Regional Airport in Grand Junction, Colorado, which is approximately 110 miles from Moab and is served by most major airlines.

CAR
Off U.S. 191, Canyonlands' Island in the Sky Visitor Center is 29 miles from Arches National Park and 32 miles from Moab on Highway 313 west of U.S. 191; the Needles District is 80 miles from Moab and reached via Highway 211, 34 miles west of U.S. 191.

AVERAGE HIGH/LOW TEMPERATURES					
JAN.	**FEB.**	**MAR.**	**APR.**	**MAY**	**JUNE**
44/22	52/28	64/35	71/42	82/51	93/60
JULY	**AUG.**	**SEPT.**	**OCT.**	**NOV.**	**DEC.**
100/67	97/66	88/55	74/42	56/30	45/23

Canyonlands in One Day

Your day begins with a choice: Island in the Sky or Needles. If you want expansive vistas looking across southeast Utah's canyons, head for the island, where you stand atop a giant mesa. If you want to walk among Canyonlands' spires and buttes, Needles is your destination. If you have a second or third day in the area, consider contacting an outfitter to take you on a rafting or 4X4 trip.

■TIP→ Before venturing into the park, top off your gas tank, pack a picnic lunch, and stock up on plenty of water and electrolytes.

Island in the Sky

Make your first stop along the main park road at the visitor center to learn about ranger talks or special programs. Next visit **Shafer Canyon Viewpoint**, where a short walk takes you out on a finger of land with views of the canyon over both sides. From here you can see Shafer Trail's treacherous descent as it hugs the canyon walls below.

Then drive to **Mesa Arch**. Grab your camera and water bottle for the short hike out to the arch perched on the cliff's edge. After your excursion, take the spur road to Upheaval Dome, with its picnic spot in the parking lot.

A short walk takes you to the first viewpoint of this crater. If you still have energy, 30 more minutes, and a little sense of adventure, continue to the second overlook.

Retrace your drive to the main park road and continue to **Grand View Point**. Stroll along the edge of the rim, and see how many landmarks you can spot in the distance. White Rim Overlook is the best of the scenic spots, particularly if you're not afraid of heights and venture all the way out to the end of the rocky cliffs (no guardrail here). On the way back to dinner in Moab, spend an hour in Dead Horse Point State Park.

Needles

If you can stay overnight as well, then begin the day by setting up camp at Needles Campground or one of the other wonderful group camping areas in Needles. Then hit the **Joint Trail**, or any of the trails that begin from the campground, and spend the day hiking in the backcountry. Save an hour for the brief but terrific little hike to **Cave Springs**, and be sure to drive to the end of the park road to check out Big Spring Canyon Overlook. Sleep under countless stars.

Before starting a journey to any of Canyonlands' three districts, make sure your gas tank is topped off, as there are no services inside the large park. The Maze is especially remote, 135 miles from Moab, and actually a bit closer (100 miles) to Capitol Reef National Park. In the Island in the Sky District, it's about 12 miles from the entrance station to Grand View Point, with a 5-mile spur to Upheaval Dome. The Needles scenic drive is 10 miles from the entrance station, with two spurs, about 3 miles each. Roads in the Maze—suitable only for high-clearance, four-wheel-drive vehicles—wind for hundreds of miles through the rugged canyons. Within the parks, it's critical that you park only in designated pull-outs or parking areas.

Park Essentials

ACCESSIBILITY
There are currently no trails in Canyonlands accessible to people in wheelchairs, but Grand View Point, Buck Canyon Overlook, and Green River Overlook at Island in the Sky are wheelchair accessible. In Needles, the visitor center, restrooms, Squaw Flat Campground, and Wooden Shoe Overlook are wheelchair accessible. The visitor centers at the Island in the Sky and Needles districts are also accessible, and the park's pit toilets are accessible with some assistance.

PARK FEES AND PERMITS
Admission is $30 per vehicle, $15 per person on foot or bicycle, and $25 per motorcycle, good for seven days. Your Canyonlands pass is good for all the park's districts. There's no entrance fee to the Maze District of Canyonlands. A $55 local park pass grants you admission to both Arches and Canyonlands as well as Natural Bridges and Hovenweep national monuments for one year.

You need a permit for overnight backpacking, four-wheel-drive camping, river trips, and mountain-bike camping. Online reservations can be made four months in advance on the park website (⊕ *www.nps.gov/cany*). Four-wheel-drive day use in Salt, Horse, and Lavender canyons and all motorized vehicles and bicycles on the Elephant Hill and White Rim trails also require a permit, which you can obtain online up to 24 hours before your trip or in person at visitor centers.

PARK HOURS
Canyonlands National Park is open 24 hours a day, seven days a week, year-round. It is in the Mountain time zone.

CELL PHONE RECEPTION
Cell phone reception may be available in some parts of the park, but not reliably so. Public telephones are at the park's visitor centers.

Restaurants

There are no dining facilities in the park, although Needles Outpost campground, a mile from Needles Visitor Center, has a small solar-powered store with snacks and drinks. Moab has a multitude of dining options, and there are a few very casual restaurants in Blanding (in Blanding, restaurants don't serve alcohol and are typically closed Sunday), plus a couple of excellent eateries a bit farther south in Bluff. *Restaurant reviews have been shortened. For full information, visit Fodors.com.*

Hotels

There is no lodging in the park. Most visitors—especially those focused on Island in the Sky—stay in Moab or perhaps Green River, but the small towns of Blanding and Bluff—which have a smattering of motels and inns—are also convenient for exploring the Needles District. *Hotel reviews have been shortened. For full information, visit Fodors.com.*

Tours

Redtail Air Adventures
TOUR—SPORTS | This company's daily, regional tours give you an eagle's-eye view of the park, and you'll walk away with new respect and understanding of the word "wilderness." The Canyonlands Tour, one of several flightseeing options, lasts for one hour. A two-person

Plants and Wildlife in Canyonlands

Wildlife is not the attraction in Canyonlands, as many of the creatures sleep during the heat of the day. On the bright side, there are fewer people and less traffic to scare the animals away. Cool mornings and evenings are the best time to spot them, especially in summer when the heat keeps them in cool, shady areas. Mule deer are nearly always seen along the roadway as you enter the Needles District, and you'll no doubt

see jackrabbits and small rodents darting across the roadway. Approximately 350 bighorn sheep populate the park. If you happen upon one of these regal animals, do not approach it even if it is alone, as bighorn sheep are skittish by nature and easily stressed. Also, report your sighting to a ranger, and note that some areas of the park are closed May–August, which is bighorn sheep lambing season.

minimum applies. ⊠ *Canyonlands Field Airport, 94 W. Aviation Way, Moab ✛ Off U.S. 191* ☎ *435/259–7421* ⊕ *flyredtail. com* ✈ *From $184 per person.*

Visitor Information

Stop by the **Island in the Sky Visitor Center** or **Needles District Visitor Center** for restrooms and water (water is seasonal at Island in the Sky, but there's no food service or general store in either section). In addition, the remote **Hans Glat Ranger Station** in the Maze has a pit toilet but no water or food.

PARK CONTACT INFORMATION Can-yonlands National Park. ☎ *435/719–2313* ⊕ *www.nps.gov/cany.*

Island in the Sky

Standing at one of the overlooks at Island in the Sky, it's hard to fully take in what looks like an oil painting a thousand feet below. Rivers and rain have eroded the desert floor for millennia, creating mesas, towers, and the park's famously deep canyons, all with an earthy red hue. While the view alone is worth the trip,

getting onto one of the district's hiking trails or four-wheel roads will get you up close with its rough beauty. While it's still a shade over 30 miles from Moab, this is the most accessible—and far most visited—section of the park.

Sights

SCENIC DRIVES
Island in the Sky Park Road
SCENIC DRIVE | This 12-mile-long main road inside the park is bisected by a 5-mile side road to the Upheaval Dome area. To enjoy dramatic views, including the Green and Colorado river basins, stop at the overlooks and take the short walks. Once you get to the park, allow at least two hours—and ideally four—to explore. ⊠ *Island in the Sky.*

SCENIC STOPS
Green River Overlook
VIEWPOINT | From the road it's just 100 yards to this stunning view of the Green River to the south and west. It's not far from Island in the Sky (Willow Flat) campground. ⊠ *About 1 mile off Upheaval Dome Rd., Island in the Sky ✛ 7 miles from visitor center.*

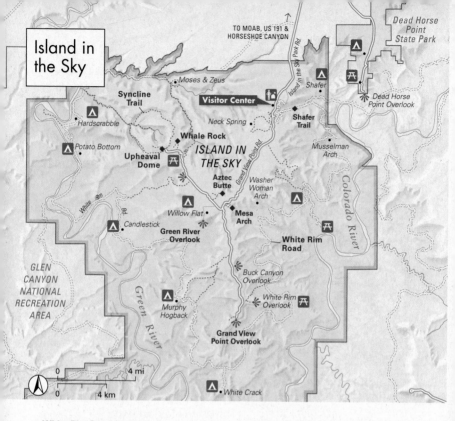

White Rim Overlook Trail

VIEWPOINT | The cliffs fall away on three sides at the end of this 1-mile level hike until you get a dramatic view of the White Rim and Monument Basin. There are restrooms at the trailhead. ⊠ *Grand View Point, Island in the Sky.*

TRAILS

Aztec Butte Trail

TRAIL | The highlight of the 2-mile round-trip hike is the chance to see Ancestral Pueblo granaries. The view into Taylor Canyon is also nice. *Moderate.* ⊠ *Island in the Sky ✛ Trailhead: Upheaval Dome Rd., about 7 miles from visitor center.*

★ Grand View Point Trail

TRAIL | This 360-degree view is the main event for many visitors to Island in the Sky. Look down on the deep canyons of the Colorado and Green rivers, which have been carved by water and erosion over the millennia. Many people just stop at the paved overlook and drive on, but you'll gain breathtaking perspective by strolling along this 2-mile round-trip, flat cliffside trail. On a clear day you can see up to 100 miles to the Maze and Needles districts of the park and each of Utah's major laccolithic mountain ranges: the Henrys, Abajos, and La Sals. *Easy.* ⊠ *End of main park road, Island in the Sky ✛ 12 miles from visitor center.*

★ Mesa Arch Trail

TRAIL | If you don't have time for the 2,000 arches in nearby Arches National Park, you should take the easy, ½-mile round-trip walk to Mesa Arch. After the overlooks this is the most popular trail in the park. The arch is above a cliff that drops 800 feet to the canyon bottom. Through the arch, views of Washerwoman Arch and surrounding buttes, spires, and canyons make this a favorite photo opportunity. ⊠ *Off main park road, Island in the Sky* ✛ *6 miles from visitor center.*

Shafer Trail

TRAIL | This rough trek that leads to the 100-mile White Rim Road was probably first established by ancient Native Americans, but in the early 1900s ranchers used it to drive cattle into the canyon. Originally narrow and rugged, it was upgraded during the uranium boom, when miners hauled ore by truck from the canyon floor. Check out the road's winding route down canyon walls from Shafer Canyon Overlook before you drive it to see why it's mostly used by daring four-wheelers and energetic mountain bikers. Off the main road, less than 1 mile from the park entrance, it descends 1,400 feet to the White Rim. Check with the visitor center about road conditions before driving the Shafer Trail. It's often impassable after rain or snow. ⊠ *Island in the Sky.*

★ Upheaval Dome Trail

TRAIL | This mysterious crater is one of the wonders of Island in the Sky. Some geologists believe it's an eroded salt dome, but others think it was made by a meteorite. Either way, it's worth the steep hike to see it and decide for yourself. The moderate hike to the first overlook is about a ½-mile; energetic visitors can continue another ½-mile to the second overlook for an even better perspective. The trail is steeper and rougher after the first overlook. Round-trip to the second overlook is 2 miles. The trailhead has restrooms and a picnic area. *Moderate.* ⊠ *End of Upheaval Dome Rd., Island in the Sky* ✛ *11 miles from visitor center.*

Whale Rock Trail

TRAIL | If you've been hankering to walk across some of that pavement-smooth stuff they call slickrock, the hike to Whale Rock will make your feet happy. This 1-mile round-trip adventure, which culminates with a tough final 100-foot climb and features some potentially dangerous dropoffs, takes you to the very top of the whale's back. Once you get there, you are rewarded with great views of Upheaval Dome and Trail Canyon. *Moderate.* ⊠ *Island in the Sky* ✛ *Trailhead: Upheaval Dome Rd., 10 miles from visitor center.*

VISITOR CENTER

★ Island in the Sky Visitor Center

INFO CENTER | The gateway to the world-famous White Rim Trail, this visitor center 21 miles from U.S. 191 draws a mix of mountain bikers, hikers, and tourists. Enjoy the orientation film, then browse the bookstore for information about the region. Exhibits help explain animal adaptations as well as some of the history of the park. Check the website or at the center for a daily schedule of ranger-led programs. ⊠ *Off Hwy. 313, Island in the Sky* ☎ *435/259–4712* ◷ *Closed late Dec.–early Mar.*

Needles

Lower in elevation than Island in the Sky, Needles is more about on-the-ground exploration than far-off vistas, but it's an especially good area for long-distance hiking, mountain biking, and four-wheel driving. The district is named for its massive sandstone spires, with hundreds of the formations poking up toward the sky. There are also several striking examples of Native American rock art here, well worth the hikes to reach them. With relatively few visitors, Needles makes for a quiet place to set up camp and recharge for a few days before returning to busy nearby Moab.

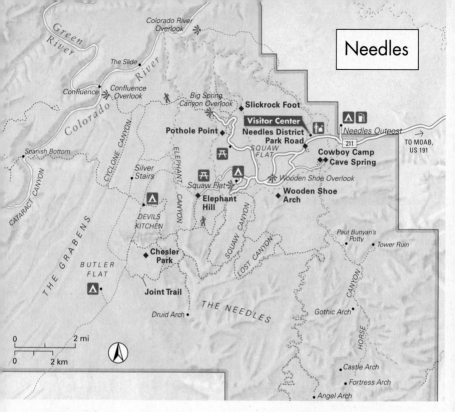

Needles

Sights

HISTORIC SIGHTS

Cowboy Camp

HISTORIC SITE | FAMILY | This fascinating stop on the 0.6-mile round-trip **Cave Spring Trail** is an authentic example of cowboy life more than a century ago. You do not need to complete the entire trail (which includes two short ladders and some rocky hiking) to see the 19th-century artifacts at Cowboy Camp. ⊠ *End of Cave Springs Rd., Needles ⊹ 2.3 miles from visitor center.*

SCENIC DRIVES

Needles District Park Road

SCENIC DRIVE | You'll feel like you've driven into a Hollywood Western as you roll along the park road in the Needles District. Red mesas and buttes rise against the horizon, blue mountain ranges interrupt the rangelands, and the colorful red-and-white needles stand like soldiers on the far side of grassy meadows. Definitely hop out of the car at a few of the marked roadside stops, including both overlooks at Pothole Point. Allow at least two hours in this less-traveled section of the park. ⊠ *Needles.*

SCENIC STOPS

Needles District Picnic Area

VIEWPOINT | The most convenient picnic spot in the Needles District is a sunny location on the way to Big Spring Canyon Overlook. There are picnic tables, but no other amenities. ⊠ *Needles ⊹ Main park road, 5 miles west of visitor center.*

Wooden Shoe Arch Overlook

VIEWPOINT | FAMILY | Kids enjoy looking for the tiny window in the rock that looks like a wooden shoe with a turned-up toe. If you can't find it on your own, there's a marker to help you. ⊠ *Off main park road, Needles ✛ 2 miles from visitor center.*

TRAILS

★ Cave Spring Trail

TRAIL | One of the best, most interesting trails in the park takes you past a historic cowboy camp, precontact rock art, and great views. Two wooden ladders and one short, steep stretch may make this a little daunting for the extremely young or old, but it's also a short hike (0.6 mile round-trip), features some shade, and has many notable features. *Moderate.* ⊠ *Needles ✛ Trailhead: end of Cave Springs Rd., 2.3 miles from visitor center.*

★ Joint Trail

TRAIL | Part of the Chesler Park Loop, this trail follows a series of deep, narrow fractures in the rock. A shady spot in summer, it will give you good views of the Needles formations for which the district is named. The loop travels briefly along a four-wheel-drive road and is 11 miles round-trip; allow at least five hours to complete it. *Difficult.* ⊠ *Needles ✛ Trailhead: Elephant Hill parking lot, 6 miles from visitor center.*

Pothole Point Trail

TRAIL | Microscopic creatures lie dormant in pools that fill only after rare rainstorms. When the rains do come, some eggs hatch within hours and life becomes visible. If you're lucky, you'll hit Pothole Point after a storm. The dramatic views of the Needles and Six Shooter Peak make this easy, 0.6-mile round-trip worthwhile. Plan for about 45 minutes. There's no shade, so wear a hat and take plenty of water. ⊠ *Off main road, Needles ✛ 5 miles from visitor center.*

Slickrock Trail

TRAIL | Wear a hat and carry plenty of water if you're on this trail—you won't find any shade along the 2.4-mile round-trip trek. This is the rare frontcountry site where you might spot one of the few remaining native herds of bighorn

sheep in the national park system. Nice panoramic views. *Easy.* ⊠ *Needles ✛ Trailhead: main park road, 6 miles from visitor center.*

VISITOR CENTER

Needles District Visitor Center

INFO CENTER | This gorgeous building is 34 miles from U.S. 191 via Highway 211, near the park entrance. Needles is remote, so it's worth stopping to inquire about road, weather, and park conditions. You can also watch the interesting orientation film, refill water bottles, and get books, trail maps, and other information. ⊠ *Off Hwy. 211, Needles* ☎ *435/259–4711* ⊘ *Closed late Nov.–early Mar.*

Maze

The most remote district of the park, the Maze is hours away from any town and is accessible only via high-clearance, four-wheel-drive vehicles. A trip here should not be taken lightly. Many of the hikes are considered some of the most dangerous in the world, and self-sufficiency is critical. But the few who do choose to visit this wild tangle of rock and desert are handsomely rewarded with unforgettable views and a silent solitude that's hard to find anywhere else. Plan to spend at least several days here, and bring all the water, food, and gas you'll need.

Sights

VISITOR CENTER

Hans Flat Ranger Station

INFO CENTER | Only experienced and intrepid visitors will likely ever visit this remote outpost—on a dirt road 46 miles east of Highway 24 in Hanksville. The office is a trove of books, maps, and other documents about the unforgiving Maze District of Canyonlands, but rangers will strongly dissuade any inexperienced off-road drivers and backpackers to proceed into this truly rugged wilderness. There's a pit toilet, but no water, food, or services of any kind. If you're headed for the backcountry, permits cost $30 per group for up to 14 days. Rangers offer guided hikes in Horseshoe Canyon on most weekends in spring and fall. ■TIP→ **Call the ranger station for road conditions leading to Horseshoe Canyon/ Hans Flat, as rain can make travel difficult.** ⊠ *Jct. of Recreation Rds. 777 and 633, Maze* ☎ *435/259–2652.*

Horseshoe Canyon

Remote Horseshoe Canyon is not contiguous with the rest of Canyon-lands National Park. Added to the park in 1971, it has what may be America's most significant surviving examples of rock art. While the canyon can usually be accessed by two-wheel drive vehicles via a graded dirt road, it's still 2½ hours from Moab. And the road conditions can change abruptly, so visitors without a four-wheel drive vehicle should always consult the park's road conditions hotline before departing. Rangers lead hikes here in the spring and fall.

Sights

Horseshoe Canyon Trail

TRAIL | This remote region of the park is accessible by dirt road, and only in good weather. Park at the lip of the canyon and hike 7 miles round trip to the Great Gallery, considered by some to be the most significant rock-art panel in North America. Ghostly life-size figures in the Barrier Canyon style populate the amazing panel. The hike is moderately strenuous, with a 700-foot descent. Allow at least six hours for the trip and take a gallon of water per person. There's no camping allowed in the canyon, although you can camp on top near the parking lot. *Difficult.* ■TIP→ **Call Hans Flat Ranger Station before heading out, because rain can make the access road a muddy mess.** ⊠ *Horseshoe Canyon* ⊕ *Trailhead: 32 miles east of Hwy. 24.*

Activities

BIKING

Mountain bikers from all over the world like to brag that they've conquered the 100 miles of White Rim Road. The trail's fame is well deserved: it traverses steep roads, broken rock, and dramatic ledges, as well as long stretches that wind through the canyons and look down onto others. If you're biking White Rim without an outfitter, you'll need careful planning, vehicle support, and much sought-after backcountry reservations. Permits are available no more than four months, and no less than two days, prior to permit start date. There is a 15-person, three-vehicle limit for groups. Day-use permits are also required and can be obtained at the Island in the Sky visitor center or reserved 24 hours in advance through the park's website. Follow the turn-off about 1 mile from the entrance, then 11 miles further along Shafer Trail in Island in the Sky.

In addition to the company listed below, **Rim Tours** and **Western Spirit Cycling Adventures** offer tours in both Arches and Canyonlands.

Magpie Cycling

BICYCLING | Professional guides and mountain biking instructors lead groups (or lone riders) on daylong and multiday bike trips exploring the Moab region's most memorable terrain, including the White Rim, Needles, and the Maze. If you need to rent a bike, Magpie can meet you at its preferred shop, Poison Spider Bicycles (☎ *800/635–1792* ⊕ *poisonspiderbicycles.com*). ⊠ *Moab* ☎ *435/259–4464* ⊕ *www.magpiecycling. com* 🚲 *Day tours from $150, multiday from $875.*

BOATING AND RAFTING

In Labyrinth Canyon, north of the park boundary, and in Stillwater Canyon, in the Island in the Sky District, the river is quiet and calm and there's plenty of shoreside camping. The Island in the Sky leg of the Colorado River, from Moab to its confluence with the Green River and downstream a few more miles to Spanish Bottom, is ideal for both canoeing and for rides with an outfitter in a large, stable jet boat. If you want to take a self-guided flat-water float trip in the park you must obtain a $30 permit, which you have to request by mail or fax. Make your upstream travel arrangements with a shuttle company before you request a permit. For permits, contact the reservation office at park headquarters (☎ 435/259–4351).

Below Spanish Bottom, about 64 miles downstream from Moab, 49 miles from the Potash Road ramp, and 4 miles south of the confluence, the Colorado churns into the first rapids of legendary Cataract Canyon. Home of some of the best white water in the United States, this piece of river between the Maze and the Needles districts rivals the Grand Canyon stretch of the Colorado River for adventure. During spring melt-off these rapids can rise to staggering heights and deliver heart-stopping excitement. The canyon cuts through the very heart of Canyonlands, where you can see this amazing wilderness area in its most pristine form. The water calms down a bit in summer. Outfitters will take you for the ride of your life in this wild canyon, where the river drops more steeply than anywhere else on the Colorado River (in ¾ mile, it drops 39 feet). You can join an expedition lasting anywhere from one to six days, or you can purchase a $20 permit for a self-guided trip from park headquarters.

Oars

WHITE-WATER RAFTING | FAMILY | This well-regarded outfitter can take you for several days of rafting the Colorado, Green, and San Juan rivers. Hiking/interpretive trips are available in Canyonlands and Arches. ✉ *Moab* ☎ *435/259–5865, 800/346–6277* ⊕ *www.oars.com/utah* ✎ *From $109.*

Sheri Griffith Expeditions

BOATING | FAMILY | In addition to trips through the white water of Cataract, Westwater, and Desolation canyons, on the Colorado and Green rivers, this company also offers specialty expeditions for women, writers, photographers, and families. One of their more luxurious expeditions features dinners cooked by a professional chef and served on linen-covered tables. Cots and other sleeping amenities also make roughing it a little more comfortable. ✉ *2231 S. U.S. 191, Moab* ☎ *435/259–8229, 800/332–2439* ⊕ *www.griffithexp.com* ✎ *From $185.*

CAMPING

Canyonlands campgrounds are some of the most beautiful in the national park system. At the Needles District, campers will enjoy fairly private campsites tucked against red rock walls and dotted with pinyon and juniper trees. At Island in the Sky, starry nights and spectacular vistas make the small campground an intimate treasure. Hookups are not available in either of the park's campgrounds; however, some sites are long enough to accommodate units up to 28 feet long.

Needles Campground. The defining features of the camp sites at Squaw Flat are house-size red rock formations, which provide some shade, offer privacy from adjacent campers, and make this one of the more unique campgrounds in the national park system. ✉ *Off main road, about 3 miles from park entrance, Needles* ☎ *435/259–4711.*

Willow Flat Campground. From this little campground on a mesa top, you can walk to spectacular views of the Green River. Most sites have a bit of shade from juniper trees. ✉ *Off main park road, about 7 miles from park entrance, Island in the Sky* ☎ *435/259–4712.*

EDUCATIONAL PROGRAMS

Just like borrowing a book from a library, kids can check out an **Explorer Pack** filled with tools for learning. The sturdy backpack includes binoculars, a magnifying glass, and a three-ring binder full of activities. These are available at Needles and Island in the Sky visitor centers.

Kids of all ages can also pick up a **Junior Ranger** booklet at the visitor centers. It's full of puzzles, word games, and fun facts about the park and its wildlife. To earn the Junior Ranger badge, they must complete several activities in the booklet.

For more information on current schedules and locations of park programs, contact the visitor centers or check the bulletin boards throughout the park. Programs change periodically and may sometimes be canceled because of limited staffing.

Grand View Point Overlook Talk

ORIENTATION | FAMILY | Spring through fall, rangers present interpretive programs at Grand View Point about the geology that created Utah's Canyonlands. ⊠ *Grand View Point, Island in the Sky.*

FOUR-WHEELING

Nearly 200 miles of challenging backcountry roads lead to campsites, trailheads, and natural and cultural features in Canyonlands. All of the roads require high-clearance, four-wheel-drive vehicles, and many are inappropriate for inexperienced drivers. The 100-mile White Rim Trail, for example, can be extremely challenging, so make sure that your four-wheel-drive skills are well honed and that you are capable of making basic vehicle repairs. Carry at least one full-size spare tire, extra gas, extra water, a shovel, a high-lift jack, and—October through April—chains for all four tires. Double-check to see that your vehicle is in top-notch condition, for you definitely don't want to break down in the interior of the park: towing expenses can exceed $1,000.

Day-use permits, available at the park visitor centers or 24 hours in advance through the park website, are required for motorized and bicycle trips on the Elephant Hill and White Rim trails. For overnight four-wheeling trips, you must purchase a $30 permit, which you can reserve no more than four months and no fewer than two days in advance by contacting the Backcountry Reservations Office (☎ *435/259–4351*). Cyclists share all roads, so be aware and cautious of their presence. Vehicular traffic traveling uphill has the right-of-way. Check at the visitor center for current road conditions before taking off into the backcountry. You must carry a washable, reusable toilet with you in the Maze District and carry out all waste.

HIKING

At Canyonlands National Park you can immerse yourself in the intoxicating colors, smells, and textures of the desert. △ **Make sure to bring water and electrolytes, as dehydration is the number-one cause of search-and-rescue calls here.**

Island in the Sky has several easy and moderate hikes that are popular with day-trippers, including the **Aztec Butte Trail, Grand View Point Trail, Upheaval Dome Trail,** and **Whale Rock Trail.** If you're up for a strenuous day of hiking, try the 8-mile **Syncline Loop Trail,** which follows the canyons around Upheaval Dome.

Both the **Cave Spring Trail** and **Slickrock Trail** are popular with day-trippers to the **Needles** section of Canyonlands, suitable for most hikers young or old, though the former requires one to climb two wooden ladders. Others are considerably more difficult and require experience.

Chesler Park is a grassy meadow dotted with spires and enclosed by a circular wall of colorful "needles." One of Canyonlands' more popular trails, the **Chesler Viewpoint Trail,** leads through the area to the famous **Joint Trail,** one of the park's star attractions, though a moderately difficult hike.

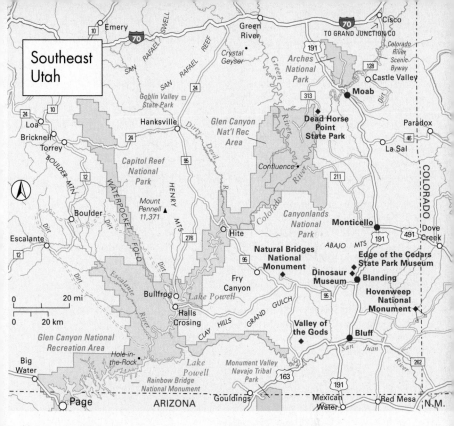

ROCK CLIMBING

Canyonlands and the surrounding area draw climbers from all over the world. Permits are not required, but because of the park's sensitive archaeological nature it's imperative that you stop at the visitor center to pick up regulations pertaining to the park's cultural resources. Popular climbing routes include Moses and Zeus towers in Taylor Canyon, and Monster Tower and Washerwoman Tower on the White Rim Road. Like most routes in Canyonlands, these climbs are for experienced climbers only. Just outside the Needles District, Indian Creek is one of the country's best traditional climbing areas.

Nearby Towns

Moab, the major gateway to both Arches and Canyonlands national parks, abounds with outfitters, shops, restaurants, and lodging options—see the Arches National Park chapter for more on this bustling, free-spirited hub of outdoor recreation. A handful of smaller communities south of Moab along U.S. 191 are closer than Moab to the Needles District and contain a smattering of amenities.

Roughly 55 miles south of Moab, **Monticello** is less than an hour from the Needles District and lies at 7,000 feet elevation, making it a cool summer refuge from desert heat. In winter it gets downright cold and sometimes receives heavy snow; the Abajo Mountains rise to 11,360 feet to the west of town. Monticello has a few basic motels and restaurants and is a good halfway point between Moab and Colorado's Mesa Verde National Park. Tiny **Blanding,** 20 miles south of Monticello, has a few bare-bones motels and prides itself on old-fashioned conservative values—it's a dry town, so alcohol sales are prohibited. It's the gateway to Edge of the Cedars State Park, Hovenweep National Monument, Natural Bridges Natural Monument, Grand Gulch, and the eastern end of Lake Powell. About 25 miles south of Blanding, tiny **Bluff** has a couple of the region's most appealing lodging and dining options and is an excellent gateway for Hovenweep, exploring the San Juan River, and visiting Monument Valley and the northern edge of the Navajo Nation.

Chapter 10

CAPITOL REEF
NATIONAL PARK

Updated by
Shelley Arenas

UTAH

⛺ **Camping**
★★☆☆☆

🛏 **Hotels**
★★☆☆☆

🏃 **Activities**
★★★★☆

👁 **Scenery**
★★★★★

🎏 **Crowds**
★★☆☆☆

WELCOME TO CAPITOL REEF NATIONAL PARK

TOP REASONS TO GO

★ **The Waterpocket Fold:** See an excellent example of a monocline—a fold in the Earth's crust with one very steep side in an area that is otherwise horizontal. This one's almost 100 miles long.

★ **Fewer crowds:** Although visitation has nearly doubled (to more than 1.2 million per year) since 2011, Capitol Reef is less crowded than nearby parks, such as Zion and Bryce Canyon.

★ **Fresh fruit:** Pick apples, pears, apricots, and peaches in season at the pioneer-planted orchards at historic Fruita. These trees still produce plenty of fruit.

★ **Rock art:** View pictographs and petroglyphs left by Native Americans who lived in this area from AD 300 to 1300.

★ **Pioneer artifacts:** Buy tools and utensils similar to those used by Mormon pioneers at the Gifford Homestead.

1 Fruita. This historic pioneer village is at the heart of what most people see of Capitol Reef. The one and only park visitor center nearby is the place to get travel and weather information and maps. Scenic Drive, through Capitol Gorge, provides a view of the Golden Throne.

2 Scenic Drive. Winding 8 miles through the park, this aptly named road is the best way to get an overview of Capitol Reef's highlights, and it's the most accessible for all vehicles. It takes about 90 minutes to drive to the end and back, but you'll want to take your time with so many interesting sights to see along the way.

3 Cathedral Valley. The views are stunning and the silence deafening in the park's remote northern section. High-clearance vehicles are required, as is crossing the Fremont River. Driving in this valley is next to impossible when the Cathedral Valley Road is wet, so ask at the visitor center about current weather and road conditions.

4 Muley Twist Canyon. At the southern reaches of the park, this canyon is accessed via Notom-Bullfrog Road from the north, and Burr Trail Road from the west and southeast. High-clearance vehicles are required for Upper Muley and Strike Valley Overlook.

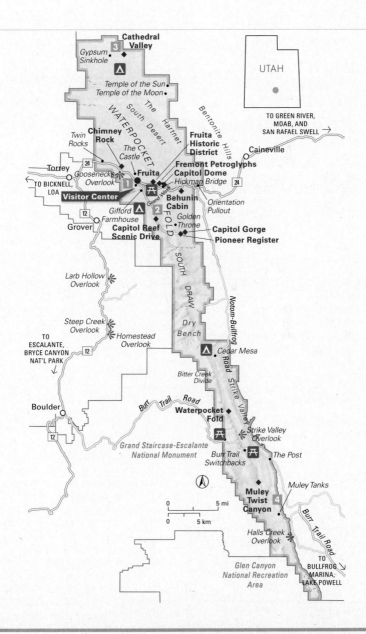

Capitol Reef National Park is a natural kaleidoscopic feast for the eyes, with colors more dramatic than anywhere else in the West. The Moenkopi rock formation is a rich, red-chocolate hue; deep blue-green juniper and pinyon stand out against it. Sunset brings out the colors in an explosion of copper, platinum, and orange, then dusk turns the cliffs purple and blue.

The park, established in 1971, preserves the Waterpocket Fold, a giant wrinkle in the earth that extends 100 miles between Thousand Lake Mountain and Lake Powell. When you climb high onto the rocks or into the mountains, you can see this remarkable geologic wonder and the jumble of colorful cliffs, massive domes, soaring spires, and twisting canyons that surround it. It's no wonder early pioneers called this part of the country the "land of the sleeping rainbow."

Beyond incredible sights, the fragrance of pine and sage rises from the earth, and canyon wrens serenade you as you sit by the water. Flowing across the heart of Capitol Reef is the Fremont River, a narrow little creek that can turn into a swollen, raging torrent during desert flash floods. The river sustains cottonwoods, wildlife, and verdant valleys rich with fruit. During the harvest, your sensory experience is complete when you bite into a perfect ripe peach or apple from the park's orchards. Your soul, too, will be gratified here. You can walk the trails in relative solitude and—except during busier periods—enjoy the beauty without confronting significant crowds on the roads or paths. All around you are signs of those who came before: ancient Native Americans of the Fremont culture, Mormon pioneers who settled the land, and other courageous explorers who traveled the canyons.

Planning

When to Go

Spring and early summer are the most bustling seasons. Some folks clear out in the midsummer heat, and then return for the apple harvest and crisp temperatures of autumn. Although the park is less crowded than nearby Zion, Bryce Canyon, and Arches, visitation has increased dramatically in recent years, and the campground fills quickly (and is by reservation only). Annual rainfall is scant, but when it does rain, flash floods can wipe out park roads. Snowfall is usually light. Sudden, short-lived snowstorms—and thunderstorms—are not uncommon in the spring.

Capitol Reef in One Day

Pack a picnic lunch, snacks, and cold drinks to take with you (there are no restaurants in the park). As you enter the park from the west, look to your left for Chimney Rock; in a landscape of spires, cliffs, and knobs, this deep-red landmark is unmistakable. Start your journey at the **visitor center**, where you can study a three-dimensional map of the area, peruse exhibits, watch a short film, and browse the many books and maps related to the park. Then head for Scenic Drive, stopping at the **Fruita Historic District** to see some of the sites associated with the park's Mormon history. Visit **Gifford Homestead** to browse the gift shop. Enjoy that lunch you packed at picnic tables on rolling green lawns lining both sides of the road by the Gifford House.

Check out the **Fremont Indian Petroglyphs,** and if you feel like some exertion, take a hike on the Hickman Bridge Trail. From the trail (or 2 miles east of the visitor center from Highway 24 if you skip the hike), you'll see **Capitol Dome.** Along this stretch of Highway 24, stop to see the old one-room **Fruita Schoolhouse**, the **petroglyphs**, and the **Behunin Cabin.** Next you'll have to backtrack west a few miles on Highway 24 to find the **Goosenecks Trail.** At the same parking lot you'll find the trailhead for **Sunset Point Trail**; take this short hike in time to watch the setting sun hit the colorful cliffs.

AVERAGE HIGH/LOW TEMPERATURES					
JAN.	**FEB.**	**MAR.**	**APR.**	**MAY**	**JUNE**
41/20	47/26	58/34	66/40	75/48	87/59
JULY	**AUG.**	**SEPT.**	**OCT.**	**NOV.**	**DEC.**
91/65	88/63	80/55	66/44	51/31	41/21

FESTIVALS AND EVENTS

Harvest Time Scarecrow Festival. Events for this month-long celebration marking the end of another busy season are held throughout Wayne County. In addition to a scarecrow contest, there are plenty of family-friendly events, including live music, arts and crafts, pumpkin carving, and a Halloween party. ⊕ www.entradainstitute.org.

Wayne County Fair. The great American county fair tradition is at its finest in Loa in mid-August. A demolition derby, rodeo, horse shows, and a parade are all part of the fun. You'll also find crafts such as handmade quilts, agricultural exhibits, children's games, and plenty of good food. ⊕ waynecountyutah.org.

Getting Here and Around

AIR

The nearest major airports are in Salt Lake City and Las Vegas, about 3½ and 5½ hours away by car, respectively. St. George Regional Airport (3½ hours away) is a handy, smaller airport with direct flights from several major cities in the West, Cedar City Municipal Airport (2¾ hours) has direct daily service on Delta from Salt Lake City, and Canyonlands Field Airport in Moab (2 hours away) has direct daily service on United Airlines from Denver.

CAR

You can approach Capitol Reef country from several routes, including highways 24 and 72 from Interstate 70 (and Moab), Highway 12 from Bryce Canyon National Park, and Highway 20 to U.S. 89 to Highway 62 from Interstate 15. All are well-maintained, safe roads that bisect rich agricultural communities steeped in Mormon history (especially in the nearby towns of Bicknell and Loa). Highway 24 runs across the middle of Capitol Reef National Park, offering scenic views the entire way.

Inspiration

The Capitol Reef Reader, edited by Stephen Trimble, shares writings about the park by almost 50 authors, and nearly 100 photos, many taken by the editor during dacades of hiking Capitol Reef's trails.

Capitol Reef: Canyon Country Eden, by Rose Houk, is an award-winning collection of photographs and lyrical essays on the park.

Dwellers of the Rainbow: Fremont Culture in Capitol Reef National Park, by Rose Houk, offers a brief background of the Fremont culture in Capitol Reef.

Red Rock Eden, by George Davidson, tells the story of historic Fruita, its settlements, and its orchards.

Park Essentials

ACCESSIBILITY

Capitol Reef doesn't have many trails that are accessible to people in wheelchairs. The visitor center, museum, film, and restrooms are all accessible, as is the campground amphitheater where evening programs are held. The Fruita Campground Loop C restroom is accessible; so is the boardwalk to the petroglyph panel on Highway 24, 1.2 miles east of the visitor center.

PARK FEES AND PERMITS

There is no fee to enter the park, but it's $20 per vehicle (or $10 per bicycle and $15 per motorcycle) to travel on Scenic Drive beyond Fruita Campground; this fee is good for one week, paid via the "honor system" at a drop box versus a staffed entry gate. Backcountry camping permits are free; pick them up at the visitor center. An annual pass that allows unlimited access to Scenic Drive is $35.

PARK HOURS

The park is open 24/7 year-round. It's in the Mountain time zone.

CELL PHONE RECEPTION

Cell phone reception is nearly nonexistent in the park, although you may pick up a weak signal in a few spots. Pay phones are at the visitor center and at Fruita Campground.

Hotels

There are no lodging options within Capitol Reef, but clean and comfortable accommodations for all budgets exist just west in nearby Torrey, and not far beyond in Bicknell and Loa. There are also a couple of options east of the park, in Hanksville. Book well ahead if visiting March through October.

Restaurants

Inside Capitol Reef you won't find any restaurants, though in summer there's a small store selling baked goods and ice cream. More dining options exist close by in Torrey, where you can find everything from creative Southwestern fusion cuisine to basic hamburger joints serving consistently good food.

Plants and Wildlife in Capitol Reef

The golden rock and rainbow cliffs are at their finest at sunset, when it seems as if they are lighted from within. That's also when mule deer wander through the orchards near the campground. The deer are quite used to people, but it's illegal to feed or even approach them. Many of the park's animals move about only at night to escape the heat, but pinyon jays and black-billed magpies flit around the park all day. The best place to see wildlife is near the Fremont River, where animals are drawn to drink. Ducks and small mammals such as the yellow-bellied marmot live nearby. Desert bighorn sheep also live in Capitol Reef, but they are elusive; your best chance for spotting them is during a long hike deep within the park. If you should encounter a sheep, do not approach it, as they've been known to charge people.

Visitor Information

PARK CONTACT INFORMATION Cap-itol Reef National Park. ☒ *Off Hwy. 24* ☎ *435/425–3791* ⊕ *www.nps.gov/care.*

Fruita

In the 1880s, Nels Johnson became the first homesteader in the Fremont River Valley, building his home near the confluence of Sulphur Creek and the Fremont River. Other Mormon settlers followed and established small farms and orchards, creating the village of Junc-tion. The orchards thrived, and by 1900 the name was changed to Fruita. The orchards, less than a mile from the visitor center, are preserved and protected as a Rural Historic District.

Sights

GEOLOGICAL LANDMARKS
Capitol Dome
NATURE SITE | One of the rock formations that gave the park its name, this giant sandstone dome is visible in the vicinity of the Hickman Bridge trailhead, 1.9 miles east of the visitor center. ☒ *Hwy. 24.*

Chimney Rock
NATURE SITE | Even in a landscape of spires, cliffs, and knobs, this deep-red landform, 3.9 miles west of the visitor center, is unmistakable. ☒ *Hwy. 24.*

HISTORIC SIGHTS
Behunin Cabin
BUILDING | FAMILY | Elijah Cutlar Behunin used blocks of sandstone to build this cabin in 1882. Floods in the lowlands made life too difficult, and he moved before the turn of that century. The house, 5.9 miles east of the visitor center, is empty, but you can peek through the window to see the interior. ☒ *Hwy. 24.*

Fremont Petroglyphs
NATIVE SITE | Between AD 300 and 1300, the Capitol Reef area was occupied by Native Americans who were eventually referred to by archaeologists as the Fremont, named after the Fremont River that flows through the park. A nice stroll along a boardwalk bridge, 1.1 miles east of the visitor center, allows close-up views of ancient rock art, which can be identified by the large trapezoidal figures often depicted wearing headdresses and ear baubles. ☒ *Hwy. 24.*

Did You Know?

The 3.5-mile round-trip trek up to Chimney Rock has some steep switchbacks, but the journey yields panoramic views. The trailhead is 3 miles from the park visitor center, near the entrance. It is forbidden to rock climb on it.

TRAILS

⭐ Chimney Rock Trail

TRAIL | You're almost sure to see ravens drifting on thermal winds around the deep-red Mummy Cliff that rings the base of this trail. This loop trail begins with a steep climb to a rim above dramatic Chimney Rock. The trail is 3.6 miles round-trip, with a 590-foot elevation change. No shade. Use caution during monsoon storms due to lightning hazards. Allow three to four hours. *Moderate–Difficult.* ⊠ *Capitol Reef National Park* ✛ *Trailhead: Hwy. 24, about 3 miles west of visitor center.*

Fremont River Trail

TRAIL | What starts as a quiet little stroll beside the river turns into an adventure. The first ½ mile of the trail wanders past orchards next to the Fremont River. After you pass through a narrow gate, the trail changes personality and you're in for a steep climb on an exposed ledge with drop-offs. The views at the top of the 480-foot ascent are worth it. It's 2 miles round-trip; allow two hours. *Moderate.* ⊠ *Capitol Reef National Park* ✛ *Trailhead: near amphitheater off Loop C of Fruita Campground, about 1 mile from visitor center.*

Golden Throne Trail

TRAIL | As you hike to the base of the Golden Throne, you may be lucky enough to see one of the park's elusive desert bighorn sheep, but you're more likely to spot their split-hoof tracks. The trail is about 2 miles of gradual rise with some steps and drop-offs. The Golden Throne is hidden until you near the end of the trail, then suddenly you see the huge sandstone monolith. If you hike near sundown, the throne burns gold. The round-trip hike is 4 miles and takes two to three hours. *Difficult.* ⊠ *Capitol Reef National Park* ✛ *Trailhead: at end of Capitol Gorge Rd., 10 miles south of visitor center.*

Goosenecks Trail

TRAIL | This nice little walk gives you a good introduction to the land surrounding Capitol Reef. You'll enjoy the dizzying views from the overlook. It's only 0.2 miles round-trip to the overlook and a very easy walk. *Easy.* ⊠ *Hwy. 24, about 3 miles west of visitor center.*

Hickman Bridge Trail

TRAIL | This trail leads to a natural bridge of Kayenta sandstone, with a 133-foot opening carved by intermittent flash floods. Early on, the route climbs a set of steps along the Fremont River. The trail splits, leading along the right-hand branch to a strenuous uphill climb to the Rim Overlook and Navajo Knobs. Stay to your left to see the bridge, and you'll encounter a moderate up-and-down trail. Up the wash on your way to the bridge is a Fremont granary on the right side of the small canyon. Allow about two hours for the 1.8-mile round-trip. Expect lots of company. *Moderate.* ⊠ *Capitol Reef National Park* ✛ *Trailhead: Hwy. 24, 2 miles east of visitor center.*

Sunset Point Trail

TRAIL | The trail starts from the same parking lot as the Goosenecks Trail, on your way into the park about 3.3 miles west of the visitor center. Benches along this easy, 0.8-mile round-trip invite you to sit and meditate surrounded by the colorful desert. At the trail's end, you will be rewarded with broad vistas into the park; it's even better at sunset. *Easy.* ⊠ *Hwy. 24.*

SCENIC DRIVES

⭐ Utah Scenic Byway 24

SCENIC DRIVE | For 75 miles between Loa and Hanksville, you'll cut right through Capitol Reef National Park. Colorful rock formations in all their hues of red, cream, pink, gold, and deep purple extend from one end of the route to the other. The closer you get to the park the more colorful the landscape becomes. The vibrant rock finally gives way to lush green hills and the mountains west of Loa.

VISITOR CENTERS

Capitol Reef Visitor Center

INFO CENTER | FAMILY | Watch a park movie, talk with rangers, or peruse the many books, maps, and materials for sale in the bookstore. Towering over the center (11 miles east of Torrey) is the Castle, one of the park's most prominent rock formations. ⊠ *Scenic Dr. at Hwy. 24* ☎ *435/425–3791* ⊕ *www.nps.gov/care.*

Scenic Drive

This 8-mile road, simply called Scenic Drive, starts at the visitor center and winds its way through the Fruita Historic District and colorful sandstone cliffs into Capitol Gorge; a side road, Grand Wash Road, provides access into the canyon. At Capitol Gorge, the canyon walls become steep and impressive but the route becomes unpaved for about the last 2 miles, and road conditions may vary due to weather and usage. Check with the visitor center before setting out.

 Sights

GEOLOGICAL LANDMARKS

The Waterpocket Fold

NATURE SITE | A giant wrinkle in the earth extends almost 100 miles between Thousand Lake Mountain and Lake Powell. You can glimpse the fold by driving south on Scenic Drive after it branches off Highway 24, past the Fruita Historic District. For complete immersion enter the park via the 36-mile Burr Trail from Boulder. Roads through the southernmost reaches of the park are largely unpaved. The area is accessible to most vehicles during dry weather, but check with the visitor center for current road conditions. ⊠ *Capitol Reef National Park.*

HISTORIC SIGHTS

Gifford House Store and Museum

NATIONAL/STATE PARK | One mile south of the visitor center in a grassy meadow with the Fremont River flowing by, this is an idyllic shady spot in the Fruita Historic District for a sack lunch, complete with tables, drinking water, grills, and a convenient restroom. The store sells reproductions of pioneer tools and items made by local craftspeople; there's also locally made fruit pies and ice cream to enjoy with your picnic. ⊠ *Scenic Dr.*

Pioneer Register

HISTORIC SITE | Travelers passing through Capitol Gorge in the 19th and early 20th centuries etched the canyon wall with their names and the date. Directly across the canyon from the Pioneer Register and about 50 feet up are signatures etched into the canyon wall by an early United States Geologic Survey crew. Though it's illegal to write or scratch on the canyon walls today, plenty of damage has been done by vandals over the years. You can reach the register via an easy hike from the sheltered trailhead at the end of Capitol Gorge Road, 10.3 miles south of the visitor center; the register is about 10 minutes along the hike to the sandstone "tanks." ⊠ *Off Scenic Dr.*

SCENIC DRIVES

★ Capitol Gorge

SCENIC DRIVE | Eight miles south of the visitor center, Scenic Drive ends, at which point you can drive an unpaved spur road into Capitol Gorge. The narrow, twisting road on the floor of the gorge was a route for pioneer wagons traversing this part of Utah starting in the 1860s. After every flash flood, pioneers would laboriously clear the route so wagons could continue to go through. The gorge became the main automobile route in the area until 1962, when Highway 24 was built. The short drive to the end of the road has striking views of the surrounding cliffs and leads to one of the park's most popular walks: the hiking trail to the water-holding "tanks" eroded into the sandstone. ⊠ *Scenic Dr.*

TRAILS

★ Capitol Gorge Trail and the Tanks

NATIONAL/STATE PARK | Starting at the Pioneer Register, about a ½ mile from the Capitol Gorge parking lot, is a ½-mile trail that climbs to the Tanks—holes in the sandstone, formed by erosion, that hold water after it rains. After a scramble up about ¼ mile of steep trail with cliff drop-offs, you can look down into the Tanks and see a natural bridge below the lower tank. Including the walk to the Pioneer Register, allow an hour or more for this interesting hike, one of the park's most popular. *Moderate.* ⊠ *Capitol Reef National Park* ⊹ *Trailhead: at end of Scenic Dr., 10 miles south of visitor center.*

Cohab Canyon Trail

TRAIL | Find rock wrens and Western pipistrelles (canyon bats) on this trail. One end is directly across from the Fruita Campground on Scenic Drive; the other is across from the Hickman Bridge parking lot. The first ¼ mile from Fruita is strenuous, but the walk becomes easier except for turnoffs to the overlooks, which are short. You'll find miniature arches, skinny side canyons, and honeycombed patterns on canyon walls where the wrens make nests. The trail is 3.2 miles round-trip to the Hickman Bridge parking lot (two to three hours). The Overlook Trail adds 1 mile. Allow two hours to overlooks and back. *Moderate.* ⊠ *Capitol Reef National Park* ⊹ *Trailheads: Scenic Dr., about 1 mile south of visitor center, or Hwy. 24, about 2 miles east of visitor center.*

Grand Wash Trail

TRAIL | At the end of unpaved Grand Wash Road you can continue on foot through the canyon to its end at Highway 24. This flat hike takes you through a wide wash between canyon walls, and is an excellent place to study the geology up close. The round-trip hike is 4.4 miles; allow two to three hours for your walk. Check at the ranger station for flash-flood warnings before entering the wash. *Easy.* ⊠ *Capitol Reef National Park* ⊹ *Trailhead: at Hwy. 24, east of Hickman Bridge parking lot, or at end of Grand Wash Rd., off Scenic Dr. about 5 miles from visitor center.*

Cathedral Valley

This primitive, rugged area was named for its sandstone geological features that are reminiscent of Gothic cathedrals. Visiting is quite the backroad adventure, so not many people make the effort to drive on roads that some have called brutal. But if you have the right vehicle and an adventurous spirit, the rewards of seeing ancient natural wonders should be worth it. The selenite crystals of Glass Mountain attract rockhounds for a closer look, but no collecting is allowed. Sunset and sunrise at the Temple of the Sun and Temple of the Moon monoliths are especially colorful and photogenic.

Sights

SCENIC DRIVES

Cathedral Valley/North District Loop

TRAIL | The north end of Capitol Reef, along this backcountry road, is filled with towering monoliths, panoramic vistas, water crossings, and a stark desert landscape. The area is remote and the road through it unpaved, so do not enter without a suitable mountain bike or high-clearance vehicle, some planning, and a cell phone (although reception is virtually nonexistent). The trail through the valley is a 58-mile loop that you can begin at River Ford Road, 11¾ miles east of the visitor center off Highway 24; allow half a day. If your time is limited, you can tour only the Caineville Wash Road, which takes about two hours by ATV or four-wheel drive vehicle. If you are planning a multiday trip, there's a

Temple of the Sun, a monolith in Capitol Reef's Cathedral Valley, is a favorite with photographers.

primitive campground about halfway through the loop. Pick up a self-guided tour brochure at the visitor center. ⊠ *River Ford Rd., off Hwy. 24.*

Muley Twist Canyon

This long canyon runs 12 miles north to south at the south end of park. It was used as a pass by pioneers traveling by wagon through the Waterpocket Fold and got its name because it was so narrow that it could "twist a mule." Park visitors typically explore Lower Muley Twist Canyon on long day hikes or overnight (a permit is required for overnight camping). Upper Muley Twist Canyon has some shorter trails, including a one-mile hike to an overlook. Trails are not maintained, so bring a map, along with plenty of water as the area is quite hot in summer. High-clearance vehicles are necessary for most of the roads.

Activities

BIKING

Bicycles are allowed only on established roads in the park. Highway 24 is a state highway and receives a substantial amount of through traffic, so it's not the best place to pedal. Scenic Drive is better, but the road is narrow, and you have to contend with drivers dazed by the beautiful surroundings. In fact, it's a good idea to traverse it in the morning or evening when traffic is reduced, or in the off-season. Four-wheel-drive roads are certainly less traveled, but they are often sandy, rocky, and steep. The Cathedral Valley/North District Loop is popular with mountain bikers (but also with four-wheelers). You cannot ride your bicycle in washes or on hiking trails.

South Draw Road

BICYCLING | This is a very strenuous but picturesque ride that traverses dirt, sand, and rocky surfaces, and crosses several creeks that may be muddy. It's not recommended in winter or spring because of deep snow at higher elevations. The route starts at an elevation of 8,500 feet on Boulder Mountain, 13 miles south of Torrey, and ends 15¾ miles later at 5,500 feet in the Pleasant Creek parking area at the end of Scenic Drive. ⊠ *Bowns Reservoir Rd. and Hwy. 12.*

CAMPING

Campgrounds—both the highly convenient Fruita Campground and the backcountry sites—in Capitol Reef fill up fast between March and October. Most of the area's state parks have camping facilities, and the region's two national forests offer many wonderful sites.

Cathedral Valley Campground. This small (just six sites), basic (no water, pit toilet), no-fee campground in the park's remote northern district touts sprawling views, but the bumpy road there is hard to navigate. ⊠ *Hartnet Junction, on Caineville Wash Rd.* ☎ *435/425–3791.*

Cedar Mesa Campground. Wonderful views of the Waterpocket Fold and Henry Mountains surround this primitive (pit toilet, no water), no-fee campground with five sites in the park's southern district. ⊠ *Notom-Bullfrog Rd., 22 miles south of Hwy. 24* ☎ *435/425–3791.*

Fruita Campground. Near the orchards and the Fremont River, the park's developed (flush toilets, running water), shady campground is a great place to call home for a few days. The sites require a $20 nightly fee, and those nearest the Fremont River or the orchards are the most coveted. ⊠ *Scenic Dr., about 1 mile south of visitor center* ☎ *435/425–3791* ⊕ *www.recreation.gov.*

EDUCATIONAL PROGRAMS

RANGER PROGRAMS

In summer, ranger programs are offered at no charge. You can obtain current information about ranger talks and other park events at the visitor center or campground bulletin boards.

Evening Program. Learn about Capitol Reef's geology, Native American cultures, wildlife, and more at the campground amphitheater about a mile from the visitor center. Programs typically begin around sunset. See the schedule at the visitor center. ⊕ *www.nps.gov/care/planyourvisit/ranger-programs.htm.*

Junior Ranger Program. Each child who participates in this self-guided, year-round program completes a combination of activities in the Junior Ranger booklet and attends a ranger program or watches the park movie. ⊕ *www.nps.gov/care/planyourvisit/ranger-programs.htm.*

Ranger Talks. Typically, the park offers a daily morning geology talk at the visitor center and a daily afternoon petroglyph-panel talk. Occasional geology hikes, history tours, and moon and stargazing tours are also sometimes offered. Times vary. ⊕ *www.nps.gov/care/planyourvisit/ranger-programs.htm.*

FOUR-WHEELING

You can explore Capitol Reef in a 4X4 on a number of exciting backcountry routes, but note that all vehicles must remain on designated roadways. Road conditions can vary greatly depending on recent weather patterns. The Cathedral Valley/North District Loop is popular with four-wheelers (and also with mountain bikers).

HIKING

Many park trails in Capitol Reef include steep climbs, but there are a few easy-to-moderate hikes. A short drive from the visitor center takes you to a dozen trails near the Fruita Historic District, but there are more challenging hikes in the other areas.

HORSEBACK RIDING

Many areas in the park are closed to horses and pack animals, so it's a good idea to check with the visitor center before you set out with your animals. Day use does not require a permit, but you need to get one for overnight camping with horses and pack animals.

Hondoo Rivers & Trails in Torrey runs horseback tours into the national park. Unless you ride with a park-licensed outfitter, you have to bring your own horse, as no rentals are available.

Nearby Towns

The best home base for exploring Capitol Reef, the pretty town of **Torrey,** just west of the park, has lots of personality. Giant old cottonwood trees make it a shady, cool place to stay, and the townspeople are friendly and accommodating. A little farther west on Highway 24, tiny **Teasdale** is a charming settlement cradled in a cove of the Aquarius Plateau. The homes look out onto brilliantly colored cliffs and green fields. Quiet **Bicknell** lies another few miles west of Torrey. The Wayne County seat of **Loa,** 10 miles west of Torrey, was settled by pioneers in the 1870s. If you head south from Torrey instead of west, you can take a spectacular 32-mile drive along Highway 12 to **Boulder,** a town so remote that its mail was carried on horseback until 1940. Nearby is Anasazi State Park. In the opposite direction, 51 miles east, **Hanksville** is a place to stop for food and fuel—the small wayside en route to Moab also has a couple of decent budget motels.

Chapter 11

CARLSBAD CAVERNS NATIONAL PARK

11

Updated by
Andrew Collins

NEW
MEXICO

⛅ Camping
★☆☆☆☆

🛏 Hotels
★★☆☆☆

🤾 Activities
★★★☆☆

👁 Scenery
★★★★☆

👥 Crowds
★★★★★

WELCOME TO CARLSBAD CAVERNS NATIONAL PARK

TOP REASONS TO GO

★ **400,000 hungry bats:** From mid-May to late October, bats wing to and from the caverns in a swirling, visible tornado.

★ **Take a self-guided tour through the underworld:** Plummet 75 stories underground and step into enormous caves hung with stalactites and bristling with stalagmites.

★ **Hike through the high desert:** Several relatively uncrowded trails, including the dramatic Rattlesnake Canyon Trail, provide views of the park's stunning aboveground desert scenery.

★ **Birding at Rattlesnake Springs:** Nine-tenths of the park's 357 bird species, including roadrunners, golden eagles, and acrobatic cave swallows, visit this green desert oasis with a shaded picnic area.

★ **Living Desert Zoo and Gardens:** More preserve than zoo, this 1,500-acre state park in the nearby city of Carlsbad houses scores of rare species, including black bears, Bolson tortoises, and endangered Mexican wolves.

1 Carlsbad Cavern Aboveground. The first place to experience the park is the visitor center (and excellent museum) above the cavern, this part of the park also features scenic drives and hikes through a dramatic Chihuahuan desertscape.

2 Carlsbad Cavern Belowground. Travel 75 stories below the surface to visit the main cavern's Big Room, where you can traipse beneath a 230-foot-tall ceiling and take in immense and eerie cave formations.

3 Rattlesnake Springs and Slaughter Canyon. Reached via a different entrance, these less-visited but rewarding areas in the western half of the park are notable for their rugged canyon hikes and outstanding bird-watching.

GUADALUPE

Yucca Canyon Trail

MOUNTAINS

NEW MEXICO

TEXAS

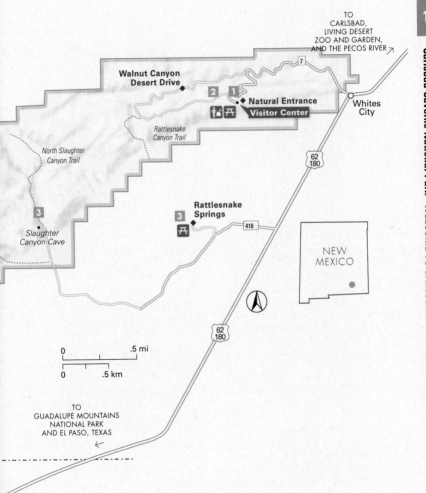

TO
CARLSBAD,
LIVING DESERT
ZOO AND GARDEN,
AND THE PECOS RIVER ↗

Walnut Canyon
Desert Drive

7

2 1

Natural Entrance

Visitor Center

Whites
City

Rattlesnake
Canyon Trail

North Slaughter
Canyon Trail

62
180

3

3

Rattlesnake
Springs

418

NEW
MEXICO

Slaughter
Canyon Cave

0   .5 mi

0   .5 km

62
180

TO
GUADALUPE MOUNTAINS
NATIONAL PARK
AND EL PASO, TEXAS
←

On the surface, Carlsbad Caverns National Park looks deceptively like the rest of southeastern New Mexico's high desert—but all bets are off once visitors set foot in the elevator, which plunges 75 stories underground into a massive cavern, part of a network of formations located within a massive reef that formed 265 million years ago when this area was covered by a vast inland sea.

Indeed, Carlsbad Caverns offers a pretty remarkable illustration of the adage "there's more than meets the eye." Wherever you go within the park's 46,766 acres, whether driving or hiking aboveground or touring subterranean areas open to visitors, it's impossible to fully grasp the sheer wonder and immensity of the area's unique geology. You'll never see more than a tiny fraction of the park from any given vantage point.

Carlsbad Cavern, whose 14-acre Big Room is the park's definitive must-see attraction, and one that you'll want to set aside at least three hours to explore. This eerie world beneath the surface is part silky darkness, part subterranean hallucination—its hundreds of formations alternately resemble cakes, ocean waves, and the face of a mountain troll. Explorer Jim White began exploring the caves in the 1890s, and in 1930 both the main cavern and a vast tract of aboveground canyons and mesas were designated Carlsbad Caverns National Park.

Remarkably, the main Carlsbad Cavern is but one of more than 110 limestone caves that have been identified within the park's boundaries. Most of them, including the largest and deepest (at 1,604 feet belowground), Lechuguilla, aren't open to the general public. Scientists only discovered Lechuguilla's huge network of rooms in 1986. So far they've mapped more than 145 miles of passages—and their work continues.

If you spend most of your first visit to the park exploring its subterranean caverns, you may be surprised to learn how much terrain there is to cover aboveground. Hikers can trek for miles across cactus-studded ridges and through wildlife-rich canyons—there's even a lush little oasis of cottonwood trees, Rattlesnake Springs, in the park's western section, which you reach by taking an entirely different road into the park.

Carlsbad Caverns is also one of two exceptional national parks within the vicinity. Just over the Texas border, a picturesque 45-minute drive to the southwest, you can investigate Guadalupe Mountains National Park, home to the highest peaks in the Lone Star State

AVERAGE HIGH/LOW TEMPERATURES					
JAN.	**FEB.**	**MAR.**	**APR.**	**MAY**	**JUNE**
56/33	60/36	66/42	75/50	83/58	91/64
JULY	**AUG.**	**SEPT.**	**OCT.**	**NOV.**	**DEC.**
91/66	89/65	83/60	75/52	64/42	58/35

and miles of rugged trails. If you have at least a week, you might even consider making a regional national parks road trip that includes the relatively nearby Big Bend (Texas) and White Sands (New Mexico) national parks. And even if you stick primarily around Carlsbad Caverns, it's worth setting aside a full day to check out the nearby city that shares the park's name, Carlsbad. With its terrific Living Desert Zoo and Gardens State Park and an attractively landscaped downtown riverfront, it makes for an enjoyable side adventure.

Planning

When to Go

While the desert above may alternately bake or freeze, the caverns remain in the mid-50s. If you're coming to see the Brazilian free-tailed bat, arrive between spring and mid-fall, keeping in mind that hiking the park's above-ground tails can be uncomfortably hot in summer.

FESTIVAL AND EVENTS

Dawn of the Bats. The third Saturday in July each year, early risers gather at the cave's entrance to watch tens of thousands of bats return home from their nocturnal search for food. Nature walks and other special ranger programs are offered as well during this free event. ⊕ *www.nps. gov/cave.*

Getting Here and Around

AIR

The nearest full-service airports are in the Texas cities of El Paso (150 miles away) and Midland (160 miles away). Cavern City Air Terminal, between Carlsbad and the park, is served by a small regional carrier, Boutique Air, with regularly scheduled service to both Albuquerque and Dallas/Fort Worth.

CAR

The park entrance is 21 miles southwest of Carlsbad, New Mexico, and 32 miles north of Guadalupe Mountains National Park via U.S. 62/180. The ascending 7-mile Carlsbad Cavern Highway from the turnoff at Whites City (which has a gas station) is paved with pull-outs that allow scenic vistas. Be alert for wildlife crossing roadways, especially in the early morning and at night.

Inspiration

Jim White's Own Story, by early explorer Jim White, tells of this cowboy's exploits into the heart of Carlsbad Caverns before it was developed as a national park.

Edward J. Greene's *Carlsbad Caverns: The Story Behind the Scenery* provides a fascinating account of the geological story behind this strange and magical landscape.

If many of the underground scenes in the classic 1959 adventure film *Journey to the Center of the Earth* look familiar, it's because they were shot inside the Big Room deep inside Carlsbad Caverns National Park.

Carlsbad Caverns in One Day

In a single day, visitors can easily view both the eerie, exotic caverns and the volcano of bats that erupts from the caverns each evening. Unless you're attending the annual Dawn of the Bats, when visitors view the early-morning bat return, go ahead and sleep past sunrise and then stroll into the caves.

For the full experience, begin by taking the **Natural Entrance Trail**, which allows visitors to trek into the cave from surface level. This tour winds past the Boneyard, with its intricate ossifications and a massive boulder called the Iceberg. After 1¼ miles, or about an hour, the trail links up with the **Big Room Trail**. If you're not in good health or are traveling with young children, you might want to skip the Natural Entrance and start with the Big Room Trail, which begins at the foot of the elevator. This underground walk extends 1¼ miles on level, paved ground, and takes about 1½ hours to complete. There is a shortcut option that's about half as long. If you have made reservations in advance or chance upon same-day availability, take the **King's Palace** guided tour for 1 mile and an additional 1½ hours. At 83 stories deep, the palace is the lowest part of the cavern open to the public. By this time, you will have spent four hours in the cavern. Take the elevator back up to the top. If you're not yet tuckered out, consider a short hike along the sunny, self-guided ½-mile **Desert Nature Walk** by the visitor center.

In the early afternoon, to experience a very different side of the park, make the 25-minute drive via Whites City to picnic by the birds, bees, and water of **Rattlesnake Springs**. You'll find old-growth shade trees, grass, picnic tables, restrooms, and water. Many varieties of birds flit from tree to tree. Return to the Carlsbad Caverns entrance road and take the 9½-mile Walnut Canyon Desert Drive loop for its panoramic views of the surrounding high desert. Leave yourself enough time to return to the **visitor center** for the evening bat flight.

Park Essentials

ACCESSIBILITY

Though the park covers a huge expanse aboveground (with key areas reached by paved roads), most of the parts you'll want to see are below the surface. Trails through the most-visited portion of the main cavern are paved and well maintained, and portions of the paved Big Room trail in Carlsbad Cavern is accessible to wheelchairs. Individuals who have difficulty walking should access the Big Room via elevator. Strollers are not permitted on any trails.

PARK FEES AND PERMITS

No fee is charged to enter the aboveground portion of the park. It costs $15 to descend into Carlsbad Caverns either by elevator or through the Natural Entrance (admission is free for kids 15 and under). Costs for guided tours of other parts of the main cavern or the other cavern in the park, Slaughter Canyon Cave, range from $7 to $20 plus general admission. For guided-tour reservations go to ⊕ www.recreation.gov or call ☎ 877/444-6777.

Those planning overnight hikes must obtain a free backcountry permit, and all hikers are advised to stop at the visitor center information desk for trail and park road conditions. Trails are marked by cairns (rock piles) and in some places can be tricky to follow; download or carry a good topographic map. Dogs are not allowed in the park, but a kennel is available at the park visitor center for a fee.

PARK HOURS

The park is open year-round, except Christmas Day, New Year's Day, and Thanksgiving. From Memorial Day weekend through Labor Day, access to the cavern is from 8:30 to 5; entrance tickets are sold until 4:45, with the last entry via the Natural Entrance at 4. After Labor Day until Memorial Day weekend, cavern access is from 8:30 to 3:30; entrance tickets are sold until 3:15, and the last entry via the Natural Entrance is at 2:30. Last-ticket times do sometimes change throughout the year due to maintenance and other causes—always confirm hours on the website before you arrive. Carlsbad Caverns is in the Mountain time zone.

CELL PHONE RECEPTION

Cell phone service is spotty in the park. It works best in the parking lots outside the visitor center. There's no Wi-Fi or cell service inside any caverns. Note that your cell phone may pick up a signal from towers in the adjacent Central time zone, giving you the incorrect impression that you're an hour ahead.

Hotels

Camping in the backcountry, at least a half mile from any trail, is your only lodging option in the park. You must obtain a backcountry camping permit at the visitor center.

Outside the park your options expand, but rates in the immediate vicinity can be steep at times due to demand by workers in the booming nearby oil-field industry—even cookie-cutter chain hotels in Carlsbad sometimes run more than

$250 a night. Whites City, just outside the park's main entrance, has a very basic and affordable motel. You can often find comparable lodgings for at least 50 percent less than Carlsbad prices farther afield, in Artesia (an hour away) and even Roswell (a little less than two hours). *Hotel reviews have been shortened. For full information, visit Fodors.com.*

What It Costs			
$	$$	$$$	$$$$
RESTAURANTS			
under $16	$16–$22	$23–$30	over $30
HOTELS			
under $120	$121–$180	$181–$240	over $240

Restaurants

Inside the park there are just two dining options—the surface-level dining room and the underground snack bar near the elevator. Everything is reasonably priced, but food quality at the park restaurants is nothing to write home about. Outside the park, skip the mediocre eatery in nearby Whites City and drive into Carlsbad, which has plenty of good options. *Hotel reviews have been shortened. For full information, visit Fodors.com.*

Tours

Carlsbad Caverns is famous for the beauty and breadth of its inky depths, as well as for the accessibility of some of its largest caves. All cave tours, except for the self-guided Natural Entrance and Big Room, are ranger-led, so you can count on a safe experience, even in remote caves. Depending on the difficulty of your cave selection (the Hall of the White Giant cavern is hardest to navigate), you'll need sturdy pants, hiking boots with ankle support, and some water. The fee for the Natural Entrance and Big Room is $15 and is good for three days. Guided tours have an additional fee of $7 to $20.

Ranger-Led Tours

SPELUNKING | FAMILY | Cavers who wish to explore both developed and wild caves can go on ranger-led tours, all of which require three AA batteries for headlamps (which will be supplied). Reservations for the five different tours (Hall of the White Giant, Lower Cave, Slaughter Canyon Cave, Left-Hand Tunnel, and King's Palace) are generally required at least a day in advance. Payment is by credit card over the phone or online. ⊠ *Carlsbad Caverns National Park* ☎ *877/444–6777 for reservations* ⊕ *www.nps.gov/cave* 🖭 *From $7.*

Visitor Information

PARK CONTACT INFORMATION Carlsbad Caverns National Park. ⊠ *Park Visitor Center, 727 Carlsbad Caverns Hwy., Carlsbad* ☎ *575/785–2232, 575/875–3012 bat flight schedule* ⊕ *www.nps.gov/cave.*

Carlsbad Cavern Aboveground

7 miles west of White City, 25 miles southwest of Carlsbad.

The eastern half of Carlsbad Caverns National Park, reached from U.S. 62/180 at Whites City via Carlsbad Caverns Highway, is where you'll find most of the key attractions, including the visitor center, which sits directly above the main cavern for which the park is named. This section of the park also contains several worthwhile hiking trails, some accessed from the visitor center and others from Walnut Canyon Desert Drive, a scenic unpaved loop road with several overlooks.

 Sights

SCENIC DRIVES

Walnut Canyon Desert Drive

SCENIC DRIVE | This scenic drive (labeled as Reef Top Cir. on some maps) begins a ½ mile from the visitor center and travels 9½ miles along the top of a ridge to the edge of Rattlesnake Canyon—which you can access via a marked trail—and sinks back down through upper Walnut Canyon to the main entrance road. The backcountry scenery on this one-way gravel loop is stunning; go late in the afternoon or early in the morning to enjoy the full spectrum of changing light and dancing colors. Along the way, you'll see Big Hill Seep's trickling water, the tall, flowing ridges of the Guadalupe mountain range, and maybe even some robust mule deer. The scenic road is not for RVs or trailers. ⊠ *Off Carlsbad Caverns Hwy.* ✥ *Just before entrance to visitor center parking lot.*

SCENIC STOPS

Bat Flight

CAVE | The 400,000-member Brazilian free-tailed bat colony here snatches up 3 tons of bugs a night. Watch them leave at dusk from the park amphitheater at the Natural Entrance, where a ranger discusses these intriguing creatures. The bats aren't on any predictable schedule, so times can be a little iffy. Ideally, viewers will first hear the bats preparing to exit, followed by a vortex of black specks swirling out of the cave mouth in search of dinner against the darkening sky. When conditions are favorable, hundreds of thousands of bats will soar off over the span of half an hour or longer. ⊠ *727 Carlsbad Caverns Hwy.*

TRAILS

Chihuahuan Desert Nature Trail

TRAIL | FAMILY | While waiting for the evening bat-flight program, take this ½-mile self-guided loop hike that begins just east of the visitor center. The tagged and identified flowers and plants make

Plants and Wildlife in Carlsbad Caverns

Without a doubt, the park's most prominent and popular residents are Brazilian free-tailed bats. Their bodies barely span the width of a hand, yet their wingspan is more than 11 inches. Female bats give birth to a single pup each year, which usually weighs more than a quarter of what an adult bat does. Their tiny noses and big ears enable them to search for the many tons of bugs they consume over their lifetime. Numbering nearly a third of a million, these tiny creatures are the park's mascot.

One of New Mexico's best birding areas is at Rattlesnake Springs. Summer and fall migrations give you the best chance of spotting the most varieties of the more than 357 species of birds. Lucky visitors may spot the occasional golden eagle or get the thrill of glimpsing a brilliant, gray-and-crimson vermilion flycatcher.

Snakes are most likely to appear late spring through early fall, especially at dusk and dawn. ■TIP➔ If you're out walking, be wary of different rattle-snake species, such as banded-rocks and diamondbacks. If you see one, don't panic. Rangers say they are more scared of us than we are of them. Just don't make any sudden movements, and slowly walk away or back around the vipers.

This area is also remarkable because of its location in the Chihuahuan Desert, which sprouts unique plant life. There are thick stands of raspy-leaved yuccas, as well as the agave (mescal) plants that were once a food source for early Native American tribes. The leaves of this leggy plant are still roasted in sand pits by tribal elders during traditional celebrations.

In spring, the stands of yucca plants unfold white flowers on their tall stalks. Blossoming cacti and desert wildflowers are among the natural wonders of Walnut Canyon. You'll see bright red blossoms adorning reach-for-the-sky ocotillo plants, and sunny yellow blooms sprouting from prickly pear cactus.

this a good place to get acquainted with local desert flora. Part of the trail is an easy stroll even for the littlest ones, and part is wheelchair accessible. The payoff is great for everyone, too: a sweeping, vivid view of the desert basin. *Easy.* ⊠ *Carlsbad Caverns National Park* ✛ *Trailhead: just east of visitor center.*

Guadalupe Ridge Trail

TRAIL | This long, winding trail extends for some 100 miles through the Chihuahuan Desert in southern New Mexico and western Texas and can be hiked from Carlsbad Caverns through to the Guadalupe Mountains. Within Carlsbad Caverns National Park, the most interesting portion runs for about 12 miles one-way from the western side of Walnut Canyon Desert Drive to the park's western boundary with Lincoln National Forest. If you hike all 12 miles and back, an overnight stay in the backcountry is strongly recommended. The hike may be long, but for serious hikers the up-close-and-personal views into Rattlesnake and Slaughter canyons are more than worth it—not to mention the serenity of being miles away from civilization. *Difficult.* ⊠ *Carlsbad Caverns National Park* ✛ *Trailhead: junction of Walnut Canyon Desert Dr. and Ridge Rd.*

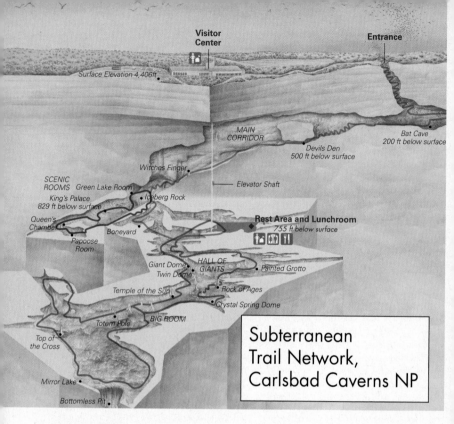

Subterranean Trail Network, Carlsbad Caverns NP

Old Guano Road Trail

TRAIL | Meandering a little more than 3½ miles one-way on steadily descending terrain (elevation gain is about 750 feet), the trail dips sharply toward its end at Whites City campground. Give yourself two to three hours to complete the walk. The high desert sun can make this hike a bit taxing any time of year, especially in summer. *Moderate.* ⊠ *Carlsbad Caverns National Park* ⊹ *Trailhead: Bat Flight Amphitheater.*

★ Rattlesnake Canyon Trail

TRAIL | Small cairns guide you along this picturesque trail, which winds 600 feet into the canyon—it's especially lush with greenery from spring through fall. Allow half a day to trek down into the canyon and make the somewhat strenuous climb out; the total trip is about 6 miles. For a look into the canyon, you can make the ¼-mile stroll to an overlook. *Moderate.* ⊠ *Carlsbad Caverns National Park* ⊹ *Trailhead: interpretive marker 9, Walnut Canyon Desert Dr.*

VISITOR CENTERS

★ Carlsbad Caverns Visitor Center

INFO CENTER | FAMILY | Within this spacious, modern facility at the top of an escarpment, a 75-seat theater offers engrossing films and ranger programs about the different types of caves. Exhibits offer a primer on bats, geology, wildlife, and the early tribes and settlers who once lived in and passed through the area. There's also an excellent exhibit on Lechuguilla, the country's deepest limestone cave, which scientists began mapping in 1986 and have located some 145 miles (it's on the park's northern border and isn't open to the general public). Friendly rangers staff an information desk, where maps are distributed and cavern tickets are sold. There's also an extensive gift shop and bookstore, and restaurant. ✉ *727 Carlsbad Caverns Hwy.* ☎ *575/785–2232* 🌐 *www.nps.gov/cave.*

🍴 Restaurants

Carlsbad Caverns Restaurant

$ | AMERICAN | This comfy, cafeteria-style restaurant in the visitor center serves basic food—hamburgers, sandwiches, some Mexican dishes—and is fine in a pinch. There are also packaged takeout items. **Known for:** close proximity to the main cavern; no alcohol; takeout options. [$] *Average main: $9* ✉ *727 Carlsbad Caverns Hwy.* ☎ *575/785–2281* 🌐 *www.nps.gov/cave* 🕑 *No dinner.*

Carlsbad Cavern Belowground

Directly beneath Carlsbad Caverns Visitor Center.

With a floor space equal to about 14 football fields, this subterranean focal point of Carlsbad Cavern clues visitors in to just how large the cavern really is. The White House could fit in one corner of the Big Room, and wouldn't come close to grazing the 230-foot ceiling. Once you buy a $15 ticket at the visitor center, you can enter the cavern by elevator or through the Natural Entrance via a 1¼-mile descending trail. Either way, at 750 feet below the surface you will connect with the self-guided 1¼-mile Big Room loop. Even in summer, long pants and long-sleeved shirts are advised for cave temperatures in the mid-50s. The main cavern also accesses the King's Palace, Left Hand Tunnel, and Hall of the White Giant caves, which can be visited only by guided tour (these all depart from the visitor center). As of this writing, tentative plans are underway to renovate and redesign some of the cavern's trails. These projects may result in the temporary closure of some portions of the cavern; check the park website for the latest advisories.

👁 Sights

GEOLOGICAL SITES

★ The Big Room

CAVE | FAMILY | A relatively level (it has some steps), paved pathway leads through these almost hallucinatory wonders of various formations and decorations. Exhibits and signage also provide a layman's lesson on how the cavern was carved (for even more details, rent an audio guide from the visitor center for $5). ✉ *Visitor Center* 🎫 *$15.*

Hall of the White Giant

SPELUNKING | Plan to squirm—and even crawl on your belly—through some tight passages for long distances to access a very remote chamber, where you'll see towering, glistening white formations that explain the name. This strenuous, ranger-led tour lasts about four hours. Steep climbs and sharp drop-offs might elate you—or make you queasy. Wear sturdy hiking shoes. No kids under 12. ✉ *Carlsbad Caverns National Park* ☎ *877/444–6777 reservations* 🌐 *www.recreation.gov* 🎫 *$20* ✍ *Reservations essential.*

★ King's Palace

SPELUNKING | FAMILY | Throughout this regal room, stunningly handsome and indeed fit for a king, you'll see leggy "soda straws" large enough for a giant to sip, plus bizarre formations that defy reality. The tour also winds through the Queen's Chamber, dressed in ladylike, multitiered curtains of stone. The mile-long walk is on a paved trail, but there's one steep hill toward the end. This ranger-guided tour lasts about 1½ hours and gives you a "look" at the natural essence of a cave—a complete blackout, when artificial lights (and sound) are extinguished. While advance reservations are highly recommended, this is the one tour you might be able to sign up for on the spot. Children younger than four aren't permitted. ✉ *Carlsbad Caverns National Park* ☎ *877/444–6777 reservations* 🌐 *www.recreation.gov* 🎫 *$8.*

Left Hand Tunnel

SPELUNKING | FAMILY | Lantern light illuminates the easy ½-mile walk on this detour in the main Carlsbad Cavern, which leads to Permian Age fossils—indicating that these caves were hollowed from the Permian Reef that still underlies the Guadalupe Mountain range above. The guided tour over a packed dirt trail lasts about two hours. It's a moderate trek that older kids can easily negotiate, but children under six aren't allowed. ✉ *Carlsbad Caverns National Park* ☎ *877/444–6777 reservations* 🌐 *www.recreation.gov* 🎫 *$7.*

Lower Cave

SPELUNKING | Fifty-foot vertical ladders and a dirt path lead you into undeveloped portions of Carlsbad Cavern. It takes about three hours to negotiate this moderately strenuous side trip led by a knowledgeable ranger. No children under 12. ✉ *Carlsbad Caverns National Park* ☎ *877/444–6777 reservations* 🌐 *www.recreation.gov* 🎫 *$20* ✍ *Reservations essential.*

★ Natural Entrance

CAVE | FAMILY | As natural daylight recedes, a self-guided, paved trail twists and turns downward from the yawning mouth of the main cavern, about 100 yards east of the visitor center. The route is winding and sometimes slick from water seepage aboveground. A steep descent of about 750 feet, much of it secured by hand rails, takes you about a mile through the main corridor and past dramatic features such as the Bat Cave and the Boneyard. (Despite its eerie name, the formations here don't look much like femurs and fibulae; they're more like spongy bone insides.) Iceberg Rock is a massive boulder that dropped from the cave ceiling millennia ago. After about a mile, you'll link up underground with the Big Room Trail and can return to the surface via elevator or by hiking back out. Footware with a good grip is recommended. ✉ *727 Carlsbad Cavern Hwy.* 🎫 *$15.*

🍴 Restaurants

Underground Lunchroom

$ | FAST FOOD | At 750 feet underground, near the elevator and entrance to the Big Room, you can grab a snack, soft drink, or club sandwich at this handy snack bar. Service is quick, even when there's a crowd, and although the food doesn't stand out, it's fun dining in this otherworldly setting. **Known for:** unusual cavern setting; quick service; convenience. [$] *Average main: $7* ✉ *727 Carlsbad Caverns Hwy.* ☎ *575/785–2232* 🌐 *www.nps.gov/cave* 🕒 *No dinner.*

Rattlesnake Springs and Slaughter Canyon

16 miles south of Carlsbad Caverns Visitor Center, 29 miles southwest of Carlsbad.

Accessed from U.S. 62/180 via Highway 418, the secluded western half of the park contains a handful of notable wilderness features, including the lush and small Rattlesnake Springs area and the visually striking Slaughter Canyon, which contains some terrific hiking trails and a popular but challenging cave accessible only by guided tour. Enormous cottonwood trees shade Rattlesnake Springs, a cool, tranquil oasis near the Black River. The rare desert wetland harbors butterflies, mammals, and reptiles, as well as 90% of the park's 357 bird species. This oasis also has a shaded picnic area, potable water, and permanent toilets, but camping and overnight parking are not allowed.

⊙ Sights

GEOLOGICAL SITES

Slaughter Canyon Cave

CAVE | Discovered in the 1930s by a local goatherd, this cave is one of the most popular secondary sites in the park, about a 40-minute drive southwest of the visitor center (you'll follow a ranger in your own vehicle to get there). Both the hike to the cave mouth and the tour will take about half a day, but it's worth it to view the deep cavern darkness as it's penetrated only by flashlights and sometimes headlamps. From the Slaughter Canyon parking area, it takes about 45 minutes to make the steep ½-mile climb up a trail leading to the mouth of the cave. You'll find that the cave consists primarily of a single corridor, 1,140 feet long, with numerous side passages.

You can take some worthwhile pictures of this cave. Wear hiking shoes with ankle support, and carry plenty of water. No kids under eight. It's a great adventure if you're in shape and love caving. ✉ End of Hwy. 418 ☎ 877/444–6777 reservations ⊕ www.recreation.gov ⊠ $15 ⌔ Reservations essential.

PICNIC AREAS

★ Rattlesnake Springs

$ | |LOCAL INTEREST | Of the several places to picnic in the park, this is the prettiest by far. There are about a dozen picnic tables and grills, many of them tree-shaded, and drinking water and restrooms are available. The seclusion of the site and the oasis-like draw add to the tranquility. Be alert to the presence of wildlife. ✉ Hwy. 418 ⌖ 8½ miles southwest of Whites City ⊕ www.nps.gov/cave.

SCENIC SPOTS

★ Rattlesnake Springs

NATURE PRESERVE | FAMILY | Enormous old-growth cottonwood trees shade the recreation area at this cool, secluded oasis near Black River. The rare desert wetland harbors butterflies, mammals, and reptiles, as well as 90% of the park's 357 bird species. Because southern New Mexico is in the northernmost region of the Chihuahuan Desert, you're likely to see birds largely unseen anywhere else in the United States outside extreme southern Texas and Arizona. If you see a flash of crimson, you might have spotted a vermilion flycatcher. Wild turkeys also flap around this oasis. Don't let the name scare you; there may be rattlesnakes here, but no more than at any similar site in the Southwest. Restroom facilities are available, but camping and overnight parking are not allowed. ✉ Hwy. 418 ⌖ 8½ miles southwest of Whites City.

TRAILS

Slaughter Canyon Trail

TRAIL | Beginning at the Slaughter Canyon Cave parking lot (four-wheel-drive or high-clearance vehicles are recommended; check with visitor center for road conditions before setting out), the trail traverses a heavily vegetated canyon bottom into a remote part of the park. As you begin hiking, look off to the east (to your right) to see the dun-colored ridges and wrinkles of the Elephant Back formation, the first of many dramatic limestone formations visible from the trail. The route travels 5½ miles one-way, the last 3 miles steeply climbing onto a limestone ridge escarpment. Allow a full day for the round-trip, and prepare for an elevation gain of 1,850 feet. Difficult. ✉ Carlsbad Caverns National Park ⌖ Trailhead: at Slaughter Canyon Cave parking lot, Hwy. 418, 10 miles west of U.S. 62/180.

★ Yucca Canyon Trail

TRAIL | Sweeping views of the Guadalupe Mountains and El Capitan give allure to this challenging but beautiful trail. Drive past Rattlesnake Springs and stop at the park boundary before reaching the Slaughter Canyon Cave parking lot (four-wheel-drive or high-clearance vehicles are recommended; check with visitor center for road conditions before setting out). Turn west along the boundary fence line to the trailhead. The 7½-mile

The Big Room is a limestone chamber in the cavern.

round-trip begins at the mouth of Yucca Canyon and climbs nearly 1,500 feet up to the top of the escarpment for a panoramic view. *Difficult.* ✉ *Carlsbad Caverns National Park* ✛ *Trailhead: at Slaughter Canyon Cave parking lot, Hwy. 418, 10 miles west of U.S. 62/180.*

Activities

BIRD-WATCHING
From redheaded turkey vultures to golden eagles, 357 species of birds have been identified in Carlsbad Caverns National Park. The park's Rattlesnake Springs area is the best for this activity. Ask for a checklist at the visitor center and then start looking for greater roadrunners, red-winged blackbirds, white-throated swifts, northern flickers, and pygmy nuthatches. Because southern New Mexico is in the northernmost region of the Chihuahuan Desert, you're likely to see birds largely unseen anywhere else in the United States outside extreme southern Texas and Arizona. If you see a flash of crimson, you might have spotted a vermilion flycatcher. Wild turkeys also flap around this oasis.

CAMPING
Backcountry camping is by permit only. No campfires are allowed in the park, and all camping is hike-to. There are commercial campgrounds in Whites City and Carlsbad, and nearby Guadalupe Mountains National Park has both designated campgrounds and backcountry sites.

HIKING
Deep, dark, and mysterious, the Carlsbad Caverns are such a park focal point that the 46,766-plus acres of wilderness above them have gone largely undeveloped, perfect for those looking for solitude—and there's no fee for accessing the park's aboveground areas. Rudimentary trails crisscross the dry, textured terrain and lead up to elevations of 6,000 feet or more. These routes often take a half day or more to travel; Guadalupe Ridge Trail is long enough that it calls for

camping overnight. Walkers who just want a little dusty taste of desert flowers and wildlife should try the Chihuahuan Desert Nature Walk.

Nearby Towns

On the Pecos River—with 3 miles of beaches, lawns, and picturesque riverside pathways—**Carlsbad** is the best base for lodging and dining near the park. At the park's main entrance road, about 7 miles from the visitor center, **Whites City** is a tiny privately owned village with a basic motel, restaurant, and gas station.

Carlsbad

25 miles north of Carlsbad Caverns National Park, 52 miles north of Guadalupe Mountains National Park.

With a few notable attractions of its own, this small city with about 29,300 residents is part–oil boom town, part–Old West, with a decided Mexican-American accent.

GETTING HERE AND AROUND

Carlsbad lies in the southeastern corner of New Mexico at the junction of U.S. 62 and 180. It's a remote part of the world, and a car is a must for getting around. The nearest good-size cities are El Paso and Lubbock, Texas, both of which are about a 2½-hour drive. It takes about 4½ hours to drive to Albuquerque.

VISITOR INFORMATION Carlsbad Chamber of Commerce. ⊠ *302 S. Canal St., Carlsbad* ☎ *575/887–6516* ⊕ *www.carlsbadchamber.com.*

Notable Quote

"The more I thought of it the more I realized that any hole in the ground which could house such a gigantic army of bats must be a whale of a big cave."

—Jim White, from *Jim White's Own Story: The Discovery and History of Carlsbad Caverns*

◉ Sights

Carlsbad Museum and Arts Center
MUSEUM | Pueblo pottery, Native American artifacts, and early cowboy and ranch memorabilia fill this downtown cultural center, along with contemporary art shows and an exhibit on Carlsbad's bats. The real treasure, though, is the McAdoo Collection, with works by painters of the Taos Society of Artists. ⊠ *418 W. Fox St., Carlsbad* ☎ *575/887–0276* ⊕ *www.cityofcarlsbadnm.com* ⊗ *Closed Sun. and Mon.*

★ **Living Desert Zoo and Gardens State Park**
GARDEN | FAMILY | More preserve than traditional zoo, this park contains an impressive collection of plants and animals native to the Chihuahuan Desert. The Desert Arboretum has hundreds of exotic cacti and succulents, and the Living Desert Zoo is home to mountain lions, javelinas, deer, elk, bobcats, bison, and a black bear. Nocturnal exhibits let you view the area's nighttime wildlife, a walk-through aviary houses birds of prey, and there's a reptile exhibit. The park also sponsors some great educational events. Though there are shaded rest areas, restrooms, and water fountains, in summer it's more comfortable to visit in the morning before the desert oven

heats up. The expansive view from here is the best in town. ✉ *1504 Miehls Dr. N, Carlsbad* ☎ *575/887–5516* ⊕ *www. livingdesertnm.org* 🎫 *$5.*

 Restaurants

★ Adobe Rose

$$ | SOUTHWESTERN | This sprawling Artesia restaurant in a restored adobe building with plenty of indoor and outdoor seating serves up hearty, creative portions of Southwestern fare. Straightforward dishes like black peppercorn filet mignon and chicken-fried chicken are flavorfully prepared, and there's an extensive wine list. **Known for:** beer-braised pot roast with brown gravy and ghost chiles; blue-corn stacked taco salads; attractive outdoor patio. ⑂ *Average main: $18* ✉ *1614 N. 13th St., Artesia* ☎ *575/746–6157* ⊕ *www.adoberoserestaurant.com* ☉ *Closed Sun. No lunch Mon.–Tues. and Sat.*

Blue House Bakery & Cafe

$ | BAKERY | This breakfast nook housed in a charming historic bungalow is a favorite of locals and a treat for travelers weary of so many generic coffee shops. Freshly squeezed juices, inventive breakfast sandwiches, homemade pastries, and arguably the best coffee in town start the day off right. **Known for:** spacious, umbrella-shaded outdoor patio; gooey cinnamon rolls; breakfast croissants filled with sausage, potatoes, and green chile. ⑂ *Average main: $7* ✉ *609 N. Canyon St., Carlsbad* ☎ *575/628–0555* ☉ *Closed Sun. No lunch. No dinner.*

Carniceria San Juan de Los Lagos

$ | MEXICAN | Equal parts butcher, bakery, and short-order restaurant, this spacious and colorfully decorated compound turns out some of the most authentic Mexican food in this corner of the state, from burritos and tacos to *chicharrón*. There's a long menu, and although alcohol isn't available, there is a selection of Mexican soft drinks and sweets. **Known**

for: carnitas-stuffed tacos and tortas; breakfast burritos; traditional house-baked Mexican pastries. ⑂ *Average main: $9* ✉ *1200 N. Pate St., Carlsbad* ☎ *575/887–0034.*

Lucky Bull

$$ | SOUTHWESTERN | Set inside the city's historic former city hall, this casual tavern serves tasty pub grub, including roasted green chile queso blanco, mammoth burgers with a range of interesting toppings, and hand-cut rib-eye steaks. An upstairs tap room carries a fine selection of craft beers, with an emphasis on New Mexico brewers. **Known for:** Pecos Valley poutine (fries topped with green chile gravy and cheddar); country-fried steak; impressive craft-beer selection. ⑂ *Average main: $17* ✉ *220 W. Fox St., Carlsbad* ☎ *575/725–5444* ⊕ *www.luckybullcarlsbad.com* ☉ *Closed Sun.*

★ Red Chimney Pit Bar-B-Q

$ | BARBECUE | FAMILY | If you hanker for sweet-and-tangy pecan wood–smoked barbecue, this homey, log-cabin-style spot serves up consistently tasty fare at reasonable prices. Sauce from an old family recipe is slathered on chicken, pork, beef brisket, turkey, and ham. **Known for:** sides of smoked mac-and-cheese and seasoned corn; charbroiled burgers; spicy jalapeño sausage. ⑂ *Average main: $14* ✉ *817 N. Canal St., Carlsbad* ☎ *575/885–8744* ⊕ *www. redchimneybbq.com* ☉ *Closed Sun. and Mon.*

★ Trinity Hotel

$$ | ITALIAN | The region's top pick for a romantic, elegant meal, this handsome dining room with vaulted ceilings, tall windows, and a long old-fashioned bar is set inside the beautifully restored 1892 Trinity Hotel. The kitchen turns out hearty and flavorful Italian fare, from traditional pastas to halibut with lemon-caper sauce, and a signature dish, chicken bolloco—essentially fettuccine Alfredo with fresh green chilies added. **Known for:** local goat cheese with blackberries and habañero sauce; an excellent selection of acclaimed New Mexico wines; biscuits and gravy at brunch. $ *Average main: $18* ✉ *201 S. Canal St., Carlsbad* ☎ *575/234–9891* ⊕ *www.thetrinityhotel.com.*

YellowBrix

$$ | MODERN AMERICAN | This attractive restaurant set in a former 1920s home has several different dining rooms as well as a breezy courtyard patio where local acoustic musicians sometimes perform. The kitchen serves eclectic fare with sophisticated flourishes, including poached-pear salads, sashimi tuna with a spicy wasabi-soy sauce, pressed Cuban sandwiches, and an extensive selection of steaks. **Known for:** Brix bacon-wrapped meat loaf; friendly and efficient service; chocolate lava cake. $ *Average main: $22* ✉ *201 N. Canal St., Carlsbad* ☎ *575/941–2749* ⊕ *www.yellowbrixrestaurant.com.*

 ## Hotels

Hampton Inn and Suites

$$ | HOTEL | On the south side of downtown leading to the Carlsbad Caverns, this well-maintained chain property lies within walking distance of a few restaurants, a gas station, and a Walmart. **Pros:** friendly staff; clean, well-kept amenities; convenient location. **Cons:** thin walls; cookie-cutter decor; on a busy road. $ *Rooms from: $160* ✉ *120 Esperanza Circle, Carlsbad* ☎ *575/725–5700* ⊕ *www.hilton.com* ⤳ *85 rooms* ⦿ *Free Breakfast.*

Hotel Artesia

$$ | HOTEL | The most distinctive lodging option in pleasant oil-refining town Artesia, about 60 miles north of the park, this striking art deco–style hotel has roomy accommodations with blond-wood furniture and the same in-room amenities you'd find at the several chain hotels in town. **Pros:** within walking distance of several restaurants and bars; great value; interesting design. **Cons:** about a 75-minute drive to the park visitor center; rooms can feel a little dark; not a lot to

do in Artesia. $ *Rooms from: $127* ✉ *203 N. 2nd St., Artesia* ☎ *575/746–2066, 888/746–2066* ⊕ *www.hotelartesia.com* ⤳ *50 rooms* ⦿ *Free Breakfast.*

Hyatt House Carlsbad

$$$ | HOTEL | This sleek, contemporary newcomer to Carlsbad's growing hotel scene has smartly appointed rooms, some with kitchens, and all furnished with large flat-screen TVs, individual climate control, laptop safes, and blackout curtains. **Pros:** stylish, contemporary design; pool and well-equipped gym; decent bar and restaurant on-site; good base for exploring Carlsbad Caverns. **Cons:** not much in the way of local ambience; on a busy road. $ *Rooms from: $189* ✉ *4019 National Parks Hwy., Carlsbad* ☎ *575/689–6700* ⊕ *www.hyatt. com* ⤳ *97 rooms* ⦿ *Free Breakfast.*

TownePlace Suites by Marriott Carlsbad

$$$$ | HOTEL | FAMILY | This attractive, contemporary outpost of Marriott's extended-stay-oriented TownPlace Suites brand has large and nicely equipped accommodations. **Pros:** convenient location; smartly designed rooms; in-room kitchens. **Cons:** it looks like any other TownePlace Suites property; can be very expensive when demand soars; on a busy road. $ *Rooms from: $309* ✉ *311 Pompa St., Carlsbad* ☎ *575/689–8850* ⊕ *www.marriott.com* ⤳ *94 rooms* ⦿ *Free Breakfast.*

★ Trinity Hotel

$$ | B&B/INN | The region's most elegant and atmospheric lodging option occupies a graceful 1892 redbrick former bank building with nine luxuriously appointed rooms with high ceilings, plush beds with pillow-top mattresses, hidden flat-screen TVs, and spacious bathrooms with glass walk-in showers. **Pros:** steps from several good restaurants; reasonable rates; terrific bar and restaurant. **Cons:** no elevator; no interior access to the lobby; no pets allowed. $ *Rooms from: $159* ✉ *201 S. Canal St., Carlsbad* ☎ *575/234–9891* ⊕ *www.thetrinityhotel. com* ⤳ *9 rooms* ⦿ *Free Breakfast.*

🍸 Nightlife

★ **Milton's Taproom and Brewery**
BREWPUBS/BEER GARDENS | This first-rate downtown craft brewery has rapidly become one of the top beer makers in southern New Mexico. There's often live music. ✉ *213 W. Mermod St., Carlsbad* ☎ *575/725–5779* 🌐 *www.miltonsbrewing.com.*

Whites City

20 miles southwest of Carlsbad, 32 miles northeast of Guadalupe Mountains National Park

It's not a city, or really even a town, but on the Western-style boardwalk of this privately owned tourist spread at the park entrance, you'll find a souvenir shop, a small grocery store, a gas station, a motel with waterslides, and a simple restaurant. It's not much, but it's close to the park entrance on U.S. 62/180.

🛏 Hotels

Whites City Cavern Inn
$ | **HOTEL** | This bland but economical two-story motel just outside the entrance to the national park has spacious rooms that have recently undergone a remodel. **Pros:** closest lodging to Carlsbad Caverns; water park is a welcome splash in summer; cheap rates. **Cons:** rooms and service are very bare-bones; often books well ahead, especially on summer weekends; few dining options nearby. [$] *Rooms from: $91* ✉ *6 Carlsbad Caverns Hwy., Whites City* ☎ *575/361–2687* 🌐 *www.whitescitynm.com* 🛏 *60 rooms* 🍴 *Free Breakfast.*

Chapter 12

CHANNEL ISLANDS NATIONAL PARK

12

Updated by
Cheryl Crabtree

CALIFORNIA

🏕 Camping	🛏 Hotels	🏃 Activities	👁 Scenery	👥 Crowds
★★★★☆	★★☆☆☆	★★★★★	★★★★☆	★★☆☆☆

WELCOME TO
CHANNEL ISLANDS NATIONAL PARK

TOP REASONS TO GO

★ **Rare flora and fauna:** The Channel Islands are home to 145 species of terrestrial plants and animals found nowhere else on Earth.

★ **Time travel:** With no cars, phones, or services and away from hectic modern life, these undeveloped islands provide a glimpse of what California was like hundreds of years ago.

★ **Underwater adventures:** The incredibly healthy channel waters rank among the top 10 diving destinations on the planet—but you can also visit the kelp forest virtually via Channel Islands Live, a live underwater program.

★ **Marvelous marine mammals:** More than 30 species of seals, sea lions, whales, and other marine mammals ply the park's waters at various times of year.

★ **Sea-cave kayaking:** Paddle around otherwise inaccessible portions of the park's 175 miles of gorgeous coastline—including one of the world's largest sea caves.

1 Anacapa. Tiny Anacapa is a 5-mile stretch of three islets, with towering cliffs, caves, natural bridges, and rich kelp forests.

2 San Miguel. Isolated, windswept San Miguel, the park's westernmost island (access permit required), has an ancient caliche forest and hundreds of archaeological sites chronicling the Native Americans' 13,000-year history on the islands. More than 30,000 pinnipeds (seals and sea lions) hang out on the island's beaches during certain times of year.

3 Santa Barbara. More than 5 miles of scenic trails crisscross this tiny island, known for its excellent wildlife viewing and native plants. It's a favorite destination for diving, snorkeling, and kayaking.

4 Santa Cruz. The park's largest island offers some of the best hikes and kayaking opportunities, one of the world's largest and deepest sea caves, and more species of flora and fauna than any other park island.

5 Santa Rosa. Campers love to stay on Santa Rosa, with its myriad hiking opportunities, stunning white-sand beaches, and rare grove of Torrey pines. It's also the only island accessible by plane.

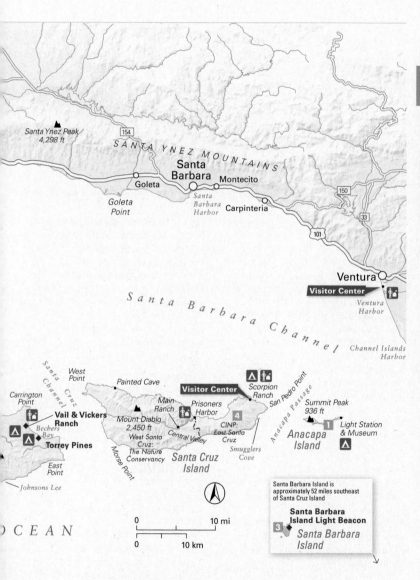

Santa Ynez Peak
4,298 ft

154

SANTA YNEZ MOUNTAINS

Santa
Barbara

Goleta

Montecito

150

Goleta
Point

Santa
Barbara
Harbor

Carpinteria

33

101

Ventura

Visitor Center

Ventura
Harbor

Santa Barbara Channel

Channel Islands
Harbor

Santa Cruz Channel

West
Point

Painted Cave

Visitor Center

Scorpion
Ranch

San Pedro Point

Carrington
Point

Main
Ranch

Prisoners
Harbor

4

Summit Peak
936 ft

Anacapa Passage

1

Light Station
& Museum

Vail & Vickers
Ranch

Bechers
Bay

Mount Diablo
2,450 ft

West Santa
Cruz:
The Nature
Conservancy

Central Valley

CINP:
East Santa
Cruz

Anacapa
Island

Torrey Pines

East
Point

Morse Point

Santa Cruz
Island

Smugglers
Cove

Johnsons Lee

OCEAN

0   10 mi

0   10 km

Santa Barbara Island is
approximately 52 miles southeast
of Santa Cruz Island

Santa Barbara
Island Light Beacon

3

Santa Barbara
Island

On crystal-clear days, the craggy peaks of Channel Islands are easy to see from the mainland, jutting from the Pacific in sharp detail. Sometimes called the North American Galápagos, they form a magnificent nature preserve, home to many native plants, land animals, and marine creatures—some found nowhere else on the planet.

Established in 1980, the national park includes five of the eight Channel Islands—ranging in size from 1-square-mile Santa Barbara to 96-square-mile Santa Cruz—and the nautical mile of ocean that surrounds them. If you visit East Anacapa in spring or summer, you'll walk through a nesting area of western gulls. If you're lucky enough to get to windswept San Miguel, you might see as many as 30,000 pinnipeds (seals and sea lions) camped out on the beach. You can kayak close to the seals (as long as you don't disturb them) or snorkel or dive amid some of the world's richest kelp forests. Even traveling on an excursion boat gives you a chance to view sea lions, brown pelicans, and spouting whales.

Scientists have uncovered many treasures during decades of research on these relatively undeveloped islands. Archaeological evidence at Santa Rosa Island's Arlington Springs site shows that people lived in coastal California 13,000 years ago and traveled by watercraft throughout the region. The native Chumash lived on the islands until the late 1700s, when Spaniards settled in California. Unfortunately, European diseases and the demise of the trade-based economy devastated the indigenous population, and the few remaining Chumash islanders left in 1816–17. Over the ensuing decades, other humans set up fishing and otter hunting camps and built ranches on the islands; the U.S. Navy also established several military installations. All commercial operations have now ceased, and the park has embarked on an ambitious project to restore the natural habitats.

Relatively few people travel out to the park. If you're among the few who do make the effort, know that a splendid land-and-sea wilderness—minus the crowds—awaits.

Planning

When to Go

Channel Islands National Park records about 410,000 visitors each year, but many never venture beyond the visitor center. During the busiest times (holidays and summer weekends) book transportation and accommodations well in advance.

AVERAGE HIGH/LOW TEMPERATURES					
JAN.	FEB.	MAR.	APR.	MAY	JUNE
66/44	66/45	66/46	68/48	69/51	71/55
JULY	AUG.	SEPT.	OCT.	NOV.	DEC.
74/57	75/59	75/57	74/53	70/48	66/44

Channel Islands in One Day

If you have a few hours or a day to visit the Channel Islands, start with viewing the exhibits at the **Channel Islands National Park Visitor Center** in Ventura. Then cruise over to **East Anacapa** for sweeping views of Santa Cruz Island and the mainland—provided it's not too foggy—and some hiking, the primary activity here. Wander through western gull rookeries, or peer down from steep cliffs and watch the antics of sea lions and seals. Alternatively, hop aboard a high-speed Island Packers catamaran, and zip out to Scorpion Landing or Prisoner's Harbor on **Santa Cruz Island** for longer hiking, snorkeling, or kayaking explorations. From March through November, Island Packers also offers day-trip transportation to **Santa Rosa Island**, where you can hike along a blufftop trail to the rare Torrey Pines grove or trek through scenic canyons. From spring through fall, when ocean conditions permit safe onshore skiff landing after your high-speed boat ride, visit **San Miguel**, and join a ranger-guided hike. Island Packers boats make the relatively long day trip to **Santa Barbara Island** several times a year; check the website for the current schedule.

The warm, dry summer and fall months are the best time to go camping. Humpback and blue whales arrive to feed from late June through early fall. The rains usually come December through March—but this is also the best time to spot gray whales and get hotel discounts. In the late spring, thousands of migratory birds descend on the islands to hatch their young, and wildflowers carpet the slopes. The water temperature is nearly always cool, so bring a wet suit if you plan to spend time in the ocean, even in the summer. Fog, high winds, and rough seas can happen any time of the year.

Getting Here and Around

AIR

You can arrange charter service to Santa Rosa and San Miguel islands. Flights depart from the Camarillo Airport, south of Ventura, or the Santa Barbara Airport.

CONTACTS Channel Islands Aviation.
✉ *305 Durley Ave., Camarillo* ☎ *805/987–1301* ⊕ *www.flycia.com.*

BOAT

The visitor center for Channel Islands National Park is on California's mainland, in the town of Ventura, off U.S. 101. From the harbors at Ventura, Santa Barbara, and Oxnard you can board a boat to one of the islands. If you have your own boat, you can land at any of the park islands without a permit, but you should visit the park website for instructions and information on restricted areas. A permit is required to land on the Nature Conservancy property on Santa Cruz Island. Boaters landing at San Miguel must contact the park ranger beforehand.

Island Packers

Sailing on high-speed catamarans from Ventura or a mono-hull vessel from Oxnard, Island Packers goes to Santa Cruz Island daily most of the year, weather permitting. The boats also go to Anacapa several days a week and to the outer islands from April through November. They also cruise along Anacapa's north shore on three-hour wildlife tours (no disembarking) several times a week. Rates start at $40 for whale-watching cruises; other types of trips start at $59. ⊠ *3550 Harbor Blvd., Oxnard* ☎ *805/642–1393* ⊕ *islandpackers.com* ✉ *$38.*

CAR

To reach the Ventura harbor, exit U.S. 101 in Ventura at Seaward Boulevard or Victoria Avenue, and follow the signs to Ventura Harbor/Spinnaker Drive. To access Channel Islands Harbor in Oxnard, exit U.S. 101 at Victoria Avenue, and head south approximately 7 miles to Channel Islands Boulevard. To access dive and whale-watching boats in Santa Barbara, exit U.S. 101 at Castillo Street, and head south to Cabrillo Boulevard, then turn right for the harbor entrance. Private vehicles are not permitted on the islands. Pets are also not allowed in the park.

TRAIN

Amtrak makes stops in Santa Barbara, Ventura, and Oxnard; from the Amtrak station, just take a taxi, rideshare service, or waterfront shuttle bus to the harbor.

Inspiration

California's Channel Islands: A History is an extensive cultural, geologic, and historical account of all eight Channel Islands by Frederic Caire Chiles, whose

Transit Times to the Islands

Island	Distance and Time by Boat	Cost (per hiker/camper)
Anacapa Island	14 miles/1 hr from Oxnard	$59/$79
San Miguel Island	58 miles/3 hrs from Ventura	$105/$147
Santa Barbara Island	55 miles/2½–3 hrs from Ventura	$82/$114
Santa Cruz Island	20 miles/1 hr from Ventura	$59/$79
Santa Rosa Island	46 miles/2 hrs from Ventura	$82/$114

pioneering great-grandfather settled Santa Cruz Island in the 1800s.

Channel Islands National Park and National Marine Sanctuary—California's Galapagos is a visual overview with more than 140 images by photographer Tim Hauf.

Diary of a Sea Captain's Wife: Tales of Santa Cruz Island is by Margaret H. Eaton, who, along with her husband, ran a camp-resort at Pelican Bay on Santa Cruz Island in the early 1900s.

Island of the Blue Dolphins, a legendary novel by Scott O'Dell that's great for kids, tells the tale of 12-year-old Karana, a native Chumash girl who must fend for herself for years after she's abandoned on one of the Channel Islands.

North America's Galapagos: The Historic Channel Islands Biological Survey, by Corinne Heyning Laverty, is a tale of the 33-member research team that chronicled the islands' history and evolution in the 1930s.

When the Killing's Done, a novel by T. Coraghessan Boyle, dives deep into the conflict between efforts to protect native wildlife by ridding the islands of invasive species and people who oppose any purposeful killing of animals.

Park Essentials

ACCESSIBILITY

The Channel Islands National Park Robert J. Lagomarsino Visitor Center is fully accessible. The islands themselves have few facilities and are not easy to navigate by individuals in wheelchairs or those with limited mobility. Limited wheelchair access is available on Santa Rosa Island via air transportation.

PARK FEES AND PERMITS

There is no fee to enter Channel Islands National Park, but unless you have your own boat, you will pay $40 or more per person for a ride with a boat operator. The cost of taking a boat to the park varies depending on which operator you choose. Also, there is a $15-per-day fee for staying in one of the islands' campgrounds.

If you take your own boat, landing permits are not required to visit islands administered by the National Park Service. However, boaters who want to land on the Nature Conservancy preserve on Santa Cruz Island must have a permit. Visit ⊕ www.nature.org/cruzpermit for permit information; allow 10 business days to process and return your permit application. If you anchor in a nearby cove at any island, at least one person should remain aboard the boat at all times. San Miguel Island is property of the U.S. Navy. To visit it, you must obtain an access permit, which is available at the boat and air concession offices and at a self-registration station on the island. To hike beyond the ranger station on San Miguel, you need a reservation and permit; call ☎ 805/658–5700 to be matched up with a ranger, who must accompany you. Anglers must have a state fishing license; for details, call the California Department of Fish and Wildlife at ☎ 916/653–7664 or visit ⊕ wildlifeca.

gov. More than a dozen Marine Protected Areas (MPAs) with special regulations surround the islands, so read the guidelines carefully before you depart.

PARK HOURS

The islands are open every day of the year. The visitor center in Ventura is closed on Thanksgiving and Christmas. Channel Islands National Park is in the Pacific time zone.

CELL PHONE RECEPTION

Reception is spotty and varies by location and service provider. Public telephones are available on the mainland near the visitor center but not on the islands.

Hotels

In the park, your only option is sleeping in a tent at a no-frills campground. If you hanker for more creature comforts, you can splurge on a bunk and meals on a dive boat.

There's a huge range of lodging options on the mainland, from seaside camping to posh international resorts. The most affordable options are in Oxnard, Ventura, and Carpinteria, a small seaside community between Santa Barbara and Ventura. Despite rates that range from pricey to downright shocking, Santa Barbara's numerous hotels and bed-and-breakfasts attract thousands of patrons year-round. Wherever you stay, be sure to make reservations for the summer and holiday weekends (especially Memorial Day, July 4, Labor Day, and Thanksgiving) well ahead of time; it's not unusual for coastal accommodations to fill completely during these busy times. Also be aware that some hotels double their rates during festivals and other events. *Hotel reviews have been shortened. For full information, visit Fodors.com.*

12

Channel Islands National Park PLANNING

Restaurants

Out on the islands, there are no restaurants, no snack bars, and in some cases, no potable water. Instead, pack a fancy picnic or a simple sandwich. For a quick meal before or after your island trip, each of the harbors has a number of decent eateries nearby.

Back on the mainland, though, it's a dining gold mine. Santa Barbara has a long-standing reputation for culinary excellence, and a "foodie" renaissance in recent years has transformed Ventura into a dining destination—with dozens of new restaurants touting nouvelle cuisine made with organic produce and meats. Fresh seafood is a standout, whether it's prepared simply in wharf-side hangouts or incorporated into sophisticated bistro menus. Dining attire is generally casual, though slightly dressy casual wear is the custom at pricier restaurants. *Restaurant reviews have been shortened. For full information, visit Fodors.com.*

What It Costs			
$	$$	$$$	$$$$
RESTAURANTS			
under $16	$16–$22	$23–$30	over $30
HOTELS			
under $120	$121–$175	$176–$250	over $250

Visitor Information

CONTACTS Channel Islands National Park Robert J. Lagomarsino Visitor Center. ⊠ *1901 Spinnaker Dr., Ventura* ☏ *805/658–5730* ⊕ *www.nps.gov/chis.* **Outdoors Santa Barbara Visitor Center.** ⊠ *113 Harbor Way, Santa Barbara* ☏ *805/456–8752* ⊕ *outdoorsb.sbmm.org.*

Anacapa Island

14 miles from Channel Islands Harbor in Oxnard.

Anacapa is actually comprised of three narrow islets. Although the tips of these volcanic formations nearly touch, the islets are inaccessible from one another except by boat. All three have towering cliffs, isolated sea caves, and natural bridges; Arch Rock, on East Anacapa, is one of the park's best-known symbols. Wildlife viewing is the main activity on East Anacapa, particularly in summer when seagull chicks are newly hatched and sea lions and seals lounge on the beaches. Exhibits at East Anacapa's compact **museum** include the original lead-crystal Fresnel lens from the 1932 lighthouse. There are picnic tables at the island's visitor center.

On West Anacapa, depending on the season, boats travel to **Frenchy's Cove.** On a voyage here you might see anemones, limpets, barnacles, mussel beds, and colorful marine algae in the pristine tide pools. The rest of West Anacapa is closed to protect nesting brown pelicans.

 Sights

TRAILS
Inspiration Point Trail
TRAIL | FAMILY | This 1½-mile hike along flat terrain takes in most of East Anacapa. There are great views from Inspiration Point and Cathedral Cove. *Easy.* ⊠ *Trailhead: at Landing Cove, Anacapa Island.*

San Miguel Island

58 miles from Ventura.

The westernmost of the Channel Islands, San Miguel Island is often battered by storms sweeping across the North Pacific. The 15-square-mile island's wild windswept landscape is lush with vegetation. Point Bennett, at the western tip, offers one of the world's most spectacular wildlife displays when more than 30,000 pinnipeds hit its beach. Explorer Juan Rodríguez Cabrillo was the first European to visit this island; he claimed it for Spain in 1542. Legend holds that Cabrillo died on one of the Channel Islands—no one knows where he's buried, but there's a memorial to him on a bluff above Cuyler Harbor. Unlike the other islands in the park, there are no picnic tables here, but there is an isolated campground.

Sights

TRAILS

Cuyler Harbor Beach Trail

TRAIL | This easy walk takes you along a 2-mile-long white sand beach on San Miguel. The eastern section is occasionally cut off by high tides. An access permit is required. *Easy.* ⊠ *Trailhead: at San Miguel Campground, San Miguel Island.*

Lester Ranch Trail

TRAIL | This short but strenuous 2-mile hike leads up a spectacular canyon filled with waterfalls and lush native plants. At the end of a steep climb to the top of a peak, views of the historic Lester Ranch and the Cabrillo Monument await. If you plan to hike beyond the Lester Ranch, you'll need a hiking permit in addition to an island-access permit; call or visit the park website for details. *Difficult.* ⊠ *Trailhead: at San Miguel Campground, San Miguel Island* ☎ *805/658–5730.*

Point Bennett Trail

TRAIL | Rangers conduct 15-mile hikes across San Miguel to Point Bennett, where more than 30,000 pinnipeds (three different species) can be seen. An access permit is required. *Difficult.* ⊠ *Trailhead: at San Miguel Campground, San Miguel Island.*

Santa Barbara Island

55 miles from Ventura.

At about 1 square mile, Santa Barbara Island is the smallest of the Channel Islands and nearly 35 miles south of the others. Triangular in shape, Santa Barbara's steep cliffs—which offer a perfect nesting spot for the Scripps's murrelet, a rare seabird—are topped by twin peaks. In spring you can enjoy a brilliant display of yellow coreopsis. Learn about the wildlife on and around the islands at the island's small **museum**.

Although the island is open to the public, access to it is difficult. Its dock was damaged in major storms, and it's uncertain when it will be repaired. In the interim, when conditions allow (i.e., the swells aren't too high and the tide is right), boats can land only at a rocky ledge near the damaged dock. Check with the park for weather conditions and updates on the dock and island landings.

◉ Sights

TRAILS

Elephant Seal Cove Trail

TRAIL | This moderate-to-strenuous, 2½-mile, round-trip walk takes you across Santa Barbara to a point where you can view magnificent elephant seals from steep cliffs. *Moderate.* ⊠ *Trailhead: at Landing Cove, Santa Barbara Island.*

Santa Cruz Island

20 miles from Ventura.

Five miles west of Anacapa, 96-square-mile Santa Cruz Island is the largest of the Channel Islands. The National Park Service manages the easternmost 24% of it; the rest is owned by the Nature Conservancy, which requires a permit to land. When your boat drops you off on a

Santa Rosa, Santa Cruz, and Anacapa Islands

PACIFIC OCEAN

Santa Cruz Island

Santa Rosa Island

Anacapa Island

Santa Barbara Channel

Santa Cruz Channel

Anacapa Passage

Ventura is approximately 28 miles
Northeast of Prisoners Harbor, Santa Cruz Island

Santa Barbara Island is
approximately 52 miles southeast
of Santa Cruz Island

San Miguel Island is
approximately 2.5 miles west
of Santa Rosa Island

West Point

Painted Cave

Mount Diablo
2,450 ft

Morse Point

CENTRAL VALLEY

West Santa
Cruz: The Nature
Conservancy

Main
Ranch

Prisoners
Harbor

Chinese Harbor

Coche Point

CINP:
East Santa
Cruz

Scorpion
Ranch

San Pedro Point

Smugglers
Cove

Sandstone Point

Summit Peak
936 ft

Frenchy's
Cove

Inspiration
Point

Arch
Rock

Light Station
and Museum

Carrington
Point

Bechers
Bay

Skunk Point

East Point

Vail & Vickers Ranch

Torrey
Pines

Black Mtn
1,298 ft

Soledad Peak
1,574 ft

Brockway
Point

Sandy Point

Johnsons
Lee

Ford Point

South Point

Cluster Point

0   5 mi

0   5 km

Plants and Wildlife on the Channel Islands

Channel Islands National Park is home to species found nowhere else on Earth: mammals such as the island fox and the island deer mouse and birds like the island scrub jay live forever on the endangered species list. Thousands of western gulls hatch each summer on Anacapa before flying off to the mainland, where they spend about four years learning all their bad habits. Then, they return to the island to roost and have chicks of their own. It all adds up to a living laboratory not unlike the one naturalist Charles Darwin discovered off the coast of South America 200 years ago, which is why the Channel Islands are often called the North American Galápagos.

portion of the 70 miles of craggy coastline, you see two rugged mountain ranges with peaks soaring to 2,500 feet and deep canyons traversed by streams. This landscape is the habitat of a remarkable variety of flora and fauna—more than 600 types of plants, 140 kinds of land birds, 11 mammal species, five varieties of reptiles, and three amphibian species live here. Bird-watchers may want to look for the endemic island scrub jay, which is found nowhere else in the world.

One of the largest and deepest sea caves in the world, Painted Cave, lies along the northwest coast of Santa Cruz. Named for the colorful lichen and algae that cover its walls, the cave is nearly ¼ mile long and 100 feet wide. In spring, a waterfall cascades over the entrance. Kayakers may see seals or sea lions cruising beside their boats in the cave.

The Channel Islands hold some of the richest archaeological resources in North America, and all artifacts are protected within the park. On Santa Cruz, you can see remnants of a dozen Chumash villages, the largest of which is at the island's eastern end in the area now called Scorpion Ranch. The Chumash mined the island's extensive chert deposits for tools to produce shell-bead money, which they traded with people on the mainland. You can learn about Chumash history and view artifacts, tools, and exhibits on native plant and wildlife at the interpretive visitor center near the landing dock. You can also explore remnants of the early-1900s ranching era in the restored historic adobe and outbuildings.

Sights

TRAILS
Cavern Point Trail
TRAIL | FAMILY | This moderate 2-mile hike takes you to the bluffs northwest of Scorpion harbor on Santa Cruz, where there are magnificent coastal views and pods of migrating gray whales from December through March. *Moderate.* ✉ *Trailhead: at Scorpion Ranch Campground, Santa Cruz Island.*

Historic Ranch Trail
TRAIL | FAMILY | This easy ½-mile walk on Santa Cruz Island takes you to a historic ranch where you can visit an interpretive center in an 1800s adobe and see remnants of a cattle ranch. *Easy.* ✉ *Trailhead: at Scorpion Beach, Santa Cruz Island.*

★ Prisoners Harbor/Pelican Cove Trail
TRAIL | Taking in quite a bit of Santa Cruz, this moderate to strenuous 3-mile trail one-way to Pelican Cove is one of the best hikes in the park. You must be accompanied by an Island Packers naturalist or secure a permit (visit ⊕ *www. nature.org/cruzpermit*; allow 10 to 15 business days to process and return

your application), as the hike takes you through Nature Conservancy property. *Moderate.* ✉ *Trailhead: at Prisoners Harbor, Santa Cruz Island.*

Santa Rosa Island

46 miles from Ventura.

Between Santa Cruz and San Miguel, Santa Rosa is the second largest of the Channel Islands. The terrain along the coast varies from broad, sandy beaches to sheer cliffs—a central mountain range, rising to 1,589 feet, breaks the island's low profile. Santa Rosa is home to about 500 species of plants, including the rare Torrey pine, and three unusual mammals: the island fox, the spotted skunk, and the deer mouse. They hardly compare, though, to their predecessors: a nearly complete skeleton of a 6-foot-tall pygmy mammoth was unearthed in 1994.

From 1901 to 1998, cattle were raised at the island's **Vail & Vickers Ranch**. The route from Santa Rosa's landing dock to the campground passes by the historic ranch buildings, barns, equipment, and the wooden pier where cattle were brought onto the island. There are picnic tables behind the ranch house here as well as at Water Canyon Beach.

Sights

TRAILS

East Point Trail

TRAIL | This strenuous 12-mile hike along beautiful white-sand beaches yields the opportunity to see rare Torrey pines. Some beaches are closed between March and September, so you have to remain on the road for portions of this hike. *Difficult.* ✉ *Trailhead: at Santa Rosa Campground, Santa Rosa Island.*

Torrey Pines Trail

TRAIL | This moderate 5-mile loop climbs up to Santa Rosa's grove of rare Torrey pines and offers stellar views of Becher's

Bay and the channel. *Moderate.* ✉ *Trailhead: at Santa Rosa Campground, Santa Rosa Island.*

Water Canyon Trail

TRAIL | Starting at Santa Rosa Campground, this 2-mile walk along a white-sand beach features some exceptional beachcombing. Frequent strong winds can turn this easy hike into a fairly strenuous excursion, though. You can extend your walk by following animal paths to Water Canyon, which is full of native vegetation. *Easy.* ✉ *Trailhead: at Santa Rosa Campground, Santa Rosa Island.*

Activities

CAMPING

Camping is the best way to experience the natural beauty and isolation of Channel Islands National Park. Unrestricted by tour schedules, you have plenty of time to explore mountain trails, snorkel in the kelp forests, or kayak into sea caves. Campsites are primitive, with no water (except on Santa Rosa and Santa Cruz) or electricity. Campfires are not allowed on the islands, though you may use enclosed camp stoves. Use bear boxes for storing your food. You must carry all your gear and pack out all trash. Campers must arrange transportation to the islands before reserving a campsite (and yes, park personnel do check).

National Park Service Reservation System
You can get specifics on each campground and reserve a campsite ($15 per night) by contacting the National Park Service Reservation System up to six months in advance. ☎ *877/444–6777* ⊕ *www.recreation.gov.*

Del Norte Campground. This remote campground on Santa Cruz offers backpackers sweeping ocean views from its 1,500-foot perch. It's accessed via a 3½-mile hike through a series of canyons and ridges. ✉ *Prisoners Harbor landing.*

East Anacapa Campground. You need to walk ½ mile and ascend more than 150 steps to reach this open, treeless camping area above Cathedral Cove. ✉ *East Anacapa landing.*

San Miguel Campground. Accessed by a steep, 1½-mile hike across the beach and through a lush canyon, this campground is on the site of the Lester Ranch; the Cabrillo Monument is nearby. Be aware that strong winds and thick fog are common here. ✉ *Cuyler Harbor landing.*

Santa Barbara Campground. This seldom-visited campground perched on a cliff above Landing Cove is reached via a challenging uphill ½-mile climb. ✉ *Landing Cove.*

Santa Cruz Scorpion Campground. In a grove of eucalyptus trees, this campground is near the historic buildings of Scorpion Ranch. It's accessed via an easy, flat ½-mile trail from Scorpion Beach landing. ✉ *Scorpion Beach landing.*

Santa Rosa Campground. Backcountry beach camping is available on this island; it's a flat 1½-mile walk to the campground. There's a spectacular view of Santa Cruz Island across the water and easy access to fantastic hiking trails. ✉ *Bechers Bay landing.*

DIVING

Island waters offer some of the world's best dives. In the relatively warm water around Anacapa and eastern Santa Cruz, you can get great photographs of rarely seen giant black bass swimming among the kelp forests. Here you also find a reef covered with red brittle starfish. If you're an experienced diver, you might swim among five species of seals and sea lions, or try your hand at spearing rockfish or halibut near San Miguel and Santa Rosa. The best time to scuba dive is in summer and fall, when the water is often clear up to a 100-foot depth.

Peace Dive Boat

SCUBA DIVING | Ventura Harbor–based Peace Dive Boat runs single-day diving adventures near all the Channel Islands. ✉ *1691 Spinnaker Dr., Dock E, Ventura* ☎ 949/247–1106 ⊕ www.peaceboat.com 🖭 *From $145.*

Raptor Dive Boat

SCUBA DIVING | The *Raptor*, a 46-foot custom boat, takes divers on two- and three-tank trips to Anacapa and Santa Cruz islands and is available for private charters. ✉ *Ventura* ☎ 805/650–7700 ⊕ www.raptordive.com 🖭 *From $140.*

Spectre Dive Boat

SCUBA DIVING | This boat runs single-day diving trips to Anacapa and Santa Cruz. Fees include three dives, air, and food. ✉ *1575 Spinnaker Dr., Dock D, Ventura* ☎ 805/486–1166 ⊕ www.spectreboat. com 🖭 *From $135.*

EDUCATIONAL PROGRAMS
RANGER PROGRAMS

Ranger programs are held at the Channel Islands National Park Robert J. Lagomarsino Visitor Center in Ventura.

Channel Islands Live Program

NATIONAL/STATE PARK | FAMILY | Want a cool sneak preview of the islands and the colorful sea life below? Experience them virtually through the Channel Islands Live Program, which takes you on interactive tours of the park. In the Live Dive Program, divers armed with video cameras explore the undersea world of the kelp forest off Anacapa Island. Images are transmitted to monitors located on the dock at Landing Cove, in the mainland visitor center, and online. The Live Hike Program takes you on a similar interactive virtual tour of Anacapa Island. Live webcams also connect you 24/7 with panoramic views of Anacapa Island, bald eagle and peregrine falcon nests, and Santa Cruz Island (from Mt. Diablo, the island's highest peak). ⊕ www.nps.gov/ chis/planyourvisit/channel-islands-live-nps.htm 🖭 *Free.*

Tidepool Talk

TOUR—SIGHT | FAMILY | Explore the area's marine habitat without getting your feet wet. Rangers at the Channel Islands Visitor Center demonstrate how animals and plants adapt to the harsh conditions found in tidal pools of the Channel Islands. The talks generally take place at 11 am and 3 pm on weekends and most holidays. ⊠ *Channel Islands National Park Visitor Center, 1901 Spinnaker Rd., Ventura* ☎ *805/658–5730* ⊕ *www.nps.gov/chis/planyourvisit/programs.htm* ☑ *Free.*

HIKING

The terrain on most of the islands ranges from flat to moderately hilly. There are no services on the islands (and no public phones; cell phone reception is dicey). You need to bring all your own food, water (except on Santa Cruz and Santa Rosa, where there are water faucets at campgrounds), and supplies.

KAYAKING

The most remote parts of the Channel Islands are accessible only by a sea kayak. Some of the best kayaking in the park can be found on Anacapa, Santa Barbara, and the eastern tip of Santa Cruz. Anacapa has plenty of sea caves, tidal pools, and even natural bridges you can paddle beneath. Santa Cruz has plenty of secluded beaches to explore, as well as seabird nesting sites and seal and sea lion rookeries. One of the world's largest colonies of Scripps's murrelets resides here, and brown pelicans, cormorants, and storm petrels nest in Santa Barbara's steep cliffs.

It's too far to kayak from the mainland out to the islands, but outfitters can take you to them year-round, though high seas may cause tour cancellations between December and March. ■TIP→ **Channel waters can be unpredictable and challenging. Don't venture out alone unless you are an experienced kayaker; guided trips are highly recommended.** All kayakers should carry proper safety gear and equipment

and be prepared for sudden strong winds and weather changes. Also refrain from disturbing wildlife. Visit the park website for kayaking rules and tips.

The operator listed here holds permits from the National Park Service to conduct kayak tours; if you choose a different company, verify that it holds the proper permits.

Channel Islands Adventure Company

KAYAKING | Full-service outfitter Channel Islands Adventure Company (an arm of Santa Barbara Adventure Company) conducts guided kayaking and snorkeling day trips from its storefront at Scorpion Anchorage on Santa Cruz Island. The company also offers chartered single- and multiday excursions to the Channel Islands. All trips depart from Ventura Harbor and include equipment, guides, and paddling lessons. There's an additional fee for transportation with an Island Packers boat. ⊠ *32 E. Haley St., Santa Barbara* ☎ *805/884–9283* ⊕ *islandkayaking.com* ☑ *From $112 plus $59 ferry.*

WHALE-WATCHING

About a third of the world's cetacean species (27 to be exact) can be seen in the Santa Barbara Channel. In July and August, humpback and blue whales feed off the north shore of Santa Rosa. From late December through March, up to 10,000 gray whales pass through the Santa Barbara Channel on their way from Alaska to Mexico and back again, and on a whale-watching trip during this time frame, you should see one or more of them. Though fewer in number, other types of whales swim the channel June through August.

Island Packers

WHALE-WATCHING | Depending on the season, you can take a three-hour tour or an all-day excursion from either Ventura or Channel Islands harbors with Island Packers. From January through March you're almost guaranteed to see gray

Inspiration point on Anacapa Island

whales in the channel. ⊠ *1691 Spinnaker Dr., Ventura* ☎ *805/642–1393* ⊕ *www.islandpackers.com* ⛴ *From $38.*

Nearby Towns

With a population of nearly 110,000, **Ventura** is the main gateway to Channel Islands National Park. It's a classic California beach town filled with interesting restaurants, shops, galleries, a wide range of accommodations, and miles of clean, white beaches. South of Ventura is **Oxnard,** a community of 208,000 boasting a busy harbor and uncrowded beaches. Known for its Spanish ambience, **Santa Barbara** has a beautiful waterfront set against a backdrop of towering mountains—plus glistening palm-lined beaches, whitewashed adobe structures with red-tile roofs, and a downtown/waterfront area with a hip, youthful vibe.

Ventura

60 miles north of Los Angeles.

Ventura Harbor is home to myriad fishing boats, restaurants, and water-activity centers where you can rent boats and take harbor cruises. The city is also very walkable. If you drive here, park your car in one of the city's free 24-hour parking lots, and explore on foot. You can also board the free trolley that cruises from downtown along the waterfront (Thursday–Sunday noon–9 pm). *See the planner section at the beginning of the chapter for Getting Here and Around information.*

 Sights

Mission San Buenaventura
HISTORIC SITE | The ninth of the 21 California missions, Mission San Buenaventura was established in 1782, and the current church was rebuilt and rededicated in 1809. A self-guided tour takes

you through a small museum, a quiet courtyard, and a chapel with 250-year-old paintings. ✉ *211 E. Main St., at Figueroa St.* ☎ *805/648–4496 gift shop* 🌐 *www.sanbuenaventuramission.org* 🎟 *$5.*

★ Ventura Oceanfront

PROMENADE | Four miles of gorgeous coastline stretch from the county fairgrounds at the northern border of the city of San Buenaventura, through San Buenaventura State Beach, down to Ventura Harbor in the south. The main attraction here is the San Buenaventura City Pier, a landmark built in 1872 and restored in 1993. Surfers rip the waves just north of the pier, and sunbathers relax on white-sand beaches on either side. The mile-long promenade and the Omer Rains Bike Trail north of the pier attract scores of joggers, surrey cyclers, and bikers throughout the year. ✉ *California St., at ocean's edge.*

🍴 Restaurants

Andria's Seafood

$$ | **SEAFOOD** | The specialties at this casual, family-oriented restaurant in Ventura Harbor Village are fresh fish-and-chips and homemade clam chowder. After placing your order at the counter, you can sit outside on the patio and enjoy the view of the harbor and marina. **Known for:** harbor views; plates with locally caught grilled fish; wide-ranging menu of salads, burgers, chicken, and sides. [$] *Average main: $18* ✉ *1449 Spinnaker Dr., Suite A* ☎ *805/654–0546* 🌐 *andriasseafood.com.*

★ Café Zack

$$$ | **AMERICAN** | A local favorite for anniversaries and other celebrations, Zack's serves classic European dishes in an intimate, two-room 1930s cottage adorned with local art. Entrées of note include seafood specials (depending on the local catch), slow-roasted boar shank, and filet mignon, the latter typically crusted in peppercorns or topped with porcini mushrooms. **Known for:** personal service; house-made desserts; excellent California wines. [$] *Average main: $30* ✉ *1095 E. Thompson Blvd., at S. Ann St.* ☎ *805/643–9445* 🌐 *cafezack.com* 🕓 *Closed Sun. No lunch Sat.*

Harbor Cove Café

$ | **CAFÉ** | Waterfront views (from beside the Channel Islands National Park Robert J. Lagomarsino Visitor Center), hearty, cooked-to-order meals, and boxed picnic lunches make this casual dockside eatery a popular spot for island travelers and beach-goers. **Known for:** hearty breakfasts; harbor views; seafood tacos. [$] *Average main: $15* ✉ *1867 Spinnaker Dr.* ☎ *805/658–1639* 🕓 *No dinner.*

Rumfish y Vino

$$$ | **CARIBBEAN** | The sibling of a popular namesake restaurant in Placencia, Belize, Rumfish y Vino serves up zesty Caribbean fare with a California Wine Country twist in a courtyard venue just off Main Street near the mission. Dine in the beach-chic dining room or on the heated patio with a roaring fireplace, and perhaps enjoy one of the live music shows offered several nights a week. **Known for:** delectable fish tacos and flatbreads; happy hour and creative cocktails; Caribbean fish stew. [$] *Average main: $26* ✉ *434 N. Palm St.* ☎ *805/667–9288* 🌐 *www.rumfishyvinoventura.com.*

🛏 Hotels

Four Points by Sheraton Ventura Harbor Resort

$$$ | **RESORT** | An on-site restaurant, spacious rooms, and a slew of amenities make this 17-acre property—which includes sister hotel Holiday Inn Express—a popular and practical choice for Channel Islands visitors. **Pros:** close to island transportation; quiet location; short drive to historic downtown. **Cons:** not in the heart of downtown; noisy seagulls sometimes congregate nearby; service can be spotty. [$] *Rooms from: $199* ✉ *1050 Schooner Dr.* ☎ *805/658–1212,*

800/368–7764 🌐 *fourpoints.com/ventura* 🛏 *106 rooms* 🍴 *No meals.*

Holiday Inn Express Ventura Harbor
$$$ | HOTEL | A favorite among Channel Islands visitors, this quiet, comfortable, lodge-inspired property sits right at the Ventura Harbor entrance. **Pros:** quiet at night; easy access to harbor restaurants and activities; five-minute drive to downtown. **Cons:** busy area on weekends; complaints of erratic service; fee for parking. [$] *Rooms from: $189* ✉ *1080 Navigator Dr.* ☎ *805/856–9533, 888/233–9450* 🌐 *hiexpress.com* 🛏 *109 rooms* 🍴 *Breakfast.*

Waypoint Ventura
$$$ | HOTEL | Stay in a meticulousy restored vintage Airstream or Spartan trailer in a landscaped park on a bluff overlooking Ventura State Beach. **Pros:** a block from Ventura Pier and a short walk to downtown; free access to fire pits, barbecues, lawn games, and house bikes; walk to craft brewery (sister business). **Cons:** near the train tracks; can be difficult to find; near several ongoing construction sites. [$] *Rooms from: $209* ✉ *398 S. Ash St., Unit E* ☎ *805/888–5750* 🌐 *www.waypointventura.com* 🛏 *19 vintage trailers* 🍴 *No meals.*

Oxnard

10 miles from downtown Ventura.

Oxnard, named for a businessman who planted sugar beets here in the late 1800s, is best known for its miles of white-sand beaches, acres of strawberry fields, and well-preserved historic downtown district. In addition, its expansive harbor is a small-craft recreation haven and the closest access point to Anacapa Island in Channel Islands National Park.

VISITOR INFORMATION Oxnard Convention & Visitors Bureau. ✉ *2775 N. Ventura Rd., Suite 204, Oxnard* ☎ *805/385–7545* 🌐 *www.visitoxnard.com.*

🍴 Restaurants

Cabo Seafood Grill and Cantina
$ | MEXICAN | A crowd of in-the-know locals gathers at this lively restaurant and bar close to downtown Oxnard for south-of-the-border seafood specialties served with fresh handmade tortillas. The rainbow-hued dining rooms and patio are casual and cheery. **Known for:** guacamole made at your table; mariachi music some days; more than a dozen types of margaritas. [$] *Average main: $15* ✉ *1041 S. Oxnard Blvd., Oxnard* ☎ *805/487–6933* 🌐 *www.caboox.com.*

Moqueca Brazilian Restaurant
$$$ | BRAZILIAN | Brazilian art and soft jazz set the mood for authentic South American feasts at this family-operated eatery on the second story of a building overlooking Channel Islands Harbor. Brazilian seafood dishes take center stage, primarily the restaurant's namesake *moquecas*, stews made of fish marinated in garlic and lime juice and then cooked in a tomato-onion-cilantro sauce in black clay pots. **Known for:** sweeping harbor and ocean views; Sunday feijoada, Brazil's national dish; exotic cocktails. [$] *Average main: $24* ✉ *3550 S. Harbor Blvd., Ste. 201, Oxnard* ✥ *In Channel Islands Harbor* ☎ *805/204–0970* 🌐 *www.moquecarestaurant.com* ⏲ *No lunch weekdays.*

🛏 Hotels

Embassy Suites by Hilton Mandalay Beach Hotel & Resort
$$$$ | HOTEL | Tropical gardens, small waterfalls, and sprawling pool areas surround this Spanish-Mediterranean complex, set on 8 acres of white-sand beach north of Channel Islands Harbor. **Pros:** on the beach; family-friendly; just a mile to island boats in Channel Islands Harbor. **Cons:** 4 miles from island transportation from Ventura Harbor; fee for parking; no full kitchens. [$] *Rooms from: $289* ✉ *2101 Mandalay Beach Rd.,*

Oxnard ☎ 805/984–2500 ⊕ www.man-
dalayembassysuites.com ➘ 250 suites
🍴 Breakfast.

Santa Barbara

*27 miles northwest of Ventura and 29
miles west of Ojai.*

Santa Barbara has long been an oasis
for Los Angelenos seeking respite from
big-city life. The attractions begin at the
ocean and end in the foothills of the
Santa Ynez Mountains. *See the planner
section at the begining of the chapter for
Getting Here and Around information.*

Sights

El Presidio State Historic Park
MILITARY SITE | FAMILY | Founded in 1782,
El Presidio was one of four military
strongholds established by the Spanish
along the coast of California. The park
encompasses much of the original site
in the heart of downtown. El Cuartel, the
adobe guardhouse, is the oldest building
in Santa Barbara and the second oldest in
California. ✉ *123 E. Canon Perdido St., at
Anacapa St., Santa Barbara* ☎ *805/965–
0093* ⊕ *www.sbthp.org* ➘ *$5.*

★ Old Mission Santa Barbara
RELIGIOUS SITE | FAMILY | Dating from 1786
and widely referred to as the "Queen of
Missions," this is one of the most beautiful and frequently photographed buildings in coastal California. The architecture
evolved from adobe-brick buildings with
thatch roofs to more permanent edifices
as the mission's population burgeoned.
An 1812 earthquake destroyed the third
church built on the site. Its replacement,
the present structure, is still a func-
tioning Catholic church. Old Mission
Santa Barbara has a splendid Spanish/
Mexican colonial art collection, as well as
Chumash sculptures and the only Native
American–made altar and tabernacle left
in the California missions. ✉ *2201 Laguna*

St., at E. Los Olivos St., Santa Barbara
☎ *805/682–4149 gift shop, 805/682–4713
tours* ⊕ *www.santabarbaramission.org*
➘ *$15 self-guided tour.*

Santa Barbara Museum of Natural History
MUSEUM | FAMILY | A gigantic blue whale
skeleton greets you at the entrance
to this 17-acre complex, whose major
draws include its planetarium, paleo and
marine life exhibits, and gem and mineral
displays. Startlingly alive-looking stuffed
specimens in the Mammal and Bird Halls
include a smiling grizzly bear and nesting
California condors. A room of dioramas
illustrates Chumash Indian history and
culture while a Santa Barbara Gallery
showcases the region's unique biodiversity. Outdoors, nature trails wind through
the serene oak woodlands and a summer
butterfly pavilion. ✉ *2559 Puesta del
Sol Rd., off Mission Canyon Rd., Santa
Barbara* ☎ *805/682–4711* ⊕ *sbnature.org*
➘ *$15; free one Sun. of month Sept.–
Apr.* ☉ *Closed Mon.–Tues.*

Stearns Wharf
MARINA | Built in 1872, Stearns Wharf is
Santa Barbara's most visited landmark.
Expansive views of the mountains,
cityscape, and harbor unfold from every
vantage point on the three-block-long
pier. Although it's a nice walk from the
Cabrillo Boulevard parking areas, you can
also park on the pier and then wander
through the shops or stop for a meal at
one of the wharf's restaurants. ✉ *Cabrillo Blvd. and State St., Santa Barbara*
⊕ *stearnswharf.org.*

Beaches

Arroyo Burro Beach
BEACH—SIGHT | FAMILY | The beach's usual-
ly gentle surf makes it ideal for families
with young children. It's a local favorite
because you can walk for miles in both
directions when tides are low. Leashed
dogs are allowed on the main stretch of
beach and westward; they are allowed
to romp off-leash east of the slough at

the beach entrance. The parking lots fill early on weekends and throughout the summer, but the park is relatively quiet at other times. Walk along the beach just a few hundreds yards away from the main steps at the entrance to escape crowds on warm-weather days. Surfers, swimmers, stand-up paddlers, and boogie boarders regularly ply the waves, and photographers come often to catch the vivid sunsets. **Amenities:** food and drink; lifeguard in summer; parking, showers, toilets. **Best for:** sunset; surfing; swimming; walking. ✉ Cliff Dr. and Las Positas Rd., Santa Barbara ⊕ countyofsb.org/parks.

🍴 Restaurants

Brophy Bros

$$$ | SEAFOOD | The outdoor tables at this casual harborside restaurant have perfect views of the marina and mountains. Staffers serve enormous, exceptionally fresh fish dishes and will text you when you're table's ready so you can stroll along the breakwater and explore the harbor while you wait. **Known for:** seafood salad and chowder; stellar clam bar; long wait times. 💲 Average main: $26 ✉ 119 Harbor Way, off Shoreline Dr., Santa Barbara ☎ 805/966–4418 ⊕ brophybros.com.

Palace Grill

$$$ | SOUTHERN | Mardi Gras energy, team-style service, lively music, and great Cajun, creole, and Caribbean food have made the Palace a Santa Barbara icon. Be prepared to wait for a table on Friday and Saturday nights (when reservations are taken for a 5:30 seating only), though the live entertainment and free appetizers, sent out front when the line is long, will whet your appetite for the feast to come. **Known for:** blackened fish and meats; Louisiana bread pudding soufflé; Cajun martini served in a mason jar. 💲 Average main: $30 ✉ 8 E. Cota St., at State St., Santa Barbara ☎ 805/963–5000 ⊕ palacegrill.com.

★ Toma

$$$ | ITALIAN | Seasonal, locally sourced ingredients and softly lit muted-yellow walls evoke the flavors and charms of Tuscany and the Mediterranean at this rustic-romantic restaurant across from the harbor and West Beach. Ahi sashimi tucked in a crisp sesame cone is a popular appetizer, after which you can proceed to a house-made pasta dish or rock shrimp gnocchi. **Known for:** house-made pastas and gnocchi; wines from Italy and California's Central Coast; romantic waterfront setting. 💲 Average main: $30 ✉ 324 W. Cabrillo Blvd., near Castillo St., Santa Barbara ☎ 805/962–0777 ⊕ www.tomarestaurant.com ⊘ No lunch.

🛏 Hotels

★ Hotel Californian

$$$$ | HOTEL | A sprawling collection of Spanish-Moorish buildings that opened in summer 2017 at the site of the historic 1925 Hotel Californian, this sophisticated hotel with a hip youthful vibe occupies nearly three full blocks just steps from Stearns Wharf and the harbor. **Pros:** steps from the waterfront, Funk Zone, and beaches; resort-style amenities; on-site parking. **Cons:** pricey; must walk or ride the shuttle to downtown attractions; train whistle noise in rooms close to station. 💲 Rooms from: $550 ✉ 36 State St. ☎ 805/882–0100 ⊕ www.thehotelcalifornian.com 🛏 121 rooms.

Hotel Indigo

$$$ | HOTEL | Artsy Hotel Indigo is a fine choice for travelers who appreciate contemporary art and want easy access to dining, nightlife, and the beach. **Pros:** multilingual staff; a block from Stearns Wharf; great value for location. **Cons:** showers only (no bathtubs); train whistles early morning; rooms on small side. 💲 Rooms from: $249 ✉ 121 State St., Santa Barbara ☎ 805/966–6586 ⊕ www.indigosantabarbara.com 🛏 41 rooms 🍴 No meals.

★ Santa Barbara Inn

$$$$ | **HOTEL** | This full-service, Spanish-Mediterranean, family-owned hotel occupies a prime waterfront corner across from East Beach. **Pros:** many rooms have ocean views; suites come with whirlpool tubs; delicious on-site restaurant Convivo. **Cons:** on a busy boulevard; limited street parking; not withing easy walking distance of downtown. [$] *Rooms from: $350* ✉ *901 E. Cabrillo Blvd., Santa Barbara* ✣ *At Milpas St.* ☎ *805/966–3636* 🌐 *www.santabarbarainn.com* 🛏 *70 rooms* 🍴 *No meals.*

Activities

BIKING

Cabrillo Bike Lane

BICYCLING | The level, two-lane, 3-mile Cabrillo Bike Lane passes the Santa Barbara Zoo, the Andree Clark Bird Refuge, beaches, and the harbor. Stop for a meal at one of the restaurants along the way, or for a picnic along the palm-lined path looking out on the Pacific.

Wheel Fun Rentals

BICYCLING | You can rent bikes, quadricycles, and skates here. ✉ *24 E. Mason St,, Santa Barbara* ☎ *805/966–2282* 🌐 *wheelfunrentalssb.com.*

BOATS AND CHARTERS

★ *Condor Express*

BOATING | From SEA Landing, the *Condor Express,* a 75-foot, high-speed catamaran, whisks up to 149 passengers toward the Channel Islands on whale-watching excursions and sunset and dinner cruises. ✉ *301 W. Cabrillo Blvd., Santa Barbara* ☎ *805/882–0088, 888/779–4253* 🌐 *condorexpress.com.*

Paddle Sports Center

WATER SPORTS | This full-service center in the harbor rents kayaks, stand-up paddleboards, surfboards, boogie boards, and water-sports gear. ✉ *117 B Harbor Way, off Shoreline Dr., Santa Barbara* ☎ *805/617–3425 rentals* 🌐 *www.paddlesportsca.com.*

CRATER LAKE NATIONAL PARK

Updated by
Andrew Collins

OREGON

🏕 Camping	🛏 Hotels	🏃 Activities	👁 Scenery	👥 Crowds
★★★☆☆	★★★☆☆	★★★★☆	★★★★★	★★★★★

WELCOME TO CRATER LAKE NATIONAL PARK

TOP REASONS TO GO

★ **The lake:** Cruise inside the caldera basin and gaze into the extraordinary sapphire-blue water of the country's deepest lake, stopping for a ramble around Wizard Island.

★ **Native land:** Enjoy the rare luxury of interacting with totally unspoiled terrain.

★ **The night sky:** Billions of stars glisten in the pitch-black darkness of an unpolluted sky.

★ **Splendid hikes:** Accessible trails spool off the main roads and wind past colorful bursts of wildflowers and cascading waterfalls.

★ **Lake-rim lodging:** Spend the night perched on the lake rim at the rustic yet stately Crater Lake Lodge.

1 Rim Village. Situated about 900 feet above the lake's south shore, this is the point from which most visitors first lay eyes on the lake. Home to historic Crater Lake Lodge, a gift shop, café, and visitor center, it's the only area along the rim with year-round access.

2 Rim Drive. This 33-mile scenic road encircles the lake and connects with Rim Village, the North Entrance road, and Cleetwood Cove's trailhead as well as some of the most popular overlooks and hikes in the park.

3 Cleetwood Cove and Wizard Island. A steep 1.1-mile trail leads down to Cleetwood Cove, which offers visitors the only access to the lake's edge; boat tours leave from the dock and circle the lake and, in some cases, ferry passengers to Wizard Island, a volcanic cinder cone on the west side of the lake.

4 Mazama Village. About 5 miles south of Rim Village and adjacent to the only year-round entrance (Annie Springs), this cluster of services is a good place to stock up on snacks, beverages, and fuel and contains the park's only other lodging.

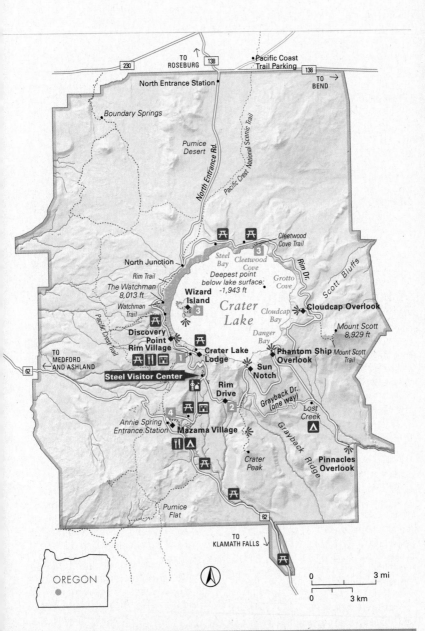

TO
ROSEBURG
230
138
TO
BEND
138
• Pacific Coast
Trail Parking
North Entrance Station •

• Boundary Springs

Pumice
Desert

North Entrance Rd.

Pacific Crest National Scenic Trail

North Junction
Steel
Bay
Cleetwood
Cove
Cleetwood
Cove Trail
Rim Dr.
Scott Bluffs
Rim Trail
The Watchman
8,013 ft
Watchman
Trail
Deepest point
below lake surface:
-1,943 ft
Grotto
Cove
Cloudcap Overlook
Wizard
Island
Crater
Lake
Cloudcap
Bay
Mount Scott
8,929 ft
Discovery
Point
Rim Village
Danger
Bay
Pacific Crest Trail
TO
MEDFORD
AND ASHLAND
62
Crater Lake
Lodge
Phantom Ship
Overlook
Mount Scott
Trail
Sun
Notch
Steel Visitor Center
1
Rim
Drive
2
Grayback Dr.
(one way)
Annie Spring
Entrance Station
4
Mazama Village
Lost
Creek
Grayback Ridge
Pinnacles
Overlook
Crater
Peak
Pumice
Flat
62
TO
KLAMATH FALLS

OREGON

0   3 mi
0   3 km

The pure, crystalline blue of Crater Lake astounds visitors at first sight. More than 5 miles wide and ringed by cliffs almost 2,000 feet high, the lake was created approximately 7,700 years ago, following Mt. Mazama's fiery explosion. Days after the eruption, the mountain collapsed on an underground chamber emptied of lava.

Rain and snowmelt filled the caldera, creating a sapphire-blue lake so clear that sunlight penetrates to a depth of 400 feet (the lake's depth is 1,943 feet). Crater Lake is both the clearest and deepest lake in the United States—and the ninth deepest in the world.

Human life has thrived around Crater Lake and the surrounding Cascade Mountains since the massive eruption of Mt. Mazama—park archaeologists have actually unearthed human-made artifacts, attributed to the region's Makalak (today's Klamath tribe) indigenous inhabitants, beneath layers of volcanic debris. Europeans, specifically a small band of ragtag prospectors in search of a fabled (and never to be found) goldmine, laid eyes on this ethereal body of water in 1853. Over the next couple of decades, more visitors arrived and a wagon road that would become today's modern Highway 62 was constructed just south of the lake en route from Prospect to Fort Klamath. Using nothing more than pipe and piano wire, surveyors were able to determine the lake's depth with surprising accuracy in 1886—they were found much more recently to be off by a mere 53 feet. Against the wishes of

local ranching and mining interests, early conservation advocate William Gladstone Steel succeeded in persuading the federal government to establish Crater Lake National Park in 1902, after many years of lobbying.

For most of today's visitors, the park's star attractions are the lake itself and the breathtakingly situated Crater Lake Lodge, which was built 12 years after the establishment of the park. The terrace outside the lodge is a particularly memorable spot to gaze out at this immense lake, but you can view it from dozens of other spots along Rim Drive, the 33-mile paved road that encircles it. A favorite overlook affords a clear view down to Phantom Ship, which vaguely resembles a ghost ship with its several vertical rock pillars. From high atop the lake's rim, Phantom Ship also looks tiny. In fact, it's the height of a 14-story building. Though it takes some effort to reach, Wizard Island is another outstanding draw.

There's more to this park than the lake, however. Other park highlights include the natural, unspoiled beauty of the forest and the geological marvels you can access by exploring the extensive

AVERAGE HIGH/LOW TEMPERATURES					
JAN.	**FEB.**	**MAR.**	**APR.**	**MAY**	**JUNE**
34/18	35/18	37/19	42/23	50/28	58/34
JULY	**AUG.**	**SEPT.**	**OCT.**	**NOV.**	**DEC.**
68/41	69/41	63/37	52/31	40/23	34/19

183,000-acre backcountry. Beyond the park borders, southern Oregon's charms are many, from wildlife refuges and outdoor recreation in Klamath Falls to acclaimed theater productions, a super wine country, and sophisticated hotels and restaurants in Ashland and Medford.

Planning

When to Go

The park's high season is July and August. September and early October are also popular but tend to draw smaller crowds. By mid-October until well into June, most of the park closes due to heavy snowfall. The road is kept open just from the South Entrance to Rim Village in winter, except during severe weather. Early summer snowmelt often creates watery breeding areas for mosquitoes. Bring lots of insect repellent in June and July to help fend off mosquito swarms in the early morning and at sunset. You might even consider a hat with mosquito netting.

Getting Here and Around

AIR

Rogue Valley International–Medford Airport (MFR) is the nearest commercial airport. About 75 miles southwest of the park, it's served by Alaska, Allegiant, American, Delta, and United Airlines and has rental car agencies. Amtrak trains stop in downtown Klamath Falls, 50 miles south of the park; car rentals are available there, too.

CAR

Crater Lake National Park's South (aka Annie Spring) Entrance, open year-round, is off southern Oregon's Highway 62, which runs northeast from Interstate 5 in Medford and northwest from U.S. 97 in Klamath Falls. From Portland, allow from 5½ to 6 hours to reach the park's South Entrance (via Interstate 5 to Medford). In summer, when the North Entrance is open, the drive from Portland takes just 4½ hours via Interstate 5 to Roseberg and then Highway 138.

Most of the park is accessible only from late June or early July through mid-October. The rest of the year, snow blocks park roadways and entrances except Highway 62 and the road from Mazama Village to Rim Village. Also in winter, no gasoline is available in the park, so be sure to top off your tank before you arrive. Beware that you may encounter icy conditions any time of year, particularly in the early morning.

Inspiration

Crater Lake National Park: A Global Treasure, by former park rangers Ann and Myron Sutton, celebrates the park's first 100 years with stunning photography, charts, and drawings.

Crater Lake: The Story Behind the Scenery, by Ronald G. Warfield, Lee Juillerat, Larry Smith, and Peter C. Howorth, creates an overview of Crater Lake's history and physical features with large photos and detailed captions that accompany the text.

Crater Lake in One Day

Begin at the **Steel Visitor Center**, a short drive from Annie Spring, the only park entrance open year-round. The center's interpretive displays and a short video describe the forces that created the lake and what makes it unique. From here begin circling the crater's rim by heading northeast on **Rim Drive**, allowing an hour to stop at overlooks—be sure to check out the Phantom Ship rock formation in the lake—before you reach the trailhead of **Cleetwood Cove Trail**, the only legal way to access the lake. Hike down the trail to reach the dock at trail's end and hop aboard a **tour boat** for a two-hour ranger-guided excursion. If you'd prefer to hike on your own, instead take the late-morning shuttle boat to **Wizard Island** for a picnic lunch and a trek to the island's summit.

Back on Rim Drive, continue around the lake, stopping at the **Watchman Trail** for a short but steep hike to this peak above the rim, which affords a splendid view of the lake and a broad vista of the surrounding southern Cascades. Wind up your visit at **Rim Village**, strolling along the rim and checking out Sinnott Memorial Overlook before continuing to **Crater Lake Lodge.** Allow time to wander the lobby of this 1915 structure that perches right on the rim. Dinner at the lodge's restaurant, overlooking the lake, caps the day—reservations are strongly advised, although you can enjoy drinks, appetizers, and desserts in the Great Hall or out on the back terrace without having booked ahead.

Wild, the acclaimed 2014 film starring Reese Witherspoon and based on Cheryl Strayed's memoir about hiking the entire Pacific Crest Trail, contains some gorgeous scenes filmed at Crater Lake.

Park Essentials

ACCESSIBILITY

All the overlooks along Rim Drive are accessible to those with impaired mobility, as are Crater Lake Lodge, the facilities at Rim Village (with the exception of Sinnott Memorial Overlook), and Steel Visitor Center. A half dozen accessible campsites are available at Mazama Campground.

PARK FEES AND PERMITS

Admission to the park is $30 per vehicle in summer, $20 in winter, good for seven days. For overnight trips, backcountry campers and hikers must obtain a free wilderness permit at Canfield Ranger Station, adjacent to Steel Visitor Center and open daily 9–5 from mid-April through early November, and 10–4 the rest of the year.

PARK HOURS

Crater Lake National Park is open 24 hours a day year-round; however, snow closes most park roadways from October to June. Lodging and most dining facilities are open usually from late May to mid-October (Rim Village Café the one year-round dining option). The park is in the Pacific time zone.

CELL PHONE RECEPTION

Cell phone reception in the park is spotty, although it's reasonably strong in Rim Village and Mazama Village.

Hotels

Crater Lake's summer season is relatively brief, and Crater Lake Lodge, the park's main accommodation, generally books up a year in advance, but it's worth checking even on short notice, as last-minute cancellations do happen on occasion. The other in-park option, the Cabins at Mazama Village, also books up early in summer. Outside the park there are a few spots in small towns near the park, like Prospect and Union Creek, and you'll find numerous lodgings in Klamath Falls, Medford, Ashland, and—worth considering if you're visting the park via the North Entrance—Roseburg. Even Bend is an option, as it's just a two-hour drive from North Entrance, which is only slightly longer than the drive from Ashland to the South Entrance. *Hotel reviews have been shortened. For full information, visit Fodors.com.*

Restaurants

There are just a few casual eateries and convenience stores within the park, all in Rim Village or Mazama Village. For a memorable meal on the caldera's rim, book a meal at Crater Lake Lodge. Outside the park, Klamath Falls has a smattering of good restaurants, and both Medford and Ashland abound with first-rate eateries serving farm-to-table cuisine and local Rogue Valley wines. *Restaurant reviews have been shortened. For full information visit Fodors.com.*

What It Costs

$	$$	$$$	$$$$
RESTAURANTS			
under $16	$16–$22	$23–$30	over $30
HOTELS			
under $150	$150–$200	$201–$250	over $250

Tours

★ **Boat Tours**

ISLAND | FAMILY | The most popular way to tour Crater Lake itself is on a two-hour ranger-led excursion aboard a 37-passenger launch. The first narrated tour leaves the dock at 9:30 am; the last departs at 3:45 pm. Several of the 10 daily boats stop at Wizard Island, where you can get off and reboard three or six hours later. Some of these trips act as shuttles, with no ranger narration. They're perfect if you just want to get to Wizard Island to hike. The shuttles leave at 8:30 and 11:30 and return to Cleetwood Cove at 12:15, 3:05, and 4:35. To get to the dock you must hike down Cleetwood Cove Trail, a strenuous 1.1-mile walk that descends 700 feet in elevation along the way; only those in excellent physical shape should attempt the hike. Bring adequate water with you. Purchase boat-tour tickets at Crater Lake Lodge, Annie Creek Restaurant and gift shop, the top of the trail, and through reservations. Restrooms are available at the top and bottom of the trail. ✉ *Crater Lake National Park* ✛ *Access Cleetwood Cove Trail off Rim Dr., 11 miles north of Rim Village* ☎ *866/292–6720* ⊕ *www.travelcraterlake.com* ≋ *$28–$55.*

Visitor Information

PARK CONTACT INFORMATION Crater Lake National Park. ☎ *541/594–3000* ⊕ *www.nps.gov/crla.*

Rim Village

7 miles north of Mazama Village and South Entrance, 15 miles south of North Entrance, 80 miles northeast of Medford.

The park's most famous man-made attraction, Crater Lake Lodge, is the centerpiece of this small cluster of buildings located just off Rim Drive and offering stupendous views of the lake. A paved promenade some 900 feet above the lake's surface runs west from the lodge past a seasonal (summer only) visitor center, Sinnott Memorial Overlook, and the Rim Village Cafe and Gift Shop, which is the only restaurant and retailer in the park open in winter. The paved walkway continues for a short distance east of the lodge before connecting to the popular Garfield Peak Trail.

Sights

HISTORIC SITES

★ Crater Lake Lodge

HOTEL—SIGHT | Built in 1915, this regal log-and-stone structure was designed in the classic style of western national park lodges, and the original lodgepole-pine pillars, beams, and stone fireplaces are still intact. The lobby, fondly referred to as the Great Hall, serves as a warm, welcoming gathering place where you can play games, socialize with a cocktail, or gaze out of the many windows to view spectacular sunrises and sunsets by a crackling fire. Exhibits off the lobby contain historic photographs and memorabilia from throughout the park's history. ✉ *Rim Village* 🌐 *www.travelcraterlake.com.*

PICNIC AREAS

★ Rim Village

LOCAL INTEREST | This is the only park picnic area with running water. The tables are set behind the visitor center, and most have a view of the lake below. There are flush toilets inside the visitor center. ✉ *Rim Dr., Rim Village* ✥ *By Crater Lake Lodge.*

TRAILS

★ Garfield Peak Trail

TRAIL | Part of the fun of this dramatic 3.6-mile round-trip scramble to a rocky summit with dazzling lake views is that the hike begins and ends along the paved walkway by Crater Lake Lodge. Keep an eye out for pikas and marmots near the summit, and when you finish, congratulate your efforts after making this 1,010-foot ascent by celebrating with a drink on the terrace of the lodge. *Difficult.* ✉ *Crater Lake National Park* ✥ *Trailhead: Crater Lake Lodge.*

VISITOR CENTERS

Rim Visitor Center

INFO CENTER | Stop here in summer for park information and to visit the neighboring Sinnott Memorial Overlook, which has a small museum with geology exhibits and a covered observation terrace 900 feet above the lake. Ranger talks take place several times a day, and although it's closed in winter, snowshoe walks leave from outside the visitor center on weekends. ✉ *Rim Dr.* ✥ *7 miles north of Annie Spring entrance station* ☎ *541/594–3000* 🌐 *www.nps.gov/crla* ⏲ *Closed Oct.–mid-May.*

Restaurants

★ Crater Lake Lodge Dining Room

$$$ | **PACIFIC NORTHWEST** | The only upscale restaurant option inside the park (dinner reservations are essential), the dining room is magnificent, with a large stone fireplace and views of Crater Lake's clear-blue waters. Breakfast and lunch are enjoyable here, but the dinner is the main attraction, with tempting dishes that emphasize local produce and Pacific Northwest seafood—think wild mushroom–and–caramelized onion flatbread and pan-seared wild salmon with seasonal veggies. **Known for:** nice selection of Oregon wines; Oregon berry cobbler; views of the lake. [$] *Average main: $29* ✉ *Crater Lake Lodge, 1 Lodge Loop Rd.* ☎ *541/594–2255* 🌐 *www.craterlakelodges.com* ⏲ *Closed mid-Oct.–mid-May.*

Hotels

★ Crater Lake Lodge

$$$ | **HOTEL** | The period feel of this 1915 lodge on the caldera's rim is reflected in its lodgepole-pine columns, gleaming wood floors, and stone fireplaces in the common areas, and the simple guest rooms. **Pros:** ideal location for watching sunrise and sunset reflected on the lake; exudes rustic charm; excellent restaurant. **Cons:** books up far in advance; rooms are small and have tubs only, no shower; no air-conditioning, phone, or TV in rooms. [$] *Rooms from: $209* ✉ *1 Lodge Loop Rd.* ✣ *Rim Village, east of Rim Visitor Center* ☎ *541/594–2255, 866/292–6720* 🌐 *www.travelcraterlake.com* ⏲ *Closed mid-Oct.–mid-May* 🛏 *71 rooms* 🍴 *No meals.*

Rim Drive

Access points are 4 miles north of Mazama Village and South Entrance, and 8 miles south of North Entrance.

There are few more scenic drives in the West than this 33-mile paved loop that encircles the rim of the lake. As you make your way around Rim Drive, you'll find pulloffs for some of Crater Lake's most exhilarating overlooks and hikes, including the parking area for Cleetwood Cove's boat cruises and the side road to dramatic Pinnacles Overlook. Keep in mind that Rim Drive (except for the short stretch connecting Rim Village to the South Entrance) is closed due to snow from late fall to late spring.

👁 Sights

PICNIC AREAS

Rim Drive

LOCAL INTEREST | About a half dozen picnic-area turnouts encircle the lake; all have good views, but they can get very windy. Most have pit toilets, and a few have fire grills, but none have running water. ✉ *Rim Dr.*

SCENIC DRIVES

★ Rim Drive

SCENIC DRIVE | Take this 33-mile scenic loop for views of the lake and its cliffs from every conceivable angle. The drive takes two hours not counting frequent stops at overlooks and short hikes that can easily stretch this to a half day. Rim Drive is typically closed due to heavy snowfall from late fall to late spring. ✉ *Crater Lake National Park* ✣ *Access points are 4 miles north of South Entrance and 8 miles south of North Entrance.*

SCENIC STOPS

Cloudcap Overlook

VIEWPOINT | The highest road-access overlook on the Crater Lake rim, Cloudcap has a westward view (best enjoyed in the morning) across the lake to Wizard Island and an eastward view of Mt. Scott, the volcanic cone that is the park's highest point. ✉ *Crater Lake National Park* ✣ *1 mile off Rim Dr.*

Discovery Point

VIEWPOINT | This overlook marks the spot at which prospectors first spied the lake in 1853. Wizard Island is just northeast, close to shore. ✉ *West Rim Dr.* ✣ *1½ miles north of Rim Village.*

Phantom Ship Overlook

VIEWPOINT | From this point you can get a close look at Phantom Ship, a rock formation that resembles a schooner with furled masts and looks ghostly in fog. ✉ *East Rim Dr.*

★ Pinnacles Overlook

VIEWPOINT | Ascending from the banks of Sand and Wheeler creeks, unearthly spires of eroded ash resemble the peaks of fairy-tale castles. Once upon a time, the road continued east to a former entrance. A path now replaces the old road and follows the rim of Sand Creek (affording more views of pinnacles) to where the entrance sign still stands. ✉ *End of Pinnacles Rd.* ✣ *6 miles from Rim Rd.*

Wildlife in Crater Lake

Wildlife in the Crater Lake area flourishes in the water and throughout the surrounding forest.

Salmon and Trout

Two types of fish swim beneath the surface of Crater Lake: kokanee salmon and rainbow trout. Kokanees average about 8 inches in length, but they can grow to nearly 18 inches. Rainbow trout are larger than the kokanee but are less abundant in Crater Lake. Trout—including bull, Eastern brook, rainbow, and German brown—swim in the park's many streams and rivers.

Elk, Deer, and More

Remote canyons shelter the park's elk and deer populations, which can sometimes be seen at dusk and dawn feeding at forest's edge. Black bears, foxes, marmots, and pine martens—cousins of the short-tailed weasel—also call Crater Lake home, as do lesser numbers of wolves, bobcats, and mountain lions. Birds such as hairy woodpeckers, California gulls, red-tailed hawks, bald eagles, and great horned owls are more commonly seen in summer in forests below the lake.

Sun Notch

VIEWPOINT | It's a relatively easy ½-mile loop hike through wildflowers and dry meadow to this overlook, which has views of Crater Lake and Phantom Ship. Mind the cliff edges. ⊠ *East Rim Dr.*

TRAILS

★ Castle Crest Wildflower Trail

TRAIL | This picturesque 1-mile round-trip trek passes through a spring-fed meadow and is one of the park's flatter hikes. Wildflowers burst into full bloom here in July. You can also access Castle Crest via a similarly easy ½-mile loop trail from East Rim Drive. *Easy.* ⊠ *Crater Lake National Park* ⊹ *Trailhead: E. Rim Dr., across road from Steel Visitor Center.*

★ Mt. Scott Trail

TRAIL | This strenuous 4½-mile round-trip trail takes you to the park's highest point—the top of Mt. Scott, the oldest volcanic cone of Mt. Mazama, at 8,929 feet. At a leisurely pace, give yourself about two hours to make the steep uphill trek—and about 60 minutes to get down. The trail starts at an elevation of about 7,679 feet, so the climb is not extreme, but the trail is steep in spots. The views

of the lake and the broad Klamath Basin are spectacular. *Difficult.* ⊠ *Crater Lake National Park* ⊹ *Trailhead: Rim Dr., across from road to Cloudcap Overlook.*

Pacific Crest Trail

TRAIL | You can hike a portion of the Pacific Crest Trail, which extends from Mexico to Canada and winds through the park for 33 miles. For this prime backcountry experience, catch the trail off Highway 138 about a mile east of the North Entrance, where it heads south and then toward the west rim of the lake and circles it for about 6 miles, then descends down Dutton Creek to the Mazama Village area. You'll need a detailed map for this hike; check online or with the PCT association. *Difficult.* ⊠ *Crater Lake National Park* ⊹ *Trailhead: at Pacific Crest Trail parking lot, off Hwy. 138, 1 mile east of North Entrance* ⊕ *www.pcta.org.*

★ Watchman Peak Trail

TRAIL | This is one of the park's best and most easily accessed hikes. Though it's just more than 1½ miles round-trip, the trail climbs more than 400 feet—not counting the steps up to the actual lookout, which has great views of Wizard

Island and the lake. *Moderate.* ⊠ *Crater Lake National Park* ✛ *Trailhead: at Watchman Overlook, Rim Dr., about 4 miles northwest of Rim Village.*

VISITOR CENTERS

Steel Visitor Center

INFO CENTER | Open year-round, the center, part of the park's headquarters, has restrooms, a small post office, and a shop that sells books, maps, and postcards. There are fewer exhibits than at comparable national park visitor centers, but you can view an engaging 22-minute film that describes the lake's formation and geology and examines the area's cultural history. ⊠ *Rim Dr.* ✛ *4 miles north of Annie Spring entrance station* ☎ *541/594–3000* ⊕ *www.nps.gov/crla.*

Cleetwood Cove and Wizard Island

11 miles north of Rim Visitor Center, 13 miles southeast of North Entrance.

Offering the only permissible way to access the lake, Cleetwood Cove and its boat dock are reached by hiking down a 1.1-mile switchback trail—it's an easy ramble down, but getting back up to the trailhead can be challenging if you're not in good shape or unused to high elevations. Boat cruises around the lake and out to Wizard Island, a craggy volcanic cinder cone that's great fun to explore, depart from the cove.

 Sights

PICNIC AREAS

★ Wizard Island

RESTAURANT—SIGHT | The park's best picnic venue is on Wizard Island; pack a lunch and book yourself on one of the early-morning boat tour departures, reserving space on an afternoon return. There are no formal picnic areas and just pit toilets, but you'll discover plenty of sunny and shaded spots where you can

enjoy a quiet meal and appreciate the astounding scene that surrounds you. ⊠ *Crater Lake* ✛ *Via boat from Cleetwood Cove* ⊕ *www.travelcraterlake.com.*

SCENIC STOPS

★ Wizard Island

BODY OF WATER | The volcanic eruption that led to the creation of Crater Lake resulted in the formation of this magical island a ¼ mile off the lake's western shore. The views at its summit—reached on a somewhat challenging 2-mile hike—are stupendous.

Getting to the island requires a strenuous 1-mile hike down (and later back up) the steep Cleetwood Cove Trail to the cove's dock. There, board either the shuttle boat to Wizard Island or a Crater Lake narrated tour boat that includes a stop on the island. If you opt for the latter, you can explore Wizard Island a bit and reboard a later boat to resume the lake tour.

The hike to Wizard Summit, 763 feet above the lake's surface, begins at the island's boat dock and steeply ascends over rock-strewn terrain; a path at the top circles the 90-foot-deep crater's rim. More moderate is the 1¾-mile hike on a rocky trail along the shore of Wizard Island, so called because William Steel, an early Crater Lake booster, thought its shape resembled a wizard's hat. ⊠ *Crater Lake National Park* ✛ *Boats lauch from foot of Cleetwood Cove Trail, off Rim Dr.* ☎ *541/594–2255, 866/292–6720* ⊕ *www.travelcraterlake. com* 🎫 *Shuttle boat $28, tour boat $55.*

TRAILS

Cleetwood Cove Trail

TRAIL | This strenuous 2¼-mile round-trip hike descends 700 feet down nearly vertical cliffs along the lake to the boat dock. Be in very good shape before you tackle this well-maintained trail—it's the hike back up that catches some visitors unprepared. Bring along plenty of water. *Difficult.* ⊠ *Crater Lake National Park* ✛ *Trailhead: on E. Rim Dr., 4½ miles east of North Entrance Rd.*

Mazama Village

7 miles south of Rim Village, 21 miles south of North Entrance, 73 miles northeast of Medford.

Adjacent to the South (Annie Spring) Entrance and offering the only park services outside of Rim Village, this quiet, shaded area contains a summer-only campground, cabin-style motel, restaurant, convenience store with a water bottle filling station, amphitheater, and gas station.

Sights

PICNIC AREAS

Godfrey Glen Trail

LOCAL INTEREST | In a small canyon abuzz with songbirds, squirrels, and chipmunks, this picnic area has a south-facing, protected location. The half dozen picnic tables here are in a small meadow; there are also a few fire grills and a pit toilet. ✉ *Munson Valley Rd.* ✣ *2½ miles south of Steel Visitor Center.*

TRAILS

Annie Creek Canyon Trail

TRAIL | This somewhat challenging 1.7-mile hike loops through a deep stream-cut canyon, providing views of the narrow cleft scarred by volcanic activity. This is a good area to look for flowers and deer. *Moderate.* ✉ *Mazama Campground, Mazama Village Rd.* ✣ *Trailhead: behind amphitheater between D and E campground loops.*

Godfrey Glen Trail

TRAIL | This 1.1-mile loop trail is an easy stroll through an old-growth forest with canyon views. Its dirt path is accessible to wheelchairs with assistance. *Easy.* ✉ *Crater Lake National Park* ✣ *Trailhead: Munson Valley Rd., 2½ miles south of Steel Visitor Center.*

Restaurants

Annie Creek Restaurant

$ | **AMERICAN** | **FAMILY** | This family-friendly dining spot in Mazama Village serves hearty if unmemorable comfort fare, and service can be hit or miss. Blue cheese–bacon burgers, Cobb salads, sandwiches, meat loaf, and a tofu stir-fry are all on the menu, and American standards are served at breakfast. **Known for:** pine-shaded outdoor seating area; convenient to lake and the park's southern hiking trails; several varieties of burgers. [$] *Average main: $13* ✉ *Mazama Village Rd. and Ave. C* ✣ *Near Annie Spring entrance station* ☎ *541/594–2255* 🌐 *www.travelcraterlake.com* 🕓 *Closed late Sept.–late May.*

Hotels

The Cabins at Mazama Village

$$ | **HOTEL** | In a wooded area 7 miles south of the lake, this complex is made up of several A-frame buildings and has modest rooms with two queen beds and a private bath. **Pros:** clean and well-kept facility; very close to the lake and plenty of hiking trails; most affordable of the park lodgings. **Cons:** lots of traffic into adjacent campground; no a/c, TVs, or phones in rooms; not actually on Crater Lake (but a short drive away). [$] *Rooms from: $172* ✉ *Mazama Village* ✣ *Near Annie Spring entrance station* ☎ *541/594–2255, 866/292–6720* 🌐 *www.travelcraterlake.com* 🕓 *Closed late Sept.–late May* 🛏 *40 rooms* 🍴 *No meals.*

Activities

BIKING

Circling the lake via 33-mile Rim Drive on a bicycle is a highly rewarding experience, so much so that the park holds a Ride the Rim bike event on two Saturdays each September. During this event the park closes a 24-mile portion of East Rim Drive to motor-vehicle traffic. Bikes are never permitted on park trails. The nearest place to the park to rent bikes is Diamond Lake Resort, 5 miles north of the park's North Entrance.

CAMPING

Tent campers and RV enthusiasts alike enjoy the heavily wooded and well-equipped setting of Mazama Campground. Lost Creek is much smaller, with minimal amenities and a more "rustic" Crater Lake experience. Pack bug repellent and patience if camping in the snowmelt season.

Lost Creek Campground. The 16 small, remote tent sites here are usually available on a daily basis; in summer arrive early to secure a spot (it's open early July–mid-October). The cost is $5 nightly. ✉ *3 miles south of Rim Rd. on Pinnacles Spur Rd. at Grayback Dr.* ☎ *541/594–3100.*

Mazama Campground. This campground open from mid-June through late September is set well below the lake caldera in the pine and fir forest of the Cascades not far from the main access road (Highway 62). Drinking water, showers, and laundry facilities help ensure that you don't have to rough it too much. About half the 214 spaces are pull-throughs, some with electricity and a few with hookups. The best tent spots are on some of the outer loops above Annie Creek Canyon. Tent sites cost $21, RV ones $31–$42. ✉ *Mazama Village, near Annie Spring entrance station* ☎ *541/594–2255, 866/292–6720* ⊕ *www. craterlakelodges.com.*

EDUCATIONAL OFFERINGS

Crater Lake Natural History Association
The association runs the bookstores at the Steel and Rim visitor centers and partners with the National Park Service to provide education about Crater Lake's natural and cultural history. ✉ *Crater Lake National Park* ☎ *541/594–3111* ⊕ *www. craterlakeoregon.org.*

Junior Ranger Program
TOUR—SIGHT | **FAMILY** | Kids ages 6–12 learn about Crater Lake while earning a Junior Ranger patch in daily activities in summer at the Rim Visitor Center, and year-round they can earn a badge by completing the Junior Ranger Activity Book, which can be picked up at either visitor center.

SKIING

Cross-country skiing is quite popular at Rim Village, along a portion of West Rim Drive going toward Wizard Island Overlook, and on East Rim Drive to Vidae Falls. Check the winter edition of the park newspaper (it's available online at ⊕ *www. nps.gov/crla*) for a map with descriptions of trails. The road is plowed to Rim Village, but it can be closed temporarily due to severe storms. There are no maintained alpine ski trails in the park, although some backcountry trails are marked with blue diamonds or snow poles—only experts should consider downhill skiing in the park. Snow tires and chains are essential when visiting in winter.

SNOWSHOEING

An increasingly popular activity here in winter, snowshoeing can be enjoyed throughout the park, especially around Rim Village, where you can rent snowshoes (at the Rim Village Gift Shop) and embark on ranger-led two-hour walks most weekends (at 1) throughout the season. There's no cost beyond the park entrance fee to join these tours, but space is limited and reservations are required (call the park visitor center at ☎ *541/594–3100*). You can find a list of trails in the park newspaper.

Nearby Towns

About 30 miles south of the main Annie Spring (South) Entrance, tiny **Prospect** is the nearest town to the park—it contains a small hotel as well as a gas station and a few basic eateries, and just about 10 miles beyond you'll find the best nearby dining option, Beckie's Cafe. The main gateways to the park's year-round South Entrance are Klamath Falls (due south) and the Ashland-Medford area (southwest), and for the summer-only North Entrance, Roseburg is a good base camp. **Klamath Falls** is an easygoing center of outdoor recreation that's close to some impressive wildlife refuges and has a handful of places to stay and eat. Although a bit farther away, both the city of **Medford,** which has the region's largest airport, and the artsy and outdoorsy university town of **Ashland** offer the greatest variety of attractions in this part of the state, from a fast-growing crop of exceptional wineries to acclaimed theater. These are also good bases if planning a visit to Oregon Caves National Monument, about 75 miles west of Medford. **Roseburg's** location at the edge of the southern Cascades led to its status as a timber-industry center—still the heart of the town's economy—but its setting along the Umpqua River also draws fishing, rafting, and hiking enthusiasts. The drive from Roseburg to Crater Lake's North Entrance takes a little under two hours.

Klamath Falls

54 miles south of Crater Lake's South (Annie Spring) Entrance, 75 miles east of Medford.

Apart from being a handy base for visiting Crater Lake as well as several different wildlife refuges, the actual town of Klamath Falls is somewhat prosaic and a bit overlooked by visitors traveling the Interstate 5 corridor, but it does have a few small but engaging museums.

GETTING HERE AND AROUND
Klamath Falls lies along U.S. 97, off which is Highway 62, the main route to Crater Lake's South Entrance. This small city is also served by Amtrak.

VISITOR INFORMATION Discover Klamath.
✉ *205 Riverside Dr.* ☎ *541/882–1501, 800/445–6728* ⊕ *www.discoverklamath. com.*

 Sights

Lava Beds National Monument
NATIONAL/STATE PARK | About midway between Crater Lake and Lassen Volcanic national parks, this 47,000-acre tract of lava beds is a popular stop among travelers taking the scenic route between these two parks. The lava beds are just down the road from the Tule Lake and Lower Klamath national wildlife refuges. Many of the top attractions at Lava Beds are underground lava tubes created 32,000 years ago during the eruptions of Mammoth Crater. You can buy lamps and hard hats in the visitor center to tour these fascinating, bat-filled caves. The park has miles of hiking trails aboveground as well. ✉ *1 Indian Well, Tulelake* ✛ *Off Hill Rd., 45 miles south of Klamath Falls via Hwy. 39* ☎ *530/667–8113* ⊕ *www.nps.gov/labe* 🎫 *$25.*

★ **Lower Klamath National Wildlife Refuge**
NATURE PRESERVE | As many as 500 bald eagles make Klamath Basin their rest stop, amounting to the largest wintering concentration of these birds in the contiguous United States. Located along the Pacific Flyway bird migration route, the nearly 40,000 acres of freshwater wetlands in this complex of six different refuges serve as a stopover for nearly 1 million waterfowl in the fall. Any time of year is bird-watching season; more than 400 species of birds—including about 30 types of raptors—have been spotted in the Klamath Basin, along with many mammals, reptiles, and amphibians. For a leisurely excursion by car, follow the tour routes in the Lower Klamath and Tule Lake refuges—the latter has a superb bookstore and visitor center and is also a short drive from Lava Beds National Monument. ✉ *Tule Lake Refuge Visitor Center, 4009 Hill Rd., Tulelake* ✛ *27 miles south of Klamath Falls via Hwy. 39* ☎ *530/667–2231* ⊕ *www.fws.gov/refuge/Lower_Klamath* 🎫 *Free.*

🍴 Restaurants

Gathering Grounds Cafe
$ | **CAFÉ** | Although this bustling coffeehouse with comfortable seating and exposed-brick walls is a hot spot for espresso drinks made from house-roasted coffee beans, it's also a great option for grabbing healthful, flavorful picnic items. Fresh-fruit parfaits and croissant and English muffin sandwiches are popular for breakfast, while lunch favorites include asparagus-prosciutto panini, sausage-lentil soup, and salads. **Known for:** panini sandwiches at breakfast and lunch; best coffee in town, roasted in-house; comfy armchairs. [$] *Average main: $9* ✉ *116 S. 11th St.* ☎ *541/887–8403* ⏲ *Closed Sun. No dinner.*

🛏 Hotels

Running Y Ranch Resort
$$ | **RESORT** | **FAMILY** | Golfers rave about the Arnold Palmer–designed course at this 3,600-acre resort in a juniper-and-ponderosa–shaded canyon overlooking Upper Klamath Lake. **Pros:** indoor pool; 8 miles of paved trails; spacious, modern rooms. **Cons:** may be too far off the beaten path for some; pricey in summer; sometimes fills up with meetings and conventions. [$] *Rooms from: $181* ✉ *5500 Running Y Rd.* ✣ *8 miles north of Klamath Falls* ☎ *541/850–5500* 🌐 *www.runningy.com* 🛏 *82 rooms* 🍴 *No meals.*

Ashland

14 miles southeast of Medford, 85 miles southwest of Crater Lake's South (Annie Spring) Entrance.

Known for its hilly streets dotted with restored Victorian and Craftsman houses, sophisticated restaurants and cafés, and surrounding natural scenery that's ideal for hiking, biking, rafting, and winery-hopping (as well as skiing in winter), Ashland's greatest claim to fame is the prestigious Oregon Shakespeare Festival, which attracts thousands of theater lovers every year, from late February to early November.

GETTING HERE AND AROUND
The southernmost community in the Rogue Valley, Ashland is also the first town off Interstate 5 driving from California. Give yourself about an hour and 45 minutes to get to Crater Lake from Ashland, via Medford.

VISITOR INFORMATION Ashland Chamber of Commerce. ✉ *110 E. Main St.* ☎ *541/482–3486* 🌐 *www.ashlandchamber.com.*

👁 Sights

★ **Lithia Park**
CITY PARK | **FAMILY** | The Allen Elizabethan Theatre overlooks this park, a wooded 93-acre jewel founded in 1916 that serves as Ashland's physical and psychological anchor. The park is named for the town's mineral springs, which supply water fountains by the band shell and on the town plaza—be warned that the slightly bubbly water has a strong and rather disagreeable taste. From morning through evening, picnickers, joggers, dog walkers, and visitors congregate in the park's most popular areas, which include dozens of paved and unpaved trails, two duck ponds, a rose garden, a Japanese garden, and ice-skating rink, and a reservoir with a beach and swimming. A great way to get a sense of Lithia Park's vastness, and just how much wilderness there is in the northern section, is to make the 3-mile loop drive around its border. On weekends from mid-March through October, the park hosts a lively artisans' market, and free concerts take place Thursday evenings in summer. Each June the Oregon Shakespeare Festival opens its outdoor season by hosting the Feast of Will in the park, with music, dancing, bagpipes, and food. Tickets ($16) are available through

the festival box office (☎ *541/482–4331* 🌐 *www.osfashland.org*). ✉ *N. Main St. at Winburn Way* 🌐 *www.ashland.or.us.*

★ Oregon Shakespeare Festival

FESTIVAL | From mid-February to early November, more than 100,000 Bard-loving fans descend on Ashland for some of the finest Shakespearean productions you're likely to see outside of London—plus works by both classic (Ibsen, O'Neill) and contemporary playwrights, including occasional world premieres. Eleven plays are staged in repertory in the 1,200-seat Allen Elizabethan Theatre, an atmospheric re-creation of the Fortune Theatre in London; the 600-seat Angus Bowmer Theatre, a state-of-the-art facility typically used for five different productions in a single season; and the 350-seat Thomas Theatre, which often hosts productions of new or experimental work. The festival, which dates to 1935, generally operates close to capacity, so it's important to book ahead. ✉ *15 S. Pioneer St.* ☎ *541/482–4331, 800/219–8161* 🌐 *www.osfashland.org.*

🍴 Restaurants

★ Amuse

$$$ | PACIFIC NORTHWEST | The Northwest-driven French cuisine served in this intimate, ivy-covered eatery, which is infused with seasonal, organic meat and produce, changes regularly but might feature charcoal-grilled prawns, duck-leg confit, or braised pork shoulder. Try to save room for one of the local-fruit desserts, such as wild huckleberry tart with a pecan crust or Gravenstein apple crisp. **Known for:** intimate, romantic setting; reasonable corkage fee to bring your own wine; delectable desserts and cheese-course options. [$] *Average main: $25* ✉ *15 N. 1st St.* ☎ *541/488–9000* 🌐 *www.amuserestaurant.com* 🕓 *Closed Mon. and Tues. No lunch.*

★ Hither Coffee & Goods

$$ | MODERN AMERICAN | Set in a minimalist downtown space with bare floors, a vaulted painted-white timber ceiling, and bounteous floral arrangements, Hither serves as an inviting coffeehouse and café by day, featuring heavenly pastries and artfully composed egg dishes and tartines. Later in the day, stop in for a light dinner of grilled duck breast with aioli and frites, or house-made pasta with 'nduja, bitter greens, and lemon bread crumbs, along with a glass or two from the well-curated natural wine list. **Known for:** clean, uncluttered aesthetic; delicious sweets and baked goods; craft coffees and local wines and beers. [$] *Average main: $20* ✉ *376 E. Main St.* ☎ *541/625–4090* 🌐 *www.hithermarket.com* 🕓 *No dinner Sun.*

Sammich

$ | DELI | In this unassuming deli tucked into a small shopping center across the street from Southern Oregon University, you'll find some of the biggest and tastiest sandwiches in the state—they've been featured on TV's *Diners, Drive-Ins and Dives,* and there's also a branch in Portland. Owner Melissa McMillan bases her menu on the Italian-style sandwiches of Chicago, where she's from, and unless you're absolutely starving, it's not a bad idea to order a half or share a whole with a friend. **Known for:** truly prodigious sandwiches; the Pastrami Zombie with Swiss, slaw, and Russian dressing on rye; grilled cheese with tomato soup. [$] *Average main: $12* ✉ *424 Bridge St.* ☎ *541/708–6055* 🌐 *www.sammichrestaurants.com* 🕓 *No dinner.*

🛏 Hotels

★ Ashland Hills Hotel & Suites

$$ | HOTEL | Hoteliers Doug and Becky Neuman (who also run the excellent Ashland Springs Hotel and Lithia Springs Resort) transformed this long-shuttered '70s-era resort into a stylish yet affordable retro-cool compound, retaining the property's fabulous globe lights, soaring lobby windows, and beam ceilings while adding many period-style furnishings. **Pros:** great rates considering all the amenities; terrific restaurant on-site; attractive grounds, including patio and sundeck. **Cons:** just off the interstate a 10-minute drive from downtown; some rooms face parking lot; fitness rooms are small and dark. $ *Rooms from: $162* ✉ *2525 Ashland St.* ☎ *541/482–8310, 855/482–8310* ⊕ *www.ashlandhillshotel. com* ⤴ *173 rooms* ❍⦿ *Free breakfast.*

Lithia Springs Resort
$$ | RESORT | Built above and named for the bubbling mineral springs that made Ashland a spa destination more than a century ago, this attractive boutique resort offers guests the chance to soak in these curative waters in their own in-room soaking tubs and mineral showers, or by booking a treatment in the enchanting day spa. **Pros:** extensive, delicious complimentary breakfast buffet; great place to rejuvenate after a hike; inviting wine garden. **Cons:** popularity with families sometimes results in noisy pool area; can book up early in summer; not within walking distance of town. $ *Rooms from: $159* ✉ *2165 W. Jackson Rd.* ☎ *541/482–7128, 800/482–7128* ⤴ *38 rooms* ❍⦿ *Free Breakfast.*

The Winchester Inn
$$$$ | B&B/INN | FAMILY | Rooms and suites in this upscale Victorian have character and restful charm—some have fireplaces, refrigerators, and wet bars, and private exterior entrances, and most are well suited to having one or two children in the room. **Pros:** outstanding restaurant; one of the more child-friendly B&Bs in town; surrounded by lush gardens. **Cons:** among the more expensive lodgings in town; downtown location can feel a bit busy in summer; some rooms are reached via steep flights of stairs. $ *Rooms from: $295* ✉ *35 S. 2nd St.* ☎ *541/488–1113* ⊕ *www.winchesterinn. com* ⤴ *24 rooms* ❍⦿ *Free breakfast.*

☕ Nightlife

★ Ostras! Tapas + Bottle Shop
TAPAS BARS | There's definitely an impressive and extensive enough selection of beautifully plated Spanish tapas—half-shell oysters with cava mignonette, braised pork cheeks—to make this sophisticated, high-ceilinged bar a dinner option (there's even paella). But it's also one of the coolest little bars in southern Oregon, offering up a stellar list of Spanish and local wines as well as fine after-dinner drinks. ✉ *47 N. Main St.* ☎ *541/708–0528* ⊕ *ostrasashland.com.*

Medford

13 miles northwest of Ashland, 72 miles southwest of Crater Lake's South (Annie Springs) Entrance.

With a population of about 82,500, Medford is the professional, retail, trade, and service hub for eight counties in southern Oregon and northern California. The historic downtown has undergone a bit of a renaissance in recent years, with a rapidly growing craft-brewing and distilling scene having taken hold, and on the outskirts you'll find several excellent wineries. Lodging tends to be cheaper in Medford than in nearby Ashland or Jacksonville, although cookie-cutter chain properties dominate the hotel landscape.

GETTING HERE AND AROUND
Medford is in the heart of the Rogue Valley on Interstate 5, and is home to the state's third-largest airport, Rogue Valley International. From downtown, it's a 90-minute drive on winding, picturesque Highway 62 to reach Crater Lake.

VISITOR INFORMATION Travel Medford. ✉ *101 E. 8th St.* ☎ *541/776–4021, 800/469–6307* ⊕ *www.travelmedford. org.*

Sights

★ Oregon Caves National Monument

CAVE | Marble caves, large calcite formations, and huge underground rooms shape this rare adventure in geology. Guided cave tours take place late March through early November. The 90-minute ½-mile tour is moderately strenuous, with low passageways, twisting turns, and more than 500 stairs; children must be at least 42 inches tall to participate. Cave tours aren't given in winter. Aboveground, the surrounding valley holds an old-growth forest with some of the state's largest trees, and offers some excellent and generally uncrowded hiking. ⚠ **GPS coordinates for the caves often direct drivers onto a mostly unpaved forest service road meant for four-wheel-drive vehicles. Instead, follow well-signed Highway 46 off U.S. 199 at Cave Junction, which is also narrow and twisting in parts; RVs or trailers more than 32 feet long are not advised.** ✉ *19000 Caves Hwy. (Hwy. 46), Cave Junction* ✣ *20 miles east of U.S. 199, 140 miles southwest of Crater Lake* ☎ *541/592–2100* 🌐 *www.nps.gov/orca* 🎟 *Park free, tours $10.*

★ Table Rock

LOCAL INTEREST | This pair of monolithic rock formations rise some 700 to 800 feet above the valley floor. Operated by a partnership between the Bureau of Land Management and the Nature Conservancy, the Table Rock formations and surrounding 4,864 acres of wilderness afford panoramic valley views from their summits, and glorious wildflower viewing and migratory bird-watching in spring. This is one of the best venues in the Rogue Valley for hiking; you can reach Lower Table Rock on a moderately challenging trail, and Upper Table Rock via a shorter, less-steep route. ✉ *Off Table Rock Rd., Central Point* ✣ *10 miles north of Medford* ☎ *541/618–2200* 🌐 *www.blm.gov.*

Restaurants

★ Elements Tapas Bar

$$$ | **TAPAS** | A stylish setting and a taste of impressively authentic Spanish fare—these are the draws of this handsome tapas restaurant in downtown Medford's turn-of-the-20th-century "Goldy" building. Pass around plates of mussels in romesco sauce, apricot-braised-pork empanadas, chorizo-studded Andalusian paella, and lamb-sausage flatbread, while sampling selections from the lengthy beer and cocktail menus. **Known for:** late-night dining; several types of paella (that serves three to four); extensive, international beer, wine, and cocktail selection. [$] *Average main: $26* ✉ *101 E. Main St.* ☎ *541/779–0135* 🌐 *www.elementsmedford.com* 🕒 *No lunch.*

Hotels

Resort at Eagle Point

$$ | **HOTEL** | The setting adjacent to one of the state's top golf courses is a major draw for this small boutique hotel with a dozen contemporary chalet-style suites featuring fireplaces and either balconies or patios. **Pros:** adjacent to and overlooking a beautiful golf course; peaceful setting; location handy for visiting Rogue Valley and Crater Lake. **Cons:** remote setting about a 20-minute drive from Medford; setting is less exciting for non-golfers; no elevator for upper-level rooms. [$] *Rooms from: $159* ✉ *Eagle Point Golf Club, 100 Eagle Point Dr., Eagle Point* ☎ *541/879–3700* 🌐 *www.resortateaglepoint.com* 🛏 *12 rooms* 🍴 *Free breakfast.*

Nightlife

Immortal Spirits & Distillery Company

BARS/PUBS | Part of the boom of craft beverage makers that's redefining downtown Medford, this inviting tasting room with tables fashioned out of barrels and rotating art exhibits offers a full bar and restaurant with creative (and big) burgers and sandwiches and creative cocktails. But you can also just stop in to sample Immortal's first-rate single-barrel whiskey, Genever-style gin, blackberry brandy, and other heady elixirs. ✉ *141 S. Central Ave.* ☎ *541/816–4344* ⊕ *www. immortalspirits.com.*

🛍 Shopping

★ Rogue Creamery
FOOD/CANDY | Just a few miles up the road from Medford in the little town of Central Point, you'll find one of the planet's most respected cheese makers (in 2019, Rogue became the first U.S. cheese maker ever to take the top prize at the prestigious World Cheese Awards). Begun in 1935 by Italian immigrants and now run by David Gremmels, this factory store sells all of the company's stellar cheeses, from Smokey Blue to a lavender-infused cheddar, and you can often watch the production through a window. Delicious grilled-cheese sandwiches and local wines and beers are also available— enjoy them at one of the sidewalk tables outside. ■**TIP→ Ardent fans of this place might want to check out Rogue Creamery Dairy Farm, outside Grants Pass, and about 30 miles away from Central Point. Tours of the milking operations and the farm are available, and you can buy cheese and other gourmet goods there as well.** ✉ *311 N. Front St., Central Point* ☎ *541/665–1155* ⊕ *www.roguecreamery.com.*

Roseburg

180 miles south of Portland, 85 miles west of Crater Lake's North Entrance.

The timber town on the Umpqua River attracts anglers in search of a dozen popular fish species, from brook trout to steelhead. The north and south branches of the Umpqua River meet up just north of town, and you can drive alongside the North Umpqua via the Rogue-Umpqua Scenic Byway en route to Crater Lake's summer-only North Entrance. Roseburg also has an attractive, historic downtown, and the surrounding countryside is also home to about 25 wineries, many of them extremely well regarded.

GETTING HERE AND AROUND
Roseburg is the first large town you'll reach driving south from Eugene on Interstate 5. To reach Crater Lake's North Entrance, it's about an hour-and-a-half drive east on Highway 138.

ESSENTIALS
VISITOR INFORMATION Roseburg Area Visitor Center. ✉ *410 S.E. Spruce St., Roseburg* ☎ *541/672–2648* ⊕ *www. roseburgchamber.com.*

👁 Sights

★ Abacela Vineyards and Winery
WINERY/DISTILLERY | The name derives from an archaic Spanish word meaning "to plant grapevines," and that's exactly what this winery's husband-wife team started doing in the late '90s. Abacela has steadily established itself as one of the best Oregon wineries outside the Willamette Valley. Hot-blooded Spanish Tempranillo is Abacela's pride and joy, though inky Malbec and a subtly floral Albariño also highlight a repertoire heavy on Mediterranean varietals, which you can sample in a handsome, eco-friendly tasting room where you can also order light appetizers to snack on. ✉ *12500 Lookingglass Rd., Roseburg* ☎ *541/679– 6642* ⊕ *www.abacela.com.*

🍴 Restaurants

★ True Kitchen + Bar
$$$ | MODERN AMERICAN | A dapper, upmarket downtown bistro with a friendly, easygoing vibe, True excels both in its gastropub menu that often draws on seasonal ingredients and arguably the region's best beverage program, which features a terrific selection of Umpqua Valley wines and Oregon craft beers. The

cuisine borrows a bit from different parts of the world, with short-rib bao buns, shrimp and grits, and adobo-lime chicken among the favorites, and several juicy burgers to choose from as well. **Known for:** generous food deals during the daily (bar-seating only) happy hour; impressive craft cocktail list; creatively topped burgers. $ *Average main: $25* ⊠ *629 S.E. Main St., Roseburg* ☎ *541/900–1000* ⊕ *www.truekitchenandbar.com* ⊘ *Closed Sun. No lunch.*

 Hotels

★ The Steamboat Inn

$$$ | **B&B/INN** | The world's top fly-fishermen converge at this secluded forest inn, high in the Cascades above the North Umpqua River; others come simply to relax in the reading nooks or on the decks of the riverside guest cabins nestled below soaring fir trees. **Pros:** good option if en route to Crater Lake; access to some of the best fishing in the West; an excellent restaurant (open to the general public; call for hours). **Cons:** far from any towns or cities; often books up well in advance in summer; no TV or Wi-Fi. $ *Rooms from: $215* ⊠ *42705 N. Umpqua Hwy., Idleyld Park* ✛ *38 miles east of Roseburg on Hwy. 138, near Steamboat Creek* ☎ *541/498–2230* ⊕ *www.thesteamboatinn.com* ⊅ *20 units* ✉ *No meals.*

Prospect

20 miles south of Crater Lake National Park's south entrance.

This secluded logging town with a peaceful and pretty setting on the Rogue River has fewer than 500 residents and not a whole lot going on, but its small, historic hotel is one of the closest lodgings to Crater Lake's only year-round entrance, making it a good base camp for park visitors.

GETTING HERE AND AROUND

Prospect is on Highway 62, about a half-hour drive from Crater Lake and an hour from Medford.

 **Restaurants**

Beckie's Cafe

$ | **AMERICAN** | **FAMILY** | You can get breakfast, lunch, or dinner at this rustic roadhouse diner 15 miles west of Crater Lake's Southern Entrance, but no one will fault you for skipping your vegetables and going straight for the dessert. Since 1926 Beckie's homemade pies have been a must-have treat for travelers on their way to or from the park. **Known for:** fresh-baked fruit pies; hearty breakfasts; barbecue wagon on summer weekends. $ *Average main: $12* ⊠ *Union Creek Resort, 56484 Hwy. 62, Prospect* ☎ *541/560–3563* ⊕ *www.unioncreekoregon.com/beckies-cafe.*

 Hotels

Prospect Historic Hotel

$$ | **B&B/INN** | The likes of Theodore Roosevelt, Zane Grey, Jack London, and William Jennings Bryan have stayed at this quaint, country-style bed-and-breakfast that's just 39 miles southwest of the park entrance on Highway 62. **Pros:** three waterfalls within walking distance; large property with beautiful grounds and creek; one of the nearest lodgings to the park. **Cons:** small, remote town; breakfast is not included for guests staying in motel units; rooms in motel units lack charm of those in main inn. $ *Rooms from: $160* ⊠ *391 Mill Creek Dr., Prospect* ☎ *541/560–3664, 800/944–6490* ⊕ *www.prospecthotel.com* ⊅ *10 main house rooms, 14 motel rooms* ✉ *Free breakfast.*

Chapter 14

DEATH VALLEY NATIONAL PARK

14

Updated by
Cheryl Crabtree

CALIFORNIA

🏕 **Camping**
★★☆☆☆

🛏 **Hotels**
★★★★☆

🤸 **Activities**
★★★☆☆

👁 **Scenery**
★★★★★

👥 **Crowds**
★★☆☆☆

WELCOME TO
DEATH VALLEY NATIONAL PARK

TOP REASONS TO GO

★ **Roving rocks:** Death Valley's Racetrack is home to moving boulders, a rare phenomenon that until recently had scientists baffled.

★ **Lowest spot on the continent:** Stand on the lowest spot on the continent at Badwater, 282 feet below sea level.

★ **Wildflower explosion:** In spring, this desert landscape is ablaze with greenery and colorful flowers, especially between Badwater and Ashford Mill.

★ **Ghost towns:** Death Valley is renowned for its Wild West heritage and is home to dozens of crumbling settlements including Chloride City, Greenwater, Harrisburg, Keeler, Leadfield, Panamint City, and Skidoo, as well as nearby Ballarat and Rhyolite.

★ **Naturally amazing:** From canyons to sand dunes to salt flats and dry lake beds, Death Valley serves up plenty of geological treasures.

1 Central Death Valley. Furnace Creek sits in the heart of Death Valley—if you have only a short time in the park, head here. You can visit gorgeous Golden Canyon, Zabriskie Point, the Salt Creek Interpretive Trail, and Artists Drive, among other popular points of interest.

2 Northern Death Valley. This region is uphill from Furnace Creek, which means marginally cooler temperatures. Be sure to stop by Rhyolite Ghost Town on Highway 374 before entering the park and exploring colorful Titus Canyon and jaw-dropping Ubehebe Crater.

3 Southern Death Valley. This is a desolate area, but there are plenty of sights that help convey Death Valley's rich history. Don't miss the Dublin Gulch Caves.

4 Western Death Valley. Panamint Springs Resort is a nice place to grab a meal and get your bearings before moving on to quaint Darwin Falls, smooth rolling sand dunes, beehive-shaped Wildrose Charcoal Kilns, and historic Stovepipe Wells Village.

Cerro Grande (ghost town)

Keeler

TO LONE PINE

Darwin

CALIFORNIA

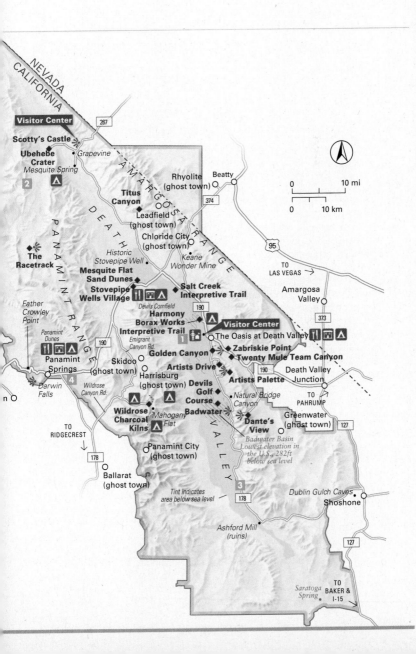

NEVADA
CALIFORNIA

Visitor Center

Scotty's Castle

Ubehebe
Crater
Mesquite Spring

2

Grapevine

267

Rhyolite
(ghost town)

Beatty

374

Titus
Canyon

Leadfield
(ghost town)

Chloride City
(ghost town)

95

TO
LAS VEGAS

Amargosa
Valley

373

The
Racetrack

Historic
Stovepipe Well

Keane
Wonder Mine

Mesquite Flat
Sand Dunes

Stovepipe
Wells Village

Salt Creek
Interpretive Trail

190

Visitor Center

The Oasis at Death Valley

Devils Cornfield

Harmony
Borax Works
Interpretive Trail

Emigrant
Canyon Rd.

1

190

Golden Canyon

Zabriskie Point
Twenty Mule Team Canyon

Father
Crowley
Point

Panamint
Dunes

190

Panamint
Springs

4

Darwin
Falls

Skidoo
(ghost town)

Harrisburg
(ghost town)

Artists Drive

Artists Palette

Death Valley
Junction

TO
PAHRUMP

Devils
Golf
Course

Natural Bridge
Canyon

Badwater

Greenwater
(ghost town)

127

TO
RIDGECREST

Wildrose
Charcoal
Kilns

Mahogany
Flat

Dante's
View

Wildrose
Canyon Rd.

178

Panamint City
(ghost town)

Badwater Basin
Lowest elevation in
the U.S., 282ft
below sea level

Ballarat
(ghost town)

Tint indicates
area below sea level

Dublin Gulch Caves

Shoshone

3

178

Ashford Mill
(ruins)

127

Saratoga
Spring

TO
BAKER &
I-15

0   10 mi
0   10 km

The natural riches of Death Valley—the largest national park outside Alaska—are overwhelming: rolling waves of sand dunes, black cinder cones thrusting up hundreds of feet from a blistered desert floor, riotous sheets of wildflowers, bizarrely shaped Joshua trees basking in the orange glow of a sunset, tiny pupfish, and a dramatic silence.

This is a land of extremes of climate (hottest and driest) and geography. The park centers around Death Valley, which extends 156 miles from north to south and includes Badwater Basin, the lowest point in the USA (282 feet below sea level). Two mountain ranges border the valley: the Panamint on the west, where Telescope Peak juts more than 11,000 feet up from the valley floor, and the Amargosa in the east. Salt basins, spring-fed oases, sand dunes, deep canyons, and more than a thousand miles of paved and dirt roads punctuate the barren landscapes.

Humans first roamed this once-lush region around 10,000 years ago. The Timbisha Shoshone have lived here for more than a thousand years, originally along the shores of a 30-foot-deep lake. They called the area Timbisha for the red-hued rocks in the hillsides. Gold-rush pioneers looking for a shortcut to California traversed the barren expanse in 1849; some met their demise in the harsh environment, and those who survived named the place Death Valley. Silver and borax mining companies soon arrived on the scene. They didn't last long (most had stopped operations by 1910), but they left ghost towns and ramshackle mines as evidence of their dreams.

In 1933, President Herbert Hoover proclaimed the area a national monument to protect both its natural beauty and its scientific importance. In 1994, Congress passed the California Desert Protection Act, adding 1.3 million acres and designating the region a national park. Today, Death Valley National Park encompasses nearly 3.5 million acres, 93 percent of which is designated wilderness.

Despite its moniker, Death Valley teems with life. More than a million visitors a year come here to view plants and animals that reveal remarkable adaptations to the desert environment, hike through deep canyons and up mountain trails, gaze at planets and stars in a vast night sky, and follow in the footsteps of ancient cultures and pioneers. They come to explore an outstanding, exceptionally diverse outdoor natural history museum, filled with excellent examples of the planet's geological history. Most of all, they come to experience peace, quiet, and solitude in a stark, surreal landscape found nowhere else on Earth.

AVERAGE HIGH/LOW TEMPERATURES					
JAN.	**FEB.**	**MAR.**	**APR.**	**MAY**	**JUNE**
65/39	72/46	80/53	90/62	99/71	109/80
JULY	**AUG.**	**SEPT.**	**OCT.**	**NOV.**	**DEC.**
115/88	113/85	106/75	92/62	76/48	65/39

Death Valley in One Day

If you begin the day in Furnace Creek, you can see several sights without doing much driving. Bring plenty of water with you and some food, too. Rise early and drive the 20 miles on Badwater Road to **Badwater**, which looks out on the lowest point in the Western Hemisphere and is a dramatic place to watch the sunrise. Returning north, stop at **Natural Bridge**, a medium-size conglomerate rock formation that has been hollowed at its base to form a span across the canyon, and then at the **Devil's Golf Course**, so named because of the large pinnacles of salt present here. Detour to the right onto **Artists Drive**, a 9-mile one-way, northbound route that passes **Artists Palette.** The reds, yellows, oranges, and greens come from minerals in the rocks and the earth. Four miles north of Artists Drive is the **Golden Canyon Interpretive Trail**, a 2-mile round-trip that winds through a canyon with colorful rock walls. Just before Furnace Creek, take Highway 190 3 miles east to **Zabriskie Point**, overlooking dramatic, furrowed red-brown hills and the **Twenty Mule Team Canyon**. Return to Furnace Creek, where you can grab a meal and visit the museum at the Furnace Creek Visitor Center. Heading north from Furnace Creek, pull off the highway and take a look at the historic **Harmony Borax Works.**

Planning

When to Go

Most of the park's 1.7 million annual visitors come between late fall and early spring, taking advantage of moderate temperatures and the lack of rainfall. During these cooler months, you will need to book a room in advance, but don't worry: the park never feels crowded. If you visit in summer, believe everything you've ever heard about desert heat—it can be brutal, with temperatures often topping 120°F. The dry air wicks moisture from the body without causing a sweat, so drink plenty of water. Bring sunglasses, a hat, and sufficient clothing to block the sun's rays and the wind. Flash floods are fairly common; sections of roadway can be flooded or washed away, as they were after a major flood in 2015. The wettest month is February, when the park receives an average of 0.3 inch of rain.

FESTIVALS AND EVENTS

Bishop Mule Days. Entertainment at this five-day festival over the Memorial Day weekend includes top country-music stars, an arts-and-crafts fair, barbecues, country dances, the longest-running non-motorized parade in the United States, and more than 700 mules competing in 181 events. Admission is free. ⊕ *www.muledays.org*

Death Valley Dark Sky Festival. A full weekend program, held in late February or early March, celebrates Death Valley's celestial distinctions with guided hikes, ranger talks, a night-sky photo session, family events, and a star party. ⊕ *www. nps.gov/deva/planyourvisit/death-valley-dark-sky-festival.htm*

Death Valley 49er Encampment Days. Originally a centennial celebration held in 1949 to honor the area's first European visitors, this five-day event draws thousands of people from around the world to the Ranch at Death Valley for art shows, a wagon train, live music, artisan booths, dancing, and even a poker tournament. ⊕ *www.deathvalley49ers.org*

Lone Pine Film Festival. Every Columbus Day weekend, this town pays tribute to its Hollywood history with three days of tours, films, lectures, and celebrity panels. ⊕ *www.museumofwesternfilm-history.org/special-events*

Shoshone Old West Days. This annual three-day festival celebrates Wild West heritage with live performances, arts-and-crafts, and a deep-pit barbecue. ⊕ *www. shoshonevillage.com*

Getting Here and Around

AIR

The closest airport to the park with commercial service, Las Vegas McCarren International Airport, is 130 miles away, so you'll still need to drive a couple of hours to reach the park. Roughly 160 miles to the west, Burbank's Bob Hope Airport is the second-closest airport.

CAR

It can take more than three hours to cross from one side of the park to another, so it's important to choose an entrance point that makes sense for what you want to see. If you're driving from Los Angeles, enter through the western portion along Highway 395; from Las Vegas, enter from the north at Beatty, Nevada, or via the central entrance at Death Valley Junction. Travelers from Orange County, San Diego, and the Inland Empire should access the park via Interstate 15 North at Baker.

Distances can be deceiving: what seems close can be very far away. Much of the park can be viewed on regularly scheduled bus tours, but these often don't allow time for hikes to sites not seen from the road, such as Salt Creek, Golden Canyon, and Natural Bridge. The best option is to drive to a number of the sites, get out of the car, and walk.

When driving in Death Valley, reliable maps are important, as signage is often limited or, in a few places, nonexistent. Bring a phone, but don't rely on cell coverage exclusively in every remote area, and pack plenty of food and water (3 gallons per person per day is recommended). Cars, especially in summer, should be prepared for the hot, dry weather, too. Some of the park's most spectacular canyons are accessible only via four-wheel-drive vehicles, but make sure the trip is well planned and use a backcountry map. Be aware of possible winter closures or driving restrictions because of snow. The National Park Service's website (⊕ *nps.gov/deva*) stays up-to-date on road closures during the wet (and popular) months. ⚠ **One of the park's signature landmarks, Scotty's Castle, and the 8-mile road connecting it to the park border may be closed until 2022 due to damage from a 2015 flood.**

CONTACTS California Highway Patrol. ☎ *800/427–7623 recorded info from CalTrans, 760/872–5900 live dispatcher at Bishop Communications Center* ⊕ *www. chp.ca.gov.* **California State Department of Transportation Hotline** ☎ *800/427–7623* ⊕ *www.dot.ca.gov.*

Inspiration

Death Valley, by Susan Perly, is a novel set in 2006 that follows a female photojournalist who travels to the desert to photograph soldiers about to deploy for combat in Iraq.

Hiking Death Valley: A Guide to Its Wonders and Mining Past, by Michel Dragonnet, offers detailed information on 57 day hikes and backpacking trips.

Survival Arts of the Primitive Paiutes, a bestseller by Margaret M. Wheat, describes how the Paiutes developed ways to survive in the harsh climate of the Death Valley and Nevada region.

Valley of Death: A Mystery in Death Valley National Park, by Gloria Skurzynski and Alane Ferguson, is the eighth book in the "Mysteries in the National Parks" series for young adults.

Park Essentials

ACCESSIBILITY

All of Death Valley's visitor centers, contact stations, and museums are accessible to all visitors. The campgrounds at Furnace Creek, Sunset, and Stovepipe Wells have wheelchair-accessible sites. Highway 190, Badwater Road, and paved roads to Dante's View and Wildrose provide access to the major scenic viewpoints and historic points of interest.

PARK FEES AND PERMITS

The entrance fee is $30 per vehicle, $25 for motorcycles, and $15 for those entering on foot or bike. The payment, valid for seven consecutive days, is collected at the park's ranger stations, self-serve fee stations, and the visitor center at Furnace Creek. Annual park passes, valid only at Death Valley, are $55.

A permit is not required for groups of 14 or fewer, but if you're planning an overnight visit to the backcountry, complete a registration form at the Furnace Creek Visitor Center. Backcountry camping is allowed in areas that are at least 2 miles from maintained campgrounds and the main paved or unpaved roads and ¼ mile from water sources. Most abandoned mining areas are restricted to day use.

PARK HOURS

The park is open day or night year-round. Most facilities operate daily 8–6.

CELL PHONE RECEPTION

Results vary, but in general you should be able to get fairly good reception on the valley floor. In the surrounding mountains, however, don't count on it.

Hotels

It's difficult to find lodging anywhere in Death Valley that doesn't have breathtaking views of the park and surrounding mountains. Most accommodations, aside from the Inn at Death Valley, are homey and rustic. Rooms fill up quickly during the fall and spring seasons, and reservations are required about three months in advance for the prime weekends.

Outside the park, head to Beatty or Amargosa Valley in Nevada for a bit of nightlife and casino action. The western side of Death Valley, along the eastern Sierra Nevada, is a gorgeous setting, though it's quite a distance from Furnace Creek. Here, you can stay in the historic Dow Villa Motel, where John Wayne spent many a night. *Hotel reviews have been shortened. For full information, visit Fodors.com.*

Restaurants

Inside the park, if you're looking for a special evening out, head to the Inn at Death Valley Dining Room, which is also a great spot to start the day with a hearty gourmet breakfast. Most other eateries within the park are mom-and-pop-type places with basic American fare. Outside the park, dining choices are much the same, with little cafés and homey diners serving up coffee shop–style burgers, chicken, and steaks. If you're vegetarian or vegan, BYOB (bring your own beans). *Restaurant reviews have been shortened. For full information, visit Fodors.com.*

What It Costs

$	$$	$$$	$$$$
RESTAURANTS			
under $12	$12–$20	$21–$30	over $30
HOTELS			
under $100	$100–$150	$151–$200	over $200

Tours

Furnace Creek Visitor Center programs

GUIDED TOURS | This center has many programs, including ranger-led hikes that explore natural wonders such as Golden Canyon, nighttime stargazing parties with telescopes, and evening ranger talks. ⊠ *Furnace Creek Visitor Center, Rte. 190, 30 miles northwest of Death Valley Junction, Death Valley* ☎ *760/786–2331* ⊕ *www.nps.gov/deva/planyourvisit/tours.htm* ☞ *Free.*

Pink Jeep Tours Las Vegas

GUIDED TOURS | A 10-passenger luxury vehicle with oversized viewing windows will pick you up at most Strip hotels for visits to park landmarks. The tours run from about 7 am to 4 pm from September through May, are professionally narrated, and include lunch and bottled water. ⊠ *3629 W. Hacienda Ave., Las Vegas* ☎ *800/873–3662* ⊕ *pinkadventuretours.com* ☞ *From $275.*

Star Wars Tour of Death Valley

DRIVING TOURS | The legendary Star Wars series filmed *Episode IV: A New Hope* and *Episode VI: Return of the Jedi* in Death Valley in the late 1970s and early 1980s. Visit the park website for details on film locations. ⊠ *Death Valley National Park* ⊕ *www.nps.gov/tripideas/star-wars-tour-of-death-valley.htm.*

Visitor Information

In addition to selling a variety of books on the area, the **Death Valley Natural History Association** (☎ *760/786–2146 or 800/478–8564* ⊕ *www.dvnha.org*) sells a waterproof, tear-proof topographical map of the entire park. Additional topo maps covering select areas are also available from the association or the visitor center.

CONTACTS Death Valley National Park. ☎ *760/786–3200* ⊕ *www.nps.gov/deva.*

Furnace Creek Visitor Center and Museum

INFO CENTER | The exhibits and artifacts here provide a broad overview of how Death Valley formed; you can pick up maps at the bookstore run by the Death Valley Natural History Association. This is also the place to find out about ranger programs (available November through April) or check out a live presentation about the valley's cultural and natural history. The helpful center offers regular showings of a 20-minute film about the park, and this is the place for children to get their free Junior Ranger booklet, packed with games and information about the park and its critters. ⊠ *Hwy. 190, Death Valley* ✛ *30 miles northwest of Death Valley Junction* ☎ *760/786–3200* ⊕ *www.nps.gov/deva.*

⚠ **The popular visitor center at Scotty's Castle is closed until at least 2022 as a result of a major flash flood in 2015 that damaged the structure and destroyed the access road.**

Central Death Valley

12 miles west of the Death Valley National Park Highway 190 entrance.

Furnace Creek village (194 feet below sea level) was once the center of mining operations for the Pacific Coast Borax Company. Today, it's the hub of Death Valley National Park, home to park headquarters and visitor center; the Timbisha Indian Village; and the Oasis at Death Valley hotels, golf course, restaurants, and market. Many

Plants and Wildlife in Death Valley

There's a general misconception that Death Valley National Park consists of mile upon endless mile of flat desert sands, scattered cacti, and an occasional cow skull. Many people don't realize that across the valley floor from Badwater—the lowest point in the Western Hemisphere—Telescope Peak towers at 11,049 feet above sea level. The extreme topography of Death Valley is a lesson in geology. Two hundred million years ago, seas covered the area, depositing layers of sediment and fossils. Between 3.5 million and 5 million years ago, faults in the Earth's crust and volcanic activity pushed and folded the ground, causing mountain ranges to rise and the valley floor to drop. The valley was then filled periodically by lakes, which eroded the surrounding rocks into fantastic formations and deposited the salts that now cover the floor of the basin.

Most animal life in Death Valley (51 mammal, 36 reptile, 307 bird, and 3 amphibian species) is found near the limited sources of water. The bighorn sheep spend most of their time in the secluded upper reaches of the park's rugged canyons and ridges. Coyotes often can be seen lazing in the shade next to the golf course and have been known to run onto the fairways to steal a golf ball. The only native fish in the park is the pupfish, which grows to slightly longer than one inch. In winter, when the water is cold, the fish burrow into the bottom mud and lie dormant, becoming active again in spring. Because they are wary of large moving shapes, you must stand quietly over a pool at Salt Creek to see them.

Botanists say there are more than 1,000 species of plants here (21 exist nowhere else in the world), though many annual plants lie dormant as seeds for all but a few months in spring, when rains trigger a bloom. The rest congregate around the few water sources. Most of the low-elevation vegetation grows around the oases at Furnace Creek and Scotty's Castle, where oleanders, palms, and salt cedar grow. At higher elevations you will find pinyon, juniper, and bristlecone pine.

major park sites are a short drive from here, including Artists Drive, Badwater Basin, Dante's View, and Zabriskie Point. Stovepipe Wells Village (where you will want to fill up at the gas station) lies 25 miles northwest of Furnace Creek.

 Sights

HISTORIC SIGHTS
Harmony Borax Works
HISTORIC SITE | Death Valley's mule teams hauled borax from here to the railroad town of Mojave, 165 miles away. The teams plied the route until 1889, when the railroad finally arrived in Zabriskie.

Constructed in 1883, one of the oldest buildings in Death Valley houses the Borax Museum, 2 miles south of the borax works at the Ranch at the Oasis at Death Valley (between the restaurants and the post office). Originally a miners' bunkhouse, the building once stood in Twenty Mule Team Canyon. Now it displays mining machinery and historical exhibits. The adjacent structure is the original mule-team barn. ⌧ *Harmony Borax Works Rd., west of Hwy. 190 at Ranch at Death Valley* ⊕ *www.nps.gov/deva/historyculture/harmony.htm.*

Keane Wonder Mine

MINE | The tram towers and cables from the old mill used to process gold from Keane Wonder Mine are still here, leading up to the mine. The access road is off the Beatty Cutoff Road, 17½ miles north of Furnace Creek. ⊠ *Access road off Beatty Cutoff Rd., Death Valley ✢ 17½ miles north of Furnace Creek* ⊕ *www. nps.gov/deva/learn/historyculture/keane-wonder-mine.htm.*

SCENIC DRIVE

Artists Drive

SCENIC DRIVE | This 9-mile, one-way route skirts the foothills of the Black Mountains and provides intimate views of the changing landscape. Once inside the palette, the valley's expanses are replaced by the small-scale natural beauty of pigments created by volcanic deposits or sedimentary layers. It's a quiet, lonely drive, and shouldn't be rushed. Reach Artists Palette by heading south on Badwater Road from its intersection with Route 190. ⊠ *Death Valley National Park.*

SCENIC STOPS

Artists Palette

NATURE SITE | So called for the contrasting colors of its volcanic deposits and sedimentary layers, this is one of the signature sights of Death Valley. Artists Drive, the approach to the area, is one-way heading north off Badwater Road, so if you're visiting Badwater from Furnace Creek, come here on the way back. The drive winds through foothills of sedimentary and volcanic rocks. About 4 miles along, a short side road veers right to a parking lot that's a few hundred feet before the "palette," whose natural colors include shades of green, gold, and pink. ⊠ *Off Badwater Rd., Death Valley ✢ 11 miles south of Furnace Creek.*

Badwater Basin

SCENIC DRIVE | At 282 feet below sea level, Badwater is the lowest spot of land in North America—and also one of the hottest. Stairs and wheelchair ramps descend from the parking lot to a wooden platform that overlooks a sodium chloride pool, a small but remarkably persistent reminder that the valley floor used to contain a lake. You can continue past the platform on a broad, white path that peters out after a ½ mile or so. Badwater is one of the most popular and easily accessible sites within the park. From this lowest point, be sure to look across to Telescope Peak, which towers more than 2 miles above the valley floor. ⊠ *Badwater Rd., Death Valley ✢ 19 miles south of Furnace Creek.*

Devil's Golf Course

NATURE SITE | Thousands of miniature salt pinnacles carved into surreal shapes by the desert wind dot this wildly varied landscape. The salt was pushed up to the surface by pressure created as underground salt- and water-bearing gravel crystallized. Get out of your vehicle, and take a closer look; you may see perfectly round holes descending into the ground. ⊠ *Badwater Rd., Death Valley ✢ 13 miles south of Furnace Creek. Turn right onto dirt road and drive 1 mile.*

Golden Canyon

NATURE SITE | Just south of Furnace Creek, these glimmering mountains are perhaps best known for their role in the original *Star Wars*. The canyon is also a fine hiking spot, with gorgeous views of the Panamint Mountains, ancient dry lake beds, and alluvial fans. ⊠ *Hwy. 178, Death Valley ✢ From Furnace Creek Visitor Center, drive 2 miles south on Hwy. 190, then 2 miles south on Hwy. 178 to parking area; the lot has kiosk with trail guides.*

Mesquite Flat Sand Dunes

NATURE SITE | These dunes, made up of minute pieces of quartz and other rock, are ever-changing products of the wind-rippled hills, with curving crests and a sun-bleached hue. The dunes are the most photographed destination in the park, and you can see them at their best at sunrise and sunset. Keep your eyes open for animal tracks—you may

The Mesquite Flat Sand Dunes

even spot a coyote or fox. Bring plenty of water, and note where you parked your car: it's easy to become disoriented in this ocean of sand. If you lose your bearings, climb to the top of a dune, and scan the horizon for the parking lot. ⊠ *Death Valley ✢ 19 miles north of Hwy. 190, northeast of Stovepipe Wells Village.*

Stovepipe Wells Village

TOWN | This tiny 1926 town, the first resort in Death Valley, takes its name from the stovepipe that an early prospector left to indicate where he found water. Although the area has a motel, restaurant, convenience store, gas station, swimming pool, and RV hookups, you're better off staying in Furnace Creek, which is more central. Off Highway 190, on a 3-mile gravel road immediately southwest, are the multicolor walls of Mosaic Canyon. ⊠ *Hwy. 190, Death Valley ✢ 2 miles from Sand Dunes, 77 miles east of Lone Pine* ☏ *760/786–7090* ⊕ *www.deathvalleyhotels.com.*

Zabriskie Point

VIEWPOINT | Although only about 710 feet in elevation, this is one of the park's most scenic spots, overlooking a striking panorama of wrinkled, multicolor hills. It's a great place to watch the sunrise, but it can be bustling any time of day. Pair it with a drive out to magnificent Dante's View. ⊠ *Hwy. 190, Death Valley ✢ 5 miles south of Furnace Creek.*

TRAILS

Keane Wonder Mine Trail

TRAIL | This fascinating relic of Death Valley's gold-mining past, built in 1907, reopened in November 2017 after nine years of repair work. Its most unique feature is the mile-long tramway that descends 1,000 vertical feet, which once carried gold ore and still has the original cables attached. From here, a network of trails leads to other old mines. A climb to the uppermost tramway terminal is rewarded by expansive views of the valley. ⊠ *Access road off Beatty Cutoff Rd., 17½ miles north of Furnace Creek, Death Valley.*

Mosaic Canyon Trail

TRAIL | FAMILY | A gradual uphill trail (4 miles round-trip) winds through the smoothly polished, marbleized limestone walls of this narrow canyon. There are dry falls to climb at the upper end. *Moderate.* ✉ *Death Valley* ✥ *Trailhead: access road off Hwy. 190, ½ mile west of Stovepipe Wells Village.*

Natural Bridge Canyon Trail

TRAIL | A rough 2-mile access road from Badwater Road leads to a trailhead. From there, set off to see interesting geological features in addition to the bridge, which is a ½ mile away. The one-way trail continues for a few hundred yards, but scenic returns diminish quickly, and eventually you're confronted with climbing boulders. *Easy.* ✉ *Death Valley* ✥ *Trailhead: access road off Badwater Rd., 15 miles south of Furnace Creek.*

Salt Creek Interpretive Trail

TRAIL | FAMILY | This trail, a ½-mile boardwalk circuit, loops through a spring-fed wash. The nearby hills are brown and gray, but the floor of the wash is alive with aquatic plants such as pickleweed and salt grass. The stream and ponds here are among the few places in the park to see the rare pupfish, the only native fish species in Death Valley. They're most easily seen during their spawning season in February and March. Animals such as bobcats, foxes, coyotes, and snakes visit the spring, and you may also see ravens, common snipes, killdeer, and great blue herons. *Easy.* ✉ *Death Valley* ✥ *Trailhead: off Hwy. 190, 14 miles north of Furnace Creek.*

🍴 Restaurants

★ Inn at the Oasis at Death Valley Dining Room

$$$$ | AMERICAN | Fireplaces, beamed ceilings, and spectacular views provide a visual feast to match this fine-dining restaurant's ambitious menu. Dinner entrées include salmon, free-range chicken, and filet mignon, and there's a seasonal menu of vegetarian dishes. **Known for:** views of surrounding desert; old-school charm; can be pricey. [$] *Average main: $42* ✉ *Inn at the Oasis at Death Valley, Hwy. 190, Furnace Creek* ☎ *760/786–3385* 🌐 *www.oasisatdeathvalley.com.*

Last Kind Words Saloon

$$$ | AMERICAN | Swing through wooden doors into a spacious dining room that recreates an authentic Old West saloon, decked out with a wooden bar and furniture, mounted animal heads, fugitive wanted fliers, film posters, and other memorabilia. The traditional steakhouse menu also includes crab cakes and other seafood, along with pastas, flatbreads, and vegan and gluten-free options. **Known for:** hefty steaks, ribs, and seasonal game dishes; extensive drinks menu, from local craft beer to whiskeys and wines; outdoor patio with fireplace. [$] *Average main: $29* ✉ *The Ranch at the Oasis at Death Valley, Hwy. 190, Furnace Creek* ☎ *760/786–3335* 🌐 *www.oasisatdeathvalley.com/dine/last-kind-words-saloon.*

19th Hole

$$ | AMERICAN | Next to the clubhouse of the world's lowest golf course, this open-air spot serves hamburgers, hot dogs, chicken, and sandwiches. **Known for:** kielbasa dog, burgers, and breakfast burrito; shaded patio; full bar. [$] *Average main: $12* ✉ *Furnace Creek Golf Course, Hwy. 190, Furnace Creek* ☎ *760/786–2345* 🌐 *www.oasisatdeathvalley.com/dining* 🕓 *Closed mid-May–mid-Oct. No service after 7 pm.*

🛏 Hotels

★ The Inn at the Oasis at Death Valley

$$$$ | HOTEL | Built in 1927, this adobe-brick-and-stone lodge in one of the park's greenest oases reopened in 2018 after a $100 million renovation, offering Death Valley's most luxurious accommodations, including 22 brand-new one- and two-bedroom casitas. **Pros:** refined;

comfortable; great views. **Cons:** services reduced during low season (July and August); expensive; resort fee. $ *Rooms from: $499* ✉ *Furnace Creek Village, near intersection of Hwy. 190 and Badwater Rd., Death Valley* ☎ *760/786–2345* ⊕ *www.oasisatdeathvalley.com* ⇆ *88 rooms* ❍ *No meals.*

The Ranch at the Oasis at Death Valley

$$$$ | **RESORT** | **FAMILY** | Originally the crew headquarters for the Pacific Coast Borax Company, the four buildings here have motel-style rooms that are a great option for families. **Pros:** good family atmosphere; central location; walk to the golf course. **Cons:** rooms can get hot in summer despite a/c; resort fee; thin walls and ceilings in some rooms. $ *Rooms from: $279* ✉ *Hwy. 190, Furnace Creek* ☎ *760/786–2345* ⊕ *www.oasisatdeathvalley.com* ⇆ *224 rooms* ❍ *No meals.*

Stovepipe Wells Village Hotel

$$ | **HOTEL** | If you prefer quiet nights and an unfettered view of the night sky and nearby Mesquite Flat Sand Dunes and Mosaic Canyon, this property is for you. **Pros:** intimate, relaxed; no big-time partying; authentic desert-community ambience. **Cons:** isolated; cheapest patio rooms very small; limited Wi-Fi access. $ *Rooms from: $144* ✉ *51880 Hwy. 190, Stovepipe Wells* ☎ *760/786–7090* ⊕ *www.deathvalleyhotels.com* ⇆ *83 rooms* ❍ *No meals.*

🛍 Shopping

Experienced desert travelers carry a cooler stocked with food and beverages. You're best off replenishing your food stash in Ridgecrest, Barstow, or Pahrump, larger towns that have a better selection and nontourist prices.

Ranch General Store

CONVENIENCE/GENERAL STORES | This convenience store carries groceries, souvenirs, camping supplies, and other basics. ✉ *Hwy. 190, Furnace Creek* ☎ *760/786–2345* ⊕ *www.oasisatdeathvalley.com.*

Northern Death Valley

6 miles west of Beatty, Nevada, via Nevada Hwy. 374, and 54 miles north of Furnace Creek via Hwy. 190 and Scotty's Castle Rd.

Venture into the remote northern region of the park to travel along the 27-mile Titus Canyon scenic drive, visit Racetrack and Ubehebe Crater, and hike along Fall Canyon and Titus Canyon Trails. Scotty's Castle, one of the park's main sights, and the 8-mile road that connects it to the park border, is currently closed to repair damage from a 2015 flood; it's expected to reopen in 2022. Check the park website for updates before you visit.

👁 Sights

SCENIC DRIVES
Titus Canyon

SCENIC DRIVE | This popular, one-way, 27-mile drive starts at Nevada Highway 374 (Daylight Pass Road), 2 miles from the park's boundary. Highlights include the Leadville Ghost Town and the spectacular limestone and dolomite narrows. Toward the end, a two-way section of gravel road leads you into the mouth of the canyon from Scotty's Castle Road (closed until at least 2022). This drive is steep, bumpy, and narrow. High-clearance vehicles are strongly recommended. ✉ *Death Valley National Park* ✛ *Access road off Nevada Hwy. 374, 6 miles west of Beatty, NV.*

SCENIC STOPS
Racetrack

NATURE SITE | Getting here involves a 28-mile journey over a washboard dirt road, but the reward is well worth the trip. Where else in the world do rocks move on their own? This mysterious phenomenon, which baffled scientists for years, now appears to have been "settled." Research has shown that the movement merely involves a rare confluence of conditions: rain and then cold to create a layer of ice that becomes a sail, thus enabling gusty winds to readily push the rocks along—sometimes for several hundred yards. When the mud dries, a telltale trail remains. The trek to the Racetrack can be made in a truck or SUV with thick tires (including spares) and high clearance; other types of vehicles aren't recommended as sharp rocks can slash tires. ⊠ *Death Valley ✛ 27 miles west of Ubehebe Crater via rough dirt road.*

Ubehebe Crater

VOLCANO | At 500 feet deep and ½ mile across, this crater resulted from underground steam and gas explosions, some as recently as 300 years ago. Volcanic ash spreads out over most of the area, and the cinders lie as deep as 150 feet near the crater's rim. Trek down to the crater's floor or walk around it on a fairly level path. Either way, you need about an hour and will be treated to fantastic views. The hike from the floor can be strenuous. ⊠ *N. Death Valley Hwy., Death Valley ✛ 8 miles northwest of Scotty's Castle.*

TRAILS

Fall Canyon Trail

TRAIL | This is a 3-mile, one-way hike from the Titus canyon parking area. First, walk ½ mile north along the base of the mountains to a large wash, then go 2½ miles up the canyon to a 35-foot dry fall. You can continue by climbing around to the falls on the south side. *Moderate.* ⊠ *Death Valley National Park ✛ Trailhead: access road off Scotty's Castle Rd., 33 miles northwest of Furnace Creek.*

Titus Canyon Trail

TRAIL | The narrow floor of Titus Canyon is made of hard-packed gravel and dirt, and it's a constant, moderate, uphill walk (3-mile round-trip is the trail's most popular tack). Klare Spring and some petroglyphs are 5½ miles from the western mouth of the canyon, but you can get a feeling for the area on a shorter walk. *Easy.* ⊠ *Death Valley National Park.*

Southern Death Valley

Entrance on Hwy. 178, 1 mile west of Shoshone and 73 miles southeast of Furnace Creek.

Highway 178 traverses Death Valley from its southern border near Shoshone, through Badwater Basin, and up to Furnace Creek.

Sights

SCENIC STOPS

★ Dante's View

VIEWPOINT | This lookout is 5,450 feet above sea level in the Black Mountains. In the dry desert air you can see across most of 160-mile-long Death Valley. The view is astounding. Take a 10-minute, mildly strenuous walk from the parking lot toward a series of rocky overlooks, where, with binoculars, you can spot some signature sites. A few interpretive signs point out the highlights below in the valley and across in the Sierra. Getting here from Furnace Creek takes about an hour—time well invested. ⊠ *Dante's View Rd., Death Valley ✛ Off Hwy. 190, 35 miles from Badwater, 20 miles south of Twenty Mule Team Canyon.*

Western Death Valley

Panamint Springs is on Hwy. 190, 30 miles southwest of Stovepipe Wells and 50 miles east of Lone Pine and Hwy. 395.

Panamint Springs, a tiny burg with a rustic resort, market, and gas station, anchors the western portion of the park. It's a good base for exploring Charcoal Kilns and hiking the Darwin Falls, Telescope Peak, and Wildrose trails. Pull over at Father Crowley Vista Point for exceptional views of the Panamint Valley and the high Sierra on Hwy. 190 if you're traveling between Lone Pine and Panamint Springs. Ballarat Canyon ghost town lies just a few miles from the southwestern border of the park.

Sights

HISTORIC SIGHTS

Ballarat Ghost Town

GHOST TOWN | Although not officially in Death Valley, Ballarat—a crusty, dusty town that saw its heyday between 1897 and 1917—might make an interesting stop during a visit to the park's western reaches. Situated 30 miles south of the Panamint Springs Resort, it has a store-museum where you can grab a cold soda before venturing out to explore the crumbling landscape. For years Ballarat's more infamous draw was **Barker Ranch,** where convicted murderer Charles Manson and his "family" were captured after the 1969 Sharon Tate murder spree; the house burned down in 2009. ✉ *Death Valley* ✣ *From Hwy. 395, Exit SR-178 and travel 45 miles to historic marker; Ballarat is 3½ miles from pavement.*

SCENIC STOPS

Father Crowley Vista Point

VIEWPOINT | Pull off Highway 190 in Western Death Valley into the vista point parking lot to gaze at the remnants of eerie volcanic flows down to Rainbow Canyon. Stroll a short distance to catch a sweeping overview of northern Panamint Valley. This is also an excellent site for stargazing. ✉ *Death Valley National Park.*

TRAILS

★ Darwin Falls

TRAIL | **FAMILY** | This lovely, 2-mile round-trip hike rewards you with a refreshing year-round waterfall surrounded by thick vegetation and a rocky gorge. No swimming or bathing is allowed, but it's a beautiful place for a picnic. Adventurous hikers can scramble higher toward more rewarding views of the falls. ⚠ **Some sections of the trail are not passable for those with mobility issues.** *Easy.* ✉ *Death Valley National Park* ✣ *Trailhead: access the 2-mile graded dirt road and parking area off Hwy. 190, 1 mile west of Panamint Springs Resort.*

★ Telescope Peak Trail

TRAIL | The 14-mile round-trip (with 3,000 feet of elevation gain) trail begins at Mahogany Flat Campground, which is accessible by a rough dirt road. The steep and at some points treacherous trail winds through pinyon, juniper, and bristlecone pines, with excellent views of Death Valley and Panamint Valley. Ice axes and crampons may be necessary in winter—check at the Furnace Creek Visitor Center. It takes a minimum of six grueling hours to hike to the top of the 11,049-foot peak and then return. *Difficult.* ✉ *Death Valley* ✣ *Trailhead: off Wildrose Rd., south of Charcoal Kilns.*

★ Wildrose Peak

TRAIL | An 8.4-mile round-trip trail leads from the Charcoal Kilns through pinyon pine and juniper woodlands up to Wildrose Peak, a 2,200-foot ascent from the trailhead. Various Death Valley views unfold along the way, and the sweeping vistas from the 9,064-foot peak include Panamint Valley and, on clear days, Mt. Whitney. *Difficult* ✉ *Death Valley National Park* ✣ *Trailhead: off Emigrant Canyon Rd., at Charcoal Kilns.*

Restaurants

Panamint Springs Resort Restaurant

$$ | **AMERICAN** | This is a great place for steak and a beer—choose from more than 150 different beers and ales—or pasta and a salad. In summer, evening meals are served outdoors on the porch, which has spectacular views of Panamint Valley. **Known for:** good burgers; extensive beer selection; great views from the porch. [$] *Average main: $15* ✉ *Hwy. 190, Death Valley* ✣ *31 miles west of Stovepipe Wells* ☎ *775/482–7680* 🌐 *www.panamintsprings.com/services/dining-bar.*

Activities

BIKING

Mountain biking is permitted on any of the back roads and roadways open to the public (bikes aren't permitted on hiking trails). Visit ⊕ *www.nps.gov/deva/ planyourvisit/bikingandmtbiking.htm* for a list of suggested routes for all levels of ability. Bicycle Path, a 4-mile round-trip trek from the visitor center to Mustard Canyon, is a good place to start. Bike rentals are available at the Oasis at Death Valley, by the hour or by the day.

Escape Adventures (*Escape Adventures*) **BICYCLING** | Ride into the heart of Death Valley on the Death Valley & Red Rock Mountain Bike Tour, a five-day trip through the national park. A customizable two-day journey (on single-track trails and jeep roads) includes accommodations (both camping and inns). Bikes, tents, and other gear may be rented for an additional price. Tours are available February–April and October only. ⊠ *Death Valley National Park* ☎ *800/596–2953, 702/596–2953* ⊕ *www.escapeadventures.com* ⤶ *From $1950.*

BIRD-WATCHING

Approximately 350 bird species have been identified in Death Valley. The best place to see them is along the Salt Creek Interpretive Trail, where you can spot ravens, common snipes, killdeer, spotted sandpipers, and great blue herons. Along the fairways at Furnace Creek Golf Course, you can see kingfishers, peregrine falcons, hawks, Canada geese, yellow warblers, and the occasional golden eagle.

You can download a complete park bird checklist, divided by season, at ⊕ *www. nps.gov/deva/learn/nature/upload/death-valley-bird-checklist.pdf.* Rangers at Furnace Creek Visitor Center often lead birding walks through various locations between November and March.

CAMPING

Camping is prohibited in historic sites and day-use spots. You'll need a high-clearance or 4X4 vehicle to reach campgrounds. For backcountry camping information, visit ⊕ *www.nps.gov/deva/ planyourvisit/camping.htm.*

Fires are permitted only in metal grates and may be restricted in summer. Wood gathering is prohibited at all campgrounds, and it's best to bring your own. Firewood is expensive and limited in supply at general stores in Furnace Creek and Stovepipe Wells. Camping is prohibited in the historic Inyo, Los Burro, and Ubehebe Crater areas, as well as all day-use spots, including Aguerberry Point Road, Cottonwood Canyon Road, Racetrack Road, Skidoo Road, Titus Canyon Road, Wildrose Road, and West Side Road.

Furnace Creek. This campground, 196 feet below sea level, has some shaded tent sites and is open all year. ⊠ *Hwy. 190, Furnace Creek* ☎ *760/786–2441.*

Mahogany Flat. If you have a four-wheel-drive vehicle and want to scale Telescope Peak, the park's highest mountain, you might want to sleep at one of the few shaded spots in Death Valley, at a cool 8,133 feet. ⊠ *Off Wildrose Rd., south of Charcoal Kilns* ☎ *No phone.*

Panamint Springs Resort. Part of a complex that includes a motel and cabin, this campground is surrounded by cottonwoods. The daily fee includes use of the showers and restrooms. ⊠ *Hwy. 190, 28 miles west of Stovepipe Wells* ☎ *775/482–7680.*

Sunset Campground. This first-come, first-served campground is a gravel-and-asphalt RV city. Closed mid-April to mid-October. ⊠ *Sunset Campground Rd., 1 mile north of Furnace Creek* ☎ *800/365–2267.*

Texas Spring. This campsite south of the Furnace Creek Visitor Center has good views and facilities and is a few dollars cheaper than Furnace Creek. It's closed mid-May to mid-October. ⊠ *Off Badwater Rd., south of Furnace Creek Visitor Center* ☎ *800/365–2267.*

EDUCATIONAL PROGRAMS

Junior Ranger Program

TOUR—SIGHT | FAMILY | Children can pick up a workbook and complete activities to earn a souvenir badge. ⊠ *Death Valley National Park.*

FOUR-WHEELING

Maps and SUV guidebooks for four-wheel-drive and other backcountry roads (including the popular Cottonwood/Marble canyons, Racetrack, Eureka Dunes, Saratoga Springs, and Warm Springs Canyon) are offered at the Furnace Creek Visitor Center. Remember: never travel alone, and be sure to pack plenty of water and snacks. Check ⊕ *www.nps. gov/deva/planyourvisit/backcountryroads. htm* for back-road conditions before setting out. Driving off established roads is strictly prohibited in the park.

Butte Valley

TOUR—SPORTS | A high-clearance, four-wheel-drive vehicle and nerves of steel are required to tackle this 21-mile road in the southwest part of the park. It climbs from 200 feet below sea level to an elevation of 4,700 feet, and the geological formations along the way reveal the development of Death Valley. It also travels through Butte Valley, passing the Warm Springs talc mine, to Geologist's Cabin, a charming and cheery little structure where you can spend the night, if nobody else beats you to it. The cabin, which sits under a cottonwood tree, has a fireplace, table and chairs, and a sink. Farther up the road, Stella's Cabin and Russell Camp are also open for public use. Keep the historic cabins clean, and restock any items that you use. The road

is even rougher if you continue over Mengel Pass. Check road conditions before heading out. ⊠ *Trailhead on Warm Spring Canyon Rd., Death Valley ✛ 50 miles south of Furnace Creek Visitor Center.*

GOLF

Furnace Creek Golf Course at the Oasis at Death Valley

GOLF | Golfers rave about how their drives carry at altitude, so what happens on the lowest golf course in the world (214 feet below sea level)? Its improbably green fairways are lined with date palms and tamarisk trees, and its level of difficulty is rated surprisingly high. You can rent clubs and carts, and there are golf packages available for resort guests. In fall and winter, reservations are essential. ⊠ *Hwy. 190, Furnace Creek* ☎ *760/786–3373* ⊕ *www.oasisatdeathvalley.com* ⌸ *From $48* ⚑ *18 holes, 6215 yards, par 70.*

HIKING

Plan to hike before or after midday in the spring, summer, or fall, unless you're in the mood for a masochistic baking. Carry plenty of water, wear protective clothing, and keep an eye out for black widows, scorpions, snakes, and other potentially dangerous creatures.

HORSEBACK AND CARRIAGE RIDES

Furnace Creek Stables

HORSEBACK RIDING | FAMILY | Set off on a one- or two-hour guided horseback, carriage, or hay wagon ride from Furnace Creek Stables. The rides traverse trails with views of the surrounding mountains, where multicolor volcanic rock and alluvial fans form a background for date palms and other vegetation. Evening carriage rides take passengers around the golf course and the Ranch at Death Valley. The stables are open October–May only. ⊠ *Hwy. 190, Furnace Creek* ☎ *760/614–1018* ⊕ *www.oasisatdeath-valley.com/plan/horseback-wagon-rides* ⌸ *From $60.*

Wildflower super-bloom in spring

Nearby Towns

Founded at the turn of the 20th century, **Beatty** sits 16 miles east of the California-Nevada border on Death Valley's northern side. Named for a single pine tree found at the bottom of the canyon of the same name, **Lone Pine,** on the park's west side, is where you'll find Mt. Whitney, the highest peak in the continental United States, at 14,496 feet. The nearby Alabama Hills have been used in many movies and TV scenes, including segments in *The Lone Ranger*. **Independence,** a well-preserved outpost that dates back to the 1860s, lies 16 miles north of Lone Pine on Highway 395. Down south, unincorporated **Shoshone,** a very small town at the edge of Death Valley, started out as a mining town.

Beatty

7 miles east of Death Valley National Park Devil's Gate entrance.

The tiny Old West town of Beatty, a northeastern gateway to Death Valley National Park, has a well-preserved historic downtown district that's worth exploring. It's also a good place to relax and refresh thanks to its cluster of hotels, restaurants, and other services. Hundreds of hiking, biking, and off-highway vehicle roads stretch out from here in all directions. Beatty is also home to the Death Valley Nut and Candy Company, Nevada's largest candy store, and the Rhyolite Ghost Town is just five miles west of downtown.

VISITOR INFORMATION
Beatty Chamber of Commerce
⊠ *119 E. Main St., Beatty* ☎ *775/553-2424* ⊕ *www.beattynevada.org.*

Sights

Rhyolite

GHOST TOWN | FAMILY | Though it's not within the boundary of Death Valley National Park, this Nevada ghost town, named for the silica volcanic rock nearby, is still a big draw. Around 1904, Rhyolite's Montgomery Shoshone Mine caused a financial boom, and fancy buildings sprung up all over town. Today you can still explore many of the crumbling edifices. The Bottle House, built by miner Tom Kelly out of almost 50,000 Adolphus Busch beer bottles, is a must-see. ✉ *Hwy. 374* ✣ *35 miles north of Furnace Creek Visitor Center and 5 miles west of Beatty* 🌐 *www.nps.gov/deva/learn/historyculture/rhyolite-ghost-town.htm.*

Restaurants

Smokin J's BBQ

$$ | **BARBECUE** | A local favorite, this central Texas–style barbecue joint slow cooks brisket, pulled pork, ribs, and chicken on an oak-fired grill and serves them in baskets heaping with fries, onion rings, and other sides. Pick up meats by the pound to feast on at your lodgings later on. **Known for:** smoked-meat sandwiches; brisket chili bowls; great-value combo plates and meals. [$] *Average main: $17* ✉ *107 West Main St., Beatty* ☎ *775/553–5160* 🌐 *www.facebook.com/Smokinjsbarbecue.*

Shoshone

1 mile from Death Valley National Park's Badwater entrance

A prospector founded this tiny burg in 1910, hoping to build businesses around a new rail stop. He and his family eventually developed the town, and his descendents still run Shoshone Village, which encompasses a hotel, general store, gas station, museum, spring-fed swimming pool, restaurant, campground, and RV park. Nearby nature trails wind through wetlands, pupfish ponds, and bird and endangered-species habitats.

VISITOR INFORMATION

Shoshone Museum Visitor Center. ✉ *Rte. 127, Shoshone* ☎ *760/852–4524* 🌐 *shoshonevillage.com/shoshone-museum.html.*

Sights

Dublin Gulch

CAVE | FAMILY | A series of caves, carved into the caliche soil by miners during the 1920s, is a great spot for exploring and is a hit with kids. Among its more famous residents were Shorty Harris and Death Valley Scotty, who spent many nights weaving tales of strikes and adventures to entertain fellow miners. You aren't allowed to walk inside, but you can view the cells—with their stone walls, sleeping platforms, and metal chimneys—from the exterior. ✉ *Shoshone* ✣ *0.3 mi southwest of Shoshone Village off Hwy. 127* 🌐 *www.shoshonevillage.com/explore-shoshone.*

Marta Becket's Amargosa Opera House

An artist and dancer from New York, Marta Becket first visited the former railway town of Death Valley Junction while on tour in 1967. Later that year, she returned to town and leased a boarded-up social hall that sat amid a group of rundown mock Spanish–colonial buildings. The nonprofit she formed in the early 1970s eventually purchased the property, where she performed for nearly 50 years. To compensate for the sparse audiences in the early days, Becket painted a Renaissance-era Spanish crowd on the walls and ceiling, turning the theater into a trompe-l'oeil masterpiece. A hotel and café still operate on-site, and the opera house presents performances from October to May. Guided tours are available year-round for a suggested $5 donation per person. ✉ *Rte. 127, Death Valley Junction* ✣ *27 miles north of Shoshone* ☎ *760/852–4441* 🌐 *www.amargosaoperahouse.org* 🎟 *Varies.*

Shoshone Museum

MUSEUM | This museum chronicles the local history of Death Valley and houses a unique collection of period items and minerals and rocks from the area. ✉ *Rte. 127, Shoshone* ☎ *760/852–4524* 🌐 *www.shoshonevillage.com/shoshone-museum.html* 🎟 *Free.*

🍴 Restaurants

Crowbar Café and Saloon

$$ | **AMERICAN** | **FAMILY** | In an old wooden building where antique photos adorn the walls and mining equipment stands in the corners, the Crowbar serves enormous helpings of regional dishes such as steak and taco salads. Home-baked fruit pies make fine desserts, and frosty beers are surefire thirst quenchers. **Known for:** home-baked fruit pies; rattlesnake chili; great breakfast spot. [$] *Average main: $15* ✉ *Rte. 127, Shoshone* ☎ *760/852–4123* 🌐 *www.shoshonevillage.com/shoshone-crowbar-cafe-saloon.html.*

🛏 Hotels

Shoshone Inn

$$ | **HOTEL** | Built in 1956, the rustic Shoshone Inn has simple, cozy rooms surrounding a motor court and a warm spring-fed swimming pool built into the foothills. **Pros:** walk to market, restaurant, museum; courtyard with firepit; peaceful retreat. **Cons:** an hour's drive to main park sights; certain rooms and beds too small for some; no room phones, spotty cell service. [$] *Rooms from: $135* ✉ *Hwy. 127, Shoshone* ☎ *760/852–4335* 🌐 *www.shoshonevillage.com/death-valley-lodging-shoshone-inn* 🛏 *18 units* 🍽 *No meals.*

Lone Pine

30 miles west of Panamint Valley.

Mt. Whitney towers majestically over this tiny community, which supplied nearby gold- and silver-mining outposts in the 1860s, and for the past century the town has been touched by Hollywood glamour: several hundred movies, TV episodes, and commercials have been filmed here.

GETTING HERE AND AROUND

Arrive via U.S. 395 from the north or south or Highway 190 or Highway 138 from Death Valley National Park. Eastern Sierra Transit buses connect Lone Pine to Reno in the north and Lancaster in the south.

VISITOR INFORMATION Lone Pine Chamber of Commerce & Visitor Center. ✉ *120 S. Main St., at Whitney Portal Rd.* ☎ *760/876–4444* 🌐 *www.lonepinechamber.org.*

👁 Sights

Alabama Hills

MOUNTAIN—SIGHT | Drop by the Lone Pine Visitor Center for a map of the Alabama Hills, and drive up Whitney Portal Road (turn west at the light) to this wonderland of granite boulders. Erosion has worn the rocks smooth; some have been chiseled into arches and other formations. The hills have become a popular location for rock climbing. Tuttle Creek Campground sits among the rocks, with a nearby stream for fishing. The area has served as a scenic backdrop for hundreds of films; ask about the self-guided tour of the various movie locations at the Museum of Western Film History. ✉ *Whitney Portal Rd., 4½ miles west of Lone Pine.*

Highway 395

SCENIC DRIVE | For a gorgeous view of the eastern Sierra, travel north of Death Valley along Highway 395 where you'll discover wandering elk herds, trout hatcheries, and breathtaking views of Mt. Whitney, the highest mountain (14,496 feet) in the continental United States. Drive south on Highway 395, between Olancha and Big Pine, and you'll notice the massive salt-crusted Owens Lake, which was drained between 1900 and 1920 as water from the Sierra was diverted to Los Angeles. Today, up to one-fourth of the water flow is being reintroduced to the lake. If you drive to the northwest end of the lake, near the abandoned Pittsburg Plate Glass Soda Ash Plant, you can see brilliant red salt flats, caused by billions of microscopic halobacteria that survive there. Revered by the National Audubon Society, the lake is home to more than 240 migrating birds, including the snowy plover, American white pelican, golden eagle, and countless grebes, bitterns, blue herons, and cranes. ✉ *Death Valley.*

Museum of Western Film History

MUSEUM | Hopalong Cassidy, Barbara Stanwyck, Roy Rogers, John Wayne—even Robert Downey Jr.—are among the celebrities who have starred in Westerns and other films shot in the Alabama Hills and surrounding dusty terrain. The marquee-embellished museum relates this Hollywood-in-the-desert tale via exhibits and a rollicking 20-minute documentary. ✉ *701 S. Main St., U.S. 395* ☎ *760/876–9909* 🌐 *www.museumofwesternfilmhistory.org* 🎟 *$5* 🕑 *Closed Tues.–Wed.*

🍴 Restaurants

Alabama Hills Café & Bakery

$$ | **AMERICAN** | The extensive breakfast and lunch menus at this eatery just off the main drag include many vegetarian items. Sandwiches are served on homemade bread; choose from up to six varieties baked fresh daily, and get a homemade pie, cake, or loaf to go. **Known for:** house-roasted turkey and beef; huge portions; on-site bakery. [$] *Average main: $13* ✉ *111 W. Post St., at S. Main St.* ☎ *760/876–4675* 🌐 *alabamahillscafe.com.*

Mt. Whitney Restaurant

$$ | **AMERICAN** | A boisterous family-friendly restaurant with four flat-screen televisions, this place serves the best burgers in town. In addition to the usual beef variety, you can choose from ostrich, elk, venison, and buffalo burgers. **Known for:** burgers; John Wayne memorabilia; convenient fuel-up stop on Highway 395. [$] *Average main: $13* ✉ *227 S. Main St.* ☎ *760/876–5751.*

Seasons Restaurant

$$$ | **AMERICAN** | This inviting, country-style diner serves all kinds of traditional American fare. For a special treat, try the medallions of Cervena elk, smothered in port wine, dried cranberries, and toasted walnuts; finish with the Baileys Irish Cream cheesecake or the Grand Marnier crème brûlée for dessert. **Known for:** high-end dining in remote area; steaks and wild game; children's menu. [$] *Average main: $27* ✉ *206 S. Main St.* ☎ *760/876–8927* 🌐 *seasonslonepine.club* 🕑 *Closed Mon. Nov.–Mar. No lunch.*

🛏 Hotels

Dow Villa Motel and Dow Hotel

$$ | **HOTEL** | Built in 1923 to cater to the film industry, the Dow Villa Motel and the historic Dow Hotel sit in the center of Lone Pine. **Pros:** clean rooms; great mountain views; in-room whirlpool tubs in some motel rooms. **Cons:** some rooms in hotel share bathrooms; sinks in some rooms are in the bedroom, not the bath; on busy highway. [$] *Rooms from: $119* ✉ *310 S. Main St.* ☎ *760/876–5521, 800/824–9317* 🌐 *www.dowvillamotel.com* 🛏 *92 rooms* 🍽 *No meals.*

Independence

17 miles north of Lone Pine.

Named for a military outpost that was established near here in 1862, sleepy Independence has some wonderful historic buildings and is worth a stop for another reason: 6 miles south of the small downtown lies the Manzanar National Historic Site, one of 10 camps in the west where people of Japanese descent were confined during World War II.

GETTING HERE AND AROUND

Eastern Sierra Transit buses pass through town, but most travelers arrive by car on U.S. 395.

Sights

Ancient Bristlecone Pine Forest

FOREST | FAMILY | About an hour's drive from Independence or Bishop you can view some of the oldest living trees on Earth, a few of which date back more than 40 centuries. The world's largest bristlecone pine can be found in Patriarch Grove, while the world's oldest known living tree is along Methusula Trail in Schulman Grove. Getting to Patriarch Grove is slow going along the narrow dirt road, especially for sedans with low clearance, but once there you'll find picnic tables, restrooms, and interpretive trails. ⊠ *Schulman Grove Visitor Center, White Mountain Rd., Bishop* ✢ *From U.S. 395, turn east onto Hwy. 168 and follow signs for 23 miles* ⊕ *www.fs.usda.gov/ main/inyo/home* 🎟 *$3.*

★ Manzanar National Historic Site

HISTORIC SITE | A reminder of an ugly episode in U.S. history, the former Manzanar War Relocation Center is where more than 11,000 Japanese-Americans were confined behind barbed-wire fences between 1942 and 1945. A visit here is both deeply moving and inspiring—the former because it's hard to comprehend that the United States was capable of confining its citizens in such a way, the latter because those imprisoned here showed great pluck and perseverance in making the best of a bad situation. Most of the buildings from the 1940s are gone, but two sentry posts, the auditorium, and numerous Japanese rock gardens remain. One of eight guard towers, two barracks, and a women's latrine have been reconstructed, and a mess hall has been restored. Interactive exhibits inside the barracks include audio and video clips from people who were incarcerated in Manzanar during WWII. You can drive the one-way road on a self-guided tour past various ruins to a small cemetery, where a monument stands. Signs mark where the barracks, a hospital, a school, and the fire station once stood. An outstanding 8,000-square-foot interpretive center has exhibits and documentary photographs and screens a short film. ⊠ *Independence* ✢ *West side of U.S. 395 between Independence and Lone Pine* ☎ *760/878– 2194* ⊕ *www.nps.gov/manz* 🎟 *Free.*

Chapter 15

GLACIER AND WATERTON LAKES NATIONAL PARKS

15

Updated by
Debbie Olsen

MONTANA

🏕 Camping	🛏 Hotels	🏃 Activities	👁 Scenery	👥 Crowds
★★★★★	★★★☆☆	★★★★★	★★★★☆	★★☆☆☆

WELCOME TO GLACIER AND WATERTON LAKES NATIONAL PARKS

TOP REASONS TO GO

★ **Witness the Divide:** The rugged mountains that weave their way through Glacier and Waterton along the Continental Divide seem to have glaciers in every hollow melting into tiny streams, raging rivers, and icy-cold mountain lakes.

★ **Just hike it:** Hundreds of miles of trails of all levels of difficulty lace the park, from flat and easy half-hour strolls to steep, strenuous all-day hikes.

★ **Go to the sun:** Crossing the Continental Divide at the 6,646-foot-high Logan Pass, Glacier's Going-to-the-Sun Road is a spectacular drive.

★ **View the wildlife:** This is one of the few places in North America where all native carnivores, including grizzlies, black bears, coyotes, and wolves, still survive.

★ **See glaciers while you still can:** Approximately 150 glaciers were present in Glacier National Park in 1850; by 2010, there were only 25 left.

1 Western Glacier National Park. Known to the Kootenai people as "sacred dancing lake," Lake McDonald is the largest glacial water basin lake in Glacier National Park and a highlight of its western reaches.

2 Along the Going-to-the-Sun Road. At 6,646 feet, Logan Pass is the highest point on, and very much a highlight of, Glacier National Park's famous (and famously beautiful) Going-to-the-Sun Road. From mid-June to mid-October, a 1½-mile boardwalk leads to an overlook that crosses an area filled with lush meadows and wildflowers.

3 Eastern Glacier National Park. St. Mary Lake and Many Glacier are the major highlights of the eastern side of Glacier National Park. Grinnell Glacier, the most accessible glacier in the park, is reached via a hike that begins near Swiftcurrent Lake in the Many Glacier region.

4 Waterton Lakes National Park. The Canadian national park is the meeting of two worlds: the flatlands of the prairie and the abrupt upthrust of the mountains. The park is also home to a vast array of wildlife, spectacular scenery, and wonderful hiking trails.

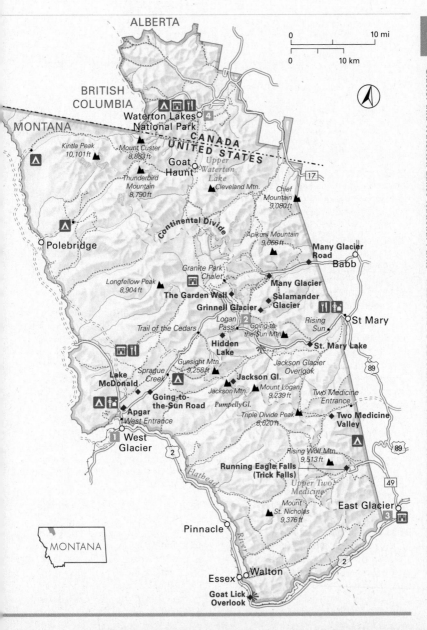

ALBERTA

BRITISH
COLUMBIA

MONTANA

Waterton Lakes
National Park

CANADA
UNITED STATES

Kintla Peak
10,101 ft

Mount Custer
8,883 ft

Goat
Haunt

Upper
Waterton
Lake

17

Thunderbird
Mountain
8,790 ft

Cleveland Mtn.

Chief
Mountain
9,080 ft

Continental Divide

Apikuni Mountain
9,068 ft

Many Glacier
Road

Babb

Polebridge

Longfellow Peak
8,904 ft

Granite Park
Chalet

The Garden Wall

Grinnell Glacier

Many Glacier

Salamander
Glacier

Logan
Pass

Going-to-
the-Sun Mtn.

Rising
Sun

St Mary

Trail of the Cedars

2

St. Mary Lake

89

Hidden
Lake

Gunsight Mtn.
9,258 ft

Jackson Glacier
Overlook

Lake
McDonald

Sprague
Creek

Jackson Mtn.

Pumpelly Gl.

Jackson Gl.

Mount Logan
9,239 ft

Two Medicine
Entrance

Going-to-
the-Sun Road

Triple Divide Peak
8,020 ft

Two Medicine
Valley

Apgar

West Entrance

89

1

West
Glacier

2

Rising Wolf Mtn.
9,513 ft

Running Eagle Falls
(Trick Falls)

49

Upper Two
Medicine

Mount
St. Nicholas
9,376 ft

East Glacier

3

Flathead

Pinnacle

River

MONTANA

2

Essex   Walton

Goat Lick
Overlook

0 ——— 10 mi

0 ——— 10 km

The astonishing landscapes at the crown of the continent know no boundaries. Here, the rugged, glacier-carved mountains span the border between the United States and Canada to form the International Peace Park, which consists of two national parks: Glacier in Montana and Waterton Lakes in Alberta.

The scenery in these parks is unparalleled: craggy peaks, thick coniferous forests, deep lakes, gleaming glaciers, wildflower-carpeted meadows, and too many stunning waterfalls to count. The animals roaming the terrain include everything from ungulates such as deer, elk, bighorn sheep, mountain goats, and moose to carnivores like mountain lions, black bears, and grizzlies.

Evidence of human use in this area dates back over 10,000 years, with the Blackfeet, Salish, and Kootenai peoples inhabiting the region long before the first Europeans came. The completion of the Great Northern Railway in 1891 allowed more people to visit and settle this region of Montana. By the late 1800s, people began to realize the land had value far beyond mining, agricultural, or other commercial endeavors.

Renowned conservationist George Bird Grinnell and other influential leaders lobbied for nearly a decade to have the so-called Crown of the Continent protected as a national park. Their efforts were rewarded when President Taft set aside 1,583 square miles (4,100 square km) to create Glacier, America's 10th national park, on May 11, 1910.

On May 30, 1895, a 140-square-km (54-square-mile) area of what is now Waterton Lakes National Park was first protected as a Dominion Forest Park. It became a national park in 1930, and today it encompasses 505 square km (195 square miles). It was Canada's fourth national park and is the smallest of those in the Canadian Rockies.

The idea of creating an International Peace Park was conceived and promoted by the Cardston Rotary Club and was unanimously endorsed in a meeting of Alberta and Montana Rotary clubs in 1931. On June 18, 1932, the two parks were officially united, establishing the world's first International Peace Park—an enduring symbol of the harmony and friendship between the United States and Canada. On December 6, 1995, the Glacier-Waterton International Peace Park was designated a UNESCO World Heritage Site.

These parks are a nature-lover's dream, filled with magnificent mountains, glaciers, lakes, and forests. There are more than 700 miles (1,127 km) of hiking trails in Glacier and another 200 km (120 miles) in Waterton Lakes. These range in difficulty from easy strolls to strenuous day hikes to multiday backpacking adventures. Other popular activities include fishing, boating, paddleboarding, cycling, mountaineering, climbing, cross-country skiing, and wildlife watching. Glacier's Going-to-the-Sun Road is considered one of the most beautiful drives on the planet, and Waterton's Crypt Lake Hike has been ranked one of the world's most thrilling. If these parks aren't on your bucket list, they should be.

Planning

When to Go

Of the 2 million annual visitors to Glacier and 400,000 to Waterton, most come between July and mid-September, when the streams are flowing, wildlife is roaming, and naturalist programs are fully underway. Snow removal on the alpine portion of Going-to-the-Sun Road is usually completed by mid-June; the opening of Logan Pass at the road's summit marks the summer opening of Glacier. Canada's Victoria Day in late May marks the beginning of the season in Waterton. Spring and fall are quieter.

FESTIVALS AND EVENTS

Canada Day. On July 1, all guests get into the national parks free of charge in honor of Canada's birthday. Waterton also has special activities for families such as treasure hunts and evening theater programs.

Montana Dragon Boat Festival. Held on Flathead Lake, this captivating event features 95 teams of 20 paddlers each racing 46-foot-long Hong Kong–style boats. ⊕ www.montanadragonboat.com.

NW Montana Antique Threshing Bee. Steam threshing machines, steam plows, antique tractors, and engines flex muscles in the Parade of Power, organized by the Northwest Montana Antique

Power Association in Kalispell. Participants challenge friends and neighbors to tractor barrel races and shingle-making events, while children of all ages enjoy miniature steam-train rides, music, food, and entertainment.

Ski Fest. This annual celebration of cross-country skiing is a great way to introduce newcomers to kick-and-glide skiing. Equipment demonstrations, free ski lessons, and family activities are scheduled at the Izaak Walton Inn in Essex, Montana, and free trail passes are dispensed. ⊕ www.izaakwaltoninn.com.

Summer Concert Series. Running each Thursday from mid-June to early August, the series is held in the Don Lawrence Amphitheater at Marantette Park in Columbia Falls. Types of music vary, but the Don Lawrence Big Band performs every year.

Waterton Wildflower Festival. Wildflower walks, horseback rides, hikes, watercolor workshops, photography classes, and family events help visitors and locals celebrate the annual blooming of Waterton's bountiful wildflowers. ⊕ www.watertonwildflowers.com.

Waterton Wildlife Weekend. Wildlife viewing is at its best in Waterton during the fall. The weekend's events include viewing on foot, on horseback, and by boat. There are also photography, drawing, and sketching courses. ⊕ www.watertonwildlife.com.

Whitefish Winter Carnival. For more than 60 years this February fest has been the scene of lively activities, including a grand parade with more than 100 entries, a torchlight parade on skis, fireworks, a penguin dip, and other family-friendly activities. ⊕ www.whitefishwintercarnival.com.

GLACIER AVERAGE HIGH/LOW TEMPERATURES IN FAHRENHEIT

JAN.	FEB.	MAR.	APR.	MAY	JUNE
28/15	35/19	42/23	53/30	64/37	71/44
JULY	AUG.	SEPT.	OCT.	NOV.	DEC.
79/47	78/46	67/39	53/32	37/25	30/18

GLACIER AVERAGE HIGH/LOW TEMPERATURES IN CELSIUS

JAN.	FEB.	MAR.	APR.	MAY	JUNE
-2/-9	2/-7	6/-5	12/-1	18/3	22/7
JULY	AUG.	SEPT.	OCT.	NOV.	DEC.
26/8	26/8	19/4	12/0	3/-4	-1/-8

WATERTON AVERAGE HIGH/LOW TEMPERATURES IN CELSIUS

JAN.	FEB.	MAR.	APR.	MAY	JUNE
0/-11	1/-10	6/-6	10/-2	15/3	19/6
JULY	AUG.	SEPT.	OCT.	NOV.	DEC.
23/8	22/7	17/3	12/1	3/-6	1/-9

WATERTON AVERAGE HIGH/LOW TEMPERATURES IN FAHRENHEIT

JAN.	FEB.	MAR.	APR.	MAY	JUNE
32/12	34/14	42/22	50/29	59/37	66/43
JULY	AUG.	SEPT.	OCT.	NOV.	DEC.
73/46	72/44	63/38	53/33	38/22	33/15

Getting Here and Around

AIR

The nearest airports to Glacier are in Kalispell (25 miles) and Great Falls (157 miles), both in Montana. The nearest airport to Waterton Lakes is in Calgary (271 km [168 miles]).

Glacier Park International Airport
Five major airlines fly into Glacier Park International Airport (FCA) and service the national park and the Flathead Valley region. ✉ 4170 Hwy. 2 E, Kalispell ☎ 406/257–5994 ⊕ iflyglacier.com.

BUS

Glacier National Park operates a free hop-on, hop-off shuttle along the Going-to-the-Sun Road from July through early September. The shuttle runs from Apgar to St. Mary Visitor Center; park visitor centers have departure information.

CAR

On the western side of Glacier National Park, U.S. 2 goes to West Glacier. At the park's northwestern edge, North Fork Road connects to Polebridge. On the park's east side, U.S. 2 goes to East Glacier and Highway 49 reaches to Two Medicine. U.S. 89 accesses St. Mary, and U.S. Route 3 connects to Many Glacier. Take the Chief Mountain Highway (Highway 17) to access Waterton Lakes in summer or U.S. 89 to Alberta Highway 2 through Cardston and then west via Highway 5 any time of the year.

In both parks, repeated freezing and thawing can cause roads—either gravel or paved—to deteriorate, so drive slowly. In summer, road reconstruction is part of the park experience as crews take advantage of the few warm months to complete projects. At any time of the year, anticipate that rocks and wildlife may be just around the bend. Gasoline is available along most paved roads. Scenic pull-outs are frequent; watch for other vehicles pulling in or out, and watch for children in parking areas. Most development and services center on Lake McDonald in the west and St. Mary Lake in the east.

BORDER CROSSINGS
A passport is required of everyone crossing the Canadian–U.S. border. When you arrive at the border crossing, customs officers will ask for information such as where you are going and where you are from. You and your vehicle are subject to random search. Firearms are prohibited, except hunting rifles, which require permission you must obtain in advance. Soil, seeds, meat, and many fruits are also prohibited. Kids traveling with only one parent need a notarized letter from the other parent giving permission to enter Canada or the United States. If you are traveling with pets, you need proof of up-to-date immunizations to cross the border in either direction. Citizens from most countries (Canada, Mexico, and Bermuda are exceptions) entering the United States from Canada must pay $6 (cash only) at the border for a required I-94 or I-94W Arrival-Departure Record form, to be returned to border officials when leaving the United States. Contact United States Customs (☎ *406/335–2611* ⊕ *www.cbp.gov*) or the Canada Border Services Agency (☎ *403/344–3767* ⊕ *www.cbsa-asfc.gc.ca*) for more information.

TRAIN
Montana's Amtrak stations are all on the *Empire Builder* route that connects Glacier National Park with Chicago and Portland/Seattle. The main stops near the park are at East Glacier Park Village, West Glacier, Essex, and Whitefish. From the stations, you can rent a car.

Inspiration

Bear Attacks: Their Causes and Avoidance, by Stephen Herrero, explores what we know about grizzly and black bears, how to avoid an incident, what to do if a bear attacks, and what the future holds for these fascinating creatures.

Charles Waterton, 1782–1865: Traveller and Conservationis, by Julia Blackburn, provides insight on Charles Waterton, the eccentric British naturalist and explorer who was one of the first conservationists of the modern age. The Waterton Lakes were named in his honor by Lieutenant Thomas Blakiston, a member of the Palliser Expedition.

Fools Crow, by James Welch and first published in 1986, is a fictional but fascinating look at what life was like for Native Americans living in this region of Montana before Glacier became a national park.

The Melting World: A Journey Across America's Vanishing Glaciers, is by Christopher White, who traveled to Montana to chronicle the work of Dan Fagre, a climate scientist and ecologist, who has spent years monitoring ice sheets in Glacier National Park.

The Wild Inside: A Novel of Suspense, by Christine Carbo, is the first in the Glacier Mystery Series of four crime novels that are set in Glacier National Park. Enjoy wonderful descriptions of the Rocky Mountains as officers follow the trail of a killer deep into the wilderness.

Park Essentials

ACCESSIBILITY

All visitor centers are wheelchair accessible, and most of the campgrounds and picnic areas are paved, with extended-length picnic tables and accessible restrooms. Three of Glacier's nature trails are wheelchair accessible: the Trail of the Cedars, Running Eagle Falls, and the Oberlin Bend Trail, just west of Logan Pass. In Waterton, the Linnet Lake Trail, Waterton Townsite Trail, Cameron Lake day-use area, and the International Peace Park Pavilion are wheelchair accessible.

PARK FEES AND PERMITS

Entrance fees for Glacier are $35 per vehicle in the summer and $25 per vehicle in the winter. The fee for motorcycles is $30 during peak season and $15 November 1–April 30. Entrance fees are good for seven days, or you can purchase a Glacier National Park annual pass for $70. An America the Beautiful Pass is $80 and covers entrance to national parks and other federal recreation sites for one year. Free entrance to the park is offered on Martin Luther King Jr. Day, the first day of national park week, National Park Service Birthday, National Public Lands Day, and Veteren's Day. A day pass to Waterton Lakes is C$7.90 for an individual or C$16 per seven people per vehicle, and a Parks Canada Discovery Pass costs C$69.19 for an individual or C$139.40 for a family and provides unlimited admission to Canada's national parks and historic sites for one year. Youth 17 and under receive free admission to all Canadian national parks and historic sites. Free entrance is offered on Canada Day (July 1). *Passes to Glacier and Waterton must be purchased separately.*

At Glacier, the required backcountry permit is $7 per person per day from the Apgar Backcountry Permit Center after mid-April for the upcoming summer. Reservations cost $40. On the park's official website (⊕ *www.nps.gov/glac/planyourvisit/ backcountry.htm*), you can find the latest backcountry information and a form that can be faxed to the backcountry office.

Waterton requires backcountry camping permits for use of its backcountry camping spots, with reservations available up to 90 days ahead at the visitor reception center. The fee is C$10.02 per person per night. A nonrefundable reservation fee of $11.96 is also charged. There is no charge for children ages 16 and under. Consult the park website or phone the visitor reception center (☎ *403/859–5133*) to find out which campgrounds are open and the condition of camping sites.

PARK HOURS

The parks are open year-round, but many roads and facilities close from October through May. The parks are in the Mountain time zone.

CELL PHONE RECEPTION

Cell phone coverage is improving, but, in mountainous terrain, it is common to have poor reception. Cell service is best available in West Glacier or St. Mary in Glacier National Park and in the Waterton Townsite in Waterton Lakes National Park. Find pay phones at Avalanche Campground, Glacier Highland Motel and Store, Apgar, St. Mary Visitor Center, Two Medicine Camp Store, and all lodges except Granite Park Chalet and Sperry Chalet. Several pay phones are also available in the townsite of Waterton Lakes National Park.

Hotels

Lodgings in the parks tend to be rustic and simple, though there are a few grand lodges. Some modern accommodations have pools, hot tubs, boat rentals, guided excursions, and fine dining. The supply of rooms within both parks is limited, but the prices are relatively reasonable. It's best to reserve well in advance, especially for July and August. *Hotel reviews have been shortened. For full information, visit Fodors.com.*

Restaurants

Steak houses serving certified Angus beef are typical of the region; in recent years, resort communities have diversified their menus to include bison, venison, elk, moose, trout, and gluten-free and vegetarian options. Small cafés offer hearty, inexpensive meals and perhaps the chance to chat with locals. In Montana, huckleberries appear on many menus. Attire everywhere is casual. *Restaurant reviews have been shortened. For full information, visit Fodors.com.*

What It Costs in U.S. Dollars

	$	$$	$$$	$$$$
RESTAURANTS				
	under $13	$13–$20	$21–$30	over $30
HOTELS				
	under $100	$100–$150	$151–$200	over $200

What It Costs in Canadian Dollars

	$	$$	$$$	$$$$
RESTAURANTS				
	under C$15	C$15–C$20	C$21–C$25	over C$25
HOTELS				
	under C$150	C$150–C$200	C$201–C$250	over C$250

Tours

Dark Sky Guides

GUIDED TOURS | A Night Sky Discovery Tour is the most popular offering from this tour company. Hike to a viewing spot, and learn about the legends associated wth constellations from a knowledgeable guide. See stars close up with powerful telescopes. The company also conducts twilight wildlife walks and starry skies strolls. ✉ *Box 56, Waterton Lakes National Park* ⊕ *darkskyguides.ca* 🔊 *From C$20 per person.*

Red Bus Tours

BUS TOURS | Glacier National Park Lodges operates driver-narrated bus tours that cover most areas of the park that are accessible by road. The tour of Going-to-the-Sun Road, a favorite, is conducted in vintage, 1936, red buses with roll-back tops—photo opportunities are plentiful. In addition to tours, which last from a few hours to a full day, hiker shuttles and transfers from the West Glacier train station to Lake McDonald Lodge or the Village Inn are available. You can catch your tour from the doorstep of Glacier Park Lodge or a few steps from Apgar Village Lodge, West Glacier Village, Motel Lake McDonald, and St. Mary Village. Reservations are essential. ☎ *855/733–4522, 303/265–7010* ⊕ *www.glaciernationalparklodges.com/red-bus-tours* 🔊 *Tours from $55; shuttles from $6.*

Sun Tours

BUS TOURS | Tour the park in an air-conditioned coach, and learn from Native American guides who concentrate on how Glacier's features are relevant to the Blackfeet Nation, past and present. These tours depart from East Glacier and the St. Mary Visitor Center. ✉ *29 Glacier Ave., East Glacier Park* ☎ *406/732–9220, 800/786–9220* ⊕ *www.glaciersuntours.com* 🔊 *From $50.*

Visitor Information

PARK CONTACT INFORMATION Glacier Country Montana. ✉ *140 N. Higgens Ave., Suite 204, Missoula* ☎ *800/338–5072* ⊕ *www.glaciermt.com.* **Glacier National Park.** ☎ *406/888–7800* ⊕ *www.nps.gov/glac.* **Waterton Lakes Chamber of Commerce.** ⊕ *www.mywaterton.ca.* **Waterton Lakes National Park.** ☎ *403/859–5133, 403/859–2224 year-round* ⊕ *www.pc.gc.ca/waterton.*

Glacier National Park

The massive peaks of the Continental Divide in northwest Montana are the backbone of Glacier National Park and its sister park in Canada, Waterton Lakes, which together make up the International Peace Park. From their slopes, melting snow and alpine glaciers yield the headwaters of rivers that flow west to the Pacific Ocean, north to the Arctic Ocean, and southeast to the Atlantic Ocean via the Gulf of Mexico. Coniferous forests, thickly vegetated stream bottoms, and green-carpeted meadows provide homes and sustenance for all kinds of wildlife.

Western Glacier National Park

35 miles northeast from Kalispell to the Apgar Visitor Center via U.S. Route 2.

The western side of the park is closest to the airport in the city of Kalispell and has the most amenities. Highlights include the bustling village of West Glacier, Apgar Village, Lake McDonald, and the tiny community of Polebridge. West Glacier Village is just over 2 miles from the Apgar Visitor Center.

Sights

HISTORIC SIGHTS

Apgar

TOWN | FAMILY | On the southwest end of Lake McDonald, this tiny village has a few stores, an ice-cream shop, motels, ranger buildings, a campground, and a historic schoolhouse. A store called the Montana House is open year-round, but except for the weekend-only visitor center, no other services remain open from November to mid-May. Across the street from the visitor center, **Apgar Discovery Cabin** is filled with animal posters, kids' activities, and maps. ⊠ *2 miles*

north of west entrance, Glacier National Park ☎ *406/888–7939.*

PICNIC AREAS

Apgar

RESTAURANT—SIGHT | In a tree-shaded area at the southern end of Lake McDonald, the Apgar Campground has tables, drinking water, and restrooms. ⊠ *Glacier National Park* ✛ *Off Going-to-the-Sun Rd., north of campground, 4 km (2½ miles) north of west entrance.*

Fish Creek

RESTAURANT—SIGHT | In a forested area adjacent to Lake McDonald, this picnic area has tables, drinking water, and restrooms. Nearby there's a swimming area and several trailheads. ⊠ *Glacier National Park* ✛ *Off Camas Rd. before Fish Creek Campground, 4 miles northwest of west entrance.*

Sprague Creek

RESTAURANT—SIGHT | This picnic site on Lake McDonald's eastern shore has tables, restrooms, and drinking water in summer. ⊠ *Glacier National Park* ✛ *Off Going-to-the-Sun Rd., adjacent to Sprague Creek Campground, 9 miles northeast of west entrance.*

SCENIC DRIVES

Apgar Village to Polebridge (Camas Road and North Fork Road)

SCENIC DRIVE | The 25-mile journey to the tiny community of Polebridge involves travel along a gravel road that has a few potholes, but the scenery along the north fork of the Flathead River makes up for the bumpy ride. Be on the lookout for wildlife, and be sure to stop for a snack at the Polebridge Mercantile and Bakery.

West Glacier Village to East Glacier Park Village (US-2 E)

SCENIC DRIVE | A paved, 57-mile, two-lane highway follows the middle fork of the Flathead River and connects West Glacier with East Glacier. Enjoy lovely mountain views, stop at Goat Lick to look for mountain goats, or consider having lunch at the Izaak Walton Inn in Essex.

Glacier in One Day

It's hard to beat the **Going-to-the-Sun Road** for a one-day trip in Glacier National Park. This itinerary takes you from west to east—if you're starting from St. Mary, take the tour backward. First, however, call the Glacier Park Boat Company (☎ 406/257–2426) to make a reservation for a boat tour on **St. Mary Lake** in the east or **Lake McDonald**, in the west, depending on your trip's end point. Then drive up Going-to-the-Sun Road to **Avalanche Creek Campground** for a 30-minute stroll along the fragrant **Trail of the Cedars**. Afterward, continue driving up—you can see views of waterfalls and wildlife to the left and an awe-inspiring, precipitous drop to the right. At the summit, **Logan Pass**, your arduous climb is rewarded with a gorgeous view of immense peaks, sometimes complemented by the sight of a mountain goat. Stop in at the **Logan Pass Visitor Center**, then take the 1½-mile **Hidden Lake Nature Trail** up to prime wildlife-viewing spots. Have a picnic at the overlook above Hidden Lake. In the afternoon, continue driving east over the mountains. Stop at the **Jackson Glacier Overlook** to view one of the park's largest glaciers. Continue down; eventually the forest thins, the vistas grow broader, and a gradual transition to the high plains begins. When you reach **Rising Sun Campground,** take the one-hour St. Mary Lake boat tour to St. Mary Falls. The Going-to-the-Sun Road is generally closed from mid-September to mid-June.

SCENIC STOPS

Goat Lick Overlook

VIEWPOINT | Mountain goats frequent this natural salt lick on a cliff above the middle fork of the Flathead River. Watch the wildlife from an observation stand. ⊠ *U.S. 2, 29 miles southeast of West Glacier Village, Glacier National Park.*

Lake McDonald

BODY OF WATER | This beautiful, 10-mile-long lake, the parks' largest, is accessible year-round from Going-to-the-Sun Road. Cruise to the middle for a view of the surrounding glacier-clad mountains. You can fish and horseback ride at either end, and in winter, snowshoe and cross-country ski. ⊠ *2 miles north of west entrance, Glacier National Park.*

Polebridge

TOWN | On the banks of the North Fork of the Flathead River on Glacier National Park's western edge, this tiny community (population 25) has just one store, one restaurant and saloon, one camp store, and one hostel, yet it is a gem in the wilderness. You can see where a massive wildfire burned up to some of the buildings in 1988 and how quickly new growth has advanced. The entrance station, staffed in summer only, is the gateway to Bowman and Kintla lakes, as well as Logging and Quartz lakes, which are in the backcountry and accessible only by hiking trails. The bakery at the Polebridge Mercantile store is amazing, with huckleberry macaroons or bear claws and hot, gooey cinnamon buns. ⊠ *Polebridge.*

TRAILS

Rocky Point Nature Trail

TRAIL | Enjoy fantastic mountain and lake views on this family friendly, 1.9-mile trail along the western shore of Lake McDonald. *Easy.* ✛ *Trailhead: near Fish Creek Campground.*

VISITOR CENTERS

Apgar Visitor Center

INFO CENTER | FAMILY | This is a great first stop if you're entering the park from the west. Here you can get all kinds of information, including maps, permits, books, and the *Junior Ranger* newspaper, and you can check out displays that will help you plan your tour of the park. There is a variety of ranger-led programs including free snowshoe walks in winter. Snowshoes can be rented for $2 at the visitor center. ✉ *2 miles north of West Glacier in Apgar Village, Glacier National Park* ☎ *406/888–7800.*

Travel Alberta West Glacier Information Center

INFO CENTER | Plan your visit to the Canadian side of the International Peace Park with the help of travel experts at this visitor center in West Glacier. You'll find maps, pamphlets, displays, and bathroom facilities here. ✉ *125 Going-to-the-Sun Rd., West Glacier* ☎ *406/888–5743* 🕒 *Mid-Sept.–mid-May.*

Restaurants

Lake McDonald Lodge Restaurants

$$$ | AMERICAN | In Russell's Fireside Dining Room, take in a great view of the lake while enjoying standards such as pasta, steak, wild game, and salmon; delicious salads; or local favorites like the huckleberry elk burger or the Montana rainbow trout. Many ingredients are locally sourced, and there is a nice selection of cocktails, wine, and craft beer. **Known for:** incredible views of Lake McDonald; hearty regional fare at main restaurant, pizza and burgers at smaller eateries; breakfast and (on request) box lunches in main restaurant. [$] *Average main: $22* ✉ *Glacier National Park* ✣ *Going-to-the-Sun Rd., 10 miles north of Apgar* ☎ *406/888–5431, 406/892–2525* 🌐 *www.glaciernationalparklodges.com/dining/lake-mcdonald-lodge* 🕒 *Closed early Oct.–early June.*

Hotels

★ **Lake McDonald Lodge**

$$$ | HOTEL | On the shores of Lake McDonald, near Apgar and West Glacier, this historic lodge—where public spaces feature massive timbers, stone fireplaces, and animal trophies—is an ideal base for exploring the park's western side. **Pros:** lakeside setting; historic property; close to Apgar, West Glacier, and Going-to-the-Sun Road. **Cons:** rustic; no TV (except in suites) and limited Wi-Fi; small bathrooms. [$] *Rooms from: $200* ✉ *Going-to-the-Sun Rd., Glacier National Park* ☎ *855/733–4522, 406/888–5431* 🌐 *www.glaciernationalparklodges.com* 🛏 *80 units* 🍴 *No meals.*

Village Inn

$$$ | HOTEL | Listen to waves gently lap the shores of beautiful Lake McDonald at this motel, which is on the National Register of Historic Places and was fully renovated in recent years, so all its rooms have Wi-Fi, new beds, and furnishings that fit with the historic style. **Pros:** great views; convenient Apgar village location; kitchenettes in some rooms. **Cons:** rustic motel; no a/c; no in-room phones. [$] *Rooms from: $165* ✉ *Apgar Village, Glacier National Park* ☎ *855/733–4522* 🌐 *www.glaciernationalparklodges.com* 🕒 *Closed Oct. 2–late May* 🛏 *36 rooms* 🍴 *No meals.*

Along the Going-to-the-Sun Road

50 miles between Glacier National Park's western and eastern reaches.

The Going-to-the-Sun Road, one of the nation's most beautiful drives, connects Lake McDonald on the western side of Glacier with St. Mary Lake on the east. Turnoffs provide views of the high country and glacier-carved valleys. Consider making the ride in one of the vintage red buses operated by Glacier National Park

Lodges (☎ 844/868–7474). Drivers double as guides, and they can roll back the tops of the vehicles for better views. Logan Pass, elevation 6,646 feet (2,026 meters), sits at the Continental Divide, the highest point on the Going-to-the-Sun Road.

◉ Sights

PICNIC AREAS

Avalanche Creek

RESTAURANT—SIGHT | This picnic area is near two popular day hikes. There are tables, restrooms, and drinking water, and shuttle transfers are available in summer. ✉ *Glacier National Park ✙ Across from Avalanche Creek Campground, off Going-to-the-Sun Rd., 25 km (15.7 miles) northeast of west entrance.*

SCENIC STOPS

The Garden Wall

NATURE SITE | An abrupt and jagged wall of rock juts above the road and is visible for about 10 miles as it follows Logan Creek from just past Avalanche Creek Campground to Logan Pass. ✉ *Going-to-the-Sun Rd., 24–34 miles northeast of West Glacier, Glacier National Park.*

Jackson Glacier Overlook

VIEWPOINT | On the eastern side of the Continental Divide, you come into view of Jackson Glacier looming in a rocky pass across the upper St. Mary River valley. If it isn't covered with snow, you'll see sharp peaks of ice. The glacier is shrinking and may disappear in another 100 years. ✉ *5 miles east of Logan Pass, Glacier National Park.*

Logan Pass

SCENIC DRIVE | At 6,646 feet, this is the park's highest point accessible by motor vehicle. Crowded in July and August, it offers unparalleled views of both sides of the Continental Divide. Mountain goats, bighorn sheep, and grizzly bears frequent the area. The Logan Pass Visitor Center is just east of the pass. ✉ *34 miles east of West Glacier, 18 miles west of St. Mary, Glacier National Park.*

TRAILS

Avalanche Lake Trail

TRAIL | From Avalanche Creek Campground, take this 3-mile trail leading to mountain-ringed Avalanche Lake. The walk is only moderately difficult (it ascends 730 feet), making this one of the park's most accessible backcountry lakes. Crowds fill the parking area and trail during July and August and on sunny weekends in May and June. *Moderate.* ✉ *Glacier National Park ✙ Trailhead: across from Avalanche Creek Campground, 15 miles north of Apgar on Going-to-the-Sun Rd.*

Baring Falls

TRAIL | **FAMILY** | For a nice family hike, try the 1.3-mile path from the Sun Point parking area. It leads to a spruce and Douglas fir woods; cross a log bridge over Baring Creek and you arrive at the base of gushing Baring Falls. *Easy.* ✉ *Glacier National Park ✙ Trailhead 11 miles east of Logan Pass on Going-to-the-Sun Rd., at Sun Point parking area.*

Hidden Lake Nature Trail

TRAIL | Hidden Lake Overlook is an easy, 1½-mile hike from the Logan Pass Visitor Center. Along the way, you'll pass through beautiful alpine meadows known as the Hanging Gardens. Enjoy incredible views of Hidden Lake, Bearhat Mountain, Mt. Cannon, Fusillade Mountain, Gunsight Mountain, and Sperry Glacier. It's common to see mountain goats near the overlook. If you want a challenge, continue hiking all the way down to the edge of the lake—a moderate 5.4-mile round-trip hike. *Easy to moderate.* ✉ *Glacier National Park ✙ Trailhead: behind Logan Pass Visitor Center.*

★ Highline Trail

TRAIL | From the Logan Pass parking lot, hike north along the Garden Wall and just below the craggy Continental Divide. Wildflowers dominate the 7.6 miles to Granite Park Chalet, a National Historic Landmark, where hikers with reservations can overnight. Return to

Logan Pass along the same trail or hike down 4½ miles (a 2,500-foot descent) on the Loop Trail. *Moderate.* ⊠ *Glacier National Park* ✛ *Trailhead: at Logan Pass Visitor Center.*

Trail of the Cedars

TRAIL | FAMILY | This ½-mile boardwalk loop through an ancient cedar and hemlock forest is a favorite of families with small children and people with disabilities (it's wheelchair accessible). Interpretive signs describe the habitat and natural history. *Easy.* ⊠ *Glacier National Park* ✛ *Trailhead: across from Avalanche Creek Campground, 15 miles north of Apgar on Going-to-the-Sun Rd.*

VISITOR CENTERS

Logan Pass Visitor Center

INFO CENTER | Built of stone, this center stands sturdy against the severe weather that forces it to close in winter. When it's open, rangers give 10-minute talks on the alpine environment and offer a variety of activities including guided hikes. You can get advice from them and buy books and maps. ⊠ *Going-to-the-Sun Rd., Glacier National Park* ✛ *34 miles east of West Glacier, 18 miles west of St. Mary* ☎ *406/888–7800.*

Hotels

Granite Park Chalet

$$ | B&B/INN | Early tourists used to ride horses 7 to 9 miles through the park each day and stay at a different chalet each night; today, the only way to reach the Granite Park, one of two such chalets that's still standing (Sperry is the other), is via hiking trails. **Pros:** beautiful scenery; secluded; historic lodging. **Cons:** difficult to access; rustic; far from services (and you must bring your own food and water). Ⓢ *Rooms from: $115* ⊠ *Going-to-the-Sun Rd., Glacier National Park* ✛ *7.6 miles south of Logan Pass* ☎ *888/345–2649* ⊕ *www.graniteparkchalet.com* ⊘ *Closed mid-Sept.–late June* ⊐ *12 rooms* ⊚ *No meals.*

Eastern Glacier National Park

Via U.S. routes 2 and 89, St. Mary is 130 miles northeast of Kalispell and 97 miles northeast of Apgar; via the Going-to-the-Sun Road, it's roughly 50 miles between Apgar and St. Mary.

The park's eastern end has historical and cultural significance to the Blackfeet Nation, and much of this region is on tribal lands. East Glacier Park Village is the hub with shops, restaurants, and hotels. Two Medicine Lake, St. Mary Lake, and Swiftcurrent Lake are scenic highlights of this area. The eastern end of the Going-to-the-Sun Road is near the tiny community of St. Mary on the western border of the Blackfeet Indian Reservation.

◉ Sights

PICNIC AREAS

Rising Sun

RESTAURANT—SIGHT | In a cottonwood grove adjacent to St. Mary Lake, this area has tables, restrooms, and drinking water in summer. ⊠ *Glacier National Park* ✛ *Off Going-to-the-Sun Rd., 6 miles southwest of St. Mary Visitor Center.*

SCENIC DRIVES

East Glacier Park Village to Two Medicine Lake and Saint Mary Lake

SCENIC DRIVE | You'll see the striking contrast of prairies and mountains as you travel northwest from East Glacier Park Village to Two Medicine Lake on MT-49. Once you turn onto Two Medicine Road, you'll be heading straight toward snowcapped peaks and lovely Two Medicine Lake. From there, head back out to MT-49 and then to US-89 North to make your way to the town of St. Mary and then onto the Going-to-the-Sun Road to reach St. Mary Lake, the park's second largest. The entire route is 49 miles one-way. (End the drive with an additional

The scenic, 50-mile Going-to-the-Sun Road takes about two hours to drive, depending on how often you stop.

stop at Swiftcurrent Lake, and you'll cover about 75 miles total.).

SCENIC STOPS

Running Eagle Falls (Trick Falls)

BODY OF WATER | Cascading near Two Medicine, these are actually two different waterfalls from two different sources. In spring, when the water level is high, the upper falls join the lower falls for a 40-foot drop into Two Medicine River; in summer, the upper falls dry up, revealing the lower 20-foot falls that start midway down the precipice. ⊠ *2 miles east of Two Medicine entrance, Glacier National Park.*

St. Mary Lake

BODY OF WATER | When the breezes calm, the park's second-largest lake mirrors the snowcapped granite peaks that line the St. Mary Valley. To get a good look at the beautiful scenery, follow the Sun Point Nature Trail (closed for renovation in 2016) along the lake's shore. The hike is 1 mile each way. ⊠ *1 mile west of St. Mary, Glacier National Park.*

Swiftcurrent Lake

BODY OF WATER | The Many Glacier Hotel is perched on the shores of Swiftcurrent Lake. The views here are some of the park's prettiest, taking in the mountains that rise more than 3,000 feet immediately west of the lake. Scenic boat tours ply the waters and transport hikers to trails that lead to other lakes and glaciers in the park's Many Glacier region.

Two Medicine Valley

NATURE SITE | Rugged, often windy, and always beautiful, the valley is a remote 9-mile drive from Highway 49 and is surrounded by some of the park's most stark, rocky peaks. Near the valley's lake you can rent a canoe, take a narrated boat tour, camp, and hike. Bears frequent the area. The road is closed from late October through late May. ⊠ *Two Medicine entrance, 9 miles east of Hwy. 49, Glacier National Park* ☎ *406/888–7800, 406/257–2426 boat tours.*

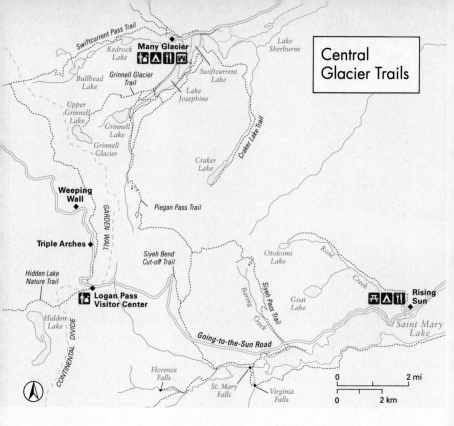

TRAILS

Grinnell Glacier Trail

TRAIL | In 1926, one giant ice mass broke apart to create the Salamander and Grinnell glaciers, which have been shrinking ever since. The 5½-mile trail to Grinnell Glacier, the park's most accessible, is marked by several spectacular viewpoints. You start at Swiftcurrent Lake's picnic area, climb a moraine to Lake Josephine, then climb to the Grinnell Glacier overlook. Halfway up, turn around to see the prairie land to the northeast. You can cut about 2 miles (each way) off the hike by taking scenic boat rides across Swiftcurrent Lake and Lake Josephine. From July to mid-September, a ranger-led hike departs from the Many Glacier Hotel boat dock on most mornings at 8:30. *Difficult.* ⊠ *Glacier National Park* ✣ *Trailheads: Swiftcurrent Lake picnic area or Lake Josephine boat dock.*

Iceberg Lake Trail

TRAIL | This moderately strenuous, 9-mile, round-trip hike passes the gushing Ptarmigan Falls, then climbs to its namesake, where icebergs bob in the chilly mountain loch. Mountain goats hang out on sheer cliffs above, bighorn sheep graze in the high mountain meadows, and grizzly bears dig for glacier lily bulbs, grubs, and other delicacies. Rangers lead hikes here almost daily in summer, leaving at 8:30 am. *Moderate.* ⊠ *Glacier National Park* ✣ *Trailhead: at Swiftcurrent Inn parking lot, off Many Glacier Rd.*

Sun Point Nature Trail

TRAIL | A stunning waterfall awaits at the end of this well-groomed, 1.3-mile trail along the cliffs and shores of picturesque St. Mary Lake. You can hike one-way and take a boat transfer back. *Easy.* ⊠ *Glacier National Park* ✣ *Trailhead: 11 miles east* *of Logan Pass on Going-to-the-Sun Rd., at Sun Point parking area.*

VISITOR CENTERS

St. Mary Visitor Center

INFO CENTER | Glacier's largest visitor complex has a huge relief map of the park's peaks and valleys and screens a 15-minute orientation video. Exhibits help visitors understand the park from the perspective of its original inhabitants—the Blackfeet, Salish, Kootenai, and Pend d'Orielle peoples. Rangers conduct evening presentations in summer, and the auditorium hosts Native America Speaks programs. The center also has books and maps for sale, backcountry camping permits, and large viewing windows facing the 10-mile-long St. Mary Lake. ⊠ *Going-to-the-Sun Rd., off U.S. 89, Glacier National Park* ☎ *406/732–7750.*

Restaurants

Ptarmigan Dining Room

$$$ | **AMERICAN** | The picturesque Ptarmigan's massive windows afford stunning views of Grinnell Point over Swiftcurrent Lake. Known for using regional, sustainably sourced ingredients, the restaurant specializes in dishes such as house-smoked Montana trout, braised bison short ribs, and roasted duck with Flathead cherry chutney. **Known for:** exceptional views; gluten-free and vegetarian options amid the regional fish-and-game mix; huckleberry cobbler (and margaritas!). ⓢ *Average main: $28* ⊠ *Many Glacier Rd., Glacier National Park* ☎ *303/265–7010* ⊕ *www.glaciernationalparklodges.com* ⊘ *Closed late Sept.–early June.*

 Hotels

Many Glacier Hotel

$$$$ | **HOTEL** | On Swiftcurrent Lake in the park's northeastern section, this is the most isolated of the grand hotels, and—especially if you are able to book a lakeview balcony room—among the most scenic. **Pros:** stunning views from lodge;

secluded; good hiking trails nearby. **Cons:** rustic rooms; no TV, limited Internet; the road leading to the lodge is very rough. ⓢ *Rooms from: $207* ⊠ *Many Glacier Rd., Glacier National Park* ⊹ *12 miles west of Babb* ☎ *855/733–4522, 406/732–4411* ⊕ *www.glaciernationalparklodges.com* ⊘ *Closed mid-Sept.–mid-June* ⇒ *214 rooms* ⏐⏐ *No meals.*

Waterton Lakes National Park

A World Heritage Site, Waterton Lakes National Park represents the meeting of two worlds—the flatlands of the prairie and the abrupt upthrust of the mountains—squeezing an unusual mix of wildlife, flora, and climate zones into its 505 square km (200 square miles). The quaint alpine town of Waterton lies just off the shore of Upper Waterton Lake, and the historic Prince of Wales Hotel sits high on a hill overlooking it all. The park is quieter than most of the other Rocky Mountain parks, but it is just as beautiful and diverse. Visitors coming from Glacier National Park typically reach Waterton via the seasonal Chief Mountain Highway border crossing, 67 miles northwest of East Glacier Park Village. It's also possible to access the park via the border crossing at Carway, which is open year-round.

In September 2017, the Kenow Wildfire burned 19,303 hectares (47,698 acres) of parkland, greatly affecting park infrastructure, including more than 80% of its hiking trail network. Through the efforts of brave firefighters, the townsite was virtually untouched. In 2018, the Boundary Wildfire burned the Boundary Creek Valley region in Glacier National Park and blazed across the U.S.–Canada border into Waterton Lakes National Park. Wildfires play an important role in a forest ecosystem, though, and the park is already recovering. Check the website to learn the status of trails before heading out.

Waterton in One Day

Begin your day with a stop at the **Waterton Information Centre** to pick up free maps and information about interpretive programs and schedules.

Stop at the **Bear's Hump Trailhead**, where you can enjoy a short and invigorating, 1.4-km (0.9-mile) hike to a beautiful scenic overlook. Afterward, drive up the hill to the historic **Prince of Wales Hotel** to enjoy the view from the hillside behind the hotel.

Next, visit **Waterton Townsite** for an early lunch. Afterward, walk the easy 3-km (2-mile) **Townsite Loop Trail**, stopping to view **Cameron Falls** and explore the trail behind the falls. Learn more about the International Peace Park and its flora and fauna by reading the interpretive signs at Peace Park Point near the marina.

End the day with a scenic two-hour **Waterton Inter-Nation Shoreline Cruise** across the border to **Goat Haunt Ranger Station** and back.

Sights

HISTORIC SIGHTS

First Oil Well in Western Canada

HISTORIC SITE | Alberta is known worldwide for its oil and gas production, and the first oil well in western Canada was established in 1902 in what is now the park. Stop at this National Historic Site to explore the wellheads, drilling equipment, and remains of the Oil City boomtown. ⊠ *Waterton Lakes National Park ⊹ Watch for sign 7.7 km (4.8 miles) up the Akamina Pkwy.* 🖘 *Free.*

Prince of Wales Hotel

HISTORIC SITE | Named for the prince who later became King Edward VIII, this hotel was constructed between 1926 and 1927 and was designated a National Historic Site in 1995. Take in the magnificent view from the ridge outside the hotel, or pop inside to enjoy the vista from the comfort of the expansive lobby, where afternoon tea is served. ⊠ *Off Hwy. 5, Waterton Lakes National Park* 🕿 *848/868–7474, 403/236–3400* ⊕ *www.glacierparkcollection.com/lodging/prince-of-wales-hotel* 🖘 *Free* ⊙ *Closed late-Sept.–mid-May.*

PICNIC AREAS

Waterton's picnic sites are in some of the most scenic areas of the park. All are equipped with tables and washroom facilities, and most have a water source nearby. Some sites are equipped with barbecues or outdoor fire pits, and you can buy firewood in the village.

Cameron Bay

RESTAURANT—SIGHT | There are several picnic shelters along Upper Waterton Lake in the Cameron Bay area. These lakefront sites are equipped with tables, water taps, and wood-burning stoves. ⊠ *Waterton Townsite ⊹ Along Upper Waterton Lake.*

SCENIC DRIVES

Akamina Parkway

BODY OF WATER | Take this winding, 16-km (10-mile) road up to Cameron Lake, but drive slowly and watch for wildlife: it's common to see bears along the way. At the lake you will find a relatively flat, paved, 1.6-km (1-mile) trail that hugs the western shore and makes a nice walk. Bring your binoculars. Grizzly bears are often spotted on the lower slopes of the mountains at the far end of the lake. ⊠ *Waterton Lakes National Park.*

Red Rock Parkway

SCENIC DRIVE | The 15-km (9-mile) route takes you from the prairie up the Blakiston Valley to Red Rock Canyon, where water has cut through the earth, exposing red sedimentary rock. It's common to see bears just off the road, especially in autumn, when the berries are ripe. ⊠ *Waterton Lakes National Park.*

SCENIC STOPS

Cameron Lake

BODY OF WATER | The jewel of Waterton, Cameron Lake sits in a land of glacially carved cirques (steep-walled basins). In summer, hundreds of varieties of alpine wildflowers fill the area, including 22 kinds of wild orchids. Canoes, rowboats, kayaks, and fishing gear can be rented here. ⊠ *Akamina Pkwy., 13 km (8 miles) southwest of Waterton Townsite, Waterton Lakes National Park.*

Goat Haunt Ranger Station

NATURE PRESERVE | Reached only by foot trail, private boat, or tour boat from Waterton Townsite, this spot on the U.S. end of Waterton Lake is the stomping ground for mountain goats, moose, grizzlies, and black bears. It is also the official border crossing for the U.S. side of Waterton Lake. In recent years, the crossing has not been staffed by U.S. Customs personnel, and, consequently, tour boats do not allow passengers to disembark at Goat Haunt as they once did. If you want to explore the trails on this end of the lake, you will need to hike or paddle in on your own. Check in before arrival by using the CBP ROAM app. Visitors to this area must carry their passports and proof of ROAM trip approval. The hikes on the U.S. side of the lake were unaffected by the wildfires of recent years. ⊠ *Southern end of Waterton Lake, Waterton Lakes National Park* ☎ *403/859–2362* ⊕ *www.watertoncruise.com* ⚓ *Tour boat C$51.*

Waterton Townsite

TOWN | In roughly the park's geographic center, this low-key townsite swells with tourists in summer, and restaurants and shops open to serve them. In winter only a few motels are open, and services are limited. ⊠ *Waterton Townsite.*

TRAILS

Bear's Hump Trail

TRAIL | This steep, 2.8-km (1.4-mile) trail climbs to an overlook with a great view of Upper Waterton Lake and the townsite. *Moderate.* ⊠ *Waterton Lakes National Park* ✛ *Trailhead: across from Prince of Wales access road. Behind site of old visitor information center.*

Bertha Lake Trail

TRAIL | This 11.4-km (7.1-mile) round-trip trail leads from Waterton Townsite through a Douglas fir forest to a beautiful overlook of Upper Waterton Lake, and on to Lower Bertha Falls. From there, a steeper climb takes you past Upper Bertha Falls to Bertha Lake. In June, the wildflowers along the trail are stunning. *Moderate.* ⊠ *Waterton Lakes National Park* ✛ *Trailhead: at parking lot off Evergreen Ave., west of Townsite Campground.*

Blakiston Falls

TRAIL | A 2-km (1.2-mi) round-trip hike will take you from Red Rock Canyon to Blakiston Falls. Several viewpoints overlook the falls. *Easy* ⊠ *Waterton Lakes National Park* ✛ *Trailhead: at Red Rock Canyon lower parking lot. Cross the bridge over Red Rock Creek, then turn left across the bridge over Bauerman Creek, and turn right to follow the trail.*

Cameron Lake Shore Trail

TRAIL | FAMILY | Relatively flat and paved, this 1.6-km (1-mile) one-way trail offers a peaceful hike. Look for wildflowers along the shoreline and grizzlies on the lower slopes of the mountains at the far end of the lake. *Easy.* ⊠ *Waterton Lakes National Park* ✛ *Trailhead: at lakeshore in front of*

15

Glacier and Waterton Lakes National Parks   WATERTON LAKES NATIONAL PARK parking lot, 13 km (8 miles) southwest of Waterton Townsite.

Crandell Lake Trail

TRAIL | This 2½-km (1½-mile) trail winds through fragrant pine forest, ending at a popular mountain lake. *Easy.* ⊠ *Waterton Lakes National Park* ⊹ *Trailhead: about halfway up Akamina Pkwy.*

★ Crypt Lake Trail

TRAIL | Awe-inspiring and strenuous, this 17.2-km (11-mile) round-trip trail is one of the most stunning hikes in the Canadian Rockies. Conquering the trail involves taking a boat taxi across Waterton Lake, climbing 700 meters (2,300 feet), crawling through a tunnel nearly 30 meters (100 feet) long, and scrambling across a sheer rock face. The reward, and well worth it: views of a 183-meter (600-foot) cascading waterfall and the turquoise waters of Crypt Lake. This hike was completely untouched by the wildfires of recent years. *Difficult.* ⊠ *Waterton Lakes National Park* ⊹ *Trailhead: at Crypt Landing, accessed by ferry from Waterton Townsite.*

VISITOR CENTERS

Waterton Information Centre

INFO CENTER | The original Waterton Information Centre was destroyed by the Kenow Wildfire in 2017, and a new building is under construction. Until it's finished, the visitor center is in the Lion's Hall in the Waterton Townsite. Stop in to pick up brochures, maps, and books. You can also pick up the booklet for the free Xplorer Program for kids between ages 6 and 11. Park interpreters are on hand to answer questions and give directions. ⊠ *Waterton Rd., before townsite, Waterton Lakes National Park* ☎ *403/859–5133.*

🍴 Restaurants

Lakeside Chophouse

$$$$ | **STEAKHOUSE** | Grab a window seat or a spot on the patio to enjoy the spectacular view from Waterton's only lakefront restaurant. This is the place in the park for a steak dinner—locally produced Alberta beef plays a starring role on the globally inspired menu. **Known for:** great steaks; lakefront views; all-day service. ⓢ *Average main: C$29* ⊠ *Bayshore Inn, 111 Waterton Ave., Waterton Townsite* ☎ *888/527–9555, 403/859–2211* ⊕ *www. bayshoreinn.com.*

Red Rock Trattoria

$$$ | **ITALIAN** | There's a large window with lovely mountain views at this intimate Italian restaurant on a quiet side street in the Waterton Townsite. The menu changes regularly, but classic starters like caprese salad and calamari are always popular, and you can't go wrong with pasta for the main course—it's all made from scratch, with sauces that are prepared à la minute. **Known for:** house-made Italian food; local ingredients; intimate dining. ⓢ *Average main: C$22* ⊠ *107 Windflower Ave., Waterton Townsite* ☎ *403/859–2004* ⊕ *www.redrockcafe.ca.*

Royal Stewart Dining Room

$$$$ | **CANADIAN** | Enjoy continental-Canadian cuisine before a dazzling view of Waterton Lake in the dining room of this century-old, hilltop chalet high above the Waterton Valley, where there's a fine selection of wines to pair with your meal. To sample locally cured meets and artisanal cheeses, start with the charcuterie board, then select from main courses that include grilled bangers and mash, pan-seared trout, and Alberta Angus beef. **Known for:** best view in town; local ingredients; British high tea. ⓢ *Average main: C$29* ⊠ *Prince of Wales Hotel, off Hwy. 5, outside Waterton Townsite, Waterton Lakes National Park* ☎ *844/868–7474 toll free, 403/236–3400* ⊕ *www.glacierparkcollection.com/lodging/prince-of-wales-hotel/dining-shopping* ⊗ *Closed Oct.–May.*

Thirsty Bear Kitchen & Bar

$$ | **AMERICAN** | Waterton's only gastropub is the place for live music most weekends and casual eats anytime. The nachos here are the best in town, and there's a wide selection of burgers, sandwiches, and wraps—all served with salad or fries. **Known for:** live music and a dance floor; great casual dining; fun atmosphere with big-screen TVs, pool tables, and foosball. $ *Average main: C$20* ✉ *111 Waterton Ave., Waterton Townsite* ☎ *403/859–2211 Ext. 309* ⊕ *www.thirstybearwaterton.com* ⊗ *Closed mid-Oct.–mid-May.*

Wieners of Waterton

$ | **HOT DOG** | **FAMILY** | If there is such a thing as a gourmet hot dog, then this is the place to find it. The buns here are baked fresh daily, and the all-beef wieners and smokies are sourced locally with one exception: the genuine Nathan's dogs are shipped from New York City. **Known for:** gourmet hot dogs; interesting toppings; fun menu. $ *Average main: C$9* ✉ *301 Wildflower Ave., Waterton Townsite* ☎ *403/859–0007* ⊕ *www.wienersofwaterton.com* ⊗ *Closed Oct.–Apr.*

 Hotels

Bayshore Inn

$$$$ | **HOTEL** | Right in town and on the shores of Waterton Lake, this inn has a lot going for it: lovely views, the only on-site spa in Waterton, multiple dining options, and easy access to many services. **Pros:** only lakefront accommodation in Waterton; plenty of on-site amenities; great townsite location. **Cons:** older-style hotel; rustic motor inn; can sometimes hear noise between rooms. $ *Rooms from: C$269* ✉ *111 Waterton Ave., Waterton Townsite* ☎ *888/527–9555, 403/859–2211* ⊕ *www.bayshoreinn.com* ⊗ *Closed mid-Oct.–Apr.* 🛏 *70 rooms* ⦿ *No meals.*

Bear Mountain Motel

$ | **HOTEL** | This classic, 1960s motel offers a variety of affordable accommodations that have painted cinder-block walls, wood-beam ceilings, and small bathrooms with shower stalls. **Pros:** most affordable accommodation in Waterton; clean,

comfortable, and very basic; family-run motel right in townsite. **Cons:** noise can be an issue with the old cinder-block construction; closed in winter; no in-room coffee or tea (available in main office). $ *Rooms from: C$149* ✉ *208 Mount View Rd., Waterton Townsite* ☎ *403/859–2366* ⊕ *bearmountainmotel.com* ⊗ *Closed Oct.–Apr.* 🛏 *36 rooms* ⦿ *No meals.*

Prince of Wales Hotel

$$$$ | **HOTEL** | A high steeple crowns this iconic, 1920s hotel, which is fantastically ornamented with eaves, balconies, and turrets; is perched between two lakes with a high-mountain backdrop; and has a lobby where two-story windows capture the views. **Pros:** spectacular valley and townsite views; historic property; bellmen wear kilts. **Cons:** very rustic rooms; no TVs; no a/c. $ *Rooms from: C$259* ✉ *Off Hwy. 5, Waterton Lakes National Park* ✛ *Turn left at marked access road at top of hill just before village* ☎ *844/868–7474, 403/859–2231* ⊕ *www.glacierparkcollection.com/lodging/prince-of-wales-hotel* ⊗ *Closed late Sept.–mid-May* 🛏 *86 rooms* ⦿ *No meals.*

Waterton Glacier Suites

$$$$ | **HOTEL** | In the heart of the townsite, this all-suite property is within walking distance of restaurants, shopping, and the dock on beautiful Waterton Lake. **Pros:** modern suites with mini-refrigerators and a/c; open year-round; convenient location. **Cons:** no views; pullout sofas uncomfortable; no on-site breakfast. $ *Rooms from: C$319* ✉ *107 Wildflower Ave., Waterton Townsite* ☎ *403/859–2004, 866/621–3330* ⊕ *www.watertonsuites.com* 🛏 *26 rooms* ⦿ *No meals.*

 Activities

The park contains numerous short hikes for day-trippers and some longer treks for backpackers. Upper and Middle Waterton and Cameron lakes provide peaceful havens for boaters. A tour boat cruises

Upper Waterton Lake, crossing the U.S.–Canada border, and the winds that rake across that lake create an exciting ride for windsurfers—bring a wet suit, though; the water remains numbingly cold throughout summer.

BIKING

Bikes are allowed on some trails, such as the 3-km (2-mile) **Townsite Loop Trail.** A great family bike trail is the paved, 6.9-km (4.3-mile) one-way **Kootenai Brown Trail,** which edges the lakes and leads from the townsite to the park gates. A ride on mildly sloping **Red Rock Canyon Road** isn't too difficult (once you get past the first hill). The **Crandell Loop** trail provides a slightly more challenging ride for mountain bikers.

Blakiston and Company

BICYCLING | Rent electric bikes, canoes, kayaks, and stand-up paddleboards through this company. ⊠ *102 Mountain Rd., Waterton Townsite* ☎ *800/456–0772* ⊕ *www.blakistonandcompany.com.*

Pat's Waterton

BICYCLING | FAMILY | Choose from surrey, mountain, and e-bikes or motorized scooters at Pat's, which also rents tennis rackets, strollers, coolers, life jackets, hiking poles, bear spray, and binoculars. ⊠ *224 Mt. View Rd., Waterton Townsite* ☎ *403/859–2266* ⊕ *www.patswaterton. com* ⬛ *From $15.*

BOATING

Nonmotorized boats can be rented at Cameron Lake in summer; private craft can be used on Upper and Middle Waterton lakes.

Cameron Lake Boat Rentals

BOATING | Rent canoes, kayaks, rowboats, pedal boats, and stand-up paddleboards right at the docks on Cameron Lake. You can also buy tackle and rent fishing rods. ⊠ *Waterton Lakes National Park* ✛ *At the boat docks at Cameron Lake, 16 km (10 miles) southwest of the townsite* ☎ *403/627–6443* ⊕ *www.cameronlake-boatrentals.com.*

Waterton Inter-Nation Shoreline Cruise Co.

BOATING | This company's two-hour round-trip boat tour along Upper Waterton Lake from Waterton Townsite to Goat Haunt Ranger Station is one of the most popular activities in Waterton. The narrated tour passes scenic bays, sheer cliffs, and snow-clad peaks. This company also offers a shuttle service for the Crypt Lake and Vimy Peak hikes. ⊠ *Waterton Townsite Marina, northwest corner of Waterton Lake near Bayshore Inn, Waterton Lakes National Park* ☎ *403/859–2362, 403/859–2362* ⊕ *www.watertoncruise. com* ⬛ *C$55.*

CAMPING

Parks Canada operates a handful of campgrounds (though one of them, the Crandell, was destroyed by the 2017 wildfire) that range from fully serviced to unserviced sites. There are also some backcountry campsites. Visitors can prebook campsites for a fee of C$11 online or C$13.50 by phone. The reservation service is available at ⊕ *www.reservation.parkscanada.gc.ca* or by phone at ☎ *877/737–3783.*

Waterton Townsite Campground. Though the campground is busy and windy, sites here are grassy and flat with access to kitchen shelters and have views down the lake into the U.S. part of the Peace Park. ⊠ *Waterton and Vimy Aves.* ☎ *877/737–3783.*

EDUCATIONAL PROGRAMS

Evening interpretive programs at Waterton Lakes National Park are offered from late June until Labor Day at the Falls Theatre, near Cameron Falls, and the townsite campground. These one-hour sessions begin at 8. A guided International Peace Park hike is held every Wednesday and Saturday in July and August. The 14-km (9-mile) hike begins at the Bertha trailhead and is led by Canadian and American park interpreters. You eat lunch at the International Border before continuing on to Goat Haunt in Glacier National Park, Montana, and returning to Waterton via

Family Fun

Opportunities for family fun at Glacier and Waterton include canoeing, climbing, hiking, biking, and touring.

Canoe Lake McDonald. Rent a canoe and paddle around the lake. If you work up a sweat, jump in. *Glacier.*

Climb Bear's Hump. This 2.8-km (1.7-mile) trail winds up a mountainside to an overlook with a great view of Upper Waterton Lake and the townsite. *Waterton.*

Hike Hidden Lake Nature Trail. A 2.4-km (1½-mile) trail runs uphill from Logan Pass to the Hidden Lake Overlook, yielding beautiful views of the lake and McDonald Valley. In spring, ribbons of water pour off the rocks surrounding the lake. A boardwalk protects the abundant wildflowers and spongy tundra on the way. *Glacier.*

Surrey Around Town. Rent a surrey bike at Pat's Waterton store and pedal around the townsite. A surrey bike has a flat seat and a canopy and can hold up to three people. *Waterton.*

Tour Going-to-the Sun in a Vintage Bus. With amazing vistas and many stops for photo ops, the Going-to-the-Sun Road tour in a vintage bus is a beloved park tradition. *Glacier.*

boat. A fee is charged for the return boat trip. You must preregister for this hike at the Waterton Information Centre.

HIKING

There are 225 km (191 miles) of trails in Waterton Lakes that range in difficulty from short strolls to strenuous treks. Some trails connect with the trail systems of Glacier and British Columbia's Akamina-Kishenina Provincial Park. The wildflowers in June are particularly stunning along most trails. In 2017, the Kenow Wildfire damaged more than 80% of the trails in Waterton Lakes National Park. The Crypt Lake and the hikes on the U.S. side of the lake that depart from the Goat Haunt Ranger Station were unaffected by the fire. Trails in other parts of the park received varying amounts of damage. Consult the park website for the latest trail reports. *Hiking Glacier and Waterton National Parks,* by Erik Molvar, has detailed information including pictures and GPS-compatible maps for 60 of the best hiking trails in both parks.

HORSEBACK RIDING

Rolling hills, grasslands, and rugged mountains make riding in Waterton Lakes a real pleasure. Scenery, wildlife, and wildflowers are easily viewed from the saddle, and horses are permitted on many park trails.

Alpine Stables

HORSEBACK RIDING | At these family-owned stables you can arrange hour-long trail rides and full-day guided excursions within the park, as well as multiday pack trips through the Rockies and foothills. They are open May through September. ⊠ *Waterton Lakes National Park* ☎ *403/859–2462, 403/653–2449* ⊕ *www. alpinestables.com* ⊠ *From C$45.*

Nearby Towns

You could easily spend a week exploring Waterton and Glacier, but you may wish to take advantage of hotels, restaurants, sights, and outfitters in nearby towns. Outside Glacier National Park's western reaches and 2½ miles south of the Apgar

Visitor Center is the gateway community of **West Glacier;** 27 miles to its southeast is **Essex.** Slightly farther afield to the southwest of West Glacier are **Columbia Falls** and **Whitefish.** Just over 40 miles southeast of the St. Mary Visitor Center on the east side of the park is the gateway of **East Glacier Park Village.** To the northeast, roughly midway between the visitor center and East Glacier, is the interesting town of **Browning.** Note that there are Amtrak stations in Whitefish, West Glacier, Essex, East Glacier Park Village, and Browning.

West Glacier

2½ miles south of Glacier National Park's Apgar Visitor Center.

The green waters of the Flathead River's Middle Fork and several top-notch outfitters make West Glacier an ideal base for river sports such as rafting, kayaking and fishing. West Glacier is one of the stops on Amtrak's nortthern route, so you can get there by train or by motor vehicle. Some accommodations and shops are open in winter, and there are snowshoe and cross-country ski trails nearby.

VISITOR INFORMATION

Glacier Area Information Center

Located in the Belton Train Depot in West Glacier, the Glacier National Park Conservancy's historic bookstore and gift shop doubles as an information center. It is open daily from Memorial Day through Labor Day. ✉ *12544 U.S. Hwy. 2 E, West Glacier* ☎ *406/888–5756* 🌐 *glacier.org.*

🍴 Restaurants

★ Belton Chalet Grill Dining Room

$$$$ | AMERICAN | The hotel's handsome restaurant still has its original wainscoting and leaded-glass windows, but in fine weather, ask to dine on the deck outside to watch the sun set behind the mountains. Bison meat loaf has been a signature dish for years, but you'll also find other unique dishes like confit duck leg with flathead cherries; house-made fettuccine with fennel, olives, and shitake mushrooms; or lamb with huckleberry jus. **Known for:** bison meatloaf; berry crisp; top-notch food. [$] *Average main: $32* ✉ *12575 U.S. Hwy. 2 E, next to railroad station, West Glacier* ☎ *406/888–5000, 844/868–7474 toll free* 🌐 *www.glacierparkcollection.com/lodging/belton-chalet/dining* 🕒 *Closed early Oct.–early Dec. and late Mar.–late May. Closed Mon.–Thurs. early Dec.–late Mar. (brunch only on Sun. Dec.–Mar.). No lunch.*

Josephine's Bar & Kitchen

$ | AMERICAN | This seasonal restaurant and bar—named for Josephine Doody, "the bootleg lady of Glacier National Park"—is a very casual spot: you order at a window beside the bar, and they bring the food to your table. For a starter, consider the fried green tomatoes with truffle caper aioli balsamic reduction; unique and delicious sandwich options include a prime rib with red onion marmalade, a smoked trout cake po' boy, and a bison gyro served in a warm pita. **Known for:** innovative cocktails; fried green tomatoes; local hangout. [$] *Average main: $12* ✉ *10245 Hwy. 2 E, Coram* ☎ *406/300–4755* 🌐 *www.josephinesbar.com* 🕒 *Closed mid-Oct.–mid-May.*

🛏 Hotels

Belton Chalet

$$$ | HOTEL | This carefully restored, 1910 railroad hotel, the original winter headquarters for the park, has a great location just outside the West Glacier entrance and cozy, bright rooms with period furnishings and original woodwork. **Pros:** excellent restaurant; wraparound decks with lovely views; historic property. **Cons:** train noise; rustic; no a/c or TVs. [$] *Rooms from: $200* ✉ *12575 U.S. Hwy. 2 E, West Glacier* ☎ *406/888–5000, 888/235–8665, 406/888-5005* 🌐 *www.beltonchalet.com* 🔑 *27 rooms* 🍽 *Breakfast.*

Glacier Guides Lodge

$$$$ | **HOTEL** | Tucked away in a forested canyon, this rustic, eco-friendly lodge is within walking distance of downtown restaurants and other amenities. **Pros:** secluded location in West Glacier; delicious included breakfast; mini-refrigerators in rooms. **Cons:** difficult to find; Wi-Fi can be slow; maximum 2 people per guest room. [$] *Rooms from: $259* ✉ *120 Highline Blvd., West Glacier* ☎ *800/521–7238 toll free, 406/387–5555* 🌐 *glacierguides.com/lodging/glacier-guides-lodge* 🕒 *Closed mid-Oct.–Apr.* 🛏 *13 units* 🍴 *Free Breakfast.*

Glacier Outdoor Center Cabins

$$$$ | **RENTAL** | **FAMILY** | Five minutes from the entrance to West Glacier, these cozy two-bedroom cabins can accommodate up to 10 people and have living rooms, barbecues, private decks, and fully equipped kitchens. **Pros:** great for families; can accommodate large groups; kitchens in cabins. **Cons:** outside the townsite; no restaurant; on the pricey side. [$] *Rooms from: $299* ✉ *12400 U.S. 2 E, West Glacier* ☎ *800/235–6781, 406/888–5454,* 🌐 *www.glacierraftco.com* 🕒 *Cabins closed Nov.–Apr.; lodge and sister Homestead property open year-round* 🛏 *26 units* 🍴 *No meals.*

Essex

27 miles southeast of West Glacier; 29 miles southeast of Apgar Visitor Center.

You can reach Essex by car or by train, as the tiny, unincorporated community is the site of the main rail terminal for park visitors. The historic Izaak Walton Inn sits right beside the tracks, and you can rent vehicles through its front desk (with advance reservations). Hiking and cross-country ski trails in the Great Bear Wilderness are nearby, as is the Walton Goat Lick Overlook, a great place to watch mountain goats. Beyond all this, there aren't many amenities or services.

🛏 Hotels

Izaak Walton Inn

$$$ | **HOTEL** | This historic lodge just south of Glacier National Park is popular with railway buffs: not only was it originally built to house rail workers (and has the industry memorabilia decor to prove it), but its lodging options include refurbished train cars, cabooses, and even a locomotive in addition to classic lodge rooms and family cabins. **Pros:** good location between East and West Glacier; Amtrak station right beside the inn; fun railway theme. **Cons:** train noise can be a problem; no phones or TVs in rooms; no cell reception and Wi-Fi signal is weak. [$] *Rooms from: $169* ✉ *290 Izaak Walton Inn Rd., off U.S. Hwy. 2, Essex* ☎ *406/888–5700, 406/888–5200* 🌐 *www.izaakwaltoninn.com* 🛏 *48 units* 🍴 *No meals.*

Columbia Falls

19 miles southwest of West Glacier.

This small town with a population of about 6,000 people is known as the "Gateway to Glacier." In addition to restaurants, accommodations, and other services in town, nearby are two excellent golf courses, a water park, and more than 80 miles of groomed snowmobile trails in winter. Interestingly, there are no falls in Columbia Falls. The word "Falls" was added to the name to avoid postal confusion with Columbus, Montana.

VISITOR INFORMATION

Columbia Falls Area Chamber of Commerce. ✉ *233 13 St. E, Columbia Falls* ☎ *406/892–2072* 🌐 *www.columbiafallschamber.org.*

Sights

Big Sky Waterpark

AMUSEMENT PARK/WATER PARK | FAMILY |
A popular summertime spot, this water
park has 10 waterslides, as well as a golf
course, arcade games, bumper cars, a
carousel, barbecue grills, a picnic area,
and food service. ⊠ *7211 U.S. Hwy. 2 E,
Columbia Falls* ✛ *at Hwy. 206* ☎ *406/892–
5025* ⊕ *www.bigskywp.com* ⊠ *$27.*

 Restaurants

Backslope Brewing

$$ | AMERICAN | Pair a great local beer with
delicious casual fare at this local brewery,
where there are always about eight
different kinds of house beer on tap as
well as kombucha, sparkling water, and
nitro iced coffee. The premium burgers
and sandwiches are exceptionally good,
especially when accompanied by hand-
cut garlic Parmesan fries. **Known for:** local
brewery; creative menu; garlic Parmesan
fries. $ *Average main: $13* ⊠ *1107 9
St. W, Columbia Falls* ☎ *406/897–2850*
⊕ *backslopebrewing.com* ☯ *Closed Sun.
Closed nightly at 8 pm.*

Hotels

Cedar Creek Lodge

$$$$ | HOTEL | If you want the atmos-
phere of a mountain lodge with modern
amenities and good connectivity, this
property is ideal. **Pros:** mountain lodge
atmosphere; modern amenities; great
included extras. **Cons:** 18 miles from
West Glacier; room price is high during
peak season for location; inside a town,
so room views are not great. $ *Rooms
from: $350* ⊠ *930 2nd Ave. W, Columbia
Falls* ☎ *855/733–4542, 406/412–4660*
⊕ *www.glaciernationalparklodges.com/
lodging/cedar-creek-lodge* ⌥ *64 rooms*
† *Free Breakfast.*

Whitefish

*10 miles northwest of Columbia Falls; 28
miles southwest of Apgar Visitor Center.*

This vibrant ski resort town, with roughly 8,500 people, sits on the shores of
Whitefish Lake at the base Big Mountain—home to Whitefish Mountain
Resort—and has a wide array of shops,
galleries, restaurants, coffeehouses,
and attractions. Amtrak's *Empire
Builder* train stops daily in Whitefish,
and the international airport in Kalispell
is just 15 minutes away. The western
entrance of Glacier National Park is
28 miles northeast of town. There is
a well-developed nighlife scene and
visitors can also enjoy live professional
theater as well as outdoor pursuits
like hiking, cycling, boating, skiing and
snowboarding.

VISITOR INFORMATION

Whitefish Chamber of Commerce. ⊠ *505
2nd St., Whitefish* ☎ *406/862–3501*
⊕ *www.whitefishchamber.org.*

Hotels

Garden Wall Inn B&B

$$$$ | B&B/INN | This 1923, antiques-
filled home has individually decorated
guest rooms with down duvets. **Pros:**
historic home; nice personal touches;
spacious rooms. **Cons:** small property;
no view; tends to book up. $ *Rooms
from: $215* ⊠ *504 Spokane Ave., White-
fish* ☎ *406/862–3440, 888/530–1700*
⊕ *www.gardenwallinn.com* ⌥ *5 rooms*
† *Breakfast.*

Good Medicine Lodge

$$$$ | B&B/INN | Built of cedar timbers
and decorated in a Western style, this
lodge-style bed-and-breakfast is warm
and inviting. **Pros:** Wi-Fi and many other
amenities; handy services for skiers; one
wheelchair-accessible room. **Cons:** no
TV in most rooms; small property; small
bathrooms. $ *Rooms from: $205* ⊠ *537*

Wisconsin Ave., Whitefish ☎ *406/862–5488, 800/860–5488* ⊕ *www.goodmedicinelodge.com* ⤶ *9 rooms* ⏏ *Breakfast.*

 ## Activities

DOGSLEDDING

Dog Sled Adventures

LOCAL SPORTS | The dogs are raring to run from late November to mid-April at Dog Sled Adventures, where the friendly mushers gear the ride to passengers ranging from kids to senior citizens. Bundled up in a sled, you'll be whisked through Stillwater State Forest on a 1½-hour ride over a 12-mile trail. Reservations are necessary. ✉ *8400 U.S. 93, Glacier National Park* ⊹ *20 miles north of Whitefish, 2 miles north of Olney* ☎ *406/881–2275* ⊕ *www.dogsledadventuresmontana.com* ⧠ *$150.*

SKIING AND SNOWBOARDING

Whitefish Mountain Resort

SKIING/SNOWBOARDING | Eight miles from Whitefish, this has been one of Montana's top ski areas since the 1930s, yet it remains comfortably small. The resort is popular among train travelers from the Pacific Northwest and the upper Midwest. The mountain has good powder skiing, nice glades, and groomed trails for all ski levels. In summer, there are bike trails, an alpine slide, an aerial adventure park, and a zip line. The terrain is 25% beginner, 50% intermediate, and 25% advanced; there are two high-speed quad chairs, one quad chair, four triple chairs, one double chair, and three surface lifts. **Facilities:** 105 trails; 3,000 acres; 2,500-foot vertical drop; 11 lifts. ✉ *1015 Glades Dr.* ☎ *406/862-2900, 406/862–7669 snow report, 877/754–3474 Toll Free* ⊕ *www.skiwhitefish.com* ⧠ *Lift ticket: $85.*

Browning

28 miles southeast of Glacier National Park's St. Mary Visitor Center.

Browning is the center of the Blackfeet Nation, whose name is thought to derive from the color of its members' painted or dyed black moccasins. At 1.5 million acres, the Blackfeet Indian Reservation is home to Montana's largest tribe by population, with about 13,000 enrolled members. The city's main attractions are the Museum of the Plains Indian, the Blackfeet Heritage Center and Art Gallery, Glacier Peaks Casino, and the Pikuni Gift Shop. If you want to really experience the culture, visit during the annual North American Indian Days celebration, which is held the second weekend in July, or during Heart Butte Indian Days the second weekend in August.

VISITOR INFORMATION

Blackfeet Country Visitor Information. ✉ *16 Old Person Rd., Browning* ☎ *406/338–7406* ⊕ *blackfeetcountry.com.*

 ## Sights

Museum of the Plains Indian

MUSEUM | The impressive collection of Blackfeet artifacts at this museum includes clothing, saddlebags, and artwork. ✉ *19 Museum Loop, Browning* ☎ *406/338–2230* ⊕ *www.doi.gov/iacb/museum-plains-indian* ⧠ *$5 June–Sept., free Oct.–May.*

East Glacier Park Village

13½ miles southwest of Browning; 42 miles southeast of St. Mary Visitor Center.

Early tourists to Glacier National Park first stopped in East Glacier, where the Great Northern Railway had established a station. Although most people coming from the east now enter by car, some still make the journey on Amtrak's *Empire Builder* train from Whitefish. With quiet, secluded surroundings and the lovely Glacier Park Lodge, East Glacier makes a great base for exploring the national park. You can golf on the oldest green grass golf course in Montana, enjoy a variety of dining options, and explore hundreds of miles of hiking trails.

VISITOR INFORMATION

East Glacier Chamber of Commerce. ✉ *909 Hwy. 49 N, East Glacier Park* ☎ *406/226–4403.*

🍴 Restaurants

Serrano's

$$ | **MEXICAN** | Mexican food in Montana! After a day on the dusty trail, Serrano's is a treat whether dining inside or on the back patio. **Known for:** excellent Mexican food; fabulous margaritas; huckleberry carrot cake. [$] *Average main: $15* ✉ *29 Dawson Ave., East Glacier Park* ☎ *406/226–9392* 🌐 *www.serranosmexican.com* 🕓 *Closed Oct.–Apr.*

Summit Mountain Steakhouse

$$$ | **STEAKHOUSE** | The slightly off-the-beaten-track drive to this steak house southwest of East Glacier is well worth it. The small dining room has large windows with mountain views that are shared by an outdoor patio with additional seating. **Known for:** grilled steaks and handmade hamburgers; huckleberry cheesecake; great views. [$] *Average main: $26* ✉ *16900 U.S. 2 W, East Glacier Park* ☎ *406/226–9319* 🌐 *www.summitmtnlodge.com* 🕓 *Closed Mon. Closed mid-Sept.–mid-June. No lunch* 💳 *No credit cards.*

🛏 Hotels

Glacier Park Lodge

$$$ | **HOTEL** | Just east of the park, across from the Amtrak station, this beautiful full-service hotel built in 1913 is supported by 500- to 800-year-old fir and 3-foot-thick cedar logs. **Pros:** golf course; scenic location; lots of activities. **Cons:** small bathrooms; no elevator; no a/c or TV. [$] *Rooms from: $179* ✉ *Off U.S. 2, East Glacier Park* ☎ *406/892–2525, 844/868–7474* 🌐 *www.glacierparkcollection.com/lodging/glacier-park-lodge* 🕓 *Closed late Sept.–May* 🛏 *161 rooms* 🍽 *No meals.*

Chapter 16

GRAND CANYON NATIONAL PARK

16

Updated by
Mara Levin

ARIZONA

⛺ Camping	🏨 Hotels	🏃 Activities	👁 Scenery	👥 Crowds
★★★★★	★★★★★	★★★★★	★★★★★	★★★★★

WELCOME TO GRAND CANYON NATIONAL PARK

TOP REASONS TO GO

★ **Its status:** This is one of those places about which you really want to say, "Been there, done that!"

★ **Awesome vistas:** The Painted Desert, sandstone canyon walls, pine and fir forests, mesas, plateaus, volcanic features, the Colorado River, streams, and waterfalls make for some jaw-dropping moments.

★ **Year-round adventure:** Outdoors enthusiasts can bike, boat, camp, fish, hike, ride mules, whitewater raft, watch birds and wildlife, cross-country ski, and snowshoe.

★ **Continuing education:** Adults and kids can have fun learning, thanks to free park-sponsored nature walks and interpretive programs.

★ **Sky-high and river-low experiences:** Experience the canyon via plane, train, and automobile, as well as by helicopter, row- or motorboat, bike, mule, or foot.

1 South Rim. The South Rim is where the action is: Grand Canyon Village's lodging, camping, eateries, stores, and museums, plus plenty of trailheads into the canyon. Four free shuttle routes cover more than 35 stops, and visitors who'd rather relax than rough it can treat themselves to comfy hotel rooms and elegant restaurant meals (lodging and camping reservations are essential).

2 North Rim. Of the nearly 5 million people who visit the park annually, 90% enter at the South Rim, but many consider the North Rim even more gorgeous— and worth the extra effort. Open only from mid-May to the end of October (or the first good snowfall), the North Rim has legitimate bragging rights: at more than 8,000 feet above sea level (1,000 feet higher than the South Rim), it has precious solitude and seven developed viewpoints. Rather than staring into the canyon's depths, you get a true sense of its expanse.

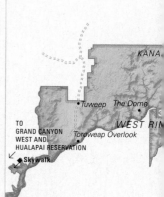

3 West Rim. Though not in Grand Canyon National Park, the far-off-the-beaten-path western end of the canyon has some spectacular scenery. At the West Rim, on the Hualapai Reservation, the Skywalk has become a major draw. This U-shape glass-floored deck juts out 3,600 feet above the Colorado River and isn't for the faint of heart.

When it comes to the Grand Canyon, there are statistics, and there are sensations. While the former are impressive—the canyon measures an average width of 10 miles, length of 277 river miles, and depth of 1 mile—they don't truly prepare you for that first impression. Viewing the canyon for the first time is an astounding experience. Actually, it's more than an experience: it's an emotion, one that only just begins to be captured with the word "Grand," the name bestowed upon the canyon by John Wesley Powell, an explorer of the American West, as he led his expedition down the Colorado River in 1869.

When President Teddy Roosevelt declared it a National Monument in 1908, he called it "the one great sight every American should see." Though many visitors do just that—stand at the rim and marvel in awe—there are manifold ways to soak up the canyon's magnificence. Hike or ride a trusty mule down into the canyon, bike or ramble along its rim, fly over, or raft through on the Colorado River.

Roughly 6 million visitors come to the park each year. You can access the canyon via two main points—the South Rim and the North Rim—but the South Rim is much easier to get to and therefore much more visited. The width from the North Rim to the South Rim varies from 600 feet to 18 miles, but traveling between rims by road requires a 215-mile drive. Hiking arduous trails from rim to rim is a steep and strenuous trek of at least 21 miles, but it's well worth the effort. You'll travel through five of North America's seven life zones. (To do this any other way, you'd have to journey from the Mexican desert to the Canadian woods.) West of Grand Canyon National Park, the tribal lands of the Hualapai and the Havasupai lie along the so-called West Rim of the canyon, where you'll find the impressive glass Skywalk.

SOUTH RIM AVERAGE HIGH/LOW TEMPERATURES					
JAN.	**FEB.**	**MAR.**	**APR.**	**MAY**	**JUNE**
41/18	45/21	51/25	60/32	70/39	81/47
JULY	**AUG.**	**SEPT.**	**OCT.**	**NOV.**	**DEC.**
84/54	82/53	76/47	65/36	52/27	43/20

NORTH RIM AVERAGE HIGH/LOW TEMPERATURES					
JAN.	**FEB.**	**MAR.**	**APR.**	**MAY**	**JUNE**
37/16	39/18	44/21	53/29	62/34	73/40
JULY	**AUG.**	**SEPT.**	**OCT.**	**NOV.**	**DEC.**
77/46	75/45	69/39	59/31	46/24	40/20

INNER CANYON AVERAGE HIGH/LOW TEMPERATURES					
JAN.	**FEB.**	**MAR.**	**APR.**	**MAY**	**JUNE**
56/36	62/42	71/48	82/56	92/63	101/72
JULY	**AUG.**	**SEPT.**	**OCT.**	**NOV.**	**DEC.**
106/78	103/75	97/69	84/58	68/46	57/37

16

Grand Canyon National Park   PLANNING

Planning

When to Go

There's no bad time to visit the canyon, though the busiest times of year are summer and spring break. Visiting the South Rim during these peak seasons, as well as holidays, requires patience and a tolerance for crowds. If you plan to hike into the canyon, be aware that temperatures rise as you descend; summer daytime highs at the bottom are often over 100° F. Fall and winter at the South Rim are spectacular and far less crowded. Note that weather changes on a whim in this exposed high-desert region. The North Rim shuts down mid-October through mid-May due to weather conditions and related road closures.

Planning Your Time

Plan ahead: Mule rides require at least a six-month advance reservation—longer for the busy season (most can be reserved up to 13 months in advance). Multiday rafting trips should be reserved at least a year in advance.

Once you arrive, pick up the free *Pocket Map and Services Guide,* a brochure with a detailed map and schedule of free programs, at the entrance gate or at any of the visitor centers. The free *Grand Canyon Accessibility Guide* is also available.

The park is most crowded on the South Rim, especially near the Visitor Center/Mather Point and in Grand Canyon Village, as well as on the scenic drives.

Grand Canyon Itineraries

Grand Canyon in One Day

Start early, pack a picnic lunch, and drive to the South Rim's **Grand Canyon Visitor Center**, just north of the south entrance, to pick up info and see your first incredible view at **Mather Point**. Continue east along **Desert View Drive** for about 2 miles to **Yaki Point**. Next, continue driving 7 miles east to **Grandview Point** for a good view of the buttes Krishna Shrine and Vishnu Temple. Go 4 miles east and catch the view at **Moran Point**, then 3 miles to the **Tusayan Ruin and Museum**, where a small display is devoted to the history of the Ancestral Pueblo. Continue another mile east to **Lipan Point** to view the Colorado River. In less than a mile, you'll arrive at **Navajo Point**, the highest elevation on the South Rim. **Desert View and Watchtower** is the final attraction along Desert View Drive.

On your return drive, stop off at any of the picnic areas if you've brought your own lunch; otherwise, there are choices ranging from food trucks to casual dining spots in Grand Canyon Village. After lunch, walk the paved **Rim Trail** west to **Maricopa Point**. Along the way, pick up souvenirs in the village and stop at the Kolb Studio and historic **El Tovar Hotel** (be sure to make reservations in advance if you want to eat dinner at El Tovar Dining Room). If you have time, drive or, during summer months, take the shuttle on **Hermit Road** to **Hermits Rest**, 7 miles away. Along that route, Hopi Point and Powell Point are excellent spots to watch the sunset.

Grand Canyon in Three Days

On Day 1, follow the one-day itinerary for the morning, but spend more time exploring Desert View Drive and enjoy a leisurely picnic lunch. Later, drive 30 miles beyond Desert View to **Cameron Trading Post**, which has a good restaurant and is an interesting side trip. Travel Hermit Road on your second morning, by car, shuttle bus, or bicycle, and drive to Grand Canyon Airport for a late-morning small plane or helicopter tour. Have lunch in **Tusayan** and cool off at the IMAX film *Grand Canyon: The Hidden Secrets*. Back in the village, take a free ranger-led program. On your third day, hike partway down the canyon on **Bright Angel Trail**. It takes twice as long to hike back up, so plan accordingly. Get trail maps at **Grand Canyon Visitor Center**, and bring plenty of water.

Alternatively, spend Days 2 and 3 exploring the remote **West Rim**, 150 miles toward Nevada or California and far away from major highways. Fill the first day with a horseback ride along the rim, a helicopter ride into the canyon, or a walk on the Skywalk. The next day, raft the Class V–VII rapids near Peach Springs. Another option, but one that would require all three days, if not more, is to get a tribal permit for a visit to **Havasu Canyon**, a truly spiritual backcountry experience. You can opt to hike or take a helicopter 8 miles down to the small village of Supai and the Havasupai Lodge.

Getting Here and Around

SOUTH RIM

CAR

The best route into the park from the east or south is from Flagstaff. Take U.S. 180 northwest to the park's southern entrance and Grand Canyon Visitor Center. From the west on Interstate 40, the most direct route to the South Rim is taking Highway 64 from Williams to U.S. 180.

PARK SHUTTLE

The South Rim is open to car traffic year-round, though access to Hermits Rest is limited to shuttle buses during summer months. There are four free shuttle routes that run from one hour before sunrise until one hour after sunset, every 15 to 30 minutes: the **Hermits Rest Route** operates March through November, between Grand Canyon Village and Hermits Rest. The **Village Route** operates year-round in the village area, stopping at lodgings, the general store, and the Grand Canyon Visitor Center. The **Kaibab Rim Route** goes from the visitor center to five viewpoints, including the Yavapai Geology Museum and Yaki Point (where cars are not permitted). The **Tusayan Route** travels between the village and the town of Tusayan from March through September. A fifth route, the **Hiker's Express,** shuttles hikers from the village to the South Kaibab Trailhead twice each morning. ■TIP→ **In summer, South Rim roads are congested and it's easier, and sometimes required, to park your car and take the free shuttle.**

TAXI AND SHUTTLE

Although there's no public transportation into the Grand Canyon, you can hire a taxi to take you to or from the Grand Canyon Village or any of the Tusayan hotels. Groome Transportation has frequent shuttle service between Flagstaff, Williams, Tusayan, and Grand Canyon Village (at Maswik Lodge); they also have connecting service from Phoenix and Sedona.

TAXI AND SHUTTLE CONTACTS Groome Transportation. ☎ *928/226–8060, 800/888–2749* ⊕ *www.groometransportation.com.* **Xanterra.** ☎ *928/638–2822, 888/297–2757* ⊕ *www.xanterra.com.*

TRAIN

Grand Canyon Railway

There's no need to deal with all of the other drivers racing to the South Rim. Sit back and relax in the comfy train cars of the Grand Canyon Railway. Live music, storytelling, and a pretend train robbery enliven the trip as you journey past the landscape through prairie, ranch, and national park land to the log-cabin train station in Grand Canyon Village. You won't see the Grand Canyon from the train, but you can walk (¼ mile) or catch the shuttle at the restored, historic Grand Canyon Railway Station. The vintage train departs from the Williams Depot every morning and makes the 65-mile journey in 2¼ hours. You can do the round-trip in a single day; however, it's a more relaxing and enjoyable strategy to stay for a night or two at the South Rim before returning to Williams. ☎ *800/843–8724* ⊕ *www. thetrain.com* ✉ *$82–$219 round-trip* ☞ *Rates do not include $35 park entry fee (for up to 9 persons).*

NORTH RIM

AIR

The nearest airport to the North Rim is **St. George Regional Airport** (☎ *435/627–4080* ⊕ *www.flysgu.com*) in Utah, 164 miles north, with regular service provided by American, Delta, and United airlines.

CAR

To reach the North Rim by car, take U.S. 89 north from Flagstaff past Cameron, turning left onto U.S. 89A at Bitter Springs. At Jacob Lake, take Highway 67 directly to the Grand Canyon North Rim. You can drive yourself to the scenic viewpoints and trailheads; the only transportation offered in the park is a shuttle twice each morning that brings eager hikers from Grand Canyon Lodge to the North Kaibab Trailhead (a 2-mile trip). Note that services on the North Rim shut down in mid-October, and the road closes after the first major snowfall (usually the end of October); Highway 67 south of Jacob Lake is closed.

SHUTTLE

From mid-May to mid-October, the **Trans Canyon Shuttle** (☏ *928/638–2820* ⊕ *www. trans-canyonshuttle.com*) travels daily between the South and North rims—the ride takes 4½ hours each way. The fare is $90 each way and reservations are required.

Inspiration

ARIZONA DOCUMENTARIES. Whether you want to learn about the Grand Canyon, Arizona's efforts to manage its water, or famous national figures such as Barry Goldwater or Sandra Day O'Connor, Arizona PBS has a collection well worth navigating ⊕ *wazpbs.org/tv/arizonacollection.*

Park Essentials

PARK FEES AND PERMITS

A fee of $35 per vehicle or $20 per person for pedestrians and cyclists is good for one week's access at both rims.

The $70 Grand Canyon Pass gives unlimited access to the park for 12 months. The annual America the Beautiful **National Parks and Recreational Land Pass** (☏ *888/275–8747* ⊕ *store.usgs.gov/ pass, $80*) provides unlimited access to all national parks and federal recreation areas for 12 months.

No permits are needed for day hikers, but **backcountry permits** (☏ *928/638–7875* ⊕ *www.nps.gov/grca, $10, plus $8 per person per night*) are necessary for overnight hikers camping below the rim. Permits are limited, so make your reservation as far in advance as possible— they're taken by fax (☏ *928/638–2125*), by mail (✉ *1824 S. Thompson St., Suite*

201, Flagstaff, AZ 86001), or in person at the Backcountry Information centers (in the village on the South Rim and near the visitor center on the North Rim) up to four months prior to your arrival. A limited number of last-minute permits are available for Indian Garden, Bright Angel, and Cottonwood campgrounds each day. Camping on the North Rim and the South Rim is restricted to designated campgrounds (☏ *877/444–6777* ⊕ *www. recreation.gov*).

PARK HOURS

The South Rim is open continuously every day of the year (weather permitting), while the North Rim is open mid-May through October. Because Arizona does not observe daylight saving time, the park is in the same time zone as California and Nevada from mid-March to early November, and in the Mountain time zone the rest of the year. Just to the east of the park, the Navajo Nation observes daylight saving time.

CELL PHONE RECEPTION

Cell phone coverage can be spotty at both the South Rim and North Rim— though Verizon customers report better reception at the South Rim. Don't expect a strong signal anywhere in the park, but Grand Canyon Village is usually the best bet.

Hotels

The park's accommodations include three "historic-rustic" facilities and four motel-style lodges, all of which have undergone significant upgrades over the past decade. Of the 922 rooms, cabins, and suites, only 203 are at the North Rim, all at the Grand Canyon Lodge. Outside El Tovar Hotel, the canyon's architectural highlight, accommodations are relatively basic but comfortable, and the most sought-after rooms have canyon views. Rates vary widely, but most rooms fall in the $175 to $250 range, though the most basic units on the South Rim go for just $125. Yavapai Lodge, on the South Rim, is the only hotel in the park that allows pets.

Reservations are a must, especially during the busy summer season. ■TIP→ **If you want to get your first choice (especially Bright Angel Lodge or El Tovar), make reservations as far in advance as possible; they're taken up to 13 months ahead. You might find a last-minute cancellation, but you shouldn't count on it.** Although lodging at the South Rim will keep you close to the action, the frenetic activity and crowded facilities are off-putting to some. With short notice, the best time to find a room on the South Rim is in winter. And though the North Rim is less crowded than the South Rim, the only lodging available is at Grand Canyon Lodge.

Just south of the South Rim park boundary, Tusayan's hotels are in a convenient location but without bargains, while Williams (about an hour's drive) and Flagstaff (about 90 minutes away) can provide price breaks on food and lodging, as well as a respite from the crowds. Extra amenities (e.g., swimming pools and gyms) are also more abundant. Even outside the park, reservations are always a good idea.

LODGING CONTACTS Xanterra Parks & Resorts. ☎ 888/297–2757 ⊕ www. grandcanyonlodges.com. **Delaware North.** ☎ 877/404–4611 ⊕ www.visitgrandcanyon.com.

Restaurants

Within the park on the South Rim, you can find everything from cafeteria food to casual café fare to creatively prepared, Western- and Southwestern-inspired American cuisine—there's even a coffeehouse with organic joe. Reservations are accepted (and recommended) only for dinner at El Tovar Dining Room; they can be made up to six months in advance with El Tovar

room reservations, 30 days in advance without. You should also make dinner reservations at the Grand Canyon Lodge Dining Room on the North Rim— as the only "upscale" dining option, the restaurant fills up quickly at dinner throughout the season (the other choice on the North Rim is a deli). The dress code is casual across the board, but El Tovar is your best option if you're looking to dress up a bit and thumb through an extensive wine list. Options for picnic supplies at the South Rim include the general store in Market Plaza and healthy grab-and-go fare at Bright Angel Bicycles' café next to the Visitor Center. Drinking water and restrooms are available only at some picnic spots.

Bring your picnic basket and enjoy dining alfresco surrounded by some of the most beautiful backdrops in the country. Be sure to bring water, as it's unavailable at many of these spots, as are restrooms. **Buggeln,** 15 miles east of Grand Canyon Village on Desert View Drive, has some secluded, shady spots. **Grandview Point** has, as the name implies, grand vistas; it's 12 miles east of the village on Desert View Drive. **Cape Royal,** 23 miles south of the North Rim Visitor Center, at the end of Cape Royal Road, is the most popular designated picnic area on the North Rim due to its panoramic views. **Point Imperial,** 11 miles northeast of the North Rim Visitor Center, has shade and some privacy.

Eateries outside the park generally range from mediocre to terrible—you didn't come all the way to the Grand Canyon for the food, did you? Our selections highlight your best options. Of towns near the park, Flagstaff definitely has the leg up on culinary variety and quality, with Tusayan (near the South Rim) and Jacob Lake (the closest town to the North Rim) offering mostly either fast food or merely adequate sit-down restaurants. Near the park, even the priciest places welcome casual dress. On the Hualapai and Havasupai reservations in Havasu Canyon and on the West Rim, dining is limited and basic.

Hotel and restaurant reviews have been shortened. For full information, visit Fodors.com.

What It Costs

	$	$$	$$$	$$$$
RESTAURANTS				
	Under $12	$12–$20	$21–$30	Over $30
HOTELS				
	Under $120	$120–$175	$176–$250	Over $250

Tours

Grand Canyon Conservancy Field Institute
GUIDED TOURS | Instructors lead guided educational tours, hikes around the canyon, and weekend programs at the South Rim. With more than 200 classes a year, tour topics include everything from archaeology and backcountry medicine to photography and natural history. Contact GCC for a schedule and price list. Private hikes can be arranged. Discounted classes are available for members; annual dues are $35. ⊠ *GCA Warehouse, 2–B Albright Ave., Grand Canyon Village* ☎ *928/638–7035, 866/471–4435* ⊕ *www.grandcanyon.org/fieldinstitute* ☎ *From $235.*

Xanterra Motorcoach Tours
GUIDED TOURS | Narrated by knowledgeable guides, tours include the Hermits Rest Tour, which travels along the old wagon road built by the Santa Fe Railway; the Desert View Tour, which glimpses the Colorado River's rapids and stops at Lipan Point; Sunrise and Sunset Tours; and combination tours. ☎ *303/297–2757, 888/297–2757* ⊕ *www.grandcanyonlodges.com* ☎ *From $40.*

Visitor Information

Grand Canyon National Park
Before you go, you can view and print the complimentary *Pocket Map and Service Guide,* updated regularly, from the Grand Canyon National Park website. You can also pick up a copy at the entrance stations and the visitor centers. ☎ *928/638–7888* ⊕ *www.nps.gov/grca.*

Grand Canyon South Rim

Visitors to the canyon converge mostly on the South Rim, and mostly in summer. Grand Canyon Village is here, with a majority of the park's lodging and camping, trailheads, restaurants, stores, and museums, along with a nearby airport and railroad depot. Believe it or not, the average stay in the park is a mere half day or so; this is not advised! You need to spend several days to truly appreciate this marvelous place, but at the very least, give it a full day. Hike down into the canyon, or along the rim, to get away from the crowds and experience nature at its finest.

Sights

HISTORIC SIGHTS

Tusayan Ruin and Museum
ARCHAEOLOGICAL SITE | This museum offers a quick orientation to the prehistoric and modern indigenous populations of the Grand Canyon and the Colorado Plateau, including an excavation of an 800-year-old Pueblo site. Of special interest are split-twig figurines dating back 2,000 to 4,000 years and other artifacts left behind by ancient cultures. A ranger leads daily interpretive tours of the Ancestral Pueblo village. ⊠ *Grand Canyon National Park* ✛ *About 20 miles east of Grand Canyon Village on E. Rim Dr.* ☎ *928/638–7888* ☎ *Free.*

Tips for Avoiding Grand Canyon Crowds

It's hard to commune with nature while you're searching for a parking place, dodging video cameras, and stepping away from strollers. However, this scenario is likely only during the peak summer months. One option is to bypass Grand Canyon National Park altogether and head to the West Rim of the canyon, tribal land of the Hualapai and Havasupai. If only the park itself will do, the following tips will help you to keep your distance and your cool.

Take Another Route

Avoid road rage by choosing a different route to the South Rim, forgoing traditional Highway 64 and U.S. 180 from Flagstaff. Take U.S. 89 north from Flagstaff instead, passing near Sunset Crater and Wupatki national monuments. When you reach the junction with Highway 64, take a break at Cameron Trading Post (1 mile north of the junction)—or stay overnight. This is a good place to shop for Native American artifacts, souvenirs, and the usual postcards, dream catchers, recordings, and T-shirts. There are also high-quality Navajo rugs, jewelry, and other authentic handicrafts, and you can sample Navajo tacos. U.S. 64 to the west takes you directly to the park's east entrance; the scenery along the Little Colorado River gorge en route is eye-popping. It's 23 miles from the east entrance to the main visitor center and Mather Point.

Explore the North Rim

Although the North Rim is just 10 miles across from the South Rim, the trip to get there by car is a five-hour drive of 215 miles. At first it might not sound like the trip would be worth it, but the payoff is huge. Along the way, you'll travel through some of the prettiest parts of the state and be granted even more stunning views than those on the more easily accessible South Rim. Those who make the North Rim trip often insist it has the canyon's most beautiful views and best hiking. To get to the North Rim from Flagstaff, take U.S. 89 north past Cameron, turning left onto U.S. 89A at Bitter Springs. En route you'll pass the area known as Vermilion Cliffs. At Jacob Lake, take Highway 67 directly to the Grand Canyon North Rim. North Rim services are closed from November through mid-May because of heavy snow, but in summer months and early fall, it's a wonderful way to beat the crowds at the South Rim.

PICNIC AREAS

Bring your picnic basket and enjoy dining alfresco surrounded by some of the most beautiful backdrops in the country. Be sure to bring water, as it's unavailable at many of these spots, as are restrooms.

Buggeln, 15 miles east of Grand Canyon Village on Desert View Drive, has some secluded, shady spots.

Grandview Point has, as the name implies, grand vistas; it's 12 miles east of the village on Desert View Drive.

SCENIC DRIVES
Desert View Drive

SCENIC DRIVE | This heavily traveled 25-mile stretch of road follows the rim from the east entrance to Grand Canyon Village. Starting from the less-congested entry near Desert View, road warriors can get their first glimpse of the canyon from the 70-foot-tall watchtower, the top

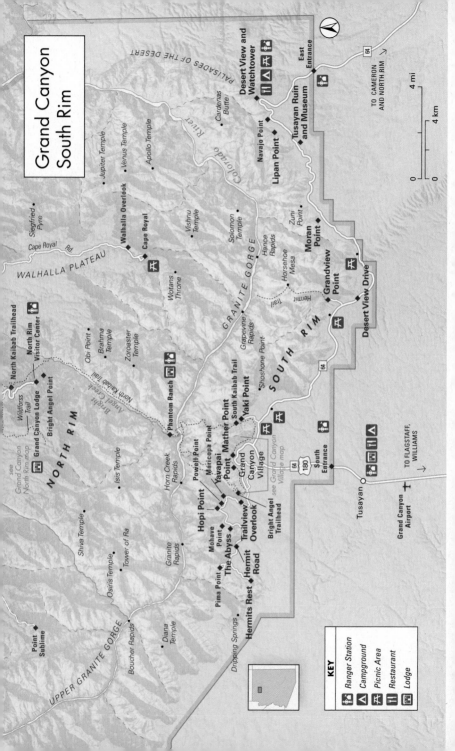

Grand Canyon South Rim

KEY

	Ranger Station
	Campground
	Picnic Area
	Restaurant
	Lodge

Point Sublime

UPPER GRANITE GORGE

Diana Temple

Boucher Rapids

Dripping Springs

Osiris Temple

Shiva Temple

Tower of Ra

Isis Temple

Granite Rapids

Horn Creek Rapids

NORTH RIM

Wildforss Trail

North Kaibab Trailhead

North Rim Visitor Center

Grand Canyon Lodge

Bright Angel Point

see Grand Canyon North Rim map

Siegfried Pyre

WALHALLA PLATEAU

Cape Royal Rd

Walhalla Overlook

Cape Royal

Jupiter Temple

Venus Temple

Apollo Temple

Obi Point

Brahma Temple

Zoroaster Temple

Wotans Throne

Vishnu Temple

Solomon Temple

Bright Angel Creek

North Kaibab Trail

Phantom Ranch

Colorado River

GRANITE GORGE

PALISADES OF THE DESERT

Carderas Butte

Desert View and Watchtower

East Entrance

TO CAMERON AND NORTH RIM

Tusayan Ruin and Museum

Navajo Point

Lipan Point

Zuni Point

Moran Point

Hance Rapids

Horsehoe Mesa

Grapevine Rapids

Shoshone Point

Yaki Point

South Kaibab Trail

Mather Point

Powell Point

Maricopa Point

Yavapai Point

Grand Canyon Village

see Grand Canyon Village map

Hopi Point

Mohave Point

The Abyss

Trailview Overlook

Hermit Road

Pima Point

Hermits Rest

Bright Angel Trailhead

SOUTH RIM

Hermit Trail

Grandview Point

Desert View Drive

64

180

South Entrance

Tusayan

Grand Canyon Airport

TO FLAGSTAFF, WILLIAMS

64

0   4 mi

0   4 km

Best Grand Canyon Views

The best time of day to see the canyon is before 10 and after 4, when the angle of the sun brings out the colors of the rock, and clouds and shadows add dimension. Colors deepen dramatically among the contrasting layers of the canyon walls just before and during sunrise and sunset.

Hopi Point is the top spot on the South Rim to watch the sun set; **Yaki** and **Pima** points also offer vivid views.

For a grand sunrise, try **Mather** or **Yaki Point**.

■TIP→ Arrive at least 30 minutes early for sunrise views and as much as 90 minutes for sunset views at these points. For another point of view, take a leisurely stroll along the Rim Trail and watch the color change along with the views. Timetables are posted at park visitor centers.

16

of which provides the highest viewpoint on the South Rim. Six developed canyon viewpoints in addition to unmarked pullouts, the remains of an Ancestral Puebloan dwelling at the Tusayan Ruin and Museum, and the secluded and lovely Buggeln picnic area make for great stops along the South Rim. The Kaibab Rim Route shuttle bus travels a short section of Desert View Drive and takes 50 minutes to ride round-trip without getting off at any of the stops: Grand Canyon Visitor Center, South Kaibab Trailhead, Yaki Point, Pipe Creek Vista, Mather Point, and Yavapai Geology Museum. ⊠ Grand Canyon National Park.

Hermit Road

SCENIC DRIVE | The Santa Fe Company built Hermit Road, formerly known as West Rim Drive, in 1912 as a scenic tour route. Nine overlooks dot this 7-mile stretch, each worth a visit. The road is filled with hairpin turns, so make sure you adhere to posted speed limits. A 1½-mile Greenway trail offers easy access to cyclists looking to enjoy the original 1912 Hermit Rim Road. From March through November, Hermit Road is closed to private auto traffic because of congestion; during this period, a free shuttle bus carries visitors to all the overlooks. Riding the bus round-trip without getting off at any of the viewpoints takes 80 minutes; the return

trip stops only at Hermits Rest, Pima, Mohave, and Powell points. ⊠ Grand Canyon National Park.

SCENIC STOPS

The Abyss

VIEWPOINT | At an elevation of 6,720 feet, the Abyss is one of the most awesome stops on Hermit Road, revealing a sheer drop of 3,000 feet to the Tonto Platform, a wide terrace of Tapeats sandstone about two-thirds of the way down the canyon. From the Abyss you'll also see several isolated sandstone columns, the largest of which is called the Monument. ⊠ Grand Canyon National Park ⊹ About 5 miles west of Hermit Rd. Junction on Hermit Rd.

Desert View and Watchtower

VIEWPOINT | From the top of the 70-foot stone-and-mortar watchtower with its 360-degree views, even the muted hues of the distant Painted Desert to the east and the Vermilion Cliffs rising from a high plateau near the Utah border are visible. In the chasm below, angling to the north toward Marble Canyon, an imposing stretch of the Colorado River reveals itself. Up several flights of stairs, the watchtower houses a glass-enclosed observatory with telescopes. ⊠ Grand Canyon National Park ⊹ Just north of East Entrance Station on Desert View Dr. ☎ 928/638–7888 ⊕ www.nps.gov/grca ≊ Free.

Grandview Point

VIEWPOINT | At an elevation of 7,399 feet, the view from here is one of the finest in the canyon. To the northeast is a group of dominant buttes, including Krishna Shrine, Vishnu Temple, Rama Shrine, and Sheba Temple. A short stretch of the Colorado River is also visible. Directly below the point, and accessible by the steep and rugged Grandview Trail, is Horseshoe Mesa, where you can see remnants of Last Chance Copper Mine. ⊠ *Grand Canyon National Park ✛ About 12 miles east of Grand Canyon Village on Desert View Dr.*

Hermits Restare

VIEWPOINT | This westernmost viewpoint and Hermit Trail, which descends from it, were named for "hermit" Louis Boucher, a 19th-century French-Canadian prospector who had a number of mining claims and a roughly built home down in the canyon. The trail served as the original mule ride down to Hermit Camp beginning in 1914. Views from here include Hermit Rapids and the towering cliffs of the Supai and Redwall formations. You can buy curios and snacks in the stone building at Hermits Rest. ⊠ *Grand Canyon National Park ✛ About 8 miles west of Hermit Rd. Junction on Hermit Rd.*

★ Hopi Point

VIEWPOINT | From this elevation of 7,071 feet, you can see a large section of the Colorado River; although it appears as a thin line, the river is nearly 350 feet wide. The overlook extends farther into the canyon than any other point on Hermit Road. The incredible unobstructed views make this a popular place to watch the sunset.

Across the canyon to the north is Shiva Temple. In 1937 Harold Anthony of the American Museum of Natural History led an expedition to the rock formation in the belief that it supported life that had been cut off from the rest of the canyon. Imagine the expedition members' surprise when they found an empty Kodak film box on top of the temple—it had been left behind by Emery Kolb, who felt slighted for not having been invited to join Anthony's tour.

Directly below Hopi Point lies Dana Butte, named for a prominent 19th-century geologist. In 1919 an entrepreneur proposed connecting Hopi Point, Dana Butte, and the Tower of Set across the river with an aerial tramway, a technically feasible plan that fortunately has not been realized. ⊠ *Grand Canyon National Park ✛ About 4 miles west of Hermit Rd. Junction on Hermit Rd.*

Lipan Point

VIEWPOINT | Here, at the canyon's widest point, you can get an astonishing visual profile of the gorge's geologic history, with a view of every eroded layer of the canyon and one of the longest visible stretches of Colorado River. The spacious panorama stretches to the Vermilion Cliffs on the northeastern horizon and features a multitude of imaginatively named spires, buttes, and temples—intriguing rock formations named after their resemblance to ancient pyramids. You can also see Unkar Delta, where a creek joins the Colorado to form powerful rapids and a broad beach. Ancestral Pueblo farmers worked the Unkar Delta for hundreds of years, growing corn, beans, and melons. ⊠ *Grand Canyon National Park ✛ About 25 miles east of Grand Canyon Village on Desert View Dr.*

★ Mather Point

VIEWPOINT | You'll likely get your first glimpse of the canyon from this viewpoint, one of the most impressive and accessible (next to the main visitor center plaza) on the South Rim. Named for the National Park Service's first director, Stephen Mather, this spot yields extraordinary views of the Grand Canyon, including deep into the inner gorge and numerous buttes: Wotans Throne, Brahma Temple, and Zoroaster Temple, among others. The Grand Canyon Lodge, on the North Rim, is almost directly north from Mather Point and only 10 miles away—yet you have to drive 215 miles to get from one spot to the other. ⊠ Near Grand Canyon Visitor Center, Grand Canyon National Park ☎ 928/638–7888 ⊕ www.nps.gov/grca.

Moran Point

VIEWPOINT | This point was named for American landscape artist Thomas Moran, who was especially fond of the play of light and shadows from this location. He first visited the canyon with John Wesley Powell in 1873. "Thomas Moran's name, more than any other, with the possible exception of Major Powell's, is to be associated with the Grand Canyon," wrote noted canyon photographer Ellsworth Kolb. It's fitting that Moran Point is a favorite spot of photographers and painters. ⊠ Grand Canyon National Park ⊹ About 17 miles east of Grand Canyon Village on Desert View Dr.

Trailview Overlook

VIEWPOINT | Look down on a dramatic view of the Bright Angel and Plateau Point trails as they zigzag down the canyon. In the deep gorge to the north flows Bright Angel Creek, one of the region's few permanent tributary streams of the Colorado River. Toward the south is an unobstructed view of the distant San Francisco Peaks, as well as Bill Williams Mountain (on the horizon) and Red Butte (about 15 miles south of the canyon rim). ⊠ Grand Canyon National Park ⊹ About 2 miles west of Hermit Rd. Junction on Hermit Rd.

Yaki Point

VIEWPOINT | Stop here for an exceptional view of Wotans Throne, a flat-top butte named by François Matthes, a U.S. Geological Survey scientist who developed the first topographical map of the Grand Canyon. The overlook juts out over the canyon, providing unobstructed views of inner-canyon rock formations, South Rim cliffs, and Clear Creek canyon. About a mile south of Yaki Point is the trailhead for the South Kaibab Trail. ■ TIP➔ The point is one of the best places on the South Rim to watch the sunrise and the sunset. ⊠ Grand

Canyon National Park ⊹ 2 miles east of Grand Canyon Village on Desert View Dr.

★ Yavapai Point

MUSEUM | Dominated by the Yavapai Geology Museum and Observation Station, this point displays panoramic views of the mighty gorge through a wall of windows. Exhibits at the museum include videos of the canyon floor and the Colorado River, a scaled diorama of the canyon with national park boundaries, fossils, and rock fragments used to re-create the complex layers of the canyon walls, and a display on the natural forces used to carve the chasm. Dig even deeper into Grand Canyon geology with free daily ranger programs. This point is also a good location to watch the sunset. ⊠ Grand Canyon Village ⊹ 1 mile east of Market Plaza.

TRAILS

★ Bright Angel Trail

TRAIL | This well-maintained trail is one of the most scenic (and busiest) hiking paths from the South Rim to the bottom of the canyon (9.6 miles each way). Rest houses are equipped with water at the 1½- and 3-mile points from May through September, and at Indian Garden (4 miles) year-round. Water is also available at Bright Angel Campground, 9¼ miles below the trailhead. Plateau Point, on a spur trail about 1½ miles below Indian Garden, is as far as you should attempt to go on a day hike; the round-trip will take six to nine hours.

Bright Angel Trail is the easiest of all the footpaths into the canyon, but because the climb out from the bottom is an ascent of 5,510 feet, the trip should be attempted only by those in good physical condition and should be avoided in midsummer due to extreme heat. The top of the trail can be icy in winter. Originally a bighorn sheep path and later used by the Havasupai, the trail was widened late in the 19th century for prospectors and is now used for both mule and foot traffic. Also note that mule trains have the right-of-way—and sometimes leave unpleasant surprises in your path. *Moderate.* ✉ *Grand Canyon National Park* ⚓ *Trailhead: Kolb Studio, Hermit Rd.*

Grandview Trail

TRAIL | Accessible from the parking area at Grandview Point, the trailhead is at 7,400 feet. The path heads steeply down into the canyon for 3 miles to the junction and campsite at East Horseshoe Mesa Trail. Classified as a wilderness trail, the route is aggressive and not as heavily traveled as some of the more well-known trails, such as Bright Angel and Hermit. There is no water available along the trail, which follows a steep descent to 4,800 feet at Horseshoe Mesa, where Hopi Indians once collected mineral paints. Hike 0.7 mile farther to Page Spring, a reliable water source year-round. Parts of this trail are icy in winter, and traction crampons are mandatory. *Difficult.* ✉ *Grand Canyon National Park* ⚓ *Trailhead: Grandview Point, Desert View Dr.*

Hermit Trail

TRAIL | Beginning on the South Rim just west of Hermits Rest (and 7 miles west of Grand Canyon Village), this steep, unmaintained, 9.7-mile (one-way) trail drops more than 5,000 feet to Hermit Creek, which usually flows year-round. It's a strenuous hike back up and is recommended for experienced long-distance hikers only; plan for six to nine hours. There's an abundance of lush growth and wildlife, including desert bighorn sheep, along this trail. The trail descends from the trailhead at 6,640 feet to the Colorado River at 2,300 feet. Day hikers should not go past Santa Maria Spring at 5,000 feet (a 5-mile round-trip).

For much of the year, no water is available along the way; ask a park ranger about the availability of water at Santa Maria Spring and Hermit Creek before you set out. All water from these sources should be treated before drinking. The route leads down to the Colorado River and has inspiring views of Hermit Gorge and the Redwall and Supai formations.

Six miles from the trailhead are the ruins of Hermit Camp, which the Santa Fe Railroad ran as a tourist camp from 1911 until 1930. *Difficult.* ✉ *Grand Canyon National Park* ⚓ *Trailhead: Hermits Rest, Hermits Rd.*

★ Rim Trail

TRAIL | The South Rim's most popular walking path is the 12-mile (one-way) Rim Trail, which runs along the edge of the canyon from Pipe Creek Vista (the first overlook on Desert View Drive) to Hermits Rest. This walk, which is paved to Maricopa Point and for the last 1½ miles to Hermits Rest, visits several of the South Rim's historic landmarks. Allow anywhere from 15 minutes to a full day, depending on how much of the trail you want to cover; the Rim Trail is an ideal day hike, as it varies only a few hundred feet in elevation from Mather Point (7,120 feet) to the trailhead at Hermits Rest (6,650 feet). The trail also can be accessed from several spots in Grand Canyon Village and from the major viewpoints along Hermit Road, which are serviced by shuttle buses during the busy summer months. On the Rim Trail, water is available only in the Grand Canyon Village area and at Hermits Rest. *Easy.* ✉ *Grand Canyon National Park.*

South Kaibab Trail

TRAIL | This trail starts near Yaki Point, 4 miles east of Grand Canyon Village, and is accessible via the free shuttle bus.

Because the route is so steep (and sometimes icy in winter)—descending from the trailhead at 7,260 feet down to 2,480 feet at the Colorado River—and has no water, many hikers take this trail down, then ascend via the less-demanding Bright Angel Trail. Allow four to six hours to reach the Colorado River on this 6.4-mile trek. At the river, the trail crosses a suspension bridge and runs on to Phantom Ranch. Along the trail there is no water and little shade. There are no campgrounds, though there are portable toilets at Cedar Ridge (6,320 feet), 1½

Grand Canyon History

The Grand Canyon's oldest layers date back to 1.8 billion years ago. The geological wonder is a prime example of arid-land erosion.

Indigenous groups inhabited the land much earlier than the first European explorers to "find" it in 1540. In fact, there's evidence of humans 12,000 years ago. Hualapai and Havasupai are among the tribes that still live in the area.

An explorer of the American West, John Wesley Powell, bestowed the name "Grand" to the canyon as he led his expedition down the Colorado River in 1869.

In 1903, train tracks were completed to Grand Canyon Village, enabling more visitors to see the Grand Canyon.

Teddy Roosevelt, a champion for protecting land with government funding, gave the Grand Canyon National Monument status in 1908.

The Grand Canyon became America's 17th National Park in 1919 under President Woodrow Wilson.

16

Grand Canyon National Park

GRAND CANYON SOUTH RIM

miles from the trailhead. An emergency phone is available at the Tipoff, 4.6 miles down the trail (3 miles past Cedar Ridge). The trail corkscrews down through some spectacular geology. Look for (but don't remove) fossils in the limestone when taking water breaks. *Difficult.* ⊠ *Grand Canyon National Park* ✛ *Trailhead: Yaki Point Rd., off Desert View Dr.*

VISITOR CENTERS

Desert View Information Center
Near the watchtower, at Desert View Point, this nonprofit Grand Canyon Association store and information center has a nice selection of books, park pamphlets, gifts, and educational materials. It's also a handy place to pick up maps and info if you enter the park at the Eastern entrance. All sales from the association stores go to support the park programs. ⊠ *Eastern entrance, Grand Canyon National Park* ☎ *800/858–2808, 928/638–7888.*

Grand Canyon Verkamp's Visitor Center
This small visitor center is named for the Verkamp family, who operated a curios shop on the South Rim for more than a hundred years. The building serves as an official visitor center, ranger station (get your Junior Ranger badges here), bookstore, and museum, with compelling exhibits on the Verkamps and other pioneers in this region. ⊠ *Desert View Dr., Grand Canyon Village* ✛ *Across from El Tovar Hotel* ☎ *928/638–7146.*

Grand Canyon Visitor Center
The park's main orientation center provides pamphlets and resources to help plan your visit. It also holds engaging interpretive exhibits on the park. Rangers are on hand to answer questions and aid in planning canyon excursions. A daily schedule of ranger-led hikes and evening lectures is available, and a 20-minute film about the history, geology, and wildlife of the canyon plays every 30 minutes in the theater. The bicycle rental office, a small café, and a huge gift store are also in this complex. It's a short walk from here to Mather Point, or a short ride on the shuttle bus, which can take you into Grand Canyon Village. The visitor center is also accessible from the village via a leisurely 1-mile walk on the Greenway Trail, a paved pathway that meanders through the forest. ⊠ *East side of Grand Canyon Village, 450 Hwy. 64, Grand Canyon* ☎ *928/638–7888* ⊕ *www.explorethe-canyon.com.*

Yavapai Geology Museum

Learn about the geology of the canyon at this Grand Canyon Association museum and bookstore. You can also catch the park shuttle bus or pick up information for the Rim Trail here. The views of the canyon and Phantom Ranch from inside this historic building are stupendous. ⊠ *1 mile east of Market Plaza, Grand Canyon Village* ☎ *928/638–7888.*

 Restaurants

Arizona Steakhouse

$$$ | STEAKHOUSE | The canyon views from this casual Southwestern-style steak house are the best of any restaurant at the South Rim. The dinner menu leans toward steak-house dishes, while lunch is primarily salads and sandwiches with a Southwestern twist. **Known for:** views of the Grand Canyon; Southwest fare; local craft beers and wines. $ *Average main: $28* ⊠ *Bright Angel Lodge, Desert View Dr., Grand Canyon Village* ☎ *928/638–2631* ⊕ *www.grandcanyonlodges.com.*

★ El Tovar Dining Room

$$$ | SOUTHWESTERN | Even at the edge of the Grand Canyon it's possible to find gourmet dining. This cozy room of dark wood beams and stone, nestled in the historic El Tovar Lodge, dates to 1905. **Known for:** historic setting with canyon views; local and organic ingredients; fine dining that's worth the splurge. $ *Average main: $28* ⊠ *El Tovar Hotel, Desert View Dr., Grand Canyon Village* ☎ *928/638–2631* ⊕ *www.grandcanyonlodges.com.*

Fred Harvey Burger

$$ | SOUTHWESTERN | FAMILY | Open for breakfast, lunch, and dinner, this casual café at Bright Angel Lodge serves basics like pancakes, salads, sandwiches, pastas, burgers, and steaks. Or you can step it up a notch and order some of the same selections straight from the neighboring Arizona Steakhouse's menu, including prime rib, baby back ribs, and

wild salmon. **Known for:** reasonably priced American fare; family-friendly menu and setting; some vegetarian and gluten-free options. $ *Average main: $14* ⊠ *Bright Angel Lodge, Desert View Dr., Grand Canyon Village* ☎ *928/638–2631* ⊕ *www.grandcanyonlodges.com.*

Maswik Food Court

$ | AMERICAN | FAMILY | You can get a burger, hot sandwich, pasta, or Mexican fare at this food court, as well as pizza by the slice and wine and beer in the adjacent Maswik Pizza Pub. This casual eatery is in Maswik Lodge, ¼ mile from the rim, and the Pizza Pub stays open until 11 pm (you can also order pizza to take out). **Known for:** good selection (something for everyone); later hours; pizza to go. $ *Average main: $10* ⊠ *Maswik Lodge, Desert View Dr., Grand Canyon Village* ⊕ *www.grandcanyonlodges.com.*

Yavapai Lodge Restaurant and Tavern

$$ | AMERICAN | If you don't have time for full-service, the restaurant in Yavapai Lodge offers cafeteria-style dining for breakfast, lunch, and dinner, including hot and cold sandwiches, pizza, barbecue ribs, and rotisserie chicken. Wine and beer, including craft brews from nearby Flagstaff, are also on the menu; or enjoy drinks on the patio at the adjacent Yavapai Tavern. **Known for:** quick bites or hearty meals; convenient dining in Market Plaza; patio with firepit at Yavapai Tavern. $ *Average main: $19* ⊠ *Yavapai Lodge, Desert View Dr., Grand Canyon Village* ☎ *928/638–4001* ⊕ *www.visitgrandcanyon.com.*

🛏 Hotels

Bright Angel Lodge

$ | HOTEL | Famed architect Mary Jane Colter designed this 1935 log-and-stone structure, which sits within a few yards of the canyon rim and blends superbly with the canyon walls; its location is similar to El Tovar's but for about half the price. **Pros:** good value for the amazing

Freebies at the Grand Canyon

While you're here, be sure to take advantage of the many complimentary services offered.

■ The most useful is the system of free shuttle buses at the South Rim; it caters to the road-weary, with four routes winding through or just outside the park—Hermits Rest Route, Village Route, Kaibab Rim Route, and Tusayan Route. Of the bus routes, the Hermits Rest Route runs only March through November and the Tusayan Route only in summer; the other two run year-round, and the Kaibab Rim Route provides the only access to Yaki Point. Hikers coming or going from the South Kaibab Trailhead can catch the Hikers Express, which departs three times each morning from the Bright Angel Lodge, makes a quick stop at the Backcountry Information Center, and then heads out to the South Kaibab Trailhead.

■ Ranger-led programs are always free and offered year-round, though more are scheduled during the busy spring and summer seasons. These programs might include activities such as stargazing and topics such as geology and the cultural history of prehistoric peoples. Some of the more in-depth programs may include a fossil walk or a condor talk. Check with the visitor center for seasonal programs including wildflower walks and fire ecology.

■ Kids ages four and older can get involved with the park's Junior Ranger program, with ever-changing activities including hikes and hands-on experiments.

■ Despite all of these options, rangers will tell you that the best free activity in the canyon is watching the magnificent splashes of color on the canyon walls during sunrise and sunset.

location; charming rooms and cabins steps from the rim; on-site Internet kiosks and transportation desk for the mule ride. **Cons:** popular lobby is always packed; parking is a bit of a hike; only some rooms have canyon views. [$] *Rooms from: $104* ✉ *Desert View Dr., Grand Canyon Village* ☎ *888/297–2757 reservations only, 928/638–2631* 🌐 *www.grandcanyonlodges.com* 🛏 *105 units* 🍴 *No meals.*

★ El Tovar Hotel

$$$$ | **HOTEL** | The hotel's proximity to all of the canyon's facilities, European hunting-lodge atmosphere, attractively updated rooms and tile baths, and renowned dining room make it the best place to stay on the South Rim. A registered National Historic Landmark, the "architectural crown jewel of the Grand Canyon" was built in 1905 of Oregon pine logs and native stone. **Pros:** historic lodging just steps from the South Rim; fabulous lounge with outdoor seating and canyon views; best in-park dining on-site. **Cons:** books up quickly; priciest lodging in the park; rooms are comfortable, not luxurious. [$] *Rooms from: $275* ✉ *Desert View Dr., Grand Canyon Village* ☎ *888/297–2757 reservations only, 928/638–2631* 🌐 *www.grandcanyonlodges.com* 🛏 *78 rooms* 🍴 *No meals.*

Kachina Lodge

$$$ | **HOTEL** | The well-appointed rooms at this motel-style lodge in Grand Canyon Village on the South Rim are a good bet for families and are within easy walking distance of dining facilities at nearby lodges. **Pros:** partial canyon views in half the rooms; family-friendly; steps from the best restaurants in the park. **Cons:** check-in at nearby El Tovar Hotel; limited parking; no air conditioning. $ *Rooms from: $232* ✉ *Desert View Dr., Grand Canyon Village* ☎ *888/297–2757 reservations only, 928/638–2631* ⊕ *www.grandcanyonlodges.com* ⇱ *49 rooms* ⎮Ⓞ⎮ *No meals.*

Maswik Lodge

$$ | HOTEL | FAMILY | Far from the noisy crowds, Maswik accommodations are in two-story, contemporary motel-style buildings nestled in a shady ponderosa pine forest. **Pros:** units are modern, spacious, and well equipped; good for families; affordable dining options. **Cons:** rooms lack historic charm; tucked away from the rim in the forest; no elevators for second-floor rooms. $ *Rooms from: $159* ✉ *Grand Canyon Village* ☎ *888/297–2757 reservations only, 928/638–2631* ⊕ *www.grandcanyonlodges.com* ⇱ *278 rooms* ⎮Ⓞ⎮ *No meals.*

Phantom Ranch

$ | B&B/INN | In a grove of cottonwood trees on the canyon floor, Phantom Ranch is accessible only to hikers, river rafters, and mule trekkers; there are 40 dormitory bunk beds and 14 beds in cabins, all with shared baths (though cabins have toilets and sinks). **Pros:** only inner-canyon lodging option; fabulous canyon views; remote access limits crowds. **Cons:** reservations are booked up to a year in advance; few amenities; shared bathrooms. $ *Rooms from: $65* ✉ *On canyon floor, Grand Canyon National Park* ✛ *At intersection of Bright Angel and Kaibab trails* ☎ *303/297–2757, 888/297–2757* ⊕ *www.grandcanyonlodges.com* ⇱ *54 beds* ⎮Ⓞ⎮ *No meals.*

Thunderbird Lodge

$$$$ | HOTEL | This motel with comfortable, simple rooms and partial canyon views has all the modern amenities you'd expect at a typical mid-price chain hotel—even pod coffeemakers. **Pros:** canyon views in some rooms; family-friendly; convenient to dining and activities in Grand Canyon Village. **Cons:** check-in at nearby Bright Angel Lodge; limited

parking nearby; no air conditioning (but some rooms have effective evaporative coolers). $ *Rooms from: $264* ✉ *Desert View Dr., Grand Canyon Village* ☎ *888/297–2757 reservations only, 928/638–2631* ⊕ *www.grandcanyonlodges.com* ⇱ *55 rooms* ⎮Ⓞ⎮ *No meals.*

Yavapai Lodge

$$ | HOTEL | The largest motel-style lodge in the park is tucked in a pinyon-pine and juniper forest at the eastern end of Grand Canyon Village, across from Market Plaza. **Pros:** transportation-activities desk in the lobby; walk to Market Plaza in Grand Canyon Village; only pet-friendly lodging at South Rim. **Cons:** farthest lodging in park from the rim (1 mile); generic appearance. $ *Rooms from: $154* ✉ *10 Yavapai Lodge Rd., Grand Canyon Village* ☎ *877/404–4611 reservations only* ⊕ *www.visitgrandcanyon.com* ⇱ *358 rooms* ⎮Ⓞ⎮ *No meals.*

🏃 Activities

BIKING

The South Rim's limited opportunities for off-road biking, narrow shoulders on park roads, and heavy traffic in summer may disappoint hard-core cyclists; for others, cycling is a fun and eco-friendly way to tour the park. Bicycles are permitted on all park roads and on the multiuse Greenway Trail System; visitors to the North Rim have Bridle Path and a 12-mile section of the Arizona Trail (⇨ *see Grand Canyon North Rim*). Bikes are prohibited on the paved portions of the Rim Trail between Mather Point and Bright Angel Trailhead. Some find Hermit Road a good biking option, especially from March through November when it's closed to cars. You can ride west 8 miles and then put your bike on the free shuttle bus back into the village (or vice versa). A shorter ride takes you east to Yaki Point (3½ miles), a great place to stop and have a picnic. Bicyclists visiting the South Rim may also enjoy meandering through the ponderosa pine forest on the Greenway Trails or the

Tusayan Bike Trail, a gentle uphill climb from Tusayan into the park. Rentals and guided bicycling tours are available mid-March through October at the South Rim from Bright Angel Bicycles (☎ 928/638–3055 ⊕ bikegrandcanyon.com) at the visitor center complex. Bicycle camping sites ($6 per person per night) are available at Mather Campground.

BOATING AND RAFTING

The National Park Service restricts the number of visitors allowed on the Colorado River each season, and seats fill up fast. Due to the limited availability, reservations for multiday trips should be made a year or two in advance. Lots of people book trips for summer's peak period: June through August. If you're flexible, take advantage of the Arizona weather; May to early June and September are ideal rafting times in the Grand Canyon.

Most trips begin at Lees Ferry, a few miles below the Glen Canyon Dam near Page. There are tranquil half- and full-day float trips from the Glen Canyon Dam to Lees Ferry, as well as raft trips that run from 3 to 18 days. For outfitters, see the boating and rafting listings under Lees Ferry in ⇨ *Nearby Towns* of this chapter. The shorter three- and four-day voyages either begin or end at Phantom Ranch at the bottom of the Grand Canyon at river mile 87. On the longer trips, you'll encounter the best of the canyon's white water along the way, including Lava Falls, listed in the *Guinness Book of World Records* as "the fastest navigable white water stretch in North America." Life jackets, beverages, tents, sheets, tarps, sleeping bags, dry bags, first aid, and food are provided—but you'll still need to plan ahead by packing clothing, a rain suit, hats, sunscreen, toiletries, and other sundries. Commercial outfitters allow each river runner two waterproof bags to store items during the day. Just keep in mind that one of the bags will be filled up with the provided sleeping bag and tarp, which leaves only one for your personal belongings.

Arranging Tours

Transportation-services desks are maintained at Bright Angel, Maswik Lodge, and Yavapai Lodge (closed in winter) in Grand Canyon Village. The desks provide information and handle bookings for sightseeing tours, taxi and bus services, and mule rides (but don't count on last-minute availability). There's also a concierge at El Tovar that can arrange most tours, with the exception of mule rides. On the North Rim, Grand Canyon Lodge has general information about local services.

CAMPING

Within the national park, there are two developed campgrounds on the South Rim and one on the North Rim. All campgrounds charge nightly camping fees in addition to the general park entrance fee; some accept reservations up to six months in advance (☎ 877/444–6777 ⊕ www.recreation.gov) and others are first-come, first-served.

Camping anywhere outside a developed rim campground, including in the canyon, requires a permit from the Backcountry Information Center, which also serves as your reservation. Permits can be requested by mail or fax only; applying well in advance is recommended. Call ☎ 928/638–7875 between 1 pm and 5 pm weekdays for information.

Bright Angel Campground. This backcountry campground is near Phantom Ranch at the bottom of the canyon. There are toilet facilities and running water, but no showers.✉ *Intersection of South and North Kaibab trails, South Rim* ☎ 928/638–7875.

Desert View Campground. Popular for spectacular views of the canyon from the nearby watchtower, this developed campground near the east entrance doesn't take reservations; show up before noon, as it fills up fast in summer. Open mid-May through mid-October, these sites have no hookups. ⊠ *Desert View Dr., 23 miles east of Grand Canyon Village off Hwy. 64, South Rim.*

Mather Campground. The largest developed campground in the park is set in a forested area near Grand Canyon Village. Open all year, Mather takes reservations from March to November and has water and toilet facilities, as well as showers and laundry (for an extra fee). There is a cofee bar/deli on-site, and the park shuttle stops here. ⊠ *Grand Canyon Village, South Rim* ☎ *877/444–6777* ⊕ *www. recreation.gov*

CROSS-COUNTRY SKIING

Tusayan Ranger District

SKIING/SNOWBOARDING | Although you can't schuss down into the Grand Canyon, you can cross-country ski in the woods near the rim when there's enough snow, usually mid-December through early March. The ungroomed trails, suitable for beginner and intermediate skiers, begin at the Grandview Lookout and travel through the Kaibab National Forest. For details, contact the Tusayan Ranger District. ⊠ *176 Lincoln Log Loop, Grand Canyon* ☎ *928/638–2443* ⊕ *www. fs.usda.gov/kaibab.*

HIKING

Although permits are not required for day hikes, you must have a backcountry permit for longer trips (⇨ *see Park Fees and Permits*). Some of the more popular trails are listed under ⇨ *Sights*, including **Bright Angel Trail, Rim Trail,** and **South Kaibab Trail;** more detailed information and maps can be obtained from the Backcountry Information centers. Also, rangers can help design a trip to suit your abilities.

Remember that the canyon has significant elevation changes and, in summer, extreme temperature ranges, which can pose problems for people who aren't in good shape or who have heart or respiratory problems. ■ TIP→ **Carry plenty of water and energy foods.** Listen to the podcast *Hiking Smart* on the Park's website to prepare for your trip. The majority of each year's 400 search-and-rescue incidents result from hikers underestimating the size of the canyon, hiking beyond their abilities, or not packing sufficient food and water.

■ TIP→ **Under no circumstances should you attempt a day hike from the rim to the river and back.** Remember that when it's 85°F on the South Rim, it's 110°F on the canyon floor. Allow two to four days if you want to hike rim to rim (it's easier to descend from the North Rim, as it's more than 1,000 feet higher than the South Rim). Hiking steep trails from rim to rim is a strenuous trek of at least 21 miles and should be attempted only by experienced canyon hikers.

HORSEBACK RIDING

Mule rides provide an intimate glimpse into the canyon for those who have the time, but not the stamina, to see the canyon on foot. ■ TIP→ **Reservations are essential and are accepted up to 13 months in advance.**

These trips have been conducted since the early 1900s. A comforting fact as you ride the narrow trail: no one's ever been killed while riding a mule that fell off a cliff. (Nevertheless, the treks are not for the faint of heart or people in questionable health.)

★ **Xanterra Parks & Resorts Mule Rides**

TOUR—SPORTS | These trips delve either into the canyon from the South Rim to Phantom Ranch, or east along the canyon's rim. Riders must be at least nine years old and 57 inches tall, weigh less than 200 pounds for the Phantom Ranch ride or less than 225 pounds for

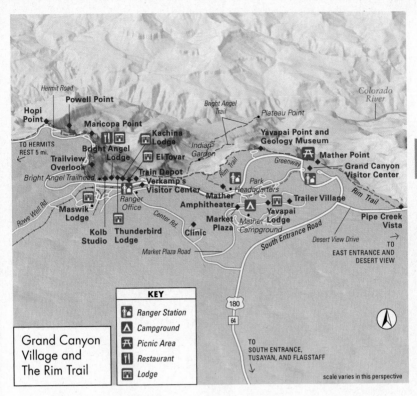

Grand Canyon Village and The Rim Trail

KEY

👫	Ranger Station
⚠	Campground
🌲	Picnic Area
🍴	Restaurant
🏨	Lodge

180
64

TO SOUTH ENTRANCE, TUSAYAN, AND FLAGSTAFF

scale varies in this perspective

the rim ride, and understand English. Children under 18 must be accompanied by an adult. Riders must be in fairly good physical condition, and pregnant women are advised not to take these trips.

The two-hour ride along the rim costs $153. An overnight mule ride with a stay in a cabin at Phantom Ranch at the bottom of the canyon, with meals included, is $693 ($1,205 for two riders). Package prices vary since a cabin at Phantom Ranch can accommodate up to four people. From November through February, you can stay for up to two nights at Phantom Ranch. Reservations are a must, but you can check at the Bright Angel Transportation Desk to see if there's last-minute availability. ☎ 888/297–2757, 303/297–2757 ⊕ www.grandcanyonlodges.com ⚴ Reservations essential.

JEEP TOURS

Jeep rides can be rough; if you have had back injuries, check with your doctor before taking a 4X4 tour. It's a good idea to book a week or two ahead, and even longer if you're visiting in summer or on busy weekends.

Buck Wild Hummer Tours

DRIVING TOURS | With this tour company, you can see majestic rim views in Grand Canyon National Park and learn about the history, geology, and wildlife of the canyon from the comfort of a 13-passenger Hummer. Daily tours run either in the morning or at sunset. ⊠ 469 AZ 64, Grand Canyon ☎ 928/362–5940 ⊕ buckwildhummertours.com 🎫 From $99.

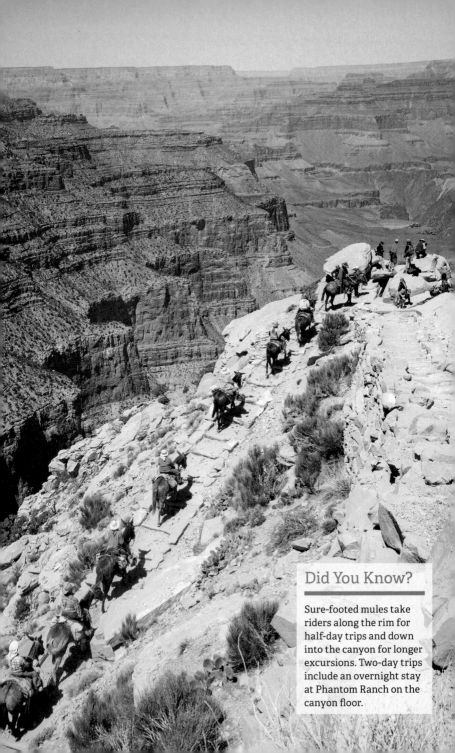

Did You Know?

Sure-footed mules take riders along the rim for half-day trips and down into the canyon for longer excursions. Two-day trips include an overnight stay at Phantom Ranch on the canyon floor.

Grand Canyon Custom Tours

TOUR—SPORTS | This tour company offers a full-day off-road adventure to the bottom of the Grand Canyon West (rather than Grand Canyon National Park) year-round in comfortable cruisers (small luxury vans with heating and air-conditioning) rather than jeeps. Tours leave from either Flagstaff or Williams. ⊠ *Williams* ☎ *928/779–3163* ⊕ *grandcanyoncustomtours.com* 💳 *From $269.*

Grand Canyon Jeep Tours & Safaris

TOUR—SPORTS | If you'd like to get off the pavement and see parts of the park that are accessible only by dirt road, a jeep tour can be just the ticket. From March through November, this tour operator leads daily three-hour off-road tours within the park, as well as jeep tours to a petroglyph site in Kaibab National Forest. Sunset tours to the canyon rim and combo tours adding helicopter or plane flights are also available. ⊠ *Grand Canyon National Park* ☎ *928/638–5337* ⊕ *grandcanyonjeeptours.com* 💳 *From $79.*

SCENIC FLIGHTS

Flights by plane and helicopter over the canyon are offered by a number of companies, departing from the Grand Canyon Airport at the south end of Tusayan. Though the noise and disruption of so many aircraft buzzing around the canyon is controversial, flightseeing remains a popular, if expensive, option. You'll have more visibility from a helicopter, but they're louder and more expensive than the fixed-wing planes. Prices and lengths of tours vary, but you can expect to pay about $159 per adult for short plane trips and approximately $300 for helicopter tours (and about $550 for combination plane and helicopter tours leaving from Vegas). These companies often have significant discounts in winter—check the company websites to find the best deals.

Grand Canyon Airlines

FLYING/SKYDIVING/SOARING | This company offers a variety of plane tours, from a 45-minute fixed-wing tour of the eastern edge of the Grand Canyon, the North Rim, and the Kaibab Plateau to an all-day tour that combines "flightseeing" with four-wheel-drive tours of Antelope Canyon and float trips on the Colorado River. They also schedule combination tours that leave from Las Vegas (plane flight from Las Vegas to Grand Canyon Airport, then helicopter flight into the canyon). ⊠ *Grand Canyon Airport, Tusayan* ☎ *702/835–8484, 866/235–9422* ⊕ *www.grandcanyonairlines.com* 💳 *From $159.*

Maverick Helicopters

FLYING/SKYDIVING/SOARING | This company offers 45-minute tours of the South Rim, North Rim, and Dragon Corridor of the Grand Canyon, as well as tours to the canyon out of Las Vegas. A landing tour option for those flying from Las Vegas to the West Rim sets you down in the canyon for champagne and a snack below the rim. ⊠ *Grand Canyon Airport, Grand Canyon* ☎ *928/638–2622* ⊕ *www.maverickhelicopter.com* 💳 *From $299.*

🛍 Shopping

Nearly every lodging facility and retail store at the South Rim stocks arts and crafts made by Native American artists and Grand Canyon books and souvenirs. Prices are comparable to other souvenir outlets, though you may find some better deals in Williams. Nevertheless, a portion of the proceeds from items purchased at Kolb Studio, Tusayan Museum, and all the park visitor centers go to the nonprofit Grand Canyon Association.

Desert View Trading Post

GIFTS/SOUVENIRS | A mix of traditional Southwestern souvenirs and authentic Native American arts and crafts are for sale here. ⊠ *Desert View Dr., Grand Canyon National Park* ✛ *Near watchtower at Desert View* ☎ *928/638–3150.*

Hopi House

CRAFTS | This two-level shop near El Tovar and Verkamp's Visitor Center has the widest selection of Native American art and handicrafts in the vicinity. ✉ *4 El Tovar Rd., Grand Canyon Village* ✛ *Across from El Tovar Hotel* ☎ *928/638–2631* ⊕ *www. grandcanyonlodges.com.*

Grand Canyon North Rim

The North Rim stands 1,000 feet higher than the South Rim and has a more alpine climate, with twice as much annual precipitation. Here, in the deep forests of the Kaibab Plateau, the crowds are thinner, the facilities fewer, and the views even more spectacular. Due to snow, the North Rim is off-limits in winter. The buildings and concessions are closed mid-October through mid-May. The road and entrance gate close when the snow makes them impassable—usually by the end of November.

Lodgings are limited in this more remote park, with only one historic lodge (with cabins and hotel-type rooms as well as a restaurant) and a single campground. Dining options have opened up a little with a deli and a coffeehouse/saloon next door to the lodge. Your best bet may be to pack your camping gear and hiking boots and take several days to explore the lush Kaibab Forest. The canyon's highest, most dramatic rim views can also be enjoyed on two wheels (via primitive dirt access roads) and on four legs (courtesy of a trusty mule).

Sights

HISTORIC SIGHTS

Grand Canyon Lodge

HISTORIC SITE | Built in 1937 by the Union Pacific Railroad (replacing the original 1928 building, which burned in a fire), this massive stone structure is listed on the National Register of Historic Places. Its huge sunroom has hardwood floors, high-beamed ceilings, and a marvelous view of the canyon through plate-glass windows. On warm days, visitors sit in the sun and drink in the surrounding beauty on an outdoor viewing deck, where National Park Service employees deliver free lectures on geology and history. The dining room serves breakfast, lunch, and dinner; the Roughrider Saloon is a bar by night and a coffee shop in the morning. ✉ *Grand Canyon National Park* ✛ *Off Hwy. 67 near Bright Angel Point* ☎ *928/638–2611 May.–Oct.* ⊕ *www. grandcanyonforever.com* ⊗ *Closed Nov.–mid-May.*

PICNIC AREAS

Cape Royal, 23 miles south of the North Rim Visitor Center, at the end of Cape Royal Road, is the most popular designated picnic area on the North Rim due to its panoramic views. **Point Imperial**, 11 miles northeast of the North Rim Visitor Center, has shade and some privacy.

SCENIC DRIVE

★ Highway 67

SCENIC DRIVE | Open mid-May to roughly mid-November (or the first big snowfall), this two-lane paved road climbs 1,400 feet in elevation as it passes through the Kaibab National Forest. Also called the North Rim Parkway, this scenic route crosses the limestone-capped Kaibab Plateau—passing broad meadows, sun-dappled forests, and small lakes and springs—before abruptly falling away at the abyss of the

Grand Canyon. Wildlife abounds in the thick ponderosa pine forests and lush mountain meadows. It's common to see deer, turkeys, and coyotes as you drive through such a remote region. Point Imperial and Cape Royal branch off this scenic drive, which runs from Jacob Lake to Bright Angel Point. ⊠ *Hwy. 67, Grand Canyon National Park.*

SCENIC STOPS

★ Bright Angel Point

TRAIL | This trail, which leads to one of the most awe-inspiring overlooks on either rim, starts on the grounds of the Grand Canyon Lodge and runs along the crest of a point of rocks that juts into the canyon for several hundred yards. The walk is only ½ mile round-trip, but it's an exciting trek accented by sheer drops on each side of the trail. In a few spots where the route is extremely narrow, metal railings ensure visitors' safety. The temptation to clamber out on precarious perches to have your picture taken should be resisted at all costs. ⊠ *North Rim Dr., Grand Canyon National Park* ✛ *Near Grand Canyon Lodge.*

Cape Royal

TRAIL | A popular sunset destination, Cape Royal showcases the canyon's jagged landscape; you'll also get a glimpse of the Colorado River, framed by a natural stone arch called Angels Window. In autumn, the aspens turn a beautiful gold, adding even more color to an already magnificent scene of the forested surroundings. The easy and rewarding 1-mile round-trip hike along **Cliff Springs Trail** starts here; it takes you through a forested ravine and terminates at Cliff Springs, where the forest opens to another impressive view of the canyon walls. ⊠ *Cape Royal Scenic Dr., Grand Canyon National Park* ✛ *23 miles southeast of Grand Canyon Lodge.*

Point Imperial

VIEWPOINT | At 8,803 feet, Point Imperial has the highest vista point at either rim; it offers magnificent views of both the canyon and the distant country: the Vermilion Cliffs to the north, the 10,000-foot Navajo Mountain to the northeast in Utah, the Painted Desert to the east, and the Little Colorado River canyon to the southeast. Other prominent points of interest include views of Mt. Hayden, Saddle Mountain, and Marble Canyon. ⊠ *Point Imperial Rd., Grand Canyon National Park* ✛ *11 miles northeast of Grand Canyon Lodge.*

★ Point Sublime

VIEWPOINT | You can camp within feet of the canyon's edge at this awe-inspiring site. Sunrises and sunsets are spectacular. The winding road, through gorgeous high country, is only 17 miles, but it will take you at least two hours one-way. The road is intended only for vehicles with high road clearance (pickups and four-wheel-drive vehicles). It is also necessary to be properly equipped for wilderness road travel. Check with a park ranger or at the information desk at Grand Canyon Lodge before taking this journey. You may camp here only with a permit from the Backcountry Information Center. ⊠ *North Rim Dr., Grand Canyon National Park* ✛ *About 20 miles west of North Rim Visitor Center.*

Roosevelt Point

VIEWPOINT | Named after the president who gave the Grand Canyon its national monument status in 1908 (it was upgraded to national park status in 1919), Roosevelt Point is the best place to see the confluence of the Little Colorado River and the Grand Canyon. The cliffs above the Colorado River south of the junction are known as the Palisades of the Desert. A short woodland loop trail leads to this eastern viewpoint. ⊠ *Cape Royal Rd., Grand Canyon National Park* ✛ *18 miles east of Grand Canyon Lodge.*

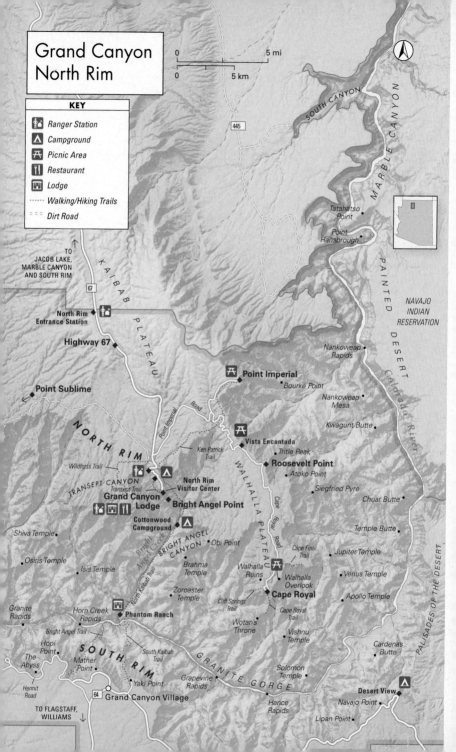

Flora and Fauna of the Grand Canyon

Eighty-nine mammal species inhabit Grand Canyon National Park, as well as 355 species of birds, 56 kinds of reptiles and amphibians, and 17 kinds of fish. The rare Kaibab squirrel is found only on the North Rim—you can recognize them by their all-white tails and black undersides. The pink Grand Canyon rattlesnake lives at lower elevations within the canyon. Hawks and ravens are visible year-round. The endangered California condor has been reintroduced to the canyon region. Park rangers give daily talks on the magnificent birds, whose wingspan measures 9 feet. In spring, summer, and fall, mule deer, recognizable by their large ears, and elk are abundant at the South Rim. Don't be fooled by gentle appearances; these guys can be aggressive. It's illegal to feed them, as it'll disrupt their natural habitats and increase your risk of getting bitten or kicked.

The best times to see wildlife are early in the morning and late in the afternoon. Look for out-of-place shapes and motions, keeping in mind that animals occupy all layers in a natural habitat and not just at your eye level. Use binoculars for close-up views. While out and about try to fade into the woodwork by keeping your movements limited and noise at a minimum.

More than 1,700 species of plants color the park. The South Rim's Coconino Plateau is fairly flat, at an elevation of about 7,000 feet, and covered with stands of piñon and ponderosa pines, junipers, and Gambel's oak trees. On the Kaibab Plateau on the North Rim, Douglas fir, spruce, quaking aspen, and more ponderosas prevail. In spring you're likely to see asters, sunflowers, and lupine in bloom at both rims.

Vista Encantada

VIEWPOINT | This point on the Walhalla Plateau offers views of the upper drainage of Nankoweap Creek, a rock pinnacle known as Brady Peak, and the Painted Desert to the east. This is an enchanting place for a picnic lunch. ⊠ *Cape Royal Rd., Grand Canyon National Park* ✛ *16 miles southeast of Grand Canyon Lodge.*

Walhalla Overlook

VIEWPOINT | One of the lowest elevations on the North Rim, this overlook has views of the Unkar Delta, a fertile region used by Ancestral Pueblo as farmland. These ancient people also gathered food and hunted game on the North Rim. A flat path leads to the remains of the Walhalla Glades Pueblo, which was inhabited from 1050 to 1150. ⊠ *Cape Royal Rd., Grand Canyon National Park* ✛ *22½ miles southeast of Grand Canyon Lodge.*

TRAILS

Cape Final Trail

TRAIL | This 4-mile (round-trip) gravel path follows an old jeep trail through a ponderosa pine forest to the canyon overlook at Cape Final with panoramic views of the northern canyon, the Palisades of the Desert, and the impressive spectacle of Juno Temple. *Easy.* ⊠ *Grand Canyon National Park* ✛ *Trailhead: dirt parking lot 5 miles south of Roosevelt Point on Cape Royal Rd.*

Ken Patrick Trail

TRAIL | This primitive trail, one of the longest on the North Rim, travels 10 miles one-way (allow six hours each way) from the trailhead at 8,250 feet to Point Imperial at 8,803 feet. It crosses drainages and occasionally detours around fallen trees. The end of the road, at Point Imperial, brings the highest views from either rim. Note that there is no water along this trail. *Difficult.* ⊠ *Grand Canyon National Park* ⊹ *Trailhead: east side of North Kaibab trailhead parking lot.*

North Kaibab Trail

TRAIL | At 8,241 feet, this trail leads into the canyon and down to Phantom Ranch. It is recommended for experienced hikers only, who should allow four days for the round-trip hike. The long, steep path drops 5,840 feet over a distance of 14½ miles to Phantom Ranch and the Colorado River, so the National Park Service suggests that day hikers not go farther than Roaring Springs (5,020 feet) before turning to hike back up out of the canyon. After about 7 miles, Cottonwood Campground (4,080 feet) has drinking water in summer, restrooms, shade trees, and a ranger. *Difficult.* ■TIP→ **A free shuttle takes hikers to the North Kaibab trailhead twice daily from Grand Canyon Lodge; reserve a spot the day before.** ⊠ *Grand Canyon National Park* ⊹ *Trailhead: about 2 miles north of Grand Canyon Lodge.*

Roosevelt Point Trail

TRAIL | FAMILY | This easy 0.2-mile round-trip trail loops through the forest to the scenic viewpoint. Allow 20 minutes for this relaxed, secluded hike. *Easy.* ⊠ *Grand Canyon National Park* ⊹ *Trailhead: Cape Royal Rd.*

Transept Trail

TRAIL | FAMILY | This 3-mile-round-trip, 1½-hour trail begins near the Grand Canyon Lodge at 8,255 feet. Well maintained and well marked, it has little elevation change, sticking near the rim before reaching a dramatic view of a large stream through Bright Angel Canyon. The trail leads to Transept Canyon, which geologist Clarence Dutton named in 1882, declaring it "far grander than Yosemite." Check the posted schedule to find a ranger talk along this trail; it's also a great place to view fall foliage. Flash floods can occur any time of the year, especially June through September when thunderstorms develop rapidly. *Easy.* ⊠ *Grand Canyon National Park* ⊹ *Trailhead: near Grand Canyon Lodge east patio.*

Uncle Jim Trail

TRAIL | This 5-mile, three-hour loop starts at 8,300 feet and winds south through the forest, past Roaring Springs and Bright Angel canyons. The highlight of this rim hike is Uncle Jim Point, which, at 8,244 feet, overlooks the upper sections of the North Kaibab Trail. *Moderate.* ⊠ *Grand Canyon National Park* ⊹ *Trailhead: North Kaibab Trail parking lot.*

Widforss Trail

TRAIL | Round-trip, Widforss Trail is 9.8 miles, with an elevation change of only 200 feet. Allow five to six hours for the hike, which starts at 8,080 feet and passes through shady forests of pine, spruce, fir, and aspen on its way to Widforss Point, at 7,900 feet. Here you'll have good views of five temples: Zoroaster, Brahma, and Deva to the southeast, and Buddha and Manu to the southwest. You are likely to see wildflowers in summer, and this is a good trail for viewing fall foliage. It's named in honor of artist Gunnar M. Widforss, renowned for his paintings of national park landscapes. *Moderate.* ⊠ *Grand Canyon National Park* ⊹ *Trailhead: off dirt road about 2 miles north of Grand Canyon Lodge.*

VISITOR CENTER

North Rim Visitor Center

View exhibits, peruse the bookstore, and pick up useful maps and brochures at this visitor center. Interpretive programs are often scheduled in summer. If you're craving refreshments, it's a short walk from here to the Roughrider Saloon at the Grand Canyon Lodge. ⊠ *Near Grand Canyon Lodge at North Rim, Grand Canyon National Park* ☎ *928/638–7864* ⊕ *www.nps.gov/grca.*

🍴 Restaurants

Deli in the Pines
$ | **AMERICAN** | Dining choices are limited on the North Rim, but this deli next to the lodge is your best bet for a meal on a budget or grabbing a premade sandwich on the go. Selections also include pizza (gluten-free or standard crust), salads, custom-made sandwiches, and soft-serve ice cream. **Known for:** convenient quick bite; sandwiches to take on the trail; outdoor seating. [$] *Average main: $9* ✉ *Grand Canyon Lodge, Bright Angel Point, North Rim* ☎ *928/638–2611* 🌐 *www.grandcanyonforever.com* 🕑 *Closed mid-Oct.–mid-May.*

★ **Grand Canyon Lodge Dining Room**
$$$ | **SOUTHWESTERN** | The high wood-beamed ceilings, stone walls, and spectacular views in this spacious, historic room are perhaps the biggest draw for the lodge's main restaurant. Dinner includes Southwestern steakhouse fare that would make any cowboy feel at home, including selections such as bison and elk. **Known for:** incredible views; charming, historic room; steaks, fish, game, and vegetarian selections. [$] *Average main: $25* ✉ *Grand Canyon Lodge, Bright Angel Point, North Rim* ☎ *928/638–2611* 🌐 *www.grandcanyonforever.com* 🕑 *Closed mid-Oct.–mid-May.*

🛏 Hotels

★ **Grand Canyon Lodge**
$$ | **HOTEL** | This historic property, constructed mainly in the 1920s and '30s, is the only lodging on the North Rim. The main building has locally quarried limestone walls and timbered ceilings. **Pros:** steps away from gorgeous North Rim views; close to several easy hiking trails; historic lodge building a national landmark. **Cons:** fills up fast; limited amenities; most cabins far from main lodge building. [$] *Rooms from: $146* ✉ *Hwy. 67, North Rim* ☎ *877/386–4383 reservations, 928/638–2611 May–Oct.* 🌐 *www.grandcanyonforever.com* 🕑 *Closed mid-Oct.–mid-May* 🛏 *218 rooms* 🍴 *No meals.*

Duffel Service: Lighten Your Load 🛏

Hikers staying at either Phantom Ranch or Bright Angel Campground can take advantage of the ranch's duffel service: bags or packs weighing 30 pounds or less can be transported to or from the ranch by mule for a fee of $81 each way. As is true for many desirable things at the canyon, reservations are a must. ☎ *303/297–2757* 🌐 *www.grandcanyonlodges.com.*

🏃 Activities

BIKING

Mountain bikers can test the many dirt access roads found in this remote area. The 17-mile trek to Point Sublime is, well, sublime; though you'll share this road with high-clearance vehicles, it's rare to spot other people on most of these primitive pathways.

Bicycles and leashed pets are allowed on the well-maintained 1.2-mile (one-way) **Bridle Trail,** which follows the road from Grand Canyon Lodge to the North Kaibab Trailhead. A 12-mile section of the **Arizona Trail** is also open to bicycles; it passes through pine forests within the park and continues north into Kaibab National Forest. Bikes are prohibited on all other national park trails.

CAMPING

North Rim Campground. The only designated campground at the North Rim of Grand Canyon National Park sits in a pine forest 3 miles north of the rim, and has 84 RV and tent sites (no hookups). Reserve in advance. ✉ *Hwy. 67, North Rim* ☎ *877/444–6777* 🌐 *www.recreation.gov.*

EDUCATIONAL PROGRAMS
Interpretive Ranger Programs
TOUR—SIGHT | Daily guided hikes and talks may focus on any aspect of the canyon—from geology and flora and fauna to history and the canyon's early inhabitants. Schedules are available online. ☎ 928/638–7967 ⊕ www.nps.gov/grca ⊠ Free.

Junior Ranger Program
TOUR—SIGHT | FAMILY | In summer, children ages four and up can take part in hands-on educational programs and earn a Junior Ranger certificate and badge. Sign up at the North Rim Visitor Center for these independent and ranger-led activities. ☎ 928/638–7967 ⊕ www.nps.gov/grca ⊠ Free.

HORSEBACK RIDING
Canyon Trail Rides
TOUR—SPORTS | FAMILY | This company leads mule rides along the easier trails of the North Rim. Options include one- and three-hour rides along the rim or a three-hour ride down into the canyon (minimum age 7 for one-hour rides, 10 for three-hour rides). The one-hour ride is $45, and the three-hour rides are $90. Weight limits are 200 pounds for canyon rides and 220 pounds for the rim rides. Available daily from May 15 to October 15, these excursions are popular, so make reservations in advance. ☎ 435/679–8665 ⊕ www.canyonrides.com ⊠ From $45.

Grand Canyon West

186 miles northwest of Williams, 70 miles north of Kingman.

The plateau-dwelling Hualapai ("people of the tall pines") acquired a larger chunk of traditional Pai lands with the creation of their reservation in 1883. Hualapai tribal lands include diverse habitats ranging from rolling grasslands to rugged canyons, and travel from elevations of 1,500 feet at the Colorado River to more than 7,300 feet at Aubrey Cliffs. In recent years, the Hualapai have been attempting to foster tourism on the West Rim—most notably with the spectacular Skywalk, a glass walkway suspended 70 feet over the edge of the canyon rim. Not hampered by the regulations in place at Grand Canyon National Park, Grand Canyon West offers helicopter flights down into the bottom of the canyon, horseback rides to rim viewpoints, ziplining, and rafting trips on the Colorado River.

The Hualapai Reservation encompasses a million acres in the Grand Canyon, along 108 miles of the Colorado River, with two main areas open to tourists. The West Rim has the Skywalk, Hualapai cultural exhibits and dancing, horseback riding, ziplining, and helicopter rides. Peach Springs, a two-hour drive from the West Rim on historic Route 66, is the tribal capital and the launch site for raft trips on this stretch of the river. Lodging is available both on the rim, at Hualapai Ranch, and in Peach Springs, at the Hualapai Lodge. Although increasingly popular, the West Rim is still relatively remote and visited by far fewer people than the South Rim—keep in mind that it's more than 120 miles away from the nearest interstate highways.

GETTING HERE AND AROUND
The West Rim is a five-hour drive from the South Rim of Grand Canyon National Park or a 2½-hour drive from Las Vegas. From Kingman, drive north 30 miles on U.S. 93, and then turn right onto Pierce Ferry Road and follow it for 28 miles. (A more scenic but slightly longer alternative is to drive 42 miles north on Stockton Hill Road, turning right onto Pierce Ferry Road for 7 miles.) Turn right (east) onto Diamond Bar Road and follow it for 21 miles to Grand Canyon West entrance.

Visitors aren't allowed to travel in their own vehicles to the viewpoints once they reach Grand Canyon West, and must purchase a tour package—which can range from day use to horseback or helicopter rides to lodging and meals—either online (⊕ *grandcanyonwest.com*) or in person from Hualapai Tourism.

TOURS

In addition to the exploring options provided by the Hualapai tribe, more than 30 tour and transportation companies service Grand Canyon West from Las Vegas, Phoenix, and Sedona by airplane, helicopter, coach, SUV, and Hummer. Perhaps the easiest way to visit the West Rim from Vegas is with a tour.

Bighorn Wild West Tours

GUIDED TOURS | This full-day tour takes you to Grand Canyon West in the comfort of a Hummer. Admission fees and lunch are included, as is a stop for photos at Hoover Dam. ☎ *702/385–4676* ⊕ *www. bighorntours.com* ✉ *From $277.*

VISITOR INFORMATION

CONTACTS Grand Canyon West.
☎ *888/868–9378, 928/769–2636* ⊕ *www. grandcanyonwest.com.*

Sights

SCENIC SPOTS

Grand Canyon Skywalk

VIEWPOINT | This cantilevered glass terrace is suspended nearly 4,000 feet above the Colorado River and extends 70 feet from the edge of the Grand Canyon. Approximately 10 feet wide, the bridge's deck, made of tempered glass several inches thick, has 5-foot glass railings on each side creating an unobstructed open-air platform. Admission to the skywalk is an add-on to the basic Grand Canyon West admission. Visitors must store personal items, including cameras, cell phones, and video cameras, in lockers before entering. A professional photographer takes photographs of visitors, which can be purchased from the gift shop. ⊕ *www. grandcanyonwest.com* ✉ *$20.*

Visiting Tribal Lands

When visiting Native American reservations, respect tribal laws and customs. Remember you're a guest in a sovereign nation. Don't wander into residential areas or take photographs of residents without first asking permission. Possessing or consuming alcohol is illegal on tribal lands. In general, the Hualapai and Havasupai are quiet, private people. Offer respect and don't pursue conversations or personal interactions unless invited to do so.

Grand Canyon West

CANYON | FAMILY | Grand Canyon West, run by the Hualapai tribe, offers a basic admission ticket ($80 per person, including taxes and fees), which includes a Hualapai visitation permit and hop-on, hop-off shuttle transportation to three sites. The shuttle will take you to Eagle Point, where you can tour authentic dwellings at the Indian Village and view educational displays on the culture of five different Native American tribes (Havasupai, Plains, Hopi, Hualapai, and Navajo). Intertribal dance performances entertain visitors at the nearby amphitheater. The shuttle also goes to Hualapai Ranch, site of ziplining, horseback rides, and the only lodging on the West Rim, and Guano Point, where the "High Point Hike" offers panoramic views of the Colorado River. At all three areas, local Hualapai guides add a Native American perspective.

For extra fees, you can add meals (there are cafés at each of the three stops), overnight lodging at Hualapai Ranch, a helicopter trip into the canyon, ziplining, a rafting trip on the Colorado, a horseback ride along the canyon rim, or a walk on the Grand Canyon Skywalk. ✉ *Grand Canyon West* ☎ *928/769–2636, 888/868–9378* ⊕ *www.grandcanyonwest.com* ✉ *$80.*

Hotels

Hualapai Lodge

$$$ | **HOTEL** | In Peach Springs on the longest stretch of the original historic Route 66, the hotel has clean, basic rooms and a comfortable lobby with a large fireplace that is welcoming on chilly nights. **Pros:** concierge desk arranges river trips with the Hualapai River Runners; good on-site restaurant with Native American dishes; Hualapai locals add a different perspective to the canyon experience. **Cons:** basic rooms lack historic charm; location off the beaten path. [$] *Rooms from: $199* ✉ *900 Rte. 66, Peach Springs* ☎ *928/769–2230, 888/868–9378* 🌐 *www.grandcanyonwest.com* 🛏 *60 rooms* 🍴 *Free breakfast.*

Hualapai Ranch

$$$ | **B&B/INN** | **FAMILY** | The only lodging on the West Rim, the comfortable cabins at Hualapai Ranch are clean and neat, but also small and unassuming. **Pros:** front porches with nice desert views; rustlers tell tall tales while you roast s'mores at the campfire; dining room and "saloon" serve all day long. **Cons:** no phones or TVs; no Internet; remote setting. [$] *Rooms from: $199* ✉ *Quartermaster Point Rd., Grand Canyon West* ☎ *928/769–2636, 888/868–9378* 🌐 *www.grandcanyonwest.com* 🛏 *26 cabins* 🍴 *Free breakfast.*

Activities

BOATING AND RAFTING

Hualapai River Runners

TOUR—SPORTS | One-, two- and five-day river trips are offered by the Hualapai Tribe through the Hualapai River Runners from mid-March through October. The trips leave from Peach Springs (a two-hour drive from the West Rim) and include rafting, hiking, and transport. Meals, snacks, and beverages are provided. Children must be at least 8 to take the one-day trip and 12 for the overnight trips; the rapids here are rated as Class III–VII, depending on the river flow. ✉ *5001 Buck N. Doe Rd., Peach Springs* ☎ *928/769–2636, 888/868–9378* 🌐 *www.grandcanyonwest.com* 🎫 *From $325.*

CAMPING

There's no camping on the West Rim, but you can pitch a tent at Diamond Creek near the Colorado River.

Diamond Creek. You can camp on the banks of the Colorado River, although this beach is a noisy launch point for river runners. You'll also need a four-wheel-drive vehicle to get here. The Hualapai permit camping on their tribal lands here, with an overnight camping permit of $27 per person per night, which can be purchased at the Hualapai Lodge. ☎ *928/769–2210, 888/255–9550* 🌐 *www.grandcanyonwest.com*

Nearby Towns

The northwest section of Arizona is geographically fascinating. In addition to the Grand Canyon, it's home to national forests, national monuments, and national recreation areas. Towns, however, are small and scattered. Many of them cater to visiting adventurers, and Native American reservations dot the map. Apart from Tusayan, located 2 miles from the South Rim, the closest town to the canyon's South Rim is Williams, the "Gateway to the Grand Canyon," 58 miles south.

The communities closest to the North Rim—all of them tiny and with limited services—include Fredonia, 76 miles north; Marble Canyon, 80 miles northeast; Lees Ferry, 85 miles east; and Jacob Lake, 45 miles north.

VISITOR INFORMATION

CONTACTS Kaibab National Forest, Tusayan Ranger District. ✉ *176 Lincoln Log Loop, Grand Canyon National Park* ☎ *928/638–2443* 🌐 *www.fs.usda.gov/kaibab.*

Tusayan

57 miles north of Williams, 2 miles south of Grand Canyon National Park.

The small hamlet of Tusayan, incorporated as a town only in 2010, is little more than a place to sleep and eat when visiting the Grand Canyon's South Rim. The main attractions here are an IMAX theater and visitor center, where you can see a film about the canyon and purchase tickets for air and jeep tours, and the Grand Canyon Airport, the takeoff point for plane and helicopter tours.

GETTING HERE AND AROUND

Tusayan's ¼-mile strip of hotels, eateries, and services sits right on Highway 64, the road leading into Grand Canyon National Park. Parking lots are plentiful.

Sights

Grand Canyon Visitor Center

INFO CENTER | Here you can get information about activities and tours, and buy a national park pass, which enables you to skip past some of the crowds and access the park by special entry lanes. Nevertheless, the biggest draw is the six-story IMAX screen that features the short movie *Grand Canyon: The Hidden Secrets.* You can learn about the geologic and natural history of the canyon, soar above stunning rock formations, and ride the rapids through the rocky gorge. The film is shown every hour on the half hour; the adjoining gift store is huge and well stocked. ⊠ *450 Hwy. 64/U.S. 180 ✛ 2 miles south of the Grand Canyon's south entrance* 🕾 *928/638–2468* ⊕ *explorethecanyon. com* 🖼 *$13 for IMAX movies.*

Restaurants

Canyon Star Steakhouse and Saloon

$$$ | **AMERICAN** | **FAMILY** | Relax in the rustic timber-and-stone dining room at the Grand Hotel for reliable if uninspired American food, with an emphasis on steaks and barbecue at dinner. Popular options include barbecue chicken and ribs, and Mexican fare. **Known for:** rollicking live music; better-than-average local dining; barbecue. $ *Average main: $26* ⊠ *Hwy. 64/U.S. 180* 🕾 *928/638–3333* ⊕ *www.grandcanyonlodges.com* ⊗ *No lunch.*

The Coronado Room

$$$ | **AMERICAN** | Inside the Best Western Grand Canyon Squire Inn is the most sophisticated cuisine in Tusayan. The menu includes well-prepared, hearty American food, with an emphasis on meat (steak, elk burgers, buffalo), plus grilled seafood, escargot, and oversize desserts. **Known for:** Tusayan's finest restaurant; splurge-worthy dining; splurge-worthy desserts. $ *Average main: $28* ⊠ *100 Hwy. 64/U.S. 180* 🕾 *928/638–2681* ⊕ *www.grandcanyonsquire.com* ⊗ *No lunch.*

🛏 Hotels

Best Western Grand Canyon Squire Inn

$$$$ | **HOTEL** | **FAMILY** | About 2 miles from the park's south entrance, this motel lacks the historic charm of the lodges at the canyon rim, but has more amenities, including pools, a bowling alley, a gym, a small cowboy museum, and one of the better restaurants in the region. **Pros:** cool pools in summer and a hot tub for cold winter nights; copious children's activities at the Family Fun Center; most rooms have refrigerators, microwaves, and coffeemakers. **Cons:** hall noise can be an issue with all of the in-hotel activities; very large (and bustling) property; rooms near pool can be especially noisy. $ *Rooms*

Continued on page 354

EXPLORING THE
COLORADO RIVER

High in Colorado's Rocky Mountains, the Colorado River begins as a catch-all for the snowmelt off the mountains west of the Continental Divide. By the time it reaches the Grand Canyon, the Colorado has been joined by multiple tributaries to become a raging river, red with silt as it sculpts spectacular landscapes. A network of dams can only partially tame this mighty river.

Snaking its way through five states, the Colorado River is an essential water source to the arid Southwest. Its natural course runs 1,450 miles from its origin in Colorado's La Poudre Pass Lake in Rocky Mountain National Park to its final destination in the Gulf of California, also called the Sea of Cortez. In northern Arizona, the Colorado River has been a powerful force in shaping the Grand Canyon, where it flows 4,000 to 6,000 feet below the rim. Beyond the canyon, the red river takes a lazy turn at the Arizona–Nevada border, where Hoover Dam creates the reservoir at Lake Mead. The Colorado continues at a relaxed pace along the Arizona–California border, providing energy and irrigation in Arizona, California, and Nevada before draining into northwestern Mexico.

A RIVER RUNS THROUGH IT

Stretching along 277 miles of the Colorado River is one of the seven natural wonders of the world: the Grand Canyon ranges in width from 4 to 18 miles, while the walls around it soar up to a mile high. Nearly 2 billion years of geologic history and majesty are revealed in exposed tiers of rock cut deep in the Colorado Plateau. What caused this incredible marvel of nature? Erosion by water coupled with driving wind are most likely the major culprits: under the sculpting power of wind and water, the shale layers eroded into slopes and the harder sandstone and limestone layers created terraced cliffs. Other forces that may have helped shape the canyon include ice, volcanic activity, continental drift, and earthquakes.

WHO LIVES HERE

Native tribes have lived in the canyon for thousands of years and continue to do so. The plateau-dwelling Hualapai ("people of the tall pines") live on a million acres along 108 miles of the Colorado River in the West Rim. The Havasupai ("people of the blue green water") live deep within the walls of the 12-mile-long Havasu Canyon—a major side canyon connected to the Grand Canyon.

ENVIRONMENTAL CONCERNS

When the Grand Canyon achieved national park status in 1919, only 44,173 people made the grueling overland trip to see it—quite a contrast from today's nearly 5 million annual visitors. The tremendous increase in visitation has greatly impacted the fragile ecosystems, as has Lake Powell's Glen Canyon Dam, which was constructed in the 1950s and '60s. The dam has changed the composition of the Colorado River, replacing warm water rich in sediments (nature's way of nourishing the riverbed and banks) with mostly cool, much clearer water. This has introduced non-native plants and animals that threaten the extinction of several native species. Air pollution has also affected visibility and the constant buzz of aerial tours has disturbed the natural solitude.

Above and right, views of Colorado River in the Grand Canyon from Toroweap.

Did You Know?

The North Rim's isolated Toroweap overlook (also called Tuweep) is perched 3,000 feet above the canyon floor: a height equal to stacking the Sears Tower and Empire State Building on top of each other.

RIVER RAFTING THROUGH THE GRAND CANYON

Viewing the Colorado River from a canyon overlook is one thing, but looking up at the canyon from the middle of the river is quite another experience. If you're ready to tackle the churning white water of the Colorado River as it rumbles and hisses its way through the Grand Canyon, take a look at this map of what you might encounter along the way.

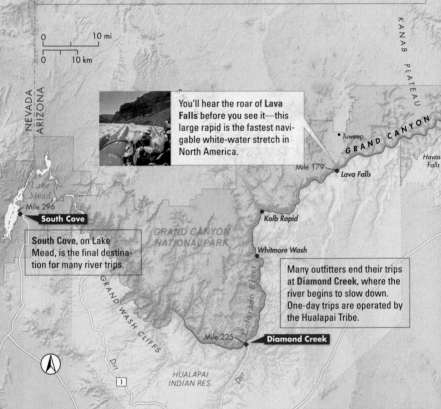

You'll hear the roar of **Lava Falls** before you see it—this large rapid is the fastest navigable white-water stretch in North America.

South Cove, on Lake Mead, is the final destination for many river trips.

Many outfitters end their trips at **Diamond Creek**, where the river begins to slow down. One-day trips are operated by the Hualapai Tribe.

COLORADO RIVER TRIPS

Time and Length	Entry and Exit points
1 day Float trip	Glen Canyon Dam to Lees Ferry (no rapids)
1 day Combo trip	Diamond Creek, then helicopter to West Rim
3–4 days	Lees Ferry to Phantom Ranch
6 days, 89 miles	Phantom Ranch to Diamond Creek
9–10 days, 136 miles	Lees Ferry to Diamond Creek
14–16 days, 225 miles	Lees Ferry to South Cove

*Trips either begin or end at Phantom Ranch/Bright Angel Beach at the bottom of the Grand Canyon, at river mile 87

Kanab

89

UTAH
ARIZONA

Lake
Powell

Glen Canyon Dam

*Direction of
Flow*

Page

89

PARIA CANYON

Lees Ferry

Mile 0

Marble Canyon

One–day float
trips (no white-
water) go
through beautiful
Glen Canyon.

VERMILION

ALT
89

CLIFFS

Bitter
Springs

*House Rock
Rapids*

MARBLE CANYON

ECHO CLIFFS

PLATEAU

89

Longer trips
begin at **Lees
Ferry**, a few
miles below the
Glen Canyon
Dam near Page.

⚠ You need to be very fit to
hike the arduous 7.8-mile
Bright Angel Trail, especially
if you choose to hike up when
departing from Phantom Ranch.

Colorado River

Deer Creek Falls

Great Thumb
Mesa

Bedrock Rapid

NORTH RIM

Point
Imperial

67

Mile 61

Phantom Ranch
allows you to begin
or end your trip
in between the
scenic North and
South Rims.

Fossil Rapid

Point
Sublime

Forester
Rapid

**Sapphire
Rapid**

Bright Angel
Point

Serpentine
Rapid

Mile 98

Crystal Rapid

Unkar Rapid

CANYON

HAVASUPAI
INDIAN RES.

Granite Rapid

Mile 87

Mather Pt

Bright
Angel
Trail

Grapevine Rapid

Grand Canyon
Village

*Hance
Rapid*

Desert View

64

Tusayan

Grandview
Point

Little Colorado River

If you begin at Phantom Ranch,
you will soon plunge through
the colossal waves of **Granite**
and **Crystal Rapids.**

Cameron

TO
FLAGSTAFF, ↓
49 Miles

COCONINO

PLATEAU

180

64

NOT JUST RAPIDS

Don't think that your experience will be
nonstop white-water adrenaline. Most of
the Colorado River features long, relaxing
stretches of water, where you drift amid
grandiose rock formations. You might
even spot a mountain goat or two. Multiday trips include camping on the shore.

PLANNING YOUR RIVER RAFTING TRIP

OAR, MOTOR, OR HYBRID?

Base the type of trip you choose on the amount of effort you want to put in. Motor rafts, which are the roomiest of the choices, cover the most miles in time and are the most comfortable. Guides do the rowing on oar boats and these smaller rafts offer a wilder ride. All-paddle trips are the most active and require the most involvement from guests. Hybrid trips are popular because they offer both the opportunity to paddle and to relax.

THE GEAR

Life jackets, beverages, tents, sheets, tarps, sleeping bags, dry bags, first aid, and food are provided—but you'll still need to plan ahead by packing clothing, hats, sunscreen, toiletries, and other sundries. Commercial outfitters allow each river runner two waterproof bags to store items during the day—just keep in mind that one of these will be filled up with the provided sleeping bag and tarp. ■TIP➜ **Bring a rain suit: summer thunderstorms are frequent and chilly.**

WHEN TO GO

Lots of people book trips for summer's peak period: June through August. If you're flexible, take advantage of the Arizona weather and go from May to early June or in September. ■TIP➜ **Seats fill up quickly; make reservations for multiday trips a year or two in advance.**

TRIP LENGTH

Rafting options on the Colorado River range from one-day trips at either the east or west end of the Grand Canyon to leisurely, two-week paddle trips through the full length of Grand Canyon National Park. If you're short on time, take a one-day trip near Grand Canyon West, where you'll run several rapids and fly back to the West Rim by helicopter. Another action-packed choice is to raft the river for 3 or 4 days, disembark at Phantom Ranch, then hike up to the Grand Canyon South Rim. "Full Canyon" rafting trips can take 9 to 16 days.

Above, Getting wet—and loving it—on an oar boat.

Did You Know?

As you're hanging on for dear life, consider this: Civil War veteran John Wesley Powell chartered these treacherous rapids in 1869—not only were conditions more dangerous then, but he had only one arm.

from: $269 ✉ 100 Hwy. 64/U.S. 180, Grand Canyon ☎ 928/638–2681, 800/622–6966 🌐 www.grandcanyonsquire.com 🛏 318 rooms 🍴 No meals.

The Grand Hotel

$$$$ | **HOTEL** | **FAMILY** | At the south end of Tusayan, this popular hotel has bright, clean, and contemporary rooms, a cozy stone-and-timber lobby, and free Wi-Fi. **Pros:** Western entertainment at restaurant; gift shop stocked with art, outdoor gear, and regional books; indoor pool and hot tub. **Cons:** somewhat generic property; on-site restaurant is uninspired and overpriced; indoor pool only. [$] *Rooms from: $272 ✉ 149 Hwy. 64/U.S. 180, Grand Canyon ☎ 928/638–3333, 888/634–7263 🌐 www.grandcanyonlodges.com 🛏 121 rooms 🍴 No meals.*

★ **Red Feather Lodge**

$$ | **HOTEL** | About 6 miles from the canyon, this clean, family-run lodge has a two-story motel building and a newer, three-story hotel building, both a good value. **Pros:** lower-priced than most lodging close to park; pet-friendly; pool and hot tub. **Cons:** stairs only in the two-story motel (the three-story hotel building has an elevator); motel rooms have showers (hotel rooms have shower/tubs); only two devices per room allowed on Wi-Fi at a time. [$] *Rooms from: $132 ✉ 300 Hwy. 64/U.S. 180 ☎ 928/638–2414, 800/538–2345 🌐 www.redfeatherlodge.com 🛏 216 rooms 🍴 No meals.*

Activities

Apache Stables

HORSEBACK RIDING | **FAMILY** | There's nothing like a horseback ride to immerse you in the Western experience. From stables near Tusayan, these folks offer gentle horses and a ride through the forest. Choose from one- and two-hour trail rides (March–October) or the popular campfire rides and horse-drawn wagon excursions (late May–early September). *✉ Forest Service Rd. 328 ✣ 1 mile north of Tusayan ☎ 928/638–2891 🌐 www.apachestables.com 🎫 From $59.*

Arizona Bike Trail

BICYCLING | Pedal the depths of the Kaibab National Forest on the Arizona Bike Trail–Tusayan Bike Trails System. Following linked loop trails at an elevation of 6,750 feet, you can bike as few as 3 miles or as many as 38 miles round-trip along old logging roads (some parts are paved) through ponderosa pine forest. Keep an eye out for elk, mule deer, hawks, eagles, pronghorn antelope, turkeys, coyote, and porcupines. Open for biking year-round (but most feasible March through October), the trail is accessed on the west side of Highway 64, a ½ mile north of Tusayan. *✉ Tusayan Ranger District ☎ 928/638–2443 🌐 www.fs.usda.gov/recarea/kaibab.*

Williams

The cozy mountain town of Williams, founded in 1882 when the railroad passed through, was once a rough-and-tumble joint, replete with saloons and bordellos. Today, it reflects a much milder side of the Wild West, with 3,300 residents and more than 25 motels and hotels. Wander along the main street—part of historic Route 66 but locally named, like the town, after trapper Bill Williams—and indulge in Route 66 nostalgia inside antiques shops or souvenir and T-shirt stores.

From Flagstaff, you can take Exit 165 to reach the historic downtown area. You'll end up on Railroad Avenue, the one-way westbound street. If you're coming from points west, take Exit 163, Grand Canyon Boulevard, into the heart of town. Most shops and restaurants are along Route 66 (also called Main Street) and Railroad Avenue, which runs parallel. The Williams Visitor Center is on the corner of Railroad Avenue and Grand Canyon Boulevard, and there's a free parking lot next to it. The Grand Canyon Railway Depot is across the tracks.

VISITOR INFORMATION **Williams Visitor Center.** ✉ *200 W. Railroad Ave., at Grand Canyon Blvd., Williams* ☎ *928/635–4061* 🌐 *experiencewilliams.com.*

🍴 Restaurants

Cruisers Café 66

$$ | **AMERICAN** | **FAMILY** | Patterned after a '50s-style high-school hangout (but with cocktail service), this diner pleases kids and adults with a large menu of family-priced American classics—good burgers and fries, barbecue pork sandwiches, salads, and ribs. A large mural of the town's heyday along the "Mother Road" and historic cars out front make this a Route 66 favorite. **Known for:** burgers and barbecue; nice patio; craft beers from local brewery. [$] *Average main: $16* ✉ *233 W. Rte. 66, Williams* ☎ *928/635–2445* 🌐 *www.cruisers66.com.*

★ **Red Raven Restaurant**

$$$ | **ECLECTIC** | This dapper bistro in the heart of downtown Williams, with warm lighting and romantic booth seating, blends American, Italian, and Asian ingredients into creative and delicious fare. Specialties include a starter of crisp tempura shrimp salad with a ginger-sesame dressing and mains like charbroiled salmon with basil butter over cranberry–pine nut couscous. **Known for:** upscale dining in Williams; good wine list; continental and Italian specialties. [$] *Average main: $27* ✉ *135 W. Rte. 66, Williams* ☎ *928/635–4980* 🌐 *www.redravenrestaurant.com* 🕐 *Closed Sun.–Tues.*

Twisters

$ | **AMERICAN** | **FAMILY** | Kick up some Route 66 nostalgia at this old-fashioned soda fountain, bar, and kitschy gift shop built in 1926. Dine on burgers and hot dogs, a famous Twisters sundae (topped with raspberry sauce, nuts, and hot fudge), Route 66 beer float, or cherry phosphate—all to the sounds of '50s tunes. **Known for:** ice cream novelties; retro decor and above-average gift shop; burgers and brews. [$] *Average main: $9* ✉ *417 E. Rte. 66, Williams* ☎ *928/635–0266* 🌐 *www.route66place.com* 🕐 *Closed Sun. Closed Jan. and Feb.*

🛏 Hotels

Canyon Motel and RV Park

$ | **HOTEL** | **FAMILY** | Sleep in a historic railcar or a stone cottage from a 1938 motor lodge at this 13-acre property at the forest's edge on the outskirts of Williams. **Pros:** family-friendly property with train cars, horseshoes, playground, and indoor swimming pool; general store; friendly and helpful owners. **Cons:** short drive to restaurants and shops; RV-park traffic; rate for train car rooms much higher. [$] *Rooms from: $107* ✉ *1900 E. Rodeo Rd., Rte. 66, Williams* ☎ *928/635–9371* 🌐 *www.thecanyonmotel.com* 🔑 *23 units* 🍽 *No meals.*

Grand Canyon Railway Hotel

$$$$ | **HOTEL** | **FAMILY** | Designed to resemble the train depot's original Fray Marcos Hotel, this upscale place features attractive Southwestern-style accommodations with large bathrooms and comfy beds with upscale linens. **Pros:** railway package options and convenience; indoor pool and outdoor playground; short walk from historic downtown restaurants and bars. **Cons:** large-scale property; pricey for these parts; pets must be boarded at on-site kennel. [$] *Rooms from: $269* ✉ *233 N. Grand Canyon Blvd., Williams* ☎ *928/635–4010, 800/843–8724* 🌐 *www.thetrain.com* 🔑 *298 rooms* 🍽 *No meals.*

The Red Garter

$$ | **B&B/INN** | This restored saloon and bordello from 1897 now houses a small, antiques-filled B&B. **Pros:** on-site coffeehouse and café; decorated in antiques and period pieces; steps from several restaurants and bars. **Cons:** all rooms are accessible only by stairs; parking is across the street; no children

under eight. [$] *Rooms from: $165* ✉ *137 Railroad Ave., Williams* ☎ *928/635–1484, 800/328–1484* 🌐 *www.redgarter.com* 🛏 *4 rooms* 🍴 *No meals.*

Sheridan House Inn

$$$ | **B&B/INN** | Nestled among 2 acres of pine trees a ½ mile uphill from Route 66, this upscale B&B has decks with good views and a flagstone patio with a hot tub. **Pros:** quiet location; scrumptious breakfasts; warm, helpful hosts. **Cons:** must drive to downtown Williams, where parking is scarce; no children under 16; some rooms are upstairs (no elevator). [$] *Rooms from: $185* ✉ *460 E. Sheridan Ave., Williams* ☎ *928/814–2809* 🌐 *www.sheridanhouseinn.com* 🛏 *8 rooms* 🍴 *Free breakfast.*

GRAND TETON NATIONAL PARK

Updated by
Andrew Collins

WYOMING

⛰ Camping
★★★★★

🛏 Hotels
★★★★★

🏃 Activities
★★★★☆

👁 Scenery
★★★★★

👥 Crowds
★★★★☆

WELCOME TO
GRAND TETON NATIONAL PARK

TOP REASONS TO GO

★ **Heavenward hikes:** Trek where grizzled frontiersmen roamed. Jackson Hole got its name from mountain man Davey Jackson; now there are hundreds of trails for you to explore.

★ **Wildlife big and small:** Keep an eye out for little fellows like short-tailed weasels and beaver, as well as bison, elk, moose, wolves, and both black and grizzly bears.

★ **Waves to make:** Float the Snake River or take a canoe, kayak, or stand-up paddleboard onto Jackson Lake or Jenny Lake.

★ **Homesteader history:** Visit the 1890s barns and ranch buildings of Mormon Row or Menor's Ferry.

★ **Cycling paradise:** Safely pedal your way to and through Grand Teton on miles of pathways and rural roads.

★ **Trout trophies:** Grab your rod and slither over to the Snake River, where cutthroat trout are an angler's delight.

1 Moose. Anchoring the southern end of the park, Moose is home to the Craig Thomas Discovery and Visitor Center, Dornan's lodgings and other services, the Menor's Ferry and Mormon Row historic districts, and Laurance S. Rockefeller Preserve. Grand Teton's nearest section to Jackson and Jackson Hole Ski Resort is laced with bike paths and both gentle and rigorous hiking trails, with mountain peaks looming on the west side and sagebrush-covered open range to the east, across the Snake River and around Antelope Flats.

2 Jenny Lake. The Teton Range reflects in this small (1,191-acre) but spectacular lake in the middle of the park that has visitor services on its developed east shore and pristine trails on its west shore—you can take a boat ride across the lake or hike entirely around it.

3 Jackson Lake. Most adventures in the northern end of the park revolve around this large alpine lake, which offers several lodging and dining options as well as marinas where you can launch or rent boats. The Snake River passes through the north end of the lake and back out to the south through Jackson Lake Dam around Oxbow Bend, a famously scenic spot for watching wildlife.

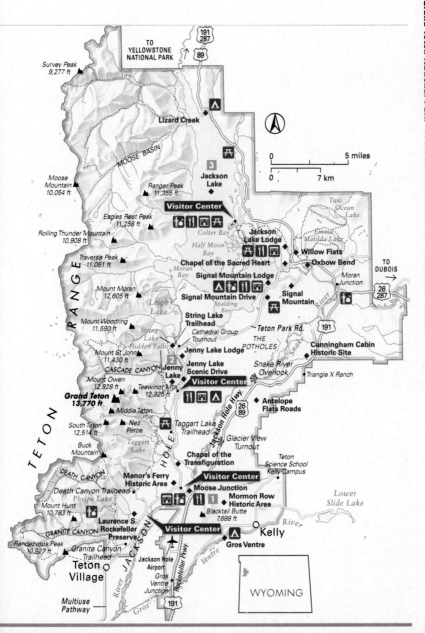

The Teton Range—dominated by the 13,770-foot Grand Teton—rises more than a mile above Jackson Hole's valley floor, with unimpeded views of its magnificent, jagged, snowcapped peaks. Mountain glaciers creep down 12,605-foot Mt. Moran, and large and small piedmont lakes gleam along the range's base. Many of the West's animals—elk, bears, bald eagles—call this park home.

First-time visitors to Grand Teton sometimes underestimate all there is to see and do here, visiting the park briefly as a detour from either its northern neighbor, Yellowstone National Park—which is seven times larger—or its southern neighbor, Jackson, a swanky year-round resort town famous for skiing and snowboarding in winter and a host of activities in summer. But it's well worth budgeting at least two or three days to fully grasp the wonder of Grand Teton National Park. With a mix of bustling recreation areas and utterly secluded wilderness, this 485-square-mile park appeals equally to active adventurers and contemplative serenity seekers.

The region's harsh winters and challenging terrain helped keep it free of permanent development until relatively recently. Nomadic indigenous groups traversed the area's meadows and streams from the end of the Pleistocene Ice Age for some 11,000 years, and early fur trappers—including the valley's namesake, Davey Jackson—began making inroads throughout the early 19th century. But the region's first year-round

ranching settlements in what would become the town of Jackson didn't occur until 1894. It wasn't long before wealthy "dudes" from the eastern United States began paying gobs of money to stay at these sprawling, scenic compounds, and thus was born the concept of the modern "dude ranch."

Jackson Hole and the Tetons began to develop at breakneck speed by the 1920s, drawing the interest of conservationists, too, including industrialist John D. Rockefeller, who toured the region in 1926 with the Superintendent of nearby Yellowstone National Park, Horace Albright. Although many locals recoiled at the thought of federal intervention, Rockefeller and other preservationists led a successful campaign for congress to establish Grand Teton National Park in 1929. Over the next 20 years, Franklin D. Roosevelt set aside additional land through the establishment of Jackson Hole National Monument, and Rockefeller donated another 35,000 acres of land that he'd steadily amassed to the federal government. All of these holdings were combined into the current Grand Teton

AVERAGE HIGH/LOW TEMPERATURES					
JAN.	**FEB.**	**MAR.**	**APR.**	**MAY**	**JUNE**
28/5	33/8	43/17	53/24	63/31	74/37
JULY	**AUG.**	**SEPT.**	**OCT.**	**NOV.**	**DEC.**
82/41	81/39	71/31	59/23	40/16	28/6

National Park in 1950. Throughout the park's evolution, Rockefeller also helped to spur its commercial and recreational development by establishing Jenny Lake and Jackson Lake lodges, along with smaller compounds of cabins and campgrounds throughout the park. And in 2001, his son donated the family's last piece of land in the area, 1,106-acre Laurance S. Rockefeller Preserve.

Although it receives the most recognition for its hulking mountain peaks, this is as much a park of scenic bodies of water and sweeping wildlife-rich meadows as it is an alpine destination. Boating, fishing, and lakeside camping are every bit as popular as hiking and climbing in the peaks, and photographers flock here from all over the world for the chance to see rare birds, lumbering moose and elk, and formidable wolves and black and grizzly bears. Some of the best terrain in the park can be accessed from well-maintained park roads and relatively short trails, but opportunities for rugged treks through miles of pristine backcountry also abound. Grand Teton offers splendid activities for a range of abilities and interests.

Planning

When to Go

In July and August all the roads, trails, and visitor centers are open, and the Snake River's float season is in full swing. You can expect smaller crowds and often lower rates in spring and fall, but some services and roads are limited.

Grand Teton Lodge Company, the park's major concessionaire, winds down its activities in late September, and most of Teton Park Road closes from November through April (U.S. 26/191/89 stays open all winter). In spring and fall, Teton Park Road is open to pedestrians, cyclists, and in-line skaters; in winter, it's transformed into a cross-country ski trail.

The towns south of the park rev up in winter. Teton Village and Jackson both buzz with the energy of Snow King Resort and Jackson Hole Mountain Resort. Prices rise for the peak winter season.

FESTIVALS AND EVENTS

ElkFest. Begun in 1967, this popular two-day festival is held the third weekend in May. Its centerpiece is the Elk Antler Auction, when thousands of pounds of naturally shed antlers are sold to the highest bidder. Get a taste of the High Noon Chili Cookoff, and enjoy the spectacle of khaki-clad lads hauling around massive racks. ⊕ *www.elkfest.org.*

Fall Arts Festival. More than 50 events celebrate art, music, food, and wine throughout Jackson Hole during this 11-day annual festival in mid-September. ⊕ *www.jacksonholechamber.com.*

Grand Teton Music Festival. Since 1962, these summer symphony concerts have been wowing audiences in the world-renowned Walk Festival Hall in Teton Village. The festival presents full orchestra concerts as smaller ensembles. ⊕ *www.gtmf.org.*

Grand Teton in One Day

Pack a picnic lunch and make your way to **Craig Thomas Discovery and Visitor Center** for a 9 am, two-hour, guided Snake River scenic float trip (book with one of the half-dozen outfitters that offer the trip). When you're back on dry ground, drive north on Teton Park Road, stopping at scenic turnouts—don't miss Teton Glacier—until you reach the Jenny Lake ranger station. Take the 20-minute boat ride to the **west shore boat dock** for a short but breathtaking hike to **Hidden Falls** and **Inspiration Point**. Return to your car by mid-afternoon, and follow Teton Park Road, detouring on Signal Mountain Road to the summit, where you can catch an elevated view of the Tetons.

Return to Teton Park Road and continue north, turning east at Jackson Lake Junction to **Oxbow Bend** or north to **Willow Flats**, both excellent spots for wildlife viewing before you backtrack to **Jackson Lake Lodge** for dinner and an evening watching the sun set over the Tetons. Or if you'd like to get back on the water, drive to **Colter Bay Village Marina**, where you can board a 1½-hour sunset cruise across Jackson Lake to Elk Island. You can reverse this route if you're heading south from Yellowstone: start the day with a breakfast cruise from Colter Bay and end it with a sunset float down the Snake River.

Getting Here and Around

AIR

Five major airlines offer service to Jackson Hole Airport (JAC), the only commercial airport inside a national park (it was established before the park opened).

CAR

Jackson Hole's main highway (U.S. 89/191) runs the length of the park, from Jackson to Yellowstone National Park's south entrance. This highway also joins with U.S. 26 south of Moran Junction and U.S. 287 north of Moran Junction. This road is open all year from Jackson to Moran Junction and north to Flagg Ranch, 2 miles south of Yellowstone. From Jackson, it's about 20-minutes to the park's southern (Moose) entrance. Coming from the north, it's about a 10-minute drive to the park's northern boundary.

Two scenic back-road entrances to Grand Teton are closed by snow from November through mid-May and can be heavily

rutted through June. Moose-Wilson Road (Hwy. 390) starts at Highway 22 in Wilson and travels 7 miles north past Teton Village to the Granite Canyon entrance station. Of the 9 miles from here to Moose, 1½ are gravel and can be a little bumpy; high-clearance vehicles are best, but you can manage this route with a regular passenger car if you take it slow. This route is closed to large trucks, trailers, and RVs. Even rougher is 60-mile Grassy Lake Road, which heads east from Highway 32 in Ashton, Idaho, through Targhee National Forest. It connects with the John D. Rockefeller, Jr. Memorial Parkway span of U.S. 89/191/287, between Grand Teton and Yellowstone.

Inspiration

A Field Guide to Yellowstone and Grand Teton National Parks, by Kurt F. Johnson, provides a comprehensive compilation of the flora and fauna of the greater Yellowstone area, including more than 1,200 color photographs.

Robert W. Righter's *Peaks, Politics, and Passion: Grand Teton National Park Comes of Age* gives the fascinating back-story behind the park's evolution since its establishment in 1950.

In Rising from the Plains, Pulitzer Prize–winning author John McPhee examines the geology of the Rocky Mountains and Wyoming through the personal history of a geologist and his family.

Windows into the Earth: The Geologic Story of Yellowstone and Grand Teton National Parks, by Robert B. Smith and Lee J. Siegel, is the best book on the market for nonspecialists hoping to grasp Teton and Yellowstone geology.

Park Essentials

ACCESSIBILITY

The frontcountry portions of Grand Teton are largely accessible to people using wheelchairs. There's designated parking at most sites, and some interpretive trails and campgrounds are easily accessible. There are accessible restrooms at visitor centers. The visitor centers also distribute an *Accessibility* brochure, which you can download from the park website.

PARK FEES AND PERMITS

Park entrance costs $35 for autos; $30 for motorcycles; and $20 per person on foot or bicycle, good for seven days in Grand Teton. The winter day-use fee is $15.

PARK HOURS

The park is open 24/7 year-round. It's in the Mountain time zone.

CELL PHONE RECEPTION

Cell phones work in most developed areas and occasionally on trails, especially at higher elevations in the park's frontcountry.

Hotels

For a park its size, Grand Teton has a tremendous variety of lodging options, from simple campgrounds, cabins, and standard motel rooms to fancier (and quite pricey) suites in historic lodges. Nearby Jackson has plenty of additional options, but rates can be steep for what you get in this upscale resort town, especially in summer and during winter ski season—if visiting during these busy times, try to book several weeks in advance in Jackson, and several months ahead for lodgings in the park. *Hotel reviews have been shortened. For full information, visit Fodors.com.*

What It Costs			
$	$$	$$$	$$$$
RESTAURANTS			
under $16	$16–$22	$22–$30	over $30
HOTELS			
under $150	$151–$225	$226–$300	over $300

Restaurants

Though the park itself has some decent, and in some cases quite good, restaurants, nearby Jackson is one of the top small towns in the Rockies when it comes to creative cooking—restaurants in both the park and Jackson are especially strong on local game, fowl, and fish dishes, and it's easier and easier to find tasty, often seasonal, vegetarian fare, too. Steaks are usually cut from grass-fed Wyoming or Montana beef, but you'll also find buffalo and elk on many menus. Rocky Mountain trout and Pacific salmon are also common. Down-home comfort fare and hearty all-American breakfasts are the norm at most casual eateries, although a handful of excellent international restaurants, mostly specializing in

Asian and Latin American cooking, are now getting notice around Jackson Hole, as are craft breweries, artisan bakeries and coffeehouses, and wine bars. Casual is the word for most dining within and outside the park, the exception being where jackets and ties for men are appreciated. *Restaurant reviews have been shortened. For full information, visit Fodors.com.*

Tours

Grand Teton Lodge Company Bus Tours

BUS TOURS | FAMILY | Half-day tours depart from Jackson Lake Lodge and include visits to scenic viewpoints, visitor centers, and other park sites. Guides provide information about park geology, history, wildlife, and ecosystems. Full-day tours continue into Yellowstone. ⊠ *Grand Teton National Park* ☎ *307/543–3100* ⊕ *www.gtlc.com* ⊒ *From $90.*

Jackson Hole Wildlife Safaris

GUIDED TOURS | Run by a staff of world-class photographers, this Jackson company offers half-, full-, and multiday tours in summer and winter that bring guests to some of the best places in Grand Teton to view elk, bison, big-horn sheep, coyotes, foxes, and other wildlife that thrives in the park. Tours to Yellowstone are offered, too. ⊠ *Jackson* ☎ *307/690–6402* ⊕ *www.jacksonholewildlifesafaris. com* ⊒ *Tours from $275.*

★ Jackson Lake Cruises

BOAT TOURS | FAMILY | Grand Teton Lodge Company runs 1½-hour Jackson Lake cruises from Colter Bay Village Marina throughout the day, as well as breakfast, lunch, and dinner cruises. Guides explain how forest fires and glaciers have shaped the Grand Teton landscape. ⊠ *Grand Teton National Park* ☎ *307/543–3100* ⊕ *www.gtlc.com* ⊒ *From $40.*

Teton Science School

SPECIAL-INTEREST | FAMILY | The school conducts guided wildlife expeditions in Grand Teton, Yellowstone, and surrounding forests—participants see and learn about wolves, bears, bighorn sheep, and other animals. Full-day and half-day excursions are offered, as well as custom trips. The bear and wolf expedition is a thrilling three-day, two-night field adventure during spring and fall. ⊠ *700 Coyote Canyon Rd., Jackson* ☎ *307/733–1313* ⊕ *www. tetonscience.org* ⊒ *Tours from $165.*

★ Teton Wagon Train and Horse Adventures

ADVENTURE TOURS | FAMILY | Unforgettable four- and seven-day covered wagon rides and horseback trips follow Grassy Lake Road on the "back side" of the Tetons. You can combine the trip with a river trip and a tour of Yellowstone and Grand Teton. ⊠ *Jackson* ☎ *307/734–6101, 888/734–6101* ⊕ *www.tetonwagontrain. com* ⊒ *From $1,095.*

Visitor Information

CONTACTS **Grand Teton National Park.** ☎ *307/739–3300* ⊕ *www.nps.gov/grte.* **Jackson Hole and Greater Yellowstone Visitor Center.** ⊠ *532 N. Cache St., Jackson* ☎ *307/733–3316* ⊕ *www.fws.gov.*

Moose

13 miles north of Jackson, 65 miles south of Yellowstone's Grant Village.

Most visitors to Grand Teton spend a good bit of time, and often begin their adventures, in and around Moose, which is the hub for exploring the southern end of the park (nearest to Jackson). The striking, contemporary Craig Thomas and Laurance S. Rockefeller Preserve visitor centers are excellent places to learn about the park's natural history and conservation efforts, and there's easy and more challenging hiking near both. Also near Moose is Dornan's service complex, with dining, lodging, gas, and a market.

Sights

HISTORIC SITES

Chapel of the Transfiguration
RELIGIOUS SITE | This tiny chapel built in 1925 on land donated by Maud Noble is still a functioning Episcopal church. Couples come here to exchange vows with the Tetons as a backdrop, and tourists snap photos of the small church with its awe-inspiring view. ⊠ *End of Menors Ferry Rd., ½ mile off Teton Park Rd., Moose* ☎ *307/733–2603* ⊕ *www.stjohns-jackson.org/chapel-of-the-transfiguration* ⊗ *Closed Sept.–late May.*

Menor's Ferry Historic Area
HISTORIC SITE | FAMILY | Down a path from the Chapel of the Transfiguration, the ferry on display here is not the original, but it's an accurate re-creation of the double-pontoon craft built by Bill Menor in 1894. That was how people crossed the Snake River before bridges were installed. While the replica ferry is no longer in operation, it's fun to see. In the cluster of turn-of-the-20th-century buildings there are displays on historical transportation methods. Pick up a pamphlet for a self-guided tour. ⊠ *End of Menors Ferry Rd.* ✛ *¼ mile off Teton Park Rd.*

Mormon Row Historic Area
HISTORIC SITE | Settled by homesteaders between 1896 and 1907, this area received its name because many of them were members of the Church of Jesus Christ of Latter-day Saints, also known as Mormons. The remaining barns, homes, and outbuildings are representative of early homesteading in the West. You can wander around, hike the row, and take photographs. The century-old T.A. Moulton Barn is said to be the most-photographed barn in the state. ⊠ *Grand Teton National Park* ✛ *Off Antelope Flats Rd., 2 miles north of Moose Junction.*

Murie Ranch
HISTORIC SITE | FAMILY | Set on a former 1930s dude ranch, this complex of historic log buildings is sometimes credited as being the home of America's conservation movement—the work of its former owners, the Muries, led to passage of the 1964 Wilderness Act. You can hike the grounds and view interpretive signs on an easy 1-mile round-trip stroll from the nearby Craig Thomas Discovery and Visitor Center. Part of the property is used as a satellite campus of the superb Teton Science School, which offers conservation and educational programs about the park. ⊠ *Moose* ✛ *Trailhead: Craig Thomas Discovery and Visitor Center.*

SCENIC DRIVES

Antelope Flats Road
SCENIC DRIVE | Off U.S. 191/26/89, about 2 miles north of Moose Junction, this narrow road wanders eastward over sagebrush flats, intersecting with the gravel lane to the Mormon Row Historic District. Less than 2 miles past here is a three-way intersection where you can turn right to loop around past the tiny hamlet of Kelly and Gros Ventre campground and rejoin the main highway at Gros Ventre Junction. Keep an eye out for abundant and swift pronghorn, along with bison, foxes, raptors, and more than a few cyclists. ⊠ *Grand Teton National Park* ⊗ *Closed winter.*

SCENIC STOPS

Laurance S. Rockefeller Preserve
NATURE PRESERVE | FAMILY | This immense 1,106-acre preserve devoted to conversation includes miles of trails. You can access it via the Valley Trail, 1¾ miles north of the Granite Canyon trailhead and ½ mile south of the Death Canyon turnoff. Hikers can admire the Phelps Lake shoreline from a loop trail beginning at the preserve's sleek, contemporary interpretive center, or climb a ridgeline with beautiful views of aspens, wildflowers, and regional birds. ⊠ *Off Moose-Wilson Rd.*

Plants and Wildlife in Grand Teton

Grand Teton's short growing season and arid climate create a complex ecosystem and hardy plant species. The dominant elements are big sagebrush—which gives the valley its gray-green cast—lodgepole pine trees, quaking aspen, and ground-covering wildflowers such as bluish-purple lupine.

Short Growing Season
In spring and early summer you will see the vibrant yellow arrowleaf balsamroot and low larkspur. Jackson Hole's short growing season gives rise to spectacular if short-lived displays of wildflowers, best seen between mid-June and early July. The changing of the aspen, willow, black hawthorn, and cottonwood leaves in early fall can be equally dazzling.

Oft and Rarely Seen Wildlife
On almost any trip to Grand Teton, you'll likely see bison, pronghorn antelope, and moose. More rarely you will see a black or grizzly bear, a fox, or a wolf. Watch for elk along the forest edge, and, in the summer, on Teton Park Road. Oxbow Bend and Willow Flats are good places to look for moose, beaver, muskrats, and otter in twilight hours any time of year. Pronghorn and bison appear in summer along the highway and Antelope Flats Road.

Smaller Animals
The park's smaller animals—yellow-bellied marmots, pikas, and Uinta ground squirrels, as well as a variety of birds and waterfowl—are commonly seen along park trails and waterways. Seek out water sources—the Snake River, the glacial lakes, and marshy areas—to see birds such as bald eagles, ospreys, Northern harriers, American kestrels, great blue herons, ducks, and trumpeter swans. Your best chance to see wildlife is at dawn or dusk.

TRAILS

Death Canyon Trail
TRAIL | This 7.9-mile round-trip trail to the junction with Static Peak Trail climbs some 2,100 feet, with lots of hills to traverse, a great view of Phelps Lake, and a final 1,061-foot climb up to a patrol cabin into this verdant glacial canyon. Give yourself about six hours to manage this rugged adventure. *Difficult.* ⊠ *Grand Teton National Park* ⊹ *Trailhead: end of White-grass Ranch Rd., off Moose-Wilson Rd.*

Lake Creek–Woodland Trail Loop
TRAIL | This relaxing, mostly level ramble alongside Lake Creek leads through a verdant forest to the southern shore of Phelps Lake, where you're rewarded with grand views up into Death Canyon. *Easy.* ⊠ *Moose* ⊹ *Trailhead: Laurence S. Rockefeller Preserve Center.*

★ Phelps Lake Overlook and Loop Trail
TRAIL | The quickest way to view this stunning lake, this 2-mile round-trip Phelps Lake Overlook Trail takes you from the Death Canyon trailhead up conifer- and aspen-lined glacial moraine to a view that's accessible only on foot. Expect abundant bird life: Western tanagers, northern flickers, and ruby-crowned kinglets thrive in the bordering woods, and hummingbirds feed on scarlet gilia beneath the overlook. From here, if you're up for a longer, enjoyable adventure, continue along the steep trail down to the north shore of the lake, where you can pick up the Phelps Loop Trail and follow it around the lake or all the way to Rockefeller Preserve. Hiking just to the overlook and back takes just over an hour, but allow four to five hours

if continuing on to the Phelps Loop Trail. *Moderate–Difficult.* ✉ *Grand Teton National Park* ✣ *Trailhead: End of Whitegrass Ranch Rd., off Moose-Wilson Rd.*

Taggart Lake Trail

TRAIL | Hike 1½ miles from the trailhead to the lake and then, optionally, you can extend your trek by continuing on a 4-mile route around the lake where the terrain becomes steeper near Beaver Creek, or making the 5-mile loop trail around Bradley Lake, just to the north. There are views of Avalanche Canyon and areas where you might see moose. Allow an hour to get to the lake and back and another two to three hours to make it around one or both lakes. *Moderate.* ✉ *Grand Teton National Park* ✣ *Trailhead: Teton Park Rd., 4.8 miles south of Jenny Lake Visitor Center.*

VISITOR CENTERS

Craig Thomas Discovery and Visitor Center

INFO CENTER | This strikingly designed contemporary building contains interactive and interpretive exhibits dedicated to themes of preservation, mountaineering, and local wildlife. There's also a 3-D map of the park and streaming video along a footpath showing the area's intricate natural features. Dozens of Native American artifacts from the David T. Vernon Collection are housed here. A plush, 155-seat theater shows a nature documentary every half hour. ✉ *Teton Park Rd., Moose* ☎ *307/739–3399* 🌐 *www.nps.gov/grte* 🕒 *Closed Nov.–late Mar.*

★ **Laurance S. Rockefeller Preserve Center**

INFO CENTER | **FAMILY** | This contemporary structure feels more like an art gallery than an interpretive facility. The elegant, eco-friendly building is more than just eye candy—you can experience the sounds of the park in a cylindrical audio chamber, and laminated maps in the reading room are great for trip planning, Rangers here promote "contemplative hiking" and are well informed about the many birds around the center's trailheads. It's best to get here in the early morning or late evening because the small parking area fills quickly. A ranger leads a hike to the lake every morning. ✉ *End of LSR Preserve Entrance Rd.* ☎ *307/739–3300* 🌐 *www.nps.gov/grte* 🕒 *Closed late Sept.–May.*

🍴 Restaurants

Dornan's Pizza & Pasta Company

$$ | **PIZZA** | Simple but hearty pizzas and pastas are the draw here, but you'll also find generous margaritas, a diverse wine list, and occasional live music. Place your order at the front counter, then head to a table inside, on the side deck, or upstairs on the roof, which has stunning mountain views. **Known for:** well-priced food; great wine shop next door (and no corkage fee); spectacular mountain views. [$] *Average main: $17* ✉ *12170 Dornan's Rd.* ☎ *307/733–2415* 🌐 *www.dornans.com.*

🛏 Hotels

★ **Dornan's Spur Ranch Cabins**

$$$ | **RENTAL** | **FAMILY** | The lodging component of Dornan's shopping, dining, and recreation development in Moose, at the south end of the park, offers one- and two-bedroom cabins with fully stocked kitchens and great views of meadows, the peaks of the Tetons, or the Snake River. **Pros:** simple, clean cabins with good Wi-Fi; great for families; you may see wildlife out your window. **Cons:** not much privacy; rustic interiors not for everyone; no pets. [$] *Rooms from: $275* ✉ *12170 Dornan's Rd., Moose* ☎ *307/733–2415* 🌐 *www.dornans.com* 🕒 *Closed Nov. and Apr.* 🔑 *12 cabins* 🍽 *No meals.*

Jenny Lake

7 miles north of Moose, 12 miles south-west of Jackson Lake Junction.

Framed to the west by Teton's magnificent peaks, Jenny Lake is one of the most picturesque—and indeed photographed—bodies of water in the Rockies. It's also the main developed area in the park's mid-section, home to a luxurious and historic lodge as well as a visitor center and ranger station, and a very popular campground. From the lake's eastern shore, you can access miles of hiking trails into the mountains across the lake, either by taking the short boat ride to the western shore or hiking there via the trail the encircles the lake. Trails also lead nearby to similarly stunning but undeveloped Leigh Lake, which is popular for paddle-sports enthusiasts and hikers.

Sights

PICNIC AREAS

Jenny Lake

LOCAL INTEREST | Shaded and pine-scented, this picnic site adjacent to the Jenny Lake shuttle boat dock is a good place to have lunch before catching a shuttle boat across the lake for some hiking. ⊠ *Grand Teton National Park* ✛ *Near Jenny Lake Visitor Center.*

SCENIC DRIVES

★ Jenny Lake Scenic Drive

SCENIC DRIVE | This 4-mile, one-way loop provides the park's best roadside close-ups of the Tetons and the eastern shore of Jenny Lake as it winds south through groves of lodgepole pine and open meadows. Roughly 1½ miles off Teton Park Road, the Cathedral Group Turnout faces 13,770-foot Grand Teton (the range's highest peak), flanked by 12,928-foot Mt. Owen and 12,325-foot Mt. Teewinot. ⊠ *Jenny Lake.*

TRAILS

★ Cascade Canyon–Hidden Falls–Inspiration Point Trail

TRAIL | FAMILY | Take Jenny Lake Boating's 20-minute boat ride or the 2¼-mile (each way) Jenny Loop Trail around the south side of the lake from the Jenny Lake Visitor Center to the start of a gentle, ½-mile climb to 200-foot Hidden Falls, the park's most popular (though crowded) hiking destination. Listen for the distinctive bleating of the rabbitlike pikas among the glacial boulders and pines. The trail continues half a mile to Inspiration Point over a moderately steep, rocky path with sweeping lake views. From here, continue west another 1½ miles into the heart of Cascade Canyon, with its dramatic views through the mountains and out toward Petersen Glacier. With the 10-minute boat shuttle ($18 round-trip), plan on a couple of hours to experience this trail—add another two hours if you hike the whole way, which is your only option from October through mid-May, when the shuttle doesn't run. *Easy–Moderate.* ⊠ *Grand Teton National Park* ✛ *Trailhead: Jenny Lake Visitor Center* ⊕ *www.jennylakeboating.com.*

Jenny Lake Loop Trail

TRAIL | FAMILY | You can walk to Hidden Falls from Jenny Lake Visitor Center by following the mostly level trail around the south shore of the lake to Cascade Canyon Trail. Jenny Lake Trail continues around the lake for a total of 6½ miles. It's an easily managed though somewhat long trail hike if you circumnavigate the whole lake—allow three hours, not counting any forays into Cascade Canyon on the west side of the lake. You'll walk through a lodgepole-pine forest, have expansive views of the lake and the land to the east, and hug the shoulder of the massive Teton range itself. Along the way you may see elk, foxes, pikas, golden-mantled ground squirrels, and a variety of ducks and water birds. *Moderate.* ⊠ *Grand Teton National Park* ✛ *Trailhead: Jenny Lake Visitor Center.*

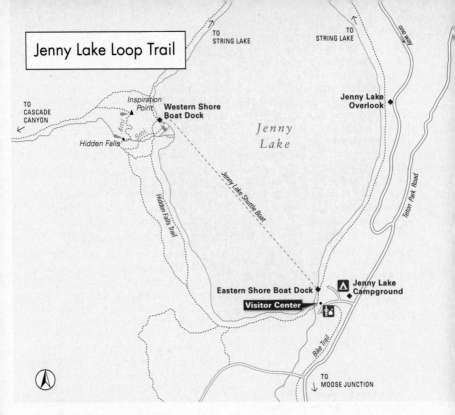

Jenny Lake Loop Trail

TO STRING LAKE

TO STRING LAKE

One Way

Inspiration Point

TO CASCADE CANYON

Western Shore Boat Dock

Jenny Lake Overlook

Hidden Falls

4mi

5mi

Jenny Lake

Hidden Falls Trail

Jenny Lake Shuttle Boat

Teton Park Road

Eastern Shore Boat Dock

Jenny Lake Campground

Visitor Center

Bike Trail

TO MOOSE JUNCTION

★ Leigh Lake Trail

TRAIL | This flat trail follows String Lake's northeastern shore to Leigh Lake's southern shore, covering 2 miles in a round-trip of about an hour. You can extend your hike into a moderate 7½-mile, four-hour round-trip by following the forested east shore of Leigh Lake to tiny but pretty Bearpaw Lake. Along the way you'll have views of Mt. Moran across the lake, and you may be lucky enough to spot a moose or a bear. Another option from Leigh Lake's southern shore is the 13-mile round-trip hike into Paintbrush Canyon to Holly Lake. *Moderate.* ⊠ *Grand Teton National Park* ⊹ *Trailhead: String Lake Picnic Area.*

String Lake Trail

TRAIL | The 3½-mile loop around String Lake lies in the shadows of 11,144-foot Rockchuck Peak and 11,430-foot Mt. Saint John. This is also a good place to see moose and elk, hear songbirds, and view wildflowers. The hike, which takes about three hours, is a bit less crowded than others in the vicinity. *Easy–Moderate.* ⊠ *Grand Teton National Park* ⊹ *Trailhead: off Jenny Lake Rd.*

Surprise and Amphitheater Lake Trails

TRAIL | A little more than 10 miles round-trip, this rigorous all-day hike starts at Lupine Meadows and switches back through steep pines and flowered meadows to Surprise Lake and the regal Amphitheater Lake, tucked away in an expansive rock basin. The trail weaves out for views of the sprawling valley, while Disappointment Peak looms above. Get to the trail early and allow at six to eight hours to tackle the 3,000-foot gain. *Difficult.* ⊠ *Jenny Lake* ⊹ *Trailhead: Lupine Meadows Trailhead.*

VISITOR CENTER

★ Jenny Lake Visitor Center and Ranger Station

INFO CENTER | Located steps from one another inside historic 1920s cabins by the Jenny Lake parking area, trailhead, and shuttle boat dock, these two ranger-staffed information centers serve different functions. The visitor center is inside a building that was once used as a studio by the park's first official park photographer, Harrison Crandall. Today it's filled with exhibits on the history of art and artists in the park. It also contains a bookstore and information about daily ranger programs. The smaller ranger station occupies a 1925 cabin that once held the park's first museum and is now a one-stop for backcountry and mountaineering advice and permits as well as boat permits. ✉ *Off Teton Park Rd., Jenny Lake* ☎ *307/739–3392* 🌐 *www.nps.gov/grte* 🕓 *Closed early Sept.–late May.*

🍴 Restaurants

★ Jenny Lake Lodge Dining Room

$$$$ | **MODERN AMERICAN** | Elegant yet rustic, Grand Teton's finest dining space is highly ambitious for a national park restaurant. For dinner, the prix-fixe, five-course menu features locally sourced ingredients and an inventive, thoughtfully assembled wine list. **Known for:** jackets encouraged for men and reservations a must; regional meats and fish, like bison, bass, and duck; lovely mountain views. [$] *Average main: $98* ✉ *Jenny Lake Rd.* ☎ *307/543–3100* 🌐 *www.gtlc.com* 🕓 *Closed early Oct.–May.*

🛏 Hotels

★ Jenny Lake Lodge

$$$$ | **RESORT** | This 1920s lodge resort, the most expensive and arguably the most elegant in any national park, is nestled off the scenic Jenny Lake Loop Road and bordering a wildflower meadow. **Pros:** ultracushy digs in a pristine setting; easy stroll from Jenny Lake trails; homey touches, like hand-made furniture and quilts. **Cons:** very expensive; not suitable for kids; often booked up months in advance. [$] *Rooms from: $555* ✉ *Jenny Lake Rd.* ☎ *307/543–3100* 🌐 *www.gtlc.com* 🕓 *Closed early Oct.–May* 🛏 *37 cabins* 🍽 *No meals.*

Jackson Lake

24 miles north of Moose, 45 miles south of Yellowstone's Grant Village.

The biggest of Grand Teton's glacier-carved lakes (it's more than 22 times the size of equally famous Jenny Lake), this body of water in the park's northern reaches was enlarged by the 1906 construction of the Jackson Lake Dam, an impressive structure that you can view from Teton Park Road just south of Jackson Lake Junction. You can fish, sail, and water ski here—three marinas (Colter Bay, Leeks, and Signal Mountain) provide access for boaters. Several picnic areas, campgrounds, and lodges overlook the lake, and vista points like Oxbow Bend, the summit of Signal Mountain, and Willow Flats are excellent places to take in the park's geological and wildlife scenery.

👁 Sights

HISTORIC SITES

Cunningham Cabin Historic Site

HISTORIC SITE | At the end of a gravel spur road, an easy ¾-mile trail runs through sagebrush around Pierce Cunningham's low-slung 1888 log-cabin homestead. Although you can peer inside, the building has no furnishings or displays. Watch for badgers, coyotes, and Uinta ground squirrels in the area. ✉ *Antelope Flats* ✢ *½ mile off U.S. 26/89/191, 5 miles south of Moran Junction.*

PICNIC AREAS

★ Colter Bay

LOCAL INTEREST | This big picnic area, spectacularly located right on the beach at Jackson Lake, gets crowded in July and August but is lovely nonetheless. It's close to flush toilets and stores. ⊠ *Grand Teton National Park* ✛ *Just north of Colter Bay Visitor Center.*

SCENIC DRIVES

Signal Mountain Summit

SCENIC DRIVE | **FAMILY** | This popular 4-mile drive climbs 700 feet along a winding forest road that offers glimpses of Jackson Lake and Mt. Moran. At the top, park and follow the well-marked path to one of the park's best panoramas. From 7,593 feet above sea level your gaze can sweep over all of Jackson Hole and the 40-mile Teton Range. The views are particularly dramatic at sunset. The road is not appropriate for long trailers and is closed in winter. ⊠ *Off Teton Park Rd.* ☉ *Closed Nov.–May.*

SCENIC STOPS

Chapel of the Sacred Heart

RELIGIOUS SITE | This small log Catholic chapel sits in the pine forest with a view of Jackson Lake. It's open only for services, but you can enjoy the view anytime, and the grounds are nice for a picnic. ⊠ *Grand Teton National Park* ✛ *Off Teton Park Rd., ¼ mile east of Signal Mountain Lodge* ☎ ⊕ *www.olmcatholic. org* ☉ *Closed Oct.–June.*

★ Oxbow Bend

VIEWPOINT | This peaceful spot overlooks a quiet backwater left by the Snake River when it cut a new southern channel. White pelicans stop here on their spring migration (many stay on through summer), sandhill cranes and trumpeter swans visit frequently, osprey nest nearby, and great blue herons nest amid the cottonwoods along the river. Use binoculars to search for bald eagles, moose, beaver, and otter. The Oxbow is known for the reflection of Mt. Moran that marks its calm waters in early morning. ⊠ *Grand Teton National Park* ✛ *U.S. 89/191/287, 2½ miles east of Jackson Lake Junction.*

Willow Flats

NATURE PRESERVE | You'll often see moose grazing in this marshy area, in part because of its flourishing willow bushes, where moose both eat and hide. Elk also graze here, and you'll occasionally see grizzly bears and wolves pursue their calves at the start of summer. This is also a good place to see birds and waterfowl, and the short Lunch Tree Hill Trail heads from the overlook parking area past beaver ponds to some vibrant bird-watching terrain. ⊠ *Grand Teton National Park* ✛ *U.S. 89/191/287, 1 mile north of Jackson Lake Junction.*

TRAILS

★ Colter Bay Lakeshore Trail

TRAIL | **FAMILY** | This easy, wonderfully picturesque 1¾-mile round-trip excursion treats you to views of Jackson Lake and the Tetons. As you follow the level trail along the rocky shore and forest's edge, you may see moose and bald eagles. Allow two hours to complete the walk. *Easy.* ⊠ *Grand Teton National Park* ✛ *Trailhead: on the beach just north of Colter Bay Visitor Center.*

Grand View Point Trail

TRAIL | Give yourself about four hours, which allows time for relaxing and soaking up dramatic views of back toward Jackson Lake and the Teton Range, to complete this moderately challenging 5.6-mile round-trip trek that starts at Jackson Lake Lodge. The trail curves around tiny Christian Pond and along the western shore of the much larger Emma Matilda Lake before climbing nearly 1,000 feet in elevation to this lovely viewpoint. ⊠ *Moran* ✛ *Trailhead: Jackson Lake Lodge.*

VISITOR CENTERS

Colter Bay Visitor Center

INFO CENTER | At this useful center near the shore of Jackson Lake, a small display shows off items from the park's collection of Native American artifacts. (Hundreds more are being conserved and stored for future displays.) In summer, rangers lead daily hikes from here. Nightly ranger talks on various topics are also offered. ✉ *Colter Bay Marina Rd., Colter Bay* ☎ *307/739–3594* 🌐 *www.nps.gov/grte* 🕒 *Closed early Oct.–mid-May.*

Flagg Ranch Information Station

INFO CENTER | This small seasonal visitor center with exhibits on John D. Rockefeller and the region's natural history is the first place you'll come to if driving south from Yellowstone. It's in the same village as Headwaters Lodge, along with a convenience store, restaurant, and gas station. ✉ *100 Grassy Lakes Rd., Moran* ✣ *20 miles north of Jackson Lake Lodge* ☎ *307/543–2372* 🌐 *www.nps.gov/grte* 🕒 *Closed early Sept.–early June.*

🍴 Restaurants

Cafe Court Pizzeria

$ | **AMERICAN** | **FAMILY** | Quick and cheap is the name of the game at this no-frills cafeteria at Colter Bay Village. The menu features pizzas, salads, and toasted subs. **Known for:** big, simple meals to eat in or take out; pizza offered by the slice or whole pie; closes later than many other options. [$] *Average main: $11* ✉ *Colter Bay Village Rd.* ☎ *307/543–2811* 🌐 *www.gtlc.com* 🕒 *Closed late Sept.–late May.*

Jackson Lake Lodge Mural Room

$$$$ | **AMERICAN** | One of the park's most picturesque restaurants gets its name from a 700-square-foot mural painted by the Western artist Carl Roters that details a Wyoming mountain man rendezvous. The menu showcases lavishly presented American fare, such as chilled prawns with a bloody Mary vinaigrette, seared King salmon with toasted-almond couscous, and grilled elk rib eye with a cherry compote. **Known for:** sumptuous mountain views; upscale lunches, dinners, and buffet breakfasts; regional favorites like bison, elk, and trout. [$] *Average main: $35* ✉ *100 Jackson Lake Lodge Rd.* ☎ *307/543–2811* 🌐 *www.gtlc.com* 🕒 *Closed early Oct.–mid-May.*

★ **Peaks Restaurant**

$$$ | **MODERN AMERICAN** | At Signal Mountain Lodge, this casual Western-style bistro offers up delectable fish and meat dishes, as well as views of Jackson Lake and the Tetons. The Trapper Grill next door also serves lunch, the adjacent Deadman's Bar is a fun spot for nachos and huckleberry margaritas, and about 10 miles north, the same concessionaire operates the popular Leek's Pizzeria, overlooking the marina of the same name. **Known for:** menu focuses on seasonal, regional ingredients; among the park's more reasonably priced restaurants; nice lake views. [$] *Average main: $27* ✉ *Signal Mountain Lodge Rd.* ☎ *307/543–2831* 🌐 *www.signalmountainlodge.com* 🕒 *Closed mid-Oct.–mid-May.*

Pioneer Grill at Jackson Lake Lodge

$$ | **AMERICAN** | With an old-fashioned soda fountain, friendly service, and seats along a winding counter, this eatery recalls a 1950s-era luncheonette. Tuck into Cobb salads, apple-cheddar burgers, banana splits, and other classic American fare. **Known for:** quick, reasonably priced food; seating is along a 200-foot-long counter; huckleberry pancakes and milkshakes. [$] *Average main: $17* ✉ *100 Jackson Lake Lodge Rd.* ☎ *307/543–2811* 🌐 *www.gtlc.com* 🕒 *Closed early Oct.–mid-May.*

Ranch House at Colter Bay Village

$$ | **AMERICAN** | The casual Ranch House offers friendly service and moderate prices, making it a good choice for travelers on a budget or families who can't take another cafeteria meal. Western-style meals—pulled pork sandwiches, smoked spare ribs, rotisserie chicken—dominate

the menu. **Known for:** traditional barbecue fare; hearty pasta dishes; gluten-free, vegetarian, and vegan. Ⓢ *Average main: $20 ✉ Colter Bay Village Rd., Colter Bay* ☎ *307/543–2811* ⊕ *www.gtlc.com* ⊗ *Closed late Sept.–late May.*

🛏 Hotels

Colter Bay Village

$$$ | HOTEL | FAMILY | A stroll from Jackson Lake, this cluster of Western-style one- and two-room cabins is close to trails, dining options, a visitor center, and plenty of other activities. **Pros:** good value; many nearby facilities; close to lake and hiking trails. **Cons:** not much privacy; no TVs or phones, and unreliable Wi-Fi; rustic feel won't appeal to everyone. Ⓢ *Rooms from: $200 ✉ Colter Bay Village Rd., Colter Bay* ☎ *307/543–3100* ⊕ *www.gtlc. com* ⊗ *Closed late Sept.–late May* ⌐ *232 cabins* 🍽 *No meals.*

Headwaters Lodge & Cabins at Flagg Ranch

$$$ | HOTEL | Set along the scenic connecting road between the north boundary of Grand Teton and the South Entrance of Yellowstone, this secluded compound offers both upscale cabins with patios, handcrafted furniture, and private baths, and less-expensive rustic camping cabins that share a common bathhouse with the campground and RV park. **Pros:** good base between Grand Teton and Yellowstone; tranquil setting; mix of upscale and budget accommodations. **Cons:** no Wi-Fi; limited dining options; remote location. Ⓢ *Rooms from: $248 ✉ 100 Grassy Lake Rd., Moran* ☎ *307/543–2861* ⊕ *www.gtlc.com* ⊗ *Closed Oct.–May* ⌐ *92 rooms* 🍽 *No meals.*

★ Jackson Lake Lodge

$$$$ | HOTEL | This sprawling resort with its distinctive mid-century modern features was designed by renowned architect Gilbert Stanley Underwood and stands on a bluff with spectacular views across Jackson Lake to the Tetons. **Pros:** in center

of Grand Teton; heated outdoor pool; great restaurants. **Cons:** some rooms don't have great views; very pricey; spotty Wi-Fi. Ⓢ *Rooms from: $346 ✉ 100 Jackson Lake Lodge Rd.* ☎ *307/543–3100* ⊕ *www.gtlc.com* ⊗ *Closed early Oct.– mid-May* ⌐ *385 rooms* 🍽 *No meals.*

★ Signal Mountain Lodge

$$$ | HOTEL | The main building of this lodge on Jackson Lake's southern shoreline has a cozy lounge and a grand pine deck overlooking the lake; stay in a traditional lodge room or a rustic cabin, some with sleek kitchens. **Pros:** excellent restaurants and bar; great lakefront location; some rooms have fireplaces. **Cons:** rustic, simple decor; not all rooms have water views; lakefront rooms are expensive. Ⓢ *Rooms from: $287 ✉ Signal Mountain Lodge Rd.* ☎ *307/543– 2831* ⊕ *www.signalmountainlodge. com* ⊗ *Closed mid-Oct.–mid-May* ⌐ *79 rooms* 🍽 *No meals.*

Activities

BIKING

Since the first paved pathways were completed in Jackson Hole in 1996, the valley has become a cyclist's paradise. Almost 60 miles of paved pathways thread through Jackson Hole, with more in the works. Those on two wheels can access Grand Teton on a path that begins at the north end of town and travels 21 miles to South Jenny Lake Junction. A bike lane permits two-way bike traffic along the one-way Jenny Lake Loop Road, a one-hour ride. The River Road, 4 miles north of Moose, is an easy four-hour mountain-bike ride along a ridge above the Snake River on a gravel road. Bicycles are not allowed on trails or in the backcountry.

Hoback Sports

BICYCLING | FAMILY | Get your own bike tuned up or rent one: road, mountain, hybrid, kids', and trailers. The shop also sells bikes, clothing, and mountain sporting accessories, as well as ski rentals and other winter-sports equipment. ✉ *520 W. Broadway, Suite 3, Jackson* ☎ *307/733–5335* ⊕ *www.hobacksports.com.*

Teton Mountain Bike Tours

BICYCLING | Mountain bikers of all skill levels can take this company's guided half-, full-, or multiday tours into Grand Teton and Yellowstone national parks, as well as winter tours of Jackson Hole on snow bikes with fat, studded tires. The outfit also rents bikes. ✉ *545 N. Cache St., Jackson* ☎ *307/733–0712* ⊕ *www.tetonmtbike.com* ✍ *Tours from $80.*

BIRD-WATCHING

With more than 300 species of birds, the Tetons make excellent bird-watching country. Here you might spot both the calliope hummingbird (the smallest North American hummingbird) and the trumpeter swan (the world's largest waterfowl). Birds of prey circle around Antelope Flats Road—the surrounding fields are good hunting turf for red-tailed hawks and prairie falcons, and Oxbow Bend, which draws white pelicans during their spring northerly migration along with bald eagles and great blue herons. At Taggart Lake and Phelps Lake you might see woodpeckers, bluebirds, and hummingbirds. Look for songbirds, such as pine and evening grosbeaks and Cassin's finches, in surrounding open pine and aspen forests.

BOATING

Water sports in Grand Teton are diverse. You can float the Snake River, which runs high and fast early in the season (May and June) and more slowly in late summer. Canoes, kayaks, and stand-up paddleboards (SUPs) dominate the smaller lakes and share the water with motorboats on large Jackson Lake and smaller Jenny Lake (which has an engine limit of 10 horsepower). You can launch your boat at Colter Bay, Leek's Marina, Signal Mountain, and Spalding Bay on Jackson Lake and at the launch on the south shore of Jenny Lake, just off Lupine Meadows Road.

Before launching on any of the state's waters, including those in the park, you must purchase a seasonal permit ($40 for motorized boats, $12 for nonmotorized, including SUPs), available year-round at Craig Thomas and Colter Bay visitor centers, where you can also check with rangers about current conditions. You also must go through an AIS (Aquatic Invasive Species) inspection, which costs $30 for motorized boats and $15 for nonmotorized; the nearest inspection sites are at the Moose and Moran park entrance stations.

Additionally, many guided float trips are offered on calm-water sections of the Snake; outfitters pick you up at the float-trip parking area near Craig Thomas Discovery and Visitor Center for a 15-minute drive to upriver launch sites. Ponchos and life preservers are provided. Early morning and evening floats are your best bets for wildlife viewing. Be sure to carry a jacket or sweater. Float season runs from mid-April to mid-October.

★ Barker-Ewing Scenic Float Trips

BOATING | FAMILY | Float along a peaceful 10-mile stretch of the Snake River within the park and look for wildlife as knowledgeable guides talk about area history, geology, plants, and animals. Private custom trips can also be arranged. ✉ *Moose* ☎ *307/733–1800, 800/365–1800* ⊕ *www.barkerewing.com* ✍ *From $80.*

★ Colter Bay Village Marina

BOATING | FAMILY | You can rent motorboats, kayaks, and canoes at Colter Bay from Grand Teton Lodge Company. Guided fishing trips are also available. ✉ *Colter Bay Village Rd.* ✛ *Off U.S. 89/191/287* ☎ *307/543–3100* ⊕ *www.gtlc.com.*

Dave Hansen Whitewater & Scenic Trips

WHITE-WATER RAFTING | Going strong since 1967, this highly respected outfit offers both rip-roaring white-water trips down class II–III Snake River rapids and more relaxing floats on calmer stretches. ⊠ *Jackson* ☎ *307/733–6295* ⊕ *www. davehansenwhitewater.com* ☞ *From $87.*

Leek's Marina

BOATING | At this Signal Mountain Lodge–operated marina on the northern end of Jackson Lake, there are boat rentals, nightly buoys, an excellent pizza restaurant, and parking for boat trailers and other vehicles for up to three nights. ⊠ *U.S. 89/191/287, 6 miles north of Jackson Lake Junction* ☎ *307/543–2831* ⊕ *www. signalmountainlodge.com.*

★ National Park Float Trips

BOATING | FAMILY | The knowledgeable and charismatic Triangle X guides will row you down 10 miles of the Snake River through pristine riparian habitat in Grand Teton National Park. For the best wildlife viewing, book a dawn or evening dinner float. ⊠ *Moose* ☎ *307/733–5500* ⊕ *nationalparkfloattrips.com* ☎ *From $82.*

★ Rendezvous River Sports

BOATING | FAMILY | However you'd like to hit the water, the river rats at Rendezvous are here to help. They offer instruction for stand-up paddleboarding and kayaking, as well as guided trips on area rivers and lakes. Or you could choose a backcountry adventure in the national parks. The shop rents kayaks, canoes, rafts, and paddleboards. ⊠ *945 W. Broadway, Jackson* ☎ *307/733–2471* ⊕ *www. jacksonholekayak.com* ☎ *From $205.*

Signal Mountain Lodge Marina

BOATING | This Jackson Lake marina rents pontoon boats, deck cruisers, motorboats, kayaks, and canoes by the hour or all day. ⊠ *Signal Mountain Lodge Rd.* ☎ *307/543–2831* ⊕ *www.signalmountainlodge.com.*

CAMPING

You'll find a variety of campgrounds, from small areas where only tents are allowed (starting from $11 nightly) to full RV parks with all services (from $64 nightly for full hookups). If you have a sleeping bag but no tent, you can take advantage of the tent cabins at Colter Bay and Headwaters Campground at Flagg Ranch. Standard campsites include a place to pitch your tent or park your trailer/camper, a fire pit for cooking, and a picnic table. All developed campgrounds have toilets and water; plan to bring your own firewood. Check in at National Park Service campsites as early as possible—sites are assigned on a first-come, first-served basis.

Colter Bay Campground and RV Park. Big, busy, noisy, and filled by noon, this centrally located campground has tent and trailer or RV sites. ☎ *307/543–2811 for tent campground, 307/543–3100 for RV Park.*

Gros Ventre. The park's second biggest campground is set in an open, grassy area on the bank of the Gros Ventre River, away from the mountains but not far from the village of Kelly, on park's southeastern edge. ☎ *307/734–4431.*

Headwaters Campground at Flagg Ranch. In a shady pine grove overlooking the headwaters of the Snake River, these sites set just north of the park border along John D. Rockefeller, Jr. Memorial Parkway provide a great base for exploring Grand Teton or Yellowstone. The showers and laundry facilities are a bonus, and camper cabins are available. ☎ *307/543–2861.*

Jenny Lake. Wooded sites and Teton views make this tent-only spot the most desirable campground in the park, and it fills early. ☎ *307/543–3390.*

Lizard Creek. Views of Jackson Lake's north end, wooded sites, and the relative isolation of this campground make it a relaxing choice. ☎ *307/543–2831.*

Signal Mountain. This campground in a hilly setting on Jackson Lake has boat access to the lake. ☎ *307/543–2831.*

You can reserve a backcountry campsite between early January and mid-May for a $45 nonrefundable fee using the online reservation system. Two-thirds of all sites are set aside for in-person, walk-in permits, so you can also take a chance on securing a site when you arrive. Obtain walk-in permits, which cost $35, from Craig Thomas Visitor and Discovery Center or Jenny Lake Ranger Station, where you can also pick up a park-required bear-proof food storage canister (these are lent out for free). The Jackson Hole Mountain Resort aerial tram provides quick access to the park's backcountry, which can also be reached on foot from various trailheads. ⊕ *www. nps.gov/grte/planyourvisit/bcres.htm.*

CLIMBING

The Teton Range has some of the nation's most diverse mountaineering. Excellent rock, snow, and ice routes abound. Unless you're already a pro, it's recommended that you take a course from one of the park's concessionaire climbing schools before tackling the tough terrain. Practice your moves at Teton Boulder Park, a free outdoor artificial climbing wall in Phil Baux Park at the base of Snow King Mountain.

Exum Mountain Guides

CLIMBING/MOUNTAINEERING | FAMILY | The climbing experiences offered by the oldest guide service in North America include one-day mountain climbs, shorter and easier adventures geared toward beginners, weeklong clinics culminating in a two-day ascent of the Grand Teton, and backcountry adventures on skis and snowboards. ⊠ *Grand Teton National Park* ☎ *307/733–2297* ⊕ *www.exumguides. com* 🎿 *From $180.*

EDUCATIONAL PROGRAMS

Check visitor centers and the park newspaper for locations and times of the park's many ranger programs.

Campfire Programs

TOUR—SIGHT | FAMILY | In summer, park rangers give free slide-show presentations, usually at Colter Bay. ⊠ *Grand Teton National Park* ⊕ *www.nps.gov/grte.*

Junior Ranger Program

TOUR—SIGHT | FAMILY | Children and even adults can earn a Junior Ranger badge or patch by picking up a Junior Ranger booklet at any park visitor center. ⊠ *Grand Teton National Park* ⊕ *www.nps. gov/grte.*

Nature Explorer's Backpack Program

INFO CENTER | FAMILY | Rangers at the Laurance S. Rockefeller Preserve Center lend a nature journal and a backpack full of activities to children ages 6 –12 before sending them out along the trails at the Rockefeller Preserve. ⊠ *Grand Teton National Park* ☎ *307/739–3654.*

FISHING

Rainbow, brook, lake, and native cutthroat trout inhabit the park's waters. The Snake's 75 miles of river and tributary are world-renowned for their fishing. To fish in the park, you need a Wyoming fishing license, which you can purchase from the state game and fish department or at Colter Bay Village Marina, Dornan's, Signal Mountain Lodge, and area sporting-goods stores. A day permit for nonresidents costs $14, and an annual permit costs $102 plus $12.50 for a conservation stamp.

Grand Teton Lodge Company Fishing Trips

FISHING | The park's major concessionaire operates guided fishing trips on Jackson Lake and guided fly-fishing trips on the Snake River. ⊠ *Grand Teton National Park* ☎ *307/543–3100* ⊕ *www.gtlc.com* 🎿 *From $115.*

Signal Mountain Lodge

FISHING | Hourly and half-day Jackson Lake guided fishing trips depart from the marina at Signal Mountain Lodge, weather permitting. The rates include equipment and tackle. ⊠ *Signal Mountain Rd.* ☎ *307/543–2831* ⊕ *www.signal-mountainlodge.com* 🍽 *From $139.*

HIKING

To fully appreciate the grandeur of the park's soaring mountains and pristine lakes, it's best to try at least one or two trails that venture well beyond the parking areas. Of Grand Teton's more than 250 miles of maintained trails, the most popular are those around Jenny Lake, the Leigh and String lakes area, and Taggart Lake Trail, with views of Avalanche Canyon.

Frontcountry or backcountry you may see all kinds of wildlife—keep your distance, at least 25 yards from bison, elk, and moose, and 100 yards from bears and wolves. Pets are not permitted on trails or in the backcountry. Many of the park's most popular trails traverse rugged, challenging terrain. If you're inexperienced, start with an easier trek. Grand Teton has several short hikes, some of them paved, in the vicinity of developed areas, such as historic sites and park visitor centers, where you can also obtain advice and good trail maps.

★ The Hole Hiking Experience

For more than three decades, guides have led hikes and wildlife tours for all ages and ability levels in the Greater Yellowstone Ecosystem. The trips have an interpretive focus, with information about the history, geology, and ecology of the area. Many excursions incorporate yoga or have a holistic bent. In winter, cross-country ski and snowshoe tours in are offered in the park. ⊠ *Jackson* ☎ *307/690–4453* ⊕ *www.holehike.com* ☞ *From $150.*

HORSEBACK RIDING

You can arrange a guided horseback tour at Colter Bay Village and Jackson Lake Lodge corrals or with private outfitters. Most offer rides from an hour or two up to all-day excursions. If you want to spend even more time riding in Grand Teton and the surrounding mountains, consider a stay at a dude ranch, such as Triangle X, on the east side of the park. Most shorter rides are appropriate for novice riders. More experienced riders will enjoy the longer journeys where the terrain gets steeper and you may wind through deep forests.

Grand Teton Lodge Company Horseback Rides

HORSEBACK RIDING | **FAMILY** | Rides start at Jackson Lake Lodge, Colter Bay Village, Headwaters Lodge, and Jenny Lake Lodge corrals. One- and two-hour trips are available, and beginners are welcome, with pony rides for small children. ⊠ *Grand Teton National Park* ☎ *307/543–3100* ⊕ *www.gtlc.com* ☞ *From $50.*

Triangle X Ranch

HORSEBACK RIDING | **FAMILY** | This classic dude ranch just south of Moran Junction on the eastern edge of the park offers day horseback trips as well as multiday experiences that include comfy cabin accommodations, meals, rides, and lots of other fun activities. ⊠ *2 Triangle X Ranch Rd., Moose* ☎ *307/733–2183* ⊕ *www.trianglex.com.*

WINTER ACTIVITES

Grand Teton has some of North America's finest and most varied cross-country skiing and snowshoeing. Try the gentle 3-mile Swan Lake–Heron Pond Loop near Colter Bay, the mostly level 10-mile Jenny Lake Trail, or the moderate 4-mile Taggart Lake–Beaver Creek Loop and 5-mile Phelps Lake Overlook Trail. Teton Park Road is groomed for classic and skate-skiing from early January to mid-March, and rangers sometimes give guided snowshoe walks from Craig Thomas Discovery and Visitor Center. The

Flagg Ranch Information Station is closed in winter, but ski and snowshoe trails are open and marked with flagging tape, and the convenience store has maps.

Nearby Towns

The major gateway to Grand Teton National Park is the famously beautiful and beautiful-peopled town of **Jackson,** along with its neighbors **Teton Village**—popular among skiers and snowboarders from all over the world as the home of Jackson Hole Mountain Resort—and the small, unincorporated community of **Wilson.** These three communities form a triangle surrounded by greater Jackson Hole, with Teton Village at the northern tip and sharing a border with the south end of the national park, and Jackson and Wilson forming the two southern points. For a small town, Jackson has an extensive array of hotels and inns, restaurants and bars, and galleries and shops. Steadily growing Wilson has a handful of additional options, while Teton Village has hundreds of hotel rooms and condos, plus several restaurants, but it's really a self-contained resort community that while close to the park doesn't have the inviting small-town character that you'll find in Jackson. What all three of these communities share is a high cost of living and visiting—hotel rates, in particular, can be very high during winter's peak ski season and also quite high in summer and—increasingly—right through October.

If you're willing to stay an hour or more from Grand Teton's southern entrance, there are some smaller towns on the region's outskirts that offer more wallet-friendly lodging options, if fewer restaurants and attractions. On the "back side of the Tetons," as eastern Idaho is known, easygoing and rural **Driggs** is western gateway to Grand Teton—it's about an hour's drive from Moose—and Yellowstone. **Dubois,** about 85 miles east of Jackson, has a smattering of hotel options, and you can usually still get a room for the night here during the peak summer travel period without making a reservation weeks or months in advance. About an hour south of Jackson, **Pinedale** is another small Wyoming town with a handful of lodging options, restaurants, and attractions.

Jackson

13 miles south of Grand Teton's Moose entrance, 90 miles east of Idaho Falls, 280 miles northeast of Salt Lake City.

A compact, charming little town anchored by a leafy square bedecked with arches woven from thousands of naturally shed elk antlers, Jackson has roughly 10,500 permanent residents but gets flooded with upwards of 4 million visitors annually. Expensive homes and fashionable shops have sprung up all over, but with its wooden boardwalks and old-fashioned storefronts, the town center still looks like a Western movie set. There's a lot to do here, both downtown and in the surrounding countryside.

GETTING HERE AND AROUND
Jackson lies at the confluence of a few key highways, U.S. 26, 89, and 191, as well as state Highway 22. It's also served by a small airport. Although downtown is quite walkable and many hotels are within steps of restaurants and shops, you'll want a car to get to the park and to explore the gorgeous surrounding scenery.

VISITOR INFORMATION Jackson Hole Chamber of Commerce. ⊠ *260 W. Broadway, Jackson* ☎ *307/733–3316* ⊕ *www. jacksonholechamber.com.*

◉ Sights

★ Jackson Hole Historical Society & Museum

MUSEUM | FAMILY | At this excellent museum you can learn about historic homesteaders, dude ranches, and hunters, as well as Jackson's all-female town government of yore—a woman sheriff of that era claimed to have killed three men before hanging up her spurs. Native American, ranching, and cowboy artifacts are on display, some of them at the summer-only second location at 105 N. Glenwood Street.

At this excellent museum you can learn about historic homesteaders, dude ranches, and hunters, as well as Jackson's all-female town government of yore—a woman sheriff of that era claimed to have killed three men before hanging up her spurs. Native American, ranching, and cowboy artifacts are on display, some of them at the summer-only second location at 105 N. Glenwood Street. ⊠ 225 N. Cache St., Jackson ☎ 307/733–2414 ⊕ www.jacksonholehistory.org ⊒ $10 ⊗ Closed Nov.–mid-Dec.

National Bighorn Sheep Center

NATURE PRESERVE | FAMILY | The local variety is known as the Rocky Mountain bighorn, but you can learn about all kinds of bighorn sheep at this nonprofit conservation center and wildlife museum about an hour east of Grand Teton National Park. Expect dioramas with full-scale taxidermy mounts that recreate bighorn habitat, as well as interactive exhibits about wildlife management and special adaptations of wild sheep. Reserve ahead for winter wildlife-viewing tours ($100) to Whiskey Mountain. ⊠ 10 Bighorn La., Dubois ☎ 307/455–3429 ⊕ www.bighorn.org ⊒ $6 ⊗ Closed Apr. and May and Sun. and Mon. in late Dec.–Mar.

National Elk Refuge

NATURE PRESERVE | FAMILY | Wildlife abounds on this 25,000-acre refuge. From late November to March, more than 7,000 elk, many with enormous antler racks, winter here. Elk can be observed from various pull-outs along U.S. 191 or by slowly driving your car on the refuge's winding, unpaved roads. Other animals that make their home here include buffalo, bighorn sheep, and coyotes, as well as trumpeter swans and other waterfowl. In summer, the refuge is light on big game, but you can tour a historic homestead from June to September. From mid-December to early April, sleigh rides operated by Bar T 5 (www.bart5.com) depart several times a day from the Jackson Hole and Greater Yellowstone Visitor Center. ⊠ E. Broadway at National Elk Refuge Rd., Jackson ☎ 307/733–9212 ⊕ www. fws.gov/refuge/national_elk_refuge ⊒ Sleigh rides $27.

★ National Museum of Wildlife Art of the United States

MUSEUM | See an impressive collection of wildlife art—most of it devoted to North American species—in 14 galleries displaying the work of artists that include Georgia O'Keeffe, John James Audubon, John Clymer, Robert Kuhn, and Carl Rungius. A deck looks out on the National Elk Refuge, where you can see wildlife in a natural habitat. An elaborate ¾-mile outdoor sculpture trail includes a monumental herd of bronze bison by Richard Loffler trudging across the butte. ⊠ 2820 Rungius Rd., Jackson ☎ 307/733–5771 ⊕ www.wildlifeart.org ⊒ $15 ⊗ Closed Sun. and Mon.

🍴 Restaurants

Bapp

$$ | **KOREAN FUSION** | Edison bulbs and wooden booths impart a simple but contemporary ambience on this modern Korean restaurant on the west side of downtown Jackson, evidence of the town's growing embrace of international cuisine. The kitchen offers up an enticing mix of classics like spicy seafood soup with udon noodles, pork-kimchi stew, and fragrant short-rib barbecue, along with some modern twists, such rare-seared ahi with bibimbap. **Known for:** kimchi–fried egg burgers; Korean chicken wings; good selection of wine and soju spirits. [$] *Average main: $20* ✉ *340 W. Broadway, Jackson* ☎ *307/201–1818* 🌐 *www.hnkim226.wixsite.com/bapp* 🕓 *Closed Sun.*

★ **Bin 22**

$$ | **MODERN AMERICAN** | Step inside this rambling wine-centric market, bar, and café to stock up on to-go bottles and finely curated picnic supplies, or dine in. The menu tends toward shareable small plates that pair well with the interesting vinos—consider a selection of imported salumi and cheeses, or Spanish- and Italian-inspired platters of patatas bravas with roasted-garlic aioli, steamed clams with chorizo, roasted bone marrow over saffron gnocchi. **Known for:** impressive list of hard-to-find wines and liquor; artisan ice cream sandwiches; deck seating with heat lamps. [$] *Average main: $22* ✉ *200 W. Broadway, Jackson* ☎ *307/739–9463* 🌐 *www.bin22jacksonhole.com.*

★ **Gather**

$$$ | **MODERN AMERICAN** | This stylish purveyor of locavore-driven modern American cuisine impresses with its deftly plated food, knowledgeable service, and light-filled dining room with a curved wall of windows and pale-green banquette seating. The menu changes seasonally but might feature Snake River Farms wagyu tartar with beet mustard and a bacon-fried egg, followed by red wine–marinated local bison or elk Bolognese. **Known for:** inventive craft cocktails; local game and produce; see-and-be-seen crowd. [$] *Average main: $27* ✉ *72 S. Glenwood St., Jackson* ☎ *307/264–1820* 🌐 *www.gatherjh.com* 🕓 *No lunch.*

★ **Hand Fire Pizza**

$$ | **PIZZA** | Set in downtown Jackon's dramatic, imaginatively retrofitted art deco cinema building, this modern high-energy pizza place has mezzanine and ground-level tables that look directly toward an open kitchen with two massive wood-fired ovens. The flavorful pies and salads abound with mostly organic, often local ingredients: slow-roasted pork shoulder, pickled jalapeños, heirloom tomatoes, house-made burrata, and the like. **Known for:** the Chew-Baca pie with herbed ricotta, bacon, caramelized onions, and local honey; Tuesday-night fundraisers that support local charities; stunning interior. [$] *Average main: $18* ✉ *120 N. Cache St., Jackson* ☎ *307/733–7199* 🌐 *www.handfirepizza.com* 🕓 *No lunch Mon.–Thurs.*

Snake River Grill

$$$$ | **MODERN AMERICAN** | One of Jackson's mainstays for special-occasion dining, this sophisticated restaurant serves creatively prepared dishes using meats and fish loved across the West. The menu changes regularly, reflecting what's available in the market, and the extensive wine list has garnered countless awards. **Known for:** log cabin–chic interior; cast-iron-seared elk steak; lavish desserts. [$] *Average main: $38* ✉ *84 E. Broadway Ave., Jackson* ☎ *307/733–0557* 🌐 *www.snakerivergrill.com* 🕓 *Closed Mon.–Tues. in Apr. and Nov. No lunch.*

Coffee and Quick Bites

Cultivate Cafe

$ | **CAFÉ** | **FAMILY** | A great option for organic breakfasts, fresh smoothies, and well-crafted coffees before setting out for a day of hiking and exploring, this popular café set inside downtown's oldest building has an Old West saloon vibe. Open-face breakfast sandwiches and waffles topped with house jam and matcha-coconut cream are among the morning specialties, while veggie-bowls and local grass-fed burgers star at lunch. **Known for:** lots of kid-friendly options; vegan and veggie fare; honey-cinnamon-vanilla lattes. [$] *Average main: $11* ✉ *135 W. Deloney Ave., Jackson* ☎ *307/200–9631* 🌐 *www.cultivate-cafe.com* 🕓 *Closed Mon. No dinner.*

★ **Persephone Bakery**

$ | **BAKERY** | The best seating at this rustic-contemporary bakery café a short stroll east of Jackson Town Square is on the spacious shaded deck overlooking lively Broadway Avenue. Choose from an extensive menu of eclectic breakfast and lunch fare, including shakshuka feta and poached eggs, bread pudding French toast with grapefruit-cranberry compote, and mortadella sandwiches with locally sauerkraut and melted fontina. **Known for:** fresh baked artisan breads and pastries; espresso drinks with house-made marshmallows; brunch cocktails. [$] *Average main: $10* ✉ *145 E. Broadway Ave., Jackson* ☎ *307/200–6708* 🌐 *www.persephonebakery.com* 🕓 *No dinner.*

Hotels

Elk Refuge Inn

$$ | **HOTEL** | This simple, two-story motel with clean, warmly furnished rooms stands out for great reason: it's set along a minimally developed stretch of U.S. 26/89/191 that overlooks Flat Creek and the National Elk Refuge. **Pros:** rooms have views of elk refuge; reasonable rates; short drive from Jackson dining and shopping. **Cons:** not within walking distance of town; rates soar in summer; parking lot partially obscures views. [$] *Rooms from: $211* ✉ *1755 U.S. 26/89/191, Jackson* ☎ *307/200–0981* 🌐 *www.elkrefugeinn.net* 🛏 *24 rooms* 🍴 *No meals.*

★ **Hotel Jackson**

$$$$ | **HOTEL** | This swank, LEED-certified hotel built of iron, repurposed barn wood, and natural stone on the site of a Victorian hotel of the same name feels at once ruggedly Western and pleasingly cosmopolitan, its guest rooms and common spaces filled with artful, comforting touches. **Pros:** opulent rooms and design; steps from Jackson Square; superb service. **Cons:** steep rates; not a great choice for families; in a busy part of town. [$] *Rooms from: $629* ✉ *120 N. Glenwood St., Jackson* ☎ *307/733–2200* 🌐 *www.hoteljackson.com* 🛏 *55 rooms* 🍴 *No meals.*

Huff House Inn & Cabins

$$$$ | **B&B/INN** | With a mix of smartly furnished rooms and suites in cabins, a historic inn, and a newer building whose rooms have views of Snow King Mountain, this cozy and cushy inn abounds with inviting touches: soft robes, tasteful furnishings, and in some cases, gas fireplaces. **Pros:** easy stroll from town square; friendly staff; enchanting garden patio with firepit and hot tub. **Cons:** pricey during summer months; no pets; often books up months in advance. [$] *Rooms from: $319* ✉ *240 E. Deloney Ave., Jackson* ☎ *307/733–7141* 🌐 *www.huffhouse-jh.com* 🛏 *25 rooms* 🍴 *Free Breakfast.*

Snow King Resort

$$$ | **HOTEL** | **FAMILY** | At the base of Snow King Mountain ski area and eight blocks from Town Square, this mid-rise resort with conventional rooms and condo rentals has a modern Western look, a popular restaurant, a cycling and ski shop, and outdoor fire pits near the beautiful pool. **Pros:** central yet away from the bustle of downtown; ski-in, ski-out;

lots of amenities. **Cons:** often booked up with large groups; pricey during peak times; daily resort fee. [$] *Rooms from: $265* ✉ *400 E. Snow King Ave., Jackson* ☎ *307/733–5200* 🌐 *www.snowking.com* 🛏 *201 rooms* 🍴 *No meals.*

★ **The Wort Hotel**

$$$$ | HOTEL | Built in 1941, this Tudor-style grande dame with a fascinating interior of priceless Western paintings and artifacts is just a block from Town Square and feels as though it's been around as long as the Tetons, but its inviting rooms feel up-to-date and feature woodsy, Western-style furnishings made locally. **Pros:** charming old building with lots of history; steps from local shopping and dining; specialty suites with one-of-a-kind designs. **Cons:** limited views; quite pricey in winter and summer; busy location. [$] *Rooms from: $449* ✉ *50 N. Glenwood St., Jackson* ☎ *307/733–2190* 🌐 *www.worthotel.com* 🛏 *55 rooms* 🍴 *No meals.*

Shopping

ART GALLERIES

★ **MADE**

CRAFTS | The whimsical, one-of-a-kind wares of more than 350 artisans, many of them from the surrounding region, are displayed in this cool and colorful little shop and gallery. ✉ *125 N. Cache St., Jackson* ☎ *307/690–7957* 🌐 *www.madejacksonhole.com.*

★ **Wild by Nature Gallery**

ART GALLERIES—ARTS | At this bright gallery you'll find wildlife and landscape photography by Henry H. Holdsworth, plus books, note cards, and gifts. Several coffee-table books contain striking Tetons imagery. Wild by Nature offers photography workshops year-round. ✉ *95 W. Deloney Ave., Jackson* ☎ *307/733–8877* 🌐 *www.wildbynaturegallery.com.*

Wilson

7 miles west of Jackson.

This smaller cousin of Jackson has no real center per se, just a handful of restaurants and businesses around where Highway 22 crosses Fish Creek on its way west over 8,431-foot Teton Pass, en route to Idaho. There are a few B&Bs and smaller accommodations in Wilson, some of them along Moose-Wilson Road, which snakes its way north alongside the Snake River toward Teton Village and one of Grand Teton's backcountry entrances.

GETTING HERE AND AROUND

From Wilson, it's a 10-minute drive on Highway 22 to get to downtown Jackson, and about the same distance on Moose-Wilson Road (Highway 390) to reach Teton Village.

Restaurants

★ **Bar J Chuckwagon**

$$$$ | BARBECUE | FAMILY | This may be the best value in Jackson Hole: you get a complete ranch-style meal plus a rollicking Western show. Served on a tin plate, the food is barbecue beef, chicken, pork ribs, or rib-eye steak with potatoes, beans, biscuits, applesauce, and spice cake, along with lemonade or coffee. **Known for:** some of the best Western music and grub around; reservations recommended; local staple for decades. [$] *Average main: $31* ✉ *4200 W Bar J Chuckwagon, Wilson* ✣ *Off Moose-Wilson Rd., 1 mile north of Hwy. 22* ☎ *307/733–3370* 🌐 *www.barjchuckwagon.com* ⏲ *Closed Oct.–late May.*

Streetfood at the Stagecoach

$ | ECLECTIC | A happy option for fans of international food and good beer, this festive miniature food hall at Wilson's famously rollicking Stagecoach bar offers well-prepared Mexican, Asian, and

American comfort foods. There's a large deck and an expansive lawn with picnic tables for al fresco dining during the warmer months, or you can dine in the lively bar. **Known for:** huge outdoor dining area; good selection of craft beers; Mexican street-food-style tacos. $ *Average main: $12* ⊠ *5755 Hwy. 22, Wilson* ☏ *307/200–6633* ⊕ *www.streetfoodjh.com.*

Shopping

Hungry Jack's General Store
CONVENIENCE/GENERAL STORES | This old-fashioned general store is a local institution with a little bit of everything—with boots, bananas and boxers all in the same aisle, and a good selection of local beer and other products. ⊠ *5655 W. Hwy. 22, Wilson* ☏ *307/733–3561* ⊕ *www.hungryjackswilson.com.*

Teton Village

9 miles southwest of Moose (summer), 25 miles southwest of Moose (in winter), 12 miles north of Jackson.

Teton Village, on the southwestern edge of Grand Teton National Park, is a cluster of businesses centered around the facilities of Jackson Hole Mountain Resort. This ski and snowboard area has the longest continuous vertical rise in the U.S. at 4,139 feet, accessed by an aerial tram to the top of Rendezvous Mountain (10,450 feet). A gondola and various other lifts take skiers to other sections of the mountain and also serve hikers, mountain-bikers, and other sightseers in summer. There are plenty of places to eat, stay, and shop in this planned resort community.

GETTING HERE AND AROUND
Give yourself about 20 to 25 minutes to drive from Jackson to Teton Village via Moose-Wilson Road (Highway 390). In summer, you can continue north another 5 minutes on Moose-Wilson Road to enter Grand Teton National Park via its southern backcountry entrance. But this is closed

to vehicles (though open to hikers, skiers, and snowshoers) from November to mid-May, at which time to enter the park by car you have to drive down to Jackson and up to Moose, a 45-minute drive.

🍴 Restaurants

Bar Enoteca
$$ | **WINE BAR** | This stylishly hip wine bar inside Hotel Terra offers a lower-keyed sipping and dining alternative to full-service Il Villagio Osteria and is great for happy hour or a late dinner after skiing or exploring nearby Grand Teton National Park. The small-plates menu focuses on raw-bar items like sea bass ceviche and yellowtail hamachi along with pork buns, salads, and crostini with creative toppings. **Known for:** chic post-industrial design; tasty breakfasts; well-chosen wine list. $ *Average main: $21* ⊠ *3335 W. Village Dr., Teton Village* ☏ *307/739–4225* ⊕ *www.enotecajacksonhole.com* ⊗ *No lunch.*

★ Teton Thai
$$$ | **THAI** | By the Ranch Lot at the base of Jackson Hole Mountain Resort, this casually smart Thai-owned restaurant serves some of the most authentic, if a bit pricey, Asian fare in the region. The pad thai and tom yum gai soups are among the specialties, and there's a full bar. **Known for:** hefty portions; can be quite spicy, as requested; coconut sticky rice with ice cream. $ *Average main: $24* ⊠ *7342 Granite Loop Rd., Teton Village* ☏ *307/733–0022* ⊕ *www.tetonthai.com* ⊗ *Closed Sun.*

🛏 Hotels

★ Hotel Terra Jackson Hole
$$$$ | **RESORT** | The opulent Hotel Terra takes green hospitality to the next level, but it's also luxe to the core, with a hip, urban feel and all the amenities the price tag suggests. **Pros:** gracious service; great dining and bar options; organic full-service spa. **Cons:** not for

budget-conscious; in a crowded corner of Teton Village; a (short) walk to ski slopes. [$] *Rooms from: $384* ✉ *3335 W. Village Dr., Grand Teton National Park* ☎ *307/739–4100* 🌐 *www.hotelterrajacksonhole.com* 🛏 *132 rooms* 🍴 *No meals.*

★ **R Lazy S Ranch**

$$$$ | **RESORT** | **FAMILY** | With the spectacle of the Tetons in the background, this classic, family-friendly dude ranch at the southern border of the national park offers a bounty of activities, with horseback riding and instruction the main attraction, and a secondary emphasis on fishing in the property's private waters. **Pros:** all-inclusive, and with great food; very popular with kids (7 and older); beautiful setting. **Cons:** no TV; 20-minute drive from Jackson; week minimum stay. [$] *Rooms from: $588* ✉ *7800 Moose-Wilson Rd., Teton Village* ☎ *307/733–2655* 🌐 *www.rlazys.com* 🕒 *Closed Oct.–mid-June* 🛏 *14 cabins* 🍴 *All-inclusive.*

Activities

SKIING

★ **Jackson Hole Mountain Resort**

SKIING/SNOWBOARDING | Skiers and snowboarders love Jackson Hole, which borders the southern end of Grand Teton National Park and offers some of the best terrain in North America. There are thousands of routes up and down the mountain, and despite Jackson's reputation not all of them are hellishly steep (although 90 percent of the terrain is intermediate or expert). There are also two terrain parks and extensive facilities. In the summer, a mountain-bike park takes advantage of the legendary terrain. **Facilities:** 116 trails; 2,500 acres; 4,139-foot vertical drop; 16 lifts. ✉ *3395 Cody La., Jackson* ☎ *307/733–2292, 888/333–7766* 🌐 *www.jacksonhole.com* 🎟 *Lift ticket regular season: from $131.*

GREAT BASIN
NATIONAL PARK

Updated by
Stina Sieg

NEVADA

⛰ Camping	🛏 Hotels	🏃 Activities	👁 Scenery	🎟 Crowds
★★☆☆☆	★☆☆☆☆	★★★☆☆	★★★★☆	★☆☆☆☆

WELCOME TO GREAT BASIN NATIONAL PARK

TOP REASONS TO GO

★ **Ancient trees:** The twisting, windswept bristlecone pines in Great Basin can live to be thousands of years old.

★ **Desert skyscraper:** Wheeler Peak rises out of the desert basin with summit temperatures often 20–30 degrees below that of the visitor center.

★ **Rare shields:** Look for hundreds of these unique disk-shape formations inside Lehman Caves.

★ **Gather your pine nuts while you may:** Come in the fall and go a little nutty, as you can gather up to three gunnysacks of pinyon pine nuts, found in abundance throughout the park. They're great on salads.

★ **Celestial show:** Pitch-dark nights make for dazzling stars. Gaze on your own or attend a seasonal nighttime talk, led by a park ranger.

1 Lehman Caves. Highlighted by the limestone caverns, this is the primary destination for many Great Basin visitors. It's located next to a popular visitor center and just past the start of Wheeler Peak Scenic Drive.

2 Wheeler Peak. This 13,063-footer is the park's centerpiece, and is especially stunning when capped with snow. Hikers can climb the mountain via strenuous, day-use-only trails, which also lead to small alpine lakes, a glacier, and some ancient bristlecone pines.

3 Snake Creek Canyon. This is the less crowded, more remote part of an already remote park. Trails follow creeks and cross meadows in the southern parts of the park, and six primitive campgrounds line Snake Creek. A bristlecone pine grove is nearby, though far off any beaten path.

4 Arch Canyon. A high-clearance, four-wheel-drive vehicle is recommended, and sturdy boots and sun protection are critical if you want to get to Lexington Arch, which is unusual in that it is formed of limestone, not sandstone as most arches are. This is a day-use-only area.

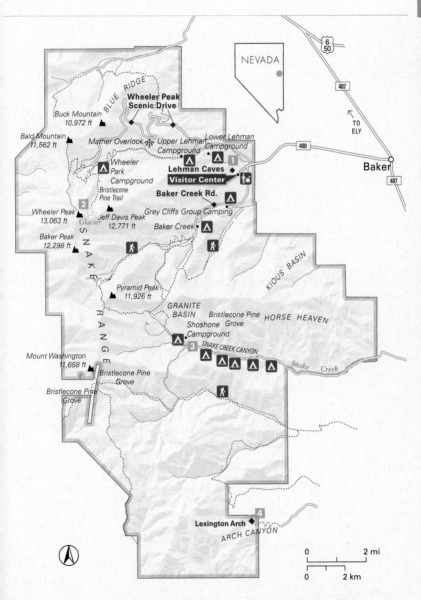

NEVADA

6
50

487

TO
ELY

488

Baker

487

BLUE RIDGE

**Wheeler Peak
Scenic Drive**

Buck Mountain
10,972 ft

Bald Mountain
11,562 ft

Mather Overlook

Upper Lehman
Campground

Lower Lehman
Campground

Wheeler
Park
Campground

Lehman Caves
Visitor Center

1

Bristlecone
Pine Trail

Baker Creek Rd.

2

Wheeler Peak
13,063 ft

Glacier

Jeff Davis Peak
12,771 ft

Grey Cliffs Group Camping

Baker Peak
12,298 ft

Baker Creek

SNAKE

KIOUS BASIN

Pyramid Peak
11,926 ft

RANGE

GRANITE
BASIN

Bristlecone Pine

HORSE HEAVEN

Shoshone Grove
Campground

3

SNAKE CREEK CANYON

Snake Creek

Mount Washington
11,658 ft

Bristlecone Pine
Grove

Bristlecone Pine
Grove

4

Lexington Arch

ARCH CANYON

0   2 mi

0   2 km

As you drive from the vast, sagebrush-dotted desert near Great Basin National Park's entrance into the cool alpine forests at the top of its signature scenic drive, you travel only a little more than 10 miles. But the change is so drastic it's like you've been transported to the Rocky Mountains, hundreds of miles away. That's a big part of why this little gem of a park exists.

Created in 1986, it preserves and highlights a sample of the incredible diversity found in the Great Basin, a gigantic arid region that spans almost all of Nevada and reaches into Utah, Oregon, California, Idaho, and Wyoming. The Lehman Caves, located in the heart of the park, went from a private tourist attraction to a national monument in 1922 until being folded into the new national park a few generations later.

Great Basin's founding came after decades of wrangling between the National Park Service, the U.S. Forest Service, local ranchers, White Pine County, and various politicians, whose compromises eventually led to the park being much smaller than originally proposed. At about 77,000 acres, it's just a sliver of the size of better-known parks like Grand Canyon and Yellowstone and gets a much smaller share of visitors, as well.

Still, those who do make the trek to Great Basin—hours from any big city in every direction—find a lot to do while surrounded by the quiet desert. Daily cave tours are one of the biggest draws, especially for families, with tickets so popular they can sell out months in advance. At night, the famously dark skies offset a sea of bright stars, and rangers lead astronomy talks and share telescopes with the public several times a week in the high season (and even host a festival in the fall). Camping and hiking are also huge, with trails to fit pretty much every ability level. Modest walks can get you to alpine lakes or a grove of bristlecone pines, some of the oldest organisms on earth. Longer, more strenuous hikes take you deep into the backcountry or the craggy top of Wheeler Peak. At more than 13,000 feet, it's the second-highest mountain in the state.

Visiting Great Basin is a rustic experience, with few amenities, little cell service, and just a speck of a town nearby. But for those in search of an earthy solitude, it's a much-needed escape from the rest of the world, and draws a certain kind of visitor back year after year.

AVERAGE HIGH/LOW TEMPERATURES

JAN.	FEB.	MAR.	APR.	MAY	JUNE
41/18	44/21	48/24	56/31	66/40	76/48
JULY	AUG.	SEPT.	OCT.	NOV.	DEC.
86/57	83/56	75/47	62/47	49/26	42/20

Planning

When to Go

Summer is when you'll find the most amenities open and also the most visitors. While Great Basin doesn't get crowded to the extent of larger parks, it has been somewhat "discovered" in recent years, leading to hard-to-find parking and camping spots between around Memorial Day and Labor Day, and sometimes beyond. In these warmer months, you should be comfortable in shorts and T-shirts during the day—though temperatures drop at night, and get colder the higher up you climb, so bring light jackets and pants. Fall and spring can be lovely times to visit, though you should plan for lower temperatures at night and fewer businesses open in Baker, the small town near the park.

A winter visit can be sublime in its solitude, but the hardy visitor must be prepared for the elements, especially if the backcountry is a destination. With temperatures hovering in the low teens, heavy coats, boots, and other appropriate winter gear are necessary. Some roads might be impassable in inclement weather; check ahead with a park ranger. No dining or groceries are available in the park during the winter, and the closest option is several miles away at the year-round Border Inn.

FESTIVALS AND EVENTS

Great Basin Astronomy Festival. In 2016, Great Basin was named a Dark Sky Park by the International Dark Skies Association. This festival, spread out over a few days every fall, is a chance to experience these famous nighttime skies, with talks, workshops, and of course, looks at the stars through park telescopes. Be sure to snag a reservation, as it can fill up fast. ⊕ www.nps.gov/grba/planyourvisit/great-basin-astronomy-festival.htm.

Silver State Classic Challenge. Twice a year, car enthusiasts of all stripes close a state highway for the country's largest (and most venerable) open-road race for amateur fast-car drivers. The event occurs the third weekend of May and the third weekend of September south of Ely on Route 318, from Lund to Hiko, and is open to just about any four-wheeled vehicle. ⊕ www.sscc.us.

White Pine County Fair. Livestock, flower, and vegetable competitions, plus horse races, food booths, dancing, and a barbecue dinner make this fair, held at the White Pine County Fairgrounds in Ely, the real thing. The dates fluctuate every August. ⊕ www.wpcfair.com.

Getting Here and Around

AIR

The nearest airport is in Cedar City (142 miles) but will likely be pricey. Salt Lake City (239 miles) and Las Vegas (303 miles) are better bets, though you'll probably get the cheapest fares (and might have the most fun) flying into Vegas.

CAR

The entrance to Great Basin is on Route 488, 5 miles west of its junction with Route 487. From Ely, take U.S. 6/50 to Route 487. From Salt Lake City or Cedar City, Utah, take Interstate 15 South to U.S. 6/50 West; from Las Vegas, drive north on Interstate 15 and then north on

Great Basin in One Day

Start your visit with the 90-minute tour of the fascinating limestone caverns of **Lehman Caves**, the park's most famous attraction (advance reservations heavily encouraged, as tours often fill up months in advance). If you have time before or after the tour, hike the short and family-friendly **Mountain View Nature Trail**, near the Lehman Caves Visitor Center, to get your first taste of the area's pinyon-juniper forests. Stop for lunch at the Lehman Caves Cafe (open April through October) or at least plan on a homemade cookie—or have a picnic near the visitor center.

In the afternoon, take a leisurely drive up Wheeler Peak Drive, with fabulous views of **Wheeler Peak**, the park's tallest mountain (and the second highest in Nevada) at just over 13,000 feet. You can stop about halfway along your drive to hike the short **Osceola Ditch Trail**, a remnant of the park's gold-mining days, or, alternatively, just enjoy the views from the two overlooks. If you're feeling energetic, when you reach the top of the winding road hike into the strange beauty of a bristlecone pine grove on the **Bristlecone Pine Trail**.

Route 93 to access U.S. 6/50. ⚠ **Don't rely on GPS to get to the park, as sometimes it sends people up remote dirt roads. The turnoff to the main section of the park is well marked in the center of Baker.**

In the park, Baker Creek Road and portions of Wheeler Peak Scenic Drive, above Upper Lehman Creek, are closed from November to June. The road to the visitor center and the roads to the developed campgrounds are paved, but two-wheel-drive cars don't do well in winter storms. RVs and trailers over 24 feet aren't allowed above Upper Lehman Creek. With an 8% grade, the road to Wheeler Peak is steep and curvy, but not dangerous if you take it slow. Motorcyclists should watch for gravel on the road's surface.

There are two gas stations located nearby. The tiny Baker Sinclair station is just outside the park entrance, while about 7½ miles farther, the Border Inn has a Phillips 66 station, open 24/7.

Inspiration

Hiking Great Basin National Park, by Bruce Grubbs, will get your Great Basin trip off on the right foot.

Trails to Explore in Great Basin National Park, by Rose Houk, is all about hiking in the park.

Geology of the Great Basin, by Bill Fiero, and *Basin and Range,* by John McPhee, present geological tours of the Great Basin.

Park Essentials

ACCESSIBILITY

Designated accessibility parking spaces are available at both visitor centers. The centers themselves are both on one level, fully accessible to those with impaired mobility, with accessible bathrooms. The park slide show is captioned. The park has two ADA-compliant trails, though both are unpaved: the Island Forest Trail (0.4 mile) at the top of Wheeler Peak Drive and the Shoshone Trail (0.1 mile) at Snake Creek. Baker Creek Campground, Upper Lehman

Creek Campground, and Wheeler Peak Campground are accessible, though the restroom access ramp at Upper Lehman Creek Campground is steep.

PARK FEES AND PERMITS

Admission to the park is free, but if you want to tour Lehman Caves there's a fee ($9–$11, depending on tour length). To fish in Great Basin National Park, those 12 and older need a state fishing license from the Nevada Department of Wildlife (⊕ www.ndow.org). The one-day nonresident license is $18, plus $7 for each additional day at time of purchase ($80 for a year). Backcountry hikers do not need permits, but for your own safety you should fill out a form at the visitor center before setting out.

PARK HOURS

The park is open 24/7 year-round; May–August, visitor center hours are 8–4:30; hours may vary from year to year. It's in the Pacific time zone.

CELL PHONE RECEPTION

There's decent coverage close to Lehman Caves; the more remote you get, the spottier it becomes. Some service is available higher portions of the Wheeler Peak hike.

SHOPS AND GROCERS

While the closest full-service grocery store is an hour away in Ely, the Stargazer Inn in Baker has a small market with some basics, including snacks, beer, and wine. Similar supplies can be found a few miles outside of town at the Border Inn's grocery section.

Hotels

There is no lodging in the park, so plan to arrive early to snag one of its coveted first-come, first-served campsites, or expect to camp in the backcountry. There is a handful of motels in nearby Baker and many more to choose from about an hour away in Ely. *Hotel reviews have been shortened. For full information, visit Fodors.com.*

What It Costs

	$	$$	$$$	$$$$
RESTAURANTS				
	under $13	$13–$20	$21–$30	over $30
HOTELS				
	under $101	$101–$150	$151–$200	over $200

Restaurants

Dining in the park itself is limited to basic but tasty breakfast and lunch fare at the Lehman Caves Cafe and Gift Shop. About 5 miles away in Baker, a town of less than 100 people, there are a few good options. Fire grates are available at each campsite in the park's four developed campgrounds for barbecuing. *Restaurant reviews have been shortened. For full information, visit Fodors.com.*

Visitor Information

PARK CONTACT INFORMATION Great Basin National Park. ⊠ Rte. 488, Baker ☎ 775/234–7331 ⊕ www.nps.gov/grba.

Lehman Caves

5½ miles from Baker.

Essentially the gateway to this small park, this area contains an in-depth visitor center and fun gift shop, the park's only restaurant (seasonal), hiking trails, and campgrounds. Perhaps most important, it's home to the Lehman Caves, the park's most well-known attraction. This is a good corner of the park to plan out your adventures or relax with a glass of wine after a day of hiking.

Sights

PICNIC AREAS

Lehman Caves Visitor Center Picnic Area
LOCAL INTEREST | FAMILY | This picnic site, with tables, water, and restrooms (the latter two available during the summer), is a short walk from the visitor center. Summer hours are often extended beyond the standard 8 am–4:30 pm. ✉ *Great Basin National Park* ⊹ *Just north of Lehman Caves Visitor Center.*

Pole Canyon Trailhead Picnic Area
LOCAL INTEREST | Inaccessible when Baker Creek Road is closed in the winter, this picnic area at the mouth of a canyon has a handful of tables and fire grills but no water. It does have a restroom. Access is via a narrow, one-lane road. ✉ *Great Basin National Park* ⊹ *East of entrance to Grey Cliffs Group Camping site, at mouth of Pole Canyon* ☾ *Closed Nov.–May.*

Upper Lehman Creek Campground
LOCAL INTEREST | There is a handful of places here where you can sit down for a bite and a breather. A group picnic site requires advance reservations, but areas near the host site and amphitheater are first come, first served. Water is available. ✉ *Great Basin National Park* ⊹ *4 miles from Lehman Caves Visitor Center on Wheeler Peak Scenic Dr.*

SCENIC DRIVES

Baker Creek Road
SCENIC DRIVE | Though less popular than the Wheeler Peak Scenic Drive, this gravel road affords gorgeous views of Wheeler Peak, the Baker Creek Drainage, and Snake Valley. Beautiful wildflowers are an extra treat in spring and early summer. The road is closed in the winter, and there are no pull-outs or scenic overlooks. ⊹ *½ mile inside park boundary off Rte. 488* ☾ *Closed Nov.–May.*

SCENIC STOPS

★ Lehman Caves
CAVE | FAMILY | While Indigenous people were the first to explore and use the caves, rancher and miner Absalom Lehman is credited with discovering this underground wonder in 1885. The single limestone and marble cavern is 2½ miles long, with stalactites, stalagmites, helictites, flowstone, popcorn, and other bizarre mineral formations that cover almost every surface. Lehman Caves is one of the best places to see rare shield formations, created when calcite-rich water is forced from tiny cracks in a cave wall, ceiling, or floor. Year-round the cave maintains a constant, damp temperature of 50°F, so wear a light jacket and nonskid shoes. Go for the full 90-minute tour if you have time; during summer, it's offered several times a day, as is the 60-minute tour. Expect daily tours during the winter. Children under age five are not allowed on the 90-minute tours, except during the winter; those under 16 must be accompanied by an adult. Take the 0.3-mile Mountain View Nature Trail beforehand to see the original cave entrance and **Rhodes Cabin,** where black-and-white photographs of the park's earlier days line the walls. ⚠ **Get tickets as far in advance as possible at recreation.gov. Tours can sell out months in advance.** ✉ *Lehman Caves Visitor Center* ☎ *775/234–7331* 💲 *From $9.*

TRAILS

Baker Lake Trail
TRAIL | This full-day, 12-mile hike can easily be made into a two-day backpacking trip. You'll gain a total of 2,620 feet in elevation on the way to Baker Lake, a jewel-like alpine lake with a backdrop of impressive cliffs. *Difficult.* ✉ *Great Basin National Park* ⊹ *Trailhead: Baker Creek Rd., going south from just east of Lehman Caves Visitor Center.*

Lehman Caves: It's amazing what a little water and air can do to a room.

Mountain View Nature Trail

TRAIL | FAMILY | Just past the Rhodes Cabin on the right side of the visitor center, this short and easy trail (0.3 mile) through pinyon pine and juniper trees is marked with signs describing the plants. The path passes the original entrance to Lehman Caves and loops back to the visitor center. It's a great way to spend a half hour or so while you wait for your cave tour to start. *Easy.* ✉ *Great Basin National Park* ✥ *Trailhead: at Lehman Caves Visitor Center.*

VISITOR CENTERS

Great Basin Visitor Center

INFO CENTER | FAMILY | Here you can see exhibits on the flora, fauna, and geology of the park, or ask a ranger to suggest a favorite hike. Books, videos, and souvenirs are for sale. Water is available. ✉ *Rte. 487 , just north of Baker* ☎ *775/234–7520* ⏲ *Closed Oct.–late Apr.*

Lehman Caves Visitor Center

INFO CENTER | FAMILY | Regularly scheduled cave tours lasting 60 or 90 minutes depart from here. Mountain View Nature Trail encircles the visitor center and includes Rhodes Cabin and the historic cave entrance. Buy gifts for friends and family back home at the bookstore, or just take in the view with a glass of wine at the adjacent café. There's also a replica of the park's famed caves you can walk through. ✉ *Rte. 488 , ½ mile inside park boundary* ☎ *775/234–7331.*

🍴 Restaurants

Lehman Caves Cafe and Gift Shop

$ | AMERICAN | This casual spot is a great place to soak in the vast desert view and offers simple breakfasts and lunches. The sandwiches, filled with meats smoked by the owner, are especially good. **Known for:** a nice place to unwind with a beer or glass of wine into the late afternoon; the only restaurant in the park; delicious cookies and other treats, baked by a local pastry chef. [$] *Average main: $10* ✉ *Next to visitor center* ☎ *775/234–7200* ⏲ *Closed Nov.–May. No dinner.*

Wheeler Peak

12 miles from the Lehman Caves Visitor Center.

You'll find some of the most dramatic scenery, including panoramic desert views, in this high-elevation section of the park. Here, hiking trails take you to some of Great Basin's most photographed spots: clear alpine lakes, a grove of bristlecone pines, and the top of Nevada's second-highest peak. This area's sole camping area, Wheeler Peak Campground, is one of the most beautiful in the park. The scenic drive that transports you from the desert to the forest is an attraction in itself but, like the campground in this prized section, is open only seasonally.

Sights

SCENIC DRIVES
★ Wheeler Peak Scenic Drive
SCENIC DRIVE | When this stunning seasonable road is open, it's a must for Great Basin visitors. Less than a mile from the visitor center off Route 488, turn onto this paved road that winds its way up to elevations of 10,000 feet. You'll go past pinyon-juniper forest in lower elevations; as you climb, the air cools as much as 20–30 degrees. Along the way, pull off at overlooks for awe-inspiring glimpses of the peaks of the South Snake Range. A short interpretive trail leads to a ditch that once carried water to the historic Osceola mining site. Turn off at Mather Overlook, elevation 9,000 feet, for the best photo ops. Wheeler Overlook is the best place to see Wheeler Peak, as well as fall colors. Allow 1½ hours for the 24-mile round-trip, not including hikes. ⊠ *Baker* ✛ *Just inside park boundary, off Rte. 488 about 5 miles west of Baker* ⊕ *www.nps.gov/grba/planyourvisit/ wheeler-peak-scenic-drive.htm* ☉ *Closed Nov.–June.*

TRAILS
Alpine Lakes Trail
TRAIL | This moderate, 2.7-mile trek loops past the beautiful Stella and Teresa lakes from the trailhead near Wheeler Peak Campground. You'll rise and fall about 600 feet in elevation as you pass through subalpine and alpine forest. The views of Wheeler Peak, amid wildflowers (in summer), white fir, shimmering aspens, and towering ponderosa pines, make this a memorable hike. The trailhead is at nearly 10,000 feet, so make sure you're adjusted to the altitude and prepared for changing weather. Allow three hours. *Moderate.* ⊠ *Great Basin National Park* ✛ *Trailhead: at Bristlecone parking area, near end of Wheeler Peak Scenic Dr.*

★ Bristlecone Pine Trail
TRAIL | **FAMILY** | Though the park has several bristlecone pine groves, the only way to see the gnarled, ancient trees up close is to hike this trail. From the parking area to the grove, it's a moderate 2.8-mile hike that takes about an hour each way. Rangers offer informative talks in season; inquire at the visitor center. The Bristlecone Pine Trail also leads to the **Glacier Trail,** which skirts the southernmost permanent ice field on the continent and ends with a view of a small rock glacier, the only one in Nevada. It's less than 3 miles back to the parking lot. Allow three hours for the moderate hike and remember the trailhead is at 9,800 feet above sea level. *Moderate.* ⊠ *Great Basin National Park* ✛ *Trailhead: Summit Trail parking area, Wheeler Peak Scenic Dr., 12 miles from Lehman Caves Visitor Center.*

Osceola Ditch Trail
TRAIL | **FAMILY** | In 1890, at a cost of $108,223, the Osceola Gravel Mining Company constructed an 18-mile-long trench. The ditch was part of an attempt to glean gold from the South Snake Range, but water shortages and the company's failure to find much gold forced the mining operation to shut down

Plants and Wildlife in Great Basin

Despite the cold, dry conditions in Great Basin, 925 plant species thrive; 13 are considered sensitive species. The region gets less than 10 inches of rain a year, so plants have developed some ingenious methods of dealing with the desert's harshness. For instance, many flowering plants will grow and produce seeds only in a year when there is enough water. Spruces, pines, and junipers have set down roots here, and the bristlecone pine has been doing so for thousands of years.

The park's plants provide a variety of habitats for animals and for more than 230 bird species. In the sagebrush are jackrabbits, ground squirrels, chipmunks, and pronghorn. Mule deer and striped skunks abound in the pygmy forest of pinyon pine and juniper trees. Shrews, ringtail cats, and weasels make their homes around the springs and streams. Mountain lions, bobcats, and sheep live on the rugged slopes and in valleys. The park is also home to coyotes, kit fox, and badgers. Treat the Great Basin rattlesnake with respect. Bites are uncommon and rarely fatal, but if you're bitten, remain calm and call 911.

in 1905. You can reach portions of the eastern section of the ditch on foot via the Osceola Ditch Trail, which passes through pine and fir trees and has interpretive signs along the way. Allow 30 minutes for this easy 0.3-mile round-trip hike. *Easy.* ⊠ *Great Basin National Park* ✛ *Trailhead: Wheeler Peak Scenic Dr.*

★ Wheeler Peak Summit Trail

TRAIL | Begin this full-day, 8.6-mile hike early in the day so as to minimize exposure to afternoon storms. Depart and return to Summit Trailhead near the end of Wheeler Peak Scenic Drive. Most of the route follows a ridge up the mountain to the summit. Elevation gain is 2,900 feet to 13,063 feet above sea level, so hikers should have good stamina and watch for altitude sickness and/or hypothermia due to drastic temperature and weather changes. The trail becomes especially steep and challenging, with lots of loose rocks, toward the summit. *Difficult.* ⊠ *Great Basin National Park* ✛ *Trailhead: Wheeler Peak Scenic Dr., Summit Trail parking area.*

Snake Creek Canyon

11 miles from Baker.

Great Basin is already far from pretty much everything, but for those who want to go just a little bit farther, Snake Creek offers true solitude. Free, primitive campsites are shaded by trees, with fire rings and picnic tables but no water or bathrooms. Snake Creek Road is open year-round, but can become snowy or muddy in the winter and spring. High-clearance vehicles are recommended, while RVs and trailers are not. A cluster of trails are at the end of the road, including routes to Johnson and Baker lakes.

Sights

SCENIC SIGHTS

Lexington Arch

NATURE SITE | Tucked far away in the rugged backcountry, Lexington Arch is six stories high, looming over Lexington Creek. While most arches are made of sandstone, this arch is limestone, more often associated with caves. That leads some to believe it was once a passage in a cave system. The 5.4-mile (round-trip) hike to the arch is challenging, with little to no shade. Hiking boots, sunscreen, water, and snacks are essential. It's one of the few trails in the park where leashed pets are allowed. The arch is actually located south of Snake Creek, outside of the small town of Garrison, Utah. Only high-clearance, four-wheel-drive vehicles are recommended on the dirt road leading to it. ⚠ **Traveling to the arch can be dangerous, as the road becomes rougher the closer you get to the trailhead. Make sure to stop driving before you get in trouble and walk the rest of the way.** ✉ *Baker* ✛ *Drive south from Baker on Rte. 487 until it becomes Utah 21. Pass through Garrison, then past Pruess Lake. Turn right at the sign for Lexington Arch, and take that dirt road about 7 miles until you reach a washed-out section. Take the south fork to reach the trailhead for the arch. Due to road damage, parking will be 1/2 to 1 mile away from the trailhead.*

Activities

Great Basin National Park is a great place for experienced outdoor adventurers. The closest outdoor store is an hour away in Ely, so bring everything you might need, and be prepared to go it alone. Permits are not required to go off the beaten path, but if you're planning a multiday hike, register with a ranger just in case. The effort is worth it, as the backcountry is pristine and not at all crowded, no matter the time of year. As is the case in all national parks, bicycling is restricted to existing roads, which can get busy with cars, especially Wheeler Peak Scenic Drive. Always be cautious, and consider biking on less popular roads.

BIRD-WATCHING
An impressive list of bird species have been sighted here—238, according to the National Park Service checklist. Some, such as the common raven and

American robin, can be seen at most locations. Others, such as the red-naped sapsucker, are more commonly seen near Lehman Creek. In the higher elevations, listen for the loud shriek of Clark's nutcracker, storing nuts.

CAMPING
Great Basin has four developed campgrounds, all easily accessible by car, but only the Lower Lehman Creek Campground is open year-round. All are first come, first served, and can be paid for on-site with cash, check, or credit card. The campgrounds do fill up, so try to snag your spot early.

Primitive campsites around Snake and Strawberry creeks are open year-round and are free; however, snow and rain can make access to the sites difficult. RVs and trailers are not recommended.

Baker Creek Campground. The turnoff is just past the park entrance, on the left as you approach the Lehman Caves Visitor Center. ✉ *2½ miles south of Rte. 488, 3 miles from visitor center in the Lehman Caves section of the park.*

Lower Lehman Creek Campground. Other than Great Basin's primitive sites, this is the only campground in the park that is open year-round. It's the first turnoff past the Lehman Caves Visitor Center. ✉ *2½ miles from visitor center on Wheeler Peak Scenic Dr. in the Lehman Caves section of the park.*

Upper Lehman Creek Campground. About a mile past the Lower Lehman Creek turnoff, this camp fills up quickly in the summer. ✉ *4 miles from visitor center on Wheeler Peak Scenic Dr. in the Lehman Caves section of the park.*

Wheeler Peak Campground. This cool high-elevation campground at the end of Wheeler Peak Scenic Drive has stunning views and is near trailheads. Many consider it the nicest in the park. ✉ *13 miles from Lehman Caves Visitor Center on*

Wheeler Peak Scenic Dr. in the Wheeler Peak section of the park.

Whispering Elms Campground. The largest camping facility close to but not inside the park is also the nearest to offer hookups for RVs. It is open year-round. ⊠ *5 miles from the park, 120 Baker Ave., Baker* ☎ *775/234–9900.*

CROSS-COUNTRY SKIING

Lehman Creek Trail

SKIING/SNOWBOARDING | In summer, descend 2,050 feet by hiking Lehman Creek Trail one-way (downhill) from Wheeler Peak campground to Upper Lehman Creek campground. In winter, it is the most popular cross-country skiing trail in the park. You may need snowshoes to reach the skiable upper section, with free rentals available at the Lehman Cave Visitor Center.

EDUCATIONAL OFFERINGS

Junior Ranger Program

TOUR—SIGHT | FAMILY | Youngsters answer questions and complete activities related to the park and then are sworn in as Junior Rangers and receive a Great Basin badge. ⊠ *Great Basin National Park* ☎ *775/234–7331* ⊕ *www.nps.gov/grba.*

Weekly Astronomy Programs

OBSERVATORY | FAMILY | You'll find some of the country's darkest skies—and brightest stars—at Great Basin. Due to its low light pollution, it was even named a Dark Sky Park by the International Dark Sky Association in 2016. As astrotourism has grown, Great Basin has responded by building a brand-new amphitheatre for these ranger-led stargazing programs. Expect to be dazzled as you get a chance to see the wild blue yonder through a telescope. It's often crowded, especially during the summer, when the program is held several times a week. It drops down to once a week in shoulder seasons. ⊠ *Lehman Caves Visitor Center, Baker* ⊕ *www.nps.gov/grba* ⊘ *Closed Nov.–Mar.*

HIKING

You'll witness beautiful views by driving along the Wheeler Peak Scenic Drive and other park roads, but hiking allows an in-depth experience that just can't be matched. Trails at Great Basin run the gamut from short, wheelchair-accessible paths to multiday backpacking excursions. Destinations include evergreen forest, flowering meadows and an extremely tall mountain peak. When you pick up a trail map at the visitor center, ask about trail conditions and bring appropriate clothing when you set out from any trailhead.

No matter the trail length, always carry water, and remember that the trails are at high elevations, so pace yourself accordingly. Never enter abandoned mineshafts or tunnels because they are unstable and dangerous. Those headed into the backcountry don't need to obtain a permit, but are encouraged to register at either of the two visitor centers. Regardless of the season, inquire about the weather, as it can be harsh and unpredictable. Since cell reception is spotty at best, a personal locator beacon can be a lifesaver when adventuring on remote trails.

Nearby Towns

An hour's drive west of the park, at the intersection of three U.S. highways, **Ely** (population 4,000) is the largest town for hours in every direction. It grew up in the second wave of the early Nevada mining boom, right at the optimistic turn of the 20th century. For 70 years copper kept the town in business, but when it ran out in the early 1980s, Ely declined fast. Then, in 1986, the National Park Service designated Great Basin National Park, and the town got a boost. Ely has since been rebuilt and revitalized, though it's kept a quirky, faded feel. If you want to stay much closer to the park, tiny **Baker** (population roughly 75) has far fewer amenities but is slowly reawakening. The cluster of homes and small businesses on Route 487 is about 5 miles from the Lehman Caves Visitor Center.

Ely

Full of rugged Americana charm, Ely is a pleasant place to bed down for the night or even spend a few days. Visitors will find several restaurants and bars to chose from, as well as a large selection of hotels and motels, many with neon signs and low prices. While the community's outskirts look generic, downtown's murals and historic buildings make it a fascinating place to stroll.

Ely prides itself on its remote location, right on a the eastern edge of two-lane highway known as "The Loneliest Road." They only way to get here is to drive, as there's no bus or train service, and the closest airport is hours away.

VISITOR INFORMATION
White Pine County Tourism and Recreation Board. ⊠ *Bristlecone Convention Center, 150 6th St., Ely* ☎ *800/496–9350, 775/289–3720* ⊕ *www.elynevada.net.*

 ## Sights

Cave Lake State Park
NATIONAL/STATE PARK | FAMILY | This is an idyllic spot 7,350 feet above sea level in the pine and juniper forest of the big Schell Creek Range that borders Ely to the east. You can spend a day fishing for rainbow and brown trout in the reservoir and a night sleeping under the stars. Arrive early; it gets crowded. Access may be restricted in winter. ⊠ *15 miles southeast of Ely via U.S. 50/6/93, Great Basin National Park* ☎ *775/296–1505* ⊕ *parks. nv.gov/parks/cave-lake* 🖼 *$5.*

Ely Renaissance Village
MUSEUM VILLAGE | FAMILY | This tiny downtown "village" gives visitors a sense of what Ely looked like more than a 100

years ago. It features a cluster of small restored homes, each representing a different ethnicity of immigrants who came to this desert outpost around the turn of the 20th century. There are also re-creations of a miner's cabin, general store, and barn. The site is open Fridays and Saturdays (seasonally), and hosts occasional re-enactments and living history presentations. ⊠ *400 Ely St., Ely* ⊕ *www. elynvarts.com* ⊙ *Closed late-Sept.–late-May and Sun.–Thurs. in season.*

★ Nevada Northern Railway Museum
MUSEUM | FAMILY | The biggest attraction in Ely draws train aficionados from near and far. During the mining boom, the Nevada Northern Railroad connected East Ely, Ruth, and McGill to the transcontinental rail line in the northeast corner of the state. The whole operation is now a museum open year-round and watched over by its famed cat mascot, Dirt, who receives food and gifts from fans across the country. You can tour the depot, offices, warehouses, yard, engine houses, and repair shops. Catch a ride on one of the vintage locomotives, and get history lessons from enthusiastic guides along the way (check website for times). You can even stay overnight in a caboose or bunkhouse. ⊠ *1100 Ave. A, Ely* ☎ *866/407–8326* ⊕ *www.nnry.com* 🖼 *$8 for museum, $31 for train ride (museum included)* ⊙ *Closed Tues. Sept.–June.*

U.S. 93 Scenic Byway
SCENIC DRIVE | The 68 miles between the park and Ely make a beautiful drive with diverse views of Nevada's paradoxical geography: dry deserts and lush mountains. You'll catch an occasional glimpse of a snake, perhaps a rattler, slithering on the road's shoulder, or a lizard sunning on a rock. Watch for deer. A straight drive to Ely takes a little more than an hour; if you have the time to take a dirt-road adventure, don't miss the Ward Charcoal Ovens or a peek at Cave Lake.

Restaurants

Cellblock Steakhouse

$$$ | STEAKHOUSE | The only fine dining in Ely, this low-lighted spot comes with a big helping of local color. Each table is its own "cell," complete with metal bars and old-timey photos on the wall—a whimsical spot to eat cowboy-size prime rib or bacon-wrapped filet mignon. **Known for:** all your favorite steak-house staples with cute, jail-themed names; crème brûlée and other desserts worth the calories; the fanciest place in Ely for a fun dinner. $ Average main: $25 ⊠ 211 5th St., Ely ☎ 775/289–3033 ⊕ www.jailhousecasino. com/dining.php ⊗ No lunch.

Mr. Gino's Restaurant & Bar

$$ | ITALIAN | Located right downtown, this spacious spot serves up generous helpings of pasta, pizza, and other Italian favorites. Also offering desserts and a full bar, this is a classy yet casual spot to chill out after the long drive to Ely. **Known for:** local favorite; large portions; expansive menu and full bar. $ Average main: $17 ⊠ 484 Aultman St., Ely ☎ 775/289–3540.

Hotels

Hotel Nevada

$ | HOTEL | One of the oldest hotels in the state, this six-story local landmark dates from 1929 and towers over Ely's historic downtown. **Pros:** bursting with historic character; in the heart of downtown; updated rooms are light, airy, and comfortable. **Cons:** can fill up quickly during busy times; no pool, hot tub, or gym; older property means small rooms and bathrooms. $ Rooms from: ⊠ 501 Aultman St., Ely ☎ 775/289–6665, 888/406–3055 ⊕ www.hotelnevada.com ➤ 64 rooms ⊗ Free Breakfast.

Jailhouse Motel and Casino

$ | HOTEL | This motel at Ely's main intersection was built near the town's old-time jail; the rooms are assigned cell numbers and there are prison bars around the booths at its fancy steak house. **Pros:** location in the center of town; on-site casino, two restaurants, and a bar; good value. **Cons:** smoke can waft from the casino adjacent to registration; not as charming as some historic options in the area; rooms are clean but no frills. $ Rooms from: $65 ⊠ 211 5th St., Ely ☎ 775/289–3033, 800/841–5430 ⊕ www.jailhousecasino.com ➤ 60 rooms ⊗ No meals.

Prospector Hotel & Gambling Hall

$ | HOTEL | One of the best bets in town, this comfortable hotel walks the line between classy and delightfully kitschy, with Western-theme rooms, on-site gambling, a pool, and a tasty Mexican restaurant. **Pros:** a good value, with quality that far surpasses many other local options; inviting, modern rooms; friendly staff. **Cons:** can book up quickly; not walking distance to downtown; having an in-house casino does not appeal to everyone. $ Rooms from: $89 ⊠ 1501 E. Aultman St., Ely ☎ 775/289–8900, 800/750–0557 ⊕ www.prospectorhotel. us ➤ 61 rooms ⊗ No meals.

Baker

5 miles from the Great Basin Visitor Center.

Located just five miles from the park's entrance, Baker is basically Great Basin's front door. The tiny desert town has a lonesome, funky charm, and is anchored by a few small motels.

Just like much of rural Nevada, Baker has no transportation services and requires a long drive from pretty much everywhere. The first stop for many visitors is the **Great Basin Visitor Center,** which lies about 5 miles northwest.

VISITOR INFORMATION
Great Basin Business and Tourism Council. ⊕ www.greatbasinpark.com.

🍴 Restaurants

★ Kerouac's

$$ | **AMERICAN** | One of the best restaurants in this corner of rural Nevada can be found in an airy, historic building that resembles an old general store on the edge of town. Expect the same caliber of burgers and artisan pizzas you'd get in a hip urban eatery, as well as incredible cocktails and luscious desserts. **Known for:** everything made from scratch, including the hamburger buns and dough for Neapolitan-style pizzas; the full bar is also a local hangout; friendly, attentive service for dinner and weekend brunch. [$] *Average main: $14* ✉ *115 S. Baker Ave., Baker* ☎ *775/234–7323* 🌐 *www.stargazernevada.com/eat-drink* 🕒 *Closed mid-Oct.–mid-Apr. No lunch.*

The Baker's Bean

$ | **BAKERY** | Two professionally trained chefs, who also happen to be twin sisters, make all the sumptuous sweet and savory treats in this compact trailer of a coffee shop in downtown Baker. Their menu is small but excellent, with an emphasis on baked goods. **Known for:** giant and rich ice cream sandwiches; tasty breakfast sandwiches with homemade English muffins; good drip coffee and various espresso drinks. [$] *Average main: $5* ✉ *40 S. Baker Ave., Baker* ☎ *719/237-5726* 🌐 *www.saltandsucre.com* 🕒 *Closed Nov.–Apr.*

🛏 Hotels

The Border Inn

$ | **HOTEL** | Located right on the border between Nevada and Utah on Route 50, the Border Inn is a reliable staple, with air-conditioned rooms, a restaurant, bar, grocery store, gas station, and small casino. **Pros:** open 24/7; low prices, with more amenities and rooms than other Baker motels; family-run business with friendly staff. **Cons:** rooms are simple and rustic; due to remote location, Wi-Fi and cell service can be iffy; a few miles farther from the park than Baker's other motels (though much closer than Ely offerings). [$] *Rooms from: $75* ✉ *U.S. 6/50, Baker* ✥ *13 miles northeast of Great Basin National Park* ☎ *775/234–7300* 🌐 *www.borderinncasino.com* 🔑 *29 rooms* 🍴 *No meals.*

★ Hidden Canyon Retreat

$$$ | **B&B/INN** | The most luxurious lodging for hours in any direction, the large rooms here have a modern serenity to them and are surrounded on all sides by hundreds of acres of rugged, high-desert beauty. **Pros:** tucked into a canyon, the setting makes this feel like a true retreat; hot tub and pool are nice for unwinding; features an extensive market, with fresh produce, ready-to-eat meals, alcohol, and more. **Cons:** no cell reception and limited Wi-Fi; far from services and a 30-minute drive to Great Basin National Park; located down a dirt road (but it is well maintained). [$] *Rooms from: $164* ✉ *2000 Hidden Canyon Pkwy., Baker* ☎ *775/234–7172* 🌐 *www.hiddencanyon-retreat.com* 🔑 *12 rooms* 🍴 *Breakfast.*

Stargazer Inn

$ | **HOTEL** | New life has been breathed into this small, quirky roadside motel, with vintage stargazing-theme art and tasteful bedspreads giving the otherwise plain, spotless rooms a rustic elegance. **Pros:** motel and small market are open year-round; great location in downtown Baker, just a few miles from the park; delicious restaurant and popular bar (seasonal). **Cons:** while rooms are comfortable, they are small and older; can fill up far in advance; some of the rooms are located on the other side of the street from motel office, about a 3-minute walk. [$] *Rooms from: $85* ✉ *115 S. Baker Ave., Baker* ☎ *775/234–7323* 🌐 *www.stargazernevada.com* 🔑 *10 rooms* 🍴 *No meals.*

Chapter 19

GREAT SAND DUNES NATIONAL PARK

Updated by
Whitney Bryen

COLORADO

⛰ Camping   🛏 Hotels   🎿 Activities   👁 Scenery   👥 Crowds
★★★☆☆   ★☆☆☆☆   ★★★★☆   ★★★★☆   ★★★☆☆

WELCOME TO GREAT SAND DUNES NATIONAL PARK

TOP REASONS TO GO

★ **Dune climbing:** Trek through the 30 square miles of main dunes in this landlocked dune field.

★ **Unrivaled diversity:** You can see eight completely different life zones in this park, ranging from salty wetlands and lush forests to parched sand sheet and frozen alpine peaks, all in a single day.

★ **Starry skies:** Gaze expansive views of the Milky Way staged above silouettes of the rolling dunes and jagged mountain peaks below.

★ **Aspens in autumn:** Take a hike—or, if you've got a high-clearance four-wheel-drive vehicle and good driving skills, take the rough road—up to Medano Pass during fall foliage season when the aspens turn gold.

★ **Vigorous hikes:** Pack a picnic lunch and climb up to High Dune, followed by the more strenuous stretch over to Star Dune. Or tackle the dramatic Music Pass Trail, which rewards you with two alpine lakes above the tree line if you can make the steep 4-mile climb.

1 **Main Use Area.** This relatively compact area contains all of the park's developed campgrounds, trails, and the visitor center.

2 **Sand Dunes.** The 30-square-mile field of sand has no designated trails. The highest dune in the park—and, in fact, in North America—is 750-foot-high Star Dune.

3 **Sangre de Cristo Mountains.** Named the "Blood of Christ" Mountains by Spanish explorers because of their ruddy color—especially at sunrise and sunset—the range contains 10 of Colorado's 54 Fourteeners (mountains taller than 14,000 feet); six within the preserve are more than 13,000 feet tall.

4 **Southern Grasslands.** Wildlife, such as elk and bison, feed on the park's grassy areas, primarily found in the park's southern area and the Great Sand Dunes National Preserve.

5 **Medano Creek Wetlands.** Popular with a variety of birds and amphibians, these seasonal wetlands form in the area around Medano Creek, where cottonwood and willow trees also thrive.

SAN LUIS VALLEY

SAND SHEET SABKHA

← TO MOSCA

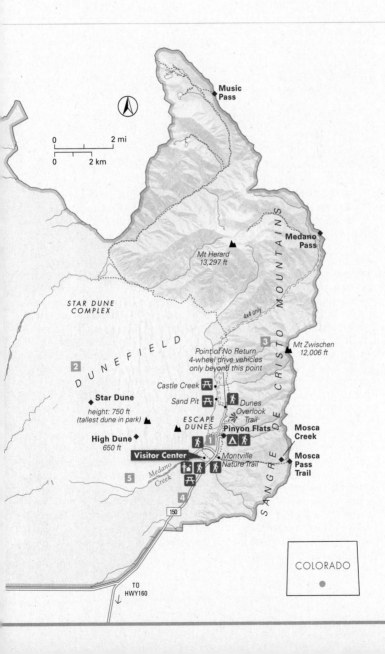

Music Pass

0   2 mi

0   2 km

Medano Pass

Mt Herard
13,297 ft

STAR DUNE COMPLEX

4x4 only

DUNEFIELD

2

Point of No Return
4-wheel drive vehicles
only beyond this point

3

Mt Zwischen
12,006 ft

Castle Creek

Sand Pit

Dunes
Overlook
Trail

Star Dune
height: 750 ft
(tallest dune in park)

ESCAPE
DUNES

Pinyon Flats

High Dune
650 ft

SANGRE DE CRISTO MOUNTAINS

Mosca Creek

Visitor Center

Montville
Nature Trail

Mosca Pass Trail

Medano
Creek

5

4

150

TO
HWY 160

COLORADO

Created by winds that sweep the San Luis Valley floor, the enormous sand dunes that form the heart of Great Sand Dunes National Park and Preserve are an improbable, unforgettable sight. The dunes stretch for more than 30 square miles, solid enough to have withstood 440,000 years of Mother Nature.

Nomadic hunters followed herds of mammoths and prehistoric bison into the San Luis Valley, making them some of the first people to visit the dunes. The hills of sand marked a common route for Native American tribes and explorers who traveled between the plains and Santa Fe. Speculation that gold was hiding under the sand attracted droves of miners in the 19th and 20th centuries. By the 1920s, operations had sprung up along the seasonal Medano Creek at the eastern base of the dunes, alarming residents of the nearby Alamosa and Monte Vista communities. Members of the Ladies Philanthropic Educational Organization lobbied politicians to protect the landmark, and in 1932 it was designated a national monument. Seventy years later, it was discovered that a large inland lake once covered the San Luis Valley, but had dried up due to climate change. Residents again rallied to protect the local resource, wildlife and unique ecosystems, and the area was expanded into a national park and preserve in 2004. Today, more than half a million visitors flock to the region annually to gawk at and play on the vast mountains of sand framed by the low grasslands and high-reaching Sangre de Cristo peaks. The tallest sand dunes in North America are nestled among diverse ecosystems of wetlands, grasslands, forests, and a towering mountain range where visitors can fish alpine lakes, walk among wildflowers, listen to songbirds, and climb the soft sand in a single day. Pronghorn, elk, and bighorn sheep call the area home, while sandhill cranes flood the area twice a year during spring and fall migrations. From star designs to sharp defined edges, the shapes of the dunes are as disparate as the geography surrounding them. Warmed by the sun or coated in snow, the sand hills, which tower as high as 750 feet, offer opportunities for sledding or climbing year-round. Adding to the awe of the unusual landscape, avalanches of sand can create a rare humming sound that inspired Bing Crosby's musical hit "The Singing Sands of Alamosa." Intrigue and inspiration continues to attract visitors from around the globe to this one-of-a-kind site.

AVERAGE HIGH/LOW TEMPERATURES					
JAN.	**FEB.**	**MAR.**	**APR.**	**MAY**	**JUNE**
35/10	39/14	47/21	56/28	66/37	77/45
JULY	**AUG.**	**SEPT.**	**OCT.**	**NOV.**	**DEC.**
81/51	78/49	71/42	60/32	46/20	36/11

Planning

When to Go

More than half a million visitors come to the park each year, most on summer weekends; they tend to congregate around the main parking area and Medano Creek. To avoid the crowds, hike away from the main area up to the High Dune. Or come in the winter, when the park is a place for contemplation and repose—as well as skiing and sledding.

Fall and spring are the prettiest times to visit, with the surrounding mountains still capped with snow in May, and leaves on the aspen trees turning gold in September and early October. In summer, the surface temperature of the sand can climb to 150°F in the afternoon, so climbing the dunes is best in the morning or late afternoon. Since you're at a high altitude—about 8,200 feet at the visitor center—the air temperatures in the park itself remain in the 70s most of the summer.

FESTIVALS AND EVENTS
Alamosa Round-Up Rodeo. The annual rodeo competition rides into Alamosa each summer with a genuine Wild West event including barrel racers, bulls, broncos, and bareback riding. ⊕ www.alamosaroundup.com

Getting Here and Around

CAR
Great Sand Dunes National Park and Preserve is about 240 miles from both Denver and Albuquerque, and roughly 180 miles from Colorado Springs and Santa Fe. The fastest route from Denver is Interstate 25 south to U.S. 160, heading west to just past Blanca, to Highway 150 north, which goes right to the park's main entrance. For a more scenic route, take U.S. 285 over Kenosha, Red Hill, and Poncha Passes, turn onto Highway 17 just south of Villa Grove, then take County Lane 6 to the park (watch for signs just south of Hooper). From Albuquerque, go north on Interstate 25 to Santa Fe, then north on U.S. 285 to Alamosa, then U.S. 160 east to Highway 150. From the west, Highway 17 and County Lane 6 take you to the park. The park entrance station is about 3 miles from the park boundary, and it's about a mile from there to the visitor center; the main parking lot is about a mile farther.

Inspiration

Great Sand Dunes: The Shape of the Wind, by Stephen Trimble, covers dune history, ecology, scenery, and wildlife.

The Essential Guide to Great Sand Dunes National Park and Preserve, by Charlie and Diane Winger, is a must-have for trip planning.

Great Sand Dunes in One Day

Arrive early in the day during the summer so you can hike up to **High Dune** and get a view of the entire dune field. Round-trip, the walk itself should take about 1½ to 2 hours (plus time to jump off or slide down the dunes). In the afternoon, hop into the car and head to Zapata Falls, hike on the short-and-shady Montville Nature Trail, or head for the longer Mosca Pass Trail, which follows a small creek through cool aspens and evergreens to one of the lower mountain passes. You can build sand castles only by the creek because you need water.

In the spring and early summer or fall, when the temperatures are cooler, first walk up to the High Dune to enjoy the view. If you're game to hike farther, head to **Star Dune** for a picnic lunch. Hike down the eastern ridge to Medano Creek, then head to the western end of the park to explore the sand sheet, grasslands, and wetlands.

Park Essentials

ACCESSIBILITY
The park has two wheelchairs with balloon tires (for the sand) that can be borrowed; someone must push them. You can reserve one by calling the visitor center. Accessible campsites are available in the park's only campground.

PARK FEES AND PERMITS
Entrance fees are $25 per vehicle and are valid for one week from date of purchase. Pick up camping permits ($20 per night per site at Pinyon Flats Campground) and backpacking permits (free) online at www.recreation.gov.

PARK HOURS
The park is open 24/7. It is in the Mountain time zone.

Hotels

There are no hotels, motels, or lodges in the park. The nearest lodge is right outside the park entrance, and there are many hotels in Alamosa and a handful of them in other surrounding towns including Salida, Walsenburg, and Monte Vista. *Hotel reviews have been shortened. For full information, visit Fodors.com.*

What It Costs

	$	$$	$$$	$$$$
RESTAURANTS				
	under $13	$13–$18	$19–$25	over $25
HOTELS				
	under $121	$121–$170	$171–$230	over $230

Restaurants

The nearest restaurant is located just outside of the park entrance. There are no dining establishments in the park. In the visitor center and at the campground there are vending machines with drinks that are stocked mid-spring through mid-fall. There is one picnic area in the park situated along the edge of the dunes and the seasonal Medano Creek. *Restaurant reviews have been shortened. For full information, visit Fodors.com.*

Visitor Information

Great Sand Dunes National Park and Preserve

✉ 11999 Hwy. 150, Mosca ☎ 719/378–6395 ⊕ www.nps.gov/grsa.

Main Use Area

There's one paved road in the park, and it goes to the park visitor center, the amphitheater, and about another mile to the Pinyon Flats Campground. Past the campground, you can take a regular car another mile on the Medano Pass Primitive Road to the Point of No Return. ⚠ Beyond the Point of No Return, only four-wheel high-clearance vehicles are allowed.

Sights

PICNIC AREAS
Mosca Creek

LOCAL INTEREST | FAMILY | Great Sand Dunes National Park's only picnic area is shaded by cottonwood trees with easy access to the sand and seasonal creek. It has a dozen places where visitors can park a car or small RV near a picnic table and a grill. ✉ Great Sand Dunes National Park ✛ South of the dunes parking lot.

TRAILS
⭐ **Mosca Pass Trail**

TRAIL | This moderately challenging route follows the Montville Trail laid out centuries ago by Native Americans, which became the Mosca Pass toll road used in the late 1800s and early 1900s. This is a good afternoon hike, because the trail rises through the trees and subalpine meadows, often following Mosca Creek. Watch for grouse and turkey along the route and listen for songbirds and owls cooing at dusk. It is 3½ miles one-way, with a 1,400-foot gain in elevation. Hiking time is about two hours each way. *Moderate.* ✉ Great

Sand Dunes National Park ✛ Trailhead: lower end of trail begins at Montville Trailhead, just north of visitor center.

VISITOR CENTER
Great Sand Dunes Visitor Center

INFO CENTER | View exhibits and artwork, browse in the bookstore, and watch a 20-minute film with an overview of the dunes. Rangers are on hand to answer questions. Facilities include restrooms and a vending machine stocked with soft drinks and snacks, but no other food. (The Great Sand Dunes Oasis, just outside the park boundary, has a café that is open generally late April through early October.) ✉ Near the park entrance ☎ 719/378–6395 ⊕ www.nps.gov/grsa/planyourvisit/visitor-center.htm.

Sand Dune Field

Seven types of sandy mounds decorate this ever-changing landscape shaped by wind and tucked into a pocket among the Sangre de Cristo mountains. The more than 30 square miles of big dunes in the heart of the park are the main attraction, although the surrounding sand sheet does have some smaller dunes. These mountains of sand range from a few feet to 750 feet into the sky, and all offer spectacular views of the dune field and the bordering peaks. You can start putting your feet in the sand 3 miles past the main park entrance.

Sights

SCENIC STOPS
High Dune

TRAIL | This isn't the park's highest dune, but it's high enough in the dune field to provide a view of all the dunes from its summit. It's on the first ridge of dunes you see from the main parking area. ✉ Great Sand Dunes National Park.

Plants and Wildlife in Great Sand Dunes

The salty wetlands are dotted with sedges, rushes, and other plants that are tolerant of changes in water salinity and levels, while the sand sheet and grasslands have prickly pear, rabbit brush, and yucca. The dune field looks barren from afar, but up close you see various grasses have rooted in swales among the dunes. Juniper, pinyon, and ponderosa pine trees grow on the lower portions of the mountain, hardy spruce and fir trees survive in the subalpine forest zone, and lichens and tiny flowers cling to the rock at the top.

Birds inhabit the wetlands; short-horned lizards, elk, and pronghorns live in the sand sheet and grassland; and Great Sand Dunes tiger beetles and Ord's kangaroo rats breed in the dune field. In the forests and on the mountainsides, raptors fly overhead, while mule deer and Rocky Mountain bighorn sheep graze.

TRAILS

Hike to High Dune

TRAIL | FAMILY | Get a panoramic view of all the surrounding dunes from the top of High Dune. Since there's no formal path, the smartest approach is to zigzag up the dune ridgelines traversing about 2½ miles round-trip. High Dune is 699 feet high, and to get there and back takes about two hours, or longer if there's been no rain for some time and the sand is soft. If you add on the walk to the 750-foot Star Dune, plan on another two or three hours and a strenuous workout up and down the dunes. *Easy to moderate.* ⊠ *Great Sand Dunes National Park* ⊹ *Start from main dune field.*

Sangre de Cristo Mountains

Stretching from central Colorado to southeast New Mexico, the Sangre de Cristo mountains contains 10 peaks that tower more than 14,000 feet. Spanish for "the blood of Christ," the range is named for the red hues reflected during sunrise and sunset. The peaks offer hundreds of miles of alpine hiking, rock climbing, and skiing and provide a home to elk and bighorn sheep.

Southern Grasslands

The less explored grasslands of the park offer solitude from the busy sand dunes. Sunflowers coat the area in mid-August, adding a colorful layer to the panoramic views of sand hills and mountain peaks offered in the distance. Keep an eye out for miniature sand-colored lizards, pronghorns and burrowing owls that live among the shrubs.

Medano Creek Wetlands

Colorado's only natural beach runs along the eastern base of the sand dunes, but it's only temporary. At the edge of the cottonwood trees, Medano Creek emerges in the spring and lingers into early summer as a result of run-off from winter snow melt. Ask a ranger where to find the hidden pools where birds can be seen chasing tadpoles—they appear in new places each year directed by the shifting sand.

Near water in the park's grasslands area is where you might see elk, mule deer, and lizards.

Activities

BIRD-WATCHING

The San Luis Valley is famous for its migratory birds, many of which stop in the park. Great Sand Dunes also has many permanent feathered residents. In the wetlands, you might see American white pelicans and the American avocet. On the forested sections of the mountains there are goshawks, northern harriers, gray jays, and Steller's jays. And in the alpine tundra there are golden eagles, hawks, horned larks, and white-tailed ptarmigan.

CAMPING

Great Sand Dunes has one campground, open April through October. During weekends in the summer, it can fill up with RVs and tents by midafternoon. Black bears live in the preserve, so when camping there, keep your food, trash, and toiletries in the trunk of your car (or use bear-proof containers). There is one campground and RV park near the entrance to Great Sand Dunes, and several others in the area.

Pinyon Flats Campground. Set in a pine forest about a mile past the visitor center, this campground has a trail leading to the dunes. Sites must be reserved online; RVs are allowed, but there are no hookups. ⊠ *On the main park road, near the visitor center* ⊕ *www.recreation.gov* ☎ *719/378–6399*.

EDUCATIONAL PROGRAMS
RANGER PROGRAMS
Interpretive Programs
TOUR—SIGHT | FAMILY | Family-friendly nature walks designed to help visitors learn more about the Great Sand Dunes National Park are scheduled most days from late May through September, and sporadically in April and October. Call or drop in to ask about sunset walks, afternoon weekend tours, and evening stargazing programs. The Junior Ranger program is a favorite for children ages 3 to 12, who can earn their badge by completing a booklet of activities.

✉ *Programs begin at the visitor center* ☎ *719/378–6395* 🏷 *Free.*

FISHING

Fly fishermen can angle for Rio Grande cutthroat trout in the upper reaches of Medano Creek, which is accessible by four-wheel-drive vehicle. It's catch-and-release only, and a Colorado license is required (☎ *800/244–5613*). There's also fishing in Upper and Lower Sand Creek Lakes, but it's a very long hike (3 or 4 miles from the Music Pass trailhead, located on the far side of the park in the San Isabel National Forest).

HIKING

Visitors can walk just about anywhere on the sand dunes in the heart of the park. The best view of all the dunes is from the top of High Dune. There are no formal trails because the sand keeps shifting, but you don't really need them: It's extremely difficult to get lost out here.

■TIP→ **Before taking any of the trails in the preserve, rangers recommend stopping at the visitor center and picking up the handout that lists the trails, including their degree of difficulty.** The dunes can get very hot in the summer, reaching up to 150°F in the afternoon. If you're hiking, carry plenty of water; if you're going into the backcountry to camp overnight, carry even more water and a water filtration system. A free permit is required to backpack in the park. Also, watch for weather changes. If there's a thunderstorm and lightning, get off the dunes or trail immediately, and seek shelter. Before hiking, leave word with someone indicating where you're going to hike and when you expect to be back. Tell that contact to call 911 if you don't show up when expected.

Nearby Towns

The vast expanse one sees from the dunes is the San Luis Valley. Covering 8,000 square miles (and with an average altitude of 7,500 feet), the San Luis Valley is the world's largest alpine valley, sprawling on a broad, flat, dry plain between the San Juan Mountains to the west and the Sangre de Cristo range to the east, and extending south into northern New Mexico. The area is one of the state's major agricultural producers.

Alamosa, the San Luis Valley's major city, is 35 miles southwest of Great Sand Dunes via U.S. 160 and Highway 150. It's a casual, central base for exploring the park and the surrounding region. The rest of the area is dotted with tiny towns, including **Mosca, Blanca, Antonito,** and **Fort Garland,** to the south of the park, and **Monte Vista** and **Hooper** to the west. They are all within an hour's drive from the park.

VISITOR INFORMATION Del Norte Chamber of Commerce. ✉ *505 Grand Ave., Del Norte* ⊕ *www.delnortechamber.org.* **Monte Vista Chamber of Commerce.** ✉ *947 1st Ave., Monte Vista* ☎ *719/852–2731* ⊕ *www.montevistachamber.org.*

Great Sand Dunes Oasis

½ mile east of Great Sand Dunes National Park Entrance; 35 miles northeast of Alamosa via Rte. 17.

The smell of country cooking welcomes visitors at the seasonal restaurant and store located just outside of the park entrance. A campground and ranch-style lodge clustered nearby make up the rest of the Great Sand Dunes Oasis. It's the only place to rent sandboards or pick up forgotten items near the park from April through mid-October.

Sights

Zapata Falls Recreation Area

TRAIL | FAMILY | If it's a hot day, take a drive to the falls section of the Zapata Falls Recreation Area, about 7 miles south of Great Sand Dunes National Park (and about 10 miles north of Alamosa). From the trailhead, it's a ½-mile hike to the 40-foot waterfall and a mildly steep trail, which can include wading in a stream and walking through a narrow gorge to view the falls (depending on water levels). Air temperatures in the gorge are always cool and inviting, and the falls are beautiful, but be careful of the current (and slippery rocks) here. A picnic area and restrooms are at the entrance. The trailhead is 3½ miles off Highway 150, between mile markers 10 and 11. ✉ *San Luis Valley Field Office, 1313 E. Highway 160, Monte Vista* ☎ *719/852–7074* 🌐 *www.blm.gov/visit/zapata-falls-special-recreation-management-area* 🎟 *Free.*

Restaurants

The Oasis Cafe

$ | AMERICAN | The no-frills restaurant in the Great Sand Dunes Oasis (which includes a grocery store and gas station as well as motel rooms and campsites), just outside the park entrance, is open for breakfast, lunch, and dinner. The Navajo taco (served on fry bread) and beef or chicken burritos are among the most popular items, although the menu ranges from grilled-cheese sandwiches to steaks. **Known for:** comfort food; right at park entrance; tacos. [$] *Average main: $11* ✉ *5400 Hwy. 150, Mosca* ☎ *719/378–2222* 🌐 *www.greatdunes.com* 🕓 *Closed Oct.– Apr.*

Hotels

Great Sand Dunes Lodge

$$ | HOTEL | Located right at the entrance of the park, behind the Oasis, this simple lodge offers clean, comfortable rooms with patios that feature great views of the dunes and mountains. **Pros:** closest hotel rooms to the dunes; great views. **Cons:** with the exception of the nearby Oasis Cafe, the nearest restaurants are more than 20 miles away. [$] *Rooms from: $165* ✉ *7900 Hwy. 150 N, Mosca* ☎ *719/378–2900* 🌐 *www.gsdlodge.com* 🕓 *Closed mid-Nov.–Feb.* 🛏 *19 rooms* 🍴 *Free Breakfast.*

Zapata Ranch

$$$$ | B&B/INN | Part of a 103,000-acre working cattle and bison ranch owned by the Nature Conservancy, the Zapata Ranch is focused mainly on all-inclusive, weeklong stays, during which guests learn about bison, land conservation, and renewable ranching practices, and participate in ranch activities (including branding cattle and mending fences). **Pros:** beautiful setting among mature cottonwoods; historic lodge buildings; terrific restaurant with indoor and outdoor seating. **Cons:** much pricier than other area accommodations; limited capacity (the ranch rents only those rooms that aren't reserved for guest ranch visitors). [$] *Rooms from: $275* ✉ *5305 State Hwy. 150, Great Sand Dunes National Park* ✥ *5 miles southwest of Great Sand Dunes National Park, 19 miles west of Mosca* ☎ *888/592–7282, 719/378–2356* 🌐 *ranchlands.com/experience/ranch-stays/zapata-ranch/* 🛏 *15 rooms* 🍴 *All-inclusive.*

Alamosa

35 miles southwest of Great Sand Dunes via U.S. 160 and Rte. 150; 163 miles southwest of Colorado Springs.

The San Luis Valley's major city is a casual, central base from which to explore the region and visit the Great Sand Dunes.

VISITOR INFORMATION
Alamosa Convention & Visitors Bureau
⊠ *610 State Ave.* ☎ *800/258–7597, 719/589–4840* ⊕ *www.alamosa.org.*

Sights

Adams State University
COLLEGE | The campus here contains several superlative examples of 1930s WPA-commissioned murals in its administrative building. The college's **Luther Bean Museum and Art Gallery** displays European porcelain and furniture collections, and exhibits of regional arts and crafts. ⊠ *Richardson Hall, Richardson and 3rd Sts.* ☎ *719/587–7151* ⊕ *www. adams.edu/lutherbean/* 🖭 *Free* ⊙ *Closed weekends.*

Alamosa National Wildlife Refuge
NATURE PRESERVE | FAMILY | Less than an hour's drive southwest of Great Sand Dunes is a sanctuary for songbirds, waterbirds, and raptors (it's also home to many other types of birds, along with mule deer, beavers, and coyotes). The Rio Grande runs through the park comprising more than 11,000 acres of natural and man-made wetlands. You can take a 4-mile hike round-trip along the river or a 3½-mile wildlife drive on the park's western side or a drive along Bluff Road to an overlook on the park's eastern side. The refuge office is staffed by volunteers sporadically from March through November and closed in winter, but a self-service kiosk provides visitor information year-round. ⊠ *9383 El Rancho La., off U.S. 160* ☎ *719/589–4021* ⊕ *www.fws.gov/refuge/alamosa/* 🖭 *Free.*

The Greenhouse at Sand Dunes Pool
HOT SPRINGS | After a long day of hiking the dunes, take a dip in the soothing soaking tubs inside the 10,000-square-foot greenhouse at the Sand Dunes Pool. Just 30 minutes northwest of the park is a sanctuary that offers 70-degree comfort year-round. Visitors 21 and older can soak in three hot tubs ranging from 103 to 110 degrees or take a dip in the large, 98-degree swimming pool surrounded by lush gardens. A bar offers cocktails and sweet and savory small plates. For families, a giant outdoor pool with views of the Sangre de Cristo mountains is a popular amenity. ⊠ *1991 County Road 63, Mosca* ☎ *719/378-2807* ⊕ *www. sanddunespool.com/greenhouse* 🖭 *$20 for adults* ⊙ *Closed Thursdays.*

Monte Vista National Wildlife Refuge
NATURE PRESERVE | FAMILY | Just west of the Alamosa wildlife refuge is its sister sanctuary, the Monte Vista National Wildlife Refuge, a 15,000-acre park that's a stopping point for more than 20,000 migrating cranes in the spring and fall. It hosts an annual Crane Festival, held one weekend in mid-March in the nearby town of Monte Vista, and a children's Crane Festival in mid-October at the park with kid-friendly activities. You can see the sanctuary by foot, bike, or car via the 4-mile Wildlife Drive. ⊠ *6120 Hwy. 15, Monte Vista* ☎ *719/589–4021* ⊕ *www. fws.gov/refuge/monte_vista* 🖭 *Free.*

🍴 Restaurants

Milagros Coffeehouse
$ | CAFÉ | The coffee is full-bodied at this coffeehouse and café where all profits go to local charities. Amish baked goods reign on the menu where local food dominates, which includes plenty of vegetarian and gluten-free options. **Known for:** vegetarian options; charitable donations; excellent coffee. 🖭 *Average main: $7* ⊠ *529 Main St.* ☎ *719/589–9299.*

Hotels

Best Western Alamosa Inn

$ | HOTEL | This sprawling, well-maintained complex is your best bet for reasonably priced lodgings. **Pros:** reliable accommodations; easy to find; good base for area activities. **Cons:** noisy street; nothing but fast food nearby; basic rooms. *$ Rooms from: $110 ⊠ 2005 Main St. ☎ 719/589–2567, 800/459–5123 ⊕ www.bestwestern.com ⇆ 53 rooms ⊙ Free Breakfast.*

Comfort Inn

$$ | HOTEL | This property is a few miles west of downtown Alamosa on a strip with other chain hotels and restaurants, several of which will deliver to the hotel. **Pros:** basic accommodations at a reasonable price; pets allowed; hot tub. **Cons:** on a noisy street; a car-ride away from downtown restaurants. *$ Rooms from: $145 ⊠ 6301 W. Hwy. 160 ☎ 800/424–6423, 719/937-4002 ⊕ www.comfortinn.com ⇆ 49 rooms, 3 suites ⊙ Breakfast.*

San Luis and Fort Garland Loop

San Luis is 50 miles from Alamosa and Great Sand Dunes National Park; Fort Garland is 16 miles from San Luis, and 30 miles from Great San Dunes National Park.

To get a real feel for this area, take an easy driving loop from Alamosa that includes San Luis and Fort Garland. In summer, take a few hours to ride one of the scenic railroads that take you into wilderness areas in this region.

◉ Sights

Cumbres & Toltec Scenic Railroad

TOUR—SIGHT | FAMILY | Take a day trip on the Cumbres & Toltec Scenic Railroad, an 1880s steam locomotive that chugs through portions of Colorado's and northern New Mexico's rugged mountains that you can't reach via roads. It's the country's longest and highest steam-operated railroad. The company offers round-trip train routes, several bus-and-train combinations, one-way trips, and themed rides. ⊠ *5234 U.S. 285, Antonito ☎ 888/286–2737 ⊕ www.cumbrestoltec.com ⊠ $110–$216.*

Fort Garland

MILITARY SITE | One of Colorado's first military posts, Fort Garland was established in 1858 to protect settlers. It lies in the shadow of the Sangre de Cristo Mountains. The mountains were named for the "Blood of Christ" because of their ruddy color, especially at dawn. The legendary Kit Carson commanded the outfit, and some of the original adobe structures are still standing. The **Fort Garland Museum** features a re-creation of the commandant's quarters and period military displays. The museum is 16 miles north of San Luis via Highway 159 and 24 miles east of Alamosa via U.S. 160. ⊠ *U.S. 160 and Hwy. 159, Fort Garland ☎ 719/379–3512 ⊕ www.museumtrail.org/fortgarlandmuseum.asp ⊠ $5.*

Manassa, San Luis, and Fort Garland Loop

SCENIC DRIVE | To get a real feel for this area, take an easy driving loop from Alamosa through much of the San Luis Valley (the whole trip is about 95 miles). Head east on U.S. 160 to Fort Garland, south on Highway 159 to San Luis, west on Highways 159 and 142 to Manassa, then north on U.S. 285 back to Alamosa.

More than half of the route is part of the Los Caminos Antiguos Drive, one of Colorado's Scenic Byways.

San Luis

TOWN | Founded in 1851, San Luis is the oldest incorporated town in Colorado. Murals depicting famous stories and legends of the area adorn several buildings in the town. A latter-day masterpiece is the **Stations of the Cross Shrine,** created by renowned local sculptor Huberto Maestas. The shrine is formally known as La Mesa de la Piedad y de la Misericordia (Hill of Piety and Mercy), and its 15 stations with bronze statutes illustrate the last hours of Christ's life. The trail leads up to a chapel called La Capilla de Todos Los Santos. ✉ *San Luis.*

Hotels

Mountain View Motor Inn

$ | **HOTEL** | This cheerful, squeaky-clean motel is just a few miles south of the Great Sand Dunes, in the tiny town of Fort Garland, and makes a great base from which to visit the park and other San Luis Valley attractions. **Pros:** spotless, comfortable rooms; 20 minutes from park. **Cons:** no pool or other recreational amenities in hotel; no great eating options nearby. [$] *Rooms from: $96* ✉ *411 U.S. 160, Fort Garland* ☎ *719/379–2993* 🛏 *22 rooms* 🍴 *No meals.*

Chapter 20

GUADALUPE MOUNTAINS NATIONAL PARK

20

Updated by
Andrew Collins

TEXAS

🏕 Camping	🏨 Hotels	🏃 Activities	👁 Scenery	👥 Crowds
★★★☆☆	★★☆☆☆	★★★★☆	★★★★☆	★☆☆☆☆

WELCOME TO GUADALUPE MOUNTAINS NATIONAL PARK

TOP REASONS TO GO

★ **Tower over Texas:**
This dramatic wilderness that nearly borders New Mexico's Carlsbad Caverns National Park is home to 8,751-foot Guadalupe Peak, the highest point in the state.

★ **Fall for fiery foliage:**
Though surrounded by the arid Chihuahuan desert, the park has miles of beautiful foliage in McKittrick Canyon. In late October and early November, it bursts with flaming colors.

★ **Hike unhindered:** The main activity at the park is hiking its rugged, remote, and often challenging trails: 80 miles' worth that are nearly always free of crowds.

★ **Marvel at wildlife:** A variety of wildlife—including shaggy brown elk, furtive mountain lions, and shy black bears—traipse the mountains, woods, and desert here, and there's fantastic bird-watching, too.

★ **The Old West whispers:**
Rock ruins and former homesteads—Frijole Ranch History Museum is a highlight—dot a hardscrabble landscape that pioneers worked hard to tame.

1 Pine Springs. The park's main visitor center, its most popular campground and trailheads, and historic sites like Frijole Ranch and the Pinery Butterfield Stage Station ruins are located in this most central unit of the park.

2 McKittrick Canyon. Beautiful year-round, the lush green foliage along McKittrick Canyon's trout-filled desert stream bursts into many hues in autumn.

3 Dog Canyon. Just over the New Mexico border, this tranquil, forested high-desert wilderness contains a scenic campground and trails, including the trek to 7,830-foot Lost Peak.

4 Salt Basin Dunes. This remote unit in the western end of the park access acres of powdery-white gypsum dunes.

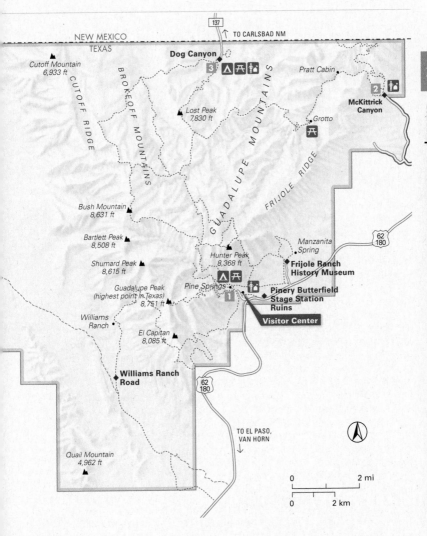

137
TO CARLSBAD NM

NEW MEXICO
TEXAS

Cutoff Mountain
6,933 ft

CUTOFF RIDGE

BROKEOFF MOUNTAINS

Dog Canyon
3

Pratt Cabin

2
McKittrick
Canyon

Lost Peak
7,830 ft

GUADALUPE MOUNTAINS

Grotto

FRIJOLE RIDGE

Bush Mountain
8,631 ft

Bartlett Peak
8,508 ft

Manzanita
Spring

62
180

Shumard Peak
8,615 ft

Hunter Peak
8,368 ft

**Frijole Ranch
History Museum**

Guadalupe Peak
(highest point in Texas)
8,751 ft

Pine Springs
1

**Pinery Butterfield
Stage Station
Ruins**

Williams
Ranch

Visitor Center

El Capitan
8,085 ft

**Williams Ranch
Road**

62
180

TO EL PASO,
VAN HORN

Quail Mountain
4,962 ft

0   2 mi

0   2 km

Guadalupe Mountains National Park is a study in extremes: it has mountaintop forests but also rocky canyons, arid desert, white gypsum sand dunes, and a stream that winds through verdant woods. It also has the loftiest spot in Texas: 8,751-foot Guadalupe Peak. The mountain dominates the view from every approach, but it's just one part of a rugged landscape carved by wind, water, and time.

This windswept stretch of the Chihuahuan Desert in far West Texas, adjacent to New Mexico's southern border, has always been a place of solitude. Roaming groups of the parepetetic Mescalero-Apache tribe hunted and harvested agave cacti in the area but never established any sizable permanent settlements. Outsiders had scarcely set foot here by 1858, the year the Butterfield Overland Mail service set up a wayside stagecoach station, the Pinery, along a route that hugged southeastern flank of soaring mountain peaks that define this stunning landscape. Just a year later, Butterfield abandoned the site for a route farther south, but remnants of Pinery Station still stand less than a mile from the park's main visitor center, Pine Springs.

Over the next century, a handful of hearty souls established lonely homesteads in the area: Felix McKittrick (for whom McKittrick Canyon is named) as well as the Rader Brothers (who built Frijole Ranch) in the 1870s, James Williams (of Williams Ranch fame) in the 1920s, and Wallace

Pratt, a geologist for the gas company that would eventually become Exxon, who built a pair of vacation homes in the 1930s in McKittrick Canyon—his handsome stone-and-wood Pratt Cabin remains a popular hiking destination to this day. Pratt was an advocate of turning this pristine landscape into a park, and in the early 1960s, he donated about 6,000 acres of McKittrick Canyon to help see his dreams come to fruition. The federal government bought a much larger tract soon after, and in 1972, Guadalupe Mountains National Park opened to the public.

In comparison to many other national parks, this 86,367-acre wilderness contains few features shaped by man—you won't find many miles of paved roads or any facilities beyond a modest visitor center and a couple of small ranger stations. To fully experience the awesome grandeur of the Guadalupe Mountains, you have to venture deep into the secluded interior. The less-visited park units, Dog Canyon and Salt Basin Dunes, are an hour or two by car from the main

AVERAGE HIGH/LOW TEMPERATURES					
JAN.	**FEB.**	**MAR.**	**APR.**	**MAY**	**JUNE**
53/30	58/35	63/38	71/46	78/55	88/63
JULY	**AUG.**	**SEPT.**	**OCT.**	**NOV.**	**DEC.**
87/63	84/62	78/57	71/49	61/38	57/33

visitor center. Unsurprisingly, the park is a favorite of long-distance hikers and backcountry campers.

That said, visitors with limited hiking experience or young kids in tow will find plenty within the park to keep them busy for at least a day, including a handful of easy nature trails and some historic buildings easily reached from U.S. 62/180, the highway that passes through the most accessible portions of the park. Head northeast on this highway, and in 45 minutes you'll reach New Mexico's Carlsbad Caverns National Park, which you might consider visiting in combination with Guadalupe Mountains. There's little else to see or do within an hour of this park, but the city of El Paso—less than two hours' drive west—has a growing art and culinary scene as well as some impressive parks and outdoor attractions.

Planning

When to Go

Trails here are rarely crowded, except in fall, when foliage changes colors in McKittrick Canyon, and during spring break in March. Still, this is a very remote area, and you probably won't find much congestion. Backcountry trails are best explored in spring and fall, when it's cooler but not too cold. Snow, not uncommon in winter, can linger in the higher elevations. The windy season is March through May, and the rainy months are July and August.

Getting Here and Around

AIR

Carlsbad's Cavern City Air Terminal, 55 miles northeast, is served by Boutique Air, with regular service from Albuquerque and Dallas/Fort Worth, but there's just one major car rental agency (Enterprise). More practical is El Paso International Airport, 100 miles west, which is served by all major air carriers and car rental companies.

CAR

Few roadways penetrate this rugged park that's primarily designated wilderness. Most sites are off U.S. 62/180, but reaching two remote park units entails long, circuitous drives: Salt Basin Dunes, on the park's western edge, is accessed from FM Road 1576 near Dell City, and Dog Canyon, on the north end of the park, is reached via Highway 137 from New Mexico.

Inspiration

The Pine Springs Visitor Center sells several excellent books on the Guadalupe Mountains' natural features and history, including the illustrated *The Guadalupes*, by Dan Murphy. Other good titles include *Trails of the Guadalupes*, by Don Kurtz and William D. Goran, and *Hiking Carlsbad Caverns and Guadalupe Mountains National Parks*, by Bill Schneider.

Guadalupe Mountains National Park in One Day

Start your tour at **Pine Springs Visitor Center**, where an exhibit and slide show introduce the park's plants, wildlife, and geology. Nearby is the ¾-mile, round-trip, wheelchair-accessible **Pinery Trail**, which rambles to the **Pinery Butterfield Stage Station** ruins (take care not to touch the fragile walls). Next, drive a couple of miles to the **Frijole Ranch History Museum**, housed in a well-preserved 1876 ranch house.

After exploring the shaded grounds and admiring the labor that built the compound, turn onto the trailhead behind the house for the 0.2-mile stroll to the calm waters of **Manzanita Spring**, one of two watering holes that gurgle within a couple of miles of the museum. These oases, called riparian zones, supply the fragile wildlife here and sometimes look like Pre-Raphaelite paintings, with mirrored-surface ponds and delicate flowers and greenery.

Afterward, visit the famed **McKittrick Canyon.** Regardless of the season, the dense foliage and basin stream are worth the hike—though it's best to visit it in late October and early November when the trees burst into color. It's about a 20-minute drive from Pine Springs Visitor Center to the contact station and trailhead. Note that the road to McKittrick Canyon closes daily around sunset.

Take your time walking the **McKittrick Canyon Trail**, which leads 2.4 miles to Pratt Cabin, or the strenuous but rewarding 8.4-mile **Permian Reef Trail**, which takes you up thousands of feet, past monumental geological formations. Or traverse the easy, short (just under 1 mile) **McKittrick Canyon Nature Trail.**

Park Essentials

ACCESSIBILITY
The wheelchair-accessible Pine Springs Visitor Center has a wheelchair available for use. The ¾-mile round-trip Pinery Trail from the visitor center to Butterfield Stage Ruins is wheelchair accessible, as is McKittrick Contact Station.

PARK FEES AND PERMITS
The $10 park fee is good for one week and payable at the visitor center and major trailheads. Camping is $15 nightly per site. For overnight backpacking trips, you must get a free permit from either the visitor center or Dog Canyon Office.

PARK HOURS
The park is open 24/7, year-round. It's in the Mountain time zone, but beware that your cell phone may pick up a signal from towers in the adjacent Central time zone, giving you the incorrect impression that you're an hour ahead.

CELL PHONE RECEPTION
Reception in the park is very spotty, but cell phones generally work around Pine Springs Visitor Center (which also has Wi-Fi) and Frijole Ranch.

Hotels

There are no hotels in or even very near the park. There's one no-frills motel in Whites City, New Mexico (35 miles), and several hotels in Carlsbad, New Mexico (55 miles), but these lodgings can be expensive because of demand by local oil-industry workers. Many visitors stay in Van Horn (60 miles), which has a cool, old historic lodging (Hotel El Capitan), and in El Paso, which is a fairly scenic

90- to 110-minute drive and has dozens of options. *Hotel reviews have been shortened. For full information, visit Fodors. com. For additional lodging options near the park, see Hotels in Big Bend National Park and Carlsbad Caverns National Park.*

What It Costs			
$	$$	$$$	$$$$
RESTAURANTS			
under $16	$16–$22	$23–$30	over $30
HOTELS			
under $101	$101–$150	$151–$200	over $200

Restaurants

Dining in the park is a do-it-yourself affair—bring a camp stove if you plan on cooking, as wood and charcoal fires aren't permitted anywhere. There are no restaurants, but the visitor center sells a few drink and snack items, and Whites City, New Mexico (35 miles), has an unremarkable restaurant and a convenience store. You'll find extensive dining options in Carlsbad, New Mexico (55 miles), and El Paso (100 miles). *Restaurant reviews have been shortened. For full information, visit Fodors.com. For additional dining options near the park, see Restaurants in Big Bend National Park and Carlsbad Caverns National Park.*

Visitor Information

The park comprises four distinct sections, with the headquarters and main visitor center located in the Pine Springs area; it and the McKittrick Canyon unit (with a small ranger station) are easily reached off U.S. 62/180. Long back-country drives are required to reach the remote Dog Canyon (also with a small ranger station) and Salt Basin Dunes sections.

CONTACTS Guadalupe Mountains National Park. ✉ *Pine Springs Visitor Center, 400 Pine Canyon Dr.* ☎ *915/828–3251* ⊕ *www.nps.gov/gumo.*

Pine Springs

55 miles southwest of Carlsbad, NM, 100 miles east of El Paso.

You'll find the park's only visitor center and the majority of its key attractions in the Pine Springs area, which is just off U.S. 62/180 in the southeastern corner of the park—it's the best place to begin your explorations of this vast wilderness. From the visitor center, it's a ½-mile walk or drive to the popular Pine Springs Campground, which is also the trailhead for such hiking highlights as Guadalupe Peak, El Capitan and Salt Basin Overlook, Devil's Hall, and the Bowl. Also nearby is Frijole Ranch and its desert springs and Williams Ranch Road.

Sights

HISTORIC SIGHTS
⭐ **Frijole Ranch History Museum**
COLLEGE | FAMILY | With its grassy, tree-shaded grounds, you could almost imagine this handsome and peaceful little 1876 ranch house somewhere other than the harsh Chihuahuan Desert. Inside what's believed to be the region's oldest intact structure, displays and photographs depict ranch life and early park history. Easy, family-friendly hiking trails lead to wildlife oases at Manzanita Spring and Smith Spring. Hours are sporadic, so check with the visitor center if you wish to go inside. Still, it's good fun just to explore the ranch grounds and outbuildings, orchard, and still-functioning irrigation system. ✉ *Frijole Ranch Rd.* ☎ *915/828–3251* ⊕ *www.nps.gov/gumo.*

Pinery Butterfield Stage Station Ruins

ARCHAEOLOGICAL SITE | FAMILY | In the mid-1800s passengers en route from St. Louis to California on the Butterfield Overland Mail stagecoach route stopped here for rest and refreshment. At more than a mile in elevation, the station was the highest on the journey, but it operated for only about a year. The ruins provide a peek into the past: the bare remains of a few buildings with rock walls (but no roofs) layered on the desert floor. Do not touch. You can drive here from U.S. 62/180, but it's more interesting to stroll over via the paved ¾-mile round-trip natural trail from the visitor center. ⊠ *U.S. 62/180 ⊹ Just east of visitor center* ⊕ *www.nps.gov/gumo.*

PICNIC AREAS

Frijole Ranch

$ | LOCAL INTEREST | | FAMILY |LOCAL INTEREST | FAMILY | It's not very secluded, but Frijole sports attractive picnic shelters near the parking area, which also has restrooms. Two picnic tables are also set up under tall trees near Frijole Ranch History Museum. ⊠ *Guadalupe Mountains National Park ⊹ Frijole Ranch Rd.*

★ Pine Springs Campground

$ | | FAMILY |LOCAL INTEREST | FAMILY | Drinking water, restrooms, and a picnic area are available at this central campground with sweeping mountain views. Shade, however, can be sparse and summer heat intense. You can walk off that hearty lunch along one of the several nearby hiking trails. ⊠ *Guadalupe Mountains National Park ⊹ ½-mile from Pine Springs Visitor Center.*

SCENIC DRIVES

Williams Ranch Road

ARCHAEOLOGICAL SITE | Although this adventure isn't for the faint of heart—a high-clearance, four-wheel-drive vehicle is required—this rough but enjoyable 7¼-mile, one-way drive over what was once the Butterfield Overland Mail Stage Line passes by dramatic limestone cliffs and offers panoramic views. Access is from U.S. 62/180 at the park's southeast border, and you must get a key at the visitor center to unlock the gate. It takes about an hour to reach the old ranch house, at the base of a 3,000-foot cliff. This is a day-trip only; overnight parking is prohibited. ⊹ *Off U.S. 62/180.*

TRAILS

★ The Bowl

TRAIL | Meandering through forests of pine and Douglas fir, this trail to an aptly named mountaintop valley is one of the most gorgeous in the park. The strenuous 9.1-mile round-trip has an elevation gain of 2,500 feet and can take up to 10 hours. It's where rangers go when they want to enjoy themselves. Bring lots of water. *Difficult.* ⊠ *Guadalupe Mountains National Park ⊹ Trailhead: Pine Springs Campground.*

★ Devil's Hall Trail

TRAIL | FAMILY | Wind through a Chihuahuan Desert habitat thick with spiked agave plants, prickly pear cacti, ponderosa pines, and a dry riverbed strewn with giant boulders to Devil's Hall, a narrow 10-foot-wide canyon with walls that soar to more than 100 feet. At a leisurely pace, this 4.2-mile round-trip jaunt will take three or four hours. *Moderate.* ⊠ *Guadalupe Mountains National Park ⊹ Trailhead: Pine Springs Campground.*

El Capitan/Salt Basin Overlook Trails

TRAIL | Several trails combine to form a popular loop through the low desert. El Capitan skirts the base of El Capitan peak for about 3.5 miles, leading to a junction with Salt Basin Overlook. The 4.7-mile Salt Basin Overlook trail begins at the Pine Springs Trailhead and has views of the stark white salt flat below and loops back onto the El Capitan Trail. The 11.3-mile round-trip is not recommended during the intense heat of summer, because there is absolutely no shade. *Moderate–Difficult.* ⊠ *Guadalupe Mountains National Park ⊹ Trailhead: Pine Springs Campground.*

Frijole/Foothills Trail

TRAIL | FAMILY | Branching off the Frijole Ranch Trail, this relatively flat hike leads to Pine Springs Campground and Visitor Center. The 5½-mile round-trip through desert vistas takes about four hours. *Moderate.* ⊠ *Guadalupe Mountains National Park* ⊹ *Trailhead: Frijole Ranch Cultural Museum.*

★ Guadalupe Peak Trail

TRAIL | An 8.4-mile workout over a steep grade to the top of Texas pays off with a passage through several ecosystems and some great views. The round-trip hike takes six to eight hours, but the trail is clearly defined and doesn't require undue athleticism. The steepest climbs are in the beginning. In summer, start this hike in early morning to allow a descent before afternoon thunderstorms flare up. Lightning targets high peaks. Be alert to changing weather and head for lower ground if conditions worsen. Also, Guadalupe Peak is considered one of the windiest points in the U.S. *Difficult, elevation gain 3,000 feet.* ⊠ *Guadalupe Mountains National Park* ⊹ *Trailhead: Pine Springs Campground.*

★ Smith Spring Trail

TRAIL | FAMILY | Departing from the Frijole Ranch, the trail heads for a shady oasis where you may spot mule deer and elk drawn to the miracle of water in the desert. As a bonus, the route passes Manzanita Spring, another wildlife refuge only 0.2 mile past Frijole Ranch. Allow 1½ hours to complete the 2.3-mile round-trip walk. This is a good hike for older kids whose legs won't tire as easily, but it's not wheelchair accessible past Manzanita Spring. *Easy–Moderate.* ⊠ *Guadalupe Mountains National Park* ⊹ *Trailhead: Frijole Ranch.*

VISITOR CENTERS

★ Pine Springs Visitor Center

INFO CENTER | You can pick up maps, brochures, and hiking permits here at the park's visitor center, just off U.S. 62/180. A slide show and a 12-minute movie provide a quick introduction to the park, half of which is protected as a designated wilderness area. Informative exhibits depict geological history, area wildlife, and flora ranging from lowland desert to forested mountaintop. You can access several trails and a lovely picnic area and campground a short ½-mile drive or stroll from the visitor center. ⊠ *400 Pine Canyon Dr.* ☎ *915/828-3251* ⊕ *www.nps.gov/gumo.*

McKittrick Canyon

12 miles northeast of Pine Springs Visitor Center.

A desert creek flows through this verdant canyon, which is easily accessed from U.S. 62/180, a 20-minute drive from the Pine Springs Visitor Center. One of the most wondrous sights of West Texas, the canyon is lined with walnut, maple, and other trees that explode into brilliant hues each autumn, from late October into early November (check with the visitor center for foliage updates). You're likely to spot mule deer here seeking water. And you'll find trailheads for several great hiking trails, including Pratt Cabin and the Grotto. The small ranger station here is staffed only part-time.

Sights

TRAILS

★ McKittrick Canyon to Pratt Cabin and Grotto

TRAIL | FAMILY | View stream and canyon woodlands along a 4.8-mile round-trip excursion that leads to the vacant Pratt Cabin (sometimes called Pratt Lodge), which was built of stone during the Great Depression in the "most beautiful spot in Texas," according to its original owner, Wallace Pratt. Perhaps he was enthralled by an oasis of running water carving through the canyon floor or a colorful riot of autumn foliage. Continue another mile each way to reach the Grotto, where you'll discover a picnic area overlooking

Plants and Wildlife in Guadalupe Mountains

Despite the constant wind and the arid conditions, more than a thousand species of plants populate the mountains, chasms, and salt dunes that comprise the park's different geologic zones. Some grow many feet in a single night; others bloom so infrequently they're called "century plants." In fall, McKittrick Canyon's oaks, bigtooth maples, and velvet ashes go Technicolor above the little stream that traverses it. Barren-looking cacti burst into yellow, red, and purple bloom in spring, and wildflowers can carpet the park for thousands of acres after unusually heavy rains.

More than 86,000 acres of mountains, chasms, canyons, woods, and deserts house an incredible diversity of wildlife, including hallmark Southwestern species like roadrunners and long-limbed jackrabbits, which run so fast they appear to float on their enormous, black-tipped ears. Other furry residents include coyotes, black bears, mountain lions, fox, deer, elk, and badgers. You may also spot numerous winged creatures: 300 different bird species, 90 types of butterflies, and 16 species of bats.

Plenty of reptiles and insects make their homes here, too: coachwhip snakes, diamondback rattlers, whiptail lizards, scorpions, and lovelorn tarantulas (the only time you might spy them is in the fall, when they search for mates), to name a few. Texas's famous (and threatened) horned lizards—affectionately called "horny toads"—can also be seen waddling across the soil in search of ants and other insects. Rangers caution parents not to let little ones run too far ahead on the trails. ■TIP➜ Rattlesnakes are common here, but they hibernate in winter. In summer, overnight campers should be cautious at dusk and dawn. The snakes are not aggressive, so try to remain calm and give a wide berth to any you spot.

a flowing stream and surface rock that resembles formations in an underground cave with jagged overhangs. Just beyond the Grotto is the historic Hunter Line Cabin. Allow two to three hours to visit Pratt Cabin and another hour or two if you go to the Grotto. *Moderate.* ⊠ *Guadalupe Mountains National Park* ✢ *Trailhead: McKittrick Contact Station.*

McKittrick Canyon Nature Trail

TRAIL | FAMILY | Signs along this nearly 1-mile loop explain the geological and botanical history of the area, and the views, while not spectacular, are engaging enough to hold your interest. You can take the loop in either of two directions when you come to a fork in the trail. *Easy–Moderate.* ⊠ *Guadalupe Mountains National Park* ✢ *Trailhead: McKittrick Contact Station.*

Permian Reef Trail

TRAIL | If you're in shape and have a serious geological bent, you may want to hike this approximately 8.5-mile round-trip climb. It heads through open, expansive desert country to a forested ridge with Douglas fir and ponderosa pines. Panoramic views of McKittrick Canyon and the surrounding mountain ranges allow you to observe many rock layers. A geology guidebook coordinated to trail makers is available at the Pine Springs Visitor Center. Set aside at least eight hours for this trek. *Difficult, elevation gain 2,000 feet.* ⊠ *Guadalupe Mountains National Park* ✢ *Trailhead: McKittrick Canyon Trailhead.*

VISITOR CENTERS

★ McKittrick Canyon Contact Station

ARCHAEOLOGICAL SITE | Poster-size illustrations on a shaded, outdoor patio of this intermittently staffed ranger station tell the geological story of the Guadalupe Mountains, believed to have been carved from an ancient sea. You can also hear the recorded memoirs of oilman Wallace Pratt, who donated his ranch and surrounding area to the federal government for preservation. Nearby trailheads access a 1-mile nature loop and lengthier hikes. ⊠ *4 miles off U.S. 62/180* ⊕ *www. nps.gov/gumo.*

Dog Canyon

102 miles northwest of Pine Springs Visitor Center.

This tranquil, wooded alpine canyon sits at an elevation of 6,300 feet and is situated at the extreme north end of the park, a two-hour drive from Pine Springs Visitor Center. Because it's such a long way to go, many who visit Dog Canyon overnight at one of the several campsites near the entrance and small ranger station. The lovely, shaded campground also has a few picnic tables—it's common to see mule deer. Drinking water and restrooms are available. This unit also has trails—popular for hiking on foot or on horseback—to several majestic vistas and is especially pleasant in summer, as it remains much cooler than the lower desert sections of the park. You get here via Highway 137 off U.S. 285 (12 miles north of Carlsbad, New Mexico) or by Highway 408 off U.S. 62/180 (9 miles south of Carlsbad). Intrepid hikers with backcountry camping experience can get to Dog Canyon from McKittrick Canyon and Pine Springs on foot; however, depending on the trail, this adventure involves at least 15 miles of hiking and a few thousand feet of elevation gain each way—those who attempt it usually allow three or four days to do so.

Sights

TRAILS

Indian Meadow Nature Trail

TRAIL | **FAMILY** | This mostly level 0.6-mile round-trip hike crosses an arroyo into meadowlands and offers a relaxing way to savor Dog Canyon's peaceful countryside in less than an hour. *Easy.* ⊠ *Guadalupe Mountains National Park* ✛ *Trailhead: Dog Canyon Office.*

Lost Peak

TRAIL | The somewhat strenuous trek from Dog Canyon into a coniferous forest is 6.4 miles round-trip and takes about five to six hours. There is no defined trail the last ¼ mile to the peak, but adventurers are rewarded with terrific views. *Moderate–Difficult, elevation gain 1,540 feet.* ⊠ *Guadalupe Mountains National Park* ✛ *Trailhead: Dog Canyon Campground.*

Marcus Overlook

TRAIL | **FAMILY** | A 4½-mile round-trip with an 800-foot elevation gain rewards you with a panoramic view of West Dog Canyon. Set aside about half a day for it. *Moderate.* ⊠ *Guadalupe Mountains National Park* ✛ *Trailhead: Dog Canyon Campground.*

VISITOR CENTERS

Dog Canyon Office

With a helpful staff who can advise you on making the most of your time in Dog Canyon, this small ranger station acts as a gateway to the vast, dramatic high country in the remote northern section of the park. ⊠ *Hwy. 137* ☎ *575/981–2418.*

Salt Basin Dunes

48 miles west of Pine Springs Visitor Center.

This little-explored unit in the remote far western edge of the park accesses stunning white gypsum dunes similar to those found about 90 miles northwest in New Mexico's White Sands National Park. But for some shaded picnic tables and pit toilets by the parking area, there are no facilities at Salt Basin Dunes, and it's about an hour's drive from Pine Springs Visitor Center via U.S. 62, FM Road 1576, and unpaved Williams Road; the nearby village of Dell City has a gas station and convenience store. This area is typically very hot in summer (and receives no shade), and fierce winds are possible in the spring, making late fall through winter the best time to go.

Sights

TRAILS

Salt Basin Dunes Trail

TRAIL | It's about a mile east of the trailhead to reach this eerily beautiful 2,000-acre expanse of gypsum sand dunes, the largest of which climbs to heights of 60 feet. Allow a couple of hours to walk three or four miles through this brilliant white-sand landscape, which also offers fine views east of the Guadalupe Mountains western escarpment. *Moderate.* ⊠ *Guadalupe Mountains National Park* ✚ *Trailhead: end of Williams Rd.*

Activities

BIRD-WATCHING

More than 300 species of birds have been spotted in the park, including the ladder-backed woodpecker, Scott's oriole, Say's phoebe, and white-throated swift. Many migratory birds—such as fleeting hummingbirds and larger but less graceful turkey vultures—stop at Guadalupe during spring and fall migrations. **Manzanita Springs,** near the Frijole Ranch History Museum, is an excellent birding spot. There aren't any local guides, but park rangers can help you spot some native species.

Books on birding are available at the visitor center, and bird lovers will find the park's birding checklist especially helpful. It's easy to spot the larger birds of prey circling overhead, such as keen-beaked golden eagles and swift, red-tailed

hawks. Watch for owls in the **Bowl** area and for swift-footed roadrunners in the desert areas (they're quick, but not as speedy as their cartoon counterpart).

CAMPING

The park has two developed campgrounds that charge $15 nightly per site, and 10 designated primitive backcountry sites where you can camp for free (you must first obtain a permit at Pine Springs Visitor Center or Dog Canyon Office) and enjoy miles of unspoiled land. In the backcountry, no restrooms are provided; visitors may dig their own privies, but toilet paper and other waste should be packed out. Wood and charcoal fires are prohibited throughout the park, but you can use a camp stove at both developed and backcountry sites.

Dog Canyon Campground. This campground is remote, but well worth the effort. The very well-maintained camping area is in a cool, high-elevation coniferous forest, with nine tent sites and four RV sites (no hookups, 23-foot maximum). ⊠ *Hwy. 137, just within park northern entrance* ☎ *575/981–2418.*

Pine Springs Campground. You'll be snuggled amid pinyon and juniper trees near the base of a tall mountain peak at this resting place a ½ mile from the Pine Springs Visitor Center. It has 20 tent sites, 19 RV sites (no hookups), one wheelchair-accessible site, and two group sites. ⊠ *U.S. 62/180* ☎ *915/828–3251.*

EDUCATIONAL PROGRAMS

Junior Ranger Program

COLLEGE | FAMILY | The park offers a self-guided Junior Ranger Program: kids choose activities from a workbook—including nature hikes and answering questions based on park exhibits—and earn a badge once they've completed four. If they complete six, they earn an additional patch. Workbooks are available at the visitor center or at the park website. ⊠ *Guadalupe Mountains National Park.*

The sun sets over the desert landscape of west Texas at Guadalupe Mountains National Park.

HIKING

No matter which trail you select, pack wisely—the visitor center carries only very limited supplies. Bring a gallon of water per day per person (there are water-filling stations at the visitor center and ranger stations), as well as sunscreen, sturdy footwear, and hats. The area has a triple-whammy regarding sun ailments: it's very open, very sunny, and has a high altitude (which makes sunburns more likely).

Nearby Towns

The Guadalupe Mountains border New Mexico to the north and are just a half-hour drive from **Whites City**, a tiny village with a few basic services that's by the entrance to Carlsbad Caverns National Park, and another 20 minutes from the small city of **Carlsbad**, which is a popular regional base but tends to have expensive lodgings; see Carlsbad Caverns National Park for more information. In Texas, although they're a bit farther away than Carlsbad, the town of **Van Horn** (an hour south) and the city of **El Paso** (90 minutes west) are handy bases. The drive from either place is picturesque and free of traffic. Van Horn is also a good stopover if making your way from Big Bend National park. El Paso, which is home to the region's major airport and has undergone an impressive downtown renaissance in recent years, offers much to see and do and is also convenient to visiting New Mexico's White Sands National Park.

El Paso

100 miles west of Guadalupe Mountains National Park, 45 miles southeast of Las Cruces, NM, 100 miles south of White Sands National Park.

With an attractive desert setting fringed by mountains, this friendly city of about 680,000 forms a culturally vibrant borderland region that encompasses neighboring Ciudad Juárez, Mexico (population 1.4 million) and Las Cruces, New Mexico (population

103,000). With distinctive hotels and restaurants (many of them set in artfully restored Victorian and early-20th-century buildings), excellent museums, and a gorgeous minor league baseball stadium, downtown El Paso is in the midst of an exciting revitalization. From here, it's an easy stroll (bring your passport) across the Rio Grande to the walkable center of Ciudad Juárez, which contains some interesting cultural draws and lively bars. Note that if affordability and convenience are your main priorities, you'll find plenty of chain hotels near El Paso's airport, an area that lacks personality but is about 15 minutes closer than downtown to both Guadalupe Mountains and White Sands national parks.

GETTING HERE AND AROUND

El Paso lies at the junction of Interstate 10, U.S. 54, and U.S. 62; the latter provides a direct and quite scenic route to Guadalupe Mountains National Park's Pine Springs Visitor Center. The city's El Paso International Airport is served by major airlines, and Amtrak stops at a historic train station downtown.

VISITOR INFORMATION Destination El Paso. ⊠ *1 Civic Center Plaza, El Paso* ☎ *915/534–0600* ⊕ *www.visitelpaso. com.*

 ## Sights

⋆ El Paso Museum of Art

MUSEUM | This superb, free museum in the heart of downtown El Paso's up-and-coming cultural district features a striking array of contemporary and historic Latin American, Spanish, and native art, as well as works by Southwest artists, such as Tom Lea and Henrietta Wyeth. ⊠ *1 Arts Festival Plaza, El Paso* ☎ *915/212–0300* ⊕ *www.epma.art* ⊠ *Free* ☉ *Closed Mon.*

⋆ Franklin Mountains State Park

NATIONAL/STATE PARK | Within this spectacular desert mountain park's 37 square miles are more than 100 miles of hiking, mountain-biking, and horseback trails, the southern section offering amazing views of the city below. This is a good place to get up close and personal with native species like foxes and kestrels and bluebirds, as well as plants found nowhere else in Texas, like the stout barrel cactus. ⊠ *2900 Tom Mays Access Rd., El Paso* ☎ *915/444–9100* ⊕ *www. tpwd.texas.gov* ⊠ *$5.*

Hueco Tanks State Park & Historic Site

NATIONAL/STATE PARK | En route between El Paso and the Guadalupe Mountains, this park, named after natural, water-holding stone basins called huecos, is internationally renowned for rock climbing and its pictographs left by the Apache, Kiowa, and Jornada Mogollon tribes who dwelt here. You can explore the park on self-guided and guided tours (book these at least a week ahead). You can also view exhibits in the visitor center, a historic ranching house, and the nearby stagecoach ruins. Because the park often fills to capacity, it's prudent to call ahead and make a reservation or arrive early. ⊠ *6900 Hueco Tanks Rd. No.1, El Paso* ✛ *Follows signs from U.S. 62/180* ☎ *915/857–1135* ⊕ *www.tpwd.texas.gov* ⊠ *$7.*

Restaurants

⋆ Anson 11

$$$ | MODERN AMERICAN | A culinary jewel of downtown's cultural district, this elegant spot with both a quieter and more refined dining room and a livelier bistro space turns out creatively prepared American cuisine. Specialties include creamy lobster risotto and grass-fed rack of lamb, while in the bistro you might opt for a flat-bread pizza or the kitchen's signature meatloaf with smoked-tomato gravy. **Known for:** one of the best wine lists in town; hand-carved steaks;

cast-iron apple cobbler. $ *Average main: $29* ✉ *303 N. Oregon St., El Paso* ☎ *915/504–6400* ⊕ *www.anson11.com.*

L&J Cafe

$ | **MEXICAN** | **FAMILY** | This rambling neighborhood spot across from historic Concordia Cemetery has been serving up big plates of delicious Tex-Mex fare since 1927. A great place to replenish your soul after a day of hiking, L&J specializes in burritos, enchiladas, tacos, and chiles rellenos smothered with red or green chile or mole sauces. **Known for:** walls hung with celebrity photos; chile con queso; steak tacos. $ *Average main: $9* ✉ *3622 E. Missouri Ave., El Paso* ☎ *915/566–8418* ⊕ *www.ljcafe.com* ⊘ *Closed Tues.*

Salt + Honey Bakery Cafe

$ | **ECLECTIC** | This bright and lively café with a mid-century modern vibe anchors the city's up-and-coming Five Points West district and is a great place to kick off your day with a well-crafted espresso drink. The all-day brunch and sandwich menu draws some of its inspiration from all over the Mediterranean, featuring novel dishes like baklava pancakes topped with house-spiced honey and poached eggs with feta, Moroccan tomato sauce, and naan bread. **Known for:** fried chicken and biscuit sandwiches; interesting beer and wine selection; heavenly baked goods. $ *Average main: $12* ✉ *801 N. Piedras St., El Paso* ☎ *915/313–4907* ⊕ *www.saltandhoneyep.com* ⊘ *Closed Mon. No dinner.*

Hotels

★ Hotel Paso Del Norte

$$$$ | **HOTEL** | Following a five-year closure and a tremendously ambitious renovation and rebranding, this 1912 grande dame with an enormous Tiffany-designed, stained-glass dome suspended above the bar reopened in 2020 as part of Marriott's posh Autograph Collection. **Pros:** stunning historic design elements; excellent restaurants and a hip bar; luxurious spa.

Cons: parking isn't free; pricey for El Paso; in a busy part of downtown. $ *Rooms from: $220* ✉ *10 Henry Trost Ct., El Paso* ☎ *915/534-3000* ⊕ *www.hotelpdn.com* ⊷ *351 rooms* ⧉ *No meals.*

★ Stanton House Hotel

$$$$ | **HOTEL** | One of the state's swankiest boutique hotels, this chic lodging set in an early 1900s building contains a remarkable contemporary art collection and spacious, light-filled rooms and suites with plush bedding and marble bathrooms. **Pros:** stunning hip-meets-antique aesthetic; exceptional restaurant; lots to see and do within walking distance. **Cons:** pricey for the area; steep fee for pets; not a great fit for kids. $ *Rooms from: $209* ✉ *209 N. Stanton St., El Paso* ☎ *915/271–3600* ⊕ *www.stanton-house.com* ⊷ *42 rooms* ⧉ *No meals.*

Nightlife

Craft and Social

BARS/PUBS | This stylish but unpretentious bar on a downtown block of eclectic and inclusive nightspots stands out for its well-curated beer and wine list as well as tasty sandwiches and charcuterie boards. ✉ *305 E. Franklin Ave., El Paso* ☎ *915/401–1909.*

Van Horn

60 miles south of Guadalupe Mountains National Park, 75 miles northwest of Marfa, 120 miles east of El Paso.

With just around 2,000 residents, this blink-and-you'll-miss-it railroad hub founded as a U.S. military outpost in the late 1850s has a small downtown with a handful of notable historic buildings, including the ornate Pueblo Revival–style Hotel El Capitan. It's also the nearest town to where Jeff Bezos's private space-tourism company, Blue Origin, soon plans to begin offering suborbital rocket flights.

GETTING HERE AND AROUND

Van Horn lies at the junction of Interstate 10, U.S. 90, and Highway 54, which leads north—via U.S. 62—to Guadalupe Mountains National Park's Pine Springs Visitor Center.

 Restaurants

Mom's Kitchen

$ | **MEXICAN** | Hearty, flavorful Mexican fare—along with a few American dishes—is the specialty in this modest diner-style eatery on the edge of tiny Van Horn, with an interior that really does look like a vintage kitchen. Specialties include chorizo-and-egg breakfast burritos, green-chile cheeseburgers, and slow-cooked-brisket tacos. **Known for:** kind staff; large portions; menudo (tripe stew) on weekends. $ *Average main: $$7 ⊠ 403 Laurel St., Van Horn* ☎ *432/283–2134* ⊗ *Closed Tues. No dinner Sun.*

Hotels

Hotel El Capitan

$$ | **HOTEL** | Famed architect Henry Trost designed this Spanish Revival hotel, which takes its place among such other glamorous Trost landmarks as the Hotel Paisano (Marfa), the Holland Hotel (Alpine), and the Gage Hotel (Marathon) and is just an hour south of Pine Springs Visitor Center via a picturesque desert drive on Highway 54. **Pros:** lovely, historic architecture; some rooms have courtyard patios; atmopsheric restaurant. **Cons:** not much to see and do in immediate vicinity; some highway noise; some rooms are quite small. $ *Rooms from: $139 ⊠ 100 E. Broadway, Van Horn* ☎ *432/283–1220, 877/283–1220* ⊕ *www.thehotelelcapitan. com* ⇆ *36 rooms* ⦿| *Free Breakfast.*

JOSHUA TREE NATIONAL PARK

Updated by
Cheryl Crabtree

CALIFORNIA

⛺ Camping
★★★★★

🛏 Hotels
★★★★☆

🏃 Activities
★★★★★

👁 Scenery
★★★★★

👥 Crowds
★★★★☆

WELCOME TO JOSHUA TREE NATIONAL PARK

TOP REASONS TO GO

★ **Rock climbing:** Joshua Tree is a world-class site with challenges for climbers of just about every skill level.

★ **Peace and quiet:** Roughly two hours from Los Angeles, this great wilderness is the ultimate escape from technology.

★ **Stargazing:** You'll be mesmerized by the Milky Way flowing across the summer sky. For spectacular natural fireworks, visit in mid-August during the Perseid meteor shower and watch shooting stars streak overhead.

★ **Wildflowers:** In spring, the hillsides explode in a patchwork of yellow, blue, pink, and white.

★ **Sunsets:** Twilight is a magical time here, especially during the winter, when the setting sun casts a golden glow on the mountains.

1 Park Boulevard. Drive the paved loop road between the west and north entrances to explore many of the park's main sights. Crawl between the big rocks at Hidden Valley, and you'll understand why this boulder-strewn area near the park's west entrance was once a cattle rustlers' hideout.

2 Keys View Road. Keys View is the park's most dramatic overlook—on clear days you can see Signal Mountain in Mexico.

3 Highway 62. Spot wildlife at Black Rock and Indian Cove (you might spy a desert tortoise). Near the park's north entrance, walk the nature trail around Oasis of Mara, which the first settlers, the Serrano, dubbed "the place of little springs and much grass."

4 Pinto Basin Road. Pull out binoculars at Cottonwood Spring, one of the best birding spots in the park. Come to Cholla Cactus Garden in the late afternoon, when the spiky stalks of the bigelow (jumping) cholla cactus are backlit against an intense blue sky.

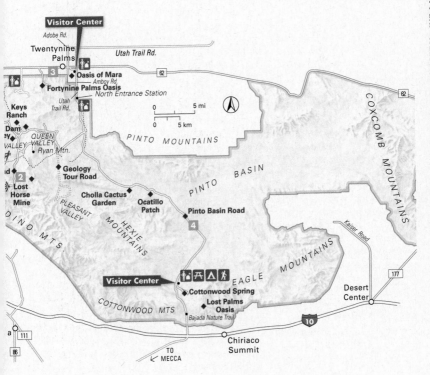

Visitor Center
Adobe Rd.
Twentynine
Palms
Utah Trail Rd.
3
Oasis of Mara
Amboy Rd.
Fortynine Palms Oasis
North Entrance Station
Utah
Trail Rd.
Keys
Ranch
Dam
QUEEN
VALLEY
VALLEY
Ryan Mtn.
Geology
Tour Road
2
Lost
Horse
Mine
PLEASANT
VALLEY
Cholla Cactus
Garden
Ocatillo
Patch
Pinto Basin Road
4
PINTO MOUNTAINS
PINTO BASIN
HEXIE
MOUNTAINS
EAGLE MOUNTAINS
COXCOMB MOUNTAINS
62
Kaiser Road
177
Desert
Center
Visitor Center
COTTONWOOD MTS.
Cottonwood Spring
Lost Palms
Oasis
Bajada Nature Trail
10
a 111
86
TO
MECCA
Chiriaco
Summit

0   5 mi
0   5 km

CALIFORNIA

Joshua Tree National Park teems with fascinating landscapes and life-forms, including its namesake trees. Dagger-like tufts grace the branches of the Yucca brevifolia, which grows in vast stands in the park's western reaches. Although nearly 3 million people visit Joshua Tree annually, it's mysteriously quiet at dawn and dusk.

The park occupies a remote area in southeastern California, where two distinct ecosystems meet: the arid Mojave Desert and the sparsely vegetated Colorado Desert—part of the Sonoran Desert, which stretches across California, Arizona, and northern Mexico. Humans have inhabited the area for at least 5,000 years, starting with the Pinto and other Native American cultures. Cattlemen, miners, and homesteaders arrived in the 1800s and early 1900s. By the 1920s, new roads lured developers and others. Pasadena resident and plant enthusiast Minerva Hoyt visited the desert often and witnessed reckless poaching and pillaging of cacti and other plants. She spearheaded studies to prove the value of regional plants and wildlife. Thanks to her dedicated efforts, Joshua Tree National Monument (825,000 acres) was established in 1936.

The 29 Palms Corporation deeded part of the historic Oasis of Mara to the National Park Service in 1950, and the monument became an official national park on October 31, 1994. Today the park encompasses about 800,000 acres (nearly 600,000 is designated wilderness). Elevation ranges from 536 feet to the peak of 5,814-foot Quail Mountain. The diverse habitats within the park protect more than 800 plant, 250 bird, and 57 mammal species, including the desert bighorn sheep and 46 reptile species, such as the endangered desert tortoise. The park also preserves numerous archaeological sites and historic structures.

You can experience Joshua Tree National Park on several levels. Even on a short excursion along Park Boulevard between the Joshua Tree entrance station and Oasis of Mara, you'll see the essence of North American desert scenery—including a staggering abundance of flora along a dozen self-guided nature trails. You'll also see remnants of homesteads from a century ago, now mostly abandoned and wind-worn. If rock climbing is your passion, this is the place for you: boulder-strewn mountaintops and slopes beckon. Nightfall brings opportunities for stellar stargazing—Joshua Tree was designated an official International Dark Sky Park in 2017. Though trails are closed after sunset, you can park at any of the road pullouts and check out the sparkling shows above. Joshua Tree National Park is a pristine wilderness where you can enjoy a solitary stroll along a trail and

AVERAGE HIGH/LOW TEMPERATURES					
JAN.	**FEB.**	**MAR.**	**APR.**	**MAY**	**JUNE**
62/32	65/37	72/40	80/50	90/55	100/65
JULY	**AUG.**	**SEPT.**	**OCT.**	**NOV.**	**DEC.**
105/70	101/78	96/62	85/55	72/40	62/31

commune with nature. Be sure to take some time to explore on your own and enjoy the peace and quiet.

Planning

When to Go

October through May, when the desert is cooler, is when most visitors arrive. Daytime temperatures range from the mid-70s in December and January to mid-90s in October and May. Lows can dip to near freezing in midwinter, and you may even encounter snow at the higher elevations. Summers can be torrid, with daytime temperatures reaching 110°F.

FESTIVALS AND EVENTS

Pioneer Days. Outhouse races, live music, and arm wrestling mark this celebration held annually, during the third full October weekend, in Twentynine Palms. The event also features a parade, carnival, chili dinner, and an old timers' gathering. ⊕ www.visit29.org.

Riverside County Fair & National Date Festival. Head to Indio for camel and ostrich races. ⊕ www.datefest.org

Getting Here and Around

AIR

Palm Springs International Airport is the closest major air gateway to Joshua Tree National Park. It's about 45 miles from the park. The drive from Los Angeles International Airport to Joshua Tree takes about two to three hours.

CAR

An isolated island of pristine wilderness—a rarity these days—Joshua Tree National Park is within a short drive of 11 million Southern California residents. Most visitors, in fact, make the two- to three-hour drive from the Los Angeles area to enjoy a weekend of solitude in 792,726 acres of untouched desert. The urban sprawl of Palm Springs (home to the nearest airport) is 45 miles away, but gateway towns Joshua Tree, Yucca Valley, and Twentynine Palms are just north of the park. If you're staying in the Palm Springs area, you can enjoy the highlights of the park in one day, including a stop for a picnic at a scenic spot. Within the park, passenger cars are fine for paved areas, but you'll need four-wheel drive for many of the rugged backcountry roadways. At the park's most popular sites, parking is limited. Joshua Tree does not have public transportation.

■ TIP→ **If you'd prefer not to drive, most Palm Springs area hotels can arrange a half- or full-day tour that hits the highlights of Joshua Tree National Park.** But you'll need to spend two or three days camping here to truly experience the quiet beauty of the desert.

Inspiration

Ingrid Goes West, a 2017 film written by director Matt Spicer and David Branson Smith, follows Ingrid (played by Aubrey Plaza) and a friend on a road trip through Joshua Tree National Park and environs.

Joshua Tree National Park Classic Rock Climbs, by Randy Vogel, is a great book

Joshua Tree in One Day

After stocking up on water, snacks, and lunch in Yucca Valley or Joshua Tree (you won't find any supplies inside the park), begin your visit at the **Joshua Tree Visitor Center**, where you can pick up maps and peruse exhibits to get acquainted with what awaits you. Enter the park itself at the nearby **West Entrance Station**, and continue driving along the highly scenic and well-maintained **Park Boulevard**. Stop first at **Hidden Valley** to relax at the picnic area or hike the easy, milelong loop trail. After a few more miles, turn left onto the spur road to the trailhead for the **Barker Dam Nature Trail**. Walk the easy 1.1-mile loop to view a water tank ranchers built to quench their cattle's thirst; along the way, you'll spot birds and a handful of cactus varieties. Return to Park Boulevard and head south; you'll soon leave the main road again for the drive to **Keys View**. The easy loop trail here is only ¼ mile, but the views extend for miles in every direction—look for the San Andreas Fault, the Salton Sea, and nearby mountains. Return to Park Boulevard, where you'll find **Cap Rock**, another short loop trail winding amid rock formations and Joshua trees.

Continuing along Park Boulevard, the start of the 18-mile self-guided **Geology Tour Road** will soon appear on your right. A brochure outlining its 16 stops is available at visitor centers; note that the round-trip will take about two hours, and high-clearance, four-wheel-drive vehicles are recommended after stop 9. ■TIP→ **Do not attempt if it has recently rained.** Back on Park Boulevard, you'll soon arrive at the aptly named **Skull Rock**. This downright spooky formation is next to the parking lot; a nearby trailhead marks the beginning of a 1.7-mile nature trail. End your day with a stop at the **Visitor Center** in Twentynine Palms, where you can stroll through the historic **Oasis of Mara**, popular with area settlers. ■TIP→ **Reverse the itinerary to avoid long lines of cars at the Joshua Tree entrance on weekends and anytime during high season.** The 29 Palms entrance is just 15 miles east, and is usually less crowded, so precious parking spots are more likely to be available.

for adventurers setting out to conquer Joshua Tree's peaks.

Keys Desert Queen Ranch, A Visual and Historical Tour, by Thomas Crochetiere, tells the history of Bill and Frances Keys' home, where they raised a family and developed what became a self-sustaining cornerstone of Joshua Tree National Park.

No Place for a Puritan: The Literature of California's Desert, edited by Ruth Nolan, is an anthology of short pieces by 80 writers, including Hunter Thompson, Joan Didion, John Hilton, and pioneer women of the 1920s and '30s.

On Foot in Joshua Tree National Monument, by Patty Furbush, lists more than 90 park trails and is a good introduction to hiking in Joshua Tree.

Wonder Valley, by Ivy Pochoa, is a thriller novel set in Twentynine Palms in 2006 that includes forays into Joshua Tree National Park and nearby towns.

Park Essentials

ACCESSIBILITY

Black Rock Canyon and Jumbo Rocks campgrounds have one accessible campsite each. Nature trails at Oasis of

Mara, Bajada, Keys View, and Cap Rock are accessible. Some trails at roadside viewpoints can be negotiated by those with limited mobility.

PARK FEES AND PERMITS

Park admission is $30 per car; $15 per person on foot, bicycle, or horse; and $25 per person by motorcycle. The Joshua Tree Pass, good for one year, is $55.

PARK HOURS

The park is open every day, around the clock, but visitor centers are staffed from approximately 8 am to 5 pm. The park is in the Pacific time one.

CELL PHONE RECEPTION

Cell phones don't work in most areas of the park, and there are no telephones in its interior.

Hotels

Lodging choices in the Joshua Tree National Park area are limited to a few motels, chain hotels, vacation rentals, and several upscale establishments in the gateway towns. In general, most offer few amenities and are modestly priced. Book ahead for the spring wildflower season—reservations may be difficult to obtain then.

For a more extensive range of lodging options, you'll need to head to Palm Springs and the surrounding desert resort communities. *Hotel reviews have been shortened. For full information, visit Fodors.com.*

Restaurants

Dining options in the gateway towns around Joshua Tree National Park are extremely limited—you'll mostly find fast-food outlets and a few casual eateries in Yucca Valley and Twentynine Palms. The exception is the restaurant at 29 Palms Inn, which has an interesting California-cuisine menu that features lots of

veggies. For the most part, though, plan on traveling to the Palm Springs desert resort area for a fine-dining experience. *Restaurant reviews have been shortened. For full information, visit Fodors.com.*

What It Costs			
$	$$	$$$	$$$$
RESTAURANTS			
under $12	$12–$20	$21–$30	over $30
HOTELS			
under $100	$100–$150	$151–$200	over $200

Tours

Big Wheel Tours

Based in Palm Desert, Big Wheel Tours offers van excursions, jeep tours, and hiking trips through the park. Bicycle tours (road and mountain bike) are available outside the park boundary. Pickups are available at Palm Springs area hotels. ✉ *41625 Eclectic St., Suite O-1, Palm Desert* ☎ *760/779–1837* ⊕ *www.bwb-tours.com* 💲 *From $169.*

Joshua Tree Adventures

GUIDED TOURS | A local family operates this well-respected tour company, which offers a range of customized private outings, from hikes and scenic tours to full- and multiday hike-and-climb combinations. ✉ *61622 El Cajon Dr., Joshua Tree* ☎ *802/673–4385* ⊕ *jtreeadventures.com* 💲 *From $70.*

★ Keys Ranch Tour

HOUSE | A guide takes you through the former home of a family that homesteaded here for 60 years. In addition to the ranch, a workshop, store, and schoolhouse are still standing, and the grounds are strewn with vehicles and mining equipment. The 90-minute tour, which begins at the Keys Ranch gate, tells the history of the family that built the ranch. Tickets are $10, and reservations are required. ⊠ *Keys Ranch gate* ☎ *760/367–5522* ⊕ *www.nps.gov/jotr.*

Mojave Guides

SPECIAL-INTEREST | Led by resident and certified climbing instructor Seth Pettit, a team of expert guides provides customized half-, full-, and multiday technical rock-climbing courses for everyone from beginners to experts. ⊠ *Joshua Tree* ☎ *760/820–2806* ⊕ *www.mojaveguides.com* 🖂 *From $100.*

Twentynine Palms Astronomy Club

SPECIAL-INTEREST | Book a private night sky experience for 2 to 10 people led by astrophotographer Steve Caron and others who have a passion for sharing the night sky. They bring high-powered telescopes and other equipment to a location of your choice in the Morongo Basin—from Morongo Valley in the west to Wonder Valley in the east, plus Pioneertown and Landers. ⊠ *Twentynine Palms* ☎ *760/401–3004* ⊕ *www.29palmsastronomy.org* 🖂 *From $250 for a two-hour session.*

Visitor Information

CONTACTS Joshua Tree National Park.
⊠ *74485 National Park Dr., Twentynine Palms* ☎ *760/367–5522* ⊕ *www.nps.gov/jotr.*

Park Boulevard

Well-paved Park Boulevard—the park's main artery—loops between the west entrance near the town of Joshua Tree and the north entrance just south of Twentynine Palms. If you have time only for a short visit, driving Park Boulevard is your best choice. It traverses the most scenic portions of Joshua Tree in the park's high-desert section. Along with some sweeping desert views, you'll see jumbles of splendid boulder formations, stands of Joshua trees, and Hidden Valley and Barker Dam, remnants of the area's

Plants and Wildlife in Joshua Tree

Joshua Tree will shatter your notions of the desert as a wasteland. Life flourishes here, as flora and fauna have adapted to heat and drought. In most areas, you'll be walking among native Joshua trees, ocotillos, and yuccas. One of the best spring desert wildflower displays in Southern California blooms here. You'll see plenty of animals—reptiles such as nocturnal sidewinders, birds like golden eagles or burrowing owls, and, occasionally, mammals like coyotes and bobcats.

wild and woolly past. From the Oasis Visitor Center, drive south. After about 5 miles, the road forks; turn right and head west toward Jumbo Rocks (clearly marked with a road sign).

Sights

HISTORIC SIGHTS

Hidden Valley

NATURE SITE | FAMILY | This legendary cattle-rustlers' hideout is set among big boulders along a 1-mile loop trail. Kids love to scramble on and around the rocks. There are shaded picnic tables here. ⊠ *Park Blvd.* ✛ *14 miles south of west entrance.*

★ Keys Ranch

This 150-acre ranch, which once belonged to William and Frances Keys and is now on the National Historic Register, illustrates one of the area's most successful attempts at homesteading. The couple raised five children under extreme desert conditions. Most of the original buildings, including the house, school, store, and workshop, have been restored to the way they were when William died in 1969.

The only way to see the ranch is on one of the 90-minute walking tours, usually offered Friday–Sunday, October–May and weekends in summer; reservations are required. ✉ *Joshua Tree National Park* ✛ *2 miles north of Barker Dam Rd.* ☏ *877/444–6777* ⊕ *www.nps.gov/jotr/ planyourvisit/ranchtour.htm* ✉ *$10, reservations through recreation.gov.*

PICNIC AREAS
Hidden Valley
RESTAURANT—SIGHT | Set among huge rock formations, with picnic tables shaded by dense trees, this is one of the most pleasant places in the park to stop for lunch. ✉ *Park Blvd.* ✛ *14 miles south of the west entrance.*

SCENIC STOPS
Barker Dam
DAM | Built around 1900 by ranchers and miners to hold water for cattle and mining operations, the dam now collects rainwater and is a good place to spot wildlife such as the elusive bighorn sheep. ✉ *Barker Dam Rd.* ✛ *Off Park Blvd., 10 miles south of west entrance.*

TRAILS
Boy Scout Trail
TRAIL | The moderately strenuous, 8-mile trail, suitable for backpackers, extends from Indian Cove to Park Boulevard. It runs through the westernmost edge of the Wonderland of Rocks (where you're likely to see climbers on the outcroppings), passing through a forest of Joshua trees, past granite towers, and around willow-lined pools. Completing the round-trip journey may require camping along the way, so you may want to hike only part of the trail or have a car waiting at the other end. *Difficult.* ✉ *Joshua Tree National Park* ✛ *Trailhead: between Quail Springs Picnic Area and Indian Cove Campground.*

Hidden Valley Trail
TRAIL | FAMILY | Crawl through the rocks surrounding Hidden Valley to see where cattle rustlers supposedly hung out on this 1-mile loop. *Easy.* ✉ *Joshua Tree*

National Park ✛ *Trailhead: at Hidden Valley Picnic Area.*

★ Ryan Mountain Trail
TRAIL | The payoff for hiking to the top of 5,461-foot Ryan Mountain is one of the best panoramic views of Joshua Tree. From here, you can see Mt. San Jacinto, Mt. San Gorgonio, Lost Horse Valley, and the Pinto Basin. You'll need two to three hours to complete the 3-mile round-trip with 1,000-plus feet of elevation gain. *Moderate.* ✉ *Joshua Tree National Park* ✛ *Trailhead: at Ryan Mountain parking area, 13 miles southeast of park's west entrance, or Sheep Pass, 16 miles southwest of Oasis Visitor Center.*

Skull Rock Trail
TRAIL | The 1.7-mile loop guides hikers through boulder piles, desert washes, and a rocky alley. It's named for what is perhaps the park's most famous rock formation, which resembles the eye sockets and nasal cavity of a human skull. Access the trail from within Jumbo Rocks Campground or from a small parking area on the highway just east of the campground. *Easy.* ✉ *Joshua Tree National Park* ✛ *Trailhead: at Jumbo Rocks Campground.*

Split Rock Loop Trail
TRAIL | Experience rocks, trees, and geological wonders along this 2½-mile loop trail (including a short spur to Face Rock) through boulder fields and oak and pine woodlands up to Joshua tree stands. *Moderate.* ✉ *Joshua Tree National Park* ✛ *Trailhead: along dirt road off main Park Blvd. (signs point the way).*

VISITOR CENTERS
Joshua Tree Visitor Center
INFO CENTER | This visitor center has maps and interesting exhibits illustrating park geology, cultural and historic sites, and hiking and rock-climbing activities. There's also a small bookstore and café. Restrooms with flush toilets are on the premises. ✉ *6554 Park Blvd., Joshua Tree* ☏ *760/366–1855* ⊕ *www.nps.gov/jotr.*

Keys View Road

Keys View Road travels south from Park Boulevard from Cap Rock up to Keys View, the best vista point in the park. If you plan to hike up to historic Lost Horse Mine, you'll find the trailhead along the way.

Sights

HISTORIC SIGHTS

Lost Horse Mine

MINE | This historic mine, which produced 10,000 ounces of gold and 16,000 ounces of silver between 1894 and 1931, was among Southern California's most productive mines. The 10-stamp mill is considered one of the best preserved of its type in the park system. The site is accessed via a fairly strenuous, 4-mile, round-trip hike. Mind the park warnings, and don't enter any mine in Joshua Tree. ⊠ *Keys View Rd. ⊹ About 15 miles south of west entrance.*

SCENIC STOPS

★ **Keys View**

VIEWPOINT | At 5,185 feet, this point affords a sweeping view of the Santa Rosa Mountains and Coachella Valley, the San Andreas Fault, the peak of 11,500-foot Mt. San Gorgonio, the shimmering surface of Salton Sea, and—on a rare clear day—Signal Mountain in Mexico. Sunrise and sunset are magical times, when the light throws rocks and trees into high relief before bathing the hills in brilliant shades of red, orange, and gold. ⊠ *Keys View Rd. ⊹ 16 miles south of park's west entrance.*

TRAILS

Cap Rock

TRAIL | This ½-mile, wheelchair-accessible loop—named after a boulder that sits atop a huge rock formation like a cap—winds through other fascinating rock formations and has signs that explain the geology of the Mojave Desert. *Easy.* ⊠ *Joshua Tree National Park ⊹ Trailhead: Keys View Rd. near junction with Park Blvd.*

Lost Horse Mine Trail

TRAIL | This fairly strenuous 4-mile round-trip hike follows a former mining road to a well-preserved mill that was used in the 1890s to crush gold-encrusted rock mined from the nearby mountain. The operation was one of the area's most successful, and the mine's cyanide settling tanks and stone buildings are the area's best-preserved structures. From the mill area, a short but steep 10-minute side trip takes you to the top of a 5,278-foot peak with great views of the valley. *Difficult.* ⊠ *Joshua Tree National Park ⊹ Trailhead: 1¼ miles east of Keys View Rd.*

Highway 62

Highway 62 stretches along the northern border of the park, from Yucca Valley in the West and Twentynine Palms in the east. Visitors can access the Black Rock, Indian Cove, Fortynine Palms, and Oasis of Mara sections of the park off this road, as well as the main visitor centers and park entrances in Joshua Tree and Twentynine Palms.

Sights

PICNIC AREAS

Black Rock Canyon

CANYON | Set among Joshua trees, pinyon pines, and junipers, this popular picnic area has barbecue grills and drinking water. It's one of the few with flush toilets. ⊠ *Joshua Tree National Park ⊹ End of Joshua La. at Black Rock Canyon Campground.*

Covington Flats

RESTAURANT—SIGHT | This is a great place to get away from crowds. There's just one table, and it's surrounded by flat, open desert dotted here and there by Joshua trees. ⊠ *La Contenta Rd. ⊹ 10 miles from Rte. 62.*

SCENIC STOPS
Fortynine Palms Oasis
NATIVE SITE | A short drive off Highway 62, this site is a bit of a preview of what the park's interior has to offer: stands of fan palms, interesting petroglyphs, and evidence of fires built by early Native Americans. Because animals frequent this area, you may spot a coyote, bobcat, or roadrunner. ⊠ *End of Canyon Rd.* ✚ *4 miles west of Twentynine Palms.*

Indian Cove
RESTAURANT—SIGHT | The view from here is of rock formations that draw thousands of climbers to the park each year. This isolated area is reached via Twentynine Palms Highway. ⊠ *End of Indian Cove Rd.*

TRAILS
California Riding and Hiking Trail
TRAIL | You'll need a backcountry camping pass to traverse this 35-mile route between the Black Rock Canyon entrance and the north entrance. You can access the trail for a short or long hike at several points. The visitor centers have trail maps. *Difficult.* ⊠ *Joshua Tree National Park* ✚ *Trailheads: at Upper Covington Flats, Ryan Campground, Twin Tanks, south of north park entrance, and Black Rock Campground.*

Fortynine Palms Oasis Trail
TRAIL | Allow three hours for this moderately strenuous, 3-mile trek. There's no shade, and the trail climbs steeply in both directions, eventually dropping down into a canyon where you'll find an oasis lined with fan palms, which can be viewed from boulders above, but not accessed. If you look carefully, you'll see evidence of Native Americans in this area, from traces of cooking fires to rocks carved with petroglyphs. *Difficult.* ⊠ *Joshua Tree National Park* ✚ *Trailhead: at end of Canyon Rd., 4 miles west of Twentynine Palms.*

Hi-View Nature Trail
TRAIL | This 1.3-mile loop climbs nearly to the top of 4,500-foot Summit Peak. The views of nearby Mt. San Gorgonio (snow-capped in winter) make the moderately steep journey worth the effort. You can pick up a pamphlet describing the vegetation you'll see along the way at any visitor center. *Moderate.* ⊠ *Joshua Tree National Park* ✚ *Trailhead: ½ mile west of Black Rock Canyon Campground.*

Indian Cove Trail
TRAIL | Look for lizards and roadrunners along this ½-mile loop that follows a desert wash. A walk along this well-signed trail reveals signs of Native American habitation, animals, and flora such as desert willow and yucca. *Easy.* ⊠ *Joshua Tree National Park* ✚ *Trailhead: at west end of Indian Cove Campground.*

Oasis of Mara Trail
TRAIL | A stroll along this short, wheelchair-accessible trail, located just outside the visitor center, reveals how early settlers took advantage of this oasis, which was first settled by the Serrano tribe. *Mara* means "place of little springs and much grass" in their language. The Serrano, who farmed the oasis until the mid-1850s, planted one palm tree for each male baby born during the first year of the settlement. *Easy.* ⊠ *Joshua Tree National Park* ✚ *Trailhead: at Oasis Visitor Center.*

VISITOR CENTERS
Oasis Visitor Center
INFO CENTER | Exhibits here illustrate how Joshua Tree was formed, reveal the differences between the park's two types of desert, and demonstrate how plants and animals eke out an existence in this arid climate. Take the ½-mile nature walk through the nearby Oasis of Mara, which is alive with palm trees and mesquite shrubs. Facilities include picnic tables, restrooms, and a bookstore. ⊠ *74485 National Park Dr., Twentynine Palms* ☎ *760/367–5500* ⊕ *www.nps.gov/jotr.*

Pinto Basin Road

This paved road takes you from high Mojave desert to low Colorado desert. A long, slow drive, the route runs from the main part of the park to Interstate 10; it can add as much as an hour to and from Palm Springs (round-trip), but the views and roadside exhibits make it worth the extra time. From the Oasis Visitor Center, drive south. After about 5 miles, the road forks; take a left, and continue another 9 miles to the Cholla Cactus Garden, where the sun fills the cactus needles with light. Past that is the Ocotillo Patch, filled with spindly plants bearing razor-sharp thorns and, after a rain, bright green leaves and brilliant red flowers. Side trips from this route require a 4X4.

 ## Sights

PICNIC AREAS

Cottonwood Spring Picnic Area

RESTAURANT—SIGHT | Shady trees make this a pleasant place to picnic. It has drinking water and restrooms with flush toilets. ✉ Joshua Tree National Park ✛ On Pinto Basin Rd., adjacent to visitor center.

SCENIC DRIVES

Geology Tour Road

SCENIC DRIVE | Some of the park's most fascinating landscapes can be observed from this 18-mile dirt road. Parts of the journey are rough; a 4X4 vehicle is required after mile marker 9. Sights to see include a 100-year-old stone dam called Squaw Tank, defunct mines, and a large plain with an abundance of Joshua trees. There are 16 stops along the way, so give yourself about two hours to complete the round-trip trek. ✉ South of Park Blvd., west of Jumbo Rocks.

SCENIC STOPS

Cholla Cactus Garden

GARDEN | This stand of bigelow cholla (sometimes called jumping cholla, because its hooked spines seem to jump

at you) is best seen and photographed in late afternoon, when the backlit spiky stalks stand out against a colorful sky. ✉ Pinto Basin Rd. ✛ 20 miles north of Cottonwood Visitor Center.

Cottonwood Spring

NATIVE SITE | Home to the native Cahuilla people for centuries, this spring provided water for travelers and early prospectors. The area, which supports a large stand of fan palms and cottonwood trees, is one of the best stops for bird-watching, as migrating birds (and bighorn sheep) rely on the water as well. A number of gold mines were located here, and the area still has some remains, including concrete pillars. ✉ Cottonwood Visitor Center.

Lost Palms Oasis

TRAIL | More than 100 fan palms comprise the largest group of the exotic plants in the park. A spring bubbles from between the rocks but disappears into the sandy, boulder-strewn canyon. The 7½-mile, round-trip hike is not for everyone, and not recommended during summer months. Bring plenty of water! ✉ Cottonwood Visitor Center.

Ocotillo Patch

GARDEN | Stop here for a roadside exhibit on the dramatic display made by the red-tipped succulent after even the shortest rain shower. ✉ Pinto Basin Rd. ✛ About 3 miles east of Cholla Cactus Gardens.

TRAILS

Bajada

TRAIL | Learn all about what plants do to survive in the Colorado Desert on this ¼-mile loop. Easy. ✉ Joshua Tree National Park ✛ Trailhead: south of Cottonwood Visitor Center, ½ mile from park entrance.

Lost Palms Oasis Trail

TRAIL | Allow four to six hours for the moderately strenuous, 7¼-mile round-trip, which leads to the most impressive oasis in the park. It's uphill on the way back to the trailhead. You'll find more

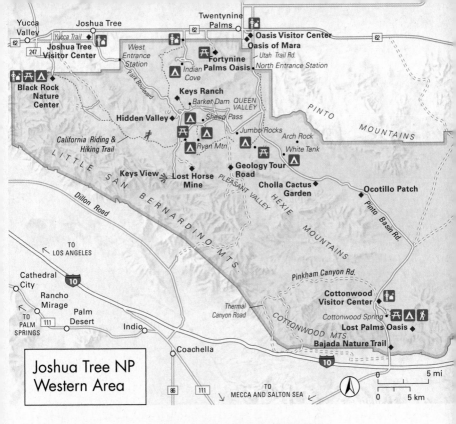

Joshua Tree NP
Western Area

than 100 fan palms and an abundance of wildflowers here. *Difficult.* ✉ *Joshua Tree National Park* ✛ *Trailhead: at Cottonwood Spring Oasis.*

Mastodon Peak Trail

TRAIL | Some boulder scrambling is optional on this 3-mile hike that loops up to the 3,371-foot Mastodon Peak, and the journey rewards you with stunning views of the Salton Sea. The trail passes through a region where gold was mined from 1919 to 1932, so be on the lookout for open mines. The peak draws its name from a large rock formation that early miners believed looked like the head of a prehistoric behemoth. *Moderate.* ✉ *Joshua Tree National Park* ✛ *Trailhead: at Cottonwood Spring Oasis.*

VISITOR CENTERS

Cottonwood Visitor Center

INFO CENTER | The south entrance is the closest to Interstate 10, the east–west highway from Los Angeles to Phoenix. Exhibits in this small center, staffed by rangers and volunteers, illustrate the region's natural history. The center also has restrooms with flush toilets. ✉ *Cottonwood Spring, Pinto Basin Rd.* ⊕ *www. nps.gov/jotr.*

Activities

BIKING

Mountain biking is a great way to see Joshua Tree. Bikers are restricted to roads that are used by motorized vehicles, including the main park roads and a few four-wheel-drive trails. Bicycling on dirt roads is not recommended during the summer. Most scenic stops and picnic areas have bike racks.

Covington Flats

BICYCLING | This 4-mile route takes you past impressive Joshua trees as well as pinyon pines, junipers, and areas of lush desert vegetation. It's tough going toward the end, but once you reach 5,518-foot Eureka Peak you'll have great views of Palm Springs, the Morongo Basin, and the surrounding mountains. ⊠ *Joshua Tree National Park* ✛ *Trailhead: at Covington Flats picnic area, La Contenta Rd., 10 miles south of Rte. 62.*

Pinkham Canyon and Thermal Canyon Roads

BICYCLING | This challenging 20-mile route begins at the Cottonwood Visitor Center and loops through the Cottonwood Mountains. The unpaved trail follows Smoke Tree Wash through Pinkham Canyon, rounds Thermal Canyon, and loops back to the beginning. Rough and narrow in places, the road travels through soft sand and rocky floodplains. ⊠ *Joshua Tree National Park* ✛ *Trailhead: at Cottonwood Visitor Center.*

Queen Valley

BICYCLING | This 13.4-mile network of mostly level roads winds through one of the park's most impressive groves of Joshua trees. You can also leave your bike at one of the racks placed in the area and explore on foot. ⊠ *Joshua Tree National Park* ✛ *Trailhead: at Hidden Valley Campground, and accessible opposite Geology Tour Rd. at Big Horn Pass.*

BIRD-WATCHING

Joshua Tree, located on the inland portion of the Pacific Flyway, hosts about 250 species of birds, and the park is a popular seasonal location for bird-watching. During the fall migration, which runs mid-September through mid-October, there are several reliable sighting areas. At Barker Dam you might spot white-throated swifts, several types of swallows, or red-tailed hawks. Lucy's warblers, flycatchers, and Anna's

hummingbirds cruise around Cottonwood Spring, a serene palm-shaded setting; occasional ducks, herons, and egrets, as well as migrating rufous and calliope hummingbirds, wintering prairie falcons, and a resident barn owl could show up. Black Rock Canyon sees pinyon jays, while Covington Flats reliably gets mountain quail, and you may see La Conte's thrashers, ruby-crowned kinglets, and warbling vireos at either locale. Rufous hummingbirds, Pacific slope flycatchers, and various warblers are frequent visitors to Indian Cove. Lists of birds found in the park, as well as information on recent sightings, are available at visitor centers.

CAMPING

Camping is the best way to experience the stark, exquisite beauty of Joshua Tree. You'll also have a rare opportunity to sleep outside in a semi-wilderness setting. The campgrounds, set at elevations from 3,000 to 4,500 feet, have only primitive facilities; few have drinking water. Most campgrounds accept reservations up to six months in advance but only for October through Memorial Day. Campsites at Belle, Hidden Valley, and White Tank are on a first-come, first-served basis. Belle and White Tank campgrounds, and parts of Black Rock Canyon, Cottonwood, and Indian Cove campgrounds, are closed from the day after Memorial Day to September. ■TIP➔ **Campgrounds fill quickly, so reserve well in advance. Also, the park may soon require reservations at all campgrounds.**

Belle Campground. This small campground is popular with families as there are a number of boulders kids can scramble over and around. ⊠ *9 miles south of Oasis of Mara* ☎ *760/367–5500* ⊕ *www.nps.gov/jotr.*

Black Rock Canyon Campground. Set among juniper bushes, cholla cacti, and other desert shrubs, Black Rock Canyon is one of the park's prettiest campgrounds. ⊠ *Joshua La., south of Hwy. 62 and Hwy. 247* ☎ *877/444–6777* ⊕ *www.recreation.gov.*

Did You Know?

Found only in Arizona, California, Nevada, and Utah, the Joshua tree (*Yucca brevifolia*) is actually a member of the agave family. Native Americans used the Joshua tree's hearty foliage like leather, forming it into everyday items like baskets and shoes. Later, early settlers used its core and limbs for building fences to contain their livestock.

Learn about the park's flora and fauna by attending the ranger programs.

Cottonwood Campground. In spring, this campground, the southernmost one in the park (and therefore often the last to fill up), is surrounded by some of the desert's finest wildflowers and is a great spot to watch the night sky. ⊠ *Pinto Basin Rd., 32 miles south of North Entrance Station* ☎ *877/444–6777* ⊕ *www.nps.gov/jotr.*

Hidden Valley Campground. This campground is a favorite with rock climbers, who make their way up valley formations that have names like the Blob, Old Woman, and Chimney Rock. ⊠ *Off Park Blvd., 20 miles southwest of Oasis of Mara* ☎ *760/367–5500* ⊕ *www.nps.gov/jotr.*

Indian Cove Campground. This is a sought-after spot for rock climbers, primarily because it lies among the 50 square miles of rugged terrain at the Wonderland of Rocks. ⊠ *Indian Cove Rd., south of Hwy. 62* ☎ *877/444–6777* ⊕ *www.nps.gov/jotr.*

Jumbo Rocks. Each campsite at this well-regarded campground tucked among giant boulders has a bit of privacy. It's a good home base for visiting many of Joshua Tree's attractions. ⊠ *Park Blvd., 11 miles from Oasis of Mara* ☎ *877/444–6777* ⊕ *www.nps.gov/jotr.*

White Tank. This small, quiet campground is popular with families because a nearby trail leads to a natural arch. ⊠ *Pinto Basin Rd., 11 miles south of Oasis of Mara* ☎ *760/367–5500* ⊕ *www.nps.gov/jotr.*

EDUCATIONAL PROGRAMS

The Desert Institute at Joshua Tree National Park

COLLEGE | The nonprofit educational partner of the park offers a full schedule of lectures, classes, and hikes. Class topics include basket making, painting, and photography, while field trips include workshops on cultural history, natural science, and how to survive in the desert. ⊠ *74485 National Park Dr., Twentynine Palms* ☎ *760/367–5535* ⊕ *www.joshuat-ree.org.*

Stargazing

COLLEGE | At Joshua Tree National Park, designated an International Dark Sky Park in 2017, you can tour the Milky Way on summer evenings using binoculars. Rangers also offer programs on some evenings when the moon isn't visible. Browse the schedule online. The park also partners with Sky's the Limit Observatory on the Utah Trail in Twentynine Palms (⊕ *www.skysthelimit29.org*); check the website for current offerings. ⊠ *Cottonwood Campground Amphitheater, Oasis Visitor Center, Sky's the Limit Observatory* ⊕ *www.nps.gov/jotr/planyourvisit/calendar.htm.*

RANGER PROGRAMS
Evening Programs

TOUR—SIGHT | Rangers present 45-minute-long programs, often on Friday or Saturday evening, at Cottonwood Amphitheater, Indian Cove Amphitheater, and Jumbo Rocks Campground. Topics range from natural history to local lore. As times and days for such offerings aren't fixed, it's best to check the online schedule. ⊠ *Joshua Tree National Park* ⊠ *Free.*

HIKING

There are more than 190 miles of hiking trails in Joshua Tree, ranging from ¼-mile nature trails to 35-mile treks. Some connect with each other, so you can design your own desert maze. Remember that drinking water is hard to come by—you won't find it in the park except at the entrances. Bring along at least a gallon per person for all but the shortest hikes, more if the weather is hot.

Before striking out on a hike or apparent nature trail, check out the signage. Roadside signage identifies hiking- and rock-climbing routes.

ROCK CLIMBING

With an abundance of weathered igneous boulder outcroppings, Joshua Tree is one of the nation's top winter-climbing destinations. There are more than 4,500 established routes offering a full menu of climbing experiences—from bouldering for beginners in the Wonderland of Rocks to multiple-pitch climbs at Echo Rock and Saddle Rock. The best-known climb in the park is Hidden Valley's Sports Challenge Rock. A map inside the *Joshua Tree Guide* shows locations of selected wilderness and nonwilderness climbs.

Joshua Tree Rock Climbing School

CLIMBING/MOUNTAINEERING | The school offers several programs, from one-day introductory classes to multiday programs for experienced climbers, and provides all needed equipment. Beginning classes, offered year-round on most weekends, are limited to six people age eight or older. ⊠ *Joshua Tree National Park* ☎ *760/366–4745* ⊕ *www.joshuatreerockclimbing.com* ⊠ *From $195.*

Vertical Adventures Rock Climbing School

CLIMBING/MOUNTAINEERING | About 1,000 climbers each year learn the sport in Joshua Tree National Park through this school. Classes, offered September–May, meet at a designated location in the park, and all equipment is provided. ⊠ *Joshua Tree National Park* ☎ *800/514–8785 office, 949/322–6108 mobile/text* ⊕ *www.vertical-adventures.com* ⊠ *From $165.*

Nearby Towns

Palm Springs, about a 45-minute drive from the North Entrance Station at Joshua Tree, serves as the home base for most park visitors. This city of 46,000 has 95 golf courses, 600 tennis courts, and 50,000 swimming pools. A hideout for Hollywood stars since the 1920s, Palm Springs also offers a glittering array of shops, restaurants, and hotels. Stroll down Palm Canyon Drive, and you're sure to run into a celebrity or two.

There are four small communities in close proximity to Joshua Tree National Park. About 9 miles north of Palm Springs

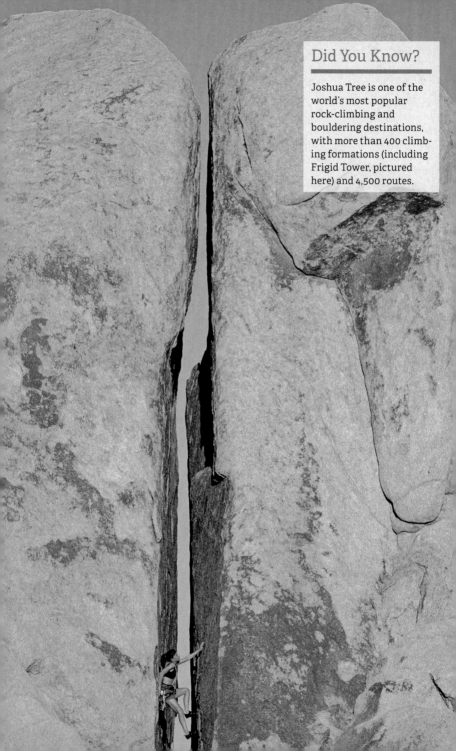

Did You Know?

Joshua Tree is one of the world's most popular rock-climbing and bouldering destinations, with more than 400 climbing formations (including Frigid Tower, pictured here) and 4,500 routes.

and closer to the park is **Desert Hot Springs,** which has more than 1,000 natural hot mineral pools and 40 health spas ranging from low-key to luxurious. **Yucca Valley** is the largest and fastest growing of the communities straddling the park's northern border. The town boasts a handful of motels, supermarkets, and a Walmart. Tiny **Joshua Tree,** the closest community to the park's west entrance, is where the serious rock climbers make their headquarters. **Twentynine Palms,** known as "two-nine" by locals, is sandwiched between the Marine Corps Air Ground Task Force Center to the north and Joshua Tree National Park to the south. Here you'll find a smattering of coffeehouses, antiques shops, and cafés.

Palm Springs

A tourist destination since the late 19th century, Palm Springs evolved into an ideal hideaway for early Hollywood celebrities who slipped into town to play tennis, lounge poolside, attend a party or two, and unless things got out of hand, steer clear of gossip columnists. But the area blossomed in the 1930s after actors Charlie Farrell and Ralph Bellamy bought 200 acres of land for $30 an acre and opened the Palm Springs Racquet Club, which soon listed Ginger Rogers, Humphrey Bogart, and Clark Gable among its members.

Today, Palm Springs is embracing its glory days. Owners of resorts, bed-and-breakfasts, and galleries have renovated mid-century modern buildings, luring a new crop of celebs and high-powered executives. LGBTQ travelers, twenty-somethings, and families also sojourn here. Pleasantly touristy Palm Canyon Drive is packed with alfresco restaurants, many with views of the bustling sidewalk, along with indoor cafés and semi-chic shops. Farther west is the Uptown Design District, the area's shopping and dining destination. Continuing

east on Palm Canyon Drive. just outside downtown lie resorts and boutique hotels that host lively pool parties and house exclusive dining establishments and trendy bars.

GETTING HERE AND AROUND
Palm Springs is 90 miles southeast of Los Angeles on Interstate 10. Most visitors arrive in the Palm Springs area by car from the Los Angeles or San Diego area via this freeway, which intersects with Highway 111 north of Palm Springs. Tahquitz Canyon Way marks the division between north and south on major streets (e.g., North and South Palm Canyon Drive).

VISITOR INFORMATION
CONTACTS Greater Palm Springs Convention & Visitors Bureau. ⊠ *Visitor Center, 70–100 Hwy. 111, at Via Florencia, Rancho Mirage* ☎ *760/770–9000, 800/967–3767* ⊕ *www.visitgreater-palmsprings.com.* **Palm Springs Visitors Center Downtown.** ⊠ *100 S. Palm Canyon Dr.* ⊹ *In Welwood Murray Memorial Library* ☎ *760/323–8296* ⊕ *www.visit-palmsprings.com.* **Palm Springs Visitors Center North.** ⊠ *2901 N. Palm Canyon Dr.* ☎ *760/778–8418, 800/347–7746* ⊕ *www. visitpalmsprings.com.*

 Sights

★ **Indian Canyons**
CANYON | FAMILY | The Indian Canyons are the ancestral home of the Agua Caliente, part of the Cahuilla people. You can see remnants of their ancient life, including rock art, house pits and foundations, irrigation ditches, bedrock mortars, pictographs, and stone houses and shelters atop cliff walls. Short easy walks through the canyons reveal palm oases, waterfalls, and, in spring, wildflowers. Tree-shaded picnic areas are abundant. The attraction includes three canyons open for touring: Palm Canyon, noted for its stand of Washingtonia palms; Murray Canyon, home of Peninsula bighorn

sheep; and Andreas Canyon, where a stand of fan palms contrasts with sharp rock formations. Ranger-led hikes to Palm and Andreas canyons are offered Friday–Sunday for an additional charge (no dogs allowed). The trading post at the entrance to Palm Canyon has hiking maps and refreshments, as well as Native American art, jewelry, and weaving. ✉ 38520 S. Palm Canyon Dr., south of Acanto Dr. ☏ 760/323–6018 ⊕ www.indian-canyons. com ✎ $9, ranger hikes $3 ⊗ Closed Mon.–Thurs. July–Sept.

★ Palm Springs Aerial Tramway

VIEWPOINT | FAMILY | A trip on the tramway provides a 360-degree view of the desert through the picture windows of rotating cars. The 2½-mile ascent through Chino Canyon, the steepest vertical cable ride in the United States, brings you to an elevation of 8,516 feet in less than 20 minutes. On clear days, which are common, the view stretches 75 miles—from the peak of Mt. San Gorgonio in the north to the Salton Sea in the southeast. Stepping out into the snow at the summit is a winter treat. At the top, a bit below the summit of Mt. San Jacinto, are several diversions. Mountain Station has an observation deck, two restaurants, a cocktail lounge, apparel and gift shops, picnic facilities, a small wildlife exhibit, and a theater that screens movies on the history of the tramway and the adjacent Mount San Jacinto State Park and Wilderness. Take advantage of free guided and self-guided nature walks through the state park, or if there's snow on the ground, rent skis, snowshoes, or snow tubes. The tramway generally closes for maintenance in mid-September. ■TIP➔ Ride-and-dine packages are available in late afternoon. The tram is a popular attraction; to avoid a two-hour or longer wait, arrive before the first car leaves in the morning. ✉ 1 Tramway Rd., off N. Palm Canyon Dr. (Hwy. 111) ☏ 888/515–8726 ⊕ www.pstramway.com ✎ From $27 ⊗ Closed 2 wks in Sept. for maintenance.

★ Palm Springs Air Museum

MUSEUM | FAMILY | This museum's impressive collection of World War II, Vietnam, and Korea aircraft includes a B-17 Flying Fortress bomber, a Bell P-63 King Cobra, and a Grumman TBF Avenger. Among the cool exhibits are model warships, a Pearl Harbor diorama, and a Mohawk into which kids can crawl. Photos, artifacts, memorabilia, and uniforms are also on display; educational programs take place on Saturday; and flight demonstrations are scheduled regularly. Rides in vintage warbirds are also available, including a T-28 Trojan, PT-17 Stearman, T-33 Shooting Star Jet, and P-51D Mustang. ✉ 745 N. Gene Autry Trail ☏ 760/778–6262 ⊕ palm-springsairmuseum.org ✎ $19.

Tahquitz Canyon

CANYON | On ranger-led tours of this secluded canyon on the Agua Caliente Reservation you can view a spectacular 60-foot waterfall, rock art, ancient irrigation systems, and native wildlife and plants. Tours are conducted several times daily; participants must be able to navigate 100 steep rock steps. (You can also take a self-guided tour of the 1.8-mile trail.) At the visitor center at the canyon entrance, watch a short video, look at artifacts, and pick up a map. ✉ 500 W. Mesquite Ave., west of S. Palm Canyon Dr. ☏ 760/416–7044 ⊕ www.tahquitzcanyon.com ✎ $13 ⊗ Closed Mon.–Thurs. July–Sept.

🍴 Restaurants

★ EIGHT4NINE

$$$ | AMERICAN | The dazzling interior design and eclectic Pacific Coast dishes made from scratch lure locals and visitors alike to this swank yet casual restaurant and lounge in the Uptown Design District. Sink into white patent leather chairs or comfy sofas in the lounge where you can gaze at historic celebrity photos, or choose a table in a grand corridor with a collection of private rooms, or in the outdoor patio with mountain

views. **Known for:** nearly everything made from scratch; four-course chef's menu; all-day happy hour in lounge. $ *Average main: $28* ⊠ *849 N. Palm Canyon Dr.* ☎ *760/325–8490* ⊕ *eight4nine.com.*

★ 4 Saints

$$$$ | CONTEMPORARY | Perched on the seventh-floor rooftop of the Kimpton Rowan Palm Springs, where stunning views unfold from nearly every table, 4 Saints serves inventive farm-to-table dishes in a slick, hipster dining room and outdoor patio. The eclectic, globally inspired menu focuses on small plates and main dishes made with locally sourced ingredients (e.g., seafood, duck, and short ribs) intended for sharing. **Known for:** creative and classic cocktails; lively social vibe; stellar seafood. $ *Average main: $43* ⊠ *100 W. Tahquitz Cyn. Way* ☎ *760/392–2020* ⊕ *www.4saint-spalmsprings.com.*

Spencer's Restaurant

$$$$ | MODERN AMERICAN | This swank dining space occupies a historic mid-century modern structure at the Palm Springs Tennis Club Resort. Crab cakes, kung pao calamari, and crispy flash-fried oysters are favorite starters. **Known for:** French–Pacific Rim influences; romantic patio; elegant dining room. $ *Average main: $35* ⊠ *701 W. Baristo Rd.* ☎ *760/327–3446* ⊕ *www.spencersrestaurant.com.*

★ Tyler's Burgers

$ | AMERICAN | FAMILY | Families, singles, and couples head to Tyler's for simple lunch fare that appeals to carnivores and vegetarians alike. Expect mid-20th-century America's greatest hits: heaping burgers, stacks of fries, root-beer floats, milkshakes; on weekends, be prepared to wait with the masses. **Known for:** house-made cole slaw and potato salad; excellent burgers and fries; delicious shakes. $ *Average main: $11* ⊠ *149 S. Indian Canyon Dr., at La Plaza* ☎ *760/325–2990* ⊕ *www.tylersburgers. com* ⊙ *Closed Sun. late May–mid-Feb. Closed mid-July–early Sept.*

 Hotels

Ace Hotel and Swim Club

$$$ | RESORT | With the hotel's vintage feel and hippie-chic decor, it would be no surprise to find guests gathered around cozy communal fire pits enjoying feel-good music. **Pros:** Amigo Room has late-night dining; poolside stargazing deck; weekend DJ scene at the pool. **Cons:** party atmosphere not for everyone; limited amenities; casual staff and service. $ *Rooms from: $189* ⊠ *701 E. Palm Canyon Dr.* ☎ *760/325–9900* ⊕ *www. acehotel.com/palmsprings* ⇆ *188 rooms* ⌾ *No meals.*

★ Kimpton Rowan Palm Springs Hotel

$$$$ | HOTEL | One of the newest arrivals on the downtown Palm Springs scene, the Rowan Palm Springs dazzles locals and guests (especially the under-40 set) with stunning views from myriad picture windows and a rooftop deck, as well as an unpretentious vibe that puts guests of all ages at ease. **Pros:** friendly, attentive service; stunning mountain and valley views; in the heart of downtown. **Cons:** rooftop pool area can get crowded; valet parking only; $35 resort fee. $ *Rooms from: $259* ⊠ *100 W. Tahquitz Canyon Way* ☎ *760/904–5015, 800/532–7320* ⊕ *www.rowanpalmsprings.com* ⇆ *153 rooms* ⌾ *No meals.*

Movie Colony Hotel

$$$ | B&B/INN | Designed in 1935 by Albert Frey, this intimate hotel evokes a mid-century minimalist ambience throughout its gleaming-white, two-story buildings—flanked with balconies—and its SoCal desert–style rooms, which are elegantly appointed and have bright mid-century color accents. **Pros:** architectural icon; in the midtown Design District; property-wide remodel in 2019. **Cons:** close quarters; basic breakfast; staff not available 24 hours. $ *Rooms from: $169* ⊠ *726 N. Indian Canyon Dr.* ☎ *760/320–6340, 888/953–5700* ⊕ *www.moviecolonyhotel.com* ⇆ *19 rooms* ⌾ *Breakfast.*

★ Orbit In Hotel

$$$ | **B&B/INN** | The exterior architectural style—nearly flat roofs, wide overhangs, glass everywhere—of this hip inn on a quiet backstreet dates back to its 1955 opening, and the period feel continues inside. **Pros:** saltwater pool; Orbitini cocktail hour; free breakfast served poolside. **Cons:** best for couples; style not to everyone's taste; staff not available 24 hours. [$] *Rooms from: $169* ✉ *562 W. Arenas Rd.* ☎ *760/323–3585, 877/996–7248* 🌐 *www.orbitin.com* 🛏 *9 rooms* 🍴 *Breakfast.*

★ The Saguaro

$$$ | **HOTEL** | A startling, rainbow-hued oasis—the brainchild of Manhattan-based architects Peter Stamberg and Paul Aferiat—the Saguaro caters to young, hip, pet-toting partygoers who appreciate its lively pool-party scene. **Pros:** lively pool scene with weekend DJ parties; daily yoga, on-site spa, 24-hour fitness center, beach cruisers; shuttle service to downtown. **Cons:** a few miles from downtown; pool area can be noisy and crowded; $33 resort fee. [$] *Rooms from: $169* ✉ *1800 E. Palm Canyon Dr.* ☎ *760/323–1711* 🌐 *thesaguaro.com* 🛏 *244 rooms* 🍴 *No meals.*

★ Willows Historic Palm Springs Inn

$$$$ | **B&B/INN** | Set in two adjacent, opulent, Mediterranean-style mansions built in the 1920s to host the rich and famous, this luxurious hillside bed-and-breakfast has gleaming hardwood and slate floors, stone fireplaces, frescoed ceilings, hand-painted tiles, iron balconies, antiques throughout, and a 50-foot waterfall that splashes into a pool outside the dining room. **Pros:** short walk to art museum, restaurants, shops; pool; expansive breakfast and afternoon wine hour. **Cons:** closed from June to September; pricey; some rooms on the small side. [$] *Rooms from: $425* ✉ *412 W. Tahquitz Canyon Way* ☎ *760/320–0771* 🌐 *www.thewillowspalmsprings.com* 🛏 *17 rooms* 🍴 *Breakfast.*

Desert Hot Springs

9 miles north of Palm Springs.

Desert Hot Springs's famous mineral waters, thought by some to have curative powers, bubble up at temperatures of 90°F to 148°F and flow into the wells of more than 40 hotel spas.

GETTING HERE AND AROUND

Desert Hot Springs lies due north of Palm Springs. Take Gene Autry Trail north to Interstate 10, where the street name changes to Palm. Continue north to Pierson Boulevard, the town's center.

Sights

Cabot's Pueblo Museum

MUSEUM | Cabot Yerxa, the man who found the spring that made Desert Hot Springs famous, built a quirky four-story, 35-room pueblo between 1939 and his death in 1965. Now a museum run by the city of Desert Hot Springs, the Hopi-inspired adobe structure is filled with memorabilia of Yerxa's time as a homesteader; his encounters with Hollywood celebrities at the nearby Bar-H Ranch; his expedition to the Alaskan gold rush; and many other events. The home, much of it crafted out of materials Yerxa recycled from the desert, can only be seen on hour-long tours. Outside, walk the grounds to a lookout with amazing desert views. ✉ *67–616 E. Desert View Ave., at Eliseo Rd.* ☎ *760/329–7610* 🌐 *www.cabotsmuseum.org* 🎟 *$13* 🕒 *Closed Mon. Oct.–May, closed Mon. and Tues. June–Sept.* ☞ *Tours 9:30, 10:30, 11:30, 1:30, 2:30 Oct.–May, and 9:30, 10:30, 11:30 June–Sept. Tours limited to 12 people.*

Hotels

The Spring

$$$$ | **HOTEL** | Designed for those who want to detox, lose weight, or chill out in the mineral pools, The Spring delivers quiet and personal service atop a Desert

Hot Springs hill. **Pros:** access to mineral pools 24 hours a day; complimentary continental breakfast; spa and lodging packages available. **Cons:** rooms lack character; no TVs or phones; not much poolside privacy. $ *Rooms from: $239* ✉ *12699 Reposo Way* ☎ *760/251–6700* ⊕ *www.the-spring.com* ⇗ *12 rooms* ⊚ *Breakfast.*

Two Bunch Palms

$$$$ | RESORT | This adults-only hotel on a gorgeous, 72-acre property with stunning views of Mt. San Jacinto provides a luxurious and relaxing experience, with access to natural hot springs. **Pros:** on-site restaurant serves breakfast, lunch, and dinner; fresh juice bar open all day; full-service spa, popular since the 1940s. **Cons:** some rooms have no TV; no pets allowed; minimum age 18. $ *Rooms from: $245* ✉ *67425 Two Bunch Palms Trail* ☎ *760/676–5000* ⊕ *twobunchpalms. com* ⇗ *68 rooms* ⊚ *No meals.*

Yucca Valley

30 miles northeast of Palm Springs.

One of the high desert's fastest-growing cities, Yucca Valley is emerging as a bedroom community for people who work as far away as Ontario, 85 miles to the west. In this suburb, you can shop for necessities, get your car serviced, grab coffee or purchase vintage furnishings, and chow down at fast-food outlets. Just up Pioneertown Road, you'll find the most-talked-about dining establishment in the desert: Pappy & Harriet's, the famed performance venue that hosts big-name talent.

GETTING HERE AND AROUND

The drive to Yucca Valley on Highway 62/Twentynine Palms Highway passes through the Painted Hills and drops down into a valley. Take Pioneertown Road north to the Old West outpost.

VISITOR INFORMATION California Welcome Center Yucca Valley. ✉ *56711 Twentynine Palms Hwy.* ☎ *760/365–5464* ⊕ *www.californiawelcomecenter. com.* **Yucca Valley Chamber of Commerce.** ✉ *56711 Twentynine Palms Hwy.* ☎ *760/365–6323* ⊕ *www.yuccavalley.org.*

Sights

Hi-Desert Nature Museum

MUSEUM | FAMILY | Natural and cultural history of the Morongo Basis and High Desert are the focus here. A small live-animal display includes scorpions, snakes, lizards, and small mammals. You'll also find gems and minerals, fossils from the Paleozoic era, taxidermy, and Native American artifacts. There's also a children's area and art exhibits. ✉ *Yucca Valley Community Center, 57090 Twentynine Palms Hwy.* ☎ *760/369–7212* ⊕ *hidesertnaturemuseum.org* ◲ *Free* ⊘ *Closed Sun.–Tues.*

Pioneertown

TOWN | In 1946, Roy Rogers, Gene Autry, the Sons of the Pioneers (the music group for whom the town is named), and Russ Hayden built Pioneertown, an 1880s-style Wild West movie set complete with hitching posts, a saloon, and an OK Corral. You can stroll past wooden and adobe storefronts and feel like you're back in the Old West. Pappy & Harriet's Pioneertown Palace, now the town's top draw, has evolved into a hip venue for indie and mainstream performers such as Dengue Fever, Neko Case, and Robert Plant. ✉ *53688 Pioneertown Rd., Pioneertown* ✛ *4 miles north of Yucca Valley* ⊕ *pappyandharriets.com.*

Restaurants

Frontier Café

$$ | CAFÉ | A cozy coffeehouse with a counterculture vibe, Frontier is a good place to stop before heading into the park or up to Pioneertown. Fill up on a breakfast bagel or fresh-baked muffin

paired with a coffee drink, and pick up a salad, hot or cold sandwich, and dessert for lunch. **Known for:** fresh bakery items; vegan, veggie, and gluten-free options; daily specials. [$] *Average main: $12* ✉ *55844 Twentynine Palms Hwy.* ☎ *760/820–1360* 🌐 *www.cafefrontier.com* 🕒 *No dinner.*

★ **Pappy & Harriet's Pioneertown Palace**
$$$ | AMERICAN | FAMILY | Smack in the middle of what looks like the set of a Western is this cozy saloon where you can have dinner, relax over a drink at the bar, and catch some great indie bands or legendary artists—Leon Russell, Lorde, Paul McCartney, and Robert Plant have all played here. Pappy & Harriet's may be in the middle of nowhere, but you'll need reservations for dinner on weekends. **Known for:** live music several days/nights a week; Tex-Mex, Santa Maria–style barbecue; fun and lively atmosphere. [$] *Average main: $25* ✉ *53688 Pioneertown Rd., Pioneertown* ☎ *760/365–5956* 🌐 *www.pappyandharriets.com* 🕒 *Closed Tues. and Wed.*

Hotels

Pioneertown Motel
$$$ | HOTEL | Built in 1946 as a bunkhouse for Western film stars shooting in Pioneertown, this motel sticks close to its roots: its clean rooms are rustic and modern, with Western-style accents and exposed-wood-beam ceilings. **Pros:** Western movie time warp; great stargazing; surrounded by mesas and protected land. **Cons:** no frills; small rooms; hot in summer. [$] *Rooms from: $180* ✉ *5040 Curtis Rd., Pioneertown* ☎ *760/365–7001* 🌐 *www.pioneertown-motel.com* 🛏 *19 rooms.*

Rimrock Ranch
$$ | RENTAL | The quiet beauty of the surrounding desert attracts Hollywood writers, artists, and musicians to circa-1940s housekeeping cabins, an Airstream trailer, the Hatch House duplex, and lodge rooms. **Pros:** quiet desert hideaway; outdoor fireplaces and fully equipped kitchens; rich music heritage on site. **Cons:** rustic cabins will not appeal to resort seekers; far from most services; some units are sparsely furnished. [$] *Rooms from: $120* ✉ *53688 Pioneertown Rd., Pioneertown* ☎ *760/228–0130* 🌐 *www.rimrockranchpioneertown.com* 🛏 *7 rental units* 🍴 *No meals.*

Joshua Tree

12 miles east of Yucca Valley.

Artists and renegades have long found solace in the small upcountry desert town of Joshua Tree, home to artsy vintage shops, cafés, and B&Bs and a gateway to Joshua Tree National Park. Those who zip through town might wonder what all the hype is about, but if you slow down and spend time chatting with the folks in this funky community, you'll find much to love.

GETTING HERE AND AROUND

Highway 62 is the main route to and through Joshua Tree. Most businesses are here or along Park Boulevard as it heads toward the park.

Sights

★ **Noah Purifoy Desert Art Museum of Assemblage Art**
ARTS VENUE | This vast, 10-acre art installation full of "assemblage art" on a sandy tract of land in the town of Joshua Tree honors the work of artist Noah Purifoy. The sculptures blend with the spare desert in an almost postapocalyptic way. Purifoy lived most of his life in this desert until his death is 2004. He used found materials to make commentary on social issues. His art has been showcased at LACMA, J. Paul Getty Museum, MOCA, and many more. ✉ *63030 Blair La.* 🌐 *www.noahpurifoy.com* 🎫 *Free* 🕒 *Closes at sunset.*

Restaurants

Crossroads Cafe

$$ | AMERICAN | Mexican breakfasts, chicken-cilantro soup, and hearty sandwiches are among the draws at this Joshua Tree institution for pre-hike breakfasts, birthday lunches, and early dinners. Taxidermied animals and beer-can lights hint at the community's consciousness, while the tattooed waitresses and slew of veggie options make it clear that the Crossroads is unlike anywhere else in San Bernardino County. **Known for:** rustic wooden interior and bar; hearty and affordable meals; vegetarian and vegan dishes. $ *Average main: $12* ✉ *61715 Twentynine Palms Hwy.* ☎ *760/366–5414* ⊕ *crossroadscafejtree.com.*

Twentynine Palms

12 miles east of Joshua Tree.

The main gateway town to Joshua Tree National Park, Twentynine Palms is also the location of the U.S. Marine Air Ground Task Force Training Center. You can find services, supplies, and lodging in town.

GETTING HERE AND AROUND

Highway 62 is the main route to and through Twentynine Palms. Most businesses here center around Highway 62 and Utah Trail, 3 miles north of Joshua Tree's entrance.

VISITOR INFORMATION Twentynine Palms Visitor Center and Gallery. ✉ *73484 Twentynine Palms Hwy.* ⊕ *www.visit29.org.*

Sights

Oasis of Murals

PUBLIC ART | Twenty-six murals painted on the sides of buildings depict the history, wildlife, and landscape of Twentynine Palms. You can't miss the art on a drive around town, but you can also pick up a free map from the visitor center.

✉ *Twentynine Palms* ⊕ *www.action-29palmsmurals.com.*

Sky's the Limit Observatory & Nature Center

OBSERVATORY | Run by a dedicated, local nonprofit, this 15-acre park near the northern entrance to Joshua Tree National Park educates visitors on the region's celestial and terrestial attributes. It has an observatory dome with a 14-inch telescope, nature trails that feature desert plants, a meditation garden, and an orrery (a scaled rendition of what's happening in the night sky). The public is invited to free star parties every Saturday night (except when the moon is full) and to join classes, clinics, and special programs. ✉ *9697 Utah Trail* ☎ *760/490–9561* ⊕ *www.skysthelimit29.org.*

Restaurants

Campbell Hill Bakery

$$ | BAKERY | Prepare to wait in line to order from the counter at this tiny but exceedingly popular eatery, owned and operated by professionals in the bakery business who escaped from New York City to the California high desert. Delectable loaves of bread, scones, muffins, and other sweet and savory treats take center stage, but you can also pick up sandwiches and various entrées—from beef pot pie and flatbreads to pizza and lasagna. **Known for:** hefty Cubano, Philly cheesesteak, and Italian subs; daily specials; good place to pick up food before touring the park. $ *Average main: $12* ✉ *73491 Twentynine Palms Hwy.* ☎ *760/401–8284* ⊕ *campbellhillbakery.com* ⊗ *No dinner. Closed Sun.*

Kitchen in the Desert

$$ | AMERICAN | This popular spot in a renovated courtyard complex with murals and mining artifacts serves comfort food with a Caribbean flair. The chef, who hails from Trinidad, creates artful dishes derived from family recipes with dashes of American and global influences—for example, Trinidadian doubles (curried chickpeas with dahl bread, cucumbers, and tamarind sauce), Dan Dan noodles (cumin-spiced pork and soba noodles with tahini), bacon burgers, and fried Oreos and donuts for dessert. **Known for:** convenient location near the junction of Highway 62 and National Park Drive; meats grilled or smoked outdoors over a mesquite fire; vegetarian and gluten-free dishes. $ *Average main: $15* ⊠ *6427 Mesquite Ave.* ☎ *760/865–0245* ◷ *No lunch.*

Hotels

Harmony Motel

$ | **HOTEL** | In 1987, the rock band U2 stayed at the roadside Harmony Motel—set on two acres of natural desert with onubstructed views of the mountains of Joshua Tree National Park—while posing for images to adorn their legendary album *U2: The Joshua Tree.* **Pros:** cactus gardens and nature trail; outdoor pool and hot tub; close to Fortynine Palms Oasis and Indian Cove. **Cons:** small property that books quickly; not close to restaurants or entertainment; on a busy highway. $ *Rooms from: $95* ⊠ *71161 Twentynine Palms Hwy.* ☎ *760/367–3351* ⊕ *www.harmonymotel.com* ⇨ *11 units* ☉l *No meals.*

Sunnyvale Garden Suites

$$ | **HOTEL** | Bay Area retirees transformed this former 1990s condominium complex into an all-suite hotel with paths that meander through carefully tended desert gardens that have sitting areas. **Pros:** outdoor hot tub, game room, community patio with fire pit, exercise room; close to national park entrance and military base; personal attention from owners and staff. **Cons:** noise can travel through thin walls and ceilings; no breakfast included; 3 miles to nearest grocery store. $ *Rooms from: $111* ⊠ *73843 Sunnyvale Dr.* ☎ *760/361–3939* ⊕ *sunnyvalesuites.com* ⇨ *21 suites.*

★ 29 Palms Inn

$$ | **B&B/INN** | **FAMILY** | The closest lodging to the entrance to Joshua Tree National Park, the funky 29 Palms Inn scatters a collection of adobe and wood-frame cottages, some dating back to the 1920s and 1930s, over 70 acres of grounds that include the ancient Oasis of Mara, a popular destination for birds and bird-watchers year-round. **Pros:** gracious hospitality; exceptional bird-watching; art gallery, pool, and on-site restaurant. **Cons:** rustic accommodations; limited amenities; no in-room Wi-Fi. $ *Rooms from: $140* ⊠ *73950 Inn Ave.* ☎ *760/367–3505* ⊕ *www.29palmsinn.com* ⇨ *24 units* ☉l *Breakfast.*

Chapter 22

LASSEN VOLCANIC NATIONAL PARK

Updated by
Andrew Collins

CALIFORNIA

⛰ Camping	🛏 Hotels	🏃 Activities	👁 Scenery	👥 Crowds
★★★★★	★★★☆☆	★★★★★	★★★★☆	★★★☆☆

WELCOME TO
LASSEN VOLCANIC NATIONAL PARK

TOP REASONS TO GO

★ **Hike a volcano:** The 2½-mile trek up Lassen Peak rewards you with a spectacular view of far northern California.

★ **Spot a rare bloom:** The Lassen Smelowskia, a small white-to-pinkish flower, which grows only in the Cascade Mountains, is especially prolific on Lassen Peak.

★ **View volcano varieties:** All four types of volcanoes found in the world—shield, plug dome, cinder cone, and composite—are represented here.

★ **Listen to the Earth:** The park's thumping mud pots and venting fumaroles roil, gurgle, and belch a raucous symphony, their actions generated by heat from beneath the Earth's crust.

★ **Escape the crowds:** Lassen, in sparsely populated far northern California, is one of the lesser-known national parks.

1 Southwest. Hydrothermal activity is greatest in the park's most-visited area; you'll see evidence on the hike to Bumpass Hell and strolling along the sidewalks at the Sulphur Works, just beyond the Kohm Yah-mah-nee Visitor Center.

2 Manzanita and Summit Lakes. The northern half of Lassen Park Highway, starting around Summit Lake, winds past the forested Devastated Area and Chaos Jumbles before reaching lush, wooded Manzanita Lake, near the park's northwest entrance.

3 Warner Valley and Juniper Lake. In the park's southeastern quadrant, Warner Valley has dazzling hydrothermal features and the park's only lodging, historic Drakesbad Guest Ranch. Juniper Lake has relaxing hikes and nonmotorized boating fishing and boating.

4 Butte Lake. Located in the park's rugged and less-visited northeast corner, Butte and Snag lakes were formed by lava from a cinder cone whose summit you can hike to.

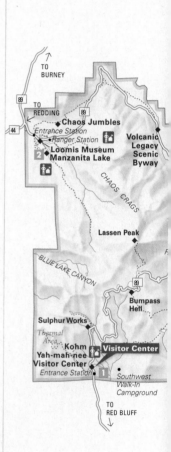

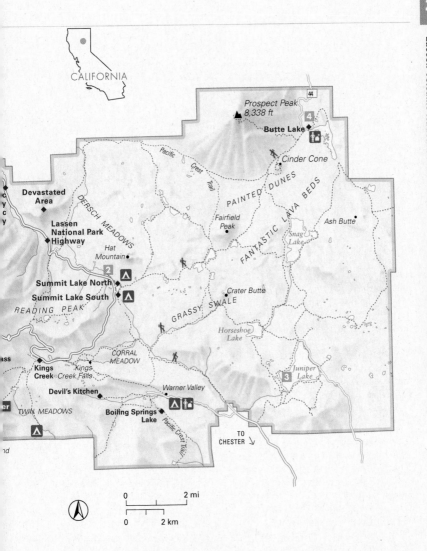

CALIFORNIA

Prospect Peak
8,338 ft

44

Butte Lake

Cinder Cone

Devastated
Area

DERSCH MEADOWS

Lassen
National Park
Highway

Pacific Crest Trail

PAINTED DUNES

Fairfield
Peak

FANTASTIC LAVA BEDS

Snag
Lake

Ash Butte

Hat
Mountain

Summit Lake North

Summit Lake South

READING PEAK

GRASSY SWALE

Crater Butte

Horseshoe
Lake

Juniper
Lake

CORRAL
MEADOW

Kings
Creek

Kings
Creek Falls

Devil's Kitchen

Warner Valley

Boiling Springs
Lake

Pacific Crest Trail

TWIN MEADOWS

TO
CHESTER ↓

0   2 mi

0   2 km

Lassen Peak, a plug dome, is the most famous feature of this 166-square-mile tract of coniferous forests and alpine meadows. Its most spectacular outburst occurred in 1915, when it blew a cloud of ash almost 6 miles high. The resulting mudflow destroyed vegetation for miles and the evidence is still visible. The volcano finally came to rest in 1921 but is not considered dormant.

Prior to Lassen's eruptions, which were the most recent of any volcano in the contiguous United States until Mt. St. Helens in 1980, the area contained a pair of neighboring national monuments, each designated by President Theodore Roosevelt in 1907: Lassen Peak and Cinder Cone. The massive eruptions brought such attention to the region that in August 1916, the federal government combined the national monuments and a significant chunk of land around them to create 106,452-acre Lassen Volcanic National Park.

Despite being located in populous California, Lassen ranks among the less-visited national parks in the West. Farther from the state's bigger cities than Yosemite, Joshua Tree, and other buzzier parks, it requires a bit of time and effort to get to. And then there's the name, Lassen Volcanic, which misleadingly gives many the impression that the park is focused on one singular feature, the peak for which it's named.

In fact, this underrated park contains tremendously varied and utterly stunning natural scenery and is surprisingly lush for a landscape devastated by volcanic blasts in relatively recent times. Lassen Peak is an undeniably impressive sight (and great fun to hike), but arguably even more memorable are the three areas of active hydrothermal activity within its shadow—Sulphur Works, Bumpass Hell, and Devils Kitchen—which delight visitors with up-close views of frothy mudpots, steamy fumaroles, and boiling springs reminiscent of those found at Yellowstone, only minus the jostling crowds.

The Cinder Cone, in the park's remote but very accessible northeastern corner, is another star feature, and in several other areas you can explore landscapes formed by and gradually adapting to the effects of volcanic activity. One byproduct of the area's eruptions are its numerous lakes, from hot and forbidding Boiling Springs Lake to the refreshing, deep-blue waters of Manzanita, Summit, Butte, and Juniper lakes, all of which are ideal for fishing, swimming, and nonmotorized boating. Well-marked hiking trails connect these marvelous lakes and hydrothermal areas with lofty peaks, wildflower-strewn

AVERAGE HIGH/LOW TEMPERATURES					
JAN.	**FEB.**	**MAR.**	**APR.**	**MAY**	**JUNE**
50/13	51/13	53/16	61/23	70/29	79/34
JULY	**AUG.**	**SEPT.**	**OCT.**	**NOV.**	**DEC.**
84/40	85/40	78/36	69/30	56/21	50/14

meadows, and alpine forests rife with Western hemlocks, Douglas firs, and Ponderosa pines.

One other reason the park receives a bit less attention than others is that it contains relatively few visitor services. But Lassen's handful of manmade structures, including the 1909 Drakesbad Guest Ranch and the 1927 Loomis Museum, are quite pleasing. An original park lodge and cabins built in the 1930s around Manzanita Lake were removed in 1974 out of fear that a rockslide in the volcanic Chaos Crags area could catastrophically overcome the village. Scientists eventually determined that such an event won't ever happen, and in 2011, the park service unveiled 20 beautiful new camping cabins around the lake's southern shore. At the park's southwestern entrance, a bland 1960s ski lodge was torn down in 2005 and replaced with airy and contemporary Kohm Yah-mah-nee Visitor Center, a LEED-certified building that's a joy to spend time in.

In the age of social media and renewed interest in camping and off-the-beaten-path adventures, Lassen's reputation for awesome beauty and geographical diversity is spreading more than ever. Annual visitor numbers have been climbing gradually since 2010. But for the foreseeable future, the chance to explore one of California's greatest natural wonders while still enjoying ample solitude remains one of the park's top draws.

Planning

When to Go

The park is open year-round, though most roads—the main exception being Lassen Park Highway up to Kohm Yah-mah-nee Visitor Center—are closed from late October to mid-June due to snow. The park's high elevation offers a cool respite in summer from California's hot central valley, while spring and fall are typically mild during the day, but you should prepare for lows below freezing at night even in June and September.

Getting Here and Around

AIR

Redding Municipal Airport (RDD), about an hour's drive west, provides the nearest commercial air service, with regular flights on United Express from San Francisco and Los Angeles. Most major airlines serve the airports in Reno, a 2½-hour drive, and Sacramento, a three-hour drive.

CAR

From the north, take the Highway 44 exit off Interstate 5 in Redding and drive east about 50 miles to the park's northwest entrance, at Highway 89. From the south, take Exit 649 off Interstate 5 and follow Highway 36 northeast 45 miles, turning left onto Highway 89 to reach the southwest (and only year-round) entrance. The 30-mile main park road, officially called Lassen National Park Highway but often called simply Lassen Park Highway, skirts around the southern,

Lassen Volcanic in One Day

Start your day early at the park's northwest entrance, accessible via Highway 44 from Redding. Stop at the **Loomis Museum** to view exhibits before taking the easy, ½-mile loop **Lily Pond Nature Trail.** Back at the museum, drive or walk to **Manzanita Lake.** Take a mid-morning break and pick up supplies at the **Camper Store** for a picnic lunch before taking the park highway toward **Lassen Peak.** As you circle the peak on its northern flank, behold **Devastated Area,** testimony to the damage done by the 1915 eruptions. Continue to **Kings Creek,** an area of lush meadows where you can hike to **Kings Creek Falls.** Allow at least two hours to make the 3-mile round-trip hike, which ends in a 700-foot ascent to the falls. If time permits, make the two-hour 3-mile round-trip hike to **Bumpass Hell,** a basin containing some of the park's most eye-popping hydrothermal activity. Or if time is short, continue to the **Sulphur Works,** where you can view sulfur-emitting steam vents from sidewalks along the park road.

eastern, and northern sides of Lassen Peak, connecting the southwest and northwest entrances. Take Highway 36 from the southwest entrance to Chester to reach Warner Valley and Juniper Lake, in the remote southeastern side of the park, and follow Highway 44 east from Manzanita to reach the similarly secluded Butte Lake area.

Inspiration

Lassen Volcanic National Park & Vicinity, by Jeffrey P. Schaffer, is a comprehensive book about the park.

Park Essentials

ACCESSIBILITY
Kohm Yah-mah-nee Visitor Center, the Loomis Museum, and the Manzanita Camper Store are fully accessible to those with limited mobility. The Devastated Area Interpretive Trail and the Sulphur Works wayside exhibits are accessible, as are most ranger programs. Butte Lake, Manzanita Lake, and Summit Lake North have some accessible camp sites.

PARK FEES AND PERMITS
From mid-April through November the fee to enter the park is $30 per car ($25 for motorcycles); the rest of the year the fee is $10 for cars and motorcycles. The fee covers seven consecutive days. Those entering by bus, bicycle, horse, or on foot pay $15. An annual park pass costs $55. For backcountry camping, pick up a free permit at the Loomis Museum or Kohm Yah-mah-nee Visitor Center, or request an application online at ⊕ *www. nps.gov/lavo.*

PARK HOURS
The park is open 24/7 year-round. It is in the Pacific time zone.

CELL PHONE RECEPTION
Cell phones don't work in most parts of the park, although you can usually pick up a signal near the Bumpass Hell parking area and the north shore of Manzanita Lake.

Hotels

Other than the inviting camping cabins at Manzanita Lake, Drakesbad Guest Ranch is the only lodging available inside Lassen. It's rustic (no electricity, just old-fashioned kerosene lamps), expensive, and tends to book up a year or more in advance for summer stays. You'll find a handful of smaller lodging options relatively near the park's southwest entrance, and a few more options nearby in Chester and a bit beyond in Susanville. Off Interstate 5, about an hour east, Red Bluff and Redding have a number of chain properties. *Hotel reviews have been shortened. For full information, visit Fodors.com.*

What It Costs

$	$$	$$$	$$$$
RESTAURANTS			
under $16	$16–$22	$22–$30	over $30
HOTELS			
under $125	$126–$175	$176–$225	over $225

Restaurants

Dining options within the park are limited to simple fare at Lassen Café & Gift in Kohm Yah-mah-nee Visitor Center and at the Manzanita Lake Camper Store, and the delicious meals at Drakesbad Guest Ranch, which does offer meals to nonguests by reservation only. The nearest community with a good mix of mostly casual dining options is Chester, about a half-hour drive from the southwest entrance station. About an hour away, the town of Susanville and the small city of Redding have more extensive restaurant selections. *Restaurant reviews have been shortened. For full information, visit Fodors.com.*

Visitor Information

CONTACTS Lassen Volcanic National Park. ⊠ *Kohm Yah-mah-nee Visitor Center, 21820 Lassen National Park Hwy., Mineral* ☎ *530/595–4480* ⊕ *www.nps.gov/lavo.*

Southwest

30 miles south of Manzanita Lake, 30 miles west of Chester, 52 miles east of Red Bluff.

Home to the park's only year-round entrance and visitor center, Lassen's southwest quadrant also contains the span of Lassen Park Highway that's likely to evoke the most oohs and aahs, as the road twists, turns, rises, and dips sharply to the south and then east of the soaring volcanic peak for which the park is named. You could spend a full day exploring this part of the park, with its fascinating hydro-thermal features and breathtaking, though sometimes quite arduous, hiking trails. It's also the most popular and accessible part of the park in winter, a great time for snowshoeing and cross-country skiing.

◉ Sights

PICNIC AREAS
Kings Creek
$ | **LOCAL INTEREST** | |**LOCAL INTEREST** | Trees shade these creekside picnic tables located at a popular trailhead. ⊠ *Lassen Park Hwy.* ✛ *11½ miles north of southwest entrance.*

Lake Helen
$ | **LOCAL INTEREST** | |**LOCAL INTEREST** | This site with picnic tables and vault toilets has views of several summits, including Lassen Peak. ⊠ *Lassen Park Hwy.* ✛ *near Bumpass Hell trailhead.*

SCENIC STOPS
★ **Lassen Peak**
NATURE SITE | When this plug dome volcano erupted in 1915, it spewed a huge mushroom cloud of debris almost 6 miles into the air. You can admire the peak from a number of points along the park road, and a fabulous panoramic view rewards those who make the strenuous 2½-mile hike to the 10,457-foot summit. ⊠ *Lassen Park Hwy.* ✛ *7 miles north of southwest entrance.*

Plants and Wildlife in Lassen Volcanic

Because of its varying elevations, Lassen has several different ecological habitats.

Below 6,500 Feet

Below 6,500 feet you can find Ponderosa pine, Jeffrey pine, sugar pine, white fir, and several species of manzanita, gooseberry, and Ceanothus. Wildflowers—wild iris, spotted coralroot, pyrola, violets, and lupine—surround the hiking trails in spring and early summer.

Manzanita Lake Area

The Manzanita Lake area has the best bird-watching opportunities, with yellow warblers, pied-billed grebes, white-headed and hairy woodpeckers, golden-crowned kinglets, and Steller's jays. The area is also home to rubber boas, garter snakes, brush rabbits, Sierra Nevada red foxes, black-tailed deer, coyotes, and the occasional mountain lion.

From 6,500 to 8,000 Feet

At elevations of 6,500 to 8,000 feet are red fir forests populated by many of the same wildlife as the lower regions, with the addition of black-backed three-toed woodpeckers, blue grouse, snowshoe hare, pine martens, and the hermit thrush.

Above 8,000 Feet

Above 8,000 feet the environment is harsher, with bare patches of land between subalpine forests. You'll find whitebark pine, groves of mountain hemlock, small pikas, yellow-bellied marmots, and the occasional black bear. Bird-watchers should look for gray-crowned rosy finches, rock wrens, golden eagles, falcons, and hawks. California tortoiseshell butterflies are found on the highest peaks. If you can visit in winter, you'll see one of the park's most magnificent seasonal sights: massive snowdrifts up to 30 and 40 feet high.

Sulphur Works Thermal Area

NATURE SITE | FAMILY | Proof of Lassen Peak's volatility becomes evident shortly after you enter the park at the southwest entrance. Sidewalks skirt boiling springs and sulfur-emitting steam vents. This area is usually the last site to close in winter, but even when the road is closed, you can access the area via a 2-mile round-trip hike through the snow. ⊠ *Lassen Park Hwy.* ⊕ *1 mile from southwest entrance.*

TRAILS

★ Bumpass Hell Trail

TRAIL | FAMILY | This 3-mile round-trip hike leads to arguably the park's most mesmerizing feature, a wondrous landscape of hydrothermal activity characterized by boiling springs, hissing steam vents, and roiling gray mud pots. Give yourself about two hours to complete the loop, which involves a gradual 300-foot descent into the Bumpass Hell basin, and be sure to venture to the basin's several upper viewpoints, which provide amazing views of the entire scene. Stay on trails and boardwalks near the thermal areas, as what appears to be firm ground may be only a thin crust over scalding mud. From the basin, you have the option of continuing another 1.9 miles along a scenic ridge to Cold Boiling Lake, from which you can trek farther to Kings Creek Picnic Area or Crumbaugh Lake. *Moderate.* ⊠ *Lassen Park Hwy.* ⊕ *Trailhead: 6 miles from southwest entrance.*

Crumbaugh Lake Trail

TRAIL | This 2.6-mile round-trip hike through meadows and forests to Cold Boiling and Crumbaugh lakes presents an excellent opportunity to view spring wildflowers, but it's quite pretty throughout summer and fall. At Cold Lake, it's possible to detour to Bumpass Hell (thereby adding 3.8 miles round-trip to your trek). *Moderate.* ✉ *Lassen Park Hwy.* ✥ *Trailhead: Kings Creek picnic area, 13 miles north of southwest entrance.*

Kings Creek Falls Trail

TRAIL | Nature photographers love this 2.3-mile loop hike through forests dotted with wildflowers. A steady 700-foot ascent leads to the spectacular falls. It can be slippery in spots, including along a stone staircase, so watch your step. *Moderate.* ✉ *Lassen Park Hwy.* ✥ *Trailhead: 3 miles south of Summit Lake.*

★ Lassen Peak Trail

TRAIL | This trail winds 2½ miles to the mountaintop. It's a tough climb—2,000 feet uphill on a steady, steep grade—but the reward is a spectacular view. At the peak you can see into the rim and view the entire park (and much of California's Far North). Give yourself about five hours to complete this climb, and bring sunscreen, water, snacks, a first-aid kit, and a jacket—it can be windy and cold at the summit. *Difficult.* ✉ *Lassen Park Hwy.* ✥ *Trailhead: 7 miles north of southwest entrance.*

Mill Creek Falls Trail

TRAIL | This 2½-hour 3.8-mile round-trip hike through forests and wildflowers takes you to where East Sulphur and Bumpass creeks merge to create the park's highest waterfall. For a longer adventure, you can continue past the falls for 2.5 miles to Crumbaugh Lake, and another 1.3 miles past Cold Boiling Lake to Kings Creek Picnic Area. *Moderate.* ✉ *Lassen Park Hwy.* ✥ *Trailhead: Southwest Walk-In Campground parking lot.*

VISITOR CENTERS

★ Kohm Yah-mah-nee Visitor Center

INFO CENTER | **FAMILY** | A handsome, contemporary LEED-certified structure at the southwest entrance, this helpful year-round resource is a good place to pick up maps, inquire about kids' activities and ranger programs, view an engaging park film, and check out the well-conceived interactive exhibits. There's also an excellent bookstore and a casual café. ✉ *21820 Lassen National Park Hwy.* ☎ *530/595–4480* 🌐 *www.nps.gov/lavo.*

🍴 Restaurants

Lassen Café & Gift

$ | **CAFÉ** | Coffee and hot cocoa, wine and beer (including local brews from Lassen Ale Works), and sandwiches, burgers, soups, salads, bagels, and pizzas are served in this casual eatery inside the park's only year-round visitor center. Indoors, there's a fireplace, but if the weather is fine, the patio with its mountain views is the place to be. **Known for:** local beers; stunning mountain views from the outdoor patio; gift shop with local art and crafts. [$] *Average main: $9* ✉ *Kohm Yah-mah-nee Visitor Center, 21820 Lassen National Park Hwy.* ☎ *530/595–3555* 🌐 *www.lassenrecreation.com* ⏲ *Closed weekdays mid-Oct.–late May.*

Manzanita and Summit Lakes

30 miles north of southwest entrance, 50 miles east of Redding.

The most recognizable landmarks in the park's vast northwestern quadrant, Manzanita and Summit lakes are connected by the Lassen Park Highway, which continues south toward Lassen Peak and the southwest entrance. As the road passes through Devasted Area, it offers an up-close glimpse of the destruction wrought by the 1915 eruption. Both lakes are popular for swimming and boating, and Manzanita Lake is just beyond the park's northwest entrance and adjacent to its largest cluster of facilities, including Loomis Museum, tent and cabin camping, and a camper store.

Sights

HISTORIC SITES

★ Loomis Museum

MUSEUM | FAMILY | In this handsome building constructed of volcanic rock in 1927, you can view artifacts from the park's 1914 and 1915 eruptions, including dramatic original photographs taken by Benjamin Loomis, who was instrumental in the park's establishment. The museum also has a bookstore, excellent exhibits about the area's Native American heritage, and a helpful staff who can recommend hikes and points of interest on this side of the park. ✉ *Lassen Park Hwy.* ✛ *Next to Manzanita Lake* ☎ *530/595–6140* ✉ *Free* ✆ *Closed late Oct.–late May.*

SCENIC DRIVES

★ Lassen National Park Highway

SCENIC DRIVE | This 30-mile scenic route, the main thoroughfare through the park, passes by such prominent sites as Lassen Peak, Bumpass Hell, Sulphur Works, Kings Creek, Devastated Area, and Chaos Crags, connecting the southwest entrance with Manzanita Lake and the northwest entrance. It's often referred to simply as Lassen Park Highway. ✉ *Lassen Volcanic National Park.*

SCENIC STOPS

Chaos Jumbles

NATURE SITE | More than 350 years ago, an avalanche from the Chaos Crags lava domes scattered hundreds of thousands of rocks—many of them from 2 to 3 feet in diameter—over a couple of square miles. ✉ *Lassen Park Hwy.* ✛ *2 miles east of northwest entrance.*

Devastated Area

NATURE SITE | FAMILY | Lassen Peak's 1915 eruptions cleared this area, which makes up a good chunk of the center of the park, of all vegetation, though after all these years the forest has gradually returned. The easy ½-mile interpretive trail loop is wheelchair accessible. ✉ *Lassen Park Hwy.* ✛ *2½ miles northwest of Summit Lake.*

Manzanita Lake

BODY OF WATER | Lassen Peak is reflected in the waters of this rippling lake, which has good catch-and-release trout fishing and a pleasant trail for exploring the area's abundant wildlife. ✉ *Lassen Park Hwy.* ✛ *Near northwest entrance station.*

Summit Lake

BODY OF WATER | The midpoint between the northern and southern entrances, Summit Lake is a good place to take an afternoon swim. A trail leads around the lakeshore, and several other trails lead east—for quite a few miles—toward a cluster of smaller lakes in the park's more remote northeastern quadrant. ✉ *Lassen Park Hwy.* ✛ *17½ miles from southwest entrance.*

TRAILS

Lily Pond Nature Trail

TRAIL | FAMILY | This ½-mile jaunt loops past a small lake and through a wooded area, ending at a pond that is filled with yellow water lilies in summer. Marked with interpretive signs, it's a good choice for families. *Easy.* ✉ *Lassen Park Hwy.* ✛ *Trailhead: across from Loomis Museum.*

☕ Coffee and Quick Bites

Manzanita Lake Camper Store

$ | CAFÉ | Pick up simple prepared foods, groceries, and beverages—local wines and beers among them—at the store, which has an ATM and a pay phone.
Known for: good local craft beer selection; supplies for a picnic by the lake; hearty deli sandwiches. Ⓢ *Average main: $7* ✉ *Manzanita Lake Campground, Lassen Park Hwy.* ☎ *530/335–7557* ⊕ *www.lassenrecreation.com* ✆ *Closed mid-Oct.–mid-June.*

Did You Know?

"I took this photo on a camping trip to Lake Manzanita in Lassen Volcanic National Park. The log in the water seemed to point towards the partly snow-covered Lassen Peak." —photo by Shyam Subramanyan, Fodors.com member

Hotels

Manzanita Lake Camping Cabins
$ | **RENTAL** | **FAMILY** | This lakeside compound of 20 rustic but handsomely designed modern cabins provides the only roof-over-your-head lodgings on the main park highway, but this is a camping experience, albeit a nicely outfitted one. **Pros:** only lodgings on Lassen Park Highway; picturesque setting; guests can purchase amenity packages, including sleeping bags. **Cons:** must supply your own bedding; rustic; open only seasonally. [$] *Rooms from: $76* ✉ *Manzanita Lake, Lassen Park Hwy.* ☎ *530/779–0307* 🌐 *www.lassenlodging.com* 🕓 *Closed mid-Oct.–mid-June* 🛏 *20 cabins* 🍴 *No meals.*

Warner Valley and Juniper Lake

18 miles northwest of Chester (to Warner Valley), 12 miles north of Chester (to Juniper Lake), 47 miles east of the park's southwest entrance.

Relatively few visitors explore the park's south-central and southeastern sections, home to the sunny meadows and impressive hydrothermal features of the Warner Valley—which also contains the park's only lodging (historic Drakesbad Guest Ranch)—and the azure waters of Juniper Lake. It takes a little effort to get to both areas, which are set along unpaved gravel roads reached by way of the small town of Chester. Although it's also possible to make your way to Warner Valley on foot from Kings Creek Trailhead in the park's Southwest area, you need to be in good shape or plan to spend a night camping if you attempt this hike that's 11 miles round-trip, not including potential side hikes to Boiling Lake or Devils Kitchen.

Sights

SCENIC STOPS

★ **Juniper Lake**
BODY OF WATER | The park's largest body of water, Juniper Lake is accessible only in summer and sits at an elevation of nearly 7,000 feet in the little-visited eastern section of the park, about a 90-minute drive—the last span of it on a gravel road—from the Southwest Entrance and a half-hour north of Chester. The reward for making your way here is the chance for swimming and kayaking or canoeing in a pristine lake, which is also a lovely spot for a picnic, perhaps before or after hiking up to the fire tower atop nearby Mt. Harkness. There's a small seasonal ranger station and a primitive campground here, as well. ✉ *Juniper Lake Rd.* ✣ *12 miles north of Chester* 🕓 *Road to lake closed Nov.–June.*

TRAILS

Boiling Springs Lake Trail
TRAIL | **FAMILY** | This worthwhile 3-mile loop leads from the Warner Valley Trailhead to Boiling Springs Lake, which is surrounded by high bluffs topped with incense cedar, Douglas fir, and other conifers. Vents beneath the milky gray-green lake release bubbles into it, heating it to a temperature of 125°F. Most who come all the way to Warner Valley combine this hike with one of the others that it connects with, typically either Devils Kitchen or Terminal Geyser. *Easy–Moderate.* ✉ *Warner Valley Rd.* ✣ *Trailhead: across the street from Warner Valley Campground.*

★ **Devils Kitchen Trail**
TRAIL | A moderately hilly 4.2 mile round-trip hike through open meadows and conifer forest leads to the least-frequented of the park's three main hydrothermal areas, the others being Sulphur Works and Bumpass Hell. The lack of crowds makes this an especially enjoyable place to view burping mud pots, misty steam vents, hot boiling pools, and even Lassen

Peak in the distance. *Moderate–Difficult.* ✉ *Warner Valley Rd.* ✣ *Trailhead: across the street from Warner Valley Campground.*

Mount Harkness Trail

TRAIL | Because of its 1,250-foot elevation change, this is the most strenuous but also rewarding of the handful of hikes from quiet Juniper Lake. Your reward for making your way through forest groves and lupine meadows to the summit of a dormant 8,046-foot shield volcanic are panoramic views from a handsome stone-and-wood fire tower built in 1930. ✉ *Lassen Volcanic National Park* ✣ *Trailhead: Juniper Lake Ranger Station.*

Hotels

★ Drakesbad Guest Ranch

$$$$ | **B&B/INN** | With propane furnaces and kerosene lamps, everything about this century-old property in the Lassen Volcanic National Park's remote but beautiful southeastern corner harks back to a simpler time. **Pros:** back-to-nature experience; great for family adventures; only full-service lodging inside the park. **Cons:** on a remote partially paved road 45 minutes' drive from nearest town (Chester); rustic, with few in-room frills; not open year-round. [$] *Rooms from: $384* ✉ *14423 Warner Valley Rd., Chester* ☎ *866/999–0914* 🌐 *www.drakesbad.com* 🕒 *Closed mid-Oct.–early June* 🛏 *19 rooms* 🍴 *All meals.*

Butte Lake

33 miles east of Manzanita Lake, 47 miles northwest of Susanville, 55 miles north of Chester.

Even more isolated and less-visited than Warner Valley, Butte Lake anchors the park's northeastern corner and is at least an hour's drive from any other parts of the park. A lot of folks don't come here until their second or third visit to Lassen, but if you're able to find the time, it's worth making the effort just to view the lake's lava-rock shoreline and, ideally, to hike to the Cinder Cone that had itself been designated a national monument prior to becoming part of Lassen Volcanic National Park. ■ **TIP→ Come prepared: there are no facilities in this areas except for vault toilets and potable water, although the tent campground here is one of the park's largest.**

Sights

SCENIC STOPS

Butte Lake

BODY OF WATER | Dark, dramatic lava beds form the western shore of this peaceful body of water in the park's secluded northeastern corner. It's a great destination for kayaking and canoeing, and trails run alongside the lake's northern and eastern shores (eventually to Widow Lake), and a short loop leads to tiny, neighboring Bathtub Lake, which is nice for a quick swim on hot days. Amenities, which are open early June through mid-October, include a boat launch, campground, and ranger station. ✉ *End of Butte Lake Rd.* ✣ *6 miles from Hwy. 44.*

TRAILS

★ Cinder Cone Trail

TRAIL | Though set in the park's remote northeastern corner, this is one of its most fascinating trails, as it offers views of a dazzling variety of volcanic features, including Painted Dunes, Fantastic Lava Beds, and Prospect Peak. It's a somewhat challenging undertaking, because the 4-mile round-trip hike to the cone summit requires a steep 845-foot climb over ground that's slippery in parts with loose cinders. For a better understanding of the geology along this hike, pick up an interpretive brochure at the trailhead or visitor centers. *Moderate–Difficult.* ✉ *Boat ramp at end of Butte Lake Rd.* ✣ *Trailhead: off Hwy. 44, 33 miles east of Manzanita Lake.*

Activities

Lassen is a rugged adventurer's paradise, but be prepared for sudden changes in the weather: fierce thunderstorms sometimes drench the mountains and produce lightning, which poses a threat to hikers above the tree line, and blizzard conditions can develop quickly in winter or even early spring and late fall. In summer, hot temperatures and limited shade can pose a threat, especially for hikers unused to high altitudes.

BIKING

Biking is prohibited on trails and can be a bit nerveracking on Lassen Park Highway because of the lack of shoulders and guardrails, and due to—on the southern half of Lassen Park Highway—some steep grades. Only experienced cyclists should attempt this drive. The gravel roads to Warner Valley and both Butte and Juniper lakes are open to cyclists and receive far less auto traffic than Lassen Park Highway. For casual cyclists, the area around Lake Almanor in Chester is quite appealing.

BOATING

People are sometimes surprised that a park named for a volcanic peak abounds with lakes. Among these, kayakers and canoers favor Manzanita, Summit, Butte, and Juniper lakes, all of which have good road access (Butte and Manzanita have actual boat launches). Motorized watercraft are not permitted anywhere in the park, and none of the park's other lakes with road access allow boating of any kind.

CAMPING

Lassen's seven campgrounds draw a broad range of campers, from large groups singing around a mesmerizing fire to solitary hikers seeking a quiet place under the stars. You can drive a vehicle to all campgrounds except the Southwest Walk-In, which is a very short stroll from Kohm Yah-mah-nee Visitor Center. This is the only campground open year-round;

the others usually open in June and close in early fall. Overnight fees range from $12 to $26. Butte Lake, Juniper, Southwest Walk-In, and Warner Valley are first-come, first served. For reservations at the other campgrounds, visit www.recreation.gov or call 877/444–6777.

Butte Lake. Situated near the edge of a lake flanked by lava rocks, this peaceful area with 101 sites is in the secluded northeastern corner of the park. ⊠ *End of Butte Lake Rd.*

Juniper Lake. On the east shore of the park's largest lake, these campsites are close to the water in a wooded area. To reach them, you have to take a rough gravel road 13 miles north of Chester to the park's southeast corner; trailers are not advised. There is no potable water here. ⊠ *Chester Juniper Lake Rd.*

Manzanita Lake. The largest of Lassen campgrounds accommodates RVs up to 35 feet and has 20 rustic cabins. Many ranger programs begin here, and a trail nearby leads to the crater that holds Crags Lake. ⊠ *Off Lassen Park Hwy., near park's northwest entrance.*

Southwest Walk-In. Relatively small and Lassen's only campground open year-round, Southwest lies within a conifer forest and has views of Brokeoff Peak. Snow camping is allowed, and drinking water is available at visitor center entry-way. ⊠ *Near southwest entrance, beside Kohm Yah-mah-nee Visitor Center.*

Summit Lake North. This completely forested campground has easy access to backcountry trails. You'll likely observe deer grazing. ⊠ *Lassen Park Hwy., 17½ miles north of southwest entrance..*

Summit Lake South. Less crowded than its neighbor to the north, this campground has wet meadows where wildflowers grow in the spring. No potable water is available after mid-September. ⊠ *Lassen Park Hwy., 17½ miles north of southwest entrance.*

Warner Valley. You'll find 17 sites at this quite, rustic campground near the trailhead for Boiling Lake, Devils Kitchen, and several other notable hydrothermal features in this breathtaking valley in the park's somewhat remote southeastern quadrant. ⊠ *Off Warner Valley Rd., just before Drakesbad Guest Ranch.*

EDUCATIONAL PROGRAMS

If you're wondering why fumaroles fume, how lava is formed, or which critter left those tracks beside the creek, check out the array of ranger-led programs. Most groups meet outside Loomis Museum or near Manzanita Lake. See the park bulletin boards for daily topics and times.

RANGER PROGRAMS
Kids Program

TOUR—SIGHT | FAMILY | Junior Rangers, ages 5 to 12, meet for 45 minutes three times a week with rangers, including for talks about the role wildfires have in shaping our national parks. Kids can earn patches by completing an activity book, or joining the Chipmunk Club and earning a sticker by completing various activities. ⊠ *Lassen Volcanic National Park.*

FISHING

The best place to fish is in Manzanita Lake, though it's catch and release only. Butte, Juniper, Snag, and Horseshoe lakes, along with several creeks and streams, are also popular fishing destinations within the park. Anglers will need a California freshwater fishing license, which you can obtain at most sporting-goods stores or through the California Department of Fish and Wildlife's website (⊕ *www.dfg.ca.gov*).

The Fly Shop
FISHING | Famous among fly fishers, the Fly Shop carries tackle and equipment and offers guide services. ⊠ *4140 Churn Creek Rd., Redding* ☎ *530/222-3555, 800/669-3474* ⊕ *www.flyshop.com.*

HIKING

Of the 150 miles of hiking trails within the park, 17 miles are part of the interstate Pacific Crest Trail, which accesses Warner Valley on its way through the park. Trails in Lassen offer an astounding range of scenery, some winding through coniferous forest and others across rocky alpine slopes, along meandering waterways, or through basins of dazzling hydrothermal boiling springs and steam vents.

HORSEBACK RIDING
Drakesbad Guest Ranch

HORSEBACK RIDING | FAMILY | This property in the park's Warner Valley offers guided rides to nonguests by reservation. Among the options is a two-hour loop to Devils Kitchen. There's also an eight-hour five-lake loop for advanced riders. ⊠ *End of Warner Valley Rd., Chester* ☎ *530/524-2841* ⊕ *www.drakesbad.com* 🎫 *From $45.*

SNOWSHOEING

You can snowshoe anywhere in the park. The gentlest places are near the northwest entrance, while more challenging terrain is in the Southwest corner of the park but is easier to access because the park road stays open here all winter. Cross-country skiing is also popular in these areas.

■**TIP→ Beware of hidden cavities in the snow. Park officials warn that heated sulfur emissions, especially in the Sulphur Works Area, can melt out dangerous snow caverns, which may be camouflaged by thin layers of fresh snow that skiers and snowshoers can easily fall through.**

Bodfish Bicycles & Quiet Mountain Sports
SNOW SPORTS | You can rent snowshoes, skis, boots, and poles at this popular shop 30 miles from the park's Southwest Entrance. ⊠ *149 Main St., Chester* ☎ *530/258-2338* ⊕ *www.bodfishbicycles.com.*

Lassen Mineral Lodges

SNOW SPORTS | This lodge near the park rents snowshoes as well as cross-country skis and poles. ✉ *38348 Hwy. 36, Mineral* ☎ *530/595–4422* ⊕ *www.minerallodge.com.*

Snowshoe Walks

SNOW SPORTS | On weekend afternoons from January through March, park rangers lead two-hour snowshoe walks that explore the park's geology and winter ecology. The hikes require moderate exertion at an elevation of 7,000 feet; children under age eight are not allowed. If you don't have snowshoes you can borrow a pair; $1 donation suggested. Walks are first come, first served; free tickets are issued beginning at 9 am (try to arrive by 11 am to be sure to secure a spot) the day of the hike at the Kohm Yah-mah-nee Visitor Center. ✉ *21820 Lassen National Park Hwy.* ☎ *530/595–4480* ⊕ *www.nps. gov/lavo* 🎫 *Free.*

Nearby Towns

Located in remote northeastern California, Lassen has few towns of any real size around it, although you will find a smattering of places to stay in unincorporated areas near the park's southwest and northwest entrances. The nearest actual town is the small logging center of **Chester,** which has a handful of eateries and lodgings and is about a 40-minute drive from the southwest entrance. You'll find more options another 35 miles east in the larger high-desert town of **Susanville.** About an hour west of the park in the northern reaches of the state's Central Valley, the small city of **Red Bluff** (population 14,300) and the area's largest metropolis, **Redding** (population 92,000), have a wide variety of restaurants and hotels. Redding, in particular, has a handful of distinctive places to stay and eat and some notable attractions—it's also a gateway for visiting beautiful **Shasta Lake,** about 10 miles north.

Chester

30 miles southeast of Lassen's southwest entrance, 71 miles east of Red Bluff.

A gateway to Lassen Volcanic National Park as well as a popular spot for fishing and boating on Lake Almanor, modest but pleasant Chester sees its population swell from 2,500 to nearly 5,000 in summer as tourists come to visit.

GETTING HERE AND AROUND

Chester is on Highway 36, the main route from Red Bluff, at the junction of Highway 89, which leads northwest to Lassen.

VISITOR INFORMATION Lake Almanor Area Chamber of Commerce. ✉ *278 Main St.* ☎ *530/258–2426* ⊕ *www.lakealmanorarea.com.*

👁 Sights

Lake Almanor

BODY OF WATER | This lake's 52 miles of forested shoreline are popular with hikers, campers, swimmers, waterskiers, and anglers. At an elevation of 4,500 feet, the lake warms to above 70°F for about eight weeks in summer. ✉ *Off Hwys. 89 and 36* ☎ *530/258–2426* ⊕ *www.lakealmanorarea.com.*

Restaurants

★ **Cravings Cafe Espresso Bar & Bakery**

$ | CAFÉ | This casual breakfast and lunch place inside a white clapboard house satisfies diners' cravings with dishes like homemade slow-cooked corned-beef hash topped with two eggs and accompanied by a slice of sourdough bread. You can get breakfast and excellent pastries all day, with soups, salads, sandwiches, and burgers on the menu for lunch. **Known for:** waffles with applewood-smoked bacon in the batter; attached bookstore has great selection of hiking and nature titles; outdoor patio. $ *Average main: $10* ✉ *278 Main St.* ☎ *530/258–2229* 🌐 *hwww.stoverlanding.com* 🕘 *Closed Tues. and Wed. No dinner.*

★ Highlands Ranch Restaurant and Bar
$$$ | **AMERICAN** | Dining at the Highlands Ranch Resort's contemporary roadhouse restaurant is in a stained-wood, high-ceilinged room indoors, or out on the deck, which has views of a broad serene meadow and the hillside beyond. Among the few sophisticated eating options within Lassen Volcanic National Park's orbit, the restaurant serves updated classics like rib-eye steak (up to 22 ounces), balsamic-marinated Muscovy duck, and blackened ahi with carrot-cucumber slaw. **Known for:** striking views inside and out; small plates and burgers in the bar; inventive sauces and preparations. $ *Average main: $29* ✉ *41515 Hwy. 36, Mill Creek* ☎ *530/595–3388* 🌐 *www.highlandsranchresort.com/restaurant* 🕘 *Closed Mon.–Wed. in Nov.–late May.*

Ranch House Pub & Grill
$$ | **AMERICAN** | **FAMILY** | This convivial neighborhood pub stands out because of its abundance of shaded patio seating—and full horseshoes pit—set in the restaurant's landscaped backyard. It's a reliable bet for filling up on hearty comfort fare after a long day of hiking and exploring—consider the decadent "loaded" fries with cheese, bacon, and pulled pork. **Known for:** a substantial kids' menu; tasty sides of garlic or sweet potato fries; molten lava chocolate cake. $ *Average main: $17* ✉ *669 Main St.* ☎ *530/258–4226* 🕘 *Closed Mon. and Tues. No dinner Sun.*

Hotels

Antlers Motel
$ | **HOTEL** | A spotlessly clean, simple, and affordable option in downtown Chester, this homey two-story 20-room motel is a handy base for exploring both Warner Valley and the southern end of Lassen Park Highway. **Pros:** reasonable rates; coffeemakers and refrigerators in every room; short walk from several restaurants and bars. **Cons:** no on-site breakfast option; pretty basic decor; parking can be a little tight when the motel is fully booked. $ *Rooms from: $90* ✉ *268 Main St.* ☎ *530/258–2722* 🌐 *www.antlersmotel.com* 🛏 *20 rooms* 🍴 *No meals.*

Best Western Rose Quartz Inn
$$ | **HOTEL** | Down the road from Lake Almanor and close to Lassen Volcanic National Park, this mid-range chain property is basically a motel, but the helpful staff (especially with touring plans) and amenities like good Wi-Fi, comfortable bedding, and spacious breakfast area make it a good choice for a short stay. **Pros:** within easy walking distance of town's restaurants; convenient to Lassen Volcanic National Park's southwest entrance; good Wi-Fi and other amenities. **Cons:** a little pricey for what you get; cookie-cutter decor; noise audible between rooms. $ *Rooms from: $165* ✉ *306 Main St.* ☎ *530/258–2002* 🌐 *www.bestwestern.com* 🛏 *50 rooms* 🍴 *Free Breakfast.*

Bidwell House
$$$ | **B&B/INN** | Some guest rooms at this 1901 ranch house near Lake Almanor have wood-burning stoves, claw-foot or Jacuzzi tubs, and antique furnishings; a separate cottage with a kitchen sleeps six. **Pros:** individually decorated rooms; beautiful wooded setting; excellent full breakfast. **Cons:** not ideal for kids; may be too remote for some guests; a little pricey. $ *Rooms from: $185* ✉ *1 Main St.* ☎ *530/258–3338* 🌐 *www.bidwellhouse.com* 🛏 *14 rooms* 🍴 *Breakfast.*

★ Highlands Ranch Resort
$$$$ | **B&B/INN** | On a gorgeous 175-acre alpine meadow 10 miles from Lassen's southwest entrance, this cluster of smartly designed upscale bungalows is peaceful and luxurious. **Pros:** stunning views; most luxurious accommodations near the park; friendly and helpful staff.

Cons: pricey for the area; remote location; books up months ahead for summer stays. $ *Rooms from: $299* ✉ *41515 Hwy. 36, Mill Creek* ☎ *530/595–3388* 🌐 *www.highlandsranchresort.com* 🕑 *Closed Mon.–Wed. in Nov.–late May* 🛏 *7 cottages* 🍴 *Free Breakfast.*

Mill Creek Resort

$ | **RESORT** | **FAMILY** | Set amid towering evergreens in a tranquil patch of Lassen National Forest, this delightfully unfussy 1930s cabin and camping resort feels as though it could be inside the national park, although it's actually about 10 miles south, on a scenic country road. **Pros:** utterly peaceful, wooded setting; one of the closest lodging options to Lassen's southwest entrance; old-fashioned, family-friendly summer-camp vibe. **Cons:** remote location is a bit of a drive from other restaurants and services; bedrooms and bathrooms in each cabin are quite cozy; there's no cell reception or Wi-Fi (although cell phones work 2 miles away). $ *Rooms from: $120* ✉ *40271 Hwy. 172, Mill Creek* ☎ *530/595–4449* 🌐 *www.millcreekresort.net* 🕑 *Closed mid-Oct.–Apr.* 🛏 *9 cabins* 🍴 *No meals.*

Susanville

35 miles east of Chester, 47 miles east of Butte Lake, 85 miles northwest of Reno, NV.

From Susanville, established as a trading post in 1854, you have an easy, though at least hour-long, approach to Lassen's northeastern (Butte Lake) and south-central and southeastern (Warner Valley and Juniper Lake) areas. The town tells the tale of its rich history through murals painted on buildings in the historic uptown area.

GETTING HERE AND AROUND

U.S. 395 leads from Reno to Susanville, where Highway 36 continues west through Chester to Lassen's southern entrances. Just west of town, you can also pick up Highway 44 to get to Lassen's Butte Lake and Manzanita Lake (northwest) entrances.

VISITOR INFORMATION Lassen County Chamber of Commerce. ✉ *156 Main St.* ☎ *530/257–4323* 🌐 *www.lassencountychamber.org.*

🍴 Restaurants

★ Lassen Ale Works Boardroom

$ | **PIZZA** | This popular craft brewery stands out because of its airy, modern interior and for turning out some of the best pizzas in the area. But you can also enjoy a great selection of perennial and seasonal ales, from the Lassen-inspired Volcanic Double IPA to rich Devil's Corral Imperial Stout. **Known for:** ales named for local sites; made-from-scratch pizzas with inventive toppings; chocolate martinis. $ *Average main: $14* ✉ *702–000 Johnstonville Rd.* ☎ *530/257–4443* 🌐 *www.lassenaleworks.com* 🕑 *Closed Mon. and Tues. No lunch Wed.–Thurs.*

White House

$ | **THAI** | Options for Asian cuisine are limited around here, which makes the consistently tasty cuisine at this homey Thai restaurant on the east side of downtown Susanville all the more surprising—and appreciated. Expect an extensive selection of traditional dishes, including fragrant *tom kha gai* soup, mango curry with chicken and shrimp, and stir-fried rice and noodle dishes. **Known for:** hearty soups large enough to make a meal out of; plenty of vegetarian options; mango sticky rice. $ *Average main: $15* ✉ *3085 Johnstonville Rd.* ☎ *530/257–6666* 🕑 *Closed Sun. and Mon.*

🛏 Hotels

Red Lion Inn & Suites Susanville

$ | **HOTEL** | Spacious, pleasant if generically furnished rooms and proximity to Lassen Volcanic National Park's eastern sections are the main draw at this mid-range chain property in the center of downtown Susanville. **Pros:** great mountain views; seasonal heated pool; handy downtown location. **Cons:** in a busy part of town; more than an hour's drive from Lassen's main entrances; cookie-cutter decor. [$] *Rooms from: $115* ✉ *3015 Riverside Dr.* ☎ *530/257–3450* 🌐 *www.redlion.com* 🛏 *67 rooms* 🍴 *Free Breakfast.*

Redding

50 miles west of Manzanita Lake, 135 miles south of Ashland, OR, 160 miles north of Sacramento.

The largest city in far northern California, Redding sits along the busy Interstate 5 corridor and is a handy gateway for visiting Lassen, especially if approaching the seasonal northwest entrance by Manzanita Lake. Although a bit sprawly and suburban, Redding does have a few notable attractions, including Turtle Bay Exploration Park, and it's a good base for visiting Shasta Lake to the north. It's also a good stopover is you're traveling from Lassen west to Redwood National and state parks on the coast.

GETTING HERE AND AROUND

Interstate 5 is the major north–south route through Redding. Highway 299 bisects the city east–west, and Highway 44 connects Redding and Lassen Park's northwest entrance.

VISITOR INFORMATION Visit Redding. ✉ *1448 Pine St.* ☎ *530/225–4100* 🌐 *www.visitredding.com.*

Sights

★ Lake Shasta Caverns National Natural Landmark

NATURE SITE | FAMILY | Stalagmites, stalactites, flowstone deposits, and crystals entice visitors to the Lake Shasta Caverns. To see this impressive spectacle, you must take the two-hour tour, which includes a catamaran ride across the McCloud arm of Lake Shasta and a bus ride up North Grey Rocks Mountain to the cavern entrance. The temperature in the caverns is 58°F year-round, making them a cool retreat on a hot summer day. The most awe-inspiring of the limestone rock formations is the glistening Cathedral Room, which appears to be gilded. **■ TIP→ In summer it's wise to purchase tickets online a day or more ahead of your visit.** ✉ *20359 Shasta Caverns Rd., Lakehead* ✣ *20 miles north of Redding* ☎ *530/238–2341, 800/795–2283* 🌐 *www.lakeshastacaverns.com* 🎟 *$30.*

★ Turtle Bay Exploration Park

CITY PARK | FAMILY | This peaceful downtown park has 300 acres of walking trails, an aquarium, an arboretum and botanical gardens, and many interactive exhibits for kids. The main draw is the stunning Santiago Calatrava–designed **Sundial Bridge,** a metal and translucent glass pedestrian walkway, suspended by cables from a single tower, spanning a broad bend in the Sacramento River. On sunny days the 217-foot tower lives up to the bridge's name, casting a shadow on the ground below to mark time. Access to the bridge and arboretum is free, but there's a fee for the museum and gardens. ✉ *844 Sundial Bridge Dr.* ☎ *530/243–8850* 🌐 *www.turtlebay.org* 🎟 *Museum $18* 🕐 *Museum closed Mon. and Tues. early Sept.–mid-Mar.*

Restaurants

From the Hearth Artisan Bakery & Café

$ | AMERICAN | A homegrown variation on the Panera theme, this extremely popular operation (as in expect a wait at peak dining hours) serves pastries, eggs and other hot dishes, and good coffee drinks, juices, and smoothies for breakfast, adding a diverse selection of wraps, panini, sandwiches, burgers, rice bowls, and soups the rest of the day. Some sandwiches are made with a bread that FTH bills as "Redding's original sourdough." **Known for:** baked goods; pork breakfast tacos; two other Redding locations (one downtown) plus another in Red Bluff. [$] *Average main: $11* ✉ *2650 Churn Creek Rd.* ☎ *530/424–2233* 🌐 *www.fthcafe.com.*

Jack's Grill

$$$ | **STEAKHOUSE** | The original Jack opened his grill (and an upstairs brothel) in 1938. Tamer these days but often jam-packed and noisy, this place is famous for its 16-ounce steaks and deep-fried shrimp and chicken dishes. **Known for:** 1930s atmosphere; great martinis; thick slabs of beef. [$] *Average main: $29* ✉ *1743 California St.* ☎ *530/241–9705* 🌐 *www.jacksgrillredding.com* 🕒 *Closed Sun. No lunch.*

Hotels

★ Bridgehouse Bed & Breakfast

$ | **B&B/INN** | In a residential area a block from the Sacramento River and a ½-mile from downtown Redding, this inn contains six rooms in two side-by-side homes. **Pros:** easygoing hospitality; proximity to downtown and Turtle Bay; freshly baked scones at full breakfast. **Cons:** lacks pool, fitness center, and other standard hotel amenities; the two least expensive rooms are small; books up well ahead in summer. [$] *Rooms from: $119* ✉ *1455 Riverside Dr.* ☎ *530/247–7177* 🌐 *www.bridgehousebb.com* 🛏 *6 rooms* 🍴 *Free Breakfast.*

Grace Lake Resort

$$ | **B&B/INN** | Set in on a grassy plot amid towering shade trees about midway between Redding and Lassen's summer-only northwest entrance, this cluster of individually furnished country cabins—plus one three-bedroom bungalow with a full kitchen—is great for families or groups of friends traveling together. **Pros:** Near Lassen's northwest entrance; pretty tree-shaded grounds with an outdoor pool; every unit has charcoal grills, kitchenettes, and picnic tables. **Cons:** a 75-minute drive from park's only winter entrance (in Mineral); need to call or email for rates and availability; few dining options nearby. [$] *Rooms from: $130* ✉ *31853 Hwy. 44, Shingletown* ☎ *707/499–3604* 🌐 *www.gracelakeresort.com* 🛏 *7 cabins* 🍴 *No meals.*

★ Sheraton Redding Hotel at Sundial Bridge

$$$ | **HOTEL** | **FAMILY** | This stylish, modern hotel opened next to Redding's famed Sundial Bridge and engaging Turtle Bay Exploration Park in 2018, and makes a great, family-friendly base for visiting Lassen as well as Whiskeytown and Shasta lakes. **Pros:** Adjacent to Turtle Bay Exploration Park; excellent pool and gym; excellent restaurant on-site. **Cons:** fee for parking; not in a very walkable neighborhood; nearly an hour's drive to Lassen Volcanic NP. [$] *Rooms from: $209* ✉ *820 Sundial Bridge Dr.* ☎ *530/364–2800* 🌐 *www.marriott.com* 🛏 *130 rooms* 🍴 *No meals.*

Chapter 23

MESA VERDE NATIONAL PARK

Updated by
Aimee Heckel

COLORADO

⛰ Camping	🛏 Hotels	🏃 Activities	👁 Scenery	👥 Crowds
★★★☆☆	★★☆☆☆	★★★★☆	★★★★★	★★★☆☆

WELCOME TO MESA VERDE NATIONAL PARK

TOP REASONS TO GO

★ **Ancient artifacts:** Mesa Verde is a time capsule for the Ancestral Pueblo culture; more than 4,000 archaeological sites and 3 million objects have been unearthed here.

★ **Bright nights:** Mesa Verde's lack of light and air pollution, along with its high elevation, make for spectacular views of the heavens.

★ **Active adventures:** Get your heart pumping outdoors with hiking, biking, and exploring on trails of varying difficulties.

★ **Cliff dwellings:** Built atop the pinyon-covered mesa tops and hidden in the park's valleys are 600 ancient dwellings, some carved directly into the sandstone cliff faces.

★ **Geological marvels:** View the unique geology that drew the Ancient Pueblo to the area: protected desert canyons, massive alcoves in the cliff walls, thick bands of sandstone, continuous seep springs, and soils that could be used for both agriculture and architecture.

1 Morefield. The only campground in Mesa Verde, Morefield includes a village area with a gas station and store, and is close to the main visitor center and some of the best hiking trails in the park.

2 Far View. Almost an hour's drive from Mesa Verde's entrance, Far View is the park's epicenter, with several restaurants and the park's only overnight lodge. The fork in the road here takes you west toward the sites at Wetherill Mesa or south toward Chapin Mesa.

3 Chapin Mesa. Home to the park's most famous cliff dwellings and archaeological sites, the Chapin Mesa area includes the famous 150-room Cliff Palace and Spruce Tree House dwellings and other man-made and natural wonders, as well as the Chapin Mesa Archaeological Museum.

4 Wetherill Mesa. See Long House, Two Raven House, Kodak House, and the Badger House Community.

COLORADO

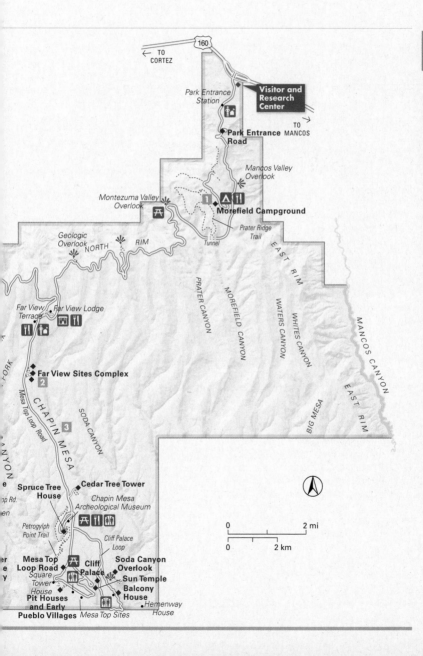

Unlike the other national parks, Mesa Verde earned its status from its ancient cultural history rather than its geological treasures. President Theodore Roosevelt established it in 1906 as the first national park to "preserve the works of man," in this case that of the Ancestral Pueblo, previously known as the Anasazi.

They lived in the region from roughly 550 to 1300; they left behind more than 4,000 archaeological sites spread out over 80 square miles. Their ancient dwellings, set high into the sandstone cliffs, are the heart of the park. Mesa Verde (which in Spanish means, literally, "Green Table," but translates more accurately to something like "green flat-topped plateau") is much more than an archaeologist's dreamland, however. It's one of those windswept places where man's footprints and nature's paintbrush—some would say chisel—meet. Rising dramatically from the San Juan Basin, the jutting cliffs are cut by a series of complex canyons and covered in several shades of green, from pines in the higher elevations down to sage and other mountain brush on the desert floor. From the tops of the smaller mesas, you can look across to the cliff dwellings in the opposite rock faces. Dwarfed by the towering cliffs, the sand-color dwellings look almost like a natural occurrence in the midst of the desert's harsh beauty.

Planning

When to Go

The best times to visit the park are late May, early June, and most of September, when the weather is fine but the summer crowds have thinned. Mid-June through August is Mesa Verde's most crowded time. In July and August, lines at the museum and visitor center may last half an hour. Afternoon thunderstorms are common in July and August.

The park gets as much as 100 inches of snow in winter. Snow may fall as late as May and as early as October, but there's rarely enough to hamper travel. In winter, the Wetherill Mesa Road is closed, but you can still get a glimpse of some of the Wetherill Mesa sandstone dwellings, sheltered from the snow in their cliff coves, from the Chapin Mesa area.

Ute Mountain Ute Bear Dance. This traditional dance, the local version of a Sadie Hawkins (in which the women choose their dance partners—and the selected men can't refuse), is held in May or June on the Towaoc Ute reservation south of Cortez. The event celebrates spring and

AVERAGE HIGH/LOW TEMPERATURES					
JAN.	**FEB.**	**MAR.**	**APR.**	**MAY**	**JUNE**
37/16	41/20	49/26	57/31	67/39	79/49
JULY	**AUG.**	**SEPT.**	**OCT.**	**NOV.**	**DEC.**
84/55	81/53	74/46	61/36	48/25	38/18

the legacy of a mythical bear that taught the Ute people her secrets. It's part of a multiday festival that includes music, races, and softball games, and culminates with an hour-long dance that's over when only one couple remains. ⊕ www.utemountainutetribe.com

Durango Fiesta Days. A parade, one of the oldest rodeos in the state, barbecue, street dance, cook-offs, live music, and more come to the Durango Fairgrounds in July. ⊕ www.downtowndurango.org

Durango Cowboy Poetry Gathering. A parade accompanies art exhibitions, poetry readings, music, theater, and storytelling in this four-day event run by the Durango Cowboy Poetry Gathering, a nonprofit set up to preserve the traditions of the American West. It's held the first weekend in October. ⊕ www.durangocowboypoetrygathering.org

Getting Here and Around

AIR
The cities of Durango (36 miles east of the park entrance) and Cortez (11 miles to the west) have airports.

CAR
The park has just one entrance, off U.S. 160, between Cortez and Durango in what's known as the Four Corners area (which spans the intersection of Colorado, New Mexico, Arizona, and Utah). Most of the roads at Mesa Verde involve steep grades and hairpin turns, particularly on Wetherill Mesa. Vehicles over 8,000 pounds or 25 feet are prohibited on this road. Trailers and towed vehicles are prohibited past Morefield Campground.

Check the condition of your vehicle's brakes before driving the road to Wetherill Mesa. For the latest road information, tune to 1610 AM, or call ☎ 970/529-4461. Off-road vehicles are prohibited in the park. At less-visited Wetherill Mesa, you must leave your car behind and hike or bike to the Long House, Kodak House, and Badger House Community.

Inspiration

Mesa Verde National Park: Shadows of the Centuries, by Duane A. Smith, discusses the history and current issues facing the park.

Ancient Peoples of the American Southwest, by Stephen Plog, is an archaeologist's account of the Ancestral Pueblo people and two other cultures.

Mesa Verde: Ancient Architecture, by Jesse Walter Fewkes, tells the stories behind the park's dwellings.

Park Essentials

PARK FEES AND PERMITS
Admission is $25 per vehicle for a seven-day permit. An annual pass is $40. Ranger-led tours of Cliff Palace, Long House, and Balcony House are $5 per person. You can also take ranger-guided bus tours from the Far View Lodge, which last between 3½ and 4 hours and cost $55 ($33 for kids; under five free). Backcountry hiking and fishing are not permitted at Mesa Verde.

Mesa Verde in One Day

For a full experience, take at least one ranger-led tour of a major cliff dwelling site, as well as a few self-guided walks. Arrive early and stop first at the Visitor and Research Center, where you can purchase tickets for Cliff Palace and Balcony House tours on Chapin Mesa. If it's going to be a hot day, you might want to take an early-morning or late-afternoon bus tour. Drive to the **Chapin Mesa Museum** to watch a 25-minute film introducing you to the area and its history. Just behind the museum is the trailhead for the ½-mile-long **Spruce Tree House Trail**, which normally leads to the best-preserved cliff dwelling in the park. While the Spruce Tree House is temporarily closed for restabilization, you can still view it from up top. Then drive to **Balcony House** for an hour-long, ranger-led tour.

Have lunch at the Spruce Tree Terrace Café or the Cliff Palace picnic area. Afterward take the ranger-led tour of **Cliff Palace** (one hour). Use the rest of the day to explore the overlooks and trails off the 6-mile loop of **Mesa Top Loop Road**. Or when the Spruce Tree House is open, head back to the museum and take **Petroglyph Point Trail** to see a great example of Ancestral Pueblo rock carvings. A leisurely walk along the Mesa Top's **Soda Canyon Overlook Trail** (off Cliff Palace Loop Road) gives you a beautiful bird's-eye view of the canyon below. On the drive back toward the park entrance, be sure to check out the view from **Park Point.**

PARK HOURS

Mesa Verde's facilities each operate on their own schedule, but most are open daily, from Memorial Day through Labor Day, between about 8 am and sunset. The rest of the year, they open at 9. In winter, the Spruce Tree House is open only to offer a few scheduled tours each day. Wetherill Mesa (and all the sites it services) is open from May through October, weather depending. Far View Center, Far View Terrace, and Far View Lodge are open between April and October. Morefield Campground and the sites nearby are open from mid-April through mid-October (and until early November for limited camping with no services). Specific hours are subject to change, so check with the visitor center upon arrival.

CELL-PHONE RECEPTION AND INTERNET

You can get patchy cell service in the park. Best service is typically at the Morefield Campground area, which is the closest to the neighboring towns of Cortez and Mancos. Public telephones can be found at all the major visitor areas (Morefield, Far View, and Spruce Tree). You can get free Wi-Fi throughout the Far View Lodge and at the Morefield Campground store.

Hotels

All 150 rooms of the park's Far View Lodge, open mid-April through late October, fill up quickly—so reservations are recommended, especially if you plan to visit on a weekend in summer. Options in the surrounding area include chain hotels, cabins, and bed-and-breakfast inns. Although 40 minutes away, Durango in particular has a number of hotels in fine old buildings reminiscent of the Old West. *Hotel reviews have been shortened. For full information, visit Fodors.com.*

What It Costs			
$	$$	$$$	$$$$
RESTAURANTS			
under $13	$13–$18	$19–$25	over $25
HOTELS			
under $121	$121–$170	$171–$230	over $230

Restaurants

Dining options in Mesa Verde are limited inside the park, but comparatively plentiful and varied if you're staying in Cortez, Mancos, or Durango. In surrounding communities, Southwestern restaurants, farm-fresh eateries, and steak houses are common options. *Restaurant reviews have been shortened. For full information, visit Fodors.com.*

Tours

BUS TOURS
Aramark Tours
GUIDED TOURS | **FAMILY** | If you want a well-rounded visit to Mesa Verde's most popular sites, consider a group tour. The park concessionaire provides all-day and half-day guided tours of the Chapin Mesa and Far View sites, departing in buses from either Morefield Campground or Far View Lodge. Tours are led by Aramark guides or park rangers, who share information about the park's history, geology, and excavation processes. Cold water is provided, but you'll need to bring your own snacks. Buy tickets at Far View Lodge, the Morefield Campground, or online. Tours sell out, so reserve in advance. ⌂ *Far View Lodge, 1 Navajo Hill, mile marker 15* ☎ *970/529–4422 Far View Lodge, 800/449–2288 Aramark* ⊕ *www.visitmesaverde.com* ⌂ *From $41* ☉ *700 Years Tour closed late Oct.–mid-Apr. Far View Explorer Tour closed mid-Aug.–late May.*

GUIDED TOURS
Ranger-Led Tours
GUIDED TOURS | The cliff dwellings known as Balcony House, Cliff Palace, and Long House can be explored only on ranger-led tours; the first two last about an hour, the third is 90 minutes. Buy tickets at the Mesa Verde Visitor and Research Center. These are active tours and may not be suitable for some children; each requires climbing ladders without handrails and squeezing through tight spaces. Be sure to bring water and sunscreen. Site schedules vary so check ahead. ⌂ *Mesa Verde National Park* ☎ *970/529–4465* ⊕ *www.nps.gov/meve/planyourvisit/visit-cliffdwelling.htm* ⌂ *$5 per site* ☉ *Closed: Cliff Palace: Oct./Nov.–late May. Balcony House: early Oct.–late Apr. Long House: mid-Oct.–mid-May.*

Visitor Information

PARK CONTACT INFORMATION Mesa Verde National Park. ☎ *970/529–4465* ⊕ *www.nps.gov/meve.*

Morefield
Sights

PICNIC AREAS
Montezuma Valley Overlook Picnic Area
$ | **LOCAL INTEREST** | **FAMILY** |**LOCAL INTEREST** | **FAMILY** | There is only one picnic table (and no services) here, but the view is excellent. ⌂ *5 miles west of park entrance.*

SCENIC DRIVES
Park Entrance Road
NATIONAL/STATE PARK | The main park road, also known as SH 10, leads you from the entrance off U.S. 160 into the park. As a break from the switchbacks, you can stop at a couple of pretty overlooks along the way, but hold out for Park Point, which, at the mesa's highest elevation (8,572 feet), gives you unobstructed,

360-degree views. Note that trailers and towed vehicles are not permitted beyond Morefield Campground. ✉ *Mesa Verde National Park.*

TRAILS

Knife Edge Trail

TRAIL | Perfect for a sunset stroll, this easy 2-mile (round-trip) walk around the north rim of the park leads to an overlook of the Montezuma Valley. If you stop at all the flora identification points that the trail pamphlet suggests, the hike takes about 1½ to 2 hours. The patches of asphalt you spot along the way are leftovers from old Knife Edge Road, built in 1914 as the main entryway into the park. *Easy.* ✉ *Mesa Verde National Park* ✥ *Trailhead: Morefield Campground, 4 miles from park entrance.*

Prater Ridge Trail

TRAIL | This 7.8-mile round-trip loop, which starts and finishes at Morefield Campground, is the longest hike you can take inside the park. It provides fine views of Morefield Canyon to the south and the San Juan Mountains to the north. About halfway through the hike, you'll see a cutoff trail that you can take, which shortens the trip to 5 miles. *Difficult.* ✉ *Mesa Verde National Park* ✥ *Trailhead: west end of Morefield Campground, 4 miles from park entrance.*

VISITOR CENTERS

Mesa Verde Visitor and Research Center

INFO CENTER | **FAMILY** | The visitor center is the best place to go to sign up for tours, get the information you need to plan a successful trip, and buy tickets for the Cliff Palace, Balcony House, and Long House ranger-led tours. The sleek, energy-efficient research center is filled with more than three million artifacts and archives. The center features indoor and outdoor exhibits, a gift shop, picnic tables, and a museum. Find books, maps, and videos on the history of the park. ✉ *Park entrance on the left, 35853 Rd H.5, Mancos* ☎ *970/529–4465* 🌐 *www.nps.gov/meve/planyourvisit/meve_vc.htm.*

🍴 Restaurants

Knife Edge Cafe

$ | **CAFÉ** | **FAMILY** | Located in the Morefield Campground, this simple restaurant in a covered outdoor terrace with picnic tables serves a hearty all-you-can-eat pancake breakfast with sausage every morning. Coffee and beverages are also available. **Known for:** lively gathering spot; breakfast burritos; large coffees with free refills all day. [$] *Average main: $10* ✉ *4 miles south of park entrance* ☎ *970/565–2133* 🌐 *www.nps.gov/meve/planyourvisit/restaurants.htm* ⏲ *Closed mid-Sept.–late Apr.*

Far View

👁 Sights

HISTORIC SITES

Far View Sites Complex

ARCHAEOLOGICAL SITE | **FAMILY** | This was probably one of the most densely populated areas in Mesa Verde, comprising as many as 50 villages in a ½-square-mile area at the top of Chapin Mesa. Most of the sites here were built between 900 and 1300. Begin the self-guided tour at the interpretive panels in the parking lot, then proceed down a ½-mile, level trail. ✉ *Park entrance road, near the Chapin Mesa area* 🌐 *www.nps.gov/meve* 🎟 *Free* ☞ *In winter, access by parking at the gate and walking in.*

TRAILS

Farming Terrace Trail

TRAIL | **FAMILY** | This 30-minute, ½-mile loop begins and ends on the spur road to Cedar Tree Tower, about 1 mile north of the Chapin Mesa area. It meanders through a series of check dams, which the Ancestral Pueblo built to create farming terraces. *Easy.* ✉ *Mesa Verde National Park* ✥ *Trailhead: park entrance road, 4 miles south of Far View Center.*

Plants and Wildlife in Mesa Verde

Mesa Verde is home to 640 species of plants, including a number of native plants found nowhere else. Its lower elevations feature many varieties of shrubs, including rabbitbrush and sagebrush. Higher up, you'll find mountain mahogany, yucca, pinyon, juniper, and Douglas fir. During warmer months, brightly colored blossoms, like the yellow perky Sue, blue lupines, and bright-red Indian paintbrushes, are scattered throughout the park.

The park is also home to a variety of migratory and resident animals, including 74 species of mammals. Drive slowly along the park's roads; mule deer are everywhere. You may spot wild turkeys, and black bear encounters are not unheard of on the hiking trails. Bobcats, coyotes, and mountain lions are also around, but they are seen less frequently. About 200 species of birds, including threatened Mexican spotted owls, red-tailed hawks, golden eagles, and noisy ravens, also live here. On the ground, you should keep your eyes and ears open for lizards and snakes, including the poisonous—but shy—prairie rattlesnake. As a general rule, animals are most active in the early morning and at dusk.

Many areas of the park have had extensive fire damage over the years. In fact, wildfires here have been so destructive they are given names, just like hurricanes. For example, the Bircher Fire in 2000 consumed nearly 20,000 acres of brush and forest, much of it covering the eastern half of the park. It will take several centuries for the woodland there to look as verdant as the area atop Chapin Mesa, which escaped the fire. But in the meantime, you'll have a chance to glimpse nature's powerful rejuvenating processes in action; the landscape in the fire-ravaged sections of the park is already filling in with vegetation.

Restaurants

Far View Terrace Café

$ | **AMERICAN** | This full-service cafeteria offers great views, but it's nothing fancy. Grab a simple coffee here or head across the dining room to Mesa Mocha for a latte. **Known for:** beautiful views; lattes; great gift shop. $ *Average main: $12* ✉ *Across from Far View Center* ☎ ⊕ *www.visitmesaverde.com/lodging-camping/dining/far-view-terrace-cafe* ☾ *Closed late Oct.–mid-Apr.*

Metate Room Restaurant

$$$ | **AMERICAN** | The park's rugged terrain contrasts with this relaxing space just off the lobby of the Far View Lodge. The well-regarded dining room is upscale, but the atmosphere remains casual.

Known for: Native American artwork; cheese and cured meats board; great views. $ *Average main: $25* ✉ *Far View Lodge, 1 Navajo Rd., across from Far View Center, 15 miles southwest of park entrance* ☎ *970/529–4422* ⊕ *www.visitmesaverde.com/lodging-camping/dining/metate-room-restaurant* ☾ *Closed late Oct.–mid-Apr. No lunch.*

🛏 Hotels

★ Far View Lodge

$$ | **HOTEL** | Talk about a view—all rooms have a private balcony, from which you can admire views of the neighboring states of Arizona, Utah, and New Mexico up to 100 miles in the distance. **Pros:** close to the key sites; views are spectacular; small on-site fitness center. **Cons:**

The Cliff Palace illuminated at night

simple rooms and amenities, with no TV; walls are thin and less than soundproof; no cell-phone service. $ *Rooms from: $151* ✉ *Across from Far View Center, 1 Navajo Rd., 15 miles southwest of park entrance* ☎ *800/449–2288* ⊕ *www.visit-mesaverde.com* ✆ *Closed late Oct.–mid-Apr.* 🛏 *150 rooms* 🍽 *No meals.*

Shopping

Far View Terrace Shop

CLOTHING | In the same building as the Far View Terrace Café, this is the largest gift shop in the park, with gifts, souvenirs, Native American art, toys, and T-shirts galore. ✉ *Mesa Top Loop Rd. , 15 miles south of park entrance* ☎ *800/449–2288 Aramark* ✆ *Hrs vary seasonally.*

Chapin Mesa

Sights

HISTORIC SIGHTS

★ **Balcony House**

ARCHAEOLOGICAL SITE | The stonework of this 40-room cliff dwelling is impressive, but you're likely to be even more awed by the skill it must have taken to reach this place. Perched in a sandstone cove 600 feet above the floor of Soda Canyon, Balcony House seems suspended in space. Even with modern passageways and trails, today's visitors must climb a 32-foot ladder and crawl through a narrow tunnel. Look for the intact balcony for which the house is named. The dwelling is accessible only on a ranger-led tour. ✉ *Cliff Palace/Balcony House Rd., 10 miles south of Far View Center, Cliff Palace Loop* ⊕ *www.nps.gov/meve/learn/historyculture/cd_balcony_house.htm* 🎫 *$5* ✆ *Closed early Oct.–late Apr.*

★ Cliff Palace

ARCHAEOLOGICAL SITE | This was the first major Mesa Verde dwelling seen by cowboys Charlie Mason and Richard Wetherill in 1888. It is also the largest, containing about 150 rooms and 23 kivas on three levels. Getting there involves a steep downhill hike and three ladders. ■ **TIP→ You may enter Balcony House or Cliff Palace by ranger-guided tour only so purchase tickets in advance.** The 90-minute, small-group "twilight tours" at sunset present this archaeological treasure with dramatic sunset lighting. Tour tickets are only available in advance at the Visitor and Research Center, Morefield Ranger Station, Durango Welcome Center, and online at ⊕ *www.recreation.gov.* ⊠ *Mesa Verde National Park* ✛ *Cliff Palace Overlook, about 2½ miles south of Chapin Mesa Archeological Museum* ⊕ *www. nps.gov/meve/learn/historyculture/ cd_cliff_palace.htm* ▤ *Regular tickets $5; twilight tours $20.* ⊗ *Closed Oct./Nov.– late May; loop closes at sunset.*

Pit Houses and Early Pueblo Villages

ARCHAEOLOGICAL SITE | Three dwellings, built on top of each other from 700 to 950, at first look like a mass of jumbled walls, but an informational panel helps identify the dwellings—and the stories behind them are fascinating. The 325-foot trail from the walking area is paved, wheelchair accessible, and near a restroom. ⊠ *Mesa Top Loop Rd. , about 2½ miles south of Chapin Mesa Archeological Museum* ▤ *Free.*

Spruce Tree House

ARCHAEOLOGICAL SITE | FAMILY | This 138-room complex is the best-preserved site in the park; however, the alcove surrounding Spruce Tree House became unstable in 2015 and was closed to visitors. Until alcove arch support is added, visitors can view but not enter this site. You can still hike down a trail that starts behind the Chapin Mesa Archeological Museum and leads you 100 feet down into the canyon to view the site from a distance. Because of its location in the heart of the Chapin Mesa area, the Spruce Tree House trail and area can resemble a crowded playground during busy periods. When allowed inside the site, tours are self-guided (allow 45 minutes to an hour), but a park ranger is on-site to answer questions. ⊠ *Mesa Verde National Park* ✛ *At the Chapin Mesa Archeological Museum, 5 miles south of Far View Center* ⊕ *www.nps. gov/meve/learn/historyculture/cd_spruce_ tree_house.htm* ▤ *Free* ⊗ *Tours closed for reconstruction.*

Sun Temple

ARCHAEOLOGICAL SITE | Although researchers assume it was probably a ceremonial structure, they're unsure of the exact purpose of this complex, which has no doors or windows in most of its chambers. Because the building was not quite half-finished when it was left in 1276, some researchers surmise it might have been constructed to stave off whatever disaster caused its builders—and the other inhabitants of Mesa Verde—to leave. ⊠ *Mesa Top Loop Rd. , about 2 miles south of Chapin Mesa Archeological Museum* ⊕ *www.nps.gov/meve/history-culture/mt_sun_temple.htm* ▤ *Free.*

PICNIC AREAS

Chapin Mesa Picnic Area

LOCAL INTEREST | FAMILY | This is the nicest and largest picnic area in the park. It has about 40 tables under shade trees and a great view into Spruce Canyon, as well as flush toilets. ⊠ *Mesa Verde National Park* ✛ *Near Chapin Mesa Archeological Museum, 5 miles south of Far View Center.*

SCENIC DRIVES

Mesa Top Loop Road

SCENIC DRIVE | This 6-mile drive skirts the scenic rim of Chapin Mesa and takes you to several overlooks and short, paved trails. You'll get great views of Sun Temple and Square Tower, as well as Cliff

Palace, Sunset House, and several other cliff dwellings visible from the Sun Point Overlook. ⊠ *Mesa Verde National Park.*

SCENIC STOPS
Cedar Tree Tower
ARCHAEOLOGICAL SITE | A self-guided tour takes you to, but not through, a tower and kiva built between 1100 and 1300 and connected by a tunnel. The tower-and-kiva combinations in the park are thought to have been either religious structures or signal towers. ⊠ *Mesa Verde National Park* ✛ *Near the four-way intersection on Chapin Mesa; park entrance road, 1½ miles north of Chapin Mesa Archeological Museum* ⊕ *www.nps.gov/meve/learn/historyculture/mt_cedar_tree_tower.htm* 🖼 *Free.*

Soda Canyon Overlook
CANYON | Get your best view of Balcony House here. You can also read interpretive panels about the site and the surrounding canyon geology. ⊠ *Cliff Palace Loop Rd. , about 1 mile north of Balcony House parking area* ☞ *Access in winter by walking the Cliff Palace Loop.*

TRAILS
★ Petroglyph Point Trail
TRAIL | Scramble along a narrow canyon wall to reach the largest and best-known petroglyphs in Mesa Verde. If you pose for a photo just right, you can manage to block out the gigantic "don't touch" sign next to the rock art. A map—available at any ranger station—points out three dozen points of interest along the trail. However, the trail is not open while Spruce Tree House is closed; check with a ranger for more information. *Moderate.* ⊠ *Mesa Verde National Park* ✛ *Trailhead: at Spruce Tree House, next to Chapin Mesa Archeological Museum.*

Soda Canyon Overlook Trail
TRAIL | FAMILY | One of the easiest and most rewarding hikes in the park, this little trail travels 1½ miles round-trip through the forest on almost completely level ground. The overlook is an excellent

point from which to photograph the Chapin Mesa–area cliff dwellings. *Easy.* ⊠ *Mesa Verde National Park* ✛ *Trailhead: Cliff Palace Loop Rd., about 1 mile north of Balcony House parking area* ☞ *Access in winter via Cliff Palace Loop.*

Spruce Canyon Trail
TRAIL | While Petroglyph Point Trail takes you along the side of the canyon, this trail ventures down into its depths. It's only 2.4 miles long, but you descend about 600 feet in elevation. Remember to save your strength; what goes down must come up again. The trail is open even while Spruce Tree House is closed. Still, check with a ranger. *Moderate.* ⊠ *Mesa Verde National Park* ✛ *Trailhead: at Spruce Tree House, next to Chapin Mesa Archeological Museum* ☞ *Registration required at trailhead.*

VISITOR CENTERS
Chapin Mesa Archeological Museum
MUSEUM | This is an excellent first stop for an introduction to Ancestral Pueblo culture, as well as the area's development into a national park. Exhibits showcase original textiles and other artifacts, and a theater plays an informative film every 30 minutes. Rangers are available to answer your questions. The shop focuses on educational materials, but you can also find park-themed souvenirs. The museum sits at the south end of the park entrance road and overlooks Spruce Tree House. Nearby, you'll find park headquarters, a gift shop, a post office, snack bar, and bathrooms. ⊠ *Park entrance road, 5 miles south of Far View Center, 20 miles from park entrance* ☏ *970/529–4465 General information line* ⊕ *www.nps.gov/meve/planyourvisit/museum.htm* 🖼 *Free.*

🍴 Restaurants

Spruce Tree Terrace Café
$ | AMERICAN | This small cafeteria has a limited selection of hot food, coffee, salads, burgers, and sandwiches. The patio is pleasant, and it's conveniently located

across the street from the museum. **Known for:** Southwest specialties; soup of the day specials; Navajo tacos. [$] *Average main: $10* ✉ *Near Chapin Mesa Archeological Museum, 5 miles south of the Far View Center* ☎ *970/529–4465* 🌐 *www.visitmesaverde.com/lodging-camping/dining/spruce-tree-terrace-cafe* ⏲ *No dinner in off-season.*

Shopping

Chapin Mesa Archeological Museum Shop
BOOKS/STATIONERY | Books and videos are the primary offering here, with more than 400 titles on Ancestral Pueblo and Southwestern topics. You can also find a selection of touristy T-shirts and hats. Hours vary throughout the year. ✉ *Spruce Tree Terrace , near Chapin Mesa Archeological Museum* ✣ *5 miles from Far View Center* ☎ *970/529–4445* 🌐 *www.nps.gov/meve/planyourvisit/museum.htm.*

Wetherill Mesa

Sights

HISTORIC SIGHTS

Badger House Community
ARCHAEOLOGICAL SITE | A self-guided walk along paved and gravel trails takes you through a group of four mesa-top dwellings. The community, which covers nearly 7 acres, dates back to the year 650, the Basketmaker Period, and includes a primitive, semisubterranean pit house and what's left of a multistory stone pueblo. Allow about 45 minutes to see the sites. The trail is 2.4 miles round-trip. ✉ *Wetherill Mesa Rd., 12 miles from Far View Center* 🌐 *www.nps.gov/meve/historyculture/mt_badger_house.htm* 🎫 *Free* ⏲ *Closed late Oct.–early May; road closes at 6 pm.*

Long House
ARCHAEOLOGICAL SITE | This Wetherill Mesa cliff dwelling is the second largest in Mesa Verde. It is believed that about 150 people lived in Long House, so named because of the size of its cliff alcove. The spring at the back of the cave is still active today. The in-depth, ranger-led tour begins a short distance from the parking lot and takes about 90 minutes. You hike about 2 miles, including two 15-foot ladders. ✉ *On Wetherill Mesa, 29 miles past the visitor center, near mile marker 15* 🌐 *www.nps.gov/meve/learn/history-culture/cd_long_house.htm* 🎫 *Tours $5* ⏲ *Closed mid-Oct.–mid-May.*

Step House
ARCHAEOLOGICAL SITE | So named because of a crumbling prehistoric stairway leading up from the dwelling, Step House is reached via a paved (but steep) trail that's ¾ mile long. The house is unique in that it shows clear evidence of two separate occupations: the first around 626, the second a full 600 years later. The self-guided tour takes about 45 minutes. ✉ *Wetherill Mesa Rd., 12 miles from Far View Center* 🌐 *www.nps.gov/meve/historyculture/cd_step_house.htm* 🎫 *Free* ⏲ *Closed mid-May–mid-Oct.; hrs vary seasonally.*

PICNIC AREAS

Cliff Palace Picnic Area
$ | LOCAL INTEREST | | FAMILY |LOCAL INTEREST | FAMILY | At this picnic area, there are several wooden tables under shade trees, plus restrooms, but no running water. The area is wheelchair accessible, although the nearby Cliff Palace dwellings are not. ✉ *2½ miles south of Chapin Mesa Archeological Museum* 🌐 *www.nps.gov/meve* ⏲ *Not plowed in the winter. Closed after sunset.*

Wetherill Mesa Picnic Area

LOCAL INTEREST | FAMILY | A handful of benches and tables near drinking water, a covered kiosk, and restrooms make this a pleasant spot for lunch in the Wetherill area. ✉ *Mesa Verde National Park* ✣ *12 miles southwest of Far View Center.*

SCENIC DRIVES

Wetherill Mesa Road

SCENIC DRIVE | This 12-mile mountain road, stretching from the Far View Center to the Wetherill Mesa, has sharp curves and steep grades (and is restricted to vehicles less than 25 feet long and 8,000 pounds). Roadside pull-outs offer unobstructed views of the Four Corners region. At the end of the road, you can access Step House, Long House, and Badger House. ✉ *Mesa Verde National Park* ⏲ *Closed late Oct.–early May.*

SCENIC STOPS

Kodak House Overlook

VIEWPOINT | Get an impressive view into the 60-room Kodak House and its several small kivas from here. The house, closed to the public, was named for a Swedish researcher who absentmindedly left his Kodak camera behind here in 1891. ✉ *Wetherill Mesa Rd.* 🌐 *www.nps.gov/meve* ⏲ *Closed late Oct.–May.*

☕ Coffee and Quick Bites

Wetherill Mesa Snack Bar

$ | AMERICAN | There's little on offer here, just chips, soft drinks, and concessions served on picnic tables under an awning, but it's the only choice on Wetherill Mesa. [$] *Average main: $7* ✉ *12 miles southwest of the park entrance* ☎ *970/529–4465* 🌐 *www.nps.gov/meve* 💳 *No credit cards* ⏲ *Closed Sept.–May.*

Activities

At Mesa Verde, outdoor activities are restricted, due to the fragile nature of the archaeological treasures here. Hiking (allowed on marked trails only) is the best option, especially as a way to view some of the Ancestral Pueblo dwellings.

BIKING

Bicycles are allowed on paved roads in the park except the twisty Wetherill Mesa Road, but there are no bike lanes and very narrow shoulders. During periods of low visibility (or when traveling through the tunnel on the main park road), bicycles must be fitted with a white light on the front and a red light (or reflector) on the back. Bikes are not allowed off-road or on trails.

BIRD-WATCHING

Turkey vultures soar between April and October, and large flocks of ravens hang around all summer. Among the park's other large birds are red-tailed hawks, great horned owls, and a few golden eagles. The Steller's jay (the male looks like a blue jay with a dark hat on) frequently pierces the pinyon-juniper forest with its cries, and hummingbirds dart from flower to flower in the summer and fall. Any visit to cliff dwellings late in the day will include frolicking white-throated swifts, which make their home in rock crevices overhead.

Pick up a copy of the park's "Checklist of the Birds" brochure or visit the National Park Service's website (🌐 *www.nps.gov/meve/planyourvisit/birdwatching.htm*) for a detailed listing of the feathered inhabitants here.

CAMPING

Morefield Campground is the only option within the park, and it's an excellent one. Reservations are accepted; it's open mid-April through mid-October, and through early November with no services. In nearby Mancos, just across the highway from the park entrance, there's a campground with full amenities (but no electrical hookups), while the San Juan National Forest offers backcountry camping.

Morefield Campground and Village. With 267 campsites, including 15 full-hookup RV sites, access to trailheads, a pet kennel, and plenty of amenities (including a gas station and a grocery store), the only campground in the park is an appealing mini-city for campers. It's a 40-minute drive to reach the park's most popular sites. Reservations are recommended, especially for RVs. ⊠ *4 miles south of park entrance* ☏ *970/564–4300, 800/449–2288* ⊕ *www.visitmesaverde.com.*

EDUCATIONAL PROGRAMS
RANGER PROGRAMS
Evening Ranger Campfire Program
TOUR—SIGHT | FAMILY | Every night in summer at the Morefield Campground Amphitheater, park rangers present a different 45- to 60-minute program on topics such as stargazing, history, wildlife, and archaeology. ⊠ *Morefield Campground Amphitheater, 4 miles south of park entrance* ☏ *970/529–4465* ⊠ *Free* ⊗ *Closed early Sept.–late May.*

Junior Ranger Program
TOUR—SIGHT | FAMILY | Children ages 4 through 12 can earn a certificate and badge for successfully completing at least three activities in the park's Junior Ranger booklet (available at the park or online). ⊠ *Mesa Verde Visitor and Research Center or Chapin Mesa Archeological Museum* ☏ *970/529–4465* ⊕ *www.nps.gov/meve/ forkids/beajuniorranger.htm.*

HIKING
A handful of trails lead beyond Mesa Verde's most visited sites and offer more solitude than the often-crowded cliff dwellings. The best canyon vistas can be reached if you're willing to huff and puff your way through elevation changes and switchbacks. Carry more water than you think you'll need, wear sunscreen, and bring rain gear—cloudbursts can come seemingly out of nowhere. Certain trails are open seasonally, so check with a ranger before heading out. No backcountry hiking is permitted in Mesa Verde, and pets are prohibited.

STARGAZING
There are no large cities in the Four Corners area, so there is little artificial light to detract from the stars in the night sky. Far View Lodge and Morefield Campground are great for sky watching.

Nearby Towns

A onetime market center for cattle and crops, **Cortez,** 11 miles west of the park, is now the largest gateway town to Mesa Verde and a base for tourists visiting the Four Corners region. You can still see a rodeo here at least once a year. **Dolores,** steeped in a rich railroad history, is on the Dolores River, 19 miles north of Mesa Verde. Near both the San Juan National Forest and McPhee Reservoir, Dolores is a favorite of outdoor enthusiasts. East of Mesa Verde by 36 miles, **Durango,** the region's main hub, comes complete with a variety of restaurants and hotels, shopping, and outdoor-equipment shops. Durango became a town in 1881 when the Denver and Rio Grande Railroad pushed its tracks across the neighboring San Juan Mountains.

Durango

47 miles south of Silverton via U.S. 550; 45 miles east of Cortez via U.S. 160; 60 miles west of Pagosa Springs via U.S. 160.

Wisecracking Will Rogers had this to say about Durango: "It's out of the way and glad of it." His statement is a bit unfair, considering that as a railroad town Durango has always been a cultural crossroads and melting pot (as well as a place to raise hell). Resting at 6,500 feet along the winding Animas

River, with the San Juan Mountains as backdrop, the town was founded in 1879 by General William Palmer, president of the all-powerful Denver & Rio Grande Railroad, at a time when nearby Animas City haughtily refused to donate land for a depot. Within a decade, Durango had completely absorbed its rival. The booming town quickly became the region's main metropolis and a gateway to the Southwest.

A walking tour of the historic downtown offers ample proof of Durango's prosperity during the late 19th century, although the northern end of Main Avenue has the usual assortment of cheap motels and fast-food outlets.

About 27 miles north of town, the down-home ski resort of Purgatory welcomes a clientele that includes cowboys, families, and college students. The mountain is named for the nearby Purgatory Creek, a tributary of the River of Lost Souls.

GETTING HERE AND AROUND

Durango Transit operates regular trolleys and bus service throughout town. Purgatory Resort runs a $10 skier shuttle between the town and the mountain on weekends and holidays during the winter. Buck Horn Limousine is your best bet for airport transfers.

CONTACTS Buck Horn Limousine. ☎ 970/769–0933 ⊕ www.buckhornlimousine.com. **Durango Transit.** ☎ 970/259–5438 ⊕ www.durangotransit.com. **Purgatory Resort Skier Shuttle.** ☎ 970/426–7282 ⊕ www.purgatoryresort.com.

VISITOR INFORMATION

CONTACTS Durango Welcome Center. ⊠ 802 Main Ave. ☎ 970/247–3500, 800/525–8855 ⊕ www.durango.org.

 # Sights

★ Durango & Silverton Narrow Gauge Railroad

TRANSPORTATION SITE (AIRPORT/BUS/FERRY/TRAIN) | FAMILY | The most entertaining way to relive the Old West is to take a ride on the Durango & Silverton Narrow Gauge Railroad, a nine-hour round-trip journey along the 45-mile railway to Silverton. Travel in comfort in restored coaches or in the open-air cars called gondolas as you listen to the train's shrill whistle. A shorter excursion to Cascade Canyon in heated coaches is available in winter. The train departs from the Durango Depot, constructed in 1882 and beautifully restored. Next door is the Durango & Silverton Narrow Gauge Railroad Museum, which is free and well worth your time. ⊠ 479 Main Ave. ☎ 970/247–2733, 877/872–4607 ⊕ www.durangotrain.com ☎ $91–$199.

Durango Hot Springs Resort & Spa

HOT SPRINGS | FAMILY | Come to this newly renovated, luxurious hot springs resort to soak your aching bones after a day of hiking or skiing. The complex includes an Olympic-size, saltwater swimming pool infused with aquagen and 27 total natural mineral pools ranging from 98°F to 110°F; all are open year-round. The pools are outdoors, perched at the base of the mountain and thoughtfully designed to blend in with nature. The grounds also feature a spa, sauna, reflexology path, food carts and fire pit, stage for live music, stream, separate adult-only area, and a hydrotherapy "yin-yang" pool. ⊠ 6475 County Rd. 203 ✛ About 5 miles north of Durango ☎ 970/247–0111 ⊕ www.durangohotspringsresortandspa.com ☎ $20.

Main Avenue National Historic District

HISTORIC SITE | The intersection of 13th Street and Main Avenue marks the northern edge of Durango's Main Avenue National Historic District. Old-fashioned streetlamps line the streets, casting a warm glow on the elegant buildings filled with upscale galleries, restaurants, and shops. Dating from 1887, the Strater Hotel is a reminder of the time when this town was a stop for many people headed west. ✉ *Main Ave., between 13th St. and 12th St.* 🌐 *www.durango.org.*

★ Purgatory Resort

Purgatory does summer better than just about any Colorado ski resort, especially for kids. In the past, activities have included a new mountain coaster, an off-road go-kart track, an alpine slide, a family-friendly ropes course, a short zipline, pony rides, bungee trampolines, an airbag jump, lift-served hiking and biking, and, of course, the obligatory climbing wall and mini-golf course. ✉ *1 Skier Pl., Purgatory* ☎ *970/247–9000* 🌐 *www.purgatoryresort.com* 🎟 *$79 for 10 activities, $59 for 5, or choose à la carte pricing. Subject to change.*

🍴 Restaurants

Carver Brewing Co.

$$ | **AMERICAN** | The "Brews Brothers," Bill and Jim Carver, have about 12 beers on tap at any given time at this Durango favorite. If you're hungry, try one of the signature handmade bread bowls filled with green chile, soup, or chicken stew. **Known for:** hearty, creative breakfasts; lovely shaded patio out back; elevated pub cuisine. [$] *Average main: $15* ✉ *1022 Main Ave.* ☎ *970/259–2545* 🌐 *www.carverbrewing.com.*

Chimayo Stone Fired Kitchen

$$$$ | **CONTEMPORARY** | The former chef for Michael Andretti's racing team runs this trendy bistro, in which every dish is cooked in one of two stone-fired ovens. The house specialty is artisan pizza (try the four-mushroom variety and add the house fennel sausage), although pizza is only a small part of the menu. **Known for:** delectable corn bread and focaccia bread; specialty cocktails; classy decor. [$] *Average main: $28* ✉ *862 Main Ave.* ☎ *970/259–2749* 🌐 *www.chimayodurango.com* 🕒 *Dinner from 4 pm Wed.–Sun.*

Dandelion Cafe

$$$ | **MEDITERRANEAN** | In warm weather you can sit on the large garden patio, and the rest of the year you'll have to cozy up to your fellow diners in the 10-table Dandelion Cafe, housed in a quaint, sparsely decorated Victorian a block off Main Avenue. Mediterranean food receives a fresh and healthy treatment, including free-range chicken, sustainably sourced seafood, and locally grown ingredients whenever possible. **Known for:** live music; falafel and gyros; outdoor dining in summer. [$] *Average main: $23* ✉ *725 E. 2nd Ave.* ☎ *970/385–6884* 🌐 *www.dandelioncafedurango.com* 🕒 *Closed Sun. in winter.*

East by Southwest

$$$ | **ASIAN FUSION** | Asian food gets a bit of a Latin treatment in this inviting space. The menu has a strong Japanese bent, with sushi and sashimi, tempura, beef, and other traditional dishes elegantly presented and layered with complementary, often Southwest-inspired flavors. **Known for:** vegan and vegetarian options; bento boxes and poke bowls for lunch; sake, beer, wine, and tea lists. [$] *Average main: $23* ✉ *160 E. College Dr.* ☎ *970/247–5533* 🌐 *www.eastbysouthwest.com* 🕒 *No lunch Sun.*

11th Street Station

$ | **FAST FOOD** | Seven locally owned food trucks, serving cuisine from Thailand to breakfast burritos to pizza to sushi, surround an outdoor courtyard with picnic-table seating. Ernie's Bar anchors the eating collective and offers craft beers, tap cocktails, and a wide tequila and mezcal selection. **Known for:** moderately priced eats; variety; fresh, contemporary vibes. [$] *Average main: $12* ✉ *1101 Main Ave.* ☎ *970/422–8482* 🌐 *www.11thstreetstation.com.*

Ken & Sue's

$$ | **MODERN AMERICAN** | Plates are big and the selection is creative at Ken & Sue's, one of Durango's favorite restaurants. Locals are wild for the contemporary American cuisine with an Asian flair, served in an intimate space. **Known for:** large, pretty patio out back; worth-it desserts; pistachio-crusted grouper with vanilla-rum butter. $ *Average main: $18* ⊠ *636 Main Ave.* ☎ *970/385–1810* ⊕ *www.kenandsues.com* ⊗ *No lunch weekends.*

★ Ore House

$$$$ | **STEAKHOUSE** | Durango is a meat-and-potatoes kind of town, and the rustic Ore House is a splurge-worthy place to indulge (just ask the locals). The steaks are fantastic, and there are plenty of expertly prepared seafood and vegetarian selections as well. **Known for:** chateaubriand; cornbread with bacon butter; deep whiskey and wine lists. $ *Average main: $39* ⊠ *147 E. College Dr.* ☎ *970/247–5707* ⊕ *www.orehous-erestaurant.com.*

★ Sow's Ear

$$$$ | **STEAKHOUSE** | This airy eatery in Silverpick Lodge is known for providing "the best steaks on the mountain," topped with incredible au poivre, which it does with aplomb. It also serves up the best views of thick aspen groves. **Known for:** lovely views of mountains and cliffs; three-season alfresco patio open nightly, weather permitting; steak au poivre. $ *Average main: $30* ⊠ *48475 U.S. 550* ☎ *970/247–3527* ⊕ *www.sowseardurango.com* ⊗ *No lunch. Closed Mon.–Tues.*

Steamworks Brewing Co.

$$ | **AMERICAN** | Widely acclaimed craft brews and above-standard sandwiches, burgers, pizzas, and salads raise Steamworks beyond usual pub grub. It's no surprise that the large, high-ceilinged venue is nearly always overflowing and has been a Durango favorite for more than two decades. **Known for:** skillfully brewed beer; daily drink specials ($3 pints, $11 pitchers, and more); back patio with mountain views. $ *Average main: $16* ⊠ *801 E. 2nd Ave.* ☎ *970/259–9200* ⊕ *www.steamworksbrewing.com.*

☕ Coffee and Quick Bites

James Ranch Grill

$$ | **AMERICAN** | **FAMILY** | For a delicious summer detour, head 10 miles north of town to James Ranch, where you'll find a pleasant organic farm, with an outdoor grill that features homemade cheeses and home-grown meats and produce grown on-site. The menu keeps things simple, featuring a short list of burgers, sandwiches, and salads. **Known for:** ample outdoor seating; organic, home-grown ingredients; Signature Burger with rosemary garlic mayo. $ *Average main: $13* ⊠ *33846 U.S. Hwy. 550* ☎ *970/676–1023* ⊕ *www.jamesranch.net.*

🛏 Hotels

Apple Orchard Inn

$$ | **B&B/INN** | This quiet B&B sits on five acres in the lush Animas Valley with an apple orchard, flower gardens, and trout ponds on the grounds. **Pros:** beautiful views; peaceful and quiet setting; cottages are intimate and romantic. **Cons:** no dinner on-site; several miles from town; rooms in the house are all upstairs (no elevator). $ *Rooms from: $160* ⊠ *7758 County Rd. 203* ✛ *About 8 miles north of downtown Durango* ☎ *970/247–0751, 800/426–0751* ⊕ *www.appleorchardinn. com* ⇄ *4 rooms, 6 cottages* ⦿⏐ *Free Breakfast.*

General Palmer Hotel

$$$ | **HOTEL** | The General Palmer Hotel is a faithfully restored historic property in downtown Durango with a clean, bright look, as well as period furniture and Victorian touches that reinforce an old-timey feel. **Pros:** central location; some rooms have balconies; free off-street parking.

Cons: no restaurant or bar; cramped elevator; pricey in season. [$] *Rooms from: $200* ✉ *567 Main Ave.* ☎ *970/247–4747* 🌐 *www.generalpalmer.com* 🛏 *39 rooms* 🍴 *Free Breakfast.*

Purgatory Lodge
$$$$ | **HOTEL** | **FAMILY** | This mountain-luxe slopeside hotel provides an upscale retreat at a down-home resort, featuring roomy two- to four-bedroom suites decorated with contemporary furnishings. **Pros:** slopeside location; good restaurants; ample amenities. **Cons:** can be pricey; far from town; no meals included. [$] *Rooms from: $350* ✉ *Purgatory Resort, 24 Sheol St.* ☎ *970/385–2100, 800/525–0892* 🌐 *www.purgatoryresort.com* 🛏 *37 suites* 🍴 *No meals.*

Rochester Hotel & Leland House
$$$ | **B&B/INN** | The Rochester Hotel is a historic, boutique hotel that features paraphernalia and posters from movies filmed in the Durango area. **Pros:** free guest parking; amazing outdoor space; close to the action, yet off the main drag. **Cons:** no on-site food; no counter space in bathrooms; no pool or hot tub. [$] *Rooms from: $199* ✉ *726 E. 2nd Ave.* ☎ *970/385–1920, 800/664–1920* 🌐 *www.rochesterhotel.com* 🛏 *27 rooms* 🍴 *Free Breakfast.*

★ **Strater Hotel**
$$$ | **HOTEL** | Still the hottest spot in town, this Western grande dame opened for business in 1887 and has been visited by Butch Cassidy, Louis L'Amour (he wrote many of the *Sacketts* novels here), Francis Ford Coppola, John Kennedy, and Marilyn Monroe (the latter two stayed here at separate times). **Pros:** right in the thick of things; free guest parking; filled with gorgeous antiques. **Cons:** breakfast not included in all rates; noisy bar; Wi-Fi is spotty. [$] *Rooms from: $220* ✉ *699 Main Ave.* ☎ *970/247–4431, 800/247–4431* 🌐 *www.strater.com* 🛏 *88 rooms* 🍴 *No meals.*

Nightlife

BARS AND CLUBS

★ **Ska Brewing Company**
BARS/PUBS | Beer fans shouldn't miss Ska Brewing, a home-grown brewery that boasts a large "tasting room" with 20 taps. The decor is bowling-alley inspired, including tables crafted with wood from former lanes at a Denver bowling alley. If the weather allows, you can sip your beer of choice on the park-like patio or second-story deck, beneath enormous, metal brew tanks. Pair your beer with a sandwich or artisan pizza from The Container restaurant, made from two repurposed shipping containers attached to the brewery.
TIP→ Stop by on a Thursday night for live music or 4 pm Monday through Saturday for a brewery tour. ✉ *225 Girard St.* ☎ *970/247–5792* 🌐 *www.skabrewing.com.*

Performing Arts

DINNER SHOWS

Bar D Chuckwagon Suppers
MUSIC | **FAMILY** | This old-style-cowboy venue, about 10 miles from Durango, serves steaks, barbecued beef and chicken, and biscuits under the stars every summer evening. After supper, the Bar D Wranglers entertain the crowd with guitar music, singing, and corny comedy. Reservations are required. ✉ *8080 County Rd. 250* ☎ *970/247–5753* 🌐 *www.bardchuckwagon.com* 🎫 *From $29* 🕒 *Closed Labor Day–Memorial Day.*

Cortez

45 miles west of Durango via U.S. 160; 78 miles southwest of Telluride via Hwy. 145.

The northern escarpment of Mesa Verde to the southeast and the volcanic blisters of La Plata Mountains to the east dominate the views around sprawling Cortez. With its Days Inns, Dairy Queens, and Best Westerns, the town has a layout that seems to have been determined by neon-sign and aluminum-siding salesmen of the 1950s. Hidden among these eyesores, however, are fine galleries, shops showcasing Native American art, and a host of secondhand shops that can yield surprising finds.

The gently rising hump to the southwest of town is Sleeping Ute Mountain, which resembles the reclining silhouette of a Native American, complete with headdress. This site is sacred to the Ute Mountain tribe, as it represents a great warrior god who, after being mortally wounded in a titanic battle with evil gods, lapsed into eternal sleep, his flowing blood turning into the life-giving Dolores and Animas rivers.

GETTING HERE AND AROUND

Cortez sits at the junction of Highway 160 and Highway 145, making it a busy town for people heading north to Dolores and Telluride, south into New Mexico and Arizona, and east to Durango. Highway 491 turns into Broadway heading north, and Highway 160 splits off due east, turning into Main Street as it passes through the center of town on its way to Durango.

VISITOR INFORMATION Colorado Welcome Center. ⊠ *928 E. Main St.* ☎ *970/565–4048.*

Sights

Cortez Cultural Center

ART GALLERIES—ARTS | The cultural center has exhibits on regional artists and Ancestral Pueblo culture, as well as events and fairs. Summer evening programs may include Native American dances and storytelling. ⊠ *25 N. Market St.* ☎ *970/565–1151* ⊕ *www.cortezculturalcenter.org* ⊗ *Closed Sun.*

Four Corners Monument

LOCAL INTEREST | This interesting landmark is located about 42 miles from Cortez, 65 miles southeast of Bluff, and 6 miles north of Teec Nos Pos, Arizona. The Four Corners Monument Navajo Tribal Park is owned and operated by the Navajo Nation. On the Colorado side is the Ute Mountain Ute of the Corners. Primarily a photo op, you'll also find Navajo and Ute artisans selling authentic jewelry and crafts, as well as traditional foods. It's the only place in the United States where you can be in six places at one time: four states and two tribal parks meet at one single point. Bring plenty of water. ⊠ *Four Corners Monument Rd., off U.S. 160, Teec Nos Pos* ⊕ *www.navajonationparks.org* 🎟 *$5–$10.*

Ute Mountain Ute Tribal Park

ARCHAEOLOGICAL SITE | The only way to see this spectacular 125,000-acre park, located inside the Ute reservation, is by taking a guided tour. Expert tribal guides lead strenuous daylong hikes into this dazzling repository of Ancestral Pueblo ruins, including beautifully preserved cliff dwellings, pictographs, and petroglyphs. There are also less-demanding half-day tours, as well as private and custom tour options. Tours meet at the Tribal Park Visitor Center at the junction of highways 160 and 491, 20 miles south of Cortez. ⊠ *Hwy. 160/491* ☎ *970/565–9653* ⊕ *www.utemountaintribalpark.info* 🎟 *From $29* ⊗ *Closed Sun. and major tribal and national holidays.* ☞ *No pets allowed.*

Restaurants

Absolute Bakery and Cafe

$ | **CAFÉ** | It's 20 minutes east of Cortez, but this from-scratch bakery and café is absolutely worth the drive. Breakfast offerings are traditional and scrumptious; lunch options include flavorful soups, salads, pastas, and sandwiches; and the home-baked breads, pastries, and desserts are heavenly. **Known for:** local, organic ingredients; house-specialty gluten-free macaroons; great value. $ *Average main: $10* ⊠ *110 S. Main St., Mancos* ☎ *970/533–1200* ⊕ *www.absolutebakery. com* ☾ *Closed Mon. No lunch Sun.*

Dolores

11 miles northeast of Cortez via Highway 145.

On the bank of the Dolores River, just downstream from the McPhee Reservoir, the tiny town of Dolores is midway between Durango and Telluride on State Highway 145. The river runs along the south edge of town, while beautiful cliffs flank the northern edge. Dolores attracts visitors with its spectacular scenery, fabulous fly-fishing, water sports, mountain hiking, biking, and other outdoor adventures.

◉ Sights

Canyons of the Ancients National Monument

ARCHAEOLOGICAL SITE | Spread across 176,000 acres of arid mesa and canyon country, the Canyons of the Ancients National Monument holds more than 20,000 archaeological sites, the greatest concentration anywhere in the United States. Some sites, like apartment-style cliff dwellings and hewn-rock towers, are impossible to miss. Others are as subtle as evidence of agricultural fields, springs, and water systems. They are powerful evidence of the complex civilization of the Ancestral Pueblo people. **Lowry**

Pueblo, in the northern part of the monument, is a 40-room pueblo with eight kivas (round chambers used for sacred rituals). Its Great Kiva is one of the largest known in the Southwest.

Exploring the monument area can be a challenge: roads are few, hiking trails are sparse, and visitor services are all but nonexistent. The visitors center, which is also a museum, is 3 miles west of Dolores on Highway 184. The best bet is a guided hike with the nonprofit Southwest Colorado Canyons Alliance. ⊠ *27501 State Hwy. 184* ⊹ *3 miles west of Dolores* ☎ *970/882–5600* ⊕ *www. blm.gov* ▨ *Monument admission is free; museum is $3.*

Galloping Goose Historical Museum

MUSEUM | Housed in a replica of the town's 1880s-era train station, this museum displays Galloping Goose No. 5, one of only seven specially designed engines built in the 1930s. The "Geese" were motored vehicles built from touring-car bodies that could operate for much less than steam-powered engines. ⊠ *421 Railroad Ave.* ☎ *970/882–7082* ⊕ *www. gallopinggoose5.com* ▨ *Free* ☾ *Closed Sun. mid-May–mid-Oct.; closed Fri.–Mon. mid-Oct.–mid-May.*

Hovenweep National Monument

ARCHAEOLOGICAL SITE | Straddling the Colorado–Utah border, this monument is known for distinctive square, oval, round, and D-shape towers that were engineering marvels when they were built around AD 1200. The buildings are spread throughout a series of ancient villages, once home to 2,500 people. The visitor center is on the Utah side of the monument. ▰**TIP→** **Per rangers, don't attempt to use your GPS to find Hovenweep. Most devices will take you either over rough dirt roads or to more remote parts of the monument.** ⊹ *From Dolores, take Hwy. 184 west to U.S. 491, then head west onto County Rd. CC for 9 miles* ☎ *970/562–4282* ⊕ *www. nps.gov/hove* ▨ *Free.*

McPhee Reservoir

BODY OF WATER | In 1985, crews completed construction of an irrigation dam across the Dolores River, forming the McPhee Reservoir, the second largest in the state. It draws anglers looking to bag a variety of warm- and cold-water fish along its 50 miles of shoreline, which is surrounded by spectacular specimens of juniper and sage as well as large stands of pinyon pine. There are two boat ramps. The area also has camping, hiking, and a relatively easy mountain-bike trail, and the mesa offers panoramic views of the surrounding San Juan National Forest. ✉ *Forest Service Rd. 271, off State Hwy. 184* ✣ *About 9 miles northwest of Dolores* 🎟 *Free* ⏲ *Marina closed Nov.–Apr.*

🍴 Restaurants

Dolores River Brewery

$$ | **AMERICAN** | Stop in here for what's fittingly billed as "thought-provoking beer." Choose from a wide selection of craft ales and stouts to wash down a slice of tasty wood-fired pizza. **Known for:** house-brewed craft ales; live, local bands–especially in summer; pleasant back patio. [$] *Average main: $15* ✉ *100 S. 4th St.* ☎ *970/882–4677* 🌐 *www.doloresriverbrewery.com* ⏲ *Closed Mon. No lunch.*

Chapter 24

MOUNT RAINIER NATIONAL PARK

24

Updated by
Shelley Arenas

🏕 Camping	🏨 Hotels	🏃 Activities	👁 Scenery	👫 Crowds
★★★★★	★★★☆☆	★★★★☆	★★★★★	★★★☆☆

WELCOME TO MOUNT RAINIER NATIONAL PARK

TOP REASONS TO GO

★ **The mountain:** Some say Mt. Rainier is the most magical mountain in America. At 14,411 feet, it is a popular peak for climbing, with more than 10,000 attempts per year—nearly half of which are successful.

★ **The glaciers:** About 35 square miles of glaciers and snowfields encircle Mt. Rainier, including Carbon Glacier and Emmons Glacier, the largest glaciers by volume and area, respectively, in the continental United States.

★ **The wildflowers:** More than 100 species of wildflowers bloom in the park's high meadows; the display dazzles from midsummer until the snow flies.

★ **Fabulous hiking:** More than 240 miles of maintained trails provide access to old-growth forest, river valleys, lakes, and rugged ridges.

★ **Unencumbered wilderness:** Under the provisions of the 1964 Wilderness Act and the National Wilderness Preservation System, 97% of the park is preserved as wilderness.

1 Longmire. Inside the Nisqually Gate explore Longmire historic district's museum and visitor center, ruins of the park's first hotel.

2 Paradise. The park's most popular destination is famous for wildflowers in summer and skiing in winter.

3 Ohanapecosh. Closest to the southeast entrance and the town of Packwood, the giant old-growth trees of the Grove of the Patriarchs are a must-see.

4 Sunrise and White River. Sunrise is the highest stretch of road in the park and a great place to take in the alpenglow—reddish light on the peak of the mountain near sunrise and sunset. Mt. Rainier's premier mountain-biking area, White River, is also the gateway to more than a dozen hiking trails.

5 Carbon River and Mowich Lake. Near the Carbon River Entrance Station is a swath of temperate forest, but to really get away from it all, follow the windy gravel roads to remote Mowich Lake.

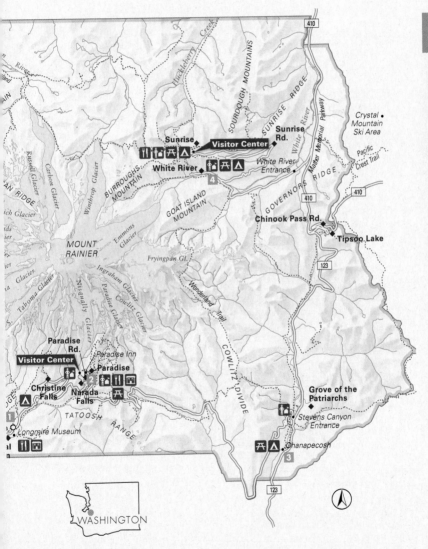

Mt. Rainier is the centerpiece of its namesake park. The impressive volcanic peak stands at an elevation of 14,411 feet, making it the fifth-highest peak in the lower 48 states. More than 2 million visitors a year enjoy spectacular views of the mountain and return home with a lifelong memory of its image.

On the lower slopes you find silent forests made up of cathedral-like groves of Douglas fir, western hemlock, and western red cedar, some more than 1,000 years old. Water and lush greenery are everywhere in the park, and dozens of thundering waterfalls, accessible from the road or by a short hike, fill the air with mist.

Established in 1899, it's the fifth-oldest national park in the U.S., created to preserve opportunities for generations to experience nature's beauty and outdoor recreation. Conservationists including John Muir lobbied for its protection as wilderness, saving its flora and fauna from the ravages of logging and mining. You can explore the park's early history in the Longmire Historic District, the location of its original headquarters, which includes a museum in one of the original early 1900 buildings and an inn in another. Further up the mountain, the historic national park lodge architecture style is on full display in the iconic Paradise Inn, built in 1917. It's definitely worth a visit even if you're not spending the night, though an overnight stay will let you enjoy the park more without worries of traffic or parking. The Paradise area is the park's most visited and parking lots often fill up early on weekends and in the summer.

As the fifth highest mountain in the contiguous U.S., Mt. Rainier is renowned as a premier climbing destination—more than 10,000 people attempt to reach the summit every year. Climbers are strongly encouraged to go with a guide service for at least their first climb, and mountain safety practices are important for all visitors to follow when exploring the park. And there is a lot to explore—369 square miles, 275 trails, 120 miles of roads, and 97% designated as wilderness. Stopping at a visitor center is highly recommended, both to learn more about the park and also to get helpful advice and information on current road and trail conditions. Guided ranger programs and self-guided "Citizen Ranger Quests" are fun ways to make the most of your visit, too. Scenic drives are fabulous for photography, for spur-of-the-moment stops at intriguing spots and getting up close to immerse in the wonder of nature, and for taking in the vastness of this stunning park.

AVERAGE HIGH/LOW TEMPERATURES					
JAN.	**FEB.**	**MAR.**	**APR.**	**MAY**	**JUNE**
36/24	40/26	44/28	53/32	62/37	66/43
JULY	**AUG.**	**SEPT.**	**OCT.**	**NOV.**	**DEC.**
75/47	74/47	68/43	57/38	45/31	39/28

Planning

When to Go

Rainier is the Puget Sound's weather vane: if you can see it, skies will be clear. Visitors are most likely to see the summit July through September. Crowds are heaviest in summer, too, meaning the parking lots at Paradise and Sunrise often fill before noon, campsites are reserved months in advance, and other lodgings are reserved as much as a year ahead.

True to its name, Paradise is often sunny during periods when the lowlands are under a cloud layer. The rest of the year, Rainier's summit gathers flying-saucer-like lenticular clouds whenever a Pacific storm approaches; once the peak vanishes from view, it's time to haul out rain gear. The rare periods of clear winter weather bring residents up to Paradise for cross-country skiing.

Getting Here and Around

AIR
Seattle–Tacoma International Airport, 15 miles south of downtown Seattle, is the nearest airport to the national park.

CAR
The Nisqually entrance is on Highway 706, 14 miles east of Route 7; the Ohanapecosh entrance is on Route 123, 5 miles north of U.S. 12; and the White River entrance is on Route 410, 3 miles north of the Chinook and Cayuse passes. These highways become mountain roads as they reach Rainier, winding up and down

many steep slopes, so cautious driving is essential: use a lower gear, especially on downhill sections, and take care not to overheat brakes by constant use. These roads are subject to storms any time of year and are repaired in the summer from winter damage and washouts.

Side roads into the park's western slope are narrower, unpaved, and subject to flooding and washouts. All are closed by snow in winter except Highway 706 to Paradise and Carbon River Road, though the latter tends to flood near the park boundary. (Route 410 is open to the Crystal Mountain access road entrance.)

Park roads have a maximum speed of 35 mph in most places, and you have to watch for pedestrians, cyclists, and wildlife. Parking can be difficult during peak summer season, especially at Paradise, Sunrise, Grove of the Patriarchs, and at the trailheads between Longmire and Paradise; arrive early if you plan to visit these sites. All off-road-vehicle use—4X4 vehicles, ATVs, motorcycles, snowmobiles—is prohibited in Mount Rainier National Park.

Inspiration

The Ledge: An Adventure Story of Friendship and Survival on Mount Rainier, by Jim Davidson, details the ill-fated trip of two friends.

Road to Rainier Scenic Byway, by Donald M. Johnstone and the South Pierce County Historical Society and part of the Images of America Series, documents how a Native American trail became a modern scenic route. *The Road to*

24

Mount Rainier National Park PLANNING

Mt. Rainier in One Day

The best way to get a complete overview of Mt. Rainier in a day is to enter via Nisqually and begin your tour by browsing in **Longmire Museum.** When you're done, get to know the environment in and around Longmire Meadow and the overgrown ruins of Longmire Springs Hotel on the ½-mile **Trail of the Shadows** nature loop.

From Longmire, Highway 706 East (Paradise Valley Road) climbs northeast into the mountains toward Paradise. Take a moment to explore two-tiered **Christine Falls,** just north of the road 1½ miles past Cougar Rock Campground, and the cascading **Narada Falls,** 3 miles farther on; both are spanned by graceful stone footbridges. Fantastic mountain views, alpine meadows crosshatched

with nature trails, a welcoming lodge and restaurant, and the excellent **Jackson Memorial Visitor Center** combine to make lofty Paradise the primary goal of most park visitors. One outstanding (but challenging) way to explore the high country is to hike the 5-mile round-trip **Skyline Trail** to Panorama Point, which rewards you with stunning 360-degree views.

Continue eastward on Stevens Canyon Road for 21 miles and leave your car to explore the incomparable, 1,000-year-old **Grove of the Patriarchs.** Afterward, turn your car north toward White River and **Sunrise Visitor Center,** where you can watch the alpenglow fade from Mt. Rainier's domed summit.

Paradise, by Karen Barnett, is a romance novel set in 1927 that tells the tale of a young woman who follows her naturalist inclinations to start a new life in Mount Rainier during the early days of the National Park Service.

Tahoma and Its People: A Natural History of Mount Rainier National Park, by Jeff Antonelis-Lapp, focuses on the park's nature and environment from the perspectives of Native Americans, park rangers, archaeologists, and others.

Park Essentials

ACCESSIBILITY

The only trail in the park that is fully accessible to those with impaired mobility is Kautz Creek Trail, a ½-mile boardwalk that leads to a splendid view of the mountain. Parts of the Trail of the Shadows at Longmire and the Grove of the Patriarchs at Ohanapecosh are also

accessible. Campgrounds at Cougar Rock and Ohanapecosh have several accessible sites. All main visitor centers, as well as National Park Inn at Longmire, are accessible. Wheelchairs are available at the Jackson Visitor Center for guests to use in the center.

PARK FEES AND PERMITS

The entrance fee of $30 per vehicle and $15 for those on foot, motorcycle, or bicycle is good for seven days. Annual passes are $55. Climbing permits are $51 per person per climb or glacier trek. Wilderness camping permits must be obtained for all backcountry trips, and advance reservations are highly recommended.

PARK HOURS

Mount Rainier National Park is open 24/7 year-round, but with limited access in winter. Gates at Nisqually (Longmire) are staffed year-round during the day; facilities at Paradise are open daily from late

May to mid-October; and Sunrise is open daily July to early September. During off-hours you can buy passes at the gates from machines that accept credit and debit cards. Winter access to the park is limited to the Nisqually entrance, and the Jackson Memorial Visitor Center at Paradise is open on weekends and holidays in winter. The Paradise snowplay area is open when there is sufficient snow.

CELL PHONE RECEPTION

Cell phone reception is unreliable throughout much of the park, although access is clear at Paradise, Sunrise, and Crystal Mountain. Public telephones are at all park visitor centers, at the National Park Inn at Longmire, and at Paradise Inn at Paradise.

Hotels

The Mt. Rainier area is remarkably bereft of quality lodging. Rainier's two national park lodges, at Longmire and Paradise, are attractive and well maintained. They exude considerable history and charm, especially Paradise Inn, but unless you've made summer reservations a year in advance, getting a room can be a challenge. Dozens of motels, cabin complexes, and private vacation-home rentals are near the park entrances; while they can be pricey, the latter are convenient for longer stays. *Hotel reviews have been shortened. For full information, visit Fodors.com.*

What It Costs			
$	$$	$$$	$$$$
RESTAURANTS			
under $16	$16–$22	$23–$30	over $30
HOTELS			
under $150	$150–$200	$201–$250	over $250

Restaurants

A limited number of restaurants are inside the park, and a few worth checking out lie beyond its borders. Mt. Rainier's picnic areas are justly famous, especially in summer, when wildflowers fill the meadows. Resist the urge to feed the yellow pine chipmunks darting about. *Restaurant reviews have been shortened. For full information, visit Fodors.com.*

Park picnic areas are usually open only from late May through September.

Visitor Information

PARK CONTACT INFORMATION Mount Rainier National Park. ⊠ *55210 238th Ave. East, Ashford* ☎ *360/569–2211, 360/569–6575* ⊕ *www.nps.gov/mora.*

Longmire

12 miles east of Ashford via Hwy. 706; 6 miles east of Nisqually Entrance.

Established in 1899 as the original park headquarters, this area is designated a national historic district. One of its first buildings (from 1916) is now a museum, and the circa-1917 National Park Inn is open year-round with basic accommodations, dining, and winter recreation equipment rentals.

Sights

HISTORIC SITES
National Park Inn
BUILDING | Even if you don't plan to stay overnight, you can stop by year-round to view the architecture of this inn, built in 1917 and on the National Register of Historic Places. While you're here, relax in front of the fireplace in the lounge, stop at the gift shop, or dine at the restaurant. ⊠ *Longmire Visitor Complex, Hwy. 706, 10 miles east of Nisqually*

entrance, Longmire ☎ *360/569–2411* 🌐 *www.mtrainierguestservices.com/accommodations/national-park-inn.*

TRAILS

Trail of the Shadows

TRAIL | This ¾-mile loop is notable for its glimpses of meadowland ecology, its colorful soda springs (don't drink the water), James Longmire's old homestead cabin, and the foundation of the old Longmire Springs Hotel, which was destroyed by fire around 1900. *Easy.* ✉ *Mt. Rainier National Park* ✥ *Trailhead: at Hwy. 706, 10 miles east of Nisqually entrance* 🌐 *www.nps.gov/mora/planyourvisit/day-hiking-at-mount-rainier.htm.*

VISITOR CENTERS

Longmire Museum and Visitor Center

INFO CENTER | Glass cases inside this museum preserve the park's plants and animals, including a stuffed cougar. Historical photographs and geographical displays provide a worthwhile overview of the park's history. The adjacent visitor center has some perfunctory exhibits on the surrounding forest and its inhabitants, as well as pamphlets and information about park activities. ✉ *Hwy. 706, 10 miles east of Ashford, Longmire* ☎ *360/569–6575* 🌐 *www.nps.gov/mora/planyourvisit/longmire.htm.*

🍴 Restaurants

National Park Inn Dining Room

$$$ | **AMERICAN** | Photos of Mt. Rainier taken by top photographers adorn the walls of this inn's large dining room, a bonus on the many days the mountain refuses to show itself. Meals are simple but tasty: flat iron steak, bison meatloaf, rosemary grilled salmon, and blackberry cobbler à la mode. **Known for:** only restaurant open year-round in the park; hearty breakfast options; nice dessert choices. [$] *Average main: $25* ✉ *Hwy. 706, Longmire* ☎ *360/569–2411* 🌐 *www.mtrainierguestservices.com.*

👁 Plants and Wildlife

Wildflower season in the meadows at and above timberline is mid-July through August. Large mammals like deer, elk, black bears, and cougars tend to occupy the less accessible wilderness areas of the park and thus elude the average visitor. The best times to see wildlife are at dawn and dusk at the forest's edge, though you'll occasionally see bears ambling through meadows in the distance during the day. Fawns are born in May, and the bugling of bull elk on the high ridges can be heard in late September and October.

🛏 Hotels

National Park Inn

$$$ | **B&B/INN** | A large stone fireplace warms the common room of this country inn, the only one of the park's two inns that's open year-round, while rustic details such as wrought-iron lamps and antique bentwood headboards adorn the small rooms. **Pros:** classic national park lodge ambience; on-site restaurant with simple American fare; winter packages with perks like breakfast and free snowshoe use. **Cons:** jam-packed in summer; must book far in advance; some rooms have a shared bath. [$] *Rooms from: $224* ✉ *Longmire Visitor Complex, Hwy. 706, 6 miles east of Nisqually entrance, Longmire* ☎ *360/569–2275, 855/755–2275* 🌐 *www.mtrainierguestservices.com* 🔑 *43 rooms* 🍽 *No meals.*

Paradise

11 miles northeast of Longmire; 18 miles from Nisqually Entrance

The most popular area of the park has something for everyone—an impressive and informative visitor center with guided ranger programs, wildflower-filled meadows, trails that range from easy nature walks to steep hikes, and a historic national park lodge for dining and overnighting in the park. In winter there's a snowplay area open when there's enough snow; patches of snow sometimes linger well into summer.

Sights

PICNIC AREAS
Paradise Picnic Area
LOCAL INTEREST | This site has great views on clear days. After picnicking at Paradise, you can take an easy hike to one of the many waterfalls in the area—Sluiskin, Myrtle, or Narada, to name a few. ⊠ *Hwy. 706, Mt. Rainier National Park* ✛ *11 miles east of Longmire* ⊕ *www.nps.gov/mora.*

SCENIC DRIVES
Paradise Road
SCENIC DRIVE | This 9-mile stretch of Highway 706 winds its way up the mountain's southwest flank from Longmire to Paradise, taking you from lowland forest to the ever-expanding vistas of the mountain above. Visit early on a weekday if possible, especially in peak summer months, when the road is packed with cars. The route is open year-round, though there may be some weekday closures in winter. From November through April, all vehicles must carry chains. ⊠ *Mt. Rainier National Park* ⊕ *www.nps. gov/mora/planyourvisit/paradise.htm.*

SCENIC STOPS
Christine Falls
BODY OF WATER | These two-tiered falls were named in honor of Christine Louise Van Trump, who climbed to the 10,000-foot level on Mt. Rainier in 1889 at the age of nine, despite having a crippling nervous-system disorder. ⊠ *Mt. Rainier National Park* ✛ *4 miles north of Longmire via Paradise Valley Road, about 2½ miles east of Cougar Rock Campground* ⊕ *www.nps.gov/mora/learn/ nature/waterfalls.htm.*

Narada Falls
BODY OF WATER | A steep but short trail leads to the viewing area for these spectacular 168-foot falls, which expand to a width of 75 feet during peak flow times. In winter the frozen falls are popular with ice climbers. ⊠ *Paradise Valley Rd., Mt. Rainier National Park* ✛ *1 mile west of turnoff for Paradise, 6 miles east of Cougar Rock Campground* ⊕ *www.nps.gov/ mora/planyourvisit/longmire.htm.*

TRAILS
Nisqually Vista Trail
TRAIL | Equally popular in summer and winter, this trail is a 1¼-mile round-trip through subalpine meadows to an overlook point for Nisqually Glacier. The gradually sloping path is a favorite venue for cross-country skiers in winter; in summer, listen for the shrill alarm calls of the area's marmots. *Easy.* ⊠ *Mt. Rainier National Park* ✛ *Trailhead: at Jackson Memorial Visitor Center, Rte. 123, 1 mile north of Ohanapecosh, at high point of Hwy. 706* ⊕ *www.nps.gov/mora/plan-yourvisit/day-hiking-at-mount-rainier.htm.*

★ **Skyline Trail**
TRAIL | This 5-mile loop, one of the highest trails in the park, beckons day-trippers with a vista of alpine ridges and, in summer, meadows filled with brilliant flowers and birds. At 6,800 feet, Panorama Point, the spine of the Cascade Range, spreads away to the east, and Nisqually Glacier tumbles downslope. *Moderate.* ⊠ *Mt. Rainier National Park* ✛ *Trailhead: Jackson Memorial Visitor Center, Rte. 123, 1 mile north of Ohanapecosh at high point of Hwy. 706* ⊕ *www.nps.gov/mora/ planyourvisit/skyline-trail.htm.*

Van Trump Park Trail

TRAIL | You gain an exhilarating 2,200 feet on this route while hiking through a vast expanse of meadow with views of the southern Puget Sound and Mt. Adams and Mt. St. Helens. On the way up is one of the highest waterfalls in the park, Comet Falls. The 5¾-mile track provides good footing, and the average hiker can make it up and back in five hours. *Moderate.* ✉ *Mt. Rainier National Park* ✣ *Trailhead: Hwy. 706 at Christine Falls, 4½ miles east of Longmire* 🌐 *https://www.nps.gov/mora/planyourvisit/comet-falls-van-trump-park-trail.htm.*

VISITOR CENTERS

Jackson Memorial Visitor Center

INFO CENTER | High on the mountain's southern flank, this center houses exhibits on geology, mountaineering, glaciology, and alpine ecology. Multimedia programs are staged in the theater; there's also a snack bar and gift shop. This is the park's most popular visitor destination, and it can be quite crowded in summer. ✉ *Hwy. 706 E, 19 miles east of Nisqually park entrance, Mt. Rainier National Park* ☎ *360/569–6571* 🌐 *www.nps.gov/mora/planyourvisit/paradise.htm* 🕒 *Closed weekdays mid-Oct.–Apr.*

🍴 Restaurants

Paradise Camp Deli

$ | **AMERICAN** | Grilled meats, sandwiches, salads, and soft drinks are served daily from May through early October and on weekends and holidays the rest of the year. **Known for:** a quick bite to eat; family-friendly cuisine; mountain-size deli sandwiches. [$] *Average main: $10* ✉ *Jackson Visitor Center, Paradise Rd. E, Paradise* ☎ *360/569–6571 visitor center, 855/755–2275 guest services* 🌐 *www.mtrainierguestservices.com* 🕒 *Closed weekdays early Oct.–Apr.*

Paradise Inn Dining Room

$$$ | **AMERICAN** | Tall windows in this historic timber lodge provide terrific views of Rainier, and the warm glow of native wood permeates the large dining room, where hearty Pacific Northwest fare is served. Sunday brunch is legendary and served during the summer months; on other days and during the shoulder season there's a breakfast buffet. **Known for:** locally sourced ingredients; warm liquor drinks; great Sunday brunch. [$] *Average main: $27* ✉ *E. Paradise Rd., near Jackson Visitor Center, Paradise* ☎ *360/569–2275, 855/755–2275* 🌐 *www.mtrainierguestservices.com* 🕒 *Closed Oct.–mid-May.*

🛏 Hotels

★ Paradise Inn

$$$ | **HOTEL** | With its hand-carved Alaskan cedar logs, burnished parquet floors, stone fireplaces, and glorious mountain views, this 1917 inn is a classic example of a national park lodge. **Pros:** central to trails; pristine vistas; nature-inspired details. **Cons:** rooms are small and basic; many rooms have shared bathrooms; no elevators, air-conditioning, cell service, TV, or Wi-Fi. [$] *Rooms from: $226* ✉ *E Paradise Rd., near Jackson Visitor Center, Paradise* ☎ *360/569–2275, 855/755–2275* 🌐 *www.mtrainierguestservices.com* 🕒 *Closed mid-Oct.–mid-May* 🔑 *121 rooms* 🍽 *No meals.*

Ohanapecosh

12 miles north of Packwood, via Hwy. 123; 3 miles north of park boundary; 42 miles east of the park's Nisqually Entrance.

The Ohanapecosh River runs through this old-growth forest area in the southeastern corner of the park. It's less crowded than the Paradise and Longmire areas, so it can be a good option to visit when their parking lots fill up. The Grove of the

Patriarchs is a must-see. The area is not accessible by vehicle in winter.

Sights

SCENIC DRIVES

Route 123 and Stevens Canyon Road

SCENIC DRIVE | At Chinook Pass you can pick up Route 123 and head south to its junction with Stevens Canyon Road. Take this road west to its junction with the Paradise–Nisqually entrance road, which runs west through Longmire and exits the park at Nisqually. The route winds among valley-floor rain forest and uphill slopes; vistas of Puget Sound and the Cascade Range appear at numerous points along the way. ⊠ *Mt. Rainier National Park.*

SCENIC STOPS

★ **Grove of the Patriarchs**

TRAIL | Protected from the periodic fires that sweep through the surrounding areas, this small island of 1,000-year-old trees is one of Mount Rainier National Park's most memorable features. A 1½-mile loop trail heads through the old-growth forest of Douglas fir, cedar, and hemlock. ⊠ *Rte. 123, west of the Stevens Canyon entrance, Mt. Rainier National Park* ⊕ *www.nps.gov/mora/planyourvisit/ohanapecosh.htm.*

VISITOR CENTERS

Ohanapecosh Visitor Center

INFO CENTER | Learn about the region's dense old-growth forests through interpretive displays and videos at this visitor center, near the Grove of the Patriarchs. ⊠ *Rte. 123, 11 miles north of Packwood, Mt. Rainier National Park* ☎ *360/569–6581* ⊕ *www.nps.gov/mora/planyourvisit/ohanapecosh.htm* ⊙ *Closed mid-Oct.–May.*

Sunrise and White River

17 miles from Ohanapecosh to the Sunrise/White River Road cutoff from Hwy. 410; 14 miles from Crystal Mountain.

This area on the northeast side of the park has a short season (generally open only July–September) yet is the second most popular part of the park. Visitors come especially for the stunning views and the thrill of being at the highest drivable point in the park, as well as access to trails and stops along Chinook Pass (Hwy. 410). Intrepid trekkers on the Wonderland Trail can start or end their 93-mile journey around the mountain here.

Sights

PICNIC AREAS

Sunrise Picnic Area

LOCAL INTEREST | Set in an alpine meadow that's filled with wildflowers in July and August, this picnic area provides expansive views of the mountain and surrounding ranges in good weather. ⊠ *Sunrise Rd., Mt. Rainier National Park* ⊹ *11 miles west of White River entrance* ⊕ *www.nps.gov/mora/planyourvisit/sunrise.htm* ⊙ *Road to Sunrise usually closed Oct.–June.*

SCENIC DRIVES

Chinook Pass Road

SCENIC DRIVE | Route 410, the highway to Yakima, follows the eastern edge of the park to Chinook Pass, where it climbs the steep 5,432-foot pass via a series of switchbacks. At its top, take in broad views of Rainier and the east slope of the Cascades. The pass usually closes for the winter in November and reopens by late May. During that time, it's not possible to drive a loop around the park. ⊠ *Mt. Rainier National Park* ⊕ *www.wsdot.wa.gov/traffic/passes/chinook-cayuse.*

Sunrise Road

SCENIC DRIVE | This popular (and often crowded) scenic road to the highest drivable point at Mt. Rainier carves its way 11 miles up Sunrise Ridge from the White River Valley on the northeast side of the park. As you top the ridge, there are sweeping views of the surrounding lowlands. The road is usually open July through September. ⊠ *Mt. Rainier National Park* ⊕ *www. nps.gov/mora/planyourvisit/sunrise.htm* ⊗ *Usually closed Oct.–June.*

SCENIC STOPS

Tipsoo Lake

BODY OF WATER | **FAMILY** | The short, pleasant trail that circles the lake—ideal for families—provides breathtaking views. Enjoy the subalpine wildflower meadows during the summer months; in late summer to early fall there is an abundant supply of huckleberries. ⊠ *Mt. Rainier National Park* ⊕ *Off Cayuse Pass east on Hwy. 410* ⊕ *www.nps.gov/mora/ planyourvisit/sunrise.htm.*

TRAILS

Burroughs Mountain Trail

TRAIL | Starting at the south side of the Sunrise parking area, this 2½-hour, 4¾-mile round-trip hike offers spectacular views of the peak named in honor of naturalist and essayist John Burroughs. The challenging trail passes Shadow Lake before climbing to an overlook of the White River and Emmon's Glacier. Continue on and you reach First Burroughs Mountain and Second Burroughs Mountain. This area on the northeast slope of Mt. Rainier has some of the most accessible tundra in the Cascades, and you can observe the delicate slow-growing plants that survive in this harsh environment. Early season hiking on this trail can be particularly hazardous due to snow and ice on the steep mountain slopes; check conditions before starting out. *Difficult.* ⊠ *Mt. Rainier National Park* ⊕ *Trailhead: at south side of Sunrise parking area* ⊕ *www.nps.gov/mora/planyourvisit/burroughs-mountain.htm.*

Sunrise Nature Trail

TRAIL | The 1½-mile-long loop of this self-guided trail takes you through the delicate subalpine meadows near the Sunrise Visitor Center. A gradual climb to the ridgetop yields magnificent views of Mt. Rainier and the more distant volcanic cones of Mt. Baker, Mt. Adams, and Glacier Peak. *Easy.* ⊠ *Mt. Rainier National Park* ⊕ *Trailhead: at Sunrise Visitor Center, Sunrise Rd., 15 miles from White River park entrance* ⊕ *www.nps. gov/mora/planyourvisit/sunrise.htm.*

★ Wonderland Trail

TRAIL | All other Mt. Rainier hikes pale in comparison to this stunning 93-mile trek, which completely encircles the mountain. The trail passes through all the major life zones of the park, from the old-growth forests of the lowlands to the alpine meadows and goat-haunted glaciers of the highlands—pick up a mountain-goat sighting card from a ranger station or visitor center if you want to help in the park's effort to learn more about these elusive animals. Wonderland is a rugged trail; elevation gains and losses totaling 3,500 feet are common in a day's hike, which averages 8 miles. Most hikers start out from Longmire or Sunrise and take 10–14 days to cover the 93-mile route. Snow lingers on the high passes well into June (sometimes July); count on rain any time of the year. Campsites are wilderness areas with pit toilets and water that must be purified before drinking. Only hardy, well-equipped, and experienced wilderness trekkers should attempt this trip, but those who do will be amply rewarded. Wilderness permits are required, and reservations are strongly recommended. *Difficult.* ⊠ *Mt. Rainier National Park* ⊕ *Trailheads: Longmire Visitor Center, Hwy. 706, 17 miles east of Ashford; Sunrise Visitor Center, Sunrise Rd., 15 miles west of White River park entrance* ⊕ *www.nps.gov/mora/planyourvisit/the-wonderland-trail.htm.*

VISITOR CENTERS

Sunrise Visitor Center

INFO CENTER | Exhibits at this center explain the region's sparser alpine and subalpine ecology. A network of nearby loop trails leads you through alpine meadows and forest to overlooks that have broad views of the Cascades and Rainier. The visitor center has a snack bar and gift shop. ⊠ *Sunrise Rd., 15 miles from White River park entrance, Mt. Rainier National Park* ☎ *360/663–2425* ⊕ *www.nps.gov/ mora/planyourvisit/sunrise.htm* ☽ *Closed mid-Sept.–June.*

🍴 Restaurants

Sunrise Day Lodge Food Service

$ | **AMERICAN** | **FAMILY** | A cafeteria and grill serve tasty hamburgers, chili, hot dogs, and soft-serve ice cream from July through September. **Known for:** only food service in this part of the park; often busy. Ⓢ *Average main: $10* ⊠ *Sunrise Rd., 15 miles from White River park entrance, Mt. Rainier National Park* ☎ *360/663–2425 visitor center, 855/755– 2275 guest services* ⊕ *www.mtrainier- guestservices.com* ☽ *Closed Oct.–June.*

Carbon River and Mowich Lake

24 miles from Wilkeson to park entrance, via Hwy 165.

The northwest corner of the park has some unique features, including the Carbon Glacier, which is the lowest-elevation glacier in the continental U.S. It also has a rainforest climate and because of past floods and road damage, vehicle access is limited past the Carbon River Ranger Station, though this is the one area of the park where mountain bikes are allowed. The road to Mowich Lake, also via Hwy. 165, leads to the deepest and biggest lake in the park.

👁 Sights

SCENIC DRIVES

Mowich Lake Road

SCENIC DRIVE | In the northwest corner of the park, this 24-mile mountain road begins in Wilkeson and heads up the Rainier foothills to Mowich Lake, traversing beautiful mountain meadows along the way. Mowich Lake is a pleasant spot for a picnic. The road is open mid-July to mid-October. ⊠ *Mt. Rainier National Park* ⊕ *www.nps.gov/mora/planyourvisit/ carbon-river-and-mowich.htm* ☽ *Closed mid-Oct.–mid-July.*

Activities

BIRD-WATCHING

Be alert for kestrels, red-tailed hawks, and, occasionally, golden eagles on snags in the lowland forests. Also present at Rainier, but rarely seen, are great horned owls, spotted owls, and screech owls. Iridescent rufous hummingbirds flit from blossom to blossom in the drowsy summer lowlands, and sprightly water ouzels flutter in the many forest creeks. Raucous Steller's jays and gray jays scold passersby from trees, often darting boldly down to steal morsels from unguarded picnic tables. At higher elevations, look for the pure white plumage of the white-tailed ptarmigan as it hunts for seeds and insects in winter. Waxwings, vireos, nuthatches, sapsuckers, warblers, flycatchers, larks, thrushes, siskins, tanagers, and finches are common throughout the park.

CAMPING

Three drive-in campgrounds are in the park—Cougar Rock, Ohanapecosh, and White River—with almost 500 sites for tents and RVs. None has hot water or RV hookups. The nightly fee is $20. The more primitive Mowich Lake Campground has 10 walk-in sites for tents only; no fee is charged. For backcountry camping, get a free wilderness permit at a visitor

Mount Rainier, Looking North

MOUNT RAINIER

Little Tahoma Peak
11,138 ft

Disappointment
Cleaver

Anvil Rock
9,584 ft

Ingraham Glacier

CATHEDRAL ROCKS

Paradise Glaciers

McClure Rock
7,385 ft

Camp Muir
10,188 ft

Muir

Snowfield

Columbia Crest
14,410 ft

Gibraltar Rock
12,660 ft

Panorama Point
6,800 ft

Skyline Trail

Alta
Vista

Paradise

Louise
Lake

Point Success
14,153 ft

Nisqually Glacier

Henry M. Jackson Memorial
Visitor Center

The Castle

Reflection
Lakes

Liberty Cap
14,122 ft

Wilson Glacier

Pinnacle
Peak
6,562 ft

SUNSET
AMPHITHEATER

Van Trump Glaciers

CUSHMAN CREST

T A T O O S H   R A N G E

Unicorn Peak
6,917 ft

St. Andrews Rock
10,992 ft

SUCCESS CLEAVER

Success Glacier

Kautz Glacier

WAPOWETY CLEAVER

Plummer Peak
6,370 ft

Lane Peak
6,012 ft

SUCCESS CLEAVER

Tahoma Glacier

South Tahoma Glacier

SUCCESS DIVIDE

Pyramid Glaciers

VAN TRUMP
PARK

Mildred Point

Wahpenayo Peak
6,231 ft

Tokaloo Rock
7,684 ft

PUYALLUP CLEAVER

GLACIER
ISLAND

PYRAMID
PARK

Chutla Peak

EMERALD   RIDGE

Pyramid Peak
6,937 ft

Eagle Peak
5,958 ft

Iron Mountain
6,263 ft

Pyramid

Creek

Rampart Ridge Trail

RIDGE

Cougar Rock

RAMPART
THE RAMPARTS

Longmire

KEY

———	Paved Roads
– – –	Hiking Trails
··········	Climbing Routes

center on a first-come, first-served basis. Primitive sites are spaced at 7- to 8-mile intervals along the Wonderland Trail.

Cougar Rock Campground. A secluded, heavily wooded campground with an amphitheater, Cougar Rock is one of the first to fill up. Reservations are accepted for summer only. ⊠ *2½ miles north of Longmire* ☎ *877/444–6777* ⊕ *www.recreation.gov* for reservations.

Mowich Lake Campground. This is Rainier's only lakeside campground and has just 10 primitive campsites. At 4,959 feet, it's also peaceful and secluded. ⊠ *Mowich Lake Rd., 6 miles east of park boundary* ☎ *360/569–2211.*

Ohanapecosh Campground. This lush, green campground in the park's southeast corner has an amphitheater and self-guided trail. It's one of the first campgrounds to open for the season. ⊠ *Rte. 123, 1½ miles north of park boundary* ☎ *877/444–6777* ⊕ *www.recreation.gov* for reservations.

White River Campground. At an elevation of 4,400 feet, White River is one of the park's highest and least wooded campgrounds. Here you can enjoy campfire programs, self-guided trails, and partial views of Mt. Rainier's summit. ⊠ *5 miles west of White River entrance* ☎ *360/569–2211.*

EDUCATIONAL OFFERINGS
RANGER PROGRAMS
Citizen Ranger Quests

NATIONAL/STATE PARK | FAMILY | Older kids and adults can do their own version of the Junior Ranger program by exploring the park on various learning adventures that take from 30 minutes to two hours to complete. After doing at least four activities (from more than a dozen choices), participants earn a Citizen Ranger patch and certificate. ⊠ *Mt. Rainier National Park* ☎ *360/569-2211* ⊕ *www.nps.gov/mora/planyourvisit/citizen-ranger.htm.*

Junior Ranger Program

Youngsters ages 6 to 11 can pick up an activity booklet at a visitor center and fill it out as they explore the park. When they complete it, they can show it to a ranger and receive a Mount Rainier Junior Ranger badge. ⊠ *Visitor centers, Mt. Rainier National Park* ☎ *360/569–2211* ⊕ *www.nps.gov/mora/planyourvisit/rangerprograms.htm* ⊠ *Free with park admission.*

Ranger Programs

Park ranger-led activities include **guided snowshoe walks** in the winter (most suitable for those older than eight) as well as **evening programs** during the summer at Longmire/Cougar Rock, Ohanapecosh, and White River campgrounds, and at the Paradise Inn. Evening talks may cover subjects such as park history, its flora and fauna, or interesting facts on climbing Mt. Rainier. There are also daily guided programs that start at the Jackson Visitor Center, including meadow and vista walks, tours of the Paradise Inn, a morning ranger chat, and evening astronomy program. ⊠ *Visitor centers, Mt. Rainier National Park* ☎ *360/569–2211* ⊕ *www.nps.gov/mora/planyourvisit/rangerprograms.htm* ⊠ *Free with park admission.*

HIKING

Although the mountain can seem remarkably benign on calm summer days, hiking Rainier is not a city-park stroll. Dozens of hikers and trekkers annually lose their way and must be rescued—and lives are lost on the mountain each year. Weather that approaches cyclonic levels can appear quite suddenly, any month of the year. All visitors venturing far from vehicle access points, with the possible exception of the short loop hikes listed here, should carry day packs with warm clothing, food, and other emergency supplies.

Did You Know?

Named after British admiral Peter Rainier in the late 18th century, Mt. Rainier was originally called Tahoma (or Takhoma) by native Salishan speakers, meaning "the mountain that was God." Attempts to restore the peak's indigenous name have been unsuccessful, although most Puget Sound residents simply call it "the mountain."

MOUNTAIN CLIMBING

Climbing Mt. Rainier is not for amateurs; each year adventurers die on the mountain, and many get lost and must be rescued. Near-catastrophic weather can appear quite suddenly any month of the year. If you're experienced in technical, high-elevation snow, rock, and ice-field adventuring, Mt. Rainier can be a memorable adventure. Climbers can fill out a climbing card at the Paradise, White River, or Carbon River ranger station and lead their own groups of two or more. Climbers must register with a ranger before leaving and check out on return. A $51 annual climbing fee applies to anyone heading above 10,000 feet or onto one of Rainier's glaciers. During peak season it is recommended that climbers make their camping reservations ($20 per site) in advance; reservations are taken by fax and mail beginning in mid-March on a first-come, first-served basis (find the reservation form at ⊕ www.nps.gov/mora/planyourvisit/climbing.htm).

MULTISPORT OUTFITTERS

RMI Expeditions

CLIMBING/MOUNTAINEERING | Reserve a private hiking guide through this highly regarded outfitter, or take part in its one-day mountaineering classes (mid-May through late September), where participants are evaluated on their fitness for the climb and must be able to withstand a 16-mile round-trip hike with a 9,000-foot gain in elevation. The company also arranges private cross-country skiing and snowshoeing guides. ⊠ 30027 Hwy. 706 E, Ashford ☎ 888/892–5462, 360/569–2227 ⊕ www.rmiguides.com ⬛ From $1,222 for 4-day package.

Whittaker Mountaineering

CLIMBING/MOUNTAINEERING | You can rent hiking and climbing gear, cross-country skis, snowshoes, and other outdoor equipment at this all-purpose Rainier Base Camp outfitter, which also arranges for private cross-country skiing and hiking guides. If you forget to bring tire chains (which all vehicles are required to carry in the national park in winter), they rent those too. ⊠ 30027 SR 706 E, Ashford ☎ 800/238–5756, 360/569–2982 ⊕ www.whittakermountaineering.com.

SKIING AND SNOWSHOEING

Mt. Rainier is a major Nordic ski center for cross-country and telemark skiing. Although trails are not groomed, those around Paradise are extremely popular. If you want to ski with fewer people, try the trails in and around the Ohanapecosh–Stevens Canyon area, which are just as beautiful and, because of their more easterly exposure, slightly less subject to the rains that can douse the Longmire side, even in the dead of winter. Never ski on plowed main roads, especially around Paradise—the snowplow operator can't see you. Rentals aren't available on the eastern side of the park.

Deep snows make Mt. Rainier a snowshoeing pleasure. The Paradise area, with its network of trails, is the best choice. The park's east-side roads, Routes 123 and 410, are unplowed and provide other good snowshoeing venues, although you must share the main routes with snowmobilers.

General Store at the National Park Inn

SKIING/SNOWBOARDING | The store at the National Park Inn in Longmire rents cross-country ski equipment and snowshoes. It's open daily in winter, depending on snow conditions. ⊠ National Park Inn, Longmire ☎ 360/569–2411 ⊕ www.mtrainierguestservices.com/activities-and-events/winter-activities/cross-country-skiing.

Paradise Snowplay Area and Nordic Ski Route

SKIING/SNOWBOARDING | Sledding on flexible sleds (no toboggans or runners), inner tubes, and plastic saucers is allowed only in the Paradise snowplay area adjacent to the Jackson Visitor Center. The area is open when there is sufficient snow, usually from late December through mid-March. The easy 3½-mile Paradise Valley Road Nordic ski route begins at the Paradise parking lot and follows Paradise Valley/Stevens Canyon Road to Reflection Lakes. Equipment rentals are available at Whittaker Mountaineering in Ashford or at the National Park Inn's General Store in Longmire. ✉ *Adjacent to Jackson Visitor Center at Paradise, Mt. Rainier National Park* ☎ *360/569–2211* ⊕ *www.nps.gov/ mora/planyourvisit/winter-recreation.htm.*

Nearby Towns

Ashford sits astride an ancient trail across the Cascades used by the Yakama tribe to trade with the coastal tribes of western Washington. The town began as a logging railway terminal; today it's the main gateway to Mt. Rainier—and the only year-round access point to the park—with lodges, restaurants, grocery stores, and gift shops. Surrounded by Cascade peaks, **Packwood** is a pretty mountain village on U.S. 12, below White Pass and less than 12 miles from the Ohanapecosh area of the national park. It's a perfect jumping-off point for exploring local wilderness areas. Near the Sunrise entrance on the northeast side of the park, the **Crystal Mountain** area provides lodging, dining, and year-round outdoor recreation options, including a popular resort for snow sports.

Ashford

60 miles east of Olympia; 85 miles south of Seattle; 130 miles north of Portland.

Adjacent to the Nisqually (Longmire) entrance to Mount Rainier National Park, Ashford draws around 2 million visitors every year. Long a transit route for local indigenous tribes, its more recent history began when it became a logging terminal on the rail line and developed into a tourism hub with lodges, restaurants, groceries, and gift shops along Highway 706.

GETTING HERE AND AROUND
Ashford is easiest to reach from Seattle via Interstate 5 southbound to Highway 7, then driving southeast to Highway 706. An alternate route is via Interstate 5 southbound to Highway 167, then continuing south to Highway 161 through Eatonville to Highway 7, then east to Highway 706. From Portland, follow Interstate 5 northbound, then head east on Highway 12 to Morton and north via Highway 7 to Highway 706.

VISITOR INFORMATION Mount Rainier Visitor Association. ⊕ *www.mt-rainier.com.*

 Sights

Northwest Trek Wildlife Park
NATURE PRESERVE | FAMILY | This spectacular, 723-acre wildlife park 30 miles southeast of Tacoma is devoted to native creatures of the Pacific Northwest. Walking paths wind through natural surroundings— so natural that a cougar once entered the park and started snacking on the deer (it was finally trapped and relocated to the North Cascades). See beavers, otters, and wolverines; get close to wolves, foxes, coyotes; and observe several species of big cats and bears in wild environments. Admission includes a 40-minute tram ride through fields of wandering moose, bighorn sheep, elk, bison, and mountain goats. The most adventurous way to see the park is via ziplines, which traverse the park canopy and are part of a series of different adventure courses. ✉ *11610 Trek Dr. E, Eatonville* ⊕ *23 miles northwest of Ashford via Hwy. 706 and 161* ☎ *360/832– 6117* ⊕ *www.nwtrek.org* ⌚ *$25* ⊙ *Closed Mon.–Thurs. in Oct.–mid-Mar.*

 **Restaurants**

Copper Creek Restaurant
$$ | AMERICAN | FAMILY | This old-fashioned roadhouse, with rough-hewn fir floors and knotty-pine walls, is nestled beneath towering trees along the main road to Mt. Rainier from Eatonville. It's been a

favorite lunch and dinner stop since it opened in the 1940s, and these days parkgoers still come by in droves to fill up on hearty, straightforward comfort fare, such as biscuits and gravy and chicken-fried steak and eggs in the morning, bacon-and-blue-cheese burgers at lunch, and wild Alaskan salmon with blackberry vinaigrette in the evening. **Known for:** save room for the blackberry pie à la mode; hearty, stick-to-your-ribs fare; rustic, family-friendly vibe. $ *Average main: $18* ⊠ *35707 Hwy. 706, Ashford* ☎ *360/569–2799* ⊕ *www.coppercreekinn.com* ⊗ *No breakfast weekdays in off-season.*

Scaleburgers
$ | **BURGER** | **FAMILY** | Once a 1939 logging-truck weigh station, the building is now a popular restaurant serving homemade hamburgers, fries, and shakes. Eat outside on tables overlooking the hills. **Known for:** handy location on the way to Mt. Rainier; luscious milkshakes. $ *Average main: $10* ⊠ *54109 Mountain Hwy. E, Elbe* ✛ *11 miles west of Ashford* ☎ *360/569–2247* ▭ *No credit cards.*

Wildberry
$ | **NEPALESE** | Owned and operated by a Himalayan mountain guide, this casual café features the flavors of Nepal as well as more standard American-mountain fare. Nepalese offerings include *thali* (full meals served on metal school-lunch style platters with curry, rice, vegetables, soup, and roti bread). **Known for:** Nepalese-American fusion cuisine; colorful decor; tasty pies. $ *Average main: $15* ⊠ *37718 WA-706, Ashford* ☎ *360/569–2277* ⊕ *www.rainierwildberry.com* ⊗ *Closed Oct.–Apr.*

 Hotels

Alexander's Lodge
$$ | **B&B/INN** | A mile from Mt. Rainier's Nisqually entrance, this ideally located lodging's vintage furnishings lend romance to rooms in the main building, which dates back to 1912; there are also two adjacent guesthouses at the charming property. **Pros:** plenty of historical character; in-room spa services available; some rooms are pet-friendly. **Cons:** steep stairs to some units; decor is a bit old-fashioned; some rooms are quite small. $ *Rooms from: $169* ⊠ *37515 Hwy. 706, Ashford* ☎ *360/569–2300* ⊕ *www.alexanderslodge.com* ⟿ *21 rooms* ⦿ *Free Breakfast.*

★ Mountain Meadows Inn
$ | **B&B/INN** | This homey woodland hideaway, 6 miles southwest of Mount Rainier National Park's Nisqually entrance, includes a lovingly restored Craftsman-style home with gorgeous Douglas fir floors, interesting antiques, and three guest rooms, as well as a separate modern chalet with three suites that have private entrances and kitchenettes. **Pros:** reasonable rates; thoughtful and friendly owners; lush grounds include a hot tub. **Cons:** no restaurants within walking distance; suites lack historic charm of main house; rooms in main house don't have TVs. $ *Rooms from: $140* ⊠ *28912 Hwy. 706, Ashford* ☎ *360/569–0507* ⊕ *www.mountainmeadows-inn.com* ⟿ *6 rooms* ⦿ *Free Breakfast.*

Paradise Village Hotel
$ | **HOTEL** | A young Ukranian bought and completely revamped what had been a dated little lodging in the center of Ashford, giving it a fresh, distinctive look and a fun energy. **Pros:** restaurant and bakery serving hearty Eastern European and American dishes; great room amenities, from Bluetooth speakers to flat-screen TVs; has a young, hip vibe. **Cons:** some rooms are a little small; hourly charge for the hot tub; traffic noise, especially in summer. $ *Rooms from: $129* ⊠ *31811 Hwy. 706, Ashford* ☎ *360/255–0070* ⊕ *www.paradisevillagelodge.com* ⟿ *12 units* ⦿ *No meals.*

★ Stormking Spa and Cabins
$$$ | **B&B/INN** | In a forest setting a mile from the Nisqually entrance of Mount Rainier National Park, Stormking features

four luxury cabins for adults; all are shaped like yurts and have cozy gas fireplaces, hot tubs, private outdoor seating areas, and natural finishes of wood and stone. **Pros:** very romantic and secluded; reasonably priced for special occasion getaways; deer and other wildlife frequent the property. **Cons:** no check-ins on Sunday; Wi-Fi available at spa but not in cabins; two-night minimum stay. $ Rooms from: $240 ⊠ 37311 SR 706 E, Ashford ☎ 360/569–2964 ⊕ www.storm-kingspa.com ☞ 4 cabins ⏍ No meals.

Packwood

25 miles southeast of Ashford via Skate Creek Rd. (closed in winter); 62 miles southeast of Ashford via Morton in winter.

Its location near the southeast entrance to Mount Rainier National Park makes this delightful mountain village on U.S. 12 an attractive destination for those who plan to explore the nearby wilderness areas.

GETTING HERE AND AROUND

From Seattle (about 120 miles away), take Interstate 5 south to Highway 167 near Renton, then south via Highway 161 through Eatonville and southeast on Highway 7 through Morton, then east on U.S. 12. Packwood is about 140 miles from Portland via Interstate 5 northbound to Exit 68, then 64 miles east via U.S. 12 (also called the White Pass Scenic Byway).

Sights

Goat Rocks Wilderness

NATIONAL/STATE PARK | The crags in Gifford Pinchot National Forest, south of Mt. Rainier, are aptly named. You often see mountain goats here in this vast and unspoiled 108,000-acre wilderness, especially when you hike into the backcountry. Goat Lake is a particularly good spot for viewing these elusive creatures. See the goats without backpacking by taking Forest Road 21 to Forest Road 2140, south from

U.S. 12. The goats will be on Stonewall Ridge looming up ahead of you. ⊠ NF-21 and NF-2140, Randle ☎ 360/891–5000 ⊕ www.fs.usda.gov/giffordpinchot.

 Restaurants

Cliff Droppers

$ | **BURGER** | **FAMILY** | This casual burger joint with a small but decent beer list and an outdoor space draws hikers, skiers, and other outdoors enthusiasts on their way to Mt. Rainier and Gifford Pinchot National Forest. Fish-and-chips, vegan bean burgers, and BLTs share the menu with a variety of hearty meat patties, including some wild-game options, with a wide variety of toppings. **Known for:** jalapeño burger topped with Swiss cheese and a tangy secret sauce; your chance to sample buffalo and elk burgers; berry milkshakes. $ Average main: $11 ⊠ 12968 U.S. 12, Packwood ☎ 360/494–2055 ⊕ www.facebook.com/Cliff-Droppers-182896865057151 ⏍ Closed Mon. and Tues. in winter.

Hotels

Cowlitz River Lodge

$$ | **HOTEL** | A large stone fireplace in the great room adds some character at this lodge—a good thing, since guest rooms have updated but fairly standard motel furniture. **Pros:** convenient to scenic areas; knowledgeable staff; inviting common areas. **Cons:** no pool; no restaurant; basic rooms. $ Rooms from: $160 ⊠ 13069 U.S. 12, Packwood ☎ 360/494–4444, 888/305–2185 ⊕ www.whitepasstravel.com/cowlitz ☞ 31 rooms ⏍ Free Breakfast.

★ Packwood Lodge

$ | **HOTEL** | This thoughtfully updated motel offers reasonable rates and a peaceful location along U.S. 12, a bit north of downtown Packwood and within easy striking distance of the Stevens Canyon Entrance to Mt. Rainier National Park. **Pros:** convenient to Mt. Rainier and White Pass Ski Area; cabins have rustic but contemporary vibe; pets are welcome. **Cons:** not within walking distance of town; no fitness center or pool; can hear trucks on highway. *$ Rooms from: $119* ✉ *13807 U.S. 12, Packwood* ☎ *360/496–5333* ⊕ *www.packwoodlodge. com* ⮑ *25 rooms* ⭑◯❙ *No meals.*

Nightlife

★ Packwood Brewing

BREWPUBS/BEER GARDENS | With picnic tables and firepits outside and a gas fireplace surrounded by wooden chairs and benches in the rustic-industrial interior, this upbeat craft brewer is a comfy place to sip rich Butter Peak Porter or hoppy Tree Line IPA any time of year. The taproom occupies a smartly restored 1930s mercantile store, and the kitchen serves tasty guacamole, poblano-chicken tacos, and a few other Mexican-influenced snacks. ✉ *12298 U.S. 12, Packwood* ☎ *360/496–0845* ⊕ *www. packwoodbrewingco.com.*

Crystal Mountain

5 miles north of the Sunrise/White River cutoff from Hwy. 410.

Just outside the park, close to the Sunrise entrance, this year-round mountain resort area provides convenient lodging and dining options for visitors exploring the east side of Mt. Rainier. Stunning views of the mountain beckon from Washington's highest-elevation restaurant and gondola rides to the top, and snow sports are so popular at the ski area that lift tickets generally need to be purchased in advance.

 Restaurants

Summit House

$$ | **PACIFIC NORTHWEST** | On top of Crystal Mountain at 6,872 feet is Washington's highest-elevation restaurant with stunning views of Mt. Rainier; the Summit House is a popular stop for skiers, hikers, and summer tourists, too. The menu features Northwest cuisine, including wild Pacific cod fish-and-chips in summer (halibut in winter), elk and bison chili, burgers, and huckleberry ice cream. **Known for:** mountain views; leisurely dining experience; accessible only by gondola (tickets sold separately). *$ Average main: $22* ✉ *33914 Crystal Mountain Blvd., Crystal Mountain* ☎ *360/663–3050* ⊕ *crystalmountainresort.com* ⊙ *Open seasonally during summer and ski season; check website or call for current hrs.*

Hotels

Alta Crystal Resort

$$$$ | **B&B/INN** | **FAMILY** | In the national forest, this small resort with family-friendly amenities feels remote yet is very close to Mt. Rainier's Sunrise entrance and Crystal Mountain Ski Resort. **Pros:** fun, nightly activities; mini-grocery store and movie library; several standalone cabins for added privacy. **Cons:** not close to restaurants or grocery store; cell phone and Internet can be spotty; pool area gets noisy, especially for first-floor units. *$ Rooms from: $259* ✉ *68317 SR 410 E, Greenwater* ☎ *360/663–2556, 800/277–6475, 360/663–2500* ⊕ *www.altacrystal-resort.com* ⮑ *27 rooms* ⭑◯❙ *No meals.*

Activities

Crystal Mountain Ski Area

SKIING/SNOWBOARDING | Washington State's biggest and best-known ski area has nine lifts (plus a children's lift and a gondola) and 57 runs. In summer, it's open for hiking, rides on the Mt. Rainier Gondola, and meals at the Summit House, all providing sensational views of Rainier and the Cascades. ■**TIP→ Because of recent episodes of overcrowding at the ski resort, during which many people were turned away, Crystal no longer sells day-of tickets during peak winter season. Facilities:** 57 trails; 2,600 acres; 3,100-foot vertical drop; 11 lifts. ✉ *33914 Crystal Mountain Blvd., off Rte. 410, Crystal Mountain* ☎ *360/663–2265* ⊕ *www. crystalmountainresort.com* 🎫 *From $25 (gondola), $80 (day ski ticket).*

NORTH CASCADES NATIONAL PARK

Updated by
Shelley Arenas

WASHINGTON

⛰ **Camping**
★★★★★

🏨 **Hotels**
★★★☆☆

🏃 **Activities**
★★★★☆

👁 **Scenery**
★★★★★

👥 **Crowds**
★☆☆☆☆

WELCOME TO NORTH CASCADES NATIONAL PARK

TOP REASONS TO GO

★ **Pure wilderness:** Spot bald eagles, deer, elk, and other wildlife on nearly 400 miles of mountain and meadow hiking trails.

★ **Majestic glaciers:** The North Cascades are home to several hundred moving ice masses, more than half of the glaciers in the United States.

★ **Splendid flora:** A bright palette of flowers blankets the hillsides in midsummer, while October's colors paint the landscape in vibrant autumn hues.

★ **Thrilling boat rides:** Lake Chelan, Ross Lake, and the Stehekin River are the starting points for kayaking, white-water rafting, and ferry trips.

★ **19th-century history:** Delve into the state's farming, lumber, and logging pasts in clapboard towns and homesteads around the park.

1 **North Cascades Scenic Highway and Ross Lake National Recreation Area.** The North Cascades Scenic Highway (State Highway 20), which runs west–east between the park's North and South units, is dotted with scenic viewpoints, trailheads, and towns that have visitor centers and other amenities. The route also runs through the Ross Lake National Recreation Area, whose eastern end stretches north toward British Columbia and whose placid lake is edged with pretty bays that draw summer swimmers and boaters.

2 **Lake Chelan National Recreation Area.** Ferries cruise between small waterfront villages along this pristine waterway, while kayakers and hikers follow quiet trails along its edges. This is one of the Northwest's most popular summer escapes, with nature-bound activities and rustic accommodations.

NORTH CASCADE NATIONAL PARK NORTH UNIT

North Cascades National Park Wilderness Information Center

Marblemount

| 0 | | 5 mi |
| 0 | | 5 km |

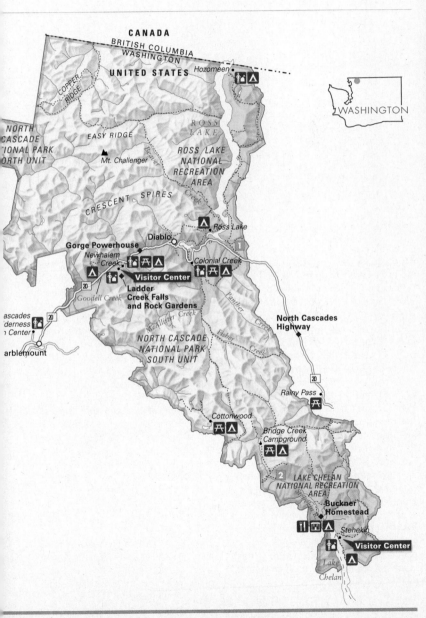

Countless snow-clad mountain spires dwarf narrow glacial valleys in this 684,000-acre expanse of the North Cascades, which encompasses three diverse natural areas. North Cascades National Park is the core of the region. The Ross Lake National Recreation Area cuts through its middle and also runs north to the Canadian border; Lake Chelan National Recreation Area flanks the park to the south.

This combined area is known as the North Cascades National Park Service Complex, and much of it is remote and inaccessible to all but the most intrepid explorers—just as wilderness is meant to be. The park has the most glaciers in the nation outside of Alaska, and the peaks of its mountains, nicknamed the "American Alps," were some of the last to be climbed in the contiguous United States (in the 1970s). But you don't have to be a hardcore adventurer to appreciate the mountain grandeur: State Highway 20—also known as the North Cascades Scenic Highway and part of the greater Cascades Loop—traverses the park, providing wide-open views and well-placed overlooks where you can stop to take it all in. Miles of trails offer more vistas and a closer look at the flora, which is among the most diverse of all the national parks. Wildlife is prevalent too; rangers and nature guides can advise on how to best interact if you have a surprise encounter.

Starting in the late 1800s, conservationists sought to have this area named as

a national park. Despite many efforts over the decades, this didn't happen until 1968, when Congress designated the park to preserve "certain majestic mountain scenery, snowfields, glaciers, alpine meadows, lakes and other unique glaciated features ... for the benefit, use and inspiration of present and future generations." Expansion of the highway in the early 1970s made it easier to reach the park, but the mountain pass still closes from late fall until the road is free of snow in mid-spring (it's stayed open all winter only once, in 1976).

Planning

When to Go

The spectacular, craggy peaks of the North Cascades—often likened to the Alps—are breathtaking anytime. Summer is peak season, especially along the alpine stretches of Highway 20;

AVERAGE HIGH/LOW TEMPERATURES					
JAN.	FEB.	MAR.	APR.	MAY	JUNE
39/30	43/32	49/34	56/38	64/43	70/49
JULY	AUG.	SEPT.	OCT.	NOV.	DEC.
76/52	76/53	69/49	57/42	45/36	39/31

weekends and holidays can be crowded. Summer is short and glorious in the high country, extending from snowmelt (late May to July) to early September.

The North Cascades Scenic Highway is a popular drive in September and October, when the changing leaves put on a colorful show. The lowland forest areas, such as the complex around Newhalem, can be visited almost any time of year. These are wonderfully quiet in early spring or late autumn on mild rainy days. Snow closes the North Cascades Scenic Highway from mid-November through mid-April, and sometimes longer.

Getting Here and Around

AIR
The closest airports to the western gateway town of Sedro-Woolley are Bellingham International Airport, 31 miles to the northwest; Paine Field Airport in Everett, 52 miles to the south; and Seattle-Tacoma International Airport, 87 miles to the south—all via Interstate 5. On the eastern side of park, Pangborn Memorial Airport in Wenatchee is 45 miles south of Chelan via US 97.

BOAT
If you're not up for a lengthy hike, you can reach Stehekin and other remote spots along Lake Chelan by boat.

Lake Chelan Boat Co
TRANSPORTATION SITE (AIRPORT/BUS/FERRY/TRAIN) | The *Lady of the Lake II* makes journeys from May to October, departing Chelan at 8:30 and returning at 6 ($45 round-trip). The *Lady Express,* a speedy catamaran, runs between Stehekin,

Holden Village, the national park, and Lake Chelan year-round; schedules vary with the seasons, with daily trips during summer and three to five trips weekly the rest of the year. Tickets are $68 round-trip May to October and $45 round-trip the rest of the year. The vessels also can drop off and pick up at lakeshore trailheads. ⊠ *1418 Woodin Ave., Chelan* ☎ *509/682–4584, 888/682–4584* ⊕ *ladyofthelake.com.*

CAR
Highway 20, the North Cascades Scenic Highway, splits the park's North and South units. It runs through the park's Ross Lake National Recreation Area, connecting towns like Sedro-Woolley, Newhalem, and Marblemount in the west with (in warmer months) Mazama, Winthrop, and Twisp in the east. This route is part of a greater Cascades Loop (www.cascadeloop.com), which continues to Chelan (via Methow, along WA 153 and US 97) and loops south and west again (along US 97 and Route 2).

The gravel Cascade River Road, which runs southeast from Marblemount, peels off Highway 20, and Sibley Creek/Hidden Lake Road (USFS 1540) turns off Cascade River Road to the Cascade Pass trailhead. Thornton Creek Road is another rough four-wheel-drive track. For the northern reaches of Ross Lake, the unpaved Hozomeen Road (Silver–Skagit Road) provides access between Hope, British Columbia, and Silver Lake and Skagit Valley provincial parks. From Stehekin, the Stehekin Valley Road continues to High Bridge and Car Wash Falls—although seasonal floods may cause washouts. Note that roads are narrow

North Cascades in One Day

The **North Cascades Scenic Highway**, with its breathtaking mountain and meadow scenery, is one of the most memorable drives in the United States. Although many travelers first head northeast from Seattle into the park and make this their grand finale, if you start from Winthrop and travel west, traffic is lighter and there's less morning fog. Either way, the main highlight is **Washington Pass**, the road's highest point, where an overlook affords a sensational panorama of snow-covered peaks.

Rainy Pass, where the road heading north drops into the west slope valleys, is another good vantage point. Old-growth forest begins to appear, and after about an hour you reach **Gorge Creek Falls overlook** with its 242-foot cascade. Continue west to Newhalem and stop for lunch, then take a half-hour stroll along the **Trail of the Cedars**. Later, stop at the **North Cascades Visitor Center** and take another short hike. It's an hour drive down the Skagit Valley to Sedro-Woolley, where bald eagles are often seen along the river in winter.

and some are closed seasonally, many sights are off the beaten path, and the scenery is so spectacular that you'll want to make more than a day trip.

Inspiration

Crown Jewel Wilderness: Creating North Cascades National Park, by Laura Danner, offers an in-depth look at how this national park came to be and highlights the tireless efforts of conservationists.

Hiking Naked: A Quaker Woman's Search for Balance, by Iris Graville, is a memoir about the author and her family's choice to leave city life behind and move to the remote village of Stehekin.

Legends of the North Cascades, by Jonathan Evison, tells the story of an Iraq War veteran and his young daughter and what happens when they go live in a cave in the North Cascades.

The North Cascades: Finding Beauty and Renewal in the Wild Nearby, by William Dietrich, is filled with stunning photos from 20 photographers and park essays by the author and others.

This Boy's Life (1993) brings Tobias Wolff's noted memoir to the big screen, starring Robert De Niro, Ellen Barkin, and Leonardo DiCaprio. It's set in the 1950s in the town of Concrete, near the western entrance to the national park.

Park Essentials

ACCESSIBILITY

Visitor centers along North Cascades Scenic Highway are accessible by wheelchair. Hikes include Sterling Munro, Skagit River Loop, and Rock Shelter, three short trails into lowland old-growth forest, all at mile 120 along Highway 20 near Newhalem, and the Happy Creek Forest Trail at mile 134.

PARK FEES AND PERMITS

There are no entrance fees to the national park and no parking fees at trailheads on park land. A Northwest Forest Pass, required for parking at Forest Service trailheads, is $5 per vehicle for a calendar day or $30 for a year. A free wilderness permit is required for all overnight stays in the backcountry; these are available in person only. Dock permits for boat-in campgrounds are $5 per day. Car camping is $10 per night at Gorge Lake Campground and $16 per night at Colonial Creek, Goodell Creek, and Newhalem Creek campgrounds during the summer and free off-season; the primitive Hozomeen Campground is free all year. Passes and permits are sold at visitor centers and ranger stations.

PARK HOURS

The park never closes, but access is limited by snow in winter. Highway 20 (North Cascades Scenic Highway), the major access to the park, is partially closed from mid-November to mid-April, depending on snow levels.

CELL PHONE RECEPTION

Cell reception in the park is unreliable. Public telephones are found at the North Cascades Visitor Center and Skagit Information Center in Newhalem and the Golden West Visitor Center and North Cascades Lodge in Stehekin.

Hotels

Accommodations in North Cascades National Park are rustic, cozy, and comfortable. Options range from remote inns and homey cabin rentals to spartan campgrounds. Expect to pay roughly $50 to $200 per night, depending on the rental size and the season. Book at least three months in advance, or even a year for popular accommodations in summer. Outside the park are numerous resorts, motels, bed-and-breakfasts, and even overnight boat rentals in Sedro-Woolley, Concrete, Marblemount, Mazama, Winthrop, Twisp, and Chelan. *Hotel reviews have been shortened. For full information, visit Fodors.com.*

Restaurants

There are no formal restaurants in North Cascades National Park, just a lakeside café at the North Cascades Environmental Learning Center. Stehekin has three options: the Stehekin Valley Ranch dining room, North Cascades Lodge, or the Stehekin Pastry Company; all serve simple, hearty, country-style meals and sweets. Towns within a few hours of the park on either side have a couple of small eateries, and a few lodgings have dining rooms with skilled chefs who craft high-end meals of locally grown products matched with extensive wine lists. Otherwise, don't expect fancy decor or gourmet frills—just friendly service and delicious homemade stews, roasts, soups, salads, and baked goods.

Developed picnic areas at both Rainy Pass (Highway 20, 38 miles east of the park visitor center) and Washington Pass (Highway 20, 42 miles east of the visitor center) have a half-dozen picnic tables, drinking water, and pit toilets. The vistas of surrounding peaks are sensational at these two overlooks. More picnic facilities are located near the visitor center in Newhalem and at Colonial Creek Campground, 10 miles east of the visitor center on Highway 20. *Restaurant reviews have been shortened. For full information, visit Fodors.com.*

What It Costs in U.S. Dollars			
$	$$	$$$	$$$$
RESTAURANTS			
under $12	$12–$20	$21–$30	over $30
HOTELS			
under $100	$100–$150	$151–$200	over $200

Tours

★ North Cascades Environmental Learning Center

ECOTOURISM | FAMILY | This is the spot for information on hiking, wildlife watching, horseback riding, climbing, boat rentals, and fishing in the park, as well as classroom education and hands-on nature experiences. Guided tours from the center include lake and dam visits, mountain climbs, pack-train excursions, and guided canoe trips on Diablo Lake. Other choices range from forest ecology and backpacking trips to writing and art retreats. Family getaway weekends in summer are a fun way to unplug from technology and introduce kids to nature. There's also a research library, a dock on Diablo Lake, an amphitheater, and overnight lodging. The center is operated by the North Cascades Institute in partnership with the National Park Service and Seattle City Light. ⊠ *1940 Diablo Dam Rd., Diablo* ☎ *360/854–2599 headquarters, 206/526–2599 environmental learning center* ⊕ *www.ncascades.org* ✍ *Day programs from $110; overnight lodging (including meals) from $256 per couple* ☉ *Closed during winter months.*

Visitor Information

PARK CONTACT INFORMATION North Cascades National Park. ⊠ *810 Rte. 20, Sedro-Woolley* ☎ *360/854–7200* ⊕ *www.nps.gov/noca.* **Glacier Public Service Center.** ⊠ *10091 Mt. Baker Hwy., Glacier* ☎ *360/599–2714* ⊕ *www.nps.gov/noca/planyourvisit/visitorcenters.htm.*

North Cascades Scenic Highway and Ross Lake National Recreation Area

Entrance to national recreation area is about 50 miles east of Sedro-Woolley and 40 miles west of Mazama via the 140-mile North Cascades Scenic Highway (Highway 20).

Perhaps the easiest way to experience the park's breathtaking scenery (and, perhaps, just a bit of its wilderness) is on a drive along North Cascades Scenic Highway (Highway 20), which traverses

the national park's Ross Lake National Recreation Area from west to east—or vice versa if you prefer. North and west of the Ross Lake NRA is the national park's North Unit. Inaccessible by roads, this unit's seemingly endless landscape of pine-topped peaks and ridges centers on snowy Mt. Challenger and stretches over the Picket Range toward the Canadian border.

On the other side of the highway, the national park's South Unit—with its lake-filled mountain foothills and flower-filled meadows—is rife with waterfalls and wildlife. Like its northern sibling, the unit doesn't have any services, but it does offer scenic outlooks and trailheads near the highway, some of which are just outside the park and and accessed via side roads.

In addition to running the length of the North Cascades Scenic Highway, Ross Lake National Recreation Area also runs along the Skagit River north to the U.S.–Canada border, encompassing the three lake reservoirs created by the power projects on the river. The largest reservoir, Ross Lake, is popular for on-the-water recreation. A water taxi shuttles hikers to remote trails in the north end of the park.

Sights

HISTORIC SIGHTS
Diablo Dam

DAM | The Diablo Dam is one of three in the area that collectively produce hydroelectric power for Seattle City Light. Although its powerhouse can only be visited on bus tours that are sometimes offered (check at the Skagit Information Center), the experience of driving across a dam makes the short detour off Highway 20 worthwhile. To see the dam from the water, continue a mile farther east along Diablo Dam Road to the North Cascades Environmental Learning Center, which offers Diablo Lake boat tours. Guides share the secret of how the lake gets its vibrant turquoise color as you cruise past Diablo Dam and then north to Ross Dam, where guides can sometimes take visitors into the powerhouse for a closer look. ⊠ *Diablo Dam Rd., Diablo ⊹ Turnoff is off North Cascades Scenic Hwy. (Hwy. 20), 7 miles northeast of Newhalem.*

Gorge Powerhouse

DAM | Built in 1917 to support the Skagit River Hydroelectric Project—three dams (Gorge, Diablo, and Ross) that work together to provide power—this art-deco structure has a visitor gallery with displays on project operations and history. Currently about 20% of Seattle's electricity comes from here. The best way to visit is on one of the summer tours operated by Skagit Tours in partnership with Seattle City Light and the North Cascades Environmental Learning Center. ⊠ *Rockport ⊹ Off Hwy. 20, 5-minute walk from Skagit Info Center in Newhalem.*

SCENIC DRIVES

North Cascades Scenic Highway

SCENIC DRIVE | Also known as Highway 20, this classic scenic route, part of the greater Cascades Loop, runs roughly 140 miles between Sedro-Woolley and Twisp. Heading west to east, the highway first winds through the green pastures and woods of the upper Skagit Valley, with mountains looming in the distance. Beyond Concrete, a former cement-manufacturing town, the highway climbs into the mountains, passes the Diablo and Ross dams, and traverses the park's Ross Lake National Recreation Area. Here several pull-outs offer great views of the lake and the surrounding snow-capped peaks. From June to September, the meadows are covered with wildflowers, and from late September through October, the mountain slopes glow with fall foliage. The pinnacle of this stretch is 5,477-foot-high Washington Pass: look east, to where the road descends quickly into a series of hairpin curves between Early Winters Creek and the Methow

Valley. Remember, this section of the highway is closed from roughly November to April, depending on snowfall, and sometimes closes temporarily during the busy summer season due to mudslides from storms. From the Methow Valley, Highway 153 travels along the Methow River's apple, nectarine, and peach orchards to Pateros, on the Columbia River; from here, you can continue east to Grand Coulee or south to Lake Chelan. ⊕ *www.cascadeloop.com.*

SCENIC STOPS

Diablo Lake Vista Point

This is a must-stop photo opp: indeed, countless photos of the gorgeous lake have been taken from here over the decades. ⊠ *North Cascades Scenic Hwy. (Hwy. 20) ⊹ 11 miles east of Newhalem.*

Ladder Creek Falls and Rock Gardens

TOUR—SIGHT | The rock gardens overlooking Ladder Creek Falls, 7 miles west of Diablo, are beautiful and inspiring. In summer, a slide show about the powerhouse and the area's history is offered at 8 pm on Thursday and Friday evenings in Currier Hall in Newhalem, followed by a free guided walk to the falls; visitors can reserve in advance for a chicken dinner at 7 pm. Skagit Information Center has maps for a self-guided walk. ⊠ *North Cascades Hwy., Newhalem ⊹ 2 miles east of North Cascades Visitor Center* ☎ *360/854–2589* ⊕ *www.seattle.gov/ light/tours/skagit* ⊠ *$19/dinner; walking tour free* ⊘ *Closed Oct.–Apr.*

Newhalem

TOWN | Home base for both the national park's main North Cascades Visitor Center and the Skagit Information Center—run by the park service, the North Cascades Institute, and Seattle City Light—the tiny, unincorporated hamlet of Newhalem is tucked between the North and South units of the park, amid the Ross Lake National Recreation Area. Stop at the centers for maps and permits and to get information on area tours and nearby trails. ⊠ *North Cascades Scenic Hwy. (Hwy. 20).*

TRAILS

★ Cascade Pass

TRAIL | This extremely popular, 3¾-mile, four-hour trail is known for stunning panoramas from the great mountain divide. Dozens of peaks line the horizon as you make your way up the fairly flat, hairpin-turn track, the scene fronted by a blanket of alpine wildflowers from July to mid-August. Arrive before noon if you want a parking spot at the trailhead. If you're feeling fit (and ambitious), a much longer hike (23 miles) goes all the way to High Bridge, where you can catch a shuttle to Stehekin in the Lake Chelan National Recreation Area. *Moderate.* ✉ *North Cascades National Park* ✛ *Trailhead: at end of Cascade River Rd., 14 miles from Marblemount off Highway 20* ⊕ *www. nps.gov/noca/planyourvisit/cascade-pass-trail.htm.*

Diablo Lake Trail

TRAIL | Explore nearly 4 miles of waterside terrain on this route, which is accessed from the Sourdough Creek parking lot. An excellent alternative for parties with young hikers is to take the Seattle City Light Ferry one-way. *Moderate.* ✉ *North Cascades National Park* ✛ *Trailhead: at milepost 135, Hwy. 20* ⊕ *www.nps.gov/noca.*

Happy Creek Forest Walk

TRAIL | FAMILY | Old-growth forests are the focus of this kid-friendly boardwalk route, a ½-mile loop through the trees off the North Cascades Scenic Highway. Interpretive signs provide details about flora along the way. *Easy.* ✉ *North Cascades National Park* ✛ *Trailhead: at milepost 135, North Cascades Scenic Hwy.* ⊕ *www.nps.gov/noca.*

Rainy Lake Trail

TRAIL | An easy, accessible, 1-mile paved trail leads to Rainy Lake, a waterfall, and a glacier-view platform. *Easy.* ✉ *North Cascades National Park* ✛ *Trailhead: off Hwy. 20, 35 miles west of Winthrop* ⊕ *www.fs.usda.gov/recarea/okawen/recarea/?recid=59385.*

Wildlife in North Cascades 👁

Bald eagles are present year-round along the Skagit River and the lakes—in December, hundreds flock to the Skagit to feed on a rare winter salmon run, and remain through January. Spring and early summer bring black bears to the roadsides in the high country. Deer and elk can often be spotted in early morning and late evening, grazing and browsing at the forest's edge. Other mountain residents include beaver, marmots, pika, otters, skunks, opossums, and other smaller mammals, as well as forest and field birds.

River Loop Trail

TRAIL | Take this flat and easy, 1¾-mile, wheelchair-accessible trail through stands of huge old-growth firs and cedars toward the Skagit River. *Easy.* ✉ *North Cascades National Park* ✛ *Trailhead: near North Cascades Visitor Center* ⊕ *www. nps.gov/noca/planyourvisit/newhalem-area-trails.htm.*

Rock Shelter Trail

TRAIL | This short trail—partly boardwalk—leads to a campsite used 1,400 years ago by Native Americans; interpretive signs tell the history of human presence in the region. *Easy.* ✉ *North Cascades National Park* ✛ *Trailhead: off Hwy. 20 near Newhalem Creek Campground* ⊕ *www. nps.gov/noca/planyourvisit/newhalem-area-trails.htm.*

Sterling Munro Trail

TRAIL | Starting from the North Cascades Visitor Center, this popular introductory stroll follows a short 300-foot path over a boardwalk to a lookout above the forested Picket Range peaks. *Easy.* ✉ *North Cascades National Park* ✛ *Trailhead:*

North Cascades National Park

LAKE CHELAN NATIONAL RECREATION AREA

milepost 120, near Newhalem Creek Campground ⊕ www.nps.gov/noca/planyourvisit/newhalem-area-trails.htm.

Thornton Lakes Trail

TRAIL | A 5-mile climb into an alpine basin with three pretty lakes, this steep and strenuous hike takes five to six hours round-trip. *Difficult.* ⊠ *Thornton Lake Rd.* ⊹ *3 miles west of Newhalem* ⊕ *www.nps.gov/noca/planyourvisit/ thornton-lake-trail.htm.*

Trail of the Cedars

TRAIL | Less than a ½ mile long, this trail winds its way through one of the finest surviving stands of old-growth western red cedar in Washington. Some of the trees along the path are more than 1,000 years old. *Easy.* ⊠ *Newhalem* ⊹ *Trailhead: near North Cascades Visitor Center, milepost 120, Hwy. 20* ⊕ *www.nps.gov/noca/ planyourvisit/newhalem-area-trails.htm.*

VISITOR CENTERS

North Cascades Visitor Center

INFO CENTER | The main visitor facility for the park has extensive displays on the surrounding landscape. Learn about the history and value of old-growth trees, the many creatures that depend on the rain-forest ecology, and the effects of human activity on the ecosystem. Check bulletin boards for special programs with park rangers. ⊠ *Milepost 120, North Cascades Hwy., Newhalem* ☎ *206/386–4495* ⊕ *www.nps.gov/noca/planyourvisit/visitorcenters.htm* ⊘ *Closed Oct.–mid-May.*

Skagit Information Center

INFO CENTER | This center is operated by Seattle City Light, North Cascades Institute, and the national park. It's the gathering point for various tours run by Seattle City Light and has exhibits about the utility's hydroelectric projects in the North Cascades. Pick up a map to a self-guided walking tour of historic Newhalem, as well as other park information. ⊠ *Hwy. 20 and Main St., Newhalem* ☎ *360/854–2589* ⊘ *Closed Oct.–mid-May.*

Hotels

Ross Lake Resort

$$$$ | **HOTEL** | Remote and unique, it's not easy to snag a booking at the only lodging in the Ross Lake area, but it's worth the effort for a chance to immerse yourself in nature in a lakefront cabin. **Pros:** spectacular setting; plenty of recreational equipment to rent; worth a day visit if you can't get lodging. **Cons:** not accessible by road; short season and books up fast; no food services but cabins have kitchens. $ *Rooms from: $220* ⊠ *Ross Lake Resort, 503 Diablo St.* ☎ *206/486–3751* ⊕ *www.rosslakeresort.com* ⊘ *Closed Nov.–June* ⇝ *15 units* ❌ *No meals.*

Lake Chelan National Recreation Area

Accessed via boat from Chelan to Stehekin.

This area includes the north end of Lake Chelan and the Stehekin Valley and river. Access from the north is by trail (on foot or horseback). The small village of Stehekin is a favorite tourist stop for its peaceful isolation; without road connections, your easiest option for getting there is a scenic boat ride on one of the vessels that runs regularly between Chelan and Stehekin. (In the past, a seaplane company provided faster service and a fun adventure, but it is temporarily closed.)

Sights

HISTORIC SITES

Buckner Homestead

FESTIVAL | Dating from 1889, this restored pioneer farm includes an apple orchard, farmhouse, barn, and many ranch buildings. You can pick up a self-guided tour booklet from the drop box. Feel free to enjoy apples from the trees in season. A harvest festival is held in October. ⊠ *Stehekin Valley Rd., 3½ miles northwest of Stehekin Landing, Stehekin* 🌐 *www.bucknerhomestead.org.*

SCENIC STOPS

★ Stehekin

TOWN | One of the most beautiful and secluded valleys in the Pacific Northwest, Stehekin was homesteaded by hardy souls in the late 19th century. It's actually not a town, but rather a small community set at the scenic northeast end of Lake Chelan, and it's accessible only by boat or trail. Year-round residents—there's about 100 of them—enjoy a wilderness lifestyle. They have intermittent outside communications, boat-delivered supplies, and just two-dozen cars among them—vehicles must be barged in, after all. Even on a peak summer season day, only around 200 visitors make the trek here. ✉ *Stehekin* 🌐 *www.stehekin.com.*

VISITOR CENTERS

Chelan Ranger Station

INFO CENTER | The base for the Chelan National Recreation Area and Wenatchee National Forest has an information desk and a shop selling regional maps and books. ✉ *428 W. Woodin Ave., Chelan* ☎ *509/682–4900* 🌐 *www.fs.usda.gov/detail/okawen/about-forest/offices* 🕒 *Closed weekends.*

Golden West Visitor Center

INFO CENTER | Maps and concise displays at this visitor center explain the layered ecology of the valley, which encompasses virtually every ecosystem in the Northwest. Rangers offer guidance on hiking, camping, and other activities and arrange bike tours. There is also an arts-and-crafts gallery and audiovisual and children's programs. Campers can pick up free backcountry permits. Note that access to Stehekin is by boat or trail only. ✉ *Stehekin Valley Rd., Stehekin* ✣ *¼ mile north of Stehekin Landing* ☎ *509/699–2080* 🌐 *www.nps.gov/noca/planyourvisit/visitorcenters.htm* 🕒 *Closed Oct.–mid-May.*

🍴 Restaurants

Restaurant at Stehekin Valley Ranch

$$ | **AMERICAN** | **FAMILY** | Meals in the rustic log ranch house, served at polished wood tables, include buffet dinners of steak, ribs, hamburgers, fish, salad, beans, and dessert. Note that breakfast is served 7 to 9, lunch is noon to 1, and dinner is 5:30 to 7; show up later than that, and you'll find the kitchen is closed. **Known for:** hearty meals; fresh berries, fruit, and produce; communal dining. [$] *Average main: $20* ✉ *Stehekin Valley Rd., 9 miles north of Stehekin Landing, Stehekin* ☎ *509/682–4677,* 🌐 *www.stehekinvalleyranch.com* 🕒 *Closed Oct.–mid-June.*

☕ Coffee and Quick Bites

Stehekin Pastry Company

$ | **BAKERY** | As you enter this lawn-framed timber chalet, you're immersed in the tantalizing aromas of a European bakery. Glassed-in display cases are filled with trays of homemade baked goods, and the pungent espresso is eye-opening. **Known for:** fruit pie; amazing pastries; hearty lunch food. [$] *Average main: $9* ✉ *Stehekin Valley Rd., Stehekin* ✣ *About 2 miles north of Stehekin Landing* ☎ *509/682–7742* 🌐 *www.stehekinpastry.com* 🕒 *Closed mid-Oct.–mid-May.*

🛏 Hotels

North Cascades Lodge at Stehekin

$$$ | **HOTEL** | Crackling fires and Lake Chelan views are provided both in standard rooms in the Alpine House, with its shared lounge and lakeside deck, and in larger rooms in the Swiss Mont building, with its private decks overlooking the water. **Pros:** on the water; recreation center with pool table; kayak and canoe rentals. **Cons:** no air-conditioning; TV is available only in the recreation building; limited Internet service and no cell phone service. [$] *Rooms from: $154* ✉ *955 Stehekin Valley Rd., Stehekin* ☎ *509/699–2056, 855/685–4167* reservations ⊕ www.lodgeatstehekin. com ☉ Closed Nov.–Jan. ⇦ 29 units ☉ No meals.

Stehekin Valley Ranch

$$$$ | ALL-INCLUSIVE | FAMILY | Alongside pretty meadows at the edge of pine forest, this rustic ranch is a center for hikers and horseback riders, who stay in barnlike cabins with cedar paneling, tile floors, and a private bath or in canvas-roof tent cabins with bunk beds, kerosene lamps, and shared bathrooms. **Pros:** easy access to recreation; playground and outdoor game fields; hearty meals included. **Cons:** no bathrooms in tent cabins; many repeat guests so book early; short opening season. $ Rooms from: $290 ⊠ Stehekin Valley Rd., Stehekin ✛ 9 miles north of Stehekin Landing ☎ 509/682–4677, ⊕ stehekinvalleyranch.com ☉ Closed Oct.–mid-June ⇦ 15 cabins ☉ All meals.

Activities

BIKING

Mountain bikes are permitted on highways, unpaved back roads, and a few designated tracks around the park; however, there is no biking on footpaths. Ranger stations have details on the best places to ride in each season, as well as notes on spots that are closed due to weather, mud, or other environmental factors. It's $31 round-trip to bring a bike on the Lake Chelan ferry to Stehekin.

Discovery Bikes

BICYCLING | You can rent mountain bikes and helmets by the hour at a self-serve rack in front of the Stehekin Log office in Stehekin. For a longer excursion, meet up at 8 am for a van ride and narrated tour to the Stehekin Valley Ranch. After enjoying a full breakfast, hop on a bike to explore the trails and sites. ⊠ Stehekin Valley Rd., Stehekin ✛ 5-min walk from boat landing ☎ ⊕ www.stehekindiscoverybikes.com ✉ From $5 per hr; $38 for ranch breakfast ride.

BOATING AND RAFTING

The boundaries of North Cascades National Park touch two long and sinewy expanses: Lake Chelan in the far south and Ross Lake, which runs north toward the Canadian border. Boat ramps, some with speed- and sailboat, paddleboat, kayak, and canoe rentals, can be found all around Lake Chelan, and passenger ferries cross between towns and campgrounds. Hozomeen, accessible via a 39-mile dirt road from Canada, is the boating base for Ross Lake. The site has a large boat ramp, and a water taxi makes drops at shoreline campgrounds. Diablo Lake, in the center of the park, also has a ramp at Colonial Creek. Gorge Lake has a public ramp near the town of Diablo, just off Highway 20.

June through August is the park's white-water season, and rafting trips run down the lower section of the Stehekin River. Along the way take in views of cottonwood and pine forests, glimpses of Yawning Glacier on Magic Mountain, and placid vistas of Lake Chelan.

North Cascades River Expeditions

WHITE-WATER RAFTING | From April to September, North Cascades River Expeditions offers whitewater rafting on the Upper Skagit and other area rivers. November to early March, you can take an easy paddle through the Skagit River Bald Eagle Natural Area for great opportunities to photograph these majestic birds in their habitat. ☎ 800/634–8433 ⊕ www. riverexpeditions.com ✉ From $60.

Orion River Expeditions

WHITE-WATER RAFTING | FAMILY | Family-oriented floats are offered in August on the Skagit River for ages six and up. More lively white-water tours run on other area rivers April to September. ☎ 509/548–1401, 509/881–9556 ⊕ www.orionexp. com ✉ From $90.

Ross Lake Resort

BOATING | From mid-June through October, the resort rents motorboats, kayaks, and canoes. It also operates a water taxi taking hikers to and from eight trailheads. The taxi is available by reservation and can accommodate up to six passengers. ⊠ *503 Diablo St., Rockport* ☎ *206/486–3751* ⊕ *www.rosslakeresort.com.*

CAMPING

Tent campers can choose between forest sites, riverside spots, lake grounds, or meadow spreads encircled by mountains. Camping here is as easy or challenging as you want to make it; some campgrounds are a short walk from ranger stations, while others are miles from the highway. Note that many remote campsites, particularly those around Stehekin, lack road access, so you have to hike, boat, or ride a horse to reach them. Most don't accept reservations, and spots fill up quickly May through September. If there's no ranger on-site, you can often sign yourself in—and always check in at a ranger station before you set out overnight. Note that some areas are occasionally closed due to flooding, forest fires, or other factors.

Lake Chelan National Recreation Area.

Many backcountry camping areas are accessible via park shuttles or boat. All require a free backcountry permit. Purple Point, the most popular campground due to its quick access to Stehekin Landing, has six tent sites, bear boxes, and nearby road access. ⊠ *Stehekin Landing, Stehekin* ☎ *509/699–2080.*

Ross Lake National Recreation Area. The

National Park Service maintains three upper Skagit Valley campgrounds; some are open fully or partially year round, with the rest open mid-May through mid-October. You can make reservations for the seasonal Newhalem Creek Campground, which has 107 sites (some suitable for RVs of up to 45 feet), drinking water, and flush toilets but not showers or hookups. Ten of the 93 sites in the South Loop of the Colonial Creek Campground are open year-round. Reservations are accepted here but not at the campground's North Loop, which has 42 seasonal sites. Both sections can accommodate tents and small RVs (no hookups or showers) and have flush toilets and drinking water. The main Goodell Creek Campground is open year round and has 19 sites (some suitable for small RVs, though no hookups or showers), pit toilets, and drinking water (seasonal). Aside from a few group sites, camping here is first come, first served. ⊠ *North Cascades National Park* ☎ *877/444–6700* ⊕ *recreation.gov.*

EDUCATIONAL OFFERINGS

In summer, rangers conduct programs at the visitor centers, where you also can find exhibits and other park information. At the North Cascades Visitor Center in Newhalem you can learn about rain-forest ecology, while at the Golden West Visitor Center in Stehekin there's an arts-and-crafts gallery as well as audiovisual and children's programs. Check center bulletin boards for schedules.

Seattle City Light Information and Tour Center

TOUR—SIGHT | Based at a history museum that has exhibits about the introduction of electric power through the Cascade ranges, Seattle's public electric company offers tours and programs during summer. Several trails start at the building, and the group offers sightseeing excursions on Diablo Lake during the summer in partnership with the North Cascades Institute, Thursday through Monday lunch cruises by advance reservation, and afternoon cruises Friday through Sunday. The boat tour includes a visit to the Diablo Dam. Other tours include a visit to the powerhouse (with picnic lunch) on weekends, and an evening dinner and guided walk to Ladder Creek Falls on Thursday and Friday. Free 45-minute walking tours through the historic town of Newhalem are offered daily from July through Labor Day. ⊠ *Milepost 120, North Cascades Hwy.,*

Newhalem ☎ 360/854–2589 ⊕ www. skagittours.com ✉ Walking tour free, other tours from $19 ⊗ Closed Oct.–Apr.

HIKING

⚠ **Do not approach the black bears that are often sighted along trails in the summer. Back away carefully, and report sightings to the Golden West Visitor Center.** Cougars, which are shy of humans and well aware of their presence, are rarely sighted in this region. Still, keep kids close, and don't let them run too far ahead or lag behind on a trail. If you do spot a cougar, pick up children, have the whole group stand close together, and make yourself look as large as possible.

HORSEBACK RIDING

Many hiking trails and backwoods paths are also popular horseback-riding routes, particularly around the park's southern fringes.

Stehekin Outfitters

HORSEBACK RIDING | Since 1947, the Courtney family has been guiding adventures in the Stehekin Valley. Departing from Stehekin Valley Ranch, 2½-hour horseback trips head to Howard Lake, while full-day rides (lunch included) take you to Bridge Creek. Stehekin Outfitters also offers tent rentals at two local campgrounds and multiday hiking adventures from June to mid-September. ✉ *North Cascades National Park ☎ 509/682–7742 ⊕ stehekinoutfitters.com ✉ From $95.*

KAYAKING

The park's tangles of waterways offer access to remote areas inaccessible by road or trail; here are some of the most pristine and secluded mountain scenes on the continent. Bring your own kayak, and you can launch from any boat ramp or beach; otherwise, companies in several nearby towns offer kayak and canoe rentals, portage, and tours. The upper basin of Lake Chelan (at the park's southern end) and Ross Lake (at the northern edge of the park) are two well-known kayaking expanses, but there are dozens of smaller lakes and creeks in between. The Stehekin River also provides many kayaking possibilities.

Ross Lake Resort

BOATING | The resort, open mid-June to October, rents kayaks, motor boats, canoes, and fishing equipment, and offers a water taxi and portage service for exploring Ross Lake. The resort is not accessible by road. ✉ *503 Diablo St., Rockport ☎ 206/486–3751 ⊕ www. rosslakeresort.com.*

Stehekin Valley Ranch

KAYAKING | Kayak tours of the upper estuary of Lake Chelan are offered every morning during the summer. ✉ *Stehekin Valley Rd., Stehekin ✛ 3½ miles from Stehekin Landing ☎ 509/682–4677 ⊕ www.stehekinvalleyranch.com ✉ $50.*

SKIING

Mt. Baker, just off the park's far northwest corner, is one of the Northwest's premier skiing, snowboarding, and snowshoeing regions—the area set a world record for most snow in a single season during the winter of 1998–99 (1,140 inches).

Stehekin is another base for winter sports. The Stehekin Valley alone has 20 miles of trails; some of the most popular are around Buckner Orchard, Coon Lake, and the Courtney Ranch (Cascade Corrals).

Mt. Baker Ski Area

SNOW SPORTS | This is the closest winter-sports area, with facilities for downhill and cross-country skiing, snowboarding, and other recreational ventures. The main base is the town of Glacier, 17 miles west of the slopes, where lodging is available. Equipment rental and food service are onsite. **Facilities:** 38 trails; 1,000 acres; 1,500-foot vertical drop; 10 lifts (8 quad chairs, 2 rope tows). ✉ *Hwy. 542, Glacier ✛ 52 miles east of Bellingham ☎ 360/734–6771, 360/671–0211 for snow reports ⊕ www.mtbaker.us ✉ Lift ticket: weekdays $62, weekends and holidays $69.*

Nearby Towns

Heading into North Cascades National Park from Seattle on Interstate 5 to Highway 2, **Sedro-Woolley** (pronounced "*see*-droh *wool*-lee") is the first main town you encounter. A former logging and steel-mill base settled by North Carolina pioneers, the settlement still has a 19th-century ambience throughout its rustic downtown area. It's also home to the North Cascades National Park Headquarters. From here, it's about 40 miles to the park's western edges. Along the way, you can stop for supplies in tiny Concrete, about 20 miles from the park along Highway 20. **Marblemount** is 10 miles farther east, about 12 miles west of the North Cascades Visitor Center. It's another atmospheric former timber settlement nestled in the mountain foothills, and its growing collection of motels, cafés, and tour outfitters draws outdoors enthusiasts each summer.

The village of **Mazama,** in the Methow Valley, is the closest town to the park's eastern entrance and the first place you can stop for gas and food when coming down the mountain from the west. It's about 24 miles from Washington Pass. **Winthrop,** a relaxed, riverside, rodeo town—complete with clapboard cafés and five-and-dime charm—is about 20 minutes east of Mazama. This is also an outdoor-recreation base. Less than 10 miles southeast of Winthrop, the tiny town of **Twisp** is settled in the farmlands and orchards, its streets lined with a few small lodgings and eateries. The resort town of **Chelan,** nestled around its serene namesake lake, lies about 60 miles due south of Winthrop along Highway 153.

Sedro-Woolley

5 miles east of Interstate 5 (Exit 232).

On its way east from Interstate 5, Highway 20 skirts Burlington and Sedro-Woolley, the latter a former mill and logging town now considered the gateway to the Cascades. It's also home to the national park headquarters.

GETTING HERE AND AROUND
Sedro-Woolley is roughly 1½ hours from Seattle via Interstate 5 north to Burlington (Exit 230), then 5 miles east via Highway 20.

Sights

VISITOR CENTERS
North Cascades Park & Forest Information Center
INFO CENTER | This is the park's major administrative center and the place to pick up passes, permits, and information about current conditions. ⊠ *810 Rte. 20, Sedro-Woolley* ☎ *360/854–7200* ⊕ *www. nps.gov/noca/planyourvisit/visitorcenters. htm* ⊘ *Closed weekends and federal holidays Oct.–mid-May.*

Marblemount

40 miles east of Sedro-Woolley.

Like Sedro-Woolley, Marblemount is a former logging town now dependent on outdoor recreation for its fortunes. Anglers, campers, hikers, bird-watchers, and hunters come and go from the town's collection of motels, cafés, and stores, while day-trippers head in for sips at the area's small wineries.

GETTING HERE AND AROUND
Marblemount is about two hours northeast of Seattle. It can be reached via Interstate 5 north to Burlington, then east past Sedro-Woolley on Highway 20. An alternate route is to take the exit from

Interstate 5 to Arlington/Darrington and proceed on Highway 530 until it reaches Highway 20, then continue east.

Sights

Skagit River Bald Eagle Interpretive Center
TOUR—SIGHT | Open on weekends in December and January to highlight the winter migration of bald eagles, the center offers guided hikes and educational presentations about the Skagit ecosystem. ✉ *52809 Rockport Park Rd., Rockport* ☎ *306/853–7626* 🌐 *www.skagiteagle.org*.

Wilderness Information Center
INFO CENTER | The main stop to secure backcountry and climbing permits for North Cascades National Park and the Lake Chelan and Ross Lake recreational areas, this office has maps, a bookshop, and nature exhibits. If you arrive after hours or during winter, there's a self-register permit stop outside. ✉ *7280 Ranger Station Rd., Marblemount* ✣ *Off milepost 105.9, N. Cascades Hwy.* ☎ *360/854–7245* 🌐 *www.nps.gov/noca/planyourvisit/visitor-centers.htm* ⏲ *Closed Oct.–mid-May.*

Restaurants

5B's Bakery and Eatery
$$ | **BAKERY** | **FAMILY** | If you need a handy stop for breakfast or lunch, or takeout provisions for a picnic in the North Cascades, this gluten-free bakery featuring tasty, made-from-scratch baked goods and hearty meals is definitely worth a quick detour off the highway between Sedro-Woolley and Marblemount. The breakfast menu lists the usual quiches, hot cakes, and waffles, along with three-potato hash (with eggs, corned beef, veggies, or andouille sausage). **Known for:** gluten-free pastries, cookies, and breads; plenty of takeout options; locally sourced ingredients. [$] *Average main: $13* ✉ *45597 Main St., Concrete* ✣ *16 miles west of Marblemount* ☎ *360/853–8700* 🌐 *www.5bsbakery.com* ⏲ *Closed Tues.*

Mazama

47 miles east of North Cascades National Park west entrance.

The closest village east of the national park, Mazama is popular with mountaineers, cross-country skiers, and other visitors wanting more secluded lodging options than nearby Winthrop.

GETTING HERE AND AROUND

Mazama is about 3½ hours from Seattle via Interstate 5 and the North Cascades Scenic Highway (when it's open); it's about 20 minutes west of Winthrop.

Hotels

★ **Freestone Inn**
$$$ | **RESORT** | **FAMILY** | At the heart of the 120-acre, historic Wilson Ranch, amid more than 2 million acres of forest, this upscale mountain retreat embraces the pioneer spirit in spacious rooms, suites, and cabins snuggled up to Early Winters Creek. **Pros:** two-story river-rock fireplace highlights the great room; groomed trails are used for year-round recreation; proximity to North Cascades National Park. **Cons:** limited cell phone and Wi-Fi service; amenities limited in shoulder season; cabins can be quite rustic. [$] *Rooms from: $179* ✉ *31 Early Winters Dr., Mazama* ☎ *509/996–3906, 800/639–3809* 🌐 *www.freestoneinn.com* 🛏 *31 rooms* 🍴 *Free Breakfast.*

Mazama Country Inn
$$ | **B&B/INN** | Ideal as a base for outdoor-recreation enthusiasts, the inn offers clean, no-frills accommodations and nearby access to the Pasayten Wilderness and North Cascades National Park. **Pros:** inclusive meal option available in winter; off-season specials; rooms very clean. **Cons:** no TV; basic rooms are small; pets allowed in cabins only. [$] *Rooms from: $145* ✉ *15 Country Rd., Mazama* ☎ *800/843–7951, 509/996–2681* 🌐 *www.mazamacountryinn.com* 🛏 *18 rooms* 🍴 *No meals.*

Shopping

★ Mazama Store

GIFTS/SOUVENIRS | At this legendary, family-run, general store in tiny Mazama, the eastern gateway to North Cascades National Park, you'll find array of both practical and whimsical goods. Think organic soaps, outdoor gear (across the courtyard in the related Goat's Beard Mountain Supplies shop), and interesting gourmet snacks. You can also pick up espresso drinks, sweets, and sandwiches in the in-house bakery. ⊠ *50 Lost River Rd., Mazama* ☎ *509/996–2855* ⊕ *www.themazamastore.com*.

Winthrop

153 miles east of Bellingham, 240 miles northeast of Seattle.

As an eastern gateway to North Cascades National Park, Winthrop is an outdoor mecca with amazing hiking, mountain biking, rock climbing, and fishing, as well as cross-country skiing along the 120-mile Methow Trails network in winter. Methow Valley was historically a favorite gathering place for indigenous tribes, who dug the plentiful and nutritious bulbs and hunted deer while their horses fattened on the tall native grasses. Pioneering settlers began to arrive in the 1800s, when this burgeoning riverside settlement grew into a cattle-ranching town whose residents inspired some of Owen Wister's colorful characters in his novel *The Virginian*. In 1972, spurred by Bavarian theme developments in the nearby town of Leavenworth, Winthrop business owners enacted a plan to market the town's Old West feel, and many of the original, turn-of-the-20th-century buildings were restored or given vintage facades. Pedestrian bridges cross the Chewuch and Methow rivers on either side of this village's bustling commercial district, and from viewing platforms on both bridges, you can watch salmon spawn in May and June.

GETTING HERE AND AROUND

When the North Cascades Scenic Highway is open, Winthrop can be reached via that scenic route; it takes about 3¾ hours from Seattle. The rest of the year, it will take about an extra hour via Stevens Pass (U.S. 2) or Snoqualmie Pass (Interstate 90 then Highway 970 to Highway 2) to Wenatchee, then north via Highways 97, 153, and 20. From Spokane, Winthrop is about 3½ hours west via Highway 2, then Highways 174, 17, 97, 153, and 20.

VISITOR INFORMATION Winthrop Chamber of Commerce. ⊠ *202 Hwy. 20, Winthrop* ☎ *509/996–2125* ⊕ *www.winthropwashington.com*.

◉ Sights

Shafer Historical Museum

HISTORIC SITE | The museum is made up of several downtown buildings that nod to Winthrop's colorful mining and ranching past, including "the castle," a late-19th-century log house built by one of the town's founding fathers. Other structures include a country store, print shop, school house, women's dress shop, and an open-air display of vintage mining equipment. Although you can go inside the buildings in summer only, the grounds alone are worth a stroll and are open year-round. ⊠ *285 Castle Ave., Winthrop* ☎ *509/380–9911* ⊕ *www.shafermuseum.org* ⊠ *$5 donation suggested* ☉ *Buildings closed early Sept.–late May.*

🍴 Restaurants

★ Arrowleaf Bistro

$$$$ | **PACIFIC NORTHWEST** | Locally sourced farm-to-table meals are the draw in this airy, casually elegant restaurant on the edge of downtown Winthrop. Notable examples of the deftly plated fare you might find here include parsnip bisque with curry oil, wild boar Bolognese, and smoked duck breast with Methow huckleberry sauce. **Known for:** great happy-hour deals on craft cocktails; nightly sustainable-seafood special; sleek but unpretentious dining room. $ *Average main: $31* ✉ *207 White Ave., Winthrop* ☎ *509/996–3919* ⊕ *www.arrowleafbistro. com* ⊗ *Closed Mon. and Tues. No lunch.*

★ Dining Room at Sun Mountain Lodge

$$$$ | PACIFIC NORTHWEST | A sylvan hilltop overlooking the Methow Valley sets the scene for an extraordinary dining experience featuring upscale Pacific Northwest cuisine with local and often organic ingredients. Exquisite flavors match the artful presentation and elegant yet unpretentious lodgelike atmosphere. **Known for:** sophisticated Pacific Northwest fare; sweeping mountain views; extensive wine list. $ *Average main: $36* ✉ *604 Patterson Lake Rd., Winthrop* ☎ *509/996–4707, 800/572–0493* ⊕ *www. sunmountainlodge.com/dining* ⊗ *Limited hrs in winter and spring. No lunch.*

Methow Valley Ciderhouse

$$ | AMERICAN | This chatter-filled, wood-paneled ciderhouse and taproom on the road to North Cascades National Park stands out for both its bright, crisp ciders and its elevated pub grub. Tuck into a plate of baby back ribs, Thai chicken sausage, or pulled-pork pizza, and consider a sampler of ciders—all of these sippers are produced with apples and other fruit grown in the immediate vicinity. **Known for:** mountain views from the patio; elevated comfort food; laid-back atmosphere. $ *Average main: $12* ✉ *28 Hwy. 20, Winthrop* ☎ *509/341–4354* ⊕ *www.methowvalleyciderhouse.com* ⊗ *Closed Wed.*

Old Schoolhouse

$$ | AMERICAN | Located in a long red building designed to resemble an old-time, one-room schoolhouse, this craft brewpub sits between the town's main drag and the Chewuch River. While waiting for a burger or a bowl of chili, sip an Epiphany Pale, Hooligan Stout, or Ruud Awakening IPA. **Known for:** breezy rear deck is popular in summer; festive atmosphere; hearty pub grub. $ *Average main: $14* ✉ *155*

Riverside Ave., Winthrop ☎ *509/996–3183* ⊕ *www.oldschoolhousebrewery.com* ⊗ *No lunch Mon.–Thurs.*

☕ Coffee and Quick Bites

Sheri's Sweet Shoppe

$ | AMERICAN | FAMILY | Tucked into this Wild West–style clapboard building is a haven of treats: myriad candy bins, boxes of chocolate bars, and—behind the glass case—all kinds of house-made chocolates and fudge. Customers rave about the cinnamon rolls and pastries. **Known for:** house-made ice cream, fudge, and chocolates; delectable cinnamon rolls; hand-dipped caramel apples. $ *Average main: $5* ✉ *207 Riverside Ave., Winthrop* ☎ *509/996–3834* ⊕ *www.sherissweet-shoppe.com* ⊗ *Closed Jan.–mid-Apr. and weekdays in Nov. and Dec.*

🛏 Hotels

Mt. Gardner Inn

$$ | HOTEL | With great views of the mountains to the west, this small hotel less than a mile from Winthrop's funky downtown sits just across Highway 20 from the scenic Methow River. **Pros:** close to several appealing restaurants; reasonable rates; friendly, thoughtful service. **Cons:** least expensive rooms are close to slightly busy road; two-night minimum stay on weekends; no breakfast. $ *Rooms from: $119* ✉ *611 Hwy. 20, Winthrop* ☎ *509/996–2000* ⊕ *www.mtgardnerinn. com* 🛏 *11 rooms* ⊗ *No meals.*

★ River's Edge Resort

$$ | B&B/INN | FAMILY | With an enviable location overlooking the Chewuch River and just a stone's throw from Winthrop's quirky shops and eateries, this small compound of one- to three-bedroom cabins with kitchens—and in most cases hot tubs and river views—is a terrific find and a great value. **Pros:** spacious accommodations with kitchens and living rooms; steps from village dining and shopping; great for families and groups. **Cons:** in the

center of a sometimes busy village; two-night minimum stay on many weekends; no pets. $ *Rooms from: $140* ⊠ *115 Riverside Ave., Winthrop* ☎ *509/996–8000* ⊕ *www.riversedgewinthrop.com* ⇄ *6 cabins* ⦿ *No meals.*

River Run Inn

$$$ | B&B/INN | FAMILY | The rooms and cabins are comfortable but not fancy here, but the inn's riverfront location and amenities—including picnic tables, hammocks, a playground, lawn games, and an indoor pool—make it a popular place to stay. **Pros:** free use of bikes; serene riverfront setting; free DVD library. **Cons:** hot tub is only big enough for a few people; bathrooms are small; just a few pet-friendly rooms. $ *Rooms from: $170* ⊠ *27 Rader Rd., Winthrop* ☎ *800/757–2709, 509/996–2173* ⊕ *www.riverrun-inn.com* ⇄ *16 rooms (plus 1 house)* ⦿ *No meals.*

Sun Mountain Lodge

$$$$ | RESORT | The stunning North Cascades and all its attractions are the stars of this outdoor-oriented resort replete with luxurious accommodations, spectacular mountain views, and a range of activities that make it a year-round destination, whether the peaks are covered in snow or wildflowers. **Pros:** stunning setting with panoramic views; a wide array of outdoor activities year-round; warm hospitality and award-winning dining. **Cons:** limited cell service; roundabout route from Seattle in winter; isolated from town. $ *Rooms from: $287* ⊠ *604 Patterson Lake Rd., Winthrop* ☎ *509/996–2211, 800/572–0493* ⊕ *www.sunmountainlodge.com* ⇄ *112 rooms* ⦿ *Free Breakfast.*

Chelan

60 miles south of Winthrop, 180 miles east of Seattle.

Lake Chelan, a sinewy, 50½-mile-long fjord—Washington's deepest lake—works its way from the town of Chelan (pronounced shuh- **lan**), at its south end, to Stehekin, on the northwest shore and located within North Cascades National Park. The surrounding mountains rise from a height of about 4,000 feet near Chelan to 8,000 and 9,000 feet closer to Stehekin—just south of the lake, 9,511-foot Bonanza Peak is Washington's tallest nonvolcanic peak. The scenery around the region is unparalleled, the lake's flat blue water encircled by plunging gorges, with a vista of snow-capped mountains beyond. The region serves as a favorite lake resort of western Washingtonians, with most visitors staying in vacation homes and condo rentals, although there are a few casual resorts and hotels.

A growing number of acclaimed wineries dot the warmer eastern shores, where temperatures often soar above 100° in summer. Chelan is one of the state's newest American Viticultural Areas, and has more than two-dozen tasting rooms, located both in the town of Chelan and in the village of Manson.

GETTING HERE AND AROUND

From Seattle, allow between 3½ and 4 hours to reach Chelan by either U.S. 2 or Interstate 90, then north via Highway 97.

VISITOR INFORMATION Lake Chelan Chamber of Commerce & Visitor Center.

⊠ *216 E. Woodin Ave., Chelan* ☎ *509/682–3503* ⊕ *www.lakechelan.com.*

● Sights

Benson Vineyards

WINERY/DISTILLERY | The excellent wine is part of the reason to drop by this vineyard hugging a hillside on the north shore of the lake. You'll also want to soak up the sweeping Lake Chelan and mountain views, both from the tasting room—with its large south-facing windows—and the terrace. ✉ *754 Winesap Ave., Manson* ☎ *509/687–0313* ⊕ *www.bensonvineyards.com.*

★ Hard Row to Hoe Vineyards

WINERY/DISTILLERY | One of Chelan's several acclaimed operations with female winemakers, this upper North Shore winery with a bordello-inspired tasting has a helpful staff and a pretty outdoor picnic area. The winery's playful approach extends to the interesting lineup, from spicy Gewürztraminer to a creamy yet lively *méthode champenoise* Brut rosé to a velvety red blend aptly called "The Coquette." There's also an aromatic Vermouth aperitif that's a perfect match with light tapas. ✉ *300 Ivan Morse Rd., Manson* ☎ *509/687–3000* ⊕ *www.hardrow.com.*

★ Karma Vineyards

WINERY/DISTILLERY | With a gracious patio, koi pond, and fireplace overlooking the lake as well as a dark and inviting wine cave, this first-rate winery on the South Shore stands out for its superb Brut de Brut Champagne-style wine as well as for its Alsatian grapes, including Gewürztraminer and Riesling (and a pretty solid Pinot Noir). ✉ *1681 S. Lakeshore Rd., Chelan* ☎ *509/682–5538* ⊕ *www.goodkarmawines.com* ⊙ *Closed Mon.–Wed.*

★ Lake Chelan

BODY OF WATER | Tremendously popular in summer, this narrow, 50-mile-long fjord—Washington's largest natural lake—offers striking scenery year-round. The views include sparkling blue water with snowcapped peaks in the distance. The lake offers swimming, boating, fishing, and a chance to soak up the sun. By road, the only access to the shore is its southeastern end, but you can explore the rest of the lake by boat. ✉ *U.S. 97A, Chelan.*

Lake Chelan State Park

NATIONAL/STATE PARK | On the lake's less crowded southwest shore, 9 miles northwest of Chelan, this 127-acre park with 6,000 feet of shoreline is a favorite hangout for soaking up sunshine and accessing the water. There are docks, a boat ramp, campsites, boat rentals, food service, and plenty of picnic areas. ✉ *7544 S. Lakeshore Rd., Chelan* ☎ *509/687–3710* ⊕ *www.parks.wa.gov* ⊜ *$10 parking.*

Nefarious Cellars

WINERY/DISTILLERY | An intimate boutique winery on the South Shore with a devoted—and growing—following, especially for its compelling blends, like the bright and zesty off-dry Consequence (Sauvignon Blanc, Pinot Grigio, and Riesling) and the classic Rhône red, called RX. This estate with sweeping lake vistas also rents out a stunning two-bedroom guesthouse. ✉ *495 S. Lakeshore Rd., Chelan* ☎ *509/682–9505* ⊕ *www.nefariouscellars.com* ⊙ *Closed weekdays.*

Wapato Point Cellars

WINERY/DISTILLERY | Home to the popular Winemaker's Grill restaurant, which serves dinner daily, this well-respected operation with a tasting room and wine bar is in the small North Shore town of Manson and makes a great stop whether you're thirsty, hungry, or both. In warm weather, have a seat on the patio and drink up the mountain views. ✉ *200 S. Quetilquasoon Rd., Manson* ☎ *509/687–4000* ⊕ *www.wapatopointcellars.com.*

⊕ Restaurants

The Bistro at Lake Chelan

$$$ | **ECLECTIC** | This new bistro, in a historic, downtown brick house, has the largest outdoor seating area in town and features a small but diverse menu for lunch and dinner. Dishes change seasonally, with several salads, steaks, burgers, pasta, and chicken pot pie during the cooler months. **Known for:** expansive outdoor seating; nice selection of drinks, including pitchers of champagne; tasty Sunday brunch options. $ *Average main: $22* ⊠ *303 E. Wapato Ave., Chelan* ☎ *509/699–7233* ⊕ *www. chelanbistro.com* ⊗ *Closed Mon. and Tues., brunch only on Sun.*

★ Riverwalk Inn & Cafe

$$ | **AMERICAN** | The cheerful café at this budget-minded downtown inn is open only seasonally, but it's one of the very best spots in the area for lunch and, especially, breakfast. Bagel sandwiches, smashed avocado on sage bread, a choice of four scrambles, and several kinds of burrito wraps are the perfect sustenance for a day of hiking, boating, or wine-touring. **Known for:** hearty yet healthy breakfast fare; Blue Star coffee served here; good list of local wines. $ *Average main: $13* ⊠ *204 E. Wapato Ave., Chelan* ☎ *509/682–2627* ⊕ *www. riverwalkinnchelan.com* ⊗ *Closed Jan.– Mar. and Mon.–Wed. No dinner.*

Vin du Lac Winery

$$$$ | **BISTRO** | Head to this north shore winery and bistro for wine tasting and dining on the terrace overlooking the Spaders Bay section of Lake Chelan. The lunch and dinner menus feature herbs and produce grown in Vin du Lac's own gardens, as well as meats, cheeses, and seafood sourced regionally as much as possible. **Known for:** tasting room with house-made wines; pretty patio with lake views; live music on Saturday. $ *Average main: $36* ⊠ *105 Hwy. 150, Chelan* ☎ *509/682–2882* ⊕ *www.vindulac.com* ⊗ *Closed Mon. and Tues.*

Hotels

Campbell's Resort

$$$$ | **RESORT** | **FAMILY** | Each room at this sprawling resort—a family favorite since 1901 and situated on beautifully landscaped grounds alongside a marina and a pristine, 1,200-foot, Lake Chelan

beach—has balcony views of the lake or mountains; some rooms also have a kitchen or fireplace. **Pros:** short walk to dining and shopping; large private beach; lake and mountain views. **Cons:** pricey in summer; lots of families and groups; needs some updating. $ *Rooms from: $285* ⊠ *104 W. Woodin Ave., Chelan* ☎ *509/682–2561, 800/553–8225* ⊕ *www.campbellsresort. com* ⇝ *170 rooms* ◎ *No meals.*

Howard's on the River

$$$ | **HOTEL** | Located on a breathtaking bend in the Columbia River about 20 miles north of Chelan, this three-story, motel-style property has handsome rooms, all of them with fireplaces and generously sized balconies with water views. **Pros:** dazzling river views from rooms and patios; good base for exploring Methow Valley; short walk to a couple of good restaurants. **Cons:** room decor isn't especially memorable; not much to do in the tiny town of Pateros; can get a little pricey on summer weekends. $ *Rooms from: $180* ⊠ *233 Lakeshore Dr., Pateros* ☎ *509/923–9555* ⊕ *www. howardsontheriver.com* ⇝ *29 rooms* ◎ *Free Breakfast.*

Lakeside Lodge & Suites

$$$$ | **HOTEL** | **FAMILY** | In addition to family friendly facilities (including two pools and two hot tubs), this four-story resort, adjacent to Lakeside Park and a couple miles from downtown Chelan, has comfortable, well-equipped rooms that all face the lake and take advantage of spectacular sunsets. **Pros:** lake views; next to park with beach, playground, and sports courts; hot breakfast included. **Cons:** some room views are blocked by a giant tree; rooms open to outside (no halls); no on-site restaurant. $ *Rooms from: $260* ⊠ *2312 W. Woodin Ave., Chelan* ☎ *800/468–2781, 509/682–4396* ⊕ *www. lakesidelodgeandsuites.com* ⇝ *93 rooms* ◎ *Free Breakfast.*

OLYMPIC NATIONAL PARK

Updated by
Shelley Arenas

WASHINGTON

🏕 Camping	🛏 Hotels	🤾 Activities	👁 Scenery	👥 Crowds
★★★★★	★★★★★	★★★★★	★★★★★	★★★☆☆

WELCOME TO
OLYMPIC NATIONAL PARK

TOP REASONS TO GO

★ **Exotic rain forest:** A rain forest in the Pacific Northwest? Indeed, Olympic National Park is one of the few places in the world with this unique temperate landscape.

★ **Beachcombing:** Miles of rugged, spectacular coastline hemmed with sea stacks and tidal pools edge the driftwood-strewn shores of the Olympic Peninsula.

★ **Nature's hot tubs:** A dip in Sol Duc's natural geothermal mineral pools offers a secluded spa experience in the wooded heart of the park.

★ **Lofty vistas:** The hardy can hike up meadowed foothill trails or climb the frosty peaks throughout the Olympics—or just drive up to Hurricane Ridge for endless views.

★ **A sense of history:** Native American history is key to this region, where eight tribes have traditional ties to the park lands—there's 12,000 years of history to explore.

1 Coastal Olympic. The ocean has carved some of the park's most memorable scenes into the rugged coastline, and provided the beaches and tide pools with sea stars, crabs, and anemones.

2 Rain Forests. Centered on the Hoh, Queets, and Quinault river valleys, this is the region's most unique landscape: Douglas firs and Sitka spruces coexist with fern- and moss-draped cedars, maples, and alders.

3 Lake Crescent and Sol Duc Valley. At the park's northern flank, old-growth forests frame stunning Lake Crescent, the state's second-deepest lake. Nearby, the Sol Duc Valley beckons with waterfalls, hot springs, the salmon-filled Sol Duc River, and hiking trails.

4 Mountains. Craggy gray peaks and snow-covered summits dominate the skyline, while low-level foliage and wildflower meadows make for excellent plateau hiking, but temperatures can be brisk; some roads are closed in winter.

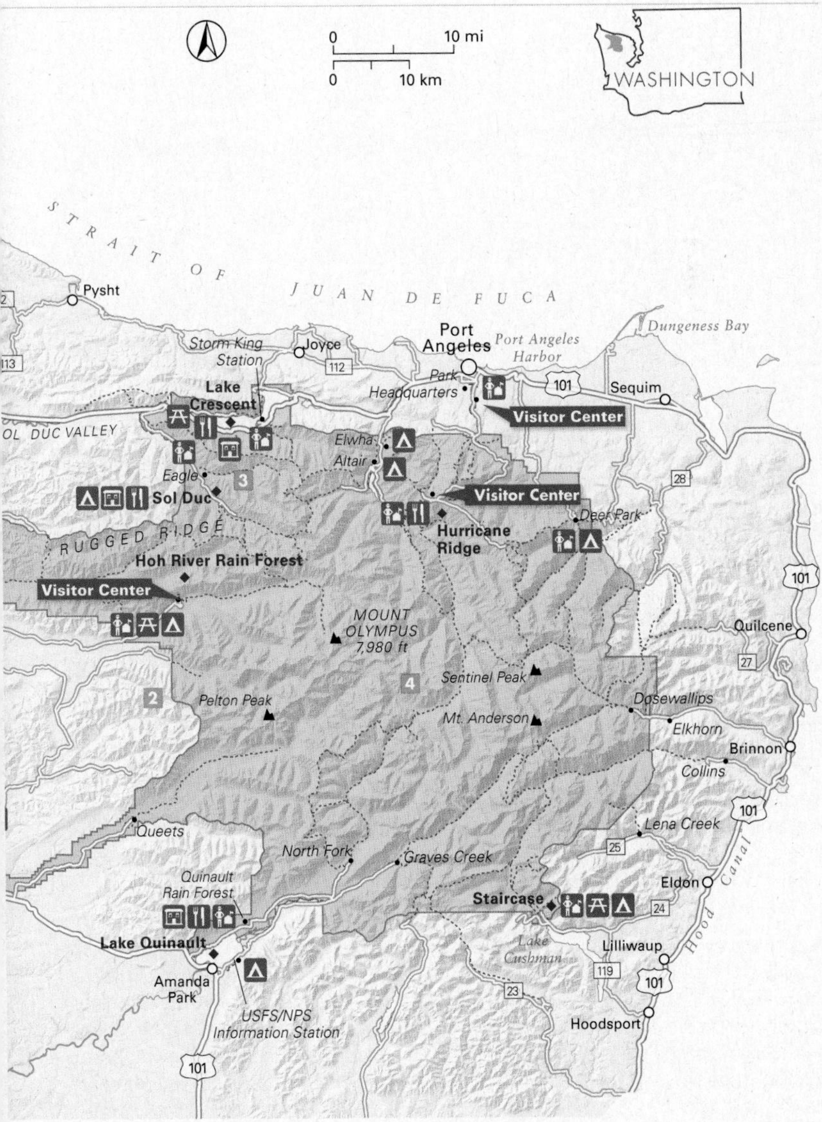

0   10 mi

0   10 km

WASHINGTON

STRAIT   OF   JUAN   DE   FUCA

Pysht

Dungeness Bay

Storm King Station

Joyce

Port Angeles

Port Angeles Harbor

Sequim

112

113

Lake Crescent

Park Headquarters

Visitor Center

OL DUC VALLEY

Elwha

Altair

28

Eagle

Visitor Center

Sol Duc

Deer Park

RUGGED RIDGE

Hurricane Ridge

101

Hoh River Rain Forest

Visitor Center

Quilcene

MOUNT OLYMPUS 7,980 ft

27

2

Pelton Peak

4

Sentinel Peak

Dosewallips

Mt. Anderson

Elkhorn

Brinnon

Collins

Queets

North Fork

Graves Creek

Lena Creek

25

Staircase

Eldon

24

Lake Quinault

Quinault Rain Forest

Lake Cushman

Lilliwaup

Amanda Park

119

101

USFS/NPS Information Station

23

Hoodsport

101

Hood Canal

Edged on all sides by water, the forested landscape is remote and pristine, and works its way around the sharpened ridges of the snowcapped Olympic Mountains. Big lakes cut pockets of blue in the rugged blanket of pine forests. From towering trees in mossy green rain forests to sea stacks jutting from ocean shores, nature puts the awe in awesome here.

The region has been described as magical by many a visitor for more than a century, and appreciated by the Native Americans that lived here for centuries before. In the late 1800s efforts began to preserve this unique area of mountains, rain forest, coast, and the diverse flora and fauna that thrive in its environment. Responding to conservationist John Muir's encouragement to save the old growth forests, President Cleveland created the Olympic Forest Reserve in his final days in office in 1897. In 1909 President Theodore Roosevelt designated the area as the Mount Olympus National Monument, in part to protect the native elk that were later renamed in his honor and still roam in the Hoh Rain Forest.

Nearly 30 years later, another President Roosevelt (Franklin) visited the area, staying overnight at the Lake Crescent Lodge (which now has cabins named after him) and lunching at the Lake Quinault Inn. In 1938 he redesignated the federal lands as Olympic National Park. Some years later, a coastal section was added.

The park gets more than 3 million visitors annually and covers a lot of area—nearly 1,500 square miles. There are more than 600 miles of trails, 168 miles of roads, 73 miles of shoreline… in other words, a lot to see and do! Most of the park's attractions are found either off U.S. Hwy. 101 or down trails that require hikes of 15 minutes or longer. The coastal beaches are linked to the highway by downhill tracks; the number of cars parked alongside the road at the start of the paths indicates how crowded the beach will be.

Five in-park lodging options—including two historic lodges on sparkling lakes and one perched above the Pacific Ocean—make it possible to take your time and really immerse yourself in this wondrous place, while gazing out at the same views that have been inspiring awe for generations. It can be an exercise in patience to try and book a room during the high season at these very popular lodges, where some families return every year. Plan ahead, visit midweek, or consider a spring or fall stay (especially fun if you like storm-watching).

AVERAGE HIGH/LOW TEMPERATURES					
JAN.	FEB.	MAR.	APR.	MAY	JUNE
45/33	48/35	51/36	55/39	60/44	65/48
JULY	AUG.	SEPT.	OCT.	NOV.	DEC.
68/50	69/51	66/48	58/42	50/37	45/34

Planning

When to Go

Summer, with its long stretches of sun-filled days, is prime touring time for Olympic National Park. June through September are the peak months; Hurricane Ridge, the Hoh Rain Forest, Lake Crescent, and Ruby Beach are bustling by 10 am.

Late spring and early autumn are also good bets for clear weather; anytime between April and October, you'll have a good chance of fair skies. Between Thanksgiving and Easter, it's a toss-up as to which days will turn out fair; prepare for heavy clouds, rain showers, and chilly temperatures, then hope for the best.

Winter is a great time to visit if you enjoy isolation. Locals are usually the only hardy souls here during this time, except for weekend skiers heading to the snowfields around Hurricane Ridge. Many visitor facilities have limited hours or are closed from October to April, and some of the park lodgings close for the winter, too.

Getting Here and Around

You can enter the park at a number of points, but because the park is 95% wilderness, access roads do not penetrate far. The best way to get around and to see many of the park's top sights is on foot.

AIR

Seattle–Tacoma International Airport is the nearest airport to Olympic National Park. It's roughly a two-hour drive from the park.

BOAT

Ferries provide another unique (though indirect) link to the Olympic area from Seattle; contact **Washington State Ferries** (☎ 888/808–7977, 206/464–6400 ⊕ www.wsdot.wa.gov/ferries) for information.

BUS

Grays Harbor Transit runs buses Monday through Saturday from Aberdeen and Hoquiam to Amanda Park, on the west end of Lake Quinault. Jefferson Transit operates a Forks–Amanda Park route Monday through Saturday.

BUS CONTACTS Grays Harbor Transit. ☎ 360/532–2770, 800/562–9730 ⊕ www.ghtransit.com. **Jefferson Transit.** ☎ 800/371–0497, 360/385–4777 ⊕ www.jeffersontransit.com.

CAR

U.S. 101 essentially encircles the main section of Olympic National Park, and a number of roads lead from the highway into the park's mountains and toward its beaches. You can reach U.S. 101 via Interstate 5 at Olympia, via Route 12 at Aberdeen, or via Route 104 from the Washington state ferry terminals at Bainbridge or Kingston.

Olympic in One Day

Start at the **Lake Quinault Lodge** in the park's southwest corner. From here, drive a half hour into the Quinault Valley via **South Shore Road**. Tackle the forested **Graves Creek Trail**, then head up **North Shore Road** to the Quinault Rain Forest Interpretive Trail. Next, head back to U.S. 101 and drive to **Ruby Beach**, where a shoreline walk presents a breathtaking scene of sea stacks and sparkling, pink-hue sands.

Forks and its **Timber Museum** are your next stop; have lunch here, then drive 20 minutes to the beach at **La Push**. Next, head to **Lake Crescent** around the corner to the northeast, where you can rent a boat, take a swim, or enjoy a picnic next to the sparkling teal waters. Drive through **Port Angeles** to **Hurricane Ridge**; count on an hour's drive from bottom to top if there aren't too many visitors. At the ridge, explore the visitor center or hike the 3-mile loop to **Hurricane Hill**, where you can see over the entire park north to Vancouver Island and south past Mt. Olympus.

Inspiration

Robert L. Wood's *Olympic Mountains Trail Guide* is a great resource for both day hikers and those planning longer excursions.

Craig Romano's *Day Hiking Olympic Peninsula: National Park/Coastal Beaches/Southwest Washington* is a detailed guide to day hikes in and around the national park.

Rob Sandelin and Stephen Whitney's *A Field Guide to the Cascades and Olympics* is an excellent trailside reference, covering more than 500 plant and animal species found in the park.

The park's newspaper, the *Olympic Bugler*, is a seasonal guide for activities and opportunities in the park. You can pick it up at the visitor centers.

A handy online catalog of books, maps, and passes for northwest parks is available from Discover Your Northwest (● *www.discovernw.org*).

Park Essentials

ACCESSIBILITY

There are wheelchair-accessible facilities—including trails, campgrounds, and visitor centers—throughout the park; contact visitor centers for information.

ADMISSION FEES AND PERMITS

Seven-day vehicle admission is $30; an annual pass is $50. Individuals arriving on foot, bike, or motorcycle pay $15. An overnight wilderness permit, available at visitor centers and ranger stations, is $8 per person per night plus a $6 per night reservation fee. An annual wilderness camping permit costs $45. Fishing in freshwater streams and lakes within Olympic National Park does not require a Washington state fishing license; however, anglers must acquire a salmon-steelhead catch record card when fishing for those species. Ocean fishing and harvesting shellfish require licenses, which are available at sporting-goods and outdoor-supply stores.

ADMISSION HOURS

Six park entrances are open 24/7; gate kiosk hours (for buying passes) vary according to season and location, but most are staffed during daylight hours. Olympic National Park is in the Pacific time zone.

CELL PHONE RECEPTION

Note that cell reception is sketchy in wilderness areas. There are public telephones at the Olympic National Park Visitor Center, Hoh Rain Forest Visitor Center, and lodging properties within the park—Lake Crescent, Kalaloch, and Sol Duc Hot Springs. Fairholme General Store also has a phone.

Hotels

Major park resorts run from good to terrific, with generally comfortable rooms, excellent facilities, and easy access to trails, beaches, and activity centers. Midsize accommodations, like Sol Duc Hot Springs Resort, are often shockingly rustic—but remember, you're here for the park, not for the rooms.

The towns around the park have motels, hotels, and resorts for every budget. For a full beach-town vacation experience, base yourself in a home or cottage in the coastal community of Seabrook (near Pacific Beach). Sequim, Port Angeles, and Port Townsend have many attractive, friendly B&Bs, plus lots of inexpensive chain hotels and motels. Forks has mostly motels, with a few guesthouses on the fringes of town.

Hotel reviews have been shortened. For full information, visit Fodors.com.

What It Costs			
$	$$	$$$	$$$$
RESTAURANTS			
under $16	$16–$22	$23–$30	over $30
HOTELS			
under $150	$150–$200	$201–$250	over $250

Restaurants

The major resorts are your best bets for eating out in the park. Each has a main restaurant, café, and/or kiosk, as well as casually upscale dinner service, with regional seafood, meat, and produce complemented by a range of microbrews and good Washington and international wines. Reservations are either recommended or required.

All Olympic National Park campgrounds have adjacent picnic areas with tables, some shelters, and restrooms, but no cooking facilities. The same is true for major visitor centers, such as Hoh Rain Forest. Drinking water is available at ranger stations, interpretive centers, and inside campgrounds.

Outside the park, small, easygoing cafés and bistros line the main thoroughfares in Sequim, Port Angeles, Port Townsend, and Forks, offering cuisine that ranges from hearty American-style fare to more eclectic local flavor. *Restaurant reviews have been shortened. For full information, visit Fodors.com.*

Visitor Information

PARK CONTACT INFORMATION Olympic National Park. ⊠ *Olympic National Park Visitor Center, 3002 Mount Angeles Rd., Port Angeles* ☎ *360/565–3130* ⊕ *www. nps.gov/olym.*

Coastal Olympic

15 miles from Forks.

Olympic National Park's coastal region showcases the powerful Pacific Ocean coastline and the unique geology created over centuries where the sea meets the shore. Some beaches are as close as a walk from a (sometimes crowded) parking lot, while others are reached via longer trails. Sea life is abundant, in tide pools and offshore. The area is also rich in history from the Native American tribes that have lived off these lands for generations.

Sights

HISTORIC SITES

La Push

BEACH—SIGHT | At the mouth of Quileute River, La Push is the tribal center of the Quileute people. In fact, the town's name is a variation on the French *la bouche,* which means "the mouth." Offshore rock spires known as sea stacks dot the coast here, and you may catch a glimpse of bald eagles nesting in the nearby cliffs. ⊠ *Rte. 110, La Push ⊹ 14 miles west of Forks* ⊕ *www.nps.gov/olym/planyourvisit/upload/mora.pdf.*

Lake Ozette

BEACH—SIGHT | The third-largest glacial impoundment in Washington anchors the coastal strip of Olympic National Park at its north end. The small town of Ozette, home to a coastal tribe, is the trailhead for two of the park's better one-day hikes. Both 3-mile trails lead over boardwalks through swampy wetland and coastal old-growth forest to the ocean shore and uncrowded beaches. ⊠ *Ozette ⊹ At end of Hoko-Ozette Rd., 26 miles southwest of Hwy. 112 near Sekiu* ☎ *360/565–3130* ⊕ *www.nps.gov/olym/planyourvisit/visiting-ozette.htm.*

PICNIC AREAS

Rialto Beach Picnic Area

LOCAL INTEREST | Relatively secluded at the end of the road from Forks, this is one of the premier day-use areas in the park's Pacific coast segment. This site has 12 picnic tables, fire grills, and vault toilets. ⊠ *Rte. 110, Forks ⊹ 14 miles west of Forks.*

SCENIC STOPS

Kalaloch

BEACH—SIGHT | With a lodge and restaurant, a huge campground, miles of coastline, and easy access from the highway, this is a popular spot. Keen-eyed beachcombers may spot sea otters just offshore. ⊠ *Hwy. 101, Kalaloch ⊹ 43 miles southwest of Forks* ☎ *360/565–3130 visitor center, 360/962–2283 ranger station* ⊕ *www.nps.gov/olym/planyourvisit/visiting-kalaloch-and-ruby-beach.htm.*

★ Ruby Beach

BEACH—SIGHT | The northernmost and arguably the most breathtaking of Olympic National Park's Kalaloch area beaches, this wild and windswept swath of shoreline is named for the rosy fragments of garnet that color its sands. From an evergreen-shaded bluff, a short trail winds down to the wave-beaten sands where Cedar Creek meets the ocean, and you may spy sea otters along with bald eagles, oystercatchers, cormorants, and other birdlife. Driftwood separates the woods from the sand—it's a good spot to set up a picnic blanket and watch the sun fall over the pounding surf. Up and down the coast, dramatic sea stacks and rock cairns frame the beach, which is a favorite place for beachcombers, artists, and photographers. **Amenities:** toilets. **Best for:** sunset; walking. ⊠ *U.S. 101, Kalaloch ⊹ 28 miles southwest of Forks* ⊕ *www.nps.gov/olym.*

Second and Third Beaches

BEACH—SIGHT | During low tide these flat, driftwood-strewn expanses are perfect for long afternoon strolls. Second Beach, accessed via an easy forest trail through Quileute lands, opens to a vista of the

Plants and Wildlife in Olympic

Along the high mountain slopes, hardy cedar, fir, and hemlock trees stand tough on the rugged land; the lower montane forests are filled with thickets of silver firs; and valleys stream with Douglas firs and western hemlock. The park's famous temperate rain forests are on the peninsula's western side, marked by broad western red cedars, towering red spruces, and ferns festooned with strands of mosses and patchwork lichens. This lower landscape is also home to some of the Northwest's largest trees: massive cedar and Sitka spruce near Lake Quinault can measure more than 700 inches around, and Douglas firs near the Queets and Hoh rivers are nearly as wide.

These landscapes are home to a variety of wildlife, including many large mammals and 15 creatures found nowhere else in the world. Hikers often come across Roosevelt elk, black-tailed deer, mountain goats, beavers, raccoons, skunks, opossums, and foxes; Douglas squirrels and flying squirrels populate the heights of the forest. Less common are black bears (most prevalent from May through August); wolves, bobcats, and cougars are rarely seen. Birdlife includes bald eagles, red-tailed hawks, osprey, and great horned owls. Rivers and lakes are filled with freshwater fish, while beaches hold crabs, sea stars, anemones, and other shelled creatures. Get out in a boat on the Pacific to spot seals, sea lions, and sea otters—and perhaps a pod of porpoises, orcas, or gray whales.

Beware of jellyfish around the shores—beached jellyfish can still sting. In the woods, check for ticks after every hike and after each shower. Biting nasties include black flies, horseflies, sand fleas, and the ever-present mosquitoes. Yellow jacket nests populate tree hollows along many trails; signs throughout the Hoh Rain Forest warn hikers to move quickly through these sections. If one or two chase you, remain calm and keep walking; these are just "guards" making sure you're keeping away from the hive. Poison oak is common, so familiarize yourself with its appearance. Bug repellent, sunscreen, and long pants and sleeves will go a long way toward making your experience more comfortable.

Pacific Ocean and sea stacks. Third Beach offers a 1¼-mile forest hike for a warm-up before reaching the sands. ✉ Hwy. 101 ✛ 14 miles west of Forks ☎ 360/565–3130 ⊕ www.nps.gov/olym.

TRAILS

Cape Alava Trail

TRAIL | Beginning at Ozette, this 3-mile boardwalk trail leads from the forest to wave-tossed headlands. *Moderate.* ✉ Ozette ✛ Trailhead: end of Hoko-Ozette Rd., 26 miles south of Hwy. 112, west of Sekiu ⊕ www.nps.gov/olym/planyourvisit/lake-ozette-area-brochure.htm.

🍴 Restaurants

Creekside Restaurant

$$$ | AMERICAN | A tranquil country setting and ocean views at Kaloch Lodge's restaurant create the perfect backdrop for savoring Pacific Northwest dinner specialties like grilled salmon, fresh shellfish, and elk burgers. Tempting seasonal desserts include local fruit tarts and cobblers in summer and organic winter-squash

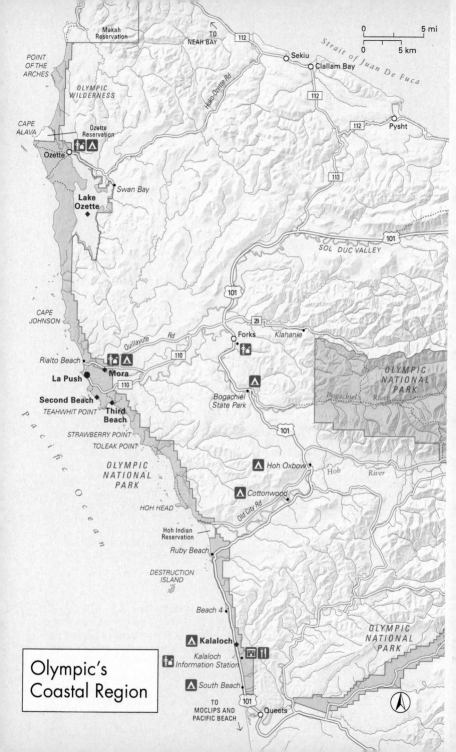

Olympic's Coastal Region

bread pudding in winter; flourless chocolate torte is enjoyed year-round. **Known for:** locally sourced food; Washington wines; stunning setting. $ *Average main: $28* ✉ *157151 Hwy. 101, Forks* ☎ *866/662–9928, 360/962–2271* ⊕ *www.thekalalochlodge.com/dine-and-shop/creekside-restaurant.*

Hotels

★ Kalaloch Lodge

$$$$ | **HOTEL** | **FAMILY** | Overlooking the Pacific, Kalaloch has cozy lodge rooms with sea views and separate cabins along the bluff. **Pros:** ranger tours; clam digging; supreme storm-watching in winter. **Cons:** no Wi-Fi and most units don't have TVs; some rooms are two blocks from main lodge; limited cell phone service. $ *Rooms from: $251* ✉ *157151 U.S. 101, Forks* ☎ *360/962–2271, 866/662–9928* ⊕ *www.thekalalochlodge.com* ⤴ *64 rooms* ⦿ *No meals.*

Rain Forests

Hoh Rain Forest is 31 miles south of Forks via Hwy. 101.

The National Park is best known as the home to one of the few temperate rain forest ecosystems in the U.S. There are actually four rain forests here; most people go to the Hoh, which has a visitor center and trails that are filled in summer with visitors from around the world. For the most serene experience, visit during the shoulder season or as early in the day as you can.

Sights

SCENIC STOPS

★ Hoh Rain Forest

FOREST | South of Forks, an 18-mile spur road links Highway 101 with this unique temperate rain forest, where spruce and hemlock trees soar to heights of more than 200 feet. Alders and big-leaf maples are so densely covered with mosses they look more like shaggy prehistoric animals than trees, and elk browse in shaded glens. Be prepared for precipitation: the region receives 140 inches or more each year. ✉ *Upper Hoh Road* ☎ *360/374–6925* ⊕ *www.nps.gov/olym/planyourvisit/visiting-the-hoh.htm.*

Lake Quinault

BODY OF WATER | This glimmering lake, 4½ miles long and 300 feet deep, is the first landmark you'll reach when driving the west-side loop of U.S. 101. The rain forest is thickest here, with moss-draped maples and alders, and towering spruce, fir, and hemlock. Enchanted Valley, high up near the Quinault River's source, is a deeply glaciated valley that's closer to the Hood Canal than to the Pacific Ocean. A scenic loop drive circles the lake and travels around a section of the Quinault River. ✉ *Hwy. 101* ⊹ *38 miles north of Hoquiam* ☎ *360/565–3131 Quinault Rain Forest ranger station* ⊕ *www.nps.gov/olym/planyourvisit/visiting-quinault.htm.*

TRAILS

★ Hoh River Trail

TRAIL | **FAMILY** | From the Hoh Visitor Center, this rain-forest jaunt takes you into the Hoh Valley, wending its way for 17½ miles alongside the river, through moss-draped maple and alder trees and past open meadows where elk roam in winter. *Easy.* ✉ *Olympic National Park* ⊹ *Trailhead: Hoh Visitor Center, 18 miles east of U.S. 101* ⊕ *www.nps.gov/olym/planyourvisit/hoh-river-trail.htm.*

VISITOR CENTERS

Hoh Rain Forest Visitor Center

INFO CENTER | Pick up park maps and pamphlets, permits, and activities lists in this busy, woodsy chalet; there's also a shop and exhibits on natural history. Several short interpretive trails and longer wilderness treks start from here. ✉ *Hoh Valley Rd., Forks* ⊹ *31 miles south of Forks* ☎ *360/374–6925* ⊕ *www.nps.gov/olym/planyourvisit/visitorcenters.htm* ⦿ *Closed Jan.–Feb., and Mon.–Thurs. off-season.*

Did You Know?

Encompassing more than 70 miles of beachfront, Olympic is one of the few national parks of the West with an ocean beach (Redwood, Channel Islands, and some of the Alaskan parks are the others). The park is therefore home to many marine animals, including sea otters, whales, sea lions, and seals.

South Shore Quinault Ranger Station
INFO CENTER | The National Forest Service's ranger station near the Lake Quinault Lodge has maps, campground information, and program listings. ✉ *353 S. Shore Rd., Quinault* ☎ *360/288–2525* 🌐 *www.fs.usda.gov/main/olympic/home* 🕒 *Closed weekends after Labor Day until Memorial Day weekend.*

Hotels

Lake Quinault Lodge
$$$ | **HOTEL** | On a lovely glacial lake in Olympic National Forest, this beautiful early-20th-century lodge complex is within walking distance of the lakeshore and hiking trails in the spectacular old-growth forest. **Pros:** boat tours of the lake are interesting; family-friendly ambience; year-round pool and sauna. **Cons:** no TV in some rooms; some units are noisy and not very private; Wi-Fi is expensive after first 30 minutes free. $ *Rooms from: $215* ✉ *345 S. Shore Rd., Quinault* ☎ *360/288–2900, 888/896–3818* 🌐 *www.olympicnationalparks.com/lodging/lake-quinault-lodge/* 🛏 *92 rooms* 🍴 *No meals.*

Lake Crescent and Sol Duc Valley

Lake Crescent is 22 miles west of Port Angeles via Hwy. 101; Sol Duc Valley is about 20 miles south of Lake Crescent via Sol Duc-Hot Springs Road.

North of the rain forest region, the sparkling blue waters of Lake Crescent and the verdant Sol Duc Valley abound with water activities and hiking trails. Historic and rustic accommodations make overnight stays in the sprawling national park convenient and memorable.

Sights

PICNIC AREAS

East Beach Picnic Area
LOCAL INTEREST | Set on a grassy meadow overlooking Lake Crescent, this popular swimming spot has six picnic tables and vault toilets. ✉ *E. Beach Rd., Port Angeles* ✣ *At far east end of Lake Crescent, off Hwy. 101, 17 miles west of Port Angeles.*

La Poel Picnic Area
LOCAL INTEREST | Tall firs lean over a tiny gravel beach at this small picnic area, which has several picnic tables and a splendid view of Pyramid Mountain across Lake Crescent. It's closed October to April. ✉ *Olympic National Park* ✣ *Off Hwy. 101, 22 miles west of Port Angeles* 🕒 *Closed mid-Oct.–mid-May.*

North Shore Picnic Area
LOCAL INTEREST | This site lies beneath Pyramid Mountain along the north shore of Lake Crescent; a steep trail leads from the eight-table picnic ground to the mountaintop. ✉ *Port Angeles* ✣ *3 miles east of Fairholm.*

SCENIC STOPS

Lake Crescent
BODY OF WATER | Visitors see Lake Crescent as Highway 101 winds along its southern shore, giving way to gorgeous views of teal waters rippling in a basin formed by Tuscan-like hills. In the evening, low bands of clouds caught between the surrounding mountains often linger over its reflective surface. ✉ *Hwy. 101* ✣ *16 miles west of Port Angeles and 28 miles northeast of Forks* ☎ *360/565–3130 visitor center* 🌐 *www.nps.gov/olym/planyourvisit/visiting-lake-crescent.htm.*

Sol Duc Valley
BODY OF WATER | Sol Duc Valley is one of those magical places where all the Northwest's virtues seem at hand: lush lowland forests, sparkling river scenes, salmon runs, and serene hiking trails. Here, the

popular Sol Duc Hot Springs area includes three attractive sulfuric pools ranging in temperature from 98°F to 104°F (admission to the pools costs $15). ✉ *Sol Duc Rd.* ✣ *South of U.S. 101, 12 miles past west end of Lake Crescent* ☎ *360/565–3130* 🌐 *www.nps.gov/olym/planyourvisit/visiting-the-sol-duc-valley.htm.*

★ Hoh Rain Forest

FOREST | South of Forks, an 18-mile spur road links Highway 101 with this unique temperate rain forest, where spruce and hemlock trees soar to heights of more than 200 feet. Alders and big-leaf maples are so densely covered with mosses they look more like shaggy prehistoric animals than trees, and elk browse in shaded glens. Be prepared for precipitation: the region receives 140 inches or more each year. ✉ *Upper Hoh Road* ☎ *360/374–6925* 🌐 *www.nps.gov/olym/planyourvisit/visiting-the-hoh.htm.*

TRAILS

Graves Creek Trail

TRAIL | This 6-mile-long moderately strenuous trail climbs from lowland rain forest to alpine territory at Sundown Pass. Due to spring floods, a fjord halfway up is often impassable in May and June. *Moderate.* ✉ *Olympic National Park* ✣ *Trailhead: end of S. Shore Rd., 23 miles east of U.S. 101* 🌐 *www.nps.gov/olym.*

★ Sol Duc River Trail

TRAIL | **FAMILY** | The 1½-mile gravel path off Sol Duc Road winds through thick Douglas fir forests toward the thundering, three-chute Sol Duc Falls. Just off the road, below a wooden platform over the Sol Duc River, you'll come across the 70-foot Salmon Cascades. In late summer and autumn, thousands of salmon negotiate 50 miles or more of treacherous waters to reach the cascades and the tamer pools near Sol Duc Hot Springs. The popular 6-mile **Lovers Lane Loop Trail** links the Sol Duc falls with the hot springs. You can continue up from the falls 5 miles to the **Appleton Pass Trail,** at 3,100 feet. From there you can hike on to the 8½-mile mark, where views at the High Divide are from 5,050 feet. *Moderate.* ✉ *Olympic National Park* ✣ *Trailhead: Sol Duc Rd., 12 miles south of U.S. 101* 🌐 *www.nps.gov/olym/planyourvisit/sol-duc-river-trail.htm.*

🍴 Restaurants

Lake Crescent Lodge

$$$ | **AMERICAN** | Part of the original 1916 lodge, the fir-paneled dining room overlooks the lake; you won't find a better spot for sunset views. Dinner entrées include wild salmon, brown butter–basted halibut, grilled steak, and roasted chicken breast; the lunch menu features elk cheeseburgers, inventive salads, and a variety of sandwiches. **Known for:** award-winning Pacific Northwest wine list; house-made lavender lemonade; lovely setting. [$] *Average main: $29* ✉ *416 Lake Crescent Rd., Port Angeles* ☎ *360/928–3211* 🌐 *www.olympicnationalparks.com/lodging/dining/lake-crescent-lodge/* ⏲ *Closed Jan.–Apr.*

The Springs Restaurant

$$$ | **AMERICAN** | The main Sol Duc Hot Springs Resort restaurant is a rustic, fir-and-cedar-paneled dining room surrounded by trees. In summer big breakfasts are turned out daily—hikers can fill up on biscuits and sage-pork-sausage gravy, bananas foster French toast, and omelets before hitting the trails; for lighter fare, there's steel cut oatmeal and yogurt and granola parfaits. **Known for:** three breakfast mimosa choices; boxed lunches. [$] *Average main: $24* ✉ *12076 Sol Duc Rd. , at U.S. 101, Port Angeles* ☎ *360/327–3583* 🌐 *www.olympicnationalparks.com/dining/sol-duc-hot-springs-resort/* ⏲ *Closed Nov.–late Mar.*

🛏 Hotels

Lake Crescent Lodge

$$$ | **HOTEL** | Deep in the forest at the foot of Mt. Storm King, this 1916 lodge has a variety of comfortable accommodations,

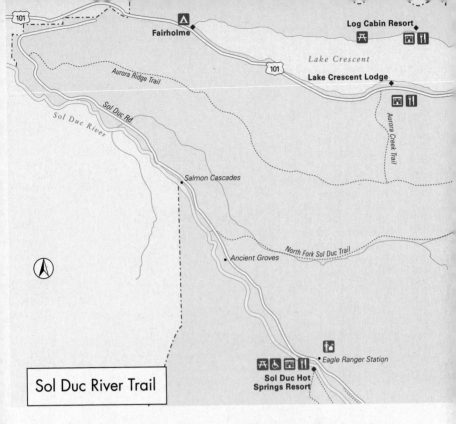

Sol Duc River Trail

from basic rooms with shared baths to spacious two-bedroom fireplace cottages. **Pros:** gorgeous setting; free wireless access in the lobby; lots of opportunities for off-the-grid fun outdoors. **Cons:** no laundry; Roosevelt Cottages often are booked a year in advance for summer stays; crowded with nonguest visitors. $ *Rooms from: $218* ✉ *416 Lake Crescent Rd., Port Angeles* ☎ *360/928–3211, 888/896–3818* ⊕ *www.olympicnational-parks.com/lodging/lake-crescent-lodge/* ⊙ *Closed Jan.–Apr., except Roosevelt fireplace cabins open weekends* ⤵ *52 rooms* ◎ *No meals.*

Log Cabin Resort

$$$ | **HOTEL** | **FAMILY** | This rustic resort has an idyllic setting at the northeast end of Lake Crescent with lodging choices that include A-frame chalet units, standard cabins, small camper cabins, motel units,

and RV sites with full hookups. **Pros:** boat rentals available on-site; convenient general store; pets allowed in some cabins. **Cons:** cabins are extremely rustic; no plumbing in the camper cabins; no TVs. $ *Rooms from: $161* ✉ *3183 E. Beach Rd., Port Angeles* ☎ *888/896–3818, 360/928–3325* ⊕ *www.olympicnational-parks.com* ⊙ *Closed Oct.–late May* ⤵ *24 rooms* ◎ *No meals.*

Sol Duc Hot Springs Resort

$$$$ | **HOTEL** | Deep in the brooding forest along the Sol Duc River and surrounded by 5,000-foot-tall mountains, the main draw of this remote 1910 resort is the pool area, with soothing mineral baths and a freshwater swimming pool. **Pros:** nearby trails; peaceful setting; some units are pet-friendly. **Cons:** units are dated and very basic; no air-conditioning, TV, or Wi-Fi; pools get crowded. $ *Rooms*

Did You Know?

Olympic National Park is home to 13 species of amphibians (frogs, toads, and salamanders), including the Pacific tree frog. The park is a rare refuge for these animals, whose world populations have been declining due to air and water pollution (amphibians live in both environments, making them doubly susceptible).

from: $230 ✉ 12076 Sol Duc Hot Springs Rd. ☎ 888/896–3818, 360/327–3583 ⊕ www.olympicnationalparks.com/lodging/sol-duc-hot-springs-resort/ ⊗ Closed Oct.–late May ⤳ 33 rooms ❖ No meals.

The Mountains

Hurricane Ridge is 17 miles north of Port Angeles.

Providing a stunning backdrop for sunsets visible from the Seattle area, the Olympic Mountain range encompasses more than a dozen mountains within Olympic National Park and adjacent Olympic National Forest. Hurricane Ridge is the most accessible by car and offers views of other mountains that can't easily be seen from elsewhere, including the highest peak in the range, Mt. Olympus. On winter weekends, snow sports are often an option at Hurricane Ridge too.

Sights

SCENIC DRIVES

★ Port Angeles Visitor Center to Hurricane Ridge

VIEWPOINT | The premier scenic drive in Olympic National Park is a steep ribbon of curves that climbs from thickly forested foothills and subalpine meadows into the upper stretches of pine-swathed peaks. At the top, the visitor center at Hurricane Ridge has some spectacular views over the heart of the peninsula and across the Strait of Juan de Fuca. A mile past the visitor center, there are picnic tables in open meadows with photo-worthy views of the mountains to the east. Hurricane Ridge also has an uncommonly fine display of wildflowers in spring and summer. In winter, vehicles must carry chains, and the road is usually open Friday to Sunday only (call first to check conditions). ✉ Olympic National Park ⊕ www.nps.gov/olym.

SCENIC STOPS

★ Hurricane Ridge

MOUNTAIN—SIGHT | The panoramic view from this 5,200-foot-high ridge encompasses the Olympic range, the Strait of Juan de Fuca, and Vancouver Island. Guided tours from the visitor center are given in summer along the many paved and unpaved trails, where wildflowers and wildlife such as deer and marmots flourish. ✉ Hurricane Ridge Rd. ✛ 17 miles south of Port Angeles ☎ 360/565–3130 ⊕ www.nps.gov/olym/planyourvisit/visiting-hurricane-ridge.htm ⊗ Closed when road is closed.

Mt. Olympus

MOUNTAIN—SIGHT | The highest peak in the Olympic Mountain range, Mt. Olympus towers over the park at 7,980 feet. It gets 50–70 feet of snow every year, supporting several glaciers including Blue Glacier, which has been one of the most-studied glaciers in the world. That glacier and others in the mountain range have been retreating rapidly in recent decades due to climate change. Because of its location in the park, the best view of Mt. Olympus is from Hurricane Ridge. Unlike other major mountains in Washington state, it can't be seen from major cities or even nearby towns. ✉ Olympic National Park ⊕ www.nps.gov/olym.

Staircase

INFO CENTER | Unlike the forests of the park's south and west sides, Douglas fir is the dominant tree on the east slope of the Olympic Mountains. Fire has played an important role in creating the majestic forest here, as the Staircase Ranger Station explains in interpretive exhibits. ✉ Olympic National Park ✛ At end of Rte. 119, 15 miles from U.S. 101 at Hoodsport ☎ 360/565–3130 ⊕ www.nps.gov/olym/planyourvisit/visiting-staircase.htm.

TRAILS

High Divide Trail

TRAIL | A 9-mile hike in the park's high country defines this trail, which includes some strenuous climbing on its last 4 miles before topping out at a small alpine lake. A return loop along High Divide wends its way an extra mile through alpine territory, with sensational views of Olympic peaks. This trail is only for dedicated, properly equipped hikers who are in good shape. *Difficult.* ⊠ *Olympic National Park* ✛ *Trailhead: end of Sol Duc River Rd., 13 miles south of U.S. 101* ⊕ *www.nps.gov/olym/planyourvisit/high-divide-loop.htm.*

Hurricane Ridge Meadow Trail

TRAIL | A ¼-mile alpine loop, most of it wheelchair accessible, leads through wildflower meadows overlooking numerous vistas of the interior Olympic peaks to the south and a panorama of the Strait of Juan de Fuca to the north. *Easy.* ⊠ *Olympic National Park* ✛ *Trailhead: Hurricane Ridge Rd., 17 miles south of Port Angeles* ⊕ *www.nps.gov/olym/planyourvisit/visiting-hurricane-ridge.htm.*

VISITOR CENTERS
Hurricane Ridge Visitor Center

INFO CENTER | The upper level of this visitor center has exhibits and nice views; the lower level has a gift shop and snack bar. Guided walks and programs start in late June. In winter, find details on the surrounding ski and sledding slopes and take guided snowshoe walks. ⊠ *Hurricane Ridge Rd.* ☎ *360/565–3131 for road conditions* ⊕ *www.nps.gov/olym/planyourvisit/visitorcenters.htm* ⊗ *Operating hrs/days vary off-season.*

Olympic National Park Visitor Center

INFO CENTER | This modern, well-organized facility, staffed by park rangers, provides everything: maps, trail brochures, campground advice, weather forecasts, listings of wildlife sightings, educational programs and exhibits, information on road and trail closures, and a gift shop. ⊠ *3002 Mount Angeles Rd., Port Angeles* ☎ *360/565–3130* ⊕ *www.nps.gov/olym/planyourvisit/visitorcenters.htm.*

Wilderness Information Center (WIC)

INFO CENTER | Located behind Olympic National Park Visitor Center, this facility provides all the information you'll need for a trip in the park, including trail conditions, safety tips, and weather bulletins. The office also issues camping permits, takes campground reservations, and loans bear-proof food canisters. ⊠ *3002 Mount Angeles Rd., Port Angeles* ☎ *360/565–3100* ⊕ *www.nps.gov/olym/planyourvisit/wic.htm* ⊗ *Hrs vary during off-season.*

Activities

BIKING

The rough gravel car tracks to some of the park's remote sites were meant for four-wheel-drive vehicles but can double as mountain-bike routes. The Quinault Valley, Queets River, Hoh River, and Sol Duc River roads have bike paths through old-growth forest. Graves Creek Road, in the southwest, is a mountain-bike path; Lake Crescent's north side is also edged by the bike-friendly Spruce Railroad Trail. More bike tracks run through the adjacent Olympic National Forest. Note that U.S. 101 has heavy traffic and isn't recommended for cycling, although the western side has broad roads with beautiful scenery and can be biked off-season. Bikes are not permitted on foot trails.

Ben's Bikes

BICYCLING | This bike, gear, and repair shop is a great resource for advice on routes around the Olympic Peninsula, including the Olympic Discovery Trail. They can deliver bikes to local lodgings and to the ferry docks in Port Angeles and Port Townsend. They rent a variety of different styles, with rentals starting at $30 per day and $110 per week. ⊠ *1251 W. Washington St., Sequim* ☎ *360/683–2666* ⊕ *www.bensbikessequim.com.*

Sound Bike & Kayak

This sports outfitter rents and sells bikes, and sells kayaks, climbing gear, and related equipment. They offer several guided mountain climbs, day hikes, and custom trips, and a climbing wall to practice skills. Bike rentals start at $10 per hour and $45 per day. ⊠ *120 E. Front St., Port Angeles* ☎ *360/457–1240* ⊕ *www. soundbikeskayaks.com.*

CAMPING

Note that only a few places take reservations; if you can't book in advance, you'll have to arrive early to get a place. Each site usually has a picnic table and grill or firepit, and most campgrounds have water, toilets, and garbage containers; for hookups, showers, and laundry facilities, you'll have to head into the towns or stay at a privately owned campground. Firewood is available from camp concessions, but if there's no store, you can collect dead wood within 1 mile of your campsite. Dogs are allowed in campgrounds, but not on most trails or in the backcountry. Trailers should be 21 feet long or less (15 feet or less at Queets Campground), though a few campgrounds can accommodate up to 35 feet. There's a camping limit of two weeks. Nightly rates run $15–$22 per site.

If you have a backcountry pass, you can camp virtually anywhere throughout the park's forests and shores. Overnight wilderness permits are $8 per person per night and are available at visitor centers and ranger stations. Note that when you camp in the backcountry, you must choose a site at least ½ mile inside the park boundary.

Kalaloch Campground. Kalaloch is the biggest and most popular Olympic campground, and it's open all year. Its vantage of the Pacific is unmatched on the park's coastal stretch. ⊠ *U.S. 101, ½ mile north of Kalaloch Information Station, Olympic National Park* ☎ *877/444–6777* or ⊕ *www.recreation.gov* for reservations.

Lake Quinault Rain Forest Resort Village Campground. Stretching along the south shore of Lake Quinault, this RV campground has many recreation facilities, including beaches, canoes, ball fields, and horseshoe pits. The 31 RV sites, which rent for $45 per night, are open year-round, but bathrooms are closed in winter. The resort also rents motel rooms and cabins. ⊠ *3½ miles east of U.S. 101, S. Shore Rd., Lake Quinault* ☎ *360/288–2535, 800/255–6936* ⊕ *www. rainforestresort.com.*

Mora Campground. Along the Quillayute estuary, this campground doubles as a popular staging point for hikes northward along the coast's wilderness stretch. ⊠ *Rte. 110, 13 miles west of Forks* ☎ *No phone.*

Ozette Campground. Hikers heading to Cape Alava, a scenic promontory that is the westernmost point in the lower 48 states, use this lakeshore campground as a jumping-off point. ⊠ *Hoko-Ozette Rd., 26 miles south of Hwy. 112* ☎ *No phone.*

Sol Duc Campground. Sol Duc resembles virtually all Olympic campgrounds save one distinguishing feature—the famed hot springs are a short walk away. ⊠ *Sol Duc Rd., 11 miles south of U.S. 101* ☎ *877/444–6777* or ⊕ *www.recreation. gov* for reservations.

Staircase Campground. In deep woods away from the river, this campground is a popular jumping-off point for hikes into the Skokomish River Valley and the Olympic high country. ⊠ *Rte. 119, 16 miles northwest of U.S. 101* ☎ *No phone.*

CLIMBING

At 7,980 feet, Mt. Olympus is the highest peak in the park and the most popular climb in the region. To attempt the summit, climbers must register at the Glacier Meadows Ranger Station. Mt. Constance, the third-highest Olympic peak at 7,743 feet, has a well-traversed climbing route that requires technical experience; reservations are recommended for the Lake Constance stop, which is limited to 20 campers. Mt. Deception is another possibility, though tricky snows have caused fatalities and injuries in the last decade.

Climbing season runs from late June through September. Note that crevasse skills and self-rescue experience are highly recommended. Climbers must register with park officials and purchase wilderness permits before setting out. The best resource for climbing advice is the Wilderness Information Center in Port Angeles.

Mountain Madness

CLIMBING/MOUNTAINEERING | Adventure through the rain forest to the glaciated summit of Mt. Olympus on a five-day trip, offered several times per year by Mountain Madness. ☎ 800/328–5925, 206/937–8389 ⊕ www.mountainmadness.com ⌛ From $1,390 for 5-day climb.

EDUCATIONAL OFFERINGS

CLASSES AND SEMINARS

NatureBridge

COLLEGE | FAMILY | This rustic educational facility offers talks and excursions focusing on park ecology and history. Trips range from canoe trips to camping excursions, with a strong emphasis on family programs. ⊠ 111 Barnes Point Rd., Port Angeles ☎ 360/928–3720 ⊕ www. naturebridge.org/olympic.

RANGER PROGRAMS

Junior Ranger Program

TOUR—SIGHT | FAMILY | Anyone can pick up the booklet at visitor centers and ranger stations and follow this fun program, which includes assignments to discover park flora and fauna, ocean life, and Native American lore. Kids get a badge when they turn in the finished work. Kids can also earn an "Ocean Steward" badge by doing activities in another booklet that teaches about the park's coastal ecosystem. ⊠ Olympic National Park ☎ 360/565–3130 ⊕ www.nps.gov/olym/ learn/kidsyouth/beajuniorranger.htm.

FISHING

There are numerous fishing possibilities throughout the park. Lake Crescent is home to cutthroat and rainbow trout, as well as petite kokanee salmon; lakes Cushman, Quinault, and Ozette have trout, salmon, and steelhead. As for rivers, the Bogachiel and Queets have steelhead salmon in season. The glacier-fed Hoh River is home to Chinook salmon April to November, and coho salmon from August through November; the Sol Duc River offers all five species of salmon. The Elwha River has been undergoing restoration since two dams were removed; strong salmon and steelhead runs have returned, although a fishing moratorium has been in place for several years. Other places to go after salmon and trout include the Dosewallips, Duckabush, Quillayute, Quinault, Salmon, and Skokomish rivers. A Washington state punch card is required during salmon-spawning months; fishing regulations vary throughout the park, and some areas are for catch and release only. Punch cards are available from sporting-goods and outdoor-supply stores.

Piscatorial Pursuits

FISHING | This company, based in Forks, offers salmon and steelhead fishing trips around the Olympic Peninsula from October through mid-May. ⊠ Forks ☎ 866/347–4232 ⊕ www.piscatorialpursuits.com ⌛ From $225 (rate per person for parties of two or more).

HIKING

Know your tides, or you might be trapped by high water. Tide tables are available at all visitor centers and ranger stations. Remember that a wilderness permit is required for all overnight backcountry visits.

KAYAKING AND CANOEING

Lake Crescent, a serene expanse of teal-color waters surrounded by deep-green pine forests, is one of the park's best boating areas. Note that the west end is for swimming only; no speedboats are allowed here.

Lake Quinault has boating access from a gravel ramp on the north shore. From U.S. 101, take a right on North Shore Road, another right on Hemlock Way, and a left on Lakeview Drive. There are plank ramps at Falls Creek and Willough- by campgrounds on South Shore Drive, 0.1 mile and 0.2 mile past the Quinault Ranger Station, respectively.

Lake Ozette, with just one access road, is a good place for overnight trips. Only experienced canoe and kayak handlers should travel far from the put-in, since fierce storms occasionally strike—even in summer.

Adventures Through Kayaking

KAYAKING | FAMILY | This outfitter offers lake kayak rentals (from $64/day), two-hour sea kayaking tours along the Whale Trail (from $79), and three-hour kayak tours on Lake Crescent (from $79). Children as young as four years old can participate. ⊠ 2358 Hwy. 101, Port Angeles ☎ 360/417–3015 ⊕ www.atkayaking.com.

Fairholme General Store

CANOEING/ROWING/SKULLING | Kayaks and canoes on Lake Crescent are available to rent from $20 per hour to $60 for eight hours. The store is at the lake's west end, 27 miles west of Port Angeles. ⊠ 221121 U.S. 101, Port Angeles ☎ 360/928–3020 ⊕ www.olympicnationalparks.com ⊙ Closed after Labor Day until Memorial Day weekend.

Lake Crescent Lodge

CANOEING/ROWING/SKULLING | You can rent kayaks and paddleboards here for $25 per hour and $60 for a half day; canoes are $35/hour, $70/half day. ⊠ 416 Lake Cres- cent Rd. ☎ 360/928–3211 ⊕ www.olympic- nationalparks.com ⊙ Closed Jan.–Apr.

Log Cabin Resort

CANOEING/ROWING/SKULLING | This resort, 17 miles west of Port Angeles, has pad- dleboat, kayak, canoe, and paddleboard rentals for $20 per hour and $60 per day. The dock provides easy access to Lake Crescent's northeast section. ⊠ 3183 E.

Beach Rd., Port Angeles ☎ 360/928–3325 ⊕ www.olympicnationalparks.com ⊙ Closed Oct.–mid-May.

RAFTING

Olympic has excellent rafting rivers, with Class II to Class V rapids. The Elwha River is a popular place to paddle, with some exciting turns. The Hoh is better for those who like a smooth, easy float.

Hoh River Rafters

WHITE-WATER RAFTING | Local guides lead Class II rafting trips down the Hoh. The three-hour trips run twice daily from March through August and cost $75. All equipment is provided and no experience is needed. ⊠ 4883 Upper Hoh Rd., Forks ☎ 360/683-9867 ⊕ www. hohriverrafters.com.

WINTER ACTIVITIES

Hurricane Ridge is the central spot for winter sports. Miles of downhill and Nordic ski tracks are open late December through March, and a ski lift, towropes, and ski school are open 10 to 4 week- ends and holidays. A snow-play area for children ages eight and younger is near the Hurricane Ridge Visitors Center. Hur- ricane Ridge Road is open Friday through Sunday in the winter season; all vehicles are required to carry chains.

Hurricane Ridge Visitor Center

SNOW SPORTS | Rent snowshoes and ski equipment here December through March. ⊠ Hurricane Ridge Rd., Port Angeles ☎ 360/565–3131 road condition information ⊕ www.nps.gov/olym/plan- yourvisit/hurricane-ridge-in-winter.htm ⊙ Closed Mon.–Thurs.

Nearby Towns

Although most Olympic Peninsula towns have evolved from their exclusive reliance on timber, **Forks,** outside the national park's northwest tip, remains one of the region's logging capitals. Washington state's wettest town (100 inches or

Scenic Drives and Vistas

Seiku to Neah Bay Few travelers make it out to the far northwestern tip of the continental United States, but the drive is well worth the time. From Seiku, Highway 112 meanders west along the coastline in roller-coaster dips, rises, and curves, which make the two-lane route seem all too narrow. Right-side passengers have the best views heading toward Neah Bay, as the road hugs the rocky coastline and its frothing, salty bays; the forest is thick and towering on the other side. The drive is best made in the late afternoon, when summer sunlight brings out the colors of the water and trees, or when winter clouds show just how foreboding this edge of the country can be.

more of rain a year), it's a small, friendly place with just over 3,800 residents and a modicum of visitor facilities. South of Forks and Lake Quinault, Washington's newest beach community (established in 2004), **Seabrook,** near the tiny village of **Pacific Beach**, is 25 miles from the southwest corner of the national park via the Moclips Highway. Created as a planned community mainly for vacationers, it's convenient for visiting both the park and the state's ocean beaches to the south. **Port Angeles,** a city of around 20,000, focuses on its status as the main gateway to Olympic National Park and Victoria, British Columbia. Set below the Strait of Juan de Fuca and looking north to Vancouver Island, it's an enviably scenic settlement filled with attractive, Craftsman-style homes.

The Pacific Northwest has its very own "Banana Belt" in the waterfront community of **Sequim,** 17 miles east of Port Angeles along U.S. 101. The town of 7,500 is in the rain shadow of the Olympics and receives only 16 inches of rain per year (compared with the 140 to 170 inches that drench the Hoh Rain Forest just 40 miles away). The Victorian-era town of **Port Towsend**, in the northeast corner of the Olympic Peninsula, has around 9,700 residents. It's a popular destination for day trips, romantic getaways to the many historic B&Bs, families exploring

the old military forts and aquatic learning centers, and anyone looking for an interesting detour before or after a trip to the national park.

Forks

35 miles southwest of Lake Crescent.

The former logging town of Forks is named for two nearby river junctions: the Bogachiel and Calawah Rivers merge west of town, and a few miles farther they are joined by the Sol Duc to form the Quillayute River, which empties into the Pacific at the Native American village of La Push. Forks is small and quiet with no major attractions per se, but is the gateway town for visiting the Hoh River valley and the Pacific beaches of Olympic National Park. As the setting for the popular *Twilight* movie series, the town has become a favorite destination for fans.

GETTING HERE AND AROUND
You definitely need a car to explore this rugged, rural area. Forks is a little more than an hour from Port Angeles and about two hours north of Aberdeen, by way of Lake Quinault.

VISITOR INFORMATION Forks Chamber of Commerce. ✉ *1411 S. Forks Ave., Forks* ☎ *360/374–2531, 800/443–6757* ⊕ *www. forkswa.com.*

🍴 Restaurants

Blakeslee's Bar and Grill

$ | **AMERICAN** | In an area with precious few dining options, this casual tavern just a little south of downtown Forks is a sight for sore eyes and hungry stomachs, offering up big portions of reliably good pub food. After a day of hiking in the national park, tuck into the half-pound Mill Creek bacon and cheeseburger, a rib-eye steak, or a platter of batter-fried local seafood. **Known for:** nachos (both traditional and Irish-style); craft beer and creative cocktails; popular place for pool. [$] *Average main: $14* ✉ *1222 S. Forks Ave., Forks* ☎ *360/374–5003* 🌐 *www.facebook.com/bbgforkswa/* ⏲ *Closed Mon.*

🛏 Hotels

★ **Miller Tree Inn Bed and Breakfast**

$$ | **B&B/INN** | With country antiques, fluffy quilts, and big windows overlooking peaceful pastures, this 1916 farmhouse on the east side of downtown Forks is nicknamed the "Cullen House" for its resemblance to the description in Stephenie Meyer's *Twilight* books. **Pros:** some rooms have whirlpool tubs and gas fireplaces; nearby rivers offer prime salmon and steelhead fishing; children are welcome in some rooms. **Cons:** lots of Twilight-related tchotchkes; some rooms require climbing stairs; pricey in summer. [$] *Rooms from: $190* ✉ *654 E. Division St., Forks* ☎ *360/374–6806, 800/943–6563* 🌐 *www.millertreeinn.com* 🛏 *8 rooms* 🍽 *Free Breakfast.*

Pacific Inn Motel

$ | **HOTEL** | It may not look like much from the outside, but the only motel for 50 miles in either direction is a comfortable and clean budget choice and a handy base for exploring Olympic National Park, with spacious rooms with modern furnishings and framed landscape photos. **Pros:** cheap rates; central location; immaculately kept. **Cons:** no breakfast; low on frills; not in a scenic part of town. [$] *Rooms from: $134* ✉ *352 Forks Ave., Forks* ☎ *360/374–9400, 800/235–7344* 🌐 *www.pacificinnmotel.com* 🛏 *34 rooms* 🍽 *No meals.*

Seabrook and Pacific Beach

30 miles southwest of Lake Quinault.

Created in 2004 as a pedestrian-friendly beach town, Seabrook has more than 400 Cape Cod–style cottage homes and many are available for short-term rentals. The community has parks, swimming pools, bike trails, beach access, special events, and a growing retail district. Nearby Pacific Beach is the original beachfront town in the area, but with just under 500 residents it's a pretty basic place with just a few small shops and eateries, not the touristy upscale vibe of Seabrook. It does have a gas station and a state park with a campground right on the beach.

GETTING HERE AND AROUND

A car is necessary to get here, either via Hwy. 101 and the Moclips Hwy. from the north, or Hwy. 101 and Ocean Beach Road from the south. Hwy. 109 from Ocean Shores and Aberdeen is a slightly longer but more scenic route along the ocean from the south. Once in Seabrook, it's easy and preferable to get around on foot or bike.

VISITOR INFORMATION Seabrook. ☎ *877/779–9990* 🌐 *www.seabrookwa.com.*

🛏 Hotels

Ocean Crest Resort

$ | **RESORT** | Set on a forested bluff above the Pacific Ocean, 30 minutes from Olympic National Park and Lake Quinault, Ocean Crest has small budget studios, large studios with ocean views, and one- and two-bedroom units. **Pros:** windows open to hear the ocean's roar; some rooms are pet-friendly; off-season specials. **Cons:** restaurant prices may be too high for budget travelers; some rooms are quite dated; the budget studios are tiny. [$] *Rooms from: $87* ✉ *4651 Rte. 109, Moclips* ✥ *1 mile north of Pacific Beach* ☎ *360/276–4465* 🌐 *www.oceancrestresort.com* 🛏 *45 rooms* 🍴 *No meals.*

Seabrook Cottage Rentals

$$ | **RENTAL** | **FAMILY** | Crushed seashells line pathways throughout the dapper planned beach resort town of Seabrook, where you'll find a collection of some 450 Cape Cod–style homes, more than half of which are available to rent. **Pros:** beach and forest within easy walking distance; attractive contemporary homes with lots of bells and whistles; some pet-friendly lodgings. **Cons:** homes are closely spaced on small lots; minimum two-night stay; quality of homes can vary depending on owner upkeep. [$] *Rooms from: $155* ✉ *Hwy. 109 at Front St., Pacific Beach* ☎ *360/276–0265* 🌐 *www.seabrookwa.com* 🛏 *260 homes* 🍴 *No meals.*

Port Angeles

22 miles east of Lake Crescent, 17 miles west of Sequim.

Sprawling along the hills above the deep-blue Strait of San Juan de Fuca, this logging and fishing town on the water's edge is drawing a steady stream of independently owned restaurants, shops, and bars, as well as a smattering of hotels (including a brand-new one built by the Lower Elwha Klallam tribe and slated to open in 2022). It's all set around a modern marina and the terminal for ferries bound for Victoria, British Columbia, 20 miles across the strait. With a population of about 20,000, the town is the largest on the Olympic Peninsula and the most prominent gateway to Olympic National Park. Summer foot traffic is shoulder-to-shoulder downtown, with travelers rushing to and from the ferry, strolling the waterfront, and relaxing at outdoor cafés and pubs.

GETTING HERE AND AROUND

Port Angeles lies about an hour's drive west of Port Townsend and is most easily reached by car, although there are several car rental agencies in town, if you arrive here by ferry and bus and need a set of wheels to visit Olympic National Park or explore the shoreline.

VISITOR INFORMATION Port Angeles Chamber of Commerce Visitor Center. ✉ *121 E. Railroad Ave., Port Angeles* ☎ *360/452–2364* 🌐 *www.portangeles.org.*

🍴 Restaurants

Dupuis Restaurant

$$ | **SEAFOOD** | This dimly lighted roadside log cabin, painted a cheery yellow, evokes the feeling of a bygone era with its wood paneling, exposed beams, and bric-a-brac-filled dining room. Local sustainable seafood, often with modern preparations, dominates the menu—consider Dungeness crab cakes with pineapple-cranberry compote, gnocchi with wild shrimp and shellfish, or cioppino with a side of creamy oyster stew. **Known for:** old-fashioned ambience; local-cod fish-and-chips; classic cocktails in the Forest Room lounge. [$] *Average main: $22* ✉ *256861 U.S. 101, Port Angeles* ☎ *360/457–8033* 🌐 *www.dupuis-restaurant.com* ⏲ *Closed Sun.–Tues. No lunch.*

Toga's Soup House Deli & Gourmet

$ | **ECLECTIC** | Toga's serves an eclectic menu of casual fare, ranging from housemade soups and fresh salads to hearty sandwiches. The many windows provide views of the Olympic Mountains, and there's also an open-air patio. **Known for:** pork schnitzel sandwich; variety of soups, chili, and chowders; decadent desserts. [$] *Average main: $13* ✉ *122 W. Lauridsen Blvd., Port Angeles* ☎ *360/452–1952* 🌐 *www.togassouphouse.com* ⏲ *Closed weekends.*

Hotels

★ Colette's Bed & Breakfast

$$$$ | B&B/INN | This contemporary ocean-front mansion set on a 10-acre sanctuary of gorgeous gardens offers a level of service and luxury that's unmatched in the area, with water-view suites that have fireplaces, patios, and two-person spa tubs, and multicourse breakfasts featuring organic fresh local produce, decadent baked goods, and house specialties like Dungeness crab hash, smoked salmon frittata, and dill crepes. **Pros:** sweeping water views; highly professional staff; lush gardens and grounds. **Cons:** not suitable for kids; 15-minute drive from town; a bit spendy for the area. ⓢ *Rooms from: $325* ✉ *339 Finn Hall Rd., Port Angeles* ☎ *360/457–9197, 888/457–9777* ⊕ *www.colettes.com* 🛏 *5 suites* ⦿| *Free Breakfast.*

★ Sea Cliff Gardens Bed & Breakfast

$$$$ | B&B/INN | A gingerbread-style porch fronts this Victorian on two landscaped acres of lush perennial gardens and a grand lawn dotted with Adirondack chairs that ends on a bluff overlooking Vancouver Island. **Pros:** sumptuous, romantic accommodations; gorgeous flower gardens; spectacular water views. **Cons:** a bit off the beaten path; among the most expensive lodgings in the area; not a good option for children. ⓢ *Rooms from: $295* ✉ *397 Monterra Dr., Port Angeles* ☎ *360/452–2322* ⊕ *www.seacliffgardens. com* 🛏 *5 suites* ⦿| *Free Breakfast.*

Sequim

17 miles east of Port Angeles.

Sequim (pronounced *skwim*), incorporated in 1913, is an endearing old mill town and farming center between the northern foothills of the Olympic Mountains and the southeastern stretch of the Strait of Juan de Fuca. The youthful vibe of neighboring Port Townsend has crept this way,

and a growing number of urbane eateries and hip boutiques have opened throughout Sequim's walkable downtown, which is marked by a historic grain elevator. A few miles to the north is the shallow and fertile Dungeness Valley, which enjoys some of the lowest rainfall in western Washington. Fragrant purple lavender flourishes in local fields.

GETTING HERE AND AROUND

You'll want a car to explore this relatively rural community that easy to reach from both Port Townsend and Port Angeles.

VISITOR INFORMATION Sequim-Dungeness Valley Chamber of Commerce. ✉ *1192 E. Washington St., Sequim* ☎ *360/683–6197,* ⊕ *www.sequimchamber.com.*

 Sights

★ Dungeness Spit

NATURE PRESERVE | FAMILY | Curving nearly 6 miles into the Strait of Juan de Fuca, the longest natural sand spit in the United States is a wild, beautiful section of shoreline. More than 30,000 migratory waterfowl stop here each spring and fall, but you'll see plenty of birdlife any time of year. The entire spit is part of the **Dungeness National Wildlife Refuge** (⊕ *www.fws.gov/refuge/dungeness*). You can access it from the trail that begins in the 216-acre **Dungeness Recreation Area,** which serves as a portal to the shoreline. At the end of the spit is the towering white 1857 **New Dungeness Lighthouse** (⊕ *www.newdungenesslighthouse. com).* Tours, including a 74-step climb to the top, are available, though access is limited to those who can hike 5½ miles or paddle about 3½ miles out to the end of the spit—the closest launch is from Cline Spit County Park. You can also enroll to serve a one-week stint as a lighthouse keeper. If you'd prefer not to make the long trek all the way out to the lighthouse, an endeavor you should only attempt at low tide to avoid having to climb over massive driftwood logs, you can still take in plenty of beautiful scenery and spot myriad wildlife by hiking just a mile or so out along the spit and back. ✉ *554 Voice of America Rd. W, Sequim* ☎ *360/683–5847* 🌐 *www.clallam.net/Parks/Dungeness.html.*

★ Railroad Bridge Park

CITY PARK | On 25 acres along the Dungeness River, this beautifully serene park is centered on a lacy ironwork bridge that was once part of the coastal rail line between Port Angeles and Port Townsend. The River Walk hike-and-bike path leads from the Dungeness River Audubon Center—which has excellent natural history exhibits—into the woods, and a horseback track links Runnion Road with the waterway. In summer, you might picnic at the River Shed pavilion, and watch performances at the River Stage amphitheater. There are free guided bird walks Wednesday mornings from 8:30 to 10:30. ✉ *2151 W. Hendrickson Rd., Sequim* ☎ *360/681–4076* 🌐 *www.dungenessrivercenter.org* 🎟 *Free.*

🍴 Restaurants

★ Nourish

$$$ | **PACIFIC NORTHWEST** | This greenhouse-enclosed restaurant with a sunny garden patio overlooks one of the region's oldest lavender and herb farms and features a seasonally inspired menu. The specialties change often but might include lamb burgers with turmeric-pickled onions and Dijon aioli, seared pork belly with tamari-ginger sauce, and chili-seared halibut with a rhubarb-tarragon salsa. **Known for:** rich selection of vegetarian, vegan, and gluten-free options; craft cocktails with herbal and fresh-fruit infusions; leisurely Sunday brunches. [$] *Average main: $25* ✉ *101 Provence View La., Sequim* ☎ *360/797–1480* 🌐 *www.nourishsequim.com* 🕒 *Closed Mon. and Tues.*

★ Salty Girls Seafood

$$ | **SEAFOOD** | This hip, counter-service seafood bar with a mod-industrial vibe serves Puget Sound oysters and clams on the half shell—either raw or baked with seasonal compound butters—and several beers and ciders on tap to wash them down. Oyster shooters are another favorite, and there's a short menu of additional fish-centric dishes, from steamed Dungeness crab with clarified butter to chowder made with local clams, but nothing fried. **Known for:** "grown-up" grilled cheese with bacon and shrimp; exceptional craft cocktails; sea-salt chocolate-chip cookies. [$] *Average main: $18* ✉ *210 W. Washington St., Sequim* ☎ *360/775–3787* 🌐 *www.saltygirlsseafood.com* 🕒 *Closed Weds.*

🛏 Hotels

Greenhouse Inn by the Bay

$$ | **B&B/INN** | All five rooms in this sweet, upscale B&B on a bluff overlooking the Strait of Juan de Fuca and Vancouver Island, just a short stroll from Cline Spit County Park, have private balconies with dramatic vistas, and some have fireplaces and soaking tubs. **Pros:** idyllic setting on Dungeness Bay; breakfast ingredients grown on property; rooms have sweeping views. **Cons:** not actually on the beach; 10-minute drive from downtown; least expensive room has two twins and bath is on different floor. [$] *Rooms from: $165* ✉ *630 Marine Dr., Sequim* ☎ *360/504–2489* 🌐 *www.greenhousebythebay.com* 🔑 *5 rooms* 🍽 *Free Breakfast.*

★ Lost Mountain Lodge

$$$$ | **B&B/INN** | In a beautiful foothills setting with Olympic Mountains views, this sumptuous 10-acre retreat offers tranquil grounds, spacious accommodations with luxe furnishings, and extras like in-room couples massage and other spa options. **Pros:** hearty breakfasts (for the suites without kitchens); quiet mountain-view setting; in-room spa services. **Cons:**

10-minute drive to downtown; books up well in advance in summer; not for families with small kids. [$] *Rooms from: $269* ✉ *303 Sunny View Dr., Sequim* ☎ *360/683–2431* 🌐 *www.lostmountainlodge.com* 🛏 *6 rooms* 🍴 *Free Breakfast.*

Port Townsend

31 miles east of Sequim.

On its own rugged peninsula—the small, crooked arm of the Quimper on the northeastern tip of the larger, torch-shaped Olympic—Port Townsend is a center of maritime activity, artistic expression, entrepreneurial spirit, and natural beauty. But the town's maritime setting and its proliferation of handsome Victorian buildings imbue it with a sense of romance that makes it popular as both a place to visit and live—a different kind of city of dreams—to this day.

GETTING HERE AND AROUND
From Seattle, it's fastest to get here via the Washington State Ferry, via Bainbridge Island or Kingston, and then drive northwest across the upper Kitsap Peninsula to the floating bridge near Port Ludlow. Both routes run roughly an hour and 45 minutes, not including waits for the ferries. From Olympia and points south, take U.S. 101 along Hood Canal to Highway 14. It's relatively easy to get here without a car, but driving is the best way to explore the greater area.

VISITOR INFORMATION Port Townsend Visitor Information Center. ✉ *2409 Jefferson St., Port Townsend* ☎ *360/385–2722* 🌐 *www.enjoypt.com.*

Sights

★ Fort Worden State Park
BEACH—SIGHT | FAMILY | With restored Victorian officers' houses and pre–World War I-era bunkers, this fascinating 432-acre park served as the filming location for the 1982 film *An Officer and a Gentleman.* Built on Point Wilson in 1896 to guard the mouth of Puget Sound, the old fort provides myriad outdoor and cultural activities for kids and adults. A sandy beach leads to the graceful 1913 Point Wilson Lighthouse. Memory's Vault, a series of pillars hidden in the hill above the inlet, features inscriptions of works from local poet Sam Hamill. Touch tanks at Port Townsend Marine Science Center on the pier offer an up-close look at sea anemones and other underwater life. Kayak tours and rentals are also available. The fort also hosts music festivals in an old military balloon-hangar-turned-performing-arts-pavilion and exhibits in an artillery museum. Many of the old buildings can now be booked as overnight accommodations, and there are a couple of excellent dining options in the park: Reveille at the Commons serves breakfast, lunch, and coffee, and Taps at the Guardhouse is known for lunch, happy hour, and early dinners. ✉ *200 Battery Way, Port Townsend* ☎ *360/344–4400* 🌐 *parks.state.wa.us/511/Fort-Worden* 🎟 *$10 parking.*

★ Northwest Maritime Center
COLLEGE | Port Townsend is one of only three Victorian-era seaports on the register of National Historic Sites, and you can learn all about it at this handsome building on the waterfront. It's the center of operations for the Wooden Boat Foundation, which stages the annual Wooden Boat Festival each September. The center has interactive exhibits, hands-on sailing instruction, boatbuilding workshops, a wood shop, and a pilot house where you can test navigational tools. You can launch a kayak or watch sloops and schooners gliding along the bay from the boardwalk, pier, and beach that fronts the buildings. There's also an excellent gift shop, The Chandlery, with a coffee bar. ✉ *431 Water St., Port Townsend* ☎ *360/385–3628* 🌐 *www.nwmaritime.org* 🎟 *Free.*

🍴 Restaurants

★ Finistère

$$$ | **MODERN AMERICAN** | In an uncluttered, light-filled storefront space in Uptown, this hip neighborhood bistro opened by a husband-wife team with experience at some of New York City's and Seattle's top restaurants turns out some of the most flavorful locavore-driven cuisine on the peninsula. You might start with a bowl of sunchoke soup with chives and truffle oil, before graduating to rabbit lasagna with sofrito and mustard greens, or seared scallops with romesco, cauliflower, and Meyer lemon. **Known for:** romantic, candlelit dining room; chicken liver pâté on toast with roasted-onion jam; house-made pastas with inventive sauces. $ *Average main: $27 ⊠ 1025 Lawrence St., Port Townsend ☎ 360/344–8127 ⊕ www. restaurantfinistere.com ⊗ Closed Mon. and Tues. No lunch weekdays.*

★ Fountain Café

$$ | **MEDITERRANEAN** | Local artwork lines the walls of this cozy, eclectic bistro tucked inside a historic clapboard building a block off the main drag, near the foot of the Taylor Street staircase. The delicious seafood- and pasta-intensive menu reveals Mediterranean and Pacific Northwest influences—think cioppino with local shellfish in a tomato-saffron broth, and roasted walnut and gorgonzola penne with wild boar. **Known for:** friendly, unpretentious service; fresh-baked baguette with herbed butter; warm gingerbread with vanilla custard. $ *Average main: $20 ⊠ 920 Washington St., Port Townsend ☎ 360/385–1364 ⊕ www. fountaincafept.com.*

Hudson Point Cafe

$ | **PACIFIC NORTHWEST** | Views of its namesake marina account for part of the popularity of this inviting spot with leather booths, local artwork, and a wall of windows overlooking the water. It's the creative cooking that keeps folks coming back, however, with a seasonally rotating menu including waffles with rhubarb syrup, smoked-salmon polenta hash, and regional oyster scrambles. **Known for:** crab cakes topped with poached eggs; excellent craft beer selection; well-prepared espresso drinks. $ *Average main: $13 ⊠ 130 Hudson St., Port Townsend ☎ 360/379–0592 ⊕ www.facebook.com/Hudson-Point-Cafe-111918065505876 ⊗ No dinner.*

☕ Coffee and Quick Bites

Elevated Ice Cream Company

$ | **CAFÉ** | This venerable ice-cream parlor and candy shop has been a fixture downtown since 1977, doling out small-batch ice creams and Italian ices, and always featuring at least 30 flavors—many, such as pink gooseberry and strawberry-rhubarb, featuring ingredients sourced from local farms. If it's a warm day, bring your cone, shake, or sundae (or bag of chocolates) next door to Pope Marine Park and enjoy your dessert while watching ships in the bay. **Known for:** signature Swiss orange chocolate chip ice cream; old-timey atmosphere; classic banana splits. $ *Average main: $5 ⊠ 627 Water St., Port Townsend ☎ 360/385–1156 ⊕ www. elevatedicecream.com.*

🛏 Hotels

★ Ravenscroft Inn

$$ | **B&B/INN** | This eight-room inn situated in a fairly peaceful residential neighborhood a short walk from both uptown and downtown eateries stands out for its sweeping double veranda, gracious gardens and lawns, and views of the bay and distant Cascade Mountains. **Pros:** hospitable innkeeper really knows the area; walking distance from many restaurants; some rooms have bay views. **Cons:** two- or three-night minimum during busy times; no TVs in rooms; not a good choice for kids. $ *Rooms from: $155 ⊠ 533 Quincy St., Port Townsend ☎ 360/205–2147, 855/290–8840 ⊕ www.ravenscroftinn.com ⇴ 8 rooms ⊚ Free Breakfast.*

Chapter 27

PETRIFIED FOREST NATIONAL PARK

27

Updated by
Elise Riley

ARIZONA

🏕 Camping	🛏 Hotels	🤸 Activities	👁 Scenery	🎭 Crowds
★☆☆☆☆	★☆☆☆☆	★★☆☆☆	★★★★★	★★☆☆☆

WELCOME TO
PETRIFIED FOREST NATIONAL PARK

TOP REASONS TO GO

★ **Terrific timber:** Be mesmerized by the clusters of petrified (fossilized) wood. The trees look like they're made of colorful stone.

★ **Walls with words:** Don't scratch the surface, but see how others did. Ancestors of the Hopi, Zuni, and Navajo left their mark in petroglyphs cut, scratched, or carved into stone.

★ **Route 66 kicks:** A section of the fabled road is preserved in the park, the only section of the highway protected in a national park.

★ **Triassic treasures:** Find an oasis of water in the desert, or at least evidence that it once existed. Clam fossils in the park indicate that waterways once prevailed where sand, stone, and trees now define the land.

★ **Corps creations:** The Painted Desert Inn, a National Historic Landmark, was modernized by the Civilian Conservation Corps (CCC) during the throes of the Great Depression. It is now a museum and bookstore.

1 Petrified Forest National Park. In the park's northern section, its main area, the Painted Desert is where the park headquarters, the Painted Desert Inn National Historic Landmark, and Route 66 are located. It's also the best place for hiking. The 28-mile park road begins here, off Interstate 40. In the heart of the Painted Desert, the 1-mile Blue Mesa trail begins off a loop road accessed from the park road. Petrified trees lie among hills of bluish bentonite clay. Get a trail guide at the Rainbow Forest Museum for the short Giant Logs Trail located behind the museum, and keep an eye out for Old Faithful, a log almost 10 feet wide. The southern terminus for the park road is here.

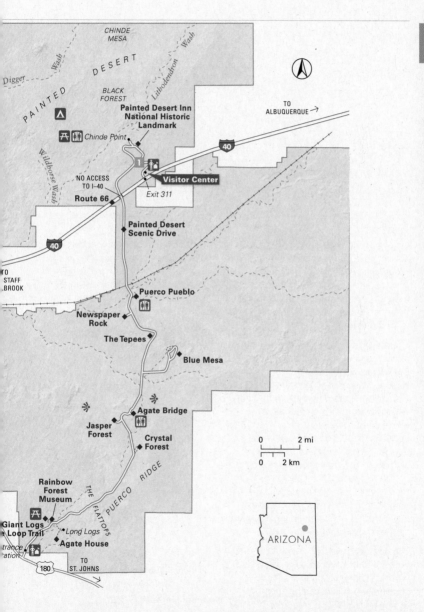

CHINDE MESA

DESERT

PAINTED

Digger Wash

Wash

Lithodendron Wash

BLACK FOREST

Chinde Point

Painted Desert Inn National Historic Landmark

TO ALBUQUERQUE →

40

Wildhorse Wash

NO ACCESS TO I–40

Route 66

40

Visitor Center

Exit 311

Painted Desert Scenic Drive

TO STAFF BROOK

Puerco Pueblo

Newspaper Rock

The Tepees

Blue Mesa

Agate Bridge

Jasper Forest

Crystal Forest

THE FLATTOPS

PUERCO RIDGE

0   2 mi

0   2 km

Rainbow Forest Museum

Giant Logs Loop Trail

Long Logs

Agate House

trance ation

180

TO ST. JOHNS

ARIZONA

Petrified Forest National Park's 221,390 acres, which include portions of the Painted Desert, are covered with petrified tree trunks whose wood cells were fossilized over centuries by brightly hued mineral deposits—silica, iron oxide, carbon, manganese, aluminum, copper, and lithium. Remnants of humans and their artifacts have been recovered at more than 500 sites in the park.

Only about 1½ hours from Show Low and the lush, verdant forests of the White Mountains, Arizona's diverse and dramatic landscape changes from pine-crested mountains to sunbaked terrain. Inside the lunar landscape of the Painted Desert is the Petrified Forest.

There are few places where the span of geologic and human history is as wide or apparent as it is at Petrified Forest National Park. Fossilized trees and countless other fossils date back to the Triassic Period, while a stretch of the famed Route 66 of more modern lore is protected within park boundaries. Ancestors of the Hopi, Zuni, and Navajo left petroglyphs, pottery, and even structures built of petrified wood. Nine park sites are on the National Register of Historic Places; one, the Painted Desert Inn, is one of only 3% of such sites that are also listed as National Historic Landmarks.

The good thing is that most of Petrified Forest's treasures can easily be viewed without a great amount of athletic conditioning. Much can be seen by driving along the main road, from which

historic sites are readily accessible. By combining a drive along the park road with a short hike here and there and a visit to one of the park's landmarks, you can see most of the sights in as little as half a day.

Planning

When to Go

The park is rarely crowded. Weatherwise, the best time to visit is autumn, when nights are chilly but daytime temperatures hover near 70°F. Half of all yearly rain falls between June and August, so it's a good time to spot blooming wildflowers. The park is least crowded in winter because of cold winds and occasional snow, though daytime temperatures are in the 50s and 60s.

FESTIVALS AND EVENTS
National Wildflower Week. Activities include wildflower walks and an interactive wildflower display.

AVERAGE HIGH/LOW TEMPERATURES					
JAN.	**FEB.**	**MAR.**	**APR.**	**MAY**	**JUNE**
48/21	54/25	60/29	70/35	79/43	89/52
JULY	**AUG.**	**SEPT.**	**OCT.**	**NOV.**	**DEC.**
92/60	89/59	84/52	72/40	59/28	48/22

Petrified Forest Park Anniversary. A national monument since 1906 and a national park since 1962, Petrified Forest throws a party for its birthday, with homemade cider, cookies, and cultural demonstrations.

Getting Here and Around

AIR

The nearest major airports are in Phoenix, Arizona (259 miles away via U.S. 17 and U.S. 40), and Albuquerque, New Mexico (204 miles via U.S. 40).

CAR

Holbrook, the nearest large town with services such as gas or food, is on U.S. 40, 27 miles from the park's north entrance and 18 miles from its south entrance.

Parking is free, and there's ample space at all trailheads, as well as at the visitor center and the museum. The main park road extends 28 miles from the Painted Desert Visitor Center (north entrance) to the Rainbow Forest Museum (south entrance). For park road conditions, call ☎ *928/524–6228.*

Inspiration

When Wood Turns to Stone: The Story of the Arizona National Petrified Forest, by K.S. Tankersley, explains the science behind petrified wood, as well as the park's origin.

While not a story about the national park itself, *The Petrified Forest,* a 1936 film starring Bette Davis, Leslie Howard, and Humphrey Bogart tells the story of a drifter, a waitress, and a gangster who cross paths in the Petrified Forest area.

Park Essentials

ACCESSIBILITY

The visitor center, museum, and overlooks on the scenic drive are wheelchair accessible. All trails are paved, although they are uneven, rough, and sometimes steep. Check the park website (⊕ *nps. gov/pefo*) for information on accessibility. The park's visitor centers, as well as some picnic areas, have accessible restrooms.

PARK FEES AND PERMITS

Entrance fees are $25 per car for seven consecutive days or $15 per person on foot or bicycle, or $20 per motorcycle. Backcountry hiking and camping permits are free (15-day limit) at the Painted Desert Visitor Center or the Rainbow Forest Museum before 4 pm.

PARK HOURS

It's a good idea to call ahead or check the website, because the park's hours vary so much; as a rule of thumb, the park is open daily from sunrise to sunset or approximately 8 am–5 pm. Keep in mind that the area does not observe daylight saving time.

Hotels

There is no lodging within Petrified Forest. Outside the park, lodging choices include modern resorts, rustic cabins, and small bed-and-breakfasts. Note that air-conditioning is not a standard amenity in the mountains, where the nights are cool enough for a blanket even in

Petrified Forest in One Day

A nonstop drive through the park (28 miles) takes only 45 minutes, but you can spend half a day or more exploring if you stop along the way. From almost any vantage point you can see the multicolor rocks and hills, where small Triassic dinosaurs once roamed (a few of their fossils have been unearthed here).

Entering from the north, stop at **Painted Desert Visitor Center** for a 20-minute introductory film. Two miles in, the **Painted Desert Inn National Historic Landmark** provides guided ranger tours. Drive south 8 miles to reach **Puerco Pueblo**, a 100-room pueblo built before 1400. Continuing south, you'll encounter **Newspaper Rock**, marked with Pueblo petroglyphs, and, just beyond, **the Tepees**, cone-shaped rock formations.

Blue Mesa is roughly the midpoint of the drive, and the start of a 1-mile, moderately steep loop hike that leads you around badland hills made of bentonite clay. Drive on for 5 miles until you come to **Jasper Forest**, just past **Agate Bridge**, with views of the landscape strewn with petrified logs. **Crystal Forest**, about 20 miles south of the north entrance, is named for the smoky quartz, amethyst, and citrine along the 0.8-mile loop trail. **Rainbow Forest Museum**, at the park's south entrance, has restrooms, a bookstore, and exhibits. Just behind Rainbow Forest Museum is **Giant Logs**, a 0.4-mile loop that takes you to "Old Faithful," the largest log in the park, estimated to weigh 44 tons.

summer. Closer to the Navajo and Hopi reservations many establishments are run by Native Americans, tribal enterprises intent on offering first-class service and hospitality. Nearby Holbrook offers some national chain motels and comfortable accommodations. *Hotel reviews have been shortened. For full information, visit Fodors.com.*

What It Costs			
$	$$	$$$	$$$$
RESTAURANTS			
under $13	$13–$20	$21–$30	over $30
HOTELS			
under $101	$101–$150	$151–$200	over $200

Restaurants

Dining in the park is limited to a cafeteria in the Painted Desert Visitor Center and snacks in the Rainbow Forest Museum. In and around the Navajo and Hopi reservations, be sure to sample Indian tacos, an authentic treat made with scrumptious fry bread, beans, and chilies. If you're searching for burger-and-fries fare, Holbrook is your best bet. *Restaurant reviews have been shortened. For full information, visit Fodors.com.*

Visitor Information

PARK CONTACT INFORMATION Petrified Forest National Park. ⊠ 1 Park Rd. ☎ 928/524–6228 ⊕ www.nps.gov/pefo

Sights

Though named for its famous fossilized trees, Petrified Forest has something to see for history buffs of all stripes, from a segment of Route 66 to ancient dwellings to even more ancient fossils. And the good thing is that most of Petrified Forest's treasures can easily be viewed without a great amount of athletic conditioning. Much can be seen by driving along the main road, from which historic sites are readily accessible. By combining a drive along the park road with a short hike here and there and a visit to one of the park's landmarks, you can see most of the sights in as little as half a day.

HISTORIC SITES

Agate House

ARCHAEOLOGICAL SITE | This eight-room pueblo is thought to have been built entirely of petrified wood 700 years ago. Researchers believe it might have been used as a temporary dwelling by seasonal farmers or traders from one of the area tribes. ⊠ *Rainbow Forest Museum parking area.*

Newspaper Rock

ARCHAEOLOGICAL SITE | See huge boulders covered with petroglyphs believed to have been carved by the Pueblo people more than 500 years ago. ■TIP→ **Look through the binoculars that are provided here—you'll be surprised at what the naked eye misses.** ⊠ *Main park road ⊹ 6 miles south of Painted Desert Visitor Center.*

Painted Desert Inn National Historic Landmark

MUSEUM | A nice place to stop and rest in the shade, this site offers vast views of the Painted Desert from several lookouts. Inside, cultural history exhibits, murals, and Native American crafts are on display. ⊠ *Main park road ⊹ 2 miles north of Painted Desert Visitor Center.*

Touch—But Don't Take

One of the most commonly asked questions about the Petrified Forest is, "Can I touch the wood?" Yes! Feel comfortable to touch anything, pick it up, inspect it ... just make sure you put it back where you found it. It's illegal to remove even a small sliver of fossilized wood from the park.

Puerco Pueblo

ARCHAEOLOGICAL SITE | This is a 100-room pueblo, built before 1400 and said to have housed Ancestral Pueblo people. Many visitors come to see the petroglyphs, as well as a solar calendar. ⊠ *Main park road ⊹ 10 miles south of Painted Desert Visitor Center.*

PICNIC AREAS

Chinde Point Picnic Area

$ | LOCAL INTEREST | |LOCAL INTEREST | Near the north entrance, this small spot has tables and restrooms. ⊠ *Petrified Forest National Park ⊹ 2 miles north of Painted Desert Visitor Center.*

Rainbow Forest Museum Picnic Area

$ | LOCAL INTEREST | |LOCAL INTEREST | There are restrooms and tables at this small picnic area near the south entrance. ⊠ *Petrified Forest National Park ⊹ Off I–40, 27 miles east of Holbrook.*

SCENIC DRIVES

Painted Desert Scenic Drive

SCENIC DRIVE | A 28-mile scenic drive takes you through the park from one entrance to the other. If you begin at the north end, the first 5 miles take you along the edge of a high mesa, with spectacular views of the Painted Desert. Beyond lies the desolate Painted Desert Wilderness Area. After the 5-mile point, the road crosses Interstate 40, then swings south toward the Puerco River across a landscape covered with sagebrush,

Different minerals in different concentrations cause the rich colors in petrified wood and in the Painted Desert.

saltbrush, sunflowers, and Apache plume. Past the river, the road climbs onto a narrow mesa leading to Newspaper Rock, a panel of Pueblo rock art. Then the road bends southeast, enters a barren stretch, and passes tepee-shaped buttes in the distance. Next you come to Blue Mesa, roughly the park's midpoint and a good place to stop for views of petrified logs. The next stop on the drive is Agate Bridge, really a 100-foot log over a wide wash. The remaining overlooks are Jasper and Crystal forests, where you can get further glimpses of the accumulated petrified wood. On your way out of the park, stop at the Rainbow Forest Museum for a rest and to shop for a memento. ⊠ *Begins at Painted Desert Visitor Center.*

SCENIC STOPS

Agate Bridge

NATURE SITE | Here you'll see a 100-foot log spanning a 40-foot-wide wash. ⊠ *Main park road ⊹ 19 miles south of Painted Desert Visitor Center.*

Crystal Forest

NATURE SITE | The fragments of petrified wood strewn here once held clear quartz and amethyst crystals. ⊠ *Main park road ⊹ 20 miles south of Painted Desert Visitor Center.*

Giant Logs Interpretive Loop Trail

NATURE SITE | A short walk leads you past the park's largest log, known as Old Faithful. It's considered the largest because of its diameter (9 feet 9 inches), as well as how tall it once was. ⊠ *Main park road ⊹ 28 miles south of Painted Desert Visitor Center.*

Jasper Forest

VIEWPOINT | More of an overlook than a forest, this spot has a large concentration of petrified trees in jasper or red. ⊠ *Main park road ⊹ 17 miles south of Painted Desert Visitor Center.*

The Tepees

NATURE SITE | Witness the effects of time on these cone-shape rock formations colored by iron, manganese, and other

Flora and Fauna

Engelmann's asters and sunflowers are among the blooms in the park each summer. Juniper trees, cottonwoods, and willows grow along Puerco River wash, providing shelter for all manner of wildlife. You might spot mule deer, coyotes, prairie dogs, and foxes, though other inhabitants, like porcupines and bobcats, tend to hide. Bird-watchers should keep an eye out for mockingbirds, red-tailed and Swainson's hawks, roadrunners, swallows, and hummingbirds. Look for all three kinds of lizards—collared, side-blotched, and southern prairie—in rocks.

Beware of rattlesnakes. They're common but can generally be easily avoided: watch where you step, and don't step anywhere you can't see. If you do come across a rattler, give it plenty of space, and let it go its way before you continue on yours. Other reptiles are just as common but not as dangerous. The gopher snake looks similar to a rattlesnake, but is nonvenomous. The collared lizard, with its yellow head, can be seen scurrying out of your way in bursts measured at up to 15 mph. They aren't venomous, but they will bite if caught.

minerals. ☒ *Main park road ✛ 8 miles south of Painted Desert Visitor Center.*

TRAILS
Agate House
TRAIL | A fairly flat 1-mile trip takes you to an eight-room pueblo sitting high on a knoll. *Moderate.* ☒ *Petrified Forest National Park ✛ Trailhead: 26 miles south of Painted Desert Visitor Center.*

★ Blue Mesa
TRAIL | Although it's only 1 mile long and significantly steeper than the rest, this trail at the park's midway point is one of the most popular and worth the effort. *Moderate.* ☒ *Petrified Forest National Park ✛ Trailhead: 14 miles south of Painted Desert Visitor Center.*

Crystal Forest Trail
TRAIL | This easy ¾-mile loop leads you past petrified wood that once held quartz crystals and amethyst chips. *Easy.* ☒ *Petrified Forest National Park ✛ Trailhead: 20 miles south of Painted Desert Visitor Center.*

Giant Logs Trail
TRAIL | At 0.4 mile, Giant Logs is the park's shortest trail. The loop leads you to Old Faithful, the park's largest petrified log—9 feet, 9 inches at its base, weighing an estimated 44 tons. *Easy.* ☒ *Petrified Forest National Park ✛ Trailhead: directly behind Rainbow Forest Museum, 28 miles south of Painted Desert Visitor Center.*

Kachina Point
TRAIL | This is the trailhead for wilderness hiking at Petrified Forest National Park. A 1-mile trail leads to the Wilderness Area, but from there you're on your own. There are no developed trails, so hiking here is cross-country style. Expect to see strange formations, beautifully colored landscapes, and maybe, just maybe, a pronghorn antelope. *Difficult.* ☒ *Petrified Forest National Park ✛ Trailhead: on northwest side of Painted Desert Inn National Historic Landmark.*

Long Logs Trail
TRAIL | Although barren, this easy 1.6-mile loop passes the largest concentration of wood in the park. *Easy.* ☒ *Petrified Forest National Park ✛ Trailhead: 26 miles south of Painted Desert Visitor Center.*

Petroglyphs: The Writing on the Wall

The rock art of early Native Americans is carved or painted on basalt boulders, on canyon walls, and on the underside of overhangs throughout the area. No one knows the exact meaning of these signs, and interpretations vary; they've been seen as elements in shamanistic or hunting rituals, as clan signs, maps, or even indications of visits by extraterrestrials.

Where to Find Them

Susceptible to (and often already damaged by) vandalism, many rock-art sites aren't open to the public. Two good petroglyphs to check out at **Petrified Forest National Park** are Newspaper Rock, an overlook near mile marker 12, and Puerco Pueblo, near mile marker 11. Other sites in Arizona include **Hieroglyphic Point** in Salt River Canyon and **Deer Valley Petroglyph Preserve** north of Phoenix.

Determining Its Age

It's just as difficult to date a "glyph" as it is to understand it. Archaeologists try to determine a general time frame by judging the style, the date of the ruins and pottery in the vicinity, the amount of patination (formation of minerals) on the design, or the superimposition of newer images on top of older ones. Most of Eastern Arizona's rock art is estimated to be at least 1,000 years old, and many of the glyphs were created even earlier.

Varied Images

Some glyphs depict animals like bighorn sheep, deer, bear, and mountain lions; others are geometric patterns. The most unusual are the anthropomorphs, strange humanlike figures with elaborate headdresses. Concentric circles are a common design. A few of these circles served as solstice signs, indicating the summer and winter solstices and other important dates. At the solstice, when the angle of the sun is just right, a shaft of light shines through a crack in a nearby rock, illuminating the center of the circle. Archaeologists believe that these solar calendars helped determine the time for ceremonies and planting.

Many solstice signs are in remote regions, but you can visit Petrified Forest National Park around June 20 to see a concentric circle illuminated during the summer solstice. The glyph, reached by a paved trail just a few hundred yards from the parking area, is visible year-round, but light shines directly in the center during the week of the solstice. The phenomenon occurs at 9 am.

■ TIP➡ **Do not touch petroglyphs or pictographs—the oil from your hands can damage the images.**

Painted Desert Rim

TRAIL | The 1-mile trail is at its best in early morning or late afternoon, when the sun accentuates the brilliant red, blue, purple, and other hues of the desert and petrified forest landscape. *Moderate.* ☒ *Petrified Forest National Park ✛ Trail runs between Tawa Point and Kachina Point, 1 mile north of Painted Desert Visitor Center; drive to either point from visitor center.*

Puerco Pueblo Trail

TRAIL | FAMILY | A relatively flat and interesting 0.3-mile trail takes you past remains of a home of the Ancestral Pueblo people, built before 1400. The trail is paved and

The stones tell a story with ancient etchings on Newspaper Rock.

wheelchair accessible. *Easy.* ⊠ *Petrified Forest National Park* ⊹ *Trailhead: 10 miles south of Painted Desert Visitor Center.*

VISITOR CENTERS

Painted Desert Inn National Historic Landmark

INFO CENTER | This visitor center isn't as large as the other two, but here you can get information as well as view cultural history exhibits. ⊠ *Main park road* ⊹ *2 miles north of Painted Desert Visitor Center* ☎ *928/524–6228.*

Painted Desert Visitor Center

INFO CENTER | This is the place to go for general park information and an informative 20-minute film. Proceeds from books purchased here will fund continued research and interpretive activities for the park. ⊠ *North entrance* ⊹ *Off I–40, 27 miles east of Holbrook* ☎ *928/524–6228.*

Rainbow Forest Museum and Visitor Center

INFO CENTER | View displays of prehistoric animals, watch an orientation video, and—perhaps most important—use the restroom facilities at this visitor center

at the southern end of the park. ⊠ *South entrance* ⊹ *Off U.S. 180, 18 miles southeast of Holbrook* ☎ *928/524–6228.*

🍽 Restaurants

Dining in the park is limited to a cafeteria in the Painted Desert Visitor Center and snacks in the Rainbow Forest Museum. You may want to pack a lunch and eat at one of the park's picnic areas.

Painted Desert Visitor Center Cafeteria

$ | AMERICAN | Serving standard (but pretty decent) cafeteria fare, this is the only place in the park where you can get a full meal. **Known for:** closest restaurant to the park; gift shop; excellent lamb stew and Navajo tacos. $ *Average main: $7* ⊠ *North entrance* ☎ *928/524–6228.*

Activities

Because the park goes to great pains to maintain the integrity of the fossil- and artifact-strewn landscape, sports and

Arizona's Other Grand Canyon

About 100 miles north of Petrified Forest National Park via US-191 N, the nearly 84,000-acre Canyon de Chelly is one of the Southwest's most spectacular natural wonders rivaling the Grand Canyon—on a smaller scale, of course—for beauty. If you have the time, it's worth checking out.

Canyon de Chelly Home to Ancestral Pueblo from AD 350 to 1300, the nearly 84,000-acre Canyon de Chelly (pronounced d'*shay*) is one of the most spectacular natural wonders in the Southwest. On a smaller scale, it rivals the Grand Canyon for beauty. Its main gorges—the 26-mile-long Canyon de Chelly ("canyon in the rock") and the adjoining 35-mile-long Canyon del Muerto ("canyon of the dead")—comprise sheer, heavily eroded sandstone walls that rise to 1,100 feet over dramatic valleys. Ancient pictographs and petroglyphs decorate some of the cliffs, and within the canyon complex there are more than 7,000 archaeological sites. Stone walls rise hundreds of feet above streams, hogans, tilled fields, and sheep-grazing lands.

You can view prehistoric sites near the base of cliffs and perched on high, sheltering ledges, some of which you can access from the park's two main drives along the canyon rims. The dwellings and cultivated fields of the present-day Navajo lie in the flatlands between the cliffs, and those who inhabit the canyon today farm much the way their ancestors did. Most residents leave the canyon in winter but return in early spring to farm.

Canyon de Chelly's South Rim Drive (37 miles round-trip with seven overlooks) starts at the visitor center and ends at **Spider Rock Overlook,** where cliffs plunge nearly 1,000 feet to the canyon floor. The view here is of two pinnacles, Speaking Rock and Spider Rock. Other highlights on the South Rim Drive are Junction Overlook, where Canyon del Muerto joins Canyon de Chelly; White House Overlook, from which a 2½-mile round-trip trail leads to the **White House Ruin,** with remains of nearly 60 rooms and several kivas; and Sliding House Overlook, where you can see dwellings on a narrow, sloped ledge across the canyon. The carved and sometimes narrow trail down the canyon side to White House Ruin is the only access into Canyon de Chelly without a guide—if you have a fear of heights, this may not be the hike for you.

The only slightly less breathtaking **North Rim Drive** (34 miles round-trip with three overlooks) of Canyon del Muerto also begins at the visitor center and continues northeast on Indian Highway 64 toward the town of Tsaile. Major stops include **Antelope House Overlook,** a large site named for the animals painted on an adjacent cliff; **Mummy Cave Overlook,** where two mummies were found inside a remarkably unspoiled pueblo dwelling; and **Massacre Case Overlook,** which marks the spot where an estimated 115 Navajo were killed by the Spanish in 1805. (The rock walls of the cave are still pockmarked by the Spaniards' ricocheting bullets.) ⊠ *Indian Hwy. 7, Chinle* ✛ *3 miles east of U.S. 191* ☎ *928/674–5500 visitor center* ⊕ *www. nps.gov/cach* ⊜ *Free.*

outdoor options in the park are limited to on-trail hiking.

CAMPING

There are no campgrounds in the park. Backpacking or minimal-impact camping is allowed in a designated zone north of Lithodendron Wash in the Wilderness Area; a free permit must be obtained (pick up at the visitor center or museum), and group size is limited to eight. RVs are not allowed. There are no fire pits or designated sites, nor is any shade available. Note that if it rains, that pretty Painted Desert formation turns to sticky clay.

EDUCATIONAL OFFERINGS

Ask at either park visitor center for the availability of special ranger-led tours, such as the after-hours lantern tour of the Painted Desert Inn Museum.

Junior Ranger

TOUR—SIGHT | FAMILY | Children 12 and younger can learn more about the park's extensive human, animal, and geologic history as they train to become a Junior Ranger. ⊠ *Petrified Forest National Park.*

Ranger Walks and Talks

TOUR—SIGHT | Park rangers lead regular programs along the Great Logs Trail, inside the Painted Desert Inn Museum, and to the Puerco Pueblo. You can view which ranger programs are currently being offered at the visitor centers or online at *www.nps.gov/pefo.* ⊠ *Petrified Forest National Park.*

HIKING

All trails begin off the main road, with restrooms at or near the trailheads. Most maintained trails are relatively short, paved, clearly marked, and, with a few exceptions, easy to moderate in difficulty. Hikers with greater stamina can make their own trails in the wilderness area, located just north of the Painted Desert Visitor Center. Watch your step for rattlesnakes, which are common in the park—if left alone and given a wide berth, they're passed easily enough.

Nearby Towns

Located in eastern Arizona just off Interstate 40, Petrified Forest National Park is set in an area of grasslands, overlooked by mountains in the distance. At nearly an hour from **American Indian Nations,** nearly two hours from **Flagstaff,** and three hours from the **Grand Canyon,** the park is relatively remote and separated from many comforts of travel. Just a half hour away, **Holbrook,** the nearest town, is the best place to grab a quick bite to eat or take a brief rest.

Holbrook

27 miles west of the Northern Entrance of the Petrified Forest on I-40; 18 miles west of the Southern Entrance of the Petrified Forest on U.S. 180.

Downtown Holbrook is a monument to Route 66 kitsch. The famous "Mother Road" traveled through the center of Holbrook before Interstate 40 replaced it as the area's major east–west artery, and remnants of the "good ole days" can be found all over town. Navajo Boulevard, the town's main thoroughfare, is known for its cartoonish models of brightly colored dinosaurs. If you're looking for a memorable photo op, it's here. Although it's probably not worth staying overnight, the town's iconic Wigwam Motel is a quirky and highly iconic option if you do find yourself needing a rest.

GETTING HERE AND AROUND

Holbrook is on Interstate 40, approximately 90 miles east of Flagstaff and 30 miles west of Petrified Forest National Park. You can access AZ 77, en route to Snowflake, Taylor, and other Eastern Arizona recreation towns, directly from Interstate 40 in Holbrook.

Hotels

Wigwam Motel
$ | **HOTEL** | On the National Register of Historic Places, the iconic Wigwam consists of 15 bright-white concrete tepees. **Pros:** impeccably kitschy; one of the signature spots along Route 66; a travel bucket-list item. **Cons:** very sparse accommodations that can fit no more than two; awkward bathroom configuration; spotty Wi-Fi. [$] *Rooms from: $79* ✉ *811 West Hopi Dr., Holbrook* ☎ *928/524–3048* 🌐 *www.sleepinawigwam.com* 🛏 *15 rooms* 🍴 *No meals.*

Winslow

47 miles west of the Northern Entrance of the Petrified Forest on I-40.

Traveling to the Petrified Forest from Flagstaff, Winslow is home to the 18th-century Spanish hacienda-style La Posada Hotel and the Homolovi State Park, which has pueblo sites that were occupied between AD 1200 and 1425.

GETTING HERE AND AROUND

On Interstate 40, Winslow is approximately 110 miles east of Flagstaff and 50 miles west of Petrified Forest National Park.

Sights

Homolovi State Park
ARCHAEOLOGICAL SITE | *Homolovi* is a Hopi word meaning "place of the little hills." The pueblo sites here are thought to have been occupied between AD 1200 and 1425, and include 40 ceremonial kivas and two pueblos containing more than 1,000 rooms each. The Hopi believe their immediate ancestors inhabited this place, and they consider the site sacred. Many rooms have been excavated and recovered for protection. The Homolovi Visitor Center has a small museum with Hopi pottery and Ancestral Pueblo artifacts; it also hosts workshops on native art, ethnobotany, and traditional foods. Campsites with water and hookups are nearby. ✉ *AZ 87, Winslow* ✥ *4 miles northeast of Winslow* ☎ *928/289–4106, 877/697–2757 for camping reservations* 🌐 *azstateparks.com/homolovi* 🎟 *$7 per vehicle.*

Rock Art Ranch
ARCHAEOLOGICAL SITE | The 3,000 Ancestral Pueblo petroglyphs on this working cattle ranch in Chevelon Canyon are startlingly vivid after more than 1,000 years. Ranch owner Brantly Baird and family will guide you down to the canyon, explaining Western and archaeological history. It's mostly an easy driving and walking tour, except for the climb in and out of Chevelon Canyon, where there are handrails. Baird houses his Native American artifacts and pioneer farming implements in his own private museum. It's out of the way and on a dirt road, but you'll see some of the best rock art in northern Arizona. Reservations are required. ✉ *Off AZ 99, Winslow* ✥ *15 miles southeast of Winslow* ☎ *928/386–5047* 🎟 *From $35 per person* 🕒 *Closed Sun. Closed Feb.–Apr.*

Hotels

★ **La Posada Hotel**
$$ | **HOTEL** | One of the great railroad hotels, La Posada ("resting place") exudes the charm of an 18th-century Spanish hacienda, and its restoration has been a labor of love. **Pros:** historic charm; unique architecture; impressive restaurant. **Cons:** mazes of staircases aren't wheelchair-friendly (but ground floor rooms and restaurant are); an hour's drive from Flagstaff; little to do in the town of Winslow. [$] *Rooms from: $129* ✉ *303 E. 2nd St., Winslow* ☎ *928/289–4366* 🌐 *www.laposada.org* 🛏 *51 rooms* 🍴 *No meals.*

Chapter 28

PINNACLES NATIONAL PARK

28

Updated by
Andrew Collins

CALIFORNIA

🏕 Camping	🏨 Hotels	🏃 Activities	👁 Scenery	👥 Crowds
★★★☆☆	★★☆☆☆	★★★☆☆	★★★★☆	★★★☆☆

WELCOME TO PINNACLES NATIONAL PARK

TOP REASONS TO GO

★ **Condor encounters:** This is one of the few places to potentially view these critically endangered birds flying overhead; of the few hundred California condors alive in the wild today, about 65 have been released or hatched in Pinnacles or nearby along the coast.

★ **Cave exploring:** The park contains two talus caves—a unique type of cave formed when boulders fall into narrow canyons, creating ceilings, passageways, and small chambers.

★ **Hiking the pinnacles:** The best way to see the otherworldly rock formations of the ancient volcano at the park's center is to hike the more than 30 miles of trails.

★ **Climbing sans crowds:** Pinnacles receives relatively few visitors because of its out-of-the-way location, leaving the hundreds of rock-climbing routes crowd-free.

★ **Star appeal:** Far from cities, the park is a popular stargazing destination, especially during the annual Perseid meteor shower.

1 East Side. Of the park's two entrances to Pinnacles, the East Side is best for families and first-time visitors. It has the park's only visitor center and campground—which includes a modest grocery store and a small swimming pool that's especially inviting on hot days. This entrance also offers the best access to both easy and more challenging hikes, including the highly popular trek to Bear Gulch Cave.

2 West Side. The park's quieter side has fewer amenities, but entering here and driving to the Chaparral Parking Area provides the best way to sneak a glimpse of the high-peak formations without having to walk anywhere. Hikers, however, will find some of the park's most rugged and exciting trails, including treks to Balconies Cave and up into the High Peaks.

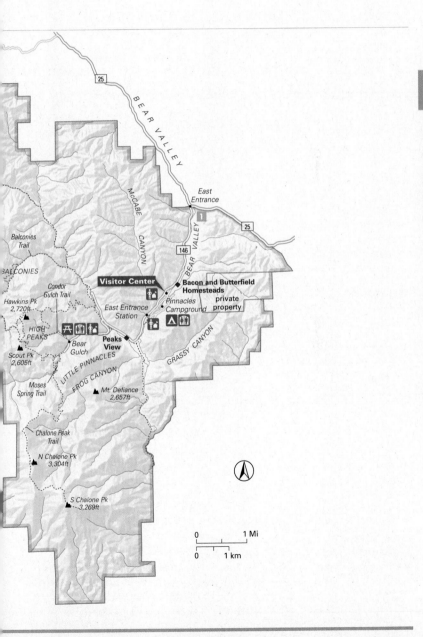

President Theodore Roosevelt recognized the uniqueness of the Pinnacles Volcanic Formation—its jagged spires and monoliths thrusting upward from chaparral-covered mountains—when he made it a national monument in 1908. Legends abound of robbers and banditos who used talus caves as hideouts, though the most famous denizens of the park today are the California condors.

The Pinnacles volcanic field formed some 23 million years ago and has slowly shifted to the northwest nearly 200 miles as a result of tectonic shifting of the Pacific plate. The peaks rise beside the San Andreas Rift Zone, which slices through Bear Valley just east of the park boundary. Highway 25 roughly parallels the faultline. Indigenous people have lived in the valleys that bracket the park for centuries, and members of the Chalon and Amah Matsun still work closely with park staff, volunteering their time and expertise on cultural and environmental projects at Pinnacles. Spanish settlers established the mission system through the region in 1769—settlements and churches from the period still stand just west of the park in Soledad as well as nearby in San Juan Bautista and out on the coast in Carmel and Santa Cruz.

Native peoples, Spaniards, and—following California statehood in 1850—white homesteaders farmed, worked, and occasionally battled over the land throughout the 19th century. A settler from Michigan, Schuyler Hain began promoting the beauty of Pinnacles around the turn

of the 20th century, leading visitors on hikes up into talus caves in Bear Valley. Word spread, which led to the park's national monument designation. In the 1930s, the federal government hired hundreds of CCC (Civilian Conservation Corps) workers to further develop the monument—they carved out many miles of the trails that still extend through the park today, along with several buildings, including Bear Gulch Nature Center and the stone restroom at Scout Peak. In 2013, Pinnacles received a major status upgrade, becoming the country's 59th national park. Although it lacks the singular thrills and sheer immensity of many of California's other national parks, this 26,000-acre park (it's less than 1 percent the size of Death Valley) offers plenty of wonder and magnificent photo ops, all of them contained within a manageable package that's at once secluded yet relatively easy to get to.

The park encompasses a cluster of craggy volcanoes flanked by scenic, sparsely populated valleys and contains no park lodgings or restaurants, but it's also within day-tripping distance of Monterey

AVERAGE HIGH/LOW TEMPERATURES					
JAN.	**FEB.**	**MAR.**	**APR.**	**MAY**	**JUNE**
62/27	63/30	67/32	72/33	80/37	88/41
JULY	**AUG.**	**SEPT.**	**OCT.**	**NOV.**	**DEC.**
95/45	95/45	90/42	81/36	69/31	61/27

Bay, San Francisco, and San Luis Obispo County. If it's your first time visiting the park, however, consider spending the night somewhere relatively near the park, such as King City, Salinas, or Hollister, or overnighting in the park's picturesque campground. Local options are neither fancy nor distinctive, but this strategy will allow you to explore each side of the park at a leisurely pace.

What's remarkable about visiting Pinnacles from anywhere on the coast is the chance to experience such a strikingly different landscape within about 35 miles of the ocean. The park's soaring golden peaks and rocky spires and comparatively arid, sunny climate look and feel a world away. The signature attractions are the high peaks and the intriguing caves, which are in the middle of the park and can be hiked to in a half-day from either side. However you approach Pinnacles, you'll find opportunities to spy rare California condors flying overhead and to soak up a breathtaking landscape.

Planning

When to Go

Triple-digit temperatures are not uncommon in summer; luckily this means fewer crowds, especially on weekdays. Spring, particularly March and April, is the most popular season—a prime time to view spectacular displays of lupine, poppies, and other wildflowers. October through December is a great time to visit if you want to enjoy cooler temperatures and smaller crowds. Winters are cold by

California standards, but this is an opportune time to hike, especially the High Peaks, where most of the trails are in the sun. Just keep in mind that temperatures in the deeply shaded areas such as the Balconies Trail can reach below freezing.

Note that Bear Gulch Cave is hugely popular but also home to a large colony of Townsend's big-eared bats. This protected species raises its young in late spring and summer, so the cave is closed from about mid-May to mid-July. Check the park website for the latest information on closures.

Getting Here and Around

AIR

It's about a 90-minute drive north to reach the nearest major airport in San Jose, and about two hours to the airports in San Francisco and Oakland. Pleasantly compact Monterey Regional Airport is about a 75-minute drive west and is served by Alaska, Allegiant, American, and United.

CAR

One of the first things you need to decide when visiting Pinnacles is whether to arrive through the east or west entrance. There is no road through the park, although it's possible to hike across the park in an hour or two and to reach the key attractions—the High Peaks and two talus caves—from either side. If you've never been to the park, entering the east side is a good strategy as it contains the main visitor center and a convenience store as well as access to more trailheads. On the other hand, if you're making just a short visit while driving up

U.S. 101 or looking for the quickest hiking access to the High Peaks, the west entrance makes sense. It takes roughly the same amount of time to reach each entrance, whether you approach from San Jose, the coast, or San Luis Obispo. The east side is accessed via Highway 146 from rural and scenic Highway 25, and the west side is reached from a different—narrow, hilly, and one-way in places—section of Highway 146 from the town of Soledad, just off the U.S. 101 freeway. RVs and trailers are advised not to use the west entrance. To drive to either entrance, without heavy traffic, allow 1½–2½ from San Jose and the Bay Area, 1½–2 hours from San Luis Obispo County, and just 1–1½ hours from the Monterey Peninsula and Santa Cruz.

By car, to get from one entrance to the other, you must exit the park, and then drive about 75 to 90 minutes. The fastest and most direct route is to the south, via U.S. 101 through King City and Highways G13 and 25. A wonderfully scenic and adventuresome option, however, is to take unpaved but generally well-maintained La Gloria Road, which curves through the mountains just north of the park boundary. Your GPS may tell you it's possible to access La Gloria Road by cutting north through the western edge of the park, but this is *not possible*. Instead, from the western entrance, follow Highway 146 west to Soledad, take U.S. 101 north to exit 305, and follow Camphora Gloria Road north to Gloria Road, which becomes unpaved and rather rugged once it passes through Henry Sands Canyon. Continue another 12 miles, taking your time to enjoy the stunning views of the mountains and wine country, before turning right (south) onto Highway 25 and continuing another 4½ miles to Highway 146 and the east entrance. The whole drive takes about 90 minutes and should be avoided after rain, when La Gloria Road can become very muddy.

Inspiration

The landscape around Pinnacles and the adjacent farming town of Soledad figured prominently in the writings of the great American novelist John Steinbeck. His 1937 novella *Of Mice and Men* took place in Soledad, but it's his epic 1952 novel *East of Eden* that most poignantly describes Pinnacles' majestic, mountainous landscape.

Shirlaine Baldwin's lushly photographed 2016 book *California Condors: A Day at Pinnacles National Park* offers a beautiful and informative look at these huge birds that had become extinct in the wild by the early 1980s but that are slowly making a comeback in the skies above the park.

Watch John Ford's gripping 1962 Western *How The West Was Won*, starring Henry Fonda and John Wayne, for a memorable cinematic view of the park.

Park Essentials

PARK FEES AND PERMITS
Park admission—good for seven days—is $30 per car, $25 for motorcycles, $15 per person on foot or bicycle.

PARK HOURS
The east entrance is always open. The west entrance is open daily 7:30 am–8 pm, but cars can exit the park through an automatic gate anytime after closing time.

CELL PHONE RECEPTION
The closer you get to Pinnacles, the less reliable the cell phone service; it's nearly nonexistent within the park. There's a pay phone at the visitor center at the east entrance, and here you can also purchase Wi-Fi from the visitor center.

Pinnacles in One Day

Although the park's two sides aren't connected by road, it is possible to visit them in one fairly long but rewarding day. Enter the west side early and stop briefly for maps and advice at the **West Pinnacles Visitor Contact Station** before continuing 2 miles to the **Chaparral Trailhead** parking lot, where you can view the park's impressive peaks. Grab your flashlight and some water and follow the **Balconies Trail** from the parking lot. This mostly level 1-mile hike takes you along the shaded canyon floor to the **Balconies Cave**, where you must duck under boulders and sometimes squeeze through talus passages. From the cave you can hike an extra ½-mile on the **Balconies Cliff Trail**, climbing to fantastic views east to Machete Ridge. Follow the trail down to the back side of the caves, and return through the caves to the original trail.

Exit the park and drive to the park's east entrance via King City or, for an even more scenic though slow and bumpy route, by way of unpaved La Gloria Road, which winds over the mountains north of the park. Stop at the **Pinnacles Visitor Center** to pick up snacks at the adjacent convenience store before driving 3 miles to the Bear Gulch Day Use Area, where you'll find a serene picnic area with shaded tables. If the seasonal **Bear Gulch Nature Center** is open, check out its displays, which include a seismograph (the park lies near the San Andreas Fault). Make sure you have your water and flashlight with you as you take the **Bear Gulch Trail** to the **Moses Spring Trail** and on to the Bear Gulch cave system (about a ½ mile). Upon entering the caves, you'll scramble through until you come to a long staircase cut into the stone, which leads to the Bear Gulch Reservoir. Follow the **Rim Trail** as it leaves the reservoir for views of the peaks to the east and west. After a switchback descent, it connects again with the Moses Spring Trail, which returns to the parking lot.

Hotels

Although there aren't any lodgings in the park, the Pinnacles Campground is right by the east entrance and offers everything from primitive tent sites to newer tent cabins with electricity. The nearest communities to the park, Soledad, King City, Hollister, and Salinas, have mostly budget- and mid-priced chain accommodations. If you're seeking luxury or character, consider staying in one of the famously scenic communities near or on the coast—such as Carmel and Carmel Valley, Monterey, and Santa Cruz—which are 60 to 90 minutes away.

Note that hotels in this part of the state, even in the sleepy towns near the park, are a bit spendy. *Hotel reviews have been shortened. For full information, visit Fodors.com.*

What It Costs			
$	$$	$$$	$$$$
RESTAURANTS			
under $16	$16–$22	$22–$30	over $30
HOTELS			
under $150	$151–$225	$226–$300	over $300

28

Pinnacles National Park PLANNING

Restaurants

The park has no restaurants—just a tiny convenience store (with bags of ice and basic snacks) next to the visitor center on the east side. So plan accordingly, and pack a cooler if you plan on picnicking or camping. The nearest communities with grocery stores and a limited selection of restaurants are Hollister to the north, King City to the south, and Soledad just outside the western entrance. It's just over an hour, however, to some of the most varied and often superb dining scenes in Monterey, Carmel Valley, and Santa Cruz. *Restaurant reviews have been shortened. For full information, visit Fodors.com.*

Visitor Information

CONTACTS **Pinnacles National Park.**
✉ *5000 Hwy. 146, Paicines* ☎ *831/389–4486* ⊕ *www.nps.gov/pinn.*

East Side

31 miles southeast of Hollister, 31 miles north of King City.

The larger of the park's two sides has a visitor center, campground, and convenience store. It also has a bit more infrastructure and roadway to explore, including the Bear Gulch Day Use Area, which has a small nature center, one of the best picnic spots in the park, and access to many of the park's top trails.

 Sights

HISTORIC SITES
Bacon and Butterfield Homesteads
HISTORIC SITE | On the park's eastern side, these two preserved homesteads are in the heart of the 331-acre Ben Bacon Ranch Historic District, which the park acquired in 2006. A walk along the former road through this section illustrates what subsistence farming in the area looked like from 1865 to 1941, before large-scale agriculture and ranching became the norm. You reach the area by way of the gravel road that starts just east of the Pinnacles Visitor Center; it then continues north about 1.3 miles by the old homesteads. ✉ *Off Hwy. 146.*

Bear Gulch Nature Center
MUSEUM | FAMILY | This small stone building constructed by the CCC (Civilian Conservation Corps) in the 1930s makes for a short but engaging stop while hiking from or picnicking in the Bear Gulch Day Use Area. Inside you can watch a film and view interpretive displays about the park, and the rangers can offer advice about nearby trails and talus caves. ✉ *Bear Gulch Day Use Area, Paicines* ☎ *831/389–4486.*

PICNIC AREAS
Bear Gulch Picnic Area
LOCAL INTEREST | The park's most pleasant picnic area, shaded by live oaks, sits alongside a seasonal creek. It's a convenient spot to picnic before or after a hike to the reservoir via the Moses Spring or Rim trail. The nearby Bear Gulch Day Use Area has bathrooms and drinking water. ✉ *Pinnacles National Park ✛ Bear Gulch Day Use Area.*

★ **Peaks View Picnic Area**
LOCAL INTEREST | Short of hiking up to the rugged High Peaks, this picturesque picnic area is the best place to catch a glimpse of them (off to the west). You might spot hawks and other birds as well. The area has restrooms and a few picnic tables, and drinking water is available. ■TIP➔ **Here you'll also find the beginning of a section of the Bench Trail that's been graded and resurfaced for wheelchair accessibility—it winds through a shady stand of oak.** ✉ *Hwy. 146 ✛ About 1.5 miles southwest of visitor center.*

TRAILS

★ Bear Gulch Cave–Moses Spring–Rim Trail Loop

TRAIL | FAMILY | Perhaps the most popular hike at Pinnacles, this relatively short (2.2-mile) loop trail is fun for kids and adults. It leads to the Bear Gulch cave system, and if your timing is right, you'll pass by several seasonal waterfalls inside the caves (flashlights are required). If it's been raining, check with a ranger, as the caves can flood. The upper side of the cave is usually closed in spring and early summer to protect the Townsend's big-ear bats and their pups. *Easy.* ✛ *Trailhead: Bear Gulch Day Use Area.*

Chalone Peak Trail

TRAIL | If you choose this strenuous 9-mile round-trip hike (2,040 feet of elevation gain), you'll be rewarded with views of the surrounding valleys from the highest point in the park at 3,304 feet, North Chalone Peak (where there are pit toilets). If you want to extend the hike, proceed south along the unmaintained portion of the trail for 1.6 miles to South Chalone Peak (3,269 feet). *Difficult.* ✉ *Pinnacles National Park* ✛ *Trailhead: Bear Gulch Reservoir, off Moses Spring Trail.*

★ Condor Gulch Trail

TRAIL | The trailhead starts at the Bear Gulch Day Use area, and it's a short but somewhat strenuous 1-mile hike uphill to the Condor Gulch Overlook, where you can get a good view of the High Peaks above. You can turn back the same way you came, or continue another 0.7 mile up to the High Peaks Trail (a total elevation gain of 1,100 feet)—and extend your hike by following it in either direction. If you're feeling ambitious, continue into the park's west side, to the Balconies Cliffs Trail, returning back via the level Old Pinnacles Trail. *Moderate–Difficult.* ✉ *Pinnacles National Park* ✛ *Trailhead: Bear Gulch Day Use Area.*

Pinnacles Visitor Center to Bear Gulch Day Use Area

TRAIL | This 4.6-mile round-trip hike (allow about three hours) follows the Chalone and Bear creeks first along the level Bench Trail for about 1½ miles, where it meets up with the Sycamore Trail, which ascends gradually through a tree-shaded ravine on its way to Bear Gulch. Purchase an interpretive map at the visitor center and keep your eyes open for signs pointing out where you might be able to spot the rare red-legged frog or the native three-spined stickleback fish. *Moderate.* ✉ *Pinnacles National Park* ✛ *Trailhead: Pinnacles Visitor Center.*

Pinnacles Visitor Center to South Wilderness Trail

TRAIL | This 6½-mile round-trip hike with no elevation gain is an easy if somewhat long stroll, first on the Bench Trail and then alongside the Chalone River to the park's southeastern boundary. A favorite of wildlife-watching enthusiasts, it's a lovely trail for listening to birds sing along the creek, and it leads through magnificent groves of valley oaks. *Easy–Moderate.* ✉ *Pinnacles National Park* ✛ *Trailhead: Pinnacles Visitor Center.*

VISITOR CENTERS

Pinnacles Visitor Center

At the park's main visitor center, near the eastern entrance, you'll find a helpful selection of maps, books, and gifts. The adjacent campground store sells light snacks. ✉ *5000 Hwy. 146, Paicines* ☎ *831/389–4485* ⊕ *www.nps.gov/pinn.*

West Side

10 miles east of Soledad, 25 miles north of King City,

Although more accessible from the coast and bigger highways and towns, the west side of Pinnacles is actually the quieter and more secluded of the two halves. You enter it via a beautiful, winding country road, and once inside the park you'll find the contact ranger station and a parking area that serves as the trailhead to several outstanding hikes.

 Sights

PICNIC AREAS

★ Chaparral Trailhead Picnic Area

LOCAL INTEREST | The west side's only picnic area offers stunning views of the High Peaks and access to some key trailheads. Look for knifelike Machete Ridge looming in the distance. There are few trees for shade, however, and it can get hot in summer. Restrooms and drinking water are available. ⊠ *End of Hwy. 146 ⊹ 2 miles northeast of West Pinnacles Visitor Contact Station.*

TRAILS

★ Balconies Cliffs–Cave Loop

TRAIL | FAMILY | Grab your flashlight before heading out from the Chaparral Trailhead parking lot for this 2.4-mile loop that takes you through the Balconies Caves. This trail is especially beautiful in spring, when wildflowers carpet the canyon floor. About 0.6 mile from the start of the trail, turn left to begin ascending the Balconies Cliffs Trail, where you'll be rewarded with close-up views of Machete Ridge and other steep, vertical formations; you may run across rock climbers testing their skills before rounding the loop and descending back through the cave. *Easy–Moderate.* ⊠ *Pinnacles National Park ⊹ Trailhead: Chaparral Parking Area.*

High Peaks to Balconies Cave Loop

TRAIL | One of the more ambitious hikes in the park, this 8.4-mile round-trip adventure also takes in some of the most dramatic scenery in the park, including its jagged spires and rock formations and the popular Balconies Cave. Start with the hard part, the 1,540-foot ascent into the majestic High Peaks, then scamper east and downhill via the 2-mile Blue Oak Trail, which leads into the park's east side, before returning via the Old Pinnacles and Balconies Cliffs trails. *Difficult.*

⊠ *Pinnacles National Park ⊹ Trailhead: Chaparral Parking Area.*

★ Juniper Canyon Loop

TRAIL | This steep 4.3-mile loop climbs into the heart of the dramatic High Peaks with a 1,215-foot elevation gain. Summer temps can soar, so bring plenty of water. From the trailhead follow the switchbacks up for 1.2 miles, where the trail veers right; stop at Scout Peak, where you'll find restrooms and fantastic views in all directions—keep an eye out for the occasional California condor in flight. Follow the High Peaks Trail north through a steep and narrow section, where you hug the side of rock faces until reaching a short, nearly vertical staircase that has a railing to help you up. Then pick up the Tunnel Trail to complete your loop back to the trailhead via the Juniper Canyon Trail. *Difficult.* ⊠ *Pinnacles National Park ⊹ Trailhead: Chaparral Parking Area.*

Prewett Point to Jawbone Trail

TRAIL | FAMILY | You can hike these two connected trails, starting with the 0.9-mile wheelchair-accessible Prewett Point hike, from the West Pinnacles Visitor Contact Station. It leads to an impressive overlook and offers panoramic views of the High Peaks, Balconies Cliffs, and Hain Wilderness. It's mostly exposed, however, so avoid it during midday in summer. The easy-to-moderate Jawbone Trail extends from Prewett Point, descending 1.2 miles through the hills to the Jawbone Parking Area, which is another 0.3 miles to Chaparral Parking Area. Allow about 45 minutes to hike to Prewett Point and back, and up to two hours round-trip if you tackle both trails. *Easy–Moderate.* ⊠ *Pinnacles National Park ⊹ Trailhead: West Pinnacles Visitor Contact Station.*

VISITOR CENTERS

West Pinnacles Visitor Contact Station

This small ranger station is just past the park's western entrance, about 10 miles east of Soledad. Here you can get maps and information, watch a 13-minute film about Pinnacles, and view interpretive

Plants and Wildlife in Pinnacles National Park

Pinnacles doesn't have the wildlife superstars found at other national parks—bison, bear, elk, bighorn sheep. Here, California condors rule the roost.

Magnificent Birds

These magnificent birds, which when fully grown have wingspans approaching 10 feet, were nearly extinct in the 1980s. Only 22 remained in the world just three decades ago, but thanks to an intensive captive breeding program, there are now more than 400, with 240 of them in the wild. Pinnacles is one of the five release locations for California condors, and about 30 make their home in the park. It is also the preferred habitat for prairie falcons, which breed here in one of the highest densities in the world.

From Bobcats to Beetles

Bobcats and cougars also roam Pinnacles, and California quail are abundant. In addition, there are 14 species of bats, including a colony of Townsend's big-eared bats in Bear Gulch Cave, hibernating in winter and raising their young throughout the summer. The park has the most

bee species—400 per unit area—of any place ever studied. It's also an essential refuge for native species, among them the big-eared kangaroo rat, the Gabilan slender salamander, the Pinnacles shield-back katydid, and the Pinnacles riffle beetle, that have been challenged by nearby human encroachment.

Wildflowers and Chaparral

Springtime sets the stage for a wildflower extravaganza, especially from March through early May, when more than 80% of the park's plants are in bloom. The most prodigious early bloomers include manzanita, shooting stars, and Indian warriors; by March the park is awash in California poppies, bush poppies, buck brush, fiesta flower, and monkey flower. Late bloomers include suncups, bush lupine, and Johnny-jump-ups. Most of the park is covered in chaparral, which has adapted to the high-heat, low-moisture conditions. This particular plant community is mostly shrubs that grow to around 6 feet tall; the dominant species is chamise, which grows alongside buck brush, manzanita, black sage, and holly-leaved cherry.

28

Pinnacles National Park ACTIVITIES

exhibits. No food or drink is available here. ⊠ Hwy. 146, Soledad ☎ 831/389–4427 ⊕ www.nps.gov/pinn.

Activities

BIRD-WATCHING

You don't have to be an avid bird-watcher to appreciate the diversity of birds at Pinnacles, so don't forget to bring your binoculars, especially for that charged moment when you realize you've spotted a rare California condor. You're most likely

to see a condor in the early morning or in the early evening in the relatively remote High Peaks area, on the Balconies Cliff Trail as you look toward Machete Ridge, or just southeast of the campground. There are two spotting scopes in the campground that may help you get a closer look. Do not under any circumstances approach these federally protected birds—you can be fined for doing so.

The High Peaks are a good place to spot other raptors, such as prairie and peregrine falcons, golden eagles, red-tailed hawks, and American kestrels. Also keep on the lookout around the campground and visitor center, which are at a convergence of habitats—riparian, oak/pine trees, chaparral, and human-made. The paved road past the parking lot is a prime habitat for coveys of California quail and wild turkeys.

CAMPING

Pinnacles has only one camping option, on the park's eastern side, next to the Pinnacles Visitor Center.

Pinnacles Campground. Set under a canopy of live oaks that provides welcome shade over most of its 134 sites, this year-round campground has flush toilets and showers and a seasonal swimming pool and camp store. Each tent ($35), RV ($45), and glamping-style tent cabin ($115–$125) has a picnic table and a fire ring. ☎ 877/444–6777 ⊕ www.visitpinnacles.com.

EDUCATIONAL PROGRAMS

Illustrated Ranger Talks

COLLEGE | On some weekend evenings, rangers give free presentations at the east entrance's campground amphitheater. The topics depend on the ranger's particular interests but always relate to the park's main stories and its geology, plants, or wildlife. Times vary, so check the Pinnacles website or the Activity Boards at the east or west entrances or the Bear Gulch Nature Center. ✉ 5000 Hwy. 146 ☎ 831/389–4486 ⊕ www.nps.gov/pinn/planyourvisit/programs.htm.

Junior Ranger Program

LOCAL INTEREST | FAMILY | Kids can pick up a free Junior Ranger booklet at Bear Nature Center and the park visitor centers and earn a badge for completing a series of fun educational activities. ✉ Pinnacles National Park.

HIKING

Hiking is by far the park's most popular activity, and the only way to get between its east and west sides, as no roads traverse the Pinnacles. There are some 30 miles of trails, most of them starting from the west side's Chaparral Parking Area and the east side's Bear Gulch Day Use Area. The best hikes across the park are either the flat and easy 3-mile Old Pinnacles Trail or by climbing up and through the High Peaks, which can entail anything from a 5- to 8-mile trek and some serious elevation gains. In summer when it can get very hot in the park, try to tackle the steeper, more arduous trails in the morning or early evening.

Flashlights are required in the Bear Gulch and Balconies cave systems—you won't be able to get through the caves without one. Penlights won't do the job; the best choice is a hands-free, head-mounted light. Also, although the hikes to the caves themselves are easy and short, getting through the caves requires much scrambling, ducking, climbing, and squeezing. Make sure you have suitable, closed-toe shoes.

GUIDED HIKES

★ **Ranger-Guided Hikes and Activities**
Ranger programs and guided hikes, including occasional and very popular full-moon night hikes, are offered on weekends, fall–spring. For details, check activity boards or talk with staff at the visitor centers. ✉ Pinnacles National Park.

ROCK CLIMBING

Although a favorite of Bay Area and Central Coast climbers for years, Pinnacles luckily remains relatively free of crowds compared with better-known parks like Yosemite and Joshua Tree. One important thing to consider is that Pinnacles is largely made of volcanic rock that can be soft and crumbly. Beginners should check with rangers for advice on climbing in this terrain. In general, the east side has stronger rock, but the west side has much higher peaks.

A good resource for first-time climbers is the nonprofit Friends of Pinnacles (⊕ www.pinnacles.org), which provides useful tips, guidelines, and updates regarding climbing closures due to nesting raptors. Some formations can be closed January–July to protect nesting falcons and eagles.

STARGAZING

Despite its proximity to the populous Bay Area, Pinnacles remains nearly untouched by light pollution, making it an outstanding place to watch meteor showers, stars, or the full moon. It's popular with astronomy clubs, whose members occasionally set up their telescopes for public use. Park rangers sometimes lead nighttime activities (reservations required; call or check the park website a few days ahead), usually on the weekends, that include dark-sky and full-moon hikes and "star parties" to watch meteor showers and other celestial phenomena.

Nearby Towns

The small town of **Soledad,** just outside the park's western entrance, is most famous as the setting of John Steinbeck's *Of Mice and Men,* but it's also in the heart of the Monterey County wine region and has some excellent wineries with tasting rooms, though few amenities beyond these. A short drive south, the similarly agricultural community of **King City** has a few modest lodgings and good restaurants—it's a good base for visiting either park entrance.

To the north, you'll find a larger though still mostly chain-oriented selection of hotels and eateries in **Salinas,** a once-gritty city of about 155,000 that's lately begun undergoing a downtown renaissance and is home to the famed National Steinbeck Center, and **Hollister,** a farming town and bedroom community with some good wineries in the countryside; the historic neighboring hamlet of San Juan Bautista has plenty of charm.

The famous Pacific coastal communities of the **Monterey Peninsula,** including Carmel Valley and Monterey, as well as **Santa Cruz** at the top of Monterey Bay, are just a 60- to 90-minute drive, yet feel like a world away, with world-class beaches, golf course, winery tasting rooms, boutiques, and distinctive dining and lodging options.

Soledad

10 miles miles west of Pinnacles' west entrance.

An agricultural center with outstanding wineries and a small but bustling downtown, Soledad has about 26,000 residents, nearly 90 percent of whom identify as Hispanic or Latino. It's a good stop for wine-tasting and to stock up on picnic supplies and fill your gas tank before visiting the park's west side.

GETTING HERE AND AROUND

The U.S. 101 passes through Soledad on its way up through inland central California from San Luis Obispo to San Jose.

VISITOR INFORMATION Soledad Visitors and Gateway Center. ⊠ *502 Front St., Soledad* ☎ *831/204–7208* ⊕ *www.soledadca. org.*

Sights

★ **Chalone Vineyard**

WINERY/DISTILLERY | Monterey County's longest-running winery is set along the sunny hills that adjoin the west entrance of Pinnacles National Park, making it an ideal stop before or after a hike. Taste Chalone's superb Pinot Noir and Chardonnay on the peaceful patio overlooking the stunning landscape. ⊠ *32020 Stonewall Canyon Rd., Soledad* ☎ *707/933–3235* ⊕ *www.chalonevineyard.com* ☉ *Closed Mon.–Thurs.*

Hahn Estate Winery

WINERY/DISTILLERY | Situated a bit south of downtown Soledad in Monterey County's renowned Santa Lucia Highlands wine country, this exceptional Pinot Noir producer with a second tasting room in downtown Carmel offers both traditional tastings and highly informative and fun ATV tours through the property's vineyards. ✉ *37700 Foothill Rd., Soledad* ☎ *831/678–4555* 🌐 *www.hahnwines.com* ⏲ *Closed Tues.–Wed.*

Mission Nuestra Señora de la Soledad
BUILDING | A worthwhile stop along the state's historic mission trail, this 1791 compound is set in the foothills of Santa Lucia Highlands' venerable wine country. There's a small museum, and you can take a self-guided tour of the church and grounds. ✉ *36641 Fort Romie Rd., Soledad* ☎ *831/678–2586* 🌐 *www.soledad-mission.com.*

🍴 Restaurants

Restaurant Plaza Garibaldi
$ | **MEXICAN** | Great Mexican food is an asset of this valley with a pronounced Mexican-American population, and this festive spot filled with colorful murals stands out from the pack for its friendly service and generous portions. Kick things off with a bowl of steaming-hot *choriqueso* (melted cheese with chorizo), followed by platters of shrimp with garlic, grilled salmon, lengua burritos, tacos al pastor. **Known for:** friendly staff; molcajete mixed-meat platters; micheladas with all the garnishes. [$] *Average main: $14* ✉ *707 Front St., Soledad* ☎ *831/237–5232* ⏲ *Closed Wed.*

🛏 Hotels

★ Inn at the Pinnacles
$$$ | **B&B/INN** | Set amid 160 acres of hilltop vineyards overlooking the Salinas Valley and the coastal Santa Lucia Mountains, this Mediterranean-style bed-and-breakfast is an oasis of comfort just off the winding road leading to the park's western entrance. **Pros:** gorgeous vineyard setting and sunset views; tasty breakfast; close to the park. **Cons:** few dining options in area; not a good fit for kids; a bit isolated. [$] *Rooms from: $260* ✉ *3025 Stonewall Canyon Rd., Soledad* ☎ *831/678–2400* 🌐 *www.innatthepinnacles.com* 🔑 *6 rooms* 🍽 *Free Breakfast.*

King City

25 miles south of Pinnacles' west entrance, 30 miles south of Pinnacles' east entrance.

With about 13,000 residents, King City shares Soledad's laid-back vibe, largely Latino population, and agricultural economy. Although lacking wineries and attractions, it does have a few places to stay, making it a good choice if you want to be near either of Pinnacles' entrances.

GETTING HERE AND AROUND
Located on the U.S. 101 freeway, King City is just a half-hour drive south of Soledad and the park's west entrance, and a 40-minute drive—via Highways G13 and 25—from the park's eastern entrance.

VISITOR INFORMATION King City Visitors Center. ✉ *200 Broadway St.* ☎ *831/385–3814* 🌐 *www.kingcity.com.*

🍴 Restaurants

★ Cork & Plough
$$ | **MODERN AMERICAN** | This stylish space on King City's main drag with a pair of outdoor dining areas pays homage to the region's bounty of fresh produce and fine wines with its creative, seasonally sourced contemporary American cooking. Good bets include whiskey-marinated bone-in pork chops and braised-oxtail rosemary gnocchi. **Known for:** burgers with interesting toppings; flights of local wines; seasonal cheesecake. [$] *Average main: $17* ✉ *200 Broadway St.* ☎ *831/386–9491* 🌐 *www.thecorkandplough.com.*

Tacos La Potranca De Jalisco
$ | **MEXICAN** | Fans of authentic, street-food-style soft tacos travel for miles to this no-frills taqueria in the center of King City. Favorite fillings include tripe, lengua, carnitas, and pork al pastor, and in addition to tacos you can enjoy your protein in a burrito, torta, or sope. **Known for:** outdoor picnic-table seating; overstuffed

burritos; horchata and jamaica agua frescas. $ *Average main: $7* ✉ *201 Broadway St.* ☎ *831/385–7500* ⊕ *www.tacoslapotrancadejalisco.com.*

Hotels

Keefer's Inn
$ | HOTEL | This no-frills budget motel just off U.S. 101 in King City, owned by the same family since 1947, has compact but pleasant rooms with wood-laminate floors, as well as a pool and hot tub. **Pros:** affordable rates; good Mexican restaurant; relatively close to both entrances of Pinnacles. **Cons:** plain decor; no pets; bland location. $ *Rooms from: $104* ✉ *615 Canal St.* ☎ *831/385–4843* ⇌ *47 rooms* ⦿ *Free Breakfast.*

Hollister

32 miles north of Pinnacles' east entrance, 45 miles southeast of San Jose.

The hub of San Benito County, this pleasant if prosaic bedroom community whose population has doubled to about 40,000 since 1990 is the large town you'll hit en route to the park from the Bay Area, making it a good place to stock up on gas and supplies. The area's charms are mostly on the outskirts of town, from a handful of choice dining options in historic neighboring communities like Tres Pinos and San Juan Bautista to several notable wineries southwest of town.

GETTING HERE AND AROUND
Hollister is at the junction of Highways 25 and 156, a 40-minute drive from the park's east entrance and a 45-minute to one-hour drive from San Jose and Monterey Bay.

VISITOR INFORMATION San Benito County
Chamber of Commerce. ✉ *243 6th St., Suite 100, Hollister* ☎ *831/637–5315* ⊕ *www.sanbenitocountychamber.com.*

Sights

★ Calera Wine Company
WINERY/DISTILLERY | One of the Central Coast's exemplars when it comes to Burgundy-style Pinot Noir and Chardonnay, Calera is set high in the foothills of the Gabilan Mountains, about 10 miles south of Hollister. Tastings are in an airy, high-ceilinged space with a breezy patio. ✉ *11300 Cienega Rd., Hollister* ☎ *831/637–9170* ⊕ *www.calerawine.com* ⊘ *Closed Tues.–Wed.*

 Restaurants

★ Inn at Tres Pinos
$$$ | STEAKHOUSE | This humble-appearing roadhouse in a tiny village 7 miles south of Hollister serves up some of the tastiest modern American food in San Benito County, with pistachio-mustard-crusted rack of lamb and filet mignon among the standouts. With a refined but easygoing vibe, the inn offers plenty of seafood and pasta options, too, along with an extensive California wine list. **Known for:** steak and seafood grills with interesting preparations; great selection of Central California wines; vanilla focaccia-bread pudding. $ *Average main: $27* ✉ *6991 Airline Hwy., Tres Pinos* ✛ *on Hwy. 25, about 25 miles north of Pinnacles' east side* ☎ *831/628–3320* ⊕ *www.trespinosinn.com* ⊘ *Closed Mon. No lunch.*

Hotels

Hacienda de Léal
$$ | HOTEL | Set just off Hwy. 156 a few blocks from San Juan Bautista's Plaza Historic District and 45 minutes to an hour from either of Pinnacles National Park's entrances, this attractive Spanish Colonial-style boutique hotel has simply but smartly furnished rooms set around a pretty courtyard with lighted trees and a fire pit. **Pros:** reasonable rates for the area; close to historic Mission San Juan Bautista; gorgeous courtyard. **Cons:** no

restaurant on-site; some traffic noise from Hwy. 156; sometimes booked up with weddings. $ *Rooms from: $143* ✉ *410 The Alameda, San Juan Bautista* ☎ *831/623–4380* 🌐 *www.liveloveleal.com* 🛏 *43 rooms* 🍴 *Free Breakfast.*

Nightlife

★ **Brewery Twenty Five Taproom**
BREWPUBS/BEER GARDENS | Tucked into a quaint red-tile-roof courtyard in San Juan Bautista's historic downtown, this casual little taproom is a sweet spot for a well-crafted hazy IPA or coffee porter after a day exploring Pinnacles. ✉ *106 3rd St., San Juan Bautista* ☎ *831/636–7640* 🌐 *www.shop.brewerytwentyfive.com.*

Salinas

35 miles northwest of Pinnacles' west entrance.

Salinas, a working-class, midsize city surrounded by vineyards and fruit and vegetable fields, honors the memory and literary legacy of John Steinbeck, its most famous native, with the National Steinbeck Center. The facility is in Old Town Salinas, where renovated turn-of-the-20th-century stone buildings house a growing number of notable restaurants, bars, and shops. The several chain hotels in town make it a good base for visiting either side of Pinnacles National Park.

GETTING HERE AND AROUND

Salinas is right on the U.S. 101, about an hour south of San Jose, 20–30 minutes east of Monterey Bay, and 45 minutes from the west entrance to Pinnacles (and 20 minutes farther from the east entrance). It's also served by Amtrak.

VISITOR INFORMATION California Welcome Center. ✉ *1213 N. Davis Rd.* ☎ *831/757–8687* 🌐 *www.visitcalifornia.com.*

Sights

★ **National Steinbeck Center**
MUSEUM | The center's exhibits document the life of Pulitzer- and Nobel-prize winner John Steinbeck and the history of the nearby communities that inspired novels such as *East of Eden*. Highlights include reproductions of the green pickup-camper from *Travels with Charley* and the bunk room from *Of Mice and Men*. **Steinbeck House,** the author's Victorian birthplace, at 132 Central Avenue, is two blocks from the center. Now a popular (lunch-only) restaurant and gift shop with docent-led tours, it displays memorabilia. ✉ *1 Main St.* ☎ *831/775–4721* 🌐 *www.steinbeck.org* 🎟 *$15.*

Restaurants

Salinas City BBQ
$ | **BARBECUE** | With a very simple, small dining area and tables covered with plastic checked cloths, this hole-in-the-wall on the west side of downtown Salinas might not look like much, but the kitchen turns out seriously tasty barbecue that's smoked for six to eight hours. Specialties include the smoked tri-tip and pulled pork, and the barbecue sauce is spicy and flavorful. **Known for:** fall-off-the-bone tender barbecue; mac-and-cheese and cornbread sides; good selection of local beers. $ *Average main: $11* ✉ *700 W. Market St.* ☎ *831/758–2227* 🌐 *www.salinascitybbq.com.*

Steinbeck House Restaurant
$ | **AMERICAN** | This delightful restaurant, housed in a beautifully restored 1897-era Queen Anne Victorian, was home to author John Steinbeck for the first 17 years of his life. Since 1974, the Steinbeck House, as it's known, has been serving lunch (and monthly Sunday-afternoon teas and Friday-night dinners) thanks to a passionate staff of volunteers who not only manage the restaurant (and gift shop), but serve the guests as well. **Known for:** antiques-filled dining

room; literary memorabilia; Steinbeck's signature brownie pie. $ *Average main: $13 ⊠ 132 Central Ave.* ☎ *831/424–2735* ⊕ *www.steinbeckhouse.com* ⊗ *Closed Sun. No dinner.*

 Hotels

Hampton Inn & Suites Salinas

$$ | **HOTEL** | Sure, this modern low-rise looks like most other Hampton Inns, but it's still a clean, comfortable place to stay near the center of Salinas, and its proximity to U.S. 101 makes it easy to get to Pinnacles National Park. **Pros:** closest nicest chain option to Pinnacles National Park; indoor pool; close to downtown restaurants and Steinbeck Center. **Cons:** bland design; overlooks U.S. 101 freeway; no pets. $ *Rooms from: $189 ⊠ 523 Work St.* ☎ *831/754–4700* ⊕ *www.hilton. com* ⊐ *105 rooms* |⊙| *Free Breakfast.*

Monterey Peninsula

50 miles west of Pinnacles' west entrance.

Natural beauty is at the heart of the Monterey Peninsula's enormous appeal—it's everywhere, from the emerald wooded hillsides to the pristine shoreline with miles of walking paths and bluff-top vistas. Nature even takes center stage indoors at the world-famous Monterey Bay Aquarium, but history also draws visitors, most notably to Monterey's well-preserved waterfront district. Quaint, walkable towns and villages such as Carmel-by-the-Sea and Carmel Valley lure with smart restaurants and galleries.

GETTING HERE AND AROUND

Highway 1 cuts through the peninsula's main communities from Santa Cruz down to Big Sur. To get to Pinnacles' west entrance, it's about a little over an hour's drive from Monterey by taking Highways 68 and G17 inland to U.S. 101. Alternately, if you're up for a longer but stunningly scenic

drive through the Santa Lucia Mountains, follow Highway G16 east through Carmel Valley through the edge of Los Padres National Forest to Greenfield, and then catch U.S. 101 north to Soledad. This 72-mile partially unpaved (but well-maintained) drive takes a little under two hours.

VISITOR INFORMATION Visit Monterey. ⊠ *401 Camino El Estero, Monterey* ☎ *888/221–1010* ⊕ *www.seemonterey. com.*

 Sights

★ Monterey Bay Aquarium

ZOO | **FAMILY** | Sea creatures surround you the minute you hand over your ticket at this extraordinary facility: right at the entrance dozens of them swim in a three-story-tall, sunlit kelp-forest tank. All the exhibits here provide a sense of what it's like to be in the water with the animals—sardines swim around your head in a circular tank, and jellyfish drift in and out of view in dramatically lighted spaces that suggest the ocean depths. A petting pool puts you literally in touch with bat rays, and the million-gallon Open Seas tank illustrates the variety of creatures, from sharks to placid-looking turtles, that live in the eastern Pacific. At the Splash Zone, which has 45 interactive bilingual exhibits, kids can commune with African black-footed penguins, potbellied seahorses, and other creatures. The only drawback to the aquarium experience is that it must be shared with the throngs that congregate daily, but most visitors think it's worth it. ⊠ *886 Cannery Row, Monterey* ☎ *831/648–4800 info, 866/963–9645 for advance tickets* ⊕ *www.montereybayaquarium.org* ⊐ *$50.*

★ 17-Mile Drive

SCENIC DRIVE | Primordial nature resides in quiet harmony with palatial, mostly Spanish Mission–style estates along 17-Mile Drive, which winds through an 8,400-acre microcosm of the Pebble Beach coastal landscape. Dotting the drive are rare Monterey cypresses, trees so gnarled and twisted that Robert Louis Stevenson described them as "ghosts fleeing before the wind." The most famous of these is the **Lone Cypress**. Other highlights include **Bird Rock** and **Seal Rock,** home to harbor seals, sea lions, cormorants, and pelicans and other sea creatures and birds, and the **Crocker Marble Palace,** inspired by a Byzantine castle and easily identifiable by its dozens of marble arches.

■ **TIP→ If you spend $35 or more on dining in Pebble Beach and show a receipt upon exiting, you'll receive a refund off the drive's $10.50 per car fee.** ✉ *Hwy. 1 Gate, 17-Mile Dr., at Hwy. 68, Pebble Beach* 🎫 *$10.50 per car, free for bicyclists.*

🍴 Restaurants

Corkscrew Café

$$ | **MODERN AMERICAN** | Farm-fresh food is the specialty of this casual, Old Monterey–style bistro. Herbs and seasonal produce come from the Corkscrew's own organic gardens, the catch of the day comes from local waters, and the meats are hormone-free. **Known for:** wood-fired pizzas; fantastic regional wine list; garden patio. [$] *Average main: $21* ✉ *55 W. Carmel Valley Rd., Carmel Valley* ☎ *831/659–8888* 🌐 *www.corkscrewcafe.com* 🕓 *Closed Jan.*

★ Passionfish

$$$ | **MODERN AMERICAN** | South American artwork and artifacts decorate Passionfish, and Latin and Asian flavors infuse the dishes. The chef shops at local farmers' markets several times a week to find the best produce, fish, and meat available, then pairs it with creative sauces like a caper, raisin, and walnut relish. **Known for:** sustainably sourced seafood and organic ingredients; reasonably priced wine list that supports small producers; slow-cooked meats. [$] *Average main: $28* ✉ *701 Lighthouse Ave., Pacific Grove* ☎ *831/655–3311* 🌐 *www.passionfish.net* 🕓 *No lunch.*

☕ Coffee and Quick Bites

Captain + Stoker

$ | **CAFÉ** | This sleek, modern cafe with hand-carved wooden tables, Edison bulbs, and bikes hanging from the ceiling opens early every morning to dispense house-roasted-espresso drinks and healthy breakfast nibbles. Banana–peanut butter toast, yogurt parfaits, and both conventional and vegan pastries provide delicious sustenance before a day of exploring. **Known for:** avocado toast and bowls; matcha lattes; raspberry-crumble cake. [$] *Average main: $9* ✉ *398 E. Franklin St., Monterey* ☎ *831/901–3776* 🕓 *No dinner.*

🛏 Hotels

★ Bernardus Lodge & Spa

$$$$ | **RESORT** | The spacious guest rooms at this luxury spa resort have vaulted ceilings, French oak floors, featherbeds, fireplaces, patios, and bathrooms with heated-tile floors and soaking tubs for two. **Pros:** exceptional personal service; outstanding food and wine; serene, cushy full-service spa. **Cons:** hefty rates; can feel a little snooty; resort fee. [$] *Rooms from: $435* ✉ *415 W. Carmel Valley Rd., Carmel Valley* ☎ *831/658–3400* 🌐 *www.bernarduslodge.com* 🛏 *73 rooms* 🍴 *No meals.*

Captain's Inn

$$ | **B&B/INN** | Commune with nature and pamper yourself with upscale creature comforts at this green-certified complex in the heart of town. **Pros:** walk to restaurants and shops; tranquil natural setting; closest Monterey Bay hotel to Pinnacles National Park. **Cons:** rooms in historic building don't have water views; far from urban amenities; not appropriate for young children. [$] *Rooms from: $189* ✉ *8122 Moss Landing Rd., Moss Landing* ☎ *831/633–5550* 🌐 *www.captainsinn.com* 🛏 *10 rooms* 🍴 *Free Breakfast.*

Spindrift Inn
$$$ | HOTEL | This boutique hotel on Cannery Row has beach access and a rooftop garden that overlooks the water. **Pros:** close to aquarium; steps from the beach; friendly staff. **Cons:** throngs of visitors outside; can be noisy; not good for families. [$] *Rooms from: $234* ✉ *652 Cannery Row, Monterey* ☎ *831/646–8900, 800/841–1879* 🌐 *www.spindriftinn.com* 🛏 *45 rooms* 🍴 *Free Breakfast.*

Santa Cruz

70 miles west of Pinnacles' west entrance and east entrances.

Long known for its surfing culture and its amusement-filled beach boardwalk, this laid-back and progressive city of about 65,000 fringes both lush redwood forests inland and miles of gorgeous beaches. Midway between the Bay Area and Pinnacles National Park, but with a cool climate and offbeat personality all its own, this slice of coastal California abounds with fun diversions, from hiking and beachcombing to checking out art galleries and wineries.

GETTING HERE AND AROUND
At the junction of Highways 17 and 1, Santa Cruz just 40-minutes south of San Jose and about 1½ hours from either entrance of Pinnacles.

VISITOR INFORMATION Visit Santa Cruz County. ✉ *303 Water St., Suite 100, Santa Cruz* ☎ *831/425–1234, 800/833–3494* 🌐 *www.visitsantacruz.org.*

Sights

★ Henry Cowell Redwoods State Park
NATIONAL/STATE PARK | FAMILY | Just 7 miles north of downtown Santa Cruz you'll find an impressive 40-acre stand of old-growth redwoods, some towering higher than 250 feet and dating back 1,500 years. An easy and fun 0.8-mile loop trail brings you directly beneath some of the most impressive trees. The historic Roaring Camp Railroad adjoins the park and offers rides through the San Lorenzo Valley. You'll find more impressive redwoods 18 miles north in Big Basin Redwoods State Park; alas, that park was closed until further notice after receiving heavy damage during 2020's CZU Lightning Complex wildfires. ✉ *101 Big Trees Park Rd., Felton* ☎ *831/335–7077* 🌐 *www.parks.ca.gov* 🎟 *$10.*

★ Seacliff State Beach
BEACH—SIGHT | FAMILY | Sandstone bluffs tower above this popular beach with a long fishing pier. The 1.5-mile walk north to adjacent New Brighton State Beach in Capitola is one of the nicest on the bay. Leashed dogs are allowed on the beach. **Amenities:** food and drink; lifeguards; parking (fee); showers; toilets. **Best for:** sunset; swimming; walking. ✉ *201 State Park Dr., Aptos* ☎ *831/685–6500* 🌐 *www.parks.ca.gov* 🎟 *$10 per vehicle.*

Restaurants

★ Mentone
$$ | MODERN ITALIAN | A casual outpost of Michelin-chef David Kinch's mini empire, this cheerful spot in hip Aptos Village, a short drive from Seacliff State Beach and the Corralitos Wine Trail, Mentone serves creatively topped pizzas and modern Italian bites. The tagliatelle pasta with shaved white truffles is a standout, and there's house-made gelato for dessert. **Known for:** thin-crust soppressata pizzas with Calabrian chiles; aperol spritz cocktails; inviting outdoor dining. [$] *Average main: $20* ✉ *174 Aptos Village Way, Aptos* ☎ *831/708–4040* 🌐 *www.mentonerestaurant.com* 🕒 *Closed Mon.–Tues.*

★ Soif
$$$ | MEDITERRANEAN | Wine reigns at this sleek bistro and wineshop that takes its name from the French word for thirst—the selections come from near and far, and you can order many of them by the taste or glass. Mediterranean-inspired

small plates and entrées are served at the copper-top bar, the big communal table, and private tables. **Known for:** Mediterranean-style dishes; diverse, interesting wine selection; jazz combo or solo pianist plays on some evenings. [$] *Average main: $24* ✉ *105 Walnut Ave., Santa Cruz* ☎ *831/423–2020* 🌐 *www.soifwine.com* 🕑 *Closed Mon. and Tues. No lunch.*

Coffee and Quick Bites

Gayle's Bakery & Rosticceria
$$ | **CAFÉ** | **FAMILY** | Whether you're in the mood for an orange-olallieberry muffin, a wild rice and chicken salad, or tri-tip on garlic toast, this bakery-deli's varied menu is likely to satisfy. Munch on your lemon meringue tartlet or chocolate brownie on the shady patio, or dig into the daily blue-plate dinner—teriyaki grilled skirt steak with edamame-shiitake sticky rice, perhaps, or roast turkey breast with Chardonnay gravy—amid the whirl of activity inside. **Known for:** prepared meals to go; on-site bakery and rosticceria; deli and espresso bar. [$] *Average main: $17* ✉ *504 Bay Ave., Capitola* ☎ *831/462–1200* 🌐 *www.gaylesbakery.com.*

Hotels

★ **Chaminade Resort & Spa**
$$$ | **RESORT** | **FAMILY** | Secluded on 300 hilltop acres of redwood and eucalyptus forest with hiking trails, this Mission-style complex also features a lovely terrace restaurant with expansive views of Monterey Bay. Guest rooms are furnished in an eclectic, bohemian style that pays homage to the artsy local community and the city's industrial past. **Pros:** peaceful, verdant setting; full-service spa and large pool; ideal spot for romance and rejuvenation. **Cons:** not within walking distance of downtown; not near the ocean; resort fee. [$] *Rooms from: $279* ✉ *1 Chaminade La., Santa Cruz* ☎ *800/283–6569, 831/475–5600* 🌐 *www.chaminade.com* 🛏 *156 rooms* 🍴 *No meals.*

Dream Inn Santa Cruz
$$$$ | **HOTEL** | A short stroll from the boardwalk and wharf, this full-service luxury hotel is the only lodging in Santa Cruz directly on the beach, and its rooms all have private balconies or patios overlooking Monterey Bay. Accommodations have contemporary furnishings, bold colors, and upscale linens, but the main draw here is having the ocean at your doorstep. **Pros:** restaurant with sweeping views of Monterey Bay; cool mid-century modern design; walk to boardwalk and downtown. **Cons:** expensive; area gets congested on summer weekends; pool area and hallways can be noisy. [$] *Rooms from: $324* ✉ *175 W. Cliff Dr., Santa Cruz* ☎ *831/740–8141, 844/510–1746* 🌐 *www.dreaminnsantacruz.com* 🛏 *165 rooms* 🍴 *No meals.*

REDWOOD NATIONAL AND STATE PARKS

Updated by
Andrew Collins

CALIFORNIA

🏕 **Camping**
★★★☆☆

🛏 **Hotels**
★★★★☆

🤸 **Activities**
★★★★☆

👁 **Scenery**
★★★★★

👥 **Crowds**
★★★★☆

WELCOME TO REDWOOD NATIONAL AND STATE PARKS

TOP REASONS TO GO

★ **Giant trees:** These mature coastal redwoods, which you can hike beneath in numerous groves throughout the park, are the tallest trees in the world.

★ **Hiking along the sea:** The park offers many miles of ocean access, including the Coastal Trail, which runs along the western edge of the park.

★ **Rare wildlife:** Mighty Roosevelt elk favor the park's flat prairie and open lands; seldom-seen black bears roam the backcountry; trout and salmon leap along streams; and Pacific gray whales swim along the coast during their spring and fall migrations.

★ **Stepping back in time:** Hike mossy and mysterious Fern Canyon Trail and explore a prehistoric scene of lush vegetation and giant ferns—a memorable scene in *Jurassic Park 2* was shot here.

★ **Getting off-the-grid:** Amid the majestic redwoods you're usually out of cell phone range and often free from crowds, offering a rare opportunity to disconnect.

1 South. The highlights of the parks' southern section are the hikes and scenic driving along Bald Hills Road, including the Lady Bird Johnson Grove, and the beautiful coastal scenery at Thomas H. Kuchel Visitor Center and the estuarial lagoons to the south. This section encompasses much of the original Redwood National Park and is where you'll find the small village of Orick, which has a gas station and a few other basic services.

2 Middle. Here in the span of park that extends from north of Orick to the Yurok tribal community of Klamath, you'll find some of the most magnificent and accessible stands of old-growth redwoods. Start your adventures at Prairie Creek Redwoods State Park's visitor center, from which several trails emanate. Also set aside time to explore the meadows inhabited by Roosevelt elk, the trail to Fern Canyon from Gold Bluffs Beach, and the gorgeous drives along Newton B. Drury Scenic Parkway and Klamath's Coastal Drive Loop

3 North. Anchored by the region's largest community, Crescent City, the park's northern third encompasses the rugged, pristine forests of Jedediah Smith Redwoods State Park, which is slightly inland, and Del Norte Coast Redwoods State Park, which also offers visitors the chance to visit stretches of windswept beaches, steep sea cliffs, and forested ridges. On a clear day it's postcard-perfect; with fog, it's mysterious and mesmerizing.

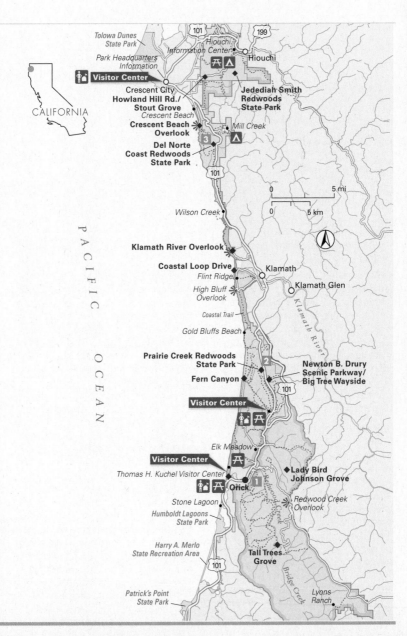

Soaring more than 375 feet high, California's coastal redwoods are miracles of efficiency—some have survived hundreds of years, a few more than two millennia. These massive trees glean nutrients from the rich alluvial flats at their feet and from the moisture and nitrogen trapped in their uneven canopy. Their thick bark can hold thousands of gallons of water, which has helped them withstand centuries of fires.

Redwood differs from other national parks, in that it's administered by a joint partnership between the National Park Service and the California Department of Parks and Recreation. This sprawling 139,000-acre park system has a footprint that extends nearly 50 miles up the coast, encompasses three state parks, and snakes in and around a handful of towns and small cities, including Orick, Klamath, and Crescent City.

Indigenous people have been stewards of this special ecosystem for millennia—hunting, fishing, and foraging the land early on, and in more recent centuries harvesting timber from downed redwoods to build homes. Despite the cruel efforts of gold prospectors and loggers who in the 1850s arrived and swiftly began trying to eradicate them, the region's native communities survived and continue to this day to thrive here. Both the Yurok and Tolowa tribes have large land holdings within the borders of the Redwood National and State Parks (RNSP) system.

Northern California's gold rush immediately transformed the natural landscape. Large-scale logging, aided by rapid technological advances, reduced the region's 2 million acres of old-growth redwoods by nearly 90 percent in a little over a century—only about 5 percent of the old-growth forest remains today. Fortunately, by the 1910s, a small but determined conservation-minded minority began lobbying to protect these special trees, beginning with the formation of the Save-the-Redwoods League, whose efforts helped to establish Del Norte Coast Redwoods and Prairie Creek Redwoods state parks in 1925, and Jedediah Smith Redwoods State Park in 1939 (these successes came on the heels of the 1921 designation of Humboldt Redwoods State Park, which is about 30 miles southeast of Eureka and not part of RNSP). A huge demand for lumber, particularly following World War II, continued to deplete the unprotected tracts of forest, which led the federal government to establish Redwood National Park in 1968. Finally, in 1994,

AVERAGE HIGH/LOW TEMPERATURES					
JAN.	**FEB.**	**MAR.**	**APR.**	**MAY**	**JUNE**
54/39	56/41	57/41	59/42	62/45	65/48
JULY	**AUG.**	**SEPT.**	**OCT.**	**NOV.**	**DEC.**
67/51	67/51	68/49	64/46	58/43	55/40

federal and state agencies officially joined forces to manage the newly designated Redwood National and State Parks, whose mission is both to preserve uncut old-growth redwood forest and to restore and replant some significant sections that have already been logged.

The easiest way to approach exploring the rather vast and complex RNSP system is to divide it geographically into North, Middle, and South sections, each of which contains at least one visitor center. Crescent City is in the North, as are two of the three state parks—Jedediah Smith Redwoods and Del Norte Coast Redwoods. The town of Klamath is in the Middle section, as is Prairie Creek Redwoods State Park. And the village of Orick is in the South, which also contains much of the original national park, although you'll find other sections of it in the Middle and North sections, too. Additionally, there are four coastal parks just south of RNSP: Humboldt Lagoons State Park, Harry A. Merlo State Recreation Area, Big Lagoon Beach and County Park, and Patrick's Point State Park. U.S. 101 is the main north-south route through the park, but the northern section is also bisected by a short stretch of U.S. 199 east of Crescent City.

Some park attractions, scenic drives, and trails are in the national park, and others are in state parks, but as you explore, it's difficult—and not particularly important—to know which section you're in. Just adhere to the excellent map in the free park brochure and visitor guide newspaper, and you'll easily figure out where you're going and how to get around this magnificent preserve that aims to protect one of the world's oldest and largest living things.

Planning

When to Go

Campers and hikers flock to the park from mid-June to early September. The crowds disappear in winter, but you'll have to contend with frequent rains and nasty potholes and even occasional closures on side roads. Temperatures fluctuate widely: the foggy coastal lowland is much cooler than the higher-altitude interior.

The average annual rainfall is between 60 and 80 inches, most of it falling between November and April. During the dry summer, thick fog rolling in from the Pacific can veil the forests, providing the redwoods a large portion of their moisture intake.

Getting Here and Around

AIR

United Airlines flies a few times daily between San Francisco and the most practical gateway, California Redwood Coast–Humboldt County Airport, between Trinidad and Arcata, about 16 miles north of Eureka. The regional carrier Contour offers daily service from Oakland to Del Norte County Regional Airport in Crescent City. Another option is Oregon's Rogue Valley International Medford Airport, which is served by Alaska, Allegiant, American, Delta, and United, and is about a two-hour drive from the northern end of the park in Crescent City.

Redwood in One Day

From Crescent City head south on U.S. 101, pausing for a stroll overlooking the ocean either at **Crescent Beach** or a little farther south with a short stroll along the **Yurok Loop Trail**. A mile south of Klamath, detour onto the 9-mile-long, narrow, and mostly unpaved **Coastal Drive** loop. Along the way, you'll pass the old **Douglas Memorial Bridge**, destroyed in the 1964 flood. Coastal Drive turns south above Flint Ridge. In less than a mile you'll reach the **World War II B-71 Radar Station**, which looks like a farmhouse, its disguise in the 1940s. Continue south to the intersection with Alder Camp Road, stopping at the **High Bluff Overlook**—keep an eye out for whales during the winter and spring migrations.

Back on U.S. 101, head south to reach **Newton B. Drury Scenic Parkway**, a 10-mile drive through one of the park's best and most accessible expanses of old-growth redwood forest. Stop at **Prairie Creek Visitor Center**, housed in a small redwood lodge. Enjoy a picnic lunch and an engaging tactile walk in a grove behind the lodge on the Revelation Trail, which was designed for vision-impaired visitors, or if you have an hour or two, hike the stunning 3½-mile **Prairie Creek–Big Tree–Cathedral Trees Loop**. Return to U.S. 101, and turn west on mostly

unpaved **Davison Road**, checking out **Elk Meadow** on your left, where you'll sometimes see a portion of the park's Roosevelt elk herd roaming about. In about 30 minutes you'll curve right to **Gold Bluffs Beach.** Continue north a short way and make the hike into lush and spectacular **Fern Canyon**. Return to U.S. 101, and drive south to the turnoff onto **Bald Hills Road**, and follow it for 2 miles to the **Lady Bird Johnson Grove Nature Loop Trail**. Take the footbridge to the easy 1.4-mile loop, which follows an old logging road through a mature redwood forest. If you have an extra hour, continue south on Bald Hills Road to **Redwood Creek Overlook** or even all the way to 3,097-foot **Schoolhouse Peak**, before backtracking to U.S. 101 and driving south through Orick to the **Thomas H. Kuchel Visitor Center.** This is a beautiful spot late in the day to watch the sunset over the ocean. Note that if you're approaching the park from Trinidad or Eureka, it's easy to undertake this itinerary in reverse. ■ TIP → Motor homes/RVs and trailers are not allowed on Coastal Drive or Davison Road and are not advised on Bald Hills Road. Conditions on these roads can sometimes lead to closures or the requirement of high-clearance vehicles—check with the visitor centers before you set out.

CAR

U.S. 101 runs north–south nearly the entire length of the park. You can access all the main park roads via U.S. 101 and U.S. 199, which runs east–west through the park's northern portion. Many roads within the park aren't paved, and winter rains can turn them into obstacle courses; sometimes they're closed completely. Motor homes/RVs and trailers aren't permitted on some routes. The drive from San Francisco to the park's southern end takes about six hours via U.S. 101. From Portland it takes roughly the same amount of time to reach the park's northern section via Interstate 5 to U.S. 199. ■ TIP → Don't rely solely on GPS, which is inaccurate in parts of the park; closely consult official park maps.

Inspiration

The *Redwood Official National and State Parks Handbook,* published by the Redwood Parks Association, covers the area's ecology, botany, natural and cultural history, and wildlife.

Richard Preston's *The Wild Trees: A Story of Passion and Daring* chronicles the redwood-climbing exploits of several botanists fiercely passionate about the endangered tall trees and the ecosystem that supports them.

The parks' larger-than-life landscapes have made their way into a handful of movies. Most famously, in 1997, Steven Spielberg filmed portions of *The Lost World: Jurassic Park* amid the verdant rainforest foliage of Fern Canyon. Perhaps he was inspired by his friend George Lucas's decision 15 years earlier to film in a grove of redwoods just outside Jedediah Smith Redwoods State Park in the famed Ewoks chase scene in *Return of the Jedi.*

Park Essentials

PARK FEES AND PERMITS

Admission to Redwood National Park is free; a few areas in the state parks collect day-use fees of $8, including the Gold Bluffs Beach and Fern Canyon sections of Prairie Creek Redwoods State Park, and the day-use areas accessed via the campground entrances in Jedediah Smith and Del Norte Coast state parks (the fee for camping overnight is $35). To visit the popular Tall Trees Grove, you must get a free permit at the Kuchel Visitor Center in Orick. Free permits, available at the Kuchel, Crescent City, and (summer only) Hiouchi visitor centers, are needed to stay at all designated backcountry camps.

PARK HOURS

The park is open year-round, 24 hours a day.

CELL PHONE RECEPTION

It's difficult to pick up a signal in much of the park, especially in the camping areas and on many hiking trails. The Prairie Creek and Jedediah Smith visitor centers have pay phones.

What It Costs			
$	$$	$$$	$$$$
RESTAURANTS			
under $16	$16–$22	$23–$30	over $30
HOTELS			
under $125	$125–$175	$176–$225	over $225

Hotels

The only lodgings within park grounds are the Elk Meadow Cabins, near Prairie Creek Redwoods Visitor Center. Orick, to the south of Elk Meadow, and Klamath, to the north, have basic motels, and in Klamath there's also the charming and historic Requa Inn. Elegant Victorian inns, seaside motels, and fully equipped vacation rentals are among the options in Crescent City to the north, and Eureka and to a more limited extent Trinidad and Arcata to the south. In summer, try to book at least a week ahead at lodgings near the park. *Hotel reviews have been shortened. For full information, visit Fodors.com.*

Restaurants

The park has no restaurants, but Eureka and Arcata have diverse dining establishments—everything from hip oyster bars to some surprisingly good ethnic restaurants. The dining options are more limited, though decent, in Crescent City and Trinidad, and there are just a couple of very basic options in Klamath and tiny Orick. Most small-town restaurants close early, around 7:30 or 8 pm. *Restaurant reviews have been shortened. For full information, visit Fodors.com.*

Visitor Information

CONTACTS Redwood National and State Parks Headquarters. ✉ *1111 2nd St., Crescent City* ☎ *707/465–7306* ⊕ *www.nps. gov/redw.*

South

19 miles north of Trinidad, 8 miles south of Prairie Creek Visitor Center, 44 miles south of Crescent City.

This is the section of the park system that you'll reach if driving up the coast from Eureka and Trinidad, and it's home to one of the largest visitor information resources, the beachfront Thomas H. Kuchel Visitor Center, which is on U.S. 101 shortly after you enter the park. For the purposes of this chapter, this section includes the town of Orick and everything else south of the turnoff onto Bald Hills Road, which leads to some of the largest stands of redwoods in the park, including the Lady Bird Johnson and Tall Trees groves.

Sights

PICNIC AREAS
Redwood Creek Overlook Picnic Area
LOCAL INTEREST | At an elevation of 2,100 feet, this impressive vista point with interpretive signs and picnic tables is a nice spot to break for a meal while driving picturesque Bald Hills Road. It can get foggy up here, so check weather conditions ahead of time. ✉ *Bald Hills Rd., Orick* ✛ *6.6 miles southeast of U.S. 101.*

SCENIC DRIVES
Bald Hills Road
SCENIC DRIVE | A winding, steep, and dramatic road that stretches into the park's southernmost section and highest elevations, Bald Hills Road accesses some great hikes—Lady Bird Johnson Grove and Lyons Ranch among them—as well as the access road to the Tall Trees Grove. But it's also wondrously scenic route all on its own, passing through sometimes misty patch of redwoods before entering a stretch of open meadows with wildflowers in spring and the chance to see Roosevelt elk and bears any time of year. Do stop at Redwood Creek Overlook, a 2,100-foot elevation pullout at mile 6.6. Bald Hills Road is paved for the first 13 miles. It continues another 4 miles unpaved to the park's southern boundary, and it's then possible to continue another 20 miles or so to the small village of Weitchpec and then onward inland toward Redding or Yreka. ✉ *Off U.S. 101, Orick.*

TRAILS
★ **Lady Bird Johnson Grove Trail**
TRAIL | One of the park's most accessible spots to view big trees, this impressive grove just a short drive northeast of Orick was dedicated by, and named for, the former first lady. A level 1.4-mile nature loop crosses a neat old wooden footbridge and follows an old logging road through this often mist-shrouded forest of redwoods. *Easy.* ✉ *Orick* ✛ *Trailhead: Bald Hills Rd., 2 miles east of U.S. 101.*

Lyons Ranch Trail
TRAIL | You won't see redwoods on this open upper-elevation 3.7-mile round-trip trail, but on summer days when the coast is socked in with rain or fog, an adventure to this typically sunny prairie at the park's southeastern boundary is highly rewarding, as is the steep—but slow—17-mile drive on Bald Hills Road. The trail leads hikers to a former sheep and cattle ranch with a few interesting old outbuildings that date to the turn-of-the-20th-century. *Moderate.* ✉ *Redwood National Park* ✛ *Trailhead: off Bald Hills Rd., 17 miles south of U.S. 101.*

Tall Trees Trail
TRAIL | Although every bit as beautiful as the other stands of old-growth redwood in the park, getting to this

roughly 30-acre grove requires a steep and windy 14-mile drive, followed by a somewhat rigorous 4-mile round-trip hike that involves an 800-foot descent into the Redwood Creek flood plain. Additionally, you must obtain a free permit at the Kuchel Visitor Center to access the unpaved road off of Bald Hills Road. Rangers dispense a limited number per day, first come, first served. No trailers or RVs. Given the effort required, if you don't have a lot of time, it's best to save this one for your second or third visit. *Moderate.* ⊠ *Orick* ✛ *Trailhead: Tall Trees Access Rd., off Bald Hills Rd., 7 miles from U.S. 101, then 6½ miles to trailhead.*

VISITOR CENTERS

★ Thomas H. Kuchel Visitor Center
INFO CENTER | FAMILY | The park's southern section contains this largest and best of the Redwoods visitor centers. Rangers here dispense brochures, advice, and free permits to drive up the access road to Tall Trees Grove. Whale-watchers find the center's deck an excellent observation point, and bird-watchers enjoy the nearby Freshwater Lagoon, a popular layover for migrating waterfowl. Many of the center's exhibits are hands-on and kid-friendly. ⊠ *U.S. 101, Orick* ✛ *Redwood Creek Beach County Park* ☎ *707/465–7765* ⊕ *www.nps.gov/redw.*

Middle

8 miles north of Thomas H. Kuchel Visitor Center, 34 miles south of Crescent City.

Encompassing a relatively narrow band of coastal forest that extends north of Orick (starting around Elk Meadow) to north of Klamath (up to Requa Road), the park's middle section is home to one of the most magical places to stroll through a redwood forest, Prairie Creek State Park, which is laced with both easy and challenging trails and traversed by the stunning Newton B. Drury Scenic Parkway. Near the visitor center and in nearby Elk Meadow, you can often view herds of Roosevelt elk. The state park extends west to famously spectacular Gold Bluffs Beach and Fern Canyon on the coast. The middle section's other highlight are the sections of the park along both sides of the Klamath River, including Coastal Drive and Klamath River Overlook.

Sights

PICNIC AREAS

Elk Prairie
LOCAL INTEREST | In addition to many elk, this spot has a campground, a nature trail, and a ranger station. ⊠ *Prairie Creek Redwoods State Park, 127011 Newton B. Drury Scenic Pkwy., Orick.*

★ High Bluff Overlook
LOCAL INTEREST | This picnic area's sunsets and whale-watching are unequaled. A ½-mile trail leads from here to the beach. ⊠ *Coastal Dr. loop, Klamath* ✛ *Off U.S. 101 and Klamath Beach Rd.*

SCENIC DRIVES

★ Coastal Drive Loop
SCENIC DRIVE | The 9-mile, narrow, and partially unpaved Coastal Drive Loop takes about 45 minutes to traverse. Weaving through stands of redwoods, the road yields close-up views of the Klamath River and expansive panoramas of the Pacific. Recurring landslides have closed sections of the original road; this loop, closed to trailers and RVs, is all that remains. Hikers access the Flint Ridge section of the Coastal Trail off the drive. ⊠ *Klamath* ✛ *Off Klamath Beach Rd. exit from U.S. 101.*

★ Newton B. Drury Scenic Parkway
SCENIC DRIVE | This paved 10-mile route threads through Prairie Creek Redwoods State Park and old-growth redwoods. It's open to all noncommercial vehicles. Great stops along the route include the 0.8-mile walk to Big Tree Wayside and observing Roosevelt elk in the prairie—both of these are near the Prairie Creek Visitor Center. ⊠ *Orick* ✛ *Entrances off*

U.S. 101 about 5 miles south of Klamath and 5 miles north of Orick.

SCENIC STOPS

★ Fern Canyon

CANYON | Enter another world and be surrounded by 50-foot canyon walls covered with sword, deer, and five-finger ferns. Allow an hour to explore the ¼-mile-long vertical garden along a 0.7-mile loop. From the northern end of Gold Bluffs Beach it's an easy walk, although you'll have to wade across or scamper along planks that traverse a small stream several times (in addition to driving across a couple of streams on the way to the parking area). But the lush, otherworldly surroundings, which appeared in *Jurassic Park 2,* are a must-see when creeks aren't running too high. Motor homes/RVs and all trailers are prohibited. You can also hike to the canyon from Prairie Creek Visitor Center along the challenging West Ridge–Friendship Ridge–James Irvine Loop, 12½ miles round-trip. ⊠ *Orick ⊹ 2¾ miles north of Orick, take Davison Rd. northwest off U.S. 101 and follow signs to Gold Bluffs Beach.*

Klamath River Overlook

VIEWPOINT | This grassy, windswept bluff rises 650 feet above the confluence of the Klamath River and the Pacific. It's one of the best spots in the park for spying migratory whales in early winter and late spring, and it accesses a section of the Coastal Trail. Warm days are ideal for picnicking at one of the tables. ⊠ *End of Requa Rd., Klamath ⊹ 2¼ miles west of U.S. 101.*

TRAILS

★ Coastal Trail

TRAIL | This gorgeous 70-mile trail, much of it along dramatic bluffs high above the crashing surf, can be tackled in both short, relatively easy sections and longer, strenuous spans that entail backcountry overnight camping. Here are some of the most alluring smaller sections, listed in order from north to south, which are accessible at well-marked trailheads.

The moderate-to-difficult **DeMartin section** (accessed from mile marker 15.6 on U.S. 101) leads south past 6 miles of old-growth redwoods and through sweeping prairie. It connects with the moderate 5½-mile-long **Klamath section,** which proceeds south from Wilson Creek Picnic Area to Klamath River Overlook, with a short detour to Hidden Beach and its tide pools, providing coastal views and whale-watching opportunities. If you're up for a real workout, hike the brutally difficult but stunning **Flint Ridge section** (accessed from the Old Douglas Memorial Bridge Site on Klamath Beach Rd.), with its 4½ miles of steep grades and numerous switchbacks past Marshall Pond and through stands of old-growth redwoods. There are additional spans at the northern and southern ends of the park. *Moderate.* ⊠ *Klamath.*

★ Prairie Creek–Big Tree–Cathedral Trees Loop

TRAIL | FAMILY | This flat, well-maintained 3½-mile loop starts and ends at the Prairie Creek Visitor Center and passes beneath some of the most awe-inspiring redwoods in the park. The 1-mile section along the Prairie Creek Trail fringes a babbling brook; you then cross Newton B. Drury Scenic Parkway, turn south onto the Cathedral Trees Trail and make a short detour along the 0.3-mile Big Tree Loop before meandering south and west through yet more gorgeous old-growth forest. Options for extending your hike include walking 1½ miles up Cal-Barrel Road (an old, unpaved logging route), and then looping back 2 miles on the Rhododendron Trail to rejoin Cathedral Trees. *Easy–Moderate.* ⊠ *Orick ⊹ Trailhead: Prairie Creek Visitor Center.*

Trillium Falls Trail

TRAIL | FAMILY | On this lush trek through a mix of old-growth redwoods, ferns, smaller deciduous trees, and some clusters of trillium flowers, you'll encounter the pretty cascades that give the hike its name after the first ½ mile. It's worth continuing on, though, and making the full 2.8-mile loop, as the southern end of the hike offers the best views of soaring redwoods. Herds of elk sometimes roam in the meadow by the trailhead. *Easy–Moderate.* ✉ *Orick* ✣ *Trailhead: Elk Meadow parking lot, Davison Rd., just west of U.S. 101.*

West Ridge–Friendship Ridge–James Irvine Loop

TRAIL | For a long, moderately strenuous trek, try this 12½-mile loop. The difficult West Ridge segment passes redwoods looming above a carpet of ferns. The slightly less taxing Friendship Ridge portion slopes down toward the coast through forests of spruce and hemlock and accesses iconic Fern Canyon. And the moderate James Irvine Trail portion winds along a small creek and amid dense stands of redwoods. Each of these segments can be hiked separately, a good plan if you're seeking a shorter and less intensive trek. *Difficult.* ✉ *Orick* ✣ *Trailhead: Prairie Creek Visitor Center.*

VISITOR CENTERS

★ **Prairie Creek Visitor Center**

INFO CENTER | FAMILY | A massive stone fireplace anchors this small redwood lodge with wildlife displays that include a section of a tree a young elk died beside. Because of the peculiar way the redwood grew around the elk's skull, the tree appears to have antlers. The center has information about interpretive programs as well as a gift shop, a picnic area, restrooms, and exhibits on flora and fauna. Roosevelt elk often roam the vast field adjacent to the center, and several trailheads begin nearby. Stretch your legs with an easy stroll along **Revelation Trail,** a short loop that starts behind the lodge. ✉ *Prairie Creek Rd., Orick* ✣ *Off southern end of Newton B. Drury Scenic Pkwy.* ☎ *707/488–2039* 🌐 *www.nps.gov/redw.*

Hotels

★ **Elk Meadow Cabins**

$$$$ | B&B/INN | FAMILY | From the porches of these beautifully restored 1,200-square-foot former mill workers' cottages, guests often see Roosevelt elk meandering in the meadows—or even their backyards. **Pros:** elks frequently congregate on the grounds; perfect for groups or families; adjacent to stunning Prairie Creek State Park. **Cons:** a bit of a drive from most area restaurants; expensive for just two occupants, though reasonable for families or groups; furnishings are comfortable but plain. [$] *Rooms from: $314* ✉ *7 Valley Green Camp Rd., off U.S. 101 north of Davison Rd., Orick* ☎ *707/488–2222, 866/733–9637* 🌐 *www.elkmeadowcabins.com* 🛏 *9 cabins* 🍴 *No meals.*

North

34 miles north of Prairie Creek Redwoods State Park, 84 miles north of Eureka, 73 miles south of Grants Pass, OR, 133 miles south of Coos Bay, OR,

Home to the small city of Crescent City, which is also where you'll find the Redwood National and State Parks headquarters, the North is home to two state parks: Del Norte Redwoods and Jedediah Smith Redwoods. Del Norte lies 5 miles south of Crescent City on U.S. 101 and contains 15 memorial redwood groves and 8 miles of pristine coastline, which you can most easily access at Crescent Beach and Wilson Beach. Jedediah Smith is 5 miles east of Crescent City on U.S. 199 and is home to the legendary Stout Memorial Grove, along with some 20 miles of hiking and nature trails. The park is named after a trapper who in 1826 became the first white man to explore Northern California's interior. If coming from interior Oregon, this is your first chance to drive and hike among stands of soaring redwoods.

Plants and Wildlife in Redwood

Coast redwoods, the world's tallest trees, grow in the moist, temperate climate of California's North Coast. The current record holder, named Hyperion, tops out at 380 feet and was found in the Redwood Creek watershed in 2006. These ancient giants thrive in an environment that exists in only a few hundred coastal miles along the Pacific Ocean. They commonly live 600 years—though some have been around for more than 2,000 years.

Diverse, Complex

A healthy redwood forest is diverse and includes Douglas firs, western hemlocks, tan oaks, and madrone trees. The complex soils of the forest floor support a profusion of ferns, mosses, and fungi, along with numerous shrubs and berry bushes. In spring, California rhododendron bloom all over, providing a dazzling purple and pink contrast to the dense greenery.

Old-Growth Forests

Redwood National and State parks hold nearly 50% of California's old-growth redwood forests, but only about a third of the forests in the park are old-growth. Of the original 3,125 square miles (2 million acres) in the Redwoods Historic Range, only 4% survived logging that began in 1850. A quarter of these trees are privately owned and on managed land. The rest are on public tracts.

Wildlife Species

In the park's backcountry, you might spot mountain lions, black bears, black-tailed deer, river otters, beavers, and minks. Roosevelt elk roam the flatlands, and the rivers and streams teem with salmon and trout. Gray whales, seals, and sea lions cavort near the coastline. More than 280 species of birds have been recorded in the park, which is located along the Pacific Flyway. A plan is also underway to reintroduce California condors to the park by 2022.

Sights

PICNIC AREAS

Crescent Beach Picnic Area

LOCAL INTEREST | This spectacular stretch of sand at the northern end of Del Norte Coast Redwoods State Park has a grassy picnic area with tables, fire pits, and restrooms, and there's a stunning overlook just to the south. ⊠ *Enderts Beach Rd., Crescent City* ✛ *4 miles south of Crescent City.*

SCENIC DRIVES

⭐ **Howland Hill Road through Stout Grove**

SCENIC DRIVE | Take your time as you drive this 10-mile route along Mill Creek, which meanders within inches of the hulking trunks of old-growth redwoods and past

the Smith River. Trailers and RVs are prohibited on this route, which is unpaved but well maintained for the roughly 7 miles that pass through Jedediah Smith Redwoods State Park. There are several pull-outs along the route, including the trailheads for the Stout Grove and Boy Scout Tree trails. You can enter either from downtown Crescent Road or off U.S. 199, via South Fork and Douglas Park Roads. ✛ *Western access from Elk Valley Rd. in Crescent City.*

SCENIC STOPS

Crescent Beach Overlook

VIEWPOINT | The scenery here includes views of the ocean and, in the distance, Crescent City and its working harbor. In balmy weather this is a great place for

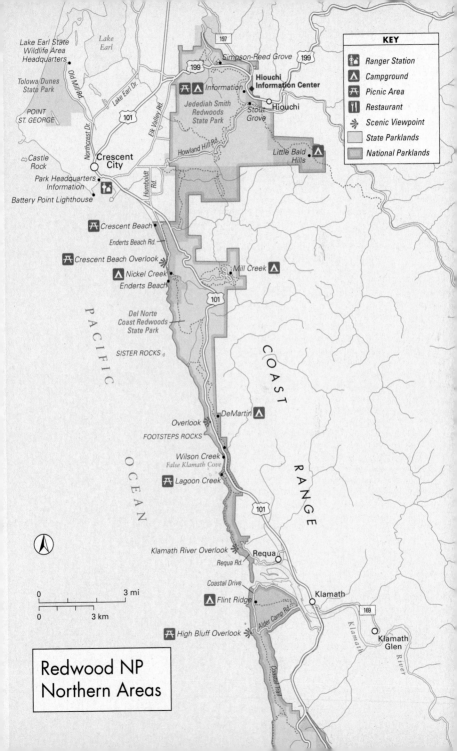

KEY

🏚 Ranger Station
⛺ Campground
🏕 Picnic Area
🍴 Restaurant
🔆 Scenic Viewpoint
State Parklands
National Parklands

Lake Earl State Wildlife Area Headquarters

Lake Earl

197

Simpson-Reed Grove

199

199

🏕 ▲ *Information*

Hiouchi Information Center

Tolowa Dunes State Park

Old Mill Rd.

Lake Earl Dr.

POINT ST. GEORGE

101

Elk Valley Rd.

Northcrest Dr.

Jedediah Smith Redwoods State Park

Stout Grove

🍴 *Hiouchi*

Howland Hill Rd.

Little Bald Hills ▲

Castle Rock

Crescent City

Park Headquarters Information 🏚

Battery Point Lighthouse

Humboldt Rd.

🏕 *Crescent Beach*

Enderts Beach Rd.

🏕 *Crescent Beach Overlook* 🔆

▲ *Nickel Creek*

Enderts Beach

Mill Creek ▲

101

Del Norte Coast Redwoods State Park

P A C I F I C

SISTER ROCKS

C O A S T

🔆 *DeMartin* ▲

Overlook

FOOTSTEPS ROCKS

R

Wilson Creek
False Klamath Cove

🏕 *Lagoon Creek*

A

O C E A N

101

N

G

Klamath River Overlook 🔆

E

Requa

Requa Rd.

Coastal Drive

▲ *Flint Ridge*

Klamath

169

Alder Camp Rd.

🏕 *High Bluff Overlook* 🔆

Coastal Trail

Klamath Glen

Klamath River

0 — 3 mi
0 — 3 km

Redwood NP Northern Areas

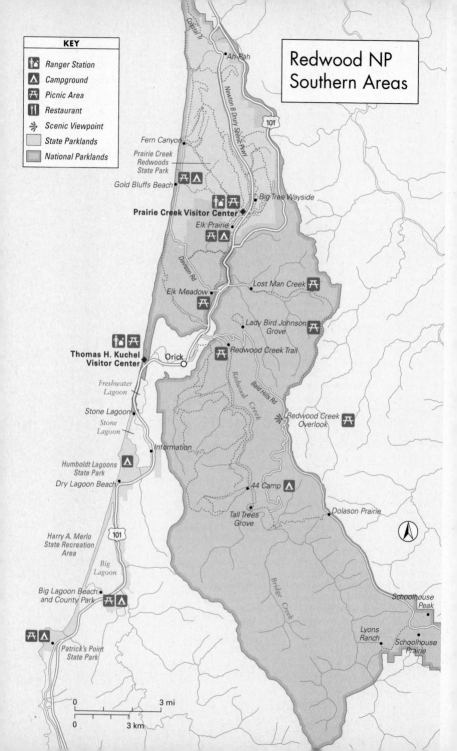

Redwood NP Southern Areas

KEY

- 🖼 Ranger Station
- ⛺ Campground
- ⛱ Picnic Area
- 🍴 Restaurant
- ⚜ Scenic Viewpoint
- State Parklands
- National Parklands

Coastal Tr

Ah-Pah

Newton B Drury Scenic Pkwy

101

Fern Canyon

Prairie Creek
Redwoods
State Park

Gold Bluffs Beach

Big Tree Wayside

Prairie Creek Visitor Center

Elk Prairie

Davison Rd

Lost Man Creek

Elk Meadow

Lady Bird Johnson
Grove

Redwood Creek Trail

**Thomas H. Kuchel
Visitor Center**

Orick

Freshwater
Lagoon

Redwood Creek

Bald Hills Rd

Stone Lagoon

Stone
Lagoon

Redwood Creek
Overlook

Information

Humboldt Lagoons
State Park

Dry Lagoon Beach

44 Camp

Tall Trees
Grove

Dolason Prairie

Harry A. Merlo
State Recreation
Area

101

Big
Lagoon

Bridge Creek

Big Lagoon Beach
and County Park

Schoolhouse
Peak

Lyons
Ranch

Schoolhouse
Prairie

Patrick's Point
State Park

0   3 mi

0   3 km

a picnic. You may spot migrating gray whales between November and April. ⊠ *Enderts Beach Rd.* ✛ *4½ miles south of Crescent City.*

TRAILS

★ Boy Scout Tree Trail

TRAIL | This is the most challenging but also the most rewarding of the hikes along Howland Hill Road. Give yourself about three hours to complete this 5.6-mile round-trip trek to verdant Fern Falls, as the old-growth redwoods along this tranquil trek are absolutely magnificent. If you don't have as much time, the easy ½-mile-loop Stout Grove Trail is a good alternative along this route. *Moderate.* ⊠ *Crescent City* ✛ *Trailhead: Howland Hill Rd., 3.7 miles east of Elk Valley Rd.*

Simpson-Reed Trail

TRAIL | FAMILY | Of the redwood hikes in Jedediah Smith Redwoods State Park, this flat and easy 1-mile loop through an incredibly dense forest is the best fit if you have only an hour or so. The trailhead is a short hop off U.S. 199 between Crescent City and Hiouchi, and interpretative signs tell a bit about the diverse flora—you'll encounter hemlocks, huckleberries, and lots and lots of ferns along this route. *Easy.* ⊠ *Crescent City* ✛ *Trailhead: Walker Rd., off U.S. 199, 2.5 miles east of U.S. 101.*

Yurok Loop Trail

BEACH—SIGHT | FAMILY | Providing a lovely opportunity to stretch your legs and breathe in the fresh sea air, this 1.2-mile loop starts at the Lagoon Creek Picnic Area on U.S. 101, at the very southern end of Del Norte Coast Redwoods State Park, and follows a short stretch of the California Coastal Trail. It then forks off toward False Klamath Cove, providing sweeping views of the ocean—keep an eye out for shore birds and migrating whales. Just to the north of False Klamath Cove, there's great beachcombing to be had along Wilson Creek Beach. *Easy.* ⊠ *Klamath* ✛ *Trailhead: Lagoon Creek Picnic Area on U.S. 101, 6.5 miles north of Klamath.*

VISITOR CENTERS

Crescent City Information Center

INFO CENTER | At the park's headquarters, this downtown Redding visitor center with a gift shop and picnic area is the main information stop if you're approaching the Redwoods from the north. ⊠ *1111 2nd St., Crescent City* ☎ *707/465–7335* ⊕ *www.nps.gov/redw* ☉ *Closed Tues.–Wed. in Nov.–Mar.*

Hiouchi Information Center

INFO CENTER | This small center at Jedediah Smith Redwoods State Park has exhibits about the area flora and fauna and screens a 12-minute park film. A starting point for ranger programs, the center has restrooms and a picnic area. ⊠ *U.S. 199* ✛ *Opposite Jedediah Smith Campground, 9 miles east of Crescent City* ☎ *707/458–3294* ⊕ *www.nps.gov/redw.*

Jedediah Smith Visitor Center

INFO CENTER | Adjacent to the Jedediah Smith Redwoods State Park main campground, this seasonal center has information about ranger-led walks and evening campfire programs. Also here are nature and history exhibits, a gift shop, and a picnic area. ⊠ *U.S. 199, Hiouchi* ✛ *At Jedediah Smith Campground* ☎ *707/458–3496* ⊕ *www.nps.gov/redw* ☉ *Closed Oct.–May.*

Activities

BIKING

Besides the roadways, you can bike on several trails, many of them along former logging roads. Best bets include the 11-mile Lost Man Creek Trail, which begins 3 miles north of Orick; the 12-mile round-trip Coastal Trail (Last Chance Section), which starts at the southern end of Enderts Beach Road and becomes steep and narrow as it travels through dense slopes of foggy redwood forests; and the 19-mile, single-track Ossagon Trail Loop in Prairie Creek Redwoods State Park, on which you're likely to see elk as you cruise through redwoods before coasting ocean side toward the end.

■ TIP → **You can rent electric bikes, which are especially nice for riding the hilly Lost Man Creek Trail, from Redwood Adventures (see Hiking, below).**

BIRD-WATCHING

Many rare and striking winged specimens inhabit the area, including chestnut-backed chickadees, brown pelicans, great blue herons, pileated woodpeckers, northern spotted owls, and marbled murrelets. By 2022, California condors are planned to be reintroduced to the park.

CAMPING

Within a 30-minute drive of Redwood National and State parks, you'll find roughly 60 public and private camping facilities. None of the primitive or backcountry areas in Redwood—DeMartin, Elam Creek, Flint Ridge, 44 Camp, Little Bald Hills, or Redwood Creek—is a drive-in site, although Flint Ridge is just a ¼-mile from the road. You must obtain a free permit from the Kuchel or Hiouchi visitor centers before camping in these areas; all are first come, first served. Bring your own drinking water—there are no sources at the sites.

Redwood has four developed, drive-in campgrounds—Elk Prairie, Gold Bluffs Beach, Jedediah Smith, and Mill Creek, all of them within the state-park boundaries. None has RV hookups, but Jedediah Smith and Mill Creek have dump stations. Fees are $35 nightly. For reservations, contact ☎ 800/444–7275 or ⊕ www.reserveamerica.com.

DEVELOPED CAMPGROUNDS

Elk Prairie Campground. Roosevelt elk frequent this popular campground adjacent to a prairie and old-growth redwoods. ⊠ Newton B. Drury Scenic Pkwy., Prairie Creek Redwoods State Park.

Gold Bluffs Beach Campground. You can camp in tents right on the beach at this Prairie Creek Redwoods State Park campground near Fern Canyon. ⊠ End of Davison Rd., off U.S. 101.

Jedediah Smith Campground. This is one of the few places to camp—in tents or RVs—within groves of old-growth redwood forest. ⊠ 9 miles east of Crescent City on U.S. 199.

Mill Creek Campground. Redwoods tower over large Mill Creek, in the remote and quiet interior of Del Norte Coast Redwoods State Park. Open mid-May–September. ⊠ U.S. 101, 7 miles southeast of Crescent City.

EDUCATIONAL PROGRAMS
RANGER PROGRAMS

All summer long, ranger-led programs explore the mysteries of both the redwoods and the sea. Topics include how the trees grow from fleck-size seeds to towering giants, what causes those weird fungi on old stumps, why the ocean fog is so important to redwoods, and exactly what those green-tentacled creatures are that float in tide pools. Campfire programs can include slide shows, storytelling, music, and games. Check with visitor centers for offerings and times.

Junior Ranger Program

Kids earn a badge by completing activity books, which are available from visitor centers. Additionally, rangers lead programs for kids throughout the summer, including nature walks and lessons in bird identification and outdoor survival.

Ranger Talks

From mid-May through mid-September, state park rangers regularly lead discussions on the redwoods, tide pools, geology, and Native American culture. Check schedules at the visitor centers.

Redwood EdVentures

TOUR—SIGHT | FAMILY | Fun and engaging Redwood EdVentures nature scavenger hunts for kids, called Quests, include ones in the park. Visit the website for "treasure map" PDFs detailing the Quests, which typically take no more than an hour. Participants receive a patch upon completion. ⊕ www.redwood-edventures.org.

FISHING

Deep-sea and freshwater fishing are popular here. Anglers often stake out sections of the Klamath and Smith rivers seeking salmon and trout. A single state license (⊕ www.wildlife.ca.gov/licensing/fishing) covers both ocean and river fishing. A two-day license costs about $27. You can go crabbing and clamming on the coast, but check the tides carefully: rip currents and sneaker waves can be deadly. No license is needed to fish from the long B Street Pier in Crescent City.

HIKING

Towering redwoods may look pretty cool from your car window, but the best way to behold their sheer immensity is the hike around and beneath. The park has miles of trails, including quite a few short, level treks just off the main roads and easily managed even if you have limited experience. Avid hikers will find plenty of fantastic rambles with serious elevation gains and thrilling flora and fauna. Note that some of the park's most delightful treks don't actually pass any big trees but rather hug Northern California's pristine and wild shoreline. Most famous is the Coastal Trail, which runs for about 70 miles from the northern to southern ends of the park. ⇨ See this chapter's Middle section for detailed descriptions of some of its best segments.

★ Redwood Adventures

HIKING/WALKING | Operated by and run out of the office of Elk Meadow Cabins, this small agency with a highly knowledgeable, passionate staff offers half- and full-day hikes through some of the park's most stunning stands of redwoods, as well as adventures exploring coastal tidepools and Fern Canyon. Backpacking with overnight camping options are also available, as are electric-bike rentals, which are great for touring around the park, especially the Lost Man Creek Trail. ⊠ 7 Valley Green Camp Rd., Orick ☎ 866/733–9637 ⊕ www.redwoodadventures.com.

KAYAKING

With many miles of often shallow rivers, streams, and estuarial lagoons, kayaking is a popular pastime in the park, especially in the southern end of the park near Kuchel Visitor Center, on Arcata and Humboldt bays near Eureka, up north along the Klamath and Smith rivers, and on the ocean in Crescent City.

Humboats Kayak Adventures

KAYAKING | You can rent kayaks and book kayaking tours that from December to June include whale-watching trips. Half-day river kayaking trips pass beneath massive redwoods; the whale-watching outings get you close enough for good photos. ⊠ Woodley Island Marina, 601 Startare Dr., Dock A, Eureka ☎ 707/443–5157 ⊕ www.humboats.com ✉ From $30 rentals, $55 tours.

★ Kayak Trinidad

KAYAKING | This respected outfitter rents kayaks and stand-up paddleboards, good for touring the beautiful estuarial and freshwater lagoons of Humboldt Lagoons State Park or sea kayaking out at sea. You can also book guided half-day paddles around Big Lagoon and Stone Lagoon, and along Trinidad Bay. The lagoons are stunning. Herds of Roosevelt elk sometimes traipse along the shoreline of Big Lagoon; raptors, herons, and waterfowl abound in both lagoons; and you can paddle across Stone Lagoon to a spectacular secluded Pacific-view beach. ⊠ Trinidad ☎ 707/329–0085 ⊕ www.kayaktrinidad.com.

WHALE-WATCHING

Good vantage points for whale-watching include Crescent Beach Overlook, the Kuchel Visitor Center in Orick, points along the Coastal Trail, Klamath Beach Road, and Klamath River Overlook. From late November through January is the best time to see their southward migrations; from February through April the whales return, usually passing closer to shore.

Nearby Towns

The North Coast's largest city is **Eureka,** population 27,000 and the Humboldt County seat. Its Old Town has an alluring waterfront boardwalk, several excellent restaurants and shops, and the region's largest selection of lodgings. It borders and forms a small metro area with the progressive college town of **Arcata,** just to the north, which has a handsome little downtown and a bevy of hip cafés and bars. Both Eureka and Arcata make good practical bases for touring the South and Middle portions of Redwood National and State Park, especially if you want to stay someplace with plenty of other diversions. A quieter and absolutely stunning little gem of a town that's 15 miles closer to the park than Arcata, **Trinidad** has a cove harbor that attracts fishermen and photographers and a few notable dining and lodging options.

Once you enter the park, as you continue north up U.S. 101 you'll come first to tiny Orick, which has but 300 residents and just a few businesses, and then to slightly larger **Klamath,** where you'll discover a handful of worthwhile places to stay and eat as well as a modern casino resort operated by the local Yurok tribe.

Crescent City, close to its Del Norte Redwoods and Jedediah Smith Redwoods state parks, is the largest town (population about 6,800) up north and home to the Redwood National and State parks headquarters as well as a good supply of restaurant and lodging options. Though it curves around a beautiful stretch of ocean, rain and bone-chilling fog often prevail.

Eureka

40 miles south of Kuchel Visitor Center, 270 miles north of San Francisco.

An excellent place to fuel up, buy groceries, and learn a little about the region's mining, timber, and fishing pasts, historic Eureka was named after a gold miner's hearty exclamation. The county visitor center has maps of self-guided walking tours of the town's nearly 100 Victorians. Art galleries and antiques stores liven up the vibrant Old Town district from C to N Street between the waterfront and 4th Street, and a walking pier extends into the harbor.

GETTING HERE AND AROUND
Eureka is set along the North Coast's main north-south highway, U.S. 101, which continues north into Redwood National and State Park. Give yourself about 45 minutes to drive to Kuchel Visitor Center, at the park's south end.

VISITOR INFORMATION Humboldt County Visitors Bureau. ⊠ *322 1st St.* ☎ *707/443–5097, 800/346–3482* ⊕ *www.visitredwoods.com.*

 Sights

Blue Ox Millworks
FACTORY | This wood-shop is among a handful in the country specializing in Victorian-era architecture, but what makes it truly unique is that its craftspeople use antique tools to do the work. Visitors can watch artisans use printing presses, lathes, and other equipment to create gingerbread trim, fence pickets, and other signature Victorian embellishments. The shop is less interesting on Saturday, when most craftspeople take the day off. ⊠ *1 X St.* ☎ *707/444–3437, 800/248–4259* ⊕ *www.blueoxmill.com* 💲 *$12* 🕐 *Closed Sun. and, in Dec.–Mar., Sat.*

Sequoia Park Zoo
ZOO | FAMILY | Animal lovers of all ages appreciate visiting California's oldest zoo (it opened in 1907). A highlight here is strolling high above the forest on the nation's only redwood canopy walk. Although it's a relatively small zoo, it is conservation-focused and fully accredited, and it's developed a number of excellent new exhibits in recent years. Favorite areas for wildlife viewing include the red

panda exhibit, a barnyard petting zoo, and a walk-in aviary with both local and exotic birds. ✉ *3414 W St.* ☎ *707/441–4263* 🌐 *www.sequoiaparkzoo.net* 🎟 *$10* 🕓 *Closed Mon.*

🍴 Restaurants

★ Brick & Fire Bistro

$$ | **MODERN AMERICAN** | Just about every seat in the darkly lighted, urbane dining room has a view of this downtown bistro's most important feature, a wood-fired brick oven used to prepare everything from roasted local Kumamoto oysters to a wild-mushroom cobbler topped with a cheesy biscuit—even the "fries," char-roasted potatoes tossed in olive oil and spices, come out of the oven. Creatively topped pizzas, sandwiches, and grilled meats and seafood round out the menu. **Known for:** house-made sausage pizzas; eggplant, brisket, and other sandwich fillings char-grilled in a wood-fired oven; house-made ginger ale. [$] *Average main: $20* ✉ *1630 F St.* ☎ *707/268–8959* 🌐 *www.brickandfirebistro.com* 🕓 *Closed Tues. No lunch weekends.*

Café Waterfront

$$ | **SEAFOOD** | Amid Old Town's vibrant dining district, this rollicking spot in what served as a saloon and brothel in the 1950s turns out consistently fresh locally caught seafood. Steamed clams, grilled snapper, oyster burgers, and chowders are all on the menu—one of the West Coast's top oyster beds, in the bay across the street, supplies the oysters on the half shell. **Known for:** historic vibe and Old Town setting; excellent locally sourced oysters (raw and grilled); homemade clam chowder. [$] *Average main: $21* ✉ *102 F St.* ☎ *707/443–9190* 🌐 *www.cafewaterfronteureka.com.*

🛏 Hotels

★ Carter House Inns

$$$ | **HOTEL** | Richly painted and aglow with wood detailing, the rooms, in two main Victorian buildings and several historic cottages, contain a mix of modern and antique furnishings; some have whirlpool tubs and separate sitting areas. **Pros:** elegant ambience; attention to detail; superb on-site Restaurant 301. **Cons:** not suitable for children; restaurant is a bit pricey; two-night minimum on weekends. [$] *Rooms from: $180* ✉ *301 L St.* ☎ *707/444–8062, 800/404–1390* 🌐 *www.carterhouse.com* 🛏 *32 rooms* 🍴 *Free Breakfast.*

Inn at 2nd and C

$$ | **B&B/INN** | By the bustling waterfront and steps from Old Town's inviting shops and restaurants, this towering 1880s Victorian inn exudes character and abounds with opulent architectural details and florid period-style bedding, wallpapers, and furnishings. **Pros:** close to Old Town Eureka dining and shopping; fascinating old building; reasonable rates. **Cons:** thin walls; some rooms don't have flat-screen TVs; least expensive rooms are small. [$] *Rooms from: $139* ✉ *139 2nd St.* ☎ *707/444–3344* 🌐 *www.historiceaglehouse.com/the-inn-at-2nd-c* 🛏 *23 rooms* 🍴 *Free Breakfast.*

Arcata

8 miles north of Eureka, 33 miles south of Kuchel Visitor Center.

Begun in 1850 as a base camp for miners and lumberjacks, Arcata is today an artsy, progressive college town. Activity centers on the grassy Arcata Plaza, which is surrounded by restored buildings containing funky bars, cafés, and indie shops.

GETTING HERE AND AROUND

Set along U.S. 101, Arcata also lies just south of the junction with the main road, Highway 299, that connects the region to the east with Redding and Interstate 5. Highway 299 is a windy, hilly route—allow about two hours and 45 minutes to make the 135-mile drive to Redding.

VISITOR INFORMATION Arcata Humboldt Visitor Center. ✉ *1635 Heindon Rd., Arcata* ☎ *707/822–3619* ⊕ *www.arcatachamber. com.*

 Restaurants

Cafe Brio

$$ | AMERICAN | With an inviting indoor dining room and outside seating over-looking bustling Arcata Plaza, this artisan bakery and restaurant is known for its savory and sweet breads. Notable nosh-es include ham-and-cheese breakfast croissants, focaccia sandwiches with avocado and Humboldt Fog goat cheese from Arcata's Cypress Grove creamery, and farm-to-table dinner fare. **Known for:** lemon cream tarts and other pastries available all day; small but terrific wine selection; Blue Bottle coffees. $ *Average main: $14* ✉ *791 G St., Arcata* ☎ *707/822–5922* ⊕ *www.cafebrioarcata. com* ⊘ *No dinner.*

★ Salt Fish House

$$$ | SEAFOOD | Just a couple of blocks from Arcata's festive Plaza, this hip seafood restaurant inside a beautifully converted old machine shop offers seating in both an airy dining room and on a large side patio. Specialties include classic panko-crusted cod and chips and seared-rare steelhead with polenta cakes, but you could also make a meal of small plates from the raw bar—octopus ceviche, scallop crudo, and grilled Pacific oysters with *nuoc cham* (dipping sauce) among them. **Known for:** sharable raw-seafood trays and towers; superb wine and cocktail list; house-made ice cream in seasonal flavors.

$ *Average main: $25* ✉ *935 I St., Arcata* ☎ *707/630–5300* ⊕ *www.saltfishhouse. com* ⊘ *Closed Mon. No lunch.*

☕ Coffee and Quick Bites

Wildberries Marketplace

$ | DELI | This market with juice and salad bars and a small café carries a great selection of deli items, cheeses, and picnic provisions, many of them produced regionally. There's a good selection of local wine and beer, too. **Known for:** burgers and jerk chicken sandwiches; organic produce; excellent pizzas, tarts, pies, and other baked goods. $ *Average main: $8* ✉ *747 13th St., Arcata* ☎ *707/822–0095* ⊕ *www. wildberries.com* ▭ *No credit cards.*

Trinidad

15 miles north of Arcata, 18 miles south of Kuchel Visitor Center.

A mellow base for exploring the southern portion of Redwood National and State Parks, coastal Trinidad got its name from the Spanish mariners who entered the bay on Trinity Sunday, June 9, 1775. For-merly the principal trading post for min-ing camps along the Klamath and Trinity rivers, these days Trinidad is a quiet and genuinely charming community with sev-eral beaches and a small but impressive selection of distinctive eateries, romantic inns, and rustic cabin compounds.

GETTING HERE AND AROUND

Trinidad sits right off U.S. 101, about 10 miles north of the junction with Highway 299, which leads to east to Redding.

Sights

Patrick's Point State Park

BEACH—SIGHT | This park on a forested plateau almost 200 feet above the surf offers stunning views of the Pacific, great whale- and sea lion–watching spots, campgrounds, picnic areas, bike paths, and hiking trails through old-growth spruce forest. There are also tidal pools at Agate Beach, a re-created Yurok Indian village, and a small visitor center with exhibits. It's uncrowded and sublimely quiet here. Dogs are not allowed on trails or the beach. ⊠ *4150 Patricks Point Dr.* ✛ *Off U.S. 101, 5 miles north of town* ☎ *707/677–3570* ⊕ *www.parks.ca.gov* ⬚ *$8 parking.*

🍴 Restaurants

★ Larrupin' Cafe

$$$$ | **AMERICAN** | Set in a two-story house on a quiet country road north of town, this casually sophisticated restaurant— one of the best places to eat on the North Coast—is often thronged with people enjoying mesquite-grilled fresh seafood, beef brisket, St. Louis–style ribs, and vegetarian dishes. The garden setting and candlelight stir thoughts of romance. **Known for:** refined but friendly service; rosemary-crusted garlic, camba-zola cheese, and toast points appetizer; super wine list. 💲 *Average main: $36* ⊠ *1658 Patricks Point Dr.* ☎ *707/677– 0230* ⊕ *www.larrupin.com* ☾ *No lunch.*

Trinidad Bay Eatery & Gallery

$$ | **SEAFOOD** | A short stroll from Trinidad's bay front, this unpretentious combination gallery and seafood-oriented restau-rant cooks up tasty meals. Buttermilk pancakes and Dungeness crab Benedict are among the favorites for breakfast; at lunchtime burgers, crab Louie salads, and clam chowder are great bets. **Known for:** well-curated wine list; cioppino in chipot-le broth; blackberry cobbler. 💲 *Average main: $21* ⊠ *607 Parker St.* ☎ *707/677– 3777* ⊕ *www.trinidadeatery.com.*

☕ Coffee and Quick Bites

Beachcomber Cafe

$ | **BAKERY** | Before a day of hiking and exploring, fuel up in downtown Trinidad on organic espresso or coffee drinks, freshly baked breads and pastries, house-made granola, frittatas, and bagels with lox, chèvre, local jams, poached eggs, and other toppings. The lineup for lunch includes soups, salads, and panini. **Known for:** bagels with creative top-pings; strong, organic coffee; vegetarian options. 💲 *Average main: $9* ⊠ *363 Trinity St.* ☎ *707/677–0106* ⊕ *www.beachcomb-ertrinidad.com* ☾ *No dinner.*

Hotels

Emerald Forest Cabins

$$$ | **B&B/INN** | **FAMILY** | Set in a grove of towering redwoods yet within a short drive of both the town of Trinidad and its harbor and beach, this well-kept RV and tent campground also offers 21 beautifully designed rustic cabins with bathrooms, knotty-pine walls, decks, and a mix of handy amenities, depending on the unit: kitchens, gas or wood stoves, heated natural-stone bathroom floors, and other nice touches. **Pros:** peaceful redwood-forest setting; just a mile from downtown Trinidad; lots of kid-friendly diversions. **Cons:** cabins are quite small; weak to nonexistent Wi-Fi; some road noise. 💲 *Rooms from: $179* ⊠ *753 Pat-ricks Point Dr.* ☎ *707/677–3554* ⊕ *www. emeraldforestcabins.com* ⤳ *21 cabins* ⦿l *No meals.*

Lost Whale Inn

$$$$ | **B&B/INN** | For a romantic, special-oc-casion getaway near the park, look to this intimate, luxurious inn perched on a sea-side bluff near Patrick's Point State Park in Trinidad. **Pros:** stunning ocean views; elaborate and delicious breakfast spread; spa services, in-room or out on the lawn, are offered. **Cons:** no pets allowed (but you'll find a few adorable pets residing at the inn); two-night minimum on summer weekends; sometimes books up fully for weddings. 💲 *Rooms from: $300* ⊠ *3452 Patricks Point Dr.* ☎ *707/677–3425* ⊕ *www.lostwhaleinn.com* ⤳ *8 rooms* ⦿l *Free Breakfast.*

Redwood trees, and the moss that often coats them, grow best in damp, shady environments.

Trinidad Inn

$$ | HOTEL | FAMILY | These quiet cottage rooms nestled in the evergreens are 2 miles north of Trinidad Bay's harbor, restaurants, and shops. **Pros:** idyllic setting; walking path through adjacent redwood grove; good for kids. **Cons:** older property; no breakfast in off-season; reservations can be made only by phone. [$] *Rooms from: $155* ✉ *1170 Patricks Point Dr.* ☎ *707/677–3349* 🌐 *www.trinidadinn.com* 🛏 *10 rooms* 🍴 *Free Breakfast.*

Turtle Rocks Oceanfront Inn

$$$$ | B&B/INN | This comfortable inn has the best view in Trinidad, with the ocean and sunning sea lions seen from private, glassed-in decks in each room. **Pros:** great ocean views; comfortable king beds; surrounding landscape left natural and wild. **Cons:** no restaurants within walking distance; often books well in advance; can be foggy here in summer. [$] *Rooms from: $280* ✉ *3392 Patricks Point Dr.* ☎ *707/677–3707* 🌐 *www.turtlerocksinn.com* 🛏 *6 rooms* 🍴 *Free Breakfast.*

Klamath

13 miles north of Prairie Creek Redwoods Visitor Center, 22 miles south of Crescent City, 64 miles north of Eureka.

A low-key, unincorporated community surrounded by Redwood parkland on all sides, Klamath is a hub of the Yurok indigenous tribe, which makes up nearly 50 percent of the town's population and operates a casino resort in its center. There are a few mostly inexpensive, no-frills motels and eateries in town and nearby along with the inviting and historic Requa Inn.

VISITOR INFORMATION

Yurok Country Visitor Center. ✉ *101 Klamath Blvd., Klamath* ☎ *707/482–1555* 🌐 *www.visityurokcountry.com.*

Sights

Trees of Mystery

FOREST | FAMILY | Since opening in 1946, this unabashedly goofy but endearing roadside attraction has been doling out family fun. From the moment you pull your car up to the 49-foot-tall talking statue of Paul Bunyan (alongside Babe the Blue Ox), the kitschy thrills begin. You can then explore a genuinely informative museum of Native American artifacts, admire intricately carved redwood figures, and browse tacky souvenirs. For a fee you can ride a six-passenger gondola over the redwood treetops for a majestic view of the forest canopy, and stroll along several mostly easy trails through the adjacent forest of redwoods, Sitka spruce, and Douglas firs. ✉ *15500 U.S. 101 N , between Klamath and Del Norte Coast Redwoods State Park, Klamath* ☎ *800/638–3389* 🌐 *www.treesofmystery.net* 🎫 *Museum free, trails and gondola $20.*

Restaurants

Woodland Villa Restaurant

$ | AMERICAN | This homey diner-style café just north of Klamath serves the sort of hearty American fare that'll fuel you up before a big day of hiking. There's breakfast sandwiches, Belgian waffles, and chicken-fried steaks in the morning, and deli sandwiches, salads, and pizzas offered throughout the rest of the day. **Known for:** big portions; good selection of craft beer and cider; local smoked-salmon in the adjacent market. [$] *Average main: $9* ✉ *15870 U.S. 101, Klamath* ☎ *707/482–2081* 🌐 *www.woodlandvillacabins.com* 🕓 *Closed Mon.*

Hotels

★ **Historic Requa Inn**

$$ | B&B/INN | This serene 1914 inn overlooks the Klamath River a mile east of where it meets the ocean. **Pros:** serene; relaxing yet central location with river views; excellent restaurant. **Cons:** least expensive rooms are quite small; not a good choice for families with kids; not many dining options in the area. [$] *Rooms from: $132* ✉ *451 Requa Rd., Klamath* ☎ *707/482–1425* 🌐 *www.requainn.com* 🛏 *16 rooms* 🍴 *Free Breakfast.*

Motel Trees

$ | HOTEL | Operated by and adjacent to the joyfully kitschy Trees of Mystery roadside attraction, this casual mid-century motel has simply furnished rooms brightened with paintings and in some cases wall-length photographic murals of local redwoods and coastal scenes. **Pros:** very affordable; close to park beaches and trails; fun retro-'50s vibe. **Cons:** not a lot of frills; on-site restaurant is just so-so; some highway noise from U.S. 101. [$] *Rooms from: $89* ✉ *15495 U.S. 101, Klamath* ☎ *707/482–3152, 800/848–2982* 🌐 *www.moteltrees.com* 🛏 *23 rooms* 🍴 *No meals.*

Crescent City

5 miles north of Del Norte Coast Redwoods State Park, 5 miles west of Jedediah Smith Redwoods State Park, 25 miles south of Brookings, OR, 82 miles southwest of Grants Pass, OR.

The northern gateway to and headquarters of Redwood National and State Parks, this small oceanfront city just below the Oregon border offers close access to many of the park's key features, from the redwoods of Stout and Simpson-Reed groves in Jedediah Smith park to the sweeping, boulder-strewn beaches of Del Norte Coast park. The town itself enjoys a remarkable scenic setting overlooking the Pacific and contains several mostly mid-priced places to eat and stay, although it's often socked in by fog in summer or pelted by big storms in winter.

VISITOR INFORMATION

Visit Del Norte County. ✉ *1001 Front St., Crescent City* ☎ *707/464–3174* 🌐 *www.visitdelnortecounty.com.*

🍴 Restaurants

Good Harvest Cafe

$$ | **AMERICAN** | **FAMILY** | This cheerful café, which serves great breakfasts and espresso drinks, lives up to its name with ample use of locally grown and organic ingredients. For lunch and dinner there are salads, burgers, sandwiches, vegetarian specialties, and several fish entrées, plus a nice range of local beers and West Coast wines. **Known for:** fish-and-chips and other local seafood; hearty, delicious breakfasts; plenty of vegetarian items. [$] *Average main: $17* ✉ *575 U.S. 101 S, Crescent City* ☎ *707/465–6028* 🌐 *www.goodharvest-cafe.com.*

★ **SeaQuake Brewing**

$$ | **PIZZA** | Water from the cool and clean Smith River goes into the dozen or so beers poured at this microbrewery with a spacious modern-industrial interior. They pair well with wood-fired thin-crust pizzas that include one with grilled chicken, bacon, artichoke hearts, garlic cream sauce, and cheeses from the local Rumiano Cheese Company. **Known for:** attractive patio with heat lamps; well-crafted beers on tap; the caramel stout sundae. [$] *Average main: $15* ✉ *400 Front St., Crescent City* ☎ *707/465–4444* 🌐 *seaquakebrewing.com* 🕒 *Closed Sun. and Mon.*

🛏 Hotels

Curly Redwood Lodge

$ | **HOTEL** | A single redwood tree produced the 57,000 board feet of lumber used to build this budget 1957 motor lodge. **Pros:** large rooms; several restaurants within walking distance; cool retro furnishings. **Cons:** road noise can be bothersome; very basic amenities; no breakfast. [$] *Rooms from: $75* ✉ *701 U.S. 101 S, Crescent City* ☎ *707/464–2137* 🌐 *www.curlyredwoodlodge.com* 🛏 *36 rooms* 🍴 *No meals.*

Ocean View Inn & Suites

$$ | **HOTEL** | This clean, comfortable, and reasonably priced hotel doesn't have a lot of bells and whistles, but it does enjoy a great location on the edge of downtown Crescent City very close to the water. **Pros:** views of the water; many restaurants nearby; good value. **Cons:** on a busy road; cookie-cutter furnishings; nearby foghorn can be a little noisy. [$] *Rooms from: $125* ✉ *270 U.S. 101, Crescent City* ☎ *707/465–1111, 855/623–2611* 🌐 *www.oceanviewinncrescentcity.com* 🛏 *65 rooms* 🍴 *Free Breakfast.*

ROCKY MOUNTAIN NATIONAL PARK

Updated by
Lindsey Galloway

COLORADO

⛰ **Camping**
★★★☆☆

🏨 **Hotels**
★★☆☆☆

🤸 **Activities**
★★★★☆

👁 **Scenery**
★★★★★

👥 **Crowds**
★★★★★

WELCOME TO
ROCKY MOUNTAIN NATIONAL PARK

TOP REASONS
TO GO

★ **Awesome ascents:**
Seasoned climbers can trek to the summit of 14,259-foot Longs Peak or attack the rounded granite domes of Lumpy Ridge. Novices can summit Twin Sisters Peaks or Mt. Ida, both reaching more than 11,000 feet.

★ **Continental Divide:**
Straddle this great divide, which cuts through the western part of the park, separating water's flow to either the Pacific or Atlantic Ocean.

★ **Gorgeous scenery:** Peer out over more than 100 lakes, gaze up at majestic mountain peaks, and soak in the splendor of lush wetlands, pine-scented woods, forests of spruce and fir, and alpine tundra in the park's four distinct ecosystems.

★ **More than 355 miles of trails:** Hike on dozens of marked trails, from easy lakeside strolls to strenuous mountain climbs.

★ **Wildlife viewing:** Spot elk and bighorn sheep, along with moose, otters, and more than 280 species of birds.

1 Moraine Park. This area offers easy access to several trailheads, the park's largest campground, and the Beaver Meadows Visitor Center near the east-side entrance.

2 Bear Lake. One of the park's most photographed places is the hub for many trailheads and a stop on the park's shuttle service.

3 Longs Peak. The park's highest (and toughest to climb) peak, this Fourteener pops up in many park vistas. A round-trip summit trek takes 10 to 15 hours; most visitors opt for a (still spectacular) partial journey.

4 Trail Ridge Road. Alpine tundra is the highlight here, as the road—the nation's highest continuous highway—climbs to over 12,000 feet (almost 700 feet above timberline).

5 Timber Creek. The park's far western area is much less crowded than other sections, though it has evening programs, 98 camping sites, and a visitor center.

6 Wild Basin Area. Far from the crowds, this southeastern quadrant has lovely subalpine forest punctuated by streams and lakes.

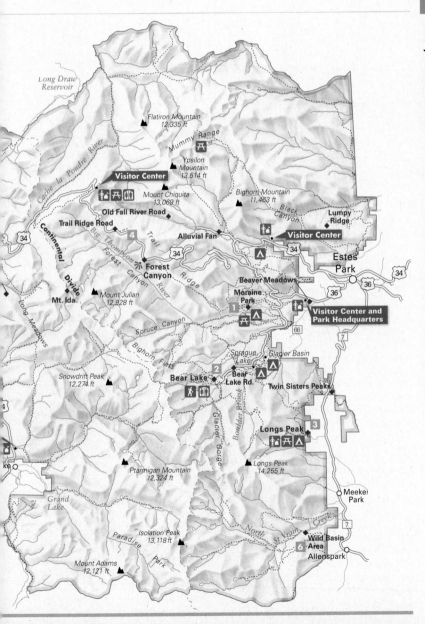

Long Draw
Reservoir

Flatiron Mountain
12,335 ft

Mummy Range

Ypsilon
Mountain
13,514 ft

Cache la Poudre River

Visitor Center

Mount Chiquita
13,069 ft

Bighorn Mountain
11,463 ft

Black
Canyon

Lumpy
Ridge

Old Fall River Road

Trail Ridge Road

Continental

34

Big Thompson River

Forest Canyon

4

Trail

Alluvial Fan

34

Visitor Center

34

Estes
Park

34

Divide

**Forest
Canyon**

Ridge

36

36

Mt. Ida

Mount Julian
12,928 ft

Beaver Meadows

**Moraine
Park**

**Visitor Center and
Park Headquarters**

Spruce Canyon

1

66

7

Long Meadows

Bighorn Flats

Sprague
Lake

Glacier Basin

Snowdrift Peak
12,274 ft

4

Bear Lake

2

Bear
Lake Rd.

Twin Sisters Peaks

Boulder Brook

3

Glacier Gorge

Longs Peak

ke

Ptarmigan Mountain
12,324 ft

Longs Peak
14,255 ft

Meeker
Park

Grand
Lake

7

Paradise Park

Isolation Peak
13,118 ft

North St. Vrain Creek

**Wild Basin
Area**
Allenspark

6

Mount Adams
12,121 ft

With its towering mountains, active and abundant wildlife, and crystal clear lakes and rivers, Rocky Mountain attracts nearly 5 million visitors per year, trailing only the Grand Canyon and the Great Smoky Mountains in the country's most visited National Parks. Established as the 10th National Park in 1915, the picturesque land has attracted humans since at least 11,000 years ago, based on the archaeological artifacts like shelters and speartips that have been found throughout the park.

These ancient people used the very same trail as today's visitors: the 48-mile Trail Ridge Road. With an apex of 12,183 feet, the road travels from the east-side Estes Park entrance, across the Continental Divide, to the west-side Grand Lake entrance, giving even nonhikers a close look at the Montane, Supalpine, and Alpine ecosystems found at different areas of the park.

Those who do hike have their pick of more than 355 miles of trails, with paths suited for every ability level. The park's high altitude—the lowest elevation starts at 7,000 feet above sea level—often affects out-of-towners, but a good night's sleep and healthy hydration go a long way. The park is famous for its robust elk population, especially active in "Elk-to-ber" when the elk come to lower elevations for their annual mating season. Moose are more common on the west side near the Kawuneeche Visitor Center and near rivers and lakes, while bighorn sheep are best spotted in late spring and early summer at the appropriately named Sheeps Lake in Horseshoe Park.

Rocky Mountain has more than 1,000 archaeological sites and 150 buildings of historic significance; 47 of the buildings are listed in the National Register of Historic Places. Most buildings at Rocky Mountain are done in the rustic style, which strives to incorporate nature into man-made structures.

Though the park has year-round access and activities, most visitors come between late spring and mid-autumn when Trail Ridge Road remains open. In the high summer months, the east side entrance and lower elevation trails can become quite congested, so beat the crowds by using the west entrance or

AVERAGE HIGH/LOW TEMPERATURES					
JAN.	FEB.	MAR.	APR.	MAY	JUNE
39/16	41/17	45/21	53/27	62/34	73/41
JULY	AUG.	SEPT.	OCT.	NOV.	DEC.
78/46	76/45	70/38	60/30	46/23	40/18

arriving before 8 am. *In 2020, a pair of devastating fires swept across approximately 30,000 acres, around 9 percent of the park, primarily in the west and far north part of the park, so check the latest conditions and closures on the park's website before setting off.*

Planning

When to Go

More than 80% of the park's annual 4.7 million visitors come in summer and fall. For thinner high-season crowds, come in early June or September. But there is a good reason to put up with summer crowds: only from late May to mid-October will you get the chance to make the unforgettable drive over Trail Ridge Road (note that the road may still be closed during those months if the weather turns bad).

Spring is capricious—75°F one day and a blizzard the next (March sees the most snow). June can range from hot and sunny to cool and rainy. July typically ushers in high summer, which can last through September. Up on Trail Ridge Road, it can be 15°F–20°F cooler than at the park's lower elevations. Wildlife viewing and fishing is best in any season but winter. In early fall, the trees blaze with brilliant foliage. Winter, when backcountry snow can be 4 feet deep, is the time for cross-country skiing, snowshoeing, and ice fishing.

FESTIVALS AND EVENTS

Rooftop Rodeo. Consistently ranked one of the top small rodeos in the country (and a tradition since 1908), this six-day event features a parade and nightly rodeo events, such as barrel racing and saddle bronc riding. ⊕ *www.rooftoprodeo.com.*

Elk Fest. In early autumn, the calls of bulls fill the forest as elk head down from the mountains for mating season. Estes Park celebrates with elk bugle contests, live music, and elk educational seminars. ⊕ *www.visitestespark.com/events-calendar/special-events/elk-fest.*

Longs Peak Scottish-Irish Highland Festival. A traditional tattoo (drum- and bugle-filled parade) kicks off this fair of ancient Scottish athletic competitions. There's also Celtic music, Irish dancing, and events for dogs of the British Isles (such as terrier racing and sheepdog demonstrations). ⊕ *www.scotfest.com.*

Getting Here and Around

AIR

The closest commercial airport is **Denver International Airport** (DEN). Its **Ground Transportation Information Center** (☎ 800/247–2336 or 303/342–4059 ⊕ *www.flydenver.com*) assists visitors with car rentals, door-to-door shuttles, and limousine services. From the airport, the eastern entrance of the park is 80 miles (about two hours). **Estes Park Shuttle** (☎ 970/586–5151 ⊕ *www.estesparkshuttle.com*; reservations essential) serves Estes Park and Rocky Mountain from both Denver International Airport and Longmont/Boulder.

Rocky Mountain in One Day

Starting out in Estes Park, begin your day at the **Bighorn Restaurant**, a classic breakfast spot and a local favorite. While you're enjoying your short stack with apple-cinnamon-raisin topping, you can put in an order for a packed lunch (it's a good idea to bring your food with you, as dining options in the park consist of a single, seasonal snack bar at the top of Trail Ridge Road).

Drive west on U.S. 34 into the park, and stop at the **Beaver Meadows Visitor Center** to watch the orientation film and pick up a park map. Also inquire about road conditions on Trail Ridge Road, which you should plan to drive either in the morning or afternoon, depending on the weather. If possible, save the drive for the afternoon, and use the morning to get out on the trails, before the chance of an afternoon lightning storm.

For a beautiful and invigorating hike, head to Bear Lake and follow the route that takes you to **Nymph Lake** (an easy 1/2-mile hike), then onto **Dream Lake** (an additional 0.6 miles with a steeper ascent), and finally to **Emerald Lake** (an additional 0.7 miles of moderate terrain). You can stop at several places along the way. The trek down is much easier, and quicker, than the climb up. ■TIP→ **If you prefer a shorter, simpler (yet still scenic) walk, consider the Bear Lake Nature Trail, a 0.6-mile loop that is wheelchair and stroller accessible.**

You'll need the better part of your afternoon to drive the scenic **Trail Ridge Road.** Start by heading west toward Grand Lake, stop at the lookout at the Alluvial Fan, and consider taking Old Fall River Road the rest of the way across the park. This single-lane dirt road delivers unbeatable views of waterfalls and mountain vistas. You'll take it westbound from Horseshoe Park (the cutoff is near the Endovalley Campground), then rejoin Trail Ridge Road at its summit, near the Alpine Visitor Center. If you're traveling on to Grand Lake or other points west, stay on Trail Ridge Road. If you're heading back to Estes Park, turn around and take Trail Ridge Road back (for a different set of awesome scenery). End your day with a ranger-led talk or evening campfire program.

BUS

Rocky Mountain has limited parking, but offers three free shuttle buses, which operate daily from 7 am to 8 pm, late May to early October. All three shuttles can be accessed from a large Park & Ride located within the park, 7 miles from the Beaver Meadows entrance. Visitors who don't want to drive into the park at all can hop on the Hiker Shuttle at the Estes Park Visitor Center. The shuttle, which runs every half hour during peak times, makes stops at the Beaver Meadows Visitor Center and the Park & Ride, where visitors can switch to one of the other two shuttles, which head to various trailheads. The Moraine Park Route shuttle runs every 30 minutes and stops at the Moraine Park Visitor Center and then continues on to the Fern Lake Trailhead. The Bear Lake Route shuttle runs every 10 to 15 minutes from the Park & Ride to the Bear Lake Trailhead.

CAR

Estes Park and Grand Lake are the Rocky Mountains' gateway communities; from these you can enter the park via U.S. 34 or 36 (Estes Park) or U.S. 34 (Grand

Lake). U.S. 36 runs from Denver through Boulder, Lyons, and Estes Park to the park; the portion between Boulder and Estes Park is heavily traveled—especially on summer weekends. Though less direct, Colorado Routes 119, 72, and 7 have much less traffic (and better scenery). If you're driving directly to Rocky Mountain from the airport, take the E-470 tollway from Peña Boulevard to Interstate 25.

The **Colorado Department of Transportation** (for road conditions ☎ 303/639–1111 ⊕ www.cotrip.org) plows roads efficiently, but winter snowstorms can slow traffic and create wet or icy conditions. In summer, the roads into both Grand Lake and Estes Park can see heavy traffic, especially on weekends.

WITHIN THE PARK

The main thoroughfare in the park is Trail Ridge Road (U.S. 34); in winter, it's closed from the first storm in the fall (typically in October) through the spring (depending on snowpack, this could be at any time between May and June). During that time, it's plowed only up to Many Parks Curve on the east side and the Colorado River trailhead on the west side. (For current road information: ☎ 970/586–1222 ⊕ www.codot.gov.)

The spectacular Old Fall River Road runs one-way between the Endovalley Picnic Area on the eastern edge of the park and the Alpine Visitor Center at the summit of Trail Ridge Road, on the western side. It is typically open from July to September, depending on snowfall. It's a steep, narrow road (no wider than 14 feet), and trailers and vehicles longer than 25 feet are prohibited, but a trip on this 100-year-old thoroughfare is well worth the effort. For information on road closures, contact the park: ☎ 970/586–1206 ⊕ www.nps.gov/romo.

Inspiration

A Lady's Life in the Rocky Mountains, by Isabella L. Bird, has long been a favorite with Colorado residents and visitors to the park.

Hiking Rocky Mountain National Park: The Essential Guide, by Erik Stensland, matches your hiking ability and time alloted to find the perfect trail.

The Magnificent Mountain Women, by Janet Robertson, gives historical accounts of early pioneers.

Park Essentials

ACCESSIBILITY

All visitor centers are accessible to wheelchair users. The Sprague Lake, Coyote Valley, Lily Lake, and Bear Lake trails are all accessible loops of hard-packed gravel, ½ to 1 mile long. The Bear Lake trail is not entirely flat and is considered the most challenging of the accessible trails. A backcountry campsite at Sprague Lake accommodates up to 12 campers, including six in wheelchairs. The Moraine Park and Timber Creek campgrounds also offer some accessible sites and restroom facilities. All in-park shuttles and bus stops are wheelchair accessible.

PARK FEES AND PERMITS

Entrance fees are $25 per automobile for a one-day pass or $35 for a seven-day pass. Those who enter via foot or bicycle can get a seven-day pass for $20. Motorcyclists can get a seven-day pass for $30. An annual pass to Rocky Mountain costs $70, while the National Parks' America The Beautiful pass costs $80 and grants admission to more than 2,000 sites across the U.S.

Wilderness camping requires a permit that's $30 per party from May through October, and free the rest of the year. Visit ⊕ www.nps.gov/romo/planyourvisit/

wilderness-camping.htm before you go for a planning guide to backcountry camping. You can get your permit online, by phone (☎ 970/586–1242), or in person. In person, you can get a day-of-trip permit year-round at one of the park's two backcountry offices, located next to the Beaver Meadows Visitor Center and in the Kawuneeche Visitor Center.

PARK HOURS

The park is open 24/7 year-round; some roads close in winter. It is in the Mountain time zone.

CELL PHONE RECEPTION

Cell phones work in some sections of the park, and free Wi-Fi can be accessed in and around the Beaver Meadows Visitor Center, Fall River, and the Kawuneeche Visitor Center.

Hotels

Bed-and-breakfasts and small inns in north central Colorado vary from old-fashioned fluffy cottages to sleek, modern buildings with understated lodge themes. If you want some pampering, guest ranches and spas will fit the bill.

In Estes Park, Grand Lake, and other nearby towns, the elevation keeps the climate cool, and you'll scarcely need (and you'll have a tough time finding) air-conditioned lodging. For a historic spot, try the Stanley Hotel in Estes Park, which dates to 1909. The park itself has no hotels or lodges. *Hotel reviews have been shortened. For full information, visit Fodors.com.*

Restaurants

Restaurants in north central Colorado run the gamut from simple diners with tasty, homey basics to elegant establishments with extensive wine lists. Some restaurants take reservations, but many—particularly midrange spots—seat on a first-come, first-served basis. In

the park itself, the Trail Ridge Store next to the Alpine Visitor Center has a café and coffee bar open from late May to October. The park also has a handful of scenic picnic areas, all with tables and pit or flush toilets. *Restaurant reviews have been shortened. For full information, visit Fodors.com.*

What It Costs			
$	$$	$$$	$$$$
RESTAURANTS			
under $13	$13–$18	$19–$25	over $25
HOTELS			
under $121	$121–$170	$171–$230	over $230

Tours

Green Jeep Tours

ADVENTURE TOURS | FAMILY | From the back of an open-air, neon-green Jeep on these tours, you can enjoy the majestic scenery while your experienced guide points out wildlife along the way. Green Jeep Tours also offers a three-hour tour in September and October that focuses on finding elk. Admission includes the cost of the one-day pass into the park. ⊠ 157 Moraine Ave., Estes Park ☎ 970/577–0034 🖾 From $90.

Wildside 4x4 Tours

DRIVING TOURS | This company's most popular tour, the "Top of the World," takes visitors in an open-top vehicle all the way to Old Fall River Road and back down Trail Ridge. A waterfall tour and sunset valley tour offer great wildlife spottings at lower elevations. ⊠ 212 E. Elkhorn Ave., Estes Park ☎ 970/586–8687 ⊕ www.wildside4x4tours.com 🖾 From $80.

★ Yellow Wood Guiding

ADVENTURE TOURS | Guided photo safaris, offered year-round, ensure visitors leave the Rocky Mountain National Park with more than just memories. Customized

Plants and Wildlife in Rocky Mountain

Volcanic uplifts and the savage clawing of receding glaciers created Rocky Mountain's majestic landscape. You'll find four distinct ecosystems here—a riparian (wetland) environment with 150 lakes and 450 miles of streams; verdant montane valleys teeming with proud ponderosa pines and lush grasses; higher and colder subalpine mountains with wind-whipped trees (krummholz) that grow at right angles; and harsh, unforgiving alpine tundra with dollhouse-size versions of familiar plants and wildflowers. Alpine tundra is seldom found outside the Arctic, yet it makes up one-third of the park's terrain. Few plants can survive at this elevation of 11,000–11,500 feet, but many beautiful wildflowers—including alpine forget-me-nots—bloom here briefly in late June or early July.

The park has so much wildlife that you can often enjoy prime viewing from the seat of your car. Fall, when many animals begin moving down from higher elevations, is an excellent time to spot some of the park's animal residents. This is also when you'll hear the male elk bugle mating calls (popular spots to see and hear bugling elk are Kawuneeche Valley, Horseshoe Park, Moraine Park, and Upper Beaver Meadows).

May through mid-October is the best time to see the bighorn sheep that congregate in the Horseshoe Park/Sheep Lakes area, just past the Fall River entrance. If you want to glimpse a moose, try Kawuneeche Valley. Other animals in the park include mule deer, squirrels, chipmunks, pikas, beavers, and marmots. Common birds include broad-tailed and rufous hummingbirds, peregrine falcons, woodpeckers, mountain bluebirds, and Clark's nutcracker, as well as the white-tailed ptarmigan, which live year-round on the alpine tundra.

Mountain lions, black bears, and bobcats also inhabit the park but are rarely seen by visitors. Altogether, the park is home to roughly 60 species of mammals and 280 bird species.

for either beginners or experts, the tours offer the use of professional digital cameras for visitors who don't have their own. ✉ 404 Driftwood Ave., Estes Park ☎ 303/775-5484 ⊕ www.ywguiding.com ⛁ From $175.

Visitor Information

CONTACT Rocky Mountain National Park. ✉ 1000 U.S. 36, Estes Park ☎ 970/586–1206 ⊕ www.nps.gov/romo.

Moraine Park

3 miles from Estes Park.

The starting point for most first-timers, the easternmost part of the park is easy to access via car or park shuttle. A number of popular trailheads originate here, particularly suited for half-day hikes, and a large campground accommodates those who want to stay overnight. It's also where you'll find the Beaver Meadows Visitor Center.

⊙ Sights

PICNIC AREAS

Hollowell Park

LOCAL INTEREST | In a meadow near Mill Creek, this lovely spot for a picnic has 10 tables and is open year-round. It's also close to the Hollowell Park and Mill Creek Basin Trailheads. ⊠ *Off Bear Lake Rd., about 2½ miles from Moraine Park Visitor Center.*

TRAILS

Cub Lake Trail

TRAIL | This 4.6-mile, three-hour (round-trip) hike takes you through meadows and stands of aspen trees and up 540 feet in elevation to a lake with water lilies. *Moderate.* ⊠ *Rocky Mountain National Park ✛ Trailhead: at Cub Lake, about 1¾ miles from Moraine Park Campground.*

Deer Mountain Trail

TRAIL | This 6-mile round-trip trek to the top of 10,083-foot Deer Mountain is a great way for hikers who don't mind a bit of a climb to enjoy the views from the summit of a more manageable peak. You'll gain more than 1,000 feet in elevation as you follow the switchbacking trail through ponderosa pine, aspen, and fir trees. The reward at the top is a panoramic view of the park's eastern mountains. *Difficult.* ⊠ *Rocky Mountain National Park ✛ Trailhead: at Deer Ridge Junction, about 4 miles west of Moraine Park Visitor Center, U.S. 34 at U.S. 36.*

Fern Lake Trail

TRAIL | Heading to Odessa Lake from the north involves a steep hike, but on most days you'll encounter fewer other hikers than if you had begun the trip at Bear Lake. Along the way, you'll come to the Arch Rocks; the Pool, an eroded formation in the Big Thompson River; two waterfalls; and Fern Lake (3.8 miles from your starting point). Less than a mile farther, Odessa Lake itself lies at the foot of Tourmaline Gorge, below the craggy summits of Gabletop Mountain, Little Matterhorn, Knobtop Mountain, and Notchtop Mountain. For a full day of spectacular scenery, continue past Odessa to Bear Lake (9 miles total), where you can pick up the shuttle back to the Fern Lake Trailhead. *Moderate.* ⊠ *Rocky Mountain National Park ✛ Trailhead: off Fern Lake Rd., about 2½ miles south of Moraine Park Visitor Center.*

Sprague Lake

TRAIL | With virtually no elevation gain, this ½-mile, pine-lined looped path near a popular backcountry campground is wheelchair accessible and provides views of Hallet Peak and Flattop Mountain. *Easy.* ⊠ *Rocky Mountain National Park ✛ Trailhead: at Sprague Lake, Bear Lake Rd., 4½ miles southwest of Moraine Park Visitor Center.*

VISITOR CENTERS

Alpine Visitor Center

INFO CENTER | At 11,796 feet above sea level, this is the highest visitor center in the National Park Service. Open only when Trail Ridge Road is navigable, the center also houses the park's only gift shop and snack bar. ⊠ *Fall River Pass, at junction of Trail Ridge and Old Fall River Rds., 22 miles from Beaver Meadows entrance* ☎ *970/586–1206.*

Beaver Meadows Visitor Center

INFO CENTER | Housing the park headquarters, this visitor center was designed by students of the Frank Lloyd Wright School of Architecture at Taliesin West using the park's popular rustic style. The center has a terrific 20-minute orientation film and a large relief map of the park. ⊠ *U.S. 36, 3 miles west of Estes Park and 1 mile east of Beaver Meadows Entrance Station* ☎ *970/586–1206.*

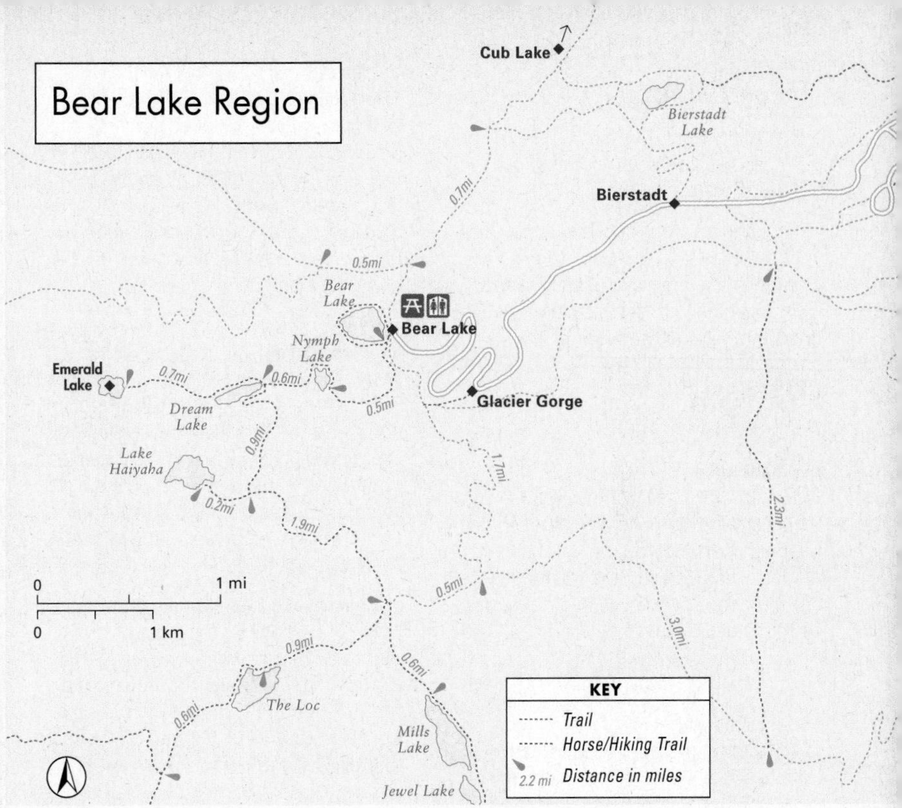
Bear Lake Region
Cub Lake
Bierstadt Lake
Bierstadt
0.7mi
0.5mi
Bear Lake
Bear Lake
Nymph Lake
Emerald Lake
0.7mi
0.6mi
0.5mi
Glacier Gorge
Dream Lake
Lake Haiyaha
0.9mi
0.2mi
1.9mi
1.7mi
2.3mi
0
1 mi
0
1 km
0.5mi
3.0mi
0.9mi
0.6mi
The Loc
0.6mi
Mills Lake
Jewel Lake
KEY
Trail
Horse/Hiking Trail
2.2 mi Distance in miles

🍴 Restaurants

Café at Trail Ridge

$ | **AMERICAN** | The park's only source for food, this small café offers snacks, sandwiches, hot dogs, and soups. A coffee bar also serves fair-trade coffee, espresso drinks, and tea, plus water, juice, and salads. **Known for:** quick bite; fair-trade coffee; no-frills food. [$] *Average main: $7* ✉ *Trail Ridge Rd., at Alpine Visitor Center* ☎ *970/586–3097* 🌐 *www.trailridgegiftstore.com* 🕑 *Closed mid-Oct.–late-May. No dinner.*

🛍 Shopping

Trail Ridge Store

CLOTHING | This is the park's only official store (though you'll find a small selection of park souvenirs and books at the visitor centers). Trail Ridge stocks sweatshirts and jackets, postcards, and assorted craft items. ✉ *Trail Ridge Rd., adjacent to Alpine Visitor Center* 🌐 *www.trailridgegiftstore.com* 🕑 *Closed mid-Oct.–late May (when Trail Ridge Rd. is closed).*

Bear Lake

7 miles southwest of Moraine Park Visitor Center.

Thanks to its picturesque location, easy accessibility, and the good hiking trails nearby, this small lake below Flattop Mountain and Hallett Peak is one of the park's most popular destinations.

 Sights

PICNIC AREAS

Sprague Lake

LOCAL INTEREST | FAMILY | With 27 tables and 16 pedestal grills, this alfresco dining spot is open year-round, with flush toilets in the summer and vault toilets the rest of the year. ⊠ *About ½ mile from intersection of Bear Lake Rd. and U.S. 36, 4 miles from Bear Lake.*

SCENIC DRIVES

Bear Lake Road

SCENIC DRIVE | This 23-mile round-trip drive offers superlative views of Longs Peak (14,259-foot summit) and the glaciers surrounding Bear Lake, winding past shimmering waterfalls shrouded with rainbows. You can either drive the road yourself (open year-round) or hop on one of the park's free shuttle buses. ⊠ *Runs from the Beaver Meadow Entrance Station to Bear Lake.*

SCENIC STOPS

Farview Curve Overlook

VIEWPOINT | At an elevation of 10,120 feet, this lookout affords a panoramic view of the Colorado River near its origin and the Grand Ditch, a water diversion project dating from 1890 that's still in use today. You can also see the once-volcanic peaks of Never Summer Range along the park's western boundary. ⊠ *Trail Ridge Rd., about 14 miles north of Kawuneeche Visitor Center.*

Forest Canyon Overlook

VIEWPOINT | Park at a dedicated lot to disembark on a wildflower-rich, 0.2-mile trail. Easy to access for all skill levels, this glacial valley overlook offers views of ice-blue pools (the Gorge Lakes) framed by ragged peaks. ⊠ *Trail Ridge Rd., 6 miles east of Alpine Visitor Center.*

TRAILS

Bear Lake Trail

TRAIL | The virtually flat nature trail around Bear Lake is an easy, 0.6-mile loop that's wheelchair and stroller accessible. Sharing the route with you will likely be plenty of other hikers as well as songbirds and chipmunks. *Easy.* ⊠ *Rocky Mountain National Park* ✛ *Trailhead: at Bear Lake, Bear Lake Rd.*

★ Bear Lake to Emerald Lake

TRAIL | This scenic, calorie-burning hike begins with a moderately level, ½-mile journey to **Nymph Lake.** From here, the trail gets steeper, with a 425-foot elevation gain, as it winds around for 0.6 miles to **Dream Lake.** The last stretch is the most arduous part of the hike, an almost all-uphill 0.7-mile trek to lovely **Emerald Lake,** where you can perch on a boulder and enjoy the view. All told, the hike is 3.6 miles, with an elevation gain of 605 feet. Allow two hours or more. *Moderate.* ⊠ *Rocky Mountain National Park* ✛ *Trailhead: at Bear Lake, off Bear Lake Rd., 8 miles southwest of the Moraine Park Visitor Center.*

★ Glacier Gorge Trail

TRAIL | The 2.8-mile hike to **Mills Lake** can be crowded, but the reward is one of the park's prettiest lakes, set against the breathtaking backdrop of Longs Peak, Pagoda Mountain, and the Keyboard of the Winds. There's a modest elevation gain of 750 feet. On the way, about 1 mile in, you pass **Alberta Falls,** a popular destination in and of itself. The hike travels along Glacier Creek, under the shade of a subalpine forest. Give yourself at least four hours for hiking and lingering. *Easy.* ✉ *Rocky Mountain National Park* ✛ *Trailhead: off Bear Lake Rd., about 1 mile southeast of Bear Lake.*

Mills Lake

TRAIL | From this popular spot, you can admire the Keyboard of the Winds, a jagged ridge connecting Pagoda and Longs Peaks that looks like the top of a spiny reptile's back. The 5.6-mile hike gains 750 feet in elevation as it takes you past Alberta Falls and Glacier Falls en route to the shimmering lake at the mouth of Glacier Gorge. *Moderate.* ✉ *Rocky Mountain National Park* ✛ *Trailhead: at Glacier Gorge Junction, about 1 mile from Bear Lake.*

Longs Peak

10.5 miles from Estes Park; trailhead at Longs Peak Ranger Station.

At 14,259 feet above sea level, Longs Peak has long fascinated explorers to the region. Longs Peak is the northernmost of the Fourteeners—the 53 mountains in Colorado that reach above the 14,000-foot mark—and one of more than 114 named mountains in the park that are higher than 10,000 feet. The peak, in the park's southeast quadrant, has a distinctive flat-topped, rectangular summit that is visible from many spots on the park's east side and on Trail Ridge Road.

Explorer and author Isabella L. Bird wrote of it: "It is one of the noblest of mountains, but in one's imagination it grows to be much more than a mountain. It becomes invested with a personality." It was named after Major Stephen H. Long, who led an expedition in 1820 up the Platte River to the base of the Rockies. Long never ascended the mountain—in fact, he didn't even get within 40 miles of it—but a few decades later, in 1868, the one-armed Civil War veteran John Wesley Powell climbed to its summit.

The ambitious climb to Longs summit is recommended only for those who are strong climbers and well acclimated to the altitude. If you're up for the 10- to 15-hour climb, begin before dawn so that you're down from the summit prior to typical afternoon thunderstorms.

◉ Sights

TRAILS

Chasm Lake Trail

TRAIL | Nestled in the shadow of Longs Peak and Mt. Meeker, Chasm Lake offers one of Colorado's most impressive backdrops, which also means you can expect to encounter plenty of other hikers on the way. The 4.2-mile Chasm Lake Trail, reached via the Longs Peak Trail, has a 2,360-foot elevation gain. Just before the lake, you'll need to climb a small rock ledge, which can be a bit of a challenge for the less sure-footed; follow the cairns for the most straightforward route. Once atop the ledge, you'll catch your first memorable view of the lake. *Difficult.* ✉ *Rocky Mountain National Park* ✛ *Trailhead: at Longs Peak Ranger Station, off Rte. 7, 10 miles from the Beaver Meadows Visitor Center.*

Longs Peak Trail

TRAIL | Climbing this 14,259-foot mountain (one of 53 "Fourteeners" in Colorado) is an ambitious goal for almost anyone—but only those who are very fit and acclimated to the altitude should attempt it. The 16-mile round-trip climb requires a predawn start (3 am is ideal), so that you're off the summit before the typical summer afternoon thunderstorm hits. Also, the last 2 miles or so of the trail are very exposed—you have to traverse narrow ledges with vertigo-inducing drop-offs. That said, summiting Longs can be one of the most rewarding experiences you'll ever have. The Keyhole route is the most popular means of ascent, and the number of people going up it on a summer day can be astounding, given the rigors of the climb. Though just as scenic, the Loft route, between Longs and Mt. Meeker from Chasm Lake, is less crowded but not as clearly marked and therefore more difficult to navigate. *Difficult.* ⊠ *Rocky Mountain National Park* ⊕ *Trailhead: at Longs Peak Ranger Station, off Rte. 7, 10 miles from Beaver Meadows Visitor Center.*

Trail Ridge Road

Also known as U.S. 34 runs between Estes Park and Grand Lake.

The park's star attraction and the world's highest continuous paved highway (topping out at 12,183 feet), this 48-mile road connects the park's gateways of Estes Park and Grand Lake. The views around each bend—of moraines and glaciers, and craggy hills framing emerald meadows carpeted with columbine —are truly awesome. As it passes through three ecosystems—montane, subalpine, and arctic tundra—the road climbs 4,300 feet. You can complete a one-way trip across the park on Trail Ridge Road in two hours, but it's best to give yourself three or four hours to allow for leisurely breaks at the overlooks. Note that the middle part of the road closes with the first big snow (typically by mid-October) and most often reopens around Memorial Day, though you can still drive up about 10 miles from the west and 8 miles from the east.

 Sights

HISTORIC SIGHTS
Lulu City
ARCHAEOLOGICAL SITE | The remains of a few cabins are all that's left of this onetime silver-mining town, established around 1880. Reach it by hiking the 3.6-mile Colorado River Trail. Look for wagon ruts from the old Stewart Toll Road and mine tailings in nearby Shipler Park (this is also a good place to spot moose). ⊠ *Off Trail Ridge Rd., 9½ miles north of Grand Lake Entrance Station.*

PICNIC AREAS
Endovalley
LOCAL INTEREST | With 32 tables and 30 fire grates, this is the largest picnic area in the park. Here, you'll find aspen groves, nice views of Fall River Pass—and lovely Fan Lake a short hike away. ⊠ *Rocky Mountain National Park* ⊕ *Off U.S. 34, at beginning of Old Fall River Rd., about 4½ miles from Fall River Visitor Center.*

SCENIC DRIVES
Old Fall River Road
SCENIC DRIVE | More than 100 years old and never more than 14 feet wide, this road stretches from the park's east side to the Fall River Pass (11,796 feet above sea level) on the west. The drive provides a few white-knuckle moments, as the road is steep, serpentine, and lacking in guardrails. Start at West Horseshoe Park, which has the park's largest concentrations of sheep and elk, and head up the gravel road, passing Chasm Falls. ⊠ *Runs north of and roughly parallel to Trail Ridge Road, starting near Endovalley Campground (on east) and ending at Fall River Pass/Alpine Visitor Center (on west).*

TRAILS
Chapin Pass
TRAIL | This is a tough hike, but it comes with great views of the park's eastern lower valleys. It's about 3½ miles one-way, including a 2,874-foot gain in elevation to the summit of Ypsilon Mountain (elevation 13,514 feet); you pass the summits of Mt. Chapin and Mt. Chiquita on the way. From the trailhead, the path heads downhill to Chapin Creek. For a short distance after leaving the trailhead, keep a sharp eye out to the right for a less obvious trail that heads uphill to the treeline and disappears. From here head up along the steep ridge to the summit of Mt. Chapin. Chiquita and Ypsilon are to the left, and the distance between each peak is about 1 mile and involves a descent of about 400 feet to the saddle and an ascent of 1,000 feet along the

ridge to Chiquita. From Ypsilon's summit you'll look down 2,000 feet at Spectacle Lakes. You may wish to bring a topo map and compass. *Difficult.* ✉ *Rocky Mountain National Park* ✛ *Trailhead: at Chapin Pass, off Old Fall River Rd., about 6½ miles from the Endovalley Picnic Area.*

VISITOR CENTERS
Fall River Visitor Center
INFO CENTER | **FAMILY** | The Discovery Room, which houses everything from old ranger outfits to elk antlers, coyote pelts, and bighorn sheep skulls for hands-on exploration, is a favorite with kids at this visitor center. ✉ *U.S. 34, at the Fall River Entrance Station* ☎ *970/586–1206.*

Timber Creek

10 miles north of Grand Lake.

Located along the Colorado River, the west part of the park attracts fewer people and more wildlife in its valleys, especially moose. The towering mountain vistas are fewer here than in the east, but the expansive meadows, rivers, and lakes offer their own peaceful beauty. Unfortunately, wildfires in 2020 destroyed many acres of forest and damaged trails here, so check conditions and closures before setting off.

◉ Sights

HISTORIC SIGHTS
Holzwarth Historic Site
ARCHAEOLOGICAL SITE | **FAMILY** | A scenic ½-mile interpretive trail leads you over the Colorado River to the original dude ranch that the Holzwarth family, some of the park's original homesteaders, ran between the 1920s and 1950s. Allow about an hour to view the buildings—including a dozen small guest cabins—and chat with a ranger. Though the site is open year-round, the inside of the buildings can be seen only June through

Elk Bugling

In September and October, there are traffic jams in the park as people drive up to listen to the elk bugling. Rangers and park volunteers keep track of where the elk are and direct visitors to the mating spots. The bugling is high-pitched, and if it's light enough, you can see the elk put their heads in the air.

early September. ✉ *Off U.S. 34, about 8 miles north of Kawuneeche Visitor Center, Estes Park.*

TRAILS
Colorado River Trail
TRAIL | This walk to the ghost town of Lulu City on the west side of the park is excellent for looking for the bighorn sheep, elk, and moose that reside in the area. Part of the former stagecoach route that went from Granby to Walden, the 3.7-mile trail parallels the infant Colorado River to the meadow where Lulu City once stood. The elevation gain is 350 feet. *Moderate.* ✉ *Rocky Mountain National Park* ✛ *Trailhead: at Colorado River, off Trail Ridge Rd., 1¾ miles north of the Timber Creek Campground.*

Continental Divide National Scenic Trail
TRAIL | This 3,100-mile corridor, which extends from Montana's Canadian border to the southern edge of New Mexico, enters Rocky Mountain National Park in two places, at trailheads only about 4 miles apart and located on either side of the Kawuneeche Visitor Center on Trail Ridge Road, at the park's southwestern end. Within the park, it covers about 30 miles of spectacular montane and subalpine terrain and follows the existing Green Mountain, Tonahutu Creek, North Inlet, and East Shore Trails. *Moderate.* ✉ *Rocky Mountain National Park* ✛ *Trailheads: at Harbison Meadows Picnic Area, off Trail Ridge Rd.,*

about 1 mile inside park from Grand Lake Entrance, and at East Shore Trailhead, just south of Grand Lake.

East Inlet Trail

TRAIL | An easy hike of 0.3 miles from East Inlet trailhead, just outside the park in Grand Lake, will get you to **Adams Falls** in about 15 minutes. The area around the falls is often packed with visitors, so if you have time, continue east to enjoy more solitude, see wildlife, and catch views of **Mt. Craig** from near the East Meadow campground. Note, however, that the trail beyond the falls has an elevation gain of between 1,500 and 1,900 feet, making it a more challenging hike. *Easy. ⊠ Grand Lake ✛ Trailhead: at East Inlet, end of W. Portal Rd. (CO 278) in Grand Lake.*

VISITOR CENTERS

Kawuneeche Visitor Center

INFO CENTER | FAMILY | The only visitor center on the park's far west side, Kawuneeche has exhibits on the plant and animal life of the area, as well as a large three-dimensional map of the park and an orientation film. *⊠ U.S. 34, 1 mile north of Grand Lake and ½ mile south of Grand Lake Entrance Station ☎ 970/586–1206.*

Wild Basin

13 miles south of Estes Park, off Rte 7.

This section in the southeast region of the park consists of lovely expanses of subalpine forest punctuated by streams and lakes. The area's high peaks, along the Continental Divide, are not as easily accessible as those in the vicinity of Bear Lake; hiking to the base of the divide and back makes for a long day. Nonetheless, a visit here is worth the drive south from Estes Park, and because the Wild Basin trailhead is set apart from the park hub, crowding isn't a problem.

Sights

TRAILS

Bluebird Lake Trail

TRAIL | The 6-mile climb from the Wild Basin trailhead to Bluebird Lake (2,478-foot elevation gain) is especially scenic. You pass Copeland Falls, Calypso Cascades, and Ouzel Falls, plus an area that was burned in a lightning-instigated fire in 1978—today it's a mix of bright pink fireweed and charred tree trunks. *Difficult. ⊠ Rocky Mountain National Park ✛ Trailhead: at Wild Basin Ranger Station, about 2 miles west of Wild Basin Entrance Station off Rte. 7, 12¾ miles south of Estes Park.*

Copeland Falls

TRAIL | FAMILY | The 0.3-mile hike to these Wild Basin Area falls is a good option for families, as the terrain is relatively flat (there's only a 15-foot elevation gain). *Easy. ⊠ Rocky Mountain National Park ✛ Trailhead: at Wild Basin Ranger Station.*

Activities

BIKING

There are no bike paths in the park, and bikes are not allowed on trails. Bicyclists are permitted on Trail Ridge Road, but it's too strenuous for most people due to its enormous changes in elevation. Those who have an extra lung or two to spare, however, might tackle a ride up the gravel 9-mile Old Fall River Road, then a ride down Trail Ridge Road.

BIRD-WATCHING

Spring and summer, early in the morning, are the best times for bird-watching in the park. **Lumpy Ridge** is a nesting ground for several kinds of birds of prey. Migratory songbirds from South America have summer breeding grounds near the **Endovalley Picnic Area.** The **alpine tundra** is habitat for white-tailed ptarmigan. The **Alluvial Fan** is the place for viewing broad-tailed hummingbirds, hairy woodpeckers, ouzels, and the occasional raptor.

CAMPING

The park's five campgrounds accommodate campers looking to stay in a tent, trailer, or RV (only three campgrounds accept reservations—up to six months in advance at ⊕ *www.recreation.gov* or ⊕ *www.reserveamerica.com*; the others fill up on a first-come, first-served basis).

Aspenglen Campground. This quiet, eastside spot near the north entrance is set in open pine woodland along Fall River. There are a few excellent walk-in sites for those who want to pitch a tent away from the crowds but still be close to the car. Reservations are recommended in summer. ⊠ *Drive past Fall River Visitor Center on U.S. 34 and turn left at the campground road.*

Wilderness Camping, Rocky Mountain National Park. Experienced hikers can camp at one of the park's many designated backcountry sites with advance reservations or a day-of-trip permit (which comes with a $30 fee in May through October). Contact the Wilderness Office before starting out to get a sense of current conditions. ⊠ *Beaver Meadows Visitor Center, Kawuneeche Visitor Center* ☎ *970/586–1242.*

Glacier Basin Campground. This spot offers expansive views of the Continental Divide, easy access to the free summer shuttles to Bear Lake and Estes Park, and ranger-led evening programs in the summer. Reservations are essential. ⊠ *Drive 5 miles south on Bear Lake Rd. from U.S. 36* ☎ *877/444–6777.*

Longs Peak Campground. Open May to November, this campgound is only a short walk from the Longs Peak trailhead, making it a favorite among hikers looking to get an early start there. The tent-only sites, which are first come, first served, are limited to eight people; firewood, lighting fluid, and charcoal are sold in summer. ⊠ *9 miles south of Estes Park on Rte. 7.*

Moraine Park Campground. The only campground in Rocky Mountain open year-round, this spot connects to many hiking trails and has easy access to the free summer shuttles. Rangers lead evening programs in the summer. You'll hear elk bugling if you camp here in September or October. Reservations are essential from mid-May to late September. ⊠ *Drive south on Bear Lake Rd. from U.S. 36, 1 mile to campground entrance.*

Timber Creek Campground. Anglers love this spot on the Colorado River, 10 miles from Grand Lake village and the only east-side campground. In the evening you can sit in on ranger-led campfire programs. The 98 campsites are first come, first served. ⊠ *1 Trail Ridge Rd., 2 miles west of Alpine Visitor Center.*

EDUCATIONAL PROGRAMS

RANGER PROGRAMS

Junior Ranger Program

TOUR—SIGHT | FAMILY | Stop by the Junior Ranger Headquarters at Hidden Valley off Trail Ridge Road for ranger-led talks during the summer months. You can also pick up a Junior Ranger activity book (in English or Spanish) at any visitor center in the park, or download it from the park's website in advance. With different activity books aimed at children of different ages, the material focuses on environmental education, identifying birds and wildlife, and outdoor safety skills. Once a child has completed all of the activities in the book, a ranger will look over his or her work and award a Junior Ranger badge. ⊠ *Rocky Mountain National Park* ☎ *970/586–1206* ⊕ *www.nps.gov/romo/forkids* 🎫 *Free.*

Ranger Programs

TOUR—SIGHT | FAMILY | Join in on free hikes, talks, and activities about wildlife, geology, vegetation, and park history. In the evening, rangers lead twilight hikes, stargazing sessions, and storytelling around the campfire. Look for the extensive program schedule in the park's newspaper available at the main

Did You Know?

A pine beetle epidemic that is affecting forests nationwide has caused some of the Rocky Mountain National Park's trees to turn a reddish color and eventually die. The mitigation efforts of the park service are to remove hazard trees and protect "high value" trees near campgrounds, picnic areas, and visitor centers.

entrances. ✉ *Rocky Mountain National Park* ☎ *970/586–1206* 🔗 *Free.*

FISHING

Rocky Mountain is a wonderful place to fish, especially for trout—German brown, brook, rainbow, cutthroat, and greenback cutthroat—but check at a visitor center about regulations and closures. No fishing is allowed at Bear Lake. To avoid the crowds, rangers recommend angling in the more-remote backcountry. To fish in the park, anyone 16 and older must have a valid Colorado fishing license, which you can obtain at local sporting-goods stores. See ⊕ *www.cpw.state.co.us* for details.

Estes Angler

FISHING | This popular fishing guide arranges fly-fishing trips from two to eight hours into the park's quieter regions, year-round. The best times for fishing are generally from April to mid-November. Equipment is also available for rent. ✉ *338 W. Riverside Dr., Estes Park* ☎ *970/586–2110, 800/586–2110* ⊕ *www.estesangler.com* 🔗 *From $149.*

Kirks Fly Shop

CAMPING—SPORTS-OUTDOORS | This Estes Park outfitter offers various guided fly-fishing trips, as well as backpacking, horseback, and llama pack trips. The store also carries fishing and backpacking gear. ✉ *230 E. Elkhorn Ave., Estes Park* ☎ *970/577–0790, 877/669–1859* ⊕ *www.kirksflyshop.com* 🔗 *From $149.*

Scot's Sporting Goods

FISHING | This shop rents and sells fishing gear, and provides instruction trips daily from May through mid-October. Clinics, geared toward first-timers, focus on casting, reading the water, identifying insects for flies, and properly presenting natural and artificial flies to the fish. ✉ *870 Moraine Ave., Estes Park* ☎ *970/586–2877 May–Sept., 970/443–4932 Oct.–Apr.* ⊕ *www.scotssportinggoods.com* 🔗 *From $220.*

HIKING

Rocky Mountain National Park contains more than 355 miles of hiking trails, so you could theoretically wander the park for weeks. Most visitors explore just a small portion of these trails—those that are closest to the roads and visitor centers—which means that some of the park's most accessible and scenic paths can resemble a backcountry highway on busy summer days. The high-alpine terrain around Bear Lake is the park's most popular hiking area, and although it's well worth exploring, you'll get a more frontierlike experience by hiking one of the trails in the less-explored sections of the park, such as the far northern end or in the Wild Basin area to the south.

Keep in mind that trails at higher elevations may have some snow on them, even in late summer. And because of afternoon thunderstorms on most summer days, an early morning start is highly recommended: the last place you want to be when a storm approaches is on a peak or anywhere above the tree line.

HORSEBACK RIDING

Horses and riders can access 260 miles of trails in Rocky Mountain National Park.

Glacier Creek Stable

HORSEBACK RIDING | FAMILY | Located within the park near Sprague Lake, Glacier Creek Stable offers two- to 10-hour rides to Glacier Basin, Odessa Lake, and Storm Pass. ✉ *Glacier Creek Campground, off Bear Lake Rd. near Sprague Lake* ☎ *970/586–3244 stables, 970/586–4577 off-season reservations* ⊕ *sombrero.com* 🔗 *From $70.*

Moraine Park Stable

HORSEBACK RIDING | FAMILY | Located inside the park just before the Cub Lake Trailhead, Moraine Park Stable offers two- to eight-hour trips to Beaver Meadows, Fern Lake, and Tourmaline Gorge. ✉ *549 Fern Lake Rd.* ☎ *970/586–2327 stables, 970/586–4577 off-season reservations* ⊕ *www.sombrero.com* 🔗 *From $70.*

National Park Gateway Stables

HORSEBACK RIDING | FAMILY | Guided trips into the national park range from two-hour rides to Little Horseshoe Park to half-day rides to Endo Valley and Fall River. The six-hour ride to the summit of Deer Mountain is a favorite. Preschool-aged children can take a 10- or 30-minute pony ride on nearby trails. ⊠ *4600 Fall River Rd., Estes Park* ☎ *970/586–5269* ⊕ *www.skhorses. com* ⊠ *From $80.*

ROCK CLIMBING

Experts as well as novices can try hundreds of classic and big-wall climbs here (there's also ample opportunity for bouldering and mountaineering). The burgeoning sport of ice climbing also thrives in the park. The Diamond, Lumpy Ridge, and Petit Grepon are the places for serious rock climbing, while well-known ice-climbing spots include Hidden Falls, Loch Vale, and Emerald and Black lakes.

★ Colorado Mountain School

CLIMBING/MOUNTAINEERING | FAMILY | Guiding climbers since 1877, Colorado Mountain School is the park's only official provider of technical climbing services. They can teach you rock climbing, mountaineering, ice climbing, avalanche survival, and many other skills. Take introductory half-day and one- to five-day courses on climbing and rappelling technique, or sign up for guided introductory trips, full-day climbs, and longer expeditions. Make reservations a month in advance for summer climbs. ⊠ *341 Moraine Ave., Estes Park* ☎ *720/387-8944, 303/447–2804* ⊕ *coloradomountainschool.com* ⊠ *From $199.*

WINTER ACTIVITIES

Each winter, the popularity of snowshoeing in the park increases. It's a wonderful way to experience Rocky Mountain's majestic winter side, when the jagged peaks are softened with a blanket of snow and the summer hordes are non-existent. You can snowshoe any of the summer hiking trails that are accessible by road; many of them also become well-traveled cross-country ski trails. Two trails to try are Tonahutu Creek Trail (near Kawuneeche Visitor Center) and the Colorado River Trail to Lulu City (start at the Timber Creek Campground).

Estes Park Mountain Shop

CLIMBING/MOUNTAINEERING | You can rent or buy snowshoes and skis here, as well as fishing, hiking, and climbing equipment. The store is open year-round and gives four-, six-, and eight-hour guided snowshoeing, fly-fishing, and climbing trips to areas in and around Rocky Mountain National Park. ⊠ *2050 Big Thompson Ave., Estes Park* ☎ *970/586–6548, 866/303–6548* ⊕ *www.estesparkmountainshop.com* ⊠ *From $95.*

Never Summer Mountain Products

CAMPING—SPORTS-OUTDOORS | This well-stocked shop sells and rents all sorts of outdoor equipment, including cross-country skis, hiking gear, kayaks, and camping supplies. ⊠ *919 Grand Ave., Grand Lake* ☎ *970/627–3642* ⊕ *www.neversummermtn.com.*

Nearby Towns

Location is just one reason why **Estes Park** is the most popular RMNP gateway (both the Beaver Meadow and Fall River entrances are 4 miles away). The town is also very family oriented, with lots of stores selling Western-theme trinkets and sweets. Many of the mom-and-pop businesses lining its streets have been passed down through several generations.

Estes Park's smaller cousin, **Grand Lake,** 1½ miles outside the park's west entrance, gets busy in summer, but has a low-key, quintessentially Western graciousness. Even with its wooden boardwalks and Old West–style storefronts, Grand Lake seems less spoiled than many other resorts.

At the park's southwestern entrance are the Arapaho and Roosevelt national forests, the Arapaho National Recreation Area, and the small town of **Granby,** the place to go for golf, mountain biking, and skiing.

Estes Park

2 miles east of Rocky Mountain National Park via U.S. 36E.

The vast scenery on the U.S. 36 approach to Estes Park gives little hint of the grandeur to come, but if ever there was a classic picture-postcard Rockies view, Estes Park has it. The town sits at an altitude of more than 7,500 feet, at the foot of a stunning backdrop of 14,259-foot Longs Peak, the majestic Stanley Hotel, and surrounding mountains.

GETTING HERE AND AROUND
To get to Estes Park from Boulder, take U.S. 36 north through Lyons and the town of Pinewood Springs (about 38 miles). You can also reach Estes Park via the Peak to Peak Scenic and Historic Byway. To reach the byway from Boulder, take Highway 119 west to Nederland and turn right (north) onto Highway 72, or follow Sunshine Canyon Drive/Gold Hill Road into Ward, and pick up Highway 72 there.

Estes Park's main downtown area is walkable, which is good news on summer weekends, when traffic can be heavy (and parking can be challenging). Keep an eye out for parking signs throughout town, as the public lots are your best chance for a close-in spot.

The National Park Service operates a free bus service in and around Estes Park and between Estes Park and Rocky Mountain National Park. Buses operate daily from early June to Labor Day, then on weekends until the end of September.

VISITOR INFORMATION Estes Park Visitor Center. ✉ *500 Big Thompson Ave.* ☎ *970/577–9900, 800/443–7837* 🌐 *www.visitestespark.com.*

Sights

Estes Park Museum
MUSEUM | The museum showcases Ute and pioneer artifacts, displays on the founding of Rocky Mountain National Park, and changing exhibits. It also publishes a self-guided walking tour of historic sites, which are mostly clustered along Elkhorn Avenue downtown. ✉ *200 4th St.* ☎ *970/586–6256* 🌐 *www.estes.org/museum* 🎟 *Free.*

MacGregor Ranch Museum
HISTORIC SITE | This working ranch, homesteaded in 1873, is on the National Register of Historic Places and provides a well-preserved record of typical ranch life. Take a guided tour of the 1896 ranch house, then explore the outbuildings and machinery on your own as you take in views of the Twin Owls and Longs Peak. ✉ *180 MacGregor La.* ✣ *1½ miles north of town on U.S. 34. Turn right on MacGregor La., a dirt road* ☎ *970/586–3749* 🌐 *www.macgregorranch.org* 🎟 *$7.*

Restaurants

Bighorn Restaurant
$ | **AMERICAN** | **FAMILY** | An Estes Park staple since 1972, this family-run outfit is where the locals go for breakfast. Try a double-cheese omelet, huevos rancheros, or grits before heading into the park in the morning. **Known for:** hearty breakfast; huge portions; picnic lunches to-go. [$] *Average main: $12* ✉ *401 W. Elkhorn Ave.* ☎ *970/586–2792* 🌐 *www.estesparkbighorn.com.*

Estes Park Brewery
$ | **AMERICAN** | If you want to sample some local brews, check out the Estes Park Brewery, which has been crafting beer since 1993. The food is no-frills (beer chili is the specialty), and the menu includes things like pizza, burgers, sandwiches, and house-made bratwurst. **Known for:** local beer; pool tables; laid-back atmosphere. [$] *Average main: $11*

✉ *470 Prospect Village Dr.* ☎ *970/586–5421* 🌐 *www.epbrewery.com.*

Mama Rose's
$$ | **ITALIAN** | **FAMILY** | An Estes Park institution since 1989, Mama Rose's consistently serves no-nonsense Italian meals, including the house specialty: hearty lasagna concocted with house-made meatballs and sausage. There are also plenty of lighter options, including vegetarian and gluten-free entrées, as well as build-your-own pasta from three noodles, six sauces, and nine meats and vegetables. [$] *Average main: $16* ✉ *338 E. Elkhorn Ave.* ☎ *970/586–3330* 🌐 *www.mamarosesrestaurant.com* 🕓 *Closed Jan.*

Poppy's Pizza & Grill
$ | **PIZZA** | **FAMILY** | This casual riverside eatery serves creative signature pizzas. Try the spinach, artichoke, and feta pie made with sun-dried tomato pesto. **Known for:** create-your-own pizza; riverfront patio; vegan- and gluten-free-friendly. [$] *Average main: $10* ✉ *342 E. Elkhorn Ave.* ☎ *970/586–8282* 🌐 *www.poppyspizzaandgrill.com* 🕓 *Closed Jan.*

★ **Seasoned**
$$$$ | **AMERICAN** | With a menu that changes monthly, Seasoned takes its name to heart with its always-changing ingredients from local farms. The creative dishes, created by chef-owner and Michelin-star veteran Rob Corey, reflect influences from North, South, and Central America and feature Colorado specialties like lamb, trout, and bass. **Known for:** creative cuisine; Colorado lamb, trout, and bass; attentive service. [$] *Average main: $30* ✉ *205 Park La.* ☎ *970/586-9000* 🌐 *seasonedbistro.com* 🕓 *Closed Mon.*

🛏 Hotels

Boulder Brook
$$$$ | **HOTEL** | Watch elk stroll past your spacious luxury suite at this smart, secluded spot on the river amid towering pines. **Pros:** scenic location; quiet area; attractive grounds. **Cons:** not within walking distance of attractions; no nearby dining. [$] *Rooms from: $250* ✉ *1900 Fall River Rd.* ☎ *970/586–0910, 800/238–0910* 🌐 *www.boulderbrook.com* 🛏 *20 suites* 🍴 *No meals.*

Glacier Lodge
$$ | **RESORT** | **FAMILY** | Families are the specialty at this secluded, 22-acre guest resort on the banks of the Big Thompson River. **Pros:** great place for families; attractive grounds on the river; on free bus route. **Cons:** not within walking distance of attractions; along rather busy road. [$] *Rooms from: $160* ✉ *2166 Hwy. 66* ☎ *800/523–3920* 🌐 *www.glacierlodgeonline.com* 🕓 *Closed Nov.–Apr.* 🛏 *30 cabins* 🍴 *No meals.*

★ **The Maxwell Inn**
$$ | **HOTEL** | Within walking distance of downtown, this family-run spot features small but comfortable rooms decorated with arts and crafts–style furnishings and locally built custom wood furniture. **Pros:** walking distance to downtown; relatively affordable for Estes Park; clean and comfortable. **Cons:** rooms are small; fairly basic accommodations. [$] *Rooms from: $145* ✉ *553 W. Elkhorn Ave.* ☎ *970/586-2833* 🌐 *www.themaxwellinn.com* 🕓 *Closed Jan. and Feb.* 🛏 *21 rooms* 🍴 *Free Breakfast.*

★ **Stanley Hotel**
$$$$ | **HOTEL** | Perched regally on a hill, with a commanding view of town, the Stanley is one of Colorado's great old hotels, featuring Georgian colonial–style architecture and a storied, haunted history, inspiring Stephen King's novel *The Shining* and daily "ghost" tours. **Pros:**

historic hotel; many rooms have been updated; good restaurant. **Cons:** some rooms are small and tight; building is old; no air-conditioning. $ *Rooms from: $299* ⊠ *333 Wonderview Ave.* ☎ *970/577–4000, 800/976–1377* ⊕ *www.stanleyhotel.com* ⊐ *140 rooms* |◯| *No meals.*

YMCA of the Rockies – Estes Park Center
$$ | RESORT | FAMILY | Surrounded on three sides by Rocky Mountain National Park, this 860-acre family-friendly property has attractive, clean lodge rooms (with either queen, full, or bunk beds), simple cabins for two to four people, and larger cabins that can sleep as many as 88 people. **Pros:** good value for large groups and longer stays; lots of family-oriented activities and amenities; stunning scenery. **Cons:** very large, busy, and crowded property; fills fast; location requires vehicle to visit town or the national park. $ *Rooms from: $169* ⊠ *2515 Tunnel Rd.* ☎ *970/586–3341, 888/613–9622 family reservations, 800/777–9622 group reservations* ⊕ *www.ymcarockies.org* ⊐ *770 rooms* |◯| *Some meals.*

Grand Lake

1½ miles west of Rocky Mountain National Park via U.S. 34.

The tiny town of Grand Lake, known to locals as Grand Lake Village, is doubly blessed by its surroundings. It's the western gateway to Rocky Mountain National Park and also sits on the shores of its namesake, the state's largest natural lake and the highest-altitude yacht anchorage in America. With views of snowy peaks and verdant mountains from just about any vantage point, Grand Lake is adored by Coloradans for sailing, canoeing, waterskiing, and fishing. In winter it's *the* snowmobiling and ice-fishing destination.

GETTING HERE AND AROUND

Grand Lake is about 60 miles from Boulder or 96 miles from Denver, as the crow flies, but to get here by car you have to circle around the mountains and travel more than 100 miles from Boulder and 171 miles from Denver. You've got two options: Take the highway the whole way (U.S. 36, CO Highway 93, I–70, U.S. 40, and U.S. 34) or take the scenic route (U.S 36 north to Estes Park, then U.S. 34 across Rocky Mountain National Park). The section of U.S. 34 that passes through Rocky Mountain National Park, known as Trail Ridge Road, is the highest paved road in America, and you can stop for a photo op at the Continental Divide sign. Trail Ridge Road closes every winter, typically between mid-October and late May.

You can explore most of the town on foot, including the historic boardwalk on Grand Avenue, with more than 70 shops and restaurants. Traffic and parking aren't a problem here.

VISITOR INFORMATION Grand Lake Chamber of Commerce and Visitor Center. ⊠ *14700 U.S. 34* ☎ *970/627–3402, 800/531–1019* ⊕ *www.grandlakechamber. com.*

 Sights

Colorado River Headwaters Scenic & Historic Byway
SCENIC DRIVE | Whether you're staying in Grand Lake or merely stopping on your way to another destination, the 80-mile (one-way) Colorado River Headwaters Scenic & Historic Byway between Grand Lake and State Bridge is worth a side trip. The route takes you along the Colorado River, past hot springs, ranches, and reservoirs, through wide spaces with views of mountains, along deep canyons, and through a seemingly incongruous

sage-covered desert. Along the turnouts within Gore Canyon, you can get a good look at the roaring Colorado River and train tracks below. Stop by the viewing platform at the Gore Canyon Whitewater Park at Pumphouse to see paddlers and boarders playing in the waves. ✉ *Grand Lake* ☎ *303/757–9786.*

Grand Lake

BODY OF WATER | According to Ute legend, the fine mists that shroud Grand Lake at dawn are the risen spirits of women and children whose raft capsized as they were fleeing a marauding party of Cheyennes and Arapahos. Grand Lake is the largest and deepest natural lake in Colorado. It feeds into two much larger man-made reservoirs, Lake Granby and Shadow Mountain Lake, and these three water bodies as well as Monarch Lake and Willow Creek and Meadow Creek reservoirs are called the "Great Lakes of Colorado." ✉ *Grand Lake.*

🍴 Restaurants

Cy's Deli

$ | **DELI** | The aroma of homemade bread and soup hint at the loving care this sandwich shop infuses into its food. Grab a quick breakfast burrito or sandwich to take out on the trail, or stay and snag a table inside the cheerful blue deli or on the sunny patio. **Known for:** quick lunch; green and red chile breakfast burritos; fresh-bread sandwiches. [$] *Average main: $9* ✉ *717 Grand Ave.* ☎ *970/627–3354* 🌐 *www.cysdeli.com* 🕒 *Closed Nov.–mid-May.*

★ **Fat Cat Cafe**

$ | **CAFÉ** | Located on the boardwalk, this cozy family-run café serves up hearty helpings, as well as advice on local sightseeing. The weekend breakfast buffet includes nearly 50 items—including biscuits and gravy, huevos rancheros casserole with house-made green chile sauce, and a wide selection of scones, pastries, and pies that are baked in-house. **Known for:** sprawling brunch buffet; homemade pies; homey decor. [$] *Average main: $10* ✉ *916 Grand Ave.* ☎ *970/627–0900* 🕒 *Closed Tues. No dinner.*

★ **Sagebrush BBQ & Grill**

$ | **SOUTHERN** | Falling-off-the-bone, melt-in-your-mouth barbecue pork, chicken, and beef draw local and out-of-town attention to this homey café. Munch on peanuts (and toss the shells on the floor) while dining at tables with cowhide-patterned tablecloths set against a backdrop of license plates from across the country. **Known for:** peanut shell–lined floor; wild game burgers and sausage; rotating daily specials. [$] *Average main: $12* ✉ *1101 Grand Ave.* ☎ *970/627–1404* 🌐 *www.sagebrushbbq.com.*

🛏 Hotels

Grand Lake Lodge

$$ | **HOTEL** | Built in 1920 and on the National Register of Historic Places, this lodge is perched on the hillside overlooking Grand Lake and has 70 cabins, a swimming pool, hot tub, picnic tables, a playground, and sundecks. **Pros:** stunning views of Grand Lake; historic charm; near Rocky Mountain National Park. **Cons:** service can be lacking; some rooms are small. [$] *Rooms from: $170* ✉ *15500 U.S. Hwy. 34* ✥ *Drive up Trail Ridge Rd. toward Rocky Mountain National Park and turn right on Tonahutu Ridge Rd.* ☎ *970/627–3967, 855/585–0004* 🌐 *www.highwaywestvacations.com/properties/grand-lake-lodge* 🕒 *Closed mid-Oct.–mid-May* 🛏 *70 cabins* 🍴 *No meals.*

★ **Historic Rapids Lodge & Restaurant**

$ | **HOTEL** | This handsome lodgepole-pine structure, which dates to 1915, is tucked on the banks of the Tonahutu River and features seven lodge rooms decorated with antique furnishings. **Pros:** in-house restaurant; condos are great for longer stays; quiet area of town. **Cons:** unpaved parking area; lodge rooms are above restaurant; all lodge rooms are on second floor and there's no elevator. $ *Rooms from: $98 ⊠ 210 Rapids La. ☎ 970/627–3707 ⊕ www.rapidslodge.com ⊗ Closed Apr. and Nov. ⇴ 31 rooms ⊙ No meals.*

Mountain Lakes Lodge

$ | **HOTEL** | **FAMILY** | Families and dog-lovers enjoy these comfortable, charming, whimsically decorated log cabins, which have such unique touches as cow-spotted walls, canoe-paddle headboards, and wooden ducks swimming on the ceiling. **Pros:** dog-friendly; close to fishing; good value. **Cons:** outside of town (and services); two-night minimum; no daily housekeeping. $ *Rooms from: $99 ⊠ 10480 U.S. 34 ☎ 970/627–8448 ⊕ www.grandlakelodging.net ⊗ Closed for 10 days in Apr. ⇴ 12 rooms ⊙ No meals.*

Western Riviera Lakeside Lodging and Events

$$$ | **HOTEL** | This friendly property offers lakeside motel rooms, cabins, and condos, as well as a second block of cabins clustered around a courtyard a few blocks up the road. **Pros:** helpful and friendly staff; lake views; clean rooms. **Cons:** rooms and bathrooms can be a little cramped; lobby is a bit small; no elevator. $ *Rooms from: $175 ⊠ 419 Garfield Ave. ☎ 970/627–3580 ⊕ www.westernriv.com ⇴ 40 units ⊙ No meals.*

Granby

20 miles south of Grand Lake via U.S. 34.

The small, no-nonsense town of Granby (elevation 7,935 feet) serves the working ranches in Grand County, and you'll see plenty of cowboys. What the town lacks in attractions it makes up for with its views of Middle Park and the surrounding mountains of the Front and Gore ranges, and with its proximity to outdoor activities, particularly its top-class golf courses just south of town.

GETTING HERE AND AROUND

Granby is 20 minutes from Rocky Mountain National Park and 15 minutes from the ski resorts Winter Park and Mary Jane and the mountain-biking trails of the Fraser Valley.

To get here from Grand Lake, take U.S. 34 south for 20 miles. From Boulder, you'll drive about 18 miles south on CO–93, 28 miles west on I–70, then take U.S. 40 north about 46 miles. From Denver, take I–70 west (about 30 miles) to U.S. 40, then drive north about 45 miles. The town is pretty small, and you can easily find a parking spot and walk from one end to the other.

Sights

Arapaho and Roosevelt National Forests and Pawnee National Grassland

FOREST | The Arapaho and Roosevelt National Forests and Pawnee National Grassland, an enormous area that encompasses 1.5 million acres, has fishing, sailing, canoeing, and waterskiing, as well as hiking, mountain biking, birding, and camping. Contained within the Arapaho National Forest is the **Arapaho National Recreation Area (ANRA)**, a 35,000-acre expanse adjacent to Rocky Mountain National Park that contains Lake Granby, Shadow Mountain Lake, Monarch Lake, and Willow Creek and Meadow Creek reservoirs. Toss in neighboring Grand Lake and you have what's known as Colorado's Great Lakes. ⊠ *USDA Forest Service Sulphur Ranger District, 9 Ten Mile Dr. ☎ 970/887–4100 ⊕ www.fs.usda.gov/main/arp.*

Hotels

C Lazy U Ranch

$$$$ | **RESORT** | **FAMILY** | Secluded in a broad, verdant valley, this deluxe dude ranch offers a smorgasbord of activities as well as plush, Western-style accommodations with wood-paneled walls,

beautiful furnishings, and bathrooms with copper sinks and custom vanities. **Pros:** kid- and family-friendly; helpful staff; deluxe in every respect. **Cons:** distant from other area attractions; strict meal times; very expensive. [$] *Rooms from: $600* ✉ *3640 Hwy. 125* ✣ *3½ miles north on Hwy. 125 from U.S. 40 junction* ☎ *970/887–3344* 🌐 *www.clazyu.com* 🛏 *40 rooms* 🍴 *All-inclusive.*

Activities

RODEO

Flying Heels Arena

RODEO | Watch cowboys demonstrate their rodeo skills at the Flying Heels Arena, held a couple of weekends in early summer. The rodeo finale and fireworks show is on the Saturday nearest July 4. ✉ *63032 U.S. 40, 1½ miles east of Granby* ☎ *970/887–2311* 🌐 *www.granbyrodeo.com* 🎟 *$10.*

Chapter 31

SAGUARO
NATIONAL PARK

Updated by
Elise Riley

ARIZONA

🏕 Camping 🛏 Hotels 🏃 Activities 👁 Scenery 👥 Crowds
★★★☆☆ ★★★☆☆ ★★☆☆☆ ★★★★☆ ★☆☆☆☆

WELCOME TO
SAGUARO NATIONAL PARK

TOP REASONS TO GO

★ **Saguaro sightseeing:** Hike, bike, or drive through dense saguaro stands for an up-close look at this king of all cacti.

★ **Wildlife-watching:** Diverse wildlife roams through the park, including such ground dwellers as javelinas, coyotes, and rattlesnakes, and winged residents ranging from the migratory lesser long-nosed bat to the diminutive elf owl.

★ **Ancient artwork:** Get a glimpse into the past at the numerous petroglyph rock-art sites where ancient peoples etched into the stones as far back as 5000 BC.

★ **Desert hiking:** Take a trek through the undisturbed and magical Sonoran Desert, and discover that it's more than cacti.

★ **Two districts, one park:** Split into two districts, the park offers a duo of separate experiences on opposite sides of Tucson.

1 Saguaro East. This area, known as the Rincon Mountain District, encompasses 57,930 acres of designated wilderness area, an easily accessible scenic loop drive, several easy and intermediate trails through the cactus forest, and opportunities for adventure and backcountry camping at six rustic campgrounds.

2 Saguaro West. Also called the Tucson Mountain District, this is the park's smaller, more-visited section. At the visitor center is a video about saguaros; also in the park's western part are hiking trails, an ancient Hohokam petro-glyph site at Signal Hill, and a scenic drive through the park's densest desert growth. This section is near the Arizona–Sonora Desert Museum in Tucson's Westside, and many visitors combine these sights.

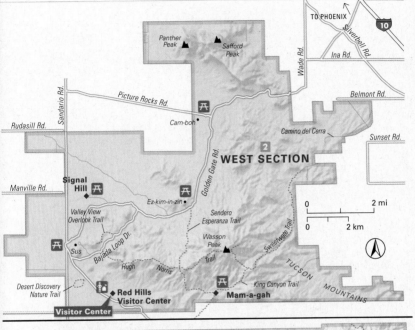

TO PHOENIX

Silverbell Rd.

Wade Rd.

Ina Rd.

Belmont Rd.

Camino del Cerra

Sunset Rd.

Picture Rocks Rd.

Rudasill Rd.

Sandario Rd.

Panther Peak

Safford Peak

Cam-boh

Golden Gate Rd.

WEST SECTION

Manville Rd.

Signal Hill

Ez-kim-in-zin

Valley View Overlook Trail

Sus

Bajada Loop Dr.

Hugh

Norris

Desert Discovery Nature Trail

Red Hills Visitor Center

Visitor Center

Sendero Esperanza Trail

Wasson Peak

Trail

Sweetwater Trail

King Canyon Trail

Mam-a-gah

TUCSON MOUNTAINS

0   2 mi
0   2 km

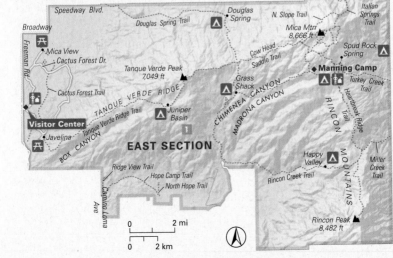

Speedway Blvd.

Broadway

Freeman Rd.

Mica View

Cactus Forest Dr.

Douglas Spring Trail

Douglas Spring

N. Slope Trail

Italian Springs Trail

Mica Mtn 8,666 ft

Spud Rock Spring

Cow Head Saddle Trail

Cactus Forest Trail

Visitor Center

Tanque Verde Peak 7,049 ft

TANQUE VERDE RIDGE

Tanque Verde Ridge Trail

BOX CANYON

Javelina

Juniper Basin

EAST SECTION

Grass Shack

CHIMENEA CANYON

MADRONA CANYON

Manning Camp

Turkey Creek Trail

Heartbreak Ridge Trail

RINCON MOUNTAINS

Ridge View Trail

Hope Camp Trail

North Hope Trail

Camino Loma Ave.

Happy Valley

Rincon Creek Trail

Miller Creek Trail

Rincon Peak 8,482 ft

0   2 mi
0   2 km

Standing sentinel in the desert, the towering saguaro is perhaps the most familiar emblem of the Southwest. Known for their height (often 50 feet) and arms reaching out in weird configurations, a saguaro can survive more than 200 years. They are found only in the Sonoran Desert, and the largest concentration is in Saguaro National Park.

Saguaro National Park's two distinct sections flank the city of Tucson. Perhaps the most familiar emblem of the Southwest, the towering saguaros are found only in the Sonoran Desert. Saguaro National Park preserves some of the densest stands of these massive cacti.

Known for their height (often 50 feet) and arms reaching out in weird configurations, these slow-growing giants can take 15 years to grow a foot high and up to 75 years to grow their first arm. The cacti can live up to 200 years and weigh up to 2 tons. In late spring (usually May), the succulent's top is covered with tiny white blooms—the Arizona state flower. The cacti are protected by state and federal laws, so don't disturb them.

Planning

When to Go

Saguaro never gets crowded. Nevertheless, most people visit in milder weather, October through May. December through February can be cool and are likely to see gentle rain showers. The spring days of March through May are bright and sunny with wildflowers and cacti in bloom. Because of high temperatures, from June through September it's best to visit the park in the early morning or late afternoon. Cooler temperatures return in October and November, providing perfect weather for hiking and camping throughout the park.

Getting Here and Around

AIR
Both districts of Saguaro National Park are approximately a 30-minute drive from the Tucson International Airport.

CAR
Both districts are about a half-hour drive from Central Tucson. To reach the Rincon Mountain District (East section) from Interstate 10, take Exit 275, then go north on Houghton Road for 10 miles. Turn right on Escalante and left onto Old Spanish Trail, and the park will be on the right side. If you're coming from town, go

AVERAGE HIGH/LOW TEMPERATURES					
JAN.	**FEB.**	**MAR.**	**APR.**	**MAY**	**JUNE**
63/38	66/40	72/44	80/50	89/57	98/67
JULY	**AUG.**	**SEPT.**	**OCT.**	**NOV.**	**DEC.**
98/73	96/72	93/67	84/57	72/45	65/39

east on Speedway Boulevard to Houghton Road. Turn right on Houghton and left onto Old Spanish Trail.

To reach the Tucson Mountain District (West section) from Interstate 10, take Exit 242 or Exit 257, then go west on Speedway Boulevard (the name will change to Gates Pass Road), follow it to Kinney Road, and turn right.

As there's no public transportation to or within Saguaro, a car is a necessity. In the western section, Bajada Loop Drive takes you through the park and to various trailheads; Cactus Forest Drive does the same for the eastern section.

Inspiration

The *Tucson Hiking Guide,* by Betty Leavengood, is a useful and entertaining book with day hikes in the park.

Books that give a general introduction to the park include *Saguaro National Park,* by Doris Evans, and *Sonoran Desert: The Story Behind the Scenery,* by Christopher L. Helms.

All About Saguaros, by Carle Hodge and published by Arizona Highways Books, includes fabulous color photos of the cactus.

For a poetic take by a naturalist, try Gary Nabhan's *Saguaro: A View of Saguaro National Monument and the Tucson Basin.*

Park Essentials

ACCESSIBILITY
In the western section, the Red Hills Visitor Center and two nearby nature trails are wheelchair accessible. The eastern district's visitor center is accessible, as are the paved Desert Ecology and Cactus Garden Trails.

CELL PHONE RECEPTION
Cell phone reception is generally good in the eastern district but is unreliable in the western district. The visitor centers have pay phones.

PARK FEES AND PERMITS
Admission to Saguaro is $25 per vehicle and $15 for individuals on foot or bicycle; it's good for seven days from purchase at both park districts. Annual passes cost $45. For hike-in camping at one of the primitive campsites in the eastern district (the closest campsite is 6 miles from the trailhead), obtain a required backcountry permit ($8 per night) up to three months in advance. ⊕ *www.recreation.gov*

PARK HOURS
The park opens at sunrise and closes at sunset every day but Christmas day. It's in the Mountain time zone. Arizona (excluding the Navajo Nation) does not observe daylight saving time. The visitor center is open daily from 9 to 5.

31

Saguaro National Park PLANNING

What It Costs			
$	$$	$$$	$$$$
RESTAURANTS			
under $13	$13–$20	$21–$30	over $30
HOTELS			
under $101	$101–$150	$151–$200	over $200

Hotels

Although there are no hotels within the park, its immediate proximity to Tucson makes finding a place to stay easy. A couple of B&Bs are a short drive from the park. Some ranches and smaller accommodations close during the hottest months of summer, but many inexpensive B&Bs and hotels are open year-round, and offer significantly lower rates from late May through August. *Hotel reviews have been shortened. For full information, visit Fodors.com.*

Restaurants

At Saguaro, you won't find more than a sampling of Southwest jams, hot sauces, and candy bars at the two visitor centers' gift shops. Vending machines outside sell bottled water and soda, but pack some lunch for a picnic if you don't want to drive all the way back into town. Five picnic areas in the west district, and two in the east, offer scenery and shade. However, the city of Tucson, sandwiched neatly between the two park districts, offers some of the best Mexican cuisine in the country. A genuine college town, Tucson also has excellent upscale Southwestern cuisine, as well as good sushi, Thai, Italian, and Ethiopian food. *Restaurant reviews have been shortened. For full information, visit Fodors.com.*

Visitor Information

PARK CONTACT INFORMATION Saguaro National Park. ⊠ *3693 S. Old Spanish Trail, Tucson* ☎ *520/733–5158 for Saguaro West, 520/733–5153 for Saguaro East* ⊕ *www.nps.gov/sagu.*

Saguaro East

12 miles east of Central Tucson.

In the Rincon Mountains, Saguaro East encompasses nearly 60,000 acres of designated wilderness area, an easily accessible scenic loop drive, several easy and intermediate trails through the cactus forest, and opportunities for adventure and backcountry camping at six rustic campgrounds.

 Sights

HISTORIC SITES
Manning Camp

HOUSE | The summer home of Levi Manning, onetime Tucson mayor, was a popular gathering spot for the city's elite in the early 1900s. The cabin can be reached only on foot or horseback via one of several challenging high-country trails: Douglas Spring Trail to Cow Head Saddle Trail (12 miles), Turkey Creek Trail (7.5 miles), or Tanque Verde Ridge Trail (15.4 miles). The cabin itself is not open for viewing. ⊠ *Saguaro East ✛ Douglas Spring Trail (6 miles) to Cow Head Saddle Trail (6 miles).*

PICNIC AREAS
Mica View

LOCAL INTEREST | Talk about truth in advertising: this picnic area gives you an eyeful of Mica Mountain, the park's highest peak. None of the tables are in the shade. ⊠ *Cactus Forest Dr., Saguaro East ✛ 2 miles north of Rincon Mountain Visitor Center.*

Saguaro in One Day

Before setting off, choose which section of the park to visit and pack a lunch (there's no food service in either park district).

In the western section, start out by watching the 15-minute video at the **Red Hills Visitor Center**, then stroll the ½-mile-long **Desert Discovery Trail**. Drive north along Kinney Road, then turn right onto the graded dirt **Bajada Loop Drive**. Before long you'll see a turnoff for the **Hugh Norris Trail** on your right. If you're game for a steep 45-minute hike uphill, this trail leads to a perfect spot for a picnic. Hike back down and drive along the Bajada Loop Drive until you reach the turnoff for **Signal Hill**. From here it's a short walk to the **Hohokam petroglyphs.**

Alternatively, in the eastern section, pick up a free map of the hiking trails at the **Rincon Mountain Visitor Center.** Drive south along the paved **Cactus Forest Drive** to the Javelina picnic area, where you'll see signs for the **Freeman Homestead Trail**, an easy 1-mile loop that winds through a stand of mesquite as interpretive signs describe early inhabitants in the Tucson basin. If you're up for more difficult hiking, you might want to tackle part of the **Tanque Verde Ridge Trail**, which affords excellent views of saguaro-studded hillsides. Along the northern loop of Cactus Forest Drive is **Cactus Forest Trail**, which branches off into several fairly level paths. You can easily spend the rest of the afternoon strolling among the saguaros.

SCENIC DRIVES

★ Cactus Forest Drive

SCENIC DRIVE | This paved 8-mile drive provides a great overview of all Saguaro East has to offer. The one-way road, which circles clockwise, has several turnouts with roadside displays that make it easy to pull over and admire the scenery; you can also stop at two picnic areas and three easy nature trails. This is a good bicycling route, but watch out for snakes and javelinas crossing in front of you. ⊠ *Cactus Forest Dr., Saguaro East.*

TRAILS

Cactus Forest Trail

TRAIL | This 2½-mile one-way loop is a moderately easy walk along a dirt path that passes historic lime kilns and a wide variety of Sonoran Desert vegetation. It's one of the only off-road trails for bicyclists. *Moderate.* ⊠ *Saguaro East* ✛ *Trailhead: 2 miles south of Rincon Mountain Visitor Center, off Cactus Forest Dr.*

Cactus Garden Trail

TRAIL | This 100-yard paved trail in front of the Rincon Mountain Visitor Center is wheelchair accessible and has resting benches and interpretive signs about common desert plants. *Easy.* ⊠ *Saguaro East* ✛ *Trailhead: next to Rincon Mountain Visitor Center.*

Desert Ecology Trail

TRAIL | **FAMILY** | Exhibits on this ¼-mile loop near the Mica View picnic area explain how local plants and animals subsist on limited water. Dogs on leash are permitted. *Easy.* ⊠ *Saguaro East* ✛ *Trailhead: 2 miles north of Rincon Mountain Visitor Center.*

Douglas Spring Trail

TRAIL | This challenging 6-mile trail, steep in some parts, leads almost due east into the Rincon Mountains. After a half mile through a dense concentration of saguaros, you reach the open desert. About 3 miles in is Bridal Wreath Falls, worth a slight detour in spring when melting snow creates a larger cascade. *Moderate.* ⊠ *Saguaro East ⊹ Trailhead: eastern end of Speedway Blvd.*

Freeman Homestead Trail

TRAIL | Learn a bit about the history of homesteading in the region on this 1-mile loop. Look for owls living in the cliffs above as you make your way through the lowland vegetation. *Easy.* ⊠ *Saguaro East ⊹ Trailhead: next to Javelina picnic area, 2 miles south of Rincon Mountain Visitor Center.*

★ Hope Camp Trail

TRAIL | Well worth the 5-mile round-trip trek, this Rincon Valley route rewards hikers with gorgeous views of the Tanque Verde Ridge and Rincon Peak. The trail is also open to mountain bicyclists. *Moderate.* ⊠ *Saguaro East ⊹ Trailhead: from Camino Loma Alta trailhead to Hope Camp.*

Tanque Verde Ridge Trail

TRAIL | Be rewarded with spectacular scenery on this 18-mile round-trip trail that takes you through desert scrub, oak, alligator juniper, and pinyon pine at the 6,000-foot peak, where views of the surrounding mountain ranges from both sides of the ridge delight. *Difficult.* ⊠ *Saguaro East ⊹ Trailhead: Javelina picnic area, 2 miles south of Red Hills Visitor Center.*

VISITOR CENTERS

Rincon Mountain Visitor Center

INFO CENTER | Stop here to pick up free maps and printed materials on various aspects of the park, including maps of hiking trails and backcountry camping permits. Exhibits at the center are comprehensive, and a relief map of the park lays out the complexities of this protected landscape. Two 20-minute slide shows explain the botanical and cultural history of the region, and there is a short self-guided nature walk along the paved Cactus Garden Trail. A select variety of books and other gift items,

along with energy bars, beef jerky, and refillable water bottles, are sold here. ⊠ *3693 S. Old Spanish Trail, Saguaro East* ☎ *520/733–5153* ⊕ *www.nps.gov/sagu.*

Saguaro West

14 miles west of Central Tucson

This popular district makes up less than one-third of the park. Here you'll find a native American video orientation to saguaros at the visitor center, hiking trails, an ancient Hohokam petroglyph site at Signal Hill, and a scenic drive through the park's densest desert growth.

Sights

PICNIC AREAS

Mam-A-Gah

LOCAL INTEREST | This is the most isolated picnic area in Saguaro West. It's on King Canyon Trail, a good area for birding and wildflower viewing. It's about a mile walk to reach the site, and the undeveloped trail isn't wheelchair accessible. ⊠ *King Canyon Trail, Saguaro West ⊹ 1 mile from Kinney Rd.*

Signal Hill

LOCAL INTEREST | Because of the nearby petroglyphs, this is the park's most popular picnic site. Its many picnic tables, sprinkled around paloverde and mesquite trees, can accommodate large groups. ⊠ *Bajada Loop Dr., Saguaro West ⊹ 4½ miles north of Red Hills Visitor Center.*

SCENIC DRIVES

★ Bajada Loop Drive

SCENIC DRIVE | This 6-mile drive winds through thick stands of saguaros and past two picnic areas and trailheads to a few short hikes, including one to a petroglyph site. Although the road is unpaved and somewhat bumpy, it's a worthwhile trade-off for access to some of the park's densest desert growth. It's one-way between Hugh Norris Trail and Golden

Plants and Wildlife in Saguaro

The saguaro may be the centerpiece of Saguaro National Park, but more than 1,200 plant species, including 50 types of cactus, thrive in the park. Among the most common cacti here are the prickly pear, barrel cactus, and teddy bear cholla—so named because it appears cuddly, but rangers advise packing a comb to pull its barbed hooks from unwary fingers.

For many of the desert fauna, the saguaro functions as a high-rise hotel. Each spring the Gila woodpecker and gilded flicker create holes in the cactus and then nest there. When they give up their temporary digs, elf owls, cactus wrens, sparrow hawks, and other birds move in, as do dangerous Africanized honeybees.

You may not encounter any of the park's six species of rattlesnake or the Gila monster, a venomous lizard, but avoid sticking your hands or feet under rocks or into crevices. Look where you're walking; if you do get bitten, get to a clinic or hospital as soon as possible. Not all snakes pass on venom; 50% of the time the bite is "dry" (nonvenomous).

Wildlife, from bobcats to jackrabbits, is most active in early morning and at dusk. In spring and summer, lizards and snakes are out and about but tend to keep a low profile during the midday heat.

Gate Road, so if you want to make the complete circuit, travel counterclockwise. The road is susceptible to flash floods during the monsoon season (July and August), so check road conditions at the visitor center before proceeding. This loop route is also popular among bicyclists, and dogs on leash are permitted along the road. ⊠ *Saguaro West.*

SCENIC STOPS
Signal Hill

ARCHAEOLOGICAL SITE | FAMILY | The most impressive petroglyphs, and the only ones with explanatory signs, are on the Bajada Loop Drive in Saguaro West. An easy five-minute stroll from the signposted parking area takes you to one of the largest concentrations of rock carvings in the Southwest. You'll have a close-up view of the designs left by the Hohokam people between AD 900 and 1200, including large spirals some believe are astronomical markers. ⊠ *Bajada Loop Dr., Saguaro West* ✛ *4½ miles north of visitor center.*

TRAILS
Desert Discovery Trail

TRAIL | FAMILY | Learn about plants and animals native to the region on this paved path in Saguaro West. The ½-mile loop is wheelchair accessible, and has resting benches and ramadas (wooden shelters that supply shade). Dogs on leash are permitted here. *Easy.* ⊠ *Saguaro West* ✛ *Trailhead: 1 mile north of Red Hills Visitor Center.*

★ Hugh Norris Trail

TRAIL | This 10-mile trail through the Tucson Mountains is one of the most impressive in the Southwest. It's full of switchbacks, and some sections are moderately steep, but the top of 4,687-foot Wasson Peak treats you to views of the saguaro forest spread across the *bajada* (the gently rolling hills at the base of taller mountains). *Difficult.* ⊠ *Saguaro West* ✛ *Trailhead: 2½ miles north of Red Hills Visitor Center on Bajada Loop Dr.*

King Canyon Trail

TRAIL | This 3.5-mile trail is the shortest, but steepest, route to the top of Wasson Peak in Saguaro West. It meets the Hugh Norris Trail less than half a mile from the summit. The trail, which begins across from the Arizona–Sonora Desert Museum, is named after the Copper King Mine. It leads past many scars from the search for mineral wealth. ■TIP→ **Look for petroglyphs in this area.** *Difficult.* ⊠ *Saguaro West* ⊹ *Trailhead: 2 miles south of Red Hills Visitor Center.*

★ Signal Hill Trail

TRAIL | FAMILY | This ¼-mile trail in Saguaro West is a simple, rewarding ascent to ancient petroglyphs carved a millennium ago by the Hohokam people. *Easy.* ⊠ *Saguaro West* ⊹ *Trailhead: 4½ miles north of Red Hills Visitor Center on Bajada Loop Dr.*

Sendero Esperanza Trail

TRAIL | Follow a sandy mine road for the first section of this 6-mile trail in Saguaro West, then ascend via a series of switchbacks to the top of a ridge and cross the Hugh Norris Trail. Descending on the other side, you'll meet up with the King Canyon Trail. The Esperanza ("Hope") Trail is often rocky and sometimes steep, but rewards include ruins of the Gould Mine, dating back to 1907. *Moderate.* ⊠ *Saguaro West* ⊹ *Trailhead: 1½ miles east of the intersection of Bajada Loop Dr. and Golden Gate Rd.*

Sweetwater Trail

TRAIL | Though technically within Saguaro West, this trail is on the eastern edge of the district, and affords access to Wasson Peak from the eastern side of the Tucson Mountains. After gradually climbing 3.4 miles, it ends at King Canyon Trail (which would then take you on a fairly steep 1.2-mile climb to Wasson Peak). Long and meandering, this little-used trail allows more privacy to enjoy the natural surroundings than some of the more frequently used trails. *Moderate.*

⊠ *Saguaro West* ⊹ *Trailhead: western end of El Camino del Cerro Rd.*

★ Valley View Overlook Trail

TRAIL | On clear days you can spot the distinctive slope of Picacho Peak from this relatively easy 1½-mile trail with a gentle ascent in Saguaro West. There are splendid vistas of Avra Valley and signs describing the flora along the way. *Moderate.* ⊠ *Saguaro West* ⊹ *Trailhead: 3 miles north of Red Hills Visitor Center on Bajada Loop Dr.*

VISITOR CENTERS

Red Hills Visitor Center

INFO CENTER | Take in gorgeous views of nearby mountains and the surrounding desert from the center's large windows and shaded outdoor terrace. A spacious gallery is filled with educational exhibits, and a lifelike display simulates the flora and fauna of the region. A 15-minute slide show, "Voices of the Desert," provides a poetic, Native American perspective on the Saguaro. Park rangers and volunteers hand out maps and suggest hikes to suit your interests. The bookstore sells books, trinkets, a few local items like honey and prickly pear jellies, and reusable water bottles that you can fill at water stations outside. ⊠ *2700 N. Kinney Rd., Saguaro West* ☎ *520/733–5158* ⊕ *www.nps.gov/sagu.*

Activities

BIKING

Scenic drives in the park—Bajada Loop in the West and Cactus Forest Drive in the East section—are popular among cyclists, though you'll have to share the roads with cars. Bajada Loop Drive is a gravel and dirt road, so it's quite bumpy and only suitable for mountain bikers; Cactus Forest Drive is paved. In the East section, Cactus Forest Trail (2.5 miles) is a great unpaved path for both beginning and experienced mountain bikers who don't mind sharing the trail with hikers and the occasional horse; Hope Camp Trail is also open to mountain bikes.

Fair Wheel Bikes

BICYCLING | Mountain bikes and road bikes can be rented by the day or week here. The company also organizes group rides of varying difficulty. ⊠ *1110 E. 6th St., University* ☎ *520/884–9018* ⊕ *fairwheelbikes.com.*

BIRD-WATCHING

To check out the more than 200 species of birds living in or migrating through the park, begin by focusing your binoculars on the limbs of the saguaros, where many birds make their home. In general, early morning and early evening are the best times for sightings. In winter and spring, volunteer-led birding hikes begin at the visitor centers.

The finest areas to flock to in Saguaro East (the Rincon Mountain District) are the Desert Ecology Trail, where you may find rufous-winged sparrows, verdins, and Cooper's hawks along the washes, and the Javelina picnic area, where you'll most likely spot canyon wrens and black-chinned sparrows. At Saguaro West (the Tucson Mountain District), sit down on one of the visitor center benches and look for ash-throated flycatchers, Say's phoebes, curve-billed thrashers, and Gila woodpeckers. During the cooler months, keep a lookout for wintering neotropical migrants such as hummingbirds, swallows, orioles, and warblers.

Wild Bird Store

BIRD WATCHING | This shop is an excellent resource for birding information, feeders, books, and trail guides. Free bird walks are offered most Sundays October–May. ⊠ *3160 E. Fort Lowell Rd., Central* ☎ *520/322–9466* ⊕ *www.wildbirdsonline.com.*

CAMPING

There's no drive-up camping in the park. All six primitive campgrounds are in the eastern district and require a hike to reach—the shortest hikes are to Douglas Spring Campground (6 miles) and to Happy Valley (5 miles). All are open year-round. Pick up your backcountry camping permit ($6 per night) at the Rincon Mountain Visitor Center. Before choosing a camping destination, look over the relief map of hiking trails and the book of wilderness campground photos taken by park rangers. You can camp in the backcountry for a maximum of 14 days. Each site can accommodate up to six people. Reservations can be made via mail or in person up to two months in advance. Hikers are encouraged to set out before noon. If you haven't the time or the inclination to hike in, several more camping opportunities exist within a few miles of the park.

Douglas Spring. Getting to this 4,800-foot-elevation campground takes a not-too-rough 6-mile hike up the Douglas Spring Trail. ⊠ *6 miles on Douglas Spring Trail, off Speedway Blvd.* ☎ *No phone.*

Grass Shack. This pretty campground is among juniper and small oak trees in a transitional area midway up Mica Mountain. ⊠ *10.3 miles via Douglas Spring Trail to Manning Camp Trail* ☎ *No phone.*

Juniper Basin. Vegetation here is oak forest, and the expansive views are worth the challenging 7-mile ascent. ⊠ *7 miles on Tanque Verde Ridge Trail.* ☎ *No phone.*

EDUCATIONAL OFFERINGS

Junior Ranger Program

TOUR—SIGHT | FAMILY | In the Junior Ranger Discovery program, young visitors can pick up an activity pack any time of the year at either visitor center and complete it within an hour or two. During June, there also are daylong camps for kids ages 5 through 12 in the East district. ⊠ *Rincon Mountain and Red Hills visitor centers* ☎ *520/733–5153* ⊕ *nps.gov/sagu.*

Orientation Programs

TOUR—SIGHT | Daily programs at both park districts introduce visitors to the desert. You might find presentations on bats, birds, or desert blooms, and naturalist-led

A saguaro grows under the protection of another tree, such as a paloverde or mesquite, before superseding it.

hikes (including moonlight hikes). Check online or call for the current week's activities. ⊠ *Rincon Mountain and Red Hills visitor centers* ☎ *520/733–5100* ⊕ *nps. gov/sagu* ⌷ *Free.*

Ranger Talks

TOUR—SIGHT | The assortment of talks by national park rangers are a great way to hear about wildlife, geology, and archaeology. ⊠ *Rincon Mountain and Red Hills visitor centers* ☎ *520/733–5100* ⌷ *Free.*

HIKING

The park has more than 100 miles of trails. The shorter hikes, such as the **Desert Discovery** and **Desert Ecology** trails, are perfect for those looking to learn about the desert ecosystem without expending too much energy. The **Hope Camp Trail, Hugh Norris Trail,** and **Signal Hill Trail** are also excellent for hiking. For more information see the trail listings under ⇨ *Sights.*

■ TIP→ **Rattlesnakes are commonly seen on trails; so are coyotes, javelinas, roadrunners, Gambel's quail, and desert spiny lizards. Hikers should keep their distance from all wildlife.**

Nearby Towns

Saguaro stands as a protected desert oasis, with metropolitan **Tucson,** Arizona's second-largest city, lying between the two park sections. Spread over 227 miles, and with a population of nearly a half million, Tucson averages 340 days of sunshine a year.

Tucson

Metropolitan Tucson has more than 850,000 residents, including thousands of snowbirds who flee colder climes to enjoy the sun that shines on the city more than 340 days out of 365. The city's tricultural population (Hispanic, Anglo, Native American) offers visitors the chance to see how these cultures interact and to sample their flavorful cuisine.

The city also has a youthful energy, largely due to the population of students attending the University of Arizona. Although high-tech industries have moved into the area, the economy still relies heavily on the university and tourism. Come summer, though, you'd never guess; when the snowbirds and students depart, Tucson can be a sleepy place.

The metropolitan area covers more than 500 square miles in a valley ringed by mountains—the Santa Catalinas to the north, the Santa Ritas to the south, the Rincons to the east, and the Tucson Mountains to the west. Saguaro National Park bookends Tucson, with one section on the far east side and the other out west near the Arizona–Sonora Desert Museum. The central portion of the city has most of the shops, restaurants, and businesses, but not many tourist sites. Downtown's historic district and the neighboring university area are much smaller and easily navigated on foot. Up north in the Catalina Foothills are first-class resorts, restaurants, and hiking trails, most with spectacular views of the entire valley.

GETTING HERE AND AROUND

You'll need a car to get around Tucson and the surrounding area, and it makes sense to rent at the airport; all the major car-rental agencies are represented. A few rental agencies have additional locations in Central Tucson, and the larger resorts arrange rental-car pickups on-site.

You can fly to Tucson International Airport (TUS), which is 8½ miles south of Downtown, off the Valencia exit of Interstate 10, but cheaper, nonstop flights into Phoenix—a two-hour drive away on Interstate 10—are often easier to find. Once in town, a car is essential to get to the outlying tourist sights.

Driving time from the airport to the center of town varies, but it's usually less than a half hour; add 15 minutes to any destination during rush hours (7:30 to 9 am and 4:30 to 6 pm). Parking isn't a problem in most parts of town, except near the university and downtown, where there are multiple pay lots and parking garages as well as meters.

VISITOR INFORMATION

CONTACTS Southern Arizona Heritage and Visitor Center. ⊠ *115 N. Church Ave., Suite 200, Downtown* ☎ *800/638–8350* ⊕ *www.visittucson.org.*

◉ Sights

★ Arizona–Sonora Desert Museum

MUSEUM | FAMILY | The name "museum" is a bit misleading, since this delightful site is actually a zoo, aquarium, and botanical garden featuring the animals, plants, and even fish of the Sonoran Desert. Hummingbirds, coatis, rattlesnakes, scorpions, bighorn sheep, bobcats, and Mexican wolves all busy themselves in ingeniously designed habitats.

An Earth Sciences Center has an artificial limestone cave to climb through and an excellent mineral display. The coyote and javelina (a wild, piglike mammal with an oddly oversize head) exhibits have "invisible" fencing that separates humans from animals, and at the Raptor Free Flight show (October through April, daily at 10 and 2), you can see the powerful birds soar and dive, untethered, inches above your head.

The restaurants are above average, and the gift shop, which carries books, jewelry, and crafts, is outstanding. ■ **TIP→ June through August, the museum stays open until 10 pm every Saturday, which provides a great opportunity to see nocturnal critters.** ⊠ *2021 N. Kinney Rd., Westside* ☎ *520/883–2702* ⊕ *www. desertmuseum.org* 🎟 *$22.*

★ Bear Canyon Trail

Also known as Seven Falls Trail, this favorite route in Sabino Canyon is a three- to four-hour, 7.8-mile round-trip that

31

Saguaro National Park NEARBY TOWNS

is moderate and fun, crossing the stream several times on the way up the canyon. Kids enjoy the boulder-hopping, and all hikers are rewarded with pools and waterfalls as well as views at the top. The trailhead can be reached from the parking area by either taking a five-minute Bear Canyon Tram ride ($6) or walking the 1.8-mile tram route. *Moderate.* ⊠ *Sabino Canyon Rd., at Sunrise Dr., Foothills* 🕾 *520/749–2861* ⊕ *www.fs.usda.gov/coronado.*

Colossal Cave Mountain Park
CAVE | FAMILY | This limestone grotto 20 miles southeast of Tucson is the largest dry cavern in the world. Guides discuss the fascinating crystal formations and relate the many romantic tales surrounding the cave, including the legend that an enormous sum of money stolen in a stagecoach robbery is hidden here.

Forty-five-minute cave tours begin every hour on the hour and require a ½-mile walk and a climb of 363 steps. The park includes a ranch area with trail rides through saguaro forests (from $38), hiking trails, a gemstone-sluicing area, a petting zoo, a gift shop, and a café. ⊠ *16721 E. Old Spanish Trail, Eastside* 🕾 *520/647–7275* ⊕ *www.colossalcave. com* 🖾 *$18.*

St. Augustine Cathedral
RELIGIOUS SITE | Although the imposing white-and-beige, late-19th-century, Spanish-style building was modeled after the Cathedral of Queretaro in Mexico, a number of its details reflect the desert setting. For instance, above the entryway, next to a bronze statue of St. Augustine, are carvings of local desert scenes with saguaro cacti, yucca, and prickly pears—look closely and you'll find the horned toad. Compared with the magnificent facade, the modernized interior is a bit disappointing. ■TIP➔ **For a distinctly Southwestern experience, attend the mariachi Mass celebrated Sunday at 8 am.** ⊠ *192 S. Stone Ave., Downtown*

🕾 *520/623–6351* ⊕ *cathedral-staugustine.org* 🖾 *Free.*

🍴 Restaurants

Beyond Bread
$ | CAFÉ | Twenty-seven varieties of bread are made at this bustling bakery with Central, Eastside, and Northwest locations, and highlights from the menu of generous sandwiches include Annie's Addiction (hummus, tomato, sprouts, red onion, and cucumber) and Brad's Beef (roast beef, provolone, onion, green chiles, and Russian dressing); soups, salads, and desserts are equally scrumptious. Eat inside or on the patio, or order takeout, but either way, splurge on one of the incredible desserts. **Known for:** stellar breads and pastries; large portions; friendliness. Ⓢ *Average main: $10* ⊠ *3026 N. Campbell Ave., Central* 🕾 *520/322–9965* ⊕ *www.beyondbread. com* ☾ *No dinner Sun.*

★ Café Poca Cosa
$$ | MEXICAN | At what is arguably Tucson's most creative Mexican restaurant, the chef prepares recipes inspired by different regions of her native country in a modern, vibrant setting. The menu, which changes daily, is listed on a chalkboard brought around to each table. **Known for:** innovative Mexican cooking; generous portions; lively energy. Ⓢ *Average main: $19* ⊠ *110 E. Pennington St., Downtown* 🕾 *520/622–6400* ⊕ *www. cafepocacosatucson.com* ☾ *Closed Sun. and Mon.*

The Grill at Hacienda del Sol
$$$$ | SOUTHWESTERN | Tucked into the foothills and surrounded by spectacular flowers and cactus gardens, this special-occasion restaurant, a favorite among locals hosting out-of-town visitors, provides an alternative to the chili-laden dishes of most nouvelle Southwestern cuisine. Wild-mushroom bisque, grilled buffalo in dark-chocolate mole, and pan-seared sea bass are among the

menu choices at this luxurious guest ranch resort. **Known for:** romantic dining; outstanding wine list; beautiful setting. $ *Average main: $32* ✉ *Hacienda del Sol Guest Ranch Resort, 5501 N. Hacienda Del Sol Rd., Foothills* ☎ *520/529–3500* ⊕ *www.haciendadelsol.com/dining/the-grill.*

★ Mi Nidito

$ | MEXICAN | A perennial favorite among locals (the wait is worth it), Mi Nidito ("my little nest") has also hosted its share of visiting celebrities: following President Clinton's lunch here, the rather hefty Presidential Plate (bean tostada, taco with barbecued meat, chiles rellenos, chicken enchilada, and beef tamale with rice and beans) was added to the menu. Top that off with the mango chimichangas for dessert, and you're talkin' executive privilege. **Known for:** reliably delicious Mexican food; festive atmosphere; great margaritas. $ *Average main: $12* ✉ *1813 S. 4th Ave., South* ☎ *520/622–5081* ⊕ *www.miniditorestaurant.com* ⊘ *Closed Mon. and Tues.*

Vivace

$$$ | ITALIAN | A modern Italian bistro in a lovely Foothills setting, Vivace has long been a favorite with Tucsonans. Wild mushrooms and goat cheese in puff pastry is hard to resist as a starter, and the fettuccine with grilled salmon is a nice, lighter alternative to such entrées as a rich osso buco. **Known for:** Italian fine dining; lovely patios with mountain and city views; a popular spot (reservations are a must on weekends). $ *Average main: $30* ✉ *6440 N. Campbell Ave., Foothills* ☎ *520/795–7221* ⊕ *www.vivacetucson.com* ⊘ *Closed Sun.*

Zinburger

$ | AMERICAN | Have a glass of wine or a cocktail with your gourmet burger and fries at this high-energy, somewhat noisy, and unquestionably hip burger joint. Zinburger delivers tempting burgers—try the Kobe beef with cheddar and wild mushrooms—and decadent milkshakes

made of creative combinations like dates and honey or melted chocolate with praline flakes. **Known for:** gourmet burgers and fries; innovative shakes; lively atmosphere. $ *Average main: $12* ✉ *1865 E. River Rd., Foothills* ☎ *520/299–7799* ⊕ *www.zinburgeraz.com.*

Hotels

★ Arizona Inn

$$$$ | HOTEL | Although near the university and many sights, the beautifully landscaped lawns and gardens of this 1930 inn seem far from the hustle and bustle. **Pros:** unique historical property; emphasis on service; gorgeous gardens and common areas. **Cons:** rooms may not be modern enough for some; close to University Medical Center but long walk (1½ miles) from the main campus; too sedate and posh for some. $ *Rooms from: $359* ✉ *2200 E. Elm St., University* ☎ *520/325–1541, 800/933–1093* ⊕ *www.arizonainn.com* ⤳ *94 rooms* ⦿ *No meals.*

★ Casa Tierra

$$$$ | B&B/INN | For a real desert experience, head to this lovely B&B on 5 acres near the Desert Museum and Saguaro National Park West, the last 1½ miles on a dirt road. **Pros:** serene Southwest getaway; hot tub; copious complimentary snacks. **Cons:** far from town (30-minute drive); two-night minimum stay; no TV in some rooms. $ *Rooms from: $225* ✉ *11155 W. Calle Pima, Westside* ☎ *520/578–3009* ⊕ *www.casatierratucson.com* ⤳ *3 rooms* ⦿ *Free breakfast.*

Hacienda del Sol Guest Ranch Resort

$$$$ | RESORT | This 32-acre hideaway in the Santa Catalina Foothills is a charming and more intimate alternative to the larger resorts, combining luxury with Southwestern character. **Pros:** outstanding restaurant and bar; historic and stunningly beautiful property; quieter than the larger resorts. **Cons:** golfers must be shuttled to a nearby course; some historic rooms are smaller; may feel too posh for some.

[$] *Rooms from: $225* ✉ *5501 N. Hacienda Del Sol Rd., Foothills* ☎ *520/299–1501, 800/728–6514* 🌐 *www.haciendadelsol.com* 🛏 *59 rooms* 🍴 *No meals.*

★ Hotel Congress

$$ | **HOTEL** | This hotel, built in 1919, has been artfully restored to its original Western version of art deco; it's now the center of Tucson's hippest scene and a great place for younger and adventurous travelers to stay. **Pros:** prime location; good restaurant and bars; historic, funky, and fun. **Cons:** no elevator to guest rooms; no TVs in rooms (only in common areas); noise from nightclub in some rooms. [$] *Rooms from: $119* ✉ *311 E. Congress St., Downtown* ☎ *520/622–8848, 800/722–8848* 🌐 *www.hotelcongress.com* 🛏 *40 rooms* 🍴 *No meals.*

Tanque Verde Ranch

$$$$ | **RESORT** | **FAMILY** | The most upscale of Tucson's guest ranches and one of the oldest in the country, the Tanque Verde sits on 640 beautiful acres in the Rincon Mountains next to Saguaro National Park East. **Pros:** authentic Western experience, including great riding; loads of all-inclusive activities; bed-and-breakfast-only is an economical option. **Cons:** at the eastern edge of town; all-inclusive package excludes alcohol. [$] *Rooms from: $250* ✉ *14301 E. Speedway Blvd., Eastside* ☎ *520/296–6275, 800/234–3833* 🌐 *www.tanqueverderanch.com* 🛏 *74 rooms* 🍴 *Free breakfast.*

★ White Stallion Ranch

$$$$ | **RESORT** | **FAMILY** | A 3,000-acre working cattle ranch run by the hospitable True family since 1965, this place is the real deal, satisfying for families as well as singles or couples. **Pros:** solid dude-ranch experience with exceptional riding program; plentiful ranch activities and evening entertainment; charming hosts. **Cons:** no TV in rooms; alcohol not included in the rate—pay extra or bring your own; rustic, rather than luxurious. [$] *Rooms from: $468* ✉ *9251 W. Twin Peaks Rd., Northwest* ☎ *520/297–0252* 🌐 *www.whitestallion.com* 🛏 *41 rooms, 1 house* 🍴 *All-inclusive.*

Activities

BALLOONING

Fleur de Tucson Balloon Tours

BALLOONING | Operating out of Northwest Tucson from October through April, this company flies over the Tucson Mountains and Saguaro National Park West. Flights include photos as well as a continental champagne brunch after you arrive back on the ground. ✉ *Northwest* ☎ *520/403–8547* 🌐 *www.fleurdetucson.net* 🎟 *From $250.*

Chapter 32

SEQUOIA AND KINGS CANYON NATIONAL PARKS

Updated by
Cheryl Crabtree

CALIFORNIA

🏕 Camping	🛏 Hotels	🤸 Activities	👁 Scenery	👥 Crowds
★★★★☆	★★★★☆	★★★★☆	★★★★★	★★★☆☆

WELCOME TO SEQUOIA AND KINGS CANYON NATIONAL PARKS

TOP REASONS TO GO

★ **Gentle giants:** You'll feel small—in a good way—walking among some of the world's largest living things in Sequoia's Giant Forest and Kings Canyon's Grant Grove.

★ **Because it's there:** You can't even glimpse it from the main part of Sequoia, but the sight of majestic Mt. Whitney is worth the trip to the eastern face of the High Sierra.

★ **Underground exploration:** Far older even than the giant sequoias, the gleaming limestone formations in Crystal Cave will draw you along dark, marble passages.

★ **A grander-than-Grand Canyon:** Drive the twisting Kings Canyon Scenic Byway down into the jagged, granite Kings River canyon, deeper in parts than the Grand Canyon.

★ **Regal solitude:** To spend a day or two hiking in a subalpine world of your own, pick one of the many trailheads at Mineral King.

1 Giant Forest–Lodgepole Village. One of Sequoia's most visited areas has major sights such as Giant Forest, General Sherman Tree, Crystal Cave, and Moro Rock.

2 Grant Grove Village–Redwood Canyon. The "thumb" of Kings Canyon is its busiest section, where Grant Grove, General Grant Tree, Panoramic Point, and Big Stump are the main draws.

3 Cedar Grove. The drive through the high-country of Kings Canyon to Cedar Grove Village, on the canyon floor, reveals magnificent granite formations of varied hues. Rock meets river in breathtaking fashion at Zumwalt Meadow.

4 Mineral King. In Sequoia's southeast section, the highest road-accessible part of the park is a good place to hike, camp, and soak up the grandeur of the Sierra Nevada.

5 Mt. Whitney. The highest peak in the Lower 48 stands on the eastern edge of Sequoia; to get there from Giant Forest you must either backpack eight days through the mountains or drive nearly 300 miles around the park to its other side.

The word "exceptional" best describes these two parks, which offer some of the nation's greatest escapes. Drives along their byways deliver stunning vistas at nearly every turn. Varied ecosystems provide opportunities for repeat adventures, among them hikes to groves of giant sequoias—some of the planet's largest, and oldest, living organisms.

This rare species of tree grows only at certain elevations and in particular environments on the Central Sierra's western slopes. Their monstrously thick trunks and branches, remarkably shallow root systems, and neck-craning heights really are almost impossible to believe, as is the fact they can live for more than 2,500 years. Several Native American groups lived among these magnificent trees for thousands of years before modern visitors arrived. By the late 1800s, word of the giant sequoias (*Sequoiadendron giganteum*) had spread, attracting logging enterprises and mobilizing those who wanted to protect these living treasures.

Sequoia National Park—the nation's second oldest after Yellowstone—was established in 1890, officially preserving the world's largest sequoia groves in the Giant Forest and other areas of the park. At first, visitors traveled along a pack road to view the towering marvels. In 1903, a road into the Giant Forest allowed access by wagon. It wasn't until 1926, with the opening of the General's Highway, that autos could chug up the mountain. Kings Canyon National Park, which included the General Grant

National Park formed a week after Sequoia, was established in 1940.

Today, the two parks, which share a boundary and have been administered jointly since World War II, encompass 865,964 wild and scenic acres between the foothills of California's Central Valley and its eastern borders along the craggy ridgeline of the Sierra's highest peaks. Next to or a few miles off the 46-mile Generals Highway are most of Sequoia National Park's main attractions, as well as Grant Grove Village, the orientation hub for Kings Canyon National Park.

Sequoia includes Mt. Whitney, the highest point in the lower 48 states (although it is impossible to see from the western part of the park and is a chore to ascend from either side). Kings Canyon has two portions: the smaller is shaped like a bent finger and encompasses Grant Grove Village and Redwood Mountain Grove (both with many sequoias), and the larger is home to stunning Kings River Canyon, where unspoiled peaks and valleys are a backpacker's dream.

AVERAGE HIGH/LOW TEMPERATURES					
JAN.	**FEB.**	**MAR.**	**APR.**	**MAY**	**JUNE**
42/24	44/25	46/26	51/30	58/36	68/44
JULY	**AUG.**	**SEPT.**	**OCT.**	**NOV.**	**DEC.**
76/51	76/50	71/45	61/38	50/31	44/27

Planning

When to Go

The best times to visit are spring and fall, when temperatures are moderate and crowds thin. Summertime can draw hordes of tourists to see the giant sequoias, and the few, narrow roads mean congestion at peak holiday times. If you must visit in summer, go during the week. By contrast, in wintertime you may feel as though you have the parks all to yourself. But because of heavy snows, sections of the main park roads can be closed without warning, and low-hanging clouds can move in and obscure mountains and valleys for days. From early October to late April, check road and weather conditions before venturing out. ■TIP→ **Even in summer, you can escape hordes of people just walking ¼ to ½ mile off the beaten path on a less-used trail.**

Temperatures in the chart below are for the mid-level elevations, generally between 4,000 and 7,000 feet.

FESTIVALS AND EVENTS
Annual Trek to the Tree. On the second Sunday of December, visitors and carolers gather at the base of General Grant Tree for a nondemoninational celebration that has taken place for nearly a century.

Big Fresno Fair. Over 12 days in October, agricultural, home-arts, and other competitions—plus horse racing and a carnival—make for a lively county fair. ⊕ *www.fresnofair.com*

Blossom Days Festival. On the first Saturday of March, communities along Fresno County's Blossom Trail celebrate the flowering of the area's orchards, citrus groves, and vineyards. ⊕ *www.goblossomtrail.com*

Three Rivers Jazzaffair. On the second weekend of April, a festival of mostly traditional jazz takes place at several venues just south of the parks. ⊕ *www.threeriversjazzaffair.com*

Woodlake Rodeo. The local Lions Club sponsors this rousing rodeo, which draws large crowds to Woodlake on Mother's Day weekend. ⊕ *www.woodlakelionsclub.com*

Getting Here and Around

AIR
The closest airport to Sequoia and Kings Canyon national parks is Fresno Yosemite International Airport (FAT).

AIRPORT CONTACTS Fresno Yosemite International Airport. *(FAT)* ⊠ *5175 E. Clinton Way, Fresno* ☎ *800/244–2359 automated info, 559/621–4500* ⊕ *www.flyfresno.com.*

CAR
Sequoia is 36 miles east of Visalia on Route 198; Grant Grove Village in Kings Canyon is 56 miles east of Fresno on Route 180. There is no automobile entrance on the eastern side of the Sierra. Routes 198 and 180 are connected by Generals Highway, a paved two-lane road (also signed as Highway 198) that sometimes sees delays at peak times due to ongoing improvements. The road is extremely narrow and steep from Route 198 to Giant Forest, so keep an eye on your engine temperature gauge,

as the incline and congestion can cause vehicles to overheat; to avoid overheated brakes, use low gears on downgrades.

If you are traveling in an RV or with a trailer, study the restrictions on these vehicles. Do not travel beyond Potwisha Campground on Generals Highway (Route 198) with an RV longer than 22 feet; take straighter, easier Route 180 through the Kings Canyon park entrance instead. Maximum vehicle length on Generals Highway is 40 feet, or 50 feet combined length for vehicles with trailers.

Generals Highway between Lodgepole and Grant Grove is sometimes closed by snow. The Mineral King Road from Route 198 into southern Sequoia National Park is closed 2 miles below Atwell Mill either on November 1 or after the first heavy snow. The Buckeye Flat–Middle Fork Trailhead road is closed from mid-October to mid-April when the Buckeye Flat Campground closes. The lower Crystal Cave Road is closed when the cave closes (typically in November). Its upper 2 miles, as well as the Panoramic Point and Moro Rock–Crescent Meadow roads, close with the first heavy snow. Because of the danger of rockfall, the portion of Kings Canyon Scenic Byway east of Grant Grove closes in winter. For current road and weather conditions, call ☎ 559/565–3341 or visit the park website: ⊕ www.nps.gov/seki.

■TIP➔ **Snowstorms are common from late October through April. Unless you have a four-wheel-drive vehicle with snow tires, you should carry chains and know how to install them.**

Inspiration

5th of July, a 2019 film shot in Sequoia National Park, highlights a young, Black, French professor who encounters trouble when he heads to the mountains to spread his father's ashes at a lake.

King Sequoia: The Tree That Inspired a Nation, Created Our National Park System, and Changed the Way We Think about Nature, by naturalist and former park ranger William C. Tweed, dives deep into the story of human discovery and connection with giant sequoias.

The Overstory: A Novel, by Richard Powers, includes tales rooted around timber wars and characters who become champions of the natural world. The book won the 2019 Pulitzer Prize in fiction.

Wild: From Lost to Found on the Pacific Crest Trail is by Cheryl Strayed, whose thousand-mile solo trek at age 26 took her through Sequoia and Kings Canyon.

Park Essentials

ACCESSIBILITY

All the visitor centers, the Giant Forest Museum, and Big Trees Trail are wheelchair accessible, as are some short ranger-led walks and talks. General Sherman Tree can be reached via a paved, level trail near a parking area. None of the caves is accessible, and wilderness areas must be reached by horseback or on foot. Some picnic tables are extended to accommodate wheelchairs. Many of the major sites are in the 6,000-foot range, and thin air at high elevations can cause respiratory distress for people with breathing difficulties. Carry oxygen if necessary. Contact the park's main number for more information.

PARK FEES AND PERMITS

The admission fee is $35 per vehicle, $30 per motorcycle, and $20 per person for those who enter by bus, on foot, bicycle, horse, or any other mode of transportation; it is valid for seven days in both parks. U.S. residents over the age of 62 pay $80 for a lifetime pass, and permanently disabled U.S. residents are admitted free.

If you plan to camp in the backcountry, you need a permit, which costs $15 for hikers or $30 for stock users (e.g., horseback riders). One permit covers the

Seeing the Parks in One Day

Sequoia National Park in One Day

After overnighting in Visalia or Three Rivers, take off early on Route 198 to the **Sequoia National Park entrance**. Pull over at the **Hospital Rock** picnic area to gaze up at the imposing granite Moro Rock, which you later will climb. Heed signs that advise "10 mph" around tight turns as you climb 3,500 feet on **Generals Highway** to the **Giant Forest Museum**. Spend a half hour here, then examine trees firsthand by circling the lovely **Round Meadow** on the **Big Trees Trail**, to which you must walk from the museum or its parking lot across the road.

Get back in your car, and continue a few miles north on Generals Highway to see the jaw-dropping **General Sherman Tree**. Then set off on the **Congress Trail** so that you can be further awed by the Senate and House big-tree clusters. Buy lunch at the **Lodgepole** complex, 2 miles to the north, and eat at the nearby **Pinewood** picnic area. Now you're ready to climb **Moro Rock**.

You can drive there or, if it is summer, park at the museum lot and take the free shuttle. Count on spending at least an hour for the 350-step ascent and descent, with a pause on top to appreciate the 360-degree view. Next, proceed past the **Tunnel Log** to **Crescent Meadow**. Spend a relaxing hour or two strolling on the trails that pass by, among other things, **Tharp's Log**. By now you've probably renewed your appetite; head to **Lodgepole Grill & Market** or the restaurant at **Wuksachi Lodge**.

Kings Canyon National Park in One Day

Enter the park via the **Kings Canyon Scenic Byway** (Route 180), having spent the night in Fresno or Visalia. Or wake up already in **Grant Grove Village**, perhaps in the **John Muir Lodge**. Stock up for a picnic with takeout from the **Grant Grove Restaurant** or with food from the nearby market. Drive east a mile to see the **General Grant Tree** and compact **Grant Grove's** other sequoias. If it's no later than mid-morning, walk up the short trail at **Panoramic Point**, for a view of Hume Lake and the High Sierra. Either way, return to Route 180, and continue east. Stop at Junction View to take in several peaks towering over Kings Canyon. From here, visit **Boyden Cavern** or continue to **Cedar Grove Village**, pausing along the way at **Grizzly Falls**. Eat at a table by the **South Fork of the Kings River** or on the Cedar Grove Snack Bar's deck. Now you are ready for the day's highlight: strolling **Zumwalt Meadow**, which lies a few miles past the village.

After you have enjoyed that short trail and its views of **Grand Sentinel** and **North Dome**, head to **Roads End**, where backpackers embark for the High Sierra wilderness. Make the return trip—with a stop at **Roaring River Falls**—past Grant Grove and briefly onto southbound **Generals Highway**. Stop at **Redwood Mountain Overlook**, and use binoculars to look down upon the world's largest sequoia grove. Drive another couple of miles to the **Kings Canyon Overlook** to survey some of what you have done today. Make reservations for a late dinner at **Wuksachi Lodge**.

group. Availability of permits depends upon trailhead quotas. Reservations are accepted by mail or email for a $15 processing fee, beginning March 1, and must be made at least 14 days in advance (☎ 559/565–3766). Without a reservation, you may still get a permit on a first-come, first-served basis starting at 1 pm the day before you plan to hike. For more information on backcountry camping or travel with pack animals (horses, mules, burros, or llamas), contact the Wilderness Permit Office (☎ 530/565–3766).

PARK HOURS

The parks are open 24/7 year-round. They are in the Pacific time zone.

CELL PHONE RECEPTION

Cell phone reception is poor to nonexistent in the higher elevations and spotty even on portions of Generals Highway, where you can (on rare clear days) see the Central Valley. Public telephones may be found at the visitor centers, ranger stations, some trailheads, and at all restaurants and lodging facilities in the park.

Hotels

Hotel accommodations in Sequoia and Kings Canyon are limited, and, although they are clean and comfortable, they tend to lack much in-room character. Keep in mind, however, that the extra money you spend on lodging here is offset by the time you'll save by being inside the parks. You won't be faced with a 60- to 90-minute commute from the less-expensive motels in Three Rivers (by far the most charming option), Visalia, or Fresno. Reserve as far in advance as you can, especially for summertime stays. *Hotel reviews have been shortened. For full information, visit Fodors.com.*

Restaurants

In Sequoia and Kings Canyon national parks, you can treat yourself (and the family) to a high-quality meal in a wonderful setting in the Peaks restaurant at Wuksachi Lodge, but otherwise you should keep your expectations modest. You can grab bread, spreads, drinks, and fresh produce at one of several small grocery stores for a picnic, or get takeout food from the Grant Grove Restaurant, the Cedar Grove Grill, or one of the two small Lodgepole eateries. *Restaurant reviews have been shortened. For full information, visit Fodors.com.*

What It Costs

	$	$$	$$$	$$$$
RESTAURANTS				
	under $12	$12–$20	$21–$30	over $30
HOTELS				
	under $100	$100–$150	$151–$200	over $200

Tours

★ Sequoia Parks Conservancy Field Institute

TOUR—SIGHT | The Sequoia Parks Conservancy's highly regarded educational division conducts half-, single-, and multiday tours that include backpacking hikes, natural-history walks, astronomy programs, snowshoe treks, and custom adventures. ☒ *47050 Generals Hwy., Unit 10, Three Rivers* ☎ *559/565–4251* ⊕ *www.sequoiaparksconservancy.org* ⊠ *From $150 for two-hour guided tour.*

Sequoia Sightseeing Tours

TOUR—SIGHT | This locally owned operator's friendly, knowledgeable guides conduct daily interpretive sightseeing tours in Sequoia and Kings Canyon. Reservations are essential. The company also offers private tours. ☒ *Three Rivers* ☎ *559/561–4189* ⊕ *www.sequoiatours.*

com ✉ From $79 tour of Sequoia; from $169 tour of Kings Canyon.

Visitor Information

NATIONAL PARK SERVICE Foothills Visitor Center. ✉ 47050 Generals Hwy., Rte. 198, 1 mile north of Ash Mountain entrance, Sequoia National Park ☎ 559/565–3341. **Sequoia and Kings Canyon National Parks.** ✉ 47050 Generals Hwy. (Rte. 198), Three Rivers ☎ 559/565–3341 ⊕ nps.gov/seki.

Sequoia National Park

Sequoia National Park is all about the trees, and to understand the scale of these giants you must walk among them. If you do nothing else, get out of the car for a short stroll through one of the groves. But there is much more to the park than the trees. Try to access one of the vista points that provide a panoramic view over the forested mountains. Generals Highway (which connects Routes 198 and 180) will be your route to most of the park's sights. A few short spur roads lead from the highway to some sights, and Mineral King Road branches off Route 198 to enter the park at Lookout Point, winding east from there to the park's southernmost section.

Giant Forest— Lodgepole Village

Giant Forest is 16 miles from the Sequoia National Park Visitor Center

The Sequoia National Park entrance at Ash Mountain is the main gateway to the Giant Forest and many of the park's major sights. From there, the narrow, twisty General's Highway snakes up the mountain from a 1,700-foot elevation through the Giant Forest (a 45-minute drive from the entrance) up to 6,720 feet at Lodgepole Village.

Sights

HISTORIC SIGHTS
Giant Forest Museum
MUSEUM | Well-imagined and interactive displays at this worthwhile stop provide the basics about sequoias, of which there are 2,161 with diameters exceeding 10 feet in the approximately 2,000-acre Giant Forest. ✉ Sequoia National Park ✛ Generals Hwy., 4 miles south of Lodgepole Visitor Center ☎ 559/565–4436 ✉ Free ✎ Shuttle: Giant Forest or Moro Rock–Crescent Meadow.

PICNIC AREAS
Take care to dispose of your food scraps properly (the bears might not appreciate this short-term, but the practice helps ensure their long-term survival).

Crescent Meadow
RESTAURANT—SIGHT | A mile or so past Moro Rock, this comparatively remote picnic area has meadow views and is close to a lovely hiking trail. Tables are under the giant sequoias, off the parking area. There are restrooms and drinking water. Fires are not allowed. ✉ Sequoia National Park ✛ End of Moro Rock–Crescent Rd., 2.6 miles east off Generals Hwy. (Rte. 198).

Foothills Picnic Area
RESTAURANT—SIGHT | Near the parking lot at the southern entrance of the park, this area has tables, drinking water, and restrooms. ✉ Sequoia National Park ✛ Across Generals Hwy. from Foothills Visitor Center.

Hospital Rock
RESTAURANT—SIGHT | Native Americans once ground acorns into meal at this site; outdoor exhibits tell the story. The picnic area's name, however, stems from a hunter/trapper who was treated for a leg wound here in 1873. Look up, and you'll see Moro Rock. Grills, drinking water, and restrooms are available. ✉ Sequoia National Park ✛ Generals Hwy. (Rte. 198), 6 miles north of Ash Mountain entrance.

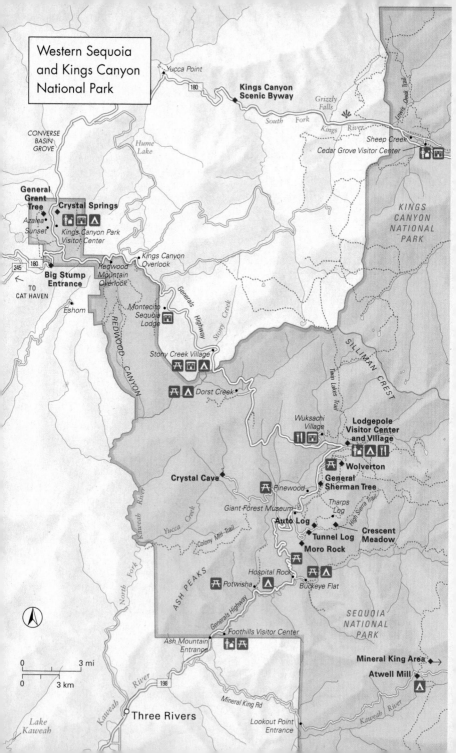

Western Sequoia and Kings Canyon National Park

CONVERSE BASIN GROVE

Yucca Point

Kings Canyon Scenic Byway

Grizzly Falls

Hume Lake

South Fork Kings River

Sheep Creek

Cedar Grove Visitor Center

Lewis Creek Trail

KINGS CANYON NATIONAL PARK

General Grant Tree

Azalea Sunset

Crystal Springs

King's Canyon Park Visitor Center

245
180

TO CAT HAVEN

Big Stump Entrance

Eshom

Redwood Mountain Overlook

Kings Canyon Overlook

REDWOOD CANYON

Generals Highway

Stony Creek

Montecito Sequoia Lodge

Stony Creek Village

Dorst Creek

SILLIMAN CREST

Twin Lakes Trail

Wuksachi Village

Lodgepole Visitor Center and Village

Wolverton

Crystal Cave

Pinewood

Giant Forest Museum

General Sherman Tree

Tharps Log

Kaweah River

Marble Fork

Yucca Creek

Colony Mill Trail

Auto Log

Tunnel Log

Moro Rock

High Sierra Trail

Crescent Meadow

ASH PEAKS

Hospital Rock

Potwisha

Buckeye Flat

SEQUOIA NATIONAL PARK

North Fork Kaweah River

Generals Highway

Foothills Visitor Center

Ash Mountain Entrance

198

Mineral King Rd

Three Rivers

Lookout Point Entrance

Mineral King Area →

Atwell Mill

Kaweah River

Lake Kaweah

0   3 mi

0   3 km

Pinewood Picnic Area

RESTAURANT—SIGHT | Picnic in Giant Forest, in the vicinity of sequoias if not actually under them. Drinking water, restrooms, grills, and wheelchair-accessible spots are provided in this expansive setting near Sequoia National Park's most popular attractions. ⊠ *Sequoia National Park* ⊹ *Generals Hwy. (Rte. 198), 2 miles north of Giant Forest Museum, halfway between Giant Forest Museum and General Sherman Tree.*

Wolverton Meadow

RESTAURANT—SIGHT | At a major trailhead to the backcountry, this is a great place to stop for lunch before a hike. The area sits in a mixed-conifer forest adjacent to parking. Drinking water, grills, and restrooms are available. ⊠ *Sequoia National Park* ⊹ *Wolverton Rd., 1½ miles northeast off Generals Hwy. (Rte. 198).*

SCENIC DRIVES

★ Generals Highway

SCENIC DRIVE | One of California's most scenic drives, this 46-mile road (also signed as Route 198) is the main asphalt artery between Sequoia and Kings Canyon national parks. Named after the landmark Grant and Sherman trees that leave so many visitors awestruck, Generals Highway runs from Sequoia's Foothills Visitor Center north to Kings Canyon's Grant Grove Village. Along the way, it passes the turnoff to Crystal Cave, the Giant Forest Museum, Lodgepole Village, and other popular attractions. The lower portion, from Hospital Rock to the Giant Forest, is especially steep and winding. If your vehicle is 22 feet or longer, avoid that stretch by entering the parks via Route 180 (from Fresno) rather than Route 198 (from Visalia or Three Rivers). Take your time on this road—there's a lot to see, and wildlife can scamper across at any time. ⊠ *Sequoia National Park.*

SCENIC STOPS

Auto Log

FOREST | Before its wood showed signs of severe rot, cars drove right on top of this giant fallen sequoia. Now it's a great place to pose for pictures or shoot a video. ⊠ *Sequoia National Park* ⊹ *Moro Rock–Crescent Meadow Rd., 1 mile south of Giant Forest.*

Crescent Meadow

TRAIL | A sea of ferns signals your arrival at what John Muir called the "gem of the Sierra." Walk around for an hour or two, and you might decide that the Scotland-born naturalist was exaggerating a bit, but the verdant meadow is quite pleasant, and you just might see a bear. Wildflowers bloom here throughout the summer. ⊠ *Sequoia National Park* ⊹ *End of Moro Rock–Crescent Meadow Rd., 2.6 miles east off Generals Hwy.* ☞ *Shuttle: Moro Rock–Crescent Meadow.*

★ Crystal Cave

CAVE | One of more than 200 caves in Sequoia and Kings Canyon, Crystal Cave is composed largely of marble, the result of limestone being hardened under heat and pressure. It contains several eye-popping formations. There used to be more, but some were damaged or obliterated by early-20th-century dynamite blasting. You can see the cave only on a tour. The Daily Tour ($17), a great overview, takes about 50 minutes. To immerse yourself in the cave experience—at times you'll be crawling on your belly—book the exhilarating Wild Cave Tour ($140). Availability is limited—reserve tickets at least 48 hours in advance at ⊕ *www.recreation.gov* or stop by either the Foothills or Lodgepole visitor center first thing in the morning to try to nab a same-day ticket; they're not sold at the cave itself. ⊠ *Crystal Cave Rd., off Generals Hwy.* ☎ *877/444–6777* ⊕ *www.sequoiaparksconservancy.org/ crystalcave.html* 🎫 *$17* ⏱ *Closed Oct.– late May.*

★ General Sherman Tree

LOCAL INTEREST | The 274.9-foot-tall General Sherman is one of the world's tallest and oldest sequoias, and it ranks No. 1 in volume, adding the equivalent of a 60-foot-tall tree every year to its approximately 52,500 cubic feet of mass. The tree doesn't grow taller, though—it's dead at the top. A short, wheelchair-accessible trail leads to the tree from Generals Highway, but the main trail (½ mile) winds down from a parking lot off Wolverton Road. The walk back up the main trail is steep, but benches along the way provide rest for the short of breath. ⊠ *Sequoia National Park* ✛ *Main trail Wolverton Rd. off Generals Hwy. (Rte. 198)* ⌕ *Shuttle: Giant Forest or Wolverton–Sherman Tree.*

★ Moro Rock

NATURE SITE | This sight offers panoramic views to those fit and determined enough to mount its 350 or so steps. In a case where the journey rivals the destination, Moro's stone stairway is so impressive in its twisty inventiveness that it's on the National Register of Historic Places. The rock's 6,725-foot summit overlooks the Middle Fork Canyon, sculpted by the Kaweah River and approaching the depth of Arizona's Grand Canyon, although smoggy, hazy air often compromises the view. ⊠ *Sequoia National Park* ✛ *Moro Rock–Crescent Meadow Rd., 2 miles east off Generals Hwy. (Rte. 198) to parking area* ⌕ *Shuttle: Moro Rock–Crescent Meadow.*

Tunnel Log

LOCAL INTEREST | This 275-foot tree fell in 1937, and soon a 17-foot-wide, 8-foot-high hole was cut through it for vehicular passage (not to mention the irresistible photograph) that continues today. Large vehicles take the nearby bypass. ⊠ *Sequoia National Park* ✛ *Moro Rock–Crescent Meadow Rd., 2 miles east of Generals Hwy. (Rte. 198)* ⌕ *Shuttle: Moro Rock–Crescent Meadow.*

★ Big Trees Trail

TRAIL | The 0.7-mile, wheelchair-accessible portion of this path is a must, as it does not take long, and the setting is spectacular: beautiful Round Meadow, surrounded by many mature sequoias. Well-thought-out interpretive signs along the way explain the ecology on display. Parking at the trailhead lot off Generals Highway is for cars with handicap placards only. The full, round-trip loop from the Giant Forest Museum is about a mile long. *Easy.* ⊠ *Sequoia National Park* ✛ *Trailhead: off Generals Hwy. (Rte. 198), near the Giant Forest Museum* ⌕ *Shuttle: Giant Forest.*

★ Congress Trail

TRAIL | This 2-mile trail, arguably the best hike in the parks in terms of natural beauty, is a paved loop that begins near General Sherman Tree. You'll get close-up views of more big trees here than on any other Sequoia hike. Watch for the clusters known as the House and Senate. The President Tree, also on the trail, supplanted the General Grant Tree in 2012 as the world's second largest in volume (behind the General Sherman). An offshoot of the Congress Trail leads to Crescent Meadow, where, in summer, you can catch a free shuttle back to the Sherman parking lot. *Easy.* ⊠ *Sequoia National Park* ✛ *Trailhead: off Generals Hwy. (Rte. 198), 2 miles north of Giant Forest* ⌕ *Shuttle: Giant Forest.*

Crescent Meadow Trails

TRAIL | A 1-mile trail loops around lush Crescent Meadow to Tharp's Log, a cabin built from a fire-hollowed sequoia. From there you can embark on a 60-mile trek to Mt. Whitney, if you're prepared and have the time. Brilliant wildflowers bloom here in midsummer. *Easy.* ⊠ *Sequoia National Park* ✛ *Trailhead: the end of Moro Rock–Crescent Meadow Rd., 2.6 miles east off Generals Hwy. (Rte. 198)* ⌕ *Shuttle: Moro Rock–Crescent Meadow.*

Little Baldy Trail

TRAIL | Climbing 700 vertical feet in 1¾ miles of switchbacking, this trail ends at a granite dome with a great view of the peaks of the Mineral King area and the Great Western Divide. The walk to the summit and back takes about four hours. *Moderate.* ✉ *Sequoia National Park* ✣ *Trailhead: Little Baldy Saddle, Generals Hwy. (Rte. 198), 9 miles north of General Sherman Tree* ☞ *Shuttle: Lodgepole-Wuksachi-Dorst.*

Marble Falls Trail

TRAIL | The 3.7-mile trail to Marble Falls crosses through the rugged foothills before reaching the cascading water. Plan on three to four hours one-way. *Moderate.* ✉ *Sequoia National Park* ✣ *Trailhead: off dirt road across from concrete ditch near site 17 at Potwisha Campground, off Generals Hwy. (Rte. 198).*

Muir Grove Trail

TRAIL | You will attain solitude and possibly see a bear or two on this unheralded gem of a hike, a 4-mile round-trip from the Dorst Creek Campground. The remote grove is small but lovely, its soundtrack provided solely by nature. The trailhead is subtly marked. In summer, park in the amphitheater lot and walk down toward the group campsite area. *Easy.* ✉ *Sequoia National Park* ✣ *Trailhead: Dorst Creek Campground, Generals Hwy. (Rte. 198), 8 miles north of Lodgepole Visitor Center* ☞ *Shuttle: Lodgepole-Wuksachi-Dorst.*

Tokopah Falls Trail

TRAIL | This trail with a 500-foot elevation gain follows the Marble Fork of the Kaweah River for 1¾ miles one-way and dead-ends below the impressive granite cliffs and cascading waterfall of Tokopah Canyon. The trail passes through a mixed-conifer forest. It takes 2½ to 4 hours to make the round-trip journey. *Moderate.* ✉ *Sequoia National Park* ✣ *Trailhead: off Generals Hwy. (Rte. 198), ¼ mile north of Lodgepole Campground* ☞ *Shuttle: Lodgepole-Wuksachi-Dorst.*

VISITOR CENTERS

Lodgepole Visitor Center

INFO CENTER | Along with exhibits on the area's history, geology, and wildlife, the center screens an outstanding 22-minute film about bears. You can buy books, maps, wilderness permits, and tickets to cave tours here. ✉ *Sequoia National Park* ✣ *Generals Hwy. (Rte. 198), 21 miles north of Ash Mountain entrance* ☎ *559/565–3341* 🕐 *Closed Oct.–Apr.* ☞ *Shuttle: Giant Forest or Wuksachi-Lodgepole-Dorst.*

🍴 Restaurants

Lodgepole Market and Café

$$ | CAFÉ | The choices here run the gamut from simple to very simple, with several counters only a few strides apart in a central eating complex. The café also sells fresh and prepackaged salads, sandwiches, and wraps. **Known for:** quick and convenient dining; many healthful options; grab-and-go items for picnics. [$] *Average main: $12* ✉ *Next to Lodgepole Visitor Center* ☎ *559/565–3301* 🌐 *www.visitsequoia.com/dine/lodgepole-dining.*

The Peaks

$$$ | MODERN AMERICAN | Huge windows run the length of the Wuksachi Lodge's high-ceilinged dining room, and a large fireplace on the far wall warms both body and soul. The diverse dinner menu—by far the best at both parks—reflects a commitment to locally sourced and sustainable products. **Known for:** seasonal menus with fresh local ingredients; great views of sequoia grove; box lunches. [$] *Average main: $28* ✉ *Wuksachi Lodge, 64740 Wuksachi Way, Wuksachi Village* ☎ *559/625–7700* 🌐 *www.visitsequoia.com/dine/the-peaks-restaurant.*

Hotels

★ Wuksachi Lodge
$$$$ | **HOTEL** | The striking cedar-and-stone main building is a fine example of how a structure can blend effectively with lovely mountain scenery. **Pros:** best place to stay in the parks; lots of wildlife; easy access to hiking and snowshoe/ski trails. **Cons:** rooms can be small; main lodge is a few-minutes' walk from guest rooms; slow Wi-Fi. [$] *Rooms from: $229* ✉ *64740 Wuksachi Way, Wukasachi Village* ☎ *559/625–7700, 888/252–5757 reservations* 🌐 *www.visitsequoia.com/lodging/wuksachi-lodge* 🛏 *102 rooms* 🍴 *No meals.*

Shopping

Lodgepole Market Center
GIFTS/SOUVENIRS | You'll find gifts, toys, books, souvenirs, and outdoor equipment in Sequoia National Park's largest store. Its grocery department has a fairly wide selection of items, some of them organic, including grab-and-go items for hikes and picnics. Across the hall is a café with various dishes for breakfast, lunch, and dinner. ✉ *63204 Lodgepole Rd., next to Lodgepole Visitor Center* ☎ *559/565–3301* 🌐 *www.visitsequoia.com.*

Wuksachi Gift Shop
GIFTS/SOUVENIRS | Souvenir clothing, Native American crafts, postcards, and snacks are for sale at this tasteful shop off the Wuksachi Lodge lobby. ✉ *Wuksachi Village* ☎ *559/625–7700.*

Mineral King

25 miles east of Generals Hwy. (Rte. 198) via Mineral King Rd.

A subalpine valley of fir, pine, and sequoia trees with myriad lakes and hiking trails, Mineral King sits at 7,500 feet at the end of a steep, winding road. This is the highest point to which you can drive in the park. It is open only from Memorial Day through late October.

Sights

SCENIC DRIVES

Mineral King Road
SCENIC DRIVE | Vehicles longer than 22 feet are prohibited on this side road into southern Sequoia National Park, and for good reason: it's smaller than a regular two-lane road, some sections are unpaved, and it contains 589 twists and turns. Anticipating an average speed of 20 mph is optimistic. The scenery is splendid as you climb nearly 6,000 feet from Three Rivers to the Mineral King Area. In addition to maneuvering the blind curves and narrow stretches, you might find yourself sharing the pavement with bears, rattlesnakes, and even softball-size spiders. Allow 90 minutes each way. ✉ *Sequoia National Forest* ✥ *East off Sierra Dr. (Rte. 198), 3 1/2 miles northeast of Three Rivers* ⏲ *Road typically closed Nov.–late May.*

TRAILS

Mineral King Trails
TRAIL | Many trails to the high country begin at Mineral King. Two popular day hikes are Eagle Lake (6.8 miles round-trip) and Timber Gap (4.4 miles round-trip). At the Mineral King Ranger Station (☎ *559/565–3768*) you can pick up maps and check about conditions from late May to late September. *Difficult.* ✉ *Sequoia National Park* ✥ *Trailheads: at end of Mineral King Rd., 25 miles east of Generals Hwy. (Rte. 198).*

VISITOR CENTERS

Mineral King Ranger Station
INFO CENTER | The station's small visitor center has exhibits on area history. Wilderness permits and some books and maps are available. ✉ *Sequoia National Park* ✥ *Mineral King Rd., 24 miles east of Rte. 198* ☎ *559/565–3341* ☞ *Typically closed mid-Sept.–mid-May.*

Hotels

Silver City Mountain Resort

$$$ | **RESORT** | High on Mineral King Road, this privately owned resort has rustic cabins and deluxe chalets—all with a stove, refrigerator, and sink—plus three hotel rooms with private baths. **Pros:** rustic setting; friendly staff; great location for hikers. **Cons:** long, winding road is not for everybody; not much entertainment except hiking; some units have shared baths. [$] *Rooms from: $170* ✉ *Sequoia National Park* ✣ *Mineral King Rd., 21 miles southeast of Rte. 198* ☎ *559/242–3510, 559/561–1322 reservations* 🌐 *www.silvercityresort.com* 🕒 *Closed Nov.–late May* 🛏 *16 units* 🍴 *No meals.*

Mt. Whitney

276 miles by car from Sequoia National Park/Foothills Visitor Center (looping around the Sierra Nevada) on US-395; 60 miles on foot (an 8-day trek) along Mt. Whitney Trail.

At 14,494 feet, Mt. Whitney is the highest point in the contiguous United States and the crown jewel of Sequoia National Park's wild eastern side. The peak looms high above the tiny, high-mountain desert community of Lone Pine, where numerous Hollywood Westerns have been filmed. The high mountain ranges, arid landscape, and scrubby brush of the eastern Sierra are beautiful in their vastness and austerity.

Despite the mountain's scale, you can't see it from the more traveled west side of the park because it is hidden behind the Great Western Divide. The only way to access Mt. Whitney from the main part of the park is to circumnavigate the Sierra Nevada via a 10-hour, nearly 400-mile drive outside the park. No road ascends the peak; the best vantage point from which to catch a glimpse of the mountain is at the end of Whitney Portal Road. The 13 miles of winding road leads from U.S. 395 at Lone Pine to the trailhead for the hiking route to the top of the mountain. Whitney Portal Road is closed in winter.

Sights

TRAILS

Mt. Whitney Trail

TRAIL | The most popular route to the summit, the Mt. Whitney Trail can be conquered by very fit and experienced hikers. If there's snow on the mountain, this is a challenge for expert mountaineers only. All overnighters must have a permit, as must day hikers on the trail beyond Lone Pine Lake, about 2½ miles from the trailhead. From May through October, permits are distributed via a lottery run each February by 🌐 *recreation.gov*. The Eastern Sierra Interagency Visitor Center (☎ *760/876–6200*), on Route 136 at U.S. 395 about a mile south of Lone Pine, is a good resource for information about permits and hiking. ✉ *Kings Canyon National Park* ☎ *760/873–2483 trail reservations* 🌐 *www.fs.usda.gov/inyo.*

Activities

BIKING

Steep, winding roads and shoulders that are either narrow or nonexistent make bicycling here more of a danger than a pleasure. Outside of campgrounds, you are not allowed to pedal on unpaved roads.

BIRD-WATCHING

More than 200 species of birds inhabit Sequoia and Kings Canyon national parks. Not seen in most parts of the United States, the white-headed woodpecker and the pileated woodpecker are common in most mid-elevation areas here. There are also many hawks and owls, including the renowned spotted owl. Due to the changes in elevation, both parks have diverse species ranging from warblers, kingbirds, thrushes, and sparrows in the foothills to goshawk, blue grouse, red-breasted nuthatch, and brown creeper at the highest elevations. The Sequoia Parks Conservancy (☎ 559/565–4251 ⊕ www.sequoiaparksconservancy.org) has information about bird-watching in the southern Sierra.

CAMPING

Some campgrounds are open year-round, others only seasonally. Except for Bearpaw (around $350 a night including meals), fees at the campgrounds range from $22 to $45, depending on location and size. There are no RV hookups at any of the campgrounds. Expect a table and a fire ring with a grill at standard sites. You can make reservations (book as far ahead as possible) at Bearpaw, Dorst Creek, Lodgepole, and Potwisha. The rest are first come, first served. The Lodgepole and Dorst Creek campgrounds can be quite busy in the summer and are popular with families. Black bears are prevalent in these areas; carefully follow all posted instructions about food storage. Bear-proof metal containers are provided at many campgrounds.

Atwell Mill Campground. At 6,650 feet, this peaceful, tent-only campground is just south of the Western Divide. ⊠ Mineral King Rd., 20 miles east of Rte. 198 ☎ 559/565–3341.

Bearpaw High Sierra Camp. Classy camping is the order of the day at this tent hotel and restaurant. Make reservations starting on January 2. ⊠ High Sierra Trail, 11.5 miles from Lodgepole Village ☎ 866/807–3598 ⊕ www.visitsequoia.com.

Buckeye Flat Campground. This tents-only campground at the southern end of Sequoia National Park is smaller—and consequently quieter—than campgrounds elsewhere in the park. Because of its low elevation (2,800 feet), it's hot in summer. ⊠ Generals Hwy., 6 miles north of Foothills Visitor Center ☎ 559/784–1500.

Dorst Creek Campground. Wildlife sightings are common at this large campground at elevation 6,700 feet. ⊠ Generals Hwy., 8 miles north of Lodgepole Visitor Center ☎ 559/565–3341 or 877/444–6777.

Lodgepole Campground. The largest Lodgepole-area campground is also the noisiest, though things quiet down at night. ⊠ Off Generals Hwy. beyond Lodgepole Village ☎ 559/565–3341 or 877/444–6777.

Potwisha Campground. On the Marble Fork of the Kaweah River, this midsize, year-round campground at an elevation of 2,100 feet gets no snow in winter and can be hot in summer. ⊠ Generals Hwy., 4 miles north of Foothills Visitor Center ☎ 559/565–3341 or 877/444–6777.

CROSS-COUNTRY SKIING

For a one-of-a-kind experience, cut through the groves of mammoth sequoias in Giant Forest. Some of the Crescent Meadow trails are suitable for skiing as well; none of the trails is groomed. You can park at Giant Forest. Note that roads can be precarious in bad weather. Some advanced trails begin at Wolverton.

Alta Market and Ski Shop

SKIING/SNOWBOARDING | Rent cross-country skis and snowshoes here. Depending on snowfall amounts, instruction may also be available. Reservations are recommended. Marked trails cut through Giant Forest, about 5 miles south of Wuksachi Lodge. ⊠ Sequoia National Park ✛ At Lodgepole, off Generals Hwy. (Rte. 198) ☎ 559/565–3301 ☞ Shuttle: Wuksachi-Lodgepole-Dorst.

EDUCATIONAL PROGRAMS

Educational programs at the parks include museum-style exhibits, ranger- and naturalist-led talks and walks, film screenings, and sightseeing tours, most of them conducted by either the park service or the nonprofit Sequoia Parks Conservancy. Exhibits at the visitor centers and the Giant Forest Museum focus on different aspects of the park: its history,

wildlife, geology, climate, and vegetation—most notably the giant sequoias. Weekly notices about programs are posted at the visitor centers and elsewhere.

Grant Grove Visitor Center at Kings Canyon National Park has maps of self-guided park tours. Ranger-led walks and programs take place throughout the year in Grant Grove. Cedar Grove and Forest Service campgrounds have activities from Memorial Day to Labor Day. Check bulletin boards or visitor centers for schedules.

Free Nature Programs

Almost any summer day, ½-hour to 1½-hour ranger talks and walks explore subjects such as the life of the sequoia, the geology of the park, and the habits of bears. Giant Forest Museum, Lodgepole Visitor Center, and Wuksachi Village are frequent starting points. Look for less frequent tours in the winter from Grant Grove. Check bulletin boards throughout the park for the week's offerings. ⊕ *www.sequoiaparksconservancy.org.*

Junior Ranger Program

Children over age five can earn a patch upon completion of a fun set of age-appropriate tasks outlined in the Junior Ranger booklet. Pick one up at any visitor center. ☎ *559/565–3341.*

Sequoia Parks Conservancy Evening Programs

The Sequoia Parks Conservancy offers hikes and evening lectures during the summer and winter. The popular Wonders of the Night Sky programs celebrate the often stunning views of the heavens experienced at both parks year-round. ⊠ *Sequoia National Park* ☎ *559/565–4251* ⊕ *www.sequoiaparksconservancy.org.*

Sequoia Parks Conservancy Seminars

Expert naturalists lead seminars on a range of topics, including birds, wildflowers, geology, botany, photography, park history, backpacking, and pathfinding. Reservations are required. Information about times and prices is available at the visitor centers or through the Sequoia Parks Conservancy. ⊠ *Sequoia National Park* ☎ *559/565–4251* ⊕ *www.sequoiaparksconservancy.org.*

FISHING

There's limited trout fishing in the creeks and rivers from late April to mid-November. The Kaweah River is a popular spot; check at visitor centers for open and closed waters. Some of the park's secluded backcountry lakes have good fishing. A California fishing license, required for persons 16 and older, costs about $16 for one day, $24 for two days, and $48 for 10 days (discounts are available for state residents and others). For park regulations, closures, and restrictions, call the parks at ☎ *559/565–3341* or stop at a visitor center. Licenses and fishing tackle are usually available at Hume Lake.

California Department of Fish and Game

FISHING | The department supplies fishing licenses and provides a full listing of regulations. ☎ *916/928–5805* ⊕ *www.wildlife.ca.gov.*

HIKING

The best way to see the park is to hike it. The grandeur and majesty of the Sierra is best seen up close. Carry a hiking map and plenty of water. Visitor center gift shops sell maps and trail books and pamphlets. Check with rangers for current trail conditions, and be aware of rapidly changing weather. As a rule of thumb, plan on covering about a mile per hour.

HORSEBACK RIDING

Trips take you through forests and flowering meadows and up mountain slopes.

Grant Grove Stables

HORSEBACK RIDING | Grant Grove Stables isn't too far from parts of Sequoia National Park and is perfect for short rides from June to September. Reservations are recommended. ☎ *559/335–9292 summer* ⊕ *www.nps.gov/seki/planyourvisit/horseride.htm* ☒ *From $50.*

Horse Corral Packers

HORSEBACK RIDING | One- and two-hour trips through Sequoia are available for beginning and advanced riders. ✉ *Big Meadow Rd., 12 miles east of Generals Hwy. (Rte. 198) between Sequoia and Kings Canyon national parks* 📞 *559/565–3404 summer, 559/565–6429 off-season,* 🌐 *hcpacker.com* ✉ *From $50.*

SLEDDING AND SNOWSHOEING

The Wolverton area, on Generals Highway (Route 198) near Giant Forest, is a popular sledding spot, where sleds, inner tubes, and platters are allowed. You can buy sleds and saucers, with prices starting at $15, at the Alta Market and Ski Shop (📞 *559/565–3301*) at the Lodgepole Visitor Center. The shop also rents snowshoes ($18–$24). Naturalists lead snowshoe walks around Giant Forest and Wuksachi Lodge, conditions permitting, on Saturday and holidays. Make reservations and check schedules at Giant Forest Museum (📞 *559/565–3341*) or Wuksachi Lodge.

Kings Canyon National Park

Kings Canyon National Park consists of two sections that adjoin the northern boundary of Sequoia National Park. The western portion, covered with sequoia and pine forest, contains the park's most visited sights, such as Grant Grove. The vast eastern portion is remote high country, slashed across half its southern breadth by the deep, rugged Kings River canyon. Separating the two is Sequoia National Forest, which encompasses Giant Sequoia National Monument. The Kings Canyon Scenic Byway (Route 180) links the major sights within and between the park's two sections.

Grant Grove Village—Redwood Canyon

56 miles east of Fresno on Route 180; 26 miles north of Lodgepole Village in Sequoia National Park.

Grant Grove Village, home to the Kings Canyon Visitor Center, Grant Grove Cabins, John Muir Lodge, a market, and two restaurants, anchors the northwestern section of the park. Nearby attractions include the General Grant Tree and Redwood Canyon sequia grove. The Kings Canyon Scenic Byway begins here and travels 30 miles down to the Kings River Canyon and Cedar Grove.

👁 Sights

HISTORIC SIGHTS

Fallen Monarch

TOUR—SIGHT | This toppled sequoia's hollow base was used in the second half of the 19th century as a home for settlers, a saloon, and even a U.S. Cavalry stable. As you walk through it (assuming entry is permitted, which is not always the case), notice how little the wood has decayed, and imagine yourself tucked safely inside, sheltered from a storm or protected from the searing heat. ✉ *Kings Canyon National Park* ✛ *Grant Grove Trail, 1 mile north of Kings Canyon Park Visitor Center.*

Gamlin Cabin

BUILDING | Despite being listed on the National Register of Historic Places, this replica of a modest 1872 pioneer cabin is only borderline historical. The structure, which was moved and rebuilt several times over the years, once served as U.S. Cavalry storage space and, in the early 20th century, a ranger station. ✉ *Grant Grove Trail.*

Plants and Wildlife in Sequoia and Kings Canyon

The parks can be divided into three distinct zones. In the west (1,500–4,500 feet) are the rolling, lower-elevation foothills, covered with shrubby chaparral vegetation or golden grasslands dotted with oaks. Chamise, red-barked manzanita, and the occasional yucca plant grow here. Fields of white popcorn flower cover the hillsides in spring, and the yellow fiddleneck flourishes. In summer, intense heat and absence of rain cause the hills to turn golden brown. Wildlife includes the California ground squirrel, noisy blue-and-gray scrub jay, black bears, coyotes, skunks, and gray fox.

At middle elevation (5,000–9,000 feet), where the giant sequoia belt resides, rock formations mix with meadows and huge stands of evergreens—red and white fir, incense cedar, and ponderosa pines, to name a few. Wildflowers like yellow blazing star and red Indian paintbrush bloom in spring and summer. Mule deer, golden-mantled ground squirrels, Steller's jays, and black bears (most active in fall) inhabit the area, as does the chickaree.

The high alpine section of the parks is extremely rugged, with a string of rocky peaks reaching above 13,000 feet to Mt. Whitney's 14,494 feet. Fierce weather and scarcity of soil make vegetation and wildlife sparse. Foxtail and whitebark pines have gnarled and twisted trunks, the result of high wind, heavy snowfall, and freezing temperatures. In summer, you can see yellow-bellied marmots, pikas, weasels, mountain chickadees, and Clark's nutcrackers.

PICNIC AREAS

Big Stump

RESTAURANT—SIGHT | Some trees still stand at this site at the edge of a sequoia grove logged in the 1800s. Near the park's entrance, the area is paved and next to the road. It's the only picnic area in either park that is plowed in the wintertime. Toilets, grills, and drinking water are available, and the area is entirely accessible. ⊠ *Kings Canyon National Park* ✢ *Generals Hwy. (Rte. 180), just inside Big Stump entrance.*

Columbine Picnic Area

RESTAURANT—SIGHT | This shaded picnic area near the sequoias is relatively level. Tables, restrooms, drinking water, and grills are available. ⊠ *Kings Canyon National Park* ✢ *Grant Tree Rd., just off Generals Hwy. (Rte. 198), ½ mile northwest of Grant Grove Visitor Center.*

SCENIC DRIVES

★ Kings Canyon Scenic Byway

SCENIC DRIVE | The 30-mile stretch of Route 180 between Grant Grove Village and Zumwalt Meadow delivers eye-popping scenery—granite cliffs, a roaring river, waterfalls, and Kings River canyon itself—much of which you can experience at vista points or on easy walks. The canyon comes into view about 10 miles east of the village at **Junction View.** Five miles beyond, at **Yucca Point,** the canyon is thousands of feet deeper than the more famous Grand Canyon. **Canyon View,** a special spot 1 mile east of the Cedar Grove Village turnoff, showcases evidence of the area's glacial history. Here, perhaps more than anywhere else, you'll understand why John Muir compared Kings Canyon vistas with those in Yosemite. ■TIP➜ **Note that this byway is a dead-end road—you have to turn** around and head back the way you came. The drive takes about an hour each way without stops. ✉ *Kings Canyon National Park* ✛ *Rte. 180 north and east of Grant Grove village.*

SCENIC STOPS
Boyden Cavern
NATURE SITE | The Kings River has carved out hundreds of caverns, including Boyden, which brims with stalagmite, stalactite, drapery, flowstone, and other formations. In summer, the Bat Grotto shelters a slew of bats. If you can't make it to Crystal Cave in Sequoia, Boyden is a reasonable substitute. Regular tours take about 45 minutes and start with a steep walk uphill. ✉ *Sequoia National Forest, 74101 E. Kings Canyon Rd. (Rte. 180), between Grant Grove and Cedar Grove* ☎ 888/965–8243 ⊕ *boydencavern.com* 🎟 $16.

General Grant Tree
LOCAL INTEREST | President Coolidge proclaimed this to be the "nation's Christmas tree," and, 30 years later, President Eisenhower designated it as a living shrine to all Americans who have died in wars. Bigger at its base than the General Sherman Tree, it tapers more quickly. It's estimated to be the world's third-largest sequoia by volume. A spur trail winds behind the tree, where scars from a long-ago fire remain visible. ✉ *Kings Canyon National Park* ✛ *Trailhead: 1 mile north of Grant Grove Visitor Center.*

Project Survival's Cat Haven
ZOO | Take the rare opportunity to glimpse a Siberian lynx, a clouded leopard, a Bengal tiger, and other endangered wild cats at this conservation facility that shelters more than 30 big cats. A guided hour-long tour along a ¼-mile walkway leads to fenced habitat areas shaded by trees and overlooking the Central Valley. ✉ *38257 E. Kings Canyon Rd. (Rte. 180), 15 miles west of Kings Canyon National Park, Dunlap* ☎ 559/338–3216 ⊕ *cathaven.com* 🎟 $15 ⊗ *Closed Tues. May–Sept. Closed Tues.–Weds. Oct.–Apr.*

Redwood Mountain Sequoia Grove
FOREST | One of the world's largest sequoia groves, Redwood contains within its 2,078 acres nearly 2,200 specimens whose diameters exceed 10 feet. You can view the grove from afar at an overlook or hike 6 to 10 miles via meadow loop trails down into the richest regions, which include two of the world's 25 heaviest trees. ✉ *Kings Canyon National Park* ✛ *Drive 6 miles south of Grant Grove on Generals Hwy. (Rte. 198), then turn right at Quail Flat; follow it 2 miles to the Redwood Canyon trailhead.*

TRAILS
Big Baldy Trail
TRAIL | This hike climbs 600 feet and 2 miles up to the 8,209-foot summit of Big Baldy. Your reward is the view of Redwood Canyon. Round-trip, the hike is 4 miles. *Moderate.* ✉ *Kings Canyon National Park* ✛ *Trailhead: 8 miles south of Grant Grove on Generals Hwy. (Rte. 198).*

Big Stump Trail
TRAIL | From 1883 until 1890, logging was done here, complete with a mill. The 1-mile loop trail, whose unmarked beginning is a few yards west of the Big Stump entrance, passes by many enormous stumps. *Easy.* ✉ *Kings Canyon National Park* ✛ *Trailhead: near Big Stump Entrance, Generals Hwy. (Rte. 180).*

Buena Vista Peak Trail
TRAIL | For a 360-degree view of Redwood Canyon and the High Sierra, make the 2-mile ascent to Buena Vista. *Difficult.* ✉ *Kings Canyon National Park* ✛ *Trailhead: off Generals Hwy. (Rte. 198), south of Kings Canyon Overlook, 7 miles southeast of Grant Grove.*

★ Grant Grove Trail
TRAIL | Grant Grove is only 128 acres, but it's a big deal. More than 120 sequoias here have a base diameter that exceeds 10 feet, and the **General Grant Tree** is the world's third-largest sequoia by volume. Nearby, the Confederacy is represented

32

Sequoia and Kings Canyon National Parks **KINGS CANYON NATIONAL PARK** by the **Robert E. Lee Tree,** recognized as the world's 11th-largest sequoia. Also along the easy-to-walk trail are the **Fallen Monarch** and the **Gamlin Cabin,** built by 19th-century pioneers. *Easy.* ✉ *Kings Canyon National Park* ✣ *Trailhead: off Generals Hwy. (Rte. 180), 1 mile north of Kings Canyon Park Visitor Center.*

Panoramic Point Trail

TRAIL | You'll get a nice view of whale-shape Hume Lake from the top of this Grant Grove path, which is paved and only 300 feet long. It's fairly steep—strollers might work here, but not wheelchairs. Trailers and RVs are not permitted on the steep and narrow road that leads to the trailhead parking lot. *Moderate.* ✉ *Kings Canyon National Park* ✣ *Trailhead: at end of Panoramic Point Rd., 2.3 miles from Grant Grove Village.*

Redwood Canyon Trails

TRAIL | Two main trails lead into Redwood Canyon grove, the world's largest sequoia grove. The 6.5-mile **Hart Tree and Fallen Goliath Loop** passes by a 19th-century logging site, pristine Hart Meadow, and the hollowed-out Tunnel Tree before accessing a side trail to the grove's largest sequoia, the 277.9-foot-tall Hart Tree. The 6.4-mile **Sugar Bowl Loop** provides views of Redwood Mountain and Big Baldy before winding down into its namesake, a thick grove of mature and young sequoias. *Moderate.* ✉ *Kings Canyon National Park* ✣ *Trailhead: off Quail Flat. Drive 5 miles south of Grant Grove on Generals Hwy. (Rte. 198), turn right at Quail Flat and proceed 1½ miles to trailhead.*

VISITOR CENTERS

Kings Canyon Visitor Center

INFO CENTER | The center's 15-minute film and various exhibits provide an overview of the park's canyon, sequoias, and human history. Books, maps, and weather advice are dispensed here, as are (if available) $15 wilderness permits. ✉ *Kings Canyon National Park* ✣ *Grant Grove Village, Generals Hwy. (Rte. 198), 3 miles northeast of Rte. 180, Kings Canyon National Park entrance at Big Stump* ☎ *559/565–3341.*

🍴 Restaurants

Grant Grove Restaurant

$$ | **AMERICAN** | Gaze at giant sequoias and a verdant meadow while enjoying a meal in this eco-friendly restaurant's spacious dining room with a fireplace or on its expansive deck. The menu centers around locally sourced natural and organic ingredients and offers standard American fare. **Known for:** takeout service year-round; walk-up window for pizza, sandwiches, coffee, ice cream; picnic tables on outdoor deck. [$] *Average main: $16* ✉ *Grant Grove Village* ☎ *559/335–5500.*

🛏 Hotels

Grant Grove Cabins

$$ | **HOTEL** | Some of the wood-panel cabins here have heaters, electric lights, and private baths, but most have woodstoves, battery lamps, and shared baths. **Pros:** warm, woodsy feel; clean; walk to Grant Grove Restaurant. **Cons:** can be difficult to walk up to if you're not in decent physical shape; costly for what you get; only basic amenities. [$] *Rooms from: $135* ✉ *Kings Canyon Scenic Byway in Grant Grove Village* ☎ *866/807–3598* 🌐 *www.visitsequoia.com/Grant-Grove-Cabins.aspx* 🔑 *50 units* 🍴 *No meals.*

John Muir Lodge

$$$$ | **HOTEL** | In a wooded area in the hills above Grant Grove Village, this modern, timber-sided lodge has rooms and suites with queen- or king-size beds and private baths. **Pros:** open year-round; common room stays warm; quiet. **Cons:** check-in is down in the village; spotty Wi-Fi; remote location. [$] *Rooms from: $210* ✉ *Kings Canyon Scenic Byway, ¼ mile north of Grant Grove Village, 86728 Hwy. 180* ☎ *866/807–3598* 🌐 *www.visitsequoia.com/john-muir-lodge.aspx* 🔑 *36 rooms* 🍴 *No meals.*

Montecito-Sequoia Lodge

$$$$ | **HOTEL** | **FAMILY** | Outdoor activities are what this year-round family resort is all about, including many that are geared toward teenagers and small children. **Pros:** friendly staff; great for kids; lots of fresh air and planned activities. **Cons:** can be noisy with all the activity; no TVs or phones in rooms; not within national park. ⓈⓇ *Rooms from: $229* ✉ *63410 Generals Hwy., 11 miles south of Grant Grove, Sequoia National Forest* ☎ *559/565–3388, 800/227–9900* ⊕ *www. mslodge.com* ⊙ *Closed 1st 2 wks of Dec.* ⏚ *52 rooms* �“❝ *All meals.*

Shopping

Cedar Grove Gift Shop and Market

GIFTS/SOUVENIRS | This place is small, but it's stocked with the essentials for RV and auto travelers. ✉ *Cedar Grove Village* ☎ *559/565–3096* ⊙ *Closed late Oct.–mid-May.*

Grant Grove Gift Shop

GIFTS/SOUVENIRS | This shop sells park-related gifts and souvenirs. ✉ *Grant Grove Village* ☎ *559/335–5500.*

Cedar Grove

35 miles east of Grant Grove Village.

The Cedar Grove section of Kings Canyon National Park bears many similarities to Yosemite Valley: a mighty river flowing through a verdant valley, ringed by massive glacier-hewn granite cliffs that loom several thousand feet above. Drive along the Kings Canyon Scenic Byway to access this relatively uncrowded wonderland, where you can hike excellent backcountry trails, stroll around lush Zumwalt Meadows, and take a break in Cedar Grove Village.

Sights

HISTORIC SIGHTS

Knapp's Cabin

BUILDING | Stop here not so much for the cabin itself, but as an excuse to ogle the scenery. George Knapp, a Santa Barbara businessman, stored gear in this small wooden structure when he commissioned fishing trips into the canyon in the 1920s. ✉ *Kings Canyon National Park* ✛ *Kings Canyon Scenic Byway, 2 miles east of Cedar Grove Village turnoff.*

PICNIC AREAS

Grizzly Falls

RESTAURANT—SIGHT | This little gem is worth a pull-over, if not a picnic at the roadside tables. A less-than-a-minute trek from the parking lot delivers you to the base of the delightful, 100-foot-plus falls. On a hot day, nothing feels better than dipping your feet in the cool water. An outhouse is on-site, but grills are not, and water is not available. ✉ *Kings Canyon National Park* ✛ *Off Rte. 180 in Sequoia National Forest, 2½ miles west of Cedar Grove entrance.*

TRAILS

Don Cecil Trail

TRAIL | This trail climbs 4,000 feet up the cool north-facing slope of the Kings River canyon, passing Sheep Creek Cascade and providing several fine glimpses of the canyon and the 11,000-foot Monarch Divide. The trail leads to Lookout Peak, which affords a panorama of the park's backcountry. This strenuous, all-day hike covers 13 miles round-trip. *Difficult.* ✉ *Kings Canyon National Park* ✛ *Trailhead: at Sentinel Campground, Cedar Grove Village.*

Hotel Creek Trail

TRAIL | For gorgeous canyon views, take this trail from Cedar Grove up a series of switchbacks until it splits. Follow the route left through chaparral to the forested ridge and rocky outcrop known as Cedar Grove Overlook, where you can see the Kings River canyon stretching

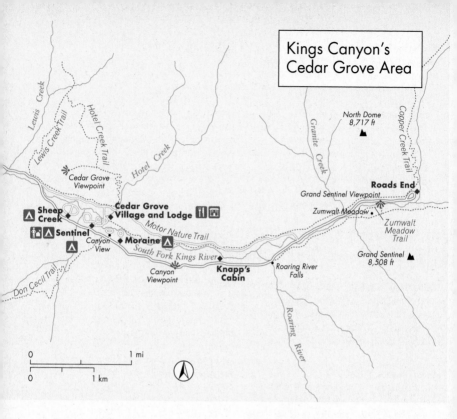

Kings Canyon's Cedar Grove Area

below. This strenuous, 5-mile round-trip hike gains 1,200 feet and takes three to four hours to complete. *Difficult.* ⊠ *Kings Canyon National Park* ✛ *Trailhead: at Cedar Grove Pack Station, 1 mile east of Cedar Grove Village.*

Mist Falls Trail

TRAIL | This sandy trail follows the glaciated South Fork Canyon through forest and chaparral, past several rapids and cascades, to one of the largest waterfalls in the two parks. Nine miles round-trip, the hike is relatively flat, but climbs 600 feet in the last 2 miles. It takes from four to five hours to complete. *Moderate.* ⊠ *Kings Canyon National Park* ✛ *Trailhead: at end of Kings Canyon Scenic Byway, 5½ miles east of Cedar Grove Village.*

Roaring River Falls Walk

TRAIL | Take a shady five-minute walk to this forceful waterfall that rushes through a narrow granite chute. The trail is paved and mostly accessible. *Easy.* ⊠ *Kings Canyon National Park* ✛ *Trailhead: 3 miles east of Cedar Grove Village turnoff from Kings Canyon Scenic Byway.*

★ Zumwalt Meadow Trail

TRAIL | Rangers say this is the best (and most popular) day hike in the Cedar Grove area. Just 1½ miles long, it offers three visual treats: the South Fork of the Kings River, the lush meadow, and the high granite walls above, including those of Grand Sentinel and North Dome. *Easy.* ⊠ *Kings Canyon National Park* ✛ *Trailhead: 4½ miles east of Cedar Grove Village turnoff from Kings Canyon Scenic Byway.*

VISITOR CENTERS
Cedar Grove Visitor Center
INFO CENTER | Off the main road and behind the Sentinel Campground, this small ranger station has books and maps, plus information about hikes and other activities. ✉ *Kings Canyon National Park* ✛ *Kings Canyon Scenic Byway, 30 miles east of Rte. 180/198 junction* ☎ *559/565–3341* ⊙ *Closed mid-Sept.–mid-May.*

🍴 Restaurants

Cedar Grove Grill
$$ | AMERICAN | The menu here is surprisingly extensive, with dinner entrées such as pasta, pork chops, trout, and steak. For breakfast, try the egg burrito, French toast, or pancakes; sandwiches, wraps, burgers (including vegetarian patties) and hot dogs dominate the lunch choices. **Known for:** scenic river views; extensive options; alfresco dining on balcony overlooking the Kings River. $ *Average main: $16* ✉ *Cedar Grove Village* ☎ *886/807–3598* ⊕ *www.visitsequoia.com/dine/cedar-grove-grill* ⊙ *Closed Oct.–May.*

🛏 Hotels

Cedar Grove Lodge
$$ | HOTEL | Backpackers like to stay here on the eve of long treks into the High Sierra wilderness, so bedtimes tend to be early. **Pros:** a definite step up from camping in terms of comfort; great base camp for outdoor adventures; on-site snack bar. **Cons:** impersonal; not everybody agrees it's clean enough; remote location. $ *Rooms from: $147* ✉ *Kings Canyon Scenic Byway* ☎ *866/807–3598* ⊕ *www.visitsequoia.com/lodging/cedar-grove-lodge* ⊙ *Closed mid-Oct.–mid-May* ⤴ *21 rooms* ⧫ *No meals.*

Activities

BIKING
Bicycles are allowed only on the paved roads in Kings Canyon. Cyclists should be extremely cautious along the steep highways and narrow shoulders.

CAMPING
Campgrounds in Kings Canyon occupy wonderful settings, with lots of shade and nearby hiking trails. All are first come, first served, and the campgrounds around Grant Grove get busy in summer with vacationing families. Keep in mind that this is black-bear country and carefully follow posted instructions about storing food. Bear-proof metal containers are provided at many campgrounds.

Azalea Campground. Of the three campgrounds in the Grant Grove area, Azalea is the only one open year-round. It sits at 6,500 feet amid giant sequoias. ✉ *Kings Canyon Scenic Byway, ¼ mile north of Grant Grove Village* ☎ *559/565–3341.*

Canyon View Campground. The smallest and most primitive of four campgrounds near Cedar Grove, this one is near the start of the Don Cecil Trail, which leads to Lookout Point. The elevation of the camp is 4,600 feet along the Kings River. There are no wheelchair-accessible sites. ✉ *Off Kings Canyon Scenic Byway, ½-mile east of Cedar Grove Village* ☎ *No phone.*

Crystal Springs Campground. Near the Grant Grove Village and the towering sequoias, this camp is at 6,500 feet. There are accessible sites here. ✉ *Off Generals Hwy. (Rte. 198), ¼ mile north of Grant Grove Visitor Center* ☎ *No phone.*

Sentinel Campground. At 4,600 feet and within walking distance of Cedar Grove Village, Sentinel fills up fast in summer. ✉ *Kings Canyon Scenic Byway, ¼ mile west of Cedar Grove Village* ☎ *559/565–3341.*

Sheep Creek Campground. Of the overflow campgrounds, this is one of the prettiest. ✉ *Off Kings Canyon Scenic Byway, 1 mile west of Cedar Grove Village* ☎ *No phone.*

Sunset Campground. Many of the easiest trails through Grant Grove are adjacent to this large camp, near the giant sequoias at 6,500 feet. ✉ *Off Generals Hwy., near Grant Grove Visitor Center* ☎ *No phone.*

CROSS-COUNTRY SKIING

Roads to Grant Grove are accessible even during heavy snowfall, making the trails here a good choice over Sequoia's Giant Forest when harsh weather hits.

Grant Grove Ski Touring Center

SKIING/SNOWBOARDING | The Grant Grove Market doubles as the ski-touring center, where you can rent cross-country skis or snowshoes in winter. This is a good starting point for a number of marked trails, including the Panoramic Point Trail and the General Grant Tree Trail. ✉ *Grant Grove Market, Generals Hwy. (Rte. 198), 3 miles northeast of Rte. 180, Big Stump entrance* ☎ *559/335–5500* ⊕ *www. visitsequoia.com/cross-country-skiing. aspx* 🎫 *$15–$20.*

FISHING

There is limited trout fishing in the park from late April to mid-November, and catches are minor. Still, Kings River is a popular spot. Some of the park's secluded backcountry lakes have good fishing. Licenses are available, along with fishing tackle, in Grant Grove and Cedar Grove. *See Activities, in Sequoia National Park, above, for more information about licenses.*

HIKING

You can enjoy many of Kings Canyon's sights from your car, but the giant gorge of the Kings River canyon and the sweeping vistas of some of the highest mountains in the United States are best seen on foot. Carry a hiking map—available at any visitor center—and plenty of water. Check with rangers for current trail conditions, and be aware of rapidly changing weather. Except

for one trail to Mt. Whitney, permits are not required for day hikes.

Roads End Permit Station

You can obtain wilderness permits, maps, and information about the backcountry at this station, where bear canisters, a must for campers, can be rented or purchased. When the station is closed (typically October–mid-May), complete a self-service permit form. ✉ *Kings Canyon National Park* ⊹ *Eastern end of Kings Canyon Scenic Byway, 6 miles east of Cedar Grove Visitor Center.*

HORSEBACK RIDING

One-day destinations by horseback out of Cedar Grove include Mist Falls and Upper Bubb's Creek. In the backcountry, many equestrians head for Volcanic Lakes or Granite Basin, ascending trails that reach elevations of 10,000 feet. Costs per person range from $40 for a one-hour guided ride to around $300 per day for fully guided trips for which the packers do all the cooking and camp chores.

Cedar Grove Pack Station

HORSEBACK RIDING | Take a day ride or plan a multiday adventure along the Kings River canyon with Cedar Grove Pack Station. Popular routes include the Rae Lakes Loop and Monarch Divide. Closed early September–late May. ✉ *Kings Canyon National Park* ⊹ *Kings Canyon Scenic Byway, 1 mile east of Cedar Grove Village* ☎ *559/565–3464 summer, 559/337–2413 off-season* ⊕ *www.nps.gov/seki/planyourvisit/horseride.htm* 🎫 *From $50 per hr or $90 per day.*

Grant Grove Stables

HORSEBACK RIDING | A one- or two-hour trip through Grant Grove leaving from the stables provides a taste of horseback riding in Kings Canyon. The stables are closed October–early June. ✉ *Kings Canyon National Park* ⊹ *Rte. 180, ½ mile north of Grant Grove Visitor Center* ☎ *559/335–9292* ⊕ *www.nps.gov/seki/ planyourvisit/horseride.htm* 🎫 *From $50 per hour, $90 for two hours.*

SLEDDING AND SNOWSHOEING

In winter, Kings Canyon has a few great places to play in the snow. Sleds, inner tubes, and platters are allowed at both the Azalea Campground area on Grant Tree Road, ¼ mile north of Grant Grove Visitor Center, and at the Big Stump picnic area, 2 miles north of the lower Route 180 entrance to the park.

Snowshoeing is good around Grant Grove, where you can take occasional naturalist-guided snowshoe walks from mid-December through mid-March as conditions permit. Grant Grove Market rents sleds and snowshoes.

Nearby Towns

Numerous towns and cities tout themselves as "gateways" to the parks, with some more deserving of the title than others. One that certainly merits the name is **Three Rivers**, a Sierra foothills hamlet (population 2,200) that's along the Kaweah River and close to Sequoia's Ash Mountain and Lookout Point entrances.

Visalia, a Central Valley city of about 128,000 people, lies 58 miles southwest of Sequoia's Wuksachi Village and 56 miles southwest of the Kings Canyon Park Visitor Center. Its vibrant downtown contains several good restaurants. If you're into Victorian and other old houses, drop by the visitor center and pick up a free map of them. A clear day's view of the Sierra from Main Street is spectacular, and even Sunday night can find the streets bustling with pedestrians. Visalia provides easy access to grand Sequoia National Park and the serene Kaweah Oaks Preserve.

Closest to Kings Canyon's Big Stump entrance, **Fresno**, the main gateway to the southern Sierra region, is about 55 miles west of Kings Canyon and about 85 miles northwest of Wuksachi Village. This Central Valley city of nearly a half-million people is sprawling and unglamorous, but it has all the cultural and other amenities you'd expect of a major crossroads.

Three Rivers

7 miles south of Sequoia National Park's Foothills Visitor Center.

Three Rivers is a good spot to find a room when park lodgings are full. Either because residents here appreciate their idyllic setting or because they know that tourists are their bread and butter, you'll find them eager to share tips about the best spots for "Sierra surfing" the Kaweah's smooth, moss-covered rocks or where to find the best cell reception (it's off to the cemetery for Verizon customers).

GETTING HERE AND AROUND

Driving is the easiest way to get to and around Three Rivers, which straddles a stretch of Highway 198. In summer, the Sequoia Shuttle connects Three Rivers to Visalia and Sequoia National Park.

CONTACTS Sequoia Shuttle. ☎ 877/287–4453 ⊕ www.sequoiashuttle.com.

Sights

Sequoia National Forest and Giant Sequoia National Monument

FOREST | Delicate spring wildflowers, cool summer campgrounds, and varied winter-sports opportunities—not to mention more than half of the world's giant sequoia groves—draw outdoorsy types year-round to this sprawling district surrounding the national parks. Together, the forest and monument cover nearly 1,700 square miles, south from the Kings River and east from the foothills along the San Joaquin Valley. The monument's groves are both north and south of Sequoia National Park. One of the most popular is the **Converse Basin Grove,** home of the Boole Tree, the forest's largest sequoia. The grove is accessible by car on an unpaved road.

The Hume Lake Forest Service District Office, at 35860 Kings Canyon Scenic Byway (Route 180), has information about the groves, along with details about recreational activities. In springtime, diversions include hiking among the wildflowers that brighten the foothills. The floral display rises with the heat as the mountain elevations warm up in summer, when hikers, campers, and picnickers become more plentiful. The abundant trout supply attracts anglers to area waters, including 87-acre **Hume Lake,** which is also ideal for swimming and nonmotorized boating. By fall, the turning leaves provide the visual delights, particularly in the Western Divide, Indian Basin, and the Kern Plateau. Winter activities include downhill and cross-country skiing, snowshoeing, and snowmobiling. ✉ *Sequoia National Park* ✥ *Northern Entrances: Generals Hwy. (Rte. 198), 7 miles southeast of Grant Grove; Hume Lake Rd. between Generals Hwy. (Rte. 198) and Kings Canyon Scenic Byway (Rte. 180); Kings Canyon Scenic Byway (Rte. 180) between Grant Grove and Cedar Grove. Southern Entrances: Rte. 190 east of Springville; Rte. 178 east of Bakersfield* ☎ *559/784–1500 forest and monument, 559/338–2251 Hume Lake* 🌐 *www.fs.usda.gov/sequoia.*

🍴 Restaurants

Sierra Subs and Salads

$$ | **AMERICAN** | This well-run sandwich joint satisfies carnivores and vegetarians alike with crispy-fresh ingredients prepared with panache. Depending on your preference, the centerpiece of the Bull's Eye sandwich, for instance, will be roast beef or a portobello mushroom; whichever you choose, the accompanying flavors—of ciabatta bread, horseradish-and-garlic mayonnaise, roasted red peppers, Havarti cheese, and spinach—will delight your palate. **Known for:** many vegetarian, vegan, and gluten-free options; weekly specials; Wi-Fi. [$] *Average main: $12* ✉ *41651 Sierra Dr.* ☎ *559/561–4810* 🌐 *www.sierrasubsandsalads.com* ⏲ *Closed Sun.–Mon. No dinner.*

🛏 Hotels

Buckeye Tree Lodge

$$$ | **B&B/INN** | Every room at this two-story motel has a patio facing a sun-dappled grassy lawn, right on the banks of the Kaweah River; individually decorated cottages and cabins across the river have private outdoor spaces with barbecue grills. **Pros:** near the park entrance; fantastic river views; kitchenette in some rooms. **Cons:** can fill up quickly in the summer; could use a little updating; some rooms are tiny. [$] *Rooms from: $200* ✉ *46000 Sierra Dr., Hwy. 198* ☎ *559/561–5900* 🌐 *www.buckeyetree.com* 🔑 *22 units* 🍽 *Breakfast* ☞ *2-night minimum on summer weekends.*

Lazy J Ranch Motel

$$ | **B&B/INN** | Surrounded by 12 acres of green lawns and a split-rail fence, the Lazy J is a modest compound of one-story motel buildings and freestanding cottages near the banks of the Kaweah River. **Pros:** pleasant landscaping; quiet rooms; friendly staff. **Cons:** on the far edge of town; can't see the river from most rooms; dated style and fixtures. [$] *Rooms from: $150* ✉ *39625 Sierra Dr., Hwy. 198* ☎ *559/561–4449* 🌐 *www.lazyjranchmotel.com* 🔑 *18 units* 🍽 *Breakfast.*

★ **Rio Sierra Riverhouse**

$$$$ | **B&B/INN** | Guests at Rio Sierra come for the river views, the sandy beach, and the proximity to Sequoia National Park (6 miles away), but invariably end up raving equally about the warm, laid-back hospitality of proprietress Mars Roberts. **Pros:** seductive beach; river views from all rooms; contemporary ambience. **Cons:** books up quickly in summer; some road noise audible in rooms; long walk or drive to restaurants. [$] *Rooms from: $275* ✉ *41997 Sierra Dr., Hwy.*

198 ☎ 559/561–4720 ⊕ www.rio-sierra. com ⇝ 3 rooms ⦿ No meals ⌣ 2-night min stay on summer weekends. Closed Jan.–mid-March.

Activities

HORSEBACK RIDING

Wood 'n' Horse Training Stables

HORSEBACK RIDING | For hourly horseback rides, riding lessons, or trail rides in the foothills, contact this outfit. Rates start at $50 for lessons and $70 for trail rides. ⊠ 42846 N. Fork Dr. ☎ 559/561–4268 ⊕ www.wdnhorse.com.

RAFTING

Kaweah White Water Adventures

BOATING | Kaweah's trips include a two-hour excursion (good for families) through Class III rapids, a longer paddle through Class IV rapids, and an extended trip (typically Class IV and V rapids). ⊠ 40443 Sierra Dr. ☎ 559/740–8251 ⊕ www.kaweah-whitewater.com ⊠ From $50 per person.

Visalia

35 miles west of the Sequoia National Park entrance.

Visalia's combination of a reliable agricultural economy and civic pride has produced the Central Valley's most vibrant downtown, with numerous restaurants, craft breweries, and cafés. If you're into history, drop by the visitor center and pick up a free map of a self-guided historic downtown walking tour. A clear day's view of the Sierra from Main Street is spectacular, and even Sunday night can find the streets bustling with pedestrians. Visalia provides easy access to grand Sequoia National Park and the serene Kaweah Oaks Preserve.

GETTING HERE AND AROUND

Highway 198, just east of its exit from Highway 99, cuts through town (and proceeds up the hill to Sequoia National Park). Greyhound stops here, but not Amtrak. KART buses serve the locals, and, in summer, the Sequoia Shuttle ($20) travels among Visalia, Three Rivers, and Sequoia National Park with a stop in Three Rivers.

VISITOR INFORMATION

CONTACTS Visalia Convention & Visitors Bureau (Visit Visalia). ⊠ 112 E. Main St. ☎ 559/334–0141, 800/524–0303 ⊕ www. visitvisalia.com.

Sights

Bravo Farms Traver

FACTORY | FAMILY | For one-stop truck-stop entertainment, pull off the highway in Traver, where at Bravo Farms you can try your luck at an arcade shooting gallery, watch cheese being made, munch on barbecue and ice cream, play a round of mini golf, peruse funky antiques, buy produce, visit a petting zoo, and climb a multistory tree house. Taste a few "squeakers" (fresh cheese curds, so named because chewing them makes your teeth squeak), and then be on your way. ⊠ 36005 Hwy. 99, 9 miles north of Hwy. 198 and Visalia, Traver ☎ 559/897–5762 ⊕ www.bravofarms.com ⊠ Free.

★ Colonel Allensworth State Historic Park

HISTORIC SITE | It's worth the slight detour off Highway 99 to learn about and pay homage to the dream of Allen Allensworth and other Black pioneers who in 1908 founded Allensworth, the only California town settled, governed, and financed by African Americans. At its height, the town prospered as a key railroad transfer point, but after cars and trucks reduced railroad traffic and water was diverted for Central Valley agriculture, the town declined and was eventually deserted. Today, the restored and rebuilt schoolhouse, library, and other structures commemorate Allensworth's heyday, as do festivities that take place each October. ⊠ 4129 Palmer Ave.,

48 miles south of Visalia, Allensworth
⊹ From Visalia, take Hwy. 99 south to
Earlimart, and then turn west toward
Allensworth ☎ 661/849–3433 ⊕ www.
parks.ca.gov ✑ $6 per car.

Kaweah Oaks Preserve

NATURE PRESERVE | Trails at this 344-acre
wildlife sanctuary off the main road to
Sequoia National Park lead past majestic
valley oak, sycamore, cottonwood, and
willow trees. Among the 134 bird species
you might spot are hawks, hummingbirds, and great blue herons. Bobcats,
lizards, coyotes, and cottontails also
live here. The Sycamore Trail has digital
signage with QR codes you can scan
with your smartphone to access plant
and animal information. ✉ Follow Hwy.
198 for 7 miles east of Visalia, turn north
on Rd. 182, and proceed ½ mile to gate
on left side ☎ 559/738–0211 ⊕ www.
sequoiariverlands.org ✑ Free.

Lake Kaweah

BODY OF WATER | The Kaweah River rushes
out of the Sierra from high above Mineral
King in Sequoia National Park. When it
reaches the hills above the Central Valley,
the water collects in Lake Kaweah, a
reservoir operated by the Army Corps
of Engineers. You can swim, sail, kayak,
water ski, hike, camp, fish, and picnic
here. The visitor center at Lemon Hill
has interesting exhibits about the dam
that created the lake. ✉ 34443 Sierra
Dr. (Rte. 198), about 20 miles east of
Visalia ☎ 559/597–2301, 877/444–6777
campground reservations, 559/597–2005
Lemon Hill visitor center ✑ $5 day use.

★ McKellar Family Farms

FARM/RANCH | FAMILY | Taste, touch,
and feel your way through orange and
mandarin groves on a guided tour of this
180-acre working citrus farm. Tours last
60 minutes; tractor-pulled wagon tours
are also available. Kids and adults love
the challenge of navigating the nation's
only orange-grove maze, answering questions at a series of checkpoints to earn a
prize at the end. ✉ 32985 Rd. 164, north

of Hwy. 216, Ivanhoe ☎ 559/731–7925
⊕ www.mckellarfamilyfarms.com ✑ Tour
$100 for up to two persons, $10 for each
additional person.

🍴 Restaurants

Fugazzi's Bistro

$$ | ITALIAN | An upscale restaurant in
Visalia's downtown hub, Fugazzi's serves
up Italian-American and international-fu-
sion dishes in a slick, contemporary
space with leather booths and shiny met-
al tables. The extensive lunch and dinner
menus feature everything from quinoa-
and-kale salad and Thai chicken wraps to
traditional Italian dishes and filet mignon.
Known for: full bar with classic and
creative cocktails; house-made sauces;
upscale yet casual vibe. $ Average main:
$19 ✉ 127 W. Main St. ☎ 559/625–0496
⊕ www.fugazzisbistro.com.

Pita Kabob Gastropub

$$ | MEDITERRANEAN | A large and
ever-changing selection of craft beers,
a lively dining garden, and authentic
Mediterranean and fusion dishes—from
kabobs, shawarma, hummus, and gyros
to rice bowls and burgers—lure locals
and visitors to this popular downtown
eatery. Pack in multiple flavors by
ordering a combination or sampler plate.
Known for: daily specials; 31 beers on tap;
veggie and vegan options. $ Average
main: $12 ✉ 227 N. Court St. ☎ 559/627–
2337 ⊕ pitakabob.com ⊗ Closed Mon.

★ The Vintage Press

$$$$ | EUROPEAN | Established in 1966,
this is one of the best restaurants in the
Central Valley. The California–continental
cuisine includes dishes such as crispy
veal sweetbreads with a port-wine sauce
and filet mignon with a cognac-mustard
sauce. **Known for:** wine list with more
than 900 selections; chocolate Grand
Marnier cake and other house-made
desserts; sophisticated vibe. $ Average
main: $32 ✉ 216 N. Willis St. ☎ 559/733–
3033 ⊕ www.thevintagepress.com.

Hotels

★ The Darling Hotel
$$$ | **HOTEL** | Developers meticulously restored a dilapidated, three-story, 1930s building to create this hotel, where rooms have a modern take on art-deco style, with plush furnishings, 12-foot ceilings, and spacious bathrooms with period accents. **Pros:** in the heart of downtown; outdoor pool; rooftop lounge and restaurant with panoramic mountain and city views. **Cons:** some rooms on the small side; fronts a busy street; vintage single-pane glass windows don't block urban noise. [$] *Rooms from: $179* ✉ *210 N. Court St.* ☎ *559/713–2113* 🌐 *thedarlingvisalia.com* 🛏 *32 rooms.*

Lamp Liter Inn
$ | **HOTEL** | **FAMILY** | A classic, 1960s, roadside motel, Lamp Liter Inn has basic but comfy rooms in several two-story buildings that surround tree-studded gardens and a spacious outdoor pool and terrace. **Pros:** family-owned and operated, personal service; on-site restaurant with full bar; convenient lodging for Sequoia National Park visitors. **Cons:** rooms could use updating; not near downtown; outdoor noise travels through thin walls in some rooms. [$] *Rooms from: $96* ✉ *3300 W. Mineral King Ave.* ☎ *559/732–4511, 800/662–6692* 🌐 *www.lampliter.net* 🛏 *100 rooms.*

Fresno

44 miles north of Visalia.

Fresno, with half a million people, is the center of the richest agricultural county in the United States. Cotton, grapes, and tomatoes are among the major crops; poultry and milk are also important. About 75 ethnic groups, including Armenians, Laotians, and Indians, live here. The city has a relatively vibrant arts scene, several public parks, and many low-price restaurants. The **Tower District**—with its restaurants, coffeehouses, and performance venues—is the town's arts and nightlife nexus. It's the closest large city to Sequoia National Park, though at some 78 miles away it's not that close, so it's an option if there's nothing available in the park itself, Three Rivers, or Visalia.

GETTING HERE AND AROUND

Highway 99 is the biggest road through Fresno. Highways 41 and 180 also bisect the city. Amtrak trains stop here daily (and often).

VISITOR INFORMATION Fresno / Clovis Convention & Visitors Bureau. ✉ *1180 E. Shaw Ave.* ☎ *559/981–5500, 800/788–0836* 🌐 *playfresno.org.*

Sights

★ Forestiere Underground Gardens
GARDEN | **FAMILY** | Sicilian immigrant Baldassare Forestiere spent four decades (1906–46) carving out an odd, subterranean realm of rooms, tunnels, grottoes, alcoves, and arched passageways that once extended for more than 10 acres between Highway 99 and busy, mall-pocked Shaw Avenue. Though not an engineer, Forestiere called on his memories of the ancient Roman structures he saw as a youth and on techniques he learned digging subways in New York and Boston. Only a fraction of his prodigious output is on view, but you can tour his underground living quarters, including bedrooms (one with a fireplace), the kitchen, living room, and bath, as well as a fishpond and auto tunnel. Skylights allow exotic full-grown fruit trees to flourish more than 20 feet belowground. ✉ *5021 W. Shaw Ave., 2 blocks east of Hwy. 99* ☎ *559/271–0734* 🌐 *www.undergroundgardens.com* 🎟 *$19* 🕒 *Closed Dec.–Mar.*

🍴 Restaurants

School House Restaurant & Tavern
$$$ | **MODERN AMERICAN** | A Wine Country–style establishment that sources ingredients from the on-site gardens and surrounding farms and orchards, this popular restaurant occupies a redbrick 1921 schoolhouse in the town of Sanger. Chef Ryan Jackson, who grew up on local fruit farms, creates seasonal menus from the bounty of familiar backyards, mostly filled with classic American dishes with a contemporary twist. **Known for:** fresh ingredients from neighboring farms and orchards; historic country setting; convenient stop between Kings Canyon and Fresno. [$] *Average main: $29* ✉ *1018 S. Frankwood Ave., at Hwy. 180 (King's Canyon Rd.), 20 miles east of Fresno, Sanger* ☎ *559/787–3271* 🌐 *schoolhousesanger.com* 🕒 *Closed Mon. and Tues.*

🛏 Hotels

Best Western Plus Fresno Inn
$$ | **HOTEL** | With a location near Highway 41 (the main route to Yosemite), Fresno State, and a big mall, this well-run hotel is popular with families, businesspeople, and parents with offspring at the university. **Pros:** convenient location; attentive staff; 24-hour business center. **Cons:** mildly sterile feel; on a busy street; small pool. [$] *Rooms from: $130* ✉ *480 E. Shaw Ave.* ☎ *559/229–5811* 🌐 *bestwestern.com* 🔑 *55 rooms* 🍴 *Breakfast.*

Hotel Piccadilly
$$ | **HOTEL** | This two-story property has 7½ attractively landscaped acres and a big swimming pool. **Pros:** big rooms; nice pool; on-site restaurant/pub. **Cons:** some rooms show mild wear; neighborhood is somewhat sketchy; no elevator. [$] *Rooms from: $119* ✉ *2305 W. Shaw Ave.* ☎ *559/348–5520* 🌐 *hotel-piccadilly.com* 🔑 *187 rooms* 🍴 *Breakfast.*

THEODORE ROOSEVELT NATIONAL PARK

Updated by
Carson Walker

NORTH
DAKOTA

☁ Camping
★★★☆☆

🛏 Hotels
★★★★☆

🏃 Activities
★★★☆☆

◉ Scenery
★★★★★

👥 Crowds
★★★★★

WELCOME TO THEODORE ROOSEVELT NATIONAL PARK

TOP REASONS TO GO

★ **The "Granddaddy Trail":** Hike the Maah Daah Hey Trail, which means "grandfather" or "been here long." It's one of the most popular and well-maintained trails in western North Dakota.

★ **Views from above:** Get an encompassing 360-degree view of the badlands from Buck Hill.

★ **History lessons from the frontier:** View Maltese Cross Ranch Cabin, which once belonged to Theodore Roosevelt.

★ **Badlands Broadway:** Come experience a theatrical tribute to the history and personalities that make up the Old West at the Medora Musical, located in the town, not the park.

★ **Great clubbing—golf, that is:** Perfect your swing at Bully Pulpit Golf Course in Medora, one of America's premier courses near the national park.

★ **Away from it all:** As this is not a heavily visited park, you'll likely encounter more wild horses than people here.

1 North Unit. Visitors looking to enjoy the great outdoors should be sure to travel along the 14-mile scenic drive and stop at one of the many hiking trailheads along the way. These trailheads give easy access to the backcountry of the North Unit.

2 South Unit. Often considered the main unit of Theodore Roosevelt National Park and adjacent to the famous town of Medora, the South Unit is home to some of the former president's personal artifacts, as well as his cabin, the Maltese Cross Ranch Cabin, and the 218-acre Elkhorn, which started it all.

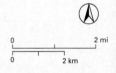

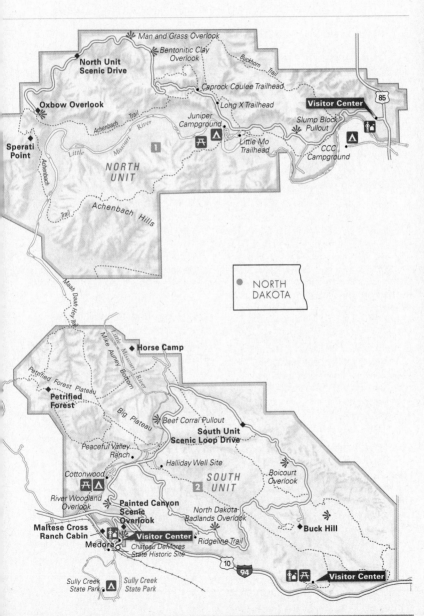

Man and Grass Overlook

Bentonitic Clay Overlook

Buckhorn Trail

North Unit Scenic Drive

Caprock Coulee Trailhead

Long X Trailhead

Visitor Center

85

Oxbow Overlook

Juniper Campground

Slump Block Pullout

Achenbach Trail

Little Missouri River

Little Mo Trailhead

CCC Campground

Sperati Point

Achenbach

NORTH UNIT

1

Trail

Achenbach Hills

Maah Daah Hey Trail

NORTH DAKOTA

Mike Auney Bottom

Little Missouri River

Horse Camp

Petrified Forest Plateau

Petrified Forest

Big Plateau

Beef Corral Pullout

South Unit Scenic Loop Drive

Peaceful Valley Ranch

Halliday Well Site

Boicourt Overlook

Cottonwood

SOUTH UNIT

2

River Woodland Overlook

Painted Canyon Scenic Overlook

North Dakota Badlands Overlook

Buck Hill

Maltese Cross Ranch Cabin

Medora

Visitor Center

Chateau DeMores State Historic Site

Ridgeline Trail

10

94

Visitor Center

Sully Creek State Park

Sully Creek State Park

The solitude that a young Theodore Roosevelt sought after the deaths of his wife and mother is also what draws many of the 750,000 visitors to this rugged swath of North Dakota every year. The 110-square-mile national park, named in honor of the former president, lacks something plentiful at other parks: people.

Roosevelt arrived in 1883 to hunt bison and fell in love with the land. Within weeks, he invested in an open range cattle ranch and came back the next year to establish a second. At the time, there were no fence lines in the prairie, and as the influx of settlers brought more livestock, the prairie became overgrazed. Roosevelt advocated for grazing and hunting regulations that protected both the land and wildlife, giving the park the nickname "cradle of conservation." Contrary to what many believe, Roosevelt established the U.S. Forest Service to regulate the use of land and wildlife (conservation), not the National Park Service, which is dedicated to preservation.

Established in 1947, the park preserves the history of the land's influence on Roosevelt. The park service also has plans to create new museum exhibits that tell an equally important story: that of the Native Americans, the region's original caretakers, who foraged and hunted here long before European settlers arrived. Some of the last untouched mixed prairie grasses in the United States grow wild here, protected by the craggy ravines, tablelands and gorges of the otherworldly moonscape that made the badlands

unsuited for crops but ideal for cattle grazing. The badlands of North Dakota are twice as old as South Dakota's, so they are more rounded and less sharp geographically, have more vegetation on the buttes, and attract more wildlife than their cousins to the south.

That wildlife (bison, elk and feral horses) is one of the main draws of the park's South Unit, largely thanks to the prairie dogs that keep the grass short and growing, which is also good for grazing. Unfortunately, erosion washed away part of the roadway that created a loop around the unit, but the park still offers a very worthwhile out-and-back drive. Roosevelt's North Unit is best known for its scenery and its solitude, and a day trekking its backcountry trails or remote gravel roads can be uninterrupted by any other humans. The area is also more stunning than the South Unit. The Little Missouri River, one of a few waterways to flow north, creates a true riparian forest with cottonwood trees that regenerate naturally because the river isn't dammed.

AVERAGE HIGH/LOW TEMPERATURES					
JAN.	FEB.	MAR.	APR.	MAY	JUNE
27/1	34/8	43/18	58/30	71/40	79/50
JULY	AUG.	SEPT.	OCT.	NOV.	DEC.
87/55	87/52	75/41	62/30	43/17	32/7

Planning

When to Go

The park is open year-round, but North Dakota winters can be extremely cold and windy. Portions of some roads close during winter months, depending on snowfall. Rangers discontinue their outdoor programs when autumn comes, and they recommend that only experienced hikers do any winter explorations. Check the park's website for current conditions.

■ TIP➜ **Although July and August tend to be the busiest months, the park is rarely crowded.** About 750,000 people visit each year, with the South Unit receiving the greatest number of visitors. The best times to see wildlife and hike comfortably are May through October. The park is all but desolate December through February, but it's a beautiful time to see the wildlife—also, winter sunsets can be very vivid as the colors reflect off the snow and ice. The park gets an average of 30 inches of snow per year.

Killdeer Mountain Roundup Rodeo. Begun in 1923, this is North Dakota's oldest rodeo sanctioned by the Professional Rodeo Cowboys Association. The community goes all out, hosting a parade, street dance, community barbecue, and fireworks displays on July 3 and 4. ⊕ killdeermountainrounduprodeo.com.

Dakota Nights Astronomy Festival. Without light pollution from nearby towns, Theodore Roosevelt National Park is ideal for astronomical observation any cloudless night of the year. To enjoy the stars with others, come during the annual Dakota Nights Astronomy Festival in September (dates vary). Check the park website for a current schedule, which includes day and evening activities in the park and in the town of Medora. ⊕ www.nps.gov/thro

Getting Here and Around

AIR

Planes fly into Bismarck, North Dakota (147 miles east of park's South Unit along Interstate 94), and Billings, Montana (295 miles west). There's also some service to even smaller airports in the North Dakota towns of Dickinson (50 miles east) and Williston (60 miles north of North Unit, 140 miles north of South Unit).

CAR

Despite its somewhat remote location, getting to and from the park is relatively easy. The South Unit entrance and visitor center is just off Interstate 94 in the tiny but lively town of Medora at Exits 24 and 27. The Painted Canyon Visitor Center is 7 miles east of Medora on Interstate 94 at Exit 32. The North Unit entrance is south of Williston and Watford City on U.S. 85 and Interstate 94.

There's ample parking space at all trailheads, and parking is free. Some roads are closed in winter. You may encounter bison and other wildlife on the roadway.

Theodore Roosevelt in One Day

With just one day, focus on the South Unit. Arrive early at the **Painted Canyon Scenic Overlook**, near the visitor center, for a sweeping and colorful vista of the canyon's rock formations. Stay awhile to watch the effect of the sun's progress across the sky, or come back in the evening to witness the deepening colors and silhouettes in the fading sunlight.

Continue to the **South Unit Visitor Center** in Medora, spending about an hour here touring the Theodore Roosevelt exhibit and the Maltese Cross Ranch Cabin. Then venture out on the 24-mile **Scenic Drive**. On the way out, stop at all the short, scenic trails, which include Wind Canyon and Coal Vein. After turning around at the Badlands Overlook, where the road ends due to erosion, stop at the Boicourt and Beef Corral Bottom overlooks, where you can gaze at the strange, ever-changing terrain before heading back to the visitor center. When you pass through **Peaceful Valley Ranch**, make sure you stop by the house, barn, and other buildings that were recently rehabilitated, before stopping for lunch—make sure to bring food with you—at the **Cottonwood picnic area**. After lunch, spend a couple of hours hiking **Jones Creek Trail** or **Lower Paddock Creek Trail**.

Return to your car at least an hour before sunset, and drive slowly on the Scenic Drive, to view the wildlife. Plan to be at **Buck Hill** for one of the most spectacular sunsets you'll ever see. Bring a jacket, because it's a bit windy and it gets chilly as the sun sets. After dark, drive carefully out of the park—elk and other animals may still be on the road.

Inspiration

Leave It as It Is: A Journey Through Theodore Roosevelt's American Wilderness, by David Gessner, documents the intrepid president's experiences in the badlands and other wild American places.

The Wilderness Warrior: Theodore Roosevelt and the Crusade for America, by best-selling historian David Brinkley, is an epic, compelling biography of the "naturalist president."

Park Essentials

ACCESSIBILITY
The visitor centers, campgrounds, and historic sites such as Roosevelt's cabin, are all wheelchair accessible, and the film at the South Unit Visitor Center is captioned. The first part of the Little Mo Nature Trail in the North Unit and the ¼-mile Skyline Vista Trail in the South Unit are both paved.

PARK FEES AND PERMITS
The entrance pass is $30 per vehicle, $25 per motorcycle, and $15 for an individual, good for seven days. A variety of annual passes are available. A backcountry permit, free from the visitor centers, is required for overnight camping away from campgrounds.

PARK HOURS
The park is open year-round. The North Unit is in the Central time zone. The South Unit and the Painted Canyon Visitor Center are in the Mountain time zone. Keep the locale in mind when checking schedules for park programs, which reflect these time differences. The South Unit Visitor Center is open year-round. The North Unit Contact Station is open daily April through October, and Thursday

through Sunday the rest of the year; the Painted Canyon Visitor Center operates from early May through late October. Check the park website for current operating hours.

CELL PHONE RECEPTION

Cell phone reception occurs in some areas of the park, but many places receive no signal. Public telephones can be found at the South Unit's Cottonwood Campground and at the Painted Canyon Visitor Center.

Hotels

If you're set on sleeping within the park, be sure to pack your tent. Outside the park are mostly small chain hotels catering to interstate travelers—largely retired couples in RVs and young families in minivans. However, there is a handful of historic properties and working ranches that offer guests a truly Western experience. *Hotel reviews have been shortened. For full information, visit Fodors.com.*

What It Costs			
$	**$$**	**$$$**	**$$$$**
RESTAURANTS			
under $13	$13–$20	$21–$30	over $30
HOTELS			
under $101	$101–$150	$151–$200	over $200

Restaurants

One does not visit Theodore Roosevelt National Park for the fine dining. In fact, the only venues within the park are the picnic areas, and provided you're prepared, this can be a perfectly simple and satisfying way to experience the open spaces and natural wonder of the badlands. In the towns near the park you'll find casual, down-to-earth family establishments that largely cater to the

locals. Expect steak and potatoes, and lots of them. Fortunately, the beef here is among the best in the country. *Restaurant reviews have been shortened. For full information, visit Fodors.com.*

Visitor Information

PARK CONTACT INFORMATION Theodore Roosevelt National Park. ☎ *701/623–4466 South Unit* ⊕ *www.nps.gov/thro.*

North Unit

69 miles north of the South Unit via Hwy 85 and I-94; 11 miles south of Watford City vis Hwy. 85.

Fewer people visit the North Unit (rather than the South Unit) because it's more than an hour's drive off Interstate 94, but that's changing. Visitation has increased from about 10% to 15% of the park's total because more people are searching for a true wilderness experience. The unit's isolated hiking trails offer otherworldly views of stunning buttes, which are also visible along the 28-mile-roundtrip scenic drive. One stop along the drive, the River Bend Overlook, provides expansive views of the Little Missouri floodplain. The Oxbow Overlook, at the halfway point, shows the bend where the river turns to the east.

Sights

PICNIC AREAS
Juniper
LOCAL INTEREST | This area has restrooms, grills, drinking water, and 28 tables (eight with shelter). ⊠ *Theodore Roosevelt National Park* ⊕ *5 miles west of North Unit Visitor Center.*

SCENIC DRIVES
North Unit Scenic Drive
SCENIC DRIVE | The 14-mile, two-way drive follows rugged terrain above spectacular views of the canyons, and is flanked by

Plants and Wildlife in Theodore Roosevelt

The park's landscape is one of prairies marked by cliffs and rock chasms made of alternating layers of sandstone, siltstone, mudstone, and bentonite clay. In spring the prairies are awash with tall grasses, wildflowers, and shrubs including the ubiquitous poison ivy. The pesky plant also inhabits the forests, where you find box elders, ash, and junipers among the trees. To avoid the rash-inducing plant—and scrapes and bruises that may come from rocks and thick undergrowth—it's always advisable to hike with long pants and sturdy boots.

More than 400 American bison live in the park. These normally docile beasts look tame, but with a set of horns, up to a ton of weight, and legs that will carry them at speeds in excess of 35 mph, they could be the most dangerous animals within park boundaries. Rangers tell visitors repeatedly not to approach them. Some mountain lions also live in the park but are rarely seen. The same goes for prairie rattlers.

On the less threatening side of the park's fauna, a herd of more than 200 to 300 elk live in the South Unit. As many as 150 feral horses are also in the South Unit. The North Unit has some longhorn steers, which are often found in the bison corral area, about 2½ miles west of the visitor center.

more than a dozen turnouts with interpretive signs. Notice the slump blocks, massive segments of rock that have slipped down the cliff walls over time. Farther along pass through badlands coulees, deep-water clefts that are now dry. There's a good chance of meeting bison, mule deer, and bighorn sheep along the way, also keep an eye out for longhorn steers, just like the ones you would see in Texas. ⊠ *From unit entrance to Oxbow Overlook, North Unit.*

SCENIC STOPS
Oxbow Overlook
VIEWPOINT | The view from this spot at the end of the North Unit drive looks over the unit's westerly badlands and the Little Missouri River, where it takes a sharp turn east. This is the place to come for stargazing. ⊠ *Theodore Roosevelt National Park ✛ 14 miles west of North Unit Visitor Center.*

River Bend Overlook
VIEWPOINT | The National Park Service calls this the North Unit's most iconic view. Take the short walk off the parking area to see the Little Missouri River floodplain and a 1930s stone shelter. ⊠ *Theodore Roosevelt National Park ✛ Midway through the 28-mile scenic drive.*

Sperati Point
VIEWPOINT | For a great view of the Missouri River's 90-degree angle, hike a 1½-mile round-trip stretch of the much longer Achenbach Trail to this spot 430 feet above the riverbed. ⊠ *Theodore Roosevelt National Park ✛ 14 miles west of North Unit Visitor Center.*

TRAILS
Achenbach Trail
TRAIL | This 18-mile round-trip trail climbs through the Achenbach Hills, descends to the river, and ends at Oxbow Overlook. Check with rangers about river-fording conditions. For a shorter (6-mile) hike to Oxbow, begin at the River Bend Overlook. This is an all-day trail. *Moderate–Difficult.* ⊠ *Theodore Roosevelt National Park ✛ Trailhead: Juniper Campground in the North Unit.*

Buckhorn Trail

TRAIL | FAMILY | A thriving prairie-dog town is just 1 mile from the trailhead of this 11.4-mile round-trip North Unit trail. It travels over level grasslands, then it loops back along the banks of Squaw Creek. If you're an experienced hiker, you'll complete the entire trail in about half a day. Novices or families might want to plan on a whole day, however. *Moderate–Difficult.* ⊠ *Theodore Roosevelt National Park* ✛ *Trailhead: Caprock Coulee Nature Trail, 1½ miles west of Juniper Campground.*

Little Mo Nature Trail

TRAIL | FAMILY | The unpaved but flat outer loop of this 1.1-mile trail passes through badlands and woodlands to the river's edge. The trail's paved 0.7-mile inner loop is wheelchair accessible. It's a great way to see the park's diverse terrain and wildlife, and because it shouldn't take you longer than an hour, it's a great trail for families with children. *Easy.* ⊠ *Theodore Roosevelt National Park* ✛ *Trailhead: Juniper Campground in the North Unit.*

Upper Caprock Coulee Trail

TRAIL | The first ¾-mile of this 4.3-mile round-trip trail takes you along a nature trail. It then loops around the pock-marked lower-badlands coulees. There's a slow incline that takes you up 300 feet. Portions of the trail are slippery. Beginners should plan a half day for this hike. *Moderate–Difficult.* ⊠ *Theodore Roosevelt National Park* ✛ *Trailhead: 8 miles west of North Unit Visitor Center.*

VISITOR CENTERS

North Unit Contact Station

INFO CENTER | While planning for a new visitor center facility is underway, this unit is being housed in temporary trailers. It still offers park information and a park film. Amenities include restrooms and a gift shop. It's open daily between April and October and Friday through Monday the rest of the year. ⊠ *North Unit entrance, off U.S. 85, North Unit* ☎ *701/623-4466* ⊕ *www.nps.gov/thro* 🎫 *Free.*

South Unit

69 miles south of the North Unit via Hwy 85 and I-94.

Visitors who have limited time to spend in Roosevelt should consider visiting only the South Unit because it offers a taste of the park's unique landscapes, wildlife, and rich history. Part of the park's main road closed in 2019 because of erosion and won't reopen for the foreseeable future because major repairs are needed, but it's still possible to see much of the park. The full trip out and back is still 24 miles one way, so it takes about two hours. If you can't afford that amount of time, a must-see stop is the Wind Canyon Trail, 11 miles into the unit. It's a short hike that offers gorgeous views of the river corridor from the top of a butte, a well-known sunset-viewing location, as well as wildlife along the way. The main entrance into the South Unit is on the northwest end of Medora, where the visitors center and Roosevelt's original cabin, the Maltese Cross, are also located.

Sights

HISTORIC SIGHTS

Elkhorn Ranch

NATURE PRESERVE | This remote unit of the park is composed of the 218 acres of ranchland where Theodore Roosevelt ran cattle on the open range. Today there are no buildings, but foundation blocks outline the original structures. ■TIP→ **Visitors who have two to three days in the park or are diehard "Rooseveltians" should make this trek, and then only when it hasn't been raining because most of the route is on unpaved roads; check with visitor center staff about road conditions.** This area truly encapsulates the spirit of why this is called Roosevelt National Park. ⊠ *Theodore Roosevelt National Park* ✛ *35 miles north of South Unit Visitor Center* ☎ *701/623–4466 South Unit* 🎫 *Free.*

Maltese Cross Ranch Cabin

BUILDING | About 7 miles from its original site in the river bottom sits the cabin Theodore Roosevelt commissioned to be built on his Dakota Territory property. Inside is Roosevelt's travel trunk. Interpretive tours are scheduled every day May through August. ⊠ *South Unit entrance, Exits 24 and 27 off I–94* ☎ *701/623–4466 South Unit* ⌨ *Free.*

PICNIC AREAS

Cottonwood

LOCAL INTEREST | This picnic area is in a lovely valley near the river. There are grills, drinking water, restrooms, eight open tables, eight covered tables, and two shelters. ⊠ *Theodore Roosevelt National Park* ✛ *5½ miles north of South Unit Visitor Center.*

Painted Canyon Scenic Overlook

LOCAL INTEREST | This area has eight covered tables, drinking water, restrooms, and a spectacular view. ⊠ *Exit 32 off I–94.*

SCENIC DRIVES

South Unit Scenic Drive

SCENIC DRIVE | A 24-mile, one-way scenic loop takes you past prairie-dog towns, coal veins, trailheads, and panoramic views of the badlands. Information on the park's natural history is posted at the various overlooks—stop at all of the interpretive signs to learn about the park's natural and historical phenomena. Some of the best views can be seen from Boicourt Overlook, Badlands Overlook, Skyline Vista Trail, and Buck Hill. If you hit the road at dusk, be prepared to get caught in a bison jam, as the huge creatures sometimes block the road and aren't in any hurry to move. Don't get out of your car or honk at them—they don't like it. ⊠ *Begins at South Unit Visitor Center in Medora.*

SCENIC STOPS

Badlands Overlook

VIEWPOINT | This stop is a great place to spend time taking in the panoramic view looking north. It's also where the park's main road was closed in 2019 because of erosion, so you'll have to turn around for the 24-mile return trip to the visitor center. ⊠ *Theodore Roosevelt National Park* ✛ *End of the main park road, 24 miles from South Unit Visitor Center.*

Boicourt Overlook

VIEWPOINT | This stop is on the northeast end of the South Unit, so it looks south onto one of the best views of the badlands. There's an easy 15-minute hike, and it's a great place to watch the sunset over the South Unit. ⊠ *Theodore Roosevelt National Park* ✛ *Northeast side of South Unit road.*

★ Buck Hill

VIEWPOINT | At 2,855 feet, this is one of the highest points in the park and provides a spectacular 360-degree view of the badlands. Come here for the sunset. ⊠ *Theodore Roosevelt National Park* ✛ *17 miles east of South Unit Visitor Center.*

Painted Canyon Scenic Overlook

VIEWPOINT | Catch your first glimpse of badlands majesty here—the South Unit canyon's colors change dramatically with the movement of the sun across the sky. ⊠ *South Unit* ✛ *Exit 32 off I–94.*

Petrified Forest

NATURE SITE | Although bits of petrified wood have been found all over the park, the densest collection is in the South Unit's west end, accessible via the Petrified Forest Loop Trail from Peaceful Valley Ranch (10 miles round-trip) or from the park's west boundary (3 miles round-trip), which is the most recommended route ⊠ *Theodore Roosevelt National Park* ✛ *Trailheads: Peaceful Valley Ranch, 7 miles north of South Unit Visitor Center; west boundary, 10 miles north of Exit 23 off I–94/U.S. 10.*

TRAILS

Jones Creek Trail

TRAIL | This out-and-back 7-mile trail runs east-west across the South Unit's Jones Creek with close-up views of the vegetation on the badlands floor. For a longer trek, head south on the Lower Talkington and Lower Paddock Creek trails, which loop back to the park road on the west. *Moderate.* ⊠ *Theodore Roosevelt National Park* ⚕ *Accessible from the west or east side of the park road.*

Lower Paddock Creek Trail

TRAIL | Trail access is located on the west end of the park at one of the South Unit's few public restrooms. The 3½-mile trail runs along Paddock Creek and provides access to a couple of other good hikes. Take the Upper Paddock Creek Trail to the far southeast corner of the South Unit, or head north on the Badlands Spur and Lower Talkington trails and connect with Jones Creek Trail, which loops you back to the west. *Moderate.* ⊠ *Theodore Roosevelt National Park* ⚕ *Trailhead is near the restrooms south of Peaceful Valley Ranch.*

★ Maah Daah Hey Trail

TRAIL | FAMILY | Traversing the full length of the 144-mile Maah Daah Hey Trail is a true multiday wilderness adventure. A popular and well-maintained route, it runs through private and public lands—including the Little Missouri Grasslands and both the North and South units of the national park—with several access points and numerous campgrounds. Maps are available at the park visitor centers and through the U.S. Forest Service and the Maah Daah Hey Trail Association. The 7.1-mile one-way segment that runs through the park's South Unit will take you three or four hours; plan on a full day out and back. *Moderate–Difficult.* ⊠ *Theodore Roosevelt National Park* ⚕ *Trailhead: Sully Creek State Park, 3 miles south of South Unit Visitor Center* ⊕ *mdhta.com.*

Ridgeline Nature Trail

TRAIL | Before heading out along this short (0.6-mile) loop pick up the accompanying map and brochure with information designed to enlighten you on the ecology of the badlands. The first few yards are steep and difficult, and there's a steep descent at the end, but otherwise the trail is even. You'll complete this trail in about a half hour. *Moderate.* ⊠ *Theodore Roosevelt National Park* ⚕ *Trailhead at River Bend Overlook.*

Skyline Vista Trail

TRAIL | This short, wheelchair-accessible trail is one of the first stops on the South Unit's main road after you leave the visitor center. It's on top of a plateau that overlooks the Little Missouri River valley. *Easy.* ⊠ *Theodore Roosevelt National Park* ⚕ *West side of the park road near the visitor center entrance.*

Wind Canyon Trail

TRAIL | This short hike is one of the must-see stops in the South Unit because of the views it offers of the Little Missouri River as well as canyons shaped by the wind. It's also one of the best places to watch a sunset. *Easy.* ⊠ *Theodore Roosevelt National Park* ⚕ *About 11 miles north of the visitor center.*

VISITOR CENTERS

Painted Canyon Visitor Center

INFO CENTER | Easily reached off Interstate 94, this South Unit Visitor Center has an information desk, exhibits, a Theodore Roosevelt Nature and History Association bookstore, a picnic area, restrooms, vending machines, water fountains, and vending phones. ⊠ *South Unit* ⚕ *Exit 32 off I–94* ☎ *701/575–4020* ⊕ *www.nps.gov/thro* 🖾 *Free* ⊘ *Closed late Oct.–early May.*

South Unit Visitor Center

INFO CENTER | This building houses a large auditorium screening the 17-minute film *Refuge of the American Spirit.* There's also an excellent exhibit on Theodore Roosevelt's life with artifacts such as the clothing he wore while ranching in the

Dakota Territory, his firearms, and several writings in his own hand reflecting his thoughts on the nation's environmental resources. Be sure to stop in the Theodore Roosevelt Nature and History Association bookstore. Restrooms and a drinking fountain are also available. ⊠ *Theodore Roosevelt National Park* ✛ *South Unit entrance, Exits 24 and 27 off I–94* ☎ *701/623–4466* ⊕ *www.nps. gov/thro* ✉ *Free*.

Activities

BIKING

Bikes are allowed on interior roads but not off-road. On the multiuse Maah Daah Hey Trail you aren't allowed to ride (or even carry or walk your bike) along the portions of the trails within the park. Alternate cycling routes off this trail include the Buffalo Gap Trail near the park's South Unit and existing roadways outside the North Unit.

Dakota Cyclery Mountain Bike Adventures
BICYCLING | This company rents bikes and provides shuttle service to the Maah Daah Hey Trail, a 144-mile-long trail that connects the north and south units on U.S. Forest Service land. There's a full-service shop with sales and service that's open May to mid-October. ⊠ *365 Main St., Medora* ☎ *701/623–4808*, ⊕ *www.dakotacyclery.com* ✉ *Check out the website for updated prices on fees and services*.

BIRD-WATCHING

Theodore Roosevelt has a recorded 185 observed species of birds and 22 species that are suspected to be in the park but have yet to be observed. Bird-watchers are asked to report to park officials if they spot a bird that is new to the list.

CAMPING

For the adventurous traveler, camping in Theodore Roosevelt is well worth the effort. The unadulterated isolation, epic views, and relationship with nature afforded by the Spartan campgrounds within the park create an experience you'll be hard-pressed to find elsewhere in the United States. Just remember that the park's campgrounds are relatively undeveloped—you'll have to pack in everything you need. If you pick a campsite in the surrounding wilderness, you must obtain a backcountry camping permit (available free) from a visitor center first.

Cottonwood Campground. Nestled under juniper and cottonwood trees on the bank of the Little Missouri River, this is a wonderful place to watch buffalo, elk, and other wildlife drink from the river at sunrise and just before sunset. ⊠ *½ mile north of South Unit Visitor Center* ☎ *701/623–4466*.

Juniper Campground. The sites here are surrounded by junipers, hence the name. Don't be surprised if you see a bison herd wander through on its way to the Little Missouri River. ⊠ *5 miles west of North Unit Visitor Center* ☎ *701/842–2333*.

EDUCATIONAL OFFERINGS
RANGER PROGRAMS
Evening Programs
Rangers host a variety of 15- to 45-minute presentations and discussions on such subjects as park history, astronomy, fires, and wildlife. Also check to see if your visit coincides with one of the park's Full Moon hikes, held several evenings each summer. Look for times and subjects posted at park campgrounds and visitor centers. ⊠ *Cottonwood Campground, South Unit; Juniper Campground, North Unit* ☎ *701/623–4466* ⊕ *www.nps.gov/thro*.

Junior Ranger Adventure
On Saturday from May through August, rangers lead a short hike (just under a mile). Kids also get an activity book and can earn a badge. Bring water; as the route is dusty, wear closed-toe shoes. ⊠ *South Unit Visitor Center* ☎ *701/623–4466* ⊕ *www.nps.gov/thro* ✉ *Free*.

Ranger-Led Talks and Walks

Rangers take visitors on the trails of both units, discussing such subjects as geology, paleontology, wildlife, and natural history. There are also tours of Roosevelt's Maltese Cross Cabin, Geology Talks, and special Bison Chats. Check at campground entrances or at the visitor centers for times, topics, departure points, and destinations. ⊠ *Theodore Roosevelt National Park* ☎ *701/623–4466* ⊕ *www.nps.gov/thro* 🔁 *Free.*

FISHING

Catfish, northern pikes, and saugers are among the underwater inhabitants of the Little Missouri River. If you wish to fish in the park or elsewhere in the state and are over age 16, you must obtain a North Dakota fishing license. For out-of-state residents, a three-day permit is $28, a 10-day permit is $38, and a one-year permit is $48. For in-state residents, a one-year permit is $18.

HIKING

During the summer months, the park is best seen by hiking its many trails. Particularly in the South Unit, there are numerous opportunities to jump on a trail right from the park road. The North and South units are connected by the 144-mile Maah Daah Hey Trail. Backcountry hiking is allowed, but you need a permit (free from any visitor center) to camp in the wild. Park maps are available at all three visitor centers. If you plan to camp overnight, let several people know about where you plan to pitch your tent, and inquire about river conditions, maps, regulations, trail updates, and additional water sources before setting out.

HORSEBACK RIDING

Although there aren't any guided trail rides in the park, you can still see some of its terrain on horseback. If you're traveling with your own animal, the South Unit's Roundup Group Horse Camp has sites that accommodate horse trailers.

It's open May through October and reservations (through ⊕ *recreation.gov*) are required. Be sure to bring enough water for the animals and certified weed-free hay. As horses are allowed only on backcountry trails or cross-country, you'll need a backcountry-use permit. Check with the park about routes. In addition to staying off park roadways and nature trails, avoid picnic areas and developed campgrounds (other than the horse camp), and keep your horse tied securely when it's not being ridden.

Medora Riding Stables

GUIDED TOURS | FAMILY | While you won't ride in Roosevelt National Park on this tour, your trail guide will take you on buttes and canyons around the park that offer spectacular views. Riders must be at least 7 years old and 45 inches tall. Kids 12 and younger have to wear a helmet that's provided. ⌖ *East end of Medora* ☎ *701/623–4444* ⊕ *medora.com.*

Nearby Towns

Medora is the gateway to the park's South Unit and it has plenty of restaurants and places to stay. Roughly 50 miles to the east is **Dickinson** (population 28,000), the largest town near the national park. North of Dickinson and about 35 miles east of the park's North Unit, **Killdeer** (pop. about 825) is known for its Roundup Rodeo—North Dakota's oldest—and its gorgeous scenery. Killdeer is the place to fill your tank, because there isn't another gas station around for 40 miles. **Williston** (pop. about 30,000) is 60 miles north of the North Unit (141 miles from the South Unit), just over the Missouri River. The Amtrak stop nearest to the national park is here.

Medora

To get to the South Unit's visitor center and entrance, you go through the town of Medora (pop. 128), off I-94 exits 24 or 27. Its sole purpose is serving visitors to Roosevelt National Park, with a very intentional Old West feel. The walkable town hosts several museums and restaurants, tiny shops, and places to stay. Its Wild West history is reenacted in a madcap musical production each night in summer. The town's convention and visitors bureau is a great resource, but you can also book lodging, show tickets, horseback riding excursions, and other activities through the nonprofit Theodore Roosevelt Medora Foundation.

VISITOR INFORMATION

Medora Convention & Visitors Bureau. ✉ *475 4th St., Medora* ☎ *701/623–4830* 🌐 *www.medorand.com.* **Theodore Roosevelt Medora Foundation.** ☎ *800/633–6721, 701/623–4444* 🌐 *medora.com.*

Sights

Chateau de Mores State Historic Site

HOUSE | The French nobleman for whom the chateau is named erected this 26-room hunting cabin in 1883 with his wife, Medora, for whom the town was named. He also built a meatpacking plant and encouraged other cattle ranchers to settle in the area. Though their cattle empire was never realized, the couple hosted extravagant hunting parties and even entertained Theodore Roosevelt during his Dakota ranching days. You can tour the restored chateau between May and October, when weekend history programs and carriage rides are also offered. The site's interpretive center is open year-round. ✉ *3426 Chateau Rd., Medora* ☎ *701/623–4355* 🌐 *www.history.nd.gov/historicsites/chateau* 🎫 *$10 adults; $3 children* 🕓 *Closed mid-Oct.–Apr.*

North Dakota Cowboy Hall of Fame

MUSEUM | This museum features six galleries and rotating exhibits, hosts special events, and is dedicated to the horse culture of the plains. ✉ *250 Main St., Medora* ☎ *701/623–2000* 🌐 *www.northdakotacowboy.com* 🎫 *$9.*

Restaurants

Boots Bar and Grill

$$ | STEAKHOUSE | FAMILY | This watering hole has Medora's largest tavern, an upstairs dining room, and breezy patios, as well as live music, dancing, and microbrews. Diners feast primarily on pizzas, burgers, and steak, and it's kid-friendly until 10 pm. **Known for:** good burgers; lively atmosphere; family-friendly. [$] *Average main: $20* ✉ *300 Pacific Ave., Medora* ☎ *701/623–2668* 🌐 *www.bootsbarmedora.com* 🕓 *Closed Dec.–Apr.*

Cowboy Cafe

$ | AMERICAN | This locally owned-and-operated café specializes in homemade soups, caramel rolls, and delicious roast beef sandwiches and chicken-fried steak. Be prepared for a (short) wait, since the cozy dining room is popular with both locals and visitors. **Known for:** great breakfast and lunch spot; cash-only; local flavor. [$] *Average main: $10* ✉ *215 4th St., Medora* ☎ *701/623–4343* 💳 *No credit cards* 🕓 *Closed Nov.–May.*

Pitchfork Steak Fondue

$$$ | AMERICAN | Steaks are prepared on the tines of pitchforks in classic Western style. A full buffet accompanies the meat, all of it served with a view of the badlands and live musical entertainment. **Known for:** authentic experience; family-friendly; good value for money. [$] *Average main: $30* ✉ *Tjaden Terrace, 3422 Chateau Rd., Medora* ☎ *701/623–4444, 800/633–6721* 🌐 *medora.com* 🕓 *Closed mid-Sept.–late-May. No lunch.*

★ Theodore's

$$$$ | AMERICAN | Theodore's offers the best fine dining in Medora and, perhaps, in western North Dakota. The lunch menu features salads, prime-rib sandwiches, and buffalo burgers, while dinner fare includes shrimp with lemon risotto, a hickory-seasoned rib eye, and tenderloin with Gorgonzola cream sauce. **Known for:** great service; varied menu; convenient location. $ *Average main: $45 ☒ Rough Riders Hotel, 301 3rd Ave., Medora ☎ 701/623–4433, 800/633–6721 ⊕ medora.com ☉ Closed Labor Day–Memorial Day.*

Hotels

AmericInn by Wyndham Medora

$$$ | HOTEL | A Western theme, complete with mounted animals, dominates the public areas of this contemporary hotel. **Pros:** near shops and restaurants; indoor pool; ideal after long hikes in the park. **Cons:** right on the railroad tracks; on the pricey side; chain-hotel feel. $ *Rooms from: $190 ☒ 75 E. River Rd. S, Medora ☎ 701/623–4800, ⊕ www.wyndhamhotels.com/americinn ⊅ 78 rooms ⦿ Free Breakfast.*

Buffalo Gap Guest Ranch and Steakhouse

$$ | RESORT | With a great view of the Badlands 8 miles west of Medora, this rustic property has access to the Maah Daah Hey Trail. **Pros:** great prices on lodging and food; exceptional view; large outdoor patio. **Cons:** 10 minutes from town; in need of facelift; very basic. $ *Rooms from: $150 ☒ 3100 Buffalo Gap Rd., Medora ☎ 701/623–4200 ⊕ www.buffalogapguestranch.com ⊅ 27 cabins, 50 RV sites ⦿ No meals.*

★ Rough Riders Hotel

$$$$ | HOTEL | Renovations over the years have made this place decidedly posh, but the historic section, which includes eight rooms, retains the red velvet chairs, antique armoires, and iron-rod and oak bed frames that have made this property a favorite for decades. **Pros:** historic, downtown location; dining on the premises; updated property with charming details. **Cons:** relatively expensive; occasional railroad noise; no on-site pool. $ *Rooms from: $230 ☒ 301 3rd Ave., Medora ☎ 701/623–4444, 800/633–6721 ⊕ medora.com ⊅ 76 rooms ⦿ No meals.*

🎭 Performing Arts

Burning Hills Amphitheatre

ARTS CENTERS | FAMILY | This seven-story amphitheater, located 1 mile west of Medora, is the area's most beloved performance space, hosting all kinds of concerts and performances. If you sit near the top, you can enjoy the best panoramic view of the badlands. ☒ *3422 Chateau Rd., Medora ☎ 701/623–4444, 800/633–6721 ⊕ medora.com.*

Medora Musical

THEATER | FAMILY | Well worth your while in summer is this theatrical tribute to the Old West, its history, and its personalities. It's been in operation for five decades and is held nightly early June through early September at the 2,852-seat, open-air Burning Hills Amphitheater. Doors open at 6:45; the show starts at 7:30. Book tickets in advance through the Theodore Roosevelt Medora Foundation, or stop by the Ticket Junction or Medora Musical Welcome Center on the day of the show. ☒ *3422 Chateau Rd., Medora ☎ 701/623–4444, 800/633–6721 ⊕ medora.com ⊠ From $43.*

🛍 Shopping

Prairie Fire Pottery

CERAMICS/GLASSWARE | The stoneware pottery and terra-cotta tiles made by local potter Tama Smith are prized for their high, high-fired-glaze colors reminiscent of the rugged badlands, blazing sunsets, and brilliant prairie skies of western North Dakota. The shop is just a mile off Interstate 94, in the small town of Beach. Studio tours are available.

✉ *127 Main St. E, Beach* ☎ *701/872–3855*
⊕ *www.prairiefirepottery.com.*

Sacajawea Trading Post

GIFTS/SOUVENIRS | This shop specializes in
artwork, gifts (including Montana silver),
and food items. Next door at the White
House, owned by the same proprietor,
you can shop for clothing, jewelry, shoes,
and other accessories. ✉ *245 Broadway,
Medora* ☎ *701/623–5050.*

Western Edge Books, Artwork, Music

BOOKS/STATIONERY | For books on Western
regional history, legend, and lore as well
as natural history and other topics, stop
by this bookstore in downtown Medora.
✉ *425 4th St., Medora* ☎ *701/623–4345*
⊕ *www.westernedgebooks.com.*

Activities

CAMPING

Bar X Guest Ranch. Catering to horseback
riding, mountain biking, and hiking enthusiasts, this guest ranch and campground
is 9 miles south of Medora via West
River Road and adjacent to the Maah
Daah Hey Trail. On cool nights, soothe
your muscles in the hot tub. ✉ *3566 W.
River Rd., 9 miles south of town, Medora*
☎ *701623–4300* ⊕ *barxguestranch.com
20 tent/RV sites, 5 cabins.*

Medora Campground. This shaded campground in west Medora is within walking
distance of downtown. Basketball and vol-
leyball courts are nearby. ✉ *195 3rd Ave.,
off Pacific Ave., Medora* ☎ *701/623–4444
or 800/633–6721* ⊕ *medora.com/stay/
camping/medora-campground/ 200 tent/
RV sites (105 with hookups).*

Red Trail Campground. Live country music is
performed every night from June through
Labor Day in front of the store at this
campground six blocks from downtown
Medora. It was built especially for RVs.
✉ *Red Trail St., off East River Rd. S, Medora* ☎ *701/623–4317 or 800/621–4317 120
tent/RV sites (110 with hookups).*

Dickinson

*About 50 miles to the east of the South
Unit.*

Dickinson (pop. 23,000) is the largest city
near the South Unit. It's home to a dozen
hotel chains as well as numerous local
restaurants that offer a variety of menus.
Several museums and other points
of interest offer history on the area's
agriculture and North Dakota's prehistoric
past, including the Badlands Dinosaur
Museum, part of the Dickinson Museum
Center, and the Theodore Roosevelt
Center at Dickinson State University.

VISITOR INFORMATION

Dickinson Convention and Visitors Bureau.
✉ *72 E. Museum Dr., Dickinson*
☎ *701/483–4988* ⊕ *www.visitdickinson.
com.*

 ## Sights

Badlands Dinosaur Museum

MUSEUM | FAMILY | A huge triceratops—
whose complete skull was excavated
in 1992 west of Dickinson—greets you
at the entrance of this museum, which
houses dozens of dinosaur bones, fossilized plants and seashells, and rocks and
minerals collected from around the world.
The museum, which is part of the greater
12-acre Dickinson Museum Center complex with the Joachim Regional Museum, Prairie Outpost Park, and Pioneer
Machinery Hall, has North Dakota's largest
dinosaur display. ✉ *188 Museum Dr. E,
Dickinson* ☎ *701/456–6225* ⊕ *dickinson-
museumcenter.com* 🎟 *$6.*

Little Missouri National Grasslands

NATURE PRESERVE | This is the largest and
most diverse of 19 national grasslands in
the western United States, spanning a
million acres in western North Dakota. It takes three hours to complete a
self-guided 58-mile driving tour known
as the Custer Auto Trail, beginning and
ending in Medora. The best time to

see wildlife is in early morning or late afternoon. Don't forget a camera and binoculars. In addition to stretches of the lengthy Maah Daah Hey Trail, which runs through the grasslands, there are seven designated trails, and back-country hiking is permitted. Little Missouri Grassland trails are open to all nonmotorized activities, including horseback riding and cycling as well as hiking. For a copy of the driving tour and trail maps, contact the U.S. Forest Service office in Dickinson or the South Unit Visitor Center. ⊠ *U.S. Forest Service, 99 23rd Ave. W, Dickinson* ☎ *701/227–7800* ⊕ *www. fs.usda.gov/dpg* 🎫 *Free.*

Roadside Art

PUBLIC ART | Known as the "Enchanted Highway," this self-guided 30-mile driving tour east of Dickinson features seven giant metal sculptures designed by a local artist, including a 51-foot Teddy Roosevelt. Massive sculptures include a deer crossing, grasshopper family, pheasants on the prairie, a 150-foot-long gaggle of geese, and a tin family with a 45-foot father, 44-foot mother, and 23-foot son. ⊠ *Exit 72 off I–94, Dickinson* ☎ *701/563–6400, 701/483–4988 to Dickinson Convention and Visitors Bureau* 🎫 *Free.*

Hotels

Roosevelt Grand Dakota Hotel

$ | **HOTEL** | Across from the Prairie Hills Mall, this three-story hotel lets you relax on couches before the fireplace in the huge lobby, and the mezzanine overlooks the pool. **Pros:** on-site grill offers steaks, burgers and pizza; great customer service. **Cons:** can be busy; pool can be quite popular, particularly in the summer. 🟍 *Rooms from: $99* ⊠ *532 15th St. W, Dickinson* ☎ *701/483–5600,* ⊕ *www. bestwestern.com* 🛏 *192 rooms* ¶⊘ *No meals.*

Killdeer

About 35 miles east of the North Unit.

North of Dickinson, Killdeer (pop. 894) is known for its Mountain Roundup Rodeo—North Dakota's oldest—and its gorgeous scenery. The rodeo is held over the Fourth of July weekend and features the usual horse-riding competitions as well as a street dance and fireworks display.

VISITOR INFORMATION

City of Killdeer. ⊠ *165 Railroad St., Killdeer* ☎ *701/764–5295* ⊕ *www.killdeer.com.*

Sights

Little Missouri State Park

NATIONAL/STATE PARK | Called *Makoshika* or "Bad Land" by the Sioux, the Little Missouri State Park has unusual land formations that create the state's most awe-inspiring scenery. The beehive-shaped rock formations resulted from the erosion of sedimentary rock deposited millions of years ago by streams flowing from the Rocky Mountains. Undeveloped and rugged, this wilderness area has both primitive and modern camping and 50 miles of horse trails. ⊠ *Killdeer* ⊕ *Off Rte. 22, 18 miles north and 2 miles east of Killdeer* ☎ *701/764–5256, 701/794–3731 winter* ⊕ *www.parkrec.nd.gov/parks/ lmosp/lmosp.html* 🎫 *$7 per vehicle* ⊘ *Closed Nov.–Apr.*

Activities

CAMPING

East View Campground. Deer and wild turkey are your neighbors in this extremely secluded campground with incredible views of buttes and badlands. Sites are first come, first served. ⊠ *10456 10th St.NW, Killdeer* ☎ *701764–8000* ⊕ *www.badlandstrailrides.com 15 tent/ RV sites (10 with full hookups).*

Williston

60 miles north of the North Unit.

Just over the Missouri River, this on-again, off-again oil boom town (pop. 29,000) offers a wide variety of lodging and restaurant options. Families looking for a break from travel and sight-seeing will appreciate the ARC, a recreational park. This is also where the Amtrak stop nearest to the national park is located.

VISITOR INFORMATION

Williston Convention and Visitors Center. ✉ *212 Airport Rd., Williston* ☎ *701/774–9041, 800/615–9041* 🌐 *www.visitwilliston.com.*

👁 Sights

Fort Buford State Historic Site

MILITARY SITE | Built in 1866 near the confluence of the Missouri and Yellowstone rivers, this military post was the site of Sitting Bull's surrender in 1881. In summer, you can take a self-guided tour of the restored officers' quarters as well as the unusual, sometimes humorous, tombstones in the soldiers' cemetery. The site grounds and adjoining Missouri-Yellowstone Confluence Interpretive Center are open year-round. ✉ *15349 39th La. NW, Williston* ☎ *701/572–9034* 🌐 *www.history.nd.gov/historicsites/buford/index.html* 🎫 *$5* ⏲ *Closed early Sept.–late May (except by appointment).*

Fort Union Trading Post National Historic Site

MEMORIAL | Built by John Jacob Astor's American Fur Company, the fort was the most important fur and bison hide trading center on the upper Missouri River between 1828 and 1867. Walk around the reconstructed grounds, which include the Trade House, teepees, and the reconstructed palisade and three-story bastions of Fort Union. Follow the easy 1-mile trail to Bodmer Overlook, named for the artist Karl Bodmer, who painted the fort from this vantage point in the early 1830s. June sees a traditional Rendezvous, with fur-trade reenactors and period music, crafts, and other demonstrations. In early August, the site also hosts a Native American arts showcase and a traditional powwow. ✉ *15550 Hwy. 1804, Williston* ☎ *701/572–9083* 🌐 *www.nps.gov/fous* 🎫 *Free.*

🍴 Restaurants

Dakota Farms

$ | **AMERICAN** | **FAMILY** | With a local reputation for fair prices and good service, Dakota Farms serves breakfast all day and all-you-can-eat fish on Friday. It has a kids' menu, and no alcohol is served. **Known for:** comfort food; good value for money; local chain with four North Dakota locations. [$] *Average main: $11* ✉ *1906 2nd Ave. W, Williston* ☎ *701/572–4480* 🌐 *www.facebook.com/dakotafarmswilliston.*

Gramma Sharon's Cafe

$ | **AMERICAN** | For great omelets and other breakfast fare, try Gramma's. Locals go for the biscuits and gravy, as well as the burgers. **Known for:** great service; generous portions; very family-friendly. [$] *Average main: $10* ✉ *1501 16th St. W, Williston* ☎ *701/572–1412* ⏲ *No dinner.*

Chapter 34

WHITE SANDS NATIONAL PARK

Updated by
Andrew Collins

NEW
MEXICO

☁ Camping	🛏 Hotels	🏃 Activities	👁 Scenery	🎎 Crowds
★★★☆☆	★★☆☆☆	★★☆☆☆	★★★★★	★★★★☆

WELCOME TO
WHITE SANDS NATIONAL PARK

TOP REASONS TO GO

★ **Wander the dunes:** Slip off your shoes and walk—or run—barefoot up and down snow-white-colored gypsum dunes, some as high as 60 feet.

★ **Walk with a ranger:** The best way to understand this peculiar landscape and its amazing geology is by taking one of the park's popular ranger-led hikes—the nightly sunset strolls are especially fun.

★ **Hit the boardwalk:** Lined with fascinating interpretative signs, the short and scenic Interdune Boardwalk Trail is fully accessible for wheelchairs and strollers.

★ **Lunch with a view:** Enjoy lunch at one of the dozens of covered mid-century-modern-style shelters with tables and grills, set among three dune-side picnic areas along the park's main drive.

★ **Go sledding:** Buy a plastic sled from the park gift shop and hit the slopes—you'll get the hang of sledding down these soaring dunes in no time.

1 Dunes Drive. An attraction in its own right, this 8-mile loop route—part of it with a hard-packed white-sand surface—also accesses all of the park's sites and attractions, starting with the visitor center and continuing past all of the picnic areas and trailheads.

Lake Lucero

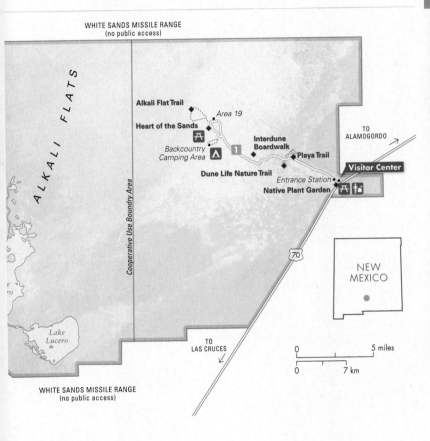

WHITE SANDS MISSILE RANGE
(no public access)

ALKALI FLATS

Alkali Flat Trail

Area 19

Heart of the Sands

Backcountry
Camping Area

Interdune
Boardwalk

1

Playa Trail

Dune Life Nature Trail

Entrance Station

Native Plant Garden

Visitor Center

TO
ALAMOGORDO

Cooperative Use Boundry Area

Lake
Lucero

WHITE SANDS MISSILE RANGE
(no public access)

70

NEW
MEXICO

TO
LAS CRUCES

0   5 miles

0   7 km

Stretching across a 275-square-mile swath of the Tularosa Basin, half of it protected within the national park, this surreal landscape is the largest gypsum dune field on earth. Located in the northern tip of the Chihuahuan Desert and framed by dramatic mountain ranges, White Sands National Park shimmers beneath the big, blue southern New Mexico sky. A wonderland for photographers, it's also a playground for outdoors lovers who come for dune-sledding, hiking, and picnicking—you can even pitch a tent and camp beneath the region's dark, starry canopy.

Indigenous tribes began farming in the Tularosa Basin following the end of the last Ice Age some 11,000 years ago, and European Americans arrived in the late 19th century. By the 1940s, the U.S. military had discovered a new use for this isolated landscape: testing weapons. On July 16, 1945, scientists from New Mexico's Los Alamos National Laboratory detonated the first atomic bomb in a lonely, arid patch of desert about 75 miles north of the park, now known as the Trinity Site. The site is part of the vast White Sands Missile Range, which forms the park's western border and still conducts missile tests that result in the temporary closure of both the park and a stretch of U.S. 70—these pauses usually take place for about an hour or two, up to twice a week. Holloman Air Force Base is just beyond the range.

As the region's military importance grew, so too did the reputation of its astounding white dunes, which began to draw tourists from far and near. The dunes also drew commercial interest, as mining companies saw the potential value in extracting the vast stores of gypsum sand, the primary ingredient in plaster and wallboard. Conservationists ultimately convinced the federal government of the need to protect this unique natural resource, and in 1933, President Herbert Hoover designed White Sands National Monument. In December 2019, White Sands achieved full national park status.

AVERAGE HIGH/LOW TEMPERATURES					
JAN.	**FEB.**	**MAR.**	**APR.**	**MAY**	**JUNE**
57/22	63/27	71/32	79/40	88/50	97/59
JULY	**AUG.**	**SEPT.**	**OCT.**	**NOV.**	**DEC.**
97/64	94/62	89/55	79/41	67/28	57/21

Visitors who spend even a couple of hours exploring the undulating white-sand dunes often come away transformed by the experience. Beyond the sheer grandeur of the endless dunes, one of the park's most amazing attributes is that it supports a habitat of plants and animals that can be found only here. These flora and fauna have thrived through ingenious adaptation—sand verbena that spread its seeds quickly, shrubs with dense root systems that take hold in the sand, and lizards and mice whose light coloring both camouflage and cool them down amid the shifting white dunes. As enormous as it is, White Sands is a relatively straightforward park to visit, as the portion of it accessible to the public is relatively small and can be fully experienced in a full day. A single 8-mile park road leads through the heart of the park, which has only a handful of marked trails and no lodgings or restaurants—just a gift shop that also sells a few snacks. You will find an impressive visitor center, however, that's noteworthy both for its historic Pueblo Revival design and the engaging exhibits in its museum.

Planning

When to Go

White Sands National Park is a year-round destination, but summer can be uncomfortably hot at midday, when temperatures can climb into the 90s and 100s. Try to plan your mid-June–mid-September visits for morning or late afternoon, keeping in mind that thunderstorms are common late in the day in summer. Days are temperate and sunny throughout the winter, but from December to February nights are often below freezing, and it does snow here occasionally—usually not more than an inch or two, once or twice a year. Seeing snow over the white sand adds an extra layer of surrealness.

FESTIVALS AND EVENTS

Hatch Green Chile Festival. Green chiles are New Mexico's signature food, and those produced in the small town of Hatch, about 35 miles north of Las Cruces, are said to be the tastiest anywhere. You can try them during this late August weekend party featuring a carnival, beer and chile-roasting gardens, and lots of great food. ⊕ www.hatchchilefest.com.

Los Cruces Wine Festival. During this late May event, you can taste for yourself why New Mexico's reputation as an emerging winemaking region continues to grow. ⊕ www.nmwine.com.

Southern NM State Fair. One of the largest agricultural fairs in the southwest, this family-friendly event with a rodeo, amusements, and live music takes place in Las Cruces at the end of September. ⊕ www.snmstatefairgrounds.net.

Trinity Site Tour. Typically twice a year, once in April and again in October, you can visit the spot at the northern end of White Sands Missile Range where a nuclear device was detonated for the first time in history. ⊕ www.wsmr.army.mil/Trinity.

White Sands Hot Air Balloon Invitational.
The park's brilliant white landscape is all the more striking when dozens of colorful hot-air balloons soar overhead during this weekend festival each September. ⊕ *www.alamogordo.com.*

Getting Here and Around

AIR
The nearest major airport to the park is in El Paso, about 100 miles south, and it's served by all major airlines and car rental companies. Another option is Albuquerque, 225 miles north.

CAR
The entrance to White Sands is along a well-traveled four-lane highway, U.S. 70, about an hour's drive northeast of Las Cruces and a 20-minute drive southwest of Alamogordo, which is also where you'll find the nearest gas stations and other services.

Inspiration

Among the several photo books that have been produced about the park, *Into The Great White Sands,* by Craig Varjabedian, is particularly impressive.

The Geology of Southern New Mexico's Parks, Monuments, and Public Lands (GSNM), published by the New Mexico Bureau of Geology and Mineral Resources, conveys a thorough understanding of how White Sands formed and came to look as it does today. It's also a great resource for learning about the many other remarkable parks and natural attractions in the southern half of the state.

The singularly surreal landscape of White Sands has appeared in countless films, fashion shoots, and music videos (Solange's 2016 "Cranes in the Sky" video is but one memorable example of the latter). You can see the park in the 1950 adventure film *King Solomon's Mines,* which one a Best Color Cinematography Oscar, as well as in 2007's *Transformers,* but its most striking and inventive use is its appearance as the distant home planet of Thomas Newton (played by David Bowie), in Nicolas Roeg's 1976 sci-fi yarn, *The Man Who Fell to Earth.*

Park Essentials

ACCESSIBILITY
The park's gift shop and visitor center are fully accessible for wheelchairs, and there are several accessible tables and vault toilets at the three designated picnic areas. Most importantly, the outstanding Interdune Boardwalk Trail is fully accessible and provides an up-close view of some of the park's biggest dunes.

PARK FEES AND PERMITS
The park fee of $25 per vehicle, $20 per motorcycle, and $15 per pedestrian or cyclist is good for one week and payable at the entrance station to Dunes Drive; there's no fee just to enter the visitor center and see its exhibits. Backcountry camping is $3 nightly per person.

PARK HOURS
The park is open year-round except on Christmas Day, and the gate opens each morning at 7. It closes in the evening generally between 6 and 9 pm, depending on the season (later in summer, earlier in winter). Visitor center hours are 9–5 most of the year, but until 6 pm from Memorial Day to early September. The park is in the Mountain time zone.

CELL PHONE RECEPTION
Cell coverage is generally good around the visitor center and the first few miles of Dunes Drive, but the signal fades a bit the farther into the park you go, depending on your carrier.

Hotels

There are no hotels or RV/car camping sites within White Sands National Park. The nearest accommodations are 20 minutes away in Alamogordo, but an hour away in Las Cruces you'll find many more options. *Hotel reviews have been shortened. For full information, visit Fodors.com. For additional lodging options near the park, see Hotels in Guadalupe Mountains National Park.*

What It Costs			
$	$$	$$$	$$$$
RESTAURANTS			
under $16	$16–$22	$23–$30	over $30
HOTELS			
under $120	$120–$180	$181–$240	over $240

Restaurants

The park has no restaurants or markets, just a gift shop with a very limited selection of packaged snacks. It's a 20-minute drive to the nearest dining options and grocery stores in Alamogordo. *Restaurant reviews have been shortened. For full information, visit Fodors.com. For additional dining options near the park, see Restaurants in Guadalupe Mountains National Park.*

Visitor Information

CONTACTS White Sands National Park.
✉ 19955 U.S. 70 W, Alamogordo ☎ 575/479–6124 ⊕ www.nps.gov/whsa.

Dunes Drive

16 miles southwest of Alamogordo, 52 miles northeast of Las Cruces.

This 8-mile loop drive provides access to all of the park's attractions, from the visitor center at the start of the road to several hiking trails and three picnic areas. Just making your way along this road, which has a hard-packed white-sand surface along the section in the heart of the park, is great fun and yields astonishing views.

◉ Sights

PICNIC AREAS
Primrose and Roadrunner Picnic Areas
LOCAL INTEREST | These two picnic areas adjoin one another on the northeast side of Dunes Drive, right after the road becomes one-way. You'll find rows of covered metal picnic tables with grills, and great views east toward the Sacramento Mountains. ✉ *Northeast side of Dunes Dr., Alamogordo.*

Yucca Picnic Area
LOCAL INTEREST | You come to this large picnic area toward the end of the one-way section of Dunes Drive, a good spot for a meal after hiking the Alkali Flat Trail or climbing and sledding on the larger dunes on this side of park drive. The picnic tables here are covered and have grills. ✉ *Southwest side of Dunes Dr., Alamogordo.*

SCENIC DRIVES
★ **Dunes Drive**
SCENIC DRIVE | FAMILY | This gorgeous drive through the heart of White Sands accesses virtually every part of the park that's accessible to visitors, including all of the trails and picnic areas. It's an 8-mile drive from the visitor center and entrance gate to the one-way loop at the end. The first 5 miles are paved, and as you

White Sands National Park in One Day

You can enjoy and get a good sense of the park in as little as a couple of hours, and in a full day you can fully acquaint yourself with this strange, spectacular landscape.

Before making your way here, pack a cooler with picnic supplies and drinks, as there are no dining options and only very limited snacks available in the park gift shop. When you arrive, spend an hour or so at the historic **White Sands Visitor Center**, watching the short film about the park and checking out the well-designed and informative exhibits. Go for a short stroll through the **Native Plant Garden**, which is next to the visitor center, and then drop by the adjacent park gift shop to buy a plastic sled if you don't already have one.

Make your way along the park's scenic main road, **Dunes Drive**. A little over 2 miles after paying your fee at the entrance station, you'll come to the parking area for the short and enjoyable **Dune Life Nature Trail**, a 1-mile loop with interpretative signs that'll also provide you with the first up-close look at the stunning white dunes. Continue a short way along Dunes Drive to **Interdune Boardwalk Trail**, a very short and level wheelchair- and stroller-friendly trail that offers a look at some of the larger

dunes for which the park is known. Afterward, as you continue your drive you'll soon reach the unpaved section of the road, and this is where the otherwordly whiteness of the landscape truly takes hold. Just after entering the one-way section of Dunes Drive, pull over and enjoy that hopefully extensive lunch you packed earlier and eat it at one of the two adjacent picnic areas, Primrose or Roadrunner.

In the early afternoon, continue around the one-way Dunes Drive loop to the parking area for the **Alkali Flat Trail**. You have a couple of options here, depending on your energy level. You can undertake the full 5-mile Alkali Flat loop hike, keeping in mind that this is a somewhat strenuous undertaking. Or just stay closer by and scamper among the huge dunes that rise above the edge of the parking area. This is a great place to try out that sled you bought (be sure to wax it first) at the gift shop. If you'd stayed long enough, about an hour before sunset, make your way to the marked meeting area (4.7 miles north of the entrance station) to join a ranger-led **Sunset Stroll**. These free hour-long rambles go at a relaxed pace and are a great way to learn about everything you've been viewing and exploring throughout the day.

make your way from the park entrance, the landscape becomes steadily more dominated by higher and whiter dunes, until you reach the final 3 miles, which are unpaved along smooth, hard-packed gypsum. This is where the experience starts to feel truly surreal, as it's easy to feel as though you're driving through a winter wonderland—the gypsum really does look like snow (which feels

particularly odd if you're driving this route on a hot summer day). You'll come to the Primrose and Roadrunner picnic areas, on the right, as you enter the one-way loop portion of Dunes Drive, and you'll come to several larger parking areas that access some of the park's biggest dunes as the road curves back around at the Alkali Flat Trailhead. It takes only about 45 minutes to drive the entire route, round-trip, but you'll want to stop and explore the dunes on foot. Part of the fun is watching park visitors, especially kids, riding sleds down the dunes. Groups of friends and families also regularly come and set up tents and umbrellas on the dunes nearest the parking areas and bask in the sun all day. It's quite a sight. Do obey speed limits, which are 45 mph as you enter but drop to 15 mph along the unpaved loop in areas with lots of pedestrian traffic. It may look tempting to zip around, but the sand can get slippery, and the road curves in places, limiting visibility. ⊠ *Alamogordo.*

SCENIC STOPS

Native Plant Garden

GARDEN | FAMILY | Located in front of the park visitor center, which is outside the entrance station (and thus free of charge), this small garden that's especially colorful and fragrant from mid-March through November (even more so after it rains) provides an up-close look at plant life—including soaptree yucca, ocotillos, myriad wildflowers, and cottonwood trees (which have beautiful foliage in autumn)—that's native to the Chihuahuan Desert. You can download a plant guide from the park website or pick one up in the visitor center. ⊠ *White Sands Visitor Center, Alamogordo* ☎ *505/479–6124.*

TRAILS

★ Alkali Flat Trail

TRAIL | The park's most ambitious trail is arguably its most rewarding, too, as it crosses an ancient lakebed now piled high with dunes, and once you're about a mile into it, it can feel as though you're on another planet, as you'll see almost nothing but white sand. Despite the name, it's actually an undulating 5-mile round-trip route over sometimes quite steep dunes. It's not the distance that makes it challenging but those hills, and that walking on dunes is slower going, and more taxing—especially in summer—than over conventional terrain. Along the way, you'll cross ridges and

pinnacles, and see some of the biggest dunes in the park. Pack lots of water, hike with at least one buddy, and keep an eye out for the bright red trail markers—it can be easy to get disoriented if there's a lot of wind (common in spring), which can greatly reduce visibility. *Difficult.* ⊠ *Alamogordo* ✛ *Trailhead: just past the 8-mile mark of Dunes Dr.*

★ Dune Life Nature Trail

TRAIL | FAMILY | Give yourself about an hour to complete this 1-mile self-guided loop trail that, while short, does climb over a couple of pretty tall dunes. This hike offers an interesting contrast with other parts of the park, as there's quite a lot of flora along it—you can really learn about the unusual plants that thrive in this harsh environment. Keep an eye out for the series of 14 interpretive signs that discuss the foxes, birds, reptiles, and other wildlife that live in the park. *Easy– Moderate.* ⊠ *Alamogordo* ✛ *Trailhead: 2.3 miles north of entrance station on Dunes Dr.*

★ Interdune Boardwalk

TRAIL | FAMILY | Along this easy 0.4-mile boardwalk trail, the only one in the park fully accessible to wheelchairs and strollers, you can read about the park's fascinating geology and ecosystem at 10 different signed interpretive stations along the route. The trail provides a fun and simple way to observe the dunes up close without having to walk through the sand itself. *Easy.* ⊠ *Alamogordo* ✛ *Trailhead: Just before the end of the paved section of Dune Dr.*

Playa Trail

TRAIL | FAMILY | This short and level ½-mile round-trip ramble is the first one you'll come to along Dunes Drive after passing through the entrance station. It's not as exciting as some of the other park trails, although it is interesting in summer when the otherwise dry lake bed it leads to usually fills with rain water. *Easy.* ⊠ *Alamogordo* ✛ *Trailhead: about 2 miles past entrance station on Dunes Dr.*

VISITOR CENTERS

★ White Sands Visitor Center

BUILDING | FAMILY | The centerpiece of
the small White Sands Historic District,
a complex of park buildings constructed
by the WPA in New Mexico's distinctive
Spanish–Pueblo Revival style in the mid-
1930s, the park's only visitor center is built
of thick adobe (mud and straw) bricks and
has a traditional *viga* (beam) and *savina*
(also called latilla) aspen-pole ceiling and
architectural details typical of the period
and style, like punched-tin light fixtures
and hand-carved wooden benches. Inside
you'll find an info desk and an array of
excellent, modern, interactive exhibits
as well as a small theater that shows a
short film about the dunes. Walk out back
to reach the park gift shop, which has
books, souvenirs, water, a very limited
assortment of snacks, and sleds with
which to careen down the park's dunes.
The district's other seven buildings include
a visitor restroom, ranger residences,
and various utility buildings. ✉ *19955
U.S. 70W, Alamogordo* ☎ *575/479–6124*
⊕ *www.nps.gov/whsa.*

Activities

BIKING

Cyclists are welcome on Dunes Drive,
and this flat loop route is pretty easy
to manage on two wheels, even the
unpaved portion, as the white-sand
surface is hard-packed. That said, because
drifting sand can be an issue, especially
during the windy spring months, and the
road can be bumpy after rainy periods, a
mountain bike or a bike with fat tires (such
as a beach cruiser) is ideal. Biking on the
dunes or anywhere off-road is strictly
prohibited, and violators will be fined.

CAMPING

Although there are no campgrounds
inside the park, you can set up a tent
at one of the primitive sites along the
short backcountry camping loop trail
just off Dunes Drive (about 6 miles from

the entrance station). You must obtain
a permit—the cost is $3 per person per
night—at the entrance station.

EDUCATIONAL PROGRAMS

★ Full Moon Hikes

TOUR—SIGHT | FAMILY | Once a month from
April through October, the park offers
ranger-led full-moon hikes along the
Dune Life Nature Trail. These nocturnal
adventures are fun for the whole family
and show the landscape in a fascinating, luminous perspective. Tickets are
required and can be purchased online
for $8; it's a good idea to book at least
a week ahead, as space is limited.
✉ *Alamogordo* ☎ *877/444–6777* ⊕ *www.
recreation.gov.*

Lake Lucero Tours

NATURE SITE | Just once a month, and only
from November through April, the park
offers up to 50 participants the chance
to visit Lake Lucero, in the southwest
corner of the park. This generally dry lake
bed is fascinating because of what it
shows us about how the park formed—a
story that rangers tell during these tours,
which cost $8 per person and must
be booked in advance (up to 30 days
ahead). The lake bed is filled with selenite
crystals, which over time erode and
break, forming ever smaller fragments
and eventually forming the bright white
dunes for which the park is famous.
Tours begin at the White Sands Missile
Range "Small Missile" Gate at mile marker 174 on U.S. 70, about 25 southwest
of the park entrance. ✉ *Alamogordo*
☎ *877/444–6777* ⊕ *www.recreation.gov.*

★ Sunset Stroll

TRAIL | FAMILY | One of the most enjoyable
ways to get to know the park is to take a
45-minute to 1-hour ranger-guided sunset
stroll, which takes place nightly year-
round and departs from the signed parking area along Dunes Drive 4.7 miles past
the park's entrance station. The exact
departure times vary according to, drum
roll please, the time the sun sets, which
you can find out each day at the visitor

center, but plan to get to the departure point about an hour before sunset. Along this leisurely 1-mile trek, you'll see dunes similar to those on the Alkali Flat Trail but with a local expert to fill you in on the plants, animals, and geology you encounter. ✉ *Dunes Dr., Alamogordo*.

HIKING

Although there are only a few marked trails in the park, you can easily hike short distances over any dune field adjoining the several parking areas along Dunes Drive. Traipsing through this strangely gorgeous landscape can take some getting used to, however, and despite the fact that the park's gently rolling dunes look about as threatening as a big sandbox, this terrain is deceptively dangerous, and you should take its potential hazards seriously. Because the dunes shift constantly and are sometimes buffeted by high winds (especially in spring), which can severely reduce visibility, it's relatively easy to get lost. Take it slow, bring lots of water, and always have a compass and a charged cell phone with you (cell service is a little uneven but it generally works on and near Dunes Drive). Although the park is in a broad basin, it's still at a lofty elevation of 4,235 feet. It's also completely unshaded, and temperatures can exceed 100 degrees in summer—it's rare, but visitors have been injured and even died from heat exhaustion after becoming disoriented. Unless you're on a marked trail, always stay within view of Dunes Drive, or at the very least other people. The good news: you don't have to scamper far from Dunes Drive to encounter mesmerizing views of seemingly endless dunes framed against majestic mountain peaks. Also, the white gypsum sand is cool to the touch, which makes it pleasant to walk barefoot through even on hot days. However, if hiking more than a few hundred feet, and especially on the longer Alkali Flat Trail, wear hiking boots, as your feet will appreciate the extra support after a mile or so of trekking over sometimes steep dunes.

SLEDDING

Further contributing to the sensation at times that you've entered an enormous landscape of snow rather than white sand, as you make your way along Dunes Drive into the heart of the park, you'll see kids and adults sledding down the dunes on plastic sleds, or snow saucers, which—if you don't have your own—you can buy at the gift shop attached to the visitor center for about $20, plus a couple of bucks for wax, which you'll need to coat your sled for it to work on the sand. Used sleds cost less but aren't always available; you can also return your new sled for $5 when you're finished. Park staffers are great with tips on how to sled on gypsum sand and also the best areas to do it, but a good place to start is the dunes adjacent either to the Interdune Boardwalk or beside the Alkali Flat Trailhead parking lot. There's also a good "how to" video on the park website.

Nearby Towns

Because White Sands National Park has no dining or lodging facilities, most visitors stay in one of three nearby communities. The military town of **Alamogordo** is closest, just 15 miles away, but it's also a somewhat prosaic, suburban community with mostly middle-of-the-road chain hotel and restaurant options. Far more charming and just 20 miles farther away (up a spectacular scenic highway), tiny **Cloudcroft** is situated high in the cool and crisp-aired Sacramento Mountains and is home to a famous old hotel, the Lodge Resort, plus a bunch of vacation-rental cabins and bungalows. Although it's nearly an hour west of the park, **Las Cruces** is actually the most popular base for visiting. It's big, located at the junction of two big interstate freeways, has plenty of hotels (although again, most are chains) and an increasingly noteworthy dining and nightlife scene, and is home to another remarkable constituent of the federal park system, Organ Mountains–Desert Peaks National Monument. One other possible option is **El Paso, Texas,** which is an easy 90-minute drive south of White Sands and has much to offer in the way of services and attractions; *see the Guadalupe Mountains National Park chapter for more on this city of 681,000.*

Alamogordo

15 miles northeast White Sands National Park, 90 miles north of El Paso, Texas, 208 miles southeast of Albuquerque.

Defense-related activities are vital to small city of Alamogordo (population 32,000) and surrounding Otero County, which covers much of the Tularosa Basin desert and White Sands National Park.

GETTING HERE AND AROUND

Located at the junction of U.S. 70, 54, and 82, this crossroads community of south-central New Mexico is just a 15-minute drive from White Sands National Park. Alamogordo is suburban in character, and a car is needed to get around.

VISITOR INFORMATION Alamogordo Chamber of Commerce. ✉ *1301 N. White Sands Blvd., Alamogordo* ☎ *575/437–6120* 🌐 *www.alamogordo.com.*

👁 Sights

New Mexico Museum of Space History
MUSEUM | FAMILY | The exhibits at this museum in the foothills on Alamogordo's east side highlight southern New Mexico's extensive and ongoing history of rocket launches, test flights, and space exploration. On the way in, check out the various rockets and other craft in the adjacent John P. Stapp Air & Space Park, and pay your respects to the gravesite of Ham the chimpanzee, who became the first hominid in space in 1961 and is now buried under a plaque dedicated to the "world's first astrochimp." The museum's highlights include the International Space Hall of Fame, a planetarium and dome theater, and a simulated Martian landscape. ✉ *3198 Hwy. 2001, Alamogordo* ☎ *575/437–2840* 🌐 *www.nmspacemuseum.org* 🎟 *$8* 🕒 *Closed Tues.*

Oliver Lee Memorial State Park
NATIONAL/STATE PARK | Just south of Alamogordo at the base of the Sacramento Mountains, this 640-acre expanse of Chihuahuan Desert offers both a short ½-mile hike along the Riparian Nature Trail and a strenuous 10-mile round-trip climb up through steep but stunning Dog Canyon—give yourself the better part of the day, as the elevation gain of about 3,500 feet is demanding. Even along the shorter trail, however, you'll be treated to good views back across the Tularosa Basin and White Sands National Park. ✉ *409 Dog Canyon Rd., Alamogordo* ☎ *575/437–8284* 🎟 *$5 per vehicle.*

🍴 Restaurants

★ Nuckleweed Place
$$$$ | AMERICAN | It takes a little effort to get to what's quite possibly the best restaurant in the region—it's set in a cheerfully decorated prefab house deep in La Borcita Canyon, about midway between Alamogordo and Cloudcroft. Open for dinner as well as weekend brunch, this quirky spot with a friendly staff turns out delicious biscuits and gravy and eggs Benedict for brunch, and choice steaks and grilled seafood at night. **Known for:** sticky pecan cinnamon rolls; tranquil, out-of-the-way setting; steak verde (with green chiles and havarti cheese). [$] *Average main: $34* ✉ *526 LaBorcita Canyon Rd., Alamogordo* ☎ *575/434–0000* 🕒 *Closed Mon.–Wed. No lunch.*

★ Waffle and Pancake Shoppe
$ | AMERICAN | This bustling restaurant is on the short list of locals and visitors in the know for tasty, and big, breakfasts and early lunches (they close at 1). Aside from fluffy waffles and pancakes

(which can come loaded with all sorts of toppings), they serve very good Mexican breakfasts and lunches—the chile verde plate for breakfast is great, as are the chicken enchiladas for lunch. **Known for:** friendly down-home service; huge portions; strawberry French toast. [$] *Average main: $8* ✉ *950 S. White Sands Blvd., Alamogordo* ☎ *575/437–0433* ⏲ *No dinner.*

Hotels

Holiday Inn Express
$ | **HOTEL** | The most pleasant and contemporary of Alamogordo's several chain hotels, this centrally located mid-rise offers friendly, professional service, immaculate grounds and interior spaces, and spacious, comfortable rooms. **Pros:** close to several restaurants; generous breakfast included; good proximity to White Sands National Park. **Cons:** looks like any other Holiday Inn Express; overlooks parking lot; on busy road. [$] *Rooms from: $115* ✉ *100 Kerry Ave., Alamogordo* ☎ *575/434–9773* 🌐 *www.ihg.com* 🛏 *80 rooms* 🍴 *Free Breakfast.*

Cloudcroft

20 miles east of Alamogordo.

Established in 1898 when the El Paso–Northeastern Railroad crew laid out the route for the Cloud Climbing Railroad, this little mountain town promotes itself these days with the slogan "9,000 feet above stress level," and from its perch nearly a mile high above the Tularosa desert basin and White Sands National Park, Cloudcroft lives up to the claim. Flowers and ponderosa and other greenery give the air an intoxicating mountain fragrance, and the boardwalks lining the main street, Burro Avenue, lend the town a kitschy Old West atmosphere that's a bit contrived, though still charming. Despite a significant influx of retirees and big-city expats over the past few years, this town of about 700 has held onto its country friendliness.

GETTING HERE AND AROUND

During the scenic half-hour drive up from Alamogordo, U.S. 82—the main route through town—climbs nearly 5,000 feet in elevation on its way to Cloudcroft.

VISITOR INFORMATION Cloudcroft Chamber of Commerce. ✉ *1001 James Canyon Hwy., Cloudcroft* ☎ *575/682–2733* 🌐 *www.coolcloudcroft.com.*

Sights

★ **Bridal Veil Falls and Grand View Trail**
TRAIL | If you have time for just one hike around Cloudcroft, make it this 7.7-mile loop, which takes in a 45-foot waterfall, a restored railroad trestle, and a steep desert landscape that offers a rugged contrast to the dune hikes down at White Sands. The trail is just off scenic U.S. 82 between Alamogordo and Cloudcroft. Farther up the hill in Cloudcroft, at the Mexican Canyon Trestle Overlook, you can get a better look at the old railroad tracks—and impressive wooden trestle—that from 1898 to 1945 carried trains up the canyon and across the chasm. The 32-mile trip from Alamogordo to Cloudcroft entails a dizzying elevation gain of about 4,700 feet. *Moderate.* ✉ *County Rd. A60, off U.S. 82 in High Rolls, Cloudcroft.*

Restaurants

★ **Cloudcroft Brewing Company**
$ | **AMERICAN** | Superb wood-fired pizzas and craft beer are the draw at this friendly, rustic brewery with reclaimed-wood walls, high ceilings, and a large side patio. The Zia Pie with chorizo, green chiles, and sharp cheddar is a local favorite, best enjoyed with a pint of Trainwreck IPA. **Known for:** cheerful, social vibe; rotating seasonal taps; pizzas with creative toppings. [$] *Average main: $14* ✉ *1301 Burro Ave., Cloudcroft*

☎ *575/682–2337* 🌐 *www.cloudcroftbrewing.com* ⏲ *Closed Tues.*

★ **Mad Jack's Mountaintop Barbecue**
$ | BARBECUE | FAMILY | This down-home joint set amid the pine-scented air of Cloudcroft is revered for its Texas-style brisket, which is best enjoyed at the outside picnic tables. The extra-cooked burnt ends get raves from people who know their barbecue, which explains the often long lines snaking around the building, especially on weekends. **Known for:** slow-smoked brisket, pulled pork, and turkey; jalapeño-cheddar sausage; fresh berry cobbler. [$] *Average main: $12* ✉ *105 James Canyon Hwy., Cloudcroft* ☎ *575/682–7577* ⏲ *Closed Mon.–Wed. No dinner.*

Hotels

★ **The Lodge Resort and Spa**
$$ | HOTEL | Extensive renovations completed in 2020 expanded the size of many rooms and added plush bedding, heated bathroom floors, and other comforts to most of the rooms and suites in this historic—reputedly haunted—Bavarian-style grand dame situated at 9,000 feet in elevation, high in the piney, rarefied air of Cloudcroft. **Pros:** exudes historic charm; full-service spa, outdoor pool, and seasonal 9-hole golf course; atmospheric restaurant. **Cons:** chilly and sometimes closed due to snow in winter; 45-minute drive from White Sands ; a bit old-fashioned for some tastes. [$] *Rooms from: $135* ✉ *601 Corona Pl., Cloudcroft* ☎ *800/395–6343* 🌐 *www.thelodgeresort.com* 🛏 *59 rooms* 🍴 *No meals.*

Las Cruces

52 miles southwest of White Sands National Park, 45 miles north of El Paso, Texas, 220 miles south of Albuquerque

The largest city in the Mesilla Valley, which has been populated for centuries, fast-growing Las Cruces (population 104,000) is part of a vibrant and diverse bi-national metro area that includes El Paso, Texas and Ciudad Juárez, Mexico. Home to New Mexico State University and adjacent to the small, historic village of Mesilla, this friendly city is also the eastern gateway to White Sands National Park as well as nearby—and quite underrated—Organ Mountains–Desert Peaks National Monument.

GETTING HERE AND AROUND

At the junction of Interstates 10 and 25, Las Cruces is also connected to Alamogordo and White Sands National Park—which is a little less than an hour away—via U.S. 70. Although downtown and neighboring Old Mesilla are quite walkable, you'll need a car to get around much of this somewhat sprawling city.

VISITOR INFORMATION Visit Las Cruces. ✉ *336 S. Main St., Las Cruces* ☎ *575/541–2444* 🌐 *www.lascrucescvb.org.*

Sights

★ **Organ Mountains–Desert Peaks National Monument**
NATIONAL/STATE PARK | Established as a national monument in 2014 on the eastern outskirts of Las Cruces, this dramatic 496,000-acre expanse of jagged spirelike peaks—which in the distance resembles a giant pipe organ—is one of the region's natural treasures. Although it receives relatively few visitors, especially compared with the more famous White

Sands, it's laced with more than 18 well-marked trails, ranging from the relatively easy 3-mile round-trip trek around Dripping Springs waterfall to longer and more strenuous hikes that traverse the mountain range's spiny backbone and offer dazzling views in every direction. The park has two main sections, Dripping Springs, which is on the western slope and closer to Las Cruces and also has a visitor center with exhibits about the park's vast trove of archaeological sites, and Aguirre Springs, which lies on the eastern slope and is more remote but also has the park's only campground and is closer to White Sands (and generally has less-crowded trails). Both sides have picnic areas and plenty of easy and challenging trails—good bets on the Aguirre Springs side are the 4-mile Pine Tree Loop and 4.1-mile round-trip Baylor Canyon Pass Trail. It's a 35-minute drive between the two sections, via U.S. 70, which runs just along the park's northern border. ✉ *15000 Dripping Springs Rd., Las Cruces* ☎ *575/522–1219* 🌐 *www.organmountains.org* 🎫 *$5 per vehicle.*

🍴 Restaurants

★ Luna Rossa Winery & Pizzeria

$ | ITALIAN | Skeptics are sometimes surprised by the high quality of southern New Mexico wines, with Mimbres Valley's Luna Rossa among the region's most impressive vintners, specializing in estate-grown, mostly Italian and Spanish, varietals like Dolcetto and Tempranillo. Here at the winery's casual restaurant in Mesilla, you can sample the wines while enjoying terrific pizzas, pastas, panini sandwiches, and house-made gelato. **Known for:** romantic enclosed patio; extensive selection of local wines; green chile-prosciutto pizzas. [$] *Average main: $15* ✉ *1321 Ave. de Mesilla, Mesilla* ☎ *575/526–2484* 🌐 *www.lunarossawinery.com.*

★ Salud! de Mesilla

$$ | BISTRO | Close to Old Mesilla Plaza, this stylish neighborhood bistro is filled with local art for sale and has several different dining areas, including a lively little bar and a covered patio. Known for its all-day, everyday brunch menu (try the French toast with berry compote, perhaps with a Prosecco mimosa) as well as a selection of international tapas, it's a welcoming venue for a leisurely meal. **Known for:** market selling local wines, gourmet snacks, and gifts; build-your-own Benedicts with creative toppings; crème brûlée. [$] *Average main: $19* ✉ *1800 Ave. de Mesilla, Mesilla* ☎ *575/323–3548* 🌐 *www.saludmesilla.com* 🕓 *Closed Mon.–Tues.*

Taqueria Las Catrinas

$ | MEXICAN | FAMILY | This inexpensive and festively decorated Mexican restaurant opened inside a former gas station on U.S. 70 several miles east of town, making it one of the last and best dining options en route to White Sands and the Aguirre Springs side of Organ Mountains–Desert Peaks National Monument. The specialty is tacos al pastor, made with tender pork marinated with a recipe from the restaurant's original sister location in Michoacán, Mexico, but you can also savor sirloin steak quesadillas and chicken flautas. **Known for:** fresh house-made tortillas; volcán-style (topped with gooey cheese) tacos al pastor tostadas; jamaica (hibiscus) and horchata agua frescas. [$] *Average main: $8* ✉ *5580 Bataan Memorial Hwy., Las Cruces* ☎ *575/382–5641* 🌐 *www.lascatrinastacos.com* 🕓 *Closed Mon.*

Hotels

Courtyard by Marriott Las Cruces

$$ | **HOTEL** | A short way from the attractive campus and museums of New Mexico State University, this contemporary low-rise opened in 2019 and offers some of the comfiest rooms in the city, plus a good-size pool and a patio with a firepit. **Pros:** sleek, modern design; well-equipped 24-hour gym; quiet but convenient location. **Cons:** not within walking distance of downtown or Old Mesilla; a chain hotel without a ton of character; can get crowded during college weekends. [$] *Rooms from: $156* ✉ *456 E. University Ave., Las Cruces* ☎ *575/526–1722* 🌐 *www.marriott.com* 🛏 *126 rooms* 🍴 *No meals.*

Hotel Encanto

$$ | **HOTEL** | A striking, contemporary hotel high on a bluff on the east side of town channels a gracious hacienda with its colorful common spaces and restaurants. **Pros:** reasonable prices; nice pool and good dining options; good base for visiting Organ Mountains and White Sands. **Cons:** rooms are a little dark; perfunctory bathrooms; on a busy road next to a shopping center. [$] *Rooms from: $130* ✉ *705 S. Telshor Blvd., Las Cruces* ☎ *575/522–4300, 866/383–0443* 🌐 *www.hotelencanto.com* 🛏 *210 rooms* 🍴 *No meals.*

Nightlife

Broken Spoke Taphouse

BREWPUBS/BEER GARDENS | More than 60 beers are on tap, many of them local, at this lively downtown ale house with an expansive beer garden that often features live music. There's good pub food, too. ✉ *302 S. Main St., Las Cruces* ☎ *575/323–8051* 🌐 *www.thebroken-spoketaphouse.com.*

WIND CAVE
NATIONAL PARK

Updated by
Carson Walker

SOUTH
DAKOTA

🏕 Camping   🛏 Hotels   🏃 Activities   👁 Scenery   🎡 Crowds

★★★☆☆   ★★★★★   ★★★★★   ★★★★★   ★★★★☆

WELCOME TO WIND CAVE NATIONAL PARK

TOP REASONS TO GO

★ **Underground exploring:** Wind Cave offers visitors the chance to get their hands and feet dirty on guided tours through long and complex caves.

★ **The call of the wild:** Wind Cave National Park boasts a wide variety of animals: bison, coyote, deer, antelope, elk, and prairie dogs.

★ **Education by candlelight:** Wind Cave offers numerous educational and interpretive programs, including the Candlelight Cave Tour, which allows guests to explore the cave by candlelight only.

★ **Historic cave:** On January 9, 1903, President Theodore Roosevelt signed a bill that made Wind Cave the first cave in the U.S. to be named a national park.

★ **Noteworthy neighbors:** With its proximity to national parks, state parks, and other monuments, Wind Cave is situated perfectly to explore some of America's greatest national treasures.

1 Wind Cave. With an explored maze of caverns of more than 150 miles, Wind Cave is considered one of the world's longest caves. Notably, scientists estimate that only 10% of the cave has been explored to date. Most of the world's known boxwork formations are found here, which means that visitors are treated to some of the rarest geological features on the planet. The cave lies at the confluence of western mountains and central plains, which blesses the park with a unique landscape. A series of established trails weave in and out of forested hillsides and grassy prairies, providing treks of varying difficulty.

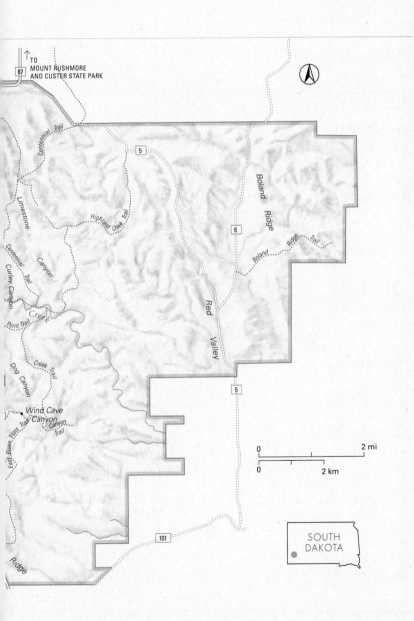

TO
MOUNT RUSHMORE
AND CUSTER STATE PARK
87

Centennial Trail

5

Boland Ridge

6

Highland Creek Trail

Boland Ridge Trail

Limestone

Centennial Trail

Curley Canyon

Canyon

Creek

Red Valley

Point Trail

5

Creek Trail

Dog Canyon

Wind Cave
Canyon

Canyon Trail

East Bison Flats Trail

0   2 mi
0   2 km

101

Ridge

SOUTH
DAKOTA

Wind Cave has 148 miles of underground passageways. Cave formations include 95% of the world's mineral boxwork, and gypsum beard so sensitive it reacts to the heat of a lamp. This underground wilderness is part of a giant limestone labyrinth beneath the Black Hills.

Wind Cave ranks as the sixth-longest cave in the world, but experts believe 90% of it has yet to be mapped. On the surface, bison, elk and other wildlife roam the rolling hills that demonstrate the biodiversity of grasslands and forest.

One of the country's oldest parks—President Theodore Roosevelt established it in 1903—the National Park Service says it's the world's most complex three-dimensional maze cave with the best boxwork, a rare honeycombed formation of calcite that hangs from the walls and ceilings. Wind Cave's name comes from the air that howls at the natural entrances because of differences in barometric pressure between the cave below and atmosphere above.

Though the underground cavern is the star of the show, make sure you also build in time to explore the park's 44 square miles of surface. The largest natural opening to the cave is located near the visitor center entrance and is accessible on a self-guided tour. The park has more than 30 miles of hiking trails, open year-round, that offer a close-up view of the forest and rolling prairies as well as bison, elk, pronghorn, prairie dogs, and the black-footed ferret. Bird-watching

is popular because the park is home to more than 100 different permanent species as well as others during spring and fall migration. If you visit in mid-September to early October, you'll see fall colors on display and maybe hear the elk bugling. A 20-mile scenic driving tour is a another great way to see the geology of the pristine Black Hills.

The area known as the Black Hills is sacred to Native Americans. Lakota culture believes that humans and bison came from the spirit world in the earth through the natural entrance of the cave, referred to as a "hole that breathes cool air." In 1881, brothers Tom and Jesse Bingham heard the sound of wind coming from one of the holes which, as the story goes, blew Jesse's hat off when he peered inside. Charlie Crary is credited with the first entry into the cave that year. After several legal fights over ownership to the land and cave below, Congress and President Roosevelt created the 10,522-acre Wind Cave National Park, making it the world's first cave to be designated as a national park. Tours of the cave started that year for 50 cents.

AVERAGE HIGH/LOW TEMPERATURES					
JAN.	**FEB.**	**MAR.**	**APR.**	**MAY**	**JUNE**
37/8	41/14	49/21	58/30	67/40	77/49
JULY	**AUG.**	**SEPT.**	**OCT.**	**NOV.**	**DEC.**
84/55	84/53	76/44	63/32	46/20	39/12

Planning

When to Go

The biggest crowds come to Wind Cave from June to September, but the park and surrounding Black Hills are large enough to diffuse the masses. Neither the cave nor grounds above are ever uncomfortably packed, although on busy summer days tours sometimes sell out over an hour ahead of time, so come early in the day and reserve your spot. Park officials contend it's actually less busy during the first full week in August, when the Sturgis Motorcycle Rally brings roughly a half-million bikers to the region, clogging highways for miles around. Most hotels within a 100-mile radius are booked up to a year in advance.

The colder months are the least crowded, though you can still explore underground, thanks to the cave's constant 54°F temperature. The shoulder seasons are also quieter, though autumn is a perfect time to visit. The days are warm, the nights are cool, and in late September/early October the park's canyons and coulees display incredible colors.

FESTIVALS AND EVENTS

Crazy Horse Volksmarch. This 6.2-mile hike up the mountain where the massive Crazy Horse Memorial is being carved is the largest event of its kind and gives hikers the opportunity to stand on the Lakota leader's outstretched arm. It's held the first full weekend in June. Another one-day Volksmarch is held in late September, timed to coincide with the Custer State Park Buffalo Roundup. ⊕ crazyhorsememorial.org.

Custer State Park Buffalo Roundup & Arts Festival. The nation's largest buffalo roundup is one of South Dakota's most exciting events. Early on a Friday morning in late September, cowboys, cowgirls, and rangers saddle up to corral and vaccinate the park's 1,300 head of bison. You'll hear the thunder of more than 5,000 hooves before you even see the bison. Before, during, and after the roundup, a three-day festival showcases works by South Dakota artists and artisans. ⊕ gfp. sd.gov/parks/detail/custer-state-park.

Days of '76. This outdoor, award-winning, Professional Rodeo Cowboys Association (PRCA) event includes the usual riding, roping, and bull riding, as well as two parades with vintage carriages and coaches and Western arts and crafts. This five-day affair is one of the state's most popular, featuring the top cowboys and cowgirls in the sport. ⊕ daysof76.com.

Deadwood Jam. A quarter-century strong and still filling the streets of Deadwood with live music, the Black Hills' premier music festival showcases an eclectic collection of country, rock, and blues for two days in mid-September. ⊕ www. deadwood.com/event/deadwood-jam.

Gold Discovery Days. A parade, carnival, car show, stick-horse rodeo, hot-air balloon rally, hunt for gold nuggets, and bed races are all part of the fun at this three-day event in late July in Custer. ⊕ www. visitcuster.com/gold-discovery-days.

Sturgis Motorcycle Rally. This 10-day event held in early August regularly draws more than 500,000 bikers and nonbikers alike who pack the Black Hills town's streets. It features a variety of food, music, T-shirt

Wind Cave in One Day

Pack a picnic lunch, then head to the visitor center to purchase tickets for a morning tour of Wind Cave. Visit the exhibit rooms in the center afterward. Then drive or walk the ¼ mile to the picnic area north of the visitor center. The refreshing air and deep emerald color of the pine woodlands will flavor your meal.

In the afternoon, take a leisurely drive through the parklands south of the visitor center, passing through **Bison Flats** and **Gobbler Pass**, for an archetypal view of the park and to look for wildlife. On the way back north, follow U.S. 385 east toward **Wind Cave Canyon**. If you enjoy bird-watching, park at the turnout and hike the 1.8-mile trail into the canyon, where you can spot swallows and great horned owls in the cliffs and woodpeckers in the trees.

Get back on the highway going north, take a right on Highway 87, and continue ½-mile to the turnout for **Centennial Trail**. Hike the trail about 2 miles to the junction with **Lookout Point Trail**, turn right and return to Highway 87. The whole loop is about 43.4 miles. As you continue driving north to the top of Rankin Ridge, a pull-out to the right serves as the starting point for 11.4-mile **Rankin Ridge Trail**. It loops around the ridge, past **Lookout Tower**—the park's highest point—and ends up back at the pull-out. This trail is an excellent opportunity to enjoy the fresh air, open spaces, and diversity of wildlife in the park.

stands and, of course, motorcycles of all varieties. ⊕ *www.sturgismotorcyclerally. com*.

Getting Here and Around

AIR
The nearest commercial airport is in Rapid City.

BUS
Bus lines serve Rapid City and Wall.

CAR
Wind Cave is 56 miles from Rapid City, via U.S. 16 and Highway 87, which runs through the park, and 73 miles southwest of Badlands National Park.

U.S. 385 and Highway 87 travel the length of the park on the west side. Additionally, two unpaved roads, NPS Roads 5 and 6, traverse the northeastern part of Wind Cave. NPS Road 5 joins Highway 87 at the park's north border.

Inspiration

Wind Cave National Park is one of the featured destinations in the 2001 IMAX movie *Journey Into Amazing Caves.* Narrated by Liam Neeson, with music by The Moody Blues, the immersive film follows scientists into unique underground worlds.

Wind Cave National Park: The First 100 Years includes more than 200 historic images as well as history and stories about the cave and park.

Wind Cave: The Story Behind the Scenery provides good photos and information about the park; it can be purchased at the visitor center.

Park Essentials

ACCESSIBILITY

The visitor center is entirely wheelchair accessible, but only a few areas of the cave itself are navigable by those with limited mobility. Arrangements can be made in advance for a special ranger-assisted tour for a small fee. The Elk Mountain Campground has two accessible sites.

PARK FEES AND PERMITS

There's no fee to enter the park; cave tours cost $10–$30. The requisite backcountry camping and horseback-riding permits are both free from the visitor center. Rates at Elk Mountain Campground are $18 a night per site early spring through late fall (when the water is turned on in the restroom facility); $9 a night per site the rest of the year.

PARK HOURS

The park is open year-round, though visitor center hours and tour schedules vary seasonally. It is in the Mountain time zone.

CELL PHONE RECEPTION

Cell phone reception is hit and miss in the park. You will find a public phone outside the visitor center.

Hotels

Wind Cave has only one campground, and you'll have to look outside park boundaries if you want to bed down in something more substantial than a tent. New chain hotels with modern amenities are plentiful in the Black Hills, but when booking accommodations consider a stay at one of the area's historic properties. From grand brick downtown hotels to intimate Queen Anne homes converted to bed-and-breakfasts, historic lodgings are easy to locate. Other distinctive lodging choices include the region's mountain lodges and forest retreats.

It may be difficult to obtain quality accommodations during summer—and downright impossible during the Sturgis Motorcycle Rally, held the first full week of August every year—so plan ahead and make reservations (three or four months out is a good rule of thumb) if you're going to travel during peak season. To find the best value, choose a hotel far from Interstate 90. *Hotel reviews have been shortened. For full information, visit Fodors.com.*

What It Costs			
$	$$	$$$	$$$$
RESTAURANTS			
under $13	$13–$20	$21–$30	over $30
HOTELS			
under $101	$101–$150	$151–$200	over $200

Restaurants

If you're determined to dine in Wind Cave National Park, be sure to pack your own meal, because other than vending machines, the only dining venues inside park boundaries are the two picnic areas, one near the visitor center and the other at Elk Mountain Campground. The towns beyond the park offer additional options. Deadwood claims some of the best-ranked restaurants in South Dakota. Buffalo, pheasant, and elk are relatively common ingredients in the Black Hills. No matter where you go, beef is king. *Restaurant reviews have been shortened. For full information, visit Fodors. com.*

Tours

Candlelight Cave Tour

GUIDED TOURS | Available once or twice daily, mid-June through Labor Day, this tour goes into a section of the cave with no paved walks or lighting. Everyone on the tour carries a lantern similar to those used in expeditions in the 1890s. The tour lasts two hours, covers 2/3 mile, and is limited to 10 people, so reservations are essential. Children younger than eight are not admitted. *Moderate.* ⊠ *26611 U.S. 385* ⊹ *Starts at visitor center* ⊕ *www.nps.gov/wica* ✉ *$12.*

Fairgrounds Cave Tour

GUIDED TOURS | View examples of nearly every type of calcite formation found in the cave on this 1½-hour, 2/3-mile tour, available at the visitor center from early June through mid-August. There are some 450 steps, leading up and down. *Moderate.* ⊠ *26611 U.S. 385* ⊹ *Off U.S. 385, 3 miles north of the park's southern boundary* ⊕ *www.nps.gov/wica/planyour-visit/tour-fairgrounds.htm* ✉ *$12.*

Fort Hays and Mount Rushmore Tours

TOUR—SIGHT | FAMILY | This nine-hour tour amid the Black Hills begins at Fort Hays on the *Dances with Wolves* film set and visits Mount Rushmore, Custer State Park, and the Crazy Horse Memorial. Guests are responsible for their own lunches at the State Game Lodge; a pre-trip breakfast and a post-trip cowboy dinner show are add-on options. ⊠ *2255 Fort Hayes Dr., Rapid City* ☎ *605/343–3113* ⊕ *www.mountrushmoretours.com* ✉ *From $90.*

Garden of Eden Cave Tour

GUIDED TOURS | You don't need to go far to see boxwork, popcorn, and flowstone formations. Just take the relatively easy, one-hour tour, which covers 1/3 mile and 150 stairs. It's available one to four times daily in summer. *Easy.* ⊠ *26611 U.S. 385* ⊹ *3 miles north of park's southern border* ⊕ *www.nps.gov/wica/planyourvisit/tour-garden-of-eden.htm* ✉ *$10.*

Natural Entrance Cave Tour

GUIDED TOURS | This 1¼-hour tour takes you 2/3 miles into the cave, onto more than 300 stairs (most heading down), and out an elevator exit. Along the way are some significant boxwork deposits on the middle level. The tour leaves several times daily year-round. *Easy.* ⊠ *26611 U.S. 385* ⊹ *Off U.S. 385, 3 miles north of park's southern border* ⊕ *www.nps.gov/wica/planyourvisit/tour-natural-entrance.htm* ✉ *$12.*

Visitor Information

PARK CONTACT INFORMATION Wind Cave National Park. ⊠ *26611 U.S. 385, Hot Springs* ☎ *605/745–4600* ⊕ *www.nps.gov/wica.*

 Sights

PICNIC AREAS

Elk Mountain Campground Picnic Area

LOCAL INTEREST | You don't have to be a camper to use this well-developed picnic spot, with more than 70 tables, fire grates (some of them heightened to accommodate people with disabilities), and restrooms. Some of the tables are on the prairie; others sit amid the pines. ⊠ *Wind Cave National Park* ⊹ *½ mile north of visitor center.*

Wind Cave Picnic Area

LOCAL INTEREST | On the edge of a prairie and grove of ponderosa, this is a peaceful, pretty place ¼ mile from the visitor center. Small and simple, it's equipped with 12 tables and a potable-water pump. ⊠ *Wind Cave National Park* ⊹ *¼ mile north of visitor center* ⊕ *www.nps.gov/wica.*

SCENIC DRIVES

Bison Flats Drive (South Entrance)

SCENIC DRIVE | Entering the park from the south on U.S. 385 takes you past Gobbler Ridge and into the hills commonly found in the southern Black Hills region. After

Plants and Wildlife in Wind Cave

About three-quarters of the park is grassland. The rest is forested, mostly by the ponderosa pine. Poison ivy is common in wetter, shadier areas, so wear long pants and boots when hiking. The convergence of forest and prairies makes an attractive home for bison, elk, coyotes, pronghorn antelope, prairie dogs, and mule deer. Wild turkey and squirrels are less obvious in this landscape, but commonly seen by observant hikers.

Mountain lions also live in the park; although usually shy, they will attack if surprised or threatened. Make noise while hiking to prevent chance encounters. Bison appear docile, but can be dangerous. The largest land mammal in North America, they weigh up to a ton and run at speeds in excess of 35 mph.

a couple of miles, the landscape gently levels onto the Bison Flats, one of the mixed-grass prairies on which the park prides itself. You might see a herd of grazing buffalo (the park has roughly 400 of them) between here and the visitor center. You can also catch panoramic views of the parklands, surrounding hills, and limestone bluffs. ⊠ Hwy. 385.

★ Rankin Ridge Drive (North Entrance)

SCENIC DRIVE | Entering the park across the north border via Highway 87 is perhaps the most beautiful drive into the park. As you leave behind the grasslands and granite spires of Custer State Park and enter Wind Cave, you see the prairie, forest, and wetland habitats of the backcountry and some of the oldest rock in the Black Hills. The silvery twinkle of mica, quartz, and feldspar crystals dots Rankin Ridge east of Highway 87, and gradually gives way to limestone and sandstone formations. ⊠ Hwy. 87.

SCENIC STOPS

Rankin Ridge Lookout Tower

VIEWPOINT | Although some of the best panoramic views of the park and surrounding hills can be seen from this 5,013-foot tower, it's typically not staffed or open to the public. Still, if you want to stretch your legs on a car ride along Rankin Ridge Drive, consider following the 1-mile Rankin Ridge loop to the tower and back. ⊠ Wind Cave National Park ⊕ 6 miles north of the visitor center on Hwy. 87.

★ Wind Cave

CAVE | Known to Native Americans for centuries, Wind Cave was named for the strong air currents that alternately blow in and out of its entrances. The cave's winds are related to the difference in atmospheric pressure between the cave and the surface. When the atmospheric pressure is higher outside than inside, the air blows in, and vice versa. With more than 150 miles of known passageway divided into three different levels, Wind Cave ranks among the longest in the world. It's host to an incredibly diverse collection of geologic formations, including more boxwork than any other known cave, plus a series of underground lakes, though they are located in the deepest parts of the cave not seen on any tours. All tours are led by National Park Service rangers and leave from the visitor center. These tours allow you to see the unusual and beautiful formations with names such as popcorn, frostwork and boxwork. The cave remains a steady 54°F year-round, so wear closed-toe shoes and bring along a jacket or sweater. Tickets are sold at the visitor center and typically sell out two hours before each tour during summer, so plan accordingly. Check out the park website for the different tours, times, and pricing. ⊠ *Wind Cave National Park* ✛ *U.S. 385 to Wind Cave Visitor Center* ⊕ *www.nps. gov/wica/planyourvisit/guidedtours.htm.*

TRAILS

Boland Ridge Trail

TRAIL | Get away from the crowds for a half day via this strenuous, 2.6-mile (one way) hike. The panorama from the top is well worth it, especially at night. *Difficult.* ⊠ *Wind Cave National Park* ✛ *Trailhead: off Park Service Rd. 6, 1 mile north of junction with Park Service Rd. 5.*

Centennial Trail

TRAIL | Constructed to celebrate South Dakota's centennial in 1989, this trail bisects the Black Hills, covering 111 miles from north to south, from Bear Butte State Park through Black Hills National Forest, Black Elk Wilderness, Custer State Park, and into Wind Cave National Park. Designed for bikers, hikers, and horses, the trail is rugged but accommodating (note, however, that bicycling on the trail is not allowed within park boundaries). It will take you at least a half day to cover the 6-mile Wind Cave segment. *Moderate.* ⊠ *Wind Cave National Park* ✛ *Trailhead: off Hwy. 87, 2 miles north of visitor center.*

Cold Brook Canyon Trail

TRAIL | FAMILY | Starting on the west side of U.S. 385, 2 miles south of the visitor center, this 1.4-mile (one way), mildly strenuous hike runs past a former prairie-dog town, the edge of an area burned by a controlled fire in 1986, and through Cold Brook Canyon to the park boundary fence. Experienced hikers can conquer this trail and return to the trailhead in an hour or less, but more leisurely visitors will probably need more time. *Moderate.* ⊠ *Wind Cave National Park* ✛ *Trailhead: west side of U.S. 385, 2 miles south of visitor center.*

Highland Creek Trail

TRAIL | This difficult, roughly 8.6-mile (one way) trail is the longest and most diverse trail within the park, traversing mixed-grass prairies, ponderosa pine forests, and the riparian habitats of Highland Creek, Beaver Creek, and Wind Cave Canyon. Even those in good shape will need a full day to cover this trail round-trip. *Difficult.* ⊠ *Wind Cave National Park* ✛ *Southern trailhead stems from Wind Cave Canyon trail 1 mile east of U.S. 385. Northern trailhead on Forest Service Rd. 5.*

Wind Cave Canyon Trail

TRAIL | This easy 1.8-mile (one way) trail follows Wind Cave Canyon to the park boundary fence. The canyon, with its steep limestone walls and dead trees, provides the best opportunity in the park for bird-watching. Be especially vigilant for cliff swallows, great horned owls, and red-headed and Lewis woodpeckers. Deer, least chipmunks, and other small animals also are attracted to the sheltered environment of the canyon. Even though you could probably do a round-trip tour of this trail in less than an hour and a half, be sure to spend more time here to observe the wildlife. *Easy.* ⊠ *Wind Cave National Park* ✛ *Trailhead: east side of Hwy. 385, 1 mile north of southern access road to visitor center.*

VISITOR CENTERS

Wind Cave Visitor Center

INFO CENTER | The park's sole visitor center is the primary place to get park information and embark on cave tours. Located on top of the cave, it has three exhibit rooms, with displays on cave exploration, Native American culture, and prairie management. The center also hosts ranger programs and has an auditorium that presents the film, *Wind Cave, Two Worlds.* Other than vending machines, there's no coffee or snacks here or elsewhere in the park. ⊠ *26611 U.S. 385, Hot Springs* ✛ *Off U.S. 385, 3 miles north of park's southern border* ☎ *605/745–4600* ⊕ *www.nps.gov/wica* 🎫 *Free.*

Common Cave Terms

Sound like a serious spelunker with this cavemen cheat sheet for various *speleothems* (cave formations).

Boxwork: Composed of interconnecting thin blades that were left in relief on cave walls when the bedrock was dissolved away.

Cave balloons: Thin-walled formations resembling partially deflated balloons, usually composed of hydromagnesite.

Flowstone: Consists of thin layers of a mineral deposited on a sloping surface by flowing or seeping water.

Frostwork: Sprays of needles that radiate from a central point that are usually made of aragonite.

Gypsum beard: Composed of bundles of gypsum fibers that resemble a human beard.

Logomites: Consist of popcorn and superficially resemble hollowed-out stalagmites.

Pool Fingers: Deposited underneath water around organic filaments.

Stalactites: Carrot-shape formations formed from dripping water that hang down from a cave ceiling.

Stalagmites: Mineral deposits from dripping water built up on a cave floor.

Activities

Many visitors come to Wind Cave solely to descend into the park's underground passages. While there are great ranger-led tours for casual visitors—and more daring explorations for experienced cavers—the prairie and forest above the cave shouldn't be neglected.

EDUCATIONAL OFFERINGS

Adventures in Nature

TOUR—SIGHT | Although annual themes and individual program topics vary, nature is always the focus on these seasonally offered adventures held at the visitor center. They're open to children ages 3 to 12, who are divided into groups that participate in age-appropriate activities. ✉ *26611 Hwy. 385* ☎ *605/745–4600* ⊕ *www.nps.gov/wica.*

Junior Ranger Program

TOUR—SIGHT | FAMILY | Kids 12 and younger (and adults too) can earn a Junior Ranger badge by completing activities that teach them about the park's ecosystems, the cave, the animals, and protecting the environment. Pick up the Junior Ranger guidebook for free at the Wind Cave Visitor Center. ✉ *Wind Cave National Park, 26611 Hwy. 385* ☎ *605/745–4600.*

BIKING

Bikes are prohibited on all of the park's trails and in the backcountry. Cyclists may ride on designated roads, and on the 111-mile Centennial Trail, once it passes the park's northern border.

Two Wheeler Dealer Cycle and Fitness

BICYCLING | Family-owned and-operated Two Wheeler Dealer Cycle and Fitness, based in Spearfish, stocks hundreds of bikes for sale and plenty of them to rent.

The service is exceptional. Get information for the Mickelson Trail and other Black Hills routes at the counter. ⊠ *305 Main St., Spearfish* ☎ *605/642–7545* ⊕ *www.twowheelerdealer.com.*

BIRD-WATCHING

Rankin Ridge

BIRD WATCHING | See large birds of prey here, including turkey vultures, hawks, and golden eagles. ⊠ *Wind Cave National Park* ✛ *6 miles north of the visitor center on Hwy. 87.*

★ Wind Cave Canyon

BIRD WATCHING | Here's one of the best birding areas in the park. The limestone walls of the canyon are ideal nesting grounds for cliff swallows and great horned owls, while the standing dead trees on the canyon floor attract red-headed and Lewis woodpeckers. As you hike down the trail, the steep-sided canyon widens to a panoramic view east across the prairies. ⊠ *Wind Cave National Park* ✛ *About ½ mile east of visitor center* ⊕ *www.nps.gov/wica.*

CAMPING

Camping is one of this region's strengths. While there is only one primitive campground within the park, there are countless campgrounds in the Black Hills. The public campgrounds in the national forest are accessible by road but otherwise secluded and undeveloped; private campgrounds typically have more amenities, as do some of those in Custer State Park, which has numerous options.

Elk Mountain Campground. If you prefer a relatively developed campsite and relative proximity to civilization, Elk Mountain is an excellent choice. You can experience the peaceful pine forests and wild creatures of the park without straying too far from the safety of the beaten path. ⊠ *½ mile north of visitor center* ☎ *605/745–4600.*

HIKING

There are more than 30 miles of hiking trails within the boundaries of Wind Cave National Park, covering ponderosa forest and mixed-grass prairie. The landscape has changed little over the past century, so a hike through the park is as much a historical snapshot of pioneer life in the 1890s as it is exercise. Be sure to hit the Wind Cave Canyon Trail, where limestone cliffs attract birds like cliff swallows and great horned owls, and the Cold Brook Canyon Trail, a short but fun trip past a prairie-dog town to the park's edge. Besides birds and small animals such as squirrels, you're apt to see deer and pronghorn while hiking, and probably some bison.

Hiking into the wild, untouched backcountry is perfectly safe, provided you have a map (available from the visitor center) and a good sense of direction. Don't expect any amenities, however; bathrooms and a water-bottle filling station are available only at the visitor center, and the trails are dirt or gravel. There are no easily accessible sources along the trails, and water from backcountry sources must be treated, so pack your own.

MULTISPORT OUTFITTERS

Granite Sports

TOUR—SPORTS | Several miles north of Wind Cave Park in Hill City, Granite Sports sells a wide range of hiking, climbing, and camping apparel and accessories; they also know the best local guides. ⊠ *201 Main St., Hill City* ☎ *605/574–2121* ⊕ *www.granite-sports.com.*

Scheels All Sport

In the Rushmore Crossing Mall, off Interstate 90 at East-North Street or Lacrosse Street exits, the enormous Scheels All Sport carries a wide selection of all-weather hiking gear, footwear, and clothes, as well as binoculars suitable for bird-watchers. ⊠ *1225 Eglin St., Rapid City* ☎ *605/342–9033* ⊕ *www.scheels.com.*

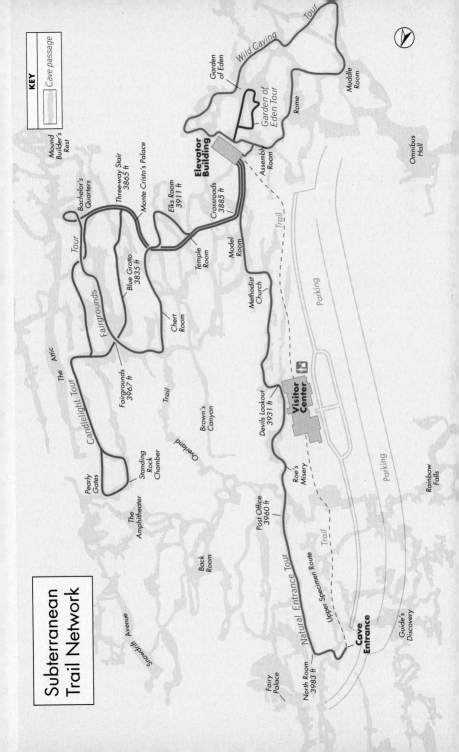

SPELUNKING

You may not explore the depths of Wind Cave on your own, but you can choose from five ranger-led cave tours, available from June through August; the rest of the year, only one or two tours are available. On each tour you pass incredibly beautiful cave formations, including extremely well-developed boxwork. The least crowded times to visit in summer are mornings and weekends.

The cave is 54°F year-round, so bring a sweater. Note that the uneven passages are often wet and slippery. Rangers discourage those with heart conditions and physical limitations from taking the organized tours. However, with some advance warning (and for a nominal fee) park rangers can arrange private, limited tours for those with physical disabilities. To prevent the spread of white-nose syndrome, a disease that is deadly to bats, don't wear any clothes or shoes or bring any equipment that you might have used to explore other caves (with the exception of the nearby Jewel Cave National Monument).

Tours depart from the visitor center. A schedule can be found online at ⊕ *www. nps.gov/wica*. To make a reservation, call ☎ 605/745–4600.

★ Wild Cave Tour

SPELUNKING | For a serious caving experience, sign up for this challenging four-hour tour. After some basic training in spelunking, you crawl and climb through fissures and corridors, most lined with gypsum needles, frostwork, and boxwork. Expect to get dirty. Wear shoes with good traction, long pants, and a long-sleeve shirt. The park provides knee pads, gloves, and hard hats with headlamps. Parents or guardians must sign a consent form for 16- and 17-year-olds. Tours, which are limited to 10 people, are available at 1 pm daily, mid-June through mid-August, and at 1 pm weekends mid-August through Labor Day. Reservations are essential. *Difficult.* ⊠ *26611 U.S. 385 ✛ Off U.S. 385, 3 miles north of park's southern boundary* ⊕ *www.nps.gov/wica/plan-yourvisit/tour-caving.htm* ⊠ *$30.*

Nearby Towns

Wind Cave is part of South Dakota's Black Hills, a diverse region of alpine meadows, ponderosa pine forests, and creek-carved, granite-walled canyons covering 2 million acres in the state's southwest quadrant. This mountain range contrasts sharply with the sheer cliffs and dramatic buttes of the Badlands to the north and east, and the wide, wind-swept plains of most of the state. Though anchored by Rapid City—the largest city for 350 miles in any direction—the Black Hills' crown jewel is Mount Rushmore National Memorial, visited by nearly 3 million people each year. U.S. 385 is the backbone of the Black Hills.

Custer

About 20 miles north of Wind Cave National Park; about 40 miles southwest of Rapid City via routes 16, 16A, and 385.

Known as the Mother City of the Black Hills, Custer is a great place to stay if you can spend a few days in the southern Black Hills. It's a short drive to world-class attractions like Mount Rushmore, Crazy Horse, Wind Cave National Park, Jewel Cave National Monument, and Custer National Park. With all the lodging, food and shopping options, you can explore all day and still find time to relax at your hotel or cabin.

Near here, George Armstrong Custer and his expedition first discovered gold in 1874, leading to the gold rush of 1875 and '76.

GETTING HERE AND AROUND

Custer is best accessed by car. It's about 20 miles north of Wind Cave National Park on US-385 and 32 miles north of Hot Springs on US-385.

TOURS

Black Hills Balloons

TOUR—SPORTS | Based in Custer, Black Hills Balloons has more than 30 years of experience providing bird's-eye views of some of the Black Hills' most picturesque locations. Tours meet up at Custer's Buffalo Ridge Theater. Reservations are essential. ⊠ *Buffalo Ridge Theater, 370 W. Mount Rushmore Rd., Custer* ☎ *605/673–2520* ⊕ *www.blackhillsballoons.com* ⊠ *$325.*

Buffalo Safari Jeep Tours

DRIVING TOURS | This open-air jeep tour is the only way you can get off-road in Custer State Park. Knowledgeable guides share historical and educational facts about the park and wildlife, while they search for pronghorns, elk, and the noble buffalo—which they almost always find. The daily tour takes about 2 hours.
■**TIP→** **If you can, plan for the Sunrise Safari (you'll be back by 8 am); it's one of the best times to see the wildlife.** ⊠ *Custer State Park Resort, Custer* ⊹ *Check in at Creekside Lodge* ☎ *605/255–4541* ⊕ *custerresorts.com/activities/activities-in-the-park/buffalo-safari-jeep-tour/* ⊠ *from $55.*

VISITOR INFORMATION

CONTACTS Visit Custer. ⊠ *615 Washington St., Custer* ☎ *605/673–2244* ⊕ *visitcuster.com.*

Sights

Crazy Horse Memorial

NATIVE SITE | FAMILY | Designed to be the world's largest work of art, this tribute to the spirit of the North American Native people depicts Crazy Horse, the legendary Lakota leader who helped defeat General Custer at Little Bighorn. A work in progress, thus far the warrior's head has been carved from the mountain, and the colossal head of his horse is beginning to emerge. Self-taught sculptor Korczak Ziolkowski started this memorial in 1948. After his death in 1982, his family carried on the project. Near the work site stands an exceptional orientation center, the Indian Museum of North America, Ziolkowski's home and workshop, and the Indian University of North America. If you're visiting in summer, come in the afternoon, and stick around for the spectacular laser-light show, held nightly from Memorial Day through late September. ⊠ *12151 Ave. of the Chiefs, Crazy Horse Memorial* ⊹ *Hwy. 385, 5 miles north of Custer* ☎ *605/673–4681* ⊕ *crazyhorsememorial.org* ⊠ *$15; $35 for 3 or more in a vehicle.*

Custer State Park

NATIONAL/STATE PARK | This 71,000-acre park is considered the crown jewel of South Dakota's state park system. Elk, antelope, mountain goats, bighorn sheep, mountain lions, wild turkey, prairie dogs, and the second-largest (behind Yellowstone National Park) publicly owned herd of bison in the world roam this pristine landscape. Scenic drives roll past fingerlike granite spires and panoramic views (try the Needles Highway). Take the 18-mile Wildlife Loop Road to see prairies teeming with animals and some of the beautiful backdrops for countless Western films. Accommodations here are outstanding, too, with numerous campgrounds and a resort network that includes five amenities-filled lodges and seven well-appointed vacation cabins.
■**TIP→** **The park is open year-round, but some amenities are closed over winter.**

⊠ *13329 U.S. 16A, Custer* ⊹ *4 miles east of Custer* ☎ *605/255–4515* ⊕ *gfp.sd.gov/parks/detail/custer-state-park* ⊠ *From $20 per vehicle.*

Jewel Cave National Monument

CAVE | Even though its more than 208 miles of surveyed passages make this cave one of the country's largest, Jewel Cave isn't renowned for its size. Rather, it's the rare crystalline formations that abound in the cave's vast passages that are the main draw. Wander the dark passageways and you'll be rewarded with the sight of tiny crystal Christmas trees, hydromagnesite balloons that would pop if you touched them, and delicate calcite deposits dubbed "cave popcorn." Year-round, you can take ranger-led tours for a fee, from a simple half-hour walk to a lantern-light tour. Surface trails and facilities are free. ⊠ 11149 U.S. Hwy. 16, Custer ✛ 15 miles west of Custer ☎ 605/673–8300 ⊕ www.nps.gov/jeca ⊠ Tours from $12.

Restaurants

Blue Bell Lodge Restaurant

$$ | AMERICAN | Feast on fresh walleye or buffalo, which you can have as a steak or a stew, in this rustic log building within the boundaries of Custer State Park. There's also a good selection of salads as well as kid-friendly burgers, sandwiches, and wraps. **Known for:** park setting; interesting dining experiences; family-friendly. $ Average main: $20 ⊠ Custer State Park, 25453 S.D. 87, Custer ☎ 605/255–4531 ⊕ www.custerresorts.com/blue-bell-lodge ⊗ Closed late Oct.–late Apr.

Bobkat's Old Fashion Purple Pie Place

$ | BAKERY | This seasonal bakery serves homemade pies and ice cream, as well as lunchtime fare like salads and paninis. Believe us when we say, the peach pie is divine, but if you're looking for something more exotic, there's rhubarb, strawberry rhubarb, cherry, blueberry, bumbleberry (that's everything together), raspberry rhubarb jalapeño, peanut butter, and a daily cream pie. **Known for:** its purple exterior; pie by the slice or whole; ice cream sundaes. $ Average main: $7 ⊠ 19 Mt Rushmore Rd., Custer ☎ 605/673–4070 ⊕ purplepieplace.com ⊗ Closed winter and spring.

Laughing Water

$ | AMERICAN | FAMILY | With windows facing the mountain sculpture, this airy pine restaurant is noted for its fry bread and buffalo burgers. There's a soup-and-salad bar, but you'd do well to stick to the Native American offerings. **Known for:** monumental views; generous portions; amazing fry bread. $ Average main: $10 ⊠ 12151 Ave. of the Chiefs, Custer ☎ 605/673–4681 ⊕ crazyhorsememorial. org/laughing-water-restaurant.html.

Hotels

State Game Lodge and Resort

$$$ | RESORT | Once the "Summer White House" for President Calvin Coolidge, this classic stone-and-wood lodge is the largest of Custer State Park's hotels. **Pros:** historic; has the regal feel of some of America's great Western lodges; park location. **Cons:** often booked up; small lobby can get busy; must drive to other restaurants. $ Rooms from: $180 ⊠ U.S. 16A, Custer ✛ 16 miles east of Custer ☎ 605/255–4541, 888/875–0001 ⊕ www. custerresorts.com ⤳ 47 rooms, 33 cabins ⊗ No meals.

Sylvan Lake Resort

$$$ | RESORT | FAMILY | This spacious stone-and-wood lodge in Custer State Park affords fantastic views of pristine Sylvan Lake and Harney Peak, the highest point in the U.S. east of the Rockies. **Pros:** wonderful views; multitude of lodging options; alpine atmosphere. **Cons:** on a winding road; limited dining options; can be pricey. $ Rooms from: $160 ⊠ 24572 S.D. 87, Custer ☎ 605/574–2561, 888/875–0001 ⊕ www.custerresorts. com ⊗ Closed Oct.–Mother's Day ⤳ 66 accommodations ⊗ No meals.

Deadwood

56 miles north of Custer on US-385; 42 miles northwest of Rapid City via I-90 W and US-14 ALT W.

In one of America's longest ongoing historic preservation projects, you'll discover brick streets fronted by Victorian architecture, with Main Street shops, restaurants, and gaming halls. Deadwood owes its historical character to gold and gaming halls, just as it did in its late-19th-century heyday. You can walk in the footsteps of Wild Bill Hickok and Calamity Jane, who swore she could out-drink, outspit, and outswear any man—and usually did. Both of the Western legends are buried in Deadwood's Boot Hill–Mt. Moriah Cemetery.

GETTING HERE AND AROUND
Deadwood is another town that's best reached by car, which you can rent at the Rapid City Airport (the closest airport).

VISITOR INFORMATION Visit Deadwood.
⊕ *www.deadwood.com.*

Sights

Adams House
HOUSE | A tour of the restored Adams House includes an explanation of the tragedies and triumphs of two of the community's founding families (the Franklins and the Adamses) who lived here. The 1892 Queen Anne–style mansion was closed in the mid-1930s and sat empty for more than 50 years, preserving the original furniture and decor that you see today. ✉ *22 Van Buren Ave., Deadwood* ☎ *605/578–3724* ⊕ *www. deadwoodhistory.com* 💲 *$10.*

Adams Museum
MUSEUM | FAMILY | Between the massive stone-block post office and the old railroad depot, there are three floors of displays at the Adams Museum, including the region's first locomotive, photographs of the town's early days, and an exhibit featuring Potato Creek Johnny's Gold Nugget, the second-largest nugget ever discovered in the Black Hills. The Adams Museum is affiliated with Deadwood History, Inc., which also oversees the Days of 76 Museum, the Historic Adams House, and a cultural center and archives. ✉ *54 Sherman St., Deadwood* ☎ *605/578–1714* ⊕ *www. deadwoodhistory.com* 💲 *Free but $5 suggested donation.*

Broken Boot Gold Mine
MINE | FAMILY | You're guaranteed to find gold on a panning experience here. If you take the short, guided mine tour, you'll also get a souvenir stock certificate. ✉ *U.S. 14A, 1200 Pioneer Way, Deadwood* ☎ *605/578–9997* ⊕ *www. brokenbootgoldmine.com* 💲 *Tour $8; gold panning from $10* ⊗ *Closed early Sept.–late May.*

Days of '76 Museum
MUSEUM | Days of '76 Museum began almost by accident as the horse-drawn carriages and stagecoaches used in the event's parade became an attraction in their own right. Over the years cowboy memorabilia, photographs, and historical clothing have been added to the collection, and the museum is currently trying to raise $6 million to build a world-class facility to better present the artifacts. ✉ *17 Crescent St., Deadwood* ☎ *605/578–1657* ⊕ *www.daysof76.com* 💲 *$8.*

Mount Moriah Cemetery
CEMETERY | Mount Moriah Cemetery, also known as Boot Hill, is the final resting place of Wild Bill Hickok, Calamity Jane, and other notable Deadwood residents. The aging landmark was revitalized by extensive restoration work in 2003, including the addition of a visitor center that houses a leather Bible, a stained-glass window, and pulpit chairs from the first and second Methodist churches of Deadwood, which were destroyed in 1885 and 2003, respectively. From the top of the cemetery you'll have the best panoramic view of the town. ✉ *Lincoln*

St., Deadwood ☎ *605/578–2600* ⊕ *www. cityofdeadwood.com/community/page/ mount-moriah-cemetery* ✉ *$2.*

Tatanka: Story of the Bison

MUSEUM | A heroic-scale bronze sculpture of three Native Americans on horseback driving 14 bison off a cliff is the center-piece of Tatanka: Story of the Bison, on a ridge above Deadwood. The attraction, owned by *Dances with Wolves* star Kevin Costner, also includes an interpretive center; Lakota guides explain Plains Indi-an life circa 1840. ✉ *U.S. 85, Deadwood* ☎ *605/584–5678* ⊕ *www.storyofthebi-son.com* ✉ *$12.*

 Restaurants

★ Deadwood Social Club

$$ | ITALIAN | On the second floor of his-toric Saloon No. 10, this warm restaurant surrounds you with wood and old-time photographs of Deadwood. Light jazz and blues play over the sound system. **Known for:** eclectic Italian menu; great martinis; historic setting. $ *Average main: $25* ✉ *657 Main St., Deadwood* ☎ *605/578–3346* ⊕ *www.saloon10.com.*

Legends Steakhouse

$$$ | STEAKHOUSE | In a place where legends aren't taken lightly, this estab-lishment in the lower level of the historic Franklin Hotel has quickly made a name for itself, beckoning back locals who like its aged beef, moderate prices, and flair. You'll find all the usual sus-pects on the menu—buffalo, beef, and chicken—but each with a flavorful twist. **Known for:** local hangout; meat-eater's dream; festive ambience. $ *Average main: $23* ✉ *Silverado Franklin Historic Hotel & Gaming Complex, 709 Main St., Deadwood* ☎ *605/578–3670* ⊕ *www. silveradofranklin.com/food-drink/leg-ends-steakhouse* ☾ *No lunch.*

Hotels

Deadwood Gulch Gaming Resort

$ | RESORT | Pine-clad hills, a creek, and a deck from which to view the mountains are at your disposal at this family-style resort about a mile from downtown Deadwood. **Pros:** away from downtown bustle; spacious rooms; attentive staff. **Cons:** more hotel than resort; busy with bus tours. $ *Rooms from: $99* ✉ *304 Cliff St., Deadwood* ☎ *605/578–1294, 800/695–1876* ⊕ *deadwoodgulchresort. com* ⤴ *87 rooms* ◉ *Free Breakfast.*

Holiday Inn Express & Suites

$$ | HOTEL | Although the exterior of this four-story hotel resembles the brick facades of Deadwood's Main Street, its interior is contemporary, with guest rooms that have Wi-Fi, free high-speed Internet connection, and other modern amenities. **Pros:** in the heart of town; contemporary comforts; reliable brand. **Cons:** street-facing rooms can be loud; no on-site parking; standard chain decor. $ *Rooms from: $169* ✉ *22 Lee St., Deadwood* ☎ *605/578–3330, 877/859–5095* ⊕ *www.ihg.com* ⤴ *100 rooms* ◉ *Breakfast.*

Mineral Palace

$$$ | HOTEL | As at the other hotels built in town since gaming was reintroduced in 1989, the architecture of Mineral Palace blends in with the historic buildings of Deadwood. **Pros:** some of the best accommodations in Deadwood; on-site steakhouse is one of the tastiest in town. **Cons:** no-smoking rooms still have a hint of smoke smell; only a small on-site parking area. $ *Rooms from: $180* ✉ *601 Main St., Deadwood* ☎ *605/578–2036, 800/847–2522* ⊕ *www.mineralpalace. com* ⤴ *71 rooms* ◉ *No meals.*

Silverado Franklin Historic Hotel & Gaming Complex

$ | HOTEL | Opened in 1903, this imposing hotel has welcomed many famous guests, including John Wayne, Teddy Roosevelt, and Babe Ruth. **Pros:** at the top of Main Street; spacious rooms; historic. **Cons:** guest rooms are tired and lack amenities; service can be patchy; casino-hotel vibe not for everyone. [$] *Rooms from: $89* ✉ *700 Main St., Deadwood* ☎ *605/578–3670, 800/584–7005* 🌐 *www.silveradofranklin.com* 🛏 *81 rooms* 🍴 *No meals.*

Nightlife

Bodega and Big Al's Buffalo Steakhouse Stockade

MUSIC CLUBS | Expect a family crowd in the day and a rowdier bunch at night at the Bodega and Big Al's Buffalo Steakhouse Stockade. Most evenings you can listen to live country or rock music; the entertainment moves outdoors in summer, when bands play in the stockade section. The Bodega has a rough past; from the 1890s until 1980, the upper floors were used as a brothel. The rooms now sit empty, although the secret buzzers and discreet back doors were removed only in the 1990s. ✉ *658 Main St., Deadwood* ☎ *605/578–1300.*

★ Old Style Saloon No. 10

BARS/PUBS | Billing itself as "the world's only museum with a bar," the Old Style Saloon No. 10 is where you want to come to drink, listen to music, and socialize. Thousands of artifacts, vintage photos, and a two-headed calf set the scene—plus the chair in which Wild Bill Hickok was supposedly shot. A reenactment of his murder takes place four times daily in summer. Upstairs, there's an exceptional restaurant, the Deadwood Social Club, with the state's premier wine and martini bar. ✉ *657 Main St., Deadwood* ☎ *605/578–3346* 🌐 *www.saloon10.com.*

Hot Springs

57 miles south of Rapid City via US 79 S; 11 miles south of the Wind Cave National Park Visitor Center via US-385.

Noted for its striking sandstone structures, the small and historic community of Hot Springs is the gateway to Wind Cave National Park. It is also the entry point to scores of other natural and historical sites, including Evans Plunge, a naturally heated indoor-outdoor pool; the Mammoth Site, where more than 50 woolly and Columbian mammoths have been unearthed; the Black Hills Wild Horse Sanctuary; and one of the region's premier golf courses.

GETTING HERE AND AROUND

Hot Springs is best reached by car, which you can rent at the Rapid City Airport (the closest one to Hot Springs).

VISITOR INFORMATION Hot Springs Area Chamber of Commerce. ☎ *605/745–4140* 🌐 *www.hotsprings-sd.com.*

Sights

Angostura Reservoir State Recreation Area

Water-based recreation is the main draw at this park 10 miles south of Hot Springs. Besides a marina, you'll find a floating convenience store, restaurant, campgrounds, and cabins. Boat rentals are available. ✉ *U.S. 385, off Rte. 79, 13157 N. Angostura Rd., Hot Springs* ☎ *605/745–6996, 800/710–2267 for reservations* 🌐 *gfp.sd.gov/parks/detail/angostura-recreation-area* 🎟 *From $8 per vehicle.*

Evans Plunge Mineral Springs

AMUSEMENT PARK/WATER PARK | **FAMILY** | The water temperature at the world's largest indoor swimming area fed by natural geothermal springs is always 87 degrees. It's also void of chemicals and the sulphur smell of other mineral springs because the pool recycles itself every 90 minutes. Established in 1890,

Evans Plunge is the oldest tourist attraction in the Black Hills. It's also kid-friendly with indoor and outdoor pools that have waterslides and tubes, and there are hot tubs, sauna, steam room, and cardio and weight rooms. Locals generally use it daily until 10 am, after which it's sanitized and opened to the public from 11 am to 4 pm. ✉ *1145 N River St., Hot Springs* ☎ *605/745–5165* 🌐 *www.evansplunge.com* 🎟 *$10.*

★ Mammoth Site

ARCHAEOLOGICAL SITE | FAMILY | While building a housing development in the 1970s, workers uncovered this sinkhole where giant mammoths came to drink, got trapped, and died. To date, 61 fossilized woolly beasts have been discovered, and most can still be seen on-site. You can watch the excavation in progress and take guided tours. ✉ *1800 W. Hwy. 18 Bypass, 15 miles south of Wind Cave National Park, Hot Springs* ☎ *605/745–6017* 🌐 *www.mammothsite.com* 🎟 *$12.*

🍴 Restaurants

Woolly's Grill and Cellar

$$ | AMERICAN | FAMILY | As it's family-owned and-operated, it's no surprise that this place caters to families. Though it specializes in hand-cut steaks and prime rib, entrées on its modestly priced menu include helpings from the 18-foot salad bar. **Known for:** family-friendly; great value for money; convenient location. [$] *Average main: $15* ✉ *1648 Hwy. 18 Bypass, Hot Springs* ☎ *605/745–6414* 🌐 *www.woollys.com* 🕒 *Closed Sun.–Wed.*

Keystone

2 miles from Mount Rushmore; 21 miles southwest of Rapid City via Rt. 16 and 16A.

Founded in the 1880s by prospectors searching for gold deposits, the small town of Keystone has an abundance of restaurants, shops, and attractions. To serve the millions of visitors passing through the area, there are more than 900 hotel rooms—that's about three times the town's number of permanent residents.

GETTING HERE AND AROUND

The best way to get to Keystone is by car, which you can rent at the Rapid City Regional Airport.

TOURS

The Keystone Visitors Information Center's website lists several helicopter and van tours.

VISITOR INFORMATION Keystone Chamber and Visitor Information Center. 🌐 *visitkeystonesd.com.*

👁 Sights

Beautiful Rushmore Cave

CAVE | FAMILY | Stalagmites, stalactites, flowstone, ribbons, columns, helictites, and the "Big Room" are all part of the worthwhile tour into this cave. In 1876, miners found the opening to the cave while digging a flume into the mountainside to carry water to the gold mines below. The cave was opened to the public in 1927, just before the carving of Mount Rushmore began. The attraction also features the Soaring Eagle Zipride, Rushmore Mountain Coaster, and Wingwalker Challenge Course. ✉ *13622 Hwy. 40, Keystone* ☎ *605/255–4384* 🌐 *www.rushmtn.com* 🎟 *From $11* 🕒 *Closed Nov.–Feb.*

In the fall, listen to elk bugling, a high-pitched whistle the animals make as they mate.

Hill City

TOWN | The small, quiet mountain town of Hill City is the gateway to Mount Rushmore. Despite having just 950 residents, the community claims four art galleries, a world-renowned dinosaur research institute, five wineries and craft breweries with tasting rooms, a vintage steam railroad, and a popular visitor center on its eastern flank. ⊠ *23935 Hwy. 385, Hill City* ☎ *800/888–1798* ⊕ *www.hillcitysd.com.*

★ Mount Rushmore

MEMORIAL | **FAMILY** | Abraham Lincoln was tall in real life—6 feet, 4 inches, though add a few more for his hat. But at one of the nation's most famous iconic sights, Honest Abe, along with presidents George Washington, Thomas Jefferson, and Theodore Roosevelt, towers over the Black Hills in a 60-foot-high likeness. The four images look especially spectacular at night, when they're always illuminated.

Follow the Presidential Trail through the forest to gain excellent views of the colossal sculpture, or stroll the Avenue of Flags for a different perspective.

Also on-site are an impressive museum, indoor theaters where films are shown, an outdoor amphitheater for live performances, an award-winning audio tour, and concession facilities. The nightly ranger program and special memorial lighting ceremony (June through mid-September) is reportedly the most popular interpretive program in all of the national parks system.

Some of the attractions at Mount Rushmore include:

Avenue of the Flags: Running from the entrance of the memorial to the museum and amphitheater at the base of the mountain, this avenue has the flag of each state, commonwealth, district, and territory—arranged alphabetically—of the United States.

Youth Exploration Area: At this stone and wood structure, along the Presidential Trail beneath the towering visage of George Washington, rangers present interactive programs for youngsters. ⊠ *13000 Hwy. 244, Mount Rushmore*

The colossal Mount Rushmore is one of the United States' most famous monuments.

☎ 605/574–2523 ⊕ *www.nps.gov/moru* ☞ *Free; parking from $10 per vehicle.*

Mount Rushmore Information Center

MEMORIAL | Between the park entrance and the Avenue of Flags, the Mount Rushmore Information Center has a small exhibit of photographs detailing the carving of the presidents' faces. The information desk is staffed by rangers who can answer questions about the area. A nearly identical building across from the information center houses restrooms, telephones, soda machines, and an award-winning audio tour by the nonprofit Mount Rushmore History Association. ✉ *13000 Hwy. 244, Keystone* ☎ 605/574–2523 ⊕ *www.nps.gov/moru* ☞ *Free; parking from $10 per vehicle.*

Peter Norbeck National Scenic Byway

SCENIC DRIVE | Although there are faster ways to get from Mount Rushmore to the southern Black Hills, this scenic drive in the Black Hills is a more stunning route. Take U.S. 16A south into Custer State Park, where bison, bighorn sheep, elk, antelope, and burros roam free. Then drive north on Highway 87 through the Needles, towering granite spires that rise above the forest. A short drive off the highway reaches 7,242-foot Harney Peak, the highest point in North America east of the Rockies. Highway 87 finally brings you to U.S. 16/U.S. 385, where you head south to the Crazy Horse Memorial. Because the scenic byway is a challenging drive (with one-lane tunnels and switchbacks) and because you'll likely want to stop a few times to admire the scenery, plan on spending two to three hours on this drive. Stretches of U.S. 16A and Highway 87 may close in winter. ✉ *Keystone* ⊕ *www. travelsouthdakota.com/trip-ideas/story/ peter-norbeck-national-scenic-byway.*

🍴 Restaurants

Alpine Inn

$$ | **STEAKHOUSE** | With its pastoral paintings, lacy tablecloths, and beer steins, the rustic Alpine Inn brings a version of old-world charm to the Old West. The lunchtime menu changes daily but always has selections of healthful sandwiches and salads—and no fried food. $ *Average main: $12* ✉ *133 Main St., Hill City* ☎ *605/574–2749* 🌐 *www.alpineinnhillcity.com* 💳 *No credit cards* 🕒 *Closed Sun.*

Carvers Cafe

$ | **AMERICAN** | The only restaurant at the Mount Rushmore Memorial affords commanding views of the memorial and the surrounding ponderosa pine forest. It serves exceptional food at reasonable prices. **Known for:** terrific park views; fantastic ice cream; sustainably sourced ingredients. $ *Average main: $10* ✉ *Ave. of Flags, Keystone* ☎ *605/574–2515* 🌐 *www.mtrushmorenationalmemorial.com/dining/carvers-cafe* 🕒 *No dinner mid-Oct.–early Mar.*

Hotels

Buffalo Rock Lodge B&B

$$$ | **B&B/INN** | A native-rock fireplace surrounded by hefty logs adds to the rustic quality of this lodge. **Pros:** quiet location; exceptional furnishings; view of Mount Rushmore from deck. **Cons:** relatively pricey; drive to shopping and dining; no TVs. $ *Rooms from: $175* ✉ *24524 Playhouse Rd., Keystone* ☎ *605/666–4781, 888/564–5634* 🌐 *www.buffalorock.net* 🛏 *7 rooms* 🍴 *No meals.*

K Bar S Lodge

$$$ | **HOTEL** | This contemporary lodge on 45 pine-clad acres feels as if it's stood here for a century. **Pros:** excellent staff; exceptional food; amid a wildlife preserve. **Cons:** quite a walk to dining options; pricey rates; often full. $ *Rooms from: $180* ✉ *434 Old Hill City Rd., Keystone* ☎ *866/522–7724, 605/666–4545* 🌐 *www.kbarslodge.com* 🕒 *Closed Nov.–Mar.* 🛏 *96 rooms* 🍴 *Free Breakfast.*

Spearfish

Spearfish is 48 miles northwest of Rapid City on I-90.

Spearfish is one of those Western towns that still maintains much of its Old West charm in downtown buildings and storefronts that now house shops, restaurants, coffee shops, and bars. The D.C. Booth National Historic Fish Hatchery, established in 1896, no longer produces trout for area streams, but it does demonstrate how it operated with underwater trout viewing, ponds, hiking trails, and historical artifacts. A must-do is the self-guided driving tour of Spearfish Canyon Scenic Byway. Leave plenty of time to take in the waterfalls, trees, plants and amazing views as well as the site where the winter camp scene was shot for the 1990 film *Dances With Wolves*. Hiking and fishing are also popular activities around Spearfish.

VISITOR INFORMATION

Visit Spearfish. ✉ *603 N Main St., Spearfish* ☎ *800/344–6181* 🌐 *visitspearfish.com.*

Sights

High Plains Western Heritage Center

MUSEUM | **FAMILY** | Focusing on a region now covered by five states—the Dakotas, Wyoming, Montana, and Nebraska—this center features artifacts such as a Deadwood-Spearfish stagecoach. Outdoor exhibits include a log cabin, a one-room schoolhouse, and, in summer, an entire farm set up with antique equipment. Often on the calendar are cowboy poetry, a cowboy supper and show, live music, and historical talks. ✉ *825 Heritage Dr., Spearfish* ☎ *605/642–9378* 🌐 *www.westernheritagecenter.com* 🎟 *$10.*

Spearfish Canyon Scenic Byway

SCENIC DRIVE | The easiest way to get from Deadwood to Rapid City is east through Boulder Canyon on U.S. 14A. However, it's worth looping north and taking the long way around on Spearfish Canyon Scenic Byway, a 20-mile scenic route past 1,000-foot limestone cliffs and some of the most breathtaking scenery in the region. Cascading waterfalls quench the thirst of quaking aspen, gnarled oaks, sweet-smelling spruce, and the ubiquitous ponderosa pine. The canyon is home to deer, mountain goats, porcupines, and mountain lions. Near its middle is the old sawmill town of Savoy, a jumping-off point for scenic hikes to Spearfish Falls and Roughlock Falls. In fall, changing leaves rival any found in New England. ✉ *10619 Roughlock Falls Rd.* 🌐 *https://www.blackhillsbadlands.com/scenic-drives/spearfish-canyon-scenic-byway.*

🍴 Restaurants

Nonna's Kitchen

$$ | **ITALIAN** | Finding a good Italian restaurant can be challenging in some cities, but not in Spearfish. Nonna's (Italian for grandmother) Kitchen opened in 2020 in an 1895 building that's full of character and good, authentic Italian food. **Known for:** authentic food; unique experience; exceptional service. [$] *Average main: $18* ✉ *544 N Main St., Spearfish* ☎ *605/307–1345* 🌐 *nonnaskitchensd.com.*

🛏 Hotels

Spearfish Canyon Lodge

$$$ | **RESORT** | Midway between Spearfish and Deadwood, this lodge-style hotel commands some of the best views in the Black Hills. **Pros:** wonderful location; lots of good-value outdoor-activity packages; as pretty as it gets. **Cons:** remote location; half-hour drive to restaurants; standard rooms. [$] *Rooms from: $174* ✉ *10619 Roughlock Falls Rd., Lead* ☎ *877/975–6343, 605/584–3435* 🌐 *www.spfcanyon.com* 🔑 *55 rooms* 🍽 *No meals.*

🏃 Activities

Heavy snowfalls and lovely views make the Black Hills prime cross-country skiing territory. Many trails are open to snowmobilers as well as skiers.

Terry Peak Ski Area

SNOW SPORTS | Perched on the sides of a 7,076-foot mountain, Terry Peak claims the Black Hills' second-highest summit and high-speed quad lifts. The runs are challenging for novice and intermediate skiers and should also keep the experts entertained. From the top, on a clear day, you can see Wyoming, Montana, and North Dakota. **Facilities:** 28 trails; 450 acres; 1,100-foot vertical drop; 5 lifts. ✉ *21120 Stewart Slope Rd., Lead* ✥ *2 miles south of Lead on U.S. 85* ☎ *800/456–0524, 605/584–2165* 🌐 *www.terrypeak.com* 🎟 *Lift ticket: $60.*

Trailshead Lodge

SNOW SPORTS | Near the Wyoming border, this lodge has a small restaurant and bar, cabins, a gas station and garage, and dozens of brand-new snowmobiles for rent by the day. This is a favorite pit-stop for snowmobilers exploring the popular Black Hills' 400-mile trail network. ✉ *22075 U.S. 85 S, Lead* ✥ *21 miles southwest of Lead on U.S. 85* ☎ *605/584–3464* 🌐 *www.trailsheadlodge.com.*

Chapter 36

YELLOWSTONE NATIONAL PARK

Updated by
Andrew Collins

WYOMING

🏕 Camping
★★★★★

🛏 Hotels
★★★★★

🏃 Activities
★★★★☆

👁 Scenery
★★★★★

👥 Crowds
★★★★★

WELCOME TO
YELLOWSTONE NATIONAL PARK

TOP REASONS TO GO

★ **Hot spots:** Thinner-than-normal crust depth and a huge magma chamber beneath the park explain Yellowstone's abundant geysers, steaming pools, hissing fumaroles, and bubbling mud pots.

★ **Bison sightings:** They're just one of many species that roam freely here (watch for moose and wolves, too). Seemingly docile, the bison make your heart race if you catch them stampeding across Lamar Valley.

★ **Hike for days:** Yellowstone has more than 900 miles of trails, along which you can summit a 10,000-foot peak, follow a trout-filled creek, or descend into the Grand Canyon of the Yellowstone.

★ **Lakefront leisure:** Here you can fish, boat, kayak, stargaze, bird-watch on black obsidian beaches, and stay in a grand historic hotel—just don't stray too far into the frigid water.

★ **Canyon adventures:** The Yellowstone River runs through the park, creating a deep yellow-tinged canyon with two impressive waterfalls.

1 **Mammoth Hot Springs.** This full-service area has an inn, restaurants, campsites, a visitor center, and general stores.

2 **Norris.** This is the hottest and most changeable part of Yellowstone National Park.

3 **Madison.** Here the Madison River is formed by the joining of the Gibbon and Firehole rivers. Anglers will find healthy stocks of brown and rainbow trout and mountain whitefish.

4 **Old Faithful.** Old Faithful erupts every 90 minutes or so. The geyser site is a full-service area with inns, restaurants, and general stores.

5 **Grant Village and West Thumb.** Named for President Ulysses S. Grant, Grant Village is on the western edge of Yellowstone Lake.

6 **Yellowstone Lake.** This is the largest body of water within the park. This is a full-service area.

7 **Canyon.** The Yellowstone River runs through the canyon, exposing geothermally altered rock.

8 **Tower-Roosevelt.** The least-visited area of the park is the place to go for horseback riding and animal sightings.

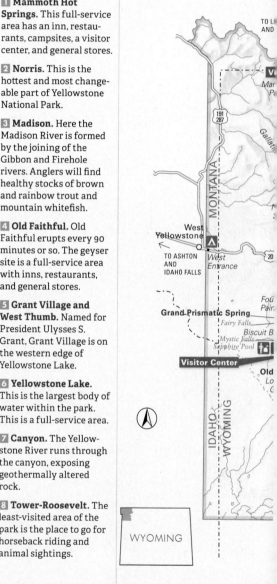

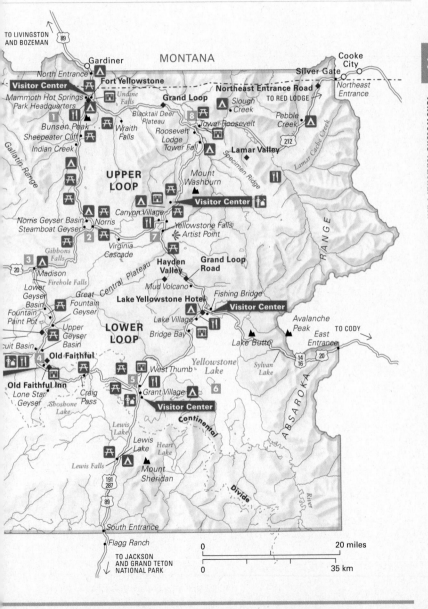

TO LIVINGSTON
AND BOZEMAN

89

MONTANA

Gardiner

North Entrance

Fort Yellowstone

Visitor Center

Mammoth Hot Springs
Park Headquarters

Cooke
City

Silver Gate

Northeast Entrance Road

Northeast
Entrance

TO RED LODGE

Bunsen Peak
Sheepeater Cliff
Indian Creek

Wraith
Falls

Undine
Falls

Blacktail Deer
Plateau

Grand Loop

Slough
Creek

Pebble
Creek

Roosevelt
Lodge

Tower Fall

Tower-Roosevelt

212

Lamar Valley

UPPER
LOOP

Mount
Washburn

Specimen Ridge

Gallatin Range

Norris Geyser Basin
Steamboat Geyser

Norris

Canyon Village

Visitor Center

Yellowstone Falls

Artist Point

RANGE

Gibbons
Falls

20

Madison

Virginia
Cascade

Central Plateau

Hayden
Valley

Grand Loop
Road

Firehole Falls

Lower
Geyser
Basin

Great
Fountain
Geyser

Mud Volcano

Lake Yellowstone Hotel

Fishing Bridge

Visitor Center

Fountain
Paint Pot

Upper
Geyser
Basin

Lake Village

Avalanche
Peak

cuit Basin

LOWER
LOOP

Bridge Bay

Lake Butte

East
Entrance

TO CODY

Old Faithful

14
16

20

Old Faithful Inn

Lone Star
Geyser

Craig
Pass

West Thumb

Grant Village

Yellowstone
Lake

Sylvan
Lake

ABSAROKA

Shoshone
Lake

Visitor Center

Continental

Lewis
Lake

Lewis
Lake

Heart
Lake

Divide

Lewis Falls

Mount
Sheridan

River

191
287

89

South Entrance

Flagg Ranch

TO JACKSON
AND GRAND TETON
NATIONAL PARK

0   20 miles

0   35 km

A landscape of astonishing beauty that's captured the imagination of visitors for many generations, this magma-filled pressure cooker of a park contains the world's greatest concentration of geysers, mud pots, fumaroles, and hot springs. But Yellowstone's unparalleled diversity makes it truly special—here you'll also find a massive river canyon, meadows teeming with bison and wolves, a huge and pristine alpine lake, and some of the country's most striking national park architecture.

Yellowstone was established in 1872 by President Ulysses S. Grant as America's first national park. At 3,472 square miles, it's also the second largest national park in the Lower 48, trailing only Death Valley. It's named for the roaring, north-flowing river that indigenous Minnetaree inhabitants called Mi tse a-da-zi, or Yellow Rock River, for the yellow bluffs that flank it— early-19th-century French trappers adapted that name, calling the entire region Yellowstone. Only one small Shoshone band, the Sheepeaters, ever settled permanently on the land now framed by the park, but for thousands of years the Blackfeet, Crow, Bannock, Flathead, Nez Perce, and Northern Shoshone frequented the area for its plentiful wildlife.

Legendary mountain man John Colter, who arrived here in 1807, was the first white American known to explore the area. His descriptions of geysers and boiling rivers prompted some mapmakers to dub the uncharted region Colter's Hell. Reports by subsequent explorers and trappers continued to spread around the country over the next few decades, eventually spurring both privately and federally funded expeditions in the 1860s. The Hayden Geological Survey of 1871 produced the most detailed report yet, complete with the still-iconic photographs by William Henry Jackson and paintings by Thomas Moran. Members of Congress were so impressed that they felt compelled to preserve this awe-inspiring land as a national park, most of it in the then territory of Wyoming (with smaller sections in Montana and Idaho). For its first 45 years, the park was administered by the U.S. Army, whose Fort Yellowstone headquarters in Mammoth Hot Springs remain a popular attraction. The National Park Service came into

AVERAGE HIGH/LOW TEMPERATURES					
JAN.	**FEB.**	**MAR.**	**APR.**	**MAY**	**JUNE**
30/10	33/12	42/17	49/28	60/32	71/41
JULY	**AUG.**	**SEPT.**	**OCT.**	**NOV.**	**DEC.**
81/45	79/45	67/37	56/30	38/22	30/12

existence in 1916 and has been overseeing the park ever since.

Although enormous, Yellowstone National Park has been developed with a visitor-friendly logic that makes it surprisingly easy to explore. The five different entrances access 310 miles of picturesque paved roads, including the Grand Loop Road, which connects the park's most popular features. A network of historic villages with lodgings, restaurants, services, and well-maintained trails provides the opportunity for overnight stays in different sections of the park. And if you get an early start, it's possible to cover quite a lot of ground each day, especially during the longer days of summer.

That said, because there's so much to see, park lodgings book months in advance, and it can take two or three hours to travel between park entrances, it's wise to prepare a strategy before visiting. The park's geothermal features—including the geyser basins around Old Faithful and Norris and the western half of Yellowstone Lake—are a must, and they're mostly situated within or adjacent to Yellowstone Caldera, the still very active supervolcano whose three massive eruptions over the past 2.1 million years created the otherworldly landscape that makes the park so famous today. You can see much of the caldera in one long day, and each subsequent day in the park will allow you to enjoy other key attractions and activities: the Grand Canyon of the Yellowstone, Mammoth Hot Springs, Lamar Valley, and the many opportunities for viewing unusual geological features and mesmerizing wildlife, from lake cruises to snowcoach tours to both easy and rugged hikes.

Planning

When to Go

There are two major seasons in Yellowstone: summer (May–October), the only time when most of the park's roads are open to cars; and winter (mid-December–February), when over-snow travel—on snowmobiles, snow coaches, and skis—delivers a fraction of the number of summer visitors to a frigid, bucolic sanctuary. Except for services at park headquarters at Mammoth Hot Springs, the park closes from mid-October to mid-December and from March to late April or early May.

You'll find the biggest crowds in July and August. If planning to visit at this time, book hotel accommodations inside or even near the park months in advance, and prepare for heavy traffic on park roads and parking areas. There are fewer people in the park the month or two before and after this peak season, but there are also fewer facilities open. In spring, there's also more rain, especially at lower elevations. Except for holiday weekends, there are few visitors in winter. Snow is possible year-round at high elevations.

FESTIVALS AND EVENTS

Cody Stampede Rodeo. The "Rodeo Capital of the World" has hosted the Stampede, one of the most important stops on the rodeo circuit, since 1919. The main event takes place at Cody Rodeo Grounds for several days around the July 4 holiday, and there are nightly performances at the Cody Nite Rodeo. ⊕ *www.codystampederodeo.com.*

Livingston Roundup Rodeo. Since the 1920s, the lively Montana town of Livingston has celebrated July 4 with riding, roping, bull-dogging, and barrel racing at the Roundup Rodeo. The revelry includes a parade, a three-day art show, and the crowning of the rodeo queen. ⊕ *www. livingstonroundup.com.*

Rendezvous Royale. Thomas Molesworth and his renowned Western furniture helped put Cody on the map when he moved here in the 1930s. This multiday festival held in late September celebrates his legacy with an art show, auctions, a quick-draw competition, and a major furniture exhibition. ⊕ *www.rendezvousroyale.org.*

Getting Here and Around

AIR

The closest airports to Yellowstone National Park served by most major airlines are in Cody, Wyoming, an hour from the East Entrance; Jackson, Wyoming, an hour from the South Entrance; and Bozeman, Montana, 90 minutes from the North and West entrances. Additionally, the tiny airport in West Yellowstone, Montana, just outside the park's west gate, has summer-only service on Delta from Salt Lake City.

CAR

Yellowstone is well away from the interstates—the nearest is Interstate 90, which passes through Livingston, Montana just 53 miles north of the park's North Entrance. You generally make your way here on scenic two-lane highways. Yellowstone has five road entrances. Many visitors arrive through the South Entrance, 57 miles north of Jackson and just 7 miles north of Grand Teton National Park. Other entrances are the East Entrance, 53 miles from Cody, Wyoming; the West Entrance at West Yellowstone, Montana (90 miles south of Bozeman), the North Entrance at Gardiner, Montana (80 miles south of Bozeman); and the Northeast Entrance at Cooke City, Montana, which can be reached from either

Cody, Wyoming, via the Chief Joseph Scenic Highway (81 miles), or from Red Lodge, Montana, over the Beartooth Pass (67 miles). ■TIP→ **You'll find gas stations at most of the main villages inside the park, although it's not a bad idea to fill your tank whenever you're outside Yellowstone, and gas is often cheaper in these areas.**

■TIP→ **The best way to keep your bearings in Yellowstone is to remember that the major roads form a figure eight, known as the Grand Loop, which all entrance roads feed into. It doesn't matter at which point you begin, as you can hit most of the major attractions if you follow the entire route.**

The 466 miles of public roads in the park (310 miles of them paved) used to be riddled with potholes and hemmed in by narrow shoulders. But the park greatly upgraded its roads, and most are now smooth, if still narrow. Roadwork is likely every summer in some portion of the park. Remember, snow is possible at any time of year in almost all areas of the park. Also, never—under any circumstances—stop your car on the road any place that isn't designated. Instances of drivers blocking traffic and potentially causing accidents are rampant on park roads. Don't be a part of this problem.

Inspiration

The Yellowstone Story, by Aubrey L. Haines, is a classic, providing an illuminating and thorough history of the park, from prehistory to the present.

Decade of the Wolf, by Douglas Smith and Gary Ferguson, is the most comprehensive and gripping account of the reintroduction of wolves into the park in the 1990s.

A book that does a terrific job explaining the park's geological processes is Robert B. Smith and Lee J. Siegel's *Windows into the Earth: The Geologic Story of Yellowstone and Grand Teton National Parks.*

Plants and Wildlife in Yellowstone

Eighty percent of Yellowstone is forest, and the great majority of it is lodgepole pine. Miles and miles of the "telephone pole" pines were lost in a 1988 fire that burned more than 35% of the park. The fire's heat created the ideal condition for the lodgepole pine's serotinous cones to release their seeds—which now provides a stark juxtaposition between 35-year-old and 110-year-old trees.

Astonishing Scenery

Yellowstone's scenery astonishes at any time of day, though the play of light and shadow makes the visuals most appealing in early morning and late afternoon. That's exactly when you should be looking for wildlife, as most are active around dawn and dusk, moving out of the forest in search of food and water. May and June are the best months for seeing baby bison, moose, and other recent arrivals. Look for glacier lilies among the spring wildflowers and goldenrod amid the changing foliage of fall. Winter visitors see the park at its most magical, with steam billowing from geyser basins to wreath trees in ice, and elk foraging close to roads transformed into ski trails.

Where the Animals Roam

Bison, elk, and coyotes populate virtually all areas; elk and bison particularly like river valleys and the geyser basins. Moose like the marshy areas along Yellowstone Lake and in the park's northeastern corner. Wolves are most common in the Lamar Valley and areas south of Mammoth; bears are most visible in the Pelican Valley–Fishing Bridge area, near Dunraven Pass, and near Mammoth. Watch for trumpeter swans along the Yellowstone River and for sandhill cranes near the Firehole River and in Madison Valley.

36

Yellowstone National Park PLANNING

Lost in My Own Backyard, by Tim Cahill, is a hilarious account of one person's experiences in the park over more than 25 years.

Alston Chase's controversial *Playing God in Yellowstone* chronicles a century of government mismanagement in asserting that the National Park Service has ultimately damaged the park's ecosystem in its efforts to protect it.

Park Essentials

ACCESSIBILITY

Yellowstone has long been a National Park Service leader in providing access to visitors with disabilities. Restrooms with sinks and flush toilets designed for those in wheelchairs are in all developed areas except West Thumb, whose facilities are quite rustic. Accessible campsites and restrooms are at every park campground except Fishing Bridge RV Park. An accessible fishing platform is about 3½ miles west of Madison at Mt. Haynes Overlook. For more information, pick up a free copy of the *Visitor Guide to Accessible Features in Yellowstone National Park* at any visitor center.

PARK FEES AND PERMITS

Entrance fees of $35 per vehicle, $30 per motorcycle or snowmobile, or $20 per visitor 16 and older entering by foot, bike, ski, and so on, are good for seven days. See Activities for details on boating, camping, fishing, and horseback permits and fees.

PARK HOURS

At least some part of Yellowstone is open year-round, with 24-hour access. But many areas and entrances are closed in winter or during fall and spring shoulder seasons, and the exact times can vary depending on the weather, so it's important to check the park website for the latest details if you're planning to visit anytime from mid-October to early May. Conventional vehicles can always access the North Entrance at Gardiner, Montana, to Mammoth Hot Springs, and from Mammoth Hot Springs to the Northeast Entrance and the town of Cooke City (with no through-travel beyond Cooke City). Only over-snow vehicles can travel other parts of the park in winter. The park is in the Mountain time zone.

CELL PHONE RECEPTION

Most of the park's developed villages have (sometimes spotty) cell service, including Mammoth Hot Springs, West Yellowstone, Old Faithful, Grand Village, Lake Village, and Mt. Washburn. However, especially in the summer, crowds can overwhelm cellular capacity and greatly slow things down. Don't expect cell service on roads between these main developed areas or in the backcountry. There are public phones near visitor centers.

Hotels

Accommodations in the park continue to undergo significant upgrades, and overall, Yellowstone's lodgings are above average in quality and with rates that are comparable to many other national parks. Options range from a pair of magnificent historic hotels—the Old Faithful Inn and Lake Yellowstone Hotel—to simple cabins and utilitarian modern motels. Make reservations at least four months ahead for all park lodgings in July and August, although if planning a trip on shorter notice, it's still worth a try, as cancellations do happen. Old Faithful Snow Lodge and Mammoth Hot Springs Hotel are the only accommodations open in winter; rates are the same as in summer. There are no TVs in any park hotels. *Hotel reviews have been shortened. For full information, visit Fodors.com.*

What It Costs			
$	$$	$$$	$$$$
RESTAURANTS			
under $16	$16–$22	$22–$30	over $30
HOTELS			
under $150	$151–$225	$226–$300	over $300

Restaurants

The park's main developed areas all have at least one cafeteria or casual restaurant and typically a convenience store with limited groceries and deli items, but distances between these places can be considerable, and crowds during busy periods can result in long wait times for a table. For more flexibility and to be able to take advantage of the huge supply of park picnic areas, it's a good idea to fill a cooler with groceries in one of the larger towns outside the park. In addition to standard comfort fare—soups, salads, burgers, sandwiches, pizzas, ice cream—available in the park's casual eateries, you'll also encounter increasingly more sophisticated regional cuisine—with a focus on elk, bison, trout, and other game and seafood—at several more upscale restaurants, including the Old Faithful Inn, Lake Yellowstone Hotel, Grant Village Old Faithful Snow Lodge, and Mammoth Hotel dining rooms; reservations are advised, particularly in summer, at these venues. Given the park's remote location, prices at park restaurants can be a bit steep. *Restaurant reviews have been shortened. For full information, visit Fodors.com.*

Yellowstone in One Day

If you have just one full day in the park, concentrate on the two biggest attractions: Old Faithful geyser and the Grand Canyon of the Yellowstone. En route between these places, you can see geothermal activity and most likely some wildlife.

Allow at least two hours to explore **Old Faithful** and the surrounding village. Eruptions occur approximately 90 minutes apart but can vary, so check with the visitor center for predicted times. Be sure to explore the surrounding geyser basin, including the 1½-mile **Geyser Hill Loop**, and **Old Faithful Inn**, from which you can watch the geyser erupt from the hotel's rear deck. A short drive north, make **Grand Prismatic Spring** in **Midway Geyser Basin** your can't-miss geothermal stop; farther north, near Madison, detour to the west along short **Firehole Canyon Drive** to see the Firehole River cut a small canyon and waterfall (Firehole Falls).

If arriving from the east, start with sunrise at **Lake Butte, Fishing Bridge**, and the wildlife-rich **Hayden Valley** as you loop through the park counterclockwise to Old Faithful. If you're entering through the North or Northeast Entrance, begin at dawn looking for wolves and other animals in **Lamar Valley**, then continue west to **Mammoth Hot Springs**, where you can walk the **Lower Terrace Interpretive Trail** past Liberty Cap and other strange, brightly colored travertine formations, before making your way south to Old Faithful. Keep an eye out for wildlife as you go—you're almost certain to see elk, bison, and possibly a bear. Once you've finished at Old Faithful, make your way east through Madison and Norris to **Canyon Village** to see the north or south rim of the **Grand Canyon of the Yellowstone** and its waterfalls. Alternatively, you could see the Canyon area earlier in the day and save Old Faithful for last—both of these areas are gorgeous at sunset.

PICNIC AREAS

You'll find more than 50 designated picnic areas in the park, ranging from secluded spots with a couple of tables to more popular stops with a dozen or more tables. ■TIP➡ **Keep an eye out for wildlife.** You never know when a herd of bison might decide to march through. If this happens, it's best to leave your food and move a safe distance away from them.

Tours

★ Historic Yellow Bus Tours

BUS TOURS | FAMILY | Tours by park concessionaire Xanterra on restored bright-yellow buses from as far back as the 1930s offer more than a dozen itineraries throughout Yellowstone. It's an elegant way to learn about the park, and on warm days, the driver–tour narrator rolls back the convertible top. The tour lineup includes Evening Wildlife Encounters, Picture Perfect Photo Safari, and Wake Up to Wildlife, all longtime crowd-pleasers. Other tours, including some all-day ones that efficiently cover huge swaths of the park, are on newer buses. Tours depart from several park hotels. Xanterra also gives a variety of bus, boat, stagecoach, and other tours. ☎ 307/344–7311 ⊕ www.yellowstonenationalparklodges. com ✉ From $42.

See Yellowstone

ADVENTURE TOURS | In summer this company conducts tours that might include day hiking in the backcountry, fly-fishing in Yellowstone, and horseback riding across wildflower meadows. The company also offers snowmobile and snowcoach excursions to Old Faithful and Lower Geyser Basin as well as cross-country skiing, snowshoeing, and dogsledding adventures. ✉ 211 Yellowstone Ave., West Yellowstone ☎ 800/221–1151 ⊕ www.seeyellowstone.com ✉ From $95.

Visitor Information

PARK CONTACT INFORMATION Yellowstone National Park. ☎ 307/344–7381 ⊕ www.nps.gov/yell.

Mammoth Hot Springs

6 miles south of Gardiner, 51 miles north of Old Faithful.

This park's northernmost community— which is just south of the North Entrance in Gardiner, Montana—is known for its massive natural travertine terraces, where mineral water flows continuously, building an ever-changing display. The entire complex of terraces, which is laced with boardwalks and pathways, is within walking distance of the area's historic village, which contains some charming mid-priced (by Yellowstone standards) lodging and dining options as well as the historic buildings of Fort Yellowstone, which are lovely to walk by. You will often see elk grazing in the village.

Sights

HISTORIC SIGHTS

★ Fort Yellowstone

MILITARY SITE | The oldest buildings here served as Fort Yellowstone from 1891 to 1918, when the U.S. Army managed the park. The redbrick buildings cluster around an open area reminiscent of a frontier-era parade ground. Pick up a self-guided tour map of the area from the Albright Visitors Center on Officers Row, and start your walking tour there. ✉ Mammoth Hot Springs.

SCENIC DRIVES

Upper Terrace Drive

SCENIC DRIVE | This popular 1½-mile drive at the top of the Mammoth Terraces will take you back into the woods, where you can see some impressive thermal features, among them White Elephant Back and Orange Spring Mound, that aren't visible from the main road. Park at the top of the Terraces for views of Fort Yellowstone, a short walk along the boardwalk to Canary Springs, or hike down into the Lower Terraces Area. RVs aren't permitted along this drive. ✉ Grand Loop Rd. ⊙ Closed Dec.–Apr.

SCENIC STOPS

★ Mammoth Hot Springs Terraces

BODY OF WATER | **FAMILY** | Multicolor travertine terraces formed by slowly escaping hot mineral water mark this unusual geological formation, one of the most remarkable sights in the park. You can explore the terraces via an elaborate network of boardwalks, the best of which is the Lower Terrace Interpretive Trail. If you head uphill from Liberty Cap, near the lower parking area, in a half-hour you'll pass bright and ornately terraced Minerva Spring, and in an hour you can make your way up to the Main Terrace Overlook and the side trail to Canary Spring. Along the way you might spot elk grazing nearby. Alternatively, you can drive up to the Main Terrace Overlook on Upper Terrace Drive and hike down to the Lower

Terrace. Distances are fairly short amid these terraces, but give yourself at least a couple of hours to thoroughly explore them—especially if you enjoy taking lots of pictures. ⌧ *Grand Loop Rd.*

TRAILS

Beaver Ponds Loop Trail

TRAIL | This 2½-hour, 5-mile loop starts at Liberty Cap in the busy Lower Terrace of Mammoth Hot Springs. Within minutes you'll find yourself amid the park's dense backcountry as you climb 400 feet through spruce and fir, passing several ponds and dams, as well as a glacier-carved moraine, before emerging on a windswept plain overlooking the Montana–Wyoming border. Look up to see Everts Peak to the east, Bunsen Peak to the south, and Sepulcher Mountain to the west. Your final descent into Mammoth Springs has great views of Mammoth Springs. *Moderate.* ⌧ *Mammoth Hot Springs* ⊹ *Trailhead: Lower Terrace parking area.*

★ Bunsen Peak Trail

TRAIL | Past the entrance to Bunsen Peak Road, this moderately challenging 4.4-mile round-trip trek climbs 1,280 feet to 8,527-foot Bunsen Peak for a dramatic panoramic view of Blacktail Plateau, Mammoth Hot Springs, the Gallatin Mountains, and the Yellowstone River valley. Allow about three hours. *Moderate–Difficult.* ⌧ *Yellowstone National Park* ⊹ *Trailhead: Grand Loop Rd., 1½ miles south of Mammoth Hot Springs.*

VISITOR CENTERS

Albright Visitor Center

INFO CENTER | **FAMILY** | Bachelor quarters for U.S. Army cavalry officers from 1909 to 1918, the carefully renovated red-roof visitor center is a great source for maps, advice, permits, and free Wi-Fi. This hefty stone structure also contains a bookstore and exhibits about the park's history, flora, and fauna, including displays of bears and wolves that kids love. ⌧ *Grand Loop Rd., Mammoth Hot Springs* ☎ *307/344–2263* ⊕ *www.nps.gov/yell.*

Restaurants

Mammoth Hotel Dining Room

$$$ | **AMERICAN** | A wall of windows in the handsome art deco–style restaurant overlooks an expanse of green that was once a military parade and drill field. While enjoying breakfast, lunch, or dinner you might catch a glimpse of elk grazing on the lawn. **Known for:** bison burgers; creative appetizers; views of roaming elk. $ *Average main: $24* ⌧ *305A Albright Ave., Mammoth Hot Springs* ☎ *307/344–7311, 866/439–7375* ⊕ *www.yellowstonenationalparklodges.com* ⊘ *Closed mid-Oct.–mid-Dec. and Mar.–late Apr.*

Mammoth Terrace Grill

$ | **AMERICAN** | **FAMILY** | Although the exterior looks rather elegant, this is actually the casual option at Mammoth Hot Springs, a good bet for simple fare like hot dogs, hamburgers, and chicken tenders. Continental breakfast is offered all day. **Known for:** biscuits and gravy in the morning; smoked-bison bratwurst sandwiches; pretty good beer and wine selection. $ *Average main: $9* ⌧ *305B Albright Ave., Mammoth Hot Springs* ☎ *307/344–7311* ⊕ *www.yellowstonenationalparklodges.com* ⊘ *Closed mid-Oct.–late Apr.*

Hotels

★ Mammoth Hot Springs Hotel and Cabins

$$ | **HOTEL** | The rooms at this 1936 lodge are smaller and simpler than those at the park's other historic hotels, but this one is less expensive; the surrounding cabins look like tiny, genteel summer homes. **Pros:** good rates for a historic property; wake up to an elk bugling outside your window; cabins are among the park's nicest. **Cons:** least expensive rooms lack bathrooms; in one of the busier parts of the park; Wi-Fi is spotty. $ *Rooms from: $197* ⌧ *2 Mammoth Hotel Ave.* ☎ *307/344–7311* ⊕ *www.yellowstonenationalparklodges.com* ⊘ *Closed mid-Oct.–mid Dec. and early Mar.–late Apr.* ⇆ *216 rooms* ⦿ *No meals.*

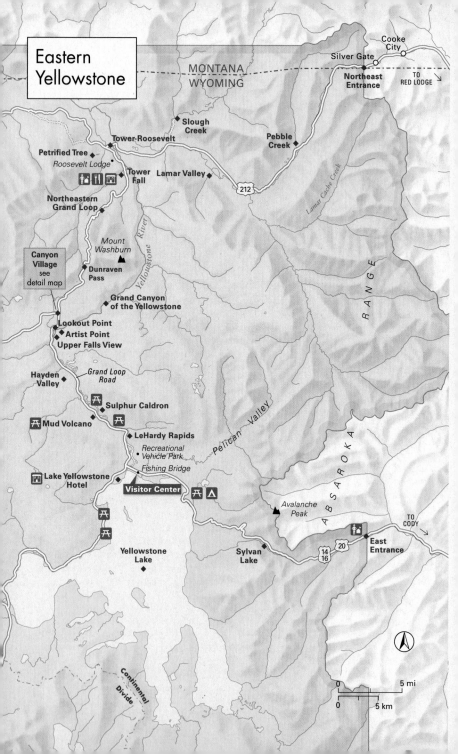

Norris

21 miles south of Mammoth Hot Springs, 13 miles west of Canyon Village.

The area at the western junction of the Upper and Lower Loops has the most active geyser basin in the park. The underground plumbing occasionally reaches such high temperatures—the ground itself has heated up in areas to nearly 200°F—that a portion of the basin is periodically closed for safety reasons. There are limited visitor services: two small museums, a bookstore, and a picnic area. The 21-mile span of Grand Loop Drive from Mammoth Hot Springs to Norris is quite dramatic, passing groves of aspens that explode with fall color just south from Upper Terrace Drive and traversing a hillside of giant boulders through the Golden Gate section.

■TIP➔ **Ask rangers at the Norris Geyser Basin Museum when different geysers are expected to erupt and plan your walk accordingly.**

Sights

PICNIC AREAS

Gibbon Meadows

LOCAL INTEREST | **FAMILY** | You may see elk or buffalo along the Gibbon River from one of the several tables at this picturesque spot, which has a wheelchair-accessible pit toilet. ⊠ *Grand Loop Rd.*

SCENIC STOPS

Museum of the National Park Ranger

MUSEUM | **FAMILY** | This historic ranger station housed soldiers from 1908 to 1918. The six-room log building is now an engaging museum where you can watch a movie telling the history of the National Park Service and visit with the retired rangers who volunteer here. Other exhibits relate to Army service in Yellowstone and early park rangers. ⊠ *Norris Campground Rd.* ☾ *Closed late Sept.–late May.*

Norris Geyser Basin

NATURE SITE | **FAMILY** | From the 1930 Norris Ranger Station, which houses a small museum that helps to explain the basin's geothermal activity, you can stroll a network of short boardwalk trails—some of them suitable for wheelchairs—to Porcelain Basin, Back Basin, and several geysers and other interesting and constantly evolving thermal features. ⊠ *Grand Loop Rd. at Norris Canyon Rd.* ⊕ *www.nps.gov/yell* ☾ *Ranger station closed mid-Oct.–mid-May.*

TRAILS

Back Basin–Porcelain Basin Loops

TRAIL | You can hike these two easy loops, which both leave from the Norris Ranger Station, in under two hours. The 1½-mile Back Basin loop passes Emerald Spring, Steamboat Geyser, Cistern Spring, and Echinus Geyser. The latter was long known as Norris's most dependable big geyser, but its schedule has become much more erratic. The ¾-mile Porcelain Basin loop leads past whitish geyserite stone and extremely active Whirligig and other small geysers. *Easy.* ⊠ *Norris* ⊹ *Trailhead: at Grand Loop Rd. at Norris Canyon Rd.*

Madison

14 miles southwest of Norris, 15 miles east of West Yellowstone, Montana.

The area around the junction of the West Entrance Road and the Lower Loop is a good place to take a break as you travel through the park, because you will almost always see bison grazing along the Madison River, and elk are often in the area, too. The only visitor services in Madison are a small information station.

◉ Sights

SCENIC DRIVES
★ Firehole Canyon Drive
SCENIC DRIVE | FAMILY | The 2-mile narrow asphalt road twists through a deep canyon of curving lava-rock formations and passes the 40-foot Firehole Falls, which are most scenic in the morning when you're not looking into the afternoon sun. In summer look for a sign marking a pull-out and swimming hole. This is one of only two places in the park (Boiling River on the North Entrance Road is the other) where you can safely and legally swim in the thermally heated waters. Look for osprey and other raptors. ⊠ *Yellowstone National Park* ✛ *1 mile south of Madison junction, off Grand Loop Rd.* ☉ *Closed early Nov.–early Apr.*

SCENIC STOPS
Gibbon Falls
BODY OF WATER | FAMILY | The water of this 84-foot fall on the Gibbon River rushes over the caldera rim. Driving east from Madison to Norris, you can see it on your right, but the angle is even better from the paved trail adjacent to the canyon's edge. ⊠ *Yellowstone National Park* ✛ *Grand Loop Rd., 4 miles east of Madison.*

VISITOR CENTERS
Madison Information Station and Trailside Museum
INFO CENTER | FAMILY | In this handsome 1930s stone-and-timber structure, knowledgeable rangers share space with a store that sells books, maps, and learning aids, and a museum with exhibits on the thermal features in the vicinity. Spotting scopes are sometimes set up for viewing eagles, bison, and elk out the rear window. You can pick up backcountry camping and fishing permits, too. Picnic tables, toilets, and an amphitheater for summer-evening ranger programs are shared with the nearby campground. ⊠ *Grand Loop Rd. at West Entrance Rd.* ☎ *307/344–2876* ⊕ *www.nps.gov/yell* ☉ *Closed early Oct.–early June.*

Old Faithful

17 miles south of Madison, 40 miles west of Fishing Bridge Village.

The world's most famous geyser is the centerpiece of this area that includes one of the largest villages in the park and three prominent geyser basins: Upper, Midway, and Lower. The 1-square-mile Upper Geyser Basin is arguably the park's most famous draw, home to Old Faithful as well as 140 different geysers—one-fifth of the known geysers in the world. It's an excellent place to spend a day or more exploring, with a complex system of boardwalks and trails—some of them suitable for bikes—and equally extensive visitor services, including several lodging and dining choices, and a very fine visitor center. In winter you can dine and stay in this area and cross-country ski or snowshoe through the geyser basin. This smaller Midway and Lower geyser basins each have their own must-see features, including Grand Prismatic Spring and Fountain Paint Pots.

Sights

HISTORIC SIGHTS
★ Old Faithful Inn
HOTEL—SIGHT | FAMILY | It's hard to imagine how any work could be accomplished with snow and ice blanketing the region, but this truly iconic hotel was constructed over the course of a single winter. Completed in 1904, what's believed to be the world's largest log structure is one of the most recognizable, and impressive, buildings in the national park system. Even if you don't spend the night, walk through or take the free 45-minute guided tour to admire its massive open-beam lobby and rock fireplace. There are antique writing desks on the second-floor balcony. You can watch Old Faithful geyser from two second-floor decks. ⊠ *3200 Old Faithful Inn Rd., Old Faithful* ☎ *307/344–7311*

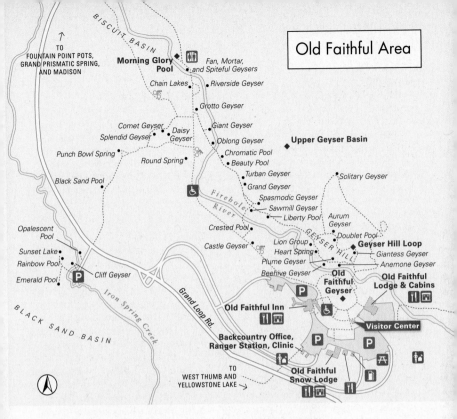

Old Faithful Area

TO FOUNTAIN POINT POTS, GRAND PRISMATIC SPRING, AND MADISON

BISCUIT BASIN

Morning Glory Pool

Fan, Mortar, and Spiteful Geysers

Chain Lakes

Riverside Geyser

Grotto Geyser

Comet Geyser
Splendid Geyser
Daisy Geyser
Giant Geyser
Oblong Geyser

Upper Geyser Basin

Punch Bowl Spring
Round Spring
Chromatic Pool
Beauty Pool

Black Sand Pool
Turban Geyser
Grand Geyser
Solitary Geyser

Firehole River

Spasmodic Geyser
Sawmill Geyser
Liberty Pool
Aurum Geyser

Opalescent Pool
Crested Pool

Sunset Lake
Castle Geyser
Lion Group
Heart Spring
Doublet Pool
Geyser Hill Loop
Giantess Geyser

Rainbow Pool
Plume Geyser
Anemone Geyser

Emerald Pool
Cliff Geyser
Beehive Geyser
Old Faithful Geyser

Old Faithful Lodge & Cabins

Iron Spring Creek

BLACK SAND BASIN

Grand Loop Rd.

Old Faithful Inn

Backcountry Office, Ranger Station, Clinic

Visitor Center

TO WEST THUMB AND YELLOWSTONE LAKE →

Old Faithful Snow Lodge

⊕ www.yellowstonenationalparklodges.com ☾ Closed early Oct.–early May.

PICNIC AREAS

Firehole River

LOCAL INTEREST | FAMILY | This scenic picnic area overlooks the roaring Firehole River, a place where you might see elk grazing along the river's banks. There's a pit toilet. ⊠ Grand Loop Rd., Madison.

SCENIC DRIVES

Firehole Lake Drive

SCENIC DRIVE | This one-way, 3-mile-long road takes you past Great Fountain Geyser, which shoots out jets of water reaching as high as 200 feet about twice a day. Rangers' predictions provide a two-hour window of opportunity. Should you witness an eruption, you'll see waves of water cascading down the terraces that form the geyser's edges. ⊠ Firehole Lake Dr., Old Faithful ☾ Closed early Nov.–early Apr.

SCENIC STOPS

Biscuit Basin

NATURE SITE | A short drive north of Old Faithful and accessed via an easy ⅔-mile loop stroll, this basin is also the trailhead for the Mystic Falls Trail. The namesake "biscuit" formations were reduced to crumbs when Sapphire Pool erupted after the 1959 Hebgen Lake earthquake. Now, Sapphire is a calm, beautiful blue pool again, but that could change at any moment. ⊠ Grand Loop Rd., Old Faithful.

Black Sand Basin

NATURE SITE | FAMILY | There are a dozen hot springs and geysers nearly opposite the cloverleaf entrance from Grand Loop Road to Old Faithful. Emerald Pool is one of the prettiest. It's an easy 1½-mile walk, ski, or bike ride from the Old Faithful area, or you can drive and

park right in the middle of the basin.
⊠ *Grand Loop Rd., Old Faithful.*

Geyser Hill Loop

TRAIL | FAMILY | Along the easy 1.3-mile Geyser Hill Loop boardwalk, accessed from the Old Faithful Boardwalk, you'll see active thermal features such as violent Giantess Geyser. Erupting only a few times each year (but sometimes going quiet for several years), Giantess spouts from 100 to 250 feet in the air for five to eight minutes once or twice hourly for a few to as long as 48 hours. Nearby Doublet Pool's two adjacent springs have complex ledges and deep blue waters that are highly photogenic. Starting as a gentle pool, Anemone Geyser overflows, bubbles, and finally erupts 10 feet or more, every three to eight minutes. The loop boardwalk brings you close to the action, making it especially fun for kids. ⊠ *Old Faithful* ⊹ *Trailhead: Old Faithful Visitor Center.*

★ Grand Prismatic Spring

NATURE SITE | FAMILY | You can reach Yellowstone's largest hot spring, 370 feet in diameter and arguably an even more dazzling sight than Old Faithful, by following a ⅓-mile boardwalk loop. The spring, in the Midway Geyser Basin, is deep blue in color, with yellow and orange rings formed by bacteria that give it the effect of a prism. For a stunning perspective, view it from the overlook along the Fairy Falls Trail. ⊠ *Midway Geyser Basin, Grand Loop Rd.*

Lower Geyser Basin

NATURE SITE | With its mighty blasts of water shooting as high as 200 feet, the Great Fountain Geyser is this basin's superstar. When it spews, waves cascade down the terraces that form its edge. Check at the Old Faithful Visitor Center for predicted eruption times. Less impressive but more regular is White Dome Geyser, which shoots from a 20-foot-tall cone. You'll also find pink mud pots and blue pools at the basin's Fountain Paint Pots, a unique spot because visitors encounter all four of Yellowstone's hydrothermal features: fumaroles, mud pots, hot springs, and geysers. ⊠ *Grand Loop Rd.*

Midway Geyser Basin

NATURE SITE | Called "Hell's Half Acre" by writer Rudyard Kipling, Midway Geyser Basin contains the breathtaking Grand Prismatic Spring and is an even more interesting stop than Lower Geyser Basin. Boardwalks wind their way to the Excelsior Geyser, which deposits 4,000 gallons of vivid blue water per minute into the Firehole River. ⊠ *Grand Loop Rd.*

Morning Glory Pool

NATURE SITE | Shaped somewhat like a morning glory, this pool once was a deep blue, but the color is no longer as striking as before due to tourists dropping coins and other debris into the hole. To reach the pool, follow the boardwalk past Geyser Hill Loop and stately Castle Geyser, which has the biggest cone in Yellowstone. Morning Glory is the inspiration for popular children's author Jan Brett's story *Hedgie Blasts Off,* in which a hedgehog travels to another planet to unclog a geyser damaged by space tourists' debris. ⊠ *Yellowstone National Park* ⊹ *North end of Upper Geyser Basin.*

★ Old Faithful

NATURE SITE | FAMILY | Almost every park visitor makes it a point to view the world's most famous geyser, at least once. Yellowstone's most predictable big geyser—although neither its largest nor most regular—sometimes shoots as high as 180 feet, but it averages 130 feet. The eruptions take place every 50–120 minutes, the average is around 94 minutes. Check the park website, visitor center, or the lobbies of the Old Faithful hotels for predicted times. You can view the eruption from a bench just yards away, from the dining room at the lodge cafeteria, or the second-floor deck of the Old Faithful Inn. The 1.6-mile loop hike to Observation Point yields yet another view—from above—of the geyser and the surrounding basin. ⊠ *Grand Loop Rd.*

A Good Tour: Old Faithful Area

Begin your tour at the impressive **Old Faithful Visitor Education Center.** Pick up the Old Faithful–area trail guide and check a bulletin board with the latest predictions for six geyser eruptions.

The Main Attraction

Concentrate first on the main attraction: **Old Faithful** spouts from 130 to 180 feet high approximately every 94 minutes. You don't need to jockey for position on the boardwalk directly in front of the visitor center to enjoy the geyser. It's impressive from any angle on the boardwalk surrounding it. The view from the second-floor deck of the **Old Faithful Inn** is glorious, too. Speaking of that famous, century-old structure, check out its massive log-construction interior.

Exploring the Basins

At Old Faithful Village you're in the heart of the **Upper Geyser Basin,** the densest concentration of geysers on Earth, with about 140 geysers within a square mile. Once you've watched Old Faithful erupt, explore the larger basin with a hike around **Geyser Hill,** where you may see wildlife as well as thermal features. Follow the trail north to the **Morning Glory Pool,** with its unique flower shape. Along this trail are Castle, Grand, and Riverside geysers. Return to the village and continue by car to **Black Sand Basin** or **Biscuit Basin.** At Biscuit Basin, follow the boardwalks to the trailhead for the Mystic Falls Trail, where you can get views of the Upper Geyser Basin.

Paint Pots and a Spring

Take a break from geyser watching with a packed lunch at the Whiskey Flat picnic area. Afterward, continue your drive toward **Lower Geyser Basin,** with its colorful **Fountain Paint Pots.** Then, on the way back to Old Faithful, stop at **Midway Geyser Basin,** where steaming runoff from the colorful 370-foot **Grand Prismatic Spring** crashes continuously into the Firehole River.

Relax and Celebrate

Relax and celebrate your day's accomplishments with dinner (reservations required) at the Old Faithful Inn, or enjoy drinks on the second floor.

TRAILS

★ Fairy Falls Trail

TRAIL | Rewarding trekkers with the chance to view Grand Prismatic Spring from high up on a bluff and to gaze up at 200-foot-tall Fairy Falls cascade from a pool of mist down below, this mostly level 5.4-mile round-trip hike is one of the highlights of the Midway Geyser Basin. *Easy.* ✉ Old Faithful ⊹ *Trailhead: Fairy Falls Trail parking lot, Midway Geyser Basin.*

Fountain Paint Pots Nature Trail

TRAIL | FAMILY | Take the ½-mile loop boardwalk to see the fumaroles (steam vents), blue pools, pink mud pots, and mini-geysers in this thermal area. The trail is popular, and sometimes a bit overcrowded, in summer and winter because it's so accessible. *Easy.* ✉ *Yellowstone National Park ⊹ Trailhead: at Lower Geyser Basin.*

Lone Star Geyser

TRAIL | FAMILY | A little longer, at 4.8 miles round-trip, than many of the other trails in the vicinity of Upper Geyser Basin, this enjoyable ramble along a level, partially paved trail that parallels the Firehole River leads to an overlook where you can watch Lone Star Geyser erupt up to 45 feet into the sky. Eruptions take place every three hours or so,and the trail is also popular with cyclists. *Easy–Moderate.* ✥ *Trailhead: Just south of Kepler Cascades parking area, 3½ miles south of Old Faithful.*

Mystic Falls Trail

TRAIL | From the west end of Biscuit Basin boardwalk, this 2.4-mile round-trip trail climbs gently for a mile through heavily burned forest to the lava-rock base of 70-foot Mystic Falls. It then switchbacks up Madison Plateau to a lookout with the park's least-crowded view of Old Faithful and the Upper Geyser Basin. *Easy–Moderate.* ✉ *Old Faithful* ✥ *Trailhead: Biscuit Basin.*

★ **Observation Point Loop**

TRAIL | A 2-mile round-trip route leaves Geyser Hill Loop boardwalk and becomes a trail shortly after the Firehole River; it circles a picturesque overview of Geyser Hill with Old Faithful Inn as a backdrop. You may also see Castle Geyser erupting. Even when 1,000-plus people are crowded on the boardwalk to watch Old Faithful, expect to find fewer than a dozen here. *Easy–Moderate.* ✉ *Old Faithful* ✥ *Trailhead: Old Faithful Visitor Center.*

VISITOR CENTERS

★ **Old Faithful Visitor Education Center**

INFO CENTER | FAMILY | At this impressive, contemporary, LEED-certified visitor center that's a jewel of the national park system, you can check out the interactive exhibits and children's area, read the latest geyser-eruption predictions, and find out the schedules for ranger-led walks and talks. Backcountry and fishing permits are dispensed at the ranger station adjacent to the Old Faithful Snow Lodge, across the street. ✉ *Old Faithful Bypass Rd.* ☎ *307/344–2751* 🌐 *www.nps.gov/yell* 🕒 *Closed mid-Nov.–mid-Dec. and mid-Mar.–mid-Apr.*

🍴 Restaurants

Bear Paw Deli

$ | AMERICAN | FAMILY | You can grab a quick bite and not miss a geyser eruption at this snack shop in the Old Faithful Inn. Salmon, black-bean, and beef burgers as well as several sandwiches are available throughout the day, as is hand-dipped ice cream. **Known for:** inexpensive, no-frills meals; opens early, closes late (by park standards); great location by geyser. [$] *Average main: $9* ✉ *3200 Old Faithful Inn Rd., Old Faithful* ☎ *307/344–7311* 🌐 *www.yellowstonenationalparklodges.com* 🕒 *Closed early Oct.–early May.*

★ **Old Faithful Inn Dining Room**

$$$ | AMERICAN | The Old Faithful Inn's original dining room—designed by Robert Reamer in 1903 and expanded by him in 1927—has lodgepole-pine walls and ceiling beams and a giant volcanic rock fireplace. Note the whimsical etched-glass panels that separate the dining room from the Bear Pit Lounge; the images of partying animals were commissioned by Reamer in 1933 to celebrate the end of Prohibition. **Known for:** gorgeous interior; buffet options offered at every meal; extensive wine list. [$] *Average main: $24* ✉ *3200 Old Faithful Inn Rd., Old Faithful* ☎ *307/344–7311* 🌐 *www.yellowstonenationalparklodges.com* 🕒 *Closed early Oct.–early May.*

Old Faithful Snow Lodge Obsidian Dining Room

$$$ | MODERN AMERICAN | From the wood-and-leather chairs etched with animal figures to the intricate lighting fixtures that resemble snowcapped trees, there's ample Western atmosphere at this relatively intimate dining room inside the Old Faithful

Snow Lodge. The huge windows give you a view of the Old Faithful area, and you can sometimes see the famous geyser as it erupts. **Known for:** hearty regional wild game dishes; open in winter; lounge offering microbrews and lighter fare. [$] *Average main: $26* ✉ *2051 Snow Lodge Ave.* ☎ *307/344–7311* 🌐 *www.yellowstonenationalparklodges.com* 🕓 *Closed late-Oct.–mid-Dec. and Mar.–late Apr.*

Hotels

★ Old Faithful Inn

$$$ | **HOTEL** | **FAMILY** | Easily earning its National Historic Landmark status, this jewel of the national park system has been a favorite since the original Old House section opened in 1904—it's worth a visit whether or not you stay here. **Pros:** a one-of-a-kind property; rooms at a range of price points; incredible location near geyser. **Cons:** thin walls; waves of tourists in the lobby; least expensive rooms lack private baths. [$] *Rooms from: $272* ✉ *3200 Old Faithful Inn Rd., Old Faithful* ☎ *307/344–7311* 🌐 *www.yellowstonenationalparklodges.com* 🕓 *Closed mid-Oct.–early May* 🛏 *329 rooms* 🍴 *No meals.*

Old Faithful Lodge Cabins

$$$ | **HOTEL** | There are no rooms inside the Old Faithful Lodge, but close to 100 rustic cabins can be found at the village's northeastern end. **Pros:** affordable; stone's throw from Old Faithful; services within walking distance. **Cons:** some cabins lack private bathrooms; pretty basic; few views from cabins. [$] *Rooms from: $183* ✉ *725 Old Faithful Lodge Rd.* ☎ *307/344–7311* 🌐 *www.yellowstonenationalparklodges.com* 🕓 *Closed early Oct.–mid-May* 🛏 *96 cabins* 🍴 *No meals.*

Old Faithful Snow Lodge

$$$$ | **HOTEL** | This large, contemporary lodge brings back the grand tradition of park lodges by making good use of heavy timber beams and wrought-iron accents in its distinctive facade, guest rooms that combine traditional style with up-to-date amenities. **Pros:** the park's most modern hotel; inviting common spaces; open in both summer and winter. **Cons:** pricey, but you're paying for location; rooms don't have a ton of character; busy part of the park. [$] *Rooms from: $324* ✉ *2051 Snow Lodge Ave., Old Faithful* ☎ *307/344–7311* 🌐 *www.yellowstonenationalparklodges.com* 🕓 *Closed late Oct.–mid-Dec. and mid-Mar.–late Apr.* 🛏 *100 rooms* 🍴 *No meals.*

Old Faithful Snow Lodge Cabins

$$$ | **HOTEL** | **FAMILY** | Just yards from Old Faithful, the Western Cabins feature bright interiors and a modern motel ambience, while the Frontier Cabins are simple pine structures. **Pros:** reasonably priced; close to geyser; open during winter. **Cons:** no amenities beyond the basics; small rooms; very rustic. [$] *Rooms from: $233* ✉ *2051 Snow Lodge Ave., Old Faithful* ☎ *307/344–7311* 🌐 *www.yellowstonenationalparklodges.com* 🕓 *Closed late Oct.–mid-Dec., early Mar.–late Apr.* 🛏 *34 cabins* 🍴 *No meals.*

Shopping

Old Faithful Basin Store

FOOD/CANDY | **FAMILY** | Recognizable by the wooden "Hamilton's Store" sign over the entrance, this shop dates to 1897 and is the second-oldest building in the park. The old-fashioned soda fountain serves up all your ice-cream favorites, including beloved huckleberry shakes. ✉ *1 Old Faithful Loop Rd.* ☎ *307/545–7282* 🌐 *www.yellowstonevacations.com.*

Grant Village and West Thumb

22 miles southeast of Old Faithful, 78 miles north of Jackson.

Along the western edge of Yellowstone Lake, called the West Thumb, Grant Village is the first community you encounter if entering the park from the South Entrance. It has some basic lodging and dining facilities and other services, but the real draw here is the geothermal activity in the West Thumb Geyser Basin.

👁 Sights

SCENIC DRIVES

South Entrance Road

SCENIC DRIVE | The sheer black lava walls and boulder-strewn landscape of the deep Lewis River canyon make this somewhat underrated drive toward Grand Teton National Park highly memorable. Turn into the parking area at the highway bridge for a close-up view of the spectacular Lewis River Falls, one of the park's most photographed sights. There are several pulloffs along the shore of Lewis Lake that are ideal for a picnic or just to stretch your legs. ✉ *Yellowstone National Park.*

SCENIC STOPS

★ West Thumb Geyser Basin

NATURE SITE | FAMILY | The primary Yellowstone caldera was created by one massive volcanic eruption, but a later eruption formed the West Thumb, an unusual and particularly photogenic geyser basin because its active geothermal features are on the shore of Yellowstone Lake. Two boardwalks loop through the basin and showcase a number of sites, including the stunning blue-green Abyss Pool and Fishing Cone, where fishermen used to drop their freshly caught fish straight into boiling water without ever taking it off the hook. This area is popular in winter, when you can take advantage of the nearby warming hut and stroll around the geyser basin before continuing your trip via snow coach or snowmobile. ✉ *Grand Loop Rd., West Thumb.*

VISITOR CENTERS

Grant Village Visitor Center

INFO CENTER | FAMILY | Exhibits at each visitor center describe a small piece of Yellowstone's history—the ones here provide details about the 1988 fire that burned more than a third of the park's total acreage and forced multiple federal agencies to reevaluate their fire-control policies. Watch an informative video, and learn about the 25,000 firefighters from across the United States who battled the blaze. Bathrooms and a backcountry office are here. ✉ *2 Grant Village Loop Rd., Grant Village* ☎ *307/242–2650* 🌐 *www.nps.gov/yell* 🕒 *Closed early Oct.–late May.*

West Thumb Information Station

INFO CENTER | This 1925 log cabin houses a bookstore and doubles as a warming hut in winter. There are restrooms in the parking area. In summer, check for informal ranger-led discussions beneath the old sequoia tree. ✉ *West Thumb Basin, West Thumb* ☎ *307/344–2650* 🌐 *www.nps.gov/yell* 🕒 *Closed early Oct.–late May.*

🍴 Restaurants

Grant Village Dining Room

$$$ | AMERICAN | Although the passable food here isn't the main event, the floor-to-ceiling windows of this waterfront restaurant provide dazzling views of Yellowstone Lake through the thick stand of pines. The pine-beam ceilings, cedar-shake walls, and contemporary decor lend the place a homey feel. **Known for:** sweeping water views; reliable breakfast fare; vanilla bean crème brûlée cheesecake. [$] *Average main: $25* ✉ *550 Sculpin La., Grant Village* ☎ *307/344–7311* 🌐 *www.yellowstonenationalparklodges.com* 🕒 *Closed Oct.–late May.*

"This was a magical moment that I captured at West Thumb Geyser Basin—the sunset reflecting off the rain clouds, steam rising from the geyser basin, and an elk drinking." —photo by Paul Stoloff, Fodors.com member

 Hotels

Grant Village Lodge

$$$ | HOTEL | Grant Village is an excellent location for touring the southern half of the park, but this 1980s lodge itself feels like a bit dormlike, its rooms furnished like their counterparts at a big-city motel, with beds, nightstands, and tables, and not much else. **Pros:** near Lake Yellowstone; many facilities nearby; closest Yellowstone lodge to Grand Teton. **Cons:** expensive for what you get; small rooms without character; spotty Wi-Fi. $ *Rooms from: $291* ⊠ *24 Rainbow Loop* ☎ *307/344–7311* ⊕ *www.yellowstonenationalparklodges. com* ⊘ *Closed late Sept.–late May* 🛏 *300 rooms* ⦿l *No meals.*

Lake Yellowstone

22 miles northeast of West Thumb and Grant Village, 80 miles west of Cody.

In the park's southeastern quadrant, this section is closest to the East Entrance and is dominated by the tranquil beauty of massive Yellowstone Lake. One of the world's largest alpine bodies of water, the 132-square-mile Yellowstone Lake was formed when the glaciers that once covered the region melted and filled a caldera—a crater formed by a volcano. The lake has 141 miles of shoreline, along which you will often see moose, elk, waterfowl, and other wildlife. In winter you can sometimes see otters and coyotes stepping gingerly onto the ice at the lake's edge. Many visitors head here for the excellent fishing—streams flowing into the lake provide an abundant

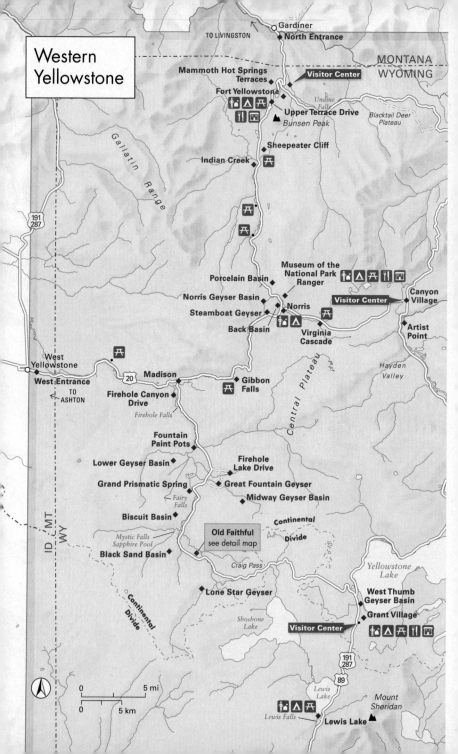

Western Yellowstone

TO LIVINGSTON
Gardiner
North Entrance

MONTANA
WYOMING

Mammoth Hot Springs Terraces
Visitor Center

Fort Yellowstone

Undine Falls

Upper Terrace Drive
Bunsen Peak

Blacktail Deer Plateau

Gallatin Range

Sheepeater Cliff

Indian Creek

Porcelain Basin

Museum of the National Park Ranger

Norris Geyser Basin

Norris
Visitor Center

Canyon Village

Steamboat Geyser

Back Basin

Virginia Cascade

Artist Point

191 287

Hayden Valley

West Yellowstone
West Entrance
TO ASHTON

20
Madison

Gibbon Falls

Central Plateau

Firehole Canyon Drive
Firehole Falls

Fountain Paint Pots

Lower Geyser Basin

Firehole Lake Drive

Grand Prismatic Spring

Great Fountain Geyser

Midway Geyser Basin

Fairy Falls

Biscuit Basin

Continental Divide

Mystic Falls
Sapphire Pool

Old Faithful
see detail map

Black Sand Basin

Craig Pass

Yellowstone Lake

Lone Star Geyser

West Thumb Geyser Basin

Grant Village

Shoshone Lake

Visitor Center

Continental Divide

ID MT WY

191 287

89

Lewis Lake

Mount Sheridan

0   5 mi
0   5 km

Lewis Falls
Lewis Lake

supply of trout. There are also three small villages near the northern tip of the lake: Fishing Bridge, which has a visitor center and the park's largest campground (you may see grizzly bears hunt for fish spawning or swimming near the lake's outlet to the Yellowstone River); Lake Village, home to the striking Lake Yellowstone Hotel and the more modest Lake Lodge; and Bridge Bay, which has a marina and boat launch.

Sights

HISTORIC SIGHTS

Lake Yellowstone Hotel

HOTEL—SIGHT | Completed in 1891 and meticulously restored in recent years, the oldest lodging in Yellowstone National Park is a splendid wedding cake of a building with a gorgeous setting on the water. Casual daytime visitors can lounge in white wicker chairs in the sun room and watch the waters of Yellowstone Lake through massive windows. Robert Reamer, the architect of the Old Faithful Inn, added a columned entrance in 1903 to enhance the original facade of the hotel. ⊠ *235 Yellowstone Lake Rd., Lake Village* ☎ *307/344–7901* ⊕ *www.yellowstonenationalparklodges.com* ⊘ *Closed late Sept.–mid-May.*

PICNIC AREAS

★ Sedge Bay

LOCAL INTEREST | **FAMILY** | On the northern end of this volcanic beach, look carefully for the large rock slabs pushed out of the lake bottom. Nearby trees offer shade and a table, or you can hop onto the level rocks for an ideal lakeside picnic. You may see bubbles rising from the clear water around the rocks—these indicate an active underwater thermal feature. The only company you may have here could be crickets, birds, and bison. ⊠ *East Entrance Rd.*

SCENIC DRIVES

★ Hayden Valley on Grand Loop Road

SCENIC DRIVE | Bison, bears, coyotes, wolves, and birds of prey all call Hayden Valley home almost year-round. Once part of Yellowstone Lake, the broad valley now contains peaceful meadows, rolling hills, and a serene stretch of the Yellowstone River. There are multiple turnouts and picnic areas on this 16-mile drive. Ask a ranger about "Grizzly Overlook," an unofficial site where wildlife watchers, including NPS rangers with spotting scopes for the public to use, congregate in summer. North of Mud Volcano are 11 unsigned turnouts. Look for the telltale timber railings, and be prepared to get caught in a traffic-stopping "bison jam" along the way. ⊠ *Grand Loop Rd. between Canyon and Fishing Bridge* ⊘ *Closed early Nov.–early Apr.*

SCENIC STOPS

LeHardy Rapids

BODY OF WATER | Witness one of nature's epic battles as cutthroat trout migrate upstream by catapulting themselves out of the water to get over and around obstacles in the Yellowstone River. The ¼-mile forested loop takes you to the river's edge. Look for waterfowl and bears, which feed on the trout. ⊠ *Fishing Bridge* ⊹ *3 miles north of Fishing Bridge.*

TRAILS

★ Avalanche Peak Trail

TRAIL | On a busy day in summer, only a handful of parties will fill out the trail register at the Avalanche Peak trailhead, so if you're seeking solitude, this is your hike. Starting across from a parking area on the East Entrance Road, this rigorous 4.2-mile, four-hour round-trip climbs 2,150 feet to the peak's 10,566-foot summit, from which you'll see the rugged Absaroka Mountains running north and south. Look around the talus and tundra near the top of Avalanche Peak for alpine wildflowers and butterflies. From early

Continued on page 793

YELLOWSTONE'S GEOTHERMAL WONDERS

Steaming, bubbling,
and erupting
throughout the day
like giant teapots.

Yellowstone's geothermal features are constantly putting on a show. The 10,000 hot springs, mud pots, and fumaroles, plus 500 or so active geysers within the park comprise more than half the entire world's thermal features. You'd need to search two or three other continents for as many geysers as you can see during a single afternoon around Old Faithful.

HEATING UP

Past eruptions of cataclysmic volcanoes brought about the steaming, vaporous landscape of Yellowstone today. The heat from the magma (molten rock) under the Yellowstone Caldera, an active volcano, continues to fuel the park's geyser basins, such as the Upper Geyser Basin, where more than 200 spouters cram into less than two square miles; and Norris, where water 1,000 feet below ground is 450° F. The complex underground plumbing in these geyser basins is affected by earthquakes and other subterranean hijinks that geologists are only beginning to understand. Some spouters spring to life, while others fall dormant with little or no warning.

HOT SPOT TIPS

■ **Stay on trails and boardwalks.** In some areas, like in Norris, water boils at temperatures of more than 200°. If you want to venture into the back country, where there are no boardwalks, consult a ranger first.

■ **Leave the area if you feel sick or dizzy.** You might be feeling this way due to overexposure to various thermal gases.

■ **These hot springs aren't for bathing.** The pH levels of some of these features are extremely acidic.

■ **They also aren't wishing wells.** In the past people threw hundreds of coins into the bright blue Morning Glory Pool. The coins clogged the pool's natural water vents, causing it to change to a sickly green color.

(left) Old Faithful. (above) Punch Bowl Spring.

HOW DO GEYSERS WORK?

A few main ingredients make geysers possible: abundant water, a heat source, a certain kind of plumbing system, and rock strong enough to withstand some serious pressure. The layout of any one geyser's underground plumbing may vary, but we know that below each vent is a system of fissures and chambers, with constrictions here and there that prevent hot water from rising to the surface. As the underground water heats up, these constrictions and the cooler surface water "cap" the whole system, keeping it from boiling over and ratcheting up the underground pressure. When a few steam bubbles eventually fight their way through the constrictions, the result is like uncapping a shaken-up soda bottle, when the released pressure causes the soda to spray.

FUN FACTS

■ A cone geyser (like Lone Star Geyser in Yellowstone's backcountry) has a spout-like formation around its vent, formed by silica particles deposited during eruptions.

■ A fountain geyser (like Daisy Geyser in the Old Faithful area) erupts from a vent submerged in a hot spring-like pool. Eruptions tend to be smaller and more sporadic.

■ Yellowstone's tallest geyser is Steamboat, in Norris, shooting up to 350 feet high.

■ When they erupt, geysers sometimes create rainbows amid their spray.

❶ RECHARGE STAGE

Groundwater accumulates in plumbing and is heated by the volcano. Some hot water flashes to steam and bubbles try to rise toward surface.

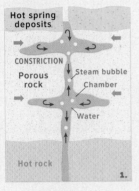

❷ PRELIMINARY ERUPTION STAGE

Pressure builds as steam bubbles clog at constriction. High pressure raises the boiling point, preventing superheated water from becoming steam.

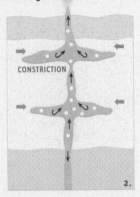

❸ ERUPTION STAGE

Bubbles squeeze through constriction, displacing surface water and relieving pressure. Trapped water flashes to steam, forcing water out of the chambers and causing a chain reaction.

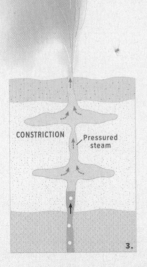

❹ RECOVERY STAGE

Eruption ends when the chambers are emptied or the temperature falls below boiling. Chambers begin to refill with ground water and the process begins again.

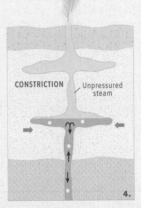

(left) Lone Star Geyser.

HOW DO HOT SPRINGS WORK?

Essentially, what keeps a hot spring from becoming a geyser is a lack of constriction in its underground plumbing. Like their more explosive cousins, hot springs consist of water that seeps into the earth, only to simmer its way back up through fissures after it's heated by hot volcanic rocks. Unlike in constricted geysers, water in a hot spring can circulate by convection. Rising hot water displaces cooling surface water, which then sinks underground to be heated and eventually rise again. Thus the whole mixture keeps itself at a gurgly equilibrium. As it rises, superheated water dissolves some subterranean minerals, depositing them at the surface to form the sculptural terraces that surround many hot springs.

The vivid colors that characterize hot springs and their terraces can be attributed alternately to minerals like sulfur and iron or to thermophiles. Thermophiles are microorganisms that thrive in extremely high temperatures. Blooming in thick bacterial mats, they convert light to energy, like plants, and their bright photosynthetic pigments help give hot springs their rainbow hues. Scientists suppose only a small percentage of Yellowstone's thermophiles have been identified. Still, these microbes have had a big impact on science. In 1965, a microorganism called Thermus aquaticus, or Taq, was discovered in the Lower Geyser Basin. From it, scientists extracted an enzyme that revolutionized molecular biology, ultimately making possible both DNA fingerprinting and the mapping of the human genome. NASA is among those performing research in the park today, studying thermophiles to gain insight on extraterrestrial life.

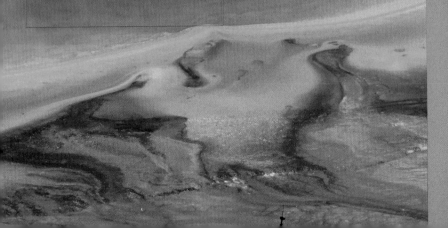

WHAT'S THAT SMELL?

Most people think hot springs smell like rotten eggs; some even say "burnt gunpowder" and "paper mill smokestack." Whatever simile you settle on, there's no question that hot springs and other thermal features stink to high heaven. Sulphur gases escaping from the volcano produce distinctive smells. Other gases are reduced to the stinky chemical hydrogen sulfide, which bubbles up to the surface. In high concentration, hydrogen sulfide can actually kill you, but the small amounts released by thermals can only kill your appetite. It's because hydrogen sulfide is often present in volcanic areas that we associate brimstone (or sulfur) with the underworld.

Did You Know?

Grand Prismatic Spring (pictured here) is the world's third-largest hot spring, at more than 370 feet across. The pool's vivid red and orange colors drizzle down its runoff channels, but from the boardwalk you can only glimpse a portion of these psychedelic tentacles. Thank the little guys: heat-loving microorganisms (bacteria and algae) tint the Grand Prismatic Spring with a rainbow of colors.

THE INNER WORKINGS OF HOT SPRINGS

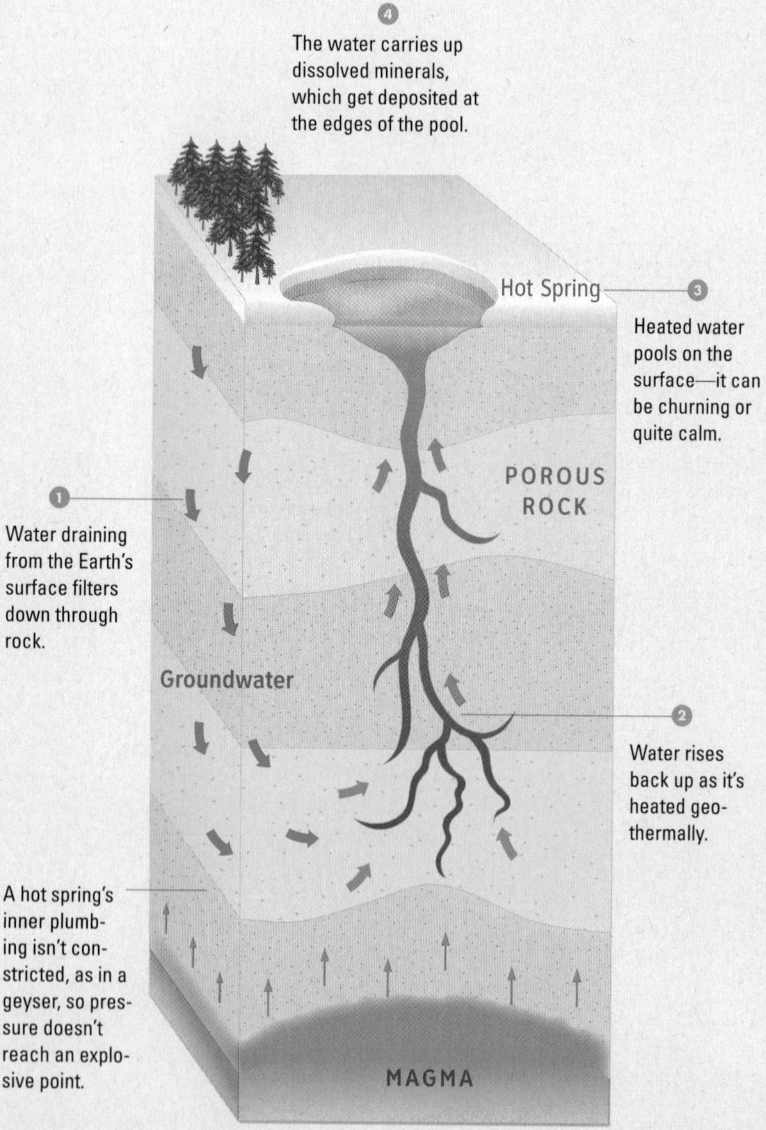

4 The water carries up dissolved minerals, which get deposited at the edges of the pool.

Hot Spring — **3**

3 Heated water pools on the surface—it can be churning or quite calm.

POROUS ROCK

1 Water draining from the Earth's surface filters down through rock.

Groundwater

2 Water rises back up as it's heated geothermally.

A hot spring's inner plumbing isn't constricted, as in a geyser, so pressure doesn't reach an explosive point.

MAGMA

WHAT ARE FUMAROLES?

Take away the water from a hot spring and you're left with steam and other gas, forming a fumarole. Often called steam vents, these noisy thermals occur when available water boils away before reaching the surface. All that escapes the vent is heat, vapor, and the whisper-roar of a giant, menacing teakettle. Fumaroles are often found on high ground. The gases expelled from fumaroles might include carbon dioxide, sulfur dioxide, and hydrogen sulfide. Some hot spots, like Red Spouter in the Lower Geyser Basin, can exhibit different behaviors depending on the seasonal water table, so what's a fumarole today could be a hot spring in a few months.

FUN FACTS

■ The word fumarole comes from the Latin *fumus*, which means "smoke."

■ Fumaroles are also known as steam vents and solfataras, from *sulpha terra*, Latin for "land of sulfur."

■ Yellowstone's hottest fumarole is *Black Growler*, at Norris, which heats up to 280°F.

■ About 4,000 fumaroles are in Yellowstone.

Fumarole

WHAT ARE MUD POTS?

Mud pots in Lower Geyser Basin.

Might as well say it up front: mud pots are great because their thick, bursting bubbles can sound like a chorus of rude noises or "greetings from the interior." That's why the few places they're found in Yellowstone are usually surrounded by gaggles of giggling visitors with video cameras rolling. A mud pot is basically just a hot spring where the water table results in a bubbling broth of water and clay. The acid gases react with surface rocks, breaking them down into silica and clay. As gases escape from below, bubbles swell and pop, flinging mud chunks onto the banks to form gloppy clay mounds. The mud's thickness varies with rainfall through the seasons.

FUN FACTS

■ Mud pots have been nicknamed "paint pots" due to iron and other metals tinting the mud.

■ The biggest cluster of mud pots in the park is in Pocket Basin in Lower Geyser Basin.

■ Before it exploded in 1872, Mud Volcano was 30 feet tall by 30 feet wide.

PHOTOGRAPHY TIPS

■ Set your alarm clock: generally, the best light for shooting the geothermal features is early in the morning. You'll avoid the thickest crowds then, too. The runner-up time is the late afternoon.

■ Breezy days are good for photographing geysers, since the steam will be blown away from the jetting water. But avoid standing downwind or your view can be clouded with steam.

■ If you get water from a thermal feature on your lens, dry it off as quickly as possible, because the water has a high mineral content that can damage your lens.

Thermal pool in the Rabbit Creek Thermal Area.

September to late June, the trail is often impassable due to snow, and fall also can see grizzly bear activity. Stick to summer. *Difficult.* ✉ *Fishing Bridge* ✣ *Trailhead: 2 miles east of Sylvan Lake on north side of East Entrance Rd.*

Storm Point Trail

TRAIL | FAMILY | Well marked and mostly flat, this 2.3-mile loop leaves the south side of the road for a perfect beginner's hike out to Yellowstone Lake, particularly with a setting sun. The trail rounds the western edge of Indian Pond, then passes moose habitat on its way to Yellowstone Lake's Storm Point, named for its frequent afternoon windstorms and crashing waves. Heading west along the shore, you're likely to hear the shrill chirping of yellow-bellied marmots. Also look for ducks, pelicans, trumpeter swans, and bison. You'll pass several small beaches that kids enjoy exploring. *Easy.* ✉ *Fishing Bridge* ✣ *Trailhead: 3 miles east of Lake Junction on East Entrance Rd.*

VISITOR CENTERS

Fishing Bridge Visitor Center

INFO CENTER | FAMILY | If you can't distinguish between a Clark's nuthatch and an ermine (one's a bird, the other a weasel), check out the exhibits about the park's smaller wildlife at this distinctive stone-and-log building, built in 1931. Step out the back door to find yourself on one of the beautiful black obsidian beaches of Yellowstone Lake. Adjacent is one of the park's larger amphitheaters. Ranger presentations take place here nightly in summer. ✉ *East Entrance Rd.* ☎ *307/242–2450* 🌐 *www.nps.gov/yell* 🕒 *Closed early Sept.–late May.*

🍴 Restaurants

★ Lake Hotel Dining Room

$$$$ | MODERN AMERICAN | Opened in 1891, this double-colonnaded dining room off the lobby of the Lake Yellowstone Hotel is the park's most elegant dining spot, and with a menu that focuses on regional ingredients. Arrive early and enjoy a beverage and the view in the airy Reamer Lounge, which debuted as a sunroom in 1928. **Known for:** elegant, old-world ambience; the park's most sophisticated and creative cuisine; excellent wine list. [$] *Average main: $31* ✉ *235 Yellowstone Lake Rd., Lake Village* ☎ *307/344–7311* 🌐 *www.yellowstonenationalparklodges.com* 🕒 *Closed early Oct.–early May.*

Wylie's Canteen at Lake Lodge

$ | AMERICAN | FAMILY | The former Lake Lodge Cafeteria was upgraded and rebranded as Wylie's Canteen in 2019 and still offers quick and casual bites with awe-inspiring Lake Yellowstone views, but the quality of food has improved. Try the breakfast burritos and breakfast sandwiches in the morning, or build-your-own burgers (bison, beef, chicken, Beyond Meat, or salmon), fried chicken, and salads later in the day. **Known for:** casual and affordable; wide variety of burgers; lake and meadow views. [$] *Average main: $12* ✉ *459 Lake Village Rd.* ☎ *307/344–7311* 🌐 *www.yellowstonenationalparklodges.com* 🕒 *Closed Oct.–early June.*

🛏 Hotels

Lake Lodge Cabins

$$ | HOTEL | FAMILY | Located just up the lake shoreline from the grand Lake Yellowstone Hotel, this 1920 lodge is one of the park's homey, hidden treasures. **Pros:** lovely lakeside location; great lobby; good for families. **Cons:** no Wi-Fi in cabins (only in main lodge); few amenities; Pioneer cabins are particularly bare bones. [$] *Rooms from: $170* ✉ *459 Lake Village Rd., Lake Village* ☎ *307/344–7311* 🌐 *www.yellowstonenationalparklodges.com* 🕒 *Closed late Sept.–early June* 🛏 *186 cabins* 🍴 *No meals.*

★ Lake Yellowstone Hotel

$$$ | **HOTEL** | Dating from 1891, the park's oldest lodge maintains an air of old-world refinement; just off the lobby, the spacious sun room offers priceless views of Yellowstone Lake at sunrise or sunset. **Pros:** relaxing atmosphere; the best views of any park lodging; charming old-world vibe. **Cons:** top rooms can be quite expensive; wired Internet, but no Wi-Fi; often books up months ahead. [$] *Rooms from: $242* ✉ *235 Yellowstone Lake Rd., Lake Village* ☎ *307/344–7311* 🌐 *www.yellowstonenationalparklodges.com* 🕒 *Closed late Sept.–mid-May* 🛏 *194 rooms* 🍴 *No meals.*

Canyon

18 miles north of Lake Yellowstone Village, 33 miles southeast of Mammoth Hot Springs.

You'll find one of Yellowstone's largest villages—with myriad lodging, dining, and other services—in this area near the geographical center of the park, which is home to the justly famous Grand Canyon of the Yellowstone, through which the Yellowstone River has formed one of the most spectacular gorges in the world, with its steep canyon walls and waterfalls. The river's source is in the Absaroka Mountains, in the park's southeastern corner. From there it winds its way north through the heart of the park, entering Yellowstone Lake, then continuing northward under Fishing Ridge and through Hayden Valley. The stunning canyon is 23 miles long; most visitors clog the north and south rims to see its dramatic Upper and Lower Falls. The red-and-ocher canyon walls are topped by emerald-green forest. It's a feast of color. Keep an eye peeled for osprey, which nest in the canyon's spires and precarious trees.

Caution: A Wild Place

As you explore the park, keep this thought in mind: Yellowstone is not an amusement park. It is a wild place. The animals may seem docile or tame, but they are wild, and every year careless visitors are injured—sometimes even killed—when they venture too close. Particularly dangerous are female animals with their young, and bison, which can turn and charge in an instant. With bison, watch their tails: if standing up or crooked like a question mark, the animal is agitated.

Sights

SCENIC STOPS

★ Artist Point

BODY OF WATER | An impressive view of the Lower Falls of the Yellowstone River can be had from this famous perch, which has two observation platforms, one accessible to wheelchairs. Rangers often give short talks on the lower platform. You can also access the South Rim Trail from here. ✉ *End of South Rim Rd.*

Lookout Point

BODY OF WATER | Midway on the North Rim Trail—also accessible via the one-way North Rim Drive—Lookout Point provides a view of the Grand Canyon of the Yellowstone. Follow the right-hand fork in the path to descend a steep trail, with an approximately 500-foot elevation change, for an eye-to-eye view of the falls from a ½ mile downstream. The best time to hike the trail is early morning, when sunlight reflects off the mist from the falls to create a rainbow. ✉ *Off North Rim Dr.*

TRAILS

Brink of the Lower Falls Trail

TRAIL | Especially scenic, this short but steep jaunt branches off of the North Rim Trail and can be accessed from either the Brink of the Upper Falls or Brink of the Lower Falls parking areas. The ½-mile one-way trail switchbacks 600 feet down to within a few yards of the top of the Yellowstone River's 308-foot Lower Falls. *Moderate.* ⊠ *Yellowstone National Park* ✢ *Trailhead: North Rim Dr., just past junction with Grand Loop Rd.*

Mt. Washburn Trail

TRAIL | One of Yellowstone's most rewarding alpine hikes, the ascent to 10,259-foot Mt. Washburn can be approached from either the south leaving from the Dunraven Pass Trailhead or the north from the Chittenden Road Trailhead. The latter approach is a bit shorter (5.6 miles round-trip) but slightly steeper with a nearly 1,500-foot elevation gain, while from Dunraven Pass the hike switchbacks through bighorn sheep habitat and is about 6 miles round-trip, with a gain of just under 1,400 feet. Either way you'll be treated to panoramic views, and you can read interpretive exhibits in the small shelter at the summit (at the base of the fire tower). *Moderate–Difficult.* ⊠ *Canyon Village* ✢ *Trailhead: Grand Loop Rd. at Dunraven Pass or Chittenden Rd.*

Mud Volcano Trail

TRAIL | FAMILY | This .6-mile loop hike in Hayden Valley curves gently around seething, sulfuric mud pots with such names as Sizzling Basin and Black Dragon's Cauldron, and around Mud Volcano itself. *Easy.* ⊠ *Canyon* ✢ *Trailhead: Grand Loop Rd., 10 miles south of Canyon Village.*

North Rim Trail

TRAIL | FAMILY | Offering great views of the Grand Canyon of the Yellowstone, the 3-mile (each way) North Rim Trail runs from Inspiration Point to Chittenden Bridge. Particularly fetching is the ½-mile section of the North Rim Trail from the Brink of the Upper Falls parking area to Chittenden Bridge that hugs the rushing Yellowstone River as it approaches the canyon. This trail is paved and fully accessible between Lookout Point and Grand View, and it can be accessed at numerous points along North Rim Drive. *Moderate.* ⊠ *Yellowstone National Park* ✢ *Trailhead: west side of Chittenden Bridge or Inspiration Point.*

Seven Mile Hole Trail

TRAIL | Give yourself the better part of a day (at least five hours) to tackle this challenging but generally uncrowded and peaceful 9.7-mile round-trip hike that begins near the North Rim's Inspiration Point, runs east for a while along the rim and then descends more than 1,000 feet to the banks of the roaring Yellowstone River. *Difficult.* ⊠ *Yellowstone National Park* ✢ *Trailhead: Glacier Boulder pullout on road to Inspiration Point.*

★ South Rim Trail

TRAIL | FAMILY | Partly paved and fairly flat, this 1¾-mile trail along the south rim of the Grand Canyon of the Yellowstone affords impressive views and photo opportunities of the canyon and falls of the Yellowstone River. It starts at Chittenden Bridge, passes by magnificent Upper Falls View and Uncle Tom's Trail, and ends at Artist Point. Beyond Artist Point, you can continue your adventures for another 1.3 miles along a less-traveled and stunning trail to Point Sublime, or cut inland through high mountain meadows along the Clear Lake–Ribbon Lake Loop. You'll see fewer humans and possibly more wildlife in this more rugged backcountry, so carry bear spray. *Moderate.* ⊠ *Canyon* ✢ *Trailhead: east side of Chittenden Bridge, off South Rim Dr.*

Uncle Tom's Trail

TRAIL | Accessed by the South Rim Drive, this spectacular and strenuous 700-step trail ½ mile east of Chittenden Bridge descends 500 feet from the parking area to the roaring base of the Lower Falls of the Yellowstone. Much of this walk is on steel sheeting, which can have a film of ice during early summer mornings or anytime in spring and fall. *Moderate–Difficult.* ✉ *Yellowstone National Park* ✣ *Trailhead: at South Rim Dr.*

VISITOR CENTERS

Canyon Visitor Center

INFO CENTER | FAMILY | This gleaming visitor center contains elaborate interactive exhibits for adults and kids. The focus here is on volcanoes and earthquakes and includes a room-size relief model of the park that illustrates eruptions, glaciers, and seismic activity. There are also exhibits about Native Americans and wildlife, including bison and wolves. The adjacent bookstore contains hundreds of books on the park, its history, and related science. ✉ *Canyon Village* ☎ *307/242–2550* 🌐 *www.nps.gov/yell* 🕒 *Closed mid-fall–late spring.*

🍴 Restaurants

Canyon Lodge Eatery

$ | ECLECTIC | FAMILY | Diners pack this mid-century-modern–inspired restaurant for casual breakfasts, as well as lunches and dinners that deviate from your standard national park fare. Design your own wok meal with veggies, meat, and toppings, or choose a protein and sauce on a three-item combo plate. **Known for:** more interesting than typical cafeteria-style fare; Asian-inspired wok stir-fries; lemon layer cake. [$] *Average main: $15* ✉ *83B Lupine Ct.* ☎ *307/344–7311* 🌐 *www.yellowstonenationalparklodges.com* 🕒 *Closed mid-Oct.–late May.*

🛏 Hotels

Canyon Lodge & Cabins

$$ | HOTEL | FAMILY | You can choose from several different types of accommodations at this large, sprawling property near the Grand Canyon of the Yellowstone, which includes a modern and attractive lodge with smartly designed and sustainable rooms, the renovated pine-frame Western Cabins, and nicely updated rooms in the historic Dunraven and Cascade Lodge buildings. **Pros:** central to different parts of the park; eco-conscious design; pretty surroundings. **Cons:** spotty Wi-Fi; a bit pricey because of location; not much dining nearby. [$] *Rooms from: $214* ✉ *41 Clover La., Canyon Village* ☎ *307/344–7311* 🌐 *www.yellowstonenationalparklodges.com* 🕒 *Closed mid-Oct.–mid-May* 🛏 *590 units* 🍴 *No meals.*

Tower-Roosevelt

20 miles north of Canyon Village, 33 miles west of Cooke City–Silver Gate.

The northeastern region of Yellowstone is the least visited part of the park, making it a great place to explore without running into as many people. Packs of wolves and herds of bison can often be spotted along the majestic drive through Lamar Valley.

👁 Sights

SCENIC DRIVES

★ **Northeast Entrance Road through Lamar Valley**

SCENIC DRIVE | This 29-mile road has the richest landscape diversity of the five entrance roads. Just after you enter the park from Cooke City, Montana, you cut between 10,928-foot Abiathar Peak and the 10,404-foot Barronette Peak. Lamar Valley is home to hundreds of bison, and the rugged peaks and ridges adjacent to it shelter some of Yellowstone's most famous wolf packs. (Wolves were reintroduced to the park in the mid-1990s.) This is the park's best place for wolf- and bison-watching, especially in the early morning and early evening. As you exit Lamar Valley, the road crosses the Yellowstone River before leading you to the rustic Roosevelt Lodge. ✉ *Yellowstone National Park.*

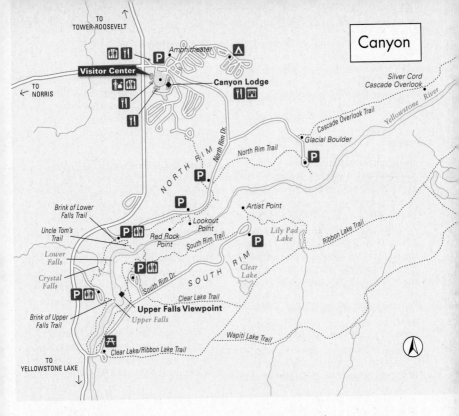

Northeastern Grand Loop

SCENIC DRIVE | Commonly called Dunraven Pass, this 19-mile segment of Grand Loop Road climbs to nearly 9,000 feet as it passes some of the park's finest scenery, including views of backcountry hot springs and abundant wildflowers. Near Tower Falls, the road twists beneath a series of leaning basalt columns from 40 to 50 feet high. That behemoth to the east is 10,243-foot Mt. Washburn. ⊠ Between Canyon Junction and Tower Falls ⊙ Closed early Nov.–early Apr.

SCENIC STOPS

Tower Fall

BODY OF WATER | FAMILY | This is one of the easiest waterfalls to see from the roadside; you can also view volcanic pinnacles here. Tower Creek plunges 132 feet at this waterfall to join the Yellowstone River. While a trail that used to go to the base of the falls has washed out, it will take trekkers down to the river. ⊠ Grand Loop Rd.

TRAILS

Slough Creek Trail

TRAIL | Starting at Slough Creek Campground, this trail climbs steeply along a historic wagon trail for 1½ miles before reaching expansive meadows and prime fishing spots, where moose are common and grizzlies occasionally wander. Allow two or three hours for the full 3.4-mile round-trip hike. Moderate. ⊠ Yellowstone National Park ⊹ Trailhead: Northeast Entrance Rd. at Slough Creek Campground.

Trout Lake Trail

TRAIL | It takes just an hour or two to enjoy this slightly elevated but generally tame 1.2-mile round-trip hike in Lamar Valley that leads through meadows and stands of Douglas fir trees and then circumnavigates pretty Trout Lake, a favorite spot for fishing. *Easy.* ✉ *Yellowstone National Park* ⊹ *Trailhead: Northeast Entrance Rd., just south of Pebble Creek Campground.*

 Restaurants

Roosevelt Lodge Dining Room

$$ | **AMERICAN** | **FAMILY** | The menu at this atmospheric log cabin in a pine forest includes appropriately rustic options like skirt steak, mesquite-smoked chicken, and blackened ruby red trout, but you'll also find simpler comfort fare, like carnitas nachos and fried-green tomatoes. For a real adventure, make a reservation for the Roosevelt Old West Dinner Cookout, which includes a horseback trail ride or a stagecoach ride. **Known for:** updated cowboy cuisine; wild-game chili; rustic setting. $ *Average main: $21* ✉ *100 Roosevelt Lodge Rd., Tower Junction* ☎ *307/344–7311* ⊕ *www.yellowstonenationalparklodges.com* ⊗ *Closed early Sept.–early June.*

Hotels

Roosevelt Lodge Cabins

$$ | **HOTEL** | Near the beautiful Lamar Valley in the park's north-central reaches, this simple lodge in a pine forest dates from the 1920s and surpasses some of the park's more expensive options when it comes to rustic tranquility. **Pros:** closest cabins to Lamar Valley and its world-famous wildlife; authentic western ranch feel; some cabins are quite affordable. **Cons:** cabins are very close together; most cabins lack private bathrooms; cabins can be chilly at night. $ *Rooms from: $209* ✉ *100 Roosevelt Lodge Rd., Tower Junction* ☎ *307/344–7901* ⊕ *www. YellowstoneNationalParkLodges.com* ⊗ *Closed early Sept.–early June* ⇌ *80 cabins* ⊗ *No meals.*

Activities

In summer, hiking, boating, and fishing are the best ways to get out and enjoy the park. During the quieter winter seasons, snowmobiling and cross-country skiing are the activities of choice.

BOATING

Motorized boats are allowed only on Lewis Lake and Yellowstone Lake. Kayaking and canoeing are allowed on all lakes except Sylvan Lake, Eleanor Lake, Twin Lakes, and Beach Springs Lagoon. Most lakes are inaccessible by car, though, so accessing them requires long portages. Boating is not allowed on any river except the Lewis between Lewis Lake and Shoshone Lake, where nonmotorized boats are permitted.

You must purchase a permit for all boats—these are available at several points in the park, including Bridge Bay Ranger Station, Grant Village Backcountry Office, and Lewis Lake Ranger Station. The cost is $5 for a week, $10 for the season, for nonmotorized boats and floatables; and $10 for a week, $20 for the season, for all others. Boat permits issued in Grand Teton National Park are honored in Yellowstone, but owners must register their vessel in Yellowstone and obtain a no-charge Yellowstone validation sticker from a permit-issuing station. Rangers inspect all boats for aquatic invasive species before issuing a permit.

Bridge Bay Marina

BOATING | Watercraft, from rowboats to powerboats, can be rented for trips on Yellowstone Lake at this well-outfitted marina, which also provides shuttle boat rides to the backcountry and dock slip rentals. Additionally, you can rent 22-foot cabin cruisers with a guide. ✉ *Grand Loop Rd., Bridge Bay* ☎ *307/344–7311* ⊕ *www. yellowstonenationalparklodges.com.*

Yellowstone Lake Scenic Cruises

BOATING | FAMILY | On one-hour cruises aboard the *Lake Queen II*, you'll learn about the park and the lake's history and have the chance to observe eagles, ospreys, and some of the park's big mammals along the shoreline. The vessel travels from Bridge Bay to Stevenson Island and back. Reservations are recommended. ⊠ *Bridge Bay Marina, Bridge Bay* ☎ *307/344–7311* ⊕ *www.yellowstonenationalparklodges.com* ⊠ *$20.*

CAMPING

Yellowstone has a dozen frontcountry campgrounds—with more than 2,000 sites—throughout the park, in addition to more than 200 backcountry sites. Most campgrounds have flush toilets; some have coin-operated showers and laundry facilities. The campgrounds run by Yellowstone National Park Lodges—Bridge Bay, Canyon, Fishing Bridge RV Park, Grant Village, and Madison—accept bookings in advance (☎ *307/344–7311* ⊕ *www.yellowstonenationalparklodges.com*); nightly rates are $27 to $32 at most of these sites, except for Fishing Bridge RV Park, which costs $79 nightly. The rest of Yellowstone's campgrounds, operated by the National Park Service, are available on a first-come, first-served basis and have rates of $15 to $20. All camping outside designated campgrounds requires a backcountry permit. For trip dates between late May (Memorial Day) and September 10, the fee is $3 per person per night; there's no charge the rest of the year.

Bridge Bay Campground. The park's largest campground, Bridge Bay rests in a wooded grove above Yellowstone Lake and adjacent to the park's major marina—the views of the water and distant Absaroka Mountains are magnificent. ⊠ *Grand Loop Rd., 3 miles southwest of Lake Village.*

Canyon Campground. A large campground with nearly 300 sites, Canyon Campground accommodates everyone from hiker/biker tent campers to large RVs. ⊠ *North Rim Dr., Canyon Village.*

Fishing Bridge RV Park. It's more of a parking lot than a campground, but services like tank filling and emptying and full hookups make this a popular—though pricey—option among RVers. ⊠ *Grand Loop Rd., 3 miles southwest of Lake Village.*

Grant Village Campground. The park's second-largest campground, with 430 sites, Grant Village has some sites with great views of Yellowstone Lake and is close to restaurants and other services. ⊠ *South Entrance Rd., Grant Village.*

Indian Creek Campground. In a picturesque setting next to a creek, this campground is in the middle of a prime wildlife-viewing area. ⊠ *Grand Loop Rd., 8 miles south of Mammoth Hot Springs.*

Lewis Lake Campground. Popular with visitors from Grand Teton, this nearest campground to the South Entrance is set among old pine trees on a bluff above beautiful and relatively uncrowded Lewis Lake. It's a quiet setting, and it has a boat launch. ⊠ *South Entrance Rd., 6 miles south of Grant Village.*

Madison Campground. The largest National Park Service–operated campground, Madison has eight loops and nearly 300 sites. It's a good central location, handy for visiting the geysers in Norris and Old Faithful. ⊠ *Grand Loop Rd., Madison.*

Mammoth Hot Springs Campground. At the base of a sagebrush-covered hillside, this campground can be crowded and noisy in the summer, but it's close to restaurants and some great attractions, and you may see bison, mule deer, and elk roaming the area. ⊠ *North Entrance Rd., Mammoth Hot Springs.*

Norris Campground. Straddling the Gibbon River, this is a quiet, popular campground. A few of its walk-in sites rank among the most desirable in the park. ⊠ *Grand Loop Rd., Norris.*

Pebble Creek. Beneath multiple 10,000-foot peaks (Thunderer, Barronette Peak, and Mt. Norris) the park's easternmost campground is set creekside in a forested canopy and is also close to the fun little hike to Trout Lake. ⊠ *Northeast Entrance Rd., 22 miles east of Tower-Roosevelt Junction.*

Slough Creek. Down the park's most rewarding 2 miles of dirt road, Slough Creek is a gem. Nearly every site is adjacent to the creek, which is prized by anglers. ⊠ *Northeast Entrance Rd., 10 miles east of Tower-Roosevelt Junction.*

Tower Falls. It's within hiking distance of the roaring waterfall, so this modest-size campground gets a lot of foot traffic but is in a somewhat remote part of the park. ⊠ *Grand Loop Rd., 3 miles southeast of Tower-Roosevelt.*

EDUCATIONAL PROGRAMS
CLASSES AND SEMINARS
Yellowstone Forever
COLLEGE | FAMILY | Learn about the park's ecology, geology, history, and wildlife from park experts, including well-known geologists, biologists, and photographers. Classes generally take place on the north side of the park, around Mammoth Hot Springs, and last from a few hours to a few days, and rates are reasonable. Some programs are designed specifically for young people and families. ⊠ *Gardiner* ☎ *406/848–2400* ⊕ *www.yellowstone.org.*

RANGER PROGRAMS
Yellowstone offers a busy schedule of guided hikes, talks, and campfire programs. For dates and times, check the park's *Yellowstone Today* newsletter, available at all entrances and visitor centers.

Daytime Walks and Talks
NATURE PRESERVE | FAMILY | Ranger-led walks are held at various locations throughout the summer. Winter programs and some walks are held at West Yellowstone, Old Faithful, and Mammoth. Check the website or park newspaper for details. ⊕ *www.nps.gov/yell.*

Evening Programs
TOUR—SIGHT | FAMILY | Gather around to hear tales about Yellowstone's fascinating history, with hour-long programs on topics ranging from the return of the bison to 19th-century photographers. Every major area hosts programs during the summer; check visitor centers or campground bulletin boards for updates. Winter programs are held at Mammoth and Old Faithful. ⊕ *www.nps.gov/yell.*

Junior Ranger Program
TOUR—SIGHT | FAMILY | Children ages 4 to 12 are eligible to earn patches and become Junior Rangers. Pick up a booklet at any visitor center for $3 and start the entertaining self-guided curriculum, or download it for free online. Kids five and older can also participate in the Young Scientist Program. Purchase a self-guiding booklet for $5 at the Canyon or Old Faithful visitor centers and solve a science mystery. ⊕ *www.nps.gov/yell.*

FISHING
Fishing season begins in late May on the Saturday of Memorial Day weekend and ends in November, and it's a highly popular activity in the park's many pristine lakes and rivers. Native cutthroat trout are among the prize catches, but four other varieties—brown, brook, lake, and rainbow—along with grayling and mountain whitefish inhabit Yellowstone's waters. Popular sportfishing opportunities include the Gardner and Yellowstone rivers as well as Soda Butte Creek, but the top fishing area is Madison River.

Yellowstone fishing permits cost $18 for three days, $25 for seven days, and $40 for the season. Anglers ages 15 and younger must have a (no-fee) permit or fish under direct supervision of an adult with a permit, which can be purchased at all ranger stations, visitor centers, and Yellowstone general stores. A state license is not needed to fish in the park.

Bridge Bay Marina Fishing Charters

FISHING | The park's largest concession-aire operates Yellowstone Lake fishing charters that can last from two to 12 hours, for up to six passengers. The fee includes gear. ✉ *Bridge Bay Marina, Bridge Bay* ☎ *307/344–7311* ⊕ *www. yellowstonenationalparklodges.com* 💲 *From $103/hr.*

HIKING

Your most memorable Yellowstone moments will likely take place along a hiking trail. Encountering a gang of elk in the woods is unquestionably more exciting than watching them graze on the grasses of Mammoth Hot Springs Hotel. Hearing the creak of lodgepole pines on a breezy afternoon feels more authentic than listening to tourists chatter as you jockey for the best view of Old Faithful. Even a one-day visitor to Yellowstone can—and should—get off the roads and into the "wilderness." Because the park is a wild place, however, even a ½-mile walk on a trail puts you at the mercy of nature, so be sure to prepare yourself accordingly. As a guide on an Old Yellow Bus Tour said, "You don't have to fear the animals—just respect them."

No matter how short the hike, the following items are essential, not dis-cretionary, especially if you're venturing into the backcountry and away from developed areas:

Bear spray. At $50 a can and sold in the park, it's not cheap, but it's a critical deterrent if you run into one. Learn how to use it, too.

Food and water. Your "meal" can be as simple as a protein bar and a bottle of water if you're hiking only a mile or two, but for hikes of an hour or longer, it's critical to head out with an ample supply of drinking water and a variety of snacks.

Appropriate clothing. Watch the forecast closely (available at every lodging office and visitor center). Bring a layer of clothing for the opposite extreme if you're hiking at least half the day. Yellowstone is known for fierce afternoon storms, so be ready with gloves, hat, and waterproof clothing.

Altitude awareness. Much of Yellowstone lies more than 7,500 feet above sea level. The most frequent incidents requir-ing medical attention are respiratory problems, not animal attacks. Be aware of your physical limitations—as well as those of your young children or elderly companions.

HORSEBACK RIDING

Reservations are recommended for horseback riding in the park. Don't worry about experience, as rangers estimate 90% of riders have not been on a horse in at least 10 years.

About 50 area outfitters lead horse-packing trips and trail rides into Yellowstone. Expect to pay from $250 to $400 per day for a backcountry trip, including meals, accom-modations, and guides. A guide must accompany all horseback-riding trips.

Private stock can be brought into the park. Horses are not allowed in front-country campgrounds but are permitted in certain backcountry campsites. Day-use horseback riding does not require a permit, but overnight trips with stock are $5 per person per night with no cap.

★ Wilderness Pack Trips

HORSEBACK RIDING | **FAMILY** | Mike and Erin Thompson at Wilderness Pack Trips have led small group trips exclusively in Yel-lowstone National Park for many years. Popular destinations include the spectac-ular remote waterfalls and wildlife-rich regions often closed to the general public. Families are welcome for these excursions. Backcountry fishing trips and other day and overnight adventures can also be arranged. ✉ *172 E. River Rd., Emigrant* ☎ *406/581–5021* ⊕ *www. yellowstonepacktrips.com* 💲 *From $375.*

Yellowstone National Park Lodges

HORSEBACK RIDING | FAMILY | The park's largest concessionaire offers one-hour horseback rides at Mammoth, and one- and two-hour rides at Tower-Roosevelt and Canyon Village. You can also book an Old West Dinner Cookout, which includes a ride. ☎ *307/344–7311* ⊕ *www. yellowstonenationalparklodges.com* ☎ *From $55.*

SKIING, SNOWSHOEING, AND SNOWMOBILING

Yellowstone can be the coldest place in the continental United States in winter, with temperatures of –30°F not uncommon. Still, winter-sports enthusiasts flock here when the park opens for its winter season during the last week of December. Until early March, the roads teem with over-snow vehicles like snowmobiles and snow coaches, and trails bristle with cross-country skiers and snowshoers. The Lone Star Geyser Trail near Old Faithful Village is a good one for skiing.

Snowmobiling is an exhilarating way to experience Yellowstone. It's also controversial: there's heated debate about the pollution and disruption to animal habitats. The number of riders per day is limited, and you must have a reservation, a guide, and a four-stroke engine, which are less polluting than the more common two-stroke variety. About a dozen companies are authorized to lead snowmobile excursions. Prices vary, as do itineraries and inclusions: ask about insurance, guides, taxes, park entrance fees, clothing, helmets, and meals.

Bear Den Ski Shops

SKIING/SNOWBOARDING | FAMILY | At Mammoth Hot Springs Hotel and Old Faithful Snow Lodge, these shops rent skis, gear, and snowshoes. Lessons, guided tours, and shuttles to trails are also available. ☒ *Mammoth Hot Springs, 1 Grand Loop Rd.* ☎ *307/344–7311* ⊕ *www.yellowstonenationalparklodges.com.*

Free Heel and Wheel

SKIING/SNOWBOARDING | This cross-country boutique outside the West Yellowstone entrance gate rents skis and other equipment and is a source for winter gear, sleds, snowshoes, and advice. Ski lessons and pull sleds for toting children are available. It also rents and repairs bicycles, and has an espresso bar to boot. ☒ *33 Yellowstone Ave., West Yellowstone* ☎ *406/646–7744* ⊕ *www. freeheelandwheel.com.*

Nearby Towns

Yellowstone National Park is itself a destination, and with its considerable size and wealth of lodging and dining options, it's easily possible—and sometimes the most enjoyable strategy—to spend nearly your entire visit within the park. That said, especially if visiting in summer without having made reservations far in advance, you may find it easier and less expensive to stay in one of the several nearby communities, which range from small villages with basic services to larger towns with swanky hotels, trendy restaurants, and the area's largest airports (which are in Cody, Jackson, and Bozeman).

In Montana, nearest to the North Entrance, are the small and bustling towns of **Gardiner,** just a short drive from Mammoth Hot Springs, and **Livingston,** a charmingly historic enclave about 53 miles north at the junction with Interstate 90. Just 25 miles west of Livingston via the interstate, the youthful and hip college town of **Bozeman** is one of the fastest-growing communities in the Rockies and a hub of art, shopping, dining, and outdoor attractions. Another popular Montana gateway, particularly in winter, is **West Yellowstone,** near the park's West Entrance. It's a small town without a ton of curb appeal, but there is a wealth of lodging and dining options. It's 50 miles south of the renowned ski resort community of **Big Sky.**

Yellowstone Today

(Old) Faithful, But Slowing Down

Though Old Faithful continues to spew routinely, even it has changed in recent years. The geyser now erupts about every 94 minutes (up from 78 minutes in 1990), and it may look different each time. Monitoring shows that Old Faithful almost always discharges the same amount of water at each eruption, but how it does so varies. Sometimes it shoots higher and faster, whereas other times the blast lasts longer but doesn't reach so high.

Less Faithful Geysers

Other geyser basin features are less faithful than Old Faithful. The force and nature of the geysers depend on several factors, but rangers say the greatest threats to the geyser basin activity are earthquakes (which occur regularly, but they are usually very small tremors) and human impact. In past years, for example, people threw hundreds of coins into the bright blue Morning Glory Pool. The coins eventually clogged the pool's water vents, causing it to turn a sickly green. Though it has been cleaned and people are warned not to throw anything into it, the pool has never regained its pristine color.

Fossils and Petrified Forests

Besides its unique geology, Yellowstone has many other faces. There are petrified forests and fossil remains of both plants and animals. The ongoing ecological development of the region draws widespread interest.

Bison on the Move

The reintroduction of wolves to the ecosystem and efforts to control the movement of bison—to keep them from wandering out of the park during the winter in search of food—are just two examples of divisive issues regarding the management of Yellowstone.

Bison leave the park in winter—mainly through the North and West entrances—in part because of overpopulation and the need to forage. Their movements are sometimes made easier by the winter grooming of Yellowstone roads for use by over-snow vehicles.

Wolves Return, But Is That Good?

Wolves were reintroduced to Yellowstone in 1995. They acclimated so well—the current population is around 530—that they quickly formed several packs, some of which have ventured outside the park's boundaries. Wolves from Yellowstone's packs have been spotted as far south as northern Utah and Colorado. The presence of wolves within the park has had a lasting effect on wildlife populations. The wolves feed on elk and buffalo, and researchers have noted a significant decline in elk calf survival as a result of wolf predation. Park rangers have also reported a significant decline in the coyote population. Since the wolves are bigger and stronger than coyotes, they kill coyotes or force them to find a new range.

In Wyoming, because of its airport and its proximity to both Grand Teton and Yellowstone national parks, **Jackson**—the closest town to Yellowstone's South Entrance—is the region's busiest community in summer and has the widest selection of dining and lodging options (⇨ *see Grand Teton National Park for more information*). The Wild West town of **Cody** lies just an hour's drive from the East Entrance and is home to one of the best museums in the Rockies as well as a number of hotels, inns, and dude ranches.

Montana is again your best bet when entering through the park's Northeast Entrance. With both Yellowstone and the Absaroka-Beartooth Wilderness at its back door, the neighboring villages of **Cooke City–Silver Gate** are good places for hiking, horseback riding, mountain climbing, and other outdoor activities. Some 50 miles to the east of Cooke City and 60 miles southeast of Billings, the small resort town of **Red Lodge** is nestled against the foot of the pine-draped Absaroka-Beartooth Wilderness and popular with skiers, anglers, golfers, and horseback riders—it has more options for dining and lodging than Cooke City.

Gardiner

1 mile north of Yellowstone's North Entrance, 77 miles south of Bozeman.

As the only entrance to Yellowstone open the entire year, Gardiner (population 971) always feels like a hive of activity, with its quaint shops and smattering of good restaurants. The town's Roosevelt Arch has marked the park's North Entrance since 1903, when President Theodore Roosevelt dedicated it. The Yellowstone River slices through town, beckoning fishermen and rafters.

GETTING HERE AND AROUND

It's about an hour's drive from Interstate 90 and Livingston via U.S. 89, and a 15-minute drive to Mammoth Hot Springs.

🍴 Restaurants

Iron Horse Bar & Grill
$ | **AMERICAN** | Vintage advertisements, street signs, and gas-station memorabilia fill the interior of this rollicking roadhouse, but the heart of this place is the huge wooden deck overlooking the Yellowstone River and the mountains in the distance. The food is simple but hearty and well-seasoned—think elk tacos, bison burgers, and panfried rainbow trout. **Known for:** wooden deck with river views; comfort fare featuring local game; nice selection of craft beers. [$] *Average main: $15* ✉ *212 Spring St., Gardiner* ☎ *406/848–7888.*

🛏 Hotels

Yellowstone Village Inn and Suites
$$ | **HOTEL** | **FAMILY** | On the west end of Gardiner across from the Yellowstone River, this mid-range hotel provides a variety of room types and plenty of amenities to keep you entertained between day trips into Yellowstone. **Pros:** great location; heated indoor pool; some suites have full kitchens. **Cons:** Wi-Fi can be spotty; breakfast is continental; 15-minute walk to downtown core. [$] *Rooms from: $220* ✉ *1102 Scott St. W, Gardiner* ☎ *406/848–7417* 🌐 *www.yellowstonevinn.com* 🛏 *45 rooms* 🍴 *Free Breakfast.*

★ **Yellowstone Riverside Cottages**
$$ | **HOTEL** | **FAMILY** | Set on a pretty bend of the Yellowstone River in the heart of downtown Gardiner, this immaculate little compound of cottages, suites, and studios that sleep from two to six guests has kitchens or kitchenettes in every unit along with good Wi-Fi and private exterior entrances. **Pros:** good variety of room configurations; within walking distance

of restaurants; short drive from Yellowstone's North Entrance. **Cons:** some rooms don't overlook river; no pets; can sometimes hear noise from rooms above. $ *Rooms from: $199* ✉ *521 Scott St. W, Gardiner* ☎ *406/848–7719* ⊕ *www.yellowstoneriversidecottages.com* ⇆ *17 rooms* ⊙⎮ *No meals.*

Livingston

53 miles north of Gardiner.

Livingston, along the banks of the beautiful Yellowstone River and set against a stunning mountain backdrop, was built to serve the railroad and the settlers it brought. The railroad still runs through this town of around 8,150, but now tourism and outdoor sports dominate the scene. Many writers and artists call Livingston home, and there are about a dozen art galleries here, along with a growing number of noteworthy restaurants. Robert Redford chose the town, with its turn-of-the-20th-century flavor, to film parts of the movie *A River Runs Through It.*

GETTING HERE AND AROUND
Livingston is at the junction of U.S. 89, which leads south to Yellowstone's North Entrance, and Interstate 90, which connects it with Bozeman to the west and Billings to the east. The historic downtown district is very walkable.

VISITOR INFORMATION Livingston Area Chamber of Commerce. ✉ *303 E. Park St., Livingston* ☎ *406/222–0850* ⊕ *www.livingston-chamber.com.*

Sights

Yellowstone River
BODY OF WATER | Just south of Livingston and north of Yellowstone National Park, the Yellowstone River comes roaring down the Yellowstone Plateau and flows through Paradise Valley. Fifteen fishing access sites are found in this area, some with primitive public campsites (available

on a first-come, first-served basis). In addition to trout fishing, rafting and canoeing are popular here. With snowcapped peaks, soaring eagles, and an abundance of wildlife, a float on this section of the Yellowstone is a lifetime experience. U.S. 89 follows the west bank of the river, and East River Road runs along the east side. ✉ *U.S. 89, Livingston.*

🍴 Restaurants

★ Faye's Cafe
$ | **MODERN AMERICAN** | Get an early start to make sure you're seated at this beloved breakfast spot—it's open only until 11 most mornings—that's operated by noted chef and cookbook author Sarah Faye. There are always plenty of delectable treats on the menu, from huevos rancheros with poached eggs and smoked chicken to fluffy waffles with whipped cream and fresh fruit; adventurers might want to go with "Faye's Choice," which lets the chef come up with a creative dish just for you. **Known for:** friendly service; Faye's "Amazeballs" made with beef, bison, and pork; Grandma's cinnamon rolls with cream cheese frosting. $ *Average main: $15* ✉ *Shane Lalani Center for the Arts, 415 E. Lewis St., Livingston* ☎ *406/223–7481* ⊕ *www.sarahfayemontana.com* ⊙ *No lunch or dinner.*

★ Mustang Fresh Food
$$$ | **MODERN AMERICAN** | Creative, contemporary regional American fare is the specialty at this romantic little bistro set inside an arresting historic downtown storefront with high pressed-tin ceilings and teal banquette seats. The menu rotates according to what's fresh but might feature pan-seared halibut with a clementine gremolata, or roasted baby carrots with a sumac-cashew sauce. **Known for:** locally, seasonally sourced cuisine; excellent vegetarian options; lemon cheesecake with salted caramel. $ *Average main: $24* ✉ *112 N. Main St.,*

Livingston ☎ *406/222–8884* 🌐 *www.mustangfreshfood.com* 🕑 *Closed Sun.*

Hotels

Chico Hot Springs Resort & Day Spa
$ | RESORT | FAMILY | This rambling, quirky spa hotel opened in 1900, offering guests leisurely soaks in its 96°F–103°F hot-spring pools and accommodations with views of 10,920-foot Emigrant Peak and the Absaroka-Beartooth Wilderness beyond. **Pros:** good restaurant; relaxing spa facilities; beautiful, quiet setting amid nature. **Cons:** remote; the least expensive rooms share a bath; sometimes books up with weddings. [$] *Rooms from: $115* ✉ *163 Chico Rd., Pray* ☎ *406/333–4933* 🌐 *www.chicohotsprings.com* 🛏 *110 rooms* 🍴 *No meals.*

★ **The Murray Hotel**
$ | HOTEL | Even cowboys love soft pillows, which is one reason so many of them favor this 1904 town centerpiece, whose floors have seen silver-tipped cowboy boots, fly-fishing waders, and the polished heels of Hollywood celebrities. **Pros:** easy stroll to shops and galleries; metal beds, claw-foot tubs, and pedestal sinks maintain period ambience; great bar and restaurant. **Cons:** elevator requires an operator; some areas show their age; thin walls. [$] *Rooms from: $139* ✉ *201 W. Park St., Livingston* ☎ *406/222–1350* 🌐 *www.murrayhotel.com* 🛏 *30 rooms.*

Nightlife

Katabatic Brewing Company
BREWPUBS/BEER GARDENS | This festive craft brewery and tap room in downtown Livingston is a great place to relax with a beer (try the Scotch Ale or Deadrock Coffee Porter) after a day of fishing or hiking. There's good pub fare, too. ✉ *117 W. Park St., Livingston* ☎ *406/333–2855* 🌐 *www.katabaticbrewing.com.*

Activities

FISHING

★ **Dan Bailey's Fly Shop**
FISHING | The fishing experts at this world-renowned shop can help you find the right fly, tackle, and outdoor clothing. Equipment is available for rental, and fly-fishing clinics and float and wade trips are conducted. ✉ *209 W. Park St., Livingston* ☎ *406/222–1673* 🌐 *www.danbaileys.com.*

Bozeman

26 miles west of Livingston, 90 miles north of West Yellowstone.

This recreation capital offers everything from trout fishing to white-water river rafting to backcountry mountain biking to skiing. The arts have also flowered in Bozeman, the home of Montana State University. The mix of cowboys, professors, students, skiers, and celebrities makes it one of the more diverse communities in the northern Rockies as well as one of the fastest-growing towns in Montana—the population has skyrocketed from 27,000 in 2000 to more than 52,000 in 2020. The boom has led to stylish new hotels and trendy eateries, but Bozeman retains a decidedly easy-going, western vibe.

GETTING HERE AND AROUND

Set along Interstate 90, Bozeman is about a 90-minute drive from Yellowstone's North Entrance (via Livingston and U.S. 89) and its West Entrance (via Big Sky and U.S. 191). Downtown is easy to get around on foot, but you'll need a car to explore farther afield. It's home to one of the region's largest airports.

VISITOR INFORMATION Bozeman Convention and Visitors Bureau. ✉ *2000 Commerce Way, Bozeman* ☎ *406/586–5421* 🌐 *www.bozemancvb.com.*

Sights

★ Museum of the Rockies

MUSEUM | **FAMILY** | Here you'll find a celebration of the history of the Rockies region, with exhibits ranging from prehistory to pioneers, plus a planetarium with laser shows. Most renowned is the museum's Siebel Dinosaur Complex housing one of the world's largest dinosaur fossil collections along with the largest-known T-rex skull, a Mesozoic Media Center, and a Hall of Giants complete with sound effects. Children love the hands-on science activities in the Explore Yellowstone Children's Discovery Center and the outdoors Tensley Homestead, with home-crafts demonstrations, including butter churning, weaving, and blacksmithing. May through mid-September, sheep, donkeys, and horses graze among the tall pasture grasses of the homestead. ✉ *600 W. Kagy Blvd., Bozeman* ✣ *south end of university campus* ☎ *406/994–2251* 🌐 *www.museumoftherockies.org* 🎫 *$14.50.*

Restaurants

Jam!

$ | **MODERN AMERICAN** | Colorful murals, high ceilings, and exposed airducts create a mod-industrial ambience in this bustling downtown café that serves breakfast all day as well as a selection of tasty lunch items. Specialties include the crab cake Benedict and challah bread French toast stuffed with jam-infused mascarpone cheese. **Known for:** mimosas and brunch cocktails; bacon–smoked bacon burgers; both sweet and savory crepes. [$] *Average main: $13* ✉ *25 W. Main St., Bozeman* ☎ *406/585–1761* 🌐 *www.jamonmain.com* 🕓 *No dinner.*

Montana Ale Works

$$ | **ECLECTIC** | A cavernous brick building, the former Northern Pacific Railroad depot houses a full bar with a huge selection of Montana microbrews, and a restaurant with a choice of quiet or boisterous seating areas. In addition to 40 beers on tap, Ale Works serves bison burgers, bison potstickers, baked pasta dishes, Caribbean and Spanish dishes, steaks, sandwiches, and salads. [$] *Average main: $21* ✉ *611 E. Main St., Bozeman* ☎ *406/587–7700* 🌐 *www.montanaaleworks.com.*

★ Whistle Pig Korean

$ | **KOREAN** | A welcome addition to Bozeman's growing selection of international restaurants, this cozy, dimly lighted Korean eatery serves delectable pork-kimchi buns, fried tofu dumplings, and bibimbap with bulgogi beef. Be sure to save room for a house-made Korean street doughnut. **Known for:** cucumber kimchi; Kalbi barbecued short ribs; short but sweet list of interesting beer and wine. [$] *Average main: $12* ✉ *25 N. Willson Ave., Bozeman* ☎ *406/404–1224* 🌐 *www.whistlepigkorean.com* 🕓 *Closed Sun.–Mon. No lunch.*

Coffee and Quick Bites

Foxtrot

$ | **CAFÉ** | This dapper counter-service café in Bozeman's eco-friendly Market Building roasts small-batch Guatemalan coffee and serves a selection of beer, wine, and cocktails, too. It's also a good bet for flavorful breakfast and lunch fare, from veggie scrambles to healthy power bowls. **Known for:** stellar espresso drinks; airy, modern design; biscuits with pork shoulder and Dijon-creme gravy. [$] *Average main: $9* ✉ *The Market Building, 730 Boardwalk Ave., Bozeman* ☎ *406/551–7438* 🌐 *www.foxtrotbzn.com* 🕓 *No dinner.*

Hotels

Gallatin River Lodge

$$$$ | **B&B/INN** | On the property of a 350-acre ranch, this full-service, year-round fly-fishing lodge has 2 miles of waterfront on the river for which it is named. **Pros:** lodge earns praise for its delicious dinners as well as matching guests with activities. **Cons:** if fly-fishing isn't your thing, not the best choice. $ *Rooms from: $375 ⊠ 9105 Thorpe Rd., Bozeman ☎ 406/388–0148, 406/388–6766 ⊕ www. grlodge.com ⟿ 12 rooms ⎮◎⎮ Breakfast.*

★ Kimpton Armory Hotel

$$$ | HOTEL | With a striking art deco design, this gorgeous nine-story hotel opened in Bozeman's former armory building in 2020, providing urbane accommodations and amenities in an appealing downtown location that's within day-tripping distance of Big Sky skiing and Yellowstone National Park adventures. **Pros:** great pool and fitness center; fantastic restaurant and roof-top bar; heart of downtown dining and shopping district. **Cons:** can be pricey at busy times; expensive valet-only parking; busy downtown location. $ *Rooms from: $250 ⊠ 24 W. Mendenhall St., Bozeman ☎ 406/551–7700, 833/549–0847 ⊕ www. armoryhotelbzn.com ⟿ 122 rooms ⎮◎⎮ No meals.*

★ Lark Bozeman Hotels

$$$ | HOTEL | Comprising a stylishly updated mid-century motel and a newly built four-story wing set around a covered courtyard with a wood-burning fireplace, this hip and contemporary hotel in the heart of downtown Bozeman feels fresh, artsy, and playful with its low-slung, light-wood furniture and bold-colored accents. **Pros:** creatively modern design; prime downtown location; guest room walls hung with installations by local artists. **Cons:** no full-service restaurant; valet parking only; a little hipster-y for some tastes. $ *Rooms from: $239 ⊠ 122 W. Main St., Bozeman ☎ 406/624–3070, 866/464–1000 ⊕ www.larkbozeman.com ⟿ 67 rooms ⎮◎⎮ No meals.*

Nightlife

★ Plonk Wine

WINE BARS—NIGHTLIFE | This long narrow bar with exposed-brick walls and an antique pressed-tin ceiling is as much fun for people-watching and gabbing with locals as it is for sipping vino from the extensive and impressive list. There's a good food menu, too, including house-made sorbets for dessert. ⊠ *29 E. Main St., Bozeman ☎ 406/587–2170 ⊕ www. plonkwine.com.*

West Yellowstone

1 mile west of Yellowstone's West Entrance, 90 miles south of Bozeman.

This western gateway to the park is where the open plains of southwestern Montana and northeastern Idaho come together along the Madison River Valley. Affectionately known among winter recreationists as the "snowmobile capital of the world," this community of 1,400 has a rather bland downtown but is a good base for fishing, horseback riding, and downhill skiing and has a couple of noteworthy attractions that tap into the area's natural and cultural history.

GETTING HERE AND AROUND

Minutes from the park's West Entrance, the town of West Yellowstone is about a 90-minute drive from Bozeman. There's a small seasonal airport served by Delta in summer.

VISITOR INFORMATION **Destination West Yellowstone.** ⊠ *30 Yellowstone Ave., West Yellowstone ☎ 406/646–7701 ⊕ www. destinationyellowstone.com.*

Sights

★ Grizzly and Wolf Discovery Center

NATURE PRESERVE | FAMILY | Home to grizzlies and grey wolves, this nonprofit wildlife park provides an up-close look at Yellowstone's largest and most powerful predators. In summer, you can also view birds of prey, and the river otter exhibit is a hit with kids. The comprehensive "Bears: Imagination and Reality" exhibit compares myths about bears to what science has revealed about them. This is the only facility that formally tests bear-resistant products such as coolers and canisters in cooperation with state and federal agencies. ✉ *201 S. Canyon St., West Yellowstone* ☎ *406/646–7001, 800/257–2570* 🌐 *www.grizzlydiscoveryctr.org* 🎫 *$15.*

Museum of the Yellowstone

MUSEUM | FAMILY | West Yellowstone's 1909 Union Pacific Depot has been transformed into a museum dedicated to the modes of travel—from stagecoaches to planes—people employed to get to Yellowstone before World War II. Films provide insight on topics such as the fire that devastated Yellowstone in 1988 and the way earthquakes affect the area's hydrothermal features. ✉ *104 Yellowstone Ave., West Yellowstone* ☎ *406/646–1100* 🌐 *www.museumoftheyellowstone.org* 🎫 *$6* 🕒 *Closed early Oct.–mid-May.*

Restaurants

Firehole Bar-B-Que

$ | BARBECUE | You'll find expertly prepared, slow-cooked, fall-off-the-bone barbecue in this no-frills barn-style restaurant a few blocks from Yellowstone's West Entrance. Order at the counter, then wait for your feast of tender brisket, pork, turkey, St. Louis–style ribs, or buffalo sausage to appear. **Known for:** smoked meats by the pound (perfect for park picnic supplies); smoked buffalo sausage links; house barbecue sauce available to go by the bottle. [$] *Average main: $11* ✉ *120 Firehole Ave., West Yellowstone* ☎ *406/641–0020* 🌐 *www.fireholebbqco.com.*

Madison Crossing Lounge

$$$ | MODERN AMERICAN | This handsome bistro and cocktail lounge set in part of West Yellowstone's 1918 former school building is an inviting spot for drinks—there's an encyclopedic wine, craft beer, and cocktail list—and appetizers. But if you're seeking a more substantial meal, consider the flat-iron steak with chimichurri sauce or a burger topped with smoked bacon and huckleberry-chipotle jam. **Known for:** nachos with bison chorizo; attractive fireplace-warmed dining room; creative cocktails. [$] *Average main: $24* ✉ *121 Madison Ave., West Yellowstone* ☎ *406/646–7621* 🌐 *www.madisoncrossinglounge.com* 🕒 *Closed mid-Oct.–mid-Dec. No lunch.*

Running Bear Pancake House

$ | AMERICAN | FAMILY | All the pies, muffins, and cinnamon rolls are made on the premises at this casual, family-friendly eatery. There are a lot of choices, but trust the name and go for the buttermilk or buckwheat pancakes topped with blueberries, strawberries, peaches, coconut, walnuts, or chocolate chips. **Known for:** several varieties of pancakes, plain and topped; espresso drinks using locally roasted beans; woodsy decor. [$] *Average main: $12* ✉ *538 Madison Ave., West Yellowstone* ☎ *406/646–7703* 🌐 *www.runningbearph.com* 🕒 *No dinner.*

Hotels

1872 Inn

$$$$ | HOTEL | This quieter, adult-oriented boutique hotel on the west side of downtown has warmly appointed rooms with leather chairs, custom wood furnishings, and Native American rugs and blankets. **Pros:** nicely designed bathrooms with heated towel racks and natural stone tiles; short walk from several restaurants; attractive common areas. **Cons:** not suitable for kids; expensive; no elevator.

$ *Rooms from: $379* ✉ *603 Yellowstone Ave., West Yellowstone* ☎ *406/646–1025* 🌐 *www.1872inn.com* 🛏 *18 rooms* 🍴 *Free Breakfast.*

★ **Explorer Cabins at Yellowstone**
$$$$ | **HOTEL** | **FAMILY** | Consisting of 50 warmly appointed, contemporary cabins set among five clusters across the street from West Yellowstone's Grizzly & Wolf Discovery Center, this family- and pet-friendly compound is an ideal base for visiting the national park. **Pros:** handy but quiet in-town location; friendly, helpful staff; most cabins can sleep 4 to 6 guests. **Cons:** no ovens or freezers in kitchenettes; cabins are close together; some cabins are a little cozy. $ *Rooms from: $383* ✉ *250 S. Canyon St., West Yellowstone* ☎ *877/600–4308* 🌐 *www.yellowstonevacations.com* 🛏 *50 cabins* 🍴 *No meals.*

Cody

53 miles east of Yellowstone's East Entrance, 60 miles southeast of Red Lodge, Montana.

Cody, founded in 1896 and named for Pony Express rider, army scout, Freemason, and entertainer William F. "Buffalo Bill" Cody, is the eastern gateway to Yellowstone National Park. But this town of 9,820 is much more than a base for exploring the surrounding area. Five excellent museums under one roof make up the outstanding Buffalo Bill Historical Center, and the Western lifestyle is alive and well on dude ranches and in colorful shops. Part of the fun in Cody is sauntering down Sheridan Avenue, stopping by the Irma Hotel (built by Buffalo Bill and named for his daughter) for a refreshment, and attending the nightly rodeo.

GETTING HERE AND AROUND
The North Fork Highway (U.S. 14)—as the route leading west to Yellowstone is locally known—follows the North Fork of the Shoshone River past barren rock formations strewn with tumbleweeds, then enters lush forests and green meadows as the elevation increases roughly 3,000 feet in 70 miles. Cody's small airport is served by Delta and United.

VISITOR INFORMATION Cody Country Chamber of Commerce. ✉ *836 Sheridan Ave.* ☎ *307/587–2777, 307/587–2777* 🌐 *www.codychamber.org.*

Sights

★ **Buffalo Bill Center of the West**
MUSEUM | **FAMILY** | This extraordinary "five-in-one" complex, an affiliate of the Smithsonian Institution, contains the Buffalo Bill Museum, the Whitney Western Art Museum, the Plains Indian Museum, the Cody Firearms Museum, and the Draper Natural History Museum. All are well organized and mount superb exhibitions in their respective subject areas. The flagship Buffalo Bill Museum puts into context the life, era, and activities of its (and its town's) namesake, William F. "Buffalo Bill" Cody (1846–1917), whose numerous careers included guide, scout, actor, and entrepreneur. If you want to understand how the myth of the American West developed, this is the place to come. The other four museums—there's also a research library—are equally absorbing. Plan to spend at least four hours here—and to discover that this isn't enough time to take it all in. Luckily, your admission ticket is good for two consecutive days. ✉ *720 Sheridan Ave.* ☎ *307/587–4771* 🌐 *www.centerofthewest.org* 🎟 *$19.75* 🕐 *Closed Mon.–Wed. in Dec.–Feb.*

★ **Heart Mountain Interpretive Center**
MUSEUM | From 1942 through 1945, nearly 14,000 Japanese Americans were relocated to this hastily constructed incarceration center—one of ten located throughout the country—at the foot of Heart Mountain, about 13 miles north of Cody. Evicted from their West Coast homes through an executive order issued by President Franklin D. Roosevelt shortly after the bombing of Pearl Harbor, the residents

lived in small, tightly spaced barracks. In 2011, a poignant museum opened on the long-abandoned site. At the Heart Mountain Interpretive Center, you can learn about this shameful episode of U.S. history by watching an excellent short movie and touring both permanent and rotating exhibits that use photographs, letters, news clippings, and other artifacts to bring to life the powerful and often inspiring stories of Heart Mountain's inhabitants, who persevered in the face of anti-Asian prejudices and unjust conditions. ✉ *1539 Rd. 19* ☎ *307/754–8000* ⊕ *www.heart-mountain.org* ☞ *$9* ⊗ *Closed Sun.–Wed. in Oct.–mid-May.*

🍽 Restaurants

Cody Steakhouse

$$$ | STEAKHOUSE | This handsome, clubby-feeling restaurant along Cody's main drag is a favorite of carnivores, but there's also a surprising variety of internationally inspired seafood and poultry dishes, including prawns with a spicy mango-jalapeño salsa. Among the meatier fare, consider the 16-ounce hand-cut buffalo rib-eye or 18-ounce T-bone Angus beef steak. **Known for:** prodigious portions; one of Cody's better wine and beer selections; rich chocolate brownie sandwiches topped with ice cream. $ *Average main: $25* ✉ *1367 Sheridan Ave.* ☎ *307/586–2550* ⊕ *www. cody-steak-house.business.site* ⊗ *Closed Mon. and Tues. No lunch.*

🛏 Hotels

Best Western Premier Ivy Inn & Suites

$$$ | HOTEL | This newer and more upscale member of the ubiquitous Best Western brand offers among the most spacious and attractive rooms in town, in a handsome stone-and-timber building on the west side of town, making it convenient for making the 50-mile drive to Yellowstone's East Entrance. **Pros:** spacious and stylish rooms; good gym and indoor

heated pool; full-service restaurant and bar. **Cons:** no pets; not within walking distance of town; on busy road. $ *Rooms from: $253* ✉ *1800 8th St.* ☎ *307/587–2572* ⊕ *www.bestwestern.com* ☞ *70 rooms* 🍴 *No meals.*

★ Chamberlin Inn

$$$ | B&B/INN | Named for Agnes Chamberlin, who opened a boardinghouse on this spot in 1904, this artfully restored redbrick inn a block off Cody's main street counts Ernest Hemingway and Marshall Field among its many past guests. **Pros:** filled with historic accents and furnishings; welcoming service; short walk to downtown dining. **Cons:** no elevator; summer rates are quite steep; no breakfast. $ *Rooms from: $285* ✉ *1032 12th St.* ☎ *307/587–0202, 888/587–0202* ⊕ *www.chamberlininn. com* ☞ *22 rooms* 🍴 *No meals.*

Cooke City–Silver Gate

2 miles east of Yellowstone's Northeast Entrance.

The tiny, neighboring communities of Cooke City and Silver Gate, are just outside the Northeast Entrance of Yellowstone and just west of the soaring Beartooth Mountains. This largely seasonal community that mostly shuts down from mid-October through early May has a handful of casual, Western-style lodgings and eateries and is a great little base camp for exploring Lamar Valley.

GETTING HERE AND AROUND
Year-round, you can get to these towns by traveling through Yellowstone's northern section from Mammoth Hot Springs past Tower Junction along Northeast Entrance Road—the drive from Gardiner takes about 90 minutes. In summer, you can continue east from town on U.S. 212 (the Beartooth Scenic Highway) to Red Lodge, which is also about a 90-minute drive.

🍴 Restaurants

★ MontAsia

$ | **ECLECTIC** | Make your way to this small log cabin with red trim for some of the tastiest and interesting fare in the region, a fusion of Asian and Montana fare (hence the restaurant's name) prepared and served by a lovely, friendly family. Made-from-scratch chili and house-roasted chicken with fries and aioli appear on the same menu as pork-cabbage potstickers with house-made ginger-soy sauce and rice noodles with tofu, nori, and Japanese sesame oil. **Known for:** outdoor seating with mountain views; Malaysian chicken rice; coconut shakes and chai brownies. $ *Average main: $15* ✉ *102 E. Main St.* ☎ *406/838–2382* ⊕ *www.montasia.ninja* ⊗ *Closed Wed.*

🛏 Hotels

Silver Gate Lodging

$$ | **RENTAL** | **FAMILY** | This friendly summer-only compound that offers everything from rustic but economical motel rooms to roomy cabins that can sleep up to 10 guests has the perfect location for exploring Lamar Valley—it's in tiny and tranquil Silver Gate, a mile from Yellowstone's Northeast Entrance. **Pros:** well-stocked general store; close proximity to Lamar Valley; good for families and larger groups. **Cons:** in a tiny town with few amenities; three-night minimum in high season; least-expensive units are quite small. $ *Rooms from: $160* ✉ *109 U.S. 212 W* ☎ *406/838–2371* ⊕ *www.silvergatelodging.com* ⊗ *Closed Nov.–Apr.* ⤳ *30 rooms* ⏺ *No meals.*

YOSEMITE NATIONAL PARK

Updated by
Cheryl Crabtree

CALIFORNIA

🏕 Camping	🛏 Hotels	🏃 Activities	👁 Scenery	👥 Crowds
★★★★★	★★★★☆	★★★★★	★★★★★	★★★★☆

WELCOME TO
YOSEMITE NATIONAL PARK

TOP REASONS
TO GO

★ **Scenic falls:** An easy stroll brings you to the base of Lower Yosemite Fall, where roaring springtime waters make for misty lens caps and lasting memories.

★ **Tunnel vision:** Approaching Yosemite Valley, Wawona Road passes through a mountainside and emerges before one of the park's most heart-stopping vistas.

★ **Inhale the beauty:** Pause to take in the light, pristine air as you travel about the High Sierra's Tioga Pass and Tuolumne Meadows, where 10,000-foot granite peaks just might take your breath away.

★ **Walk away:** Leave the crowds behind—but do bring along a buddy—and take a hike somewhere along Yosemite's 800 miles of trails.

★ **Winter wonder:** Observe the snowflakes and stillness of winter in the park.

1 **Yosemite Valley.** At an elevation of 4,000 feet, in roughly the center of the park, beats Yosemite's heart. This is where you'll find the park's most famous sights and biggest crowds.

2 **Wawona.** The park's southern tip holds Wawona, with its grand old hotel and pioneer history center, and the Mariposa Grove of Giant Sequoias. These are closest to the south entrance, 35 miles (a one-hour drive) south of Yosemite Village.

3 **Tuolumne Meadows.** The highlight of east-central Yosemite is this wildflower-strewn valley that's laced with hiking trails and nestled among sharp, rocky peaks. It's a 1½-hour drive northeast of Yosemite Valley along Tioga Road (closed mid-Oct.–late May).

4 **Hetch Hetchy.** The most remote, least visited part of Yosemite accessible by automobile, this glacial valley is dominated by a reservoir and veined with wilderness trails. It's near the park's western boundary, about a half-hour drive north of the Big Oak Flat entrance.

0   5 mi

0   5 km

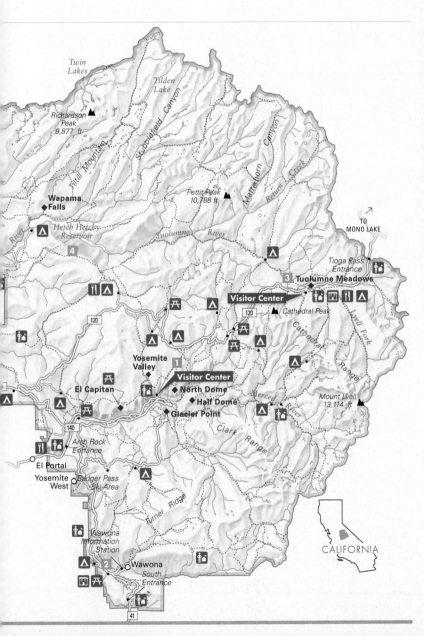

By merely standing in Yosemite Valley and turning in a circle, you can see more natural wonders in a minute than you could in a full day pretty much anywhere else. Half Dome, Yosemite Falls, El Capitan, Bridalveil Fall, Sentinel Dome, the Merced River, white-flowering dogwood trees, maybe even bears ripping into the bark of fallen trees or sticking their snouts into beehives—it's all here.

Native American nations—including the Miwok, Paiute, Mono, and Ahwahnee-chee tribes—roamed this wonderland long before other cultures. Indeed, some of the footpaths used by Native Americans to cross mountains and valleys are still used as park hiking trails today.

In the mid-1800s, the valley's special geologic qualities and the giant sequoias of Mariposa Grove 30 miles to the south began attracting visitors. The two areas so impressed a group of influential Californians that they lobbied President Abraham Lincoln to grant them to the state for protection, which he did on June 30, 1864. Further lobbying efforts by naturalist John Muir and Robert Underwood Johnson, editor of *The Century Magazine,* led Congress to set aside an additional 1,500 square miles for Yosemite National Park on October 1, 1890. The valley and Mariposa Grove, which had remained under state control, also became part of the park in 1906.

Yosemite is so large and diverse, it almost seems to be multiple parks. Many visitors spend their time along the southwestern border, between Wawona, which is open all year and is where the giant sequoias stand, and the Big Oak Flat entrance. Also very popular are Yosemite Valley, famous for its waterfalls and cliffs and also open year round, and the Badger Pass Ski Area, a winter-only destination. The seasonal, east–west Tioga Road spans the park north of the valley and bisects Tuolumne Meadows, the subalpine high country that's open for summer hiking and camping; in winter, it's accessible only via cross-country skis or snowshoes. The northwestern Hetch Hetchy district, home of less-used back-country trails, is most accessible from late spring through early fall.

Photographers, hikers, and nature enthusiasts visit again and again, lured by the seasonally changing landscapes. In spring, waterfalls are robust thanks to abundant snowmelt. In early summer, wildflowers blanket alpine meadows. In fall, the trees showcase glorious explosions of color. In winter, snows provide a magical setting for activities like ice skating in the valley or cross-country skiing to Glacier Point.

AVERAGE HIGH/LOW TEMPERATURES					
JAN.	**FEB.**	**MAR.**	**APR.**	**MAY**	**JUNE**
48/29	53/30	55/32	61/36	69/43	78/49
JULY	**AUG.**	**SEPT.**	**OCT.**	**NOV.**	**DEC.**
85/55	84/55	79/49	70/42	56/34	47/29

Planning

When to Go

During extremely busy periods—such as weekends and holidays throughout the year—you will experience delays at the entrance gates. For smaller crowds, visit midweek. Or come January through March, when the park is a bit less busy, and the days usually are sunny and clear.

Summer rainfall is rare. In winter, heavy snows occasionally cause road closures, and tire chains or four-wheel drive may be required on the routes that remain open. The road to Glacier Point beyond the turnoff for the Badger Pass Ski Area is closed after the first major snowfall. Tioga Road is closed from late October through May or mid-June. Mariposa Grove Road is typically closed for a shorter period in winter.

FESTIVALS AND EVENTS

Bluesapalooza. The first weekend of every August, Mammoth Lakes hosts a blues and beer festival—with an emphasis on the beer tasting. ⊕ www.mammoth-bluesbrewsfest.com

The Bracebridge Dinner at Yosemite. Held at The Ahwahnee hotel in Yosemite Village every Christmas since 1928, this 17th-century-theme, madrigal dinner is so popular that most seats are booked months in advance. There are also lodging packages (again, book as soon as you can). ⊕ www.travelyosemite.com

Chefs' Holidays. Celebrated chefs present cooking demonstrations and multicourse meals at The Ahwahnee hotel in Yosemite Village from mid-January to early February. You can get dinner or a dinner/room package, but space is limited. ⊕ www.travelyosemite.com

Mammoth Jazzfest. This mid-July weekend festival funded by the town of Mammoth Lakes features free jazz performances at The Village at Mammoth. ⊕ www.mammothjazzfest.org

Sierra Art Trails. The work of more than 100 artists is on display in studios and galleries throughout eastern Madera and Mariposa counties over a long weekend in early October. Purchase the catalog of locations and hours at area shops. ⊕ www.sierraarttrails.org

Vintners' Holidays. Some of California's most prestigious vintners hold two- and three-day midweek seminars in the Great Room of The Ahwahnee hotel in Yosemite Village. The event culminates with an elegant—albeit pricey—banquet dinner. Arrive early for seats; book early for the dinner or lodging and dining packages. ⊕ www.travelyosemite.com

Getting Here and Around

AIR

The closest airport to the south and west entrances is Fresno Yosemite International Airport (FAT). Mammoth Yosemite Airport (MMH) is closest to the east entrance. Sacramento International Airport (SMF) is also close to the north and west entrances.

BUS AND TRAIN

Amtrak's daily *San Joaquins* train stops in Merced and connects with YARTS buses that travel to Yosemite Valley along Highway 140 from there. Seasonal YARTS buses (typically mid-May to late September) also travel along Highway 41 from Fresno, Highway 120 from Sonora, and Highway 395 and Tioga Road from Mammoth Lakes with scheduled stops at towns along the way. Once you're in Yosemite Valley, you can take advantage of the free shuttle buses, which operate on low emissions, have 21 stops, and run from 7 am to 10 pm year-round. Buses run about every 10 minutes in summer, a bit less frequently in winter. A separate (but also free) summer-only shuttle runs out to El Capitan. Also in summer, you can pay to take the "hikers' bus" from Yosemite Valley to Tuolumne or to ride a tour bus up to Glacier Point. During the snow season, buses run regularly between Yosemite Valley and Badger Pass Ski Area.

CAR
Roughly 200 miles from San Francisco, 300 miles from Los Angeles, and 500 miles from Las Vegas, Yosemite takes a while to reach—and its many sites and attractions merit much more time than what rangers say is the average visit: four hours.

Of the park's four entrances, Arch Rock is the closest to Yosemite Valley. The road that goes through it, Route 140 from Merced and Mariposa, is a scenic western approach that snakes alongside the boulder-packed Merced River. Route 41, through Wawona, is the way to come from Los Angeles (or Fresno, if you've flown in and rented a car). Route 120, through Crane Flat, is the most direct route from San Francisco. The only way in from the east is Tioga Road, which may be the best route in terms of scenery— though due to snow accumulation it's open for a frustratingly short amount of time each year (typically early June through mid-October). Once you enter Yosemite Valley, park your car in one of the two main day-parking areas, at Yosemite Village and Yosemite Falls, then

visit the sights via the free shuttle bus system. Or walk or bike along the valley's 12 miles of paved paths.

There are few gas stations within Yosemite (Crane Flat and Wawona, none in the valley), so fuel up before you reach the park. From late fall until early spring, the weather is especially unpredictable, and driving can be treacherous. You should carry chains during this period as they are required when roads are icy and when it snows.

Inspiration

The Photographer's Guide to Yosemite, by Michael Frye, is an insider's guide to the park, with maps for shutterbugs looking to capture perfect images.

Sierra Nevada Wildflowers, by Karen Wiese, is perfect for budding botanists, indentifying more than 230 kinds of flora growing in the Sierra Nevada region.

Yosemite: Art of an American Icon, by Amy Scott, has insightful essays accompanying museum-quality artwork.

Yosemite and the High Sierra, edited by Andrea G. Stillman and John Szarkowski, features beautiful reproductions of landmark photographs by Ansel Adams, accompanied by excerpts from the photographer's journals written when he traveled in Yosemite National Park in the early 20th century.

Park Essentials

ACCESSIBILITY
Yosemite's facilities are continually being upgraded to make them more accessible. Many of the valley floor trails—particularly at Lower Yosemite Fall, Bridalveil Fall, and Mirror Lake—are wheelchair accessible, though some assistance may be required. The Valley Visitor Center is fully accessible, as are the park shuttle buses. A sign-language interpreter is available

Yosemite in One Day

Begin at the **Valley Visitor Center**, where you can watch the documentary *Spirit of Yosemite*. A minute's stroll from there is the **Native American village of the Ahwahnee**, which recalls Native American life circa 1870. Take another 20 minutes to see the **Yosemite Museum**. Then, hop aboard the free shuttle to Yosemite Falls, and hike the **Lower Yosemite Fall Trail** to the base of the falls. Have lunch at **Yosemite Valley Lodge**, which you can access via a shuttle or a 20-minute walk.

Afternoon choices include spending time in **Curry Village**—perhaps swimming or ice-skating, shopping, renting a bike, or having a beer on the deck; checking out the family-friendly **Happy Isles Art and Nature Center**

and the adjacent nature trail; or hiking up the **Mist Trail** to the Vernal Fall footbridge to admire the view.

Hop back on the shuttle, then disembark at **The Ahwahnee.** The Great Lounge here has a magnificent fireplace and Native American artwork; have a meal in the Dining Room if you're up for a splurge. Or take the shuttle to **Yosemite Village** where you can grab some fixings, then drive to **El Capitan picnic area** and enjoy an outdoor evening meal. At this time of day, "El Cap" should be sun-splashed. (You will have also gotten several good looks at world-famous **Half Dome** throughout the day.) If the sun hasn't set yet, drive to the base of **Bridalveil Fall** to take a short hike.

for ranger programs. Visitors with respiratory difficulties should take note of the park's high elevations—the valley floor is approximately 4,000 feet above sea level, but Tuolumne Meadows and parts of the high country hover around 10,000 feet.

PARK FEES AND PERMITS

The admission fee, valid for seven days, is $35 per vehicle, $30 per motorcycle, or $20 per individual.

If you plan to camp in the backcountry or climb Half Dome, you must have a wilderness permit. Availability of permits depends upon trailhead quotas. It's best to make a reservation, especially if you will be visiting May through September. You can reserve two days to 24 weeks in advance by phone, mail, or fax (preferred method) (✉ Box 545, Yosemite, CA ☎ 209/372–0826); you'll pay $5 per person plus $5 per reservation if and when your reservations are confirmed. You can apply online via the park website

(⊕ www.nps.gov/yose/planyourvisit/backpacking.htm). Without a reservation, you may still get a free permit on a first-come, first-served basis at wilderness permit offices at Big Oak Flat, Hetch Hetchy, Tuolumne Meadows, Wawona, the Wilderness Center in Yosemite Village, and Yosemite Valley in summer. From fall to spring, visit the Valley Visitor Center.

PARK HOURS

The park is open 24/7 year-round. All entrances are open at all hours, except for the Hetch Hetchy entrance, which is open roughly dawn to dusk. Yosemite is in the Pacific Time Zone.

CELL PHONE RECEPTION

Cell phone reception can be hit or miss everywhere in the park. There are public telephones at entrance stations, visitor centers, all park restaurants and lodging facilities, gas stations, and in Yosemite Village.

Hotels

Indoor lodging options inside the park appear more expensive than initially seems warranted, but that premium pays off big-time in terms of the time you'll save—unless you are bunking within a few miles of a Yosemite entrance, you will face long commutes to the park when you stay outside its borders (though the Yosemite View Lodge, on Route 140, is within a reasonable half-hour's drive of Yosemite Valley).

Because of the park's immense popularity—not just with tourists from around the world but with Northern Californians who make weekend trips here—reservations are all but mandatory. Book up to one year ahead. ■TIP➔ If you're not set on a specific hotel or camp but just want to stay somewhere inside the park, call the main reservation number to check for availability and reserve (888/413–8869 or 602/278–8888 international). Park lodgings have a seven-day cancellation policy, so you may be able to snag last-minute reservations. *Hotel reviews have been shortened. For full information, visit Fodors.com.*

Restaurants

Yosemite National Park has a couple of moderately priced restaurants in lovely (which almost goes without saying) settings: the Mountain Room at Yosemite Valley Lodge and the dining room at the Wawona Hotel. The Ahwahnee hotel provides one of the finest dining experiences in the country.

Otherwise, food service is geared toward satisfying the masses as efficiently as possible. Yosemite Valley Lodge's Base Camp Eatery is the valley's best lower-cost, hot-food option, with Italian, classic American, and world-cuisine counter options. In Curry Village, the offerings at Seven Tents are overpriced and usually fairly bland, but you can get decent pizzas on the adjacent outdoor deck. In Yosemite Valley Village, the Village Grill whips up burgers and fries, Degnan's Kitchen has made-to-order sandwiches, and The Loft at Degnan's has an open, chaletlike dining area in which to enjoy barbecue meals and appetizers.

The White Wolf Lodge and Tuolumne Meadows Lodge—both off Tioga Road and therefore guaranteed open only from early June through September—have small restaurants where meals are competently prepared. Tuolumne Meadows also has a grill, and the gift shop at Glacier Point sells premade sandwiches, snacks, and hot dogs. During ski season, you'll also find one at the Badger Pass Ski Area, off Glacier Point Road. *Restaurant reviews have been shortened. For full information, visit Fodors.com.*

What It Costs

	$	$$	$$$	$$$$
RESTAURANTS				
	under $12	$12–$20	$21–$30	over $30
HOTELS				
	under $100	$100–$150	$151–$200	over $200

Tours

★ **Ansel Adams Camera Walks**

SPECIAL-INTEREST | Photography enthusiasts shouldn't miss these guided, 90-minute walks offered four mornings (Monday, Tuesday, Thursday, and Saturday) each week by professional photographers. All are free, but participation is limited to 15 people so reservations are essential. Meeting points vary. ✉ *Yosemite National Park* ☎ *209/372–4413* ⊕ *www.anseladams.com* ⌘ *Free.*

Discover Yosemite

GUIDED TOURS | This outfit operates daily tours to Yosemite Valley, Mariposa Grove, and Glacier Point in 14- and 29-passenger vehicles. The tour travels along Highway

41 with stops in Bass Lake, Oakhurst, and Fish Camp; rates include lunch. Sunset tours to Sentinel Dome are additional summer options. ☎ 559/642–4400 ⊕ discoveryosemite.com ✆ From $158.

Glacier Point Tour

GUIDED TOURS | This four-hour trip takes you from Yosemite Valley to the Glacier Point vista, 3,214 feet above the valley floor. Some people buy a $29 one-way ticket and hike down. Shuttles depart from the Yosemite Valley Lodge three times a day. ⊠ Yosemite National Park ☎ 888/413–8869 ⊕ www.travelyosemite.com ✆ From $57 ⊗ Closed Nov.–late May ⚲ Reservations essential.

Grand Tour

GUIDED TOURS | For a full-day tour of Yosemite Valley, the Mariposa Grove of Giant Sequoias, and Glacier Point, try the Grand Tour, which departs from the Yosemite Valley Lodge in the valley. The tour stops for a picnic lunch (included) at the historic Wawona Hotel. ⊠ Yosemite National Park ☎ 209/372–1240 ⊕ www.travelyosemite.com ✆ $110 ⚲ Reservations essential.

Moonlight Tour

This after-dark version of the Valley Floor Tour takes place on moonlit nights from June through September, depending on weather conditions. ⊠ Yosemite National Park ☎ 209/372–4386 ⊕ www.travelyosemite.com ✆ $38.

Tuolumne Meadows Hikers Bus

BUS TOURS | For a full day's outing to the high country, opt for this ride up Tioga Road to Tuolumne Meadows. You'll stop at several overlooks, and you can connect with another shuttle at Tuolumne Lodge. This service is mostly for hikers and backpackers who want to reach high-country trailheads, but everyone is welcome. ⊠ Yosemite National Park ☎ 209/372–1240 ⊕ www.travelyosemite.com ✆ $15 one-way, $23 round-trip ⊗ Closed Labor Day–mid-June ⚲ Reservations essential.

Valley Floor Tour

GUIDED TOURS | Take a two-hour tour of Yosemite Valley's highlights, complete with narration on the area's history, geology, and flora and fauna. Tours (offered year round) are either in trams or enclosed motor coaches, depending on weather conditions. ⊠ Yosemite National Park ☎ 209/372–1240, 888/413–8869 reservations ⊕ www.travelyosemite.com ✆ From $38.

Visitor Information

PARK CONTACT INFORMATION Yosemite National Park. ☎ 209/372–0200 ⊕ www.nps.gov/yose.

Yosemite Valley

Yosemite Valley Visitor Center is 11.5 miles from the Arch Rock entrance and 15 miles east of El Portal.

The glacier-carved Yosemite Valley stretches nearly 8 miles along the Merced River. It holds many of the park's major sights, including El Capitan, Half Dome, Glacier Point, and famous waterfalls. The valley is accessible year-round. Park your car at Yosemite Village (home of the visitor center, museum, market, and other services), Curry Village, or near Yosemite Falls. Free shuttle buses loop through the eastern and western sections of the valley.

◉ Sights

HISTORIC SITES

The Ahwahnee

HOTEL—SIGHT | Gilbert Stanley Underwood, architect of the Grand Canyon Lodge, also designed The Ahwahnee hotel. Opened in 1927, it is generally considered his best work. You can stay here (for about $500 a night), or simply explore the first-floor shops and perhaps have breakfast or lunch in the bustling

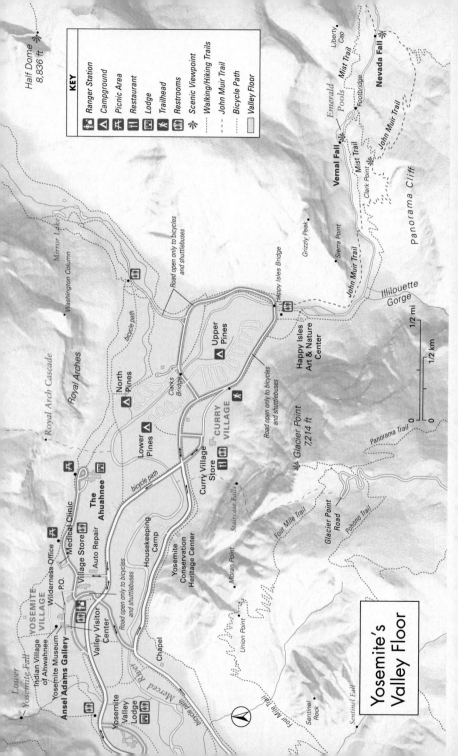

Yosemite's Valley Floor

KEY

- Ranger Station
- Campground
- Picnic Area
- Restaurant
- Lodge
- Trailhead
- Restrooms
- Scenic Viewpoint
- ·········· Walking/Hiking Trails
- – – – John Muir Trail
- ·········· Bicycle Path
- Valley Floor

Half Dome 8,836 ft

Liberty Cap

Mist Trail

Nevada Fall

Emerald Pools

Vernal Fall

Footbridge

Mist Trail

John Muir Trail

Clark Point

Panorama Cliff

Mirror Lake

Washington Column

Road open only to bicycles and shuttlebuses

Grizzly Peak

Sierra Point

Happy Isles Bridge

John Muir Trail

Illilouette Gorge

Royal Arch Cascade

Royal Arches

bicycle path

Upper Pines

North Pines

Clarks Bridge

Happy Isles Art & Nature Center

1/2 mi

1/2 km

Lower Pines

CURRY VILLAGE

Glacier Point 7,214 ft

Road open only to bicycles and shuttlebuses

Curry Village Store

Panorama trail

The Ahwahnee

Medical Clinic

bicycle path

Housekeeping Camp

Staircase Falls

Four Mile Trail

Glacier Point Road

Pohono Trail

Village Store

Auto Repair

Yosemite Conservation Heritage Center

Moran Point

Wilderness Office

P.O.

YOSEMITE VILLAGE

Indian Village of Ahwahnee

Yosemite Museum

Ansel Adams Gallery

Valley Visitor Center

Road open only to bicycles and shuttlebuses

Chapel

Union Point

Lower Yosemite Fall

Merced River

bicycle path

Yosemite Valley Lodge

Sentinel Falls

Sentinel Rock

Four Mile trail

and beautiful Dining Room or more casual bar. The Great Lounge, 77 feet long with magnificent 24-foot-high ceilings and all manner of artwork on display, beckons with big, comfortable chairs and relative calm. ⊠ *Yosemite Valley, Ahwahnee Rd., Yosemite Village* ⊹ *About ¾ mile east of Yosemite Valley Visitor Center* ☎ *209/372–1489* ⊕ *www.travelyosemite. com/lodging/the-ahwahnee.*

Curry Village

HOTEL—SIGHT | A couple of schoolteachers from Indiana founded Camp Curry in 1899 as a low-cost option for staying in the valley, which it remains today. Curry Village's 400-plus lodging options, many of them tent cabins, are spread over a large chunk of the valley's southeastern side. This is one family-friendly place, but it's more functional than attractive. ⊠ *Southside Dr.* ⊹ *About ½ mile east of Yosemite Village.*

Indian Village of Ahwahnee

MUSEUM VILLAGE | This solemn smattering of structures, accessed by a short loop trail behind the Yosemite Valley Visitor Center, offers a look at what Native American life might have been like in the 1870s. One interpretive sign points out that the Miwok people referred to the 19th-century newcomers as "Yohemite" or "Yohometuk," which have been translated as meaning "some of them are killers." ⊠ *Northside Dr., Yosemite Village* ⊲ *Free.*

Yosemite Museum

MUSEUM | This small museum consists of a permanent exhibit that focuses on the history of the area and the people who once lived here. An adjacent gallery promotes contemporary and historic Yosemite art in revolving gallery exhibits. A docent demonstrates traditional Native American basket-weaving techniques a few days a week. ⊠ *Yosemite Village* ☎ *209/372–0299* ⊲ *Free.*

PICNIC AREAS
Cathedral Beach

LOCAL INTEREST | **FAMILY** | Your alfresco meal may be quite peaceful at this area in the eastern end of the valley, which usually has fewer people than picnic spots. ⊠ *Southside Dr.* ⊹ *Underneath spirelike Cathedral Rocks.*

Church Bowl

LOCAL INTEREST | **FAMILY** | This picnic area nearly abuts the granite walls below the Royal Arches. It's also the closest area to the village—good to know if you're trekking with picnic supplies. ⊹ *Behind The Ahwahnee.*

El Capitan

LOCAL INTEREST | **FAMILY** | Come here for great views that look straight up the giant granite wall above. ⊠ *Northside Dr.* ⊹ *At western end of valley.*

Sentinel Beach

Usually crowded in season, this area is right alongside a running creek and the Merced River. ⊠ *Southside Dr.* ⊹ *Just south of Swinging Bridge.*

Swinging Bridge

LOCAL INTEREST | **FAMILY** | This picnic area is just before the little wooden footbridge that crosses the Merced River, which babbles by pleasantly. ⊠ *Southside Dr.* ⊹ *East of Sentinel Beach.*

SCENIC STOPS
Bridalveil Fall

BODY OF WATER | This 620-foot waterfall is often diverted dozens of feet one way or the other by the breeze. It is the first marvelous site you will see up close when you drive into Yosemite Valley. ⊠ *Yosemite Valley, access from parking area off Wawona Rd.*

El Capitan

NATURE SITE | Rising 3,593 feet—more than 350 stories—above the valley, El Capitan is the largest exposed-granite monolith in the world. Since 1958, people have been climbing its entire face, including the famous "nose." You can

Plants and Wildlife in Yosemite

Dense stands of incense cedar and Douglas fir—as well as ponderosa, Jeffrey, lodgepole, and sugar pines—cover much of the park, but the stellar standout, quite literally, is the *Sequoiadendron giganteum*, the giant sequoia. Sequoias grow only along the west slope of the Sierra Nevada between 4,500 and 7,000 feet in elevation. Starting from a seed the size of a rolled-oat flake, each of these ancient monuments assumes remarkable proportions in adulthood; you can see them in the Mariposa Grove of Giant Sequoias. In late May, the valley's dogwood trees bloom with white, starlike flowers. Wildflowers, such as the black-eyed Susan, bull thistle, cow parsnip, lupine, and meadow goldenrod, peak in June in the valley and in July at higher elevations.

The most visible animals in the park—aside from the omnipresent western gray squirrels, which fearlessly attempt to steal your food at every campground and picnic site—are the mule deer. Though sightings of bighorn sheep are infrequent in the park itself, you can sometimes see them on the eastern side of the Sierra Crest, just off Route 120 in Lee Vining Canyon. You may also see the American black bear, which can have a brown, cinnamon, or blond coat. The Sierra Nevada is home to thousands of these creatures, and you should take all necessary precautions to keep yourself—and them—safe. Bears that acquire a taste for human food can become very aggressive and destructive and often must be destroyed by rangers, so store all your food and even scented toiletries in the bear lockers located at many campgrounds and trailheads, or use bear-resistant canisters if you'll be hiking in the backcountry.

Watch for the blue Steller's jay along trails, near public buildings, and in campgrounds, and look for golden eagles soaring over Tioga Road.

spot adventurers with your binoculars by scanning the smooth and nearly vertical cliff for specks of color. ⊠ *Yosemite National Park ✛ Off Northside Dr., about 4 miles west of Valley Visitor Center.*

★ Glacier Point

VIEWPOINT | If you lack the time, desire, or stamina to hike more than 3,200 feet up to Glacier Point from the Yosemite Valley floor, you can drive here—or take a bus from the valley—for a bird's-eye view. You are likely to encounter a lot of day-trippers on the short, paved trail that leads from the parking lot to the main overlook. Take a moment to veer off a few yards to the Geology Hut, which succinctly explains and illustrates what the valley looked like 10 million, 3 million, and 20,000 years ago. ⊠ *Yosemite National Park ✛ Glacier Point Rd., 16 miles northeast of Rte. 41* ☎ *209/372–0200* ⊘ *Closed late Oct.–mid-May.*

★ Half Dome

NATURE SITE | Visitors' eyes are continually drawn to this remarkable granite formation that tops out at more than 4,700 feet above the valley floor. Despite its name, the dome is actually about three-quarters intact. You can hike to the top of it on an 8½-mile (one-way) trail whose last 400 feet must be ascended while holding onto a steel cable. Permits, available only by lottery, are required and are checked on the trail. Call ☎ *877/444–6777* or visit ⊕ *www.recreation.gov* well in advance of your trip for details. Back down in the valley, see Half Dome reflected in the Merced River by heading to Sentinel Bridge just before sundown. The brilliant orange light on Half Dome is a stunning sight. ⊠ *Yosemite National Park* ⊕ *www. nps.gov/yose/planyourvisit/halfdome. htm.*

Nevada Fall

BODY OF WATER | Climb Mist Trail from Happy Isles for an up-close view of this 594-foot cascading beauty. If you don't want to hike (the trail's final approach is quite taxing), you can see it—albeit distantly—from Glacier Point. Stay safely on the trail, as there have been fatalities in recent years after visitors have fallen and been swept away by the water. ⊠ *Yosemite Valley, access via Mist Trail from Nature Center at Happy Isles.*

Ribbon Fall

BODY OF WATER | At 1,612 feet, this is the highest single fall in North America. It's also the first waterfall to dry up in summer; the rainwater and melted snow that create the slender fall evaporate quickly at this height. Look just west of El Capitan for the best view of the fall from the base of Bridalveil Fall. ⊠ *Yosemite Valley, west of El Capitan Meadow.*

Sentinel Dome

VIEWPOINT | The view from here is similar to that from Glacier Point, except you can't see the valley floor. A moderately steep, 1.1-mile path climbs to the viewpoint from the parking lot. Topping out at an elevation of 8,122 feet, Sentinel is more than 900 feet higher than Glacier Point. ⊠ *Glacier Point Rd., off Rte. 41.*

Vernal Fall

BODY OF WATER | Fern-covered black rocks frame this 317-foot fall, and rainbows play in the spray at its base. You can get a distant view from Glacier Point, or hike to see it close up. You'll get wet, but the view is worth it. ⊠ *Yosemite Valley, access via Mist Trail from Nature Center at Happy Isles.*

★ Yosemite Falls

BODY OF WATER | Actually three falls, they together constitute the highest combined waterfall in North America and the fifth highest in the world. The water from the top descends a total of 2,425 feet, and when the falls run hard, you can hear them thunder across the valley. If they dry up—that sometimes happens in late summer—the valley seems naked without the wavering tower of spray. If you hike the mile-long loop trail (partially paved) to the base of the Lower Fall in spring, prepare to get wet. You can get a good full-length view of the falls from the lawn of Yosemite Chapel, off Southside Drive. ⊠ *Yosemite Valley, access from Yosemite Valley Lodge or trail parking area.*

TRAILS

Cook's Meadow Loop

TRAIL | FAMILY | Take this 1-mile, wheelchair-accessible, looped path around Cook's Meadow to see and learn the basics about Yosemite Valley's past, present, and future. A trail guide (available at a kiosk just outside the entrance) explains how to tell oaks, cedars, and pines apart; how fires help keep the forest floor healthy; and how pollution poses significant challenges to the park's inhabitants. *Easy.* ⊠ *Yosemite National Park* ⊕ *Trailhead: across from Valley Visitor Center.*

Four-Mile Trail

TRAIL | If you decide to hike up Four-Mile Trail and back down again, allow about six hours for the challenging, 9½-mile round-trip. (The original 4-mile-long trail, Yosemite's first, has been lengthened to make it less steep.) The trailhead is on Southside Drive near Sentinel Beach, and the elevation change is 3,220 feet. For a considerably less strenuous experience, you can take a morning tour bus up to Glacier Point and enjoy a one-way downhill hike. *Difficult.* ⊠ *Yosemite National Park* ⊕ *Trailheads: at Glacier Point and on Southside Dr.*

⭐ John Muir Trail to Half Dome

TRAIL | Ardent and courageous trekkers continue on from Nevada Fall to the top of Half Dome. Some hikers attempt this entire 10- to 12-hour, 16¾-mile round-trip trek in one day; if you're planning to do this, remember that the 4,800-foot elevation gain and the 8,842-foot altitude will cause shortness of breath. Another option is to hike to a campground in Little Yosemite Valley near the top of Nevada Fall the first day, then climb to the top of Half Dome and hike out the next day. Get your wilderness permit (required for a one-day hike to Half Dome, too) at least a month in advance. Be sure to wear hiking boots and bring gloves. The last pitch up the back of Half Dome is very steep—the only way to climb this sheer rock face is to pull yourself up using the steel cable handrails, which are in place only from late spring to early fall. Those who brave the ascent will be rewarded with an unbeatable view of Yosemite Valley below and the high country beyond. Only 300 hikers per day are allowed atop Half Dome, and they all must have permits, which are distributed by lottery, one in the spring before the season starts and another two days before the climb. Contact ⊕ www.recreation.gov for details. *Difficult.* ⊠ *Yosemite National Park* ⊹ *Trailhead: at Happy Isles* ⊕ *www.nps. gov/yose/planyourvisit/halfdome.htm.*

Mirror Lake Trail

TRAIL | FAMILY | Along this trail, you'll look up at Half Dome directly from its base and also take in Tenaya Canyon, Mt. Watkins, and Washington Column. The way is paved for a mile to Mirror Lake itself (total of 2 miles out and back). The trail that loops around the lake continues from there (for a total of 5 miles). Interpretive exhibits provide insight into the area's natural and cultural history. *Easy to moderate.* ⊠ *Yosemite Village* ⊹ *Trailhead: shuttle bus stop #17 on the Happy Isles Loop.*

Mist Trail

TRAIL | Except for Lower Yosemite Fall, more visitors take this trail (or portions of it) than any other in the park. The trek up to and back from Vernal Fall is 3 miles. Add another 4 miles total by continuing up to 594-foot Nevada Fall; the trail becomes quite steep and slippery in its final stages. The elevation gain to Vernal Fall is 1,000 feet, and to Nevada Fall an additional 1,000 feet. The Merced River tumbles down both falls on its way to a tranquil flow through the valley. *Moderate.* ⊠ *Yosemite National Park* ⊹ *Trailhead: at Happy Isles.*

⭐ Panorama Trail

TRAIL | Few hikes come with the visual punch that this 8½-mile trail provides. It starts from Glacier Point and descends to Yosemite Valley. The star attraction is Half Dome, visible from many intriguing angles, but you also see three waterfalls up close and walk through a manzanita grove. *Moderate.* ⊠ *Yosemite National Park* ⊹ *Trailhead: at Glacier Point.*

⭐ Yosemite Falls Trail

TRAIL | Yosemite Falls is the highest waterfall in North America. The upper fall (1,430 feet), the middle cascades (675 feet), and the lower fall (320 feet) combine for a total of 2,425 feet, and when viewed from the valley appear as a single waterfall. The ¼-mile trail leads from the parking lot to the base of the falls. Upper Yosemite Fall Trail, a strenuous 7.2-mile round-trip climb rising 2,700 feet, takes you above the top of the falls. Lower trail: *Easy.* Upper trail: *Difficult.* ⊠ *Yosemite National Park* ⊹ *Trailhead: off Camp 4, north of Northside Dr.*

VISITOR CENTERS

Valley Visitor Center

INFO CENTER | Learn about Yosemite Valley's geology, vegetation, and human inhabitants at this visitor center, which is also staffed with helpful rangers and contains a bookstore with a wide selection of books and maps. Two films, including one by Ken Burns, alternate on the half hour in the theater behind the visitor center. ✉ *Yosemite Village* ☎ *209/372–0200* 🌐 *www.nps.gov/yose.*

Yosemite Conservation Heritage Center
INFO CENTER | This small but striking National Historic Landmark (formerly Le Conte Memorial Lodge), with its granite walls and steeply pitched shingle roof, is Yosemite's first permanent public information center. Step inside to see the cathedral-like interior, which contains a library and environmental exhibits. To find out about evening programs, check the kiosk out front. ✉ *Southside Dr., about ½ mile west of Half Dome Village* 🌐 *sierraclub.org/yosemite-heritage-center* 🕑 *Closed Mon., Tues., and Oct.–Apr.*

🍴 Restaurants

★ The Ahwahnee Dining Room
$$$$ | **EUROPEAN** | Rave reviews about The Ahwahnee hotel's dining room's appearance are fully justified—it features towering windows, a 34-foot-high ceiling with interlaced sugar-pine beams, and massive chandeliers. Reservations are always advised, and the attire is "resort casual." **Known for:** lavish $56 Sunday brunch; finest dining in the park; bar menu with lighter lunch and dinner fare at more affordable prices. [$] *Average main: $39* ✉ *The Ahwahnee, Ahwahnee Rd., about ¾ mile east of Yosemite Valley Visitor Center, Yosemite Village* ☎ *209/372–1489* 🌐 *www.travelyosemite.com.*

Base Camp Eatery
$$ | **AMERICAN** | The design of this modern food court, open for breakfast, lunch, and dinner, honors the history of rock climbing in Yosemite. Choose from a wide range of menu options, from hamburgers, salads, and pizzas, to rice and noodle bowls. **Known for:** grab-and-go selections; best casual dining venue in the park; automated ordering kiosks to speed up service. [$] *Average main: $12* ✉ *Yosemite Valley Lodge, about ¾ mile west of visitor center, Yosemite Village* ☎ *209/372–1265* 🌐 *www.travelyosemite.com.*

Curry Village Seven Tents
$$ | **AMERICAN** | Formerly Curry Village Pavilion, this cafeteria-style eatery serves everything from roasted meats and salads to pastas, burritos, and beyond. Alternatively, order a pizza from the stand on the deck, and take in the views of the valley's granite walls. **Known for:** convenient eats; cocktails at Bar 1899; additional venues (Meadow Grill, Pizza Patio, Coffee Corner). [$] *Average main: $18* ✉ *Curry Village* ☎ *209/372–8303* 🕑 *Closed mid-Oct.–mid-Apr. No lunch.*

★ Mountain Room
$$$ | **AMERICAN** | Gaze at Yosemite Falls through this dining room's wall of windows—almost every table has a view—as you nosh on steaks, seafood, and classic California salads and desserts. The Mountain Room Lounge, a few steps away in the Yosemite Valley Lodge complex, has about 10 beers on tap. **Known for:** locally sourced, organic ingredients; usually there is a wait for a table (no reservations); vegetarian and vegan options. [$] *Average main: $29* ✉ *Yosemite Valley Lodge, Northside Dr., about ¾ mile west of visitor center, Yosemite Village* ☎ *209/372–1403* 🌐 *www.travelyosemite.com* 🕑 *No lunch except Sun. brunch.*

Village Grill Deck
$$ | **FAST FOOD** | If a burger joint is what you've been missing, head to this bustling eatery in Yosemite Village that serves veggie, salmon, and a few other burger varieties in addition to the usual beef patties. Order at the counter, then take your tray out to the deck, and enjoy your meal under the trees. **Known for:** burgers, sandwiches, and hot dogs; crowds; outdoor seating on expansive deck. [$] *Average main: $12* ✉ *Yosemite Village* ⊕ *100 yards east of Yosemite Valley Visitor Center* ☎ *209/372–1207* 🌐 *www.travelyosemite.com* 🕑 *Closed Oct.–Apr. No dinner.*

Hotels

★ The Ahwahnee

$$$$ | **HOTEL** | This National Historic Landmark is constructed of sugar-pine logs and features Native American design motifs; public spaces are enlivened with art-deco flourishes, Persian rugs, and elaborate iron- and woodwork. **Pros:** best lodge in Yosemite; helpful concierge; in the historic heart of the valley. **Cons:** expensive rates; some reports that service has slipped in recent years; slow or nonexistent Wi-Fi in some hotel areas. [$] *Rooms from: $581* ✉ *Ahwahnee Rd., about ¾ mile east of Yosemite Valley Visitor Center, Yosemite Village* ☎ *801/559–4884* 🌐 *www.travelyosemite.com* 🛏 *125 rooms* 🍴 *No meals.*

Curry Village

$$ | **HOTEL** | Opened in 1899 as a place for budget-conscious travelers, Curry Village has plain accommodations: standard motel rooms, simple cabins with either private or shared baths, and tent cabins with shared baths. **Pros:** close to many activities; family-friendly atmosphere; surrounded by iconic valley views. **Cons:** community bathrooms need updating; can be crowded; sometimes a bit noisy. [$] *Rooms from: $143* ✉ *South side of Southside Dr.* ☎ *888/413–8869, 602/278–8888 international* 🌐 *www.travelyosemite.com* 🛏 *583 units* 🍴 *No meals.*

Yosemite Valley Lodge

$$$$ | **HOTEL** | This 1915 lodge near Yosemite Falls is a collection of numerous two-story, glass-and-wood structures tucked beneath the trees. **Pros:** centrally located; dependably clean rooms; lots of tours leave from out front. **Cons:** can feel impersonal; high prices; no in-room a/c. [$] *Rooms from: $260* ✉ *9006 Yosemite Valley Lodge Dr., Yosemite Village* ☎ *888/413–8869* 🌐 *www.travelyosemite.com* 🛏 *245 rooms* 🍴 *No meals.*

Performing Arts

Yosemite Theater

THEATER | Various theater and music programs are held throughout the year, and one of the best loved is Lee Stetson's portrayal of John Muir in *Conversation with a Tramp* and other Muir-theme shows. Purchase tickets in advance at the Conservancy Store at the Valley Visitor Center or the Tour and Activity Desk at Yosemite Valley Lodge. Unsold seats are available at the door at performance time, 7 pm. ✉ *Valley Visitor Center, Yosemite Village* ☎ *209/372–0299* 🎟 *$10.*

Shopping

Ahwahnee Hotel Gift Shop

GIFTS/SOUVENIRS | This shop sells more upscale items, such as Native American crafts, photographic prints, handmade ceramics, and elegant jewelry. For less expensive gift items, browse the small book selection, which includes writings by John Muir. ✉ *The Ahwahnee, Ahwahnee Rd.* ☎ *209/372–1409.*

Ansel Adams Gallery

ART GALLERIES | Framed prints of the famed nature photographer's best works are on sale here, as are affordable posters. New works by contemporary artists are also available, along with Native American jewelry and handicrafts. The elegant camera shop conducts photography workshops, from free camera walks a few mornings a week to five-day courses. ✉ *Northside Dr., Yosemite Village* ☎ *209/372–4413* 🌐 *anseladams.com.*

Curry Village Gift & Grocery

CONVENIENCE/GENERAL STORES | You can pick up groceries and supplies at this bustling shop at the east end of the valley. ✉ *Curry Village* ☎ *209/372–8391.*

Housekeeping Camp General Store

You'll find the basics here for picnics, campfires, and other outdoor activities. ✉ *Southside Dr., ½ mile west of Half Dome Village* ☎ *209/372–8353.*

Village Store

CONVENIENCE/GENERAL STORES | The Yosemite Valley's largest store has an extensive selection of groceries (including many organic items), household products, and personal-care items. It also has an extensive gift and souvenir shop. ⊠ *Yosemite Village* 🕾 *209/372–1253.*

Yosemite Bookstore

BOOKS/STATIONERY | An extensive selection of maps and books is available at this store in the Valley Visitor Center. ⊠ *Valley Visitor Center, Yosemite Village* 🕾 *209/372–0299* ⊕ *shop.yosemite.org.*

Yosemite Museum Shop

CRAFTS | In addition to books on California's Native Americans, this tiny shop sells traditional arts and crafts. ⊠ *Yosemite Village* 🕾 *209/372–0295.*

Yosemite Valley Lodge Gift Shop

CONVENIENCE/GENERAL STORES | Groceries, snacks, and beverages occupy half of this large store. The other half is a gift shop. ⊠ *Yosemite Valley Lodge, Northside Dr., about ¾ mile west of visitor center, Yosemite Village* 🕾 *209/372–1205.*

Wawona

27 miles from Yosemite Valley Visitor Center; 7½ miles north of Fish Camp.

Wawona is a small village (elevation 4,000 feet) about an hours' drive south of Yosemite Valley. It's rich in pioneer history (visit the Pioneer Yosemite History Center to learn more) and is home to the Victorian-era Wawona Hotel. The park's famous Mariposa Grove of Giant Sequoias is a few miles down the road.

Sights

HISTORIC SIGHTS

Wawona Hotel

HOTEL—SIGHT | Imagine a white-bearded Mark Twain relaxing in a rocking chair on one of the broad verandas of one of the park's first lodges, a whitewashed series of two-story buildings from the Victorian era. Plop down in one of the dozens of white Adirondack chairs on the sprawling lawn, and look across the road at the area's only golf course, one of the few links in the world that does not employ fertilizers or other chemicals. ⊠ *Rte. 41, Wawona* 🕾 *209/375–1425* ⊕ *www. travelyosemite.com/lodging/wawona-hotel* ☉ *Closed Dec.–Mar. except 2 wks around Christmas and New Year's.*

Pioneer Yosemite History Center

MUSEUM | **FAMILY** | These historic buildings reflect different eras of Yosemite's history, from the 1850s through the early 1900s. They were moved to Wawona (the largest stage stop in Yosemite in the late 1800s) from various areas of Yosemite in the '50s and '60s. There is a self-guided-tour pamphlet available for 50 cents. Weekends and some weekdays in the summer, costumed docents conduct free blacksmithing and "wet-plate" photography demonstrations, and for a small fee you can take a stagecoach ride. ⊠ *Rte. 41, Wawona* 🕾 *209/375–9531* ⊕ *www. nps.gov/yose/planyourvisit/waw.htm* 🖾 *Free* ☉ *Closed Mon., Tues., and mid-Sept.–early June.*

SCENIC DRIVES

Route 41

SCENIC DRIVE | Entering Yosemite National Park via this road, which follows an ultimately curvy course 55 miles from Fresno through the Yosemite gateway towns of Oakhurst and Fish Camp, presents you with an immediate, important choice: turn right to visit the Mariposa Grove of Giant Sequoias 4 miles to the east, or turn left to travel via Wawona to Yosemite Valley, 31 miles away. Try to do both. (You can get by with an hour in Mariposa Grove if you're really pressed for time.) As you approach the valley, you will want to pull into the Tunnel View parking lot (it's on the east side of the mile-long tunnel) and marvel at what lies ahead: from left to right, El Capitan, Half

Dome, and Bridalveil Fall. From here, the valley is another 5 miles. The drive time on Wawona Road alone is about an hour. Make a full day of it by adding Glacier Point to the itinerary; get there via a 16-mile seasonal road that shoots east from Route 41 and passes the Badger Pass Ski Area. ✉ *Yosemite National Park.*

SCENIC STOPS

Mariposa Grove of Giant Sequoias

FOREST | Of Yosemite's three sequoia groves—the others being Merced and Tuolumne, both near Crane Flat and Hetch Hetchy well to the north—Mariposa is by far the largest and easiest to walk around. Grizzly Giant, whose base measures 96 feet around, has been estimated to be one of the world's largest. Perhaps more astoundingly, it's about 1,800 years old. Park at the grove's welcome plaza, and ride the free shuttle (required most of the year). Summer weekends are crowded. ✉ *Yosemite National Park* ✣ *Rte. 41, 2 miles north of south entrance station* 🌐 *www.nps.gov/yose/planyourvisit/mg.htm.*

TRAILS

Chilnualna Falls Trail

TRAIL | This Wawona-area trail runs 4 miles one-way to the top of the falls, then leads into the backcountry, connecting with other trails. This is one of the park's most inspiring and secluded—albeit strenuous—trails. Past the tumbling cascade, and up through forests, you'll emerge before a panorama at the top. *Difficult.* ✉ *Wawona* ✣ *Trailhead: at Chilnualna Falls Rd., off Rte. 41.*

🍴 Restaurants

Wawona Hotel Dining Room

$$$ | **AMERICAN** | Watch deer graze in the meadow while you dine in the romantic, candlelit dining room of the whitewashed Wawona Hotel, which dates from the late 1800s. The American-style cuisine favors fresh ingredients and flavors; trout and flatiron steaks are menu staples. **Known for:** Saturday-night barbecues on the lawn; historic ambience; Mother's Day and other Sunday holiday brunches. [$] *Average main: $28* ✉ *8308 Wawona Rd., Wawona* ☎ *209/375–1425* 🕒 *Closed most of Dec., Jan., Feb., and Mar.*

🛏 Hotels

Redwoods in Yosemite

$$$$ | **RENTAL** | This collection of more than 125 homes in the Wawona area is a great alternative to the overcrowded valley. **Pros:** sense of privacy; peaceful setting; full kitchens. **Cons:** 45-minute drive from the valley; some units have no a/c; cell phone service can be spotty. [$] *Rooms from: $260* ✉ *8038 Chilnualna Falls Rd., off Rte. 41, Wawona* ☎ *209/375–6666 international, 844/355–0039* 🌐 *www.redwoodsinyosemite.com* 🛏 *125 units* 🍴 *No meals.*

Wawona Hotel

$$$ | **HOTEL** | This 1879 National Historic Landmark at Yosemite's southern end is a Victorian-era mountain resort, with whitewashed buildings, wraparound verandas, and pleasant, no-frills rooms decorated with period pieces. **Pros:** lovely building; peaceful atmosphere; historic photos in public areas. **Cons:** few modern amenities, such as phones and TVs; an hour's drive from Yosemite Valley; shared bathrooms in half the rooms. [$] *Rooms from: $157* ✉ *8308 Wawona Rd., Wawona* ☎ *888/413–8869* 🌐 *www.travelyosemite.com* 🕒 *Closed Dec.–Mar., except mid-Dec.–Jan. 2* 🛏 *104 rooms, 50 with bath* 🍴 *Breakfast.*

🛍 Shopping

Wawona Store

The Wawona area's only market carries essentials (for some, that means ice cream) in its grocery section. There's also a gift shop. ✉ *Rte. 41 at Forest Dr., Wawona* ☎ *209/375–6574.*

Did You Know?

Waterfalls in Yosemite Valley are especially famous for their heart-stopping drops over sheer granite cliffs. At peak times, hydrologists estimate that almost 135,000 gallons of water tumble down Yosemite Falls' triple cascade every minute.

Tuolumne Meadows

56 miles from Yosemite Valley; 21 miles west of Lee Vining via Tioga Road.

The largest subalpine meadow in the Sierra (at 8,600 feet) is a popular way station for backpack trips along the Pacific Crest and John Muir trails. The setting is not as dramatic as Yosemite Valley, 56 miles away, but the almost perfectly flat basin, about 2½ miles long, is intriguing, and in July it's resplendent with wildflowers. The most popular day hike is to Lembert Dome, atop which you'll have breathtaking views of the basin below. Note that Tioga Road rarely opens before June and usually closes by November.

Sights

SCENIC DRIVES

Tioga Road

SCENIC DRIVE | Few mountain drives can compare with this 59-mile road, especially its eastern half between Lee Vining and Olmstead Point. As you climb 3,200 feet to the 9,945-foot summit of Tioga Pass (Yosemite's sole eastern entrance for cars), you'll encounter broad vistas of the granite-splotched High Sierra and its craggy but hearty trees and shrubs. Past the bustling scene at Tuolumne Meadows, you'll see picturesque Tenaya Lake and then Olmsted Point, where you'll get your first peek at Half Dome. Driving Tioga Road one way takes approximately 1½ hours. Wildflowers bloom here in July and August. By November, the high-altitude road closes for the winter; it sometimes doesn't reopen until early June. ✉ *Yosemite National Park.*

SCENIC STOPS

High Country

NATURE PRESERVE | The high-alpine region east of the valley—a land of alpenglow and top-of-the-world vistas—is often missed by crowds who come to gawk at the more publicized splendors. Summer wildflowers, which pop up mid-July through August, carpet the meadows and mountainsides with pink, purple, blue, red, yellow, and orange. On foot or on horseback are the only ways to get here. For information on trails and backcountry permits, check with the visitor center. ✉ *Yosemite National Park.*

Restaurants

Tuolumne Meadows Grill

$ | **FAST FOOD** | Serving throughout the day until 5 or 6 pm, this fast-food eatery cooks up basic breakfast, lunch, and snacks. It's possible that ice cream tastes better at this altitude. **Known for:** soft-serve ice cream; crowds; fresh local ingredients. [$] *Average main: $8* ✉ *Tioga Rd. (Rte. 120), 1½ miles east of Tuolumne Meadows Visitor Center* ☎ *209/372–8426* 🌐 *www.travelyosemite.com* 🕓 *Closed Oct.–Memorial Day. No dinner.*

Tuolumne Meadows Lodge Restaurant

$$$ | **AMERICAN** | In a central dining tent beside the Tuolumne River, this restaurant serves a menu of hearty American fare at breakfast and dinner. The red-and-white-checkered tablecloths and a handful of communal tables give it the feeling of an old-fashioned summer camp. **Known for:** box lunches; communal tables; small menu. [$] *Average main: $24* ✉ *Tioga Rd. (Rte. 120)* ☎ *209/372–8413* 🌐 *www.travelyosemite.com* 🕓 *Closed late Sept.–mid-June. No lunch.*

White Wolf Lodge Restaurant

$$$ | **AMERICAN** | Those fueling up for a day on the trail or famished after a high-country hike will appreciate the all-you-can-eat, family-style breakfasts and dinners in this tiny dining room. Mashed potatoes, big pots of curried vegetables, and heaps of pasta often grace the tables in this cozy out-of-the-way place. **Known for:** all you can eat; box lunches available; rustic vibe. [$] *Average main: $24* ✉ *Yosemite National Park* ✣ *Tioga Rd. (Rte. 120), 25 miles west of Tuolumne Meadows and*

15 miles east of Crane Flat 📞 *209/372-8416* 🌐 *www.travelyosemite.com* 🕐 *Closed mid-Sept.–mid-June. No lunch.*

 Hotels

White Wolf Lodge

$$ | **HOTEL** | Set in a subalpine meadow, the White Wolf Lodge has rustic accommodations and makes an excellent base camp for hiking the backcountry. **Pros:** quiet location; near some of Yosemite's most beautiful, less crowded hikes; good restaurant. **Cons:** far from the valley; tent cabins share bathhouse; remote setting. 💲 *Rooms from: $138* ✉ *Yosemite National Park* ✚ *Off Tioga Rd. (Rte. 120), 25 miles west of Tuolumne Meadows and 15 miles east of Crane Flat* 📞 *801/559-4884* 🕐 *Closed mid-Sept.–mid-June* 🛏 *28 cabins* 🍴 *No meals.*

 Shopping

Tuolumne Meadows Store

CONVENIENCE/GENERAL STORES | The only retailer in the high country carries backpacking and camping supplies, climbing gear, trail maps and guides, food and beverages, and fishing licenses. ✉ *Yosemite National Park* ✚ *Tioga Rd. Rte. 120, 1½ miles east of Tuolumne Meadows Visitor Center* 📞 *209/372-8096* 🕐 *Closed Oct.–early June.*

Hetch Hetchy

18 miles from the Big Oak Flat entrance station; 43 miles north of El Portal via Highway 120 and Evergreen Road.

This glacier-carved valley (now filled with water) and surrounding peaks anchor the northwestern section of the park. Drive about 2 miles west of the Big Oak Flat entrance station and turn right on Evergreen Road, which leads down to the Hetch Hetchy entrance and trails along the dam and into the mountains. Two groves of giant sequoia trees—Merced and Tuolomne—grow near Crane Flat, a tiny collection of services south of Big Oak Flat at the intersection of Highway 120 and Tioga Road.

 Sights

SCENIC STOPS

Hetch Hetchy Reservoir

BODY OF WATER | When Congress approved the O'Shaughnessy Dam in 1913, pragmatism triumphed over aestheticism. Some 2.5 million residents of the San Francisco Bay Area continue to get their water from this 117-billion-gallon reservoir. Although spirited efforts are being made to restore the Hetch Hetchy Valley to its former, pristine glory, three-quarters of San Francisco voters in 2012 ultimately opposed a measure to even consider draining the reservoir. Eight miles long, the reservoir is Yosemite's largest body of water, and one that can be seen up close from several trails. ✉ *Hetch Hetchy Rd., about 15 miles north of Big Oak Flat entrance station.*

Tuolumne Grove of Giant Sequoias

FOREST | About two dozen mature giant sequoias stand in Tuolumne Grove in the park's northwestern region, just east of Crane Flat and south of the Big Oak Flat entrance. Park at the trailhead and walk about a mile to see them. The trail descends about 500 feet down to the grove, so it's a relatively steep hike back up. Be sure to bring plenty of drinking water. ✉ *On Tioga Rd., just east of Crane Flat, about a 45-minute drive from Yosemite Valley.*

TRAILS

Merced Grove of Giant Sequoias

FOREST | Hike 1½ miles (3 miles round-trip, 500-foot elevation drop and gain) to the small and scenic Merced Grove and its approximately two dozen mature giant sequoias. The setting here is typically uncrowded and serene. Note that you can also park here and hike about 2 miles round-trip to the Tuolumne Grove. Bring plenty of water for either outing. *Moderate*. ✉ *Big Oak Flat Rd.* ✛ *East of the Big Oak Flat entrance, about 6 miles west of Crane Flat and a 45-minute drive from Yosemite Valley.*

Hotels

Evergreen Lodge at Yosemite

$$$$ | **RESORT** | **FAMILY** | Amid the trees near Yosemite National Park's Hetch Hetchy entrance, this sprawling property is perfect for families. **Pros:** cabin complex includes amphitheater, pool, and more; guided tours available; great roadhouse-style restaurant. **Cons:** no in-room TVs; long, winding access road; spotty cell service. ⓢ *Rooms from: $280* ✉ *33160 Evergreen Rd., 30 miles east of town of Groveland, Groveland* ☎ *209/379–2606* ⊕ *www.evergreenlodge.com* ⌁ *88 cabins.*

★ Rush Creek Lodge

$$$$ | **RESORT** | **FAMILY** | Occupying 20 acres on a wooded hillside, this sleek, nature-inspired complex has a saltwater pool and hot tubs, a restaurant and tavern with indoor and outdoor seating, a guided recreation program, a spa and wellness program, a general store, nature trails, and outdoor play areas that include a zip line and a giant slide. **Pros:** close to Yosemite's Big Oak Flat entrance; YARTS bus stops here and connects with Yosemite Valley and Sonora spring–fall; year-round evening s'mores. **Cons:** no in-room TVs; pricey in high season; spotty cell service. ⓢ *Rooms from: $410* ✉ *34001 Hwy. 120, Groveland* ✛ *25 miles east of Groveland, 23 miles north of Yosemite Valley* ☎ *209/379–2373* ⊕ *www.rushcreeklodge.com* ⌁ *143 rooms* ⍥ *No meals.*

Shopping

Crane Flat Store

CONVENIENCE/GENERAL STORES | This small store is a convenient place to get gas and pick up snacks and camping supplies if you're arriving via Route 120. The store is closed November–March. ✉ *Yosemite National Park* ✛ *Intersection of Big Oak Flat Rd. and Tioga Rd., 7 miles east of Big Oak Flat entrance* ☎ *209/379–2742* ⊗ *Closed Dec.–Mar.*

Activities

BIKING

One enjoyable way to see Yosemite Valley is to ride a bike beneath its lofty granite monoliths. The eastern valley has 12 miles of paved, flat bicycle paths across meadows and through woods, with bike racks at convenient stopping points. For a greater challenge, you can ride on 196 miles of paved park roads elsewhere. Note, though, that bicycles are not allowed on hiking trails or in the backcountry, and kids under 18 must wear a helmet.

Yosemite bike rentals

BICYCLING | You can arrange rentals ($12 per hour or $36 per day) at Yosemite Valley Lodge and Curry Village bike stands. Bikes with child trailers, baby-jogger strollers, and wheelchairs are also available. ✉ *Yosemite Valley Lodge or Curry Village* ☎ *209/372–4386* ⊕ *www.travelyosemite.com.*

BIRD-WATCHING

More than 250 bird species have been spotted in the park, including the sage sparrow, pygmy owl, blue grouse, and mountain bluebird. Park rangers lead free bird-watching walks in Yosemite Valley a few days each week in summer; check at a visitor center or information station for times and locations. Binoculars sometimes are available for loan.

Birding seminars

BIRD WATCHING | The Yosemite Conservancy organizes day- and weekend-long seminars for beginner and intermediate birders, as well as bird walks a few times a week. They can also arrange private naturalist-led walks any time of year. ✉ *Yosemite National Park* ⊕ *www.yosemite.org* ⍈ *From $99.*

Winter in Yosemite

CAMPING

If you are going to concentrate solely on valley sites and activities, you should endeavor to stay in one of the "Pines" campgrounds, which are clustered near Curry Village and within an easy stroll from that busy complex's many facilities. For a more primitive and quiet experience, and to be near many back-country hikes, try one of the Tioga Road campgrounds.

RESERVATIONS

National Park Service Reservations Office Reservations are required at many of Yosemite's campgrounds. You can book a site up to five months in advance, starting on the 15th of the month. Unless otherwise noted, book your site through the central National Park Service Reservations Office. If you don't have reservations when you arrive, many sites, especially those outside Yosemite Valley, are available on a first-come, first-served basis. ☎ *877/444–6777 reservations, 518/885–3639 international, 888/448–1474 customer service* ⊕ *www.recreation.gov.*

RECOMMENDED CAMPGROUNDS YOSEMITE VALLEY

Camp 4. Formerly known as Sunnyside Walk-In, this is the only valley campground available on a walk-in basis—and the only one west of Yosemite Lodge. Open year-round, it's favored by rock climbers and solo campers. From mid-September to mid-May, the camp operates on a first-come, first-served basis; it typically fills early in the morning except in winter. From mid-May to mid-September, campsites are available only by daily lottery (one day in advance via Recreation.gov from midnight to 4 pm Pacific Time) for up to 12 people per application, 6 people per campsite. This is a tents-only campground with 36 sites. ⊠ *Base of Yosemite Falls Trail, just west of Yosemite Valley Lodge on Northside Dr., Yosemite Village.*

Housekeeping Camp. Each of the 266 units here consists of three walls (usually concrete) that are covered with two layers of canvas; the open-air side can be closed off with a heavy, white-canvas curtain.

Inside, typically, are bunk beds and a full-size bed (dirty mattresses included); outside is a covered patio, fire ring, picnic table, and bear box. You rent "bedpacks," consisting of blankets, sheets, and other comforts in the main building, which also has a small grocery. Lots of guests take advantage of the adjacent Merced River. ⊠ *Southside Dr., ½ mile west of Curry Village*.

Lower Pines. This moderate-size campground with 60 small tent/RV sites sits directly along the Merced River; it's a short walk to the trailheads for the Mirror Lake and Mist trails. Expect lots of people. ⊠ *At east end of valley*.

Upper Pines. One of the valley's largest campgrounds, with 238 tent and RV sites, is also the closest one to the trailheads. Expect large crowds in the summer—and little privacy. ⊠ *At east end of valley, near Curry Village*.

CRANE FLAT
Crane Flat. This 166-site camp for tents and RVs is on Yosemite's western boundary, south of Hodgdon Meadow and just 17 miles from the valley but far from its bustle. A small grove of sequoias is nearby. ⊠ *From Big Oak Flat entrance on Rte. 120, drive 10 miles east to campground entrance on right*.

WAWONA
Bridalveil Creek. This campground sits among lodgepole pines at 7,200 feet, above the valley on Glacier Point Road. From here, you can easily drive to Glacier Point's magnificent valley views. Fall evenings can be cold. The 74 sites can accommodate tents and RVs. ⊠ *From Rte. 41 in Wawona, go north to Glacier Point Rd. and turn right; entrance to campground is 25 miles ahead on right side*.

Wawona. Near the Mariposa Grove, just downstream from a popular fishing spot, this year-round campground's 93 sites for tents and RVs are larger and less densely packed than those at campgrounds in

Yosemite Valley. The downside? It's an hour's drive to the valley's attractions. ⊠ *Rte. 41, 1 mile north of Wawona*.

TUOLUMNE MEADOWS
Porcupine Flat. Sixteen miles west of Tuolumne Meadows, this campground sits at 8,100 feet. Sites are close together, but if you want to be in the high country and Tuolumne Meadows is full, this is a good bet. There is no water available. The campground's 52 sites for tents and RVs can't accommodate rigs of 35 feet or longer. ⊠ *Rte. 120, 16 miles west of Tuolumne Meadows*.

Tuolumne Meadows. In a wooded area at 8,600 feet, just south of its namesake meadow, this is one of the most spectacular and sought-after campgrounds in Yosemite. Hot showers can be used at the Tuolumne Meadows Lodge—though only at certain times. Half the 314 tent and RV sites are first-come, first-served, so arrive early, or make reservations. The campground is open July–September. ⊠ *Rte. 120, 46 miles east of Big Oak Flat entrance station*.

White Wolf. Set in the beautiful high country at 8,000 feet, this is a prime spot for hikers from early July to mid-September. There are 87 tent and RV sites; rigs of up to 27 feet long are permitted. ⊠ *Tioga Rd., 15 miles east of Big Oak Flat entrance*.

EDUCATIONAL OFFERINGS
CLASSES AND SEMINARS
Art Classes
ARTS VENUE | Professional artists conduct workshops in watercolor, etching, drawing, and other media. Bring your own materials, or purchase the basics at the Happy Isles Art and Nature Center. Children under 12 must be accompanied by an adult. The center also offers beginner art workshops and children's art and family craft programs ($20–$40 per person). ⊠ *Happy Isles Art and Nature Center* ⊕ *www.yosemite.org* ✉ *$20* ⊙ *No classes Sun. Closed Dec.–Feb.*

Happy Isles Art and Nature Center

MUSEUM | FAMILY | This family-focused center has a rotating selection of kid-friendly activities and hands-on exhibits that teach tykes and their parents about the park's ecosystem. Books, toys, and T-shirts are stocked in the small gift shop. ⊠ *Yosemite National Park* ⊹ *Off Southside Dr., about ¾ mile east of Curry Village* 🎫 *Free* ☉ *Closed Oct.–Apr.*

Yosemite Outdoor Adventures

Naturalists, scientists, and park rangers lead multihour to multiday outings on topics from woodpeckers to fire management to day hikes and bird-watching. Most sessions take place spring through fall with just a few in winter. ⊠ *Yosemite National Park* ⊕ *www.yosemite.org* 🎫 *From $99.*

RANGER PROGRAMS

Junior Ranger Program

TOUR—SIGHT | FAMILY | Children ages 3 to 13 can participate in the informal, self-guided Junior Ranger program. Park activity handbooks ($3.50 for ages 7 to 13 and $3 for Junior Cubs ages 3 to 6) are available at the Valley Visitor Center, the Happy Isles Art and Nature Center, the Tuolumne Visitor Center, and the Wawona Visitor Center. Once kids complete the book, rangers present them with a badge and, in some cases, a certificate. ⊠ *Valley Visitor Center or the Happy Isles Art & Nature Center* ☎ *209/372–0299.*

Ranger-Led Programs

TOUR—SIGHT | Rangers lead entertaining walks and give informative talks several times a day from spring to fall. The schedule is more limited in winter, but most days you can find a program somewhere in the park. In the evenings at Yosemite Valley Lodge and Curry Village, lectures, slide shows, and documentary films present unique perspectives on Yosemite. On summer weekends, campgrounds at Curry Village and Tuolumne Meadows host sing-along campfire programs. Schedules and locations are posted on bulletin boards throughout the park as well as in the indispensable *Yosemite Guide*, which is distributed to visitors as they arrive at the park. ⊠ *Yosemite National Park* ⊕ *nps.gov/yose.*

Wee Wild Ones

TOUR—SIGHT | FAMILY | Designed for kids under 10, this 45-minute program includes naturalist-led games, songs, stories, and crafts about Yosemite wildlife, plants, and geology. The event is held outdoors before the regular Yosemite Valley Lodge evening programs in summer and fall. All children must be accompanied by an adult. ⊠ *Yosemite National Park* ☎ *209/372–1153* ⊕ *www.travelyosemite.com* 🎫 *Free.*

FISHING

The waters in Yosemite are not stocked; trout, mostly brown and rainbow, live here but are not plentiful. Yosemite's fishing season begins on the last Saturday in April and ends on November 15. Some waterways are off-limits at certain times; be sure to inquire at the visitor center about regulations.

A California fishing license is required; licenses cost around $17 for one day, $26.50 for two days, and $53 for 10 days. Full-season licenses cost $53 for state residents and $142 for nonresidents (costs fluctuate year to year). Buy your license in season at **Yosemite Mountain Shop in Curry Village** (☎ *209/372–1286*) or at the **Wawona Store** (☎ *209/375–6574*).

GOLF

The Wawona Golf Course is one of the country's few organic golf courses; it's also an Audubon Cooperative sanctuary for birds. You can play a round or take a lesson from the pro here.

Wawona Golf Course

GOLF | This organic (one of only a handful in the United States), 9-hole course has two sets of tee positions per hole to provide an 18-hole course. ⊠ *Rte. 41, Wawona* ☎ *209/375–4386* ⊕ *www.travelyosemite.com* 🎫 *$24 for 9 holes; $39*

for 18 holes 🏌 9 holes, 3011 yards, par 35
☞ Closed Nov.–early May.

HIKING

Wilderness Center

HIKING/WALKING | This facility provides free
wilderness permits, which are required
for overnight camping (advance reservations are available for $5 per person
plus $5 per reservation and are highly
recommended for popular trailheads in
summer and on weekends). The staff
here also provides maps and advice to
hikers heading into the backcountry. If
you don't have your own bear-resistant
canisters, which are required, you can
buy or rent them here. ⊠ Between Ansel
Adams Gallery and post office, Yosemite
Village ☎ 209/372–0308.

Yosemite Mountaineering School and Guide Service

HIKING/WALKING | From April to November,
you can rent gear, hire a guide, or join a
two-hour to full-day trek with Yosemite
Mountaineering School. They also lead
backpacking and overnight excursions.
Reservations are recommended. In
winter, cross-country ski programs
are available at Badger Pass Ski Area.
⊠ Yosemite Mountain Shop, Curry Village
☎ 209/372–8344 ⊕ yosemitemountain-
eering.com.

HORSEBACK RIDING

Reservations for guided trail rides must
be made in advance at hotel tour desks
or by phone. Scenic trail rides range from
two hours to a half day. Four- and six-day
High Sierra saddle trips are also available.

Wawona Stable

HORSEBACK RIDING | Two-hour rides at this
stable start at $70, and a challenging
full-day ride to the Mariposa Grove of
Giant Sequoias (for experienced riders
in good physical condition only) costs
$144. Reservations are recommended.
⊠ Rte. 41, Wawona ☎ 209/375–6502
⊕ www.travelyosemite.com/things-to-do/
horseback-mule-riding.

ICE-SKATING

Curry Village Ice Skating Rink

ICE SKATING | Winter visitors have skated
at this outdoor rink for decades, and
there's no mystery why: it's a kick to
glide across the ice while soaking up
views of Half Dome and Glacier Point.
⊠ South side of Southside Dr., Curry
Village ☎ 209/372–8319 ⊕ www.travely-
osemite.com ☜ $11 per session, $4.50
skate rental.

RAFTING

Rafting is permitted only on designated
areas of the Middle and South forks of
the Merced River. Check with the Valley
Visitor Center for closures and other
restrictions.

Curry Village Recreation Center

WHITE-WATER RAFTING | The per-person
rental fee at Curry Village Recreation
Center covers the four- to six-person
raft, two paddles, and life jackets, plus
a return shuttle after your trip. ⊠ South
side of Southside Dr., Curry Village
☎ 209/372–4386 ⊕ www.travelyosemite.
com/things-to-do/rafting ☜ From $33.

ROCK CLIMBING

The granite canyon walls of Yosemite
Valley are world renowned for rock
climbing. El Capitan, with its 3,593-foot
vertical face, is the most famous, but
there are many other options here for all
skill levels.

Yosemite Mountain Shop

SPECIALTY STORES | A comprehensive
selection of camping, hiking, backpacking, and climbing equipment, along with
experts who can answer all your questions, make this store a valuable resource
for outdoors enthusiasts. This is the best
place to ask about climbing conditions
and restrictions around the park, as well
as purchase almost any kind of climbing
gear. ⊠ Curry Village ☎ 209/372–8436.

Yosemite Mountaineering School and Guide Service

CLIMBING/MOUNTAINEERING | The one-day basic lesson offered by this outfit includes some bouldering and rappelling and three or four 60-foot climbs. Climbers must be at least 10 years old and in reasonably good physical condition. Intermediate and advanced classes include instruction in first aid; anchor building; and multipitch, summer-snow, and big-wall climbing. There's a Nordic program in the winter. ⊠ Yosemite Mountain Shop, Curry Village ☎ 209/372–8444 ⊕ www.travelyosemite.com ⌦ From $172.

SKIING AND SNOWSHOEING

The beauty of Yosemite under a blanket of snow has long inspired poets and artists, as well as ordinary folks. Skiing and snowshoeing activities in the park center on Badger Pass Ski Area, California's oldest snow-sports resort, which is about 40 minutes away from the valley on Glacier Point Road. Here you can rent equipment, take a lesson, have lunch, and join a guided excursion.

Badger Pass Ski Area

SKIING/SNOWBOARDING | California's first ski resort has 10 downhill runs and 90 miles of groomed cross-country trails. Lessons, backcountry guiding, and cross-country and snowshoeing tours are also available. You can rent downhill, telemark, and cross-country skis, as well as snowshoes and snowboards. Note that shuttle buses run twice daily between the valley and the ski area. **Facilities:** 10 trails; 90 acres; 800-foot vertical drop; 5 lifts. ⊠ Yosemite National Park ✛ Badger Pass Rd., off Glacier Point Rd., 18 miles from Yosemite Valley ☎ 209/372–8430 ⊕ www.travelyosemite.com/winter/badger-pass-ski-area ⌦ Lift ticket: from $62.

Badger Pass Ski Area Sport Shop

Stop here to gear (and bundle!) up for downhill and cross-country skiing, snowboarding, and snowshoeing adventures. ⊠ Yosemite National Park ✛ Yosemite Ski & Snowboard Area, Badger Pass Rd., off Glacier Point Rd., 18 miles from Yosemite Valley ☎ 209/372–8444 ⊕ www.travelyosemite.com/winter/badger-pass-ski-area.

Yosemite Cross-Country Ski School

SKIING/SNOWBOARDING | The highlight of Yosemite's cross-country skiing center is a 21-mile loop from Badger Pass Ski Area to Glacier Point. You can rent cross-country skis for $28 per day at the Cross-Country Ski School, which also rents snowshoes ($26.50 per day) and telemarking equipment ($36). ☎ 209/372–8444 ⊕ www.travelyosemite.com.

Yosemite Mountaineering School

SKIING/SNOWBOARDING | This branch of the Yosemite Mountaineering School, open at the Badger Pass Ski Area during ski season only, conducts snowshoeing, cross-country skiing, telemarking, and skate-skiing classes starting at $44. ⊠ Badger Pass Ski Area ☎ 209/372–8444 ⊕ www.travelyosemite.com.

Badger Pass Ski Area School

SKIING/SNOWBOARDING | The gentle slopes of Badger Pass Ski Area make the ski school an ideal spot for children and beginners to learn downhill skiing or snowboarding for as little as $75 for a group lesson. ☎ 209/372–8430 ⊕ www.travelyosemite.com.

SWIMMING

Several swimming holes with small sandy beaches can be found in mid-summer along the Merced River at the eastern end of Yosemite Valley. Find gentle waters to swim; currents are often stronger than they appear, and temperatures are chilling. To conserve riparian habitats, step into the river at sandy beaches and other obvious entry points. ■TIP➔ Do not attempt to swim above or near waterfalls or rapids; people have died trying.

Did You Know?

In the Sierra's mixed-conifer forests, telling the many types of pines apart can be difficult if you don't know the trick: sizing up the cones and examining the branches to count how many needles are in discrete clusters. If the needles are paired, you're likely looking at a lodgepole pine. If the needles are long and come in threes, chances are you've come upon a ponderosa pine.

Nearby Towns

Marking the southern end of the Sierra's gold-bearing mother lode, **Mariposa** is the last town before you enter Yosemite on Route 140 to the west of the park. In addition to a fine mining museum, Mariposa has numerous shops, restaurants, and service stations.

Motels and restaurants dot both sides of Route 41 as it cuts through the town of **Oakhurst,** a boomtown during the gold rush that is now an important regional refueling station in every sense of the word, including organic foods and a full range of lodging options. Oakhurst has a population of about 3,000 and sits 15 miles south of the park.

Almost surrounded by the Sierra National Forest, **Bass Lake** is a warm-water reservoir whose waters can reach 80°F in summer. Created by a dam on a tributary of the San Joaquin River, the lake is owned by Pacific Gas and Electric Company and is used to generate electricity as well as for recreation.

As you climb in elevation along Highway 41 northbound, you see nothing but trees until you get to **Fish Camp,** where there's a post office and general store, but no gasoline. (For gas, head 7 miles north to Wawona, in Yosemite, or 14 miles south to Oakhurst.)

Near the park's eastern entrance, the tiny town of **Lee Vining** is home to the eerily beautiful, salty Mono Lake, where millions of migratory birds nest. Visit **Mammoth Lakes,** about 40 miles southeast of Yosemite's Tioga Pass entrance, for excellent skiing and snowboarding in winter, with fishing, mountain biking, hiking, and horseback riding in summer. Nine deep-blue lakes form the Mammoth Lakes Basin, and another hundred dot the surrounding countryside. Devils Postpile National Monument sits at the base of Mammoth Mountain.

Mariposa

43 miles west of Yosemite's Arch Rock Entrance.

Mariposa marks the southern end of the Mother Lode. Much of the land in this area was part of a 44,000-acre land grant Colonel John C. Fremont acquired from Mexico before gold was discovered and California became a state. Many people stop here on the way to Yosemite National Park, about an hour's drive east on Highway 140.

GETTING HERE AND AROUND
If driving, take Highway 49 or Highway 140. YARTS (🌐 *www.yarts.com*), the regional transit system, can get you to Mariposa from the Central Valley town of Merced (where you can also transfer from Amtrak) or from Yosemite Valley. Otherwise, you'll need a car.

VISITOR INFORMATION Mariposa County Visitor Center. ✉ *5158 Hwy. 140* ☎ *866/425–3366, 209/966–7081.* **Yosemite Mariposa County Tourism Bureau.** ✉ *5065 Hwy. 140, Suite E* ☎ *209/742–4567* 🌐 *www.yosemite.com.*

🍴 Restaurants

1850 Restaurant & Brewery
$$$ | **AMERICAN** | The name, decor, and menu at this lively brewpub pay homage to California's Gold Rush era and the year the state and county were officially established. Many of the craft beers on tap come from the owners' 1850 Brewing Company, and dishes include everything from traditional Bavarian pretzels and hearty steak-and-ale pie to ahi nachos and salmon cakes. **Known for:** brine-marinated fried chicken; nearly a dozen types of burgers; rotating local seasonal beers on tap. [$] *Average main: $22* ✉ *5114 Hwy. 140* ☎ *209/966–2229* 🌐 *www.1850restaurant.com* 🕒 *Closed Mon.*

Oakhurst

40 miles north of Fresno.

Motels, restaurants, gas stations, and small businesses line Highway 41 in Oakhurst, the last sizable community before Yosemite National Park and a good spot to find provisions. The park's southern entrance is 23 miles north of Oakhurst on Highway 41.

GETTING HERE AND AROUND

At the junction of highways 41 and 49, Oakhurst is about an hour's drive north of Fresno. It's the southern gateway to Yosemite, so many people fly into Fresno and rent a car to get here and beyond.

🍴 Restaurants

★ South Gate Brewing Company

$$ | **AMERICAN** | Locals pack this family-friendly, industrial-chic restaurant to socialize and savor small-lot beers, crafted on-site, along with tasty meals. The creative pub fare runs a wide gamut, from thin-crust brick-oven pizzas to fish tacos, fish-and-chips, and vegan black-bean burgers. **Known for:** craft beer; house-made desserts; live-music calendar. [$] *Average main: $18* ✉ *40233 Enterprise Dr., off Hwy. 49, north of Von's shopping center* ☎ *559/692–2739* 🌐 *southgatebrewco.com.*

🛏 Hotels

Best Western Plus Yosemite Gateway Inn

$$$$ | **HOTEL** | **FAMILY** | Perched on 11 hillside acres, Oakhurst's best motel has carefully tended landscaping and rooms with stylish contemporary furnishings and hand-painted murals of Yosemite. **Pros:** on-site restaurant; indoor and outdoor swimming pools; frequent deer and wildlife sightings. **Cons:** some rooms on the small side; Internet connection can be slow; some rooms need updating. [$] *Rooms from: $249* ✉ *40530 Hwy. 41* ☎ *559/683–2378* 🌐 *www.yosemitegatewayinn.com* 🛏 *149 rooms* 🍴 *No meals.*

Homestead Cottages

$$$ | **B&B/INN** | Set on 160 acres of rolling hills that once held a Miwok village, these cottages (the largest sleeps six) have gas fireplaces, fully equipped kitchens, and queen-size beds. **Pros:** remote location; quiet setting; friendly owners. **Cons:** might be too quiet for some; breakfasts on the simple side; 7 miles from center of Oakhurst. [$] *Rooms from: $189* ✉ *41110 Rd. 600, 2½ miles off Hwy. 49, Ahwahnee* ☎ *559/683–0495* 🌐 *www.homesteadcottages.com* 🛏 *7 cottages* 🍴 *Breakfast.*

Sierra Sky Ranch

$$$$ | **HOTEL** | Off Highway 41 just 10 miles south of the Yosemite National Park, this 19th-century cattle ranch near a hidden grove of giant sequoia trees provides a restful, rustic retreat. **Pros:** peaceful setting; historic property; short drive to giant sequoias. **Cons:** some rooms on the small side; not in town; basic breakfast. [$] *Rooms from: $249* ✉ *50552 Rd. 632* ☎ *559/683–8040* 🌐 *www.sierraskyranch.com* 🛏 *26 rooms* 🍴 *Breakfast.*

Bass Lake

50 miles north of Fresno via Hwy. 41 to Bass Lake Road 222.

Almost surrounded by the Sierra National Forest, Bass Lake is a reservoir whose waters can reach 80°F in summer. Created by a dam on a tributary of the San Joaquin River, the lake is owned by Pacific Gas and Electric Company and is used to generate electricity as well as for recreation.

🍴 Restaurants

Ducey's on the Lake/Ducey's Bar & Grill

$$$$ | AMERICAN | With elaborate chandeliers sculpted from deer antlers, the lodge-style restaurant at Ducey's attracts boaters, locals, and tourists with its lake views and standard lamb, beef, seafood, and pasta dishes. It's also open for breakfast: try the Bass Lake seafood omelet, huevos rancheros, or the Rice Krispies–crusted French toast. **Known for:** steaks and fresh fish; lake views; upstairs bar and grill with more affordable eats. Ⓢ *Average main: $32* ✉ *Pines Resort, 54432 Rd. 432* ☎ *559/642–3131* ⊕ *www.basslake.com.*

Fish Camp

14 miles north of Oakhurst.

As you climb in elevation along Highway 41 northbound, you see nothing but trees until you get to Fish Camp, where there's a post office and general store. (For gas, head 7 miles north to Wawona, in Yosemite, or 14 miles south to Oakhurst.)

GETTING HERE AND AROUND
Highway 41 is the main drag. YARTS transit stops in Fish Camp on its route between Fresno and Yosemite Valley.

👁 Sights

Yosemite Mountain Sugar Pine Railroad

TRANSPORTATION SITE (AIRPORT/BUS/FERRY/TRAIN) | FAMILY | Travel back to a time when powerful steam locomotives hauled massive log trains through the Sierra. This 4-mile, narrow-gauge railroad excursion takes you near Yosemite's south gate. There's a moonlight special ($63), with dinner and entertainment, and you can visit the free museum. ✉ *56001 Hwy. 41, 8 miles south of Yosemite* ☎ *559/683–7273* ⊕ *www.ymsprr.com* 💰 *$28* ⏱ *Closed Nov.–Mar. Closed some weekdays Apr. and Oct.*

🛏 Hotels

Narrow Gauge Inn

$$$$ | HOTEL | Rooms at this family-owned property have balconies with views of the surrounding woods and mountains. **Pros:** close to Yosemite's south entrance; nicely appointed rooms; wonderful balconies. **Cons:** rooms can be a bit dark; dining options are limited, especially for vegetarians; housekeeping service can be spotty. Ⓢ *Rooms from: $229* ✉ *48571 Hwy. 41* ☎ *559/683–7720* ⊕ *www.narrowgauge-inn.com* 🛏 *27 rooms* 🍽 *No meals.*

★ Tenaya Lodge

$$$$ | RESORT | FAMILY | One of the region's largest hotels is ideal for people who enjoy wilderness treks by day but prefer creature comforts at night. **Pros:** close to Yosemite and Mariposa Grove of Giant Sequoias; exceptional spa and exercise facility, 36 miles of mountain bike trails; activities for all ages. **Cons:** so big it can seem impersonal; pricey during summer; daily resort fee. Ⓢ *Rooms from: $379* ✉ *1122 Hwy. 41* ☎ *559/683–6555, 888/514–2167* ⊕ *www.tenayalodge.com* 🛏 *352 rooms* 🍽 *No meals.*

El Portal

14 miles west of Yosemite Valley on Hwy. 140.

The market in town is a good place to pick up provisions before you get to Yosemite. You'll find a post office and a gas station, but not much else.

GETTING HERE AND AROUND
The drive here on Highway 140 from Mariposa and, farther west, Merced, is the prettiest and gentlest route to Yosemite National Park. Much of the road follows the Merced River in a rugged canyon. The Yosemite Area Regional Transportation System (YARTS ⊕ *www.yarts.com*) is a cheap and dependable way to go between Merced and Yosemite

Valley; all buses stop in El Portal, where many park employees reside.

Hotels

Yosemite View Lodge

$$$$ | **HOTEL** | Two miles outside Yosemite's Arch Rock entrance, this modern property is the most convenient place to spend the night if you are unable to secure lodgings in the valley. **Pros:** great location; good views; lots of on-site amenities. **Cons:** somewhat pricey; it can be a challenge to get the dates you want; rooms could use an update. [$] *Rooms from: $239* ✉ *11136 Hwy. 140* ☎ *209/379–2681, 888/742–4371* 🌐 *www.yosemiteresorts.com/yosemite-view-lodge* 🛏 *335 rooms* 🍴 *No meals.*

Lee Vining

20 miles east of Tuolumne Meadows, 30 miles north of Mammoth Lakes.

Tiny Lee Vining is known primarily as the eastern gateway to Yosemite National Park (summer only) and the location of vast and desolate Mono Lake. Pick up supplies at the general store year-round, or stop here for lunch or dinner before or after a drive through the high country. In winter, the town is all but deserted, except for the ice climbers who come to scale frozen waterfalls.

To drive from Lee Vining to Tuolumne Meadows is an unforgettable experience, but keep in mind that the road is closed for at least seven months of the year.

GETTING HERE AND AROUND

Lee Vining is on U.S. 395, north of the road's intersection with Highway 120 and on the south side of Mono Lake. In summer YARTS public transit (🌐 *yarts.com*) can get you here from Yosemite Valley, but you'll need a car to explore the area.

VISITOR INFORMATION Lee Vining Chamber of Commerce. ☎ *760/647–6629* 🌐 *www.leevining.com.* **Mono Basin National Forest Scenic Area Visitor Center.** ✉ *Visitor Center Dr., off U.S. 395, 1 mile north of Hwy. 120* ☎ *760/647–6595* 🌐 *www.fs.usda.gov/recarea/inyo/recarea/?recid=20620.*

Sights

June Lake Loop

SCENIC DRIVE | Heading south from Lee Vining, U.S. 395 intersects the June Lake Loop. This gorgeous 17-mile drive follows an old glacial canyon past Grant, June, Gull, and Silver lakes before reconnecting with U.S. 395 on its way to Mammoth Lakes. **■ TIP→ The loop is especially colorful in fall.** ✉ *Hwy. 158 W.*

★ Mono Lake

BODY OF WATER | Since the 1940s, Los Angeles has diverted water from this lake, exposing striking towers of tufa, or calcium carbonate. Court victories by environmentalists have meant fewer diversions, and the lake is rising again. Although to see the lake from U.S. 395 is stunning, make time to visit South Tufa, whose parking lot is 5 miles east of U.S. 395 off Highway 120. There, in summer, you can join the naturalist-guided **South Tufa Walk,** which lasts about 90 minutes. The **Scenic Area Visitor Center,** off U.S. 395, is a sensational stop for its interactive exhibits and sweeping Mono Lake views (closed in winter). In town, at U.S. 395 and 3rd Street, the **Mono Lake Committee Information Center & Bookstore**, open from 9 to 5 daily (extended hours in summer), has more information about this beautiful area. ✉ *Hwy. 120, east of Lee Vining* ☎ *760/647–3044 visitor center, 760/647–6595 info center* 🌐 *www.monolake.org* 🎟 *Free.*

Restaurants

Mono Cone

$ | **AMERICAN** | Get soft-serve ice cream, burgers, and fries at this hopping shack in the middle of Lee Vining, but be prepared to wait in line. There's some indoor seating, but unless the clouds are leaking, take your food to nearby (and quiet) Hess Park, whose views of Mono Lake make it one of the best picnic spots in eastern California. $ *Average main: $9* ✉ *51508 U.S. 395* ☎ *760/647–6606* ▭ *No credit cards* ⊘ *Closed in winter*.

Tioga Gas Mart & Whoa Nelli Deli

$$ | **AMERICAN** | This might be the only gas station in the United States serving craft beers and lobster taquitos, but its appeal goes beyond novelty. Order at the counter and grab a seat inside, or sit at one of the picnic tables on the lawn outside and take in the distant view of Mono Lake. **Known for:** fish tacos and barbecued ribs; regular live music; convenient location. $ *Average main: $16* ✉ *Hwy. 120 and U.S. 395* ☎ *760/647–1088* ⊕ *www. whoanelliedeli.com* ⊘ *Closed early Nov.– late Apr.*

Hotels

Lake View Lodge

$$ | **B&B/INN** | Cottages, enormous rooms, and landscaping that includes several shaded sitting areas set this motel apart from its competitors in town. **Pros:** convenient access to Yosemite, Mono Lake, Bodie State Historic Park; peaceful setting; on-site restaurant. **Cons:** could use updating; slow Wi-Fi in some areas; no views from some rooms. $ *Rooms from: $143* ✉ *51285 U.S. 395* ☎ *760/647–6543, 800/990–6614* ⊕ *www.lakeviewlodgeyo-semite.com* ⇥ *88 units*.

Bodie State Historic Park

31 miles northeast of Lee Vining.

Bodie State Historic Park's scenery is spectacular, with craggy, snowcapped peaks looming over vast prairies. The town of Bridgeport is the gateway to the park, and the only supply center for miles around. Bridgeport's claims to fame include a courthouse that's been in continuous use since 1880 and excellent fishing—the California state record brown trout, at 26 pounds 12 ounces, was caught in Bridgeport's Twin Lakes. In winter, much of Bridgeport shuts down.

GETTING HERE AND AROUND

A car is the best way to reach this area. Bodie is on Highway 270 about 13 miles east of U.S. 395.

◉ Sights

★ Bodie Ghost Town

GHOST TOWN | The mining village of Rattlesnake Gulch, abandoned mine shafts, and the remains of a small Chinatown are among the sights at this fascinating ghost town. The town boomed from about 1878 to 1881; by the late 1940s, though, all its residents had departed. A state park was established here in 1962, with a mandate to preserve everything in a state of "arrested decay." Evidence of Bodie's wild past survives at an excellent museum, and you can tour an old stamp mill where ore was crushed into fine powder to extract gold and silver. Bodie lies 13 miles east of U.S. 395 off Highway 270. The last 3 miles are unpaved, and snow may close the highway from late fall through early spring. No food, drink, or lodging is available in Bodie. ✉ *Bodie Rd., off Hwy. 270, Bodie* ☎ *760/616–5040* ⊕ *www.parks.ca.gov/bodie* 🎫 *$8.*

Chapter 38

ZION NATIONAL PARK

Updated by
Shelley Arenas

UTAH

🏕 Camping	🛏 Hotels	🤸 Activities	👁 Scenery	👥 Crowds
★★★★☆	★★★★☆	★★★★☆	★★★★★	★★★★★

WELCOME TO ZION NATIONAL PARK

TOP REASONS TO GO

★ **Eye candy:** Pick just about any trail in the park and it's all but guaranteed to culminate in an astounding viewpoint full of pink, orange, and crimson rock formations.

★ **Peace and quiet:** From February through November, cars are generally not allowed on Zion Canyon Scenic Drive, allowing this section of the park to remain relatively quiet and peaceful.

★ **Botanical wonderland:** Zion Canyon is home to more than 1,000 species of plants, more than anywhere else in Utah.

★ **Animal tracks:** Zion has expansive hinterlands where furry, scaly, and feathered residents are common. Hike long enough and you'll encounter deer, elk, rare lizards, birds of prey, and other zoological treats.

★ **Unforgettable canyoneering:** Zion's array of rugged slot canyons is the richest place on Earth for scrambling, rappelling, climbing, and descending.

1 **Zion Canyon.** This area defines Zion National Park for most people. Free shuttle buses are the only vehicles allowed February through November, the busiest months in the park. The backcountry is accessible via the West Rim Trail and the Narrows, and 2,000-foot cliffs rise all around.

2 **Kolob Canyons.** The northwestern corner of Zion is a secluded 30,000-acre wonderland that can be reached only via a special entrance. Don't miss the West Temple and the Kolob Arch, and keep looking up to spot Horse Ranch Mountain, the park's highest point.

Spendlove K

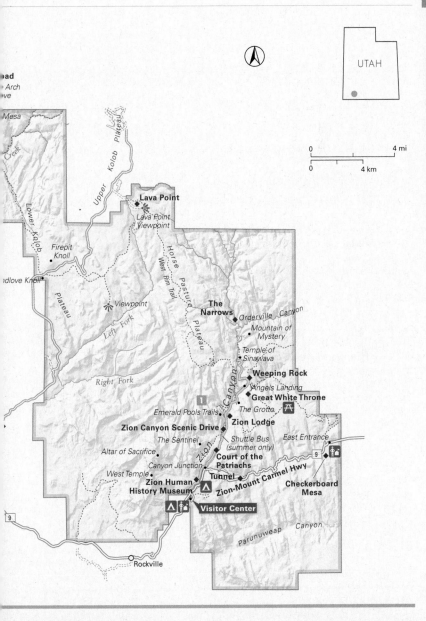

0   4 mi

0   4 km

oad
Arch
ve

Mesa

Creek

Upper Kolob Plateau

Lava Point

Lava Point
Viewpoint

Firepit
Knoll

Lower Kolob

dlove Knoll

Plateau

Horse Pasture Plateau

West Rim Trail

Viewpoint

Left Fork

Plateau

**The
Narrows**

Orderville   Canyon

Mountain of
Mystery

Temple of
Sinawava

Right Fork

Canyon

Weeping Rock

Angels Landing

Great White Throne

The Grotto

1

Emerald Pools Trails

Zion Canyon Scenic Drive   **Zion Lodge**

The Sentinel   Shuttle Bus
(summer only)   East Entrance

Altar of Sacrifice

Canyon Junction   **Court of the
Patriachs**

West Temple   9

Zion Human   Tunnel   **Checkerboard
History Museum**   Zion-Mount Carmel Hwy   **Mesa**

Z.I.O.N.

Visitor Center

Parunuweap   Canyon

9

Rockville

The walls of Zion Canyon soar more than 2,000 feet above the valley. Bands of limestone, sandstone, and lava in the strata point to the distant past. Greenery high in the cliff walls indicate the presence of water seepage or a spring. Erosion has left behind a collection of domes, fins, and blocky massifs bearing the names of cathedrals and temples, prophets and angels.

Trails lead deep into side canyons and up narrow ledges to waterfalls, serene spring-fed pools, and shaded spots of solitude. So diverse is this place that 85% of Utah's flora and fauna species are found here. Some, like the tiny Zion snail, appear nowhere else in the world.

The Colorado River helped create the Grand Canyon, while the Virgin River—the Colorado's muddy progeny—carved Zion's features. Because of the park's unique topography, distant storms and spring runoff can transform a tranquil slot canyon into a sluice, and flood damage does sometimes result in extended trail closures, as happened in summer 2018 to three trails near the Grotto and Zion Lodge sections of Zion Canyon.

Planning

When to Go

Zion is the most heavily visited national park in Utah, receiving 4.5 million visitors each year. Locals used to call the spring and fall the shoulder seasons because traffic would drop off from the highly visited summer months. Not so much anymore. These days the park is busy from March through November.

Summer in the park is hot and dry, punctuated by sudden cloudbursts that can create flash flooding and spectacular waterfalls. Expect afternoon thunderstorms between July and September. Whether the day starts out sunny or not, wear sunscreen and drink lots of water, even if you aren't exerting yourself or spending much time outside. The sun is very powerful at this elevation.

AVERAGE HIGH/LOW TEMPERATURES

JAN.	FEB.	MAR.	APR.	MAY	JUNE
52/29	57/31	63/36	73/43	83/52	93/60
JULY	AUG.	SEPT.	OCT.	NOV.	DEC.
100/68	97/66	91/60	78/49	63/37	53/30

Winters are mild at lower desert elevations. You can expect to encounter winter driving conditions from November to mid-March, and although most park programs are suspended in winter, it is a wonderful and solitary time to see the canyons.

■ TIP→ **The temperature in Zion often exceeds 100°F in July and August.**

Getting Here and Around

AIR

The nearest commercial airport, with direct flights from a number of western U.S. hubs, is an hour away in St. George, Utah. It's about a three-hour drive to the nearest major airport, McCarran in Las Vegas, Nevada, and a 4½-hour drive from Salt Lake City's airport.

CAR

Zion National Park lies east of Interstate 15 in southwestern Utah. From the interstate, head east on Highway 9. After 21 miles you'll reach Springdale, which abuts the main entrance.

From February through November, you can drive on Zion Canyon Scenic Drive only if you have reservations at the Zion Lodge. Otherwise, you must park your car in Springdale or at the Zion Canyon Visitor Center and take the shuttle. There are no car restrictions in December and January.

The Zion Canyon Visitor Center parking lot fills up quickly. You can avoid parking heartburn by leaving your car in Springdale and riding the shuttle to the park entrance. Shuttles are accessible for people with disabilities and have plenty

of room for gear. Consult the print park guide or check online at ⊕ *www.nps.gov/zion/planyourvisit/shuttle-system.htm* for the town shuttle schedule.

Inspiration

Towers of Stone, by J. L. Crawford, summarizes the essence of Zion National Park, its landscape, plants, animals, and human history.

Zion: Canyoneering, by Tom Jones, shows you how to explore the park's most dramatic landscapes.

An Introduction to the Geology of Zion, by Al Warneke, is a good pick for information on Zion's geology.

The Zion Tunnel, from Slickrock to Switchback, by Donald T. Garate, tells the fascinating story of the construction of the mile-long Zion Tunnel in the 1920s.

Zion National Park: Sanctuary in the Desert, by Nicky Leach, provides a photographic overview and a narrative journey through the park.

Park Essentials

ACCESSIBILITY

Both visitor centers, all shuttle buses, and Zion Lodge are fully accessible to people in wheelchairs. Several campsites (sites A24 and A25 at Watchman Campground and sites 103, 114, and 115 at South Campground) are reserved for people with disabilities, and two trails— Riverside Walk and Pa'rus Trail—are accessible with some assistance.

Zion in One Day

Begin your visit at the **Zion Canyon Visitor Center**, where outdoor exhibits inform you about the park's geology, wildlife, history, and trails. Get a taste of what's in store by viewing the far off Towers of the Virgin, then head to the **Court of the Patriarchs** viewpoint to take photos and walk the short path. Take the shuttle (or your car, if it's December or January) to **Zion Lodge**, where you can hike a trail to one of the park's most beautiful spots, the **Emerald Pools**. The Lower Pool Trail is the second most popular walk at Zion; the trail branches off into Middle Pool and Upper Pool trails for those with more time. Ride the next shuttle to the end of the road, where the paved, accessible **Riverside Walk**, Zion's most popular path, will deliver you to the gateway of the canyon's **Narrows**.

Reboard the shuttle to return to the Zion Canyon Visitor Center to pick up your car (or continue driving December–January). Head out onto the beautiful **Zion–Mount Carmel Highway**, with its long, curving tunnel, keeping your camera at the ready for stops at viewpoints along the road. Once you reach the park's east entrance, turn around, and on your return trip stop to take the short hike up to **Canyon Overlook**. In the evening, you might want to attend a ranger program at one of the campground amphitheaters or at Zion Lodge.

PARK FEES AND PERMITS

Entrance to Zion National Park costs $35 per vehicle for a seven-day pass. People entering on foot or by bicycle pay $20 per person for a seven-day pass; those on motorcycle pay $30.

Permits are required for backcountry camping and overnight hikes. Depending on which parts of the trails you intend to explore, you'll need a special permit for the Narrows and Kolob Creek or the Subway slot canyon. Climbing and canyoneering parties need a permit before using technical equipment.

Zion National Park limits the total number of overnight and canyoneering permits issued per day and has a reservation system with most of the permits now issued in an online lottery to apportion them fairly. Permits to the Subway, Mystery Canyon, the Narrows through-hikes, and West Rim are in short supply during high season. The maximum size of a group hiking into the backcountry is 12 people. Permits cost $15 for one or two people; $20 for three to seven; and $25 for eight or more. Permits are available at the visitor centers.

PARK HOURS

The park, open daily year-round, 24 hours a day, is in the Mountain time zone.

AUTOMOBILE SERVICE STATIONS

Just outside the park and in nearby Kanab and Springdale, you can fuel up, get your tires and oil changed, and have auto repairs done.

CELL PHONE RECEPTION

Cell phone reception is good in Springdale but spotty in the park. Public telephones can be found at Zion Canyon Visitor Center, Zion Lodge, and Zion Human History Museum.

EMERGENCIES

In the event of an emergency, dial 911, report to a visitor center, or contact a park ranger at ☎ *435/772–3322*. The nearest hospitals are in St. George, Cedar City, and Kanab.

Hotels

The Zion Lodge is rustic, designed in 1920s period style, and comfortable. Most lodging is located outside the park. Springdale has dozens of lodging options, from quaint bed-and-breakfasts to modest motels to chain hotels with riverside rooms, and farther west you'll find more options (and usually better values) in Hurricane and St. George. To the east and north, you'll find a smaller number of hotels and motels, from Kanab up to Panguitch, both of which are good bases if you're continuing on to Bryce or, in the case of Kanab, the Grand Canyon. *Hotel reviews have been shortened. For full information, visit Fodors.com.*

What It Costs			
$	$$	$$$	$$$$
RESTAURANTS			
under $16	$16–$22	$23–$30	over $30
HOTELS			
under $125	$125–$175	$176–$225	over $225

Restaurants

Only one full-service restaurant operates within the park, at the famed Zion Lodge, but in Springdale, just outside the park's South Entrance, you'll find a growing number of both casual and sophisticated eateries. To the east, options are limited, but there is a handful of options within an hour's drive. *Restaurant reviews have been shortened. For full information, visit Fodors.com.*

Visitor Information

PARK CONTACT INFORMATION Zion National Park. ✉ *Hwy. 9, Springdale* ☎ *435/772–3256* ⊕ *www.nps.gov/zion.*

Zion Canyon

Sights

GEOLOGICAL LANDMARKS

★ **The Narrows**

NATURE SITE | This sinuous 16-mile crack in the earth where the Virgin River flows over gravel and boulders is one of the world's most stunning gorges. If you hike through it, you'll find yourself surrounded—sometimes nearly boxed in—by smooth walls stretching high into the heavens. Plan to get wet, and beware that flash floods can occur here, especially in spring and summer. Check on the weather before you enter. ✉ *Zion National Park* ⊹ *Begins at Riverside Walk.*

HISTORIC SIGHTS

Zion Human History Museum

MUSEUM | This informative museum tells the park's story from the perspective of its human inhabitants, among them Ancestral Puebloans and early Mormon settlers. Permanent exhibits illustrate how humans have dealt with wildlife, plants, and natural forces. Temporary exhibits have touched on everything from vintage park employee photography to the history of Union Pacific Railroad hotels. Don't miss the incredible view of Towers of the Virgin from the back patio. ✉ *Zion Canyon Scenic Dr., ½ mile north of south entrance* ☎ *435/772–3256* ▣ *Free.*

PICNIC AREAS

The Grotto

LOCAL INTEREST | FAMILY | Get your food to go at the Zion Lodge, take a short walk to this scenic retreat, and dine beneath a shady oak. Amenities include drinking water, picnic tables, and restrooms, but there are no fire grates. A trail from here leads to the Emerald Pools. ⊠ *Off Zion Canyon Scenic Dr., at Grotto.*

Zion Nature Center

LOCAL INTEREST | FAMILY | On your way to or from the Junior Ranger Program you can feed your kids at the center's picnic area. When the center is closed, use the restrooms in South Campground. ⊠ *Zion National Park* ✣ *Near entrance to South Campground, ½ mile north of south entrance.*

SCENIC DRIVES

★ Zion Canyon Scenic Drive

SCENIC DRIVE | Vividly colored cliffs tower 2,000 feet above the road that meanders north from Springdale along the floor of Zion Canyon. As you roll through the narrow, steep canyon you'll pass the Court of the Patriarchs, the Sentinel, and the Great White Throne, among other imposing rock formations. From February through November, unless you're staying at the lodge, Zion Canyon Scenic Drive is accessed only by park shuttle. You can drive it yourself at other times. ⊠ *Off Hwy. 9.*

Zion–Mount Carmel Highway and Tunnels

SCENIC DRIVE | Two narrow tunnels as old as the park itself lie between the east entrance and Zion Canyon on this breathtaking 12-mile stretch of Highway 9. One was once the longest man-made tunnel in the world. As you travel the (1.1-mile) passage through solid rock, five arched portals along one side provide fleeting glimpses of cliffs and canyons. When you emerge you'll find that the landscape has changed dramatically. Large vehicles require traffic control and a $15 permit, available at the park entrance, and have restricted hours of travel. This includes nearly all RVs, trailers, dual-wheel trucks, and campers. The Canyon Overlook Trail starts from a parking area between the tunnels. ⊠ *Hwy. 9, 5 miles east of Canyon Junction* ⊕ *www.nps.gov/zion/planyourvisit/the-zion-mount-carmel-tunnel.htm.*

SCENIC STOPS

Checkerboard Mesa

NATURE SITE | It's well worth stopping at the pull-out 1 mile west of Zion's east entrance to observe the distinctive waffle patterns on this huge white mound of sandstone. The stunning crosshatch effect visible today is the result of eons of freeze-and-thaw cycles that caused vertical fractures, combined with erosion that produced horizontal bedding planes. ⊠ *Zion–Mount Carmel Hwy.*

Court of the Patriarchs

NATURE SITE | This trio of peaks bears the names of, from left to right, Abraham, Isaac, and Jacob. Mount Moroni is the reddish peak on the far right that partially blocks the view of Jacob. Hike the trail that leaves from the Court of the Patriarchs Viewpoint, 1½ miles north of Canyon Junction, to get a much better view of the sandstone prophets. ⊠ *Zion Canyon Scenic Dr.*

Great White Throne

NATURE SITE | Dominating the Grotto picnic area near Zion Lodge, this massive Navajo sandstone peak juts 2,000 feet above the valley floor. The popular formation lies about 3 miles north of Canyon Junction. ⊠ *Zion Canyon Scenic Dr.*

Weeping Rock

NATURE SITE | Surface water from the rim of Echo Canyon spends several thousand years seeping down through the porous sandstone before exiting at this picturesque alcove 4½ miles north of Canyon Junction. A paved walkway climbs ¼ mile to this flowing rock face where wildflowers and delicate ferns grow. In fall, the maples and cottonwoods burst with color, and lizards point the way down the path, which is too steep for wheelchairs or strollers. A major rockslide closed the Weeping Rock Trail in summer 2019; check with visitor center to see if it has reopened. ⊠ *Zion Canyon Scenic Dr.*

TRAILS

★ Angels Landing Trail

TRAIL | As much a trial as a trail, this path beneath the Great White Throne, which you access from the Lower West Rim Trail, is one of the park's most challenging hikes. Early on you work your way through Walter's Wiggles, a series of 21 switchbacks built out of sandstone blocks. From there you traverse sheer cliffs that have chains bolted into the rock face to serve as handrails in some (but not all) places. In spite of its hair-raising nature, this trail is popular. Allow 2½ hours round trip if you stop at Scout's Lookout (2 miles), and four hours if you keep going to where the angels (and birds of prey) play. The trail is 5 miles round trip and is not appropriate for children or those who are uneasy about heights. *Difficult.* ⊠ *Zion National Park* ✢ *Trailhead: off Zion Canyon Scenic Dr. at the Grotto.*

★ Canyon Overlook Trail

TRAIL | **FAMILY** | The parking area just east of Zion–Mount Carmel tunnel leads to this popular trail, which is about 1 mile round trip and takes about an hour to finish. From the breathtaking overlook at the trail's end you can see the West and East temples, the Towers of the Virgin, the Streaked Wall, and other Zion Canyon cliffs and peaks. The elevation change is 160 feet. There's no shuttle to this trail and the parking area often fills up—try to come very early or late in the day to avoid crowds. *Moderate.* ⊠ *Zion National Park* ✢ *Trailhead: off Hwy. 9 just east of Zion–Mount Carmel tunnel.*

Emerald Pools Trail

TRAIL | **FAMILY** | Multiple waterfalls cascade (or drip, in dry weather) into algae-filled pools along this trail, about 3 miles north of Canyon Junction. The path leading to the lower pool is paved and appropriate for strollers and wheelchairs. If you've got any energy left, keep going past the lower pool. The ¼ mile from there to the middle pool becomes rocky and somewhat steep but offers increasingly scenic views. A less crowded and exceptionally enjoyable return route follows the Kayenta Trail, connecting to the Grotto Trail. Allow 50 minutes for the 1¼-mile round-trip hike to the lower pool, and an hour more each round trip to the middle (2 miles) and upper pools (3 miles). *Lower, easy. Upper, moderate.* ⊠ *Zion National Park* ✢ *Trailhead: off Zion Canyon Scenic Dr., at Zion Lodge or the Grotto.*

Grotto Trail

TRAIL | **FAMILY** | This flat trail takes you from Zion Lodge, about 3 miles north of Canyon Junction, to the Grotto picnic area, traveling for the most part along the park road. Allow 20 minutes or less for the walk along the ½-mile trail. If you are up for a longer hike and have two or three hours, connect with the Kayenta Trail after you cross the footbridge, and head for the Emerald Pools. You will begin gaining elevation, and it's a steady, steep climb to the pools, which you will begin to see after about 1 mile. *Easy.* ⊠ *Zion National Park* ✢ *Trailhead: off Zion Canyon Scenic Dr. at the Grotto.*

Hidden Canyon Trail

TRAIL | This steep, 2-mile round-trip hike takes you up 850 feet in elevation. Not too crowded, the trail is paved all the way to Hidden Canyon. Allow about three hours for the round-trip hike. A massive rockfall in summer 2019 resulted in the closure of this trail—check with the visitor center for updates.

Moderate–Difficult. ✉ *Zion National Park* ✣ *Trailhead: off Zion Canyon Scenic Dr. at Weeping Rock.*

★ Narrows Trail

TRAIL | After leaving the paved ease of the Gateway to the Narrows trail behind, walk on the riverbed itself. You'll find a pebbly shingle or dry sandbar path, but when the walls of the canyon close in, you'll be forced into the chilly waters of the Virgin River. A walking stick and good shoes are a must. Be prepared to swim, as chest-deep holes may occur even when water levels are low. Check with park rangers about the likelihood of flash floods. A day trip up the lower section of the Narrows is 6 miles one-way to the turnaround point. Allow at least five hours round trip. *Difficult.* ✉ *Zion National Park* ✣ *Trailhead: off Zion Canyon Scenic Dr., at end of Riverside Walk.*

Pa'rus Trail

TRAIL | **FAMILY** | An approximately 1¾-mile, relatively flat paved walking and biking path, Pa'rus parallels and occasionally crosses the Virgin River. Starting at South Campground, ½ mile north of the South Entrance, the walk proceeds north along the river to the beginning of Zion Canyon Scenic Drive. Along the way you'll take in great views of the Watchman, the Sentinel, the East and West temples, and Towers of the Virgin. Leashed dogs are allowed on this trail. Wheelchair users may need assistance. *Easy.* ✉ *Zion National Park* ✣ *Trailhead: at Canyon Junction.*

Riverside Walk

TRAIL | **FAMILY** | This 2.2-mile round-trip hike shadows the Virgin River. In spring, wildflowers bloom on the opposite canyon wall in lovely hanging gardens. The trail, which begins 6½ miles north of Canyon Junction at the end of Zion Canyon Scenic Drive, is the park's most visited trail, so be prepared for crowds in high season. Riverside Walk is paved and suitable for strollers and wheelchairs, though some wheelchair users may need assistance. Round trip it takes about 90 minutes. At the end, the much more challenging Narrows Trail begins. *Easy.* ✉ *Zion National Park* ✣ *Trailhead: off Zion Canyon Scenic Dr. at Temple of Sinawava.*

Watchman Trail

TRAIL | For a dramatic view of Springdale and a look at lower Zion Creek Canyon and the Towers of the Virgin, this strenuous hike begins on a service road east of Watchman Campground. Some springs seep out of the sandstone, nourishing the hanging gardens and attracting wildlife. There are a few sheer cliff edges, so supervise children carefully. Plan on two hours for this 3.3-mile round-trip hike that has a 368-foot elevation change. *Moderate.* ✉ *Zion National Park* ✣ *Trailhead: at Zion Canyon Visitor Center.*

VISITOR CENTERS

Zion Canyon Visitor Center

INFO CENTER | Learn about the area's geology, flora, and fauna at an outdoor exhibit next to a gurgling stream. Inside, a large shop sells everything from field guides to souvenirs. Zion Canyon shuttle buses leave regularly from the center and make several stops along the canyon's beautiful Scenic Drive; ranger-guided shuttle tours depart once a day from Memorial Day to late September. ✉ *Zion Park Blvd. at south entrance, Springdale* ☎ *435/772–3256* 🌐 *www.nps.gov/zion.*

🍴 Restaurants

Castle Dome Café & Snack Bar

$ | **CAFÉ** | Next to the shuttle stop at Zion Lodge, this small fast-food restaurant is both convenient and enjoys a lovely shaded outdoor patio. You can grab a banana, burger, smoothie, or salad to go, order local brews from the Beer Garden cart, or enjoy a dish of ice cream while soaking up the views of the surrounding geological formations. **Known for:** quick bites; gorgeous views; nice beer selection. [$] *Average main: $6* ✉ *Zion Lodge, Zion Canyon Scenic Dr.* ☎ *435/772–7700* 🌐 *www.zionlodge.com/dining* ⏲ *Closed Dec.–Feb.*

Red Rock Grill

$$ | AMERICAN | The fare at this restaurant at Zion Lodge includes steaks, seafood, and Western specialties such as pecan-encrusted trout and jalapeño-topped bison cheeseburgers headlining the dinner menu. Photos of the surrounding landscape adorn the walls of the spacious dining room, which has enormous windows taking in the scenery, and the large patio has gorgeous views of the real thing. **Known for:** dinner reservations necessary in summer; astounding views inside and out; only full-service restaurant in the park. $ *Average main: $19* ⊠ *Zion Lodge, Zion Canyon Scenic Dr.* ☎ *435/772–7760* ⊕ *www.zionlodge.com/dining.*

 Hotels

★ **Zion Lodge**

$$$$ | HOTEL | For a dramatic location inside the park, you'd be hard-pressed to improve on a stay at the historic Zion Lodge: the canyon's jaw-dropping beauty surrounds you, access to trailheads is easy, and guests can drive their cars on the lower half of Zion Park Scenic Drive year-round. **Pros:** handsome hotel in the tradition of historic park properties; incredible views; bike rentals on-site. **Cons:** pathways are dimly lit (bring a flashlight); spotty Wi-Fi, poor cell service; books up months ahead. $ *Rooms from: $229* ⊠ *Zion Canyon Scenic Dr.* ☎ *888/297–2757 reservations only, 435/772–7700* ⊕ *www.zionlodge.com* ⇥ *122 rooms* ⊠ *No meals.*

Kolob Canyons

 Sights

SCENIC DRIVES
Kolob Canyons Road

SCENIC DRIVE | The beauty starts modestly at the junction with Interstate 15, but as you move along this 5-mile road the red walls of the Kolob finger canyons rise suddenly and spectacularly out of the earth. With the crowds left behind at Zion Canyon, this drive offers the chance to take in incredible vistas at your leisure. Trails include the short but rugged Middle Fork of Taylor Creek Trail, which passes two 1930s homestead cabins, culminating 2¾ miles later in the Double Arch Alcove. During heavy snowfall Kolob Canyons Road may be closed. ⊠ *I–15, Exit 40.*

Kolob Terrace Road

SCENIC DRIVE | This 21-mile road begins 14 miles west of Springdale at Virgin and winds north to Kolob Reservoir. The drive meanders in and out of the park boundaries, crossing several important trailheads, all the while overlooking the cliffs of North Creek. A popular day-use trail (permit required) leads past fossilized dinosaur tracks to the Subway, a stretch of the stream where the walls of the slot canyon close in so tightly as to form a near tunnel. Farther along the road you reach the Wildcat Canyon trailhead, which connects to the path overlooking the North Guardian Angel. The road terminates at the reservoir, beneath 8,933-foot Kolob Peak. Although paved, this narrow, twisting road is not recommended for RVs. Because of limited winter plowing, the road is closed from November or December through April or May. ⊠ *Zion National Park* ⊹ *Begins in Virgin at Hwy. 9.*

SCENIC STOPS

Lava Point

VIEWPOINT | Infrequently visited, this area has a primitive campground and two nearby reservoirs that offer the only significant fishing opportunities. Lava Point Overlook, one of the highest viewpoints in the park, provides a panoramic view of Zion Canyon from the north. The higher elevation here makes it much cooler than the Zion Canyon area. Park visitors looking for a respite from crowds and heat find the campground a nice change of pace, though the six sites fill up quickly and are only open May through September. ⌧ *Zion National Park ✛ Kolob Terrace Rd to Lava Point Rd then turn right.*

Kolob Canyons Viewpoint

VIEWPOINT—SIGHT | Nearly 100% of travelers along Interstate 15 from Las Vegas to Salt Lake overlook this short drive a few hundred yards from the highway. The reward is a beautiful view of Kolob's "finger" canyons from about six picnic tables spread out beneath the trees. The parking lot has plenty of space, a pit toilet, and an overlook with a display pointing out canyon features. Restrooms and drinking water are available at the Kolob Canyons Visitor Center. ⌧ *Zion National Park ✛ On Timber Creek Trail at end of Kolob Canyons Rd.*

TRAILS

Taylor Creek Trail

TRAIL | This trail in the Kolob Canyons area descends parallel to Taylor Creek, sometimes crossing it, sometimes shortcutting benches beside it. The historic Larsen Cabin precedes the entrance to the canyon of the Middle Fork, where the trail becomes rougher. After the old Fife Cabin, the canyon bends to the right into Double Arch Alcove, a large, colorful grotto with a high blind arch (or arch "embryo") towering above. To Double Arch it's 2½ miles one way—about four hours round trip. The

elevation change is 450 feet. *Moderate.* ⌧ *Zion National Park ✛ Trailhead: at Kolob Canyons Rd., about 1½ miles east of Kolob Canyons Visitor Center.*

VISITOR CENTERS

Kolob Canyons Visitor Center

INFO CENTER | Make this your first stop as you enter this remote section of the park. There are books and maps, a small gift shop, and clean restrooms here, and rangers are on hand to answer questions about Kolob Canyons exploration. ⌧ *3752 E. Kolob Canyons Rd., Exit 40 off I–15* ☎ *435/772–3256* ⊕ *www.nps.gov/zion.*

Activities

BIKING

Zion Cycles

BICYCLING | This shop just outside the park rents bikes by the hour or longer, sells parts, and has a full-time mechanic on duty. You can pick up trail tips and other advice from the staff here. They also offer guided road-biking treks in the park and mountain-biking excursions elsewhere in Southern Utah. ⌧ *868 Zion Park Blvd., Springdale* ☎ *435/772–0400* ⊕ *www. zioncycles.com* 🖃 *Guided tours from $175; bike rentals from $40/day.*

CAMPING

South Campground. All the sites here are under big cottonwood trees that provide some relief from the summer sun. The campground operates on a reservation system. ⌧ *Hwy. 9, ½ mile north of south entrance* ☎ *435/772–3256, 877/444–6777* ⊕ *www.recreation.gov.*

Watchman Campground. This large campground on the Virgin River operates on a reservation system between March and November, but you do not get to choose your site. ⌧ *Access road off Zion Canyon Visitor Center parking lot* ☎ *435/772–3256, 877/444–6777* ⊕ *www.recreation.gov.*

EDUCATIONAL PROGRAMS
CLASSES AND SEMINARS
★ Zion Natl Park Forever Project
COLLEGE | Formerly known as the Zion Natural History Association, the project conducts workshops about the park's natural and cultural history. Topics can include edible plants, bat biology, river geology, photography, and bird-watching. Most workshops include a hike. For a glimpse of Zion's inner workings, volunteer to assist with one of their ongoing projects. ⊠ *Zion National Park* ☎ *435/772-3264* ⊕ *www.zionpark.org* ☜ *From $45.*

RANGER PROGRAMS
Evening Programs
TOUR—SIGHT | Held each evening May through September in Watchman Campground and at Zion Lodge, these 45-minute ranger-led talks cover geology, biology, and history. You might learn about coyote calls, the night sky, animal hideouts, or observing nature with all your senses. Slide shows and audience participation are often part of the proceedings. Check the visitor center for schedules. ⊠ *Zion National Park.*

★ Expert Talks
TOUR—SIGHT | Informal lectures take place on the Zion Human History Museum patio. Past topics have included wildlife, geology, and the stories of early settlers. Talks usually last from 20 to 30 minutes, though some run longer. Check park bulletin boards or the visitor center for schedules. ⊠ *Zion National Park.*

Junior Ranger Program
TOUR—SIGHT | **FAMILY** | Educational activities aimed at younger visitors include the chance to earn a Junior Ranger badge. Kids do so by attending at least one nature program and completing the free Junior Ranger Handbook, available at visitor centers. ⊠ *Zion National Park* ⊕ *www.nps.gov/zion/learn/kidsyouth/bea-juniorranger.htm.*

★ Ranger-Led Hike
TOUR—SIGHT | A daily guided hike along the 1.7-mile Pa'rus Trail provides an overview of the park's geology and natural and other history. Groups meet at 2 pm at Zion Canyon Visitor Center. Wear sturdy footgear and bring a hat, sunglasses, sunscreen, and water. Wheelchairs are welcome on this paved trail but may need assistance. ⊠ *Zion National Park.*

★ Ride with a Ranger Shuttle Tours
TOUR—SIGHT | **FAMILY** | Once a day from Memorial Day through September, rangers conduct shuttle tours of points of interest along Zion Canyon Scenic Drive. In addition to learning about the canyon's geology, ecology, and history, you'll be treated to some great photo-ops. The two-hour tour takes place in the morning and departs from the Zion Canyon Visitor Center. Make reservations in person at the visitor center up to three days in advance for up to eight people in your group. ⊠ *Zion National Park* ☜ *Free.*

HORSEBACK RIDING
Canyon Trail Rides
HORSEBACK RIDING | **FAMILY** | Grab your hat and boots and see Zion Canyon the way the pioneers did—on a horse or mule. Easygoing, one-hour and half-day guided rides are available (minimum age 7 and 10 years, respectively). Maximum weight is 220 pounds. These friendly folks have been around for years, and are the only outfitter for trail rides inside the park. Reservations are recommended and can be made online. ⊠ *Across from Zion Lodge* ☎ *435/679-8665* ⊕ *www.canyonrides.com* ☜ *From $45.*

Nearby Towns

Hotels, restaurants, and shops thrive in steadily growing **Springdale,** population 581, on the southern boundary of Zion National Park, yet the town still manages to maintain its small-town charm. There are plenty of dining and lodging options, and if you take the time to stroll the main drag you can pick up souvenirs. A free shuttle carries you through town and to the park's South Entrance (which is within walking distance of the visitor center), and you can rent bikes in town.

If you have time to explore, there's always **Virgin, La Verkin,** and the ghost town of **Grafton,** which you might recognize from *Butch Cassidy and the Sundance Kid* and other films. Today there's a stone school, a dusty cemetery, and a few other restored buildings. **Hurricane,** population about 16,200, has experienced much growth since 2000 and keeps sprouting new restaurants and lodgings (many of them chains). (Locals emphasize the first syllable, barely uttering the last.) There are historical sites, a world-class golf course, and the Hurricane Canal, dug by hand and used for 80 years to irrigate fields around town. It's just up Interstate 15 from the largest city in southern Utah, **St. George** (population 82,400), a prosperous and attractive small metropolis with a dramatic red-rock setting.

Heading east from Zion is **Mount Carmel Junction,** an intersection offering a couple of funky small-town lodgings and the studio of American West artist Maynard Dixon. It's a 20-minute drive south from here to funky Kanab, a growing hub of recreation with a handful of excellent restaurants and hotels—it's an excellent base if you'll also be visiting Bryce Canyon, the Grand Canyon, and Grand Staircase–Escalante National Monument.

Index

Photo Credits

Front Cover: Denise Taylor [Description: Vertical night time image of small tent lit from within near large boulders with night sky and stars. In Joshua Tree National Park.]. **Back cover, from left to right:** Bob Pool/Shutterstock, Freebilly Photography/Shutterstock, Travel Stock/Shutterstock. **Spine:** Francesco R. Iacomino/Shutterstock. **Interior, from left to right:** Evan Spiler (1). RRuntsch/shutterstock (2). Christophe Testi/Shutterstock (5). **Chapter 1: Experience the National Parks of the West:** Jeff Vanuga (10-11). cadlikai/Shutterstock (12). Tashka | Dreamstime.com (13). Anton Foltin/Shutterstock (13). DnDavis/Shutterstock (14). Ken Wolter/Shutterstock (14). Zack Frank/Shutterstock (14). Oscity/Shutterstock (14). Sean Pavone/Shutterstock (15). sumikophoto/Shutterstock (15). Jill Krueger (15). kan_khampanya/Shutterstock (15). Mike Brake/Shutterstock (16). Matthew Connolly/Shutterstock (16). Linda Moon/Shutterstock (16). Benkrut | Dreamstime.com (16). Swdesertlover | Dreamstime.com (17). Antonel | Dreamstime.com (17). Charles Haire/Shutterstock (17). Anton Foltin/Shutterstock (17). Sergey Yechikov/Shutterstock (18). neelsky/Shutterstock (18). Nina B/Shutterstock (18). /Shutterstock (18). kojihirano/Shutterstock (19). Laurens Hoddenbagh/Shutterstock (19). Americanspirit | Dreamstime.com (19). Sebastien Burel/Shutterstock (19). Checubus/Shutterstock (20). Gestalt Imagery/Shutterstock (20). Anton Foltin/Shutterstock (20). Isu83boo | Dreamstime.com (20). Kris Wiktor/Shutterstock (21). F11photo | Dreamstime.com (22). Lorcel/Shutterstock (22). YayaErnst/iStockphoto (22). Hale Kell/Shutterstock (23). 2018 Michel Verdure (30). Courtesy of Grand Teton Lodge Company (30). Roman Khomlyak/Shutterstock (30). Asif Islam/Shutterstock (31). Kitleong | Dreamstime.com (31). Courtesy Deby Dixon (32). Swdesertlover | Dreamstime.com (32). Laurens Hoddenbagh/Shutterstock (32). Steve Lagreca/Shutterstock (33). Edmund Lowe Photography/Shutterstock (33). NPS (34). Andrey Tarantin/Shutterstock (34). Gene Lee/Shutterstock (34). Jacom Stephens/Avid Creative, Inc./iStockphoto (35). Keifer | Dreamstime.com (35). David Davis/Shutterstock (36). Dan King (36). Dan King (36). Stephen Fadem (36). Erica L. Wainer (36). Roger Bravo (37). BostonGal (37). Debbie Bowles (37). Darklich14/Wikimedia Commons (37). Bill Perry/Shutterstock (37). **Chapter 2: Planning Your Visit:** Lorcel/Shutterstock (39). **Chapter 3: Great Itineraries:** chomi (51). **Chapter 4: Arches National Park:** Evan Spiler (65). Lukas Urwyler/Shutterstock (72-73). **Chapter 5: Badlands National Park:** JOECHO-16 (81). Virrage Images/Shutterstock (90). **Chapter 6: Big Bend National Park:** Eric Foltz/iStockphoto (101). Mike Norton/Shutterstock (113). **Chapter 7: Black Canyon of the Gunnison National Park:** Tom Till / Alamy (129). Jim Parkin/Shutterstock (141). **Chapter 8: Bryce Canyon National Park:** Chris Christensen (http://AmateurTraveler.com) (155). Inc/Shutterstock (167). **Chapter 9: Canyonlands National Park:** Bryan Brazil/Shutterstock (173). **Chapter 10: Capitol Reef National Park:** Luca Moi/Shutterstock (189). Anton Foltin/Shutterstock (196). Kerrick James (200). **Chapter 11: Carlsbad Caverns National Park:** Nphoto | Dreamstime.com (203). Doug Meek/Shutterstock (216). **Chapter 12: Channel Islands National Park:** Christopher Russell/iStockphoto (221). Americanspirit | Dreamstime.com (235). **Chapter 13: Crater Lake National Park:** William A. McConnell (241). **Chapter 14: Death Valley National Park:** Bryan Brazil/Shutterstock (261). Evan Spiler, Fodors.com member (271). Phitha Tanpairoj/Shutterstock (278). **Chapter 15: Glacier and Waterton Lakes National Parks:** alfwilde (283). chip phillips/iStockphoto (297). **Chapter 16: Grand Canyon National Park:** NPS (311). Kerrick James (334). Christophe Testi/Shutterstock (346-347) Anton Foltin/Shutterstock (348). Geir Olav Lyngfjell/Shutterstock (349). Kerrick James (350, Top & Bottom). Grand Canyon NPS/Flickr, [CC BY 2.0] (351). Kerrick James (351). Pacific Northwest Photo | Shutterstock (352). Kerrick James (353). **Chapter 17: Grand Teton National Park:** Patrick Tr/Shutterstock (357). **Chapter 18: Great Basin National Park:** Dennis Frates / Alamy (385). Heeb Christian / age fotostock (393). **Chapter 19: Great Sand Dunes National Park:** Photo by J.C. Leacock/CTO (401). NPS (409). **Chapter 20: Guadalupe Mountains National Park:** Zack Frank/Shutterstock (415). Michael J Thompson/Shutterstock (427). **Chapter 21: Joshua Tree National Park:** Eric Foltz/iStockphoto (431). Pixelite/Shutterstock (445). pmphoto/Shutterstock (446). Greg Epperson/agefotostock (448). **Chapter 22: Lassen Volcanic National Park:** Zack Frank/Shutterstock (457). Shyam Subramanyan (467). **Chapter 23: Mesa Verde National Park:** Rob Crandall/Shutterstock (477). Kerrick James (486). **Chapter 24: Mount Rainier National Park:** chinana, Fodors.com member (499). zschnepf/Shutterstock (514-515). **Chapter 25: North Cascades National Park:** LoweStock / Getty Images (521). **Chapter 26: Olympic National Park:** Rita Bellanca (543). Lindsay Douglas/Shutterstock (554). SuperStock/age fotostock (558). **Chapter 27: Petrified Forest National Park:** Kerrick James (571). Clara/Shutterstock (578). Kerrick James (581). **Chapter 28: Pinnacles National Park:** yhelfman/Shutterstock (585). **Chapter 29: Redwood National and State Parks:** iStockphoto (605). Mike Norton/Shutterstock (626). **Chapter 30: Rocky Mountain National Park:** Stock Connection Distribution / Alamy (629). Harold R. Stinnette Stock Photography / Alamy (646). **Chapter 31: Saguaro National Park:** Johnny Stockshooter (655). Sasha Buzko/Shutterstock (666). **Chapter 32: Sequoia and Kings Canyon National Parks:** Robert Holmes (671). urosr/Shutterstock (687). **Chapter 33: Theodore Roosevelt National Park:** North Dakota Tourism (703). **Chapter 34: White Sands National Park:** sunsinger/Shutterstock (721). **Chapter 35: Wind Cave National Park:** South Dakota Tourism (737). South Dakota Tourism (757). Alex Pix/Shutterstock (758). **Chapter 36: Yellowstone National Park:** funtravlr (761). Paul stoloff (781). Jeff Vanuga (784-792). **Chapter 37: Yosemite National Park:** Jill Krueger (813). Nathan Jaskowiak/Shutterstock (831). Pung/Shutterstock (835). Katrina Leigh/Shutterstock (840-841). **Chapter 38: Zion National Park:** John Vaccarelli (847). **About Our Writers:** All photos are courtesy of the writers.

*Every effort has been made to trace the copyright holders, and we apologize in advance for any accidental errors. We would be happy to apply the corrections in the following edition of this publication.

Notes

Notes

Notes

Notes

Fodor's THE COMPLETE GUIDE TO THE NATIONAL PARKS OF THE WEST

Publisher: Stephen Horowitz, *General Manager*

Editorial: Douglas Stallings, *Editorial Director;* Jill Fergus, Jacinta O'Halloran, Amanda Sadlowski, *Senior Editors;* Kayla Becker, Alexis Kelly, *Editors*

Design: Tina Malaney, *Director of Design and Production;* Jessica Gonzalez, *Graphic Designer;* Mariana Tabares, *Design and Production Intern*

Production: Jennifer DePrima, *Editorial Production Manager;* Elyse Rozelle, *Senior Production Editor;* Monica White, *Production Editor*

Maps: Rebecca Baer, *Senior Map Editor;* Mark Stroud (Moon Street Cartography), *Cartographer*

Photography: Viviane Teles, *Senior Photo Editor;* Namrata Aggarwal, Ashok Kumar, Carl Yu, *Photo Editors;* Rebecca Rimmer, *Photo Intern*

Business and Operations: Chuck Hoover, *Chief Marketing Officer;* Robert Ames, *Group General Manager;* Devin Duckworth, *Director of Print Publishing;* Victor Bernal, *Business Analyst*

Public Relations and Marketing: Joe Ewaskiw, *Senior Director Communications and Public Relations*

Fodors.com: Jeremy Tarr, *Editorial Director;* Rachael Levitt, *Managing Editor*

Technology: Jon Atkinson, *Director of Technology;* Rudresh Teotia, *Lead Developer;* Jacob Ashpis, *Content Operations Manager*

Writers: Shelley Arenas, Whitney Bryen, Andrew Collins, Cheryl Crabtree, Lindsey Galloway, Aimee Heckel, Kellee Katagi, Laura M. Kidder, Mara Levin, Debbie Olsen, Elise Riley, Stina Sieg, Carson Walker

Editors: Alexis Kelly, Laura Kidder, Rachael Roth

Production Editor: Jennifer DePrima, Monica White

7th Edition

ISBN 978-1-64097-428-9

ISSN 1941–5419

SPECIAL SALES
This book is available at special discounts for bulk purchases for sales promotions or premiums. For more information, e-mail SpecialMarkets@fodors.com.

PRINTED IN THE UNITED STATES OF AMERICA

10 9 8 7 6 5 4 3 2 1

About Our Writers

Shelley Arenas grew up in eastern Washington and has lived in the Seattle area since college. She's been a regular contributor to Fodor's guidebooks for more than a decade, along with co-authoring a book about Seattle for families and writing for several regional publishers. She updated the Bryce, Capitol Reef, Mt. Rainier, North Cascades, and Zion chapters for this edition.

Whitney Bryen has been a journalist since 2010. She worked at the *Boulder Daily Camera* and *Longmont Times-Call* until 2016 when she took a year off to travel. From a 1968 Silver Streak trailer, Bryen explored national, state, and local parks across the country documenting her experiences in stories and photographs. Bryen returned to the workforce as an investigative reporter and continues to write about food, drinks, and travel as a freelancer. Follow @whitneywanders on Instagram. Whitney updated the Great Sand Dunes chapter.

Former Fodor's staff editor **Andrew Collins** is based in both Mexico City and a small village in New Hampshire's Lake Sunapee region, but he spends much of his time traveling throughout the United States. He updated the Big Bend, Carlsbad Caverns, Crater Lake, Grand Teton, Guadalupe Mountains, Lassen Volcanic, Pinnacles, Redwood, White Sands, and Yellowstone chapters. A long-time contributor to more than 200 Fodor's guidebooks, including Pacific Northwest, Utah, Santa Fe, Inside Mexico City, and New England, he's also written for dozens of mainstream and LGBTQ publications—*Travel + Leisure, New Mexico Magazine, AAA Living, The Advocate,* and *Canadian Traveller* among them. Additionally, Collins teaches travel writing and food writing for New York City's Gotham Writers Workshop. You can find more of his work at ⊕ *AndrewsTraveling.com,* and follow him on Instagram @ TravelAndrew.

Native Californian **Cheryl Crabtree**—who updated the Yosemite, Sequoia and Kings Canyon, Channel Islands, Death Valley, and Joshua Tree chapters—has worked as a freelance writer since 1987. She also contributes regularly to Fodor's California and Oahu guidebooks. Cheryl is editor of *Montecito Magazine*. She co-authors *The California Directory of Fine Wineries* hardcover book series (Napa•Sonoma and Central Coast editions). Her articles have appeared in numerous regional and national publications, and she has also authored travel apps for mobile devices and content for travel websites.

Lindsey Galloway lives in Boulder, Colorado, and has covered travel for 15 years, including the Living In column for *BBC Travel*. She loves taking new Colorado visitors to Estes Park, especially The Stanley for its Stephen King connection. She is the founder and editor of ⊕ *TravelPretty.com,* tweets too often at @savvylindz, and sometimes TikToks at @travelpretty. Lindsey updated the Rocky Mountain National Park chapter for this edition.

Aimee Heckel is honored to have been a part of the Fodor's Colorado guide books since 2013. She also published her own book, *Colorado Day Trips by Theme,* in 2020. She has more than two decades of journalism experience and has edited or contributed to more than 50 books. As a travel expert, Heckel has covered Colorado as a regular contributor for *USA Today,* 10Best.com, Culture Trip, SpaTravelGal.com, TripSavvy, Travel Boulder, and more. For this edition, she updated the Mesa Verde chapter. Visit ⊕ *AimeeHeckel.com*

Kellee Katagi Kellee Katagi has lived in eight U.S. states, but her present home of Colorado is her favorite. A former managing editor of *SKI magazine,* Katagi is now a freelance writer/editor specializing in travel, sports, fitness, health, and food in all its marvelous forms. When not at her desk, she enjoys playing in the Colorado mountains with her husband, their three teenage explorers, and their trusty raft, dubbed K-5 Shark. Katagi updated the Black Canyon of the Gunnison chapter.

New England–based freelancer **Laura M. Kidder** has been a travel editor and writer for more than 25 years, with in-house stints as editorial director at both Fodor's Travel Guides and Rand McNally. She's covered much of the United States; all of the Caribbean and Latin America; and countless destinations in Europe, Africa, Asia, and the Pacific. She updated the Experience, Planning Your Visit, and Great Itineraries chapters.

Saguaro and Grand Canyon updater **Mara Levin** divides her time between travel writing, traveling, and social work. A native of California, Mara now lives in Tucson, where the grass may not be greener, but the mountains, tranquillity, and slower pace of desert life have their own appeal.

Debbie Olsen is a gutsy granny who has snorkeled with whale sharks, hiked the Camino de Santiago, and summited five peaks in the Canadian Rockies. She and her husband, Greg, live in Alberta, Canada. They have four adult children and four grandchildren. Debbie is an award-winning writer and photographer and a national bestselling author. She has contributed to 12 Fodor's Guidebooks and writes for many other publications. Follow Debbie and Greg's adventures on Wander Woman Travel Magazine (⊕ *www. wandwerwoman.ca*) and on social media at @wwtravelmag. Debbie updated the Glacier and Waterton Lakes chapter, as well as the online content for Banff and Jasper.

A Phoenix-based freelance writer and editor, **Elise Riley** left her native Arizona to report for newspapers across the country. She quickly learned that no place had Mexican food like the Valley, and eventually found the way back to her favorite salsas and enchiladas. Today she appreciates the striking desert sunsets more than she did in her childhood, and eagerly awaits the next out-of-state visitor she can take on a tour of her favorite local restaurants. This edition, she contributed to the Petrified Forest chapter

About Our Writers

 Stina Sieg is a writer, radio reporter, knitter, baker, and happily slow hiker who has lived all over the West. Though she was born and raised by the ocean, she now feels most at home surrounded by vast desert. You can hear her reporting on Colorado Public Radio, as well as various NPR shows. She's @ StinaSieg on Twitter, where she shares Western news and many photos of her cat. She updated the Great Basin, Arches, and Canyonlands chapters for this book.

 Carson Walker worked in radio, television, newspaper, and at the Associated Press as a multiplatform reporter and photojournalist, editor, and manager. While at the AP, he had numerous stories and photos published in major online news platforms and national newspapers. He also has experience in media relations, internal communications, and currently leads crowdsourcing at the largest rural health care organization in the U.S. You can follow him on Twitter at @carsonjw and at ⊕ linkedin.com/in/carsonwalker. He updated the Badlands, Theodore Roosevelt, and Wind Cave chapters.